Annual Review of
BEHAVIOR THERAPY
THEORY AND PRACTICE
1976

ANNUAL REVIEW OF
BEHAVIOR THERAPY THEORY & PRACTICE
1976

Edited with Commentaries by

CYRIL M. FRANKS, Ph.D.

*Professor, Graduate School of Applied
and Professional Psychology,
Rutgers University (New Brunswick)*

and

G. TERENCE WILSON, Ph.D.

*Associate Professor, Graduate School of Applied
and Professional Psychology,
Rutgers University (New Brunswick)*

BRUNNER/MAZEL, *Publishers* • New York

"To the [practitioner] particularly, a scientific discipline is an incalculable gift, which leavens his whole life, giving exactness to habits of thought and tempering the mind with that judicious faculty of distrust which can alone, amid the uncertainties of practice, make him wise. . . . For perdition inevitably awaits the mind of the practitioner who has never had the full inoculation with the leaven, who has never grasped clearly the relations of science to his art, and who knows nothing, and perhaps cares less, for the limitations of either."

SIR WILLIAM OSLER
Aequanimitas
New York: McGraw-Hill, 1906, p. 92

Copyright © 1976 by Cyril M. Franks and G. Terence Wilson

Published by
BRUNNER/MAZEL, Inc
19 Union Square, New York, N. Y. 10003

Library of Congress Catalog Card No. 76-126864
SBN 87630-134-0

MANUFACTURED IN THE UNITED STATES OF AMERICA

Preface

This year's Annual Review is somewhat of a departure from previous volumes in that we are now on a truly annual basis. The articles were selected from those from January through December, 1975 with the inclusion of November and December, 1974 to ensure continuity. The Commentaries will continue to extend six months further, to the summer of the current year.

Comments about the burgeoning behavior therapy literature are now passé. What is of more interest is the nature of the discrepancies—and unfortunately, we are convinced that such discrepancies do exist—between the single growth curve with respect to quantity of output, probably exponential, and the multidimensional curves of quality, less easy to define. It is the changing nature of these relationships, expressed in nonmathematical terms, which is really what these Annual Reviews are all about. Hopefully, the modifications outlined above will make it easier for readers to evaluate the success of our endeavors at explication.

The growth curve for new behavioral journals may not be exponential but it is nevertheless impressive. As noted in our Commentaries, at least four new publications, each with editors of repute, are either in print or in the works: *Biofeedback and Self-Regulation, Addictive Behaviors, Cognitive Therapy and Research,* and *Behavior Modification.* We extend our felicitations to the editors and publishers of these journals and promise to peruse all future issues with the care and attention they merit.

Taking our cue from the noble tradition of the Chinese calendar, we are tempted to designate each volume of the Annual Review by the name of the prevailing technique or mode of thought for that year. Thus, for the theoretician, 1975 could well be the Year of the Paradigm. And for the practitioner 1975 is, without question, the Year of Assertion. How and if the paradigm will shift remains uncertain. As for "assertive training" (grammatically incorrect but perhaps descriptively more accurate than many of its fervent advocates realize; assertion trainees tend to be embarrassingly assertive at times!), it is our impression that, like the Year of the Dragon, the Year of Assertion crops up time and time again. For instance, in 1847 a treatise for young men on how to say NO with grace and dignity rather than aggression and churlishness appeared in print in Boston, Massachusetts (see Commentary, Section II).

This year could also be called the Year of Revelation. Professor Minde of South Africa* gives an engaging "insider's" account of the eventual acceptance of a thesis—"An Approach to the Problem of Neurosis Based on the Conditioned Response"—for the degree of Doctor of Medicine at the University of Witwatersrand in the year 1948. The candidate's name was Joseph Wolpe, whom Minde now describes as the "father of behavior therapy."

Turning to more contemporary events, it will be noticed that biofeedback features prominently in at least two sections of this year's Annual Review. Again, this is no coincidence, it reflects the *Zeitgeist*. Despite a certain amount of clinical overextension, the overall quality of research in this area is encouraging. Behavior therapists are rediscovering cognitive psychology (there is little that is new under the sun) and busily applying a variety of ingenious techniques to the hitherto forbidden areas of thought, attitude and feeling. In so doing, they are attempting—perhaps prematurely—to substitute cognitive models for explanation in terms of some conditioning mechanism (see Commentary, Section I). Such concepts are often neomentalistic. Physiological underpinnings tend to be neglected. Hopefully, the current surge of interest in biofeedback research and practice by traditional behavior therapists as well as others will bring about a needed infusion of physiological regulation into these cognitively based models. We look forward to the opportunity to report upon such developments in future volumes.

As always, we thank those many individuals who took time out from their busy schedules to submit articles and manuscripts for our consideration. We are also grateful to those who drew our attention to literature or areas of behavioral application we might otherwise have overlooked. One such case in point is the utilization of behavioral principles in industry, which is prominently featured in this Series for the first time this year. We are particularly grateful to Gary Yukl, Martin Greller and Tom Mawhinney, and hope that they and others will con-

---

* *South African Medical Journal*, 1975, 49, 367-374.

tinue to help us expand this important area in future volumes. Our students and colleagues also helped trigger off certain portions of the Commentaries by their stimulating interactions in the classroom and outside.

Once again, it is a pleasure to acknowledge our gratitude to those authors whose articles we have reprinted. Of equal, if less visible, significance are the many writers whose works we have had occasion to cite in our Commentaries. Reed Martin and Research Press generously granted us permission to reprint their *Review Checklist* from that fine text *Legal Challenges to Behavior Modification* in the Commentary to Section I.

Our thanks go to Barbara Honig—the stalwart Administrative Assistant to the Rutgers Alcohol Behavior Research Laboratory—and Daryl Gross—our indefatigable and incredibly efficient departmental secretary at the Carrier Clinic—for the competent manner in which they expedited the transcription and final preparation of our Commentaries and extensive list of References. Last, but in many ways foremost, we thank our wives Violet and Elaine, themselves recognized psychologists of no mean ilk, who remained constructively with us, both literally and figuratively, during the birth pangs of this volume.

The final responsibility for the contents, including any errors or other deficits, remains ours and ours alone. We hope that our readers will point out such weaknesses for correction in future issues. For ourselves, we find the yearly preparation of this Series to rank high among the more significant of our professional duties and, of even greater relevance, among the more pleasurable and stimulating of our activities. We hope that our readers will find the finished product acceptable.

CYRIL M. FRANKS
G. TERENCE WILSON

Graduate School of Applied
   and Professional Psychology
Rutgers University
August, 1976

CONTENTS

Section I

ETHICS, LAW AND MODELS
OF MAN

Commentary

Ethical and legal issues, accountability, certification, licensing and training are all inextricably related to each other, to the model of man that the behavior therapist espouses, and to the value system which he and his society generates. It is for this reason that this year's Annual Review begins with Bandura's Presidential Address to the American Psychological Association. It is important on a variety of accounts, not the least of which is that it presents social learning theory as a model for a behavior therapy of the seventies squarely in perspective. At the very outset, Bandura sets forth the position that conditioning and behavior therapy are by no means synonymous. In Bandura's provocative words, "contrary to popular belief, the fabled reflexive condition in humans is largely a myth." For Bandura, conditioning is simply a descriptive term for learning through paired experiences; it is not an explanation of how these changes came about. Conditioning is not something that occurs automatically; it is cognitively mediated—says Bandura—and people do not learn despite repetitive paired experiences unless they recognize that events are correlated. Thus, so-called conditioned reactions are largely self-activated on the basis of learned expectations rather than being automatically correlated. This comes at a time when, on the one hand, individuals are still carrying out well-designed studies to demonstrate that classical conditioning can occur without awareness (e.g., Brandeis & Lubor, 1975), while, on the other hand, acknowledged experts in the field are equally convinced that conditioning in human subjects is produced through the operation of higher mental processes, rather than

1

vice versa. For example, Brewer (1974) carried out a massive re-analysis of the conditioning literature and ended up with the remarkable and sweeping conclusion that "behavioristic psychology could not explain even simple behavior."

Traditionally, it has been hypothesized that, for classical conditioning to occur, all that is necessary is the repeated contiguous pairing of a conditional stimulus (CS) and an unconditional stimulus (UCS) and that this will cause the CS to elicit a conditional response (CR) in an unconscious, automatic fashion. Similarly, for operant behavior the traditional hypothesis is that the probability of occurrence of a response when it is followed by a reinforcer will likewise increase in an unconscious, automatic fashion. Such a point of view may be found in any of the standard texts in experimental psychology. But, as Brewer correctly points out, subjects in these studies are not really as naive as one might suppose. Perhaps it is the experimenter who is naive in failing to ask the subject what he or she thought was going on. Clearly, such experimenters believe either that higher mental processes do not exist or that they are inconsequential. Be this as it may, in his penetrating, if somewhat less than objective, analysis of an array of conditioning studies noted above, Brewer comes to the conclusion that subjects are not making unconscious automatic responses but are developing conscious hypotheses and expectations about the experiments and that it is these that produce the resulting "conditioning." Gradually, the subjects become aware of the prevailing CS-UCS relationship in classical conditioning or the reinforcement contingency in operant conditioning and make responses according to their cognitions about what is going on. Subjects respond appropriately to their "expectations" and needs to comply or otherwise with the experimenters' wishes. Thus, in operant autonomic conditioning, the subject conditions only to the extent that he or she develops a conscious cognitive strategy which allows him to bring his autonomic responses under voluntary control.

There are many critics of such an extreme position (e.g., Dulany, 1974) and it may well be that both the nonbehavioral—one might almost say antibehavioral—cognitive theory of Brewer and the traditional conditioning points of view possess plausibility or even merit. The virtue of both stances is their amenability to experimental investigation. This issue, it might be noted, is somewhat different from that which is currently engaging the attention of cognitive behavior therapists where the argument is whether some form of extra-conditioning but somehow behaviorally anchored cognitive mechanism is a better way of conceptualizing internal processes than a covert conditioning model (e.g., Mahoney, 1974). Berlyne (1975) argues that the opposing shortcomings of contemporary Skinnerian and neo-cognitivist positions might be avoided by a return to the behavior theory of Hull. As the title of his article puts it, "Behaviorism? Cognitive Theory? Humanistic Psychology?—To Hull with Them All."

To Hull or not to Hull, whether and to what extent it is now necessary to expand or go beyond a conditioning model to account for cognitive processes remain a matter of debate and accruing data. On the one hand, investigators such as Ray (1973) urge the incorporation of more ecologically oriented variables into what remains conceptually a form of conditioning paradigm. On the other hand, Jeffmar and Jeffmar (1975) suggest a system approach to cognition which bypasses a conditioning model entirely. Paivio's (1975) thoughtful and potentially important Presidential Address to the Canadian Psychological Association heralds what he calls *neomentalism* as a viable alternative to either traditional introspection or behaviorism in the study of cognitive processes. The new mentalism, defined as "the objective study of the structure, function and development of mental representations," successfully combines features from both classic introspection and behaviorism. Unlike neobehaviorism, which allows mentalistic concepts only under the guise of mediating stimulus and response events, neomentalism embraces mental phenomena as its subject matter and behavioral approaches as the method of study.

There is little doubt, however, that old distinctions between classical and instrumental conditioning are breaking down. It may well be, as Ray and Brown (1976) suggest, that classical-instrumental distinctions of any type will reduce to parametric extremes rather than being a matter of generic differences per se. Dykman (1976) does not dismiss conditioning mechanisms altogether, but suggests that they are better explained in terms of neither classical nor operant learning, but of sensitization—a term introduced by Wendt (1930) to describe a phenomenon quite distinct from conditioning and more in accord with the related concept of pseudo-conditioning. The concept of emotional sensitization seems germane to most forms of conditioning, whether operant or classical. Kimmel (1973) has described operant conditioning in terms of habituation and Dykman is merely going a step further than Kimmel in evoking a sensitization model. For Dykman, sensitization is the basis of all forms of learning, a unitary process model which is at least strategically consistent with earlier theories seeking a single principle of conditioning, whether it be Hull and drive reduction or Guthrie and contiguity. Certainly, sensitization is a physiological construct and, as such, focuses needed attention on the reflex properties of the nervous system.

Whether there are two conditioning processes, as much of current American psychological thought seems to suggest, or one process of sensitization, habituation or what have you, or whether conditioning per se is a myth, remains unresolved. Re-examination of existing data and presentation of new data offer little support for the viability of two process theories and seem to make the concept of conditioning itself suspect (see Gormezano & Tait, 1976).

Despite Bandura's position, disputes about the unconscious nature of the conditioning process or processes remain unsettled. Many an eminent learning theorist believed and probably still believes that the conditioning process is fully automatic (e.g., Crider, Schwartz & Shnidman, 1969; Greenspoon & Brownstein, 1967). It was once thought that Russian evidence in favor of interoceptive conditioning (see Razran, 1961) provided unequivocal support for conditioning without awareness. But Russian studies are notoriously difficult to replicate—a recent review of Russian psychology by Joravsky (1975) relegates much of this work, conceptually speaking that is, to the realm of mythology ("a mythic design, compounded of errors, inventions and crucial omissions")—and even Bykov (1957) had reason to suspect that the UCS was not as unconscious as it had been made out to be.

It is, of course, perfectly rational to espouse a more cognitive theory of conditioning for humans and a more automatic model of conditioning for animals. But, if it is assumed that cognitive theory cannot be applied to animals, it could equally reasonably be argued that, as a parsimonious first tactic, one should begin by attempting to use conditioning theory for both species. Brewer makes an interesting reversal of this logic and suggests that, since cognitive theory holds for humans, it is not parsimonious not to apply it to animals. Fairly recent work on thinking and language in chimpanzees does seem to suggest that cognitive theory could be a reasonable proposal at least for certain higher primates (e.g., Schrier & Stollnitz, 1971).

The debate is far from finished and the evidence is by no means all in. Almost daily, new evidence is produced in favor of one side or the other of this cognitive-conditioning battle. Sometimes an essentially integrationist position is adopted, as for example when Boneau (1974) attempts to develop what Frank (1975) calls "cognitive behaviorism."

Perhaps all we are thinking of are new metaphors and new cross-sections of one entity. The advantage of these new models is that they lend themselves to precise generation of predictions and hence to testing. As Popper (1963) suggests in his *Conjectures and Refutations,* one should not be discouraged from making mistakes in science, but one should be encouraged for detecting them. Being wrong, affirms Weimer (1976), is not an indication of failure for a field in flux and transition (such as the conditioning-cognition debate). Progress is going to be a matter of detecting mistakes—we "learn which way not to go."

If Skinner (1975) has learned beyond doubt which route to take—the "steep and thorny way to a science of behavior"—Bandura points to a scientifically equally plausible path which is probably more acceptable not only to the majority of behavior therapists, but also to mental health professionals at large. Rewards do not function as automatic strengtheners of human conduct. Behavior is not much affected by consequences without "awareness" of what is being reinforced. Reinforcement has changed from a mechanical strengthener of conduct to an informative and motivated influence. People do not function in isolation and the same outcome can become either a reward or a punishment, depending upon the reference used for social comparison.

Bandura's thesis, reaffirmed in many different ways throughout this first article, will be reassuring to the mainstream of the professional community. Adaptive social learning theory is in tune with the prevailing *Zeitgeist,* consistent with much of the evidence and worthy of detailed study, point by point. It is a model of man for all seasons, acceptable as a possible basis for *avante-garde* thinking not only in contemporary behavior therapy but in the thinking of all whose concerns are with the data oriented restructuring of society. Kunkel (1975) makes the important point that such a model does not really require that people do anything which is substantially different from what they have been doing in the past. The rationale may be more explicit and the program may be more rigorous, but the basic ideas are the same. What is different is that, when we actually want to do something and when learning principles and the present social context have shown us what to do, then we go out into the world and actually start doing it.

Probably the most controversial as well as significant alternative influence to a social learning model of man that has emerged this year is that proposed by Wilson (1975). Wilson's sociobiology, which he calls "the modern synthesis," looks at behavior from a gene's point of view. The human brain, says Wilson, has been programmed to perform as if it knows that its underlying genes will be best proliferated by certain behaviors optimizing personal survival, namely reproduction and altruism (see Asher, 1975—*APA Monitor*). In Wilson's impressive schema, Skinnerian principles become "enabling devices by which the evolved human 'biogram' is expressed." Rewards are ultimately determined by genetic fitness, and it is a matter of biological rather than social evolution. According to Wilson, sociobiology leads to a view of man as being under the influence of inherited programs of behavior and control mechanisms that are much more complex than the simple conditioning suggested by either the operant or classical conditioning schools of thought.

In many senses, Wilson's sociobiology is more consistent with the work of such thinkers as Piaget and Claud Levi-Straus. The basic tenet of sociobiology is Darwinist—social behavior evolved to increase the chances of survival of the species. His thesis, that altruism, generally considered a uniquely human type of behavior, is not, in fact, unique to man but common to many species, is well documented and compelling. His excursion into the social sciences is far less convincing. Undaunted by a gamut of impassioned refutations by vociferous critics, Wilson is attempting to develop a unified science of sociobiology which will encompass the social behavior of human beings at all levels. Politics, culture, ethics and religion all meld together into the new comprehensive science of sociobiology, doing away with the need for such discrete disciplines as ethology, sociology, animal behavior and comparative psychology—or, if not altogether taking their places, at least helping to reformulate what exactly are their places.

Wilson's many critics fall into two main categories, according to Caplan (1976). Some biologists take exception on methodological grounds, others on moral or ethical grounds. It is unfortunate that the debate is being resolved less in terms of scholarship and evidence than through invective, emotionally held belief and personal accusation—shades of Eysenck, Jensen and the race-intelligence issue! As Wilson himself would probably be the first to concur, his scientific views should not hinder efforts to legislate needed social reform and improvements any more than the genetic nature of nearsightedness should discourage people from getting glasses.

Davison and Stuart's article, reprinted next, is both an implicit affirmation of Bandura's main thesis and a sort of position paper for behavior therapy in the mid-seventies with special reference to human rights. Their point that behavior modification is a particularly unfortunate term is well taken. It refers only to the end product of an intervention and, even within the psychological domain, could apply to psychoanalysis, psychosurgery, pastoral counselling or nude encounter groups. It is for this purpose that they prefer the more generic "behavior therapy." Certainly, as far as the uninformed public are concerned, the term behavior modification applies to all kinds of drastically different procedures, including drug therapy, electroconvulsive shock treatment, solitary confinement and even psychosurgery.

In an earlier presentation, Davison and Stuart (1974) argued in favor of retaining "behavior modification," a term with a clear and precise meaning for use exclusively by applied conditioners. Unfortunately, the public at large—both the general public and our informed leaders—do not seem to appreciate this distinction. What term will eventually be used is a matter to be decided in the future. A term gaining great popularity—with good reason if one is strongly wedded to a traditional operant conditioning model—is that of behavior analyst or "applied behavior analyst." The more social learning theory oriented behavior therapist will probably not find this too acceptable.

Perhaps the most important contribution of Davison and Stuart here is their stress upon the thesis that every therapeutic intervention should begin with the least intrusive procedures from which a positive outcome can reasonably be expected—the principle of least severity. Then, as Wexler (1973) has noted, behavior therapists will be called on to use increasing ingenuity in their efforts to find meaningful incentives for behavior change within the context of the evolving guidelines of an ethically and legally acceptable practice.

Davison and Stuart affirm both the right to receive treatment and the right not to receive treatment. Here, we may note an innovative twist pointed out by Morris (1968), that prisoners have the right to receive punishment and that to deny them this right is somehow to deny them certain aspects of their humanity. This is an interesting notion which may have more to it than is at first apparent. Also of importance is Davison and Stuart's judgment that, rather than being looked at with askance as a violation of resident rights, institutional evaluative research should be regarded as a mandatory aspect of responsible institutional management. Contrary to the prevailing thrust of public opinion, they view the monitoring of existing programs and the search for more beneficial alternatives as essential activities to insure the basic rights of patients and inmates.

Ethical issues, civil liberties and the rights of patients are closely related topics. Whether behavior therapy needs its own code of ethics

over and above that of the parent profession of any particular practitioner is still a debatable issue. Many arguments have been adduced for
and against such a code and these are detailed at length by Braun
(1975). Arguments in favor may be philosophic—behavior control means
power over people, individuals can be victimized by a malevolent society, and so forth. They may be ethical or legal—if behavior modifiers
don't regulate their procedures and technology the lawyers will assume
the responsibility for us. The arguments against the development of a
code of ethics are equally varied. One somewhat naive point of view
declares that the very existence of such a code could be constituted as an
implicit admission that behavioral techniques are more unethical than
others. Another argument invokes prematurity and lack of data. Perhaps,
as behavior analysts, what we should do is pinpoint desirable and undesirable professional behaviors, define the conditions under which they
can occur and produce a demonstrably viable methodology to improve
ethical practice.

A code of ethics will need to be developed not only for clinical practice but also for research in behavior modification and it is to such
matters that Stolz (1975) addresses herself: All behavior modification
procedures, including aversive control, can be used ethically and with
concern for the subjects involved, or unethically and with insufficient
precautions. The choice is ours. If ethics are important, they can be no
more important than the training and value system of those who
develop the procedures and of those who carry them out. To this end,
Sulzer-Azaroff, Thaw, and Thomas (1975) have provided a beginning by
their analysis of the applied skills of behavior therapists and behavior
modifiers. Their questionnaire, sent to a large number of prominent
behavior therapists, yielded a list of 69 skills pertaining to the practice
of applied behavior modification. Despite the limitations of the sample
and the sometimes global nature of parts of the analysis, this is a significant endeavor—a first step in the arduous process of identifying the
requisite limits of competency of behavior modifiers. Tentatively identifying four levels of behavior modifier, ranging from the top-level con-
ceptualizer down to the day-to-day "co-technician," they make the point
that rather than await a more definitive system for identifying components of competent modifiers, something has to be done immediately,
and that a crude system is better than none.

Logan and Turnage (1975) take the position that it is insufficient for a
behavior therapist to defend himself against criticism by enumerating
successes. He has to be accountable for the work he does, aware of the

limitations of his techniques and the cautions to be applied, depending on circumstances, instruments employed and other pertinent variables. Ethical considerations extend to the individual, his training and his equipment. There is much concern now, for example, with standards of safety for electrical apparatus used in aversion therapy (e.g., Siddall, Vargas, & Adesso, 1975; Butterfield, 1975a, 1975b). Therapists using electric shock are often not aware of the dangers that the equipment they are using may pose to their patients, and sometimes hazards are due more to specific ignorance than to general incompetence.

The best of techniques or equipment can be misused by poorly trained or unqualified individuals and methodological guidelines can and should be specified. By the same token, sometimes the most ethical of individuals can behave in unethical fashion without seeming to be aware of it. Stein (1975), for example, draws to our attention the situation of the responsible and competent behavior therapist who conducts a brief one- or two-day workshop. Often, this workshop is carried out in an isolated part of the country, given to individuals unselected and unscreened and never to be seen again. Under such circumstances, says Stein, we may well be reinforcing the misapplication of behavioral principles by the relatively brief presentations that characterize such seminars. It is doubtful if enough information can be disseminated in a one- or two-day, or even a one-week workshop, to allow participants to apply the principles taught in an appropriate fashion. Either innocently, or sometimes less innocently, "graduates" of such workshops may do harm to the individuals with whom they then work, to the people they then proceed to train, and to the image of behavior therapy. If we are reinforcing the misapplication of principles in this fashion, then we may well inadvertently be contributing to the charges that behavioral methods are unethical.

The next paper to be reprinted, by the late Michael Serber, Hiller, Keith and Taylor, highlights the potential of behavior modification both for helping and for abuse. Their experiences at Atascadero State Hospital in California graphically illustrate both the positive and negative possibilities inherent in the application of behavior modification principles. They can be used to sculpt humane and effective treatment programs or they can become a tool for abuse of patient rights and human dignity.

In certain circumstances, behavior modification can become little more than a pseudoscientific rationalization for harsh and punitive methods of control within an environment which lacks the resources for more positive means of accomplishing this end. Use of the drug Anectine, which for all practical purposes simulates death in those who receive it, is an example of such an abuse. When this was officially pointed out, significant reforms were made. But aversion therapy in the form of seclusion continued to be utilized for assorted patients, and critical review procedures, both from within and without the institution, were still lacking as of the date that this article was written. A complaint about the Anectine studies was registered with the ethics committee of the American Psychiatric Association in 1971; in 1975 there was still no systematic procedure for investigating such cases. As a matter of fact, the American Psychiatric Association did not even provide a budget for such investigations, making comprehensive ethical review not feasible.

The caveats for the use of behavior modification procedures are important. Incarceration is to be used sparingly; aversive policies should be avoided; the psychiatric profession must concern itself with patients' rights by more thorough self-regulation of unethical practices. In this regard, Peck (1975) outlines the issues, the new legislation and the more important judicial decisions of the last five years with respect to involuntary civil commitments, the right to refuse treatment and the right to treatment. She also provides examples of states which have not yet reformed their laws and makes suggestions for improvement. On June 26, 1976 there was an important Supreme Court decision which upheld the District Court and the Court of Appeals rulings which freed a Florida State mental patient after 15 years of confinement. The Court of Appeals ruled that, since the patient was not dangerous and not receiving treatment, he should not be confined. This is a landmark which will have wide ramifications in the months and years to come for the large population of patients who are involuntarily committed.

In the prison system, the situation is similar in many respects and yet somewhat different. As Rangel (1975) points out, one of the major problems faced by the Bureau of Prisons is the attitude of certain inmates towards the prison system and its administrators. These inmates view themselves as political prisoners who have committed political acts in protest against an unjust society. Suffering no feeling of guilt, they tend to view the Federal Bureau of Prisons and their staff as agents of a society bent on destroying them. Understandably enough, under these circumstances they view the most benign program of behavior modification as a form of brainwashing. What they would think of programs of behavior modification that were less than benign need hardly be elaborated here.

Since many of the self-styled experts in the field of behavior modification in prison themselves tend to misinterpret what behavior modification is about, it is hardly to be expected that those who are even less informed will think otherwise. For example, Gaylin and Blatte (1975) have written an extensive article on behavior modification in prisons for the *American Criminal Law Review* and this is how they define behavior therapy as a formal treatment: "Crudely, the therapy can be seen as different from psychotherapy in that its concern and focus is the *behavior* itself—either by denying the existence of an unconscious or by feeling that 'mind' considerations are not essential. It attempts to modify directly the undesired behavior. As such, its roots lie deep in the basic research of Pavlov and the conditioned reflex. It generally eschews the consideration of motivation, purpose and dynamism." If informed individuals can write in this fashion, it is hardly surprising that the general public and nonspecialists in the field have equally erroneous notions about the use of behavior modification in prisons.

Goldberger (1975) presents a much more thoughtful and realistic consideration of the legal problems involved in the use of behavior modification programs in prisons. He describes in detail the Illinois experiment with behavior modification that began in mid-1971 at two penitentiaries primarily for members of Chicago street gangs regarded by prison guards as troublesome and dangerous to prison security. Each institution had a newly-appointed warden whose attempts to initiate reforms were—perhaps understandably—resented by the prison guards, whose fears were that these changes would interfere with security and upset control over the inmates. If prison officials did not assure adequate protection for the guards, the guards threatened to strike. The officials therefore decided to establish a multi-tiered behavior modification program to house inmates whom the guards felt were troublesome.

The events which prompted the litigation described by Goldberger began as a result of a fistfight between guards and inmates, resulting in every inmate being locked into his cell on an around-the-clock basis. Inmates solicited the help of attorneys for help in correcting the inhuman conditions to which they were subjected and an investigation soon became underway. Eventually, agreements were reached and promises made to bring about the needed reforms. However, no mention was made that one of those reforms involved the three-tier behavior modification program described above. Fortunately, or perhaps unfortunately depending on one's point of view, one of the correction social work staff anonymously outlined the program and policies of this Special Program

Unit (SPU) to the investigating lawyers. Among other details, he revealed that the principal criteria for selection of SPU candidates included street-gang affiliation and the guards' hostilities towards particular inmates. Based upon this and other information, the lawyers for the inmates drafted a complaint of a class action and filed it in a Federal District Court in Chicago. The allegations emphasized the punitive nature of the program and made the point that it and the previous conditions which accompanied the lock-up amounted to cruel and unusual punishment. Counsel filed the complaint and issued a press release in September, 1971. Examination of the data was begun shortly thereafter and several changes were immediately instigated. The correctional counselor directly in charge of implementing the behavior modification program at SPU, an individual with a Master's degree in personnel management and virtually no training of a sophisticated nature in behavior modification, was deposed. It was found that none of the SPU clinical staff had training adequate for implementation of any of the behavioral techniques central to the program.

Interestingly enough, even though the district court explicitly held that the SPU was a permissible approach to prison programming, the Illinois corrections officials quietly abandoned the behavior modification experiment. They converted the unit into a regular segregation unit with appropriate amenities and facilities. However, Goldberger warns, despite this outcome, similar behavior modification units will probably continue to be initiated or continued at other penal institutions, necessitating further litigation to challenge their existence. It is of interest to note Goldberger's observation that, as in other prison cases, lawyers challenging behavior modification programs on behalf of inmates were met with persistent delays by prison officials and their lawyers. Without the active help of a willing district judge, plaintiff's counsel may be unable to prevent delay. He also makes the surprising point that legislation in this area of behavior modification is not soon to be expected. For this reason, litigation is likely to serve as the principle safeguard against the total abrogation of an inmate's constitutional protection carried out in the name of rehabilitation.

It is perhaps in this area of prison rehabilitation that accountability is most urgently required. But this does not mean that accountability is something which can be ignored in the less involuntary area of everyday practice. Accountability in the mental health field is coming to mean that we verify and record what we do and that we justify on paper why we did it. Atthowe (1975) has made a cogent plea for legal and ethical accountability in the consulting room. To be fully accountable, he advocates what is termed a goal-oriented treatment contract, an extension of Weed's (1971) pioneering problem-oriented medical record. The goal-oriented treatment contract should specify such things as fee-schedule, length of the contract, signed consent for treatment performed, signed release for information if it is to be sent elsewhere, initial contracts and the designation of a treatment plan focusing specifically upon assessment, goals, procedures, contingencies, evaluation and re-evaluation, after-care and discharge procedures. Finally, the goal-oriented treatment contract can serve as a consent form for outpatients and for partial and full-hospital cases.

Goldberger is not a psychologist and his interest in the institution of behavior modification programs within the prison system is primarily legal. Psychologists might be more interested in the related issues of how it is that prison riots and guard dissatisfaction tend to occur whenever a strict security-minded administration is replaced by a warden interested in rehabilitation. Clinicians such as Watkins (1974) speculate in a mixture of psychodynamic and quasi-behavioral terms, but as yet hard data are lacking. According to Watkins, behavioral methods will be resisted in the prison system precisely because they are likely to work: If correction really is effective, it will disturb the status quo and create anxiety both within and outside the prison. This is an inviting hypothesis which as yet remains untested. If confirmed, its implications are far-reaching.

The final two papers in this Section also focus upon legal regulation of applied behavioral analysis in mental institutions and prisons. Friedman, an attorney whose pioneering endeavors on the behalf of mental health law reform have achieved national recognition, has presented a stimulating and detailed exposition of current developments in this area. Because of its length, we are omitting the first two portions of his penetrating analysis of the legal regulations pertaining to the application of behavior modification principles in mental institutions and hospitals.

Traditionally, society and the courts have ignored mental patients and prisoners during their confinement, focusing only upon issues of admission and release. It is only in recent years that public concern for the legal rights of mental patients and prisoners has dramatically increased. Particular attention is now being paid to the emerging concept of the right to treatment and the right to refuse treatment. Potentially hazardous or intrusive treatments have come under increasing scrutiny and attempts have been made to delimit the conditions under which

even an involuntarily committed patient or prisoner may refuse a particular treatment. It is the right to refuse treatment—or, to put it more
precisely, the nature and extent of limitations upon the state's power to
impose treatment and procedures upon unwilling or incompetent persons
—which is the subject of Friedman's extensive discussion.

First, he provides a definition of applied behavior analysis, an overview of the reasons for the current thought on the use of behavior procedures in closed institutions and a discussion of the legal and ethical
issues common to all therapies. The second section focuses upon the
applied behavior analyst's statutory and common law duties as well as
the possible legal bases for constitutional duty to refrain from using
hazardous procedures in those not exactly rare instances where a competent mental patient or prisoner withholds informed consent or where a
procedure is not in the best interest of an incompetent patient or prisoner.
Also discussed are the legal scrutiny to which behavioral programs may
be subjected and relevant legal concepts such as waiver, permissible and
compelling state interest and the least restrictive alternatives.

In the third section, reprinted here, five special problems which applied behavior analysts are likely to encounter in attempting to comply
with the constitutional duty to refrain from using hazardous or intrusive procedures except under special circumstances are explored.
Finally, in the fourth section, also reproduced here, the implications of a
recent case setting procedural limitations on the imposition of behavioral
programs are set forth. The two appendices—also reproduced—are of
considerable relevance, in that the first sets forth standards for the
regulation of behavioral programs in mental institutions and the second
—based upon an actual situation encountered by us in the Psychological
Clinic of Rutgers University (see Romanczyk & Goren, 1975; also Commentary, Section X)—demonstrates how the proposed standards for the
regulations of behavior modification should be applied in actual practice.

Friedman makes the point that behavior modification (he persists in
using the term "behavior analysis") has been singled out for current
attention more than other equally hazardous therapies such as psychosurgery or electroconvulsive therapy. His speculations as to why this
might be so and the possible reasons for the growing concern in our
society about attempts to control thoughts, feelings and actions are issues
which are very much in the forefront of both public and professional
debate these days. We still have little reliable information pertaining to
the public's belief concerning what behavior modification is all about. It
is, therefore, Friedman's legal conclusions which are most important.

While it is difficult to give precise advice to applied behavior analysts with respect to legal limitations, the proposed standards and procedures outlined in the first appendix should be acceptable because they conform with recommended standards for professional practices. But whether such standards can be implemented in practice remains to be decided.

In some respects, Friedman's choice of the term "applied behavior analysis" is a good one. It is precise and definitive. A major weakness, or so it seems to us, is that it is too closely wedded to one model of man, in particular, operant conditioning as espoused by the *Journal of Applied Behavior Analysis*. We prefer the term "social learning theory" which takes into account cognitive processes, self-control, and the active, humanistic value systems which characterize modern behavior therapy. The former term is more likely to imply (e.g., Gaylin & Blatte, 1975) that behavior therapists do not necessarily examine a person's "innermost thoughts." Behavior therapy, as we view the term, is as much concerned with the inner man as with the world around him.

In his penetrating commentary, Goldiamond (1975) takes Friedman to task on a variety of additional accounts. Perhaps because he is neither psychiatrist nor psychologist, Friedman tends to gloss over or obscure basic issues with respect to conceptual schemes for behavior change which are far more than matters of terminology. And as Goldiamond points out, one adverse consequence which could arise from Friedman's proposal is the impediment of scientific research and development. Advances in research depend to a large extent upon advances in treatment. Hindrance to treatment might well hinder advances in understanding and improved patient care. Thus Friedman's standards could stultify developments in this field for, ultimately, it is just this knowledge upon which the evaluation and adoption of any recommended treatment depend.

Psychologists as well as legal scholars are becoming increasingly concerned about the growing tendency of the courts to pass judgment upon institutional treatment programs which could conceivably deprive individuals of some of their fundamental human rights (e.g., Schwitzgebel, 1975). If elemental reinforcers such as recreational facilities and second helpings at mealtimes are classified as legal rights, then many seemingly successful token economies must come to a grinding halt. If these are the signs of the times, then alternative solutions have to be developed. The behavior therapist can use his ingenuity to invent reinforcers which are both potent and legal; the institution can set up stringent monitoring programs in those situations where searching appraisal indicates that seemingly illegal procedures are in the best interests of the subjects. Situations are rarely unequivocal and, in each instance, the letter of the law has to be balanced against the intent vis-à-vis the recipient.

Martin (1975), also a lawyer, reminds us that the law and the behavioral sciences need not be antagonistic to each other. The effective resolution of any legal challenge to the particular actions of a mental health professional is rarely the simple matter of some clear and final courtroom judgment. The real challenge, says Martin, will emerge in many arenas: in the institution, in legislative bodies, in funding, in new programs and in the formulation of new guidelines. The problem is not over once the court decision is made. Implementation necessitates difficult and often slightly different judgments in each situation, sometimes involving major institutional changes, staff retraining and continual attention to legal developments. Martin offers a convenient checklist which he suggests that everyone engaged in instituting a program consider:

1. Are the rules under which you operate written down in objective terms?
2. Are the individuals to be affected by a program given notice and an opportunity for a hearing?
3. Is the affected individual allowed the resources needed to challenge inclusion in the program if he wishes to do so?
4. Does the impact of inclusion in the program mean one group of individuals will be treated so differently from others that the distinction cannot be justified?
5. Does the participant in the program receive in services the same types of things which the institution generally provides, or does the program deprive the participants of something? If the latter, is it a constitutionally protected right or a privilege that is being withheld?
6. Is there an individual treatment program?
7. Are there periodic reviews of progress?
8. Is the least restrictive alternative explored first?
9. Are all the individuals in need of this program being offered services? If some are being excluded, can their separation be justified?
10. Is anyone's condition worsening?
11. Is anyone not receiving help because he has been assigned to a "control" group?
12. Is there a system in operation which allows those in charge to determine if something is wrong?
13. Have all funding agency guidelines been examined to determine if there are additional requirements? (p. 10 ff.).

The publication *Law and Behavior,* in its Winter, 1976 issue, spells out the doctrine of the *least restrictive alternative.* The notion that the least restrictive setting must be considered first is easy to master in theory, but is very difficult to implement in practice. The right is really to the least restrictive alternative *suitable* to the individual's need. Full compliance with this doctrine will come only as the technology of evaluation is developed, and implementation will depend on the availability of alternatives.

One possible way of determining what is the best strategy to use is by an application of the techniques of benefit cost analysis (see the National Research Council Report, 1976). There is no fully objective, scientific way of making decisions, nor is it likely that there will ever be. The temptation to oversimplify and overlook the exquisitely subtle complexities of most real life situations is strong. However, use of the techniques developed by decision theory and benefit cost analysis could provide the decision maker with a useful framework and language for describing and discussing trade-offs, noncommensurability, uncertainty and the like. It is not suggested that benefit cost analysis is anything more than a valuable aid. It does not dictate choice; it doesn't replace the ultimate authority and responsibility of the decision maker with some mechanical impersonal device. The most important and pervasive limitation of benefit cost analysis is in the role of value and this will probably always be ultimately a subjective decision of the individual directly concerned or those legally empowered to make decisions for him.

One of the few recent examples of benefit cost analysis in the field of behavior modification is offered by Foreyt, Rockwood, Davis, DesVousges, & Hollingsworth (1975). Reporting the results of a benefit cost analysis of a token economy program with adult psychiatric patients at Florida State Hospital, Chattahoochee, these authors compare the costs to government of the first year and a half of the program with the probable benefits to government produced during this same period. Economists have developed viable statistical procedures for comparing hospital costs incurred by getting patients and keeping patients out of the hospital with the extra costs to the public incurred by the patients once they have been released.

The final paper reprinted in this section is a commentary on Friedman's paper by Wexler, an attorney who needs no introduction to readers of earlier Annual Reviews. Understandably enough, since they have shared so many experiences together, Wexler agrees closely with Friedman's central thesis and orientation: An intrusive behavioral procedure cannot be thrust upon an unwilling competent person but, nevertheless, under certain appropriate circumstances, the state may disregard the supposed desire of an incompetent client and apply behavioral techniques believed to be in his best interests. This position becomes a starting off point for a brief exposition of certain notions about competence and informed consent.

Wexler has addressed himself to related legal developments elsewhere and the interested reader is advised to refer to these directly (e.g., Wexler, 1975a; Wexler, 1975b). As to be expected in areas of rapidly changing social attitudes and scientific and technological advances, the law—particularly as embodied in Supreme Court pronouncements—lags appreciably behind the pulse of the public. At present, this lag is clearly evident in the field of mental health. For example, while the Supreme Court is still pondering for the first time whether confined mental patients have a constitutionally recognized right to treatment, public attention is shifting to the question of whether patients and prisoners have a right to refuse some of the more frightening therapies that are currently dramatized in the popular press. It is such intrinsic concerns which become of increasing relevance to forward looking attorneys and mental health specialists as well as the direct issues themselves. Ultimately, it is the prevailing values of our society which will determine which direction such issues will take. And it is our responsibility as individuals to evaluate and contribute to these values.

SECTION I: ETHICS, LAW AND MODELS OF MAN

1

BEHAVIOR THEORY AND THE MODELS OF MAN

Albert Bandura

Department of Psychology
Stanford University

The views about the nature of man conveyed by behavior theory require critical examination on conceptual and social grounds. What we believe man to be affects which aspects of human functioning we study most thoroughly and which we disregard. Premises thus delimit research and are, in turn, shaped by it. As knowledge gained through study is put into practice, the images of man on which social technologies rest have even vaster implications. This is nowhere better illustrated than in growing public concern over manipulation and control by psychological methods. Some of these fears arise from expectations that improved means of influence will inevitably be misused. Other apprehensions are aroused by exaggerated claims of psychological power couched in the language of manipulation and authoritarian control. But most fears stem from views of behaviorism, articulated by popular writers and by theorists themselves, that are disputed by the empirical facts of human behavior.

In the minds of the general public, and of many within our own discipline, behavior theory is equated with "conditioning." Over the

Reprinted with permission from *American Psychologist*, Vol. 29, No. 12, December, 1974, 859-869. Copyright 1974, American Psychological Association.

Presidential Address presented at the meeting of the American Psychological Association, New Orleans, August 1974.

years, the terms *behaviorism* and *conditioning* have come to be associated with odious imagery, including salivating dogs, puppetry, and animalistic manipulation. As a result, those who wish to disparage ideas or practices they hold in disfavor need only to label them as behavioristic or as Pavlovian precursors of a totalitarian state.

Contrary to popular belief, the fabled reflexive conditioning in humans is largely a myth. *Conditioning* is simply a descriptive term for learning through paired experiences, not an explanation of how the changes come about. Originally, conditioning was assumed to occur automatically. On closer examination it turned out to be cognitively mediated. People do not learn despite repetitive paired experiences unless they recognize that events are correlated (Dawson & Furedy, 1974; Grings, 1973). So-called conditioned reactions are largely self-activated on the basis of learned expectations rather than automatically evoked. The critical factor, therefore, is not that events occur together in time, but that people learn to predict them and to summon up appropriate anticipatory reactions.

The capacity to learn from correlated experiences reflects sensitivity, but because Pavlov first demonstrated the phenomenon with a dog, it has come to be regarded as a base animalistic process. Had he chosen to study physiological hyperactivity in humans to cues associated with stress, or the development of empathetic reactions to expressions of suffering, conditioning would have been treated in a more enlightened way. To expect people to remain unaffected by events that are frightening, humiliating, disgusting, sad, or pleasurable is to require that they be less than human. Although negative effects such as fears and dislikes can arise from paired experiences of a direct or vicarious sort, so do some of the enobling qualities of man. The pejorative accounts of learning principles, which appear with regularity in professional and lay publications, degrade both the science of psychology and the audiences that the offensive rhetoric is designed to sway.

It is well documented that behavior is influenced by its consequences much of the time. The image of man that this principle connotes depends on the types of consequences that are acknowledged and on an understanding of how they operate. In theories that recognize only the role of proximate external consequences and contend they shape behavior automatically, people appear as mechanical pawns of environmental forces. But external consequences, influential as they often are, are not the sole determinants of human behavior, nor do they operate automatically.

Response consequences serve several functions. First, they impart information. By observing the effects of their actions individuals eventually discern which behaviors are appropriate in which settings. The acquired information then serves as a guide for action. Contrary to the mechanistic metaphors, outcomes change behavior in humans through the intervening influence of thought.

Consequences motivate, through their incentive value, as well as inform. By representing foreseeable outcomes symbolically, future consequences can be converted into current motivators of behavior. Many of the things we do are designed to gain anticipated benefits and to avert future trouble. Our choices of action are largely under anticipatory control. The widely accepted dictum that man is ruled by response consequences thus fares better for anticipated than for actual consequences. Consider behavior on a fixed-ratio schedule (say, 50:1) in which only every fiftieth response is reinforced. Since 96 percent of the outcomes are extinctive and only 4 percent are reinforcing, behavior is maintained despite its dissuading consequences. As people are exposed to variations in frequency and predictability of reinforcement, they behave on the basis of the outcomes they expect to prevail on future occasions. When belief differs from actuality, which is not uncommon, behavior is weakly controlled by its actual consequences until repeated experience instills realistic expectations (Bandura, 1971b; Kaufman, Baron, & Kopp, 1966).

Had humans been ruled solely by instant consequences, they would have long become museum pieces among the extinct species. Not that our future is unquestionably secure. The immediate rewards of consumptive life-styles vigorously promoted for short-term profit jeopardize man's long-term chances of survival. But immediate consequences, unless unusually powerful, do not necessarily outweigh deferred ones (Mischel, 1974). Our descendants shall continue to have a future only because those who foresee the aversive long-term consequences of current practices mobilize public support for contingencies that favor survival behavior. Hazardous pesticides, for example, are usually banned before populations suffer maladies from toxic residues. The information-processing capacities with which humans are endowed provide the basis for insightful behavior. Their capacity to bring remote consequences to bear on current behavior by anticipatory thought supports foresightful action.

Explanations of reinforcement originally assumed that consequences increase behavior without conscious involvement. The still prevalent notion that reinforcers can operate insidiously arouses fears that improved techniques of reinforcement will enable authorities to manipulate people without their knowledge or consent. Although the empirical issue is not yet completely resolved, there is little evidence that rewards function as automatic strengtheners of human conduct. Behavior is not much affected by its consequences without awareness of what is being reinforced (Bandura, 1969; Dulany, 1968). After individuals discern the instrumental relation between action and outcome, contingent rewards may produce accommodating or oppositional behavior depending on how they value the incentives, the influencers and the behavior itself, and how others respond. Thus reinforcement, as it has become better understood, has changed from a mechanical strengthener of conduct to an informative and motivating influence.

People do not function in isolation. As social beings, they observe the conduct of others and the occasions on which it is rewarded, disregarded, or punished. They can therefore profit from observed consequences as well as from their own direct experiences (Bandura, 1971c). Acknowledgment of vicarious reinforcement introduces another human dimension —namely, evaluative capacities—into the operation of reinforcement influences. People weigh consequences to themselves against those accruing to others for similar behavior. The same outcome can thus become a reward or a punishment depending upon the referents used for social comparison.

Human conduct is better explained by the relational influence of observed and direct consequences than by either factor alone. However, behavior is not fully predictable from a relational coefficient because social justifications alter the impact of outcome disparities. Inequitable reinforcement is willingly accepted when people are graded by custom into social ranks and rewarded according to position rather than by performance. Arbitrary inequities are also likely to be tolerated if the underrewarded are led to believe they possess attributes that make them less deserving of equal treatment. Persuasively justified inequities have more detrimental personal effects than acknowledged unfairness because they foster self-devaluation in the maltreated. Negative reactions to inequitable reinforcement, which is acknowledged to be unwarranted, can likely be diminished by temporizing. If people are led to expect that unfair treatment will be corrected within the foreseeable future, it becomes less aversive to them.

Theories that explain human behavior as the product of external rewards and punishments present a truncated image of man because people partly regulate their actions by self-produced consequences (Bandura, 1971c; Thoresen & Mahoney, 1973). Example and precept impart standards of conduct that serve as the basis for self-reinforcing reactions.

The development of self-reactive functions gives humans a capacity for self-direction. They do things that give rise to self-satisfaction and self-worth, and they refrain from behaving in ways that evoke self-punishment.

After self-reinforcing functions are acquired, a given act produces two sets of consequences: self-evaluative reactions and external outcomes. Personal and external sources of reinforcement may operate as supplementary or as opposing influences on behavior. Thus, for example, individuals commonly experience conflicts when rewarded for conduct they personally devalue. When self-condemning consequences outweigh rewarding inducements, external influences are relatively ineffective. On the other hand, if certain courses of action produce stronger rewards than self-censure, the result is cheerless compliance. Losses in self-respect for devalued conduct can be abated, however, by self-exonerating justifications. I shall return to this issue shortly.

Another type of conflict between external and self-produced consequences arises when individuals are punished for behavior they regard highly. Principled dissenters and nonconformists often find themselves in this predicament. Personally valued conduct is expressed provided its costs are not too high. Should the threatened consequences be severe, one inhibits self-praiseworthy acts under high risk of penalty but readily performs them when the chances of punishment are reduced. There are individuals, however, whose sense of self-worth is so strongly invested in certain convictions that they will submit to prolonged maltreatment rather than accede to what they regard as unjust or immoral.

External consequences exert greatest influence on behavior when they are compatible with those that are self-produced. These conditions obtain when rewardable acts are a source of self-pride and punishable ones are self-censured. To enhance compatiblility between personal and social influences, people select associates who share similar standards of conduct and thus ensure social support for their own system of self-reinforcement.

Individualistic theories of moral action assume that internalization of behavioral standards creates a permanent control mechanism within the person. Restraints of conscience thereafter operate as enduring controls over reprehensible conduct. The testimony of human behavior, however, contradicts this view. Much human maltreatment and suffering are, in fact, inflicted by otherwise decent moral people. And some of the most striking changes in moral conduct, as evidenced, for example, in political and military violence, are achieved without altering personality structures or moral standards. Personal control is clearly more complex and flexible than the theorizing implies.

Although self-reinforcing influences serve as regulators of conduct, they can be dissociated from censurable deeds by self-exonerating practices (Bandura, 1973). One device is to make inhumane behavior personally and socially acceptable by defining it in terms of high moral principle. People do not act in ways they ordinarily consider evil or destructive until such activities are construed as serving moral purposes. Over the years, much cruelty has been perpetrated in the name of religious principles, righteous ideologies, and regulatory sanctions. In the transactions of everyday life, euphemistic labeling serves as a handy linguistic device for masking reprehensible activities or according them a respectable status. Self-deplored conduct can also be made benign by contrasting it with more flagrant inhumanities. Moral justifications and palliative comparisons are especially effective because they not only eliminate self-generated deterrents but engage self-reward in the service of reprehensible conduct. What was morally unacceptable becomes a source of self-pride.

A common dissociative practice is to obscure or distort the relationship between one's actions and the effects they cause. People will perform behavior they normally repudiate if a legitimate authority sanctions it and acknowledges responsibility for its consequences. By displacing responsibility elsewhere, participants do not hold themselves accountable for what they do and are thus spared self-prohibiting reactions. Exemption from self-censure can be facilitated additionally by diffusing responsibility for culpable behavior. Through division of labor, division of decision making, and collective action, people can contribute to detrimental practices without feeling personal responsibility or self-disapproval.

Attribution of blame to the victim is still another exonerative expedient. Victims are faulted for bringing maltreatment on themselves, or extraordinary circumstances are invoked as justifications for questionable conduct. One need not engage in self-reproof for committing acts prescribed by circumstances. A further means of weakening self-punishment is to dehumanize the victim. Inflicting harm upon people who are regarded as subhuman or debased is less likely to arouse self-reproof than if they are looked upon as human beings with sensitivities.

There are other self-disinhibiting maneuvers that operate by misrepresenting the consequences of actions. As long as detrimental effects are ignored or minimized, there is little reason for self-censure. If consequences are not easily distortable, distress over conduct that conflicts with self-evaluative standards can be reduced by selectively remembering the benefits and forgetting the harm of one's acts.

Given the variety of self-disinhibiting devices, a society cannot rely on control by conscience to ensure moral and ethical conduct. Though personal control ordinarily serves as a self-directive force, it can be nullified by social sanctions conducive to destructiveness. Indoctrination and social justifications give meaning to events and create anticipations that determine one's actions. Control through information, which is rooted in cognitive processes, is more pervasive and powerful than conditioning through contiguity of events. Cultivation of humaneness therefore requires, in addition to benevolent personal codes, safeguards built into social systems that counteract detrimental sanctioning practices and uphold compassionate behavior.

A conceptual orientation not only prescribes what facets of man will be studied in depth but also how one goes about changing human behavior. Early applications of reinforcement principles, for example, were guided by the then prevalent belief that consequences alter behavior automatically and unconsciously. Since the process supposedly operated mechanically, the reinforcers had to occur instantly to be effective. Participants in change programs were, therefore, uninformed about why they were being reinforced, and, in an effort to ensure immediacy of effects, reinforcers were presented intrusively as soon as the requisite responses were emitted. The net effect was a tedious shaping process that produced, at best, mediocre results in an ethically questionable manner. In many public and professional circles, reinforcement still connotes furtive control even though reinforcement theory and practices have progressed well beyond this level.

Realization that reinforcement is an unarticulated way of designing appropriate conduct prompted the use of cognitive factors in the modification of behavior. Not surprisingly, people change more rapidly if told what behaviors are rewardable and punishable than if they have to discover it from observing the consequences of their actions. Competencies that are not already within their repertoires can be developed with greater ease through the aid of instruction and modeling than by relying solely on the successes and failures of unguided performance.

As further research revealed that reinforcers function as motivators, consequences were recognized as sources of motivation that depend heavily for their effectiveness upon the incentive preferences of those undergoing change. Hence, people do not indiscriminately absorb the influences that impinge upon them. Outcomes resulting from actions need not necessarily occur instantly. Humans can cognitively bridge delays between behavior and subsequent reinforcers without impairing the efficacy of incentive operations.

At this second evolutionary stage, reinforcement practices changed from unilateral control to social contracting. Positive arrangements affirm that if individuals do certain things they are entitled to certain rewards and privileges. In the case of negative sanctions, reprehensible conduct carries punishment costs. The process is portrayed in reinforcement terms, but the practice is that of social exchange. Most social interactions are, of course, governed by conditional agreements, though they usually are not couched in the language of reinforcement. Describing them differently does not change their nature, however.

Contingencies vary in the human qualities they embody and in the voice individuals have in decisions concerning the social arrangements that affect their lives. Reflecting the salient values of our society, reinforcement practices have traditionally favored utilitarian forms of behavior. But conditions are changing. With growing reservations about materialistic life-styles, reinforcement practices are being increasingly used to cultivate personal potentialities and humanistic qualities. These emerging changes in value commitments will probably accelerate as people devote fewer hours to working for income and have more leisure time for self-development.

Another change of some consequence is the renewed concern for individual rights. People are seeking a collaborative role in the development of social contingencies that affect the course and quality of their lives. As part of this social trend, even the actions taken in the name of psychotherapy are being examined for their ethics and social purposes. These concerns have provided the impetus for prescripts to ensure that reinforcement techniques are used in the service of human betterment rather than as instruments of social control.

A closely related issue is the relative attention devoted to changing individuals or to altering the institutions of society to enrich life. If psychologists are to have a significant impact on common problems of life, they must apply their corrective measures to detrimental societal practices rather than limit themselves to treating the casualties of these practices. This, of course, is easier said than done. Practitioners, whatever their specialty, are reinforced more powerfully for using their knowledge and skills in the service of existing operations than for changing them. Socially oriented efforts are hard to sustain under inadequate reinforcement supports.

The methods of change discussed thus far draw heavily upon external consequences of action. Evidence that people can exercise some control over their own behavior provided the impetus for further changes in reinforcement practices. Interest began to shift from managing conduct to developing skills in self-regulation. In the latter approach, control is vested to a large extent in the hands of individuals themselves: They arrange the environmental inducements for desired behavior; they evaluate their own performances; and they serve as their own reinforcing agents (Goldfried & Merbaum, 1973; Mahoney & Thoresen, 1974). To be sure, the self-reinforcing functions are created and occasionally supported by external influences. Having external origins, however, does not refute the fact that, once established, self-influence partly determines what actions one performs. Citing historical determinants of a generalizable function cannot substitute for contemporaneous influences arising through exercise of that function.

The recognition of self-directing capacities represents a substantial departure from exclusive reliance upon environmental control. But the emerging self-influence practices are still closely rooted in physical transactions—the self-administered consequences are, for the most part, material. Eventually changes in form, as well as source, of reinforcement will appear as the insufficiency of material outcomes is acknowledged. Most people value their self-respect above commodities. They rely extensively on their own self-demands and self-approval as guides for conduct. To ignore the influential role of covert self-reinforcement in the regulation of behavior is to disavow a uniquely human capacity of man.

Proponents who recognize only external consequences restrict their research and practice to such influences and thus generate evidence that reinforces their conceptions. Those who acknowledge personal influences as well tend to select methods that reveal and promote self-directing capabilities in man. The view of man embodied in behavioral technologies is therefore more than a philosophical issue. It affects which human potentialities will be cultivated and which will be under-developed.

The preceding remarks addressed the need to broaden the scope of research into the reinforcement processes regulating human behavior. Much the same might be said for the ways in which human learning is conceptualized and investigated. Our theories have been incredibly slow in acknowledging that man can learn by observation as well as by direct experience. This is another example of how steadfast adherence to orthodox paradigms makes it difficult to transcend the confines of conceptual commitment. Having renounced cognitive determinants, early proponents of behaviorism advanced the doctrine that learning can occur only by performing responses and experiencing their effects. This legacy is still very much with us. The rudimentary form of learning based on direct experience has been exhaustively studied whereas the more pervasive and powerful mode of learning by observation is largely ignored. A shift of emphasis is needed.

The capacity to represent modeled activities symbolically enables man to acquire new patterns of behavior observationally without reinforced enactment. From observing others, one forms an idea of how certain behavior is performed, and on later occasions the coded information serves as a guide for action. Indeed, research conducted within the framework of social learning theory shows that virtually all learning phenomena resulting from direct experience can occur on a vicarious basis by observing other people's behavior and its consequences for them (Bandura, 1969). The abbreviation of the acquisition process through observational learning is, of course, vital for both development and survival. Modeling reduces the burden of time-consuming performance of inappropriate responses. Since errors can produce costly, if not fatal, consequences, the prospects of survival would be slim indeed if people had to rely solely on the effects of their actions to inform them about what to do.

In many instances the behavior being modeled must be learned in essentially the same form. Driving automobiles, skiing, and performing surgery, for example, permit little, if any, departure from essential practices. In addition to transmitting particular response patterns, however, modeling influences can create generative and innovative behavior. In the latter process, observers abstract common features from seemingly diverse responses and formulate generative rules of behavior that enable them to go beyond what they have seen or heard. By synthesizing features of different models into new amalgams, observers can achieve through modeling novel styles of thought and conduct. Once initiated, experiences with the new forms create further evolutionary changes. A partial departure from tradition eventually becomes a new direction.

Some of the limitations commonly ascribed to behavior theory are based on the mistaken belief that modeling can produce at best mimicry of specific acts. This view is disputed by growing evidence that abstract modeling is a highly effective means of inducing rule-governed cognitive behavior (Bandura, 1971a, Zimmerman & Rosenthal, 1974). On the basis of observationally derived rules, people alter their judgmental orientations, conceptual schemes, linguistic styles, information-processing strategies, as well as other forms of cognitive functioning. Nevertheless, faulty evaluations continue to be mistaken for weaknesses inherent in theory.

Observational learning has recently come to be accepted more widely, but some theorists are willing to grant it full scientific respectability only if it is reduced to performance terms. As a result, enactment paradigms are used which are rooted in the traditional assumption that responses must be performed before they can be learned. Instant reproduction of modeled responses is favored, thereby minimizing dependence upon cognitive functions which play an especially influential role when retention over time is required. The issue of whether reinforcement enhances modeling is pursued to the neglect of the more interesting question of whether one can keep people from learning what they have seen.

When learning is investigated through observational paradigms, a broader range of determinants and intervening mechanisms gains prominence. Learning by observation is governed by four component processes: (a) attentional functions regulate sensory input and perception of modeled actions; (b) through coding and symbolic rehearsal, transitory experiences are transformed for memory representation into enduring performance guides; (c) motor reproduction processes govern the integration of constituent acts into new response patterns; and (d) incentive or motivational processes determine whether observationally acquired responses will be performed. Studied from this perspective, observational learning emerges as an actively judgmental and constructive, rather than a mechanical copying, process.

Because observational learning entails several subfunctions that evolve with maturation and experience, it obviously depends upon prior development. Differences in theoretical perspectives prescribe different methodologies for studying how the capacity for observational learning itself is acquired. When modeling is conceptualized in terms of formation of stimulus-response linkages, efforts are aimed at increasing the probability of imitative responses through reinforcement. Modeling can be increased by rewarding matching behavior, but such demonstrations are not of much help in identifying what exactly is being acquired during the process, or in explaining imitation failures under favorable conditions of reinforcement. From a social learning view, the capability for observational learning is developed by acquiring skill in discriminative observation, in memory encoding, in coordinating ideomotor and sensorimotor systems, and in judging probable consequences for matching behavior.

Understanding how people learn to imitate becomes a matter of under-standing how the requisite subfunctions develop and operate. Capacity for observational learning is restricted by deficits, and expanded by improvements, in its component functions.

Over the years, proponents of the more radical forms of behaviorism not only disclaimed interest in mentation but also marshaled numerous reasons why cognitive events are inadmissible in causal analyses. It was, and still is, argued that cognitions are inaccessible except through untrustworthy self-reports, they are inferences from effects, they are epiphenomenal, or they are simply fictional. Advances in experimental analysis of behavior, it was claimed, would eventually show them to be unnecessary. Empirical evidence, however, has shown the opposite to be true. A large body of research now exists in which cognition is activated instructionally with impressive results. People learn and retain much better by using cognitive aids that they generate than by repetitive reinforced performance (Anderson & Bower, 1973; Bandura, 1971a). With growing evidence that cognition has causal influence in behavior, the arguments against cognitive determinants are losing their force.

These recent developments have shifted emphasis from the study of response learning to analyses of memory and cognition. From this effort we have gained a better understanding of the mechanisms whereby information is acquired, stored, and retrieved. There is more to learning, however, than the acquisition and retention of information. Behavioristic theories addressed themselves to performance but deemphasized internal determinants, whereas the cognitive approaches remain immersed in thought but divorced from conduct. In a complete account of human behavior, internal processes must eventually be tied to action. Hence, explanations of how information eventuates in skilled performance must additionally be concerned with the organization and regulation of behavior. Social learning includes within its framework both the processes internal to the organism as well as performance-related determinants.

Speculations about man's nature inevitably raise the fundamental issues of determinism and human freedom. In examining these questions it is essential to distinguish between the metaphysical and the social aspects of freedom. Many of the heated disputes on this topic arise as much, if not more, from confusion over the dimensions of freedom being discussed as from disagreements over the doctrine of determinism.

Let us first consider freedom in the social sense. Whether freedom is an illusion, as some writers maintain, or a social reality of considerable importance depends upon the meaning given to it. Within the social learning framework, freedom is defined in terms of the number of options available to people and the right to exercise them. The more behavioral alternatives and social prerogatives people have, the greater is their freedom of action.

Personal freedom can be limited in many different ways. Behavioral deficits restrict possible choices and otherwise curtail opportunities to realize one's preferences. Freedom can therefore be expanded by cultivating competencies. Self-restraints arising from unwarranted fears and stringent self-censure restrict the effective range of activities that individuals can engage in or even contemplate. Here freedom is restored by eliminating dysfunctional self-restraints.

In maximizing freedom a society must place some limits on conduct because complete license for any individual is likely to encroach on the freedom of others. Societal prohibitions against behavior that is socially injurious create additional curbs on conduct. Conflicts often arise over behavioral restrictions when many members of society question conventional customs and when legal sanctions are used more to enforce a particular brand of morality than to prohibit socially detrimental conduct.

The issue of whether individuals should be allowed to engage in activities that are self-injurious but not detrimental to society has been debated vigorously over the years. Prohibitionists argue that it is difficult for a person, other than a recluse, to impair himself without inflicting secondary harm on others. Should self-injury produce incapacities, society usually ends up bearing the treatment and subsistence costs. Libertarians do not find such arguments sufficiently convincing to justify a specific prohibition because some of the self-injurious activities that society approves may be as bad or worse than those it outlaws. Normative changes over time regarding private conduct tend to favor an individualistic ethic. Consequently, many activities that were formerly prohibited by law have been exempted from legal sanctions.

Some groups have their freedom curtailed by socially condoned discrimination. Here, the alternatives available to a person are limited by skin color, sex, religion, ethnic background, or social class, regardless of capabilities. When self-determination is prejudicially restricted, those who are subordinated remove inequities by altering practices that compromise or temporize the professed values of society.

Freedom deals with rights as well as options and behavioral restraints. Man's struggle for freedom is principally aimed at structuring societal contingencies so that certain forms of behavior are exempted from aversive control. After protective laws are built into the system, there are

certain things that a society may not do to an individual, however much
it might like to. Legal prohibitions on societal control create freedoms
that are realities, not simply feelings or states of mind. Societies differ
in their institutions of freedom and in the number and types of behaviors
that are officially exempted from punitive control. Social systems that
protect journalists from punitive control, for example, are freer than
those that allow authoritative power to be used to silence critics or their
vehicles of expression. Societies that possess an independent judiciary
ensure greater social freedom than those that do not.

In philosophical discourses, freedom is often considered antithetical
to determinism. When defined in terms of options and rights, there is no
incompatibility of freedom and determinism. From this perspective,
freedom is not conceived negatively as the absence of influences or
simply the lack of external constraints. Rather, it is defined positively in
terms of the skills at one's command and the exercise of self-influence
upon which choice of action depends.

Psychological analyses of freedom eventually lead to discourses on the
metaphysics of determinism. Are people partial determiners of their own
behavior, or are they ruled exclusively by forces beyond their control?
The long-standing debate over this issue has been enlivened by Skinner's
(1971) contention that, apart from genetic contributions, human behavior
is controlled solely by environmental contingencies, for example, "A
person does not act upon the world, the world acts upon him" (p. 211).
A major problem with this type of analysis is that it depicts the environment as an autonomous force that automatically shapes and controls
behavior. Environments have causes as do behaviors. For the most part,
the environment is only a potentiality until actualized and fashioned by
appropriate actions. Books do not influence people unless someone writes
them and others select and read them. Rewards and punishments remain
in abeyance until prompted by appropriate performances.

It is true that behavior is regulated by its contingencies, but the contingencies are partly of a person's own making. By their actions, people
play an active role in producing the reinforcing contingencies that impinge upon them. Thus, behavior partly creates the environment, and
the environment influences the behavior in a reciprocal fashion. To the
oft-repeated dictum, change contingencies and you change behavior,
should be added the reciprocal side, change behavior and you change the
contingencies.

The image of man's efficacy that emerges from psychological research
depends upon which aspect of the reciprocal control system one selects

for analysis. In the paradigm favoring environmental control, investigators analyze how environmental contingencies change behavior [B = f (E)]. The personal control paradigm, on the other hand, examines how behavior determines the environment [E = f (B)]. Behavior is the effect in the former case, and the cause in the latter. Although the reciprocal sources of influence are separable for experimental purposes, in everyday life two-way control operates concurrently. In ongoing interchanges, one and the same event can thus be a stimulus, a response, or an environmental reinforcer depending upon the place in the sequence at which the analysis arbitrarily begins.

A survey of the literature on reinforcement confirms the extent to which we have become captives of a one-sided paradigm to map a bidirectional process. Environmental control is overstudied, whereas personal control has been relatively neglected. To cite but one example, there exist countless demonstrations of how behavior varies under different schedules of reinforcement, but one looks in vain for studies of how people, either individually or by collective action, succeed in fashioning reinforcement schedules to their own liking. The dearth of research on personal control is not because people exert no influence on their environment or because such efforts are without effect. Quite the contrary. Behavior is one of the more influential determinants of future contingencies. As analyses of sequential interchanges reveal, aggressive individuals actualize through their conduct a hostile environment, whereas those who display friendly responsiveness produce an amicable social milieu within the same setting (Rausch, 1965). We are all acquainted with problem-prone individuals who, through their aversive conduct, predictably breed negative social climates wherever they go.

It should be noted that some of the doctrines ascribing preeminent control to the environment are ultimately qualified by acknowledgment that man can exercise some measures of countercontrol (Skinner, 1971). The notion of reciprocal interaction, however, goes considerably beyond the concept of countercontrol. Countercontrol portrays the environment as an instigating force to which individuals react. As we have already seen, people activate and create environments as well as rebut them.

People may be considered partially free insofar as they can influence future conditions by managing their own behavior. Granted that selection of particular courses of action from available alternatives is itself determined, individuals can nevertheless exert some control over the factors that govern their choices. In philosophical analyses all events can be submitted to an infinite regression of causes. Such discussions usually emphasize how man's actions are determined by prior conditions but neglect the reciprocal part of the process showing that the conditions themselves are partly determined by man's prior actions. Applications of self-control practices demonstrate that people are able to regulate their own behavior in preferred directions by arranging environmental conditions most likely to elicit it and administering self-reinforcing consequences to sustain it. They may be told how to do it and initially be given some external support for their efforts, but self-produced influences contribute significantly to future goal attainment.

To contend, as environmental determinists often do, that people are controlled by external forces and then to advocate that they redesign their society by applying behavioral technology undermines the basic premise of the argument. If humans were in fact incapable of influencing their own actions, they could describe and predict environmental events but hardly exercise any intentional control over them. When it comes to advocacy of social change, however, thoroughgoing environmental determinants become ardent exponents of man's power to transform environments in pursuit of a better life.

In backward causal analyses, conditions are usually portrayed as ruling man, whereas forward deterministic analyses of goal setting and attainment reveal how people can shape conditions for their purposes. Some are better at it than others. The greater the foresight, proficiency, and self-influence, all of which are acquirable skills, the greater the progress toward their goals. Because of the capacity for reciprocal influence, people are at least partial architects of their own destinies. It is not determinism that is in dispute, but whether it is treated as a one-way or a two-way control process. Considering the interdependence of behavior and enivronmental conditions, determinism does not imply the fatalistic view that man is but a pawn of external influences.

Psychological perspectives on determinism, like other aspects of theorizing, influence the nature and scope of social practice. Environmental determinists are apt to use their methods primarily in the service of institutionally prescribed patterns of behavior. Personal determinists are more inclined to cultivate self-directing potentialities in man. The latter behavioral approach and humanism have much in common. Behavioral theorists, however, recognize that "self-actualization" is by no means confined to human virtues. People have numerous potentialities that can be actualized for good or ill. Over the years, man has suffered considerably at the hands of self-actualized tyrants. A self-centered ethic of self-realization must therefore be tempered by concern for the social consequences of one's conduct. Behaviorists generally emphasize environmental sources of control, whereas humanists tend to restrict their interest to personal control. Social learning encompasses both aspects of the bidirectional influence process.

When the environment is regarded as an autonomous rather than as an influenceable determinant of behavior, valuation of dignifying human qualities and accomplishments is diminished. If inventiveness emanates from external circumstances, it is environments that should be credited for people's achievements and chastised for their failings or inhumanities. Contrary to the unilateral view, human accomplishments result from reciprocal interaction of external circumstances with a host of personal determinants including endowed potentialities, acquired competencies, reflective thought, and a high level of self-initiative.

Musical composers, for example, help to shape tastes by their creative efforts, and the public in turn supports their performances until advocates of new styles generate new public preferences. Each succeeding form of artistry results from a similar two-way influence process for which neither artisans nor circumstances deserve sole credit.

Superior accomplishments, whatever the field, require considerable self-disciplined application. After individuals adopt evaluative standards, they expend large amounts of time, on their own, improving their performances to the point of self-satisfaction. At this level of functioning, persistence in an endeavor is extensively under self-reinforcement control. Skills are perfected as much, or more, to please oneself as to please the public.

Without self-generated influences most innovative efforts would be difficult to sustain. This is because the unconventional is initially resisted and gradually accepted only as it proves functionally valuable or wins prestigious advocates. As a result, the early efforts of innovators bring rebuffs rather than rewards or recognition. In the history of creative endeavors, it is not uncommon for artists or composers to be scorned when they depart markedly from convention. Some gain recognition later in their careers. Others are sufficiently convinced of the worth in their work that they labor indefatigably even though their productions are negatively received during their lifetimes. Ideological and, to a lesser extent, technological advances follow similar courses. Most innovative endeavors receive occasional social support in early phases, but environmental conditions alone are not especially conducive to unconventional developments.

The operation of reciprocal influence also has bearing on the public concern that advances in psychological knowledge will produce an increase in human manipulation and control. A common response to such apprehensions is that all behavior is inevitably controlled. Social influence, therefore, is not a question of imposing controls where none existed before. This type of argument is valid in the sense that every act has a cause. But it is not the principle of causality that worries people. At the societal level, their misgivings center on the distribution of controlling power, the means and purposes for which it is used, and the availability of mechanisms for exercising reciprocal control over institutional practices. At the individual level, they are uneasy about the implications of psychotechnology in programming human relations.

Possible remedies for exploitative use of psychological techniques are usually discussed in terms of individual safeguards. Increased knowledge about modes of influence is prescribed as the best defense against manipulation. When people are informed about how behavior can be controlled, they tend to resist evident attempts at influence, thus making manipulation more difficult. Awareness, alone, however, is a weak countervalence.

Exploitation was successfully thwarted long before there existed a discipline of psychology to formulate principles and practices of behavior change. The most reliable source of opposition to manipulative control resides in the reciprocal consequences of human interactions. People resist being taken advantage of, and will continue to do so in the future, because compliant behavior produces unfavorable consequences for them. Sophisticated efforts at influence in no way reduce the aversiveness of yielding that is personally disadvantageous. Because of reciprocal consequences, no one is able to manipulate others at will, and everyone experiences some feeling of powerlessness in getting what they want. This is true at all levels of functioning, individual and collective. Parents cannot get their children to follow all their wishes, while children feel constrained by their parents from doing what they desire. At universities, the administrators, faculty, students, and alumni all feel that the other constituencies are unduly influential in promoting their self-interests but that one's own group is granted insufficient power to alter the institutional practices. In the political arena, Congress feels that the executive branch possesses excessive power, and conversely the executive branch feels thwarted in implementing its policies by congressional counteraction.

If protection against exploitation relied solely upon individual safeguards, people would be continually subjected to coercive pressures. Accordingly, they create institutional sanctions which set limits on the control of human behavior. The integrity of individuals is largely secured by societal safeguards that place constraints on improper means and foster reciprocity through balancing of interests.

Because individuals are conversant with psychological techniques does not grant them license to impose them on others. Industrialists, for example, know full well that productivity is higher when payment is made for amount of work completed rather than for length of time at work. Nevertheless, they cannot use the reinforcement system most advantageous to them. When industrialists commanded exclusive power, they paid workers at a piece-rate basis and hired and fired them at will. Reductions in power disparity between employers and employees resulted in a gradual weakening of performance requirements. As labor gained economic coercive strength through collective action, it was able to negotiate guaranteed wages on a daily, weekly, monthly, and eventually on an annual basis. At periodic intervals new contractual contingencies are adopted that are mutually acceptable. In the course of time, as better means of joint action are developed, other constituents will use their influence to modify arrangements that benefit certain segments of labor and industry but adversely affect the quality of life for other sectors of society.

As the previous example illustrates, improved knowledge of how to influence behavior does not necessarily raise the level of social control. If anything, the recent years have witnessed a diffusion of power, creating increased opportunities for reciprocal influence. This has enabled people to challenge social inequities, to effect changes in institutional practices, to counteract infringements on their rights, and to extend grievance procedures and due process of law to activities in social contexts that hitherto operated under unilateral control. The fact that more people wield power does not in and of itself ensure a humane society. In the final analysis, the important consideration is the purposes that power serves, however it might be distributed. Nor does knowledgeability about means of influence necessarily produce mechanical responsiveness in personal relations. Whatever their orientations, people model, expound, and reinforce what they value. Behavior arising out of purpose and commitment is no less genuine than improvised action.

The cliché of *1984*, and its more recent kin, diverts public attention from regulative influences and pose continual threats to human welfare. Most societies have instituted reciprocal systems that are protected by legal and social codes to prevent imperious control of human behavior. Although abuses of institutional power arise from time to time, it is not totalitarian rule that constitutes the impending peril. The hazards lie more in the intentional pursuit of personal gain, whether material or otherwise, than in control by coercion. Detrimental social practices arise and resist change, even within an open society, when many people benefit from them. To take a prevalent example, inequitable treatment of disadvantaged groups for private gain enjoys public support without requiring despotic rule.

Man, of course, has more to contend with than inhumanities toward one another. When the average consequences of otherwise rewarding lifestyles are delayed and imperceptibly cumulative, people become willful agents of their own self-destruction. Thus, if enough people benefit from activities that progressively degrade their environment, then, barring contravening influences, they will eventually destroy their environment. Although individuals contribute differently to the problem, the harmful consequences are borne by all. With growing populations and spread of lavish life-styles taxing finite resources, people will have to learn to cope with new realities of human existence.

Psychology cannot tell people how they ought to live their lives. It can, however, provide them with the means for effecting personal and social change. And it can aid them in making value choices by assessing the consequences of alternative life-styles and institutional arrangements. As a science concerned about the social consequences of its applications, psychology must also fulfill a broader obligation to society by bringing influence to bear on public policies to ensure that its findings are used in the service of human betterment.

REFERENCES

ANDERSON, J. R. & BOWER, G. H. *Human Associative Memory*. New York: Wiley, 1973.

BANDURA, A. *Principles of Behavior Modification*. New York: Holt, Rinehart & Winston, 1969.

BANDURA, A. (Ed.). *Psychological Modeling: Conflicting Theories*. Chicago: Aldine-Atherton, 1971. (a)

BANDURA, A. *Social Learning Theory*. New York: General Learning Press, 1971. (b)

BANDURA, A. Vicarious and self-reinforcement processes. In R. Glaser (Ed.), *The Nature of Reinforcement*. New York: Academic Press, 1971. (c)

BANDURA, A. *Aggression: A Social Learning Analysis*. Englewood Cliffs, N. J.: Prentice-Hall, 1973.

DAWSON, M. E. & FUREDY, J. J. The role of relational awareness in human autonomic discrimination classical conditioning. Unpublished manuscript, University of Toronto, 1974.

DULANY, D. E. Awareness, rules, and propositional control: A confrontation with S-R behavior theory. In T. R. Dixon & D. L. Horton (Eds.), *Verbal Behavior and General Behavior Theory*. Englewood Cliffs, N. J.: Prentice-Hall, 1968.

GOLDFRIED, M. R. & MERBAUM, M. (Eds.). *Behavior Change Through Self-Control*. New York: Holt, Rinehart & Winston, 1973.

GRINGS, W. W. The role of consciousness and cognition in autonomic behavior change. In F. J. McGuigan & R. Schoonover (Eds.), *The Psychophysiology of Thinking.* New York: Academic Press, 1973.

KAUFMAN, A., BARON, A., & KOPP, R. E. Some effects of instructions on human operant behavior. *Psychonomic Monograph Supplements,* 1966, 1, 243-250.

MAHONEY, M. J. & THORESEN, C. E. *Self-Control: Power to the Person.* Monterey, Calif.: Brooks/Cole, 1974.

MISCHEL, W. Processes in delay of gratification. In L. Berkowitz (Ed.), *Advances in Experimental Social Psychology.* Vol. 7. New York: Academic Press, 1974.

RAUSCH, H. L. Interaction sequences. *J. Pers. Soc. Psychol.,* 1965, 2, 487-499.

SKINNER, B. F. *Beyond Freedom and Dignity.* New York: Knopf, 1971.

THORESEN, C. E. & MAHONEY, M. J. *Behavioral Self-Control.* New York: Holt, Rinehart & Winston, 1973.

ZIMMERMAN, B. J. & ROSENTHAL, T. L. Observational learning of rule-governed behavior by children. *Psychol. Bull.,* 1974, 81, 29-42.

2

BEHAVIOR THERAPY AND CIVIL LIBERTIES

Gerald C. Davison

State University of New York at Stony Brook

and

Richard B. Stuart

University of British Columbia

For the past two hundred to three hundred years, science has played a major role in the development of western culture. Societies have capitulated to the demands of "progress" and have disregarded the costs as expedients to the industrial revolution (Etzioni, 1968, p. 208). Unfortunately, the costs have mounted quietly, and perhaps because the awareness has been so long delayed, there is a strong feeling today that the excesses of science must be curbed immediately and completely. Current efforts to promote the rights of people over technological advances are an expression of this concern. Because behavior therapy is viewed by many as a machinelike process for use in the suppression of individual freedom, it is being placed at the center of the current controversy when psychology is discussed.

Reprinted with permission from *American Psychologist*, Vol. 30, No. 7, July, 1975, 755-763. Copyright 1975, American Psychological Association.

This article was presented at the symposium "How Does Science Threaten Liberties" as part of the biannual meeting of the American Civil Liberties Union, Milwaukee, Wisconsin, June 14, 1974. The authors are, respectively, past-president and president of the Association for Advancement of Behavior Therapy.

WHAT IS BEHAVIOR THERAPY?

Rather than being a single unitary approach, behavior therapy encompasses a wide variety of goals and techniques. Some behavior therapeutic efforts are directed toward changing the ways in which the individual responds to forces in the environment. Other approaches aim to change the environment in ways that suit the individual. Person-changing goals are sought through respondent or operant conditioning techniques and cognitive restructuring procedures, singly or in combination. Environment-changing techniques typically rely on operant conditioning and may be targeted to individuals, small groups or total social institutions (cf., Kanfer & Phillips, 1969).

Despite the range of goals and techniques falling within the rubric of behavior therapy, behavioral treatments have several important unifying characteristics. First, the focal techniques have been derived from, or consistent with, research in experimental and social psychology. Second, their intrinsic goal is the alleviation of human suffering and the enhancement of human functioning. Third, when responsibly practiced, they always involve a systematic evaluation of treatment outcome using single-subject or group designs. Fourth, they typically involve reeducational efforts intended to facilitate improved functioning as measured by increased skill, independence, and satisfaction. Fifth, the practice of behavior therapy is typically guided by a contractual agreement between both client and therapist specifying the goals and methods of intervention (e.g., Stuart, in press-b).

The techniques used by behavior therapists have much in common with those employed by most psychological care-givers. Some of these techniques involve efforts by the therapist to overcome the client's anxiety or depression and to help to clarify the client's objectives. Other techniques involve efforts by the therapist to strengthen the client's resolve to make specific changes in his or her behavior outside of the therapeutic environment. In selected instances, the therapist may help the client to restructure his or her social environment so that desired changes can be more readily made and maintained.

The goals of properly conducted behavior therapy are always explicit. There are times when there may be differences between the values of the client, significant others (e.g., parents, teachers, spouses), and the therapist. When this happens, treatment efforts are held in abeyance until consensus is achieved. The general goals accepted by most behavior therapists place primary emphasis on the achievement of positive behavioral changes, that is, the acquisition of skills that are positively valued by both society and the client. In many instances, the emergence of these desired behaviors is itself sufficient to diminish the strength of problematic responses. At times, however, behavior therapists may go on to use extinction procedures, or in extreme cases, aversive procedures, in efforts to overcome recalcitrant problems. This has been well illustrated in the work of Lovaas and Simmons (1969), for example, who showed that a small number of electric shocks to the extremities, as part of a sound, comprehensive treatment program, can terminate the savage self-mutilation of some autistic children. But whether positive behaviors are strengthened or problematic behaviors are weakened, the treatment methods should always be as explicit and negotiable as the goals, and the outcome should always be objectively monitorable. It is this explication of goals, methods, and outcomes that places behavior therapists in a unique position of accountability.

CRITIQUES OF BEHAVIOR THERAPY

There are numerous dimensions to the current stage of siege of behavior therapy. The first—and weakest—results from a confusion of terms. Behavior therapists have at times referred to themselves as "behavior modifiers," and the terms *behavior therapy* and *behavior modification* are often used interchangeably. A problem arises, however, when behavior modification is used to refer only to the end product of an intervention, a change in the client's behavior. Every intervention approach—whether psychoanalysis or psychosurgery, pastoral counseling or nude encounter group therapy—has this objective. Therefore, as a result of a definitional error, behavior therapists have been taken to task for some practices that they themselves abhor. Therefore, use of the genetic term behavior therapy or specific terms such as *systematic desensitization* can help to overcome this confusion.

A second dimension of the current problem has been exacerbated by occasional intemperate statements by behavior therapists. Behavior therapy has achieved notable success in relieving psychological problems that had hitherto been essentially immune to intervention efforts, for example, the management of obesity (Stuart, in press-a). But the technology of behavior therapy remains, and doubtless always will remain, limited in its effectiveness (Davison, 1973). Unfortunately, some behavior therapists seem to have become giddy because of their achievements and have lost sight of their limitations. For example, one of our former colleagues has said: "We should reshape our society so that we would all be trained from birth to want to do what society wants us to do. We have the techniques now to do it" (McConnell, 1970, p. 74). Many behavior therapists would question whether we should be so shaped, and virtually all of us realize the futility of such an effort, given the incompleteness of our knowledge and the imprecision of our ability to apply that knowledge. But the damage done by statements such as this is inestimable, and their very occurrence may be seen as evidence of our inability to achieve the powers claimed by the self-appointed spokesmen.

A third dimension of the attack upon behavior therapy is an outgrowth of concern with the social regulation of individual behavior. Many of us object to the increasingly obvious intrusions upon individual thoughts, feelings, and actions by governments and industry through legislation, environmental management, the mass media, and the vast increase in the monitoring of individual actions through computerized data banks (see Miller, 1971). Reacting to the seemingly unchecked growth of these influences, many citizens have come to adopt positions that are highly critical of any and all behavior influence efforts.

But it is essential that advocates of individualism not lose sight of the determinism that is basic to a lawful society. This notion has been pointedly stated by Szasz (1970), in the following terms:

> Among the many foolish things Rousseau said, one of the most foolish, and most famous is: "Man is born free, and yet everywhere he is in chains." This highflown phrase obscures the nature of freedom. For if freedom is the ability to make uncoerced choices, then man is born in chains. And the challenge of life is liberation (p. 1).

Szasz has observed that in every social organization the interactions of individuals are self-limiting in the sense that the actions of one constrain the reactions of the other in predictable ways. The perpetuation of social organization depends on an orderliness in these mutual behavioral influence patterns.

This natural regulatory process often operates to the advantage of all concerned. But there is no assurance that the spontaneous pattern will always achieve the most beneficial possible option. When organizational influences do go astray, efforts to correct them are often the object of greater concern than the original abuse. Albert Bandura, past-president of the American Psychological Association and a leading figure in behavior therapy, has characterized the attacks on behavior as follows:

It is interesting to note that . . . the conditions that are undesign-
ably imposed upon others are generally regarded with favor, whereas
identical conditions created after thoughtful consideration of their
effects on others are often considered culpable. There exists no
enterprise [other than psychotherapy] which values incognizance so
highly, often at the expense of the client's welfare (Bandura, 1969,
p. 81).

Behavior therapists have often called for change when societal practice
deviates from ethical values and goals. For example, (a) in schools, they
have directed their efforts toward the introduction of more humanistic
procedures in order to make learning both more pleasant and more
fruitful (Ulrich, Stachnik, & Mabry, 1974); (b) in public assistance
programs, they have sought to reverse contingencies that result in sustained social dependence and the disruption of family life (Miller &
Miller, 1970); and (c) they have sought to replace institutionalization
with community treatments when possible (e.g., Phillips, Phillips, Fixsen,
& Wolf, 1971) or to humanize institutional practices while awaiting the
development of alternative services (e.g., Ayllon & Azrin, 1968). Hopefully,
this sense of social consciousness and responsibility will continue inasmuch as it represents the best present hope for institutional progress.*

Another attack on behavior therapy relates to its underlying model of
human behavior. Some of the principles of learning on which contemporary behavior therapy rests have been derived from laboratory research
with infrahuman organisms. Other principles have been derived from
experimentation in social psychology laboratories. Based upon both
avenues of research, hypotheses about the biological and environmental
determinants of human behavior have been formulated for testing in
applied research settings. Theories useful in the prediction of human
behavior have been developed, and it is upon the regularities suggested
by these theories that current behavior therapeutic practices are founded.

The model of human behavior that has emerged stresses the dynamic
interplay of biological factors and experiences in the past and present

---

* The authors recognize that some social institutions such as prisons and mental
hospitals are symptomatic of the breakdown of social processes. Some attorneys, such
as those in the National Prison Project of the American Civil Liberties Union, argue
cogently that such institutions should and must be closed at the earliest possible
moment. However, it seems to us that we do not yet have the technological competence to make this possible and that every effort must therefore be made to create the
most humane and socially constructive institutional environments possible while alternative approaches are being developed. It should also be borne in mind that existing institutions *already* are strong shapers of behavior. The question is not *whether*
to influence the behavior of involuntary residents but *how* and to *what ends*.

environments. The units of measure in this study of human behavior are observable events, of which some are monitorable psychophysiological reactions and overt actions and others are verbal reports about the individual's feelings, goals, interests, and desires. Further, it is recognized that although the individual is the focal point of persistent patterns of social influence, he can also respond with "countercontrol" so that emergent behavior is a consequence of the interplay between the behaviors of the individual and those with whom he or she interacts (Bandura, 1969; Davison, 1973).

Behavior therapy utilizes a mechanistic language, conceptualizing behavior in terms such as *stimulus, response, reinforcement,* and *shaping.* These metaphors convey a detached, objective, even cold-hearted orientation to human beings, suggesting to some that behavior therapy prevents or at least discourages practitioners from relating to other people as human beings. Inasmuch as behavior therapists are themselves only human beings, it would be rash to assert categorically that there are not some people using behavior therapy procedures who do not care about the feelings and integrity of the people with whom they are dealing. However, the basic point is that words like *stimulus* and *response* are best viewed as scientific metaphors useful in understanding behavior so as to increase our ability to help people. The principles arising from a functional analysis of behavior have been used to identify environmental events that control human behavior, focusing attention on efforts to change these events so that actions can be more personally satisfying and socially constructive.

Because many behavior therapy principles are derived from laboratory research with animals, some observers mistakenly infer that behavior therapists regard people as *nothing but* animals. This unfortunately misses the point of experimental work in a science. Laboratory experiments by definition attempt to isolate a phenomenon and study it under conditions that are more controlled than is the case in everyday life. To use a pigeon in an experiment rather than a human being and then to extrapolate the findings from the pigeon to human beings is to engage in *analogue* work. Based on these experiments, inferences are drawn about human behavior. When these inferences are validated in clinical experiments with humans, they contribute to our increased clinical competence. When cross-species validation does not occur, the results of the animal research are ignored. Animal studies therefore have heuristic rather than literal implications for behavior therapists.

BEHAVIOR THERAPY AND HUMAN RIGHTS

As a group, behavior therapists subscribe to the codes of ethics of the professions from which they are drawn. But the existence of ethical guidelines does not negate the need for constant sensitivity to ethical issues any more than it guarantees that all decisions by behavior therapists will always be in keeping with ethically responsible practice.

Perhaps because of their novelty, their potency, or their accountability, behavior therapy practices have been the subject of more vocal ethical questioning than has been true of other intervention techniques that have had similar aims. Although most prominently directed toward institutional practice, many of these concerns apply equally to the practice of behavior therapy in open settings. Because of their great importance, we would like to discuss four of these issues.

Absolute Versus Contingent Rights

When an individual is convicted of violating the law or when a judgment is rendered that he or she is mentally unfit for life in the open community, a process of involuntary institutionalization is often the consequence. We are among the many who seriously question the utility and justice of involuntary mental hospitalization (Davison & Neale, 1974; Ennis & Siegel, 1973; Stuart, 1969; Szasz, 1963). But society is painfully slow to recognize that institutions expected to reduce deviance often maintain or even intensify misconduct and self-defeating behavior by prisoners or patients. This delay, combined with a covert but ever present willingness to employ punitive strategies, a reluctance to draw on more expensive alternatives to institutional care (such as the establishment of greater socioeconomic equity), and the current unavailability of clearly validated alternative intervention methods, conspires to sustain the continued use of institutions. Therefore, scores of thousands of people will be denied their freedom through institutional confinement for many years. Thus, it is now essential to develop rehabilitative methods that are consistent with the protection of the rights of prisoners and patients. (We assume that the purpose of imprisonment is not merely to punish and deter. If rehabilitation, however defined, is truly an important goal, then one necessarily is concerned with the most humane, effective, and efficient ways to change behavior.)

Recent court decisions have recognized that residents in correctional and psychiatric institutions possess a set of constitutionally protected rights. With regard to prisons, Rothman (1973) observed that: "court rulings reflected . . . an awareness that inmates were not fundamentally different from citizens" (p. 15). *Rouse* v. *Cameron* (373 F.2d 451, D.C. Cir. 1966) initially affirmed mental patients' rights to treatment, and *Wyatt* v. *Stickney** extended this doctrine to the establishment of guidelines for therapeutic services. For example, the latter decision required that individual treatment plans be prepared for all patients, that the use of aversive procedures be reviewed by a Human Rights Committee, and that basic privileges be offered without the requirement that they be earned through participation in an institution-maintaining work force. The force of these rulings promises to guarantee to institutional populations those minimal rights that permit life with at least a modicum of dignity.**

In their attempt to expedite the rehabilitative function of institutions, some behavior therapists have sought to offer inmates and patients access to the amenities of life as consequences for constructive behavioral changes. This has meant the denial of these resources at earlier stages of the program with a gradual restoration of privileges as a consequence of progress. If these programs require participation in the institutional work force as a means of securing such amenities of life as the institution provides, they may be construed as involuntary servitude and would be in violation of the principle set forth in *Jobson* v. *Henne* (335 F. 2d 129, 2d Cir. 1966) and supported in *Wyatt* v. *Stickney*. Moreover, when the entry level of privileges in these programs falls below the level at which human dignity can be maintained (admittedly a subjective judgment in some instances), these programs will require immediate reformulation.

As a general rule, it can be stated that every therapeutic intervention should begin with the least intrusive procedure from which a positive outcome can reasonably be expected. This principle of "least severity" would apply to both community- and institution-based services (Morris, 1966). In both settings it would require the exposure of clients to the least possible risk and discomfort relative to the greatest possible expected benefit. In institutions it would require that inmates or patients enter intervention programs with a level of comfort no more severe than the institutional practice which it is intended to replace. This would require a careful judgment to which client groups, institutional adminis-

---

* 344 F. Supp. 387 (M.D. Ala. 1972), aff'd *sub nom Wyatt v Anderholt.*——F. 2d—— (5th Cir. Nov. 8, 1974).

** The major right to treatment case, *Donaldson* v. *O'Connor* (493 F. 2d 507, 5th Cir. 1974), is currently before the Supreme Court. Whether the Court upholds or reverses this trend remains to be seen.

trators, laymen in the community, and professionals would all have to contribute. And as Wexler (1973; Note 1) has noted, behavior therapists would be called on to use increasing ingenuity in their efforts to find meaningful incentives for behavior change within the context of the evolving guidelines for ethically and legally acceptable practice.

Choice of Goals

Working in institutional settings, behavior therapists have often been called upon to develop incentive systems that would increase the productivity of inmates and patients in prison industries and hospital maintenance programs. This has presumably been done to provide rehabilitative experiences and to offer some distraction from the monotony of institutional life. Following the *Wyatt* v. *Stickney* decision, and consistent with many advocates of bills of rights for prisoners and patients, two changes would appear to be necessary: first, the servitude implicit in these programs would have to be replaced by compensation at or above the federal minimum wage; and second, participation would have to be voluntary. If adopted, the tasks could remain the same but the compensation and consent process would be changed.

Wexler (1973) has argued, however, that the enactment of this requirement might work to the profound disadvantage of many mental patients (and, possibly, of inmates as well). They could suffer if institutional directors, interested in maximum efficiency, were to call upon outside employees to perform essential institution maintenance services, thus denying patients access to opportunities to acquire some skills that could enhance their employability upon discharge. Although Fairweather, Sanders, Maynard, Cressler, and Bleck (1969) have shown that patients with higher level abilities can successfully participate in more demanding work efforts, a large number of chronic patients do not function beyond a very minimal level. Therefore, implementation of the *Wyatt* v. *Stickney* provision could have the stultifying impact of dooming patients to continued idleness and the odious consequences of the stimulus deprivation that this implies.

The role of work programs in institutional settings can be considered from another viewpoint. Stuart (1971) has argued that two clusters of goals exist in correctional and psychiatric settings: 1) "minimal goals—those which seek to remove the problematic response which led to identification of the individual as deviant in the first place . . . [and 2)] optimal goals—those which seek to enhance the social functioning of the individual identified as a deviant" (p. 110). More recently, Robinson (1974) has suggested that offenses can be roughly dichotomized as to whether they cause harm to others. When there is such harm, he believes that the individual "can lay no moral claim to the right not to be changed" (p. 236). Combining these two views, changes in the aggressive behavior of those who have harmed others would seem to be a minimal goal, while changes in other behaviors of these individuals or behavior change for those who have not harmed others would seem to be optimal goals.

Given these dichotomies, some would argue that patients or prisoners can be required to undergo rehabilitative treatment aimed at the attainment of minimal goals. The logical conclusion of Robinson's argument, for example, is that the commission of an offense against society denies the offender of his or her rights to remain aloof from treatment. Others, however, would argue that institutionalized persons have a right to accept or reject treatment, recognizing that the rejection of treatment would often lead to the completion of a mandatory period of incarceration. This is likely to remain a hotly debated issue in the next several years as institutional services are subjected to ever more careful scrutiny. And clearly, every therapeutic decision would require careful attention to evolving moral and legal principles.

The Right to the Best Possible Validated Treatment

A series of recent court decisions promises to establish the "patient's right to treatment." The logic of these decisions is unquestionable: If society denies citizens their freedom, it is the responsibility of society to offer such intervention as can be reasonably expected to prepare them for the resumption of lawful, socially acceptable behavior in the community upon their release. The fact that institutional programs have been catastrophic failures (Stuart, 1970) is strong evidence that this service requirement has not been met.

In order to determine treatment effects, it is necessary to define precisely all relevant dimensions of service programs as well as their short- and long-range effects. This requires a continual process of descriptive and evaluative research extending beyond the end of confinement. But descriptive research, of obvious importance (albeit infrequent occurrence), is insufficient because positive results offer no assurance that a particular program is the most effective, least drastic alternative, nor do negative results suggest alternative strategies. Therefore, responsible program administrators may have an ethical responsibility to seek and compare the effectiveness of alternate programs.

Although the right to treatment may no longer be an issue, the concept of evaluative program research is very much under attack at this time. The guidelines for research that have been proposed by the National Institutes of Health (1974) would slow research efforts because of their very broad categorization of the risks associated with participation in research. The result of enactment of these guidelines in their present form would be unfortunate indeed because countless thousands of youths and adults might be detained in institutional settings in which they are exposed to profoundly deviance-producing conditions. Research that could yield new knowledge would be virtually stymied.

Therefore, it is our judgment that rather than regarding institutional evaluative research as a potential violation of resident rights, these descriptive and comparative research efforts should be *mandatory* aspects of responsible institutional management. Thus, contrary to the present thrust of public opinion, we regard the monitoring of existing programs and the search for more beneficial alternatives as activities necessary to ensure the basic rights of patients and inmates.

Much scientific experimentation involving human subjects involves a trade-off of basic values: expected gains for the community are traded off against potential injury to individuals. Progress in the alleviation or prevention of human suffering is the community good. Exposure to experimental injury and the denial of necessary services or compromise of the subjects' rights and/or dignity are the individual risks. On the other hand, the larger community faces the risk of the erosion of morality, "possibly caused by too ruthless a pursuit of scientific progress [which] would make its most dazzling triumphs not worth having" (Jonas, 1970, p. 28). And gains can accrue to the individual in terms of satisfaction derived from the opportunity to participate in social and scientific progress and/or direct gains from the experiments themselves. Therefore, both the community and the individual face the prospect of benefit and detriment resulting from scientific research. The outcome of the process depends on the rigor with which experiments are conceived and the ethical responsibility with which they are carried out.

Although behavior therapists and researchers may not always have used the best judgment with respect to ethical decision making, their record of responsibility is at least the equal of professionals working within other theoretical perspectives. One of the cornerstones of the rights of therapy clients and research subjects is the right to offer or to

TABLE 1

Guidelines for Procedures for Protection of Subject's Right to
Participate Only in Experiments of Own Choice

Level of risk	Likelihood of free consent	High potential benefit to subject		Low potential benefit to subject/ high potential benefit to society	
		Established procedure	Experimental procedure	Established procedure	Experimental procedure
Low risk	Great freedom	2-4	4	2-4	4-5
	Some coercion	5	5	5-6	7
High risk	Great freedom	4	5	5-6	7
	Some coercion	6	6	7	8

Note. The numbers in the table refer to a proposed hierarchy of protections of the consent-giving process. See text for a complete discussion.

withhold informed consent to treatment or research participation. This protection has been expressed by the Nuremberg Code, by the Declaration of Helsinki, and by other more recent statements by professional associations throughout the world. Behavior therapists have been in the forefront of those offering protection to clients, having pioneered the use of behavioral treatment contracts (e.g., Stuart, in press-b). In contrast, some difficulty has been experienced in applying the doctrine of consent to research participation because the blanket protection does not contain within it sufficient precision to permit individual decision making. An absolute dichotomy between consent or nonconsent to research participation has made difficult the kinds of discriminations that would allow this vital protection to be guaranteed. To help in providing guidelines for implementation of the consistent doctrine, we would like to suggest the following framework. It consists of a hierarchy of constraints upon the giving of consent and a set of institutional dimensions that would point to the use of each level in the hierarchy.

The first element in this approach is *a hierarchy of protections of the consent-giving process.* Identification of the steps at each level of the hierarchy should be discussed by all concerned. One possible delineation of key points on this hierarchy, ranging from minimal to maximal protection, could take the following form:

1. *No consent by the subject is necessary.* It is sufficient to assume that the investigator, abiding by ethical research guidelines, will assure protection of the subject's rights. For example, the nonobtru-

sive observation of traffic flow in public places or other public behavior might fall into this category. Use of this procedure and the
next are permissible only when a review panel has determined that
the potential risk of harm to the anonymously observed subjects is nil.

2. *Subject is simply asked to sign a consent form for participation
in research as a subject of observation—with no explanation of the
nature of the study.* One example might be an observational study
of the supermarket shopping behavior of individuals in which an
explanation of the objectives of the study might change the relevant
behavior.

3. *Subject is asked to sign a consent form for participation in
research with "debriefing" following participation.* Such a study
might involve an examination of interpersonal behavior in public
places in which prior disclosure of the hypotheses could change the
behavior under study. For such a practice to be used, however, a
panel of experts would have to determine that there is little potential risk to the subject (including humiliation following debriefing) as a result of participation in the research.

4. *Subject is asked to sign a consent form for participation in a
project, following a full disclosure of the objectives and methods of
the research.* This procedure would be applicable in efforts to evaluate services by randomly assigning some subjects to experimental, to
placebo control, and to no-treatment control conditions. In these
situations a review panel must judge that the procedures are of
potential benefit to the experimental subjects, with the risk of harm
to control subjects being equal to or less than the dangers that
would have existed if there were no experiment.

5. *Subject is asked to sign a consent form for participation in a
project, following a full disclosure of the objectives and methods of
the research and in the presence of at least one witness who is not
involved in the research.* This procedure would be appropriate any
time the presumptive danger of coercion to participate is deemed
to exist by a review panel. For example, experimental services to
adjudicated offenders could fall into this category.

6. *Subject is asked to sign a consent form for participation in a
project, following full disclosure of the objectives and methods of
the research and in the presence of witnesses, with his or her consent
reviewed by an independent human subjects' committee to protect
the rights of subjects within the institution.* This procedure might be
used in the experimental evaluation of programs intended to contribute to the subject's development of skills relating to the attainment of institutional objectives, for example, vocational training in
prisons or mental hospitals.

7. *Subject is asked to sign a consent form for participation in a
project, following full disclosure of the objectives and methods of
the research, in the presence of witnesses, with the consent reviewed
by an independent human subjects' rights committee within the*

institution, this ruling to be reviewed by a similar committee out-side the institution. The procedure could be relevant when the research concerns behavior changes that are not strictly related to institutional objectives. This might be illustrated by efforts to train mental patients in a concept acquisition task.

8. *No consent is possible because conditions are lacking that can adequately protect the rights of subjects.*

Such a hierarchy is not exhaustive. There may be several midpoints that have been omitted, just as more permissive or more demanding protections could be designed for use at either extreme. But the hierarchy may serve to stimulate thought about a range of suitable possibilities, depending on the character of the research that is being contemplated. Such a continuum could replace the absolute dichotomy that is commonly discussed.

An analysis of the institutional factors bearing on the research would determine which level of the hierarchy is appropriate. We have identified four such factors, each of which is also a continuum. Like the hierarchy of protections just proposed, each of the following dimensions is proposed as a topic for discussion (see Table 1).

The first of these dimensions is the *level of potential benefit to the subject/client.* This can range from a high level of direct benefit to the individual to primary benefit accruing to the larger society with low direct benefit to the individual. The second dimension is the *level of risk.* This continuum ranges from the very low risk of harm associated with the nonobtrusive collection of anonymous data about a subject/client to the application of procedures that might eventuate in serious harm to the individual. The third dimension is the *validational status or novelty of the procedure to be used.* At one point on the continuum are found procedures that have been fully established and are considered to be the "treatment of choice," while at the other extreme are interventions that are purely experimental. (In institutional research, this dimension can reflect a range of programs from those that are routinely present, ethically acceptable and empirically validated to those that are considered radical departures.) Finally, it is necessary to assess the *extent to which subjects can freely offer their informed consent* to participation. In open community settings, free consent is more likely than in total institutional settings. Therefore, greater care must be taken in the protection of the right to refuse participation in the latter settings. When the guarantees have been met, an emergent contract between the parties assures the protection of the interests of both (Schwitzgebel & Kolb, 1974).

Table 1 offers one possible arrangement of these variables. The values assigned to each cell are arbitrary and should be replaced by the judgment of a great many researcher/clinicians of varying orientations and from far-ranging scientific disciplines as well as from lawyers, community leaders, laymen, and representatives of the subject/client populations. When consensus has been reached on the appropriateness of these or similar guidelines, and when they are utilized in all basic and applied research, they may help protect the rights of individuals on the one hand and yet permit the essential continuation of the discovery process on the other hand.

TOTALITARIANISM OR PLURALISM

Much of the foregoing discussion applies equally to the entire field of biological and behavioral science. One concern which has been expressed primarily about behavior therapy deserves particular mention, namely that behavior therapy seeks to achieve a cultural and societal "leveling" that would produce conformity and limit creativity (Kittrie, 1971). We believe that this fear is exaggerated. Rather than reducing the diversity of our cultures, behavior therapists have been willing to assess the impact of alternative methods of social influence and forms of social organization, thereby fostering diversity rather than uniformity.

Behavior therapists recognize that patterns of social influence reach into almost every quarter of our lives. They also realize that unless the process of this influence and its goals are made known, we will continually be subjected to covert manipulations that are planned by groups with vested interests. Drawing upon a scientific approach to the study of human behavior, behavior therapists hope to make valuable contributions to pluralism by generating a body of data describing the operation of influence processes and their consequences. Thus, if people are to make their own decisions about how to conduct their lives, is it not reasonable to provide as much knowledge as possible about how behavior is developed, maintained, and changed (London, 1964, 1969)? Based on these data, individuals and society will be able to choose alternative focuses, license the use of some techniques of persuasion, and proscribe the use of others, and to do all of this in the arena of full public discourse through a fully democratized decision-making process. Conversely, to allow these forces to remain beyond public scrutiny and to neglect the responsibility of providing direction is to allow the co-opting of these forces for potentially antisocial ends.

REFERENCE NOTE

1. WEXLER, D. B. *Of Rights and Reinforcers.* Paper presented at the Law and Society Research Group Symposium, Florida State University, May 1974.

REFERENCES

AYLLON, T. & AZRIN, N. *The Token Economy: A Motivational System for Therapy and Rehabilitation.* New York: Appleton-Century-Crofts, 1968.

BANDURA, A. *Principles of Behavior Modification.* New York: Holt, Rinehart & Winston, 1969.

DAVISON, G. C. Counter control in behavior modification. In L. A. Hamerlynck, L. C. Handy, and E. J. Mash (Eds.), *Behavior Change: Methodology, Concepts, and Practice.* Champaign, Ill.: Research Press, 1973.

DAVISON, G. C. & NEALE, J. M. *Abnormal Psychology: An Experimental Clinical Approach.* New York: Wiley, 1974.

ENNIS, B. & SIEGEL, L. *The Rights of Mental Patients.* New York: Avon Books, 1973.

ETZIONI, A. *The Active Society: A Theory of Societal and Political Processes.* New York: Free Press, 1968.

FAIRWEATHER, G., SANDERS, D., MAYNARD, H., CRESSLER, D., & BLECK, D. *Community Life for the Mentally Ill: An Alternative to Institutional Care.* Chicago: Aldine, 1969.

JONAS, H. Philosophical reflections on experimenting with human subjects. In P. A. Freund (Ed.), *Experimentation with Human Subjects.* New York: George Braziller, 1970.

KANFER, F. H. & PHILLIPS, J. S. A survey of current behavior therapies and a proposal for classification. In C. M. Franks (Ed.), *Behavior Therapy: Appraisal and Status.* New York: McGraw-Hill, 1969.

KITTRIE, N. *The Right to Be Different.* Baltimore, Md.: Johns Hopkins Press, 1971.

LONDON, P. *The Modes and Morals of Psychotherapy.* New York: Holt, Rinehart & Winston, 1964.

LONDON, P. *Behavior Control.* New York: Harper & Row, 1969.

LOVAAS, O. I. & SIMMONS, J. Q. Manipulation of self-destruction in three retarded children. *J. Appl. Behav. Anal.,* 1969, 2, 143-157.

McCONNELL, J. V. Criminals can be brainwashed—now. *Psychology Today,* April 1970, pp. 14, 16, 18, 74.

MILLER, A. *The Assault on Privacy; Computers, Data Banks, and Dossiers.* Ann Arbor: University of Michigan Press, 1971.

MILLER, L. K. & MILLER, O. L. Reinforcing self-help group activities of welfare recipients. *J. Appl. Behav. Anal.,* 1970, 3, 57-64.

MORRIS, N. Impediments to penal reform. *Univ. Chicago Law Rev.,* 1966, 33, 627-656.

National Institutes of Health. Protection of human subjects: Policies and procedures. *Federal Register,* May 30, 1974, 18914-18920.

PHILLIPS, E. L., PHILLIPS, E. A., FIXSEN, D. L., & WOLF, M. M. Achievement place: Modification of the behaviors of pre-delinquent boys within a token economy. *J. Appl. Behav. Anal.,* 1971, 4, 45-59.

ROBINSON, D. N. Harm, offense, and nuisance: Some first steps in the establishment of an ethics of treatment. *Amer. Psychol.,* 1974, 29, 233-238.

ROTHMAN, D. J. Decarcerating prisoners and patients. *Civil Liberties Review,* 1973, 1, 6-30.

SCHWITZGEBEL, R. K. & KOLB, D. A. *Changing Human Behavior: Principles of Planned Intervention.* New York: McGraw-Hill, 1974.

STUART, R. B. A critical reappraisal and reformulation of selected mental health problems. In L. A. Hamerlynck, P. O. Davidson, and L. E. Acker (Eds.), *Behavior Modification and Ideal Mental Health Services.* Calgary, Canada: University of Calgary Press, 1969.

STUART, R. B. *Trick or Treatment: How and When Psychotherapy Fails.* Champaign, Ill.: Research Press, 1970.

STUART, R. B. Behavioral control of delinquency: Critique of existing programs and recommendations for innovative programming. In L. A. Hamerlynck and F. C. Clark (Eds.), *Behavior Modification for Exceptional Children and Youth.* Calgary, Canada: University of Calgary Press, 1971.

STUART, R. B. Behavioral control of overeating: A status report. In G. R. Bray (Ed.), *Obesity: A National Symposium.* Washington, D. C.: National Institutes of Health, in press. (a)

STUART, R. B. *Treatment Contract.* Champaign, Ill.: Research Press, in press. (b)

SZASZ, T. S. *Law, Liberty and Psychiatry.* New York: Macmillan, 1963.

SZASZ, T. S. *Ideology and Insanity: Essays on the Psychiatric Dehumanization of Man.* New York: Doubleday, 1970.

ULRICH, R., STACHNIK, T., & MABRY, J. (Eds.). *Control of Human Behavior. Vol. 3: Behavior Modification in Education.* Glenview, Ill.: Scott, Foresman, 1974.

WEXLER, D. B. Token and taboo: Behavior modification, token economics and the law. *Calif. Law Rev.,* 1973, 61, 81-109.

3

BEHAVIOR MODIFICATION IN MAXIMUM SECURITY SETTINGS: ONE HOSPITAL'S EXPERIENCE

Michael Serber, Carolyn Hiller, Claudia Keith
and John Taylor

Atascadero State Hospital, California

I. INTRODUCTION

The history of behavior modification programs at the Atascadero State Hospital in California illustrates the potential of behavior modification both for helping and for abuse. This article, drawing upon the Atascadero experience, will show that behavior modification techniques can shape humane and effective treatment programs. However, it will also be shown that unless adequate mechanisms for review of treatments are available, any "therapeutic" regime can be a tool for abuse of inmates' rights.

Reprinted from *The American Criminal Law Review*, Vol. 13, 1975, 85-99. Copyright 1975, American Bar Association Section of Criminal Justice.

This paper is a composite of two papers: Problems of Behavior Modification in Maximum Security Settings—One Hospital's Experience, by Michael Serber, Claudia Keith, and John Taylor; and The Failure of Psychiatric Peer Review, A Case Study, by Michael Serber and Carolyn Hiller.

The opinions expressed within this paper are those of the authors only and are not to be construed as those of the State of California, Department of Health.

Dr. Michael Serber passed away during the formulation of this article. He formerly served as Clinical Director of the Atascadero State Hospital, Atascadera, California. Mr. Taylor is Assistant Program Director of the Community Planning Program at Atascadero. Ms. Hiller and Ms. Keith are former Research Assistants at Atascadero.

"Behavior modification" is a catch-all phrase that can be applied to the numerous ways by which human behavior can be changed. Among these are positive conditioning,[1] negative conditioning,[2] extinction,[3] desensitization,[4] assertive training,[5] and others.[6] This wide spectrum of therapies does not represent strange controlling forces, but rather attempts by behavior modifiers to systematically arrange circumstances in which normal learning takes place. The basic principles underlying behavioral treatment methods are descriptions of how people learn to respond to their environments. People have always tried to discriminate between positive and negative events, to seek reinforcement, and to avoid punitive situations.

Advocates of behavior modification typically represent it as an innovative therapy which yields positive results quickly, even in those situations where other programs have failed.[7] Opponents, however, often equate

---

[1] Positive conditioning (positive reinforcement) is an operation in which the presentation of a stimulus as the consequence of a particular response or behavior is designed to increase the strength or frequency of the response. B. Wolman, *Dictionary of Behavioral Sciences,* 1973, 320 [hereinafter cited as Wolman].

[2] Negative conditioning (negative reinforcement) involves the use of coercive stimuli to bring about a reduction or prevention of a response. *Id.*

[3] Extinction involves the withholding of the unconditioned response or the instrumental reward in order to achieve the gradual diminution of a conditioned response. *Id.,* at 134.

[4] Desensitization is a process where phobic patients are taught to relax and then mild phobic stimulations are gradually presented in a progressive manner so that patients may systematically unlearn their anxiety responses. *See* F. Kanner and J. Phillips, *Learning Foundations of Behavior Therapy,* 1970, 152-185 [hereinafter cited as Kanfer & Phillips].

[5] Assertive training is a process whereby persons are systematically taught additional or alternative behavior to increase their social and behavioral repertoire utilizing standardized learning techniques such as modeling, role training, and positive reinforcement. *See* Wolman, *supra* note 1 at 32.

[6] *See generally* A. Bandura, *Principles of Behavior Modification,* 1969 [hereinafter cited as Bandura]; Kanfer & Phillips, *supra* note 4. *See also* Note, Conditioning and Other Technologies Used to "Treat?" "Rehabilitate?" "Demolish?" Prisoners and Mental Patients, *S. Cal. L. Rev.,* 45, 616, 627 n. 60 [hereinafter cited as Note, Prisoners and Mental Patients]; Gaylin & Blatte, Behavior Modification in Prisons, *infra* at 11, in this Symposium.

[7] *E.g.,*

"For the first time in history the laws of respondent and operant conditioning, which have been derived from a sound scientific discipline, are being systematically applied in the effective and dramatic amelioration of many forms of human distress."

W. W. Wenrich, *A Primer of Behavior Modification,* 1970, 1. *See generally* T. Ayllon and N. Azrin, *The Token Economy: A Motivational System for Therapy and Rehabilitation,* 1968; A. Bandura, *supra* note 6; C. Franks, *Behavior Therapy: Appraisal and Status,* 1969; C. Franks, *Conditioning Techniques in Clinical Practice and Re-*

behavior modification with punishment.[8] These extreme views fail to account for the diversity of behavior modification techniques and the complexity of the problems to which they are applied. Some behavior modification techniques have proven more effective than others, while some behavioral treatments are more appropriate for certain situations than for others. In any discussion of behavior modification, as with any treatment, the particular technique employed must be independently evaluated to ascertain the positive or negative effects that it will have on the recipient and whether or not specific treatments may be beneficial for the recipient.

Several factors have converged to lead institutions to implement behavior modification treatments. Extensive criticism of prisons and state mental hospitals[9] has led to calls for reform. At the same time, behavior modification has been widely promoted as treatment for socially deprived individuals, especially those in institutions.[10] Since behavior modification

search, 1964; L. Krasner and L. Ullmann, *Research in Behavior Moidfication*, 1965; B. F. Skinner, *Science and Human Behavior*, 1953; L. Ullmann and L. Krasner, *Case Studies in Behavior Modification*, 1965; R. Ulrich, T. Strachnik, and J. Mabry, *Control of Human Behavior*, 1966; J. Wolpe, *The Practice of Behavior Therapy*, 1973; J. Wolpe, *Psychotherapy by Reciprocal Inhibition*, 1958; J. Wolpe and A. Lazarus, *Behavior Therapy Techniques*, 1966.

[8] *See generally* P. Hilts, *Behavior Modification*, 1974; C. Rogers, *On Becoming a Person*, 1961; Allchin, Behavior Therapy, *British J. Psychiatry*, 1964, 110, 110; Breger and McGaugh, Critique and Reformulation of "Learning Theory" Approaches to Psychotherapy and Neuroses, *Psychol. Bull.*, 1972, 63, 338; Jourad, On the Problem of Reinforcement by the Psychotherapist of Healthy Behavior in the Patient, in *Behavioristic Appriaches to Counseling and Psychotherapy: A Southeastern Psychological Association Symposium*, 1961; Keisler, Some Myths of Psychotherapy Research and the Search for a Paradigm, *Psychol. Bull*, 1966, 65, 110; Opton, Jr., Psychiatric Violence Against Prisoners: When Therapy Is Punishment, *Miss. L. J.*, 1974, 45, 605; Patterson, Control, Conditioning and Counseling, *Personnel and Guidance*, 1963, 41, 680; Rogers and Skinner, Some Issues Concerning the Control of Human Behavior: A Symposium, *Science*, 1956, 124, 1057; Sage, Crime and the Clockwork Lemon, *Human Behavior*, No. 9, 1974, 3, 16 [hereinafter cited as Sage]; Shoben, The Therapeutic Object: Men or Machines? *J. Counseling Psychology*, 1963, 10, 264; Note, Aversion Therapy: Its Limited Potential for Use in the Correctional Setting, *Stan. L. Rev.*, 1974, 26, 1327.

[9] *See, e.g.*, H. Badillo and M. Haynes, *A Bill of No Rights: Attica and the American Prison System*, 1972; K. Menninger, *The Crime of Punishment*, 1966; J. Mitford, *Kind and Usual Punishment*, 1973; *President's Commission on Law Enforcement and the Administration of Justice: The Challenge of Crime in a Free Society: A Report*, 1967.

[10] *See, e.g.*, McConnell, Criminals Can Be Brainwashed—Now, *Psychology Today*, April, 1970; Singer, Psychological Studies of Punishment, *Calif. L. Rev.*, 1970, 58, 405, 433. *See also* Wicker, Interview with Dr. Martin Groder, Director of the Federal Prison in Butner, North Carolina, *N. Y. Times*, Dec. 31, 1972, § IV, at 9 col. 5, and Jan. 2, 1973, at 35, col. 1.

technology promises to yield results where traditional therapies have failed, many behavioral regimes have been adopted in the name of reform and rehabilitation.

Far too frequently, however, behavior modification terminology as well as other psychiatric nomenclature has actually been no more than a pseudo-scientific rationalization for harsh and punitive measures of control within environments lacking resources to positively reinforce inmates.[11] Treatments such as extended solitary confinement and electroshock therapy have been labeled "behavior modification" and simplistically applied to discourage frowned-upon inmate behavior with little regard for the rehabilitative needs of the inmates.

Precautions are necessary to limit injustices that may occur when any punitive or humiliating measures are used. An attempt has been made by the United States Department of Health, Education, and Welfare (HEW) to protect the subjects of behavior modification experiments.[12] The HEW guidelines require that before certain research activities[13] may be conducted, participants who will be exposed to possible harm[14] must give their "informed consent"[15] to the project.

Unfortunately, these regulations do not adequately address the problem of potential abuse in an institutional setting. To equate informed consent in a locked institution with informed consent in a free situation

---

[11] See, e.g., J. Mitford, supra note 9, at 97; Opton, Jr., supra note 8; Sage, supra note 8, at 16; Shapiro, Legislating the Control of Behavior Control: Autonomy and the Coercive Use of Organic Therapies, S. Cal. L. Rev., 1974, 47, 237, 249. See also Knecht v. Gillman, 488 F.2d 1136 (8th Cir. 1973):

> Whether it is called "aversive stimuli" or punishment, the act of forcing someone to vomit for a 15 minute period for committing some minor breach of the rules can only be regarded as cruel and unusual unless the treatment is being administered to a patient who knowingly and intelligently has consented to it.

488 F.2d at 1139-40.

[12] See C.F.R., 1974, 45, § 46.

[13] The regulations apply to HEW funded "research, development, and related activities in which human subjects are involved." C.F.R., 1974, 45, § 46.1 (a).

[14] Individuals are covered by the regulations if they "may be exposed to the possibility of injury, including physical, psychological, or social injury." C.F.R., 1974, 45, § 46.3 (b).

[15] "Informed consent," under the regulations, means the "knowing consent of an individual . . . so situated as to be able to exercise free power of choice without undue inducement or any element of force, fraud, deceit, duress, or other form of constraint or coercion." The person must be informed of risks involved, attendant discomforts, and possible benefits. He must also be informed of his right to withdraw consent. C.F.R., 1974, 45, § 46.3 (c).

is to indulge in a civil rights fantasy.[16] It is questionable whether any prisoner has the capacity to exercise a free power of choice when he has been deprived of other basic freedoms.[17] Moreover, patients and prisoners are frequently under pressure to cooperate or face extended incarceration.[18] Patients committed until they are "cured" may in fact be facing a life sentence if they are judged uncooperative or unmotivated for treatment. Many prisoners will feel obligated to accept any "offer" of treatment when failure to cooperate might mean a prolonged prison term. Under these conditions, treatment activities often are convenient for and meet the needs of the staff more often than patient's needs. Moreover, patients in mental hospital usually have been committed at least in part because of an inability to handle their own affairs. The HEW regulations should not even apply to these patients since they are incapable of giving informed consent.[19]

II. TREATMENT PROGRAMS AT ATASCADERO STATE HOSPITAL

The 1000 patient-inmates committed to Atascadero State Hospital are primarily mentally disordered criminals.[20] The dominant form of treatment at Atascadero until 1970 consisted of milieu therapy and group psychotherapy conducted by psychiatric technicians. Chemotherapy represented one of the few individualized treatment techniques. Application of treatment, as in other facilities, was significantly affected by the attitudes and self-interests of the staff. Some members of the staff apparently felt that their responsibilities consisted of acting as custodians as well as punishing the patients. Treatment was dictated by staff interests to such

---

[16] For discussion of the consent problem with certain treatments in an institutional setting, see Mark, Brain Surgery in Aggressive Epileptics, *Hastings Center Rep.*, 1973, 3, 1, 5 n.1; Note, Prisoners and Mental Patients, *supra* note 6, at 673.

[17] J. Mitford, *supra* note 9, at 153. *See also,* Shapiro, *supra* note 11, at 276-320.

[18] It is impossible for an involuntary (sic) detained mental patient to be free of ulterior forms of restraint or coercion when his very release from the institution may depend upon his cooperating with the institutional authorities and giving consent to experimental surgery.
Kainowitz v. Dept. of Mental Health, Civ. No. 73-19434 (Cir. Ct., Wayne City, Mich., July 10, 1973), at 27. *See also* Shapiro, *supra* note 11, at 316-320; Note, Prisoners and Mental Patients, *supra* note 6, at 672-673.

[19] The regulations do allow a "legally authorized representative" to consent for a subject. *C.F.R.,* 1974, 45, § 46.3 (c). Whether such representative consent is appropriate is left to "applicable law." *C.F.A.,* 1974, 45, § 46.3 (h).

[20] Persons may be committed to Atascadero if they are mentally disordered sex offenders, *Calif. Welf. & Inst'ns Code* §§ 6300 *et seq.* (West Supp. 1974), criminally insane, *Cal. Penal Code* § 1026 (West Supp. 1970), and incompetent to stand trial, *Cal. Penal Code* §§ 1370, 1372 (West Supp. 1970).

an extent that patients from a specific geographic area were housed together regardless of their individual needs. This enabled the physician responsible for their treatment to travel to only one area of the state when required to testify in court.

An extreme example of the misuse of aversive treatment was the "Anectine" experiment. Between 1966 and 1969 over 90 male patients at Atascadero were given a drug called succinylcholine[21] as part of an "exploratory study."[22] The drug, which was administered in a nonroutine manner, was intended to induce an aversive experience.[23] All of these patients forcibly received succinylcholine without their approval—there was no signed consent.[24]

Succinylcholine has gained acceptance in the medical profession when used in moderate dosages as an adjunct to general anesthesia or electroshock therapy.[25] Here, however, the authors of the study utilized high dosages upon conscious patients. Under these circumstances the effects are severe: succinylcholine is a neuromuscular blocking agent, and high dosages of it cause paralysis of the muscles and respiratory system for two to five minutes.[26] When conscious, the patient experiences feelings of suffocating and death.

What Anectine does, in short, is to simulate death. Within 30 to 40 seconds of injection it brings on paralysis, first in the small, rapidly moving muscles in the fingers, toes and eyes, then in the diaphragm and cardiovascular system. As a result the patient cannot move or breathe, and yet remains fully conscious as though drowning, and dying.[27]

Three advocates of this so-called aversive technique, reporting on their experiment, described it as "an exploratory study to determine the effectiveness of succinylcholine as an agent in behavior modification."[28] The specific criteria for selection of subjects were not made clear, but included "persistent physical or verbal violence, deviant sexual behavior and lack of cooperation and involvement in the individual treatment

---

[21] Succinylcholine chloride is marketed under the trade name "Anectine." *Physician's Desk Reference,* 1975, 661.

[22]. Reimringer, Morgan, & Bramwell, Succinylcholine as a Modifier of Acting-Out Behavior, *Clinical Medicine,* 77 (No. 7, 1970), 28.

[23] *Id.*

[24] The researchers apparently felt that there was no need for signed consent because they did not consider anectine therapy to be "expermental." *See* Note, Prisoners and Mental Patients, *supra* note 6, at 641.

[25] Sage, *supra* note 8, at 18.

[26] Reimringer, et al., *supra* note 22.

[27] Sage, *supra* note 8, at 18.

[28] Reimringer, et al., *supra* note 22, at 28,

program prescribed by the patient's ward team."[29] The subjects were clinically described as ranging from "overtly psychotic and mentally retarded to sociopathic patients."[30] In fact, this treatment was given to patients having behavioral problems which could be described, as the records show, as any behavior which offended the staff members authorized to prescribe the aversive use of the drug.

The treatment was administered by injection. At the onset of apnea, or respiratory paralysis, the patient was given both positive and negative instructions delivered by a male technician in a confident, authoritarian manner.[31] Treatment results were then evaluated by comparing the frequency of the inmate-patient "acting out" behavior before and after treatment.[32] The authors reported that 61 subjects improved, 16 temporarily improved, 12 showed no change in behavior and one patient showed increased violence.[33] It was concluded that the general effectiveness of the succinylcholine treatment appeared to be established,[34] and the procedure was later utilized at the California Medical Facility at Vacaville.[35] There was no evaluation of positive social behavior by patients, such as cooperation with other treatment programs within the institution after treatment. Also, there was no follow-up as to inmate behavior after release form the institution.

Although described as an experiment, it is apparent from the records that the drug was used non-systematically as punishment. The physician's notes reveal the biased and arbitrary way in which patients were selected for "treatment."

> Whispers in obvious hallucinations. Irrational. Placed on Anectine because of his unpredictable behavior.
>
> Observed in active fellatio attitude with J.B. Aversion treatment ordered (Anectine).
>
> Uncooperative, disruptive in group. Pacing, Negativistic, laughs and grins inappropriately. Muslim who stirs up race hatred. Recommend Anectine.

Whatever the avowed intent of the study, the purpose and effect, shown by its actual administration, was not experimental nor individual therapy, but simply maintenance of institutional control and punishment of deviants. There was no standardized or matching procedures to pick

---

[29] *Id.*, at 28-29.
[30] *Id.*
[31] *Id.*, at 29.
[32] *Id.*

subjects, and no control groups were utilized to evaluate results.

The use of this drug for aversive therapy had never been approved by the hospital's research committee; and the California Department of Mental Hygiene did not become aware that the drug was being used in this manner until the case gained notoriety following reports in the *Medical World News*[36] and the *San Francisco Chronicle*,[37] after which the Department immediately ordered the study discontinued.

In 1972 there was a reorganization at Atascadero which provided an opportunity for those staff and administrators who were genuinely concerned with patient treatment and rights and disenchanted with the existing arbitrary system of care and evaluation to generate major changes within parts of the hospital. These changes included the grouping of patients by primary needs and the systematizing of treatment into an objective, or goal-planning format.

Dr. Serber and his staff, after studying the limited background and behavioral repertoire of the committed inmates, concluded that the best clinical and most ethical treatment program should include the teaching of additional or alternative social behaviors which could prove useful to a patient in avoiding violence or recidivism, using behavioral modification techniques. Several specialized behavioral techniques were utilized. These included: assertive training,[38] modeling,[39] direct education, role playing,[40] and vicarious conditioning[41] utilizing movies and videotapes to teach improved "how to" social skills.

A behavioral goal plan was designed for each patient, regardless of the treatment program to which he was assigned. The plan consisted of clear, objective statements of the patient's primary problems, the short term and long term goals of the treatment, and the methods the staff and patient would utilize to achieve these goals.[42] Great importance was placed upon describing problems and goals in terms of easily defined patient behavior which could be clearly understood by all concerned including the patient and the court. All patients had knowledge of the information contained in the goal plans and, if possible, participated in the formulation of those plans.

For patients who were judged to be criminally insane and who demon-

33 *Id.*
34 *Id.*
35 Sage, supra note 8, at 16; Scaring the Devil Out, *Medical World News,* 29 (October 9, 1970); Note, Prisoners and Mental Patients, *supra* note 6, at 670-672.
36 Scaring the Devil Out, *supra* note 35.
37 Schwartz, "Unwilling Patients Got Fright Drug," *San Francisco Chronicle,* October 16, 1970, at 1, col. 3.

strated acute psychiatric problems, programs were developed using other therapeutic techniques such as chemotherapy, token economies, and simple positive reinforcement treatments. Those who were committed after being charged with a crime, but found unable to stand trial, were taught trial competency through role-playing, watching mock trials, direct instruction, and traditional psychiatric treatments.

An assertive training program was developed to offer specialized skills to the socially inadequate patient who typically displayed tantrums or was verbally abusive in stressful or even slightly uncomfortable situations. Such training was also made available to the non-assertive patient who inhibited himself from expressing his true feelings. This program used teaching, modeling, discriminative learning,[42] and role playing to directly teach patients certain social skills, such as constructive criticism, complimenting, and being affectionate.

Many patients were hospitalized at Atascadero primarily as a result of family problems. A specialized program was developed to deal with these patients and the family members who were significant in their lives. Aimed at increasing family functioning skills, this program made extensive use of contingency contracting,[44] group couples therapy, family counseling, and assertive and interpersonal communication training.

A sexual orientation program was developed to aid patients experiencing problems concerning their sexuality. Such a program was thought

---

[38] See note 5 supra.

[39] Modeling occurs when the behavior of others is performed in front of the patient as an example of proper behavior to be expressed when the patient is himself confronted with similar interpersonal situations. Bandura, supra note 6, at 198.

[40] Role-playing involves the replication or simulation of significant parts of the patient's extratherapeutic environment in the therapist's presence and allows the patient to discover and try out in a supportive situation behaviors that will improve his social effectiveness. Kanfer & Phillips, supra note 4, at 232-236.

[41] Vicarious conditioning "results from observing others experience positive or negative emotional effects in conjunction with particular stimulus events." Bandura, supra note 6, at 167.

[42] The goal plan program at Atascadero closely followed the ideas developed in Houts and Scott, Goal Planning in Mental Health, 1972 (Department of Behavioral Science, Pennsylvania State University, Milton S. Hershey Medical Center). See also Schwitzgebel, The Right to Treatment for the Mentally Disabled: The Need for Realistic Standards and Objective Criteria, Harv. Civ. Rights-Civ. Lib. L. Rev., 1973, 8, 513, 521-530.

[43] Discriminative learning is the process of reinforcing responses to certain stimuli while allowing others to become extinct by not rewarding the patient when he performs them. Wolman, supra note 1, at 102.

[44] Contingency contracting involves "deliberate negotiation of contracts that demand specific behaviors of the patient and for whose successful achievement the therapist provides a predetermined reinforcement." Kanfer & Phillips, supra note 4, at 437-438.

to be helpful since it was discovered that many child molesters were simply men who felt so inferior in the company of other adults that they preferred the presence of children. An attempt was made to remedy that situation by encouraging these patients to adopt the sexual orientation of their choice, either heterosexual or homosexual, and to develop skills which would enable them to pursue their sexual interests with adults. This treatment included sexual education courses, sexual skills training through the use of vicarious training materials, and training in sexual preference and self-control.

An important facet of this treatment included the teaching of sex-related social skills. A specialized assertive training format utilizing instruction, modeling, discriminative learning, and role playing attempted to teach the patients heterosexual or homosexual social skills. For example, female volunteers participated in the heterosexual skills training program by helping the patients to learn to initiate social contracts with women, how to dance, and the appropriate signs of affection in public situations.

A homosexual social skills group used a similar format. For example, for the minority of child molesters who were homosexual in orientation, skills appropriate to the gay world were emphasized. Volunteers from a local gay students union simulated functional gay social behavior. The hospital staff was thus able to observe the interaction and isolate key behaviors that could serve as a foundation on which the essential social skills could be built. One such behavior, for example, was the ability to be sensitive to another male's glances, to learn from the quality of those glances whether one was being "cruised" or rejected.

Through role-playing, the inmate was also required to learn how to take the initiative and express his own interests through the necessary eye contact. Each session was videotaped, so that at the end it could be played back and discussed. Finally, patients were given information on contacts with gay organizations outside the hospital, and arrangements were made with gay community service centers to provide counseling, employment, and housing information in order to ease the patient's transition upon release.[45]

Despite efforts to provide innovative treatment programs designed to meet the needs of the patients, treatment was necessarily limited by the fact that it was conducted within a locked institution. Many of the behaviors that can be taught in such an institution are those essential for adapting to life within the confines of the hospital. Because of these limits, the teaching of socially appropriate behaviors can only be started in the institution. An institutionalized patient has no opportunity to practice socially appropriate behavior in an unsupervised setting since his environment is not even remotely conducive to genuine social interaction. No hospital can reproduce the stresses and various stimuli present in the outside community.

Because of the "unreal" nature of the institutional setting, it is important that patients receive follow-up treatment at the community level after release.[46] In this way, their ability to cope with the problems they may experience can be monitored and they can be provided with therapeutic support. In addition, social skills training begun within the institution must be continued so that the patient will have available to him realistic situations in which to practice and perfect these skills.

Atascadero developed a specialized exit program to smooth the patient's adjustment within the community. A patient's specific needs were assessed so that useful information could be provided to the community agency serving the patient after release.[47] When a patient was deemed to be no longer dangerous and was cooperative toward out-patient treatment, he was released under the condition that he make use of specific out-patient therapies. A continuous assessment of the patient's community behavior is maintained by the hospital when legally feasible.

---

[45] A more complete description of this program is available in Sage, *supra* note 8, at 24-25. *See also,* Serber & Keith, The Atascadero Project: Model of a Sexual Retraining Program for Incarcerated Homosexual Pedophiles, *Journal of Homosexuality,* 1974, 1, 1.

[46]

> [W]hatever fixing [of deviants] goes on in our current system disappears when the prisoner goes home. Fixing the environment within the prison with behavior modification may make a crowd of nice, sociable prisoners. But when they are back in the street their behavior is controlled by the payoffs of the street, of their friends, their work (if they can get it), and their families. There is not much chance that what behavior you fix in the prison will stay fixed. If you want to fix a criminal's behavior, you have to fix it where it counts. The criminal must be plugged into the right payoffs at home.

P. Hilts, *Behavior Modification,* 1974, 121. *See also* Shapiro, Psychiatry in the Correctional Process, *Crime & Delin.,* 1966, 12, 9, 15.

[47] One purpose of this particular plan was to alert the agency to the "environmental and behavioral events which set the stage for criminal action and serve as predictors of recidivism" so that the patient's likely problems could be forecast. If sufficient information could be provided to the agency, it would increase the effectiveness of the parole system. *See* Jenkins, et al., *The Measurement and Prediction of Criminal Behavior and Recidivism: The Environmental Deprivation Scale (EDS) and the Maladaptive Behavior Record (MBR),* 1972, 1 (Draper Correctional Center, Elmore, Alabama).

While significant reforms have been made, Atascadero, like other institutions, has far to go in identifying and treating inmate needs. The hospital has been unable to attract a psychiatric residency program because of the distance from medical schools. Aversive therapy in the form of seclusion continues to be utilized for assaultive patients, although the periods for seclusion are seldom longer than two or three days. Nevertheless, escape and staff and patient injuries occur relatively infrequently. This may be credited to high patient-staff ratios, good staff training, and release policies which permit early discharges based upon good behavior. The hospital has been remiss, due to lack of resources, in providing job training and adequate post-hospital funding for released patients.

III. SAFEGUARDING PRISONERS' RIGHTS IN BEHAVIOR MODIFICATION PROGRAMS

Perhaps the most serious deficiency in treatment programs at Atascadera and elsewhere has been the relative lack of critical review, both from within and from outside the institutions. Systematic and routine outside professional review of the adequacy of general treatment programming and of the necessity of each individual punitive therapy, including seclusion, should be carried out on a regular basis for all state agencies incarcerating inmates. University departments or professional associations could serve well in such a role and as a source of new information. All funding to medical schools and universities should be linked to these and other services including mandatory residency and other teaching programs within state hospitals or prisons.

Peer review, particularly at the institutional level, has proved inadequate. Many penal institutions seldom receive even cursory visitation by outside professional organizations, and many professionals are reluctant to point an accusing finger at a peer. Unfortunately, inadequate peer review often results in disregard for even the most basic of professional standards within these institutions.

For example, when the Anectine studies at Atascadero and Vacaville were first publicized,[48] a complaint was registered with the Ethics Committee of the American Psychiatric Association (APA), and an investigation followed. According to the then-secretary of the APA, the committee spoke with the three authors of the original study and concluded that

---

48 *See* notes 36 and 37 *supra* and accompanying text.

"no unethical behavior occurred."[49] This judgment was reached even though the entire issue of consent was generally ignored by the researchers, no patients who received the "treatment" were interviewed, and no charts were reviewed.

This investigation occurred in 1971. In 1975, there is still no systematic procedure by the APA for investigating cases such as the one described above.[50] The APA does not even provide a budget for investigative work. Thus, comprehensive ethical review is presently not feasible. This situation becomes worse when one considers that the psychiatric profession may permit abuses of the socially deprived that would never be tolerated if received by wealthier classes. It is difficult to imagine a psychiatrist forcibly giving private patients an aversive succinylcholine treatment without their consent and then getting a clean bill of health from his peers or the courts.

The APA has been reluctant to respond to these problems. In 1973, the Board of Trustees voted to disband a previously endorsed ad hoc committee which was to study conflicts of interest in psychiatry.[51] That committee intended to investigate allegations that psychiatrists employed in institutions often serve the interests of the institution and not those of the patients. Specifically, institutional psychiatric treatment has been designed to suppress behavior not approved within the institution, such as refusal to accept authority. The situation at Atascadero involved such a use of psychiatry for social control, and the subsequent action of the APA Ethics Committee is an urgent reminder that now is the time to endorse, not disband, committees established to study an unethical way in which psychiatry is sometimes practiced. If no effective mechanism for peer review within the psychiatric profession is developed, an outside agency may have to be called upon to fulfill that responsibility.

In any event, final review should be, and is, taking place in court.[52] Frequently, significant reform of social institutions occurs not through

---

49 Letter from Dr. G. Tarjan, then-Secretary of the American Psychiatric Association, to Dr. A. L. Halpern, March 10, 1971.

50 See, e.g., Board of Trustees of the American Psychiatric Association, Position Statement on Peer Review in Psychiatry, Amer. J. Psych., 1973, 130, 381; Langsley, Peer Review: Prospects and Problems, Amer. J. Psych., 1973, 130, 301.

51 For an interesting report on the Board's action, see Miller, APA: Psychiatrists Reluctant to Analyze Themselves, Science, 1973, 181, 246.

52 See, e.g., Knecht v. Gillman, supra note 11 (drug treatment without inmate consent). See also, Rouse v. Cameron, 373 F.2d 451 (D.C. Cir. 1966) (hospital inmates' right to treatment): Nelson v. Heyne. 355 F. Supp. 451 (N.D. Ind. 1973) (use of tranquilizing drugs to control behavior of juvenile inmates): Wyatt v. Stickney, 325 F. Supp. 781 (N.D. Ala. 1971) (involuntary patients' right to treatment).

the concerted action of professionals or by government administration, but through litigation. In the past, courts have been too hesitant in their questioning of mental health professionals.[53] Courts should not be reluctant to take corrective action against institutions and individual government employees who fail to provide promised treatment or who force inappropriate or punitive treatment on inmates. Mandatory, periodic legal review, including the right to an annual hearing for all judicially-committed persons, may be one mechanism to expedite this process. However, the vagueness of traditional mental health jargon makes it difficult for an inmate to contest his prescribed treatment in court. Terms like "psychopath," "deeper relationship," and "cured" offer little information into the institution's or individual practitioner's assessment of the inmate and the specific criteria used to make that assessment.[54] Behavior modification can make important contributions to the process of court evaluation of inmate treatment.

Behavior modification brings a degree of specificity to the field. At least one commentator has recognized that the identification of the goal of a therapeutic program, stated in terms of the client's improved behavior, is an important ingredient in ethical practice because the client and a reviewing court can easily understand the benefits of and evaluate a given mode of treatment.[55] The clear specification of individual treatment should also be noted. Goal attainment scaling and contingency contracting have become an integral part of the medical records kept

[53] we do not suggest that the court should or can decide

What particular treatment this patient requires. The court's function here resembles one when we review an agency action. We do not decide whether the agency has made the best decision, but only make sure that it has made a permissible and reasonable decision. . . .

Tribby v. Cameron, 379 F.2d 104, 105 (D.C. Cir. 1967). *Accord* O'Donoghue v. Riggs, 73 Wash. 2d 814, 440 P.2d 823 (1969) ("One who enters a hospital as a mentally ill person . . . impliedly consents to the use of such force as may be reasonably necessary to the proper care of the patient. . . ." 73 Wash. 2d at 820, n.2, 440 P.2d at 828 n.2). *See also*, Rothman, Decarcerating Prisoners and Patients, *Harv. Civ. Rights-Civ. Lib. L. Rev.*, 1973, 1, 8.

[54] *See, e.g., D.C. Code Ann.*, 1973, § 24—301 (e):

Where any person has been confined in a hospital for the mentally ill pursuant to subsection (d) of this section, and the superintendent of such hospital certifies (1) *that such person has regained his sanity*, (2) that, in the opinion of the superintendent, such person will not in the reasonable future be dangerous to himself or others, and (3) in the opinion of the superintendent, *the person is entitled to his unconditional release* from the hospital . . . the court [is authorized] to order the unconditional release of the person . . . (emphasis supplied).

at Atascadero State Hospital. These techniques force the treatment staff to clearly state in the patient's records which inmate behavior will be used in making judgments relating to release or findings of improvement. If the staff must base its testimony on objective events and behavioral goals, patients may be able to contest the validity of "treatments" such as washing walls or making license plates. They can also question the relationship of all phases of treatment to their release or future dangerousness.[56]

Behavior modification techniques can offer substantial improvements to the present treatment of prisoners and mental patients. These improvements are especially possible where behavior modification is viewed in terms of positive rather than aversive conditioning. On the basis of the experience at Atascadero State Hospital, behavior modification is most valuable when the following caveats are observed:

1. Incarceration should be used sparingly and only when there is a demonstrable danger that the patient will harm himself or others. The institutional setting is not suitable for most kinds of treatments. The court-imposed criterion of a "cure" as a prerequisite to release motivates patients to underestimate or deny their treatment needs in order to petition for release. Patient and staff then become antagonists since further treatment may only signify continued detention. Such a relationship makes real treatment difficult. Thus, the right to treatment under the least restrictive conditions possible should be recognized. For cooperative patients, well-supervised parole or out-patient treatment is preferable to incarceration which continues until an arbitrarily defined "cure" is made. Parole should be used with requirements attached that the patient take advantage of out-patient facilities for specified treatments as a condition of release.

2. Aversive policies and practices in locked settings should be avoided

---

55 Often, the principal aims of social change enterprises are never clearly articulated, with the result that programs remain directionless or offer learning experiences that are selected fortuitously by personal preferences of the change agents rather than specifically for the needs of the recipients. Bandura, *supra* note 6, at 70.

56 The whole concept of "dangerousness" is one that should undergo scrutiny. It appears that false labelling may occur up to 90 percent of the time. *See* Leavy, The Mentally Ill Criminal Defendant, *Crim. L. Bull.*, 1973, 9, 197; Rubin, Prediction of Dangerousness in Mentally Ill Criminals, *Arch. Gen. Psychiatry*, 1972, 27, 397; Szasz, Some Observations on the Relationship Between Psychiatry and the Law, *Arch. of Neurological Psychiatry*, 1956, 75, 297. *See also,* Gaylin & Blatte, Behavior Modification in Prisons, *infra* at 11, in this Symposium.

whenever possible. Examples of effective control of inmate behavior accompanied by reductions in violence utilizing positive reinforcement such as token economies already exist.[57]

3. Entries into medical records should be based upon behavioral goal planning formats where inmate performance is described and measured in terms of improved behavior and where treatment activities are made explicit.

The psychiatric profession could protect patients' rights by more thorough self-regulation of unethical practices. Some reforms that could be adopted include: 1) closed-door hearings, held on all complaints, before a panel minimally composed of a lawyer, a psychiatrist, and an inmate advocate, 2) testimony before the panel by witnesses representing all sides of the case, including experts called as needed to clarify the practical and theoretical issues involved in each case, 3) a complete official report of the closed-door inquiry, including the details of the investigation, and 4) publication of results of disciplinary hearings.

The techniques of behavior modification can offer a more effective and humane way of dealing with prisoners and mental patients. These techniques, however, also have great potential for abuse of the inmate's humanity. The legal profession, entrusted as it is with a special responsibility for protecting every citizen's rights, must be more responsive to the issues raised by behavior modification than the psychiatric profession has been up to now. The knowledge of both fields is essential to help society respond adequately to the task before it.

---

[57] See, J. McKee, *Applied Behavior Analysis and the Imprisoned Adult Felon*, October 1974 (Experimental Manpower Laboratory for Corrections, Rehabilitation Research Foundation, Montgomery, Alabama).

4

LEGAL REGULATION OF APPLIED BEHAVIOR ANALYSIS IN MENTAL INSTITUTIONS AND PRISONS

Paul R. Friedman

Managing Attorney, Mental Health
Law Project, Washington, D. C.

III. SPECIAL PROBLEMS WHICH THE APPLIED BEHAVIOR ANALYST
WILL ENCOUNTER IN ATTEMPTING TO IMPLEMENT
THE DUTY TO REFRAIN

A. *Determining Competency*

Most prisoners, except possibly those who are psychotic or severely retarded, are competent to make decisions about their treatment or rehabilitation. Moreover, it is now generally recognized that persons who are mentally handicapped may have impaired functioning in some areas

---

Reprinted with permission from *Arizona Law Review*, Vol. 17, No. 1, 75-104. Copyright 1975, the Arizona Board of Regents. Because of the length of this article, the Editors have eliminated Sections I and II, with the permission of the author. The numbering of footnotes has been retained from the original article.

This article has been prepared with two limited purposes in mind: first, to survey and synthesize in nontechnical language some of the relevant scientific and legal literature concerning applied behavior analysis for a mixed audience of lawyers, behaviorists, and representatives both of prisons and mental hospitals and of their inmates; second, to serve as a catalyst for a full discussion of the very difficult ethical and legal issues posed by the use of applied behavior analysis in closed institutions. In this connection, the reader should take note that many of the issues treated briefly here—for example, the theory of a constitutional right to mental privacy or the notion of capacity to consent—are sufficiently complex to have been discussed and to

but be perfectly functional and competent in others.[183] For example, the Second Circuit has noted:

> [T]he law is quite clear in New York that a finding of "mental illness" even by a judge or jury, and commitment to a hospital, does not raise even a presumption that the patient is "incompetent" or unable adequately to manage his own affairs. Absent a specific finding of incompetence, the mental patient retains the right to sue or defend in his own name, to sell or dispose of his property, to marry, draft a will, and, in general to manage his own affairs.[184]

Nevertheless, because the very nature of a total institution impairs a patient's capacity to make important decisions concerning his life, the issue of whether a prisoner or mental patient is competent to give consent is always a difficult one. For example, while recognizing that involuntarily-detained mental patients may have sufficient IQ's to intellectually comprehend their circumstances, the *Kaimowitz* court noted with concern that "the very nature of [a confined mental patient's] incarceration diminishes his capacity to consent. . . . He is particularly vulnerable as a result of his mental condition, his involuntarily [*sic*] confinement, and the effects of 'institutionalization.' "[185]

Defining capacity to consent is, along with defining voluntariness, one of the thorniest of all issues involved in the regulation of applied be-

---

warrant discussion in individual scholarly articles. Given the very early stages of evolution of the law in this area, the reader is cautioned not to rely upon the conclusions reached and the recommendations propounded as definitive. Rather, this article should be used as a starting point for what will hopefully become a more comprehensive and systematic exploration of the many issues raised by all of those who are concerned.

The author wishes to acknowledge the valuable research assistance of Steve Scott, Wendy Krasner, Michelle Moss, and Susan Fox; and the helpful comments of Dr. Saleem Shah, Dr. G. Terence Wilson, and Dr. Todd Risley; attorneys at the ACLU National Prison Project; fellow members of the American Psychological Association's Commission on Behavior Modification; Benjamin W. Heineman, Jr., Joel Klein, James W. Ellis, and other colleagues at the Mental Health Law Project. The views reflected are those of the author and do not necessarily reflect those of the Mental Health Law Project.

183 See Winters v. Miller, 446 F.2d 65, 68 (2d Cir.), *cert. denied,* 404 U.S. 985 (1971); Henry v. Ciccone, 315 F. Supp. 889 (W.D. Mo. 1970).

184 Winters v. Miller, 446 F.2d, 65, 68 (2d Cir.), *cert. denied,* 404 U.S. 985 (1971).

185 Kaimowitz v. Michigan Dep't of Mental Health, 42 U.S.L.W. 2063, 2064 (C.A. 73-19434-AW, Cir. Ct. Wayne County, Mich., July 10, 1973). As the court explained the problem:

> The fact of institutional confinement has special force in undermining the capacity of the mental patient to make a competent decision on this issue, even though he is intellectually competent to do so. . . . Institutionalization tends to strip the individual of the support which permits him to mtaintain

havior analysis. As a general proposition, it may only be stated that capacity, like voluntariness, "is a requirement of variable demands."[186] Greater care must be taken when the proposed procedure is experimental, dangerous, or intrusive than when it is routine.

The goal of choosing a standard of competency is, on the one hand, to enhance self-autonomy and guard against paternalism and, on the other, to provide for vicarious judgment in the best interest of patients when necessary. As with so many of the difficult issues in mental health law, there may be no ideal approach. Under too lax a standard of competency, persons will be allowed to act in ways which may be viewed as being contrary to their best interests. Under too strict a standard, the opportunity for self-determination may be undermined and personal integrity denigrated by the paternalism of the state. Horror story hypotheticals can be formulated to expose potential weaknesses in any standard of competency that has been proposed. The real question is under which standard will undesirable results be most effectively minimized. Unfortunately, very little attention has been devoted to this problem to date, and it is, therefore, possible only to identify some of the different standards of competency which have been used and to briefly discuss the likely effects of choosing one standard over another.

1. *Competency defined as reaching a reasonable result.* One approach to determining competency requires the reviewer to decide whether the result of the client's decision is one which a "reasonably competent man might have made."[187] Thus, "[p]ersons who, because of mental illness, would be likely to make decisions about their own interests which would result in substantial damage to their own mental or physical well-being," should be deemed incompetent.[188] This approach has been criticized as

---

his sense of self worth and the value of his own physical and mental integrity. An involuntarily confined mental patient clearly has diminished capacity for making a decision. . . .
Id. (material not reported in U.S.L.W.). For exhaustive discussion of Kaimowitz and its ramifications, see Note, *supra* note 74, at 301.

[186] *U.S.L.W.* 42, at 2063.

[187] Green, Proof of Mental Incompetency and the Unexpressed Major Premise, *Yale L.J.*, 1944, 53, 271, 306-307; Note, Civil Commitment of the Mentally Ill: Theories and Procedures, *Harv. L. Rev.*, 1966, 79, 1288.

[188] Note, *supra* note 187, at 1295. *See also Nat'l Institute of Mental Health, Draft Act Governing Hospitalization of the Mentally Ill* § 9 (g) (2) (1952), found in *Amer. Bar Foundation, supra note* 164, at 457, 459. This section proposes involuntary commitment of patients who lack "sufficient insight or capacity to make responsible decisions with respect to hospitalization." The commentary to this section, however, indicates that the authorities are concerned only with the capacity of the individual. The issue is "whether he is *capable* of making a responsible, not necessarily a wise, decision. . . ." *Id.* at 469.

being extremely paternalistic and drawing a probably unsupportable distinction between the decision-making freedom of persons with physical illnesses and mental disabilities.[189] Under this standard, a mentally ill person who decides to forego a treatment despite a substantial risk to his mental well being might be labelled incompetent and thus denied his basic right to self-determination. Any determination of the reasonableness of a result is based on the balancing of complex factors and is likely to be subjective. Thus, adoption of this standard may result in a Catch-22 logic—any decision with which the reviewer of competency disagreed would provide a basis for labelling the client incompetent and for substituting the reviewer's opinion as to the best result for the client.

2. *Competency defined as the capacity to reach a decision based on rational reasons.* Under this standard, competency is defined as the capacity to understand the nature of the behavioral procedure, to weigh the risks and benefits, and to reach a decision for rational reasons. This standard is most commonly advanced in scholarly writings.[190] While it is an improvement on the first proposed standard, it has its own difficulties. To be sure, this standard tends to protect against the paternalistic tendency to substitute the reviewer's decision for the client's by focusing on the client's overall patterns of thought rather than on the result of a particular decision.[191] Thus, the patient's total decision making process is evaluated to determine if there is evidence of incoherent reasoning or eccentricities of emotion. The insolvable problem of any rationality test, however, is that it may express a value preference for a particular kind of thinking, the results of which have not been proved to be less valid than other modes of reasoning. As is commonly observed, the line between genius and madness is a thin one, and many sound decisions have been made on the basis of unconscious or preconscious thought or on the basis of what might be characterized as irrational or intuitive reasons. Arguably, any attempt to assess the quality of reasoning, as distinguished from the ability to decide at all, carries with it the danger that the reviewer of competency will substitute his own manner of thinking and value preferences for those of the clients.

189 *See* Dix, Hospitalization of the Mentally Ill in Wisconsin: A Need for a Reexamination, *Marq. L. Rev.*, 1967, 51, 2, 26-27 & n.79; Shapiro, *supra* note 76, at 288.
190 *See, e.g.*, Dix, *supra* note 189, at 26; Postel, Civil Commitment: A Functional Analysis, *Brooklyn L. Rev.*, 1971, 38, 1; Siegel, The Justifications for Medical Commitment—Real or Illusory, *Wake Forest L. Rev.*, 1969, 6, 21, 32-33; Developments—Civil Commitment, *supra* note 165, at 1217.
191 Shapiro, *supra* note 76, at 311-313.

3. *Competency defined as the capacity to make a decision.* A minority of courts and scholarly commentators have suggested an approach to defining competency which would avoid the difficulties inherent in evaluating whether a person's thought processes are rational or irrational but which also would preclude the apparent consent of persons clearly out of touch with reality. Under this approach, so long as the client has a sufficient understanding of the nature of the procedure, its risks and benefits, and the possible alternatives, his decision, provided there is a decision, will be honored.[192] Of course, here again, the question of what constitutes sufficient understanding is highly subjective.

In re Yetter,[193] a decision by a Pennsylvania lower court, provides a good illustration of the application of this approach. Maida Yetter had been committed to Allentown State Hospital in 1971, and her diagnosis at that time was chronic undifferentiated schizophrenia. Subsequently, because Mrs. Yetter was discovered to have a breast discharge, the doctors recommended a surgical biopsy and any additional necessary corrective surgery. Mrs. Yetter refused the surgery because she was afraid of that type of operation, which she claimed had resulted in the death of her aunt. The caseworker indicated that at the time of the refusal, Mrs. Yetter was "lucid, rational, and appeared to understand the possible consequences of her refusal included death."[194] The court described Mrs. Yetter's refusal as "informed" and "conscious of the consequences," and stated:

> The ordinary person's refusal to accept medical advice based upon fear is commonly known and while the refusal may be irrational and foolish to an outside observer, it cannot be said to be incompetent in order to permit the state to override the decision.
>
> . . . .
>
> . . . Upon reflection, balancing the risk involved in our refusal to act in favor of compulsory treatment against giving the greatest possible protection to the individual in furtherance of his own desires, we are unwilling now to overrule Mrs. Yetter's original irrational but competent decision.[195]

While the *Yetter* standard of competency would appear to be more objective and less likely to provoke disagreement in its application

---

[192] *See, e.g.,* In Re Yetter, 62 D. & C. 2d 619 (C.P. Northampton County, Pa. 1973); Grannum v. Berard, 70 Wash. 2d 304, 422 P.2d 812 (1967); Note, Informed Consent and the Dying Patient, *Yale L.J.,* 1974, 83, 1366.

[193] 62 D. & C. 2d 619 (C.P. Northampton County, Pa. 1973).

[194] *Id.* at 621.

than a rationality standard, it is not without its own problems. There was, for example, evidence in the *Yetter* case that Mrs. Yetter's decision to forego corrective surgery was based not only on irrational reasons but also on fundamental misperceptions of reality. Mrs. Yetter justified her objections to surgery on the basis that her aunt had died following surgery for cancer. In fact, the aunt's death was unrelated to her cancer operation and occurred some 15 years after that operation.[196] Other evidence that Mrs. Yetter's reasoning had a delusional component came from her responses to questions by the court and counsel; she indicated that the proposed operation would interfere with her genital system, affect her ability to have children, and would prohibit a movie career.[197] At the time of these questions, Mrs. Yetter was 60 years of age. It might, therefore, have been decided that Mrs. Yetter was not competent even under this standard because she lacked sufficient understanding of the nature of the procedure, the risks and benefits, and the alternatives involved.

Clearly, if a client is psychotic or hallucinating and cannot assimilate information about a proposed procedure at all, he is incompetent to make a decision one way or the other. More difficult situations are presented where the client cannot accurately "hear" and weigh the pertinent information for delusional reasons. Consider, for example, the difference between the decision of a child molestor to reject proposed aversive conditioning on the ground that the pain of the proposed procedure is not, in his opinion, worth the possibility of a change in his behavior and the decision of a similarly situated person to refuse aversive conditioning based on a paranoid belief that all behavior modifiers are conspiring in a plot to kill him or that he has a little man inside him who is his true self and who would be fried by any electricity. What this and similar hypothetical comparisons point up is that we are dealing with a question which involves the balancing of complex factors and the delicate evaluation of personal preferences.[198] The task of fram-

---

195. *Id.* at 624.
196 *Id.* at 622.
197 *Id.*
198 An approach to defining competency which would obviate these problems would be to forego any inquiry into understanding at all, provided a client is able to hear the question of whether he is willing to consent to a particular therapy and to answer either yes or no. Barring some additional requirement of a causal connection, the response of a client who automatically said, "no, no, no," to any and all questions which he was asked would be a competent refusal. Even with a causal connection requirement, this standard would require the response of a client who could hear the information given, but whose hallucinations caused serious distortions in his thinking, to be

ing an ideal standard of competency and studying its operational effectiveness is beyond the scope of this Article. The tentative approach recommended in the proposed standards set out in an Appendix to this Article[199] removes the rationality standard from the determination of competency since rationality per se is unduly restrictive. Instead, the standards define competency to consent as the ability to understand and knowingly act upon the information provided. Meaningful decisions concerning this or any other standard, however, can be made only through a careful empirical study of operational results.

B. *Determining Whether Consent in the Institutional Context Is Truly Voluntary and Competent*

After noting that a crucial element of informed consent is voluntariness, the *Kaimowitz*[200] court also gave an informative description of the great difficulty of eliciting a truly voluntary consent in an institutional setting:

> It is impossible for an involuntarily detained mental patient to be free of ulterior forms of restraint or coercion when his very release from the institution may depend upon his cooperating with the institutional authorities and giving consent to experimental surgery.

> The privileges of an involuntarily detained patient and the rights he exercises in the institution are within the control of the institutional authorities. As was pointed out in the testimony of John Doe, such minor things as the right to have a lamp in his room, or the right to have ground privileges to go for a picnic with his family assumed major proportions. For 17 years he lived completely under the control of the hospital. Nearly every important aspect of his life was decided without any opportunity on his part to participate in the decision-making process.

> . . . .

> Involuntarily confined mental patients live in an inherently coercive institutional environment. Inidirect and subtle psychological coercion has profound effects upon the patient population. . . . They

---

honored. This very low standard for competency was adopted by the federal district court in Wyatt v. Adarholt, 368 F. Supp. 1383 (M.D. Ala. 1974), with regard to consent by the mentally retarded to sterilization. The court's order provided that even legally incompetent residents may not be sterilized unless they have "formed . . . a genuine desire to be sterilized." *Id.* at 1385.

[199] See App. I, *infra* at 95.

[200] *U.S.L.W.*, 42, 2063 (C.A. 73-19434-AW, Cir. Ct. Wayne County, Mich., July 10, 1973). For a discussion of Kaimowitz, see text & notes 94-99 *supra*.

are not able to voluntarily give informed consent because of the inherent inequality in their positions.[201]

If the *Kaimowitz* court's analysis is read to mean that no involuntarily-confined patient may ever be subjected to any treatment since he can never give legally adequate consent, the thrust of normalization theory and the attempts of advocates of the mentally handicapped to restore to them the fullest possible degree of personal autonomy would be seriously undercut. Such a reading, however, would suggest a very unsophisticated understanding of the underlying issues of voluntariness, and a failure by the court to recognize that degrees of voluntariness exist in all situations, even those outside the confines of institutions. Read this way, the *Kaimowitz* decision would appear to assume that persons in the community always act with unimpaired voluntariness. Perhaps, they do in a very general sense; however, the husband or wife seeking private psychotherapy under pressure from a spouse who has threatened separation or divorce may actually act less voluntarily than a mental patient or prisoner agreeing to undertake psychotherapy. Clearly, involuntary confinement is only one of many variables, albeit a very important one, which can and do limit the voluntariness of a person's acts.

Fortunately, the *Kaimowitz* court does not appear to have intended to suggest that confined persons may never give a valid consent. As the court itself commented:

> We do not agree that a truly informed consent cannot be given for a regular surgical procedure by a patient, institutionalized or not. The law has long recognized that such valid consent can be given.

[201] Kaimowitz v. Michigan Dep't of Mental Health, *U.S.L.W.*, 42, 2063 (C.A. 73-19434-AW, Cir. Ct. Wayne County, Mich., July 10, 1973) (material not reported in *U.S.L.W.*). The appropriateness of the court's observations about the difficulty of assuring the voluntariness of a decision made by an involuntarily-confined person was nicely illustrated by subsequent events in this very case. While he was confined in Ionia State Hospital, the patient involved in the case staunchly maintained that he genuinely and voluntarily desired to participate in the psychosurgery experiment. Two review committees pressed him on whether his decision was the result of coercion, and he convinced them that he genuinely desired to participate, even if he were released from Ionia. Nevertheless, after he was released from the institution and after the sexual psychopath statute justifying his commitment was held to be unconstitutional, he suddenly saw things very differently and withdrew all consent for the performance of the proposed experiment. *Id.* (material not reported in *U.S.L.W.*). Moreover, whether or not the hope of early freedom and improved conditions destroys decision-making capacity or constitutes duress, an explicit or implicit offer of such benefits by the state may amount to an unconstitutional condition for freedom or privileges. Shapiro, *supra* note 76, at 318.

But we do hold that informed consent cannot be given by an involuntarily detained mental patient for experimental psychosurgery. . . .[202]

The analytical framework employed by the court does not regard consent as an all or nothing concept. In deciding whether there has been voluntary consent in a particular factual setting, a number of factors must be balanced. Consent must be more carefully scrutinized if the right to be waived is constitutionally protected, if the procedure to be employed is dangerous, or if the nature of the setting in which consent is to be given undermines capacity and voluntariness.[203]

This is the approach which has been adopted by several federal courts which have scrutinized ostensibly voluntary decisions by mental patients to undergo sterilization,[204] aversive conditioning,[205] or to labor without

---

[202] Kaimowitz v. Michigan Dep't of Mental Health, *U.S.L.W.*, 42, 2063 (CA 73-19434-AW, Cir. Ct. Wayne County, Mich., July 10, 1973) (material not reported in *U.S.L.W.*).

[203] As the *Kaimowitz* court stated:

> Informed consent is a requirement of variable demands. Being certain that a patient has consented adequately to an operation, for example, is much more important when doctors are going to undertake an experimental, dangerous, and intrusive procedure than, for example, when they are going to remove an appendix. When a procedure is experimental, dangerous, and intrusive, special safeguards are necessary. The risk-benefit ratio must be carefully considered, and the question of consent thoroughly explored.

Id. at 2063-64. The result reached in *Kaimowitz* is probably correct, but the opinion is very unclear on the issue of informed consent and probably confused the understanding of this important concept. As noted above, to the extent that it suggests that mental patients or prisoners may not be able to give consent to at least some procedures, it has potential for undermining their integrity and autonomy. What the *Kaimowitz* court was actually doing was making a basic social policy judgment that the potential harms of psychosurgery were so great and the potential benefits so small that involuntarily-confined mental patients, subject to especially strong coercion, should not be allowed to give consent to such a procedure. But to say that patients or prisoners should not be allowed, as a matter of social policy, to consent to certain procedures, or, to put it another way, to erect a ban on certain procedures in certain settings for social policy reasons is significantly different from saying that patients lack the ability to give a legally valid consent. Unfortunately, informed consent was the legal handle which the court utilized to accomplish an arguably worthy result at the cost of conceptual clarity and at the risk of undermining developing public notions that mental patients and prisoners are able to exercise autonomy and should be allowed to exercise autonomy to the fullest possible extent.

[204] *See* Wyatt v. Aderholt, 368 F. Supp. 1383 (M.D. Ala. 1974); *cf.* Relf v. Weinberger, 372 F. Supp. 1196 (D.D.C. 1974).

[205] *See* Knecht v. Gillman, 488 F.2d 1136 (8th Cir. 1973).

compensation in an institutional setting.[206] In such circumstances, and
in acknowledgment of the inherently coercive pressures of an institution,
the courts have scrutinized consent with special care, but have permitted
residents to consent to procedures after ascertaining that reasonable efforts have been undertaken to ensure capacity and voluntariness.[207] These
courts recognized the fallibility of consent in a total institutional setting.
They also recognized, however, that to assume that institutionalized
populations are incompetent to make any decisions affecting their lives
would have serious consequences; it would erode the notion of personal
autonomy and might well lead to a situation in which the state would
invoke alleged incapacity to consent as justification for substituting its
own judgment on a whole range of issues personally involving a patient
or prisoner. Such a situation would not only involve bad therapy or
rehabilitation fostering dependency and loss of self-control but also might
involve an unconstitutional abridgment of the first, fifth, or fourteenth
amendment rights of prisoners and mental patients.[208] Sound public
policy requires that courts and legislators formulate standards for consent which balance the threat of coercion against the equally serious
threat of paternalism.[209]

[206] See Henry v. Ciccone, 315 F. Supp. 889 (W.D. Mo. 1970); Parks v. Ciccone, 281
F. Supp. 805 (W.D. Mo. 1968). In Henry v. Ciccone, the court denied an involuntary
servitude claim only after it found that the patient knowingly and freely signed a
form which "fully informed him of his right not to work. . . . 315 F. Supp. at 891. The
court further found that "inmates who do not sign the waiver are permitted all normal privileges and no punitive action is taken against them . . . and that the work
agreement form is not binding. . . ." Id.

[207] For example, in Knecht v. Gillman, 488 F.2d 1136 (8th Cir. 1973), the Eighth
Circuit laid down specific safeguards designed to ensure that consent to an aversive conditioning program for inmates with behavioral problems was truly voluntary. The action was brought by two residents of the Iowa Security Medical Facility who sought to
enjoin the use of apomorphine on nonconsenting residents. For a fuller discussion of
Knecht, see text & notes 115-23 supra. The court ordered that all treatment using apomorphine be enjoined unless a written consent was obtained from the inmate specifying the nature, purpose, and risks of the treatment; advising the inmate of his right
to revoke his consent at any time; and, certifying by a physician that the inmate had
read and understood the terms of the consent and that the inmate was mentally
competent to understand the consent. While a step in the right direction, these standard procedures to ensure informed consent could certainly be improved. See App. I,
infra at 97-99.

[208] For a discussion of the constitutional rights of mental patients and prisoners, see
text accompanying notes 76-144 supra.

[209] One of the most interesting and difficult issues relating to voluntariness arises in
the context of contingency contracting procedures. Simply explained these procedures
are used for clients who express a wish to change certain deep-rooted behavior, such
as excessive eating, drinking, or smoking or a sexual fetish, but who lack the "self
control" to do so by themselves. In such procedures, various reinforcements are set

forth in advance for participation in therapy. In the behavioral treatment of obesity, for example, applied behavior analysts have eliminated the notorious tendency of obese clients to drop out of on-going therapy programs by making a refundable deposit contingent upon attendance at group sessions. *See, e.g.,* Romanczyk, Tracey, Wilson & Thorpe, Behavioral Techniques in the Treatment of Obesity: A Comparative Analysis, in *Behaviour Research & Therapy*, 1973, 629-640. In another variation on the same theme, applied behavior analysts often contract with clients to have post-dated checks sent off to the client's most disliked organization if therapeutic directives which have been mutually agreed upon are not followed. Boudin, Contingency Contracting as a Therapeutic Tool in the Deceleration of Amphetamine Use, *Behavior Therapy*, 1972, 3, 604, 604-608.

Applied behavior analysts argue with much persuasion that once clients have voluntarily agreed to enter into such a contract they should be legally required to see the behavioral procedure through, even if at a subsequent time the clients express the desire to dispense with the procedure in question. Such a requirement would appear to be most necessary in connection with procedures involving aversive stimuli. A client may very desperately wish to rid himself of an alcohol addiction or a sexual fetish and may therefore agree to a program involving aversive stimuli, but when it is time for the aversive stimulus—electric shock or a nausea-inducing drug, for example—to be applied, the client may suddenly see the matter in a very different perspective and vigorously attempt to withdraw his consent.

The essential dilemma here is that the time in the presence of the aversive stimuli which will ultimately make it possible to stop drinking or having perverse sexual fantasies is the very time at which the value of being able to stop seems lowest to the client. As soon as the aversive stimuli are removed, the value of not drinking or the wish to be free of the sexual fetish assumes its usual high place. The commitment to accept the consequences in this situation must be offered and accepted at a time when the value of not smoking or not drinking is high. The effect of the commitment is to reduce the client's choice—to *compel* him to give up his addiction. Rachlin, *supra* note 8, at 100-04. Perhaps the classic expression of this commitment strategy is Homer's recounting of how Odysseus arranged to have himself bound to the mast of his ship ahead of time so that when he sailed by the island of the Sirens, he could not be tempted by their dangerous enticements.

Seen from this perspective, the attempt of the court in Knecht v. Gillman, 488 F.2d 1136 (8th Cir. 1973), to set forth specific safeguards to assure the voluntariness of resident consent to behavioral programs involving aversive stimuli is very important and controversial. In *Knecht,* the Eighth Circuit held as a matter of constitutional law that in order to ensure informed consent, an inmate must have "the right to terminate his consent at any time." Applied behavior analysis would argue that this approach might frustrate well-meaning attempts to utilize contingency contracting procedures involving aversive stimuli and would make it legally impossible for clients with self-control problems to adopt an effective "commitment" strategy. With regard to such procedures, applied behavior analysts also argue a contractual theory that once a client makes a valid "contract" to undergo such a procedure, and the applied behavior analyst goes to the trouble of designing an individualized program, they should have a right to compel the client to perform this part of the contract or at least to pay the designated forfeits.

This analysis grows out of discussion with Professor David B. Wexler and Dr. G. Terence Wilson. The problems associated with a rule of revocability have, for the past few years, been of particular interest to Professor Wexler. *See* Wexler, Foreword: Mental Health Law and the Movement Toward Voluntary Treatment, *Calif. L. Rev.,* 1974, 62, 671, 688-691; Wexler, Of Rights and Reinforcers, *San Diego L. Rev.,* 11, 957,

The problem of securing a valid informed consent from institutionalized populations has been recognized by behaviorists as well as the
courts,[210] and the meaning of informed consent has been considered in
the context of behavior therapy. One approach relies on the individuals'
ability to learn behavioral principles and understand how environmental
events can control their own behavior.[211] The hope is that behavioral
principles are more widely disseminated and understood by the public,
the client population will become increasingly sophisticated about issues
of control and will resist controls with which they are not in sympathy.

970-971; Wexler, Reflections on the Legal Regulation of Behavior Modification in
Institutional Settings, Ariz. L. Rev., 1975, 17, 132, 138-140; Wexler, Therapeutic Justice, Minn. L. Rev., 1972, 57, 289, 330-331; Wexler, supra note 12, at 108 n. 151.

[210] Some exponents of applied behavior analysis challenge the applicability of the
concept of informed consent to the treatment of institutionalized mental patients and
prisoners. See R. K. Schwitzgebel, A Contractual Model for the Protection of the Rights
of Institutionalized Patients, 1975 (unpnblished paper). They argue that informed
consent is a notion derived from the medical model of treatment. While it may be
appropriate to a decision concerning therapy, it is not a relevant concept under a
learning theiry model of behavior change. The more appropriate model, it is argued,
would be a contractual model in which the client and the therapist agree upon explicit
goals and the means by which these goals will be achieved, each undertaking specified
responsibilities in this regard. Adoption of the contractual model, however, would
give only illusory relief to the therapist who believes that under this model the nag-
ging problem of informed consent disappears. In the first place, courts have traditionally exercised their power to review and, on occasion, declare contracts void when the
bargaining was not between parties of equal status or power or where one side was
able to effectively coerce or influence the other into signing. A. Corbin, Contracts,
1952, § 228. Courts have also held contracts which are based on fraud or inaccurate
information to be voidable, id. §§ 6, 146, 228, and contracts made by minors or incompetents are voidable as a matter of public policy. Id. §§ 6, 146, 227. Thus, the issues
of knowledge, competency, and voluntariness will be just as relevant under a contractual model of behavioral therapy as under a medical model. Finally, if the Constitution
protects mentation and privacy against coercive intrusion by the state in at least some
situations, then a necessary condition for use of such therapies by the state is the informed consent of the subject. Shapiro, supra note 76, at 307.

[211] Stolz, Ethical Issues in Research on Behavior Therapy, March 28, 1974 (unpublished paper presented at the First Drake Conference on Professional Issues in Behavior
Analysis, March 28-29, 1974, Des Moines, Iowa), on file in the Arizona Law Review
office; see Davidson, Countercontrol in Behavior Modification, in L. Hamerlynck, L.
Handy, and E. Mash (Eds.), Behavior Change: Methodology, Concepts, and Practice,
1973, 153 (arguing that "nearly everything we do in behavior modification requires
the active cooperation of the client. This is especially true when the therapist cannot
be present whenever the problematic behavior may occur, and/or when the therapist's
presence cannot insure the forcing out of a particular response at any given time").
See also Freund, Some Problems in the Treatment of Homosexuality, in H. Eysenck
(Ed.), Behaviour Therapy and the Neuroses, 1960. Freund's study found that markedly
fewer homosexuals referred for therapy by the courts or coerced by relatives achieved
changes in sexual orientation than patients who seemed to have come of their own
accord.

It is recognized, however, that "until behavioral understanding is more widespread than it is at present, experimenters should be particularly sensitive to the manner in which they describe research and ask for the subject's cooperation. [Behaviorists] should help [their] subjects by making them aware of variables that may affect their decision."[212]

A third behaviorist would, however, go even further. Noting that possible remedies for exploitative use of psychological techniques are usually discussed in terms of individual safeguards and that increased knowledge about modes of influence is prescribed as the best defense to manipulation, he observes that awareness alone is insufficient.

> If protection against exploitation relies solely upon individual safeguards, people would continually be subjected to coercive pressures. Accordingly, they create institutional sanctions which set limits on the control of human behavior. The integrity of individuals is largely secured by societal safeguards that place restraints upon improper means and foster reciprocity through balancing of interests.[213]

One behaviorist has offered the following helpful definition of uncoerced consent in behavioral terms:

> We may now define contingencies of consent. The behaviors of the subject are on the left and the consequences provided are on the right. Aversive confinement is in parentheses because it may not be involved in non-penal institutions:
>
> 1. Ongoing program participation
> → Standard custodial consequences (and standard aversive confinement).
>
> 2. Program participation absent
> → Standard custodial consequences (and standard aversive confinement).

212 Stoltz, *supra* note 211, at 12-13. *See also Nat'l Prison Project, Comments on DHEW-NIH Draft and Regulations: Prisoners* (undated) (comments by Holland); Ulrich, Behavior Control and Public Concern, *Psychological Record*, 1967, 17, 229-234.

213 Bandura, *supra* note 8, at 868. It is the discussion of just such institutional sanctions and restraints, of course, which is the purpose of the conference for which this Article is written.

AND
3. Ongoing program participation
                                    → Program-specific
                                    consequences.

4. Program participation absent
                                    → No program-specific
                                    consequences.

Stated otherwise, the institution provides or eliminates no custodial (or confinement) consequences contingent on participation or non-participation in the program. What maintains participation is the delivery and nondelivery of consequences which derive from the program itself. The presence of this set of options defines a *noncoercive* situation.

. . . .

This method not only defines the options as noncoercive, but as involving full consent.[214]

The approach taken to formulating the protective standards later set forth in this Article is in harmony with that of the cases and commentators cited above. Informed consent is not treated as a unitary concept.

---

[214] Goldiamond, Toward a Constructional Approach to Social Problems: Ethical and Constitutional Issues Raised by Applied Behavior Analysis, *Behaviorism*, 1974, 2, 1-84.
    Other behaviorists offer a proposal for securing consent which involves a hierarchy of protections responsive to the level of benefit to the client; level of risk; the validational status of the procedure to be used; and the extent to which the client can freely render informed consent. G. Davison & R. Stuart, *supra* note 12, at 15-16. This proposal can be diagramed as follows:

		Level of Potential Benefit to Subject		Low Potential Benefit to Subject/High Potential Benefit to Society	
		High Potential Benefit to Subject			
	Novelty of Procedure	Established	Experimental	Established	Experimental
Level of Risk	Likelihood of Free Consent				
Low	Great Freedom	1	3	2	4
Risk	Some Coercion	4	5	7	8
High	Great Freedom	2	4	5	10
Risk	Some Coercion	6	7	9	N/A

The above graph ranks the degree of consent which is required in relation to the variable factors. The number 1 signifies that the consent can be simply verbal. The number 10 signifies that consent must be witnessed and approved by an outside review panel.

The model invoked recognizes that coercive influences[215] and diminished capacity will depend upon the setting in which consent takes place and the nature of the procedure for which consent is requested. Just as a person may be competent for some purposes but not for others, the same person may be competent to consent to some procedures and not to others. The more coercive the pressures to which a person is subjected and the more potentially harmful, intrusive, or experimental are the procedures for which consent is requested, the stricter and more numerous must be the safeguards erected to protect the person from an unwarranted intrusion. Although none of the generally accepted applied behavior techniques appear to be so offensive as to require an absolute protective ban, some are potentially abusive and require the strictest control.

C. Determining Best Interest

The functional equivalent of consent by a competent patient is the notion that the treatment of an incompetent patient must be in his best interest. The idea that a procedure is in the client's best interest would require, at a minimum, that the benefits of the contemplated procedure clearly outweigh both the known harms and the possible risks or side effects. Ideally, there should be assurance that the proposed procedure is in fact efficacious; and that where the procedure is either intrusive or hazardous, less intrusive or less hazardous procedures have first been exhausted.

---

215 The danger of abuse of prisoners' rights is obvious. Most glaring is the possibility that the degrading and depressing aspects of prison life, combined with the lure of parole, will make a truly voluntary consent impossible. Given this inherent coercion, critics have called for a temporary or permanent ban on the use of prisoners for research. See Capron, Medical Research in Prisons, Hastings Center Rep., 1973, 4.

While admitting the possibility of coercion, other critics have refused to call for an outright ban on such prison research and instead have urged greater supervision and control over the consent process. Among those proposing means for greater control are: Alberts & DeReimer, Connecticut "Watchdogs" Human Research Experiments, Amer. J. of Correction, 1973, 40; Hodges & Bean, supra note 158, at 177. Rules promulgated by HEW on May 30, 1974 adopt such a regulatory position. See 39 Fed. Reg. 18914 (1974). On August 23, 1974, HEW proposed additional regulations providing more safeguards for vulnerable groups, such as prisoners and the mentally disabled. See 39 Fed. Reg. 30647 (1974).

A Commission for the Protection of Human Patients has been recently established by Congress and charged with identifying the basic ethical principles which should underlie research, developing guidelines accordingly, and making recommendations to the Secretary of HEW concerning administrative action. See generally Human Experimentation Regulations: Too Little or Too Much? Federation of Amer. Scientists Professional Bull., Feb. 1975, 3.

Since a best interest determination requires a balancing, it must be the outcome of a decision making process and cannot be objectively described. The numerous variables, such as intrusiveness, risk, potential harm, or side effects, the degree to which the procedure is established or experimental, and the efficacy of the treatment, cannot be fully quantified. For example, a relatively safe procedure may not be in the person's best interest if there are even safer and more efficacious procedures available to effect the same behavioral change; conversely, a highly risky or intrusive procedure may be in the client's best interest if the available alternatives are even more risky, more intrusive, or less effective.

Procedures which would normally be considered intolerable may be acceptable if they are successful in eliminating even less desirable conditions:

> It can be argued . . . that elimination of severe self-abusive behavior warrants the use of painful stimuli, since the damage to the subject is relatively milder and of much shorter duration. Again, these questions are ethical rather than empirical in nature and value judgments must be made in reaching decisions. The making of value judgments is inescapable in such cases, since deciding not to use aversive conditioning is itself a decision based on value considerations which can have major consequences for the subject. For example, without recourse to aversive conditioning, prevention of self-injury or possibly death may require indefinite use of restraint which can effectively totally curtail the individual's development and freedom of action.[216]

Consequently, one must carefully balance a wide variety of factors in determining whether a particular procedure is in the best interest of an incompetent patient.

D. The Validity of Vicarious Parental Consent for Children

Traditionally, minors have been presumed to be incompetent, and parents have given vicarious consent on their behalf for various therapies

---

[216] Roos, *supra* note 12, at 3. An interesting issue relating to best interest determinations is whether prior competent indications of a desire to undertake or refuse specific procedures by a now incompetent client should be honored. The theoretical issue underlying this question is whether the purpose of substitute judgment for incompetent clients is to make the decision which they themselves would have made were they competent or whether it is to make the decision that a reasonable man would make under all the circumstances known. Those commentators who have addressed this issue seem to agree that where the essential facts remain the same and where the prior decision was competent, it should be honored even though the client is now incompetent and others may feel that a reasonable man would have made a different decision.

and even for civil commitment. Recently, however, the assumption that parents always effectively represent the best interests of their children when giving consent has been called into question.[217] With regard to civil commitment, for example, a New York federal court held that:

> There may be a fundamental conflict of interest between a parent who is ready to avoid the responsibility for caring for an abnormal child, and the best interests of the child. . . . A "voluntary admission" on the petition of the parents may quite properly be treated in the same category as an "involuntary admission," in the absence of evidence the child's interests have been fully considered.[218]

One commentator has observed that factors motivating parents to seek institutionalization of their children include the interest of other children in the family, the mental and physical frustration of the parents, economic strain resulting from caring for the child at home, the stigma of retardation, hostility resulting from the burdens of caring for the child, and the parents' success-oriented expectations of the child.[219]

At least one federal court has extended the questionability of parental consent from the civil commitment process to the intrusive surgical procedure of sterilization. In Relf v. Weinberger,[220] plaintiffs challenged the statutory authorization and constitutionality of regulations of the

See, e.g., Cantor, A Patient's Decision to Decline Life-Saving Medical Treatment: Bodily Integrity vs. The Preservation of Life, Rutgers L. Rev., 1973, 26, 228; Developments—Civil Commitment, supra note 165, at 1218 n.95; Note, An Adult's Right to Resist Blood Transfusions: A View Through John F. Kennedy Memorial Hospital v. Heston, Notre Dame Law, 1972, 47, 571. This issue is by no means academic since many mental disorders have the effect of intermittently causing their victims to become disoriented while leaving them completely lucid otherwise. See Developments—Civil Commitment, supra note 165, at 1217 n. 91.

[217] See generally J. Goldstein, A. Freud, & A. Solnit, Beyond the Best Interests of the Child, 1973; Ellis, Volunteering Children: Parental Commitment of Minors to Mental Institutions, Calif. L. Rev., 1974, 62, 840.

[218] New York State Ass'n for Retarded Children v. Rockefeller, 357 F. Supp. 752, 762 (E.D.N.Y. 1973) (citations omitted); accord, Saville v. Treadway, Civ. No. 6969 (M.D. Tenn., Mar. 8, 1974) ("possible conflicts of interest between a mentally retarded child and even a parent" render apparently "voluntary" commitments of mentally retarded children under the Tennessee statute constitutionally inadequate); see Heryford v. Parker, 396 F.2d 393, 396 (10th Cir. 1968); Horacek v. Exon, 357 F. Supp. 71 (D. Neb. 1973) (preliminary relief); Frazier v. Levi, 440 S.W.2d 393 (Tex. Civ. App. 1969); cf. Strunk v. Strunk, 445 S.W.2d 145 (Ky. Ct. App. 1969). See generally Ellis, Supra note 217, at 844-850; Herr, Retarded Children and the Law: Enforcing the Constitutional Rights of the Mentally Retarded, Syracuse L. Rev., 1972, 23, 995; Murdock, Civil Rights of the Mentally Retarded: Some Critical Issues, Notre Dame Law, 1972, 48, 133, 139-143.

[219] Murdock, supra note 217, at 139-143.

[220] 372 F. Supp. 1196 (D.D.C. 1974).

Department of Health, Education, and Welfare governing sterilizations under the programs funded by the Department of Public Health Services. The *Relf* court found uncontroverted evidence in the record that minors and other incompetents had been sterilized in a family planning program which Congress had intended to function on a purely voluntary basis. In order to ensure that sterilizations under the program were voluntary in the full sense of the term, the court found it necessary to enjoin or revise substantial portions of the regulations which had allowed the "voluntary" participation of minors and other incompetents.

An analysis of the revisions suggest that an institution utilizing constitutionally intrusive behavioral procedures on children would be advised to seek consent directly from the child as well as the parent.[221] Review of proposed procedures by a committee which would not have the possible conflict of interest problems of a parent would help protect against biased decisions. Some procedures, like sterilization, however, may be so intrusive and irreversible that they call for a per se rule enjoining their use until such time as a child becomes an adult and is capable of giving a legally valid consent.

E. *Determining Intrusiveness*

Not every behavioral procedure is sufficiently intrusive to require either waiver by competent patients or a best interest determination for incompetent patients. Where such a determination is required, however, there exists a need for criteria determining intrusiveness and a consensus about a hierarchy of alternative behavioral procedures based upon their intrusiveness. Without criteria for intrusiveness, for example, it is difficult to determine whether, in any given situation, psychoanalysis is more or less intrusive than aversive conditioning by electric shock.

One commentator has suggested the following six criteria for intrusiveness:

> (i) the extent to which the effects of the therapy upon mentation are reversible; (ii) the extent to which the resulting psychic state is "foreign," "abnormal" or "unnatural" for the person in question, rather than simply a restoration of his prior psychic state (this is closely related to the "magnitude" or "intensity" of the change); (iii) the rapidity with which the effects occur; (iv) the scope of the change in the total "ecology" of the mind's functions; (v) the ex-

---

221 *Id.* at 1204-1205.

tent to which one can resist acting in ways impelled by the psychic effects of the therapy; and (vi) the duration of the change.[222]

Even guided by these criteria of intrusiveness, deciding which treatments are more restrictive is largely a matter of subjective opinion and theoretical disposition. But the idea that some techniques may be viewed as more onerous than others and that they may be categorized may contribute to making the search for the least restrictive alternative less difficult.[223]

It is beyond the scope of this discussion to improve upon the important initial efforts made by these commentators. Ultimately, in order to make judgments about the client's right to refuse and determinations of best interest, the exponents of applied behavior analysis and other concerned individuals must systematically establish the range of specific behaviors which are presently sought to be promoted or extinguished. Then, for each specific behavior, they must list all the various techniques which are thought to promote or extinguish that behavior and must indicate for each procedure: 1) both its short and long-term effectiveness; 2) its intrusiveness upon the personal autonomy of the patient; 3) the harms and the probability of such harms resulting from its use; 4) how experimental, from a medical view, the use of the technique to promote or extinguish the specific behavior is; and 5) how the alternative procedures available to modify each specific behavior compare in terms of the above categories.

IV. PROCEDURAL LIMITATIONS ON IMPOSING TREATMENT—DUE PROCESS REVISITED

The primary focus of this Article has been the right to refuse treatment. Accordingly, primary emphasis has been placed on developing and

---

[222] Shapiro *supra* note 76, at 262.

[223] Another commentator has formulated a "coerciveness continuum" for various therapeutic techniques, ranking coerciveness according to three criteria: (1) the nature, extent, and duration of the primary and side effects of the technique; (2) the extent to which an "uncooperative" patient can avoid the effects of the technique; and (3) the extent of the physical intrusion. Note, *supra* note 10, at 619. This resulted in the following ranking of therapies from the least to the most intrusive: milieu therapy, psychotherapy, drug therapy, behavior modification, aversion therapy, electroconvulsive therapy, electronic stimulation of the brain, lobotomy, and stereotactic psychosurgery. *Id.* at 619-633. It might be questioned, however, whether behavior modification is amenable to such a ranking since it covers a small universe of different procedures, all of which have varying degrees of intrusiveness. Compare the proposed standards and procedures in Appendix I, *infra* at 95, which provide that different behavior modification techniques be ranked in three sepaarte categories calling for different protective safeguards according to their differing degrees of intrusiveness.

analyzing the possible bases for the applied behavior analyst's duty to refrain from utilizing hazardous or intrusive behavioral procedures except under special circumstances. A discussion of applied behavioral analysis in mental institutions and prisons would not be complete, however, without a brief discussion of procedural due process and the limitations which it may impose on the utilization of behavioral procedures.

Procedural due process requires that persons be given adequate notice, an opportunity to be heard, and other procedural protections where impending state action will deprive them of a significant property or liberty interest.[224] The fundamental question in each case is whether a deprivation without notice and an opportunity to be heard violate traditional notions of fairness.[225] A determination that liberty or property interests protected by due process are being invaded, however, is only the beginning of the inquiry. The nature and extent of the procedural protections required will depend on the importance of the liberty or property interests involved and the nature of the proceedings.[226]

The due process rights of prisoners and mental patients have been the subject of acute controversy. In the past, courts have ordered hearings before patients were transferred to sections of a hospital with greater security and fewer privileges[227] or were returned to prison after receiving hospital treatment.[228] Courts also have accorded prisoners the right to a hearing before allowing changes in the conditions of confinement.[229]

Of particular interest in the behavior modification areas is Clonce v. Richardson,[230] a recent right-to-refuse rehabilitation case resting on procedural due process grounds. The challenged program, Special Treatment and Rehabilitative Training [START], was developed at the Medical Center for Federal Prisoners at Springfield, Missouri, in Sep-

---

[224] See, e.g., Wolff v. McDonnell, 418 U.S. 539 (1974); Fuentes v. Shevin, 407 U.S. 67 (1972); Goldberg v. Kelley, 397 U.S. 254 (1970).

[225] See, e.g., Duncan v. Louisiana, 391 U.S. 145 (1968); Gideon v, Wainwright, 372 U.S. 335 (1963); Palko v. Connecticut, 302 U.S. 319 (1937).

[226] See, e.g., Fuentes v. Shevin, 407 U.S. 67 (1972); Cafeteria & Restaurant Workers Local 473 v. McElroy, 367 U.S. 886 (1961); Hannah v. Larche, 363 U.S. 420 (1960).

[227] Jones v. Robinson, 440 F.2d 249 (D.C. Cir. 1971).

[228] Burchett v. Bower, 355 F. Supp. 1278 (D. Ariz. 1973).

[229] Wolff v. McDonnell, 418 U.S. 539 (1974) (placement in punitive segregation); Schumate v. People, 373 F. Supp. 1166 (S.D.N.Y. 1974) (termination of work-release privileges); Cousins v. Oliver, 369 F. Supp. 553 (E.D. Va. 1974) (reclassification leading to reduced privileges); White v. Gillman, 360 F. Supp. 64 (S.D. Ia. 1973) (transfer to an institution of increased security); Park v. Thompson, 356 F. Supp. 783 (D. Hawaii 1973) (transfer to an out-of-state prison).

[230] 379 F. Supp. 338 (W.D. Mo. 1974).

tember 1972. START was an involuntary program. Prisoners who were selected for placement in START were not notified that they were being considered for the program, nor were they granted an opportunity for a hearing at the time of their selection.

The stated purpose of START was to teach participants to adjust to the requirements demanded in a prison environment, rather than to make them better adapted to life in the community after release from prison. No prisoner was permitted to leave the START unit for the purpose of attending religious services, and Muslim petitioners were not provided with an opportunity to consult with or to seek guidance from a Muslim spiritual leader. START prisoners in the "orientation" phase, the lowest level of the program, were prohibited from possessing, reading, or otherwise using political and educational literature, religious materials, and political publications. They were denied the opportunity to view television and possess or utilize a radio. Their actions, including communications with others in the START program, were under continual surveillance for the purpose of determining the inmates' rates of progress.

The START program had several ingredients of a behavior modification system, including deprivation state, reinforcement arrangement, and a graded progression of criteria for reinforcement. The program operated as a form of a token economy designed to teach prisoners to live according to the rules of a penal institution by taking away all privileges and rights, and then offering to restore them in graduated steps as the prisoner "progressed."

On the merits, the court held that "a prisoner transferred into START or into a behavior modification program like START, which . . . involves a major change in the conditions of confinement is entitled, at a minimum, to the type of hearing required by the Supreme Court's opinion in Wolff v. McDonnell."[231] The Wolff court had required prison officials to provide a hearing, written notice to a prisoner of his alleged violation, a written statement of findings of fact, and a right to call witnesses, all prior to the imposition of solitary confinement or the deprivation of good-time credits.[232]

---

[231] Id. at 348.

[232] The Clonce court declined to answer, on grounds of mootness, the questions whether a prisoner selected to participate in START had a right to freely withdraw without penalty and whether the START program, as designed and applied, violated protected constitutional rights such as freedom of religion, freedom of speech and association, the right to be free from unwarranted search and seizure, the right of privacy, and the prohibition against cruel and unusual punishment. The court's opinion, how-

Undoubtedly, *Clonce* foreshadows the application of procedural due process protections to prisoners and mental patients participating in other behavior modification programs. The limitations of the case's impact, however, should be noted. The START program involved extensive deprivations for lengthy periods and major changes in the conditions of confinement. Thus, it is unclear to what extent the requirements of *Wolff* would apply to most behavior modification programs. Further case law development will be necessary to define the scope of procedural protections required for various behavior modification programs. In this regard, a major concern of the standards proposed in this Article is the assurance of adequate procedural safeguards for mental patients prior to the imposition of behavioral treatments.

CONCLUSION

It is difficult at present to give precise advice to applied behavior analysts or other therapists as to the legal limitations on the use of behavioral or other procedures. The greater volume of legal precedent suggests an overly deferential respect by courts for the discretionary judgments of administrators and staff of mental institutions and prisons[233] Nevertheless, one senses that newer and stricter notions of accountability are gaining acceptance. Cases such as *Kaimowitz, Knecht, Mackey,* and *Wyatt* suggest a new and more activist judicial scrutiny of enforced therapy. Consequently, although it may not be stated with certainty that the following proposed standards and procedures are constitutionally required at this time, it is fair to say that an applied behavior analyst or other therapist who complies with these standards will minimize the risk of costly and vexacious litigation. The following proposed standards and procedures should be acceptable because they

---

ever, implicitly recognizes the nonfrivolity of these constitutional claims. Serious constitutional issues were clearly raised since.

> [f]orced participation in S.T.A.R.T. was obviously designed to accomplish a modification of the participant's behavior and his general motivation. He was forced to submit to procedures designed to change his mental attitudes, reactions and processes. A prisoner may not have a constitutional right to prevent such experimentation but procedures specifically designed and implemented to change a man's mind and therefore his behavior in a manner substantially different from the conditions to which a prisoner is subjected in segregation reflects a major change in the conditions of confinement.

379 F. Supp. at 350. In context, the meaning of this somewhat ambiguous statement appears to be that the court did not have to reach the issue whether other constitutional rights were denied by the START program in order to hold that due process is violated if prisoners are transferred without a notice and hearing.

comport with recommended standards for professional practice found in the literature and because similar approaches have not been deemed unduly cumbersome or restrictive by representative behavior analysts the author has had the opportunity to consult. But, whether such standards could be practically implemented is an issue which requires further debate and discussion.[234]

APPENDIX I

Proposed Standards and Procedures to Govern Applied Behavior Analysis in Mental Institutions[235]

I. *Declaration of Policy*

It is hereby recognized and declared that all persons involuntarily confined to mental institutions have a fundamental right to refuse behavioral procedures which intrude upon their first, eighth, and fourteenth amendment rights under the United States Constitution. This fundamental right

---

[233] See discussion note 3 *supra.*

[234] This is, of course, precisely the subject for full discussion and debate at the conference for which this Article has been prepared.

These proposed standards draw upon and attempt to integrate several existing models. In large part, they grow out of the author's experience as a member of a Joint Task Force on Behavioral Procedures which was assembled by the Florida Division of Retardation and the Department of Psychology of Florida State University on June 17, 1974, after some incidents of alleged abuse involving behavioral programs in Florida's institutions. Much of the credit for Task Force recommendations concerning legal rights of the clients/residents in Florida's institutions belongs to Professor David Wexler, College of Law, University of Arizona, who was also a member of the Task Force. The final report of the Task Force, entitled Florida Guidelines for the Use of Behavioral Procedures in State Programs for the Retarded, is to be published shortly in monograph form by the National Association for Retarded Citizens. Another important model which was considered and often closely followed in developing these proposed standards was the proposed California standards. *See* Shapiro, *supra* note 76, at 339-346 (analyzing the California standards). *See also* Wyatt v. Aderholt, 368 F. Supp. 1383 (M.D. Ala. 1974) (standards regulating voluntary sterilization); Wyatt v. Aderholt, Civ. No. 3195-N (M.D. Ala., Interim Order issued Feb. 25, 1975) (standards regulating the administration of psychosurgery, aversive conditioning, and electroconvulsive therapy); G. Davison & R. Stuart, *supra* note 12; M. Wolf, D. Fixsen, & E. Phillips, Some Suggestions for Accountability Procedures for Behavior Modification Treatment Programs, June 3, 1974 (unpublished paper presented at NIMH Behavior Modification Seminar), on file in the *Arizona Law Review* office.

[235] Standards for the use of applied behavior analysis in prison are not set forth. The operation of behavioral programs in prisons creates even more difficult problems than the operation of such programs in mental institutions. Of concern is the likelihood of considerable abuse of behavioral programs by prison guards, *see, e.g.,* Clonce v. Richardson, 379 F. Supp. 338 (W.D. Mo. 1974); Hilts, *supra* note 19; Opton, *supra*

requires that any person who has the capacity to give informed consent and who refuses certain behavioral procedures may not be compelled to undergo such procedures. In order to justify the use of these behavioral procedures upon a person who lacks the capacity for informed consent, the state must establish that such procedures would be in the best interest of the person and that all less onerous alternatives to the proposed procedure have been exhausted or would be ineffective. No behavioral procedure shall be applied without the prior approval of a Peer Review Committee and a Human Rights Committee.

II. *Peer Review Committee*

A. There shall be established a state-wide Peer Review Committee [PRC] which shall consist of three members, two of whom have demonstrated competence in applied behavior analysis, but with different theoretical orientations, one of whom is a physician. The PRC shall be appointed by the governor, subject to approval by the state chapters of the National Association for Retarded Citizens [NARC] and the National Association for Mental Health [NAMH]. Members of this Committee shall serve 2-year staggered terms and shall be compensated at an appropriate level.

B. New behavioral programs or particular behavioral procedures which are specifically designed for an individual or group of individuals and which are proposed for introduction in any facility shall first be submitted to the PRC for its approval. The PRC also shall review particular behavioral procedures upon request for the Human Rights Committee. Approval by the PRC shall be based on a finding that the procedure is effective for strengthening or weakening specified behaviors and that the design of the procedure is professionally sound. The PRC shall set forth all possible harms associated with the proposed procedure and the likelihood of occurrence of each harm. It also shall indicate

---

note 32, and the possibility that prison officials may alter the goal of behavioral programs to one of shaping a prisoner's behavior to the institution's needs, rather than to one of enabling the prisoner to adapt his behavior to society. Such an alteration in behavioral objectives may actually have an antirehabilitative effect. *Id.*

One possible approach to avoiding such abuses would be to require that all hazardous and intrusive behavioral programs be operated outside the prison setting by independent professionals on a subcontract basis. A primary objective of such programs must remain that of enabling an inmate to better function upon return to society, rather than to conform to the "unreal" environment of the prison. A second alternative would be to prohibit hazardous and intrusive, or perhaps all, behavioral programs in prisons on the grounds that the real purposes of criminal confinement are deterrence and retribution and that behavioral programs in the context of criminal confinement have simply not proved effective. A final alternative would be to allow behavioral programs within prisons to be run under much the same safeguards proposed for mental institutions. The approach to regulating behavioral programs in prisons is a matter of utmost complexity and importance and will hopefully receive appropriate attention at the conference for which this Article has been written.

whether there is a risk of unknown harms and the likelihood of their occurrence. The PRC also shall indicate whether there are less hazardous or intrusive procedures which would be effective to accomplish the stated behavioral objective. The PRC may disapprove the proposed procedure, approve it, or approve it with specified modifications, limitations, or restrictions.

C. The PRC shall keep a written record of the factors enumerated in paragraph (B) above and the reasons supporting these decisions.

III. *Human Rights Committee*

A. There shall be established a Human Rights Committee [HRC] for various regions in the state. Each HRC shall consist of five members unaffiliated with the Division of Mental Health or Mental Retardation, among whom shall be: an applied behavior analyst; a lawyer, preferably with experience in representing the mentally handicapped and versed in civil liberties; a representative of the consumers of behavioral services; and concerned members of the community. Members shall serve for 3-year staggered terms and shall be compensated at an appropriate level. Appointment to the HRC shall be by the governor, with the approval of the local chapters of the NARC and the NAMH. The HRC shall meet as necessary, but no less than once monthly.

B. The HRC shall receive and investigate complaints regarding behavioral programs lodged by clients, parents, staff, public officials, members of the press, or the public. The HRC also shall make periodic visits to the state's mental institutions and inspect their facilities and behavioral programs.

C. The HRC shall have responsibility for categorizing target behaviors and the procedures used to strengthen or weaken such behaviors according to the following scheme:

1) Procedures not sufficiently hazardous or intrusive to raise constitutional issues and used to modify behaviors which are clearly for the benefit of the clients/residents and not primarily for the benefit or convenience of the institution.[236] Once initially approved by the HRC and the PRC, these combinations of behaviors and procedures used to strengthen or weaken them shall be regarded as reasonable and conventional and may be employed in accordance with proper professional standards, without further notification to or approval by the HRC.

2) Procedures to strengthen or weaken behaviors specified under subparagraph (C)(1) above, which are somewhat more hazardous or intrusive but not sufficiently hazardous or intrusive to require full review under paragraph (D) below.[237] Subject to initial approval by the HRC, programs utilizing the procedures in this category shall be regarded as

---

[236] Examples would be the use of positive reinforcement involving reinforcers other than "basic" reinforcers such as regular meals or regular bedding to strengthen sensory awareness, self-help or mobility; or use of extinction to weaken self-mutilating or self-stimulating behaviors.

sometimes necessary and as relatively reasonable and conventional and may be employed to strengthen or weaken the target behaviors listed pursuant to subparagraph (C)(1) above when performed in accordance with proper professional standards without prior approval by the HRC, so long as both the PRC and the HRC are notified of the use of such procedures within a reasonable time, not to exceed 7 days after such use. The HRC shall monitor such procedures on a sampling basis.

D. The strengthening or weakening of any behaviors not listed pursuant to subparagraph (C)(1) above and the use of any procedures not specified under subparagraphs (C)(1) or (C)(2) above may be performed only after the HRC finds that the conditions set forth in subparagraphs (1)-(4) or (5) of this paragraph have been met and the PRC approves such performance.[238]

1) That the client/resident has the capacity to consent to the particular procedure and has given a valid informed consent[239] or waiver in writing to the proposed procedure, and if the client/resident is a minor, that the parent or guardian of the client/resident also has given valid informed consent or waiver in writing. Informed consent requires a decision that is: (a) based upon an understanding of the nature and consequences of the procedure; (b) wholly voluntary and free from any coercion, overt or covert;[240] and, (c) given by a person competent to make such a decision.

---

[237] Examples would be brief timeout to weaken temper tantrums or educational fines for aggression toward fellow clients/residents.

[238] Examples of procedures to strengthen or weaken behaviors which would be covered under this section would be aversive conditioning with electric shock to extinguish head banging in an autistic child and making a severely retarded nonverbal child's meals conditional upon learning language.

[239] From the legal point of view, informed consent is required only for those procedures which intrude upon legally protected rights. From a policy point of view, however, the practice of disclosing relevant information about any procedure to a client/resident and securing the client's voluntary cooperation has a sound basis in both ethics and successful practice. See, M. Wolf, S. Fixsen & E. Phillips, supra note 234. Thus, administrators of behavioral programs would be wise to comply with this section for all behavioral programs.

[240] One of the most difficult issues concerning voluntariness of consent is whether participation in a behavioral program by a mental patient or prisoner does not deserve to be a factor in decisions concerning the release or parole of such persons. In order to safeguard voluntariness, it is the position of these proposed standards that release or parole can never be made contingent upon participation in a behavioral program per se. This is not to say, of course, that if participation in a program alters the condition of a mental patient or prisoner so that, for example, a mental patient is no longer mentally ill or dangerous, the patient or prisoner should not be entitled to release on the basis of the actual change. The most difficult problems in this areas arise with respect to prisoners, in that parole boards typically make decisions for parole based upon mere participation in behavioral and other programs rather than measurable change, thus putting undue pressure on prisoners who wish to assert their legal rights to refrain from participation in such programs. This practice is presently being challenged in Taylor v. Manson, C.A. No. H 75/37 (D. Conn., filed January 29, 1975),

2. For purposes of requirement (D) (1) (a), the applied behavior analyst shall communicate directly with the client/resident and clearly and explicitly provide all the following information:

(a) The nature and seriousness of the client's behavioral problem and the proposed specific objectives for the client;

(b) The nature of the proposed procedure to accomplish these objectives, its probable duration, and intensity;

(c) The likelihood of improvement or deterioration, temporary or permanent, without the administration of the proposed procedure;

(d) The likelihood and degree of improvement, remission, or control resulting from the administration of such procedure; the likelihood, nature, and extent of changes in and intrusions upon the person's personality and patterns of behavior and thought resulting from such procedure; and the degree to which these changes may be irreversible;

(e) The likelihood, nature, extent, and duration of side effects of the proposed procedure and how and to what extent they may be controlled, if at all;

(f) The uncertainty of the benefits and hazards of the proposed procedure;

(g) The reasonable alternative therapies or procedures available and an explanation why the specific procedure recommended has been chosen. These alternatives shall be described and explained to the client/resident in the same manner as the recommended procedure;

(h) Whether the proposed procedure is generally regarded as established procedure by applied behavior analysts or is considered experimental;

(i) A description of the procedure for termination of the treatment program prior to completion and clear notification whether consent or waiver may be withdrawn at any time;

(j) The data gathering procedures which will be used to evaluate the program.

3) For purposes of requirement (D) (1) (b), the client/resident must be informed orally and in writing that no benefits or penalties will be made contingent upon participation in the proposed program or agreement to undergo the proposed procedure. Specifically, there must be an explicit understanding by the client/resident that his consent is not a precondition for release from the institution, and his decision should not be made to obtain approval or avoid reprisals from the staff. Any individual having knowledge of implicit or explicit coercion of any client/resident shall immediately bring such information to the attention of the facility's HRC. Failure to do so shall be punishable as provided by law.

---

which attacks a parole board on behalf of prisoners who allege that their chances for early release will be prejudiced because of their refusal to participate in a behavioral program involving hypnotism and aversive conditioning for recidivist child molesters at Somers State Prison in Connecticut.

4) For purposes of requirement (D) (1) (c), a person confined shall be deemed incapable of giving informed consent if such person cannot understand and knowingly act upon the information specified under provisions (D) (2) (a)-(j) above or if for any other reason he cannot manifest his consent. A client confined to a mental institution shall not be considered incompetent solely because of his institutionalization.

To aid the HRC in assessing the client's competency, the director of the facility or his designated representative shall prepare a written report evaluating the resident's understanding of the proposed procedure and describing the steps taken to inform the resident of the nature and consequences of the procedure.

5) If the client/resident has been determined to be legally incompetent by a court of competent jurisdiction, or if the director or his designated representative cannot certify without reservation that the client/resident understands the nature and consequences of the proposed procedure, the procedure may not be used unless the parents, in the case of a minor, or the guardian, in the case of an adult incompetent, of the client/resident have given informed consent and the HRC is persuaded that: the procedure complies with generally accepted professional standards; less intrusive alternatives either have been exhausted without success or would be clearly ineffective; the benefits of the procedure clearly outweigh the harms; and, the procedure would be in the best interest of the client/resident. If in rendering a decision under this paragraph the HRC finds that a less restrictive alternative is insufficient only because of the lack of staff or funds, it shall immediately notify the director, the governor, the attorney general, and the chairmen of the appropriate legislative committees, including health and appropriations.[241]

E. Prior to approving procedures under paragraph (D) above, the HRC shall review appropriate medical, social, and psychological information concerning the client/resident and shall interview the client/resident and others who in its judgment have information pertinent to its determination. The HRC shall maintain written records of its determinations and the reasons therefor, with supporting documentation. The HRC shall file a written report in the office of the state attorney general at least bimonthly indicating the number and nature of procedures approved and disapproved, the reasons for approval or disapproval, and other relevant information, including follow-up evaluations of the success of the procedures utilized. The identity of the client/resident involved shall not be disclosed in these reports. The reports shall be available to the public if they are released by a competent client/resident or by the parent or guardian and the legal representative of an incompetent client/resident.

F. Client/residents shall be assisted and represented throughout all

---

[241] Note that this paragraph takes no position on whether the HRC should rule for or against a more restrictive procedure when it finds that the only bar to less drastic measures is inadequate resources.

the processes detailed above by legal counsel or by a lay advocate recommended by the local chapter of a concerned consumer group such as the local chapters of NAMH or NARC. Such counsel shall assist competent clients/residents in deciding whether to undergo proposed procedures and shall ensure for minor and incompetent clients/residents that all considerations militating against the proposed procedure have been fully explored and resolved. No such counsel shall be an officer, employee, or agent of the treating facility or have any other conflict of interest which would impair adequate representation. If such counsel believes the HRC has made a biased or mistaken decision based on all the evidence, he shall appeal the decision to a state court of competent jurisdiction,[242] and the procedure shall not be utilized until and unless the court has given its approval.

APPENDIX II

SAMPLE APPLICATION OF SUGGESTED STANDARDS AND PROCEDURES TO A HYPOTHETICAL SITUATION[243]

Facts

At about 2½ years of age, Bob began to show mild and intermittent head tapping. The behavior gradually increased in intensity, and he was diagnosed as autistic at age 4. By the age of 7, when aversive conditioning was first considered, his head banging had reached the point where constant restraint was required. He would, if left unrestrained, beat himself at a rate of 5,000 times an hour. He is capable of splitting his head with one well-placed knee blow or knocking himself unconscious on the floor. Indeed, in the recent past he has had several trips to the hospital emergency room.

In past years, various drugs and various standard behavioral procedures, including withdrawal of attention, time-out, and reinforcement of other noninjurious behaviors, have all been tried without success. Under these circumstances, the staff recommends a program of aversive

---

242 Presumably, there is already jurisdiction for such an appeal since imposition of intrusive behavioral procedures without compliance with these provisions raises issues of violation of constitutional rights. Specific legislation providing for appeal from HRC and PRC decisions to the courts, however, would facilitate this review.

243 This hypothetical is based upon an actual case at the Psychological Clinic of Rutgers University. *See* S. Harris, Statement in Response to a Complaint Received by the Attorney General's Office by Unknown Parties with Respect to the Use of Reward-Punishment Treatment (undated) (undated paper in the Psychological Clinic of Rutgers University), on file in the *Arizona Law Review* office. The author has received assurance that this hypothetical may be used with the subject's consent.

conditioning for Bob. They propose using a standard hand-seld Sears &
Roebuck inductorium to administer an electric shock for .5 seconds to
his leg or arm each time he hits himself. The individualized treatment
plan for Bob calls for data to be kept on the frequency of his self-
injurious behavior and provides for the reinforcement of learning and
social skills at the same time the self-injurious behavior is to be extinguished by shock.

Peer Review Committee

The PRC is called together to consider this case. The first question
the Committee asks is whether there is evidence in the professional
literature that the procedure proposed would be effective to extinguish
Bob's self-injurious behavior. The committee recognizes that no one
knows what causes self-injurious behavior. Some claim that it arises out
of a need for increased stimulation, and others argue that it results
from a need for greater attention. But the members of the PRC agree
that there are ample reports in the professional literature which show
that the use of electric shock to treat self-injurious behavior can be
very effective.[244] On the basis of this review of the literature and their
own personal familiarity with the techniques, the members of the PRC
agree that the proposed procedure is likely to be effective and may be
considered therapeutic rather than experimental at this time. Upon
reviewing the history of the child and the alternative procedures which
have been tried and have proved ineffective, the PRC also decides that
there are no less intrusive procedures which have not been exhausted or
which would likely be effective.

The PRC next reviews the literature for indications of harms or side-
effects associated with the proposed procedure. The primary harm associated with the procedure is determined to be the infliction of a localized and brief, but painful, shock to the arm or leg.[245] But on the basis
of its review of the professional literature and after special review by
its physician member, the PRC decides that electric shock administered
to a physically healthy patient under controlled conditions is harmless
and produces no side effects. On the benefit side, the PRC notes first the

---

[244] *See, e.g.,* Lang & Melamed, Avoidance Conditioning Therapy of an Infant with
Chronic Ruminative Vomiting, *J. Abnormal Psychology,* 1969, 74, 1; Lovaas & Simmons, Manipulation of Self Destruction in Three Retarded Children, *J. Applied Behavior Analysis,* 1969, 2, 143; Risley, The Effects of Punishing the Autistic Behaviors
of a Deviant Child, *J. Applied Behavior Analysis,* 1968, 1, 21.

[245] *See* Lovaas & Simmons, *supra* note 244, at 149; Risley, *supra* note 244, at 25.

obvious value of the procedure which promises to be efficacious in eliminating self-injurious behavior. Moreover, the committee notes reports in the literature that self-injurious children who received aversive conditioning have become more social and appeared more at ease with themselves.

As the final task, the PRC turns to the research design proposed for the procedure. The committee approves the general research design and notes with satisfaction: 1) that a baseline of the self-destructive behavior prior to treatment had been determined so that an objective record of the client's behavior could be maintained during and after treatment to help determine when the aversive procedures should be discontinued; 2) that the contemplated level of shock will be no higher than necessary but high enough to discourage possible adaptation by Bob; and, 3) that the design for the procedure properly will call for positively reinforcing Bob with affection and attention and other appetitive reinforcers contingent upon his not hitting himself, at the same time as his self-injurious behavior is to be suppressed with shock. The PRC, however, notes one flaw in the research design. The design does not allow for the fact that there is "situation specificity" associated with the use of punishment. That is, although the client is taught to suppress his behavior in the presence of one adult, it does not necessarily follow that the behavior will not occur with other adults or in other settings. The PRC, therefore, exercises its option to approve the proposed program upon the condition that the procedure be modified to allow administration of shock by more than one person in more than one environment to ensure that Bob will learn to extinguish his self-injurious behavior not only in specific situations but in his life generally. The PRC's written findings are then passed to the Human Rights Committee.

The Human Rights Committee

At its regular monthly meeting, the HRC considers Bob's case. The members of the HRC agree that aversive conditioning is in the category of procedures which require most careful scrutiny under section III, paragraph (D) of the operative standards. Its first task, therefore, is to determine whether Bob has the capacity to consent to aversive conditioning and, if so, whether he has given a valid informed consent or waiver to the proposed procedure. After hearing from the mental health professional in charge of Bob's treatment and speaking with Bob himself, the members of the committee agree that Bob, who is autistic and a minor, is not legally competent to make a decision one way or the other on the proposed aversive procedure. The HRC then proceeds to determine: whether Bob's parents have given informed consent to the proposed procedure and to review for itself, according to its mandate; whether the procedure complies with previously adopted professional standards; whether less intrusive alternatives have either been exhausted without success or would be clearly ineffective; whether the benefits of the procedure clearly outweigh the risks; and whether the procedure would be in Bob's best interest.

The committee determines that Bob's parents have been fully informed about the nature and seriousness of Bob's behavioral problem and the specific objectives of aversive conditioning; that they understand the nature of aversive conditioning and its probable duration and intensity in Bob's case; that they are aware of the likelihood and nature of side effects, of alternative procedures, and of the reasons the procedure recommended was thought to be the best procedure; that they understand that the procedure is generally regarded as sound by applied behavior analysts and is not considered experimental; that they understand the kind of data which will be kept about Bob's behavior and are satisfied with the controls which are contemplated for this data; and that they have been apprised that their initial consent will not be binding should they decide in the process of treatment that aversive conditioning is not in Bob's best interest. Since there is no evidence to rebut the presumption of the parents' competence, and since the parents had been informed orally and in writing that no benefits or penalties will be made contingent upon their consent to the procedure, the HRC concludes that informed consent has been properly secured from the parents.

The HRC then reviews the record developed by the PRC and agrees that the proposed procedure complies with generally accepted professional standards and that less intrusive alternates have either been exhausted without success or would be clearly ineffective.

Considering the possible and probable benefits and harms from this procedure as they have been articulated by the PRC, the HRC next proceeds to its weighing function. While the members of the HRC are, like most of us, reluctant to inflict pain upon other persons, they recognize that the psychologist in charge of Bob's treatment might, like other highly respected members of our society such as surgeons and dentists, be required to inflict pain in an attempt to promote the health of his client. After some discussion, the HRC decides that use of electric shock in the manner prescribed would be ethical and humane. Although this procedure will be briefly painful to Bob, the committee determines that the duration of this pain will be relatively short and that the pain is clearly justified since the remaining alternatives are either further life-threatening self-injury or a possible lifetime of chemical or physical restraint. After weighing all of the known possible harms or side effects, which, apart from the relatively short pain of the shock itself, appear to be minimal relative to the promise of long-term freedom and improvement for Bob, the HRC unanimously agrees that the benefits of the procedure clearly outweigh the harms and that the procedure will be in Bob's best interest.

The counsel appointed by the HRC to assist in the deliberations by ensuring that all considerations militating against the proposed procedure have been fully explored and resolved is satisfied and therefore declines to appeal the HRC decision to the local court. The secretary of the HRC prepares minutes of these proceedings with supporting documentation so that the decision can be incorporated in the next bi-monthly written report which, with Bob's identity concealed and with the parents' consent, will be made available for public inspection if released.

The standards and procedures for review of aversive conditioning having been complied with, Bob's individual conditioning program is begun shortly thereafter.

5

REFLECTIONS ON THE LEGAL REGULATION OF BEHAVIOR MODIFICATION IN INSTI-TUTIONAL SETTINGS

David B. Wexler

Professor of Law, University of Arizona

These remarks are intended more to highlight certain themes in Paul Friedman's article "Legal Regulation of Applied Behavior Analysis in Mental Institutions and Prisons"[1] than they are intended to critique its principal thesis. A full-blown critique would be out of the question, for Friedman and I have attended so many meetings together recently that our intellectual behavior has obviously been shaped by similar forces! Indeed, Friedman's proposed standards derive largely from those developed for state retardation programs by the Florida Task Force on Behavioral Procedures, a task force on which we both served.

I agree with Friedman's central thesis that, as a matter of policy and quite possibly of constitutional law, the state lacks sufficient interest to justify thrusting an intrusive behavioral procedure upon an unwilling competent person, but that competent persons should be able to consent to the use of such procedures. I agree, too, that in appropriate instances, the state, upon certain findings made by a Human Rights Committee, may disregard the supposed desire of an incompetent client and may

Reprinted with permission from *Arizona Law Review*, Vol. 17, No. 1, 132-143, 1975. Copyright 1975, Arizona Board of Regents.

apply a behavioral technique believed to be in the client's best interest. Since the entire legal scheme of regulation seems dependent upon the notions of competence and informed consent, those concepts are worthy of highlighting.

Competence and Informed Consent

It is often said that informed consent is unobtainable in an instituttional setting, largely, though by no means exclusively, because the lure of release from the institution is so overpowering that any consent given must be deemed to be coerced[2] It is important to recognize, however, that neither law nor philosophy views every pressure to select a particular option as coercion. In law, for example, conditions of probation or parole must be voluntarily assumed in order to be enforceable, and pleas of guilty must be given voluntarily if they are to be upheld. Yet, the law upholds reasonable probation and parole conditions as voluntary, and similarly upholds plea bargains, even though the avoidance or reduction of incarceration is the supreme motivating force underlying those agreements. Thus, the law does not employ the concept of coercion to condemn pressure per se. Rather, coercion is employed as a normative concept to condemn pressures regarded as unfair or unreasonable.[3]

In light of this, it would be improper to hold that a resident's strong desire for release by itself impermissibly coerces the resident into agreeing to behavioral procedures. Otherwise, the logical result would be that all therapy on involuntarily-institutionalized persons would, despite their expressed desires to submit to therapy, be deemed coerced and, therefore, either prohibited altogether or referred for approval to a surrogate decisionmaker. The surrogate in this situation would surely be no better equipped than the resident to decide whether to agree to the procedure.[4]

---

[1] *Ariz. L. Rev.*, 1975, 17, 39.

[2] *See* Kaimowitz v. Michigan Dep't of Mental Health, *U.S.L.W.*, 42, 2063 (C.A. 73-19434-AW, Civ. Ct. Wayne County, Mich., July 10, 1973).

[3] *See* Wexler, Foreword: Mental Health Law and the Movement Toward Voluntary Treatment, *Calif. L. Rev.*, 1974, 62, 671, 679. Philosophers have more explicitly recognized the normative content of the coercion concept. *See* V. Haksar, Civil Disobedience Threats and Offers 49-64, 1974 (unpublished paper), on file in the *Arizona Law Review* office. *But cf.* Nozick, Coercion, in S. Morgenbesser, P. Suppes & M. White (Eds.), *Philosophy, Science, and Method: Essays in Honor of Ernest Nagel*, 1969, 440.

[4] The surrogate may well be less equipped than the resident to determine whether there should be consent to the procedure. In the ordinary situation of substituted judgment, the client is incompetent to understand and assess alternatives, and the role of the surrogate is obvious: to substitute its competent and rational judgment for that of the incompetent and irrational client. When, however, the client is presumably com-

Indeed, to deem all such therapy to be impermissibly coerced, and thereby to preclude or severely restrict its use, may well constitute improper interference with what Friedman[5] calls the freedom of mentation[6] and with what I would include under the constitutional right to privacy. Elsewhere, I have argued that the Supreme Court abortion cases,[7] which found the physician-patient decision regarding abortion to be constitutionally protected against noncompelling state interference, may well be extended to other physician-patient decisions, including consensual therapeutic procedures.[8] As with abortion, the courts could find state interference with such procedures unwarranted if interference or prohibition could lead to "the taxing of mental . . . health" and to a "distressful life and future."[9]

To comply with the various policies enumerated above, coercion ought to be defined, at least in part, in terms of unfair consequences rather than in terms of sheer pressure to avoid further incarceration. At least for openers, I would accept, as Friedman apparently does,[10] Dr. Goldiamond's interesting behavioral formulation of uncoerced consent.[11] Problems of informed consent and competence will have to be grappled with in the day-to-day administration of behavioral procedures. Two of the more troubling issues will be examined below.

1. *Minors.* Friedman's proposed standards specify that the behavioral procedures may be employed on a competent minor if consent is obtained from the minor as well as from the parents.[12] If the minor is incompetent, the minor's consent is not required, but the approval of

---

petent but is confronted with the unpleasant choice of continued confinement if his mental condition remains unchanged or the possibility of release if he submits to an intrusive procedure which ameliorates his mental condition, his autonomy ought to be respected by permitting him to make the decision. The surrogate ought not to be permitted to interfere with the client's choice and, in effect, perhaps mandate the continued confinement of the client. Of course, if a client is confronted not with the simple pressure that flows from his desire for release, but with unfair pressure, such as the prospect of punishment or the retaliatory withholding of privileges if consent is not given, a surrogate could take appropriate action to terminate the impermissible consequences. That, however, is not the present situation.

[5] Friedman, *supra* note 1, at 58.

[6] *Accord,* Shapiro, Legislating the Control of Behavior Control: Autonomy and the Coercive Use of Organic Therapies, *S. Cal. L. Rev.,* 1974, 47, 237, 255-256.

[7] Roe v. Wade, 410 U.S. 113 (1973); Doe v. Bolton, 410 U.S. 179 (1973).

[8] Wexler, *supra* note 3, at 681-683.

[9] Roe v. Wade, 410 U.S. 113, 153 (1973).

[10] Friedman, *supra* note 1, at 86 n. 214.

[11] Goldiamond, Toward a Constructional Approach to Social Problems: Ethical and Constitutional Issues Raised by Applied Behavior Analysis, *Behaviorism,* 1974, 2, 1, 60.

[12] Friedman, *supra* note 1, at 97.

the parents and of the Human Rights Committee is a prerequisite to the utilization of specified procedures.[13] In both instances the consent of the parents is required, but, because the interests of the parent might be at odds with the best interests of the minor, in neither instance is their consent sufficient.

While I have no objection to such checks on parental abuse, I suspect the potential for conflict over the submission to behavioral procedures will differ considerably from the potential for conflict over institutionalization and sterilization, the two areas in which potential parent-child conflict has been recognized in litigation.[14] Parents may obviously attempt to use institutionalization to rid themselves of a troublesome child or may attempt to use sterilization to avoid the prospect of being burdened with supporting or caring for grandchildren. It is rather unlikely, however, that parents would volunteer their resident child for behavioral therapy unless they thought that the procedure would benefit the child.

Indeed, any possible conflict would probably flow in the other direction: parents truly bent on preventing their child's return to the family might be unwilling to consent to therapy that is in the child's best interest. Moreover, even truly concerned parents of retarded children often incorrectly view retardation as a rigid, inflexible condition and thus view their children as pitiful and hopeless. Accordingly, such parents are sometimes unwilling to subject their children to intrusive, but perhaps efficacious, behavioral procedures. To the extent that conflicts in this direction are genuine and operate to frustrate the right to treatment of minors, thought might be given to removing the requirement of parental consent as an absolute prerequisite to the use of behavioral procedures on minors.[15] Perhaps the approval of an independent Human Rights Committee should, under certain circumstances, be sufficient. At the least, the issue is probably deserving of debate and ventilation.

2. *Determinations of competence.* Under Friedman's proposed stand-

---

[13] *Id.* at 99.

[14] Relf v. Weinberger, 372 F. Supp. 1196 (D.C.C. 1974) (sterilization); Saville v. Treadway, Civil No. 6969 (M.D. Tenn. Mar. 8, 1974) (institutionalization).

[15] If certain behavioral procedures are shown to be so efficacious that they stand on a par with standard medical procedures, parental refusal to consent to the behavioral procedures could be viewed as abuse, neglect, or incompetence and could lead to total or partial termination of the legal parent-child relationship, with parental decisionmaking authority being transferred to another body. *Cf.* Zaremski, Blood Transfusions and Elective Surgery: A Custodial Function of an Ohio Juvenile Court, *Clev. St. L. Rev.,* 1974, 23, 231.

ards, intrusive behavioral procedures may be employed if the Human Rights Committee finds, presumably without reservation, that the client is competent and agrees to the procedure,[16] or if the committee finds, among other things, that the client is clearly incompetent and that the procedure is in his best interest.[17] Unfortunately, many cases will not fall easily within either the "clearly competent" or "clearly incompetent" category. The Human Rights Committee's handling of these borderline cases therefore poses difficulties worthy of discussion.

If the client expresses a genuine desire to undergo the procedure, the problem for the committee will not be substantial. Approval should be given upon a finding that less restrictive procedures are unsuitable and that the proposed procedure is in the client's best interest. Under such circumstances, the issue of competency need not be definitely resolved, for whatever its resolution, the treatment is proper. If the client is competent his desire will be respected. If he is incompetent, the committee's finding that the procedure is suitable and in the client's best interest will be sufficient.

A more complicated situation is presented if the client expresses an unwillingness to submit to the procedure. Under Friedman's standards, if the client is unequivocally competent, his refusal is to be given conclusive weight. If the client is incompetent, and if certain other conditions are met, his refusal may be disregarded by the committee. But if the competency question cannot be clearly resolved, the unanswered question is whether the client's desire should be respected or overridden. Since respect for the client's autonomy requires a presumption of competence which, in this situation, has not been negated, his wishes should be complied with.

Friedman's standards, as augmented by the foregoing discussion, may be set forth diagrammatically. The diagram below represents the various possibilities of client competence and client preference and indicates whether, under the various combinations of circumstances and findings, the Human Rights Committee should approve or disapprove the use of a proposed intrusive behavioral procedure.[18]

---

16 Friedman, *supra* note 1, at 97.

17 *Id.* at 99.

18 The shaded boxes represent factual or legal rarities or impossibilities. The term Qualified Approval means approval so long as the Human Rights Committee finds that less drastic procedures are unsuitable and that the proposed procedure is, in an anticipated cost-benefit sense, in the best interest of the client. If the committee is unable to find those additional conditions satisfied, the Qualified Approval would convert to a Disapproval. The term Unstated under the Client Preference category principally in-

FIGURE 1

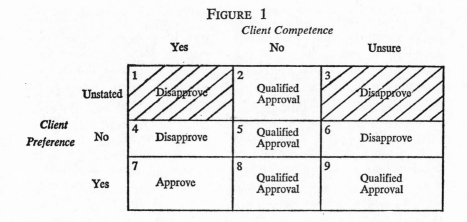

Friedman suggests that, throughout the committee proceedings, the client be represented by counsel or a lay advocate.[19] Apparently, counsel will assist competent clients in reaching a decision whether or not to undergo a proposed procedure. For incompetent clients, counsel will ensure that factors militating against the proposed procedure are fully developed. If counsel is dissatisfied with the committee's decision, he can seek judicial review.[20]

This scheme assumes that client competence has already been determined. Yet the competence or incompetence of the client is one of the crucial open issues with which the committee must grapple. Thus, counsel's role, at least in certain instances, may be more complicated and less clear-cut than Friedman's scheme suggests. The committee and counsel should begin by presuming the client's competence. If competence is presumed, counsel should strive to achieve the stated preference of his client, whether it be for or against undergoing the proposed behavioral procedure. That goal is best achieved by counsel advocating a finding of competence, for if the client is found competent, his preference will stand.

So far, counsel's role is clear. Further, if the committee in the first prong of a presumably bifurcated decisionmaking process finds the client incompetent, counsel's role will remain clear and consistent so long as

---

cludes instances where the client, presumably because of his mental condition, is unable to form or communicate a clear and specific preference.

19 Friedman, *supra* note 1, at 100.

20 *Id.*

the client's stated preference was and is against submission to the therapy. In such a situation, counsel, during the second prong of the process, will try to elicit information establishing that the proposed procedure is not in the best interest of the client[21] or that less intrusive alternatives are available.[22] But if the client is found incompetent and yet states a preference for the proposed procedure, it will be difficult and awkward for counsel suddenly to shift gears, to ignore—indeed, oppose—the stated preference of the client, and to begin eliciting factors mitigating against committee approval of the proposed procedure.[23] Moreover, if the committee rules in favor of the procedure, counsel may further ignore the client's stated preference and challenge the decision in court.[24]

Perhaps the tension and awkwardness of this situation could be eliminated by specifying that counsel argue against committee approval only in those instances where the client lacks a stated preference[25] or where the client's stated preference is in opposition to the proposed technique.[26] In situations where the client favors the proposed technique,[27] counsel could advocate the competence of the client during the first phase of committee decision-making and, win or lose at that stage, could advocate the client's stated preference during the second phase of the decision-making process. Another lawyer, perhaps serving as amicus to the committee, could, during the second phase, perform the role of fully informing the committee by eliciting information suggesting the impropriety

---

[21] The client's antagonistic feeling toward the procedure, or perhaps his anxiety over it, may constitute a significant factor to be thrown into the hopper of considerations relevant to gauging whether, in a cost-benefit sense, the proposed procedure is in the best interest of the client. By the same token, the client's strong feelings in favor of the procedure may be relevant, though not determinative, in finding the procedure to be in his best interest. *Cf.* Wexler, Therapeutic Justice, *Minn. L. Rev.*, 1972, 57, 289, 326.

[22] The lawyer's role also will be relatively straightforward and uncomplicated in instances where the client is unable to state any preference for or against the proposed procedure. In such cases, the client will almost certainly be declared incompetent, and in eliciting factors against the use of the proposed procedure, counsel will not be urging a position in conflict with the client's stated preference.

[23] It is possible, of course, that during the process of arguing that a procedure is not in the client's best interest or that less restrictive procedures are effective, counsel will discover a less restrictive procedure to which the behavior therapist and client will agree. This may alleviate the tension and eradicate any mistrust that the client would develop toward counsel.

[24] Of course, counsel may also challenge in court the committee's finding of incompetence, and that course of action would be consistent with the client's stated preference.

[25] See Figure 1, *supra* at 136, boxes 1-3.

[26] See *id.,* boves 4-6.

[27] See *id.,* boxes 7-9.

of the proposed procedure,[28] and could even participate in all first-prong proceedings by developing facts which cast doubt on the competence of the client.

Absolute and Contingent Rights

It has been recognized that it may be constitutionally impermissible, or at least constitutionally difficult, to utilize the acquisition of certain items, activities, and events as reinforcers in a behavioral procedure such as a token economy.[29] Certain personal requirements are so basic that they should seemingly be afforded to institutionalized individuals as a matter of right.[30] For example, these absolute rights might include food and a suitable place to sleep. On the other hand, other aspects of institutional life may not be constitutionally guaranteed. Thus, acquisition of the latter may be made contingent on proper behavior. To the extent that absolute rights are broadly defined, there is a conflict between them and the need for contingent rights which are essential to effective behavior modification.

Friedman contends that the conflict between absolute and contingent rights may not be as serious as is feared by some behavior modification practitioners.[31] He notes that competent patients may waive their rights, thus allowing such rights to be made available contingently.[32] He also notes that, with respect to incompetent patients, even constitutionally-guaranteed rights can be vicariously waived if the denial of those rights constitutes the least restrictive means of furthering the patient's best interest.[33] Further elaboration of several of these points should indicate that while the conflict may be somewhat less than some behavioral practioners fear, it may also be somewhat greater than Friedman assumes.

It is of course true that competent patients may waive their rights to basic items, activities, and benefits and submit to an intrusive behavioral procedure.[34] But it is also true that candidates for such behavioral

---

28 See id., boxes 8-9.

29 See Wexler, Token and Taboo: Behavior Modification, Token Economies, and the Law, Calif. L. Rev., 1973, 61, 81, 92-97.

30 See Wyatt v. Stickney, 344 F. Supp. 373 & 387 (M.D. Ala. 1972), aff'd sub nom., Wyatt v. Aderholt, 503 F.2d 1305 (5th Cir. 1974).

31 Friedman, supra note 1, at 75.

32 Id.

33 Id.

34 See, e.g., Knecht v. Gillman, 488 F.2d 1136 (8th Cir. 1973); Wyatt v. Aderholt, 368 F. Supp. 1383 (M.D. Ala. 1974); Henry v. Ciccone, 315 F. Supp. 889 (W.D. Mo. 1970), appeal dismissed, 440 F.2d 1052 (8th Cir. 1971).

procedures are often chronic patients who, while perhaps technically competent, are highly apathetic and dependent. Accordingly, they may be quite unwilling to waive the standard benefits of hospital life in order to embark upon an arduous program of self-improvement. Further, even if patients give initial consent, an emerging rule requires that clients be permitted to withdraw consent and terminate procedures at will.[35] While this free revocability principle may make sense in general, more discussion is in order concerning its applicability to behavioral procedures.

Of particular concern is the situation in which a competent client desires to attain certain target behavior but realizes that he lacks motivation for social learning. Accordingly, that client may agree to waive basic rights by entering a token economy where the items and events he has waived will be available only if earned through performance of target behaviors. A patient may waive a right to food or to a bed, but when the patient becomes hungry or tired and lacks the tokens to purchase a meal or a bed, revocation of the waiver would be, at that moment, the easiest way out of an uncomfortable situation. If the client may terminate consent and retrieve his right to these items or events at any time, the motivational force of the token economy might be sapped.[36] Thus, it may soon be necessary to discuss whether there should be certain situations in which a competent client may waive even the right of revocation. Of course, if a limited exception to revocability is contemplated, it also must be asked whether the exception could withstand the prospect of expansion by administrative abuse. In any event, under the free revocability rule, the waiver-of-rights approach to solving the absolute versus contingent right controversy will, for the above reasons, probably be unworkable in practice.

Beyond infringement by waiver, it might be permissible with respect to nonconsenting competent patients to infringe on constitutionally-guaranteed rights in order to satisfy a compelling state interest.[37] But the various basics guaranteed as constitutional rights in Wyatt v. Stickney,[38] unlike other constitutional rights, were cast by the court in terms of *minimum* constitutional standards. As such, they may fall without the

---

35 *See, e.g.,* Knecht v. Gillman, 488 F.2d 1136 (8th Cir. 1973).

36 *See* Wexler, *supra* note 29, at 108 n. 151; Wexler, Of Rights and Reinforcers, *San Diego L. Rev.,* 1974, 11, 957, 970-971.

37 Friedman, *supra* note 1, at 68-69, 71-72.

38 344 F. Supp. 373 & 387 (M.D. Ala. 1972), *aff'd sub nom.,* Wyatt v. Aderholt, 503 F.2d 1305 (5th Cir. 1974). For discussion of *Wyatt,* see Friedman, *supra* note 1, at 56-57, 74-75.

ordinary ambit of constitutional balancing. Also, even if the *Wyatt* rights are viewed as ordinary constitutional rights susceptible to negation by balancing, legislative action may secure those basics as absolute guarantees. In that event, they will be given legislative status that exceeds their constitutional status, and it will be impermissible to convert them for therapeutic purposes into mere contingent reinforcers. Finally, even if protective legislation is not enacted and even if the *Wyatt*-type rights are regarded as ordinary constitutional rights, they, as with other constitutional rights, may be denied only if less restrictive means of attaining the state's compelling interest do not exist. But there is at the moment no clear indication that procedures involving massive deprivation of basic rights achieve therapeutic outcomes superior to alternative systems which do not approach that level of deprivation.[39]

With respect to incompetent patients, problems are raised which are similar to those raised regarding nonconsenting competent patients. While incompetent patients may not waive rights, their rights may be vicariously waived, according to Friedman, if waiver would be in the patient's best interest and would be the least intrusive means to a therapeutic end.[40] Presumably, an incompetent patient's rights are also potentially subject to balancing. The minimal nature of basic rights, however, would make it difficult to contend that their denial is in the patient's best interest. Additionally, as with nonconsenting competent patients, the judicial characterization of these basics as minimal guarantees may remove those rights from the constitutional balancing process. Legislative action may also protect the basic rights of incompetents. Finally, even if basic rights may be balanced and are not legislatively protected, there is no clear indication that procedures denying basic rights are superior to systems not involving such deprivations.

The Problem of Prisoners

In his discussion of the use of intrusive behavioral procedures on prisoners, Friedman suggests several possible avenues: permit the use of such procedures to the same extent as with mental patients, ban their use altogether, or permit their use if performed by independent professionals outside the prison setting[41] A troubling prior question, however, is whether, when dealing with convicted criminals, the state has a com-

---

[39] *See* Wexler, *supra* note 29, at 104-109.
[40] Friedman, *supra* note 1, at 99.
[41] *Id.*, at 85 n. 235.

pelling interest in reformation that is sufficient to thrust intrusive behavioral procedures on prisoners even over their competent objections.

The constitutional question is more difficult in the context of convicted criminals than it is with respect to mental patients. It has been contended that there exist compelling interests permitting imposition of intrusive procedures on prisoners but not on mere mental patients.[42] While most modern commentators would not view competent prisoners as standing in a legal position any weaker than competent mental patients,[43] the constitutional issue remains unresolved. Yet, even if it is assumed that it would not be constitutionally offensive to force treatment on unwilling competent prisoners, there are legal as well as policy reasons which favor respecting the autonomy of prisoners by providing intrusive treatment only after securing informed consent.

This result would be persuasively required if needed, in depth legal and empirical research were to support the following assumptions:

(1) When dealing with experimental techniques—at least those involving possible pain, privation, or risk—rather than with techniques of demonstrated efficacy, the informed consent of competent subjects should surely be a necessary condition to the utilization of the technique, even if it is of potential, but undemonstrated, therapeutic value. That is to say, there is no overriding state interest permitting forced experimentation with prisoners.

(2) In practice, the line between experimentation and therapy, particularly with respect to behavioral procedures and perhaps with all other therapeutic techniques, is extremely difficult to draw.

(3) To date, there is no known therapeutic technique which is demonstrably efficacious in rehabilitating prisoners,[44] especially when prisoners object to the reformative effort or technique.[45]

If these assumptions are correct, then even if there were a constitutionally-recognized compelling state interest in the forced treatment of prisoners, the current absence of demonstrably efficacious procedures could lead to a successful substantive due process challenge to the pro-

---

[42] R. Schwitzgebel, *Development and Legal Regulation of Coercive Behavior Modification Techniques with Offenders*, 1971, 66.

[43] *See* Morris, The Future of Imprisonment: Toward a Punitive Philosophy, *Mich. L. Rev.*, 1974, 72, 1161.

[44] *See* Citizens' Inquiry on Parole and Criminal Justice, Inc., *Summary Report on New York Parole* (Mar. 1974), 36.

[45] See Bandura, Behavior Theory and the Models of Man, *Amer. Psychologist,* 29, 859, 860-861.

posed forcible administration of merely experimental procedures on the ground that the use of such techniques is not closely enough connected to the state's reformative goal.

Even if the suggested substantive due process right of competent prisoners to resist intrusive therapies simply reflects the momentary absence of effective rehabilitative techniques, it is not at all clear that anticipated scientific advances in therapeutic efficacy will necessarily undercut the right to resist. Scientific advances regarding therapeutic efficacy will come about only through experimentation, and the sort of prisoner experimentation that we are concerned with may, under the first assumption above, be performed only on volunteers. Further, under the third assumption, a subject's voluntary desire to change may be highly instrumental in the success of behavior modification efforts.[46] Consequently, future scientific claims of therapeutic efficacy based upon experiments performed on prison volunteers, will be limited in their demonstrated efficacy to consenting prisoners, and would therefore remain experimental—and accordingly beyond the pale of coercive administration—with respect to nonconsenting prisoners.[47]

---

[46] See id. Of course, the success of neurologically and biochemically based therapies such as psychosurgery and chemotherapy might depend less, or not at all, on the voluntary cooperation of the subjects. With behavioral procedures, however, the motivational element has been asserted as crucial. Without a thorough review of the psychological literature, it is difficult to determine whether claims that voluntary cooperation is part and parcel of successful behavior modification are scientifically grounded or whether they are made to blunt assertions that applied behavior analysts have at their disposal powerful techniques capable of altering the behavior of even unwilling subjects. Further, it may be that the therapeutic necessity of voluntary cooperation has never been a major focal point of scientific scrutiny by behavioral researchers. If the latter is the case, the law may have to rely on the conclusory assertion that voluntariness plays a key role in behavior modification, since research on the significance of voluntary cooperation will presumably be precluded, at least in this country, if we deem it improper to experiment on nonvolunteers in order to compare the therapeutic outcome of that group with a group of volunteers. Any thought of plugging the scientific void by performing motivational research in nations with fewer restrictions on experimentation will of course run into its own ethical and scientific problems: whether it is ethical to seek a laboratory that is not bound by high ethical standards, a question which should not really be open to much discussion, and whether research results obtained in such a foreign setting may be comfortably generalized to a population of nonconsenting American prisoners.

[47] The application of the arguments in this section to mental patients, while permissible, is considerably more complex. First, as to mental patients, whether competent or incompetent, there may exist demonstrably efficacious behavioral techniques. Thus, assuming the existence of an overriding state interest, a substantive due process argument could not be made in opposition to the forced application of those techniques. Of course, to the extent that other techniques are not demonstrably efficacious, due process stands as a barrier to their application. It is, however, conceivable that tech-

If this array of assumptions proves accurate, coerced treatment of prisoners may be barred, for any system which seeks to implement a purported constitutionally-authorized state interest in the coercive reformation of prisoners is likely to encounter several crippling snags. The constitutional risk need not be run, however, and the practical impediments can be avoided, if policymakers, perhaps exceeding minimal constitutional requirements, adopt a firm right of prisoners to resist intrusive treatment.[48]

---

niques whose efficacy is undemonstrated may be applied in the best interest of willing and unwilling incompetent patients. In this manner, the efficacy of those techniques may ultimately be demonstrated. Moreover, to the extent that the effectiveness of such techniques is generalizable from incompetent to competent patients, there would be no due process bar to the application of those techniques to nonconsenting competent patients.

The foregoing results presents a certain irony. It is more likely that state interests sufficient to allow coerced treatment will be recognized for prisoners than for patients. See text accompanying notes 42-43 supra. Thus, as to prisoners but not as to mental patients, the legitimate end requirement of due process might be satisfied. Yet, as to prisoners but not as to mental patients, the means may be insufficiently related to the end to satisfy due process.

48 The argument in this section was formulated by the author and others during a recent meeting of the American Psychological Association Commission on Behavior Modification. While several persons contributed to the formulation of the argument, it is advanced here for the purpose of discussion as the personal and tentative view of the author, does not represent a position of the Commission, and it is not necessarily embraced by any other member of the Commission.

Section II

SYSTEMATIC DESENSITIZATION, FLOODING, SYMBOLIC AND PARTICIPANT MODELING, COGNITIVE RESTRUCTURING, AND ASSERTION TRAINING

Commentary

Last year we noted that Wolpe's original systematic desensitization procedure was being increasingly modified and that alternative strategies for anxiety reduction and management were being developed (Franks & Wilson, 1975, p. 65 ff.). This trend, with its broadening emphasis on cognitive variables, in vivo exposure to threatening situations, and active coping with anxiety-evoking conditions, has not only continued but increased significantly. Diverse therapeutic strategies within behavior therapy are now available to the practitioner in the treatment of anxiety disorders. Some of these various treatment techniques are only variations of the same theme and differ minimally from one another in terms of procedure, whereas still others involve distinctly different procedural variations and underlying theoretical considerations. A reflection of this shifting emphasis is the fact that for the first time in this series we have not included an article specifically on systematic desensitization in this Section. As in the past years, however, systematic desensitization has been an important focus of basic and applied research, and it is with this well-known behavioral method that we commence our evaluative review of the pertinent literature in this Section.

Systematic Desensitization

Expectancy Factors in Systematic Desensitization. Two major critical reviews during the past year focused on the effects of expectancy factors

119

in systematic desensitization (Emmelkamp, 1975a; Lick & Bootzin, 1975). Both evaluated two broad categories of experimental studies: a) those that compared the efficacy of systematic desensitization to that of attention-placebo control treatments; and b) those that attempted to alter subjects' expectancies of therapeutic gain when receiving systematic desensitization.

Lick and Bootzin identified three important methodological weaknesses in the studies they reviewed. These problems—which we have previously discussed in this series (Franks & Wilson, 1974, pp. 44-46 ff.)— included the use of unconvincing placebo treatments (e.g., Nau, Caputo, & Borkovec, 1974), only mildly fearful and/or poorly motivated subjects (e.g., Borkovec, 1973), and the failure to assess adequately—if at all—the experiential impact of the therapist's or experimenter's expectancy-inducing instructions (e.g., Wilkins, 1973). These difficulties notwithstanding, Lick and Bootzin argued that four studies (Lick, 1975; Marcia, Rubin, & Efran, 1969; McReynolds, Barnes, Brooks, & Rehagen, 1973; Tori & Worell, 1973) which they considered to have met the minimal necessary methodological requirements, indicated that systematic desensitization was not significantly superior to a convincing placebo treatment in the reduction of fear.

In contrast to these four studies, both Brown (1973) and Wilson (1973) found that systematic desensitization was significantly more effective than placebo controls (see Davison & Wilson, 1973—reprinted in Franks & Wilson, 1974). Lick and Bootzin point out, however, that the placebo treatments used by Brown and Wilson were different from those employed by Lick (1975), McReynolds et al. (1973) and Tori and Worell (1973) with the result that they might have been less effective. Emmelkamp (1975b) offers essentially the same criticism in comparing the Wilson (1973) and McReynolds et al. (1973) studies. He speculates that the latter's dissonance enhancement placebo treatment, stressing "cognitive control training" and "training in body awareness" is more credible than the former's placebo which was derived from Marcia et al. (1969). Of course, this is still an empirical question, and as our discussion of the Lick (1975) and Rosen (1975) papers below makes clear, making a priori assumptions about the impact of different instructional sets can be a hazardous undertaking. However, this criticism is important, since of the three studies reviewed by Lick and Bootzin (1975) which did independently assess subjects' expectancies while they were undergoing treatment (viz. Lick, 1975; McReynolds et al. 1973; Wilson, 1973), only the Wilson study showed the superiority of systematic desensitization.

On the basis of all these studies Lick and Bootzin (1975) concluded that "it is reasonable to hypothesize that placebo influences may be more important in [systematic desensitization] than earlier writers believed" (p. 921). In a somewhat stronger statement Emmelkamp (1975a) declared that neither systematic desensitization nor flooding (in imagination) has been shown to be effective independent of expectancy factors. Although it would be difficult to disagree with Lick and Bootzin's overall thesis, the methodological adequacy of the studies they document their conclusion with can be questioned. The Marcia et al. (1969) study has been severely critiqued (Bandura, 1969; Davison & Wilson, 1973), and the McReynolds et al. (1973) study, although internally valid, may have used only mildly fearful subjects (Lick, 1975; Wilson & Davison, 1975), as the Tori and Worell (1973) study almost certainly did (Franks & Wilson, 1974). It is Lick's (1975) data, from one of the best controlled studies to date that satisfied the necessary methodological criteria, that provide strong support for Emmelkamp's (1975a) and Lick and Bootzin's (1975) position.

In this study, systematic desensitization was compared to two pseudo-therapy control treatments based on Marcia et al.'s (1969) procedure. Subjects in these control conditions were told that they would be exposed to subliminal presentations of their phobic stimuli and that their reactions would be monitored psychophysiologically. One group received fake GSR feedback after every session indicating that they were becoming less fearful, while the other group did not. Unlike the vast majority of analogue studies on fear reduction, genuinely fearful and well-motivated subjects were recruited from the community. Criteria for acceptance into the study included evidence of a specific behavioral inhibition regarding snakes or spiders, such as the inability to go camping or clean closets; failure to reach into an aquarium containing a snake or spider with a gloved hand; a willingness to participate in any one of three treatments after hearing brief descriptions thereof; and a $20 deposit to be refunded after completion of the study. Eight fortnightly treatment sessions were administered which means that the total time subjects spent in treatment compared favorably with Paul's (1966) landmark study. Even then not all desensitization subjects completed their hierarchies. This provides another index of the high intensity of the subjects' fear. Most analogue studies have typically used significantly fewer treatment sessions and still report completion of anxiety hierarchies, presumably because their subjects were not really phobic.

All three treatments were significantly superior to a no-treatment control condition in modifying behavioral, physiological, and self-report measures of fear but they did not differ from one another. The results for the three treatment groups in terms of self report of fear were maintained at a four-month follow-up. Assessment of subjects' expectancies at the end of the first session indicated that the desensitization and pseudotherapy plus fake feedback treatments induced marginally greater subject expectancies than pseudotherapy without feedback ($p < .1$). Subjects' expectancies were not significantly correlated with treatment outcome.

Attempts have been made to manipulate expectancies about the outcome of systematic desensitization in two ways. In one type of study subjects are informed that they are receiving a therapeutic technique and are then given either positive, neutral, or negative expectancies about outcome. In the other kind of study subjects receiving usually positive therapeutic instructions are compared to those who are deliberately misled about the nature of their participation (e.g., they are informed that the study is an experimental investigation of the physiology of fear). Lick and Bootzin (1975) concluded that the former group of studies "have uniformly shown no effect for expectancy-inducing instructions," whereas the latter series of studies have demonstrated that "a therapeutic versus an experimental definition of systematic desensitization is an important determinant of therapeutic effectiveness" (p. 924).

A recent exception to Lick and Bootzin's analysis is Lott and Murray's (1975) finding that snake fearful subjects who received desensitization with positive expectancy-inducing instructions improved substantially more than subjects who received neutral instructions. However, both groups improved significantly, indicating a differential effect of expectancy set on outcome. As in Lick's (1975) study, subjects' initial treatment expectancies had no measurable effect on outcome. Similarly, Borkovec (in press) reports the failure to obtain any significant correlations between expectancy ratings and outcome in three studies on the behavioral treatment of sleep disturbance. It is of interest that no correlations were found either during counterdemand or positive demand phases of these studies (see Steinmark & Borkovec, 1974—reprinted in Franks & Wilson, 1975). Addressing himself to this issue, Lick (1975) suggests that the problem might be "unreliability inherent in the simple Likert scale used to measure expectancy . . .," and the possibility "that the subject's expectancy varies considerably over time and is inadequately sampled by any one measurement" (p. 566).

A commendable feature of Lott and Murray's study was the fact that the expectancy manipulation was independently validated in a prior study with a similar subject population. Subjects in the positive expectancy condition indicated greater anticipated improvement on the behavioral avoidance test if they were to participate in the treatment procedure than subjects in the neutral expectancy condition. This methodological alternative in which the subject completes part of the actual procedure and is then assessed for expectancy, appears preferable to the customary procedures in desensitization studies in which subjects simply rate their expectancies on a Likert scale. Unfortunately, Lott and Murray's subjects seem to have been only mildly fearful, thereby undermining this study's external validity.

In attempting to account for the differences between these two groups of studies, Lick and Bootzin refer to Miller's (1972) earlier suggestion that the treatment procedures in systematic desensitization usually generate considerable positive subject expectancy when the method is left unlabeled or is defined as therapy. If this were the case additional instructional variables would be unlikely to have much effect. However, subjects who are deceived about the purpose of desensitization appear not to attribute therapeutic efficacy to the technique, with a subsequently negative influence on treatment outcome.

The importance of determining whether experimenter-administered instructional sets actually produce the intended subject expectancies is underscored by Rosen (1975). He points out that specific instructional sets will not always reliably lead to particular subject expectancies because the latter are also a function of several other influences, including prior knowledge, basic suggestibility, and so on. In a study of subjects' initial therapeutic expectancies towards systematic desensitization as a function of varied instructional sets, Rosen distributed a questionnaire containing a procedural description of desensitization to undergraduates. Instructional sets were manipulated within a 2 × 3 factorial design to provide subjects with either a therapeutic or an experimental rationale accompanied by either an additional positive, neutral, or negative expectancy set. Subjects were asked to indicate whether they would participate in the proposed project and to rate how the procedure would affect their fear of snakes if they did participate.

The results were inconsistent and unexpected. Using only those subjects who indicated "much" or "very much" fear on the Fear Survey Schedule (Wolpe & Lang, 1964), the expectancy instructions, but not the rationale factor, produced a significant effect on subjects' stated expectancies. As discussed above, it has usually been the therapeutic versus experimental rationale manipulation which has shown significant effects in analogue desensitization studies! In another puzzling finding, subjects who received the therapeutic rationale alone indicated that they were less willing to participate in the study than any other group. Although it is difficult to make sense of these results, Rosen's point that the "attitudes subjects hold in response to particular instructional manipulations must be empirically demonstrated rather than assumed" (p. 235) seems well taken.

Given that expectancy-inducing instructions influence therapeutic outcome, the critical question concerns how this change is mediated (see Wilson & Evans, Section X this volume). Lick and Bootzin propose five possible mechanisms.

1. *Positive expectancies may engender feelings of hope and optimism which facilitate counterconditioning.*

This hypothesis is similar to Rosen's (1974) suggestion that positive expectancies serve to reduce physiological arousal and thereby facilitate non-reinforced exposure to the threatening stimuli, a crucial therapy process variable (Bandura, 1969; Lang, Melamed, & Hart, 1970). Indeed, Borkovec (1974) has shown that therapeutic instructions resulted in significantly lower heart rate during treatment sessions than nontherapeutic instructions, an important finding which lends strong support to this interpretation.

2. *Therapeutic instructions might enhance compliance with basic treatment procedures.*

However, Rosen's (1974) results are inconsistent with this view.

3. *Therapeutic instructions serve a motivational rather than a counterconditioning function.*

Having experienced a "convincing therapy," subjects may be encouraged to engage in reality testing in the natural environment such that in vivo extinction occurs (cf. Leitenberg, 1976). An important aspect of this hypothesis is that in vivo extinction is facilitated by the fact that subjects are motivated *to look for improvement* in their behavior in *a persistent fashion*. Emmelkamp (1975a) offers a similar notion in emphasizing the importance of the client's *belief* that he has improved.

One of the advantages of this interpretation is that it plausibly accounts for what has been called the "transfer gap" in systematic desensitization, i.e., the incomplete generalization from imaginal to in vivo stimuli. Previous accounts have stressed a stimulus sampling theory (Davison, 1968) which predicts a generalization decrement from the imaginal to the in vivo situation. Wilson and Davison (1975) have argued that in vivo reality testing is made possible by the reduction of fear, during systematic desensitization, below a critical threshold above which clients either cannot or will not confront aversive events. The conditioning and motivational interpretations are not mutually exclusive, of course, and it is likely that both factors are important, as Emmelkamp (1975b) suggests.

4. *Therapeutic instructions create demand characteristics for improved behavioral performance.*

This hypothesis states that following participation in an "effective therapy," subjects will experience a socially mediated demand to approach the feared object during the posttreatment behavioral avoidance test. Borkovec (1973), however, has shown that these demand characteristics modify the behavior of mildly fearful but not genuinely phobic individuals. Although demand characteristics for improvement might not reduce intense physiological fear arousal (Borkovec, 1974), they might, as Lick and Bootzin suggest, motivate initial approach behavior which then facilitates in vivo extinction. Demand characteristics have often been regarded as a "source of error" in experiments on fear reduction. This might be the case in a controlled study designed to separate their effects from a basic conditioning process. In the clinical situation, however, the behavior change potential of demand characteristics is as important as formal conditioning techniques. Although long since labeled as "nonspecific" influences, their effects can be specified and usefully integrated into a comprehensive social learning treatment approach (cf. Borkovec, in press; Wilson, 1975; Wilson & Evans, in press).

5. *Therapeutic instructions modify cognitive processes which directly reduce fear responding.*

Bandura (1969) has proposed that emotional behavior may be governed by two different sources of stimuli: "One is the emotional arousal self-generated by symbolic activities in the form of emotion-provoking thoughts about frightening or pleasurable events. The second is the response evoked directly by conditioned aversive stimuli" (p. 364). In this hypothesis about the function of therapeutic instructions, Lick and Bootzin speculate that they affect the self-generated symbolic processes which determine emotional responsiveness. There is little evidence to support this view. As Lick and Bootzin observe, both systematic desensitization and pseudotherapy control treatments usually have failed to alter significantly subjects' self-report of fear arousal although overt avoidance behavior may have been modified. Moreover, false feedback designed to induce favorable cognitions about decreased fear arousal has been shown to be ineffective in reducing fear and/or avoidance in very fearful subjects (Davison & Wilson, 1973). The reduction of fear/avoidance through direct cognitive control is a demonstrably effective treatment strategy (e.g., Meichenbaum, Gilmore, & Fedoravicius, 1971—reprinted in Franks & Wilson, 1973), but more seems to be involved than the simple provision of positive expectancy-inducing instructions (see below).

Fear Reduction Research: Some Methodological Considerations. The external validity or clinical relevance of the majority of analogue fear reduction studies has been seriously questioned on several grounds, including the use of only mildly fearful subjects, assessment procedures extremely vulnerable to situational demand characteristics, and treatment procedures which differ from actual clinical methods (Bernstein & Paul, 1971—reprinted in Franks & Wilson, 1973). Lick and Unger (1975) maintain that there is yet another problem for the laboratory assessment of fear. After teatment with systematic desensitization, two phobic subjects showed substantial improvement on the typical behavioral avoidance test, being able to approach and touch a caged spider or snake. However, neither subject was able to engage in previously inhibited behaviors in the natural environment, such as camping or gardening. A second assessment in the laboratory showed that when the spider or snake was uncaged and placed on the floor, both subjects evidenced considerable physiological and subjective distress and were unable to even approach the phobic stimulus. Following Marks (1969), Lick and Unger suggest that a sense of unpredictability may be a major component of clinical fears, and since the BAT is a highly structured predictable situation, "it is impossible to predict how increased approach behavior to a feared object correlate (s) with improvement in the specific problem areas relevant to the subject's daily activities" (p. 865).

However, Lick and Unger's contention seems to overlook the purpose of analogue fear research, which is *to demonstrate* the specific behavior change properties of well-defined treatment methods. The intent is not necessarily to produce changes in the subject's daily activities as it would be in therapy. As Lick and Unger themselves note, given the situational specificity of behavioral performance, "it is not surprising that behavioral gains made in the laboratory sometimes fail to generalize to the natural environment" (p. 865). When appropriate social learning strategies designed to facilitate generalization are followed, improvement on standardized laboratory measures does transfer to the very activities addressed by Lick and Unger—see the first article in this Section by Bandura, Jeffery, and Gajdos.

Methodological criticism of analogue research on fear reduction has centered on studies on fears of small animals (e.g., Bernstein & Paul, 1971). Yet Blom and Craighead (1974) have recently shown that the same limitations may apply to studies of speech anxiety. College students selected for their reported fear of speech anxiety were randomly assigned to one of four expectancy-demand conditions in a 2×2 design. In the two situational demand conditions, subjects were informed that the study was being conducted in (a) the speech anxiety clinic, or (b) the nonverbal communication laboratory; in the instructional-expectancy conditions, subjects were told that the study was an investigation of (a) fear and anxiety, or (b) simulating the effects of relaxation training for communications skills problems. All subjects underwent a multi-response system assessment of speech anxiety using procedures based on Paul's (1966) assessment methods.

The results indicated that both the clinic setting and the fear test instructions produced significantly more anxiety than the laboratory setting and the simulated relaxation training instructions respectively. The implications of these findings are clear. Both subjective and objective measures of anxiety can be increased or decreased by providing certain stimulus settings. The problem for analogue therapy studies is that pretreatment assessment resembles their simulated relaxation training instructions. As a result, improvement as posttreatment cannot be unequivocally attributed to the efficacy of the treatment technique. The significance of Blom and Craighead's findings is enhanced by the fact that most of their subjects met one or more of Paul's (1966) criteria for inclusion in his classic study.

The lack of adequate control procedures makes it impossible to interpret some treatment studies. Zemore (1975), for example, compared traditional systematic desensitization to Goldfried's (1971) modified version of desensitization as a self-control method and a no-treatment control group in the treatment of speech and test anxiety. Flying in the face of much of the recent evidence summarized above, Zemore justified the omission of an attention-placebo condition on the basis of the "well-established finding that systematic desensitization produced significantly greater fear reduction than simple placebo treatments" (p. 158). In addition, only a single therapist was used, resulting in a major therapist × technique confound. The results, showing no difference between the two treatments although both were superior to no treatment at all, are quite uninterpretable, and render gratuitous Zemore's analysis of their implications for desensitization as a self-control method. Simple demand factors could plausibly have produced this uninformative result.

The same problem is evident in Russell, Miller, and June's (1975) comparison of systematic desensitization with a cue-controlled relaxation procedure and no treatment with test anxiety. There were no differences between the two treatment groups on any measure, although both differed from the no treatment condition. (Even then this difference was only on two of several self-report measures and not on a behavioral outcome measure.) Although the authors conclude that their data support the efficacy of cue-controlled relaxation, an alternative interpretation in terms of positive demand—especially in view of the inadequate dependent measures in this study—is more than a little plausible.

Comparative Outcome Studies. Kockott, Dittmar, and Nusselt (1975) compared systematic desensitization to "routine therapy" and a waiting list control group in the treatment of impotence. "Routine therapy" was defined as the combination of advice and medication given by general practitioners and psychiatrists in Munich, West Germany. Twenty-four patients, equally distributed across the three groups, were selected according to the following criteria: the inability to achieve intromission for at least six months prior to therapy; a cooperative partner; and no organic disorder, sexual deviation (unspecified), or endogenous depression. Patients in the desensitization condition received 14 treatment sessions, whereas those in the routine therapy were seen by psychiatrists for a total of four occasions at intervals of 3-5 weeks. A taped, semi-structured interview, subsequently scored by the interviewer and two independent psychiatrists, served as a pre-post measure of therapeutic efficacy. No reliability figures were reported. In addition, penile plethysmographic measures were obtained from 10 of the patients while they were asked to imagine two separate scenes involving sexual intercourse. All subjects provided subjective ratings of these two imagery scenes.

Although patients who received systematic desensitization reported less subjective aversion or anxiety to the thought of sexual intercourse at the end of treatment, behavioral improvements, as determined from the semistructured interviews, were minimal in both treatment groups. Only two patients in each group were judged to have been "cured"—defined as "erection maintained for at least 1 minute after intromission with intravaginal ejaculation before loss of erection" (p. 498). An increase in duration of erection up to 20 percent was observed in only four patients (at least one in each group) at posttreatment. However, there was no association between this increase in tumescence and the clinical ratings.

Kockott et al. attribute the ineffectiveness of systematic desensitization to the fact that it is a technique for "dealing with anxiety-related problems alone," whereas "during the behavior analysis of the patients it became clear that there was a great number of other factors in addition to anxiety which seemed to maintain the behavioral disturbance" (p. 499). Unimproved patients were subsequently treated with a modified Masters and Johnson program addressing some of the factors such as unrealistic standards and negative attitudes about sex. Of the 12 patients treated in this manner, eight were rated as cured, three had shown no improvement, and one had relapsed shortly after therapy.

Systematic desensitization has been applied to the treatment of heterosexual or dating anxiety in males in several studies. Curran and Gilbert (1975) found that both systematic desensitization and a comprehensive social skills training program were significantly more effective than a minimal contact control group in reducing self-report measures of anxiety at posttreatment and a six month follow-up. Only the skills training program, however, produced significant improvement on behavioral ratings of interpersonal skills. In an otherwise well-controlled study, a problem is the minimal detail reported about the minimal contact group, which, Curran and Gilbert state, was "designed to control for nonspecific effects such as the passage of time, repeated testing, and motivation" (p. 514). No data are provided to indicate that this goal was realized. Curran and Gilbert offer an important clinical observation in noting that several of their subjects were not so much deficient in social skills as they were inclined to devalue their own behavior. Glasgow and Arkowitz (1975) similarly emphasize the important role of negative, self-critical self-statements as a determinant of heterosexual anxiety—a finding which clearly argues for the use of cognitive methods such as self-instructional training.

In a second study, Curran (1975) found that both systematic desensitization and the social skill training program were significantly more effective than attention-placebo (relaxation training) and waiting list control groups on behavioral ratings of heterosexual behavior.

Also in contrast to Curran and Gilbert's (1975) results, Bander, Steinke, Allen, and Mosher (1975) found that a "reeducative" therapy featuring a hierarchical program of behavior rehearsal and in vivo interactions with women produced improvements in both interpersonal skills and heterosexual anxiety. Systematic desensitization failed to increase the efficacy of the reeducative therapy, which, in terms of client reported and behaviorally rated outcome criteria, was superior to both a microlab treatment based on group encounter techniques and an apparently convincing attention-placebo treatment.

Lastly, Orr, Mitchell, and Hall (1975) compared the effects on heterosexual anxiety of six sessions of systematic desensitization, an abbreviated four session treatment, a relaxation training condition, and no treatment. The desensitization treatments did not differ from each other in terms of self-reports of social anxiety, but both were significantly superior to the relaxation training and no treatment control conditions. As in the Curran and Gilbert study, desensitization did not effect any appreciable change in actual heterosexual behavior as measured by frequency of social activities or the type of social interactions. Aside from questions about the nature of relaxation training as an appropriate control group, the study is flawed by the use of a single therapist.

Flooding

Comparative Outcome Studies. Flooding, which involves prolonged exposure to high intensity aversive stimulation, can be differentiated from implosive therapy (Stampfl & Levis, 1967) in two ways. The latter not only includes the presentation of stimulus material based on psychodynamic concepts, but also horrifying scenes with frequently adverse consequences which unnecessarily exceed the intensity of flooding scenes (cf. Morganstern, 1973). Kirsch, Wolpin, and Knutson (1975) compared these two techniques with successive approximation and an attention-placebo condition in the treatment of speech anxiety. All treatments were carried out in vivo. The three behavioral methods proved to be more effective than the placebo in reducing anxiety, with flooding significantly superior to both implosion and successive approximation. As in other studies reviewed here, the absence of data on the credibility of the placebo treatment, taken in conjunction with the issues raised by Blom and Craighead (1974), pose problems in interpreting these findings.

There are all too few reports on long-term follow-ups of clinical patients treated by behavioral techniques. A commendable exception to this general trend is a five-year follow-up by Boudewyns (1975) of psychiatric inpatients who had originally received either implosion, desensitization using free association, or a progressive hospital milieu treatment. Based on rehospitalizations, telephone contacts, and mailed questionnaires, the implosion group appeared to have maintained previous gains and had a significantly lower re-hospitalization rate (36.36 percent) than the milieu treatment group (80 percent).

As the preceding section on systematic desensitization makes clear, numerous research studies on the behavioral treatment of anxiety continue to utilize non-clinical subject populations. One of the strong points of the research program of Emmelkamp and his associates in Holland has been the concentration on clinically phobic clients. For example, Emmelkamp and Wessels (1975) compared imaginal, in vivo, and combined imaginal and in vivo flooding treatments in the treatment of agoraphobic clients. Clients' average age was 34 years (range 16-55 years), while the average duration of their disorder was 7 years (range 2-20 years). Following four 90-minute treatment sessions, in vivo flooding was found to be marginally more effective than imaginal flooding in terms of time clients were able to spend in the phobic situation ($p <$ .10), and both therapist and client ratings of phobic anxiety and avoidance. Combined flooding was superior to imaginal flooding only on therapist ratings of anxiety and avoidance. Although Stern and Marks (1973—reprinted in Franks & Wilson, 1974) had previously shown the superiority of in vivo over imaginal flooding, the imaginal flooding in that investigation was conducted by means of tape-recordings, which, according to Stern and Marks, is less effective than flooding carried out by the therapist in person.

Subsequent to the flooding treatment, all clients were treated with 8 sessions of what Emmelkamp and Wessels call a self-observation procedure (see below). In this technique, the client is instructed to enter the phobic situation in a graduated fashion and is allowed to turn back in the face of "undue anxiety." The client systematically records the amount of time spent in the phobic situation, but is not reinforced by the therapist as in successive approximation (Emmelkamp & Ultee, 1974; Leitenberg, 1976). Indeed, the therapist was present only for the first two treatment sessions after which the clients proceeded on their own. Although self-observation resulted in little additional improvement in clients originally treated with in vivo or combined flooding, it produced significantly greater reduction of anxiety and avoidance than imaginal flooding. In contrast to the findings of Lick (1975) and Lott and Murray (1975), clients' expectancies of therapeutic gain at the beginning of treatment were positively correlated with outcome.

Emmelkamp and Wessel's clinical observations are worthy of note. A number of clients treated with flooding in imagination apparently reported an increase in ratings of "anxious mood," and found it to be an "irksome procedure." And while in vivo flooding was most effective overall, one client was sufficiently terrified at its prospect that she "hid in the cellar!" Findings of this sort emphasize the need to be able to flexibly tailor treatment techniques to different clients' problems. In view of the almost comparable efficacy of the self-observation method, which, because it is graduated and client-controlled would seem to be less taxing, it might well be preferable to flooding.

The application of flooding to obsessive-compulsive disorders (Marks, Hodgson, & Rachman, 1975) is described in the next section.

Theoretical Mechanisms in Flooding. Two well-controlled analogue studies by McCutcheon and Adams (1975) investigated competing theoretical concepts and the effects of different durations of flooding on physiological, behavioral, and subjective measures. In the first experiment, 12 subjects who were unable to watch a film showing surgical procedures on battle casualties were assigned to one of three treatment groups: a relevant imagery (RI) group, which was administered a 20-minute tape-recorded flooding session focusing on the fear-provoking imagery of witnessing surgery; an irrelevant imagery (II) group, which was given a 20-minute tape-recorded session focusing on anxiety-provoking imagery of snakes; and a control group, which was simply told to relax and saw no film. The pre-post behavioral assessment consisted of exposure to the surgical film which subjects could stop at any time. All subjects completed a 100 point fear thermometer immediately before and after the experimental sequence, and GSR was recorded continuously throughout the entire study. The results showed no difference on the behavioral test (time spent viewing the film), while GSR recordings indicated that the RI group showed significantly *increased* fear arousal during the posttreatment assessment.

The second experiment was identical to the first with the exception that the flooding session was extended to one hour. The RI group watched the film for a significantly longer time than either the II or the control group, and showed marginally significant ($p < .10$) reductions in autonomic arousal compared to the other groups. As in experiment 1, autonomic arousal increased during the first 20 minutes of the flooding session. This convincing replication of previous findings and the overall divergent outcome of the two experiments seem to rule out any interpretation in terms of demand characteristics. Theoretically, as McCutcheon and Adams note, the marked superiority of the RI over the II group discredits the exhaustion hypothesis of why flooding works (Rachman, 1969). And the fact that the surgical assessment film was rated as more anxiety-arousing than the flooding sessions argues against the behavioral contrast explanation (Hodgson & Rachman, 1972). In all, these results provide convincing support for the extinction interpretation of flooding in which repeated nonreinforced exposure to the feared stimuli is a critical process. Ornstein and Carr (1975), however, obtained evidence inconsistent with a simple extinction model. Parenthetically, it should be noted that experiment 2 showed the effective use of tape-recorded flooding.

McCutcheon and Adams' demonstration that too short a duration of flooding can exacerbate fear arousal was replicated by Stone and Borkovec (1975). Brief exposure to the feared stimulus resulted in significantly increased heart rate from pre- to posttest assessments. Moreover, among subjects categorized as high autonomic perceivers on the basis of the Autonomic Perception Questionnaire (Mandler, Mandler, & Uviller, 1958), brief exposure produced less posttreatment approach behavior to the feared stimulus than either zero or prolonged exposure. These data, Stone and Borkovec conclude, demonstrate the incubation of fear responses (Eysenck, 1968). They appropriately caution that "flooding may be harmful . . . under conditions in which patients do not receive exposure of sufficiently long duration" (p. 54).

Participant Modeling

The first article reprinted in this Section, by Bandura, Jeffery, and Gajdos, is particularly important in that it demonstrates how self-directed performance can facilitate generalization of improvement in psychological functioning. Presented here are some very real implications for the improved clinical practice of behavior therapy. Beyond these practical implications, however, seminal theoretical issues are raised about the processes which mediate generalization of behavior change. In pointing out the role of enhancement of self-adequacy and the acquisition of generalizable coping skills in addition to stimulus generalization, Bandura et al. emphasize how much more complex and cognitive current day social learning theory is compared to earlier learning models in which generalization is seen simply as a function of the similarity of stimuli in the external environment (see also Bandura, Section I this volume).

The clinical efficacy of participant modeling has been intensively investigated in the treatment of obsessive-compulsive disorders at the Maudsley Hospital in London. Recently, Marks Rachman, and Hodgson (1975) reported a two-year follow-up of 20 (3 men and 17 women) obsessive-compulsive patients who had been treated with one of the following three methods: 1) rapid exposure (in vivo flooding), in which the patient was persuaded but not forced to enter the most frightening situation first; 2) rapid in vivo exposure with prior modeling by the therapist; and 3) slow in vivo exposure with modeling (participant modeling), in which patients were encouraged to gradually enter a hierarchy of fearful situations after each step was modeled by a calm, reassuring therapist. The patient was then required to imitate the therapist under direct guidance until each step could be performed without assistance. All three groups were instructed to refrain from engaging in compulsive acts between treatment sessions. All 20 patients received 15 treatment sessions while hospitalized over a three to six week period. For 15 of the patients (5 in each treatment group), these flooding/modeling treatments were preceded by three weeks of relaxation (control) training. (The details of the treatment of 10 of these patients [the rapid exposure without modeling and the participant modeling groups, which also received relaxation training] and the initial three-month follow-up, were previously described by Rachman, Hodgson, & Marks, 1971—reprinted in Franks & Wilson, 1973).

Unlike earlier follow-ups at which blind assessments were made and avoidance tests administered, the two-year evaluation was based on self-ratings which the patients mailed in. Eleven were directly interviewed. Interviews with the relatives of nine of these 11 corroborated patient self-ratings. Retrospective analyses of these two groups of 11 and 9 patients respectively failed to show any differences in response to treatment, suggesting that they could be regarded as comparable at the two-year follow-up. Furthermore, since self-ratings were strongly correlated with other outcome interviews at the six-month follow-up, Marks et al. argue that their two-year measures were valid indices of progress. The results indicated that, based on pooled self-ratings of obsessive anxiety and avoidance behavior, 14 patients were judged to be much improved, one improved, and five unchanged. Improvement during the first few weeks of treatment predicted favorable outcome at follow-ups. Specific inter-group comparisons are not presented, although Marks et al. reiterate their earlier conclusions that relaxation training was ineffective and that modeling of exposure "conferred no advantage over exposure alone for the group as a whole, though it may help selected patients" (p. 349). Interpretation of the efficacy of the individual techniques is further complicated by the fact that many patients received booster treatments after discharge, 9 were administered anti-depressant medication, 2 required marital therapy, and one had assertion training.

In a useful series of clinical observations on the treatment of these 20 patients, Marks et al. comment on the importance of the therapist-patient relationship in prompting patients to comply with instructions to desist from their rituals, and the value of the active involvement of family members. Indeed, 11 patients in all had a mean of three home visits following discharge. And, of the patients who failed to improve, all but one refused to cooperate in following instructions once they returned home.

In another study by the Maudsley group, Roper, Rachman, and Marks (1975) assigned 10 obsessive-compulsive patients to one of two treatment groups. The first received 15 sessions of a control treatment in which patients modeled the therapist engaging in relaxation exercises, followed by 15 sessions of participant modeling. The second received 15 sessions of passive modeling in which patients observed the therapist engaging in behaviors they would normally avoid and/or be greatly distressed by, followed by 15 sessions of participant modeling. Treatment was administered on an inpatient basis for a period of five to seven weeks.

The results showed that modeling of exposure to the threatening activities produced significantly more improvement than modeled relaxation, which was ineffective in modifying compulsive rituals. Although both modeling treatments produced changes, Roper et al. concluded that "those observed after participant modeling treatment were more pronounced and were evident on a wider range of measures" (p. 274). A six-month follow-up indicated that of the 10 patients, four were much improved, four were improved, and two were unchanged—a clinical outcome similar to Marks et al.'s (1975) findings.

Methodological problems preclude parceling out the relative efficacy of passive and participant modeling. In the first place, as Roper et al. themselves point out, both modeling procedures were confounded with repeated instructions to the patients to desist from engaging in compulsive acts. In the second place, the experimental design employed does not permit an adequate evaluation of the respective modeling methods. There was no between-group comparison, and the absence of counterbalancing of the two treatments within the group that received both forms of modeling resulted in a treatment × order confound.

To summarize, the Maudsley group's findings, while they do not always permit a comparative assessment of the efficacy of individual therapeutic strategies, provide the best clinical evidence yet that obsessive-compulsive disorders can be successfully treated by behavior therapy.

The relative efficacy of modeling, participation, and the combination of the two in reducing avoidance behavior was also investigated by Lewis (1974). Using a factorial design that improved upon Roper et al.'s (1975) methodology, Lewis compared each of these three treatment conditions to a control group in decreasing children's fear of swimming.

The combined, participant modeling treatment was the most effective, although both components were individually more successful than the control group. Perhaps most importantly, the combined participant modeling group showed significant generalization of improvement on the assessment of fear of swimming in a different pool with a new instructor. In contrast to previous findings with snake phobic subjects (Blanchard, 1970), the participation component was superior to the modeling procedure. Lewis suggests that the relative contributions of these components to participant modeling may vary according to the target behavior. For example, Bandura (1971) emphasizes the importance of actual behavioral practice in the performance of inhibited activities that involve significant motor components. Fear of swimming would seem to be an excellent example of this latter type of activity.

Using a cross-over design, Hackmann and McLean (1975) treated two groups of obsessive-compulsives, each of which received four sessions of thought stopping* and in vivo exposure (participant modeling) respectively, in random order. The latter treatment was based on Rachman et al.'s (1971) in vivo exposure with modeling procedure. The authors claim that both treatments seemed to be effective, although there was no significant difference between them.

However, it is difficult to draw any meaningful conclusions from this study. Omitted from the dependent measures was a behavioral avoidance test, on the puzzling grounds that "it was felt that this might be too

---

* Rimm, Saunders, and Westel (1975) describe the use of thought stopping in the treatment of snake phobics.

similar in content to the flooding sessions to allow a fair comparison to be made" (p. 263). Aside from the usual psychiatric and self-ratings of improvement, patients were asked to self-monitor obsessional thoughts every half hour during the day. This represents a considerable advance over global rating scales. Unfortunately, there were no differences between the two treatments on this enterprising measure. And while t-tests showed several significant pre-post differences, an analysis of variance comparing the effects of treatment and order effects indicated no differences. No follow-up data were reported.

Symbolic Modeling

The second article reprinted in this Section, by Melamed and Siegel, describes the successful use of filmed modeling in reducing pre- and post-operative fear in children undergoing surgery. Behavioral principles and procedures are being increasingly applied within the field of medicine and health care. There is even a new label—behavioral medicine—to describe this interdisciplinary endeavor that is supporting a burgeoning literature (e.g., Katz & Zlutnick, 1975). Much, if not all, of behavioral medicine has thus far been concerned with the use of biofeedback methods with predominantly psychosomatic disorders (e.g., Birk, 1973) and the treatment of addictions such as cigarette smoking, alcoholism, and obesity (see Section V, this volume). In demonstrating the utility of a simple but effective modeling method for reducing fear arousal and the frequency of behavior problems associated with hospitalization, Melamed and Siegel point the way to still more extensive applications of social learning principles to medical practice. Aside from improving the psychological well-being of the patient facing surgery, the reduction of undue stress and anxiety may actually facilitate physical recovery from surgery.

The influence of model similarity on the extinction of avoidance behavior in second- and third-grade children was studied by Kornhaber and Schroeder (1975). Girls who were afraid of snakes viewed one of four types of models: a) a fearless child who performed all the tasks of the behavioral avoidance test with positive self-verbalizations such as "This is fun"; b) a fearful child who performed all the tasks hesitantly while making statements such as "This is scary"; c) a fearless adult who made positive comments such as "He's pretty"; and d) a fearful adult who performed all the tasks reluctantly while making comments such as "I don't know if I can do that." A no treatment group controlled for the effects of pre- and post-testing exposure to the snake.

Peer group models were significantly more effective than the adult models in decreasing behavioral avoidance. Model similarity on the response dimension of level of fear did not have a significant influence on behavior. With respect to measures of the children's attitude towards snakes, however, more similar models produced the greatest changes irrespective of the dimension (level of fear or age) on which similarity occurred. In a study with adult subjects, Bandura and Barab (1973) found that age similarity of models did not differentially influence avoidance behavior. Kornhaber and Schroeder point out that the discrimination view of extinction resolves the apparent discrepancy. Whereas the children might have discriminated and discounted the performance of adults from their own abilities on the basis that adults are more competent, the adults in Bandura and Barab's study were motivated to show improvement, despite residual fear, after watching child models perform the avoidance tasks. Accordingly, the authors concluded that "age dissimilarity may have either positive or negative effects on behavior depending on the age of the observer" (p. 606).

Kornhaber and Schroeder also compared their results to those of Meichenbaum (1971) that showed the superiority of a coping model who gradually became less fearful, over a mastery model who fearlessly performed the feared activities. They suggest that Meichenbaum's coping models were effective not because of their initial emotional similarity to the observers, but by virtue of the self-control coping behaviors they displayed.

In contrast to the efficacy of symbolic modeling in these and other studies (cf. Bandura, 1971), Lira, Nay, McCullough, and Etkin (1975) obtained no difference among self-regulated symbolic modeling, exposure only, and no treatment control conditions in the modification of snake avoidance behavior. A role-playing treatment, however, was significantly more effective than all other groups in terms of behavioral and attitudinal measures at posttreatment. Role-playing consisted of subjects reading a brief description of a "fearless snake hobbyist," after which they were then instructed to think, feel, and behave as this individual in role-playing approach behavior to the snake. Although Lira et al. report that treatment gains were maintained at a two-month follow-up, the fact that only 21 of the original sample of 48 subjects were evaluated vitiates the confidence that can be placed in these data.

Sarason (1975) exposed high and low test anxiety subjects to three different types of models: a) a model who disclosed feeling anxious but verbalized problem-solving strategies for coping with test anxiety; b) a model who similarly disclosed test anixety without indicating coping abilities; and c) a model who disclaimed any anxiety and described how she concentrated on the task before her instead of worrying needlessly and anticipating failure. The performance of the high test anxiety subjects on a subsequent learning task was significantly improved as a result of exposure to the self-disclosing, coping model. These findings lend further support to the notion that coping models are more effective than models displaying complete mastery in modifying fear and avoidance behavior (Meichenbaum, 1971).

Finally, Annon and Robinson (1975) described the innovative use of vicarious learning principles in the treatment of sexual dysfunction. Their results indicated that a variety of sexual behaviors could be acquired and/or increased in frequency, and more favorable attitudes towards masturbatory activities developed through symbolic modeling procedures.

Covert Modeling

The third article reprinted in this Section is the most recent of Kazdin's series of studies on a specific form of symbolic modeling, viz., covert modeling, in which the person *imagines* rather than observes a model. Among the notable features of this study are the report of a four-month follow-up (albeit only on one measure), and the assessment of subjects' actual imagery during sessions. The finding that some subjects embellished treatment scenes will come as no surprise to clinicians using directed imagery procedures, although the significance of this phenomenon remains to be demonstrated.

Kazdin's results are important for social learning theory in at least two major respects. First, they show how systematically manipulated covert processes can influence overt behavior. Secondly, by showing that the parameters of covert modeling are similar to those of overt modeling, the data provide further support for the more general hypothesis that symbolic activities are governed by the same psychological laws as are overt behaviors (Meichenbaum, 1971—in Franks & Wilson, 1973).

Self-Observation, Reinforced Practice and Feedback

In addition to flooding and participant modeling, other variations of in vivo exposure have proved effective in reducing phobic behavior. Emmelkamp and Emmelkamp-Benner (1975) compared self-observation administered on either an individual or group basis, with and without prior presentation of a film in which successful ex-clients related their experiences with self-observation treatment. Their therapy had been effective but not to the same extent in all cases, suggesting that this was an instance of coping versus mastery modeling. The authors conceptualized this procedure as historically portrayed modeling (Bandura & Barab, 1973). The patients were 34 agoraphobics (31 women and 3 men), 31 of whom completed four sessions of treatment.

Both at posttreatment and at a one-month follow-up the results on a number of behavioral and self-report measures showed that treatment had been effective, although there were no differences between individual versus group treatment, and scant effect of the film. As Emmelkamp and Emmelkamp-Benner themselves suggest, repeated exposure to the film during treatment would have constituted a better test of the modeling method. Consistent with previous findings (Emmelkamp & Wessels, 1975), patients' expectancies of therapeutic gain at the start of treatment correlated significantly with improvement.

Leitenberg, Agras, Allen, Butz, and Edwards (1975) reported a series of five single-subject experiments with phobic patients in which they systematically examined the effect of precise feedback of behavioral performance and contingent therapist praise on the reinforced practice procedure. Feedback was substantially more effective than praise in initiating approach behavior in the feared situation. However, once a certain degree of progress was made, praise and repeated graduated practice seemed to maintain improved performance. Leitenberg et al. point out that feedback per se appears capable of modifying an impressive range of problem behaviors, including psychosomatic disorders (Birk, 1973), anorexia nervosa (Agras, Barlow, Chapin, Abel, & Leitenberg, 1974—reprinted in Franks & Wilson, 1975), and obesity (Romanczyk, Tracey, Kilson, & Thorpe, 1973). In explaining this therapeutic influence the authors suggest that feedback of slight but successful changes may increase motivation and may enhance positive expectancies about outcome.

Becker and Costello (1975) showed that client-controlled, graduated in vivo exposure with therapist-administered feedback on performance was more effective than a no treatment control group in reducing avoidance behavior in snake fearful subjects. Unfortunately, the almost total lack of the minimally necessary controls in analogue research of this nature renders the findings uninterpretable. Hepner and Cauthen (1975) found that the same graduated in vivo exposure technique was significantly more effective in reducing avoidance behavior in snake fearful subjects when exposure was subject- as opposed to experimenter-controlled.

A third variation of this procedure, in which nongraduated exposure was experimenter-controlled, produced the least improvement.

Feedback of performance has also been shown to facilitate behavioral change in other treatment procedures. Christensen, Arkowitz, and Anderson (1975) demonstrated the efficacy of practice dating with reciprocal feedback between partners in the conjoint treatment of socially inhibited men and women. Specifically, after each date, subjects completed a feedback form in which they explicitly commented on positive aspects of their partners' appearance and behavior which they liked, and one aspect of behavior which they wished altered.

Sherman, Mulac, and McCann (1974) compared four groups of speech anxious subjects, each of which received one of the following four treatments: rehearsal feedback, self-relaxation, a combination of relaxation/rehearsal, and no treatment. The rehearsal feedback treatment was designed to train subjects to recognize and progressively decrease overt indications of anxiety while they were speaking. To this end, subjects were coached in identifying anxiety cues by watching selected videotape recordings demonstrating overt signs of speech anxiety, practiced their own speeches which were videotaped, and then analyzed immediate playbacks of these speeches for the presence of anxiety. Only the combined treatment group showed significantly lowered speech anxiety, on behavioral and subjective measures obtained unobtrusively outside the treatment setting in the normal context of a speech course, as compared to the no treatment control group. Neither the self-relaxation nor the rehearsal feedback condition alone was superior to the control group. In retrospective analyses, Sherman et al. suggest that the treatments given singly did reduce anxiety in the treatment laboratory, but that only the combined treatment generalized to the more natural context of the speech course. The authors advocate the advisability of using multimodal therapy approaches to effect generalizable improvement.

Cognitive Restructuring

As Bandura makes clear in his decisive statement on psychological models of man (see Section I, this volume), social learning theory places great emphasis on cognitive variables as determinants of human behavior. Accordingly, it is hardly surprising to note lively interest in the investigation and application of cognitive restructuring methods, what with a growing literature—including a new journal, *Cognitive Therapy and Research*—and The First National Conference on Cognitive Behavior Therapy Research in New York this past April.

Ellis' (1962) rational-emotive psychotherapy remains the most influential of the cognitive therapies. A fundamental tenet of this approach is that people hold certain irrational beliefs that underlie overly negative, self-defeating covert self-statements that cause emotional uspet. Goldfried and Sobocinski (1975) conducted two experiments to investigate the relationship between the 10 irrational beliefs identified by Ellis and susceptibility to emotional disturbance. In experiment 1, significant positive correlations between these irrational beliefs and questionnaire measures of interpersonal, test, and public speaking anxiety were obtained. In experiment 2, individuals scoring either extremely high or low on one particular irrational belief—the desire to be loved and appreciated by everyone—were asked to imagine specific social situations that might be interpreted as involving rejection by other people. The high irrationality group showed significantly greater emotional arousal as measured by the anxiety and hostility dimensions of the Multiple Affect Adjective Checklist. No differences were obtained on several analogue behavioral tasks (e.g., word association and speed writing) that had been predicted to reflect affective disturbance.

The primary aim of cognitive restructuring is to identify and then replace these irrational cognitions with more constructive, coping responses. In a study of the use of verbal controlling responses for overcoming fear of the dark, Kanfer, Karoly, and Newman (1975) had 5-6-year-old children rehearse one of three types of controlling response: a) sentences emphasizing active control or competence (e.g., ". . . you know where everything is . . . when the door is closed you know that nobody can come in that you would not know"); b) sentences concentrating on reducing the aversive nature of darkness (e.g., "The dark is the best place to go to sleep and have good dreams. . . . When it is dark it is nice to cuddle up to stuffed animals"); and c) neutral sentences having nothing to do with the dark. Following this training, the children were assessed for their tolerance for remaining in the dark, and for the terminal illumination intensity they eventually chose on two posttreatment trials.

Children in the competence condition displayed significantly less fear of the dark (as operationalized above) than both the other groups. The group that concentrated on reducing the aversiveness of the stimulus situation produced significantly greater tolerance for the dark than the group given neutral sentences to rehearse. An important feature of this study was that the verbal training was carried out in a well-lit room, i.e., in the absence of fear-eliciting stimuli. As a result, Kanfer et al.

conclude that the therapeutic effects are attributable to the direct mediating effects on overt behavior of the verbal controlling responses, rather than to any possible counterconditioning or nonreinforced exposure to the aversive stimuli. As an alternative interpretation, they speculate that the verbal controlling sentences might have functioned as "self-instructions to behave like a brave boy or girl, with the expectation of social approval and self-reinforcements based upon past encouragements to act competently (like a brave boy or girl)" (p. 257). From a more clinical point of view these interesting findings strongly encourage the systematic analysis and modification of clients' self-verbalizations.

Wein, Nelson, and Odom (1975) described a well-controlled investigation of a cognitive restructuring method that D'Zurilla, Wilson, and Nelson (1973) found to be more effective than either systematic desensitization or graduated prolonged exposure in reducing subjective measures of anxiety. Carefully selected snake fearful subjects were assigned to one of the following four groups: a) cognitive restructuring; b) systematic desensitization; c) verbal extinction; d) attention-placebo; and e) no treatment. The cognitive restructuring treatment was designed to engage subjects in prolonged verbalizations of snake relevant experiences, to identify irrational past associations about snakes, and by providing detailed explanations of the development of irrational fears in terms of social learning principles, to assist subjects to relabel these anxiety-provoking cognitions in a more rational manner. Wein et al. refer to this latter rational relabeling process as reattribution. The verbal extinction treatment was an attempt to evaluate independently the contribution, to the overall cognitive restructuring method, of prolonged non-reinforced verbalizations of anxiety-arousing notions about snakes. This treatment was described as "confrontation therapy" to subjects who were told that fear could be reduced by verbally recounting its origins and development. The attention-placebo condition was based on Davison's (1968) procedure which focused on childhood experiences related to sexual matters on the grounds that a fear of snakes was merely the manifest symptom of an underlying conflict. Assessment procedures included behavioral, physiological, and subjective measures of fear.

Both systematic desensitization and cognitive restructuring produced significantly greater improvement on the behavioral avoidance test than either the attention-placebo or no-treatment control groups. Cognitive restructuring was also significantly superior to no treatment in reducing subjective measures of fear. Verbal extinction demonstrated significantly more fear reduction than the attention-placebo group on one of the subjective measures. No differences were obtained on the heart rate measure. Wein et al. concluded that the reattribution component of the cognitive restructuring method contributes significantly beyond verbal extinction in modifying both behavioral and subjective indices of fear.

In contrast to several of the studies reviewed in this Section, Wein et al.'s study is distinguished by the commendable attention paid to the methodological imperatives of analogue fear research (cf. Bernstein & Paul, 1971; Borkovec, 1973). In addition to using a high-demand-for-approach pre- and posttreatment behavioral test, Wein et al. analyzed subjects' expectancies of therapeutic gain before treatment, at the end of the first session, and at the completion of therapy. There were no differences between groups on either of the first two assessments. At posttreatment, both the cognitive restructuring and systematic desensitization groups recorded significantly more favorable expectancies than the attention-placebo and no treatment groups. These data suggest that the outcome cannot be attributed to differential credibility between treatments, and that treatment-produced improvements in the cognitive restructuring and desensitization groups subsequently affected subjects' expectancies as measured at posttreatment. Interestingly, these findings on the initial expectancy-inducing properties of Davison's (1968) placebo rationale contradict Borkovec and Nau's (1972) results indicating that this treatment rationale was inferior to that of systematic desensitization in developing positive expectancies. It is possible that the same rationale might be differentially effective across different therapists and different studies, and caution should be exercised before previous placebo treatments are retrospectively dismissed as unconvincing on the basis of more recent studies (see also Osarchuk & Goldfried, 1975).

Finally, cognitive restructuring comprised a major part of Fremouw and Harmatz's (1975) broad-spectrum behavioral treatment of speech anxiety. An interesting feature of this study was that speech anxious subjects (helpers) were taught anxiety-reducing techniques with which they subsequently treated other subjects like themselves (helpees). Both helpers and helpees were significantly improved on behavioral and self-report measures compared to a waiting list control group. These findings attest further to the advantages of using nonprofessional mediators in in behavioral treatment programs (see Wilson & Evans, Section X, this volume).

A Theoretical Note. The point has been made that the maintenance of clinical anxiety reactions despite frequent nonreinforced exposure to the feared situation poses a serious dilemma for learning theory (cf.

Eysenck & Beech, 1971; Seligman, 1971). After all, nonreinforced exposure to the conditioned stimulus (CS) defines the extinction procedure. Of course, it can be argued that systematic and repeated exposure rather than haphazard encounters is necessary for extinction to occur, but this view looks suspiciously like a convenient rationalization in at least some instances. Borkovec (1975) has proposed an important theoretical explanation of this apparent exception to the extinction rule.*

In short, Borkovec suggests a cognitive extension of Mowrer's classic two-factor theory in which he asserts that physical exposure to the external CS is not sufficient to ensure extinction. Rather, *functional exposure* to the CS may be the critical ingredient, and this can be negated or interfered with by cognitive avoidance responses. This position is supported by data from Borkovec's (1972, 1974) avoidance response control condition. In this condition snake phobic subjects were imploded until they signalled anxiety, at which point they visualized an avoidance response they might have typically made in the actual situation. In marked contrast to both the desensitization and implosion therapy treatments in this study, the avoidance control condition resulted in neither improvement on the behavioral avoidance test nor reductions in heart rate during the therapy sessions.

One of the interesting implications of this view is that cognitive escape/avoidance with or without behavioral escape may result in the development of avoidance behaviors that would otherwise rapidly extinguish in the face of nonreinforced exposure. How neurotic fear/ avoidance responses are acquired in the first place remains to be adequately explained, and Borkovec's hypothesis offers a promising lead. Another implication of immediate clinical relevance is that treatment will only be effective to the extent that cognitive avoidance responses are prevented.

Assertion Training

Although Kazdin's article, reprinted here, demonstrates how assertive behavior can be increased by covert modeling procedures, assertion training has typically been carried out through the use of overt modeling and behavior rehearsal methods. The therapist models appropriate assertive behavior, the client rehearses improved performance, and

---

* Drawing upon more traditional, noncognitive learning principles, Rachman and Hodgson (1974) have also proposed an explanation for the persistence of avoidance behavior.

receives coaching and feedback from the therapist on his behavior (McFall & Twentyman, 1973—in Franks & Wilson, 1974). More recently, Twentyman and McFall (1975) identified a sample of shy male college students who reported that they were unable to interact with women. Subjects who participated in an analogue treatment program comprising behavior rehearsal, modeling, and coaching showed less physiological arousal, reported less anxiety, and were rated as more proficient in terms of interpersonal skills than an assessment control group at posttreatment. At a six-month follow-up subjects were contacted and asked to self-monitor interactions with women. Subjects who had received treatment continued to show superior improvement to control group members with respect to frequency and duration of heterosexual contacts. However, the fact that less than 50 percent of the subjects were contacted and responded at follow-up undermines the confidence that can be placed in these maintenance data.

Thorpe (1975) compared the following four treatments in the modification of unassertive behavior in college students: a) systematic desensitization; b) overt modeling and behavior rehearsal; c) self-instructional training; and d) a placebo control condition in which subjects discussed the origins of their interpersonal difficulties in terms of social learning theory. Based on Meichenbaum et al.'s (1971) technique, subjects in the self-instruction group were taught to re-evaluate self-defeating cognitions and rehearsed more rational, constructive self-statements in the context of making an assertive response. All treatments were conducted in groups for six weekly sessions. Assessment procedures were based on those employed by McFall and Lillesand (1971—in Franks & Wilson, 1973).

Results on the behavioral measures of situations in which subjects had been treated indicated that all three therapy conditions were more effective than placebo in increasing assertive responses. However, both on self-report and behavioral measures, self-instructional training was generally superior to all treatments. Modeling and behavior rehearsal were slightly less effective, but systematic desensitization fared relatively poorly. Generalization from treated to untreated situations in the laboratory, or to a novel situation outside the laboratory, was not observed. Pulse rates and finger sweat print measures showed no inter-group differences. Subjects' expectancy ratings of therapeutic gain after they heard their respective treatment rationales were not different. Posttreatment subject ratings of therapists indicated significant group differences, with self-instructional training and the placebo group members rating the therapists as less likeable and less competent than the other two groups.

Thorpe interprets these data to mean that "nonspecific" influences were not operating equally across the different treatments. However, the fact that the self-instructional group outperformed the others appears to rule out an explanation of the results in terms of these "nonspecific" factors. Although the clinical implications of this study are limited, as Ramsay (1975) notes, self-instructional training might be more widely used in the treatment of unassertive clients than has heretofore been the case in behavior therapy.

From a clinical viewpoint, the most disappointing aspect of Thorpe's results was the failure to demonstrate generalized behavior change. In an experimental analysis of generalization of assertion training, Hersen, Eisler, and Miller (1974) assessed the performance of unassertive psychiatric patients before and after therapy in 10 interpersonal situations that required an assertive response. Patients were trained on five of these situations during treatment; the remaining five served as a test of generalization. Pre- and posttreatment performance on these situations was rated on eight behavioral components of assertiveness.

Patients who were exposed to videotaped modeling of assertive behavior, and who were explicitly instructed in how to act assertively showed significantly increased assertive behavior compared to control groups that had not received modeling plus instructions. Specifically, the modeling/instructions group showed greater assertion on seven of the eight components for the five training situations, but on only five of the eight components of assertion for the five generalization situations. A novel, in vivo test of generalization of assertion showed negligible effects.

Generalization of assertion training was the subject of inquiry in two other studies. Gormally, Hill, Otis, and Rainey (1975) failed to obtain substantial generalization of assertive behavior following assertion training of students through a microtraining procedure. However, Eisler, Hersen, and Miller (1974) demonstrated that training two unassertive psychiatric patients on specific expressive deficits produced a marked improvement in overall assertion. The same study showed that training on interpersonal situations unrelated to the subjects' unassertiveness in real-life situations generalized to problem relevant situations.

Chronic hospitalized patients were administered an assertion training program consisting of modeling, coaching, and overt or covert behavior rehearsal (Longin & Rooney, 1975). In comparison to two control groups, one of which received a comprehensive behavioral treatment program without assertion training, the other representing an assessment control, assertion training produced significantly greater non-compliance with unreasonable requests then either of the two control groups. Evidence of generalization from situations used during role-played training sessions to untrained situations was obtained. Overt rehearsal was more effective than covert rehearsal.

Similarly, Field and Test (1975) found that group assertion training with severely disturbed outpatients resulted in increased assertion as compared to control subjects who showed no change. A 10-month follow-up of four of the five treatment patients indicated that they had maintained behavioral improvement.

In last year's volume (Franks & Wilson, 1975), we noted that popular books allegedly describing assertion training were becoming another "in thing." Treatises elaborated on the "technique" of how, when, and why to say No; what to say No to, and why you should not feel guilty in saying No. Landau (1976) put the count of such popular books at nine. The trend has accelerated during the past year, with assertion training hailed as "the hottest new form of behavior therapy" and "the key to the happy, nonneurotic life." Unfortunately, the procedures touted in some of these books are *not* behavior therapy; assertion training per se is *not* the "key" to blissful content; and it is certainly *not* new. Aside from the fact that assertion training was part and parcel of the contemporary origins of behavior therapy (cf. Salter, 1949; Wolpe, 1958), consider the following quote taken from a chapter entitled, On the Importance of Being Able to Say No: "If you find any difficulty in uttering (No), . . . go by yourself, and practice saying no, no, No! till you can articulate clearly, distinctly, and without hesitation; and have it always ready on your tongue's end, to utter with emphasis to every boy or girl, man or woman, or evil spirit that presumes to propose to do you anything that is wrong. Only be careful to say it respectfully and courteously, with the usual *prefixes* and *suffixes,* which properly belong to the persons to whom you are speaking" (p. 211). The chapter is in *How to Be a Man; A Book for Boys,* written by Harvey Newcomb, and published in 1847.

It is interesting to observe that this exhortation to say No was directed towards men only. Ladies would certainly not have been expected to be assertive in the mid-1800s. With the current emphasis on equality of women, we might anticipate that the sexist nature of assertion training is a thing of the past. In this respect, however, we echo Goldfried and Davison's (1976) recent concern that assertion training may still be used primarily with men. Certainly one of the reviewers of the rash of popular books on "assertion training" finds some of them unacceptably sexist (Harrison, 1975).

Indeed, the critical reviews with which these popular books have been received are not without relevance to behavior therapists (e.g., Harrison, 1975; Laudau, 1976). Perhaps most worrisome are the ethical objections these reviewers have to "assertion training." For example, Harrison declares that "In spite of the often sanctimonious disclaimers of these assertiveness-training books, I think the evidence proves that much of assertiveness training is gimmicky and glib; in dealing with surfaces, it strenuously avoids grappling with moral dilemmas; eschewing value judgments, it sidesteps, amorally, the question of whether what one wants is right or wrong, good or bad; it operates in a moral, cultural and societal vacuum, where only the clients' needs are considered and the rest of the world becomes an adversary; it ignores the rights and needs of others; it encourages artifice rather than spontaneity" (p. 32).

Clearly this position is an overstatement, and Landau (1976) is careful to differentiate books which encourage unabashed manipulation and exploitation of people from those that are more true to assertion training in emphasizing the rights of others, and the notion of personal choice rather than necessity, in acting assertively or not. Nonetheless, it would be a mistake to ignore some of the ethical considerations raised by these books.

Becoming assertive can have profound consequences not only for the individual client, but also for his/her spouse and immediate social network. In contrast to some, but not all of the authors of these popular books, it is our judgment that assertion training is best employed by professional therapists as part of a planned, integrated social learning treatment program. This is most likely to ensure that ethical/moral issues will be taken into consideration, that probable consequences of change will be carefully weighed, and that therapist and client will agree upon mutually negotiated goals with which they can both feel comfortable. Caveat emptor!

SECTION II: SYSTEMATIC DESENSITIZATION,
FLOODING, SYMBOLIC AND PARTICIPANT
MODELING, COGNITIVE RESTRUCTURING,
AND ASSERTION TRAINING

6

GENERALIZING CHANGE THROUGH PARTICIPANT MODELING WITH SELF-DIRECTED MASTERY

Albert Bandura, Robert W. Jeffery

and Eva Gajdos

Department of Psychology, Stanford University

Summary—It was hypothesized that a brief experience of self-directed mastery after phobic behavior had been eliminated by participant modeling would enhance generalized changes in psychological functioning. Adult phobics received participant modeling alone, or participant modeling followed by self-directed performance with either familiar or varied threats. Subjects who had the benefit of independent mastery experiences, compared to those who received participant modeling alone, displayed more generalized behavioral changes, greater fear reduction, higher levels of self-competency, and less fear of threats beyond the one specifically treated. Self-directed performance with a familiar threat,

Reprinted with permission from *Behaviour Research and Therapy*, Vol. 13, 141-152, 1975.

This research was supported by Public Health Research Grant M-5162 from the National Institute of Mental Health. The authors are grateful to Jan Beyer and Mary Bandura for their assistance in various phases of this research.

151

however, extinguished fear more thoroughly and induced a
stronger sense of self-competency than did coping independently with varied threats. The overall evidence indicates that
the successful transfer effects resulted from stimulus generalization, enhancement of self-adequacy, and acquisition
of a generalizable skill for coping with fear-provoking
situations.

Treatments combining modeling with guided participation have
proven highly effective in eliminating defensive conduct (Bandura, 1975).
Unlike approaches that attempt to disinhibit behavior by extinguishing
anxiety, participant modeling favors successful performance as the principal vehicle of psychological change. Avoidance of subjectively real but
objectively unwarranted threats keeps behavior out of touch with existing conditions of reinforcement. Through participant modeling it is
possible to achieve rapid reality testing, which provides the corrective
experiences for change.

People suffering from intractable fears and inhibitions are not about
to do what they dread. In implementing participant modeling the therapist, therefore, structures the environment in such a way that, despite
their incapacities, clients can perform successfully. This is achieved by
enlisting a variety of response induction aids. The therapist first models
threatening activities in easily mastered steps. Clients then enact the
modeled conduct with appropriate guidance until they can perform it
skillfully and fearlessly. If they are unable to do so, the therapist sequentially introduces performance aids that eventually ensure success. As
treatment progresses, the supplementary aids are gradually withdrawn so
that clients can cope effectively unassisted.

Previous research substantiated the paramount role of response induction aids in participant modeling (Bandura et al., 1974). Phobics with
comparable incapacities progressed rapidly when therapists had recourse
to a wide array of induction aids, but rates of improvement and attainment were much lower when therapists had only a few performance
aids at their disposal. Therapeutic efficacy, however, was not monotoni-
cally related to the number of performance facilitators. Modeling with
moderate induction procedures, though somewhat slower than the highly
aided treatment in eliminating phobic behavior, produced more generalized changes. In both forms of participant modeling, as well as in
earlier tests of this method (Bandura, Blanchard & Ritter, 1969; Blanchard, 1970b), the findings indicate that transfer effects could be further
improved.

According to social learning theory (Bandura, 1969), fearful behavior can be evoked either directly by aversive events or through an intermediary self-arousal mechanism. In the latter process, potential threats activate fear-provoking thoughts which, in turn, motivate defensive behavior. People's sense of self-competency affects their susceptibility to self-arousal. They fear and avoid threatening situations that they believe exceed their coping skills, but behave affirmatively when they judge themselves capable of managing circumstances that would otherwise be intimidating. Perceived self-competence not only reduces anticipatory fears but, through expectation of eventual success, sustains coping efforts in the face of difficulties.

Self-confidence is best enhanced by independent achievements. The reinforcing power of success, however, may be attenuated in several ways when behavior is disinhibited by strong induction procedures. The first involves discrimination processes. The consequences that individuals anticipate for threatening activities differ under circumstances which vary in safeguards. As a result, they may behave boldly when cues signifying safety are present, but respond fearfully when they are absent. In applications of participant modeling, fading techniques are used to prevent the formation of such discriminations. Nevertheless, the corrective value of unaided success may be circumscribed, if the company of the therapist itself becomes a discriminative safety feature that counteracts generalization of fear extinction.

Attributional processes may similarly delimit gains from success experiences. When disinhibition is facilitated by extensive supports, people may ascribe their success to external aids rather than to their own restored capabilities. Generalization decrements are more likely to occur if bold performances are attributed to special situational arrangements, rather than to regained personal competence.

Circumscribing processes might be minimized without sacrificing the substantial benefits of induction procedures by providing opportunities for self-directed performance after the desired behavior has been established. Any lingering doubts clients may have, either about their capabilities or about probable response consequences under unprotected conditions, can be dispelled easily in this manner. The more varied are the threats that are mastered independently, the more likely are success experiences to authenticate personal competence and to impede the formation of insulating discriminations.

The present experiment was designed to test the efficacy of participant modeling approaches when powerful induction procedures for creating change were combined with self-directed performance for reinforcing and generalizing attainments. Adult snake phobics were matched in triads and received participant modeling alone, or participant modeling followed by self-directed performance with either a single familiar snake or varied snakes. The generality and durability of changes effected through participant modeling were analyzed as a function of the amount and variety of self-directed mastery. Multiple measures of psychological effects were included to elucidate possible mechanisms responsible for transfer of change.

It was predicted that self-directed performance would enhance self-competency and produce more generalized reductions in phobic behavior and fear arousal than would participant modeling alone. Mastering diversified threats was expected to further augment positive transfer.

METHOD

Subjects

Subjects whose functioning was handicapped by their snake phobia were recruited through advertisements placed in community newspapers. Of the 30 Ss who participated in the study, four were males and the remainder were females. They came from many different backgrounds and ranged in age from 14 to 48 years, with a mean age of 29 years.

Pretreatment Measures

A multifaceted assessment procedure was used including measures of avoidance behavior, fear arousal, anxiety proneness, self-competency, and personal potency.

Behavioral avoidance. The test of avoidance behavior consisted of a series of 29 performance tasks requiring increasingly more threatening interactions with a 3-foot boa constrictor. Subjects were instructed to approach the snake in a glass cage, to look down at it, to touch and hold the snake with gloved and then bare hands, to let it loose in the room and return it to the cage, to hold it within 5 inches of their faces, and finally to tolerate the snake crawling in their laps while they held their hands passively at their sides.

A female tester administered all the assessment procedures. Prior to measuring phobic behavior, Ss were given factual information about the characteristics and habits of snakes to eliminate moderately fearful Ss who might be emboldened by information alone. Those who could not enter the room containing the snake received a score of zero; Ss who did enter were asked to perform the various tasks in the graded series. To control for any possible influence of expressive cues from the tester, she stood behind the S and read aloud the tasks to be performed.

The S's avoidance score was the number of snake-interaction tasks performed successfully. Those who could lift the snake inside the cage with a gloved hand were considered insufficiently fearful to be included in the experiment. Based on this criterion, 33 percent of the respondents were excluded. To maximize the generality of the findings, all people who were sufficiently phobic on the behavioral test were selected for study regardless of any other psychological characteristics.

Fear arousal accompanying approach responses. In addition to measuring performance capabilities, the degree of fear aroused by each approach response was also assessed. During the behavioral test, Ss rated orally, on a 10-interval scale, the intensity of fear they experienced when each snake approach task was described to them, and again while they were performing the corresponding behavior. These fear ratings were averaged across the approach tasks actually completed to provide the index of fear arousal.

Fear of snake encounters. Fear of snakes was measured on six scales portraying diverse encounters with snakes, including visiting a reptile exhibit, watching a film on the habits of snakes, suddenly encountering snakes on hikes and in the garage, visiting a household containing pet snakes and handling them. Subjects were instructed to rate each item on a 7-interval scale of fearfulness. The mean of the six ratings constituted the threat value of snakes.

Self-competency. Subjects also rated the snake encounters described above in terms of how effectively they could cope with them. The ratings were averaged to provide a score of perceived self-competence in dealing with snakes. In addition, they rated their felt adequacy in coping with other animals they feared and difficult social situations.

Personal potency. Subjects' judgments of personal potency were assessed by the semantic differential technique. The form used consisted of 6 bipolar rating scales using the following pairs of contrasting adjectives: submissive-assertive, weak-strong, inadequate-competent, fearful-bold, hesitant-self-assured, and dependent-independent. The mean of these pooled ratings provided the scores of personal potency.

Fear proneness. As the final task in the pretreatment assessment, Ss completed a comprehensive fear inventory containing 20 items in each of the following five classes of fear: animals; interpersonal encounters; physical afflictions and injuries; classical phobias; and a collection of miscellaneous fears. They rated their anxiety toward each object or situation on 5-point scales describing increasing degrees of distress. The number and mean intensity of fears were scored separately for each of the five categories and summed across all of the items to provide an overall measure of vulnerability to fear arousal.

Treatment Conditions

Subjects were individually matched in triads on the basis of their pretreatment avoidance behavior and then randomly assigned to one of three conditions. In order to evaluate the efficacy of the treatments across therapists, two experimenters, one male and one female, administered each of the methods to half of the subjects.

All Ss initially received aided participant modeling with the boa constrictor used in the pretest until they completed all the therapeutic tasks. In this approach, which is described at length elsewhere (Bandura et al., 1974), defensive behavior is rapidly eliminated by enlisting a standard series of response induction aids. To weaken inhibitions, each threatening activity was first modeled and then Ss were instructed to perform it. If they were unable to do so, the therapist sequentially introduced response aids from a preestablished hierarchy.

Intimidating performances were reduced to graduated subtasks of increasing difficulty ranging from looking at, touching, and holding the snake; placing open hands in front of its head as it moved about; holding the snake in front of their faces; allowing the snake to crawl freely in their laps; to letting the snake loose in the room and retrieving it. Joint performance with the therapist, who offered physical assistance when required, was used to facilitate actions that people could not execute on their own. Another method for overcoming inhibition was to have Ss enact the feared behavior for initially brief but increasing durations. Safeguards that reduce the likelihood of feared consequences (i.e., use of protective gloves, coats, and visors, and control of the snake by the therapist to ensure safety) were arranged as a further means of weakening dysfunctional restraints that retard change. Severely incapacitated phobics, who remained immobile even under these secure conditions, first performed the dreaded responses with appropriate aids toward a baby boa, which was much less threatening, and then with the larger boa. After the desired behavior was induced, the supportive aids and protective controls were withdrawn.

The therapists were not informed about Ss' pretreatment performances or the conditions to which they were assigned so as not to alter the manner in which they administered the participant modeling phase of the study. Subjects completed the therapeutic tasks through participant modeling within a relatively short period, requiring an average of 60.8 minutes. The durations of the participant modeling for Ss preassigned to the self-directed, varied self-directed, and participant modeling conditions were 61, 56, and 66 minutes, respectively. These small time-variations did not differ statistically. Nor did the groups diverge in the number of induction aids they required.

Subjects who received *participant modeling* alone were scheduled for posttesting after completing the therapeutic tasks. Those assigned to the *self-directed performance* condition spent an additional hour interacting on their own with the same boa constrictor used in treatment. They were instructed to perform, in the order of their own choosing, the activities they had previously executed with the therapist's assistance. The protective accouterments (gloves, visors) were available although the Ss rarely used them. During the initial part of the self-directed performance the therapist remained in the room but as a nonparticipant. In the second part, the therapist retired to an adjacent room where he observed the Ss' independent performance through a one-way mirror. If Ss expressed fear at being left entirely on their own, the therapist watched briefly from the corridor through the open door before proceeding to the observation room.

The varied self-directed performance was conducted in a manner identical to that described above except that Ss in this condition spent the hour interacting not only with the familiar boa, but also with an unfamiliar king snake markedly different in color and activity level. They handled the boa first, and then the king snake. Subjects in both self-directed treatments performed successfully all of the listed tasks with the boa, and those in the varied condition enacted 96 percent of the interaction tasks with the king snake.

In order to determine the extent to which each treatment reinforced personal adequacy, Ss were administered the measures of self-competency, and personal potency, and fear of snake encounters after the participant modeling, and again upon completing the self-directed component.

An untreated control group was not included because several previous studies, drawing Ss from the same source and using similar measurement procedures, revealed no significant changes with repeated testing alone (Bandura & Barab, 1973; Blanchard, 1970a; Bandura et al., 1969). This experiment was designed to test whether the addition of self-directed performance enhanced therapeutic changes beyond those produced by participant modeling alone. For this purpose, a no-treatment baseline is of little interest.

Posttreatment Assessment

The assessment procedures used in the pretreatment phase of the experiment were readministered to Ss in all conditions within a week after the completion of treatment.

To gauge the generality of therapeutic changes, half of the Ss in each of the conditions was tested initially with the familiar boa constrictor (B) and then with a 4-foot corn snake (C), while the remaining Ss were tested with the two snakes in the reverse order. A previous study (Bandura et al., 1974) showed the two snakes to be of equivalent threat value as measured by Ss' avoidance behavior and fear arousal.

The same female tester who conducted the pretreatment assessment administered the posttreatment measures. To control for any possible bias, she had no information on the conditions to which Ss were assigned.

Follow-up Assessments

Several follow-up assessments were conducted to evaluate further the generality and durability of changes. All Ss, except for one in the participant modeling condition who had moved elsewhere, were readministered the assessment procedures in a one-month follow-up.

After 6 months had elapsed, Ss were sent questionnaires measuring the extent to which they were able to participate in vocational, recreational, and social activities previously precluded by their snake phobia, as well as modifications in the incidence of nightmares and other frightening thoughts of snakes. These changes, if any, were rated on 5-interval scales ranging from a worsening of debilities through no improvement to substantial improvement. Subjects were requested to supplement their ratings with concrete examples of the changes they had undergone. In addition, they indicated how often, if ever, they used the method learned in treatment to eliminate fears in other areas of functioning.

To give everyone equal opportunity to profit maximally from treatment, Ss in participant modeling who displayed residual fears and inhibitions were given additional treatment with self-directed performance, if they so desired, after a 1-month follow-up assessment. Because of variations in the type and amount of supplemental treatment received by Ss

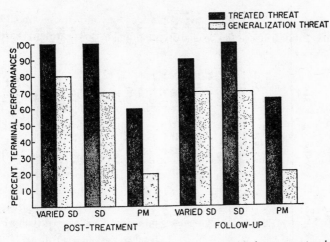

Fig. 1. Percent of subjects who achieved terminal performances with the treatment and generalization snakes depending upon whether they received participant modeling alone or supplemented with either uniform or varied self-directed performance.

in the participant modeling conditions, the 6-month data were analyzed formally only for the self-directed treatments.

Subjects in the self-directed conditions who could be located one year later appeared for a formal assessment. The multifaceted procedures were readministered by the same tester in the 1-year follow-up as in the earlier phases of the experiment.

RESULTS

Approach Behavior

The percent of Ss in the various conditions who achieved terminal performances are presented in Figure 1. The self-directed treatments eliminated phobic behavior toward both the treated and generalization threats in virtually all Ss. Because almost all of the Ss in the latter treatments achieved terminal approach scores, the differences among the three conditions were evaluated by nonparametric techniques.

The three treatments did not yield significant differences in the rates of terminal performances with the snake used in treatment. Results of the Cochran Q test, however, show that terminal performance with the generalization snake differ in the posttest ($Q = 6.20$; $p < 0.05$) and and follow-up ($Q = 6.25$; $p < 0.05$) assessments.

Intergroup differences were evaluated by the sign test. Compared to

Table 1. Significance of treatment effects on supplementary measures in the posttreatment phase

Response measure	Treatment effects	Inter-group comparisons (F test)			Within-group comparisons (t test)		
		VSD vs SD	VSD vs PM	SD vs PM	VSD	SD	PM
Fear arousal							
Initial approach (B + C)	8.59*	4.53*	4.89***	18.82***	9.07***	10.19***	5.98***
Initial approach B	7.51**	2.56	5.65**	15.81***	8.45***	10.64***	5.97***
Initial approach C	7.06**	4.34**	3.52	15.67***	8.99***	9.81***	5.54***
Total approach (B + C)	11.27***	5.13*	7.10*	24.43***	5.23***	9.27***	3.69***
Total approach B	11.72***	1.88	11.65***	22.89***	8.45***	10.53***	3.80***
Total approach C	6.44**	3.92	3.24	14.28***	3.36**	8.10***	3.32**
Failed task (B + C)	5.22*	0.11	7.09*	8.94**	14.18***	19.12***	6.51***
Failed task B	3.79*	0.01	5.67*	6.02*	20.57***	23.67***	7.23***
Failed task C	3.33†	1.03	4.16	6.14*	9.75***	15.57***	5.15***
Fear of snake encounters	12.69***	8.46**	4.84*	26.14***	8.24***	11.59***	6.00***
Self-competency (snakes)	10.09***	3.79	6.83*	20.84***	6.90***	10.15***	4.02***
Self-competency (animals)	2.25				1.12	2.48*	1.62
Self-competency (social)	0.55				2.24	0.00	0.80
Personal potency	0.21				1.86	1.96	1.94
Number of fears							
Total	0.12				2.87*	1.08	1.19
Animal	0.17				2.18	1.74	1.64
Social	1.17				3.53***	0.46	0.56
Classical	0.05				1.21	0.66	0.88
Tissue injury	0.12				1.08	1.87	1.63
Miscellaneous	1.67				1.89	0.26	0.38
Intensity of fears							
Average	1.51				3.74**	3.34**	1.69
Animal	3.51*	0.54	3.38	6.62*	3.29**	4.46**	2.40*
Social	3.42*	3.53	0.63	7.13*	0.55	2.14	1.32
Classical	0.33				1.25	1.24	1.38
Tissue injury	0.74				1.93	1.71	1.08
Miscellaneous	0.16				2.02	0.50	1.71

*$p < .005$ **$p < .001$ ***$p < .0001$

participant modeling alone, both the varied self-directed ($p = 0.035$; $p = 0.06$) and the self-directed ($p = 0.06$; $p = 0.03$) conditions produced substantially greater generalized changes in posttest and follow-up, respectively. The two self-directed treatments, however, did not differ significantly from each other.

Supplementary Measures

Effects of the treatments as revealed by the other multiple measures were evaluated by analysis of covariance with pretreatment scores serving as the covariates. The order in which the snake tests were administered failed to produce any significant differences, and the two therapists were equally effective.

Table 1 shows the significance levels of the treatment effects, the intergroup differences, and the changes that occurred within each group in the posttest assessment. The corresponding values for the follow-up assessment are presented in Table 2. The changes achieved proved highly durable and there were no significant differences on any measure between posttest and follow-up, except for a few minor variations. Subjects who had received the self-directed treatment experienced less fear arousal while responding toward the generalization snake ($t = 1.97$; $p < 0.08$) and a stronger sense of personal potency ($t = 1.89$; $p < 0.10$) 1 month later.

Fear Arousal Accompanying Approach Responses

Extinction of fear arousal accompanying approach responses was measured in several ways. The average level of fear evoked by responses that Ss performed before treatment was compared with the fear levels reported in subsequent tests for the same set of responses, and for the total number of approach responses they executed successfully. Decreases in the level of anticipatory fear evoked by the approach task that Ss could not perform in pretest provided an additional index of fear extinction that was unaffected by having enacted the behavior. These various measures were computed separately for each snake and for the pooled data, thus yielding a total of nine indices.

Inspection of Tables 1 and 2 shows that all three treatments produced considerable reduction in fear arousal. The self-directed treatment, however, extinguished fear most thoroughly. In intergroup comparisons, the latter procedure surpassed participant modeling on all nine extinction measures in the posttest and retained its superiority in the follow-up

Table 2. Significance of treatment effects on supplementary measures in the follow-up phase

Response measure	Treatment effects	Inter-group comparisons (F test)			Within-group comparisons (t test)		
		VSD vs SD	VSD vs PM	SD vs PM	VSD	SD	PM
Fear arousal							
Initial approach (B + C)	4.19*	5.83*	0.38	9.18***	8.35***	10.33***	5.54***
Initial approach B	4.28*	7.53*	0.05	8.83***	9.44***	10.68***	7.06***
Initial approach C	3.86*	4.45*	0.69	8.65***	6.80***	10.03***	4.20***
Total approach (B + C)	9.01**	5.28*	4.69*	19.90***	6.86***	9.78***	3.59***
Total approach B	9.77***	6.89*	4.21	21.89****	7.82***	10.63***	4.56***
Total approach C	5.90**	2.93	3.51	12.86**	3.95*	8.96***	2.42*
Failed task (B + C)	2.45†	1.14	1.44	5.14*	9.47***	19.33***	6.31***
Failed task B	2.98†	1.34	1.80	6.25*	14.81***	30.91***	8.36***
Failed task C	2.00				6.28***	12.24***	4.47***
Fear of snake encounters	9.52***	8.36**	2.27	19.38****	7.23***	14.08***	4.57***
Self-competency (snakes)	8.87**	9.44**	1.19	17.24****	7.77***	12.23***	5.92***
Self-competency (animals)	2.76†	2.77	0.36	5.14*	1.41	3.41*	2.25
Self-competency (social)	2.81†	5.03*	0.17	7.08*	1.96	1.50	1.00
Personal potency	1.64				2.72*	2.51*	0.71
Number of fears							
Total	0.51				4.25**	3.68**	1.94
Animal	1.24				3.50**	3.55**	1.83
Social	0.24				4.16**	1.41	2.44*
Classical	0.88				0.43	2.49*	1.28
Tissue injury	0.38				1.44	3.74**	2.80*
Miscellaneous	2.65†	0.32	3.39	5.78*	3.03*	3.24**	0.12
Intensity of fears							
Average	1.93				4.83***	2.53*	1.40
Animal	4.77**	2.85	1.95	9.52**	3.30**	4.60**	2.55*
Social	3.73*	0.77	3.67	7.80*	1.81	2.94*	1.27
Classical	0.62				1.28	2.28*	1.94
Tissue injury	1.70				3.31**	2.41*	1.72
Miscellaneous	0.79				3.04*	1.19	1.23

*p < 0.05   **p < 0.001   ***p < 0.0001   †0.05 < p < 0.10

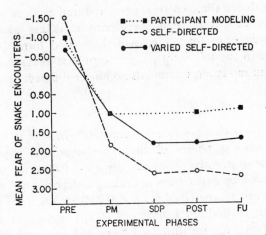

Fig. 2. Fear of encounters with snakes expressed by subjects in the different conditions before treatment (Pre), after receiving participant modeling (PM), after completing self-directed performances (SDP), and in the posttreatment (Post) and follow-up (FU) assessments.

phase. Varied self-directed treatment exceeded participant modeling in posttreatment on all of the pooled measures and on fear decrements for responses toward the treated threat, but not toward the generalization snake. By the follow-up period, the latter two conditions differed only in the pooled reactions for total approach performances, with the varied treatment achieving the greater reduction in fear arousal.

The self-directed group, in relation to Ss receiving the varied treatment, showed significantly weaker pooled reactions and less fear arousal in responding to the generalization snake. The relative superiority of the self-directed treatment for eliminating fear arousal extended in follow-up to the snake employed in therapy.

Fear of Snake Encounters

The degree to which Ss feared encounters with snakes in natural situations is shown graphically in Figure 2. Participant modeling diminished fear of snake encounters in all preassigned groups beyond the 0.001 significance levels. The addition of varied ($t = 5.62$; $p < 0.001$) and uniform ($t = 4.09$; $p < 0.003$) self-directed enactment produced further reductions in fearfulness.

Analysis of data from posttest and follow-up phases yielded a pattern of results comparable to those for response-evoked fears to the test snakes

(Table 1). Both self-directed treatments reduced anxiety over snake encounters more effectively than participant modeling alone. The self-directed procedure, in turn, surpassed the varied form. Similar results were obtained in the follow-up phase except that Ss receiving the varied and participant modeling treatments no longer differed.

Self-Competency

Figure 3 depicts changes in self-competency in coping with snakes as measured at various phases of the experiment. Participant modeling raised Ss' sense of adequacy substantially ($p < 0.001$), a change that was further enhanced by experience in dealing independently with one ($t = 2.89$; $p < 0.02$) or more ($t = 4.86$; $p < 0.001$) snakes.

The pattern of findings confirms that self-directed treatment is the method of choice for instilling a generalized sense of self-competency. Although both self-directed procedures exceeded participant modeling in posttest, the uniform version surpassed both the other two treatments at the time of follow-up. Compared to participant modeling it also increased Ss' sense of competence in coping with other feared animals.

Independent mastery of a threat, whether uniform or varied, was more effective than participant modeling alone at enhancing self-competency in coping with taxing social situations (Table 2).

Personal Potency

Subjects' sense of personal potency was initially unaffected by the treatments. In the follow-up assessment, those who had the benefit of self-directed mastery felt more affirmative compared to their pretreatment level (Table 2). The intergroup differences were not significant, however.

Fear Proneness

The treatments were differentially effective in reducing fears toward threats beyond the specifically treated phobia. Participant modeling weakened only the intensity of animal fears, whereas the self-directed treatments produced a general diminution of fears (Table 1). In addition, Ss receiving the varied self-directed treatment reported fewer social anxieties as well as fewer total anxieties.

The intragroup differences are even more marked in the follow-up assessments (Table 2). Generalizations of fear decrements accompanying participant modeling were confined to number of social and tissue

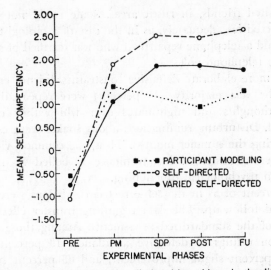

Fig. 3. Self-competency in coping with snakes displayed by subjects in the different conditions before treatment (Pre), after receiving participant modeling (PM), after completing self-directed performances (SDP), and in posttreatment (Post) and follow-up (FU) assessment.

injury anxieties, and intensity of animal fears. Varied self-directed treatment achieved broader improvements in both the number (total, animal, social, miscellaneous), and intensity (mean, animal, tissue injury, miscellaneous) of fears. The self-directed procedure, on the other hand, resulted in widespread fear reductions in virtually all areas of functioning.

In intergroup comparisons, the self-directed condition proved more effective than participant modeling in reducing the number of miscellaneous fears and in weakening fear of animals and stressful social situations.

Extended Follow-Up

Subjects' psychological functioning was adversely affected by their snake phobia in two principal ways: behaviorally and cognitively. Their lives were constricted by defensive avoidance of social, recreational, and vocational activities that might occasion exposure to a snake, however remote the possibility. All had abandoned one or more recreational activities such as camping, hiking, and swimming in rivers or lakes. They could not walk through grassy or wooded areas, or go bicycling for fear of encountering snakes. They refused to reside, and only reluctantly visited friends, in rustic areas. Some could not conduct their vocational activities adequately, as in the case of a biologist who dreaded field trips, and a telephone repairman who was terrified of snakes lurking near or atop telephone poles.

Even the more elaborate defensive constraints did not ensure serenity, however. The vast majority (85 percent) were repeatedly plagued by distressing thoughts and nightmares over which they could exercise little control. Disturbing ruminations about snakes were especially troublesome during the summer months. Thus, the common view of a snake phobia as a circumscribed inconvenience is belied by its widespread intrusions on psychological functioning.

Eighty percent of Ss in the self-directed conditions were available for the extended follow-up. The data regarding transfer effects corroborate the results of the standardized assessments. Among those in the varied condition, on ratings of defensive avoidance, 13 percent reported no change, 25 percent slight improvement, and 63 percent substantial improvement. Sixty percent experienced slight amelioration of disturbing thoughts, and 40 percent were substantially benefited in this respect. All Ss in the uniform self-directed condition, on the other hand, reported substantial improvement in both defensive behaviors (100 percent) and relief from distressing thoughts (100 percent).

Subjects' concrete descriptions of change convey more clearly than the frequency data the generalized benefits they derived from treatment. Unlike their earlier avoidance of the outdoors, they became active participants in recreational activities:

> My phobia prevented many activities that I could have enjoyed in the country. Now I can go on biology field trips, I hike, and I am willing for the first time even to try camping.

> I can now do all of the things I couldn't do before, including watching movies, walking in the rough, and roaming the trails. I am no longer troubled by snake dreams, either.

> I went hiking in the mountains and almost stepped on two snakes and didn't even freak out too much or run away or refuse to go on with the hike.

Some of the additional restored capacities illustrated individual characteristics. One woman, for example, was able to retrieve golf balls from the rough, much to the relief of her golfing companions and pocketbook. Another woman who shunned anything even remotely resembling snakes ("I avoided clothes that had any 'snaky' associations. I even had

to discard a necklace made of sequins strung together when someone
told me it reminded them of a coral snake"), could expand her ward-
robe. Some could perform tasks that they formerly avoided ("I'm not
afraid to walk in my Aunt's orchard, in fact, my husband and I pruned
the trees and I gathered the twigs in the tall grass with my bare hands
this year. I am not afraid to get wood for the fireplace or to move old
boxes stashed for years in the garage"). Still others enlarged the circle
of friends they visited and even moved to areas they previously feared
("I am now living in the foothills where I am told there are lots of
snakes. I am not preoccupied looking for snakes 'in the grass' ").

The elimination of nightmares was equally striking. Before treatment,
Ss suffered from recurring dreams in which they were dropped into
snake pits and encircled or pursued by menacing serpents. Treatment
produced welcome relief:

> All of the bad dreams and nightmares always had snakes in them.
> My bad dreams are infrequent now, and no longer have snakes in
> them.

> I have not been troubled very much lately with thoughts and visions
> of snakes. Actually, until I sat down to fill out this questionnaire, I
> had not thought of snakes for some time.

Other benefits that Ss described documented the positive transfer effects of treatment. Some of the changes reflected decreased fear toward
other animals:

> I have always had a great aversion to dogs of all kinds. Since treat-
> ment, I have overcome this to a great extent.

> Until last summer I disliked being around horses. By applying what
> I learned in treatment, I now have little or no fear of horseback
> riding—in fact, I rather enjoy it.

Social anxieties were similarly reduced:

> I'm generally somewhat less timid than I was before.

> The feeling of accomplishment I was experiencing at having over-
> come the fear of snakes gave me the confidence to overcome my
> fear of public speaking.

Some voiced their increased sense of personal competence ("The biggest benefit to me of the successfulness of the treatment was the feeling

that if I could lick snakes, I could lick anything. It gave me the confidence to tackle, also successfully, some personal stuff").

The self-report data indicate that some of the transfer effects are products of a generalizable skill rather than merely accompaniments of treatment-induced changes. Forty-four percent of the Ss in the varied condition occasionally used the method they learned in treatment to extinguish other sources of anxiety, while 22 percent in the uniform condition often did so.

Fifty percent of the Ss in the self-directed conditions could be located for the formal assessment 1 year following treatment. Over this interval Ss maintained their therapeutic gains at the same level they displayed in the posttreatment assessment. Statistical comparison of scores obtained at the completion of treatment and 1 year later revealed no significant changes in terminal performances, self-competency, personal potency or in any of the indices of fearfulness toward snakes. The reductions in fear proneness were also stably maintained with a few additional improvements over the year. Subjects reported further significant decrements in the intensity of social fears ($t = 1.95$; $p < 0.10$).

DISCUSSION

The present findings attest to the substantial therapeutic gains from self-directed performance after behavioral functioning has been restored through participant modeling. Compared to Ss who received participant modeling alone, those who had the benefit of independent mastery experiences exhibited bolder behavior toward an unfamiliar threat, weaker fear arousal, less apprehension of snake encounters, higher self-competency in coping with snakes, and less fear of threats not specifically treated. Because the induced changes were durably maintained, most of the advantages of self-directed performance persisted over time.

The oft repeated dictum that maintenance of changes depends upon environmental contingencies conveys the impression that behavior is exclusively determined by situational influences. This belief has retarded research on how supplemental experiences can be arranged in the immediate posttreatment phase to enhance psychological changes and to reduce vulnerability to defensive relearning. Environmental contingencies are not autonomous influences that inevitably impinge upon individuals to shape and control their actions. Behavior is regulated by its contingencies, but these are partly of a person's own making. People who possess effective coping skills will create different environmental experiences than those who are less adept. Results of this study show that opportunities for self-directed performance scheduled at the time when treatments are usually terminated expand the scope of psychological changes.

There is reason to believe that self-directed successes might also reduce susceptibility to defensive relearning. The capacity of aversive events to reinstate fears and defensive behavior depends upon the total pattern of experience in which they occur. Occasional mishaps among many positive or neutral experiences have little negative effect (Rescorla, 1972). Favorable experiences not only neutralize aversive events, but prevent inappropriate generalization of fearful behavior (Hoffman, 1969). Therefore, extensive performance of formerly threatening activities under favorable conditions after treatment could serve to reduce vulnerability to later mishaps. Thus, for example, dog-phobics who have many benign interactions with different dogs following treatment will not be much affected by a few unpleasant encounters. At most, such experiences will establish discriminative avoidance of realistic threats, which has adaptive value. In contrast, if people have limited contacts with previously feared objects after treatment, a few unfavorable experiences are likely to reestablish defensive behavior that generalizes inappropriately. The full value of alternative treatments should be measured in terms of vulnerability to defensive relearning as well as success in eliminating defensiveness. Some methods may leave Ss more susceptible to aversive relearning than others.

The present experiment was primarily designed to test whether self-directed performance following treatment augments generalization of induced changes. Further research is needed to identify the means by which it does so. Independent performance creates additional exposure to former threats, it provides opportunities to perfect coping skills, and it produces response feedback experiences which determine whether exposure and performance will have beneficial or adverse effects. Research in which the contributions of these factors are separated would not only elucidate the intervening processes involved in generalization, but designate optimal programs for consolidating changes in the immediate posttreatment phase when vulnerability to defensive relearning is greatest.

The timing of exposure to potential threats might well explain why varied self-directed treatment did not surpass the gains from successful coping with a familiar threat. The latter treatment extinguished fears most thoroughly and induced the strongest sense of self-competency. A number of the Ss in the varied condition were taken aback by the sudden confrontation with an unfamiliar snake. Premature performance demands in the face of severe threat can undermine self-confidence and partially reinstate fears that have been extinguished. Previously cited research would indicate that forbidding tasks are best introduced after an ample foundation of success has been established. The comparative efficacy of self-directed treatments under abrupt and gradual introduction of new threats clearly merits investigation.

Results of this, and related studies (Bandura et al., 1969; Blanchard, 1970a; Perloff, 1970), demonstrate that treatments aimed at improving behavioral functioning produce diverse collateral changes in affect, attitudes, and self-evaluation. Just as traumatic experiences simultaneously create avoidance, fear, negative attitudes, and self-perceptions of vulnerability, conversely, powerful success experiences concurrently attenuate fearfulness, and instill positive attitudes and a sense of self-competency.

Generalized reductions of fearful behavior in areas not specifically treated may result from several processes. One possibility is that fear decrements automatically transfer from events neutralized by treatment to related sources of anxiety on the basis of stimulus similarity. Evidence that fear reductions generalize most consistently to threats in the same general class—from snakes to other animals—lends support for this interpretation (Bandura & Barab, 1973; Bandura et al., 1969, Bandura et al., 1974).

The finding, however, that fears are also reduced toward unrelated threats points to other mechanisms. A second explanation, which bears on one of the propositions of this study, involves reduction in self-produced fear through changes in self-perception. Consistent with this interpretation, Ss who displayed the greatest change in perceived self-competency subsequently reported the weakest fear while responding to the generalization snake, and showed the broadest transfer effects. Supplementary data provided by the extended follow-up corroborate the Ss' affirmative approach to situations they previously feared.

A further explanation, given some weight by the self-report data, entails acquisition of a generalizable skill for coping with stress. In the course of treatment, Ss learned a serviceable method for overcoming their fears, and a number of them applied it on their own with evident success. Some of the generalized improvments may thus be products of self-administered treatment under natural circumstances. The alternative processes were undoubtedly activated in varying degrees to produce generalized changes in psychological functioning.

The disinhibitory power of performance-oriented treatments raises interesting issues concerning the determinants of defensive behavior. Snakes can become threatening through a combination of experiences in which anxiety is transmitted in early childhood by fearful parental modeling and reinforced by frightening personal experiences, grisly folklore, and filmed portrayals of the injurious nature of reptiles (Bandura et al., 1969). After snakes acquire frightening properties they become the cause of defensive behavior although the original causes have ceased to exist. These are essentially the laboratory conditions under which intractable avoidance behavior is created and maintained. A formerly innocuous event that acquires threat value through association with distressing experiences can sustain avoidance long after the aversive events have been discontinued. When historical and contemporary determinants differ, as they typically do, defensive behavior is successfully eliminated by neutralizing the acquired threats, but is little affected by insight into its origins.

Psychodynamic theories view phobic behavior as representing internally generated anxieties that are displaced and externally projected. From this perspective, the phobic actually fears his dangerous impulses rather than the phobic objects *per se*. A male who appeared at pretest, for example, was discouraged by his psychotherapist from participating in the present study on the grounds that his fear of snakes actually represented fear of himself and he was fortunate to have transferred the self-fear to snakes.

Fearful reactions to snakes are frequently interpreted to phobics as manifestations of sexual anxieties. Thereafter, fears evoked by thoughts of snakes may become associated with sexual activities. It has been shown that neutral events can become invested with frightening properties if paired with thought-provoked fears (Bandura, 1969; Grings, 1973). These findings present some basis for concern that interpreting snake threats in terms of genital fears may well condition anxiety to sexual activities without ameliorating the snake phobia.

REFERENCES

BANDURA, A. *Principles of Behavior Modification.* New York: Holt, Rinehart & Winston, 1969.

BANDURA, A. Effecting change through participant modeling. In J. D. Krumboltz and C. E. Thoresen (Eds.), *Counseling Methods.* New York: Holt, Rinehart & Winston, 1975.

BANDURA, A. & BARAB, P. G. Processes governing disinhibitory effects through symbolic modeling. *J. Abnorm. Psychol.,* 1973, 82, 1-9.

BANDURA, A., BLANCHARD, E. B., & RITTER, B. The relative efficacy of desensitization and modeling approaches for inducing behavioral, affective, and attitudinal changes. *J. Person. Soc. Psychol.*, 1969, 13, 173-199.

BANDURA, A., JEFFREY, R. W., and WRIGHT, C. L. Efficacy of participant modeling as a function of response induction aids. *J. Abnorm. Psychol.*, 1974. 83, 56-64.

BLANCHARD, E. B. The relative contributions of modeling, informational influences, and physical contact in the extinction of phobic behavior. *J. Abnorm. Psychol.*, 1970, 76, 55-61. (a)

BLANCHARD, E. B. The generalization of vicarious extinction effects. *Behav. Res. & Ther.*, 1970, 8, 323-330. (b)

GRINGS, W. W. The role of consciousness and cognition in autonomic behavior change. In F. J. McGuigan and R. Schoonover (Eds.), *The Psychophysiology of Thinking.* New York: Academic Press, 1973.

HOFFMAN, H. S. Stimulus factors in conditioned suppression. In B. A. Campbell and R. M. Church (Eds.), *Punishment and Aversive Behavior.* New York: Appleton-Century-Crofts, 1969.

PERLOFF, B. Influences of muscular relaxation, positive imagery, and neutral imagery on extinction of avoidance behavior through systematic desensitization. Unpublished doctoral dissertation, Stanford University, 1970.

RESCORLA, R. A. Information variables in Pavlovian conditioning. In G. H. Bower (Ed.), *The Psychology of Learning and Motivation*, Vol. 6. New York: Academic Press, 1972.

SECTION II: SYSTEMATIC DESENSITIZATION,
FLOODING, SYMBOLIC AND PARTICIPANT
MODELING, COGNITIVE RESTRUCTURING,
AND ASSERTION TRAINING

7

REDUCTION OF ANXIETY IN CHILDREN FACING HOSPITAL-IZATION AND SURGERY BY USE OF FILMED MODELING

Barbara G. Melamed and Lawrence J. Siegel

Case Western Reserve University

Sixty children about to undergo elective surgery for hernias, tonsillectomies, or urinary-genital tract difficulties were shown on hospital admission either a relevant peer modeling film of a child being hospitalized and receiving surgery or an unrelated control film. Both groups received extensive preparation by the hospital staff. State measures of anxiety, including self-report, behavioral observation, and Palmar Sweat Index, revealed a significant reduction of preoperative (night before) and postoperative (3-4 week postsurgery examination) fear arousal in the experimental as compared to

Reprinted with permission from *Journal of Consulting and Clinical Psychology*, Vol. 43, No. 4, 1975, 511-521. Copyright 1975, American Psychological Association.

The project was supported by funds provided by the Cleveland Foundation and the Health Sciences Communications Center of Case Western Reserve University.

Portions of the data reported in this study were included in an unpublished doctoral dissertation submitted by the second author in partial fulfillment for the doctoral degree at Case Western Reserve University, 1974.

the control film group. The parents reported a significant posthospital increment in the frequency of behavior problems in the children who had not seen the modeling film. Trait measures of anxiety did not reflect the group differences due to the hospital experience.

The literature on hospitalized children suggests that there is a consensus that all children need some kind of psychological preparation for the hospital experience, particularly when accompanied by surgery. The need for such preparation is predicted on the belief that hospitalization and surgery are stressful and anxiety-producing experiences that can lead to transient or long-term psychological disturbances in most children. A number of behavior problems have been observed in children who have been hospitalized for surgery (Chapman, Loeb, & Gibbons, 1956; Gellert, 1958) with estimates for the incidence of these problems ranging from 10 percent to 35 percent (Jessner, Blom, & Waldfogel, 1952; Prugh, Staub, Sands, Kirschbaum, & Lenihan, 1953; Schaffer & Callender, 1959). Cassell (1965) reported slight psychological upset in as many as 92 percent of the hospitalized children studied.

Skipper and Leonard (1968) noted that the hospital experience itself may produce anxiety for the child irrespective of the reason for hospitalization. In addition to its role in the development of physical and emotional problems, anxiety is of particular interest to the hospital staff because of its influence on the patient's reaction to surgery and its adverse effects on postoperative recovery. Several authors have suggested that preoperative anxiety is a significant factor in impeding recovery from surgery (Dumas, 1963; Giller, 1963; Janis, 1958).

In an attempt to alleviate the stressful effects of hospitalization, several methods of psychological preparation have been utilized. Vernon, Foley, Sipowicz, and Schulman (1965) have suggested that the major purpose of preoperative preparation is to (a) provide information to the child, (b) encourage emotional expression, and (c) establish a trusting relationship with the hospital staff.

The most frequently used method of preparing children for the hospital and surgery is preoperative instruction (Heller, 1967; Mellish, 1969). While a number of different procedures have been used to impart information to the child about the hospital and his operation, they are similar in that they attempt to correct any misinformation that he might have and to help him master the experience by enabling him to anticipate events and procedures and to understand their meaning and purpose.

Puppet therapy (Cassell, 1965) and play therapy (Dimock, 1960; Impallaria, 1955) have also been used as preoperative preparation techniques with children. The child is given the opportunity to act out, draw, or describe the events that he will experience in the hospital. It is believed that such activities permit the child to resolve his fears and concerns with the assistance of a supporting adult.

Several studies have investigated the effectiveness of various methods of preoperative preparation with children (Cassell, 1965; Jackson, Winkley, Faust, & Cermack, 1952; Lende, 1971; Prugh et al., 1953). The results of these studies, however, are equivocal in demonstrating differences between prepared and unprepared subjects on a variety of criterion measures. Most of the measures that purport to measure the child's anxiety are interview questionnaires with the parents or global ratings of the child's response to the treatment procedures. Reliability data on the use of these ratings are not reported. In addition, these investigations suffer from a number of methodological problems that make interpretation of the data difficult. Such factors as previous hospitalizations, age of the child, and prehospitalization personality, which are cited (Vernon et al., 1965) as major determinants of psychological upset, are often uncontrolled.

Recent demonstrations of the therapeutic use of modeling to effectively reduce anxiety-mediated avoidance behavior in children (Bandura, Grusec, & Menlove, 1967; Bandura & Menlove, 1968; Ritter, 1968) suggest that this procedure might also be useful for reducing children's anxiety and fears concerning the hospital and surgery. Vicarious extinction of emotional behavior is typically achieved by exposing the child to a model's approach responses toward a fearful stimulus that does not result in any adverse consequences or that may, in fact, produce positive consequences.

The purpose of this study was to investigate the efficacy of filmed modeling in reducing the emotional reactions of children admitted to the hospital for elective surgery and in facilitating their emotional adjustment during a posthospital period. While several investigations have demonstrated the successful application of therapeutic modeling in alleviating children's fears of dental treatment (Johnson & Machen, 1973; Melamed, Hawes, Heiby, & Glick, 1975; Melamed, Weinstein, Hawes, & Katin-Borland, 1975; White, Akers, Green, & Yates, 1974), there has been only one systematic investigation of this procedure in a hospital setting. Vernon and Bailey (1974) found that children who observed an experimental modeling film exhibited significantly less disruptive and fearful behaviors during induction of anesthesia than a control group that did not observe the modeling film. However, since children in the control group did not observe any film, it is not possible to determine whether the mere act of watching a movie or the content of the movie itself was the critical variable. In addition, the only measure of the film's effectiveness was a "global mood scale" that was used to rate the child's behavior during various phases of the anesthesia-induction procedure.

The current investigation attempts to avoid the methodological flaws of previous research by controlling for the age, sex, and prior hospitalization history of the subjects. The prehospital personality was assessed through measures of chronic anxiety and behavior maladjustment. The effectiveness of a peer-modeling hospital film in reducing anxiety of the experimental group was compared against a group of children matched in age, sex, and type of surgery who were also exposed to a preadmission film that was not related to the hospitalization. Both groups of children also received preoperative preparation by the hospital staff. Thus the effectiveness of the film was evaluated for its potency above that of procedures already thought to effectively reduce anxiety in these children.

Since anxiety is generally regarded as a multidimensional construct expressing itself in several response classes including physiological, skeletal-muscular, and verbal (cognitive) behavior, a number of dependent measures were used in the present study to assess the children's emotional responses to hospitalization and surgery (Cattell & Scheier, 1961; Lang, 1968). The measures were further selected in order to differentiate between the child's anxiety in specific situations (state anxiety) and his characteristic level of anxiety (trait anxiety) (Cattell & Scheier, 1961; Spielberger, 1966). In addition, these measures were assessed throughout the hospital experience and not just during certain medical procedures. A follow-up assessment of the children was conducted 3-4 weeks after discharge when they returned to the hospital for a postoperative examination by the surgeon.

METHOD

Subjects

The subjects were 60 children between the ages of 4 and 12 years old who were admitted to Rainbow Babies and Children's Hospital, Cleveland, Ohio, for elective surgery. They had no prior history of hospitalization. The subjects were selected from the Division of Pediatric Surgery and were sheduled for either tonsillectomies, hernia, or urinary-genital tract surgery.* The length of stay in the hospital for the children ranged from 2 to 3 days.

Thirty matched subjects were assigned to the experimental or control group. Group assignment was conducted in order to counterbalance for age, sex, race, and the type of operation.

Measures of Anxiety

In order to assess the various response classes considered to reflect the multidimensional nature of anxiety, a number of indices of the child's emotional behavior were employed including self-report, behavioral, and physiological measures.

Three measures were used to assess "trait" anxiety, or the long-term effects of the hospital experience. The first measure was the Anxiety scale (Klinedinst, 1971). The 30 items that comprise this scale were rationally derived from the Personality Inventory for Children (Wirt & Broen, 1958). Items on the scale, which the mother rates as true or false about her child, are intended to measure more chronic and stable anxiety.

The Children's Manifest Anxiety Scale (Castaneda, McCandless, & Palermo, 1956) was a second measure of the long-term effects of the hospital experience. The Human Figure Drawing Test (Koppitz, 1968) was the third index of trait anxiety. Koppitz has developed a set of norms for 30 "emotional indicators" that were used to score the subjects' drawings. Average interrater agreement for scoring the drawings, which was computed by dividing the number of agreements of two independent raters by the total number of agreements and disagreements, was 97 percent.

Situational, or "state," anxiety was assessed by the Palmar Sweat Index, the Hospital Fears Rating Scale, and the Observer Rating Scale of Anxiety.

The Palmar Sweat Index (Johnson & Dabbs, 1967; Thomson & Sutarman, 1953) is a plastic impression method that permits enumeration of active sweat gland activity of the hand. Since the sweat glands of the hand are primarily affected by emotional factors and not other variables such as temperature, the number of active sweat glands provides a measure of transitory physiological arousal. The Palmar Sweat Index was

* Acknowledged is the cooperation and support of Robert Izant, Jr., Howard Filston, Robert Crumrine, Dennis Drotar, Anne Godfrey, Lester Persky, Walter Maloney, Patricia Rutherford, Cindy Chessler, and Carol Cook, who provided direct patient service, as well as guidance, in the project development. The staff of Rainbow Babies and Children's Hospital and the Ethan Stein family made a significant contribution to this study.

TABLE 1

Sample Characteristics of the Experimental
and Control Groups

Variable	Experimental	Control
Age in months		
M	90.4	86.9
SD	26.85	24.97
Sex		
Male	18	19
Female	12	11
Race		
White	23	23
Black	7	7
Type of operation		
Hernia	13	13
Tonsillectomy	4	5
Urinary-genital tract	13	12
No. of mothers staying overnight	16	15

recorded from the index finger of the child's left hand. Rater reliability
for two persons independently scoring the same area of the print, as
determined by the Pearson product-moment correlation coefficient, was .93.

The second measure of situational anxiety was the Hospital Fears Rating Scale. This is a self-report measure comprised of 8 items from the
Medical Fears subscale, factor analyzed from the Fear Survey Schedule
for Children (Scherer & Nakamura, 1968). Another 8 items with the
face validity for assessing hospital fears were also included. The Hospital
Fears Rating Scale is comprised of these 16 items and 9 nonrelated
filler items. Each subject rated his degree of fear for each item on a fear
thermometer that ranged from 1 (not afraid at all) to 5 (very afraid).
The sum of the ratings on the 16 medical fear items was the subject's
score for this measure.

A third measure of situational anxiety was the Observer Rating Scale
of Anxiety. This behavioral observation scale was constructed of 29
categories of verbal and skeletal-motor behavior thought to represent
behavioral manifestations of anxiety in children. A time sampling procedure was used in which an observer indicated the presence or absence
of each response category during three intervals of time in a 9-minute
observation period. Examples of items indicative of anxiety include

"crying," "trembling hands," "stutters," and "talks about hospital fears, separation from mother, or going home." The frequency of responses observed during the total period of observation was the subject's score on the Observer Rating Scale of Anxiety. Rater reliability was assessed throughout each phase of experimental procedure. Average interrater reliability, which was computed by dividing the number of observer agreements by the total number of categories of behavior that were observed, was 94 percent.

Procedure

Each subject was asked to report to the hospital 1 hour prior to his scheduled admission time.* Upon their arrival, the child and his parents were escorted to a research area of the hospital. The parents and child were separated and taken to adjoining rooms. The parents were questioned to obtain information regarding the child's age and grade, whether he was taking medication, number of previous hospitalizations, whether other siblings had been hospitalized, and whether the mother was planning to remain overnight with the child (the hospital permitted the mother to sleep in the child's room during his stay in the hospital). A consent form was signed by the parents indicating their agreement to have their child participate in a study investigating better methods of preparing children psychologically for hospitalization and surgery.

The mother then completed the Parents' Questionnaire, which asked her to rate 10 statements pertaining to her own anxiety about being a hospital patient, how her child had reacted to past medical procedures, and how she felt her child would respond to the current hospital experience on a 5-point scale. In addition, the mother completed the Behavior Problem Checklist (Peterson, 1961; Peterson, Becker, Shoemaker, Luria, & Hellmer, 1961; Quay & Quay, 1965; Quay & Peterson, 1967), a 55-item rating scale of behavior problems frequently observed in children. She was instructed to rate the child's behavior during the last 4 weeks. Finally, the mother filled out the Anxiety scale from the Personality Inventory for Children.

The child was taken to a separate room by an experimenter dressed in a white laboratory coat who introduced himself to the child as a doctor. As soon as the child was seated, a second experimenter began observing him with the Observer Rating Scale of Anxiety. The "doctor"

* Michael Ike, Neil Haymes, and Raymond Meyer were responsible for primary data collection. Lawrence Melamed and Nancy Martin assisted in analysis.

placed electrodes on the child's left hand and chest in order to record galvanic skin response and heart rate.* The subjects were told that the purpose of the "wires" was to enable the doctor to listen to their heart while they watched a movie. In addition to recording electrophysiological activity, the placement of electrodes provided a sample of behavior with which to measure the subjects' response to an anxiety-evoking situation that closely resembled actual medical procedures encountered by the child in the hospital.

Following the attachment of the electrodes, the doctor left the room to begin the electrophysiological recording. A third experimenter administered the Children's Manifest Anxiety Scale, the Hospital Fears Rating Scale, and the Human Figure Drawing Test. Finally, the Palmar Sweat Index was recorded.

After the measures were completed, the subject was shown the experimental or control film depending on his group assignment. Each film was in the form of an 8-mm cassette that was shown on a Technicolor projector. The experimenter who recorded the behavioral observations left the room prior to the start of the film in order to remain unaware of the treatment condition to which the subject had been assigned. The third experimenter remained in the room with the child during the film.

The experimental film, entitled *Ethan Has an Operation,* depicts a 7-year-old white male who has been hospitalized for a hernia operation.** This film, which is 16 minutes in length, consists of 15 scenes showing various events that most children encounter when hospitalized for elective surgery from the time of admission to time of discharge including the child's orientation to the hospital ward and medical personnel such as the surgeon and anesthesiologist; having a blood test and exposure to standard hospital equipment; separation from the mother; and scenes in the operating and recovery rooms. In addition to explanations of the hospital procedures provided by the medical staff, various scenes are narrated by the child, who describes his feelings and concerns that he had at each stage of the hospital experience. Both the child's behavior and verbal remarks exemplify the behavior of a coping model so that while he exhibits some anxiety and apprehension, he is able to overcome his initial fears and complete each event in a successful and nonanxious manner. Meichenbaum (1971) has shown that film models who are initially anxious and overcome their anxiety (coping models)

---

* These data were not available for presentation in this article.

** *Ethan Has An Operation* may be obtained from the Health Sciences Communication Center, Case Western Reserve University, Cleveland, Ohio 44106.

result in greater reduction in anxiety than models who exhibit no fear (mastery models).

The subjects in the control group were shown a 12-minute film entitled *Living Things Are Everywhere.** The control film was similar in interest value to the experimental film in maintaining the children's attention but was unrelated in content to hospitalization. It presents the experiences of a white preadolescent male who is followed on a nature trip in the country.

Immediately following the experimental or control film, the second experimenter returned to the room to observe the subject with the Observer Rating Scale of Anxiety. The Palmar Sweat Index was recorded, and the Hospital Fears Rating Scale was readministered.

Following the postfilm assessment, the child and his parents were escorted to the hospital lobby. The child was formally admitted to the hospital in the usual manner and taken to the surgical ward.

Later in the afternoon, both the experimental and control subjects were given preoperative instruction by the hospital staff, a standard procedure at the pediatric hospital. This instruction involved a nurse who explained to the child, through pictures and demonstration, what would happen to him the day of surgery, including the things he would observe and experience. The child was also visited by the surgeon and/or anesthesiologist who explained to the child and his parents what his operation would involve, what he would see in the operating room, and the method of anesthesia that would be used. A preoperative teaching communication sheet was completed by the nurse in order to provide a record of the kind of information given to the child to insure that all subjects received similar preoperative instructions.

The subject's level of anxiety was again assessed the evening before he was scheduled for surgery and after preoperative instructions had been completed. Observations of the child with the Observer Rating Scale of Anxiety were made in the child's hospital room while the following took place: first, the child's Palmar Sweat Index was recorded; then Hospital Fears Rating Scale was readministered, a game about hospitalization and surgery called "operation" was played with all subjects. All children were premedicated with Seconal and Atropine. A xylocaine patch was routinely placed on the hand for intravenous induction.

All subjects returned to the hospital for a postoperative physical examination by the surgeon. A follow-up assessment of the child was made

---

* Appreciation is expressed to *Encyclopaedia Britannica* for use of their film *Living Things Are Everywhere* as a control in this study.

at this time. The follow-up session was 20-26 days after the child had been discharged from the hospital. The parents and child were asked to report to the hospital 15 minutes prior to the appointment with the surgeon. After the parents and child were separated, the mother again completed the Anxiety scale from the Personality Inventory for Children and the Behavior Problem Checklist. She was instructed to rate the child's behavior since he left the hospital.

The child was observed with the Observer Rating Scale of Anxiety. Following measurement of the Palmar Sweat Index, the subject was readministered the Children's Manifest Anxiety Scale, the Hospital Fears Rating Scale, and the Human Figure Drawing Test. After all of the measures were completed, the subject was taken to the surgeon's office for his appointment.

Design

A mixed design was employed to evaluate the results of the between-subjects variable and the within-subjects variable. The type of film was the between-subjects variable, with matched groups of children receiving either the hospital-relevant film or an unrelated control film. The within-subjects variable was the time of measurement. Situational measures of anxiety were assessed at four points: prefilm—as the subject was being hooked up to the polygraph; postfilm—immediately after the film viewing was completed; preoperative—the night before surgery (after all preoperative preparation had been concluded a game called operation was played with the child in an attempt to elicit his concern about the impending surgery); postoperative—immediately prior to the surgeon's follow-up examination when the child returned to the hospital 3-4 weeks after discharge. The measures of chronic anxiety and the Behavior Problems Checklist were obtained at the prefilm and postoperative assessments.

The variation in the routine time of preparing the child and the use of premedication immediately prior to surgery made assessment during preoperative medical procedures and the morning of surgery impractical. Also, since the child was discharged prior to full recovery from anesthesia and pain medication, the effect of immediate recovery from the operation was obtained on a global postoperative recovery questionnaire.

RESULTS

The state measures of anxiety consistently reflected differences between the experimental and control groups. Differences between groups

PALMAR SWEAT INDEX

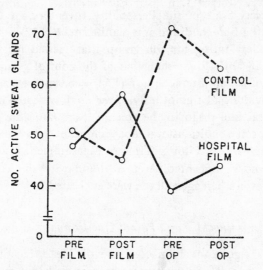

FIGURE 1. Number of active sweat glands for the experimental and control groups across the four measurement periods.

were also found on the prehospitalization to posthospitalization parental ratings of the child's behavior. Measures of trait anxiety did not demonstrate a significant effect of the treatment conditions.

Trait Anxiety Measures

There were no significant differences between prefilm and postoperative assessments between the experimental and control groups on the Children's Manifest Anxiety Scale, the Anxiety Scale of the Personality Inventory for Children, or the Human Figure Drawing Score for anxiety. Because of the wide range of ages, the data were reanalyzed with sex and age taken into account. The children were divided into two age groups defined as younger than 7 years or 7 and older.

The Children's Manifest Anxiety Scale revealed a significant effect of age, $F(1,52) = 8.39$, $p < .005$, with the younger children having higher scores on the measure. The significant Sex $\times$ Age $\times$ Time interaction,

$F(1,52) = 4.54$, $p < .04$, further revealed that young females reported more anxiety on this measure following hospitalization, whereas older females became slightly less anxious. Males reported slightly less anxiety after the hospital experience for both age groups.

On the Anxiety Scale of the Personality Inventory for Children, the main effect of the film condition was significant, $F(1,52) = 6.21$, $p < .02$. The mean anxiety rating for the group that viewed the hospital film (5.75) was significantly lower than that of the control group (8.02). The Sex $\times$ Type of Film interaction, $F(1,52) = 5.08$, $p < .03$, further revealed that females had significantly lower anxiety scores in the experimental (hospital film) than in the control (unrelated film) group. The difference between conditions was not significant for the males. There was no significant Sex $\times$ Film $\times$ Time of Measurement interaction.

There were no significant differences found with the Human Figure Drawing Task even when age and sex were evaluated.

Behavior Problems Checklist and Parent Questionnaire

There was a significant Film $\times$ Time of Measurement interaction, $F(1,58) = 5.05$, $p < .03$. Subsequent t-tests revealed that the children in the control group showed a significant increase in the degree of behavior problems from the prehospital to postoperative periods, $t(29) = 2.23$, $p < .05$. These children showed a mean rating of 10.63 prior to the hospital experience and a mean rating of 12.5 at the postoperative assessment. The experimental subjects did not show any significant increase or decrease in behavior problems across the two assessments. When the data were further evaluated for sex and age, the Film $\times$ Time interaction remained significant, $F(1,52) = 4.4$, $p < .03$. The significant Age $\times$ Sex $\times$ Film interaction, $F(1,52) = 9.13$, $p < .004$, revealed that the younger females and older males exhibited the most behavior problems in the experimental group, whereas older females had the highest number of behavior problems in the control condition. The Behavior Problem Checklist score (postoperative) correlated significantly with the Anxiety scale of the Personality Inventory for Children ($r = .446$, $p < .02$). Although there were no group differences, $t(58) = .67$, $p > .20$, of initial statement of parental anxiety, the Parents' questionnaire, a measure of parental concern, correlated significantly with the Behavior Problem Checklist (postoperative $r = .36$, $p < .05$).

Situational "State" Anxiety Measures

There were no initial differences between groups for either the Palmar Sweat Index or the Observer Rating Scale for Anxiety. Repeated measures analysis of variance were used to assess the main effects of type of film and the effect of time of measurement and the interactions between the two variables. Since there were group differences on the initial self-report ratings of anxiety on the Hospital Fears Rating Scale, a covariance analysis was employed with this dependent measure. Neuman-Keuls analyses were performed to reveal differences between group means.

Palmar Sweat Index. Figure 1 illustrates the significant Film × Time of Measurement interaction, $F(3,174) = 12.72$, $p < .0001$. The groups were significantly different the night before surgery (preoperative, $p < .01$) and at the postoperative examination ($p < .05$). The children who viewed the hospital film (experimental group) showed lower levels of sweat gland activity than those who had been exposed to an unrelated control film. Looking at the within-group differences for this same interaction, a Neuman-Keuls analysis revealed that the children who viewed the hospital film showed a significant increase ($p < .05$) in sympathetic arousal (Palmar Sweat Index) from the prefilm to postfilm assessment. However, the experimental group also showed a significant decrease ($p < .01$) in arousal from postfilm to the preoperative assessment. The significant decrease was maintained from the postfilm to the postoperative assessment ($p < .05$).

The control group (unrelated film) on the other hand, showed significant increases in physiological arousal on this measure from prefilm to postoperative ($p < .01$) and from postfilm to preoperative assessment ($p < .01$). The means within the control group were also significant (with increased palmar sweating) when the comparisons between prefilm and postoperative assessment ($p < .05$) and postfilm and postoperative assessment ($p < .01$) were examined. When the analysis was made to investigate age and sex variables, the Film × Time interaction remained significant, $F(3,156) = 14.48$, $p < .00001$, despite a significant Sex × Age interaction, $F(1,52) = 5.28$, $p < .02$. Older males exhibited more overall arousal than younger males ($p < .01$), while younger females displayed more arousal than older females ($p < .01$).

Hospital Fears Rating Scale. Figure 2 illustrates the significant Film × Time interaction, $F(2,115) = 4.74$, $p < .05$, that resulted when a covariance analysis was performed on this scale to statistically control for

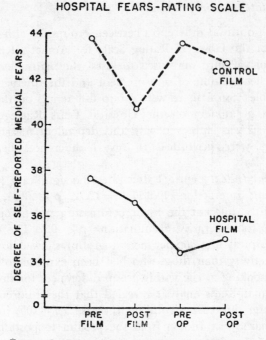

FIGURE 2. Degree of self-reported medical fears for the experimental and control groups across the four measurement periods.

the initial difference that existed between groups. The control group had a higher fear rating than the experimental group at all assessment times. Statistical significance was achieved at the preoperative $(p < .01)$ and postoperative $(p < .01)$ measurement across groups. The self-report measure did not yield significant within-group effects across measurement times. There was a significant effect of age, $F(1,52) = 4.47$, $p < .04$, with the younger children reporting greater fear regardless of film condition. This, however, did not change the significant interaction described above.

Observer Rating Scale of Anxiety. The significant differences in the frequency of observer-rated verbal and nonverbal anxiety responses that resulted between groups across the times of measurement are illustrated by Figure 3, for the Film × Time interaction, $F(3,174) = 3.33$, $p < .02$. The groups did not differ from each other at prefilm or postfilm assessments. The group that viewed the hospital film exhibited significantly

OBSERVER RATING SCALE OF ANXIETY

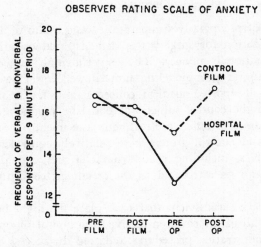

FIGURE 3. Frequency of observer-rated verbal and nonverbal anxiety responses for the experimental and control groups across the four measurement periods.

fewer ($p < .05$) anxiety-related behaviors than the control group at both preoperative and postoperative assessments.

In further evaluating the Film × Time interaction by examining the changes within each group on subsequent measurement trials, it was revealed that the experimental subjects showed a significant reduction in this measure of anxiety from both prefilm ($p < .01$) and postfilm ($p < .01$) to the preoperative measurement. There was also a significant reduction on this scale for the comparison of prefilm to postoperative assessment ($p < .05$). It should be noted that although the prefilm to postoperative assessment showed a reduction, there was a significant increase in anxiety-related responses from preoperative to postoperative assessment ($p < .05$). Both the experimental and control groups showed a significant increase in anxiety-related behavior from preoperative to postoperative assessment ($p < .05$). It is interesting to note, however, that the experimental group evidenced a significant reduction in observed anxiety from the prefilm to postoperative assessment period ($p < .05$), whereas there was no significant reduction in anxiety for the control group. There was no significant effect of age or sex on this dependent measure.

DISCUSSION

The efficacy of preoperative preparation using a film of a child undergoing hospitalization for surgery was demonstrated on all measures of transitory, situational anxiety. The experimental subjects who had viewed the hospital peer-modeling film showed lower sweat gland activity, fewer self-reported medical concerns, and fewer anxiety-related behaviors than the control subjects at both the preoperative and postoperative assessments. Since pretreatment assessment revealed that the experimental and control groups were relatively equivalent on the dependent variables, including group characteristics, any differences between groups can be attributed to the treatment conditions that were provided.

The preoperative assessment that took place the night before surgery, and only after all of the children received the typical preoperative counseling and demonstration procedures, reflected the success of the film in reducing anticipatory and situational anxiety beyond that of the staff's efforts. In fact, there was no significant reduction in anxiety for children receiving hospital-initiated preparation. The maintenance of these group differences at the postoperative examination, 3-4 weeks following discharge, further supports the need for more preparation than is ordinarily received once the child is in the hospital.

The 4-week posthospital examination by the surgeon also provided a test of generalization of the film's effectiveness since it presented the child with a similar anticipatory stressful situation that was not specifically depicted in the hospital film. Group differences were maintained on all measures of situational anxiety. Furthermore, experimental subjects showed a significant reduction in anxiety-related behaviors as compared with their initial (prefilm) hospital experience. This would support generalization of the film's effectiveness. There was, however, a significant increment in behaviorally rated anxiety in both groups from the preoperative to postoperative assessments and a trend toward a similar increase, although not significant, in self-reported medical fears and physiological arousal, for the experimental group during this same measurement period. These results may reflect the greater potency of the film under the arousal condition that was present during the initial hospitalization. Another interpretation is that the content of the film, which is specific to procedures during hospitalization, may be a major influence in the reduction of anxiety since the film did not show the child what to expect at the follow-up visit with the surgeon. Finally, the time delay between the viewing of the film and the stress condition (postoperative follow-up) may have attenuated the generalization effects that were obtained.

The specific components that made the film effective will be explored in further parametric investigation. Perhaps the film oriented the child to the hospital procedures, therefore making later preparation more meaningful. Whether the use of a peer coping model enhanced the film's effectiveness must be investigated using appropriate control groups. For instance, one may question whether the film merely familiarized the child with the experiences he would most likely encounter. An experiment comparing peer model, adult model, and demonstration-no-model conditions should be undertaken.

Although the use of the film alone was not possible in the present investigation because of the ethical considerations involved in denying a child preoperative preparation, the research is being replicated in a hospital in which staff-patient ratio does not allow for preoperative preparation. Thus the effectiveness and generalizability of this particular film will be evaluated. In addition, the effectiveness of this film with children who have already been hospitalized needs to be investigated. It would seem that children with one or more hospital experiences may differ sufficiently from the subjects employed in this study since one cannot automatically assume that the film will be equally effective with children having a prior history of hospitalization for surgery.

The increase in arousal level, as measured by the Palmar Sweat Index, for the experimental group from prefilm to postfilm lends some support for the contention of Janis (1958) that a moderate amount of arousal may facilitate response to stress in those facing impending surgery. Therefore, another variable of interest would be the time of presentation of the hospital film. In the present investigation, the children seeing the film immediately prior to admission to the hospital showed an initial increase in arousal. However, their scores on this somatic index as well as the behavioral and self-report measures of situational anxiety decreased from the initial level throughout their hospital and post-hospital experiences. Similar results are reported by Florell (1971), who found an increase in transitory anxiety in hospitalized patients immediately following treatment (emotional support and information about the hospital routine) and a decrease in anxiety following surgery, as compared with a control group who exhibited higher transitory anxiety scores after surgery. Schachter and Singer (1962) and Bandura and Rosenthal (1966) provided data that are particularly relevant to the present discussion. They found that moderate levels of physiological and emotional arousal increased imitation of a model's behavior by an observer. Taken together, these results suggest that a particular level of arousal may enhance the modeling effect, and in the case of the present investigation, it may further facilitate attention to the instructions and demonstrations provided by the hospital staff the day before surgery.

One shortcoming of the current investigation was the failure to assess the children's degree of anxiety during actual medical procedures, such as the blood test, the surgeon's examination, etc. However, the time at which these procedures took place was quite variable. In addition, the analysis would not clearly show the effectiveness of the film manipulation since the preoperative teaching by the hospital staff took place throughout the day of admission.

The measures of trait anxiety did not demonstrate a significant effect of the film manipulation. These findings are not surprising in view of the definition of trait anxiety as a stable consistent characteristic of the individual. These results are consistent with Kaplan and Hafner (1959), who found no changes on subjects' scores on the Children's Manifest Anxiety Scale during their hospitalization for surgery. Spielberger, Auerbach, Wadsworth, Dunn, and Taulbee (1973) and Auerbach (1973), using the State-Trait Anxiety Inventory, provided further data indicating the stability of trait measures of anxiety (A-Trait) with hospitalized surgical patients. A-State scores, however, were found to change from presurgery to postsurgery assessments and again during the posthospitalization period.

When the variance due to age and sex was examined in additional analyses of variances, some interesting facts were revealed. Younger children reported higher anxiety on the measure of children's manifest anxiety. Younger females in particular appeared to be more vulnerable to the hospital experience since they reported increased anxiety on this measure at the postoperative examination. When sex is also significant as a factor contributing to the variance on the Anxiety scale of the Personality Inventory for Children, it was found that lower scores for females on anxiety did occur in the experimental group. Therefore, viewing a male model did not hinder the effectiveness of this film manipulation.

It is interesting that the parents' report of behavior problems occurring 4 weeks following discharge does correspond with how the children reacted to stress during their hospitalization. The children in the control group had an increase in behavior problems during the 3-4 week posthospitalization period before they returned to the hospital for their postoperative examination by the surgeon. They also showed higher physiological arousal, greater concern about medical fears, and increased anxiety-related behaviors the night prior to surgery and at the follow-up examination. This again supports the contention that in order to avoid posthospital traumatization as observed in psychological disturbances, extensive preoperative preparation is essential.

The use of a multidimensional approach to the measurement of the anxiety proved valuable in understanding the relationships and changes between subjective (self-report), physiological, and behavioral subsystems of human fear response. At least for this sample of children between the ages of 4 and 12, the self-report measure of hospital fears was least sensitive to changes in response at various times during and after hospitalization.

The implications of the research for the measurement and alteration of the stress reaction of normal children to hospitalization and surgery are numerous. The film *Ethan Has an Operation,* which demonstrates a child going through the experiences of being hospitalized for an operation, was more effective in alleviating anxiety than simple verbal, pictorial, or actual demonstration of hospital procedures by the concerned staff. The need for a multidimensional approach to the evaluation of children's responses to stress is supported in view of the differences reflected by trait and state measures of anxiety, as well as between the measures of situational anxiety.

REFERENCES

AUERBACH, S. M. Trait-state anxiety and adjustment to surgery. *J. Cons. Clin. Psychol.,* 1973, 40, 264-271.

BANDURA, A., GRUSEC, J. E., & MENLOVE, F. L. Vicarious extinction of avoidance behaviors. *J. Pers. Soc. Psychol.,* 1967, 5, 16-23.

BANDURA, A. & MENLOVE, F. L. Factors determining vicarious extinction of avoidance behavior through symbolic modeling. *J. Pers. Soc. Psychol.,* 1968, 8, 99-108.

BANDURA, A. & ROSENTHAL, T. L. Vicarious classical conditioning as a function of arousal level. *J. Pers. Soc. Psychol.,* 1966, 3, 54-62.

CASSELL, S. Effects of brief puppet therapy upon the emotional responses of children undergoing cardiac catheterization. *J. Cons. Psychol.,* 1965, 29, 1-8.

CASTANEDA, A., McCANDLESS, B. R., & PALERMO, D. S. The children's form of the Manifest Anxiety Scale. *Child Devel.,* 1956, 27, 317-326.

CATTELL, R. B. & SCHEIER, I. H. *The Meaning and Measurement of Neuroticism and Anxiety.* New York: Ronald Press, 1961.

CHAPMAN, A. H., LOEB, D. G., & GIBBONS, M. J. Psychiatric aspects of hospitalization of children. *Arch. Pediat.,* 1956, 73, 77-88.

DIMOCK, H. G. *The Child in Hospital: A Study of His Emotional and Social Well-Being.* Philadelphia: Davis, 1960.

DUMAS, R. G. Psychological preparation for surgery. *Amer. J. Nurs.*, 1963, 63, 52-55.

FLORELL, J. Crisis intervention in orthopedic surgery. (Doctoral dissertation, Northwestern University, 1971.) *Dissert. Abs. Int.*, 1971, 32, 3633B. (University Microfilms No. 71-30799, 204.)

GELLERT, E. Reducing the emotional stress of hospitalization for children. *Amer. J. Occup. Ther.*, 1958, 12, 125-129.

GILLER, D. W. Some psychological factors in recovery from surgery. *Hosp. Topics*, 1963, 41, 83-85.

HELLER, J. A. *The Hospitalized Child and His Family*. Baltimore: Johns Hopkins Press, 1967.

IMPALLARIA, C. The contribution of social group work: The hospitalized child. *Amer. J. Orthopsychiat.*, 1955, 55, 293-318.

JACKSON, K., WINKLEY, R., FAUST, O. A., & CERMACK, E. The problem of emotional trauma in the hospital treatment of children. *J. Amer. Med. Assn.*, 1952, 149, 1536-1538.

JANIS, I. L. *Psychological Stress*. New York: Wiley, 1958.

JESSNER, L., BLOM, G. E., & WALDFOGEL, S. Emotional implications of tonsillectomy and adenoidectomy in children. In R. S. Eisslen (Ed.), *The Psychoanalytic Study of the Child*. New York: International Universities Press, 1952.

JOHNSON, R. & DABBS, J. M. Enumeration of active sweat glands: A simple physiological indicator of psychological changes. *Nurs. Res.*, 1967, 16, 273-276.

JOHNSON, R. & MACHEN, J. B. Behavior modification techniques and maternal anxiety. *J. Dent. Child.*, 1973, 40, 272-276.

KAPLAN, A. M. & HAFNER, A. J. Manifest anxiety in hospitalized children. *J. Clin. Psychol.*, 1959, 15, 301-302.

KLINEDINST, J. K. *Relationship between Minnesota Multiphasic Personality Inventory and Personality Inventory for Children Data from Mothers of Disturbed Children.* (Doctoral dissertation, University of Minnesota, 1971.) *Dissert. Abs. Int.*, 1971, 32, 4860B. (University Microfilms No. 72-05545, 116.)

KOPPITZ, E. M. *Psychological Evaluation of Children's Human Figure Drawings.* New York: Grune & Stratton, 1968.

LANG, P. J. Fear reduction and fear behavior: Problems in treating a construct. In J. M. Shlien (Ed.), *Research in Psychotherapy* (Vol. 3), 1968.

LENDE, E. W. *The Effect of Preparation on Children's Response to Tonsillectomy and Adenoidectomy Surgery.* (Doctoral dissertation, University of Cincinnati, 1971.) *Dissert. Abs., Int.*, 1971, 32, 3642B. (University Microfilms No. 72-01440, 95.)

MEICHENBAUM, D. Examination and model characteristics in reducing avoidance behavior. *J. Pers. Soc. Psychol.*, 1971, 17, 298-307.

MELAMED, B. G., HAWES, R. R., HEIBY, E., & GLICK, J. The use of filmed modeling to reduce uncooperative behavior of children during dental treatment. *J. Dent. Res.*, 1975.

MELAMED, B. G., WEINSTEIN, D., HAWES, R., & KATIN-BORLAND, M. Reduction of fear-related dental management problems using filmed modeling. *J. Amer. Dent. Assn.*, 1975, 90, 822-826.

MELLISH, R. W. Preparation of a child for hospitalization and surgery. *Pediat. Clin. N. Amer.*, 1969, 16, 543-553.

PETERSON, D. R. Behavior problems of middle childhood. *J. Consult. Psychol.*, 1961, 25, 205-209.

PETERSON, D. R., BECKER, W. C., SHOEMAKER, D. J., LURIA, Z., & HELLMER, L. A. Child behavior problems and parental attitudes. *Child Devel.*, 1961, 32, 151-162.

PRUGH, D. G., STAUB, E., SANDS, H. H., KIRSHBAUM, R. M., & LENIHAN, E. A. A study of the emotional reactions of children and families to hospitalization and illness.

Amer. J. Orthopsychiat., 1953, 23, 70-106.

QUAY, H. C. & PETERSON, D. R. *Manual for the Behavior Problem Checklist*. Unpublished manuscript, University of Illinois, 1967.

QUAY, H. C. & QUAY, L. C. Behavior problems in early adolescence. *Child Devel.*, 1965, 36, 215-220.

RITTER, B. The group desensitization of children's snake phobias using vicarious and contact desensitization procedures. *Behav. Res. & Ther.*, 1968, 6, 1-6.

SCHACHTER, S. & SINGER, J. E. Cognitive, social, and physiological determinants of emotional state. *Psychol. Rev.*, 1962, 69, 379-399.

SCHAFFER, H. R. & CALLENDER, W. H. Psychological effects of hospitalization in infancy. *Pediat.*, 1959, 24, 528-539.

SCHERER,, M. W. & NAKAMURA, C. Y. A fear survey schedule for children (FSS-FC): A factor analytic comparison with manifest anxiety (CMAS). *Behav. Res. & Ther.*, 1968, 173-182.

SKIPPER, J. & LEONARD, R. Children, stress, and hospitalization: A field experiment. *J. Health Soc. Behav.*, 1968, 9, 275-287.

SPIELBERGER, C. D. Theory and research on anxiety. In C. D. Spielberger (Ed.), *Anxiety and Behavior*. New York: Academic Press, 1966.

SPIELBERGER, C. B., AUERBACH, S. M., WADSWORTH, A. P., DUNN, T. M., & TAULBEE, E. S. Emotional reactions to surgery. *J. Cons. Clin. Psychol.*, 1973, 40, 33-38.

THOMSON, M. L. & SUTARMAN, The identification and enumeration of active sweat glands in man from plastic impressions of the skin. *Trans. Roy. Soc. Trop. Med. Hyg.*, 1953, 47, 412-417.

VAUGHAN, G. F. Children in hospital. *Lancet*, 1957, 272, 1117-1120.

VERNON, D. T. A. & BAILEY, W. C. The use of motion pictures in the psychological preparation of children for induction of anesthesia. *Anesth.*, 1974, 40, 68-72.

VERNON, D. T. A., FOLEY, J. M., SIPOWICZ, R. R., & SCHULMAN, J. L. *The Psychological Responses of Children to Hospitalization and Illness*. Springfield, Ill.: Charles C Thomas, 1965.

WIRT, R. D. & BROEN, W. E. *Booklet for the Personality Inventory for Children*. Minneapolis: Authors, 1958.

WHITE, W., AKERS, J., GREEN, J., & YATES, D. Use of imitation in the treatment of dental phobias in early childhood: A preliminary report. *J. Dent. Child.*, 1974, 26, 106.

8

COVERT MODELING, IMAGERY ASSESSMENT, AND ASSERTIVE BEHAVIOR

Alan E. Kazdin

The Pennsylvania State University

The purpose of the present investigation was (a) to examine the effect of two variables in developing assertive behavior using covert modeling and (b) to develop a technique to assess ongoing imagery during treatment. In a 2 × 2 design, the number of models imagined (imagining several models versus imagining a single model perform assertively) and model reinforcement (imagining favorable consequences following model behavior versus imagining no consequences) were combined. A nonassertive-model control group that imagined assertion-relevant scenes was included in the design. The results indicated that imagining multiple models or model reinforcement enhanced behavior change across self-report inventories and a behavioral role-playing test. Treatment effects transferred to novel role-playing situations and were maintained at a 4-month follow-up assessment. Assessment of imagery during the session corroborated the

Reprinted with permission from *Journal of Consulting and Clinical Psychology,* Vol. 43, No. 5, 1975, 716-724. Copyright 1975, American Psychological Association.

This research was supported by Grant MH23399 from the National Institute of Mental Health.

adherence of subjects to the imagery conditions to which they were assigned. However, subjects systematically introduced elaborations into the scenes. The data suggest the importance of assessing imagery in covert conditioning therapy studies.

Covert modeling is a therapy technique in which individuals imagine a model engage in the behaviors they wish to develop (Cautela, 1971). Recently, analogue studies have suggested that covert modeling is an effective technique (Kazdin, 1973, 1974a, 1974b, 1974c) that may be as effective as live modeling (Cautela, Flannery, & Hanley, 1974) in reducing subphobic levels of avoidance. Unfortunately, covert modeling has not been extensively evaluated with behaviors that more closely resemble clinical problems than do mild fears of college students. In one report (Kazdin, 1974d), covert modeling was effective in developing assertive behavior of clients carefully screened for inadequate social skills. Interestingly, the gains were maintained up to 3 months after treatment.

The present investigation extends previous work in developing assertive behavior with covert modeling and by evaluating parameters that may influence modeling effects. Specifically, two variables important in live modeling were evaluated including the number of models and the consequences that follow model behavior (Bandura, 1971; Rachman, 1972). In overt modeling, observing several models is superior to observing a single model (Bandura & Menlove, 1968). In addition, favorable consequences that follow model behavior enhance performance of the observer (Bandura, 1965; Bandura, Ross, & Ross, 1963). Previous analogue research has shown that imagining either multiple covert models or favorable consequences following model behavior tends to influence client performance (Kazdin, 1973, 1974a). The present investigation evaluated the separate and combined effects of multiple models and favorable model consequences in developing assertive behavior.

Aside from evaluating parameters of covert modeling, this study also developed a methodology to enhance evaluation of covert techniques in general. Assessing imagery is a problem for covert conditioning techniques. By their very nature, private events such as images are not readily accessible to the experimenter. Although the experimenter instructs the client to imagine specific material, there is no way to ensure that the client actually is imagining the events as presented. However, claims are frequently made about the crucial events that must be imagined to achieve behavior change via covert techniques. Depending on the specific technique, various events are assumed to be essential for behavior chance such as imagining a model (covert modeling) or reinforcing or punishing events after behavior (covert reinforcement and punishment, respectively). In fact, subjects may not consistently imagine the supposedly crucial ingredients of therapy. Informal reports sometimes reveal that imagined scenes depart from those presented verbally by the experimenter (Davison & Wilson, 1973; Weitzman, 1967). Assessment of imagery during treatment might help to determine whether subjects adhere to the scenes presented. The present investigation assessed ongoing imagery during treatment and evaluated compliance with specific imagery conditions and imaginal correlates of therapy outcome.

In summary, the purpose of the present investigation was twofold. First, the two parameters important in live modeling were examined in the context of covert modeling to develop assertive behavior. In a 2 × 2 design, the number of models (imagining a single covert model perform assertively across treatment sessions versus imagining several models) was combined with model reinforcement (imagining favorable consequences following covert model behavior versus no consequences). A nonassertive-model group was included in the design to control for imagining assertion-relevant scenes in the absence of an assertive model. The second purpose was to assess ongoing imagery during the therapy sessions. Tape-recorded narrations of imagery were analyzed across a number of dimensions.

METHOD

Subjects

Subjects were solicited from newspaper and telephone advertisements as well as by local posters offering free assertion training. Of the 74 individuals who responded, 54 participated in the project (24 females, 30 males). The participants ranged in age from 18 to 61 years (*Mdn* = 21 years). The subjects who participated met the screening requirements detailed below and submitted a refundable deposit ($10) to ensure their completion of the program.

Overview of Procedure

Individuals who responded to advertisements received an initial interview and were administered the assessment battery. Subjects were then assigned randomly to one of five treatment conditions administered individually in four therapy sessions. The stimulus material (covert modeling scenes) used in treatment was standardized across groups, varying only in the parameters under investigation, and presented on tape. During treatment the subjects described their ongoing imagery that was tape-recorded. Immediately after treatment and at a 4-month follow-up, the subjects were reassessed.

Assessment of Assertive Skills

Self-report. Four self-report pencil-and-paper measures assessed the extent to which subjects could assert themselves, refuse others, and cope with anxiety-provoking social situations. The measures included (a) the Conflict Resolution Inventory, (b) the Wolpe-Lazarus Assertive Training Scale, (c) the Rathus Assertiveness Schedule, and (d) the Willoughby Scale.

Behavioral role-playing test. After completing the self-report measures, a behavioral role-playing test was administered. The test required the subjects to respond spontaneously to prerecorded situations in which an assertive response would be appropriate (cf., McFall & Marston, 1970; Rehm & Marston, 1968). A subject was told to respond as if actually in the situation and to play the role of the person to whom the events were happening. At the end of the prerecorded situation, a bell signaled the subject to respond. All subjects' responses were recorded. Two sets of 10 role-playing situations were used. One of the sets was administered at pretest. At posttreatment, the pretest set was re-presented and followed by the new set of situations (that served as the generalization measure). The two sets were counterbalanced across subjects.

The primary dependent measure from the behavioral test was an assertiveness rating of the subject's role-playing responses (1 = not at all and 5 = very assertive). Additional measures included latency of response after the signal and the duration of the assertive response. These measures were derived from tape recordings after the experiment was terminated. Judges, unaware of the purpose of the study, rated the tapes in random order. The preassessment and postassessment data for a given subject were not on the same tape and were not rated in sequence. A final measure taken during the behavioral test was the subject's pulse rate measured by a Pulsemeter (2D16—Medical Systems Corporation) connected to the subject's left index finger.

Subject screening. To participate in the assertive training clinic, subjects had to meet at least two of the following requirements: (a) rate their lack of assertiveness as a "significant problem" (defined as 65 or greater on a scale in which 1 = no problem, 100 = very significant problem), (b) rate their assertiveness at the 25th percentile or lower relative to others in our culture, and (c) respond with a greater number of nonassertiveness than assertive responses on the 35 refusal items of the Conflict Resolution Inventory. Finally, each subject was not to reply assertively to more than one of the behavioral role-playing test situations at pretest. Global ratings of role-playing responses made at the time of assessment by a research assistant (1 = no response, 2 = inassertive, 3 = assertive) were used for *screening* only. Interrater agreement on the scoring of pretest behavioral responses was checked on four occasions across a total of 115 responses with perfect agreement for 90.4 percent of the responses. Of the initial clients, 20 failed to meet the screening requirements.

Follow-up. Approximately 4 months after treatment, the Conflict Resolution Inventory and the Wolpe-Lazarus scale were sent to each subject.

Covert Modeling Treatment Stimuli

Thirty-five treatment scenes were used during treatment. The scenes were prerecorded, and presentation was controlled by the therapist (with a remote on-off switch). Each scene consisted of three parts: (a) a description of the *context* and situation in which an assertive response was appropriate, (b) a *model* who made an assertive response, and (c) *favorable consequences* that resulted from the model's assertive response. The partitioning of scenes in this fashion permitted careful delineation of the experimental conditions. A typical scene is illustrated below:

> 1. The person (model) is eating in a restaurant with friends. He (she) orders a steak and tells the waiter he (she) would like it rare. When the food arrives the person begins to eat and apparently finds something wrong with the steak.
> 2. He (she) immediately signals the waiter. When the waiter arrives, the person says "I ordered the steak rare, and this one is medium. Please take it back and bring me one that is rare."
> 3. In a few minutes the waiter brings another steak and says he is very sorry this has happened.

Assessment of Imagined Scenes

A major purpose of the study was to assess aspects of the subjects' imagery as they imagined scenes in the treatment sessions. Subjects were instructed to verbalize or narrate the scene they were imagining aloud after the scene had been presented and clearly pictured. The verbalizations by the subjects while imagining the scenes were tape-recorded. The tapes subsequently were evaluated to assess the extent to which subjects adhered to the presented scenes and elaborated specific components of the scenes. Each scene was scored to assess the presence or absence of particular characteristics:* (a) *Scene components.* Three categories assessed whether the specific components of the scene were reported by the subject and whether the narrative was consistent with the scene as presented. The three components included the context, the model's assertive response, and whether favorable consequences followed model behavior. (b) *Elaboration of scene.* This measure assessed whether subjects elaborated or introduced additional descriptive material about the scene, model, or consequences, and (c) *completed scene.* The final measure assessed whether or not the subject was able to complete his description of the scene in the time allotted for imagery.

Treatment Conditions

Subjects were assigned randomly to one of five groups and to one of five therapists with the restriction that each therapist saw subjects in each condition. Graduate or senior undergraduate students (two females, three males) served as therapists. Treatment was administered individually in four sessions over a 2-week period. In the initial session, the therapist discussed the treatment rationale and required the subjects to practice imagining scenes in which a model similar in age and of the same sex was present. Practice material was unrelated to assertiveness but provided subjects with an opportunity to imagine scenes carefully, describe their imagery, and receive instructions and direction from the therapist.

In the first session, all subjects were told that the person imagined in the practice scenes was to be imagined in the treatment scenes. In subsequent sessions, all subjects imagined a practice scene that differed across experimental conditions, if the model was to be altered. Assertion training scenes followed the practice scenes in each session. Each scene was held for 35 seconds, beginning when the subject signaled that the image was

---

* Several additional variables other than those included here were assessed such as whether the subjects (a) imagined themselves being assertive (b) described feelings of the characters in the scenes (c) described the setting (d) described physical characteristics of people in the scenes and (e) repeated, continued, or altered the scene when it was imagined the second time. These variables did not yield significant results and are not detailed in this article.

clear. The scenes employed in each session were imagined twice. At the end of each session, subjects completed a questionnaire in which they rated their clarity of imagery, anxiety experienced during the session, the amount of the material presented that they could successfully imagine, and the various features of the model (e.g., age and sex).

The five groups included a 2 × 2 factorial combination of the number of models (imagining one model versus imagining four different models over the course of treatment) and model reinforcement (favorable consequences following model performances versus no consequences). A non-assertive-model control group was included in the design. Because previous research employing the assessment battery and screening requirements indicated no changes over time without treatment and a relatively limited number of subjects was available, a no-treatment group was not included in the design (Kazdin, 1974c, 1975). The following groups were employed.

Single model/reinforcement. Subjects (n = 11) imagined a person similar to themselves in age and of the same sex as the model in all treatment sessions. Prior to each session, subjects practiced imagining the same person at the beginning of the session. The scenes used in treatment consisted of the context in which an assertive response was appropriate, the model's assertive response, and favorable consequences following model performance.

Single model/no reinforcement. Subjects (n = 11) imagined the same model throughout treatment sessions as did the previous group. The treatment scenes employed for this group did *not* include the favorable consequences following model performance. Subjects received only the context and the model's assertive response in each scene.

Multiple models/reinforcement. Subjects (n = 11) imagined a *different* model in each treatment session. Across the four treatment sessions the models were similar in age and of the same sex, older and of the opposite sex, older and of the same sex, and similar in age and of the opposite sex, respectively. The scenes used in treatment consisted of the context, the model's assertive response, and favorable consequences.

Multiple model/no reinforcement. Subjects (n = 11) imagined a different model in each treatment session. The treatment scenes employed for this group did *not* include the favorable consequences. Only the context and the model's assertive response were presented.

Nonassertive-model/control. Subjects (n = 10) received only one portion of the treatment scenes, namely, the *context* in which an assertive response was appropriate. A person or model *was* imagined in the scene

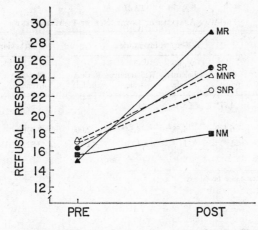

FIGURE 1. Mean refusal responses on the Conflict Resolution Inventory for single model/reinforcement (SR), single model/no-reinforcement (SNR), multiple model/reinforcement (MR), multiple model/no-reinforcement (MNR), and nonassertive-model control (NM) groups.

as the previous groups. However, *no assertive response* was made by the model *nor* did *consequences* follow performance. The person in the scene was imagined as part of the context (i.e., to whom an event occurred that provided impetus for an assertive response).

RESULTS

Treatment

Preliminary one-way analyses of variance indicated no differences among groups on any dependent measure at pretreatment nor significant differences at posttreatment resulting from therapists. Also, groups did not differ on the postsession questionnaires on rated clarity of imagery, anxiety experienced during the sessions, and in the amount of material presented that could be successfully imagined. With the exception of one dependent variable, mentioned below, sex of subject was not related to performance. Two-way analyses of covariance (using pretreatment performance as the covariate), Newman-Keuls comparisons including non-assertive-model controls, and within-group t-tests from pretreatment to posttreatment were employed to evaluate the data.

TABLE 1

Two-Way Analyses of Covariance at Posttreatment

Source	df	Self-report inventories				Behavior role-playing test		
		CRI refusal	Wolpe-Lazarus scale	Willoughby scale	Rathus schedule	Asser-tiveness	Latency	Duration
No. models (A)	1	4.77*	3.82	<1	<1	5.36*	<1	<1
Model reinforce-ment (B)	1	6.40*	4.58*	4.54*	2.00	7.39**	5.02*	1.95
A × B	1	<1	<1	<1	<1	3.32	2.83	<1
Error	39							

Note. CRI = Conflict Resolution Inventory.
* $p < .05$.
** $p < .01$.

Self-report inventories. The results for the two-way analyses of covariance for the major dependent variables appear in Table 1. The Conflict Resolution Inventory showed the effect of the number of models, and the Wolpe-Lazarus scale showed the effect of model reinforcement. Subjects who imagined several models rather than a single model or favorable consequences rather than no consequences were more assertive on both measures. The means for the Conflict Resolution Inventory data are presented in Figure 1. Multiple comparisons revealed that each covert modeling group differed from nonassertive-model controls.* Also, multiple model/reinforcement subjects were more assertive than all other groups. On the Wolpe-Lazarus scale, all groups except the single model/ no-reinforcement group were more assertive than nonassertive-model controls.

Analysis of Willoughby Scale responses also showed an effect of model reinforcement (see Table 1) indicating that imagining favorable consequences led to greater assertive behavior than imagining no consequences. Multiple comparisons indicated that all modeling groups were superior to nonassertive-model controls, but they did not differ from each other. The final self-report inventory, the Rathus Assertiveness Schedule, revealed no differences among treatment conditions.

Within-group increases in assertive behavior from pretreatment to posttreatment for the self-report inventories appear in Table 2. The *t*-tests indicated that covert modeling groups tended to show consistent

---

* All Newman-Keuls comparisons reported as significant met the .05 level of confidence.

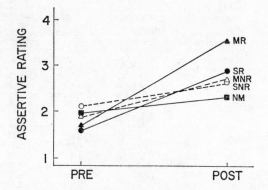

FIGURE 2. Mean assertive rating on the behavior role-playing test for single model/reinforcement (SR), single model/no-reinforcement (SNR), multiple model/reinforcement (MR), multiple model/no-reinforcement (MNR), and nonassertive-model control (NM) groups.

increases in assertive behavior across measures, whereas the nonassertive-model control group did not.

Behavior role-playing test. Responses to the behavior role-playing test were recorded and subsequently scored in random order across pretreatment and posttreatment. Two judges completed the ratings for assertiveness, latency, and duration of responses. Interjudge agreement was computed separately for each dependent variable. Ratings of assertiveness were made for each response (5 point scale: 1 = not at all, 5 = very assertive). The correlation between judges across 125 responses of 12 randomly selected subjects was .94. For latency and response duration, each situation was scored as an agreement if the estimate of both judges agreed within .5 or 1.0 seconds, respectively. A disagreement was scored if the estimate exceeded the criterion. Reliability was calculated as agreements divided by agreements plus disagreements and multiplied by 100 to form a percentage. Across 110 responses of 10 subjects, reliability was 87.3 percent for latency and 89.1 percent for duration.

For rated assertiveness, on the role-playing test both the number of models and model reinforcement were significant (see Table 1). The means for assertiveness ratings for each group appear in Figure 2. Each treatment group was more assertive at posttreatment than controls. Multiple model/reinforcement subjects were rated as more assertive than all other groups. Analysis of response latency revealed a significant effect of

TABLE 2

WITHIN-GROUP CHANGES FROM PRETEST TO POSTTEST ASSESSMENTS (t TESTS)

Response measure	Single model/ rein- forcement	Single model/ no rein- forcement	Group Multiple model/ reinforcement	Multiple model/no reinforcement	Nonassertive model
			Self-report		
Conflict resolution inventory	7.57***	4.40**	9.00***	4.42**	1.73
Wolpe-Lazarus scale	4.25**	4.00**	6.83***	5.30***	.97
Rathus schedule	1.62	2.49*	1.03	2.38	−1.77
Willoughby Scale	4.18**	3.31**	6.19***	3.19**	1.68
Assertive ability (self-rate)	4.47**	1.94	4.10**	4.20**	3.55**
Saying "no" (self-rate)	1.99	3.38**	2.44*	3.47**	1.63
Extent of problem (self-rate)	1.98	4.12**	2.79*	2.34*	2.37*
			Behavior role-playing test		
Assertiveness	7.66***	5.61***	11.25***	7.72***	2.29*
Response latency	2.82*	1.84	4.03**	3.07*	1.78
Response duration	2.61*	.95	3.61**	2.72*	.78
Pulse rate	2.67*	.61	2.25*	−.12	.34

* $p < .05$.
** $p < .01$.
*** $p < .001$.

model reinforcement with subjects imagining favorable model consequences showing a shorter response latency than nonreinforcement subjects (see Table 1). Only multiple model/reinforcement subjects were different from control subjects.

Analyses of response duration indicated no difference among treatment conditions. During the behavioral test, the pulse rate of the subjects was recorded immediately after a role-playing situation was presented. At posttreatment, groups did not differ in pulse rate.

Within-group changes on the behavior role-playing test (see Table 2) were evident for each of the treatment groups. Although the nonassertive-model control group improved in rated assertiveness, the change was markedly less than for the covert modeling groups. In any case, the within-group improvements were relatively consistent for the covert modeling groups.

Behavior role-playing test: Generalization. Subjects also responded to novel role-playing situations at posttreatment to determine whether treatment effects generalized. Performance on the novel situations was similar to performance on the previous retest situations. For ratings of assertiveness in the novel situation, significant effects were obtained for number of models, $F(1,39) = 10.22$, $p < .01$ model reinforcement, $F(1,39) = 8.68$,

$p < .01$, and the interaction, $F(1,39) = 4.90$, $p < .05$. The interaction resulted from the marked effect of favorable consequences for multiple-model subjects. Indeed, multiple model/reinforcement subjects were significantly greater in assertiveness than all other groups. Latency of responses to the novel role-playing situations yielded a significant effect of model reinforcement, $F(1,39) = 4.34$, $p < .05$, but no other effects. Reinforcement subjects showed a shorter latency than did nonreinforcement subjects. There were no differences among groups in response duration on the novel role-playing situation.

Global self-ratings. Subjects rated how assertive they were, the extent to which they could say "no" to others, and the degree to which saying "no" was a problem (each on a 1-100 point scale). Groups did not differ in global self-ratings. Each group improved on at least one of three global self-ratings (see Table 2). The only sex difference obtained in the investigation resulted from males rating themselves as having less of a problem in saying no at posttreatment than did females, $F(1,52) = 6.27$, $p < .05$.

Follow-Up

Four months after treatment, the Conflict Resolution Inventory and the Wolpe-Lazarus Assertive Training Scale were mailed to each subject. Thirty-eight (or 70.4 percent) of the subjects returned the questionnaires. Two-way analysis of variance of follow-up data (unweighted-means solution) yielded a significant effect of model reinforcement of the Conflict Resolution Inventory, $F(1,28) = 4.99$, $p < .05$. Reinforcement subjects were more assertive than nonreinforcement subjects. Both single model/reinforcement and multiple model/reinforcement subjects were significantly different from nonassertive-model controls, but they did not differ from each other. On the Conflict Resolution Inventory, within-group increases in refusal responses from pretreatment to follow-up were significant for single model/reinforcement, $t(8) = 2.32$, $p < .05$, multiple model/no-reinforcement, $t(7) = 5.18$, $p < .01$, multiple model/reinforcement, $t(8) = 8.36$, $p < .001$, and nonassertive-model control subjects, $t(5) = 3.16$, $p < .05$.

Although there were no differences among groups of the Wolpe-Lazarus scale, within-group improvements from pretreatment to follow-up were evident for single model/no-reinforcement, $t(5) = 5.72$, $p < .01$, multiple model/no-reinforcement, $t(7) = 3.31$, $p < .05$, multiple model/reinforcement, $t(8) = 3.68$, $p < .01$, and nonassertive-model control subjects, $t(5) = 3.93$, $p < .05$.

Within-Session Report of Imagery

Verbalizations of subjects during the treatment sessions while subjects were imagining the scenes were tape-recorded and evaluated by two judges (different from the judges who rated the role-playing test). Interobserver agreement was assessed by comparing agreements and disagreements for each scene across 200 scenes of 10 randomly selected subjects. An agreement was counted if observers' responses were identical for a specific category during a given scene. A disagreement was noted for non-identical scoring. Reliability was calculated by dividing agreements by agreements plus disagreements and multiplying by 100 to form a percentage. Reliability was 83.0 percent for whether subjects finished the scenes they were verbalizing, 93.2 percent for whether the model was described as asserting himself in the scenes, 88.6 percent for scoring whether the subject described consequences following model behavior, and 83.6 percent for whether the subject elaborated portions of the scenes.

Model assertiveness and consequences. One-way analyses of variance were completed across each variable. Significant differences among the groups were attained for the number of scenes in which an assertive model was included in the verbal description, $F(4,49) = 28.93$, $p < .001$. All treatment groups reported substantially more scenes with an assertive model than did nonassertive-model controls. Modeling groups did not differ from each other. This finding was expected because only the treatment groups were instructed to imagine an assertive model in the scenes. Groups also differed in their verbalizations of consequences following model behavior in the scenes, $F(4,49) = 68.87$, $p < .001$. The two reinforcement groups (not different from each other) more frequently reported consequences following model behavior relative to all other groups. This, too, was expected from implementation of the experimental manipulations. Overall, the within-session imagery data indicated that treatment conditions differed along experimentally manipulated dimensions as intended (i.e., whether an assertive model or favorable consequences were imagined).*

---

* Postsession questionnaire responses corroborated the within-session verbalizations. Questionnaire responses at the first and last sessions indicated that 90.9 percent and 95.5 percent of the model subjects, respectively, reported imagining an assertive model. In these sessions, 100 percent and 97.7 percent of the subjects, respectively, reported imagining a model appropriate in age and sex to their experimental condition. Also, 86.4 percent of the subjects (for the first and last sessions) indicated imagining consequences as appropriate to their experimental condition (i.e., favorable

Scene deviation and scene elaboration. Although subjects reported imagining material that closely adhered to the material presented, in a few instances subjects introduced material not associated with their condition. That is, subjects sometimes deviated from the condition to which they were assigned. For example, although nonassertive-model control subjects never were instructed to imagine an assertive model in the scenes, a mean of 8.9 percent of the scenes described included an assertive model. Similarly, although both groups included in the model/ no-reinforcement condition never were instructed to imagine favorable consequences, a mean of 6.2 percent of the scenes reported included favorable consequences. Overall, subjects followed the presented scenes but on some occasions added modeling material and consequences.

Aside from introducing ingredients associated with specific treatment conditions (e.g., assertive model behavior or model consequences), the verbalizations were evaluated for the extent to which subjects elaborated upon the scenes presented. Elaboration of the scenes referred to including "extra" descriptive material beyond the material presented. A two-way analysis of variance indicated that model/reinforcement subjects elaborated significantly more on the scenes presented than did nonreinforcement subjects, $F(1,40) = 6.70$, $p < .05$. Elaboration of the treatment scenes by the reinforcement subjects may explain why these subjects were scored as having completed their descriptions of fewer scenes during treatment than did nonreinforcement subjects, $F(1,40) = 6.30$, $p < .05$.

Imagery and Treatment Outcome

To evaluate the relationship between within-session verbalizations of imagery and behavior change, within-cell correlations (averaged by Fisher's z) were computed between verbalization measures and pre-post changes in assertiveness. In general, various features of imagery (e.g., describing feelings of the model or features of the setting) did not consistently relate to changes in assertive behavior. Similarly, postsession questionnaire self-ratings of clarity of imagery, anxiety while imagining treatment scenes, and amount of material that was successfully imagined did not reliably relate to increases in assertive behavior.

---

consequences or no consequences). For the nonassertive-model control subjects, 80 percent and 90 percent reported the model did not assert himself/herself during the first and last session, respectively. These results indicate that subjects reported adhering closely to the conditions to which they were assigned.

DISCUSSION

The results indicated that (a) imagining several models engage in assertive performance led to greater changes in assertive behavior than did imagining a single model, (b) imagining favorable consequences following model performance enhanced modeling effects, (c) imagining assertion-relevant scenes without an assertive model was not as consistently associated with changes in assertive behavior as were covert modeling conditions, (d) the gains effected with covert modeling transferred to novel role-playing situations and tended to be maintained for up to 4 months of follow-up on a self-report measure, and (e) the within-session reports of imagery were useful in determining the extent to which subjects adhered to the imagery conditions to which they were assigned and in revealing divergence from the scenes presented.

As expected, covert modeling groups showed consistently more assertive behavior than did nonassertive-model control subjects. Imagining multiple models and model reinforcement enhanced the effects of covert modeling. These findings are consistent with results from overt modeling (Bandura, 1971; Rachman, 1972). Favorable model consequences appeared to effect behavior change to a greater extent than did multiple models, as shown in the number of dependent variables affected and in within-group improvements from pretreatment to posttreatment assessment. These findings replicate earlier work on the effect of model consequences (Kazdin, 1975).

The present results suggest that variations of parameters of imagery influence behavior change. Future work can continue to explore features of imagery that can be manipulated to enhance treatment. However, an important priority for research is the use of direct comparative studies assessing the relative efficacy of procedures based on imagery alone with those based upon overt behavior (e.g., behavioral rehearsal). In various areas of treatment, both techniques based on imagery and overt rehearsal claim effectiveness. Some direct comparisons need to be made because there is suggestive evidence that symbolic rehearsal and imagery-based procedures are not as effective as overt behavioral rehearsal in altering behavior (e.g., Bandura, Blanchard, & Ritter, 1969). Comparative studies might reveal the priority with which imagery-based treatments should be accorded.

A major purpose of this study was to assess aspects of imagery during treatment. Within-session verbalizations were useful in determining whether subjects imagined specific features of the material presented.

Generally, subjects adhered closely to the imagery conditions to which they were assigned. However, verbalizations also revealed some changes from the scenes presented. Although the deviations were relatively infrequent, they are worth examining.

An interesting finding from the assessment of imagery was that model/reinforcement subjects added descriptive material to the treatment scenes to a greater extent than did nonreinforcement subjects. This finding leads to the interesting speculation that elaboration of scenes rather than model reinforcement mediated the superior performance on measures of assertiveness achieved by the reinforcement groups. The present investigation only raises this issue. Future research might profitably focus on manipulated and nonmanipulated aspects of imagery to determine more specific correlates of behavior change.

The extent to which scene deviation occurs in covert therapy investigations should always be determined. A failure of "different" treatment conditions to have different effects on behavior may result from relatively large subject deviations from the scenes presented. The actual imagery on the part of the subjects may make diverse experimental conditions less distinct than originally intended by the experimenter. In effect, subjects may imagine features that "alter" the treatment conditions to which they were assigned. Although this occurred infrequently in the present study, deviation from presented scenes has both methodological and substantive implications that need to be addressed.

REFERENCES

BANDURA, A. Influence of models' reinforcement contingencies on the acquisition of imitative responses. *J. Pers. Soc. Psychol.*, 1965, 1, 589-595.

BANDURA, A. Psychotherapy based upon modeling principles. In A. E. Bergin and S. L. Garfield (Eds.), *Handbook of Psychotherapy and Behavior Change*. New York: Wiley, 1971.

BANDURA, A., BLANCHARD, E. G., & RITTER, B. Relative efficacy of desensitization and modeling approaches for inducing behavioral, affective, and attitudinal changes. *J. Pers. Soc. Psychol.*, 1969, 13, 173-199.

BANDURA, A. & MENLOVE, F. L. Factors determining vicarious extinction of avoidance behavior through symbolic modeling. *J. Pers. Soc. Psychol.*, 1968, 8, 99-108.

BANDURA, A., ROSS, D., & ROSS, S. Vicarious reinforcement and imitative learning. *J. Abnorm. Soc. Psychol.*, 1963, 67, 601-607.

CAUTELA, J. R. Covert Modeling. Paper presented at the fifth annual meeting of the Association for the Advancement of Behavior Therapy, Washington, D. C., September 1971.

CAUTELA, J., FLANNERY, R., & HANLEY, E. Covert modeling: An experimental test. *Behav. Ther.*, 1974, 5, 494-502.

DAVISON, G. C. & WILSON, G. T. Processes of fear-reduction in systematic desensitization: Cognitive and social reinforcement factors in humans. *Behav. Ther.*, 1973, 4, 1-21.

KAZDIN, A. E. Covert modeling and the reduction of avoidance behavior. *J. Abnorm. Psychol.*, 1973, 81, 87-95.

KAZDIN, A. E. Comparative effects of some variations of covert modeling. *J. Behav. Ther. Exp. Psychiat.*, 1974, 5, 225-231. (a)

KAZDIN, A. E. Covert modeling, model similarity, and reduction of avoidance behavior. *Behav. Ther.*, 1974, 5, 325-340. (b)

KAZDIN, A. E. The effect of model identity and fear-relevant similarity on covert modeling. *Behav. Ther.*, 1974, 5, 624-635. (c)

KAZDIN, A. E. Effects of covert modeling and reinforcement on assertive behavior. *J. Abnorm. Psychol.*, 1974, 83, 240-252. (d)

KAZDIN, A. E. Effects of covert modeling, multiple models and model reinforcement on assertive behavior. *Behav. Ther.*, 1975.

MCFALL, R. M. & MARSTON, A. R. An experimental investigation of behavior rehearsal in assertive training. *J. Abnorm. Psychol.*, 1970, 76, 295-303.

RACHMAN, S. Clinical applications of observational learning, imitation, and modeling. *Behav. Ther.*, 1972, 3, 379-397.

REHM, L. P. & MARSTON, A. R. Reduction of social anxiety through modification of self-reinforcement: An instigation therapy technique. *J. Consult. Clin. Psychol.*, 1968, 32, 565-574.

WEITZMAN, B. Behavior therapy and psychotherapy. *Psychol. Rev.*, 1967, 74, 300-317.

Section III

BIOFEEDBACK AND OTHER STRATEGIES IN SELF-MANAGEMENT

Commentary

Self-control continues to be one of the most active and stimulating areas in behavior theory, research, and therapy. It is also one of the most controversial. The relevant clinical and experimental literature has increased dramatically, and, as in the case of cognitive research and therapy in behavior modification (see Section II), a new journal—*Biofeedback and Self-Regulation*—devoted exclusively to behavioral self-control, has been launched. As in the past volumes in this Series, the topic of self-control is not exclusive to this one particular Section that deals explicitly with it. It is a reflection of the great emphasis on self-control in behavior therapy that articles reprinted in other Sections could well have been included here (e.g., Bandura et al., Section II), and that much of the commentary throughout the book, particularly Section V, bears on the application of behavioral self-control principles to a variety of human problems.

Conceptual Issues

In his editorial to this new journal, *Biofeedback and Self-Regulation,* Stoyva (1976) identifies biofeedback as both a technology and a set of ideas, and places it in the broader context of self-regulation of behavior. However, he draws a distinction between biofeedback and other behavioral self-control techniques. The former, Stoyva argues, first modifies some physiological response and then considers the "experiential concomitants of such physiological modification" (p. 4). The latter are said

211

to assume that private events or symbolic processes can be altered directly through reinforcement methods.

A very different perspective on biofeedback is proposed by Richard Lazarus in the article in this Section. Particularly at odds with the strict operant conditioning model that has guided most biofeedback researchers is Lazarus' assertion that cognitive mediating processes are *causal* determinants of emotional responses and self-regulatory functions in general. However, his emphasis on "an active, striving, evaluating person at the helm" in self-control/biofeedback as in other learning and performance situations is a fundamental aspect of the social learning approach to behavior change (cf. Bandura, Section I, this volume; Thoresen & Mahoney, 1974). Although Lazarus does not make reference to it, the position that a person's cognitive appraisal of the events which affect him/her is decisive in determining the nature of his/her emotional response, is the very cornerstone of Ellis' (1962) system of rational-emotive therapy that has strongly influenced contemporary behavior therapy (cf. Franks & Wilson, 1973). Moreover, in quoting Schwartz on the importance of treating the "total person" with a multifaceted rather than a narrowly focused intervention program, Lazarus advocates an approach that is very much part of the clinical application of social learning principles (e.g., Franks & Wilson, 1975; Goldfried & Davison, 1976; O'Leary & Wilson, 1975).

Lazarus makes a useful distinction between the "direct action" and the "palliative" approach, categorizing biofeedback research and therapy as belonging within the latter. However, at the risk of being churlish, it is difficult to understand why the direct approach is then necessarily identified with "resolving . . . psychodynamic origins . . . of somatic turmoil." Although the palliative approach is "symptom" oriented as Lazarus suggests, it does not define behavior therapy. Behavior therapy emphasizes the multiple causes of behavior in attempting to modify, *where possible,* all the controlling variables and functional consequences of behavior disorders. Rather than viewed as a palliative alternative to more fundamental psychodynamic treatment, biofeedback might also be seen within the social learning model as an intervention that primarily reduces distress not by neutralizing controlling stimuli but by an exclusively response-directed program (Bandura, 1969). It is interesting to note that, in drawing this very distinction in terms of the therapeutic use of relaxation training, Bandura cautioned that sufficient relaxation might produce "temporary relief, but if the eliciting cues are absent (during relaxation, the client) will still remain vulnerable to the disturbing stimuli because their arousing properties have in no way been altered" (p. 478). The implication of this position is that biofeedback would be optimally used within an integrated, multifaceted social learning treatment program.

In sum, Richard Lazarus offers a stimulating paper that will provide an impetus towards investigating still more challenging theoretical questions and developing even more effective therapy methods. With the recent emphasis within behavior therapy on the notion of "coping"— the use of coping models and the teaching of generalizable coping skills —it might be well to explore Lazarus' considerable research on this topic, only briefly touched on in the article reprinted here.

Stoyva's distinction reflects the increasingly apparent schism between a narrow applied behavior analysis viewpoint and the broader social learning framework articulated by Bandura. The investigation and application of self-regulatory processes are fundamental features of this social learning framework, and among self-regulatory phenomena the concept of self-reinforcement plays a prominent role. In a recent article, however, Catania (1975), echoing many of the objections raised by Rachlin (1974), claims that self-reinforcement is a "myth" and tries to reinterpret it out of existence by finding external sources of reinforcement to account for observed effects. The implications of this view are far-reaching, and as Bandura (in press) points out in a specific commentary on this controversy, "in the final analysis, it is not the legitimacy of self-reinforcement but the nature of reinforcement itself that is in question." A detailed discussion of this important dialogue will be deferred until next year's volume and the publication of Bandura's (in press) response so that the issues can be presented and considered in their entirety.

Ainslie (1975) has provided a comprehensive and scholarly discussion of impulsiveness and self-control in the literature of economics, sociology, psychiatry, and different psychological perspectives. Impulsiveness is defined as the choice of a small, immediate reward in preference to a larger, delayed reward; impulse control is the ability to overlook the small-immediate reward that Ainslie calls "specious" with respect to the larger-delayed reward. According to Ainslie, the "majority of behavior therapists writing about impulsiveness have appealed to common knowledge of what it is and have not discussed even tangentially their assumptions about it" (p. 469).

In a far-reaching, provocative theoretical account, Ainslie attempts to explain the phenomenon of impulsiveness and its control in a consistent behavioral (operant) framework. Specifically, he appeals to the explanatory power of theoretical functions describing the decline in effectiveness of rewards as they are delayed from the time of choice between pairs of small-immediate and larger-delayed rewards. A little mentioned paper by Mowrer and Ullman (1945) is credited as having been the first explicit model of impulsiveness, showing that the effectiveness of reward is discounted as it is delayed. Rats were shocked if they ate food within 3 seconds after it became available. If the shock occurred after 3 seconds the rats learned not to eat too soon; but if the shock were delayed up to 12 seconds, the rats usually ate too soon and were shocked. This model was incomplete, however, because it failed to describe how more important but delayed consequences ever come to control behavior. The additional explanation, Ainslie argues, is provided by recent parametric choice experiments with rats that have generated the theoretical functions that predict reliable changes in choice between alternative rewards as a function of time (Rachlin & Green, 1972—reprinted in Franks & Wilson, 1973).

In emphasizing commitment strategies, decided well in advance of choice conflicts, to overcome impulsiveness, Ainslie presents little that was not discussed—at least in principle—by Rachlin (1974). In suggesting how individuals can engage in gratification-delaying behavior on their own without any other environmental intervention, Ainslie advocates that the person group sets of large-delayed rewards together because theoretically this makes them more resistant to specious rewards, even if the latter are grouped into sets, too. "Sets may be created when a person perceives his own current choice behavior as a cue predicting similar preferences in the future. Because a person who perceives himself rejecting one delayed reward in a set thereby gets a cue predicting that he will not obtain any of the delayed rewards in the set, he may come to weigh the whole set of immediate rewards at each choice point" (p. 492). In true operant fashion, Ainslie argues that "there is no need to assume that consciousness is necessary for gratification delaying behavior" (p. 475). He suggests that if appropriate commitment strategies that succeed in securing the larger-delayed reward occur on a trial and error basis, it could be expected that they would be learned on this basis alone. But, at best, this is an incomplete explanation. The consistent reference to the person grouping, perceiving, and comparing behaviors and their anticipated consequences inevitably portrays the individual attempting to exercise self-control as an actively aware initiator and appraiser of his/her interactions with the environment (see Bandura, Section I; Lazarus, this Section).

From a clinical viewpoint, Ainslie's speculations appear to be rather vague. It is never made clear how an individual who lacks impulse control can be taught to acquire it, when or how one "groups sets of delayed-rewards together." Although subsequent research might begin to provide answers to these questions, current clinical application of self-control strategies (e.g., Thoresen & Mahoney, 1974) would not be altered in any way on the basis of Ainslie's behavioral theory.

Unlike Ainslie, Meichenbaum (1975) prefers a cognitive theory of self-control, stating that "the role and significance attributed to the client's cognitions seem to be the fulcrum that truly distinguishes the various clinical approaches" (p. 4). The different ways in which cognitions have been conceptualized—as behaviors (the homogeneity assumption), faulty belief systems, and as problem solving and coping skills— are usefully summarized. However, Meichenbaum's three-stage theory does not add appreciably to his important previous contributions to the self-control literature.

The first stage is one of self-observation in which the client becomes aware of specific thoughts, feelings, and behaviors; in the second stage self-observation becomes the occasion for emitting thoughts and behaviors that are incompatible with previous maladaptive behavior; and in the third stage—that is said to determine generalization and maintenance— the client develops new self-statements and/or images about his behavior change. The critical question is how the second stage works, and Meichenbaum, emphasizing its complexity, sketches some possibilities. Thus, cognitive self-instructions are postulated to function as interpersonal instructions, to reduce egocentrism, to alter attentional behaviors, and relabel physiological arousal. Greater precision and more detail are necessary before we can talk meaningfully about a "theory" of self-control.

Biofeedback and Relaxation Training

The second article reprinted in this Section, by Cox, Freundlich and Meyer, describes a comparative outcome study of the efficacy of EMG feedback in the treatment of tension headaches. Among the distinguishing features of this study are the use of motivated clients from the general population rather than the college student volunteers, a broad range of relevant dependent measures and the inclusion of a four-month follow-up. On the negative side, however, no data are reported attesting to the adequacy of the medication placebo group in controlling for factors extraneous to the two specific techniques under investigation (see Section

II). Consequently, although both relaxation methods were significantly superior to the placebo condition, and despite the fact that they appear to have produced substantial improvement, particularly at follow-up, caution must be had in attributing these positive clinical outcomes to the specific behavioral techniques per se.

The pattern of Cox et al.'s results was duplicated by Haynes, Griffin, Mooney, and Parise (1975). Both EMG feedback and progressive relaxation were superior to a no-treatment control group in decreasing tension headaches, but did not differ from each other. Particularly encouraging is the fact that treatment gains appear to have persisted at a 5-7-month follow-up.

Tape-recorded progressive relaxation training was compared to non-continuous biofeedback therapy and a no-therapy control group in the treatment of essential hypertension (Shoemaker & Tasto, 1975). Results showed that muscle relaxation training produced the most change, significantly lowering both diastolic and systolic blood pressure as the six treatment sessions progressed. Biofeedback did produce lower diastolic blood pressure, to a lesser degree, but failed to influence systolic pressure significantly. The control group had little effect. Shoemaker and Tasto conclude that their findings justify including relaxation training in the treatment of hypertension. They discuss how it might be optimally combined with biofeedback in certain instances, and emphasize the importance of helping patients develop effective relaxation skills that generalize from the laboratory to the natural environment.

Coursey (1975) compared EMG feedback as a relaxation technique to two control treatments using normal college students as subjects. In one of these control groups subjects were told to relax, but were not given any specific instructions about how to relax, nor any feedback. The other group was given brief instructions about relaxation, without any feedback. Following seven 21-minute treatment sessions over a two-week period, the results showed that the feedback group registered significantly lower EMG scores than the control groups. A number of self-report measures of anxiety and relaxation failed, in general, to indicate differences among the three groups. Praiseworthy further analysis showed that EMG feedback training, while statistically significant, was not substantively so, accounting for only 18 percent of the variance during the final testing session. As Coursey points out, this is disappointing given that the dependent measure was the EMG of the same muscle used for feedback during training and that subjects were receiving feedback during the final measurement session. There was minimal evidence of generalized relaxation across other body muscle groups.

Reinking and Kohl (1975) examined the comparative effects of four types of relaxation training programs: a) Jacobson's (1938) progressive relaxation method; b) EMG feedback; c) progressive relaxation plus EMG feedback; and d) EMG feedback plus a monetary reward. A no-treatment control group completed the study that employed normal college students as subjects. All four relaxation training groups showed significantly lower EMG responses than the control group following training. However, the EMG feedback groups were superior to the progressive relaxation group. Whereas the latter condition produced a reduction in muscle tension level of 50 percent over the 12 training esssions, the EMG groups decreased tension levels by almost 90 percent during the same period. In view of the difficulty in producing substantive relaxation with Jacobson's method, Reinking and Kohl point out that studies that have previously included this form of relaxation training (usually analogue desensitization research), and which did not include an independent assessment of the degree of relaxation induced, might not have provided a valid test of the presumed effects of relaxation training.

The apparently superior efficacy of EMG relaxation training in this study is not consistent with the Cox et al., Haynes et al. (1975), and Shoemaker and Tasto (1975) studies described earlier in this Section. The difference may be ascribed to the use in the latter three studies of motivated clients with clinical problems. Overall it can be concluded that EMG feedback training has not been demonstrated to be more effective than the simpler progressive relaxation procedure which has the added advantage of not requiring specialized and often expensive technology.

Pertinent to this discussion is Coursey's (1975) clinical observation that EMG feedback may, on occasion, be a self-defeating technique that is not necessarily the treatment of choice with all highly anxious neurotic clients. He notes that some subjects seem to work actively at attaining the goal of relaxation, a goal-oriented striving that overly tense people might already overuse. Both Lazarus and Cox et al. similarly remark upon the possibility of subject variables moderating the effect of biofeedback training. The latter, for example, state that obsessive-compulsive characteristics often introduce a performance anxiety that interferes with the relaxation response. In these instances they suggest the use of relaxation procedures lacking an overt achievement criterion. Indicating the increasing sophistication and specification of behavioral treatment methods, Coursey echoes Paul (1967) in framing the critical question: "What sort of relaxation technique is effective with what sort of people with what sort of problems in conjunction with what other procedures?" (p. 833). In fact, Schwartz (in press) has recently proposed a model in which different relaxation techniques would be appropriate for different anxiety problems depending on the modality of the latter (cognitive or somatic). Moreover, in addition to cognitive versus somatic types of relaxation techniques, Schwartz suggests that the degree to which they are predominantly active or passive techniques might be important. It is precisely this latter point to which both Cox et al. and Coursey (1975) addressed themselves.

Feedback-assisted relaxation training has been used in the experimental treatment of chronic alcoholics (Steffen, 1975). When compared to an attention-placebo condition, EMG-induced relaxation treatment resulted in significantly lower muscle tension levels, greater reductions in reports of subjective disturbance, and lower blood alcohol levels. However, objectively measured alcohol consumption showed no difference between the relaxation and placebo treatments. The small sample size and the inconsistent findings make it difficult to interpret these results.

Progressive relaxation training is one of the most widely used behavioral techniques. Accordingly, some cautionary comments on its optimal use might be noted. Some of the studies reviewed above administered tape-recorded relaxation training. However, some investigators have claimed that tape-recorded relaxation training may be less effective than its use by a live therapist (e.g., Bernstein & Borkovec, 1973). It is possible that this may have been a factor in the failure to obtain substantially lower muscle tension levels in the Reinking and Kohl (1975) study. Moreover, progressive relaxation involves at least two different components. In omitting systematic tension-release exercises, and concentrating solely on instructions to focus on and relax away tension, many practitioners might be inappropriately applying a less effective method. Within the context of a research program on the treatment of sleep disturbance, Borkovec, Kaloupek, and Slama (1975) demonstrated that the full progressive relaxation procedure was significantly more effective than a truncated condition that did not include muscle tension-release instructions. The credibility of these findings is greatly strengthened through the clever use of counterdemand instructions to rule out factors unrelated to the relaxation technique being evaluated (Steinmark & Borkovec, 1974—reprinted in Franks & Wilson, 1975). Parenthetically, Borkovec et al., finding that improvement continued over a five-month follow-up replicated previous results from this laboratory, and indicate that progressive relaxation is an effective treatment for moderate insomnia.

Biofeedback: Modification of Gastrointestinal and Cardiovascular Responses

Welgan's article, reprinted in this Section, describes the successful modification of gastric acid secretion in patients with duodenal ulcers. An interesting feature of this study is the absence of immediate feedback about the nature of the acid secretions. Welgan addresses this issue in his discussion of the results, concluding that the duration of the gastric response can be long enough to permit conditioning to occur. Of course, this concern over the possibility that the temporal parameters of conditioning were violated is predicated on the assumption that visceral learning is best accounted for within a conditioning model. Lang (1974), however, has suggested that an operant conditioning model is not adequate to accommodate the phenomena of visceral learning, and has proposed a human skills learning model as an alternative interpretation. (See Shapiro & Surwit, 1976, for a discussion of theoretical mechanisms in the learned control of physiological functions).

The modification of human gastric acid secretion was also investigated by Whitehead, Renault, and Goldiamond (1975). In contrast to Welgan's study, Whitehead et al. used normal, volunteer subjects; coupled visual feedback with money reinforcers; and, with improved technology, provided subjects with immediate feedback of intragastric pH. A differential-reinforcement-of-high rates-schedule (DRH) produced a threefold increase in rate of secretion in three of the four subjects. A differential-reinforcement-of-other-behaviors schedule (DRO) resulted in a return to baseline in the rate of secretion in these three subjects. The fourth subject was unaffected by the DRH schedule. An attempt to establish stimulus control of differential rates of acid secretion in one of the three responding subjects was unsuccessful. Concurrent physiological measurement of heart rate, respiration, and gastric motility showed that these functions were not consistently correlated with acid secretions across subjects, although individual subjects indicated sizeable correlations between acid secretion and one or other physiological response.

Although the DRO schedule did not decrease the target response below baseline levels, Whitehead et al. reject the idea that this contingency was ineffective and that the decrease in secretion simply represented an extinction effect. This assertion is based on the observation that one of the subjects showed no decrease in rate of acid secretion following an 11-day interruption during the DRH sequence. The authors similarly argue that this subject's data provide informal evidence of the maintenance of learned control over gastric acid secretion. This latter reasoning is tenuous at best, but the general picture presented by Whitehead et al.'s and Welgan's findings strongly suggest that biofeedback may be an important technique in the treatment of duodenal ulcers.

Penile tumescence to erotic stimuli has been shown to be significantly inhibited by instrumental conditioning procedures (Rosen, 1973). In a more recent paper, Rosen, Shapiro, and Schwartz (1975) compared two groups of normal subjects: one received analogue visual feedback and money reinforcement for increases in penile diameter; the other received no feedback, noncontingent reward, and the same instructions to maximize erections in the absence of erotic stimulation. Although both groups were able to increase penile tumescence voluntarily, the feedback/ reward group showed significantly improved performance over trials.

Perhaps more important than the confirmation that penile tumescence is susceptible to biofeedback procedures is Rosen et al.'s observation of two apparently distinctive patterns of psychophysiological mediation of erection. Concurrent heart rate and respiration measurements showed a "tension" pattern in some subjects, marked by noticeable cardiac acceleration, irregular respiration, and variable penile responsiveness. Other subjects displayed a "relaxation" pattern marked by stable heart rate, regular respiration, and smooth penile tumescence response. Rosen et al. suggest that the "tension" pattern reflected a reaction to the performance demands of the situation, an inability to remain calm and relaxed, and speculate that this pattern of autonomic response might be a precursor to a sexual dysfunction such as premature ejaculation. They caution that feedback procedures of this kind are probably contraindicated in the treatment of erectile problems in highly anxious individuals who might well be prone to the "tension" pattern. The same clinical caveat about biofeedback methods has been issued by other workers, as discussed above.

Using an ABCB single-subject methodology with a primarily homosexual, impotent male, Herman and Prewett (1974) found that penile tumescence to slides of both male and female nudes increased during contingent feedback about tumescence and decreased during noncontingent feedback. Increased masturbation, more active sexual fantasies, and reports of sexual arousal outside of the laboratory accompanied treatment phases in which penile tumescence increased. However, Barlow, Agras,

Abel, Blanchard, and Young (1975) failed to find evidence that biofeedback is an effective treatment for producing clinically significant increases in heterosexual arousal. Of three homosexual patients who received treatment, two showed no effect of feedback on penile tumescence during treatment or generalization sessions. Significant increases in erection were noted in the third patient, but this improvement persisted despite the withdrawal of feedback in a single-subject design. Barlow et al. concluded that some other source of influence, such as simple exposure to heterosexual stimuli that has been shown to produce enhanced heterosexual arousal (Herman, Barlow, & Agras, 1974) may have been responsible for the observed effects. They caution against drawing premature conclusions about the causal properties of therapeutic interventions such as biofeedback on the basis of uncontrolled case studies.

Nunes and Marks (1975) supplemented the treatment of 10 women with small animal phobias with feedback of their true heart rate during in vivo exposure sessions. Each of 2-4 treatment sessions consisted of four ½ hour periods, half of which included visual heart rate feedback plus instructions to lower heart rate. Any substantial movement of heart rate in the desired direction met with therapist praise. In addition, auditory feedback was used with four of the patients. Although heart rate was reduced significantly during feedback-instructions, self-report measures of anxiety, all of which decreased over treatment, indicated no difference between feedback and non-feedback periods. The authors point out that it would be premature to conclude that feedback that reduces autonomic arousal during participant modeling is of no value, given the brevity of treatment and the unfortunate omission of an objective behavioral index of performance.

Blanchard, Young, and Haynes (1975) described a simple feedback system, based on closed circuit television, for the treatment of elevated blood pressure. Systolic blood pressure was successfully lowered to the normal range in four hypertensive or borderline hypertensive patients. Single-subject methodology indicated that the combination of instructions and feedback was the effective change agent. No data on generalization beyond the laboratory setting were provided.

Finally, two systematic case reports of problems that have proved resistant to modification were published this last year. Blanchard and Haynes (1975)—reprinted in Section X—reported the successful treatment of a patient with moderate but longstanding Raynaud's disease with a biofeedback method based on finger tip surface temperature. The use of an ABAB design enabled the authors to attribute change to the feedback procedure per se. Johnson and Turin (1975) also described the use of peripheral temperature feedback in effectively treating an individual suffering from migraine.

Self-Monitoring, Self-Reinforcement, and Self-Instruction

The fourth article in this Section, by Turkewitz, O'Leary and Ironsmith, is a systematic replication and extension of previous findings on the critically important topics of the generalization and maintenance of behavior change in the classroom (cf. Drabman, Spitalnik, & O'Leary, 1973—reprinted in Franks & Wilson, 1974). The demonstration that children maintained the low levels of disruptive behavior produced by a token economy for as long as 28 days, during which they self-imposed performance standards, strongly attests to the utility of these self-control procedures. Of considerable theoretical importance is the fact that this adherence to self-determined performance standards was maintained despite the fact that the children clearly knew that they could discard performance contingencies and freely reward themselves with impunity. Indeed, the children verbalized the understanding that they could "be bad" when external consequences were withdrawn. The possibility that subjects in previous research of a similar nature could not discriminate the presence or absence of externally-administered consequences made it difficult to unequivocally attribute outcome to the operation of self-reinforcement (cf. Franks & Wilson, 1974). Turkewitz et al. usefully discuss some reasons why the children refrained from engaging in unmerited self-reward during the no-backup phase, and point out how the development of a particular self-evaluative/self-reinforcing function does not ensure that it will be activated in different circumstances, i.e., the failure to obtain generalization to the regular classroom. This issue is elaborated by Bandura, Mahoney, and Dirks (1976).

The clinical utility of self-monitoring is further suggested by an uncontrolled but informative study by Zimmerman and Levitt (1975). Enlisting the cooperation of a wide range of therapists, they arranged to have clients systematically count a specific problem behavior and record it on a daily data sheet. The clients, whose diagnoses ranged from psychotic to various neurotic types, were provided specific guidelines on what, when, and how to self-monitor. Of the 22 clients involved, eight reported definite behavior change, and 14 indicated that they had gained important awareness and/or understanding about their problems. As the authors point out, this simple behavioral procedure that can be therapeutically reactive, adds precision to the assessment process and has the benefit of actively involving clients in their own behavior change. The reactivity of self-monitoring is influenced by several variables. Using an analogue research situation, Nelson, Lipinski, and Black (1975) investigated the effects of expectancy on the reactivity of self-monitoring of face-touching by college students. Trained, unobtrusive observers provided reliability checks of students' self-monitoring. Nelson et al.'s results showed a) that the process was reactive in that face-touching decreased; b) that self-recording was less reliable when subjects were unaware that reliability checks were being made, thereby replicating Romanczyk, Kent, Diament, and O'Leary's (1973—reprinted in Franks & Wilson, 1974) results with trained behavioral observers of other people's behavior; and c) that face-touching decreased irrespective of differential expectancies about outcome.

In a second study, Lipinski, Black, Nelson, and Ciminero (1975) found that reliable self-recording is increased if differentially reinforced. This increment in reliability did not produce a concomitant increase in reactivity. The independence between reliability and reactivity has been noted previously (Thoresen & Mahoney, 1974). The specificity of verbal feedback appeared not to effect reliability of students' face-touching behavior. Finally, Lipinski et al. showed that self-monitoring of number of cigarettes smoked over a four-week period resulted in a significant decrease in a group motivated to stop smoking but not in a group that was unmotivated to stop (see also, Commentary, Section IV).

In another demonstration of the positive behavior change potential of self-monitoring, Richards (1975a) found that self-monitoring added significantly to a self-control procedure for improving study skills in college students. Students monitored the number of pages read and hours studied on a daily basis, and plotted cumulative graphs of these data that were turned in to the therapist each week. Self-control methods were, in general, more effective than control procedures in increasing study skills. Frederiksen (1975) reported the successful treatment of ruminative thinking by an intensive self-monitoring procedure.

Self-instructional training has been shown to be effective in modifying a diverse range of behaviors in both adults and children (cf. Mahoney, 1974; Meichenbaum, 1973). Specifically, Meichenbaum and Goodman (1971) used self-instructional training in teaching impulsive children to alter their response style on standardized tests. In an extension of this research with children with writing deficiencies Robin, Armel, and O'Leary (1975) compared three treatment groups: a) direct training feedback and praise for each letter copied; b) self-instructions plus direct training—with the self-instructional procedure a slightly modified version of Meichenbaum and Goodman's method; and c) no treatment. The results showed that self-instruction was more effective than direct training, and that both treatments were superior to the control group. A generalization test to letters on which the children had not been trained showed no difference between the three groups. This failure to obtain generalization is particularly disappointing in view of Meichenbaum's (1973) conceptualization of self-instruction as a generalizable, cognitive skill.

The fact that the correlation between percent correct performance and the number of self-instructions emitted is nonsignificant and negative is theoretically puzzling. This absence of an association is inconsistent with a mediational explanation of the effects of self-instructions. The authors suggest that other subtle influences, possibly therapist enthusiasm expressed in the quality of social reinforcement, might have been responsible for the superiority of self-instructional training. Of great clinical interest is Robin et al.'s conclusion that, while statistically effective, self-instruction "may be impractical for routine use at the present time" (p. 178). Specifically, the authors comment that it was extremely difficult to teach the children self-instruction. Children would condense instructions into one word, uttered rapidly, and often not in coordination with the motor, writing response. At the end of treatment 85 percent of all verbalizations were still being prompted, seriously calling into question the degree to which the procedure can be classified as self-control. Another problem is the fact that the time required to work on self-instructional training decreased time available for writing practice. And lastly, the authors query whether a teacher in most classrooms could allow self-instructing aloud without disrupting the classroom as a whole. The latter was a particular difficulty since the therapists were unable to train the children to verbalize covertly as Meichenbaum and Goodman reported. In assessing the extent of these practical difficulties it must be remembered that self-instruction accounted for only 17 percent of the variance of behavior change. Accordingly, Robin et al. conclude that before claims for the efficacy of self-instructional training with children can be taken seriously, "more research is needed concerning both the mediational effects of self-instructions with clinical behaviors and the additional time required for teachers and therapists to get children to appropriately self-instruct" (p. 186).

SECTION III: BIOFEEDBACK AND OTHER
STRATEGIES OF SELF-MANAGEMENT

9

A COGNITIVELY ORIENTED
PSYCHOLOGIST LOOKS AT
BIOFEEDBACK

Richard S. Lazarus
University of California, Berkeley

Feedback is without a doubt one of the most profound and unifying
concepts in all the behavioral sciences. It is fundamental in biological
adaptation, being the basis of natural selection and evolution. Feedback
from the environment about the consequences of one's acts provides the
rewards and punishments that are in part responsible for learning. Maintenance of homeostasis and the neurohumoral regulation of behavior
also operate through feedback loops; the brain is, among other things, a
great feedback or servomechanism system. Social psychology too makes
use of feedback principles in viewing the interaction of persons—social
reactions feed back and modify the behavior of each party to a social
interaction. Biofeedback is a special case, referring to information the
person receives about his bodily processes. Whether and how this information may be used to regulate such processes is not yet fully
understood.

Current research in biofeedback brings together under a single rubric

Reprinted with permission from *American Psychologist*, Vol. 30, No. 5, May, 1975,
553-561. Copyright 1975, American Psychological Association.

The article is based on an invited address presented at the annual meeting of the
Biofeedback Research Society at Colorado Springs, Colorado, February 15, 1974.

a group of psychologists with very diverse objectives and interests. For some, the fundamental issue of such research is whether or not visceral reactions can be controlled through a "pure" process of operant conditioning, pure in the sense that it is said not to depend on any of several types of mediation, including extraneous cues, perceptual or cognitive process, internal muscular or respiratory ones, and so on. You realize I have in mind here the recent debate between Katkin and Murray (1968) and Crider, Schwartz, and Shnidman (1969). For still others, a key virtue of biofeedback consists of the practical possibilities it affords for the amelioration of diseases of adaptation, for example, tension headaches, hypertension, and so on (Schwartz, 1973). There is still some uncertainty about the practical potential of biofeedback procedures in the control of autonomic end-organ responses, as evidenced by Blanchard and Young's (1973) review of such work with cardiovascular measures; recent research on alpha rhythm by Lynch, Paskewitz, and Orne (1974); and an article by Miller (in press). However, my purpose is not to rehash such issues, nor to review biofeedback research or its use in clinical practice. Rather, I want to embed biofeedback research and clinical practice in what I see as a larger context, namely, adaptation and emotion. Many of the points I make here are much in accord with the valuable comments and analyses made recently by Schwartz (1973), though I was not aware of his article when I prepared this paper.

Biofeedback processes are important for three main reasons: First, the recognition that bodily processes can be volitionally regulated, even if only to a small extent, is a corrective to the partially erroneous classical position in which voluntary regulation was opposed to involuntary or autonomic regulation (Schwartz, 1973). I shall say no more about this here. Second, biofeedback seems to offer an informational aid to the person in his quest for the self-regulation of his bodily processes, particularly those that get in the way of successful behavioral adaptation or result in "diseases of adaptation." Third, biofeedback research could throw light on important theoretical and practical questions about the diverse psychological processes by which people regulate their emotional lives and how well these processes work.

In this article, there are three main, interrelated themes: (a) The somatic reactions with which biofeedback deals are really part of a much broader set of issues, namely, those related to the stress emotions and their role in human adaptation; (b) emotional processes and their self-regulation are products of mediating cognitive appraisals about the significance of an event for a person's well-being; and (c) the control of somatic processes is an integral aspect of emotional states and their self-regulation. Indeed, this self-regulation is going on all the time in day-to-day living and is accomplished through a variety of mechanisms whose workings, determinants, and consequences are badly in need of understanding. The first theme is merely an obvious assertion that requires no further elaboration, while the second and third have to do with the nature of emotions and their regulation, and hence form the crux of the argument in the remainder of the article.

COGNITIVE PROCESSES AND EMOTION

If indeed the somatic reactions dealt with in biofeedback research and therapy are aspects of emotion and adaptation, then we must consider what an emotional state is and how it is brought about and regulated. From my theoretical perspective (Lazarus, 1966, 1968; Lazarus, Averill, & Opton, 1970), the various emotions arise from and reflect the nature of a person's or animal's ongoing adaptive commerce or transactions with his environment. Each of us has special personality attributes (e.g., motives, belief systems, and competencies to cope with environmental pressures) that shape our reactions and the way we interpret and arrange these transactions.

I define and analyze emotion as a complex disturbance that includes three main components: subjective affect, physiological changes related to species-specific forms of mobilization for adaptive action, and action impulses having both instrumental and expressive qualities. The somatic disturbance arises from the impulse to act that, in part, defines biologically the particular emotion. The quality and intensity of the emotion and its action impulse all depend on a particular kind of cognitive appraisal of the present or anticipated significance of the transaction for the person's well-being. Four kinds of appraisal are critical to the emotional response, namely, that the transaction is damaging, threatening (implying the likelihood of future damage), productive of positive well-being, or challenging (implying the likelihood of overcoming obstacles in the pursuit of something). In lower animals, such as those studied by Tinbergen, the evaluative or appraisal feature of the emotion-eliciting perception is very concrete, simple, and built into the nervous system. In higher animals, such as man, symbolic thought processes and learning play a predominant role.

The historically oriented reader will recognize that this viewpoint is a specific version of numerous earlier and current attempts to develop a

metatheory of psychological activity and behavior in cognitive-phenomenological terms. It contains recognizable elements of William James
for whom emotion involved an evaluative perception, the field theoretical
approach of Lewin, and the more recent cognitive outlooks of theoreti-
cians such as Tolman, Heider, Murray, Rotter, and a current group of
attribution theorists such as Weiner (1972). Thus, cognitive approaches
are certainly not new. Bolles (1974), in summarizing the historical trend
of cognitive viewpoints, points out that psychology has always been more
or less cognitive in outlook. It has only rather recently turned to mechanistic philosophy, and for only a brief interlude in the overall history
of the field. Bolles thinks that psychology has begun to turn around
from its brief flirtation with a mechanistic approach to behavior and
that it has returned to a cognitive orientation.

In regard specifically to emotion, a cognitive-phenomenological approach was evident in the earlier writings on stress of Grinker and
Spiegel (1945) in which the term *appraisal* appeared, though somewhat
unsystematically, and in the more recent writings of Arnold (1960), who
used the term quite systematically in her analysis of emotion. The relatively recent resurgence of cognitive approaches to emotion is also
illustrated by the Loyola Symposium on Feelings and Emotions (see
Arnold, 1970), a follow-up of two earlier ones, the Wittenberg Symposium
in 1927 and the Mooseheart Symposium in 1948, which were clearly
dominated by a mechanistic orientation.

One way to highlight the importance of cognitive appraisal in the
mediation of emotional states is to point to a contrast between Hans
Selye, with his *general adaptation syndrome,* on the one hand, and John
Mason and me, on the other. Selye argued that the general adaptation
syndrome is a universal biological defensive reaction aroused by any
physically noxious agent. Mason (1971), also an endocrinologist, pointed
out, however, that the endocrine response to stressor conditions is constantly being affected by cognitive processes. To express this mediation
of the physiological response, Mason used the compound term *psycho-
endocrinology.* Mason and I have gone even further in this direction,
both having suggested (Lazarus, 1966; Mason, 1971) that the essential
mediator of the general adaptation syndrome may indeed be cognitive.
In effect, the pituitary-adrenal cortical response to disturbed commerce
with the environment may require that the animal or person somehow
recognize his plight. Any animal that has sustained an injury is apt to
sense that he is in trouble; and if he doesn't, there will be no general
adaptation syndrome. In research on the general adaptation syndrome,

cognitive mediation has almost never been ruled out. Thus, one could argue with some justification that this cognitive appraisal of harm via cerebrally controlled processes is necessary to initiate the body's defensive adrenal cortical response.

An animal that is unconscious can sustain bodily harm without the psychoendocrine mechanisms of the general adaptation syndrome becoming active. Data from Symington, Currie, Curran, and Davidson (1955), for example, suggest that unconsciousness and anesthesia eliminate the adrenal effects of physiological stress. It was observed that patients who were dying from injury or disease showed a normal adrenal cortical condition as assessed during autopsy as long as they have remained unconscious during the period of the fatal condition. In contrast, patients who were conscious during the periods of the fatal disease process and died did show adrenal cortical changes. Also relevant, Gray, Ramsey, Villarreal, and Krakaner (1956) showed that general anesthesia, by itself, does not produce a significant adrenal reaction. These studies raise the question of whether it is the psychological significance of the injury rather than the physiologically noxious effects of that injury that produces the adrenal cortical changes associated with stress.

In his recent book, *Stress without Distress,* Selye (1974) now seems to have changed his generalist, noncognitive position somewhat by suggesting that only certain kinds of stress, for example, the stress of frustration or failure, are harmful, but other kinds of stress, such as the joyful pursuit of one's occupation, are benign or even beneficial. This seems to limit the general adaptation syndrome, or at least its damaging features, to certain kinds of transactions, and gives to mediating psychological processes an essential role. Similarly, Rahe (1964), who had once emphasized that all life changes demanding adaptive effort contributed to illness regardless of whether they are regarded as positive or negative, now considers it important to consider psychological defenses and coping activities as mediators of somatic illness. There seems to be a widespread movement toward the position that cognitive processes intervening between the person's adaptive transactions with the environment and the emotional reaction (including its somatic consequences) are important determinants, though the empirical case for this position still remains somewhat uncertain.

In arguing that such a view is relevant to the biofeedback context, let me take a somewhat different tack and consider the point made recently by Janis (Note 1) that the interpersonal features of biofeedback research and therapy situations are primary sources of the mediating psychological processes responsible for successful training in the control of bodily reactions, in contrast with the conditioning paradigm variables that some biofeedback researchers think are sufficient (see also Morris & Suckerman, 1974a, 1974b). Janis quoted (see Jonas, 1972) a young woman who had undergone an arduous 10-week training period during which she succeeded temporarily in lowering her diastolic blood pressure from 97 to about 80. She stated:

> I always depend very heavily on Barry Dworkin's [her trainer] encouragement and on his personality. I think he could be an Olympic Coach. He not only seems aware of my general condition but he is never satisfied with less than my best, and I can't fool him. I feel we are friends and allies—it's really as though *we* were lowering my pressure.

In this case, one mediator of the self-control processes appears to be the quality and significance to the subject of the relationship with the therapist, a relationship that sustains her in the arduous training program and without which the self-control might have been impossible. If we can accept the statements of the young woman at face value, we must look at the components of this relationship and their determinants to understand adequately the way biofeedback procedures work, and perhaps to arrange for something to take their place outside the laboratory situation for generalization to occur. I am saying two things here: First, we cannot in our thinking isolate the somatic disturbances and their self-regulation in biofeedback from the larger context of the person's adaptive commerce with his environment. Second, this adaptive commerce is constantly being mediated by social and psychological processes.

A comparable point is implied in Marston and Feldman's (1972) analysis of the concept of self-control in the context of behavior modification. Although seeming to identify themselves as behavior modifiers, they made use of mediated psychological processes in discussing the acquisition of self-control as a two-stage process. Initially, there is the development of a general cognitive set in which the person comes to value the inhibition of the impulse and commits himself to the effort. The authors used the expression *executive response* in referring to this cognitive set. The person is described as making a commitment and evaluating the chances of success and the relative importance of the desired change against the effort required. There are surely individual differences in the motivation to do this and in the relative costs and benefits as evaluated by the person. There follow attempts by the person, with or without therapeutic guidance, to arrange the environmental contingencies that presumably will aid in overcoming the bad habit or impulse. Why not recognize at the outset that in the biofeedback situation, just as in any other situation of learning and performing, there is an active, striving, evaluating person at the helm struggling to do something for which information about his own success can be enormously useful in increasing his chances of ultimate mastery or self-control?

From this standpoint, we have a great need for an adequate transactional language to describe individual differences in the way a person relates psychologically to the environment. I have constructed a simple hypothetical example. Consider two different persons who perceive that they are facing a demand, or the juxtaposition of several demands, which seems to them to be at the borderline or beyond their capacity to master—too much is expected of them. As a result of their individual histories and particular personalities, Person A feels that failure of mastery reflects his own inadequacy, while Person B, by contrast, feels the same inadequacy but interprets the situation as one in which people are constantly trying to use or abuse him. Both experience similar degrees of anticipatory stress and are mobilized to cope with the problem. Prior to the confrontation that will reveal the success or failure of mastery, both experience anxiety, an anticipatory emotion in the context of appraised threat. In Person A, the anxiety is mixed, perhaps with anticipatory depression, while in Person B, the anxiety is mixed with external blaming and anger. Following confrontation in which, let us say, both perform badly, Person A experiences mainly loss and depression, while Person B experiences mainly anger and resentment. A similar set of overwhelming demands have been construed or appraised quite differently because of different personality dispositions. If these persons do well in the confrontation, both may experience elation because they have overcome the difficulty, depending on whether the explanation of the success is luck or their own perseverance and skill; for example, see Weiner's (1974) attribution theory approach to achievement motivation. In any case, such subtle differences in appraisal of a stressful commerce with the environment underlie variations among individuals in the severity (and possibly the pattern) of bodily reactions, the intensity and chronicity of the accompanying emotion, the quality of the effects experienced, and the types of solutions for which they opt, including seeking, accepting, and using clinical help. I don't think such personality-based variations can be ignored in biofeedback therapy setting or in any other kind, and in research on how such therapy works. As Schwartz (1973) put it:

> biofeedback should be viewed as but one approach to the treatment of the "total person," realizing that to "cure" a problem such as hypertension will require more than just the patient consciously attempting to lower his pressure (p. 670).

THE SELF-REGULATION OF EMOTION

What about the third theme, concerning self-regulation? Emotion is not a constant thing, but it ebbs and flows and changes over time, as the nature of the adaptive commerce and the information about it changes. Anger suddenly melts and changes to guilt, depression, and love; anxiety changes to euphoria; guilt changes to anger. Rarely are strong emotional states so simple that they have only one quality; more often, emotions involve complex combinations of affect, each deriving from multiple elements of cognitive appraisal—some even ambivalent— to be found in any complex human transaction with the environment. These shifts in intensity and quality over time reflect perceived and appraised changes in the person's relationship with the environment, based in part on feedback from the situation and from his own reactions. In the stress emotions, the changes reflect, in part, the person's constant efforts to master the interchange by overcoming the damage, by postponing or preventing the danger, or by tolerating it. Thus, expectations and discoveries about his power to deal with the environment and master danger are a constantly changing factor, and sometimes a stable determinant, of whether he will feel threatened, for instance, or challenged by what happens.

This latter theme is especially important for an understanding of emotional processes, and for the link between biofeedback and the study of emotion, because it places emphasis on coping processes as a central feature of the emotional state. We are, of course, sometimes accidentally confronted by a situation having major relevance for our welfare; but we also do a great deal of active regulating of our emotional reactions. To some extent, the person selects the environment to which he must respond; he shapes his commerce with it, he plans, chooses, avoids, tolerates, postpones, escapes, demolishes, and manipulates his attention, and he also deceives himself about what is happening, as much as possible casting the relationship in ways that fit his needs and premises about himself in the world. In regulating his emotional life, he is also thereby regulating the bodily reactions that are an integral part of any emotional state.

The idea of coping is hardly new. It has a considerable recent history, largely clinical in focus, although as will be seen shortly coping processes have usually been treated as consequences of an emotion rather than playing the causal role I give to them. The Freudian conception of anxiety, for example, emphasized not only its cue function but also its control by ego-defensive operations, and it helped establish a tradition of study of coping processes in adaptive functioning. It would not be fruitful here to try to summarize this history of ideas about the relationships between coping processes and emotional states. Suffice it to say now that my basic position is that we cannot hope to understand the emotions unless we also take into account the coping activities that affect them.

There are countless observations of the important role that coping or self-regulatory processes play. In a previous discussion of these (Lazarus, in press), I cited both everyday-life anecdotal examples, such as the management of grief, the escalation of discouragement of a love relationship, being a good loser; and formal research examples, such as field studies of combat stress, the psychoendocrine research of the Bethesda group on parents of children dying of leukemia, and research from my own laboratory (Koriat, Melkman, Averill, & Lazarus, 1972) dealing with the self-control of emotional states. There is insufficient time here to do full justice to the problem, but it will be useful to illustrate with some examples below.

Coping as a Causal Factor in Emotion

There would be little argument that people are capable of inhibiting emotional behaviors such as avoidance and aggression, or the behavioral expression of emotions such as grief, love, depression, and joy. I am saying, of course, more than this; namely, that intrapsychic forms of coping such as detachment and denial are also capable of modifying, eliminating, or changing the emotion itself, including its subjective affect and bodily changes. When successful, these mechanisms not only affect the visible signs of emotion but also dampen or eliminate the entire emotional syndrome. Thus, in the well-known NIH studies of parents with children dying of leukemia (Wolff, Friedman, Hofer, & Mason, 1964), by denying the fatal significance of their child's illness the NIH parents no longer felt as threatened, and in consequence they exhibited lower levels of adrenal cortical stress hormones than those parents who acknowledged the tragic implications.

Moreover, by successfully distancing themselves from the emotional features of an autopsy, the medical students observed by Lief and Fox (1963) not only behaved unemotionally but in all likelihood, if the appropriate measurements had been made, would have been shown to react with little or no affect and without the bodily disturbances that are an integral part of stress emotion. Lief and Fox (1963) conducted extensive interviews with medical students witnessing for the first time a medical autopsy. Most such students, who are probably self-selected to a high degree, achieve detachment from the experience, though there are some failures too. Certain features of the procedure itself and of the institutionalized behavior of the participants, probably evolved out of the wisdom of long professional experience, provide great help to the student in the process of achieving detachment. During the autopsy, for example, the room is immaculate and brightly lit, and the task is approached with seriousness, skill, and a professional air facilitating a clinical and impersonal attitude toward death. Certain parts of the body are kept covered, particularly the face and genitalia; and the hands, which are so strongly connected with human, person qualities, are usually not dissected. Once the vital organs are removed, the body is taken from the room, bringing the autopsy down to isolated tissues that are more easily depersonalized. Students avoid talking about the autopsy; and when they do, the discussion is impersonal and stylized. Finally, whereas in laboratory dissection humor appears to be a widespread and effective emotional control device, it is absent in the autopsy room, perhaps because the death has been too recent and joking would appear too insensitive. One senses here the process of struggling to achieve a proper balance between feeling things and looking at them objectively, in short, an effort to regulate a common and expected emotional reaction in which detachment and distancing is the mode of coping. We also recognize that some individuals in medicine and nursing overdo the coping strategy of detachment or dehumanization and appear to their patients as cold and indifferent.

Moreover, much coping activity is anticipatory; that is, the person expects a future harmful confrontation, such as failing an examination, performing in public, or confronting a flood, tornado, or a personal criticism, and this leads him to prepare against the future possibility of harm. To the extent that he prepares effectively, overcoming or avoiding danger before it materializes or being better able to function adequately in the anticipated confrontation, he thereby changes the nature of the ultimate transaction, along with the emotions that might have been experienced in the absence of such anticipatory coping. Overcoming the danger before it materializes can lead to exhilaration rather than fear, grief, depression, or whatever, depending upon the nature of the harm or loss that might have been experienced and the appraisal of the reasons for success.

You will note that this analysis reverses the usual wisdom that coping always follows emotion (or is caused by it) and suggests that coping can precede emotion and influence its form or intensity. In fact, my general position requires the assertion that coping never follows emotion in anything but a temporal sense, a stance in direct opposition to the long-standing and traditional view that emotions (such as anxiety) serve as drives or motives for adaptive behavior (Lazarus, 1968). The exception to this is when the person is trying to regulate the bodily state directly; but more about this in a moment.

Unfortunately, the psychology of coping is largely descriptive in nature, rather than systematic and predictive. People use a wide variety of coping processes, depending on their personal characteristics, the nature of the environmental demands and contingencies, and how these are appraised. They engage in a variety of preparatory activities. For example, they may worry without taking adequate steps to increase their effectiveness in confrontation; they reduce intense arousal by periodic disengagements from stressful transactions; they take tranquilizers to lower excessive levels of arousal; they use antispasmodics to quiet their bowels; they practice positive mental attitudes; they try to tell themselves that the problem will work itself out or that there is really no problem; they seek support from loved ones or those they trust; they try this or that stress-preventive fad or fashion, such as transcendental meditation, psychotherapy, relaxation, hypnosis, and yoga; they direct their attention away from the source of threat and toward benign or escapist literature or movies; they cope with loss ultimately by giving up what was previously a central portion of their psychological domain. However, we still know extremely little about the conditions, both within the person and in the stimulus configuration, that led to one or another coping process, about the relative effectiveness of such diverse coping processes in regulating emotional states, or about the comparative costs or maladaptive consequences of each form of coping.

A Typology of Self-Regulation

My earlier comment about attempts directly to regulate bodily reactions draws an implicit distinction between two kinds of emotion-regulatory or coping processes, a distinction others have made (cf. Mechanic, 1962). One type, which might properly be called *direct action,* concerns behavioral efforts by the person to deal with the problem generating the stress emotion in the first place. Whether the person attacks or avoids the harmful agency, or engages in some preparatory activity, the focus of the coping effort is on preventing or extricating himself from the plight in which he finds himself. The other type, which might be called *palliation* of emotion, is focused on reducing the visceral or motor disturbances that are a feature of the stress emotion generated by troubled commerce with the environment. Palliation includes both intrapsychic defensive modes and somatically oriented ones such as muscle-relaxant drugs and narcotics.

Thus, if a student who is facing an important and very threatening examination spends the anticipatory interval reading relevant books and articles, rehearsing his understanding of the subject matter with other students or teachers, trying to guess or find out the questions that will be asked, and so on, he is engaged in direct-action forms of coping with the problem, whether he does this effectively or ineffectively. He is attempting to alter his basic relationship with the environment, or, put differently, to change the nature of his troubled commerce with it. To the extent that such activity leads to a more benign appraisal of the potential outcome of the examination, for example, by giving him a sense of preparedness and mastery, the emotional reaction attendant on the threatening character of the situation for him is to some extent short-circuited. Anxiety is also reduced, along with its bodily concomitants, and he is better able to sleep, think, draw upon his knowledge in the examination, etc.

On the other hand, if the same student uses tranquilizers, drinks to control his disturbed bodily state, takes sleeping pills, engages in muscle relaxation, deceives himself into believing he has nothing to be concerned about, diverts his attention for a time, or tries other techniques designed to quiet his heightened arousal, he is employing palliative modes to control the emotional response itself rather than to cope actively with the environmental transaction that generated the arousal in the first place. He is dealing with the somatic reaction rather than its cause. In all likelihood, the rules by which these two divergent kinds of processes operate are quite different.

I do not intend any derogation of this latter "symptom"-oriented or peripheral approach. We all use a variety of coping devices, including palliation, and these often help greatly. Sometimes they are the only ones available, perhaps because the tendency to appraise certain situations as threatening is very deep-rooted in the person, or the source of threat is unknown to him and hence fairly refractory to change. In the case of inevitable harms such as death or imminent surgery, there is little concrete that he can do to alter his plight. Moreover, as in the handling of test anxiety, sometimes effective action in the problem-oriented sense is largely impaired by the emotion itself, as when the person finds he cannot think clearly about his problem and prepare adequately in the face of the interfering effects. Under such conditions, reducing the anxiety or the correlates of anxiety by *any* means available may serve to facilitate adaptive coping. Moreover, in chronic or repeated situations of threat, even merely lowering debilitating arousal may swing the balance of the approach-avoidance conflict in favor of approach and commitment and away from avoidance and disengagement, and this may make possible the attainment of goals of great importance.

The palliative form of control that aims at reducing somatic turmoil rather than at resolving its psychodynamic origins is the arena into which biofeedback research and its use in therapy fall. I would argue that those who want to rule out cognitive or other mediators in biofeedback research miss the central point in the self-regulation of emotion. Not only does such an effort greatly narrow the scope of such self-regulation, but it minimizes the complexity of the problem and the diverse patterns by which it typically operates in all our lives. We need to have more knowledge of the myriad forms of self-regulation that are available and serviceable to given kinds of people and in given types of situations in managing their emotional lives (see also Schwartz, 1973). As my opening statements suggest, a major virtue of the biofeedback movement lies in the opportunity it proves to test some of our ideas about the coping process used by people and about those that are capable of influencing the emotional response.

What actually mediates biofeedback effects themselves is still an open question. One possibility is that the relaxation process could serve as a means of attention deployment (Budzynski, Stoyva, Adler, & Mullaney, 1973). The person learns to focus his attention on relaxing his muscles, and his attention is turned away from the stress-producing source of the tension from which the headaches are indirectly derived. Or alternatively, such training might induce a relaxed psychological state that is incompatible with the tension, a mechanism that has been suggested by Wolpe (1958) and by Mendelsohn (1962). Or it might merely create a physiological state (muscle relaxation) that is itself incompatible with the physiological headache mechanism. If these processes could be shown to generalize to situations outside the laboratory, they might provide a powerful tool of therapy as well as research into the efficacy of various mediating self-regulatory processes.

Some of my own research (Koriat et al., 1972), in fact, has emphasized the cognitive mediators regulating autonomic nervous system activity while subjects watched a stressful movie. We asked subjects to watch the film while adopting two different attitudes, one to involve themselves more fully in the stressful episodes and the other to detach or distance themselves. Evidence that our subjects were capable of such self-control of emotional states came from autonomic as well as self-report measures. This research was also designed to discover the cognitive processes producing altered emotional arousal, though it might well have been improved by the use of biofeedback procedures to aid subjects in assessing how well they were succeeding in involving or detaching themselves from the stressful scenes. We found that certain strategies were reportedly widely used to achieve detachment, while others predominated in the effort to create emotional involvement. But we could not adequately test the effectiveness of these strategies.

Coping and Environmental Interactions

An important qualification should be made here. We should not expect given self-regulating strategies to be effective in every context of adaptive commerce. Rather, depending on the environmental demands and options open to the person, some strategies should be serviceable and others not. For example, Cohen and Lazarus (1973) found that patients who approached surgery with avoidant strategies, that is, those who did not want to know about their illness and the nature of the surgery, showed a more rapid and smoother post-surgical recovery than did patients adopting a vigilant strategy. It was speculated that vigilance might actually be a handicap for the surgical patient because there was nothing constructive he could really do in the postoperative recuperation period except simply to ignore or deny the sources of threat and pain. Trying postoperatively to pay attention vigilantly to every possible cue of danger or sign of discomfort resulted in a longer and more complicated recovery, and this appeared to be maladaptive in this situation.

However, a very different strategy seems called for in the stressful context studied by Reuven Gal (Note 2), namely, seasickness among Israeli navy personnel. Holding constant the degree of seasickness, it was found that sailors who had the trait or disposition of coping in an active, purposive, and vigilant fashion despite their sickness functioned much better at their normal jobs. Forgetting for a moment several possible sources of confounding, such as the measures of coping (trait versus state) and the type of population, the juxtaposition of these two studies points up the potential interaction that might exist bewteen type of coping and the nature of the environmental demands. Moreover, such research also points up another one of the major gaps in theory and research in the biofeedback arena, namely, the absence of evident interest in individual differences. Biofeedback procedures even when oriented to therapy seem generally to have approached normatively rather than ipsatively to assess the contribution of situations and individual differences in personality to the results. Depending on preferred coping styles and patterns of belief and expectation and on the nature of the situational demands, individuals should differ greatly in their capacity to profit from particular biofeedback procedures and to acquire control over their bodily reactions (see also Schwartz, 1973, p. 672).

CONCLUDING COMMENT

We are a long way from understanding the modes of self-regulation of emotion that are available to individuals and serviceable in any given environmental context. Indeed, this seems to me to be one of psychology's most important issues, and the biofeedback arena offers unparalleled opportunities to tackle it. I am convinced that self-regulation of emotion is a perfectly normal part of everyday living and does not emerge only in the biofeedback laboratory. We need to know more about these modes of self-regulation, their efficacy, and the rules of their operation, and biofeedback studies could provide a powerful tool to resolve these basic issues. I believe that such research will go further if it is approached within the larger context of emotion and adaptation and oriented to the wide variety of mediators that affect the reaction pattern, rather than being treated as a special or unique kind of process limited to the biofeedback laboratory.

240 ANNUAL REVIEW OF BEHAVIOR THERAPY

REFERENCE NOTES

1. JANIS, I. L. *Preventing Dehumanization: Some Comments on Howard Leventhal's Analysis.* Unpublished manuscript. (Available from Yale University, Department of Psychology.)
2. GAL, R. *Coping Processes under Seasickness Conditions.* Manuscript submitted for publication, 1975.

REFERENCES

ARNOLD, M. B. *Emotion and Personality.* New York: Columbia University Press, 1960.
ARNOLD, M. B. (Ed.). *Feelings and Emotions.* New York: Academic Press, 1970.
BLANCHARD, E. B. & YOUNG, L. D. Self-control of cardiac function: A promise yet unfulfilled. *Psychol. Bull.,* ,1973, 79, 145-163.
BOLLES, R. C. Cognition and motivation: Some historical trends. In B. Weiner (Ed.), *Cognitive Views of Human Motivation.* New York: Academic Press, 1974.
BUDZYNSKI, T. H., STOYVA, J. M., ADLER, C. S., & MULLANEY, D. J. EMG biofeedback and tension headache: A controlled outcome study. *Psychom. Med.,* 1973, 35, 484-496.
COHEN, F. & LAZARUS, R. S. Active coping processes, coping dispositions, and recovery from surgery. *Psychosom. Med.,* 1973, 35, 375-389.
CRIDER, A., SCHWARTZ, G., & SHNIDMAN, S. On the criteria for instrumental autonomic conditioning: A reply to Katkin and Murray. *Psychol. Bull.,* 1969, 71, 455-461.
GRAY, S. J., RAMSEY, C. S., VILLERREAL, R., & KRAKANER, L. J. Adrenal influences upon the stomach and the gastric response to stress. In H. Selye and G. Hensen (Eds.), *Fifth Annual Report on Stress, 1955-1956.* New York: MD Publications, 1956.
GRINKER, R. R. & SPIEGEL, J. P. *Men Under Stress.* New York: McGraw-Hill, 1945.
JONAS, G. Profiles: Visceral learning I. (On Neal E. Miller.) *New Yorker,* August 19, 1972, pp. 34-36+.
KATKIN, E. S. & MURRAY, E. N. Instrumental conditioning of autonomically mediated behavior: Theoretical and methodical issues. *Psychol. Bull.,* 1968, 70, 52-68.
KORIAT, A., MELKMAN, R., AVERILL, J. R., & LAZARUS, R. S. The self-control of emotional reactions to a stressful film. *J. Pers.,* 1972, 40, 601-619.
LAZARUS, R. S. *Psychological Stress and the Coping Process.* New York: McGraw-Hill, 1966.
LAZARUS, R. S. Emotions and adaptation: Conceptual and empirical relations. In E. J. Arnold (Ed.), *Nebraska Symposium on Motivation* (Vol. 16). Lincoln: University of Nebraska Press, 1968.
LAZARUS, R. S. The self-regulation of emotion. In L. Levi (Ed.), *Parameters of Emotion.* New York: Raven Press, in press.
LAZARUS, R. S., AVERILL, J. R., & OPTON, E. M., JR. Towards a cognitive theory of emotion. In M. B. Arnold (Ed.), *Feelings and Emotions.* New York: Academic Press, 1970.
LIEF, H. I. & FOX, R. S. Training for "detached concern" in medical students. In H. I. Lief, V. F. Lief, & N. R. Lief (Eds.), *The Psychological Basis of Medical Practice.* New York: Harper & Row, 1963.
LYNCH, J. J., PASKEWITZ, D. A., & ORNE, M. T. Some factors in the feedback control of human alpha rhythm. *Psychosom. Med.,* 1974, 36, 399-410.
MARSTON, A. R. & FELDMAN, S. E. Toward the use of self-control in behavior modification. *J. Consult. Clin. Psychol.,* 1972, 39, 429-436.
MASON, J. W. A re-evaluation of the concept of "nonspecificity" in stress theory. *J. Psychiat. Res.,* 1971, 8, 323-333.

MECHANIC, D. *Students Under Stress*. New York: The Free Press of Glencoe, 1962.
MENDELSOHN, G. A. The competition of affective response in human subjects. *J. Abnorm. Soc. Psychol.*, 1962, 65, 26-31.
MILLER, N. E. Critical issues in the therapeutic application of biofeedback. In G. E. Schwartz and J. Beatty (Eds.), *Biofeedback: Theory and Research*. New York: Academic Press, in press.
MORRIS, R. J. & SUCKERMAN, K. R. The importance of the therapeutic relationship in systematic desensitization. *J. Consult. Clin. Psychol.*, 1974, 42, 148. (a)
MORRIS, R. J. & SUCKERMAN, K. R. Therapist warmth as a factor in automated systematic desensitization. *J. Consult. Clin. Psychol.*, 1974, 42, 244-250. (b)
RAHE, R. H. The pathway between subjects' recent life changes and their near-future illness reports: Representative results and methodological issues. In B. S. Dohrenwend and B. P. Dohrenwend (Eds.), *Stressful Life Events: Their Nature and Effects*. New York: Wiley, 1974.
SCHWARTZ, G. E. Biofeedback as therapy: Some theoretical and practical issues. *Amer. Psychol.*, 1973, 28, 666-673.
SELYE, H. *Stress without Distress*. Philadelphia, Pa.: J. B. Lippincott, 1974.
SYMINGTON, T., CURRIE, A. R., CURRAN, R. S., & DAVIDSON, J. N. The reaction of the adrenal cortex in conditions of stress. In *Ciba Foundation Colloquia on Endocrinology* (Vol. 8). *The Human Adrenal Cortex*. Boston: Little, Brown, 1955.
WEINER, B. *Theories of Motivation*. Chicago: Markham, 1972.
WEINER, B. An attributional interpretation of expectancy-value theory. In B. Weiner (Ed.), *Cognitive Views of Human Motivation*. New York: Academic Press, 1974.
WOLFF, C. T., FRIEDMAN, S. B., HOFER, M. A., & MASON, J. W. Relationship between psychological defenses and mean urinary 17-hydroxycorticosteroid excretion rates: Parts I and II. *Psychosom. Med.*, 1964, 26, 576-609.
WOLPE, J. *Psychotherapy by Reciprocal Inhibition*. Stanford, Calif.: Stanford University Press, 1958.

10

DIFFERENTIAL EFFECTIVENESS OF ELECTROMYOGRAPH FEEDBACK, VERBAL RELAXATION INSTRUCTIONS, AND MEDICATION PLACEBO WITH TENSION HEADACHES

Daniel J. Cox, Andrew Freundlich

and Robert G. Meyer

Psychology Clinic, University of Louisville

Twenty-seven adults from the general population with chronic tension headaches were divided into three groups. Nine were assigned to auditory electromyograph (EMG) feedback, 9 to progressive relaxation instructions, and 9 to placebo treatment. Subjects came for 2 weeks of pre- and posttreatment assessment, with 4 intervening weeks of treatment. Measures were taken on headache frequency, intensity and duration, frontalis EMG recordings, medication intake, locus of control, and additional psychosomatic complaints. Comparison of postassessment and 4-month follow-up data indicated that biofeedback and verbal relaxation instructions were equally superior to the medicine placebo on all meas-

Reprinted with permission from *Journal of Consulting and Clinical Psychology,* Vol. 43, No. 6, 1975, 892-898. Copyright 1975, American Psychological Association.

ured variables in the direction of clinical improvement, except for shifts in locus of control. All groups experienced equally significant shifts toward internality.

Survey data (Waters & O'Connor, 1971; Wolff, 1972) indicate that between 50 percent and 70 percent of adults experience headaches, 40 percent of which are tension or muscle-contraction headaches (Kashiwagi, McClure, & Wetzel, 1972). Tension headaches are characterized by bilateral tightening sensations originating usually in the frontal or suboccipital region and are directly related to excessive and sustained contraction in scalp and/or neck muscles. Despite this high frequency of occurrence and the known mechanism of pain, traditional treatment has been restricted to symptomatic medication, for example, tranquilizers, muscle relaxants, and analgesics, or individual psychotherapy.

Recently, the self-control technique of electromyograph (EMG) biofeedback (Budzynski, Stoyva, Adler, & Mullaney, 1973; Wickramasekera, 1972) has been used in the successful training of headache victims in relaxation of relevant muscular structures for prevention of muscle-contraction headaches. However, a review by Blanchard, Young, and Jackson (1974) pointed out that biofeedback research concerning tension headaches "confirms the efficacy of the combination of feedback and home practice in relaxation; their designs do not make it possible to isolate the effects of biofeedback alone" (p. 578). The question is whether home practice of relaxation instructions is sufficient to achieve similar therapeutic effects repeatedly demonstrated by electronically sophisticated biofeedback techniques.

McKenzie, Ehrisman, Montgomery, and Barnes (1974) and Wickramasekera (1973) have combined relaxation instructions and biofeedback in the successful treatment of tension headaches. Tasto and Hinkle (1973) and Fichtler and Zimmerman (1973) have demonstrated that verbal relaxation instructions alone can produce significant reductions in headache activity. Jacobson (1935) indicated that progressive relaxation training is capable of lowering muscle activity and suggests its use in the treatment of tension headaches. In a detailed case study, Jacobson (1970) demonstrates the effective application of relaxation training in the remediation of chronic headaches. However, all of these studies were deficient in adequate controls and comparisons to answer the question of differential treatment effectiveness. This study attempts to address the question of whether biofeedback training itself makes a significant contribution to the treatment of tension headaches.

Subjects

A newspaper article generated 93 respondents. Of these, 27 were selected who most closely fit the following criteria: experienced headaches of a steady bilateral pain originating in the frontal or suboccipital region, occurred three or more times a week, and had no organic basis according to family physician.

The 27 subjects consisted of 7 males and 20 females, whose age ranged from 16 to 64 years with an average age of 39. Mean duration of headache history was 11 years, ranging from 1 to 39 years.

Procedure

During the first 2 weeks, subjects came for individual weekly pretreatment assessment. The first meeting involved signing a treatment contract, making a $20 refundable deposit, obtaining family physician's approval, recording frontalis EMG following a 20-minute rest period, and administration of the Nowicki-Strickland Locus of Control Scale (Nowicki & Duke, 1972) and the Psychosomatic Checklist. The Psychosomatic Checklist, developed for this study, lists 18 common psychosomatic complaints, each of which is given a rating by the subject on intensity and frequency. During the following week, and all subsequent weeks, subjects filled out a daily Headache Data Sheet recording intensity and duration of each headache experienced, circumstances surrounding headache onset and how it was responded to, and medication taken. The second pretreatment session included recording frontalis EMG, as did all following sessions, and a review of Headache Data Sheets. Subjects were assigned to a treatment group at the third session, with groups equated for headache frequency and locus of control scores.

Biofeedback group. Biofeedback subjects came twice weekly for eight hourly treatment sessions. Auditory analogue EMG feedback was given for 30 minutes a session. Feedback was generated from frontalis EMG monitored by three disk electrodes placed across the forehead (Budzynski et al., 1973), which was amplified and rectified allowing average peak-to-peak voltage readings over a 1-second interval.* Subjects were instructed to use cue-controlled breathing (Russell & Sipich, 1974) immediately following 30 minutes of feedback. Subjects accomplished this by

---

* For a detailed description of the EMG biofeedback unit, contact Electronic Systems, Development Corporation, P.O. Box 18223, Louisville, Kentucky.

maintaining their relaxed condition and focusing on their natural rhythmic breathing while simultaneously using the covert self-instruction, "relax."

Reduction of EMG was progressively shaped and auditory feedback systematically faded out during training. Shaping was accomplished by gradually increasing feedback gain, or sensitivity, requiring progressively lower levels of EMG to maintain low auditory feedback signals. Intervals of no feedback were introduced as subjects gained greater control of their frontalis activity in an effort to fade out feedback dependency. To further facilitate generalizing the training effect, subjects practiced relaxation in techniques learned during feedback twice daily and used cue-control breathing prior to each meal. All home practice was recorded (Tasto & Hinkle, 1973). After the third feedback session, biofeedback subjects were instructed to begin applying their relaxing skills at the first sign of a headache onset.

Verbal relaxation instruction group. Bernstein and Borkovec's (1973) procedure was used in training relaxation. The first three of the eight twice-weekly treatment sessions were concerned with tightening and relaxing 16 muscle groups. The subsequent five sessions dealt with progressively reducing the operated muscle groups until subjects only recalled feelings of relaxation and used cue-control breathing, thus eliminating the need for any vigorous exercises. Identical to biofeedback subjects, relaxation subjects engaged in cue-control self-instruction following their relaxation exercise, practiced their relaxation exercises and cued breathing at home, and began to implement their relaxation skills at initial signs of a headache following the third treatment session.

Medication placebo group. These subjects received a green and white glucose capsule administered during weekly individual hourly sessions. They were told that it was a peripheral-acting time-release muscle relaxant known to be effective.

Sessions of the 2-week posttreatment assessment, as well as the 2 weeks of follow-up occurring 4 months later, were identical to pretreatment sessions for all subjects. The Nowicki-Strickland and the Psychosomatic Checklist scales were administered during the second week of both evaluation periods.

RESULTS

Analysis of covariance (Winer, 1971) was used to analyze posttreatment levels of headache activity and frontalis EMG since it controls for group

TABLE 1

CRITICAL VALUES FROM THE COMPARISON OF TREATMENT EFFECTIVENESS

Comparison	Biofeedback vs. vs. placebo	Verbal instructions vs. placebo	Biofeedback vs. verbal instructions
Posttreatment			
H_D scores			
F	5.73**	2.95*	.81
df	1, 23	1, 23	2, 23
Frontalis EMG	41.12****	33.31****	1.69
F			
df	1, 23	1, 23	1, 23
Medication reduction			
U	21	21	39
df	9, 9	9, 9	9, 9
Psychosomatic Checklist reduction			
U	4.0****	4.5****	39.5
df	9, 9	9, 9	9, 9
Locus of control changes			
U	28	28	30
df	9, 9	9, 9	9, 9
Follow-up			
H_D scores			
F	10.10****	10.96***	.03
df	1, 20	1, 20	1, 20
Frontalis EMG			
F	3.52*	8.60***	.21
df	1, 20	1, 20	1, 20
Medication reduction			
U	15**	15**	39
df	8, 8	8, 8	8, 8
Psychosomatic Checklist reduction			
U	15**	13**	9*
df	8, 8	8, 8	8, 8
Locus of control changes			
U	28	22	30
df	8, 8	8, 8	8, 8

* $p < .10$.
** $p < .05$.
*** $p < .01$.
**** $p < .001$.

differences in pretreatment levels. The dimension of headache activity analyzed was an H_D conversion (Budzynski et al., 1973) in which hours of headache activity were weighed by intensity of headache pain.* Using pretreatment data as the covariant, an overall F of 2.86 ($df = 2,23$, $p < .10$) was obtained. Since the trend was in the predicted direction, an a priori comparison of weighted means (Winer, 1971, p. 785) was carried out. Table 1 shows biofeedback superior to placebo ($p < .05$) and equiva-

---

* $H_D = \sum (I:D)/24$ where headache intensity (I), as indicated on a 5-point scale, is multiplied by the hours of headache duration (D); these products being summed for each day and divided by 24, yielding an hourly weighted average of headache activity.

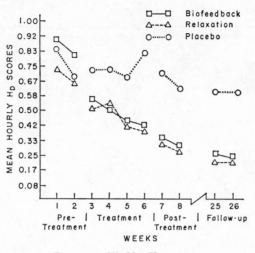

FIGURE 1. Weekly H_D scores.

lent to relaxation, whereas relaxation subjects show a trend $(p < .10)$ over placebo. This is further substantiated by inspection of Figure 1 in which biofeedback and relaxation subjects show a progressively parallel improvement rate over weeks and the placebo profile exhibits no such trend. Virtually identical results and treatment trends were obtained when analyzing unweighted hours of headache activity (Cox, 1974).

When comparing posttreatment frontalis EMG taken after a 20-minute rest interval, an overall F of 3.88 $(df = 2,23, p < .05)$ was observed. As seen in Table 1, a comparison of adjusted means shows that biofeedback $(p < .001)$ and relaxation $(p < .001)$ were superior to placebo. Biofeedback and relaxation did not differ.

Secondary effects of treatment were analyzed in terms of medication intake and additional psychosomatic complaint reductions. A Kruskal-Wallis analysis of variance yielded an H of 5.90 $(df = 2, p < .05)$ when comparing prereduction and postreduction of psychosomatic complaints. Again Table 1 shows that biofeedback $(p < .001)$ and relaxation $(p < .001)$ were superior to placebo and equivalent to one another as analyzed by the Mann-Whitney U test. Similarly, reduction in units of medication taken was found to be differentially affected, H $(2) = 14.77$, p $< .001$, with biofeedback producing significantly greater medication reduction than placebo $(p < .05)$ and equivalent reductions to relaxation, whereas

TABLE 2

MEANS AND STANDARD DEVIATIONS OF DEPENDENT MEASURES AT PREASSESSMENT, POSTASSESSMENT
AND FOLLOW-UP ASSESSMENT FOR ALL TREATMENT GROUPS

	Biofeedback		Relaxation		Placebo	
Measure	M	SD	M	SD	M	SD
H_D score						
Pre	1.69	1.14	1.35	.57	1.55	1.05
Post	.63	.77	.63	.54	1.25	.73
Follow-up	.60	.85	.46	.53	.90	.70
Improvement[a]	63%		53%		19%	
Headache frequency per week						
Pre	18.4	8.9	16.6	4.1	17.8	9.8
Post	9.1	12.4	7.9	4.0	13.9	11.4
Follow-up	7.8	12.8	8.0	6.3	14.4	13.6
Improvement	51%		52%		23%	
Hours of headaches per week						
Pre	94.7	62.0	79.7	35.4	84.4	54.4
Post	33.0	37.3	37.2	27.0	68.3	67.6
Follow-up	31.3	41.2	28.4	30.0	37.6	27.7
Improvement	65%		53%		19%	
Medication per week						
Pre	34.2	32.0	28.1	17.8	34.4	39.4
Post	14.1	26.8	11.3	11.6	33.0	42.3
Follow-up	8.5	11.6	7.0	9.1	37.4	54.8
Improvement	59%		60%		−14%	
Locus of control scores						
Pre	9.9	4.6	10.7	5.9	10.4	4.4
Post	6.8	3.1	8.9	6.9	8.7	3.2
Follow-up	7.4	3.7	8.5	6.1	11.6	3.3
Improvement	24%		17%		16%	
Psychosomatic Checklist scores						
Pre	31.9	18.3	18.9	8.2	26.9	20.2
Post	13.1	13.0	9.9	8.4	20.1	15.1
Follow-up	16.5	16.4	11.6	7.2	26.4	19.1
Improvement	58%		48%		23%	

[a] Percentage of improvement from preassessment to postassessment.

relaxation was superior to placebo ($p < .05$). Group means and standard deviations of these measures are given in Table 2.

Shifts in locus of control scores as a function of treatment were similar for all groups, as seen in Table 1. Chi-square analysis demonstrated significant pre-post shifts toward internality for biofeedback, $\chi^2 (1) = 7.08$, $p < .01$, relaxation, $\chi^2 (1) = 6.00$, $p < .05$, and placebo, $\chi^2 (1) = 6.00$, $p < .05$. There was no significant correlation between initial locus of control scores and amount of headache reduction.

Follow-Up Data

As displayed in Figure 1 and Table 2, treatment effectiveness of biofeedback and relaxation training continued to improve for the eight available subjects in each treatment at a 4-month follow-up. This is substantiated by an overall analysis of covariance F of 4.62 (df = 2, $p <$ .05) showing biofeedback and relaxation equivalently superior to placebo (see a priori F values in Table 1). This analysis was done by comparing the H_D follow-up data of treatment groups to posttreatment data of placebo. Placebo follow-up data were contaminated by the effect that two of the women had quit their stress-related jobs, another had sought relaxation training at the clinic, one had gotten a divorce, a fifth subject was in the hospital at the time, and a sixth man was undergoing twice-weekly chiropractic massages for his headaches. All this had taken place during the 4-month interim, whereas no such changes were noted with the treatment subjects as evaluated by questionnaire.

Covariance analysis of EMG data was significant, $F(2,23) = 5.61$, $p <$ .05, with the results in Table 1 suggesting that relaxation effects were more reliable than biofeedback. Psychosomatic complaints and medication intake reduction held stable as can be seen in Table 1.

DISCUSSION

EMG feedback and relaxation instructions were found to be equally superior treatments to medication placebo in reducing headache activity and frontalis EMG. These procedures were also similarly effective in producing reductions of medication intake and ancillary psychosomatic complaints. Even though the relaxation instructions did not significantly differ from placebo on reduction of headache activity at posttreatment, the continually improving profile of relaxation in Figure 1, contrasted to placebo and the clinically significant data presented in Table 3, indicate that relaxation instruction is a superior technique after only 4 weeks of treatment. This treatment effectiveness is further substantiated by placebo subjects' consistent reports of seeking alternative forms of headache relief during the 4 months following treatment, whereas no such reports were received from treatment subjects. This is not a reaction to being in a "placebo group," since the subjects were never informed that they were receiving an inert drug until after the follow-up assessment.

Reduction in medication is not surprising since with fewer headaches there should be less need for medication. This, along with the stable reduction of ancillary psychosomatic complaints, was also reported by

TABLE 3

FREQUENCY DISTRIBUTION OF (SUBJECTS') IMPROVEMENT ON H_D SCORES AT POSTTREATMENT
AND FOLLOW-UP, RELATIVE TO PRETREATMENT LEVELS

Range of % improvement	Biofeedback		Relaxation		Placebo	
	Posttreatment	Follow-up	Posttreatment	Follow-up	Posttreatment	Follow-up
0–24	1	1	2	0	4	4
25–49	0	0	3	1	3	1
50–74	5	2	2	3	1	2
75–100	3	5	2	4	1	1

Budzynski's finding of an r of .90 between reduction of headache activity and reduction of frontalis EMG, the same correlation in the present study yielded an r of .42. In other words, reduction in EMG only accounted for 18 percent of the variance in treatment effect. The difference in these two findings is possibly a consequence of EMG sampling; whereas Budzynski et al.'s EMG readings were taken during feedback sessions, relevant EMG readings in the present analysis were recorded during 2 weeks of pretreatment and posttreatment when no feedback or training was offered.

This low correlation raises the question of what else accounts for the treatment effect besides the sampled EMG reduction. It is proposed that successful treatment is dependent on four steps: (a) learning EMG reduction in treatment; (b) increased relaxation throughout daily activities; (c) recognizing early onset of a headache; and (d) adequate, early application of relaxation skills. Budzynski et al.'s procedure focused on feedback training and application and was thus concerned with a and d, whereas the present study additionally required subjects to use their relaxation skills, in the form of cue-controlled breathing, daily prior to each meal, and to record and examine conditions in which headaches arose. Hence, this study also focused on Steps b and c. The effect of incorporating additional skills in the treatment paradigm allows additional techniques to contribute to the treatment effect. This multidimensional approach achieved similar therapeutic effects in 8 hours of treatment to Budzynski's 16 hours of treatment. However, the specific relevance of this additional focus needs further research to delineate its treatment contribution.

In considering Table 3, the range of variance is observed to be large in all groups. Initial locus of control scores were anticipated to account for some of this variance, but its low correlation with percentage of reduction in H_D indicates the poor predictability of this instrument. The Nowicki-Strickland Locus of Control Scale is primarily concerned with perceived control of social interactions. Possibly, an instrument constructed to measure perception of intrapersonal self-control, specifically on a physiological dimension, would have a greater predictive value. It is apparent that additional subject dimensions should be investigated to allow greater prediction of treatment responsiveness and to permit individual tailoring of a therapeutic procedure. Subsequent research at the clinic suggests that subject variables, such as extreme obsessive-compulsive characteristics, may interfere with the effective use of biofeedback techniques; that is, excessive concern with auditory feedback may produce an interfering performance anxiety. For such subjects, a relaxation procedure absent of an overt achievement criterion, such as verbal relaxation training, may be the treatment of choice. Investigation of such a hypothesis is presently being conducted.

Recent research (Shoemaker & Tasto, 1975) supplements the present study's findings of equivalent effectiveness for a biofeedback technique and relaxation instruction in the treatment of the psychosomatic complaint essential hypertension. We also concur with their conclusion that optimal results may be obtained by combining biofeedback techniques and relaxation instructions or by using different types of biofeedback techniques.

In using intervention techniques such as EMG feedback and relaxation instructions in treatment of headaches, one must be sure that the headache source is a high level of neuromuscular activity. Additionally, it should be investigated whether maintenance of headaches is not being contributed to by secondary gains or resulting from a modeling effect.

Given these precautions, either relaxation technique is a justified intervention.

REFERENCES

BERNSTEIN, D. A. & BORKOVEC, T. D. *Progressive Relaxing Training: A Manual for the Helping Professions.* Chicago: Research Press, 1973.

BLANCHARD, E. B., YOUNG, L. C., & JACKSON. Clinical applications of biofeedback training. *Arch. Gen. Psychiat.,* 1974, 30, 573-589.

BUDZYNSKI, T. H., STOYVA, J. M., ADLER, C. S., & MULLANEY, D. J. EMG biofeedback and tension headaches: A controlled outcome study. *Sem. Psychiat.,* 1973, 5, 387-410.

COX, D. J. *Differential Effectiveness of EMG Feedback, Verbal Relaxation Instructions and Medication Placebo with Muscle Contraction Headaches* (master's thesis, University of Louisville, 1974), University Microfilms, No. 31RB2.

FICHTLER, H. & ZIMMERMAN, R. R. Changes in reported pain from tension headaches. *Percept. Mot. Skills,* 1973, 36, 712.

JACOBSON, E. *Progressive Relaxation.* Chicago: University of Chicago Press, 1935.

JACOBSON, E. *Modern Treatment of Tense Patients.* Springfield, Ill.: Charles C Thomas, 1970.

KASHIWAGI, T., McCLURE, J. N., & WETZEL, R. D. Headache and psychiatric disorders. *Dis. Nerv. Syst.,* 1972, 33, 659-663.

McKENZIE, R. E., EHRISMAN, W. J., MONTGOMERY, P. S., & BARNES, R. H. The treatment of headache by means of electroencephalographic biofeedback. *Headache,* 1974, 13, 164-172.

NOWICKI, S. & DUKE, M. A Locus of Control Scale for Adults: An Alternative to the Rotter. Unpublished manuscript, Emory University, 1972.

RUSSELL, R. K. & SIPICH, J. R. Treatment of test anxiety by cue-control relaxation. *Behav. Ther.,* 1974, 5, 673-676.

SHOEMAKER, J. E. & TASTO, D. L. The effects of muscle relaxation on blood pressure of essential hypertensives. *Behav. Res. & Ther.,* 1975, 13, 29-43.

TASTO, D. L. & HINKLE, J. M. Muscle relaxation treatment for tension headaches. *Behav. Res. & Ther.,* 1973, 11, 347-349.

WATERS, W. E. & O'CONNOR, P. J. Epidemiology of headaches and migraine in women. *J. Neurol. Neurosurg. Psychiat.,* 1971, 34, 148-155.

WICKRAMASEKERA, I. Electromyographic feedback training and tension headaches: Preliminary observations. *Amer. J. Clin. Hyp.,* 1972, 15, 83-85.

WICKRAMASEKERA, I. The application of verbal instructions and EMG feedback training to the management of tension headaches—preliminary observations. *Headache,* 1973, 13, 74-76.

WINER, R. J. *Statistical Principles in Experimental Design.* New York: McGraw-Hill, 1971.

WOLFF, R. *Headaches and Other Head Pains.* New York: Oxford University Press, 1972.

SECTION III: BIOFEEDBACK AND OTHER
STRATEGIES OF SELF-MANAGEMENT

11

LEARNED CONTROL OF GASTRIC ACID SECRETIONS IN ULCER PATIENTS

Peter R. Welgan

*Orange County Department of Mental Health and the School
of Medicine, University of California, Irvine*

The study was an attempt to train increases in the pH of
gastric acid secretions in specific ulcer patients. In Experiment 1, in the presence of pH feedback, 10 Ss showed significant increases in pH of gastric acid secretions, while acid
concentration and volume of secretions significantly declined. When feedback was subsequently withheld, no significant changes appeared in these measures. A second study
then tested if initial changes following the basal period
were experimental effects. In Experiment 2, 10 Ss were divided into two groups; one group received no feedback after
a basal condition, while a second group received feedback
after the basal condition. Results showed that significant
increases in pH and decreases in acid concentration and vol-

Reprinted from *Psychosomatic Medicine*, Vol. 36, No. 5, September-October, 1974,
411-419. Copyright 1974, American Psychosomatic Society, Inc.

This article is adapted from a dissertation submitted to the University of Wisconsin, Milwaukee, as partial fulfillment of requirements toward the Ph.D. The
author wishes to thank Thomas Stampfl for his guidance as Committee Chairman
and Walter Hogan of the Milwaukee County Hospital for his indispensable advice
and support.

253

ume occurred only after the onset of pH feedback. This preliminary work suggests that gastric acid secretions may be
altered and controlled with the appropriate feedback.

INTRODUCTION

Information or feedback to an individual of his own biological functions has become an important variable in the control of the autonomic
nervous system (ANS). Since Kimmel and Hill (17) first demonstrated
the possibility of instrumental conditioning of the galvanic skin response (GSR), investigators have reported the learned control of a
wide range of ANS responses including GSR (14, 22), heart rate (11, 12),
heart rate variable (16, 19), blood pressure (8), vasomotor responses (6,
7) and salivation (5).

Recent research in training of gastric responses by Miller (20) and
his colleagues has had significant implications for the study of several
gastrointestinal disorders. In a series of studies on the learning of visceral and glandular responses, these investigators were able to control
the blood flow and motility in the stomach of the rat.

It would seem that if similar control of gastrointestinal functions
could be obtained in humans, factors contributing to conditions such
as peptic ulcer might be controlled.

The excessive secretion of hydrochloric acid in the stomach is considered an important factor in the formation of peptic ulcer (15, 23).
Hydrochloric acid is known to produce ulceration and digestion of the
stomach tissues (9) as well as to reduce the neutralizing capability of
the stomach mucus secretions (13, 21). Feedback of the pH of stomach
contents might provide sufficient cues from the stomach to enable an
individual to control his own gastric acid secretions.

It was the purpose of this study, therefore, to attempt to reduce
stomach hydrochloric acid secretions by providing feedback to the subject of the pH of his own gastric contents. It was hypothesized that increases in the pH of gastric secretions could be obtained by permitting
the subject to monitor changes in pH and instructing him to increase
pH during the experimental period. It was further hypothesized that
during control conditions in which feedback was withheld and instructional set changed, pH would significantly decrease.

Since increases in pH are affected by either the reduction of the acid
secreted in the stomach or the increase in the volume of alkaline and
neutral fluids (e.g., mucus), it was hypothesized that increases in pH
would be associated with reductions in the volume of acid secreted.

Method

Subjects. Ten subjects (*Ss*), 8 male and 2 female, with duodenal ulcer were selected for the study. The diagnosis of previous or current ulcer was established at x-ray by the demonstration of a deformity of the duodenal bulb and/or the presence of an ulcer crater in the duodenum. All *Ss* were within a range of 35 to 60 years old, and all had previously completed a gastric secretory analysis and were accustomed to the nasogastric tube in their stomach. Subjects for this study were selected if their pH was less than or equal to 3.5, and their volume of stomach secretions was at least 10 cc/30 minutes.

Apparatus. Stomach contents were aspirated under continuous suction (3 in Hg) with a Gomco Thermotic Drainage Pump through an Anderson multilimen tube specifically designed to prevent nasogastric tube plug-up by obstructions in the stomach (e.g., mucus, stomach wall enclosures). Acid changes in the gastric secretions were monitored on a Beckman Model 76 pH meter and graphically recorded on a Beckman pH recorder interfaced with the meter. A Beckman pH glass electrode and reference electrode were mounted in the nasogastric tub, 1 foot from the *S*'s face. The electrodes were inserted vertically in the wall of a 1 × 1.5 inch collection cylinder so that the electrode tips were continuously immersed in 0.1 to 0.3 ml. of gastric secretions. Volumes exceeding this amount drained into another collection vessel. This procedure assured a reliable and continuous recording without contamination of stomach samples from residual secretions.

Changes in pH activated a tape recorder by closing a circuit to the pH recorder. The distance between contacts on the pen of the pH recorder and on a movable rail were adjusted to permit changes in the response criterion of 0.1 pH unit, that is, to allow for shaping procedures. Shaping was achieved by progressively reinforcing increases of 0.1 pH. When this was maintained for 30 seconds, criterion was increased 0.1 pH. Repeating tones (5000 Hz; 55 dB) of 0.5 second duration with 0.5 second interbeat intervals were presented when the circuit was closed and the pH reached criterion.

A portable curtain shielded the recording equipment and the experimenter (*E*) from *S*'s view.

Procedure

Preexperimental period. The study was conducted in the gastric secretory laboratory between 8:00 A.M. and 12:00 P.M., after the *S* had fasted for 12 hours. No anticholinergic drugs were given for at least 72 hours prior to the test.

An Anderson tube was passed under fluoroscopic control so that its tip was positioned in the most dependent portion of the stomach. The S was then placed on his left side on an hydraulic stretcher. During the entire experiment Ss expectorated saliva collected in their mouth.

Experimental period. During the basal period, gastric secretions were continuously aspirated for 15 minutes and the contents discarded. During the following 15 minutes, the contents were collected for analysis.

In the basal (B) period, the face of the pH meter was screened from the S, and he was instructed to relax and become comfortable.

Experimental task. The 1 hour and 15 minute experimental task consisted of three 15-minute experimental (E) periods alternated with two 15-minute rest (R) periods. During each experimental period a screen was removed from the face of the pH meter to permit feedback of the stomach pH changes on the expanded (2 pH unit range) scale of the meter.

During the R periods the meter was screened from the S although pH was continuously recorded.

Prior to the 15-minute experimental period, the S was informed of the nature of the task. The relationship was described between acid secretions, movement of the pH meter indicator needle and the presentation of the tones. Then the following instructions were given:

> During this period, you may learn to control your own stomach acid. Look at the meter in front of you. It measures the amount of acid in the contents of your stomach on a scale from very acid (point to the left side of the scale to pH 1) to less acid (point to right side of the scale of pH 14). Your task is to learn to keep the indicator needle moving toward the less acid side of the scale. Thoughts and feelings (emotions) are believed to influence stomach acidity. See if you can create the feelings and thoughts that will move the needle toward the less acid side. When your acid decreases, you will hear a repeating tone. That will indicate to you that you are reducing your acid. When the tone stops, it means that you are no longer decreasing your acid. Therefore, you should try to keep the tones on as long as possible. That will indicate to you that you are continuing to reduce your acid. You will also be able to see the needle move in front of you.

The S was then asked to repeat the instructions to insure they were understood. After each experimental period, S was instructed to stop what he was doing and merely relax. A 15-minute R period followed during which the S received no auditory or visual feedback of his acid secretions.

Measurement of Gastric Acid. Three millimeter samples of gastric secretions from collections during the treatment conditions were titrated with 0.1 N NaOH to pH 7.0 to obtain the concentration of HCl in milliequivalents (mEq), expressed as mEq of hydrochloric acid/liter.

Volume of gastric secretions was measured for each 15-minute treatment condition in cubic centimeters.

Results

pH. The 15-minute B, E and R conditions were divided into three 5-minute intervals. In each 5-minute interval, the highest pH was measured, and the three 5-minute measures were averaged to form the mean pH of each 15-minute condition.

A Cochran (3) test for homogeneity of variance between basal and treatment variances was not significant ($C = 0.2749$).

A repeated measures analysis of variance showed a significant change in pH ($F = 4.42$, $df = 5,45$; $p < 0.05$) in Table 1. A comparison of mean changes with a Newman-Keuls (18) test showed that pH increased significantly ($p < 0.05$) from the basal period to the E_2 period. However, no other changes between B, E and R conditions were significant.

Hydrochloric acid concentration. An analysis of variance of stomach secretions (Table 2) showed a significant change in acid concentration ($F = 23.85$, $df = 5,45$; $p < 0.01$) between treatments. A Newman-Keuls test showed that acid concentration dropped significantly from the basal condition to the E_1 ($p < 0.01$), E_2 ($p < 0.01$, R_2 ($p < 0.01$) and E_3 ($p < 0.01$) treatments. No differences were found between B and R_1 or between E and R conditions.

Volume of stomach secretions. Analysis of variance of volume changes in these periods (Table 3) showed significant changes between conditions ($F = 2.55$, $df = 5,45$; $p < 0.05$). A Newman-Keuls test showed a significant decline in volume from the basal condition to E_1 ($p < 0.05$), R_2 ($p < 0.05$) and R_2 ($p < 0.05$) treatments. Volume measurements did not significantly differ between E and R conditions.

A partial correlation (10) was also performed to determine the relationship between acid secretions and stomach volume changes with the variance due to nonacid secretions removed. Declines in the volume of stomach contents were found to be significantly related to declines in acid secretions in the R_1 ($r = 0.66$; $p < 0.05$), E_2 ($r = 0.77$; $p < 0.01$), R_2 ($r = 0.90$; $p < 0.01$) and E_3 ($r = 0.69$; $p < 0.01$) treatments.

TABLE 1

Means and Standard Deviations of Subjects' pH in the Basal (B)
Experimental (E) and Resting (R) Treatments

| | Treatments | | | | | |
	B	E_1	R_1	E_2	R_2	E_3
Means	1.91	2.88	1.98	2.20	1.63	1.68
Standard deviations	0.74	1.63	3.08	3.30	2.84	2.69

TABLE 2

Means and Standard Deviations of Subjects' Acid Concentration/
Liter in the Basal (B), Experimental (E) and
Resting (R) Treatments

| | Treatments | | | | | |
	B	E_1	R_1	E_2	R_2	E_3
Means	55.4	42.7	41.8	39.7	38.6	37.3
Standard deviations	35.3	28.7	32.3	37.3	36.9	35.9

TABLE 3

Means and Standard Deviations of Subjects' Stomach Secretion
Volume in the Basal (B), Experimental (E) and
Resting (R) Treatments

| | Treatments | | | | | |
	B	E_1	R_1	E_2	R_2	E_3
Means	46.2	27.3	22.6	27.5	22.9	30.1
Standard deviations	39.9	15.7	12.1	20.9	15.4	20.3

Significant changes in pH, acid concentration and volume were found between the basal and treatment conditions. However, there were no significant differences between any E and R conditions. It was difficult, therefore, to determine if the initial significant changes in acid and volume were experimental effects or normal changes that occur after a 30-minute rest period. Therefore, a second experiment was conducted to answer these qustions.

EXPERIMENT 2

It was expected that if Ss could control their stomach acid secretions, decreases in these measures would occur only after the start of pH feedback and an instructional set. Therefore a significant difference was expected between a group provided a prolonged basal period and a group provided feedback during the same period.

Method

Subjects. Ten male duodenal ulcer patients served as Ss in this study. All Ss met the same requirements as those in Experiment 1. The Ss were randomly assigned to one of two groups.

Procedure

The procedure in Experiment 1 was used in Experiment 2 with the following exceptions.

Experimental task. The experimental task consisted of a 30-minute basal period followed by three 15-minute treatment periods.

Group I. Following the 30-minute basal period, Ss continued to rest in an additional 15-minute R period. Two 15-minute periods followed during which pH feedback was provided and instructions given to increase pH. The experimental procedure was $B-R-E_1-E_2$.

Group II. Following the 30-minute basal period, pH feedback was introduced and instructions given to increase the pH in a 15-minute period. Feedback of pH was withheld in the following R control condition and S was instructed to rest. A second 15-minute E period followed in which S was given pH feedback and instructed to increase pH. The experimental procedure was $B-E_1-H-E_2$.

Results

A Cochran test for homogeneity of variance between basal and treatment variances was not significant $(C = 0.3125)$.

TABLE 4

Means and Standard Deviations of pH During Treatments for
Group I (B-R-E_1-E_2) and Group II (B-E_1-R-E_2)

Groups		Treatments			
		1	2	3	4
Group I	X̄	2.17	2.32	2.49	2.89
B-R-E_1-E_2					
	SD	3.01	2.48	1.25	1.79
Group II	X̄	1.72	1.81	1.99	2.84
B-E_1-R-E_2					
	SD	2.20	1.36	0.75	1.41

A 2 × 4 repeated measures analysis of variance showed significant changes ($F = 17.75$, $df = 3,24$; $p < 0.01$) in pH across treatments (Table 4). A Newman-Keuls test showed that pH increased significantly ($p < 0.01$) from the basal period to the E_2 treatment. The pH did not change significantly during other periods, however.

No significant differences were found ($F = 2.29$, $df = 1,8$; NS) between groups, although there was a significant Groups × Treatments interaction ($F = 6.63$, $df = 1,8$; $p < 0.01$). A further analysis of simple main effects showed that pH increased across treatments in Group I ($F = 13.00$, $df = 3,24$; $p < 0.01$) and Group II ($F = 8.14$, $df = 3,24$; $p < 0.01$). In the E_2 treatment, Group I had significantly higher pH (F 24.91, $df = 1,8$; $p < 0.01$) than Group II. However, the groups did not differ significantly in any other periods.

Hydrochloric acid concentration. An analysis of hydrochloric acid concentration showed significant decreases ($F = 14.61$, $df = 3,24$; $p < 0.01$) in acid concentration across treatments (Table 5).

A Newman-Keuls test showed acid concentration decreased significantly ($p < 0.01$) between the basal period and all treatments.

There were no significant differences ($F = 1.4$, $df = 1,8$; NS) between groups in their ability to reduce acid concentration. However, there was a significant Groups × Treatments interaction ($F = 3.94$, $df = 3,24$; $p < 0.05$). An analysis of simple main effects showed that acid concentration significantly decreased in Group I ($F = 13.00$, $df = 1,8$; $p < 0.01$) and Group II ($F < 8.42$, $df = 3,24$; $p < 0.01$). When pH feedback was introduced to Group II during E_1, acid concentration significantly decreased ($F = 3.92$, $df = 3,24$; $p < 0.05$) compared to Group I in the corresponding R treatment period. When pH feedback was withheld in

TABLE 5

Means and Standard Deviations of Stomach Secretion Volume
during Treatments for Group I (B-R-E_1-E_2)
and Group II (B-E_1-R-E_2)

Groups		Treatments			
		1	2	3	4
Group I B-R-E_1-E_2	X̄	36.22	38.10	12.63	8.69
	SD	30.00	24.38	7.67	6.12
Group II B-E_1-R-E_2	X̄	49.30	11.57	14.92	5.11
	SD	28.51	9.49	11.85	4.69

Group II during the R condition, acid concentration significantly increased compared to acid concentration in E_1 ($p < 0.05$ and E_2 ($p < 0.05$) treatments.

Volume. An analysis of variance of changes in stomach volume showed significant changes ($F = 27.34$, $df = 3,24$; $p < 0.05$) across treatments (Table 6).

A Newman-Keuls test showed that volume decreased significantly ($p < 0.01$) between the basal period and all treatment conditions. While there were no significant differences ($F = 4.24$, $df = 1,8$; NS) between groups in volume changes, there was a significant Groups × Treatments interaction ($F = 8.15$, 3, 24; $p < 0.01$). An analysis of simple main effects showed significant declines in volumes across treatments in Group I ($F = 17.90$, $df = 3,24$; $p < 0.01$) and Group II ($F = 17.62$, $df = 3,24$; $p < 0.01$). In E_1 treatment, Group II significantly ($F = 9.77$, $df = 3,24$; $p < 0.01$) reduced the volume of secretions compared to Group I in a corresponding R period. They did not differ significantly in other treatment periods, however.

Partial correlations were performed to determine the effect of acid secretion changes on the total volume of gastric secretions. In Group I, declines in the volume of secretions were significantly related to declines in acid secretions in E_1 ($r = 0.82$; $p < 0.01$) and E_2 ($r = 0.74$; $p < 0.01$). In Group II, declines in these measures were significantly related in both E_1 ($r = 0.85$; $p < 0.01$) and E_2 ($r = 0.65$; $p < 0.05$).

An examination of pH changes in this study shows a discrepancy between the highly significant F test and the relatively slight increase in mean pH over sessions seen in Table 4. This discrepancy may be ac-

TABLE 6

Means and Standard Deviations of Acid Concentration/
Liter during Treatments for Group I $(B\text{-}R\text{-}E_1\text{-}E_2)$
and Group II $(B\text{-}E_1\text{-}R\text{-}E_2)$

Groups		Treatments			
		1	2	3	4
Group I	$\bar{X}$	78.13	80.29	53.85	37.92
$B\text{-}R\text{-}E_1\text{-}E_2$	SD	52.73	39.75	41.66	19.07
Group II	$\bar{X}$	89.01	45.84	65.11	28.32
$B\text{-}E_1\text{-}R\text{-}E_2$	SD	60.15	23.08	29.77	20.46

counted for by the relatively similar performance of Ss within each group. While mean performance changed slightly over treatments, the changes were significant due to the relatively small within-group error variance during these sessions. The fact that pH did not change as markedly as acid concentration and volume may be due partly to the nature of the pH measure. Large changes in acid concentration and volume typically produce relatively small alterations in stomach pH. It can be seen in Experiment 1 that a similar relationship between pH and two measures did not exist. The inconsistency between the findings of these studies cannot easily be interpreted, and a clear explanation awaits further investigation.

DISCUSSION

The major hypothesis of this investigation, whether pH of stomach acid secretions could be learned, received partial support from this study. The findings from the two studies showed that the feedback technique used was associated with a significant increase in pH and significant decreases in both acid concentration and the volume of acid secreted.

Results of Experiment 1 supported the expectation that pH would increase and acid secretions decrease with the introduction of pH feedback and instructional set. However, the results did not support the expectation that these measures would reverse significantly when feedback was withheld and instructional set changed. It was not clear, therefore, whether declines in acid and volume after the basal period were experimental effects or normal gastric changes following a 30-minute rest period. Experiment 2 showed that these changes occurred only after the introduction of pH and an instructional set.

Experiment 2 generally supported the results of Experiment 1. Groups I and II significantly increased pH and decreased acid concentration and volume following the basal period. Unlike the first study, the second study showed that acid concentration and volume increased significantly in Group II when pH feedback was withheld and instructional set changed.

Establishing learned control of the gastric response in humans depends on the accuracy and reliability of the pH measurement. Accurate measurement of acid pH depends first on the place of the tip of the nasogastric tube in the stomach. The optimal placement of the tip of the nasogastric tube is in the most dependent portion of the stomach (i.e., antrum), an area of large parietal cell concentration where fluids tend to pool. Measurement from other areas (e.g., cardia) tend to be affected by artifact from large concentrations of mucus cells.

As a measurement of free hydrogen ion, pH independently represents the hydrochloric acid concentration in the stomach. Therefore, feedback of pH may not provide the "handle" necessary for the control of the glandular response of acid secretion. A more direct measurement such as milliequivalents of hydrochloric acid may provide a more accurate measurement of acid concentration. However, research in this area must await technological advances in biofeedback instrumentation.

The accuracy and reliability of the online measurement of pH outside the stomach was another concern of the study. The procedure eventually adopted had the advantage of continuous measurement of pH while allowing for the collection of stomach secretions for *in vitro* analyses. The problem of pH measurement outside the stomach lies in the length of time required to transport the fluids to the electrodes. Estimates of the time ranged from 2 to 15 seconds depending on the viscosity of the fluid. The viscosity was related to the amount of mucus aspirated in the fluid; the more mucus, the greater the viscosity and, therefore, the greater the time needed to transport the fluid. In view of this fact it was necessary to inform the subjects of the time interval needed to transport the gastric fluids, to provide a mediation of the response during the delay.

A more critical problem arising from the present measurement technique concerned whether the duration of the gastric response was sufficiently long (at least 15 seconds) for conditioning to occur. Although parametric studies of human gastric responses are not available, there are indications in the literature that gastric reactions associated with conditioned stimuli are sufficiently long. For example, Crawshaw, Frazier, and Wanderer (4) found that medical students, who were shown food, secreted acid at a significantly high rate for a period of at least 15 minutes. Badgley, Spiro, and Sinay (1) found significant declines in acid and volume of fluid during mental arithmetic tasks throughout a 15-minute experimental period.

While this evidence does not establish a clear relationship between a gastric response and a single stimulus, it does show that an experimental task may produce a response, the duration of which exceeds 15 seconds. Measurement problems of a temporal nature may be partly reduced through the use of an intragastric pH electrode.

Current research has shown that the apparent division between the CNS and ANS learning characteristics may result from the way the effectors of these systems relate to the environment rather than from the basic differences in the properties of these branches of the nervous system. Miller (20) has speculated that since smooth muscles and glands do not typically have an instrumental effect on the external environment, instrumental responses tend not to be reinforced. Through augmented sensory feedback of smooth muscle and gland responses, however, research tends to be showing a similarity between the two branches of the nervous system. In this regard, the present studies may provide a step toward applying these findings to the understanding of clinically related problems.

REFERENCES

1. BADGLEY, L., SPIRO, H., & SENAY, E. Effect of mental arithmetic on gastric secretions. *Psychophysiology*, 1969, 5, 633-637.
2. BARON, J. Studies of basal and peak acid with an augmented histamine test. *Gut.*, 1963, 4, 136-144.
3. COCHRAN, W. Some consequences when the assumptions for the analysis of variance are not satisfied. *Biometrics*, 1947, 3, 22-38.
4. CRAWSHAW, H., FRAZER, D., & WANDERER, T. Can psychic stimulation cause gastric acid secretion in man? *Lancet*, 1968, 1j, 66-68.
5. DELSE, C. & FEATHER, R. The effect of augmented sensory feedback on control of salivation. *Psychophysiology*, 1968, 5, 15-21.
6. DiCARA, L. & MILLER, N. Instrumental learning of peripheral vasomotor responses by curarized rat. *Commun. Behav. Biol.*, 1968, 1 (A), 209-212. (a)
7. DiCARA, L. & MILLER, N. Instrumental learning of vasomotor responses by rats: Learning to respond differentially in two ears. *Science*, 1968, 159, 1485-1486. (b)
8. DiCARA, L. & MILLER, N. Instrumental learning of systolic blood pressure responses by curarized rats: Dissociation of cardiac and vascular changes. *Psychosom. Med.*, 1968, 30, 489-494. (c)

9. DRAGSTEDT, L. R.: Contributions to the physiology of the stomach; XXXVII. Gastric juice in duodenal and gastric ulcers. *J.A.M.A.*, 1917, 68, 330-333.
10. DuBois, P. *An Introduction to Psychological Statistics.* New York: Harper and Row, 1965.
11. ENGEL, B. & CHISM, R. Operant conditioning of heart rate speeding. *Psychophysiology*, 1967, 3, 418-426.
12. ENGEL, B. & HANSEN, S. Operant conditioning of heart rate slowing. *Psychophysiology*, 1966, 3, 563-567.
13. FLOREY, H. & HARDING, H. The nature of the hormone controlling Brunner's glands. *Quart. J. Exp. Physiol.*, 1935, 25, 329-339.
14. FOWLER, R. & KIMMEL, H. Operant conditioning of GSR. *J. Exp. Psychol.*, 1962, 63, 536-567.
15. HAY, L., VARCO, R., COLE, C., ET AL.: The experimental production of gastric and duodenal ulcers in laboratory animals by the intramuscular injection of histamine in beeswax. *Surg. Gynecol. Obstet.*, 1942, 75, 170-182.
16. HNATIOW, M. & LANG, P. Learned stabilization of cardiac rate. *Psychophysiology*, 1965, 1, 330-336.
17. KIMMEL, E. & HILL, F. Operant conditioning of the GSR. *Psychol. Rep.*, 1960, 7, 555-562.
18. KIRK, R. *Experimental Design: Procedures for the Behavioral Sciences.* Belmont: Brooks/Cole Publishing Company, 1969.
19. LANG, P., SROUFE, L., & HASTINGS, J. Effects of feedback and instructional set on the control of cardiac-rate variability. *J. Exp. Psychol.*, 75, 425-431.
20. MILLER, N. Learning of visceral and glandular responses. *Science*, 1969, 163, 434-445.
21. RIDER, A., MOELLER, J., & PULETTI, E.: Pitfalls and common misconceptions in the treatment of simple peptic ulcers. *Western Med.* 1965 (Feb.), 53-62.
22. SHAPIRO, D. CRIDER, A., & TURSKY, B. Differentiation of an autonomic response through operant reinforcement. *Psychosom. Sci.*, 1964, 1, 147-148.
23. WALPOLE, S., VARCO, R., CODE, C., ET AL. Production of gastric and duodenal ulcer in the cat by intramuscular implantation of histamine. *Proc. Soc. Exp. Biol. Med.*, 1940, 44, 619-621.

SECTION III: BIOFEEDBACK AND OTHER
STRATEGIES OF SELF-MANAGEMENT

12

GENERALIZATION AND MAINTENANCE OF APPROPRIATE BEHAVIOR THROUGH SELF-CONTROL

Hillary Turkewitz, K. Daniel O'Leary

and Marsha Ironsmith

State University of New York at Stony Brook

Eight disruptive children attended an after school reading tutorial program 1 hour a day for 72 days. After baseline, the children evaluated their academic and social behavior. A token program was instituted and then modified to include the following procedures: (a) Points and backup reinforcers were made contingent upon accurate self-ratings; (b) the requirement of accurately matching teacher ratings was faded until the children had complete control over point distribution; and (c) backup reinforcers were also faded and eliminated. While there was a lack of generalization of appropriate social behavior to the regular classroom

Reprinted with permission from *Journal of Consulting and Clinical Psychology*, Vol. 43, No. 4, 1975, 577-583. Copyright 1975, American Psychological Association.

This study was supported by U.S. Office of Education Grant OEG-0-71-2872. The opinions expressed herein, however, do not necessarily reflect the position or policy of the U.S. Office of Education, and no official endorsement by the U.S. Office of Education should be inferred. We are especially grateful to Warren Lowey and Thomas Stone and the teachers of the transitional adjustment classes of the Three Village Schools, Stony Brook, New York, for referring children to us. The authors wish to thank Dennis Dubey and Ron Prinz for their helpful suggestions.

266

situation, generalization was demonstrated in the 15-minute control period of every class, and maintenance was demonstrated in the final week of the program after all backup reinforcers were withdrawn.

Many of the early classroom token programs demonstrated substantial reductions in inappropriate behavior, but when the token programs were withdrawn, this behavior change was not maintained (Birnbrauer, Wolf, Kidder, & Tague, 1965; Kuypers, Becker, & O'Leary, 1968; O'Leary, Becker, Evans, & Saudargas, 1969). Similarly, many studies have not found generalization effects of the token program to times of the day when the program was not in effect (Kuypers et al., 1968; Meichenbaum, Bowers, & Ross, 1968; O'Leary et al., 1969; Wolf, Giles, & Hall, 1968). Recently, however, there have been reports of maintenance or generalization. Bolstad and Johnson (1972) noted maintenance effects following removal of a token program, but since observers were responsible for token administration and checking of students' self-evaluative behavior, the continued observer presence during the token withdrawal phase may have had a suppressive effect on disruptive behavior (Surratt & Ulrich, 1969). Drabman (1973) had student captains or teachers evaluate student behavior following removal of the rewards associated with a token program and found that disruptive behavior remained relatively low during the reward withdrawal period. Walker and Buckley (1972) assessed various maintenance strategies following a special class token reinforcement program and found that if teachers continue to systematically apply variations of the special class behavioral interventions, the appropriate behavior is maintained at higher rates than if no maintenance intervention is used. O'Leary, Drabman, and Kass (1973) demonstrated maintenance of treatment effects in 8 weeks following withdrawal of token program where no maintenance intervention was used. Finally, Drabman, Spitalnik, and O'Leary (1973) demonstrated very clear generalization effects of a token program to times of the day when the token program was not in effect. In sum, there is accumulating evidence of maintenance and generalization, although maintenance of appropriate behavior has not been unequivocally demonstrated in the absence of some maintenance strategy.

The present study was designed to produce both generalization and maintenance of a token reinforcement effect through the use of several procedures designed to increase the probability of successful self-management. As in the Drabman et al. (1973) study, the children were taught to evaluate their own behavior, and the teachers' control over point distribution was faded and eliminated. In addition, the backup reinforcers were gradually withdrawn. Thus, this study was a systematic replication and extension of Drabman et al. (1973).

METHOD

Children and Teachers

The experimental class consisted of eight children, five girls and three boys, between 7 and 11 years of age. The children, who were in "transitional adjustment" classes for students with academic and social problems, attended an after school token reinforcement reading program at the University laboratory school. Children were referred by their teachers for the program if they displayed high rates of disruptive classroom behavior and were at least a year below grade level in reading. Two female students, an undergraduate who had completed student teaching and a graduate student, served as teachers in this study. The class met 5 days a week from 4:00 to 5:00 p.m. Parents were asked to bring their children at least four times a week.

In addition to the eight children involved in the program, eight control children, who were matched for age and California Achievement Test reading scores and who were also in "transitional adjustment" classes, were observed in their home classes and given the same preachievement and postachievement tests as the children in the program.

Procedure

This study lasted over a period of 4.5 months including 72 school days. Twelve different conditions were instituted at this time. The hour was divided into four 15 minute intervals, one of which was randomly chosen each day as a control period in which tokens were never given. The 12 conditions were as follows: (a) baseline, (b) goals, (c) self-evaluation, (d) tokens, (e) matching—100 percent, (f) matching—50 percent, (g) matching—33⅓ percent, (h) no matching, (i) fading backups—50 percent, (j) fading backups—33⅓ percent, (k) fading backups—12½ percent, and (l) no backups. These procedures are similar to those used by Drabman et al. (1973) with the exception of Phases i-l. The conditions involved the following procedures:

Baseline. In this condition, the children were given Sullivan readers (Sullivan, 1969) and asked to work as far as they could. Every 15 minutes, they were stopped and their progress was noted in their book. Throughout the program, the two teachers were continually giving individual aid to the children at their desks and having them read out loud to develop their phonic skills. During this time teachers were asked to use any form of disciplinary control they thought was appropriate. This discipline primarily involved the use of praise and ignore techniques, although reprimands were used on occasion, and if a child was disrupting the entire class he or she was asked to leave the room and sit in the "principal's" office. This isolation procedure was used four times in the first three conditions of the program; it was never necessary after tokens were introduced. Baseline lasted 4 days.

Goals. In this phase, children were assigned goals that were written on a card taped to their desks at the beginning of each 15-minute interval. Goals continued to be assigned during all subsequent phases. Disruptive behavior was handled as in baseline. This condition lasted 6 days.

Self-evaluation. In this condition, children were asked to rate themselves on their goal cards at the end of every 15-minute interval. Children were instructed to give themselves up to 5 points for their academic work and up to 5 points for their behavior during the interval. Teachers also rated students during this phase; the students were given general feedback on their self-ratings but were not informed of the exact teachers' rating. This condition was in effect for 5 days.

Tokens. During this phase the children were not asked to rate their own behavior. Instead it was explained that the teachers would be giving them points after three of the four intervals and that these points could be exchanged for candy, snacks, and small toys at the end of the hour. One randomly chosen interval served as a control period during which generalization was assessed. At the beginning of each control interval, the teachers announced that no points would be awarded during that 15-minute period. The control period during this and all subsequent phases was identical to the goal phase; i.e., children were assigned goals at the beginning of the period, but they were not asked to evaluate their behavior, and the teachers did not evaluate the children or give them rewards. During the three token intervals, the teachers were told to give the children up to 5 points for social behavior and up to 5 points for academic behavior. The teachers wrote the number of points on a card, gave the children feedback after each rating, and explained why such a rating was given. An additional contingency for cheating was instituted when it was discovered that the children were not working conscientiously on the Sullivan books but were looking at the answers beforehand. If the child was ever seen cheating during the interval, he lost all 5 academic points.

The number of points necessary to obtain any given reinforcer was determined by taking the retail price of the item and adding one-third. For example, a 15¢ candy bar could be obtained for 20 points. Teachers were advised to rate the children only on their behavior during the interval and not to be influenced by behavior during the control period. This condition lasted 12 days.

Matching—100 percent. In this condition, teachers again asked the children to rate their social and academic behavior. They were informed that if their ratings were within 1 point of the teachers' ratings, they would receive the number of points they had given themselves. If the two ratings matched exactly, they also received a bonus point. However, if there was more than a 1-point discrepancy between the ratings, they got no points for that interval. Teachers praised the students for accuracy in matching and gave feedback on inaccuracy. This phase lasted 8 days.

Matching—50 percent. In this phase, the children were informed that now only half of the children present would match their ratings with the teachers'. Names were chosen beforehand, so that in this phase each child would match an equal number of times. However, at the end of each interval, the names were put on pieces of paper and drawn out of a hat so that the children believed they were randomly chosen. Children who were not chosen to match received the number of points they gave themselves and could not receive a bonus point. Teachers rated all children but only reported their ratings to children who matched. However, they praised accuracy and gave feedback on inaccurate ratings to all children. This phase lasted 5 days.

Matching—33⅓ percent. This phase was identical to the previous phase except that one-third of the children present were chosen each day to match with the teachers'. This phase lasted 4 days.

No matching. In this condition, children were informed that no one would match with the teacher and that they would all receive whatever points they gave themselves. Feedback was still given on the accuracy of the ratings. For the remainder of the study, the children were in complete control of the number of points they received. This phase lasted 5 days.

Fading backups—50 percent. In this condition, each child rated himself and did not match with the teacher. However, at the end of the hour, names of half of the children were chosen from a hat, and only those children were allowed to exchange their points for reinforcers that day. As before, the names were prechosen so that each child would be selected an equal number of times. Teachers' instructions to the children were as follows:

> We have been very happy with the way you have been working. We would like to help you learn how to work well without getting the candy and snacks. Most of the time you have been very accurate in your ratings; we think that you don't need rewards all the time to work well.
>
> What we are going to do at the end of each day is select some of your names—the same way we did when we matched. If your name is selected, you will exchange your points for that day. Each day we will select new names.

Feedback on accuracy of ratings was always given to each child. This phase lasted 5 days.

Fading backups—33⅓ percent. In this phase, the procedures were the same as in Phase i, except that the names of one-third of the children present were chosen each day to exchange their points. This phase lasted 5 days.

Fading backups—12½ percent. This phase was identical to the previous two phases except that only one child was chosen each day to receive backups. This phase lasted 8 days.

No backups. In the final phase, a reinstitution of the self-evaluation condition, the children were informed that they had been doing good work and that we thought they would work without getting prizes. Therefore, they were told to continue to rate themselves during the three rating intervals but that they would no longer be able to trade their points for backups. Feedback on the accuracy of the children's ratings was still given. This phase lasted 5 days.

Dependent Measures

The primary dependent measure was the mean number of disruptive behaviors observed during a 20-second period. The observation code was that used by O'Leary, Kaufman, Kass, and Drabman (1970) for classroom assessment and included recordings of inappropriate verbalizations, aggression, not attending, and being out of their seats. Three trained undergraduates observed the children through a one-way mirror in the University laboratory school. Observations were made on a 20-second observe/10-second record basis. Each child was observed for one 15-minute interval each day. Reliability checks were made an average of 5.4 times per con-

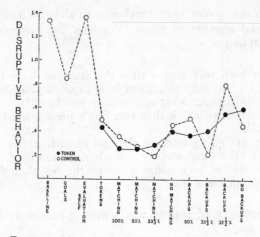

FIGURE 1. Mean number of disruptive behaviors per
20-sec interval across all phases of the study.

dition. Reliability was calculated by dividing the number of perfect
agreements on the occurrences of disruptive behaviors by the total number of agreements plus disagreements. When a reliability check was
taken, an average of the two observations was used for the data point.
Reliabilities averaged across children for the various phases were as
follows: baseline, .96; goals, .95; self-evaluation, .94; tokens, .91; matching
—100 percent, .93; matching—50 percent, .86; matching—33⅓ percent,
.79; no matching, .91; fading backups—50 percent, .95; fading backups—
33⅓ percent, 1.00; fading backups—12½ percent, .97; no backups, .96.

Changes in reading skills were assessed in the experimental and control
children through preadministrations and postadministrations of the California Achievement Test. In addition, two 15-minute class observations
were made of each of the experimental and control children in their
public school classrooms at the beginning and end of the tutorial program. Additional data available were teachers' ratings, the children's
ratings, and the daily progress of the children on the Sullivan readers.

RESULTS

The mean levels of disruptive behavior for the entire class across all
conditions are presented graphically in Figure 1. There were 4 days in
which less than four children were present in the class. The data gathered
on these occasions are not included in the analysis. A repeated-measures

TABLE 1
FREQUENCY OF DISRUPTIVE BEHAVIOR, ACADEMIC PERFORMANCE,
AND STUDENT AND TEACHER RATINGS

Phase	Average no. disruptive behaviors per 20-sec interval		Work output % of goals met	Average ratings		% self-ratings within 1 point of teachers'
	Token period	Control period		Teacher	Student	
Baseline		1.33				
Goals		.85	83.2			
Self-evaluation		1.37	58.2	2.83	8.99	14
Tokens	.43	.50	69.0	7.94		
Matching—100%	.26	.34	85.9	8.05	8.89	84
Matching—50%	.26	.27	80.4	8.60	9.45	81
Matching—33⅓%	.29	.19	93.3	8.73	9.88	81
No matching	.40	.46	86.9	8.28	9.80	61
Backups 50%	.37	.53	94.0	9.18	9.78	83
Backups 33⅓%	.40	.26	86.4	9.01	9.71	81
Backups—12½%	.56	.81	86.2	7.75	9.88	63
No backups	.60	.46	82.8	7.95	9.57	60

analysis of variance revealed a significant treatment effect, $F(11) = 13.51$, $p < .01$. There was no significant difference between the level of disruptive behavior in the control intervals and the token periods, $t(8) = .1$, $p > .7$.

Baseline data indicate that the students were extremely disruptive, averaging 1.33 disruptive behaviors in every 20-second interval. The level of disruptive behavior dropped somewhat when the children were given academic goals every 15 minutes, but the effect of this procedure was only temporary. During the 5 days of self-evaluation, the level of disruptive behavior rose to just slightly above that during baseline. In addition, during self-evaluation the children's ratings of their own behavior were extremely inaccurate; only 14 percent of their ratings fell within 1 point of the teachers'. While the mean teacher rating for this phase was 2.83 points out of a possible 10, the mean self-rating was 8.99. The mean child and teacher ratings across conditions are presented in Table 1.

The disruptive behavior decreased dramatically with the introduction of the token program, both in the control and token intervals. The mean teacher rating rose to 7.94.

The disruptive behavior during token intervals dropped from .43 to .26 during the first matching condition. A similar decrease was evidenced in the control period, from .50 during the token phase to .34 in the matching phase. The percentage of accurate matches (self-ratings within 1 point of teacher ratings) rose sharply to a mean of 84 percent. Forty-two percent of the self-ratings were in perfect agreement with the teacher ratings. The difference between the average teacher and student ratings was .8 points.

The low levels of disruptive behavior and the high degree of accuracy of self-ratings were maintained in the following two phases when the frequency of matching was faded to 50 percent and then to 33⅓ percent of the time. During these phases the children reported that they wanted to be selected to match with the teacher since they had the opportunity to earn a bonus point for perfect matches. During the no-matching condition, the level of disruptive behavior rose slightly, and the percentage of accurate matches decreased to 61 percent.

During the first 2 days of the next phase, in which only 50 percent of the children received backup reinforcers, the level of disruptive behavior during the token periods was slightly lower than it was during the initial token phase—.39 disruptive behaviors per 20-second interval. Low levels of disruptive behavior continued throughout this phase. The children continued to rate their behavior accurately; 83 percent of the ratings were within 1 point of the teachers', and 60 percent of the ratings were perfect matches. Accurate self-evaluations and low levels of disruptive behavior were also maintained when one-third of the children received backups.

During the phase in which one child received backups, the level of disruptive behavior rose to .56 during the token intervals and .81 during the control intervals, and the accuracy of the self-ratings dropped. The mean disruptive behavior in the last week of the program, when it was announced that all backup reinforcers were being withdrawn, was .60 during the intervals in which the students were self-evaluating and .46 during the control intervals.

Academic output, summarized in Table 1, is presented in terms of the percentage of intervals in which the student met the goal the teacher set for him. Although the Sullivan reader provides a precise measure of output, through the number of frames completed, this measure was confounded by the cheating the teachers found difficult to control in the early stages of the program. During the self-evaluation phase, the teachers deducted 5 points for cheating in 80 percent of their ratings; thus they saw a child cheating at least once in 80 percent of the 15-minute intervals. The children were working at a much faster rate than they would have been if they were actually reading the material instead of looking at the answers. When the token program was instituted the children were informed of the penalty for this behavior, the frequency of cheating decreased drastically. The teachers deducted the 5 points only

20 percent of the time. This lower rate of cheating was maintained throughout the program, finally decreasing to 15 percent during the no-backup phase.

The children advanced an average of 2.5 grade levels in the Sullivan readers, with the gains ranging from 1.4 to 3.9 grades. However, only a 5-month gain in reading skills was demonstrated by the pretest and post-test scores on the California Achievement Test. There were no significant differences in the academic gains between the experimental and control children.

The observations of children in the public school revealed that there was no difference in the degree of behavior change between the experimental and control students. Both groups showed slight decreases in disruptive behavior from baseline to the end of the 4.5-month period of the after school program.

DISCUSSION

This study clearly indicates that it is not necessary for a teacher to continually monitor a classroom token program, given appropriate shaping and fading procedures. In addition, the low levels of disruptive behavior in the control intervals demonstrate generalization of appropriate behavior, and the low levels of disruptive behavior following removal of the token program demonstrate maintenance of appropriate behavior.

One expectation of the investigators that was not confirmed was that the experimental subjects would demonstrate significantly greater reading gains than the control group. Throughout the token program, half of the points were contingent upon academic output and accuracy. In fact, as evidenced by the work output data, the children were advancing steadily in their workbooks throughout the program. In addition, teachers were frequently giving individual tutoring at the children's desks. However, there are several possible reasons for the lack of differential gains: (a) The opportunity to cheat undermined the utility of the workbooks; (b) there appeared to be competition among the students to finish the books quickly; and (c) some of the children tended to "beat the system" by filling in the answers from cues in the preceding frames without reading the material. The teachers felt that it was difficult to motivate some of these children to learn academic skills. This lack of motivation plus the fact that the students reported that the workbooks were very boring may have contributed to the unproductive work habits cited previously and would clearly reduce the effectiveness of the Sullivan series. Drabman et al. (1973) reported that their subjects advanced 7.2 months in reading vocabulary during the 58 days of an after school token program, but this was the only subtest of the California Achievement Test they administered, and no treatment-control comparisons were made.

The observed generalization to the nontoken interval is a replication of the results of the Drabman et al. (1973) study. It was clear that the children were aware of the change in contingencies from the token to control intervals. The control intervals were always announced by the teacher, and the children often made statements to the effect that they could "be bad" because tokens were not being given. There are several possible reasons why they did not choose to do so. It may have been that the training in self-evaluation contributed to this effect, but one cannot conclude that this training was totally responsible for the generalization because in this study, as in the Drabman et al. (1973) investigation, the generalization to the control interval occurred before matching was instituted. It may be that either the random assignment of the control interval or the ratio of token to control time is the critical variable. However, these arguments cannot explain the maintenance effect that occurred when no backups were awarded. The rate of disruptive behavior during the no-backup phase was less than half of the baseline and self-evaluation conditions, and the mean disruptive behavior during the final 2 days of the last condition was lower than during the first 2.

The maintenance of low levels of disruptive behavior when backup reinforcers were withdrawn may have been due to the gradual fading of reinforcers, which actually began when the children lost points for inaccurate matches. Another possible explanation comes from the teachers' observation that the children made statements indicating that they were monitoring and evaluating their behavior, e.g., "I was out of my seat—I'm going to lose a point," and "I should't do that or I'll lose a point." It is interesting that these statements were made during the 28 days when the children were in complete control of the points they were to receive, and even during the final week of the program when the children were evaluating themselves but the points were no longer exchangeable for backups.

One could argue that if accurate self-evaluations were a powerful change agent, then the disruptive behavior of the experimental subjects in their regular classrooms should have decreased. This negative finding underscores the difficulty of producing generalization to nontreatment settings. However, no attempt was made to prompt these children to self-evaluate in their home classes; this prompting, coupled with social reinforcement, may be necessary to produce generalized effects.

There are several important practical advantages of the treatment package presented. Less teacher time is involved in administration of the token program. The extrinsic reinforcers can be withdrawn completely without a return to baseline level of disruptive behavior. In addition, this procedure introduced self-evaluative skills that, with more extensive prompting and training, might be used by the child across various academic settings.

REFERENCES

BIRNBRAUER, J. S., WOLF, M. M., KIDDER, J. D., & TAGUE, C. E. Classroom behavior of retarded pupils with token reinforcement. *J. Exp. Child Psychol.*, 1965, 2, 219-325.

BOLSTAD, O. D. & JOHNSON, S. M. Self-regulation in the modification of disruptive classroom behavior. *J. Appl. Behav. Anal.*, 1972, 5, 443-454.

DRABMAN, R. S. Child- versus teacher-administered token programs in a psychiatric hospital school. *J. Abnorm. Child Psychol.*, 1973, 1, 68-87.

DRABMAN, R. S., SPITALNIK, R., & O'LEARY, K. D. Teaching self-control to disruptive children. *J. Abnorm. Psychol.*, 1973, 82, 10-16.

KUYPERS, D. S., BECKER, W. C., & O'LEARY, K. D. How to make a token system fail. *Except. Child.*, 1968, 35, 101-109.

MEICHENBAUM, D. H., BOWERS, K. S., & ROSS, R. R. Modification of classroom behavior of institutionalized female adolescent offenders. *Behav. Res. & Ther.*, 1968, 6, 343-353.

O'LEARY, K. D., BECKER, W. C., EVANS, M. B., & SAUDARGAS, R. A. A token reinforcement program in a public school: A replication and systematic analysis. *J. Appl. Behav. Anal.*, 1969, 2, 3-13.

O'LEARY, K. D., DRABMAN, R. S., & KASS, R. E. Maintenance of appropriate behavior in a token program. *J. Abnorm. Child Psychol.*, 1973, 1, 127-138.

O'LEARY, K. D., KAUFMAN, K. F., KASS, R. E., & DRABMAN, R. S. The effects of loud and soft reprimands on the behavior of disruptive students. *Except. Child.*, 1970, 37, 145-155.

SULLIVAN, M. W. *Reading.* Palo Alto, Calif.: Behavioral Research Laboratory, 1969.

SURRATT, P. R., ULRICH, R. E., & HAWKINS, R. P. An elementary student as a behavioral engineer. *J. Appl. Behav. Anal.*, 1969, 2, 85-92.

WALKER, H. M. & BUCKLEY, N. K. Programming generalization and maintenance of treatment effects across time and across settings. *J. Appl. Behav. Anal.*, 1972, 5, 209-224.

WOLF, M. M., GILES, D. K., & HALL, R. V. Experiments with token reinforcement in a remedial classroom. *Behav. Res. & Ther.*, 1968, 6, 51-64.

Section IV

ASSESSMENT, MEASUREMENT
AND METHODOLOGY

Commentary

Because of the very nature of behavior therapy, all its facets involve objectivity, precise measurement and an ongoing process of assessment. A specific section on assessment then becomes primarily a matter of emphasis and personal preference. For this reason, rather than attempting the virtually impossible task of making a limited report on assessment at large, we have chosen first to offer some commentaries on the relative merits of single subject and between groups designs and then to organize the subsequent discussion around the four reprinted papers which make up this Section. By way of partial compensation for this exclusion, the following readily available new articles dealing with various aspects of assessment may be noted: methodology and design (Lovitt, 1975; Kazdin & Kopel, 1975); mathematical models of evaluation (Revenstorff, 1975; Mai, 1975); marital satisfaction (Wills, Weiss & Patterson, 1974); alcoholism and the addictive behaviors (Briddell & Nathan, 1976; Jeffrey, 1975; menstrual symptom assessment (Chesney & Tasto, 1975); education (Ramp & Semb, 1975); and depression (Lewinsohn, 1974, 1975). Furthermore, some half a dozen books devoted exclusively to behavioral assessment are currently in press.

Between-group designs create special problems for applied researchers in the behavioral sciences. Gathering data can be costly and time consuming, ethical considerations are involved in withholding treatment from control groups and it is not invariably easier to make valid generalizations from between-group studies than from individual case data.

A homogeneous sample of patients for a particular study is difficult to gather together and, by the very nature of its homogeneity, generalization to other groups is limited.

Sidman (1960) points to another difficulty with group studies and this pertains to the statistical analysis. To expose the subject to different values of the independent variable could conceivably result in contamination by the earlier intervention. And to conduct a between-group experiment with each group exposed to a single value of the individual variable could still result in the masking of important individual differences. Many a group study has unwittingly obscured interesting individual effects which could be of greater potential relevance than the primary findings.

The solution does not lie in the indiscriminate use of the single subject. In the uncontrolled case study, sometimes necessary in the development of a clinical science but a stage which much of behavior therapy has long since passed, it is sufficient merely to describe before and after effects without attempting to differentiate treatment effects from extratherapeutic factors that may be operating. By contrast, the controlled single case study represents a systematic attempt to determine in individual cases the functional relationships that obtain between the observed behavior and various facets of the treatment procedure applied. Kazdin (1973) and Leitenberg (1973)—both reprinted in full in earlier volumes of the Annual Review—describe the more common and basic single-subject designs currently in use and Barlow and Hersen (1973) have discussed sophisticated variations. Leitenberg clearly distinguishes between two basic models, the reversal design (ABAB or ABA) and the withdrawal (BAB or ABAB). In the reversal design, a particular procedure is applied in the experimental phase to make the desirable behavior increase or the incompatible undesirable behavior decrease. In the next phase, the operation is reversed to demonstrate control. Hopefully the desirable behavior will decrease and the undesirable behavior increase. In the withdrawal design, a single treatment procedure is introduced, withdrawn and then reintroduced without an initial baseline assessment.

The single-subject design possesses many advantages. It is not necessary to locate a large, homogeneous—or even heterogeneous—group of patients. It is possible through the study of a single case to focus in depth upon patient characteristics of special interest. And single-subject studies can provide progressive and reactive modification of hypotheses as the the data come in. Often, treatment effects are so substantial that effectiveness is unequivocally evident by visual inspection alone; in many a group study, the changes are so small as to be, in the words of Barlow and Hersen (1973), "statistically significant but clinically useless."

Single-subject methodology is not without its limitations. It is usually applied to real people in real-life situations and, for obvious reasons, a reversal design is often inappropriate. It might be neither ethical, feasible nor possible—how, for example, can one reverse a skill learning—to engage in a reversal. A multiple baseline strategy is sometimes effective where reversal is not appropriate. In this technique, no reversal is required. Instead, a number of specific but independent behaviors can be identified and measured over time to provide baselines over which changes can be evaluated. Once these baselines are established, it is then possible to apply the intervention to any one of the behaviors. Kazdin (1973) specifically advises against the use of reversal designs when the intent is to study nontransitive effects of therapeutic intervention and identifies a variety of situations which preclude the use of even ABAB designs. Sometimes the resistance to reversal procedures comes from the professional staff themselves, especially when the study is being carried out in an institution. Understandably, the staff are often adverse to engaging in reversal procedure once they have seen how effective the new strategy can be. To promote undesirable behavior, even if temporarily and in good cause, is an ethically questionable procedure (Birnbrauer, Peterson & Solnick, 1974).

Hartmann and Atkinson (1973) point to another dilemma. On the one hand, the clinical researcher seeks to program extra-therapeutic generalization and maintenance, and yet on the other hand, he wishes to demonstrate a high degree of experimental control—two qualities which may well be incompatible. Unequivocal demonstration of behavioral control may be an indication of lack of generalization and thus predictive of long-range failure.

Bandura (1976) sums up well the limitations of single-subject designs: $N = 1$ projects involve subjective judgments of variations in individual performance, and such a design is not necessarily more stringent than simple evaluations of inter-group data in the establishment of causal relationships. There is no criterion for generalization of the findings from the individual case. It is all too easy, if treatments with the one- or two-individual cases are successful, to attribute this success to the procedure; if the treatment is ineffective, this finding can be dismissed in terms of failure to deploy the procedures correctly. Nevertheless, the single-subject design is probably one of the more powerful that we have for those situations where highly stable baselines can be obtained and the treatment effects produced so clear-cut that there is little or no over-lap between experimental and baseline performance. Such an ideal situation is rare.

As a last word, it might be pointed out that it does not have to be an either/or issue. It is possible, if sometimes complicated, to deploy both single-subject methodology and between-group designs. The addition of control groups and appropriate data analysis for single-subject methodology in no way detracts from the analysis of individual variability and offers the advantages of more cases as well as a high degree of replicability and a great ability to generalize (see Bandura, 1976; Kazdin, 1973; Leitenberg, 1973). In this way, if the clinical investigator has the necessary resources, it is possible to have one's cake and eat it, too.

Lanyon and Lanyon (1976) stress that theoretical and research foundations in behavior therapy are rapidly becoming sophisticated enough for problems of therapeutic behavior change to be approached primarily as problems in design. And the design of strategies and programs for behavior change entails both initial and ongoing periods of assessment and decision-making. Unfortunately, the design of behavior-change strategies tends to lag behind the development of behavior-change technology itself, and Lanyon and Lanyon suggest two major reasons why this may be so. The first pertains to the fact that behavior therapy originated as a series of procedures for the structuring of specific, easily defined, discrete behaviors such as phobic anxiety. Here, questions of design and assessment were not very pressing. The second pertains to the rejection by early behavior therapists of assessment in any form, perhaps because of the opprobrium associated with the centralist concepts underlying the traditional test battery. In their understandable desire to reject such an orientation to the study of man, even nonpsycho-dynamic, psychometric approaches to assessment—with a very few notable exceptions such as the work of Eysenck—were rejected. Only recently have systematic attempts been made to explore the role of psychometric technology in behavior therapy (e.g., Goldfried & Sprafkin, 1974; Wolff & Merrens, 1974).

Authorities in the field have arrived at remarkably similar views with respect to the domain of behavioral assessment (e.g., Mischel, 1968; Peterson, 1968; Kanfer & Phillips, 1970). The emphasis is always upon specific details about what the person is actually doing, overtly or covertly, the antecedents, both internal and external, of the problem behavior, the consequences of the behavior and so forth. Methodological factors in the design of an optimal treatment regimen are often overshadowed by considerations of strategy, for example the possibility that assessment will reveal the inadequacy of available resources, in which case nothing further would be attempted. The Lanyons also stress the continuous and ongoing nature of the various assessment processes, really a series of consecutive steps in which the design is constantly subject to revision.

In view of the current tendency for certain more woolly minded behavior therapists to believe that sophistication in behavior therapy means looking beyond the presenting complaint to "what is *really* going on"—shades of psychodynamic theory!—it is salutary to see Lanyon and Lanyon return squarely to some of the basic premises of behavior therapy. First, that the significant events maintaining the positive behavior are currently present in the patient's environment even though this may not be evident at first blush. The event that originally caused the development of the problem may well be different from the events that are currently maintaining it and it is the events that are currently maintaining the problem that are important to the behavior therapist. Thus, behavioral assessment should focus on the problem behaviors as presented and not on inferred happenings that speculation by the therapist raises as the "real" underlying problems. Second, it is not necessary to attempt to unravel the conditions of original learning of a problem behavior. Third, the patient's declaration that the "real" problem behavior is not what the therapist has been working on is no reason for taking the view that this more basic behavior has somehow been uncovered merely by removing the protective function of the first. All this, of course, is not meant to imply that the behavior therapist will invariably focus exclusively on the presenting problem, or that historical events are never of relevance, but that the critical data are more usually to be found in the present internal or external maintaining conditions.

As every sophisticated behavior therapist is well aware, behavioral assessment involves far more than an evaluation of the patient's overt (motoric) behavior, whether it be in the natural setting or in the more artificial environment. The interest is in what a patient says that he or she has done, or what he would do in any particular situation, as well as what he or she actually does when put to the test. Increasingly, assessment procedures involve cognitive, motoric and physiological components. No longer is the early, reductionist S-R model either adequate or appropriate (although there is little doubt that as a starting-off device this was a necessary over-simplification).

Historically, it was traditional in psychological testing to focus virtually entirely on organismic mediational variables—the O in Wood-worth's S-O-R—in the quest for predictive and explanatory concepts. Then, perhaps as an overreaction, behavior therapists rejected completely the O component, focusing equally exclusively on environmental contingencies outside the individual. It is only recently, with Kanfer and Saslow (1969) signifying a point of departure in this respect with their specific introduction of the biological condition of the organism as a pertinent variable, that the "inner" man has come into prominence. Thus, behavioral assessment and behavior therapy alike emphasize cognitive processes, self-control strategies, biofeedback and components of man's activities other than overt motoric behavior (see the Commentary to Section I). What is particularly unfortunate is that a large proportion of the seemingly informed mental health profession, not to mention the lay public, still view the simplistic and outdated S-R model as the prototype of current behavior therapy and assessment. In other words, "behavioral" is confused with "behaviorist."

So far, there is no one scholarly text available which is devoted exclusively to behavioral assessment. Several clinicians have presented a practical framework to behavioral assessment (e.g., Kanfer & Saslow, 1969; Goldfried & Pomeranz, 1968; Mischel, 1968; Goldfried & Kent, 1972). Others have stressed methodological issues (e.g., Johnson & Bolstad, 1973) and a number of recent behavior therapy texts devote small sections to this area (e.g., Rimm & Masters, 1975; O'Leary & Wilson, 1975; Gelfand & Hartman, 1975). It is probably neither easy nor desirable to combine theoretical review and practical manual in the one text, and both are needed. But before scholarly reviews can be conducted, pertinent data must be available, and these are lacking in the assessment area. Nowhere is this lacuna more evident than clinically with respect to the parameters of assertion training—probably the most controversial and "in" topic of the year—and within the burgeoning area of behavioral industrial psychology (see Commentary, Section VIII).

Traditional approaches to the study of organizational behavior viewed performance primarily in overall or global terms. Current emphasis is to think in terms of some form of multivariable construct measured along a variety of independent or partially related performance dimensions. One behavioral, or quasi-behavioral, contribution to this endeavor is to assess performance directly in terms of a series of multi-dimensional behavior-specific attributes referred to as behaviorally anchored rating scales (BARS). These scales are based upon a series of operationally defined and increasingly refined critical incidents within the industrial setting. The final BARS instrument consists of a series of vertical scales (one for each of 6 or 7 dimensions) anchored by the retained incidents (Schwab, Heneman, & DeCotiis, 1975). Thus, BARS is viewed as a step towards clarification of job dimensions and pertinent behavioral incidents that are specific and unambiguous. This offers obvious advantages with respect both to the individual using the instrument and its recipient. Cummings and Schwab (1973) suggest that BARS may be useful in providing specific feedback to appraisees with respect to concrete examples of areas where job behaviors could be improved. In a similar vein, Blood (1974) suggests that the incidents may serve as bases for training programs aimed directly at improving the employees' abilities to perform the desired behaviors. Unfortunately, when Schwab et al. review the literature they end up with conclusions about validity and reliability, not to mention general utility, which are less than encouraging. As they point out, the design of future evaluation research must move beyond manipulation of the characteristics of the instrument itself to external sources of variance.

As behavioral assessment extends its domain from the clinic to society at large, the emphasis is going to shift from the more traditional forms of interpersonal relationship, individual or group, to the evaluation of programs, systems and institutions. In so doing, it is important that replication not be neglected. For example, Liberman, Ferris, Salgado and Salgado (1975) carried out a carefully planned replication in California of Kansas' highly successful Achievement Place group home program, a venture which has seen much favorable discussion in this and previous volumes of the Annual Review. Even though exact duplication in applied studies is difficult to arrange, one should always attempt to replicate as far as possible to assess the generality of the findings. Obviously, establishing and maintaining the same environmental conditions are virtually impossible whenever there are differences—as there nearly always are— in cultural, socioeconomic or other factors in the populations being compared. Behavior change in one milieu may be less appropriate in a different setting, and it is important to establish that certain procedures are effective despite variations across population. This is particularly so when a "package" of techniques is found to be helpful in a model setting. Replication may uncover the need for additional investigation of procedures that are less well understood than originally thought. It could also help to develop assessment measures which have some degree of utility in other than the specific situations for which they were originally devised—a major problem, for example, in the seemingly

endless array of measures of assertiveness, social skills, and marital relationships, each with its own cryptic acronym and idiosyncratic purpose.

Measuring the quality of residential care is important for administrator
and professional alike. Here, again, the need is to quantify, to define
what the social ecologist Moos (1974, 1975, 1976) calls the environmental
climate of residential care, and to make situation-specific what is being
measured. Starting from Goffman's (1961) now classic description of the
total institution, King, Raynes and Tizard (1971) developed a scale
which operationally defines and measures staff practices—certainly one
way of viewing environmental climate—relating to the management of
children in residential settings. More recently, as part of an ongoing
research project aimed at the evaluation of residential services for
severely mentally handicapped children and their families, Whatmore,
Durward and Kushlick (1975) refined these earlier formulations in an
attempt to overcome some of the difficulties of applying an individualized
operant model to the evaluation of a group structure.

Future directions will almost certainly focus on institutional evaluation. And as we indicate in the Commentary to Section VIII, rigorous
cost-benefit analyses will have to be built in to these evaluations if the
programs concerned are to be made viable and acceptable to administrators as well as mental health professionals. Program evaluation is a
thriving enterprise, as many a recent conference and workshop testifies
(e.g., Davidson, Clark & Hamerlynck, 1974). Evaluation and accountability go hand-in-hand, and political and technological goals are closely
related (Weinstein, 1975; Weiss, 1973). Political evaluation is as important in its own way as technological evaluation; the existence of a
service has to be justified to the politician, the administrator and the
public at large.

Closely monitored institutional assessment is likely to be facilitated by
some form of problem record-keeping (Weed, 1971). As a number of
recent reports testify (e.g., Katz & Woolley, 1975; Klonoff & Cox, 1975;
McLean & Miles, 1974; Scales & Johnson, 1975), problem-oriented records
(POR) are being increasingly utilized in a variety of institutional settings. An integral part of the POR is the problem list, a form of behavioral assessment. However, as yet, the level of precision achieved in
describing problem behaviors does not approach that of the carefully
conducted behavioral analysis. Hopefully, as behavioral assessment extends
itself to these areas, this deficit will be corrected.

Another area where behavioral assessment can be applied with profit
pertains to the numerous behavior modification training programs which

seem to spring up everywhere. While these workshops, ranging from good to bad through the modal indifferent, are aimed at both the professional and the public at large, the majority seem geared towards programs for children rather than adults. Mazza and Pumroy (1975) surveyed some 96 researchers and practitioners in North America who were known to be actively interested in behavior modification training. From their 32 respondents, they were able to categorize the approaches to evaluating training effectiveness into three areas: the use of standardized instruments to measure personality and attitude change; written measures, including subjective opinions, various rating scales and pre- and post-measures of knowledge gained as a result of training; and direct observation of either the trainee's behavior or that of the subject the trainee is attempting to change. Direct observation seems to be the most common, and probably the most effective, method of evaluating such programs, in which case videotape might well be the method of choice for both data analysis and the provision of unbiased feedback. Children and teachers could adapt to a fixed closed-circuit TV monitor more easily than to the perhaps more intrusive presence of a few observers appearing intermittently in the classroom.

Adequate follow-up and generalization data in the area of training are the exception rather than the rule. There have been few systematic attempts to assess for how long after discontinuation of training, the traineees continue to incorporate their newly acquired behavioral approach into their everyday lives. Obviously, such follow-ups are difficult: Trainees are difficult to locate after conclusion of training and there is probably a positive bias in those individuals who can be located. As Mazza and Pumroy point out, there is a need for better fading procedures from training program to classroom or home, for continued program support over a longer period of time and for institutional reinforcers for those who continue to implement such programs. Such evaluations, if appropriately designed, could help determine which features of the training program are essential, which are redundant or overlapping with other features and which contribute little or nothing.

The first paper that we reprint in this Section examines a current controversy which is, by its very nature, not really resolvable on an either/or basis. Mariotto and Paul's concern is with the relative contributions of situational as opposed to trait approaches. Bowers (1973) reviewed 11 such studies and concluded that neither a rigid situationist nor a pure trait approach adequately accounts for the data. By happy circumstance, a long-term evaluation of the comparative milieu and learning programs for chronic hospitalized mental patients was under way and this presented Mariotto and Paul with the opportunity for a systematic assessment of the parametric characteristics of the person versus situation issue in a real-life setting with much more precision than had previously been reported in the literature.

While their findings, discussed at length in the article, are of considerable merit in their own right, it is their general methodology which is of primary interest here, and their conclusion that it is the interactive nature of the dimensions of person-behavior and situation-variables (rather than an either/or situation) that should be the focus of future investigations. Their practical recommendations are more speculative and questionable. For example, it might be premature to infer from their findings that "in-office" treatment might be as effective for some cognitive dysfunctions as "in situ" focus. By contrast, so they speculate, for effective assessment and treatment, the comparatively greater situational specificity of social interactions suggests the need for a greater concentration on the relative dimensions of the situation within which the behavior occurs.

What is really under scrutiny is the still lively issue of trait and dynamic theories of behavior and assessment on the one hand, versus situation-specific, on the other. Both trait and dynamic theories take an approach to behavior in which observable responses are viewed as signs of global personality characteristics. Dynamic theorists tend to use projective and psychodynamically oriented tests to measure personality. Both psychodynamic and trait models depend upon inference, but at different levels (Goldfried & Kent, 1972). Projective testing rests upon much more indirect and much more complex levels of influence than psychometrically standardized questionnaires such as the MMPI. Nevertheless, in both, considerable inference is necessary. It is left to Mischel to develop a model of behavioral assessment in which the emphasis is upon a functional analysis of the specific variables that are controlling or effective in specific situations.

Functional behavioral analysis is an extreme position which cannot be said to characterize behavioral assessment in terms that are universally acceptable to all behavior therapists. Behavioral assessment means different things to different people. Yates (1975) identifies four diverse frameworks: the behavioral analytic model of Goldfried and his associates (Goldfried & D'Zurilla, 1969; Goldfried & Kent, 1972; Goldfried & Pomeranz, 1968); the behavioral diagnosis model of Kanfer and Saslow (1969); the modality profile of Lazarus and his BASIC ID (Lazarus,

1976) and finally the behavioral analysis of those who employ the strictly operant approaches of applied behavior analysis (e.g., Baer, Wolf & Risley, 1968).

Leading behaviorally oriented personality theorists such as Mischel (1968) and Peterson (1968) insist that people should be assessed in terms of what they do ("do" referring both to behavioral and cognitive events) in relationship to the circumstances under which they do it rather than in terms of any putative inner processes. In Mischel's (1973) own words, "The focus shifts from describing situation-free people with broad trait adjectives to analyzing the specific interactions between conditions and the cognitions of behaviors of interest." Many terms have been coined to describe procedures derived from this social learning position; there is, for example, psychosituational assessment (Bersoff, 1973), and behavioral personality assessment (Goldfried & Sprafkin, 1974). Mash and Terdal (1974) succinctly present the essential features of the person/situation dialogue and the closely related issue of the feasibility or validity of employing standardized procedures for assessment.

Mischel's plea for an examination of specific behaviors in relation to the conditions under which they occur is convincing. However, this condition is not satisfied by studies which rest content with descriptions such as the "ward" or "classroom" without any systematic attempts to be more specific. The way we assess the meaning of stimuli can be as important as the objective stimuli themselves. To this extent, Mischel's social learning theory oriented model of behavior therapy is at variance with the more traditional Skinnerian model. Consistent with the times, it includes cognitive and mediational variables under the behavioral rubric, a conceptual extension which presents one of the more exciting and challenging issues facing us today (see Commentary, Section I). At the more practical level, Meichenbaum (in press) suggests a number of innovative assessment procedures which can be derived from such a position.

In an observational analogue situation, Mash and McElwee (1974) paid young female volunteers, mainly housewives, students or secretaries to code unpredictable audiotaped dyadic verbal interactions between a male and a female. As far as one can generalize from any analogue study, their results suggest that observer accuracy is very much situation dependent and point up the need to consider carefully the observer's training history in relation to later observational conditions. As with earlier studies by Reid (1970) and Romanczyk, Kent, Diament, and O'Leary (1973), an observer's previous accuracy level is not necessarily a good predictor of future performance when considered independently of the situation for later observation. Accuracy is not a measure reflecting some static response property of a trained observer but something which reflects the situation-specific response which is likely to be dependent upon observer characteristics, conditions of observation and recording procedure characteristics. This provides further evidence for the behavioral situation-specificity paradigm.

Mischel (1968) has rightly concluded that the empirical search for the anticipated consistencies underlying a trait assumption about a person's behavior in different situations has rarely generated a correlation coefficient above +.30. In their sophisticated and still timely analyses of the trait/situational-specificity argument, Bem (1972) and Bem and Allen (1974) come up in essence with the old Scottish verdict of "not proven" with respect to either position in the extreme: The dichotomy between those who believe that behavior is consistent across situations and those who believe that behavior is situationally specific is a false one, and it is possible to believe in both propositions. The actual cleavage is between nomothetic and idiographic criteria for consistency and inconsistency. In the words of Bem and Allen, "The failure of traditional assessment procedures and the belief that person-situation interaction will account for most of the psychologically interesting variance in behavior have led several recent writers to emphasize that personality assessment must begin to attend seriously to situations. We agree. We have merely chosen to emphasize a perfectly symmetric, but perhaps more subtle, point that personality assessments must also begin to attend seriously to persons."

The next reprinted paper, by Schnelle, Kirchner, McNees and Lawler, could well have been reproduced in Section VIII since it very much focuses upon society and the community. However, since the primary concern is the application of a quasi-experimental strategy in the area of social evaluation, it is reproduced here. As behavior therapy moves from the one-to-one situation through the study of group processes to societal intervention, so behavioral assessment mirrors these developments. We are now at the stage of beginning to apply assessment concept and procedures to the extended society (see Section VIII).

The term "behavioral community psychology" (Briscoe, Hoffman & Bailey, Section VIII) denotes an application of applied behavioral analysis to socially significant problems in institutional or community settings where the behavior of individuals is not considered deviant in the traditional sense. As we have seen, assessment is being extended to a variety of settings, to industry, to education, to social systems. Many additional examples are readily available: there is Jones and Azrin's (1973) analysis of job finding, a study which clearly demonstrates the utility of simple record-keeping in analyzing the effects of a behavioral intervention. Herman, DeMontes, Dominguez, Montes and Hopkins (1973) focused on habitual tardiness in a factory, utilizing the time-clock and punch card to assess worker punctuality. While their finding that punctuality increases with the provision of a monetary bonus is not altogether surprising, we ponder the ethics of this procedure and its potential for misuse by management (see also Commentary, Section VIII).

Pierce and Risley (1974) used direct observation to analyze the job performance of young recreation aides working in a neighborhood Youth Corps program. However, it is sometimes not very practical to sample behavior of workers directly and more indirect measures have to be employed. Indirect measures are more or less easy to come by when the task is relatively specific and circumscribed, such as the number of letters stamped by the postman, but it is much more difficult to do so when social welfare services, for example, are involved. One apparently successful strategy in the mental health setting is to appraise the work performance of the attendants by evaluating in behavioral terms the improvement of the patients, using a variety of different observational measures, depending on which aspect of the patient's behavior it is desired to evaluate (e.g., Quilitch, 1975; Pomerleau, Bobrove & Smith, 1973).

In education, assessment is extending beyond the classroom towards the educational system itself. To obtain data about pupils unobtrusively and yet ethically, especially within an inner city school system, it is necessary to be both creative and adaptive (e.g., Copeland, Brown & Hall, 1974).

A somewhat related area where assessment procedures can be valuable within the larger context of the educational system is that of racial integration. Hauserman, Walen and Behling (1973)—reported in our 1974 Annual Review—were interested in assessing voluntary interactions between children of different races during the lunch period—a program which may well be likely to produce more social integration than the mandatory school bussing which is currently the favored strategy. While their findings are mainly positive, once again it is their attempts to define, manipulate and break down the global concept of racial integration into specific components that is of most interest here.

Working at the other end of the educational spectrum, Meyers, Nathan and Kopel (in press) concentrated upon the failure to reshelve library journals in the Medical Library of Rutgers University—a common library problem which inconveniences readers and staff alike as the accumulated pile of books and journals mounts. The procedure, which rests upon a token reinforcement system, seems to be effective and of practical significance. It is economical in cost, takes little staff time and is highly acceptable to all concerned. But it is the fact of their bothering to monitor the reshelving process that singles this study out for mention in this Section of the Annual Review.

The work of Moos and his associates in the Social Ecology Laboratory at Stanford University and the Palo Alto Veterans Administration Hospital has been discussed in greater detail in the Commentary to Section VIII of this year's Annual Review. Moos (1974, 1975) defines social ecology, which deals with both human adaptation and human milieu, as the multi-disciplinary study of the impacts of physical and social environments upon human beings. Its concerns are with both the assessment and development of operant human milieu as points of entry into relevant clinical and applied problems.

In his 1974 book, *Evaluating Treatment Environments: A Social Ecological Approach,* Moos described in detail the various methods by which the social environments of psychiatric treatment facilities can be systematically assessed. In a 1975 book, *Evaluating Correctional and Community Settings,* Moos applies a similar type of strategy to correctional and community settings. Taken together, these two volumes offer an impressive array of scales—some more behavioral than others—for the assessment of various types of environments: correctional programs, families, military companies, half-way houses, community care homes, rehabilitation workshops, hospitals and the like. While unresolved conceptual and methodological issues abound, as Moos himself is well aware, we are offered here a potentially viable strategy for the massive assessment of diverse social systems on a large scale.

The assessment of living environments is becoming of increasing concern not only to psychologists, but to individuals in seemingly unrelated disciplines such as architecture, sociology and economics. In recent years, research teams have been active in developing assessment procedures which cut across disciplines. At the University of Kansas, Risley's Living Envirnoment Group has developed three major procedures applicable to assessment in quite diverse environments. Activity measures are used to assess the degree to which the individuals concerned participate in planned activities (e.g., Quilitch & Risley, 1973; Lelaurin & Risley, 1972).

Interaction measures, which tell us what the individuals in the environment are doing, are most helpful when the degree of participation in planned activity is low. Cataldo and Risley (1974) recommend the use of a continuous record-keeping system for obtaining adequate interaction measures. Stimulation measures provide data about the experiences that the individuals in the given environments are undergoing. Once again, this is a useful measure when the more formal or overt activity is limited. McClannahan and Risley (1975) use such a measure to evaluate the behavior of patients in a geriatric nursing home (see Commentary, Section VIII). All three measures are of particular interest because they can be readily applied to a variety of institutions and environments, and even to entire communities.

Sometimes behavioral community assessment can verge on the trivial, as when articles devote their entire attention to the assessment of littering behavior (e.g., Kohlenberg & Phillips, 1973; Chapman & Risley, 1974). And even at this level, or perhaps especially at this level, a variety of practical problems present themselves. For example, to ensure an acceptable response, Hayes, Johnson and Cone (1975) developed what they call the Marked Item Technique, in which special incentives are offered for the collection of distinctively marked garbage and other material.

Slightly different strategies can be applied to the monitoring of an entire community with respect to possibly more immediately pressing issues such as the conservation of energy. For example, Kohlenberg, Phillips and Proctor (1976) placed recording devices in the homes of volunteer families to monitor the amount of electrical energy consumed throughout the day. An experimenter visited the home on a weekly basis to record data. These monitoring techniques were then incorporated into a feedback program to bring about striking changes in the pattern of peak energy consumption. Everett, Hayward and Meyers (1974) made a behavioral assessment of bus ridership in an entire college community of some 40,000 people. And in Section VIII of this Annual Review we reprint a paper by Briscoe, Hoffman and Bailey in which behavioral analysis is applied to the assessment and development of problem-solving skills by low-income members of a Community Board in an impoverished area.

It is rarely possible to submit social interaction studies to those neat laboratory designs so beloved of the behavioral scientists. Neither reversal nor multiple baseline procedures are practical in most community situations. The best approximation is usually some form of quasi-experimental model involving a time-series design (e.g., Schnelle & Lee, 1974). The

paper by Schnelle, Kirschner, McNees and Lawler reprinted next is of
interest because it does manage to employ a multiple baseline design to
study the effects of police patrolling strategy. The point that Schnelle
and his associates make, that quasi-experimental designs can be successfully used as a first stage to pave the way for more sophisticated designs,
is a compelling one. As they point out, a more refined project would not
have been politically possible without this preliminary study.

Such unobtrusive experimental technology is a logical methodological
and political first step towards placing social agencies on a sounder experimental basis. In an excellent paper by Reppucci and Saunders (1974),
reprinted in full in last year's Annual Review, eight practical issues
confronting behavioral scientists in their attempts at either assessment
or intervention in the natural environment were presented in detail.
Each problem area presents distinctive issues leading to a reduction in
the effectiveness of both assessment and modification, and each reflects
the changing practical, theoretical and ethical concerns with which the
behavior therapist must constantly involve himself.

In the remaining portion of this Section and our Commentary, we
concern ourselves with assertion training and measurement. If assertion
training is one of the most popular topics of the year, the same cannot
be said about assertion research. Literally dozens of recent books deal
more or less effectively with the practical aspects of assertion training, of
which the best so far brought to our attention is almost certainly that
of Lange and Jakubowski (1976). But none of these volumes—not even
the Lange and Jakubowski text—focuses in any adequate detail upon
basic methodological, conceptual and research issues. To paraphrase a
distinguished behavior modifier on an even larger scale, we are tempted
to declare that never has so much been written by so many people based
upon so few data—except that one could possibly draw this conclusion
about too many areas in clinical psychology to warrant its unique application to assertion training. Three book chapters in press which highlight these deficits and point the way towards their remediation are by
Eisler (1976), Hersen and Bellack (1976), and Bellack and Hersey (in
press), respectively. Between them, these authors thoroughly review the
current literature and the many problems involved in the development
and assessment of social skills (see also Section II).

Self-report inventories can be used to obtain factual data about motoric
responses, physiological activities or cognitions, or to gather data about
the individual's subjective experiences or evaluation of these primary
components. It is important that the inventory not confuse the two

goals. Another difficulty stems from the fact that many of these inventories were originally devised for use in small laboratories as part of specific research projects, bringing about a proliferation of overlapping measures, with little coordination, much redundancy, and a dearth of useful validity and reliability data.

Both research and clinical application could profit from the availability of effective assessment devices. Hersen and Bellack (1976) describe 10 self-report scales that have been developed since 1966. While reliability is generally satisfactory, validity data tend to be lacking. Unlike the many scales for the measurement of fear and anxiety, there seems to be a significant relationship between scores on assertion measures and motoric responses. Thus, in the paper by Eisler, Hersen, Miller and Blanchard reprinted next in this Section, psychiatric patients rated high and low, respectively, on the behavioral components of assertion also differed significantly on the Wolpe-Lazarus assertiveness scale.

In their evaluation of the current status of self-report scales of assertion, Hersen and Bellack (1976) raise a number of focal issues. Many of the scales reviewed yield an overall assertiveness score, whereas behavioral data such as those provided by Eisler et al. in the paper reprinted here suggest that "assertiveness" consists of a number of component behaviors that are relatively independent, and that assertion skills vary across situations. Reliabilities are essentially short-term and normative data tend to be somewhat deficient with respect to sex differences. And the emphasis up to now has been predominantly upon negative assertion rather than positive response: if these are distinct entities, it may be necessary to develop separate scoring systems and norms for each.

Since there is no evidence that any one modality—self-report, overt behavior or physiological response measures—is sufficient in itself to represent the complexity of social skills, the use of a multidimensional measurement battery appears to be a necessity. The question as to which measures and in what proportions remains unresolved. Psychometric evaluation of existing devices could go hand in hand with psychometric construction of new devices, and here factor analysis might be extremely useful.

A particularly interesting facet of the Eisler et al. study is with respect to the not altogether unexpected sex differences in negative situations requiring an individual to "stand up for his rights," males evidencing greater assertion towards women than towards other men. Similarly, in situations requiring positive assertive expression, subjects are more likely to offer praise and appreciation to female rather than male partners.

While consistent with prevailing social cultural norms, it does indicate the need for differential norms for men and women. In this respect, Glasgow and Arkowitz (1975) depart radically from earlier behavioral assessment studies by involving both male and female subjects in their project and analyzing the data separately for each sex. In the Eisler study, not only did their male subjects behave more assertively towards other men, but they were also more assertive when interacting with unfamiliar persons of both sexes and towards familiar persons. This has important implications for social skills training. Such investigations point to the need for the development of norms across situation, sex, age, cultural background and as yet to be determined variables.

The College Self-Expression Scale (CSES) has probably generated the greatest amount of normative data to date. Designed for the explicit purpose of evaluating assertiveness in college students (see Galassi, Delo, Galassi & Bastien, 1974; Galassi & Galassi, 1974), the focus is upon positive assertiveness, negative assertiveness, and self-denial in relationship to family, strangers, business relations, authority figures, like- and opposite-sex peers. However, as Bodner (1975) points out in his review of the role of assessment in assertion training, it does not allow for orderly breakdown of these skills according to situation. More recently, the CSES has been modified for adults in the form of the closely related Adult Self-Expression Scale (ASES) (Gay, Hollandworth & Galassi, 1975). However, further normative validation with a clinical population is necessary before it is ready for general usage.

One advantage of self-report measures is the economy with respect to time, effort and cost. But the validity or accuracy of self-report by questionnaire is often suspect and there is always the possibility of a discrepancy between self-report and behavior. However, as we endeavor to suggest throughout this Annual Review series, as long as it is not the only measure, verbal report is not to be viewed as necessarily inferior. That is why we make a repeated plea for multi-modal assessment not only of social skills, but of all areas.

There are some populations for whom self-ratings are quite inappropriate. Institutionalized patients frequently have deficits which make it difficult for them to assess their own behavior accurately. However, apart from such specialized areas, there is little doubt that emphasis on self-recording will continue to grow both in research and in clinical practice. Self-report may well be the only way that so-called "private events" can be recorded (Zimmerman, 1975).

It is well known that the behavior of the self-recorder changes as a function of his self-recording, but the variables which influence the directions of these reactive behavior changes have not been fully investigated. Nelson, Lipinski and Black (1975) studied self-recording in 20 college students, the same data (face-touching during class) being recorded by unobtrusive independent observers. The main conclusions were that self-recording is reactive, with self-recorders being less reliable when they are unaware that a check is being made on them, and that, regardless of differential expectancies, all groups decreased face-touching while self-recording—a finding with possible therapeutic implications (see also, Commentary, Section III).

The final paper reprinted in this Section, by Gambrill and Richey, describes an Assertion Inventory which is usable with a variety of individuals, samples a range of situations, is situationally specific and provides a wide range of information. It is one of the few assertion measures to differentiate between discomfort and behavior in specific situations. All in all, despite a characteristic lack of external validation, this is a useful inventory which merits further study.

13

PERSONS VERSUS SITUATIONS IN THE REAL-LIFE FUNCTIONING OF CHRONICALLY INSTITUTIONALIZED MENTAL PATIENTS

Marco J. Mariotto

Purdue University

and

Gordon L. Paul

University of Illinois at Urbana-Champaign

The present study examined the "person versus situation" controversy regarding the contribution to variance of behavior in real-life environments of 34 severely disabled psychiatric patients, using reliable and valid observational assessment of both patient behavior and dimensions of situations. Components-of-variance analyses were performed on data for two different behavior domains (cognitive dysfunction

Reprinted with permission from *Journal of Abnormal Psychology*, Vol. 84, No. 5, 1975, 483-493. Copyright 1975, American Psychological Association.

This study was the basis of a doctoral thesis at the University of Illinois by the first author, under the direction of the second author. Appreciation is expressed to the other members of the committee, Lloyd G. Humphreys, Steven L. Golding, and Donald T. Shannon, for their suggestions. Analyses were performed on the IBM 360 computer of the University of Illinois Digital Computer Laboratory. This study was supported, in part, by Public Health Service Grant MH 15553 from the National Institute of Mental Health.

and social interaction) across two dimensions of situations (physical settings and psychological demand) on two occasions within two different treatment environments. The relation of level of functioning to behavioral consistency was investigated by correlational analyses. Results indicated that behavioral consistency was a complex function of behavior domains assessed, differing psychological demand within situations, and the overall situational characteristics of the treatment environments in which the patients lived. Practical and theoretical ramifications of these results are discussed.

The ongoing controversy between intrapersonal and situational models of human behavior has come to focus on the empirical contribution of person variables (e.g., traits, drives, habits) versus situational variables (e.g., reinforcement contingencies, demand characteristics, discriminative stimuli) in accounting for the occurrence of various classes of behavior (Bowers, 1973; Mischel, 1973). A number of studies designed to assess directly the relative contributions of person and situational variables to behavior have appeared (e.g., Endler, Hunt, & Rosenstein, 1962; Medley & Mitzel, 1963; Moos, 1968, 1969, 1970; Nelson, Grinder, & Mutterer, 1969). Bowers (1973) reviewed 11 studies in which person and situation effects were calculated via an analysis of variance model and concluded that neither a rigid situationist nor a pure trait approach adequately accounts for the data. Bowers estimated that situations accounted for an average of only 10 percent of the total variance in these studies, whereas persons and person × situation interaction effects accounted for an average of 13 percent and 21 percent, respectively. The recognition that investigations of this type could be designed to emphasize either person or situation effects has resulted in reformulations of both points of view. Proposed integrative theories of both Mischel (1973) and Bowers (1973) emphasize the interactive nature of persons and situations and, in fact, may be more similar to each other than either is to their respective theoretical predecessors.

A closer examination (Mariotto, Note 1) of much of the literature on on which the person-situation controversy is based found two major shortcomings that limit the generalizability of results: (a) a restricted range and mode of assessment of behavioral domains for person variables, and (b) inadequate specification and measurement of situational variables. Thus, there exists a lack of empirical data based on reliable and valid assessment of relevant aspects of both ongoing behavior and situational dimensions from which inferences can be drawn.

As a result of an ongoing comparative treatment project with institutionalized psychiatric patients, the opportunity was presented to systematically assess parametric characteristics of the person versus situation issue in a real-life setting with more precision than has previously been attained. The presence of reliable and valid measurement of both patient behavior and situational dimensions allowed the assessment of the consistency of two different behavior domains (cognitive dysfunction and social interaction) across two dimensions of situations (physical setting and psychological demand) within two overall environments providing known differences in situational characteristics. Additionally, independent assessments of patient behavior allowed investigation of potential moderating effects of level of functioning to relative behavioral specificity.

METHOD

Parent Project Environment

The investigation was undertaken within the context of a long-term study evaluating the comparative effectiveness of milieu and social-learning programs for chronic mental patients. The latter two programs were conducted on adjacent, identical, 28-bed units of a mental health center in which patients resided coeducationally, with one treatment program on each unit. The same staff conducted both treatment programs, equating staff time and exposure by balanced rotation. Operating principles and differences were detailed in staff manuals with specific staff behavior × resident behavior × setting instructions. Within day-to-day schedules, functional activity periods focused on specific classes of target behaviors. Trained observers continuously time-sampled both staff and patient behavior, and 6-monthly assessments of both staff and patients were obtained on standardized instruments. Details of programs, manuals, and differential effects are available elsewhere (Paul & Lentz, Note 2).

The continuous behavioral observations obtained by trained observers included the Time Sample Behavioral Checklist (TSBC) (see Mariotto & Paul, 1974) and the Staff-Resident Interaction Chronograph (SRIC) (see Paul, McInnis, & Mariotto, 1973, Paul & Lentz, Note 3). The TSBC codes all resident (patient) behavior that occurs during a 2-second observation each waking hour in behavioral classes within seven categories describing an individual's (a) physical location (e.g., bedroom, hallway), (b) position (e.g., walking, lying down), (c) awake-asleep status (i.e., eyes open, eyes closed), (d) facial expression (e.g., smiling with apparent stimulus, neutral with no apparent stimulus), (e) social orientation (e.g., alone, with staff), (f) concurrent appropriate behaviors (e.g., talking with others, watching TV), and (g) inappropriate behaviors (e.g., talking to self, posturing). Scores derived from the TSBC represent the average proportion of various classes of behavior that occur during standard observational time periods, providing specific time $\times$ setting $\times$ behavior recordings. Average interobserver reliabilities over 12 observer pairs during the period including the present study ranged from $r = .90$ to $r = 100$, with a median r of .97.

The SRIC codes all behavior of a target staff member in functional relation to the behavior of residents present during 10 sequential 1-minute periods. Interactions on the SRIC are recorded within each 1-minute period in appropriate cells of a 5×21 matrix in which the 5 columns indicate classes of resident behavior (e.g., "appropriate," "inappropriate crazy, "request") and the 21 rows indicate classes of staff behavior (e.g., "ignore," "positive prompt," "reflect; clarify"). Summarization of interactions within individual cells and across combinations of the matrix allows the derivation of both quantitative (e.g., frequency of total interactions) and qualitative (e.g., frequency of "good" programmatic interactions) scores reflecting the psychosocial climate of a unit, with time $\times$ place $\times$ staff specification. Reliabilities of the individual cells on the SRIC over 12 observer pairs for the period overlapping the present study ranged from average intraclass reliability coefficients of $r = .93$ to $r = 1.00$, with the overall average reliability of the instrument greater than $r = .99$.

The ongoing assessments via TSBC and SRIC plus the equation of staff and functional activity periods between programs thus provided for precise definition of different dimensions of situations and different classes of patient behavior. Data from the parent project master files on both patient and staff behavior were abstracted for two consecutive 4-week blocks encompassing the 8th through 16th weeks following introduction of treatment programs. The latter period provided enough time from program introduction to allow for patient exposure to situations, but it still showed a relatively high frequency of dysfunctional cognitive behaviors.

"Situations" Within Treatment Programs

The above structure provided numerous functional activity periods. Although a broader range of functional activity periods would be likely to increase situational contributions to variance, limiting analyses to only two specific activity periods on evenings and weekends provided considerably greater specification and experimental control of the dimensions of situations. In addition to complete equation of treatment staff, observers, and time periods, such selection provided two different externally validated psychological situations with equal patient access to 12 different physical settings.

Psychological situations (informal interaction and free time) shared a common expectancy for social interaction and absence of dysfunctional behavior, but they differed in the degree of staff demand ("psychological press"). During informal interaction periods all recreational facilities within each unit were available for patient use. Specific staff focus was on facilitation of appropriate social interaction and a concomitant reduction of dysfunctional "crazy" behavior. Both treatment programs shared the same focus, differing in the specific techniques applied. On the milieu unit, staff employed communication of positive and negative expectancies, interpretation of metacommunications, group pressure, and positive and negative feedback. On the social-learning unit, prompts, shaping chips (exchangeable for tokens), and social reinforcement were contingently used. Each resident was contacted at least once every 10 minutes during informal interaction. In contrast, during scheduled free times, all recreational facilities were also available; however, only the general demands of the treatment programs were present, with no specific focus on particular classes of behavior and no requirements for staff to interact with patients.

Differential demand between informal interaction and free time psychological situations during the period of the present investigation was documented to differ over threefold for both treatment programs. Total interactions from the SRIC found mean staff-resident interactions of 137-29 and 40.77 per hour, respectively, for informal interaction and free time on the milieu unit. Parallel means on the social-learning unit were 126.97 and 40.50. Qualitatively, of all interactions by staff, 95 percent were programmatic ("good") on the milieu unit and 96 percent were programmatic on the social-learning unit, without differences in quality between the two psychological situations.

Physical settings were identical on both treatment units and equally available in the two psychological situations. Each treatment unit provided 12 physical settings to which patients had open access: classroom lounge, TV room, open corridor, bedroom, other's bedroom, activity pit, open living room, hallways, dining area, restrooms, bathing area, and laundry room. Presence in any 1 of the 12 physical settings was, essentially, a free-field choice of patients in the two functional periods. Presence in the physical settings was assessed by the TSBC location category, with interobserver reliability exceeding $r = .99$.

"Persons" and Behavior Domains

Two scores of particular theoretical and empirical relevance were selected for analysis from the TSBC: Cognitive Distortion index (relative frequencies of talking to self, verbalized delusions or hallucinations, incoherent speech, crying, smiling without a stimulus, and frowning without a stimulus), and Social Interaction index (relative frequencies of watching, talking, or listening to others, playing a game, and cooperative group activity). Both of the latter scores yielded interobserver reliabilities greater than $r = .96$. The resident population in the two treatment groups of the parent project at the time period selected provided the initial population for subjects in the present study. The parent groups included 28 patients each, initially equated on 16 demographic and level-of-functioning variables. As described elsewhere (Lentz, Paul, & Calhoun, 1971; Paul, Tobias, & Holly, 1972) at initial selection the parent population was the most debilitated chronically hospitalized group ever systematically studied, functioning at such a low lovel that they had been rejected for sheltercare placement after intensive efforts to "empty the back wards." Subjects for the current analyses were selected from the parent population on the basis of individual Cognitive Distortion index scores greater than or equal to .075 for the time periods included. The latter criterion resulted in 18 persons from the milieu program and 16 persons from the social-learning program—with an average of 90 TSBC observations per person under conditions selected for analysis.

Level-of-functioning data for correlational analyses were obtained from standardized ward rating and interview scales from an assessment during the 2-week period immediately following the behavioral assessments. Ward ratings were from Paul, Lentz, and Redfield's (Note 4) Intramural Scale of Minimal Functioning (ISMF), with interrater reliability of $r = .86$. Interview ratings were from Lorr, Klett, McNair, and Lasky's (1962) Inpatient Multidimensional Psychiatric Scale (IMPS), with interrater reliability of $r = .95$ for the total morbidity score. Details of administration are published elsewhere (Lentz et al., 1971).

RESULTS

Although the time periods for the present investigation were selected, in part, due to the relative stability of behavior in the parent population, both treatment programs had already shown rapid improvement (Paul et al., 1972), with the social-learning program showing greater improvement. Therefore, prior to analysis of person versus situation effects within the two dimensions of situations, the characteristics of the lower functioning subsamples selected for the current investigation need examination. Three-way repeated-measures analyses of variance (treatment programs × psychological situations × occasions) were performed separately on raw scores of the Cognitive Distortion and Social Interaction indices. These descriptive analyses of inspection of means in Table 1 found a significant increase over occasions to have occurred for the subsamples on cognitive distortion, $F(1,32) = 4.75$, $p < .05$). Changes over time in social interaction were complex, with significant differential changes between psychological situations, treatment programs, and occasions, $F(1,32) = 7.22$, $p < .05$. Thus, these extremely low functioning patient subgroups were changing in the presence of active treatment programs, with evidence that the programs were differentially producing situational discrimination in social interaction (see Table 1).

Person Versus Situation as a Function of Psychological Demand

The relative contribution of person versus situation effects on dysfunctional cognitive behavior and social interaction as a function of psychological demand was first examined in the traditional manner, without taking physical setting specificity into account. Raw Cognitive Distortion and Social Interaction index scores were each cast into a three-way classification within each treatment program: persons (individual patients) × situations (informal interaction, free time) × occasions (Time 1, Time 2). From this completely crossed design, analyses of variance were carried out that allowed computation of components of variance from which omega-squared ratios (percentage of variance accounted for, Hays, 1964) and coefficients reflecting reliability of effects (Cronbach, Gleser, Nanda, & Rajaratnam, 1973) were calculated. Although the conditions under which data were obtained fit a mixed model (persons random, situations and occasions fixed), random-effects analyses are also presented for interpretation because the latter results are directly comparable to the model of analyses in previous person versus situation

Table 1. Average Raw Scores on Cognitive Distortion and Social Interaction Over Psychological Situations and Occasions for the Low Functioning Patients Selected from Two Treatment Programs

SCORE	OCCASION	MILIEU PROGRAM (N = 18)						SOCIAL-LEARNING PROGRAM (N = 16)					
		PSYCHOLOGICAL SITUATION						PSYCHOLOGICAL SITUATION					
		Informal Interaction		Free Time		Total		Informal Interaction		Free Time		Total	
		Mean	S.D.	Mean	S.D.	Mean	S.D.	Mean	S.D.	Mean	S.D.	Mean	S.D.
COGNITIVE DISTORTION INDEX	Time 1	.219	.1970	.199	.2543	.209	.2244	.238	.2114	.206	.1728	.222	.1906
	Time 2	.278	.1630	.291	.1334	.247	.1472	.253	.2362	.254	.1897	.254	.2107
	Total	.249	.1806	.245	.2058	.247	.1923	.246	.2206	.230	.1801	.238	.1941
SOCIAL INTERACTION INDEX	Time 1	.626	.2227	.580	.2310	.603	.2249	.663	.2416	.659	.2063	.661	.2200
	Time 2	.692	.2288	.697	.1485	.695	.1994	.679	.1751	.529	.2097	.604	.2013
	Total	.659	.2228	.639	.2008	.649	.2134	.671	.2106	.594	.2146	.633	.2137

studies. However, it should be emphasized that all comparisons across treatment programs and behavior domains under assumptions of either model are only descriptive because the sampling distribution of variance components is unknown.

The results of the above analyses are summarized in Table 2. In general, both random and mixed-effects analyses found strong person effects for cognitive distortion, with reliable individual differences over occasions and situations. Psychological situation effects for cognitive distortion were present only in the context of small, but moderately generalizable, person × situation effects which were comparatively stronger within the social-learning program. In contrast to cognitive distortion, both random- and mixed-effect analyses of social interaction suggest a difference in the relative contribution of person effects between the treatment programs: Person effects were stronger in absolute magnitude and more generalizable across situations and occasions within the milieu program in comparison to the social-learning program. The psychological situation effect on social interaction was present, though slight in absolute strength and reliability, only in the social-learning program. The relative contribution to variance of person × situation effects within programs shows considerably greater effects for the interaction within the social-learning program.

Summarizing both descriptive and component analyses on raw index scores, remarkably strong person effects, with substantial generalizability, were found in both treatment programs for dysfunctional cognitive behaviors and in the milieu progra mfor social behavior. Person effects for social behavior were relatively weaker in the social-learning program. Psychological situation effects per se were only evident in the social-learning program where significant level differences were found for social interaction rate between psychological situations (Table 1), although the absolute strength and generalizability of situation effects, even here, was small (Table 2). Person × situation effects were relatively greater for social interaction than for cognitive distortion in both programs and comparatively stronger in the social-learning program than in the milieu program. Additionally, the social-learning program showed a relatively greater proportion of unaccounted for variance in both behavior domains.

Person × occasions effects were relatively greater in the milieu program for both cognitive and social behavior. However, the person × occasion effects were as strong as or stronger than person × situation effects within both treatment programs, suggesting that other environmental (situational) events occurring within the active treatment programs over

Table 2. Relative Proportions of Variance and "Reliability" of Cognitive Distortion and Social Interaction Over Psychological Situations and Occasions for Low Functioning Patients Selected from Two Treatment Programs Analyzed Under Both Random and Mixed Effects Models

SOURCE	PROPORTION OF VARIANCE ACCOUNTED FOR (OMEGA-SQUARED)				RELIABILITY OF THE EFFECT[a]			
	MILIEU PROGRAM		SOCIAL-LEARNING PROGRAM		MILIEU PROGRAM		SOCIAL-LEARNING PROGRAM	
	RANDOM	MIXED	RANDOM	MIXED	RANDOM	MIXED	RANDOM	MIXED
Cognitive Distortion Index:								
Persons	.462	.506	.621	.597	.487	.524	.621	.600
Situations	*	*	*	*	*	*	*	*
Occasions	.051	.036	.033	.006	.095	.082	*	.017
Persons X Situations	*	.052	*	.092	.487	.578	.653	.693
Persons X Occasions	.314	.283	.138	.164	.817	.818	.759	.765
Situations X Occasions	*	*	*	*	--	--	*	*
Residual	.173	.122	.209	.142	--	--	--	--
Social Interaction Index:								
Persons	.397	.453	*	.278	.427	.477	*	.305
Situations	*	*	.017	.024	*	*	.021	.051
Occasions	.065	.048	*	.028	.122	.110	*	.057
Persons X Situations	.073	.107	.199	.203	.506	.591	.272	.527
Persons X Occasions	.307	.278	.207	.206	.757	.770	.228	.531
Situations X Occasions	.006	.004	.075	.034	.027	.020	.115	.200
Residual	.152	.110	.503	.227	--	--	--	--

NOTE.--N = 18 for Milieu Program; N = 16 for Social-Learning Program; * = .000

a. Indexed by unit sample generalizability coefficient for random effects model and modified epsilon-squared value for mixed effects model. Since the absolute magnitude of these estimates is partially a function of the number of observations in a sample, the coefficients were calculated as estimates obtained from the smallest sample size possible (persons = occasions = situations = 1) (see Golding, 1975) time had at least as great an influence as the psychological demand dimension of the situations sampled. Thus, although the absence of known sampling distributions leaves interpretation at a descriptive level, the relative contribution of individual differences and the psychological demand dimension of situations to the behavior of these extremely low-functioning patient subgroups appeared to vary as a function of both the class of behavior and the overall situational characteristics of the total treatment environment in which the patients lived.

Situational Specificity as a Function of Physical Setting

Before analyzing the specificity of cognitive and social behavior to specific physical settings, the extent to which the two treatment programs and psychological situations may have produced differences in relative utilization of physical locations per se was examined. Analyses of variance did find that social-learning patients increased the average number of locations frequented over time, $F(1,32) = 6.92$, $p < .05$, but used significantly fewer locations than milieu patients, $F(1,32) = 149.08$, $p < .001$. In order to examine the specificity of location utilization for individual patients, TSBC Location Stereotypy scores (the ratio of total observations within each location)* were calculated for each subject, within psychological situations at each occasion. The latter score provides an index of the relative specificity in utilization of the available physical locations (i.e., stereotypy of presence in a limited number of available locations), independent of the number of observations. Analysis of variance indicated that the patient subsample in the social-learning program was considerably more stereotyped in location utilization than the subsample in the milieu program, $F(1,32) = 20.67$, $p < .001$, without within-program differences in psychological situations or occasions. Thus, the overall characteristics of the treatment environments produced differences in which patients in the social-learning program showed greater specificity of location preference over a smaller number of locations than those in the milieu program.

Because the possibility of any behavior showing specificity to physical settings will be a function of the relative opportunity to perform the behavior in identified physical locations, relative differences in location stereotypy must be taken into account in the analysis of physical setting specificity. Therefore, a physical setting specificity score was developed

---

* Complete derivations of both the location stereotypy score and the physical setting specificity score are available upon request to the first author.

(see footnote 1) which reflects the specificity of occurrence of any target behavior as a function of physical locations in which the individual had the opportunity to perform, independent of both the total frequency of the target behaviors and the total observations. The latter score (the ratio of total incidence of a target behavior squared to the sum of squared incidents of a target behavior within each location in which it occurs, divided by location stereotypy, and subtracted from the quantity's theoretical maximum), under present conditions, would reflect identically equal proportions of target performance to presence in physical locations at a value of 3.395. Higher scores, to a maximum of 4.395, reflect greater setting specificity. Lower scores, to a maximum of .0, reflect less setting specificity than would be expected from the opportunity to perform. Physical setting-specificity scores for both cognitive distortion and social interaction were independently entered into three-way analyses of variance (treatment programs × psychological situations × occasions) to assess the degree to which behavioral setting specificity differed as a function of the situational dimensions of treatment programs and psychological demand.

The analysis of variance for cognitive distortion found a significant main effect for treatment programs, $F(1,32) = 10.86$, $p < .005$, and psychological situations, $F(1,32) = 4.36$, $p < .05$, without occasions main effects and without significant interactions. Inspection of means presented in Table 3 shows that greater setting specificity occurred for cognitive distortion in low-demand free-time situations than during high-demand informal-interaction situations in both treatment programs. Additionally, patients in the milieu program exhibited greater physical setting specificity in the performance of dysfunctional cognitive behavior than patients in the social-learning program. On an absolute level, the milieu subsample showed the specificity of performance of dysfunctional cognitive behavior to physical setting to be significant over both psychological situations, $ts(17) > 4.31$, $p < .01$. In contrast, the social-learning subsample did not show significant specificity of dysfunctional cognitive behavior to physical settings in the high-demand informal-interaction situation, $t(15) < 1$, and only approached significance in the low-demand free time situation, $t(15) = 1.96$, $p < .10$.

Unlike cognitive distortion, the physical setting specificity of social interaction did not show consistent differences between psychological situations. Although the analysis of variance again revealed the milieu program to produce greater physical setting specificity than the social-learning program, $F(1,32) = 6.74$, $p < .05$, the three-way interaction was signifi-

Table 3. Average Physical Setting Specificity Scores for Cognitive Distortion and Social Interaction Over Psychological Situations and Occasions for the Low Functioning Patients Selected from Two Treatment Programs

PHYSICAL SETTING SPECIFICITY SCORE	OCCASIONS	MILIEU PROGRAM (N = 18)						SOCIAL-LEARNING PROGRAM (N = 16)					
		PSYCHOLOGICAL SITUATION						PSYCHOLOGICAL SITUATION					
		Informal Interaction		Free Time		Total		Informal Interaction		Free Time		Total	
		Mean	S.D.	Mean	S.D.	Mean	S.D.	Mean	S.D.	Mean	S.D.	Mean	S.D.
COGNITIVE DISTORTION	Time 1	3.741	.3082	3.894	.3306	3.812	.3242	3.468	.2786	3.555	.4466	3.512	.3688
	Time 2	3.665	.3018	3.626	.3301	3.646	.3124	3.367	.4542	3.565	.1852	3.466	.3553
	Total	3.703	.3032	3.760	.3528	3.729	.3279	3.418	.3738	3.560	.3364	3.489	.3599
SOCIAL INTERACTION	Time 1	3.517	.2387	3.565	.2517	3.541	.2441	3.538	.1644	3.349	.3134	3.444	.2641
	Time 2	3.569	.2093	3.509	.3194	3.539	.2684	3.322	.2425	3.426	.1463	3.374	.2097
	Total	3.543	.2234	3.537	.2858	3.540	.2553	3.430	.2315	3.388	.2389	3.409	.2366

NOTE.--Higher scores reflect greater specificity of performance to specific physical locations. A mean of 3.395 reflects equal performance of the target behavior across all physical settings.

cant, $F(1,32) = 6.74$, $p < .05$. As seen in Table 3, the latter interaction reflects completely crossed and opposite changes over time periods, both within and between treatment programs for the setting specificity of social behavior. On an absolute level, the social-learning program showed significant specificity of social behavior to physical settings only at the Time 1, information-interaction situation, $t(15) = 3.479$, $p < .01$, with all other cells failing to approach significance, $ts(15) < 1.20$, $p > .20$. All milieu cells, in contrast, showed significant physical setting specificity for social behavior, $ts(17) > 2.11$, $p < .05$, as well as for dysfunctional cognitive behavior.

Components-of-variance analyses on physical setting specificity scores (paralleling those on raw indices) yielded large residual components. However, a similar patterning of effects occurred as with the components analyses of the raw index scores: Person effects was the strongest contributor to variance in setting specificity of cognitive distortion in the milieu program and situation effects were nonexistent. In contrast, the social-learning program showed less of a person effect and a slight situation effect, whereas the person × occasion effect was the most reliable contributor to variance on the setting specificity of cognitive distortion. The physical setting specificity of social interaction also showed differences as a function of treatment programs, with situation effects only present in the social-learning program. Thus, the relative contribution of the physical setting dimension of situations to the behavior of these extremely low functioning patient subgroups appeared to differ as a function of the class of behavior assessed, the psychological demand dimension of situations in which performance occurred, and the overall situational characteristics of the total treatment environment in which the patients lived. Although the relative contribution of individual differences was strong in all analyses, the absolute magnitude of person effects was also a complex function of the physical setting and psychological demand dimensions of situations, the class of behavior assessed, and the overall situational characteristics of the treatment environments.

Predictability of Situational Specificity

Multiple regression analyses were undertaken to assess the relation between level of functioning (IMPS and ISMF) and both behavioral consistency over situations and occasions (indexed by a consistency index anologous to stereotypy scores) and physical setting specificity. The only significant prediction obtained from the latter analyses was between level of functioning and consistency of social interaction across occasions and psychological situations, $R = .54$, $F(2,31) = 6.449$, $p < .01$. Inspection of the beta weights and prime correlations found this relation to be totally attributable to the correlation between the ISMF and the consistency index for social interaction within the milieu program, reflecting greater consistency for higher levels of functioning $(r = .83)$. The latter prime correlation was also significantly different $(p < .05)$ from the correlation of ISMF and consistency of social interaction within the social-learning program $(r = .08)$. Physical setting specificity scores for cognitive distortion and social interaction were found to be significantly intercorrelated in the total sample $(r = .58)$ with no significant differences or within programs across psychological situations and occasions. The extent to which either class of behavior tended to be performed specific to given physical settings was, thus, a relatively consistent personal attribute. However, the physical setting specificity of either class of behavior was not predictable from global level of functioning.

DISCUSSION

The results of the present study found that the consistency of the observed behavior of extremely low-functioning chronic mental patients in real-life environs over free-choice physical settings, psychological situations, and different occasions was a complex function of the class of behavior, differences in psychological demand between situations, and the overall situational characteristics of the treatment environment. For dysfunctional cognitive behavior, persons accounted for a large majority of total variance and were remarkably consistent across the psychological demand dimension of situations and occasions in absolute level; however, the differing demand of situations influenced the extent to which these behaviors were specific to physical settings. Further, the relative contribution of person versus situation effects to the latter setting specifically appeared to be a function of the situational characteristics of the overall treatment environments.

For appropriate social behavior, person effects were less consistent across psychological situations and occasions in absolute level, especially in one treatment environment. Psychological demand was more influential on setting specificity, and the relative contribution of person versus situation effects appeared to be an even greater function of differing treatment environments for appropriate social behavior than for dysfunctional cognitive behavior. Physical setting specificity per se was found to be a relatively consistent attribute of persons within treatment environments. However, the combined results suggest that the relative contribution of individual differences to different behavior domains may have been more a function of the overall situational characteristics of treatment environments than of the selected psychological and physical dimensions within environmental situations.

The greater precision of measurement and specification of both behavioral domains and dimensions of situations in the present study provides interesting substantive results in comparison with previous investigations of the parameters involved in the consistency of behavior issue. Person effects were substantially greater than those reported elsewhere (Bowers, 1973). Because previous investigations have found that person effects increase and situation effects lessen as the overall level of functioning of the subject sample declined (cf., Bowers, 1973; Endler, 1973), the most tenable basis for the comparatively greater person effects in the present study is the extremely low level of functioning of the subject sample. Although hospitalized psychiatric patients have previously been the focus of research on the consistency issue, the lowest functioning of earlier samples (Moos, 1968) had been hospitalized only 3 months, whereas subjects of the present investigation had been hospitalized a median of 18 years and were more debilitated than any sample previously subjected to systematic investigation. Thus, the comparative strength of person effects relative to the psychological demand dimension of situations supports the hypothesis of other writers (Alker, 1972; Mischel, 1973)—that is, that the relative situational specificity of behavior is partially related to the overall level of functioning of the subject sample. Higher functioning samples are likely to show greater situational specificity, when situations are defined on psychological dimensions.

In spite of the comparative strength of person effects, there was evidence that social interactional behaviors were more influenced by situational dimensions than were dysfunctional cognitive behaviors. The latter finding supports prior work in which cognitive behavior, in general, has been relatively more intrapersonally consistent, whereas social behavior has been relatively more situationally determined (Mischel, 1973).

If only the psychological demand dimension of the selected situations were considered, the results of the present study found much less situation effect than has previously been reported when psychological demand, physical setting, and task requirements have been confounded. Even with clear documentation of differences between psychological situations, persons were remarkably consistent over this dimension of situations. Of course, simply by selecting more situations with differing task require- ments, situation effects could be greatly enhanced. However, even within the relatively weak contribution of the demand dimension with equated task requirements and physical settings over only two situations, its effect on level of behavior appeared to be a function of the behavior domain (absent for cognitive distortion, present for social interaction) and the treatment environment (stronger within social learning).

In contrast to the weak effects of the psychological demand dimension of situations alone, the effect of the physical setting dimension, as it in- teracted with the psychological dimension, was substantial on the be- havioral consistency of cognitive distortion. Dysfunctional cognitive behavior was less a function of particular physical settings when the psy- chological situation was high rather than low in demand. The latter interactional effect of the two dimensions of situations was not apparent for social interaction. A direct comparison of person effects to physical setting effects was not possible within the design, but persons demon- strated consistency in the degree to which they were "setting bound" across behavioral domains. However, both classes of behavior were sig- nificantly tied to particular physical settings only within the milieu program.

The differential effects found for the psychological demand and the physical setting dimensions of situations are further evidence that con- founding of these dimensions in previous work may seriously limit in- terpretation of situation effects (Rauch, Dittman, & Taylor, 1959; Raush, Farbmann, & Llewellyn, 1960; Moos, Daniels, Nukowsky, Sassano, Hatton, Dueltgen, Beilin, & Moos, 1964). In the present study, the effect of the psychological demand dimension was slight, and the interaction effect of psychological demand with physical settings appeared to be stronger. However, the latter effects and the relative contribution of individual differences overall to behavioral consistency appeared to be more of a function of the third dimension of situations (treatment environment) than either of the situational parameters assessed within treatment pro- grams. Had the present study focused on a wide range of subsettings within units, thereby confounding psychological demand, physical setting, and task required (e.g., meal time, appearance checks, community meet- ings), clear situation effects would have been obtained which would have contributed heavily to variance. However, such a finding would add little regarding the basis of such situational effects.

Because the relative strength of person and situation effects which were investigated appeared to be partially a function of differing characteristics of the overall treatment environments (situation effects seeming comparatively stronger within the social-learning program than within the milieu program), differences between the programs warrant closer examination. The social-learning program was characterized by moment-to-moment individual contingency management that resulted in a highly response-contingent environment. The milieu program, in contrast, was characterized by the therapeutic community model, which resulted in a relatively noncontingent environment. The differential predictability found for behavioral consistency in the present study is in substantial agreement with other investigations from the parent population (Montgomery, Paul, & Powers, 1974; Theobald & Paul, Note 5). Specifically, level of functioning has predicted performance on a variety of laboratory tasks for subjects from the milieu program, whereas performance of subjects from the social-learning program on the same tasks was more predictable by within-program responsiveness reflecting increased attention and discriminative responding to situational cues. An increase in "discriminative facility" (Mischel, 1973) within the response-contingent environment is further suggested by the significantly greater concentration of patient locations in settings where positive consequences were more probable for patients in the social-learning program. Thus, of the documented situational dimensions in the present study, the overall characteristics of the treatment programs appear to be the most influential and the most probable factor contributing to apparent differences in the relations among the two domains of person effects and the two within-program situational dimensions.

The above findings, although limited by the descriptive level of analyses, suggest some specific recommendations. On a practical level, the extent to which various classes of behavior are more or less situationally determined might predict the degree to which changes in behavior are likely to generalize across situations and, thus, guide the focus of intervention strategies. Specifically, the extent to which dysfunctional cognitive behaviors appear to be relatively transsituational suggests that assessment and treatment techniques might be relatively effective when focused on the individual and his behavior. Thus, "in-office" focus might be as effective for treating some cognitive dysfunction as "in-situ" focus. The comparatively greater situational specificity of social interactions, in contrast, suggests the need for a greater concentration on the relevant dimensions of the situations in which the behavior occurs for effective assessment and treatment. The possible differential effectiveness of treatment modalities in fostering the development of discriminative facility further suggests that chronically hospitalized patients might emphasize moment-to-moment response-contingent consequences, if patients are expected to eventually learn to function in different environments.

In regard to the person versus situation controversy, these results clearly demonstrate that the interactive nature of dimensions of person behavior and dimensions of situation variables (rather than either/or) should be the focus of investigation for delineation of the determinants of behavior. It is, however, not sufficient to merely state that this relation exists. Demonstrations of the structure of these interactions based on reliable and valid assessment of various dimensions of person and situation variables are a necessary empirical prerequisite to the development and articulation of theoretical systems. Similarly, with regard to clinical assessment, it is the identification of the functional relation (i.e., interaction) between dimensions of patient behavior and situations within which they behave (rather than either/or) that might better be the focus of clinical assessment (Paul, 1974). Thus, the theoretical and practical value of the person *versus* situation issue seems extremely limited, not only because both persons and situations are important parameters but also because neither appears important, nor meaningfully measured, in isolation.

REFERENCE NOTES

1. MARIOTTO, M. J. *Persons versus Situations: Empirical Status and Theoretical Implications.* Manuscript submitted for publication, 1975.
2. PAUL, G. L. & LENTZ, R. J. *Psychosocial Treatment of Chronically Institutionalized Mental Patients: A Comparative Study of Milieu vs. Social-Learning Programs.* Book in preparation, 1975. (See, also, Paul, Tobias, & Holly [1972]; Paul & McInnis [1974]; Paul, McInnis, & Mariott
3. PAUL, G. L. & LENTZ, R. J. (Eds.). *Observational Assessment Instrumentation for Institutional Research and Treatment.* Book in preparation, 1975.
4. PAUL, G. L., LENTZ, R. J., & REDFIELD, J. *The Intramural Scale of Minimal Functioning: A revision of Social Breakdown Syndrome Gradient Index.* Manuscript submitted for publication, 1975.
5. THEOBALD, D. T. & PAUL, G. L. *Reinforcing Value of Praise for Chronic Mental Patients as a Function of Historical Pairing with Tangible Reinforcers in the Treatment Environment.* Manuscript submitted for publication, 1974.

REFERENCES

ALKER, H. A. Is personality situationally specific or intrapsychically consistent? *J. Pers.* 1972, 40, 1-16.
BOWERS, K. S. Situationism in psychology: An analysis and a critique. *Psychol. Review,* 1973, 80, 307-336.
CRONBACH, L. J., GLESER, G. C., NANDA, H., & RAJARATRAM, N. *The Dependability of*

Behavioral Measurements: Theory of Generalizability for Scores and Profiles. New York: Wiley, 1973.

ENDLER, N. S. The person versus the situation—a pseudoissue? A response to Alker. J. Pers., 1973, 41, 287-303.

ENDLER, N. S., HUNT, J. McV., & ROSENSTEIN, A. J. An 5-R inventory of anxiousness Psychol. Monog., 1962, 76 (17, Whole No. 536).

GOLDING, S. L. Flies in the ointment: Methodological problems in the analysis of percent of variance due to persons and situations. Psychol. Bull., 1975, 82, 278-288.

HAYS, W. L. Statistics for Psychologists. New York: Holt, Rinehart & Winston, 1964.

LENTZ, R. J., PAUL, G. L., & CALHOUN, J. F. Reliability and validity of three measures of functioning in a sample of "hard core" chronic mental patients. J. Abn. Psych., 1971, 78, 69-76.

LORR, M., KLETT, C. J., McNAIR, D. M., & LASKY, J. J. In-patient Multidimensional Psychiatric Scale. Manual. Palo Alto, Calif.: Consulting Psychologists Press, 1962.

MARIOTTO, M. J. & PAUL, G. L. A multimethod validation of the Inpatient Multidimensional Psychiatric Scale with chronically institutionalized patients. J. Consult. and Clin. Psychol., 1974, 42, 497-508.

MEDLEY, D. M. & MITZEL, H. E. Measuring classroom behavior by systematic observation. In N. L. Gage (Ed.), Handbook of Research on Teaching. Chicago, Ill.: Rand-McNally, 1963 .

MISCHEL, W. On the empirical dilemmas of psychodynamic approaches: Issues and alternatives. J. Abn. Psychol., 1973, 82, 335-344.

MONTGOMERY, G. K., PAUL, G. L., & POWERS, C. T. Influence of environmental contingency history on acquisition of new discrimination by chronic mental patients. J. Abn. Psychol., 1974, 83, 339-347.

MOOS, R. Situational analysis of a therapeutic community milieu. J. Abnorm. Psychol., 1968, 73, 49-61.

MOOS, R. H. Sources of variance in responses to questionnaires and in behavior. J. Abnorm. Psychol., 1969, 74, 405-412.

MOOS, R. H. Differential effects of psychiatric ward settings on patient change. J. Nerv. Ment. Dis., 1970, 5, 316-321.

MOOS, R. H., DANIELS, D. N., NUKOWSKY, E., SASSANO, M., HATTON, J., DUELTGEN, A., BEILLIN, L., & MOOS, B. S. The ecological assessment of behavior in a therapeutic community. Int. J. Soc. Psychiat., 1964, Special Congress Edition, 87-96.

NELSON, E. A., GRINDER, R. F., & MUTTERER, M. L. Sources of variance in behavioral measures of honesty in temptation situations. Methodological analyses. Soc. Psychol., 1969, 1, 265-179.

PAUL, G. L. Experimental-behavioral approaches to schizophrenia. In R. Cancro, N. Fox, and L. Shapiro (Eds.), Strategic Intervention in Schizophrenia: Current Development in Treatment. New York: Behavioral Publications, 1974.

PAUL, G. L. & McINNIS, T. L. Attitudinal changes associated with two approaches to training mental health technicians in milieu and social-learning programs. J. Cons. Clin. Psychol., 1974, 42, 21-33.

PAUL, G. L., McINNIS, T. L., & MARIOTTO, M. J. Objective performance outcomes associated with two approaches to training mental health technicians in milieu and social-learning programs. J. Abnorm. Psychol., 1973, 82, 523-532.

PAUL, G. L., TOBIAS, L. L., & HOLLY, B. L. Maintenance psychotropic drugs in the presence of active treatment programs: A "triple-blind" withdrawal study with long-term mental patients. Arch. Gen. Psychiat., 1972, 27, 106-115.

RAUSCH, H., DITTMAN, A. T., & TAYLOR, T. J. Person, setting, and change in social interaction. Human Relations, 1959, 12, 361-378.

RAUSCH, H. L., FARBMANN, I., & LLEWELLYN, L. G. Person, setting and change in social interactions: II. A normal control study. Human Relations, 1960, 13, 305-332.

14

SOCIAL EVALUATION RESEARCH: THE EVALUATION OF TWO POLICE PATROLLING STRATEGIES

John F. Schnelle, Robert E. Kirchner,
M. Patrick McNees and Jerry M. Lawler

*Middle Tennessee State University, Nashville Metropolitan
Police Department, and Rutherford County
Guidance Center*

In most social evaluation research it is difficult to achieve the degree of experimental rigor possible in an applied be-behavioral study. This study illustrates how the evaluation researcher can increase experimental rigor in the analysis of social interventions. In the first evaluation, a variation of the time-series design that offered maximum experimental control given the limitations of the situation, was employed to evaluate the effects of a specialized home-burglary police patrol. This design revealed that no effects could be attributed to the patrol. In the second evaluation, a multiple baseline-like design was possible in determining the effects of a

Reprinted from the *Journal of Applied Behavior Analysis*, 1975, 8, 353-365. Copyright 1975, the Society for the Experimental Analysis of Behavior, Inc.

The authors wish to thank Dr. Gene V. Glass of the Laboratory for Educational Research, University of Colorado, for the direct technical assistance and instruction he provided in statistical analyses.

police walking patrol. This design revealed that the patrol produced an increase in crime reporting but not in arrests. Social interventions often occur in a manner that allows varying degrees of experimental analysis. The evaluation researcher must attain optimal experimental analysis given the limitations of each social intervention.

Descriptors: community setting, social evaluation research, multiple baseline, walking patrol, time-series analysis

The importance of applying quasi-experimental and experimental design technology to the evaluation of legal reforms and social interventions that affect large numbers of people has been emphasized by a number of authors (Campbell, 1969; Glass, Willson, & Gottman*). Campbell** in particular has argued eloquently for an experimenting society that utilized the experimental and quasi-experimental logic to make decisions about the impact of social programs.

The design most favored in such evaluation research is familiar to the field of applied behavior analysis, *viz.*, the time-series design (Gottman, 1973; Jones, Vaught, & Reid†; Risley & Wolf, 1972). This design involves repeated measures before, during, and after intervention. Its primary strength is its applicability to many types of field situations that preclude the use of any design requiring strong treatment control. For example, Glass, Tiao, and Maguire (1971) evaluated the effects of a change in German divorce laws on divorce-rate data retrieved from archival records. In that situation, there was no possibility of randomly assigning the law change to different sections of the country, nor was it possible to stagger sequentially the intervention in multiple-baseline style. The most powerful form of analysis available was the time-series design.

Schnelle and Lee (1974) demonstrated the application of a time-series design to the evaluation of a prison disciplinary intervention. The disciplinary policy was directed toward inmate rule infractions and was applied to the entire prison at one time. There was no possibility of reversing the intervention, randomly selecting control groups, nor of

---

* G. U. Glass, U. L. Willson, and J. M. Gottman. Design and Analysis of Time Series Experiments. Unpublished manuscript, laboratory of Educational Research, University of Colorado, 1972.

** D. T. Campbell. *Methods for the Experimenting Society Evaluation Research Paper Series.* Evanston, Illinois: Northwestern University, 1971.

† R. R. Jones, R. S. Vaught, and J. R. Reid. Time-Series Analysis as a Substitute for Single Subject Analysis of Variance Designs. Paper presented at American Psychological Association Convention, Montreal, 1973.

sequentially applying the disciplinary technique to multiple baselines. In short, time-series technology offered the only means of retrieving evaluation data.

The primary disadvantage of the time-series design when compared to several stronger time-series design variations is the possibility of the existence of historical validity threats. Campbell and Stanley (1966) defined historical validity threats as "specific events occurring between the first and second measurement in addition to the independent variable." Reversal and multiple-baseline designs are variations of the time-series design that minimize such historical possibilities by controlling when treatment is delivered. With the latter designs, historical threats are rendered improbable by the fact that either the treatment is applied more than once and/or control time-series lines are present.

In addition to the reversal and multiple-baseline designs, there are three other variations of the simple time-series design that enhance interpretative power by providing a measure of control for historical threats. The first variation is labelled by Cook and Campbell* as an interrupted time series with nonequivalent dependent variables. Historical interpretations are minimized by collecting time-series data for some dependent variables that should be affected by treatment and for others that should not. The nonequivalent dependent variables should be conceptually related. Ross, Campbell, and Glass (1970) applied this design in the evaluation of a British breathalyzer crackdown, a concentrated effort to keep drunk drivers off the roads and hence hopefully to reduce automobile accidents.

The simplest analysis of the "Breathalyzer Crackdown" would be to compare measures of pre-intervention accidents to measures of postintervention accidents. Even if there were a change in accidents at the time of intervention, such a time-series analysis would not separate the effects of the intervention from historical effects such as weather conditions, safer cars, newspaper publicity, etc.

Ross et al. (1970) noted that pubs in Britain are open only during certain hours. Thus, separate time-series data could be collected on traffic accidents occurring when pubs were open and when they were closed. (The importance of the distinction between accidents when pubs are closed or open is that historical interpretations of a decrease in fatalities should apply to all fatalities, irrespective of the time of day in

---

* T. D. Cook and D. T. Campbell. The Design and Conduct of Quasi-Experiments and True Experiments in Field Settings. Unpublished manuscript, Northwestern University, 1975.

which the accident took place.) Thus, if a change in accidents took place at the time of the intervention during open hours but not during closed hours, the evidence is strong that the intervention and not historical factors produced the change.

The second time-series variation supplements the simple time-series design with data from a nonequivalent, no-treatment control group. The major difference between the latter design and the multiple-baseline design is that control-group data are eventually treated in multiple-baseline designs, but not in the time-series variation here discussed.

Lawler and Hackman (1969) illustrated this design in their evaluation of participative decision-making concerning bonus money for work attendance. In this study, one set of workers made a group decision to award themselves extra money for work attendance. The effect of this decision and bonus was evaluated by collecting time-series data on attendance before and after the decision. A second group of men who did not engage in participative decision making were awarded extra money, and served as a control for historical threats.

Campbell and Ross (1968) evaluated a crackdown on speeding in Connecticut by comparing change in time-series fatality measures in Connecticut to time-series fatality measures in several adjoining states. Once again, if change occurred at the point of intervention in Connecticut but not at the same time in the other states, it becomes unlikely that historical factors account for the change. At the very least, controls are present for historical factors common to all states.

A still stronger variation of the previous two time-series designs results when treatment is applied to several time-series lines simultaneously while control series data are collected on either conceptually related dependent measures or on no-treatment control groups. Thus, in the speeding crackdown, if several states had simultaneously initiated speeding crackdowns, then Campbell and Ross (1968) could have evaluated changes in all treated states against changes in states that did not initiate the crackdown. In such a situation, historical interpretation of change is further minimized and treatment effects are replicated.

The third variation of the time-series design is the multiple-baseline design, which involves sequential intervention on all time-series baselines. Like the second design described, treatment effects can be interpreted by comparing pretreatment time-series data to posttreatment time-series data and by comparing treated baselines to untreated baselines. Finally, in both designs there are replications of treatment effects.

The major advantage of the multiple-baseline design seems to be that the comparability of the independent baselines is demonstrated only in the multiple-baseline design. In other words, if some baselines are treated and some are not, there is always the chance that the untreated control baselines are "dead" measures, and hence insensitive to any type of influence, either treatment or historical. If this premise is true, then untreated baselines are not adequate controls for the treated baselines in the control series design.

To this point, several time-series designs have been described that are applicable to the evaluation of a wide range of social interventions. The remainder of this paper demonstrates the application of two of these designs to the evaluation of two police patrol strategies.

In neither patrol intervention was the evaluator given the opportunity to design the evaluation research strategy freely. Instead, the methods by which the intervention had to be introduced were first specified and the evaluation task was to design the most powerful research strategy given these limitations.

The first study evaluated the effect of police saturation patrolling, in which several critical patrol zones were intervened into simultaneously. The design involved comparing time-series data on the multiple treated zones to both nonequated control groups and nonequivalent dependent measures. The second study evaluated the effects of a police walking patrol that was introduced into patrol areas at separate times. A multiple-baseline design was employed in the latter situation.

EVALUATION I: THE EFFECTS OF SPECIALIZED HOME-BURGLARY SATURATION PATROLS ON BURGLARY RATES

It has been said that police burglary patrols have three functions: 1) to guard businesses and residences, 2) to watch suspected burglars, and 3) to move quickly and catch burglars on the scene (Hanna, 1974). Additionally, the Crime-Specific Handbook (Hanna, 1974) recommends that police sometimes shift normal patrol forces into target zones to provide saturation coverage for particularly troublesome areas.

The Kansas City Preventive Patrol experiment (Kelling, Pate, Deckman, & Brown*) attempted to determine the effects of varying patrol strategies and indicated the possibility that saturation patrolling would have no effect on crime rates. In five "reactive" beats, vehicles entered the

---

* G. L. Kelling, T. Pate, D. Deckman, and C. E. Brown. *The Kansas City Preventive Patrol Experiment: A Summary Report.* Police Foundation, 1909 K Street, N.W., Washington, D. C.

beat only in response to calls for service. In five control beats, the normal patrol level of one car per beat was continued. In five "proactive" beats, two or three marked cars patrolled in each beat. No effects on reported crime were found due to increasing or decreasing patrol strength in the beats.

The present investigation dealt with the effects of increasing patrol strength in particular zones, and focused on one particular type of crime, namely home burglaries. Differences between the present investigation and the Kansas City experiment are that (a) patrol strength in the present study was much higher than in the Kansas City experiment, (b) the specialized patrol focused only on home burglaries, (c) unmarked cars and plainclothes personnel were used in the target zones, and (d) before the intervention, the specialized burglary patrol received specific information about people with an arrest history for burglary.

METHOD

Setting and Subjects

This investigation was carried out in Davidson County, Tennessee. Nashville, with a population of 449,000, is the largest city in Davidson County. For police purposes, Davidson County is divided into three geographic areas called "sectors." The sectors are divided into a total of 32 zones (14, 10, 8 zones in each of the three sectors). The total Metropolitan Police force (sworn police officers) numbers 862. Thirty-five patrolmen were assembled into one group from various branches of the department to form a specialized burglary patrol.

Patrol preparation. After the 35 men had been established as a specialized burglary patrol, they were briefed on the specifications of their assignment, which included (a) the assignment of each man to one of three zones, (b) only residential burglaries during the second shift (8 a.m. to 4 p.m.) were targeted, and (c) patrolmen would work as two-man teams. Additionally, each patrolman was given a book containing the identity, pictures, and information on individuals previously arrested for burglary.

Deployment and patrolling procedures. The 35 patrolmen selected for the burglary patrol were assigned to three zones (zone 31, zone 71, and zone 91) thought by the police to be particularly "troublesome." Zone 31 was 2.96 miles from zone 71 and 4.23 miles from zone 91. Zone 71 was 6.77 miles from zone 91. Before the burglary patrol was initiated, two patrolmen (one car) covered each zone. During the saturation patrol, eight to 15 men patrolled each of the three target zones during the second shift. The variance in numbers were due primarily to court appearances by the patrolmen.

On January 23, 1974, the burglary patrol saturated the three target zones and was terminated on March 1, 1974.

Data collection. Information was gathered on home-burglary rates for the three shifts in the target zones and home-burglary rates for three randomly chosen comparison zones. Burglaries are defined by the Nashville Metropolitan Police Department as reported instances in which the following two elements are present: (a) evidence for forced entry, and (b) citizen report of missing property resulting from the forced entry. The crime monitoring system used by the Nashville Metropolitan Police Department contains inherent reliability checks that ensure accurate recording of citizens report of burglary.

A burglary complaint is initiated when a citizen calls the central police telephone number. A police radio operator receives the complaint and dispatches a squad car to the scene. All incoming calls to the police department are automatically tape recorded. This tape is periodically checked to ascertain how well citizen calls are received by the complaint clerk. The patrolmen arriving on the scene must write a general report describing the situation. In the case of burglary reports, specific mention must be made of the method of entry into the burglarized environment and a description of stolen property. These general reports are turned in to a centralized point at the end of a shift, and, based on the information specified in the general report, the incident is checked for proper classification as to the type of crime committed. Two people are responsible for making the classification independently. All situations in which forced entry was evident and in which something is reported to be missing are classified as burglaries. Periodically, classified reports are checked by the police Inspections Section for consistency and accuracy of the classification system.

Finally, in the case of burglaries, the general reports are turned in to the Detective Division, which is given seven days to make a supplementary investigation and report. This supplementary report is designed to check the information in the first general report and to add further information. In the case of minor burglary loss, the supplementary investigation may be conducted by telephone. The officer making the initial general report has no way of knowing which detective will make the supplementary report. Based on the supplementary report, the reported crime may be reclassified. These internal checks ensure that there is little chance of either fabricating a report of burglary that did not occur, or of neglecting to record a reported burglary.

RESULTS

The upper three panels in Figure 1 show the weekly home-burglary rates for the second shift in the three target zones before, during and after the burglary patrol. In all three target zones, initiation of the burglary patrol did not decrease burglaries substantially in those zones. Employing a time-series analysis computer program provided by Gene V. Glass, the data were analyzed statistically. There were no significant changes in the level of slope of the time-series lines in the point of intervention. The change in level t-tests were: $t = -1.92$, $t = 1.55$, $t = 0.52$, $df = 55$, $p > 0.05$. The means of the pre-intervention phase and intervention phase for the three target zones were 2.8, 2.9; 4.0, 3.4; and 1.9, 2.0, respectively.

The middle three panels of the figure illustrate the home-burglary rates in the target zones for a shift other than when saturation period was present.

Again, no significant changes in the level or slope of the time-series lines were found. Level change t-tests were: $t = 0.40$, $t = 0.14$, $t = -0.78$, $df = 55$, $p > 0.05$. The means of the pre-intervention phase and intervention phase were 2.3, 2.0; 1.9, 2.0; and 1.4, 1.6, respectively.

The lower three panels of the figure show home-burglary rates for the three randomly chosen control zones. No significant changes in the level or slope of burglaries occurred during the saturation of the target zones. Level change t-tests were: $t = 0.70$, $t = 1.62$, $t = 0.35$, $df = 55$, $p > 0.05$. The means of the pre-intervention and intervention phases were 2.4, 3.0; 2.06, 3.6; and 1, 0.3, respectively.

The time-series statistical analysis is necessary to test for changes in either the slope or level of data collected over time because of the typical interdependency nature of the time-series measures. This interdependency, unless corrected, would lead to deflated various estimates and hence spuriously large t or f ratios if such ratios were calculated by the usual methods. Time-series analyses leads to an adjusted t ratio in the sense that the time-series scores are transformed into scores with uncorrelated error terms. These transformed scores can then be tested for differences in level or slope between phases. The time-series analysis proceeds by first identifying the basic dependency nature of the time-series measures by mans of a correlogram. A lag 1 correlation shows the correlation between

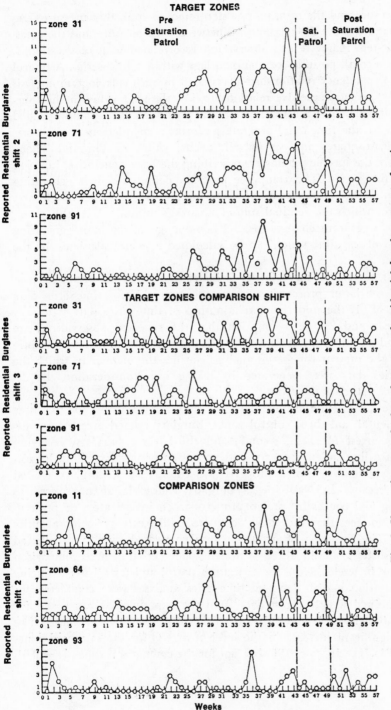

Fig. 1. Upper three panels show frequency of residential burglary reports for the three target zones and patrol shift in which the situation patrol took place. The middle three panels illustrate frequency of residential burglary reports in the three saturated patrol zones during a shift in which the saturation patrol was not present. The last three panels show frequency of residential burglaries for three randomly selected comparison zones that did not receive the saturation patrol.

each measure and the measure one step removed from that measure. Lag 2 correlations show the relationship between each measure and the measure two steps removed, i.e., observation 1 correlated with observation 3, and so on to all possible correlational lags within a time-series. A typical type of dependency relationship as revealed by such correlogram analysis would be an autoregressive relationship, i.e., the next value in the time-series is predicted by a constant times the previous score plus unpredicted noise. Next, the time-series program performs a complete normal theory, linear least-squares analysis for all specific values of Phi and Theta, which are the specific parameters describing the basic generating function of the time-series. The computer program defines the best generating function of the time-series line by showing the specific values of Phi and Theta for which the residual sum of squares is minimized. At this point, t-test for significant changes in level of slope, given the basic generating function of the time series, can be calculated and are calculated by the program.

Linear regression curve fitting is better known in the social sciences than is the latter process but is not recommended for time-series data because of: 1) the underlying relationship of time-series data is usually not linear and 2) the assumption that the repeated observations are independent samples cannot be met. The generating function procedure used in the present time-series analysis clarifies the manner in which the time-series data were generated by taking into consideration the dependency nature of the series.

Figure 2 shows the average daily burglary related arrests for the three experimental and three control zones. Burglary related arrests were defined as arrest for first-, second-, and third-degree burglary, receiving and concealing stolen property, and possession of burglary tools. Receiving and concealing stolen property was counted as a burglary related offense because in Nashville, a burglary charge is often reduced to receiving and concealing stolen property when investigators or prosecutors do not feel that they have adequate evidence to press for a guilty verdict. The frequency of arrests for burglary related crimes was collected for all shifts from the three saturated zones and the three comparison zones for 15 weeks before the saturation patrol and for all weeks during the saturation patrol. Separate time-series analyses were conducted for the combined weekly arrest data from the experimental zones and for the combined weekly arrest data from the three comparison zones. There was a significant increase in the level of arrests for the saturated zones ($t = 2.81$, $df = 16$, $p < 0.05$) but not for the comparison zones ($t = 0.61$,

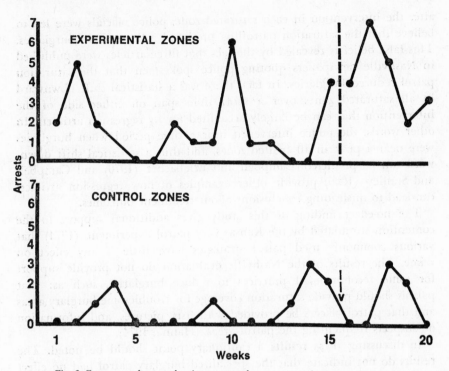

Fig. 2. Frequency of arrests for three saturated zones *versus* three control zones.

$df = 16$, $p > 0.05$). There were no changes in the slopes of the time-series lines. Once again, the tests were accomplished by time-series analysis.

DISCUSSION

In this evaluation, development and use of a specialized home-burglary patrol produced no changes in burglary rates in three zones selected for saturation. The inclusion of data on comparison shifts and comparison zones indicates no overall increase in burglary rates at the point that the target zones were saturated. The lack of change in the comparison shifts and zones rules out the possibility that the burglary patrol actually suppressed what would have been an increase in burglary rates. In other words, the effects of the patrol on burglary rates in the target zones were not obscured by general increases in burglary rates. Visual inspection of city wide time-series data on burglary rates reaffirmed the comparison zone data, which showed no increase in burglary reports.

By looking at only several data points before and several data points after the intervention in each saturated zone, police officials were led to believe that the saturation patrolling produced a decrease in burglaries. This false belief is revealed by the fact that three articles were published in Nashville newspapers quoting police spokesmen that the saturation patrol reduced burglaries. In fact, there was a statistical shift downward in all saturated zones over a short time span on either side of the intervention that can be largely accounted for by regression artifacts. In other words, the police intervened near a time period when burglaries were near a peak in all treated zones, and thus a statistical shift downward can be predicted. Campbell and Erlebacher (1970) and Campbell and Stanley (1966) provide other examples of how regression artifacts can lead to misleading conclusions about treatment outcomes.

The no-effect finding of this study gives additional support to the contention stimulated by the Kansas City patrol experiment (1974) that various commonly used patrol strategies have little if any effect on crime. The results of the Nashville evaluation do not provide support for some recommended practices to reduce burglaries, such as: that patrols should provide saturation coverage for troublesome burglary areas and that patrol officers be provided with lists, pictures, and information on suspects frequenting the patrol areas (Hanna, 1974).

In discussing these results a cautionary point should be noted. The results do not indicate that the specialized burglary patrol had no effect on people's lives in the target zone or the city. Also, generalizations to other types of crime or patrolling strategies should not be made at this point. However, the results do indicate that the specialized burglary patrol did not serve its expressed function: to reduce burglaries in the target zones.

It is interesting that the saturation patrol led to an increase in burglary arrests. The fact that arrests increased provided direct evidence that the police were actively involved in the saturated zones but also raises several unanswered questions about the relationship between arrests for specific crimes and the frequency of these crimes.

EVALUATION II: THE EFFECTS OF POLICE
WALKING PATROL ON REPORTED CRIME

A fashionable innovation in police department law enforcement work is the walking patrol. Even though there are variations in different cities, the basic idea of the walking patrol is to put police officers in personal contact with the citizens they serve (O'Connor & Vanderbosch, 1967; Whesehand & Cline, 1971).

The walking patrol in Nashville, Tennessee, involved police officers located in a centralized "storefront" office of two patrol zones from 9 a.m. to 5 p.m. The introduction of the walking patrol occurred sequentially, being started in one area some six months before being introduced in the other. This sequential introduction, made necessary by manpower limitations and cost factors, provided the opportunity to evaluate the effects of patrol by multiple-baseline technology.

METHOD

Subjects and Setting

The walking patrol experimental areas were picked by the Nashville Housing Authority as being most appropriate and most in need of the walking patrol. The Nashville Housing Authority requested that patrol area 110 be worked with first because of greater need. Statistics supported the contention that area 110 experienced more crime than the other area chosen.

The walking patrol concept was first introduced in both patrol areas in a tenants' meeting. Within two months after these tenant meetings (which occurred six months apart in the two zones), the police department rented office space within the patrol zone and walking patrol started immediately afterwards.

Population density, socioeconomic levels, and age groupings were similar in both areas, each consisting of low-income government housing with a predominantly black population. A history of poor police-community relations was evident in the two patrol zones. There were three white and three black officers in each patrol zone.

Measures. Since the police were primarily concerned with the patrol's effect on crime and arrests, the measures employed to evaluate the walking patrol were reported offenses and arrests. Before the walking patrol, offenses were reported by one method only: citizens calling the city police number to report an incident. These telephoned incidents were classified by a complaint clerk and given immediately to a dispatcher, who dispatched a patrol car to investigate. The reports of the officer were written, classified as to the type of crime committed, and fed into an information retrieval source. All calls that were dispatched required a follow-up report by the investigating patrol officer. One hundred percent of the calls resulted in matched follow-up reports. Arrest data were collected directly from arrest reports filled out by the officer at every arrest. These data were also computerized.

After the walking patrol was initiated, offense statistics were collected as usual by citizens' calls to a centralized police number. In addition, complaints could be taken directly to a patrolman working within the walking patrol zone. These complaints were written on a daily log by the walking patrolman and eventually fed into a computer system. The police radio operator and the dispatcher were not involved in the latter process. Arrest statistics were collected from arrest reports. There was no change in the method of writing arrest reports.

Reliability checks. Reliability checks of reported crime by two independent observers were not possible in this study. The two reporting sources who could be in error were the radio operator receiving the telephone complaint calls and the patrol officers receiving direct citizen complaints. The most probable recording error would be neglecting to write up a complaint, rather than writing up a complaint that did not actually occur, since a follow-up report, citing names, times, and addresses, was made for every recorded incident. These follow-up reports were often done by officers other than the officer who initially recorded the complaint information. Thus, a fake complaint write-up would be readily uncovered by a follow-up report. It was not possible for an officer to predict exactly when a follow-up would be done. Thus, the follow-up reporting procedure served as a reliability check for writing up false complaints. Throughout this study, there was no evidence of a follow-up investigation that did not confirm the fact that a citizen actually made a complaint.

In addition, a random sample of people who reported offenses was called upon by a member of the police Inspections Section, who asked a series of questions related to how satisfied the complainant was with his interaction with the police. Once again, officers could not predict when such a consumer index would be taken, and there was no instance of report falsification in the consumer surveys.

That an officer might neglect to write up a complaint was possible but improbable, because if an officer neglected to write up an offense, then the citizen reporting the offense could complain to the police department's Internal Security Section about police inactivity in regard to the complaint. There was no change in the number of such citizen complaints during this study.

Reliability checks on arrests can be made only by checking the disposition of the arrest case. If there were a change in the number of arrests disallowed for technical reasons, or a change in arrest-conviction ratios, then the hypothesis that officers changed arrest procedures would be plausible (instrumentation threat). In this particular case, there was no evidence that officers changed normal arrest procedures. Unfortunately, with social measures such as arrest statistics, it is still possible to disregard completely the possibility that subtle changes in arrest methods did occur.

RESULTS

The solid line in Figure 3 illustrates the offense reports taken over a 28-month and 34-month period before the walking patrol and for a six-month period in Zone 1 and a five-month period in Zone 2 after the walking patrol. Data collection in Zone 1 terminated six months after the walking patrol intervention because several new police interventions were undertaken in this zone.

It is obvious that reported offenses increased after the patrol was introduced in both patrol zones. Time-series analysis showed a significant change in the level of reported offenses in both zones ($t = 1.84$ and $t = 7.0$, $p < 0.05$), respectively. There were no changes in slope in either zone. The actual types of crime showing the most increase at the time of the walking patrol intervention were theft, simple assault, public drunkenness, and disorderly conduct. Major crime, such as murder, rape, and burglary, did not show such increases. The extent of this increase due to citizens reporting directly to the officers is illustrated by the dotted line after the walking patrol intervention. The solid line illustrates total offenses reported, and was computed by adding the number of complaints made directly to patrolmen in the zone to the number of telephoned complaints; there were no direct citizen reports to officers before the walking patrol.

Arrest frequencies did not change systematically at the time of the intervention in either patrol zone, and thus are not illustrated.

DISCUSSION

The walking patrol intervention produced an increase in reported crime, a large part of which was due to citizens making direct reports to patrolmen in addition to telephoning reports to the central police number. Thus, the increase in reported crime seems to be partially due to what Campbell (1969) called instrumentation factors. Instrumentation is defined by Campbell as changes in the calibration of a measuring instrument or changes in the observers or scores that may produce changes in the obtained measurements. Despite the fact that instrumentation

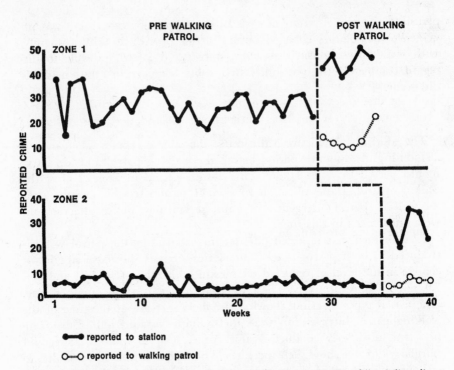

Fig. 3. Solid lines indicate total reported crime in the two walking patrol zones. Dotted lines indicate direct citizen report of crime to patrolman. Direct citizen reporting was nonexistent before the intervention.

changes can explain much of the increase in reported crime, the instrumentation in this case has applied significance, since citizens will seemingly report more crime if placed in close proximity with police officers. A survey by the Law Enforcement Assistance Administration (1974) indicated that unreported crime in several large cities exceeded actual reports of crime. The walking patrol is a logical way to increase crime reporting, even though the effect of the walking patrol on unreported crime measures was not directly evaluated in this study.

The present results were in part anticipated by Press (1972), who considered the possibility that an increased patrol strength in a precinct in New York City would produce an increase in reported crime. Likewise, Etzioni (1968) reported cases of increases in reported crime when police departments changed their reporting procedures.

It should be noted that there was a significant increase in crime reporting directly to police in both zones, but that there was a greater relative increase in telephone reports to police in Zone 2 than in Zone 1. The reasons for this difference are not apparent from this study and could logically be due to several factors, i.e., the lower overall baseline crime reporting in Zone 2 as compared to Zone 1 or possibly publicity that took place in Zone 2 but not in Zone 1. Nevertheless, it is still possible to state that the walking patrol increased overall reporting of crime in both zones only at the time of intervention. In other words, the fact that the walking patrol had a replicable effect on crime reports is incontestable.

A final point that should be made clear is the important differences between the multiple-baseline design employed to evaluate the walking patrol and multiple-baseline analysis in which the evaluator controls the treatment variable. Cook and Campbell* list a number of validity threats that are made probable by a lack of treatment control. Specific to the case of the walking patrol, it is conceivable that the area that the Nashville housing authority picked to undergo the intervention first, was at the time of the intervention experiencing large amounts of crime not reported because of citizen mistrust in the police who were immediately patrolling the area. This "historical" event could have contributed to the subsequent large increase in reports of crime only in that area and not in the comparison area. This validity threat possibility could be termed the interaction of selection and history and/or the interaction of selection and regression. In other words, perhaps the walking patrol would show dramatic change in crime reporting only if an area were immediately upset with its former patrol car officers or if crime reporting were suppressed to unusually low levels. If both the area and the time of intervention were picked randomly, then such interaction validity threats would be less probable. In addition, since both areas were not randomly picked from the total population of areas that potentially would have been amenable to walking patrol strategies, then questions can be raised about how the results from these two selected areas would generalize to other areas. In other words, the factors that led these areas to be selected could also have been the factors necessary for the increased reporting of crime that occurred when the walking patrol was initiated. The latter external validity problem would not be so obvious if the areas were randomly picked from the total population of possibilities.

GENERAL DISCUSSION

This report has demonstrated the application of the most powerful

---

* Cook and Campbell, *op. cit.*

design technology possible in two applied situations that precluded a large degree of treatment control. In other words, the police department was not engaging in research when they conceptualized the patrol strategies, but instead were reacting to political and economic realities. No financial resources were set aside to evaluate the effects of the patrol intervention.

These quasi-experimental evaluations produced the surprising conclusion (to the police) that (a) saturation patrol had no significant effect separate from regression artifacts; (b) the walking patrol produced an overall increase in the report of crime. In neither case was it necessary to fit the methods of initiating patrol intervention to the preconceived evaluation to arrive at these conclusions.

The need for simultaneous intervention into several high-rate burglary zones was largely determined by public pressure on the police administration to reduce crime rates and by the existence of three zones that were simultaneously experiencing high burglary rates. The sequential intervention into two areas by the walking patrol was made necessary by the fact that the police could not afford to start the patrol in two areas at once. The selection of the walking patrol areas was determined by a history of poor police-public relations in the two zones and requests from the Nashville Housing Authority for action.

Undoubtedly, a more powerful experimental technology could have been applied to both interventions if supplementary political and financial resources were available for a true experimental evaluation. In both cases, public opinion and victimization surveys would have been helpful. Also, in both cases it would have been more experimentally sound, and more costly, if the evaluator could have randomly determined which zones received treatment, and when the treatment was delivered.

It is the point of this report, however, that until the police are given resources necessary to place their operation on an experimental basis, an already existing evaluation technology can be used at little or no cost. This quasi-experimental technology can be applied in such a way that the usual procedures that social agencies employ in their interventions do not have to be changed. In other words, the evaluation can be largely unobtrusive.

The importance of the present study lies as much in the demonstrated application of the quasi-experimental strategy as in the information it provided about patrols, even though useful conclusions about patrols were produced. To make clearer statements about police patrols it would be necessary to have a more detailed description of what the police officers actually did in the patrols. Such research is now being conducted, and it must be said that this more refined patrol research would not have been politically possible without the preliminary research described in the present report.

This paper primarily illustrates that usable data can be immediately gained by the applied behavior analyst if efforts are directed toward the evaluation of normally occurring social interventions. It would seem that such unobtrusive experimental technology is a logical first step toward placing social agencies on a sounder experimental basis.

REFERENCES

CAMPBELL, D. T. Reforms as experiments. *Amer. Psychologist*, 1969, 24, 407-429.

CAMPBELL, D. T. & STANLEY, J. C. *Experimental and Quasi-Experimental Design for Research*. Chicago: Rand McNally, 1966.

CAMPBELL, D. T. & Ross, H. L. The Connecticut Crackdown on speeding: Time series data in quasi-experimental analysis. *Law & Soc. Rev.*, 1968, 8, 33-53.

CAMPBELL, D. T. & ERLEBACHER, A. How regression artifacts in quasi-experimental evaluations can mistakenly make compensatory education look harmful! In J. Hellmuth (Ed.), *Compensatory Education: A National Debate, Vol. III of The Disadvantaged Child*. New York: Brunner/Mazel, 1970, pp. 185-210; reply to replies, pp. 221-225.

ETZIONI, A. "Shortcuts" to social change? *The Public Interest*, 1968, 12, 40-51.

GLASS, G. U., TIAO, G. C., & MAGUIRE, T. O. Analysis of data on the 1900 revision of German divorce laws as a time-series quasi-experiment. *Law & Soc. Rev.*, 1971, 4, 539-562.

GOTTMAN, J. M. N-of one and N-of two research in psychotherapy. *Psychol. Bull.*, 1973, 80, 93-105.

HANNA, J. Crime-Specific Burglary Handbook: Evaluates reviews of O.C.J.P. Projects. *Bull. Crim. Just. Planning*, 1974, 7, 5-12.

Law Enforcement Assistance Administration, Trust and the police. *Time*, 1974, 103, 124.

LAWLER, E. E. & HACKMAN, J. R. Impact of employee participation in the development of pay incentive plans: A field experiment. *J. Appl. Psychol.*, 1969, 53, 467-471.

O'CONNOR, G. W. & VANDERBOSCH, C. G. (Eds.). *The Patrol Operation*. Washington, D. C.: Library of Congress, 1967.

PRESS, S. J. Police manpower versus crime. In J. M. Tanur (Ed.), *Statistics: A Guide to the Unknown*. San Francisco: Holden-Day, 1972.

RISLEY, T. R. & WOLF, M. M. Strategies for analyzing behavioral change over time. In J. Nesselbroade and H. Reese (Eds.), *Life-span Development Psychology: Methodological Issues*. New York: Academic Press, 1972.

Ross, H. L., CAMPBELL, D. T., & GLASS, G. U. Determining the social effects of a legal reform: The British "Breathalyzer" crackdown of 1967. *Amer. Behav. Scientist*, 1970, 13, 493-509.

SCHNELLE, J. F. & LEE, F. J. A quasi-experimental retrospective evaluation of a prior policy change. *J. Appl. Behav. Anal.*, 1974, 7, 483-496.

WHESEHAND, P. M. & CLINE, J. L. *Patrol Operations*. Englewood Cliffs: Prentice-Hall, 1971.

15

SITUATIONAL DETERMINANTS OF ASSERTIVE BEHAVIOR

Richard M. Eisler, Michel Hersen, Peter M. Miller

*Veterans Administration Center, and
University of Mississippi Medical Center, Jackson, Mississippi*

and

Edward B. Blanchard

University of Mississippi Medical Center, Jackson, Mississippi

Thirty-two assertive situations that varied in social-interpersonal context were administered to 60 hospitalized psychiatric patients via role playing. Half of the role-played situations required the expression of negative (hostile) assertiveness, and the other half required positive (commendatory) assertive expression. Situational context was varied by having the subjects respond to male and female interpersonal partners who were either familiar or unfamiliar to patients. Responses were videotaped and rated on five measures of speech content and seven measures of nonverbal behavior. Additionally, groups of high- and low-assertive patients were identified from the total sample using a behavioral measure of global assertiveness and a self-report instrument. Results indicated that interpersonal behavior in assertive situations

Reprinted with permission from the *Journal of Consulting and Clinical Psychology,* Vol. 43, No. 3, 1975, 330-340. Copyright 1975, American Psychological Association. Michel Hersen is now at the University of Pittsburgh School of Medicine.

varied as a function of social context. Further, high- and low-assertive subjects were differentiated on the basis of 9 of the 12 measures of interpersonal behavior. Support for a stimulus specific theory of assertive behaviors and implications for assertive training are discussed.

Assertive training (Wolpe, 1958, 1969; Wolpe & Lazarus, 1966), originally developed as a treatment for individuals with a passive or inhibited life style, has reportedly been successful in the treatment of various clinical problems including sexual deviation (Edwards, 1972; Stevenson & Wolpe, 1960), depression (Piaget & Lazarus, 1969), and marital conflict (Eisler, Miller, Hersen, & Alford, 1974; Fensterheim, 1972). Assertive training has also been used to improve the interpersonal functioning of schizophrenics (Weinman, Gelbart, Wallace, & Post, 1972). Recently there has been an increased interest in identifying the most effective treatment ingredients comprising assertive training. McFall and his colleagues (McFall & Lillesand, 1971; McFall & Marston, 1970) have shown that behavior rehearsal both with and without performance feedback was superior to control procedures. Studies examining acquisition of assertive responses with modeling and therapeutic instructions have also yielded positive results (Eisler, Hersen, & Miller, 1973; Goldstein, Martens, Hubben, Van Belle, Shaaf, Wiersma, & Goedhart, 1973; Hersen, Eisler, Miller, Johnson, & Pinkston, 1973; Kazdin, 1974).

Although a number of well-controlled studies attest to the efficacy of various assertive training procedures, several important issues require clarification. With respect to the scope of behaviors considered "assertive," Lazarus (1971) has pointed out that most definitions of assertiveness do not include the expression of positive emotions such as affection, empathy, admiration, and appreciation. Wolpe (1969) has also differentiated between "hostile" assertive responses such as "I insist that you come to work on time" or "Please don't stand in front of me," compared with "commendatory" remarks such as "I admire your tenacity" or "You look lovely, terrific, ravishing, glamorous, etc." Most studies to date have been concerned primarily with assertion in the narrow sense, or what Wolpe would call hostile assertion, and have failed to consider the positive aspects of assertive expression.

A second unexplored issue is delineating the role of the social-interpersonal context in determining whether or not a response is "assertive." Behaviors that are socially appropriate in one circumstance may not be so in another. For example, if one is waiting in line to purchase a ticket at a movie theater and someone cuts in front of them, the response socially sanctioned will differ depending on whether the person is a middle-aged man, a young child, or an old woman. Similarly, the assertive response required will differ depending on whether one is relatively familiar with the other person as compared with one's response to a total stranger.

Finally, development of valid measures of assertive behavior has been difficult. This is partly due to the fact that (a) assertive behavior involves many simultaneously occurring verbal and nonverbal responses; (b) there has been a confusing array of behavioral, physiological, and self-report indices used as dependent measures of assertiveness; and (c) it is not clear how these indices relate to global judgments of assertiveness. In a preliminary study, Eisler, Miller, and Hersen (1973) attempted to delineate specific behaviors related to judgments of assertive expression. These authors extended the use of McFall and Marston's (1970) role-playing technique by developing 14 standard interpersonal situations requiring negative (hostile) assertive responses. The role-playing situations were administered to 30 male psychiatric inpatients. A female assistant prompted subjects' responses to a role-played wife, waitress, saleslady, etc. These role-played interactions were videotaped and rated on various verbal and nonverbal behaviors. Global judgments of overall assertiveness were also made independently of the behavior ratings. Subjects were then dichotomized at the median into high- and low-assertive groups. t-tests performed on ratings of behavior showed that the more highly assertive patients evidenced lengthier responses, louder speech with shorter latencies, and more pronounced affect than low-assertive subjects. Additionally, the speech content of patients in the high-assertive groups exhibited less compliance and more requests for the interpersonal partner to change her behavior.

One purpose of the present investigation was to extend the previous Eisler, Miller, and Hersen (1973) study, which identified some of the behavioral components of negative assertion while adding additional situations that typically elicit positive (commendatory) responses. A second purpose was to examine more systematically the effects of social context on interpersonal behavior in assertive situations. In one instance the effects of responding assertively to a male was contrasted with assertiveness responding to a female. A second aspect of social context was varied depending on whether or not the subject had recurrent interactions with the interpersonal partner (familiarity). For example, it was presumed that a subject's responses to a person he interacted with on a day-to-day basis such as his wife or employer would differ from his responses to a less familiar person such as a waitress or the mechanic who repaired his car. Finally, an additional objective was to delineate behaviors that would differentiate high- from low-assertive patients in each of the aforementioned contexts of assertion.

METHOD

Subjects

Sixty male psychiatric patients hospitalized at the Veterans Administration Center (Jackson, Mississippi) served as subjects. While no attempt was made to select subjects on the basis of diagnosis, patients who were acutely psychotic or with evidence of organic brain syndrome were excluded. With respect to diagnostic classification, the group selected included 30 character disorders, 25 neurotics, 3 schizophrenics, and 2 with adult situational reactions. The patients ranged in age from 21 to 67 years, with a mean age of 43.4 years. Educational level ranged from 3 to 18 years, with a mean of 11.2 years.

Thirty-seven of the subjects were currently married, while the remaining 23 were either divorced, separated, or widowed. Patients who had never married were excluded since some of the scenes required assertive responding to a role-played wife.

Role-Played Assertive Situations

Thirty-two role-played situations that required assertive responding in simulated real-life encounters were used. Some of the role-played scenes that required responses to familiar and unfamiliar females were adapted from previous research on hostile assertion (Eisler, Miller, & Hersen, 1973). Additional scenes that would elicit both positive and negative assertive expressions to familiar and unfamiliar individuals of both sexes were constructed by the authors.

Sixteen of the 32 scenes required the subject to express "positive" feelings such as praise, appreciation, or liking for his interpersonal partner, while the remaining 16 required the subject to express "negative" feelings such as anger, displeasure, or disappointment toward the role-playing partner. In half of the scenes the role-playing partner was male while in the other half the partner was female. Finally one-half of the scenes required the patient to respond to a person with whom he was presumed to have a good deal of interactive experience, e.g., wife or employer (familiar). In the other 16 scenes, the patient was required to interact with a person with whom it was presumed he had little interactive experience, e.g., cashier or waitress (unfamiliar).

All three situational variables contained two levels (i.e., positive and negative, male and female, familiar and unfamiliar) that were nested. Thus, there were eight categories of stimulus scenes with four scenes in each category. The following are sample scenes from each category as narrated to the patients.*

1. Male-Positive-Familiar

Narrator: "You have been working on a difficult job all week, your boss comes over with a smile on his face." *Your boss says:* "That's a very good job you have done; I'm going to give you a raise next week."

2. Male-Positive-Unfamiliar

Narrator: "You are the leader of the company bowling team. Your team is slightly behind when one of the men on your team makes three strikes in a row to even up the score. You are really proud of him." *He says:* "How did you like that one?"

3. Male-Negative-Familiar

Narrator: "You have had a very busy day at work and are tired. Your boss comes in and asks you to stay late for the third time this week. You really feel you would like to go home on time tonight." *Your boss says:* "I'm leaving now; would you mind staying late again tonight and finishing this work for me?"

4. Male-Negative-Unfamiliar

Narrator: "You go to a ballgame with reserved seat tickets. When you arrive you find that someone has put his coat in the seat for which you have reserved tickets. You ask him to remove his coat and he tells you that he is saving that seat for a friend." *He says:* "I'm sorry, this seat is saved."

5. Female-Positive-Familiar

Narrator: "Your wife has just bought a new outfit and is trying it on. You really like it and think that she looks very nice in it." *Your wife says:* "Well, how do I look in this outfit?"

6. Female-Positive-Unfamiliar

Narrator: "You are in a restaurant and the waitress had just served you an excellent meal cooked just the way you like it. You are pleased with her prompt, efficient service." *She comes by and says:* "I hope you enjoyed your dinner, sir."

---

* Complete descriptions of the 32 role-played scenes may be obtained free of charge from the first author.

7. Female-Negative-Familiar

Narrator: "You are in the middle of watching an exciting football game on television. Your wife walks in and changes the channel as she does everytime you are watching a good game." *Your wife says:* "Let's watch the movie instead; it's really supposed to be good."

8. Female-Negative-Unfamiliar

Narrator: "You are in a crowded grocery store and are in a hurry because you are already late for an appointment. You pick up one small item and get in line to pay for it. Then a woman with a shopping cart full of groceries cuts in line right in front of you." *She says:* "You don't mind if I cut in here, do you?"

Procedure

The Wolpe-Lazarus (1966) self-report inventory of assertiveness was administered to all subjects. The 32 assertive situations were then presented via role playing in a furnished room containing a portable television camera and a two-way intercom system. An adjoining control room contained recording equipment and a television monitor for observing subjects' responses. (See Eisler, Hersen, & Agras, 1973, for details.) All instructions to the subjects were given by the experimenter in the control room through the intercom. A female research assistant was used to role play all scenes involving a woman interpersonal partner, and a male research assistant role played all interactions involving a male interpersonal partner.

One-half of the subjects were presented with all scenes involving a female interpersonal partner first, and then responded to all scenes involving a male. The remaining 30 subjects responded to all male-related scenes first and then were administered the female-related scenes. Scenes within sex of partner were presented in different random order for all 60 subjects.

Each patient was escorted into the experimental videotape studio and seated next to either the male or female interpersonal partner, both of whom had been trained to deliver a predetermined prompt to the patient following narration of each scene from the control room. Following the patient's reply the interpersonal partner made no further response until narration of the next scene when a new prompt was delivered. Instructions were given to the subjects by the experimenter as follows:

> The purpose of today's procedure is to find out how you react to some everyday situations that might occur outside the hospital. The idea is for you to respond just as if you were in that situation

at home, at work, at a store, or in a restaurant. I will describe various situations that you might find yourself in with your wife, your boss, or some other person such as a waitress or salesclerk. When each situation is described to you, try and imagine that you really are there. In order to make these situations seem more real life, Miss Jones will play the part of your wife or another woman who is in the scene. Mr. Smith will play the part of your boss or another man who is in the scene. For example, after I have described a situation, Miss Jones will say something to you. After she speaks, I want you to say what you would say if she had said this to you in the situation that was described. *This is important.* Some of the scenes will be such that you feel irritated or annoyed if you were actually in that situation.

At this point the experimenter narrated a practice scene that required expression of "negative" feelings:

> "You have just put together a new shelf which you have hung up in the kitchen. You are proud of the shelf, but your wife makes some comments to the effect that you are a poor carpenter." *Your wife says:* That shelf looks awful."

Once it appeared that the patient understood the instructions and gave an appropriate response, the experimenter gave additional instructions for the positive scenes: "In other scenes you might feel appreciative or friendly toward the other person." The experimenter then narrated the following practical scene: "You are just coming in the house after cutting the grass on a hot afternoon. Your wife meets you at the door with a glass of ice cold lemonade." *Your wife says:* "You looked so hot, I thought you'd enjoy something cold to drink." The experimenter then said, "Remember, try to express your true feelings whatever they might be. Also, be sure to express yourself as fully as possible." (Responses to the practice scenes were not included in the analysis.)

*Videotape Ratings**

All ratings of the patients' responses were made independently by two judges who observed replays of the videotaped situations. The raters had over a year of experience in rating patient behaviors that were found to be related to negative (hostile) assertiveness in previous research (Eisler, Miller, & Hersen, 1973; Hersen et al., 1973). Ratings of interactive

* The authors wish to thank Susan G. Pinkston, Harriet F. Alford, Laura S. Wooten and John G. Watts for their assistance in rating the videotapes.

behaviors from videotape have been shown to be highly reliable and equivalent to rating the same behaviors from live observation (Eisler, Hersen, & Agras, 1973). Additional measures of speech content that have been described in the literature as related to positive or commendatory assertion were further elaborated and rated in a similar manner (Lazarus, 1971; Wolpe, 1969).

Components of social interactive behavior were broadly categorized in terms of (a) nonverbal behaviors, (b) positive content, (c) negative content, and (d) overall assertiveness. They were defined as follows:

Nonverbal behaviors. (a) *Duration of eye contact:* Length of time that a subject looked at his interpersonal partner from delivery of prompt to termination of response (in seconds) was recorded for each scene. (b) *Smiles:* Smiles were recorded on a dichotomous occurrence or nonoccurrence basis for each scene from delivery of prompt to termination of response. (c) *Duration of reply:* Length of time (in seconds) that the subject spoke to his partner was recorded for each scene. Speech pauses of greater than 3 seconds terminated timing until the subject began speaking again. (d) *Latency of response:* The subject's latency of response from the time that the partner delivered his prompt to the beginning of the subject's speech was recorded for each scene. (e) *Loudness of speech:* Loudness of the subject's speech for each scene was rated on a 5-point scale from 1 (very low) to 5 (very loud). (f) *Appropriate affect:* Subject's affect was scored on a 5-point scale with 1 indicating a very flat, unemotional tone of voice and 5 indicating a full and lively intonation appropriate to each situation. (g) *Ratio of speech disturbances to duration of speech:* Frequency of speech disturbances categorized by Mahl (1956) including pauses, stutters, and expletives such as "ah," "oh," "um," etc., were recorded for each scene. The ratio was compared by dividing the number of speech disturbances by the total duration of speech (in seconds).

Negative content. (a) *Compliance:* Verbal content indicating compliance was rated on a dichotomous occurrence or nonoccurrence basis for each scene. Compliance was scored if the subject did not resist his partner's position (e.g., if he agreed to stay and work late for the boss or let his wife change the television channel). (b) *Request for new behavior:* Verbal content requesting new behavior from the interpersonal partner was scored on an occurrence or nonoccurrence basis for each scene. Responses scored in this category required more than mere noncompliance. The subject had to show evidence that he wanted his partner to change his behavior (e.g., he had to request the person at the ballgame to

TABLE 1
EFFECTS OF SITUATIONAL CONTEXT ON MEASURES OF INTERPERSONAL BEHAVIOR

Dependent variable	Situational context			Interaction effects			
	Positive vs. negative expression	Male vs. female	Unfamiliar vs. familiar	Expression × sex	Sex × Familiarity	Familiarity × expression	Expression × Sex × Familiarity
Nonverbal measure							
Duration of eye contact	13.89***	2.81	<1.00	<1.00	1.41	<1.00	1.17
No. smiles	9.25***	27.04***	11.71**	<1.00	23.05***	4.89*	<1.00
Affect	8.90**	1.00	<1.00	<1.00	24.66***	<1.00	<1.00
Duration of reply	92.08***	46.73***	<1.00	8.92**	2.51	<1.00	2.20
Latency of response	8.66**	<1.00	<1.00	12.29***	8.53**	2.36	<1.00
Loudness of speech	6.63*	<1.00	1.35	2.22	1.81	5.10*	<1.00
Speech disturbance ratio	2.53	6.43*	<1.00	6.25*	4.05*	1.29	<1.00
Content measure							
Compliance content	—	4.51*	<1.00	—	2.51	—	—
Request for new behavior	—	9.86*	<1.00	—	<1.00	—	—
Praise	—	118.06***	29.86***	—	292.69***	—	—
Appreciation	—	15.67***	28.27***	—	93.72***	—	—
Spontaneous positive behavior	—	122.02***	12.45***	—	26.54***	—	—

$* p < .05.$
$** p < .01.$
$*** p < .001.$

remove his coat or ask the woman who cut in front of him at the grocery store to step to the end of the line).

Positive content. (a) *Praise:* This consisted of verbal content indicating that the subject expressed approval, admiration, or was complimentary toward the partner's behavior (e.g., if the subject told his wife she looked very good, terrific, etc., in the new outfit.) Praise was scored on an occurrence or nonoccurrence basis for each scene. (b) *Appreciation:* This was verbal content indicating that the subject expressed gratitude or thankfulness for the partner's behavior (e.g., if the subject thanked his boss for the raise). Appreciation was scored on an occurrence or nonoccurrence basis for each scene. (c) *Spontaneous positive behavior:* This was verbal content indicating that the subject has volunteered to perform some act for the partner (e.g., if the subject offered to buy a beer for his teammate who just bowled three strikes in a row). Positive behavior was scored on the basis of occurrence or nonoccurrence for each scene.

Overall assertiveness. After all previous behaviors were rated, two individual raters who were not familiar with the purpose of the study were asked to rate the subjects' behavior on overall assertiveness, using a 5-point scale, with 1 indicating "very unassertive" and 5 indicating "very assertive." The ratings were performed independently after the raters had familiarized themselves with Wolpe's (1959) definition of "hostile" and "commendatory" assertiveness.

Scoring

For all content measures and smiles, *presence* of the behavior in each category, i.e., compliance, appreciation, request for new behavior, praise, spontaneous positive behavior, was tallied for each subject for each of the eight categories of scenes (e.g., male-positive-familiar, female-negative-unfamiliar). For all other measures the subject's score was obtained by taking the mean value averaged over the four scenes in each of the eight categories. In analyzing the data for differences between high- and low-assertive subjects, scores were combined across all categories of scenes for each subject.

Reliability of Behavioral Measures

Two judges were used to assess interrater reliability. One judge rated the 60 subjects on all behavioral measures across all scenes while the second judge rated the behavior of 20 subjects selected at random. For the five measures of speech content, number of speech disturbances, and frequency of smiles, interjudge agreement was computed by dividing the total number of agreements by the total number of judgments (agreements plus disagreements) for each context. For these measures, percentage of agreement was over 95 percent across all situational contexts. For the remaining continuous measures, Pearson product-moment correlations were computed between the two sets of ratings. Correlation coefficients were all greater than .94. The exceptionally high reliabilities obtained appear to be related to the specificity of criteria outlined for each measure, the fact that only one measure was rated for each videotape playback, and the fact that the raters had several years of experience making similar ratings.

RESULTS

Separate three-factor analyses of variance with repeated measures were used to assess the effects of situational context on each response measure. The levels of each factor were (a) positive versus negative expression, (b) male versus female interpersonal partner, and (c) unfamiliar versus familiar interpersonal partner. The results of these analyses are summarized in Table 1, which shows significance levels for situational contexts and their interactions. There were no instances of positive content occurring in any scene requiring positive assertion. This was assurance that scenes structured for positive assertive expression did in fact elicit only positive comments and scenes structured for negative assertive expression elicited only negative comments. Therefore, *content* measures were not analyzed with respect to positive or negative expression.

Effects of Situational Context

The results indicated that negative scenes elicited significantly different interpersonal behavior on all nonverbal response measures (see Table 1). In comparison to positive scenes, the responses to negative scenes could be characterized by generally longer replies, increased eye contact, greater affect, more speech volume, and increased latency of response. As expected, positive scenes elicited a greater number of smiles than did negative scenes. Finally, subjects tended to obtain higher ratings on overall assertiveness when expressing positive than negative feelings, $F(1,59) = 6.71, p < .05$.

With respect to sex of interpersonal partner, subjects tended to talk longer to other men than to women. They also evidenced a greater ratio of speech disturbances, relative to total speech, when the interpersonal partner was male as compared to female. However, subjects smiled more at women than men.

In expressing negative content, subjects complied with the wishes of men more frequently than those of female partners. They were also more likely to request that a female partner change her behavior rather than verbalize such assertions to another male. Thus, in situations requiring negative (hostile) assertion, these subjects were significantly more assertive with women than men. Similarly, in situations requiring positive assertion, subjects were more likely to deliver praise and appreciation to females than to males. However, they were more likely to offer to perform a favor (spontaneous positive behavior) to another male as opposed to a female.

In comparing responses to familiar versus unfamiliar persons, subjects were rated higher in overall assertiveness when their expressions were directed toward unfamiliar persons when compared to familiar persons, $F(1,59) = 8.56, p < .01$. In situations requiring positive expression, subjects were more likely to offer praise, appreciation, or to do a favor for a person they did not know well as compared with persons with whom they were more familiar. When in situations requiring negative expres-

TABLE 2

NEUMAN-KEULS COMPARISONS OF SITUATIONAL CONTEXT INTERACTIONS

Measure	Interaction			
	Expression × Sex			
Duration of reply	Female positive	Male positive	Female negative	Male negative
Latency	Male positive$_a$	Female positive$_{a, b}$	Female negative$_b$	Male negative
Speech disturbances	Female negative$_a$	Female positive$_a$	Male positive$_a$	Male negative
	Sex × Familiarity			
Smiles	Male familiar$_a$	Female unfamiliar$_a$	Male unfamiliar$_a$	Female familiar
Affect	Male familiar$_a$	Female unfamiliar$_a$	Male unfamiliar$_b$	Female familiar$_b$
Latency	Female familiar$_a$	Male unfamiliar$_a$	Female unfamiliar$_{a, b}$	Male familiar$_b$
Speech disturbances	Female unfamiliar	Female familiar$_a$	Male unfamiliar$_a$	Male familiar$_a$
Appreciation	Female familiar$_a$	Male unfamiliar$_a$	Male familiar	Female unfamiliar
Spontaneous positive	Female familiar	Female unfamiliar	Male unfamiliar$_a$	Male familiar
Praise	Male familiar	Female unfamiliar	Male unfamiliar	Female familiar
	Familiarity × Expression			
Smiles	Unfamiliar negative	Familiar negative$_a$	Unfamiliar positive	Familiar positive
Loudness	Familiar positive$_a$	Unfamiliar positive$_a$	Unfamiliar negative	Familiar negative

Note. Any two means with the same subscript are not significantly different, whereas any two means with different subscripts are significantly different. All differences are at $p < .05$. Means are presented in increasing order from left to right.

sion, there were no differences due to familiarity of interpersonal partner. With respect to noncontent measures, few significant differences emerged with respect to familiarity. However, as might be exepcted, subjects smiled more when talking with familiar rather than unfamiliar partners.

Interaction Effects

Significant two-way interactions obtained between the independent variables (see Table 1) were further analyzed by Newman-Keuls tests, summarized in Table 2. No higher order interactions attained significance.

Expression × Sex. With respect to interactions between sex of interpersonal partner and type of assertive expression required (positive versus negative), it was found that significant differences emerged between all possible social context combinations for "duration of reply." Subjects generally tended to talk longer in negative contexts as compared with positive contexts. Also, irrespective of whether positive or negative expression was required, subjects spoke longer to males than to females. Latency of response was significantly longer to a male in a negative context than when initiating responses to females or to males in a positive context. There were no differences in latency of response to females, irrespective of type of expression, or between males and females when the expression was positive. Finally, there was a significantly greater ratio of speech disturbances per unit of time when speaking to males in a negative context than when speaking to females, in either positive or negative contexts, or to males in a positive context.

Sex × Familiarity. Interactions between sex of partner and familiarity of partner attained significance on 7 of the 12 dependent measures. Significantly more smiles were directed toward females in a positive context than to males in either context or females in a negative context. Also significantly more affect was expressed toward familiar males and unfamiliar females (who did not differ from each other) than to familiar females and unfamiliar males (who also did not differ from each other). Latency of response was greater to familiar males than to either unfamiliar males or familiar females. No other differences were significant with respect to latency. In general, there were fewer speech disturbances to unfamiliar females than to familiar females or familiar or unfamiliar males.

Significant interactions were obtained between sex of partner and familiarity of partner in situations requiring positive but not negative expression. Familiar females elicited praise almost three times as often as familiar males. Also, familiar females received more praise than unfamiliar females, and unfamiliar males received more praise than familiar males. Both unfamiliar females and familiar males elicited significantly more appreciation than either familiar females and unfamiliar males. Unfamiliar males did not differ from familiar females in receiving appreciation. Finally, males, irrespective of familiarity, elicited more spontaneous offers for a subject to return a favor than did females. However, an unfamiliar female was more likely to elicit a favor than a familiar female.

Familiarity × Expression. There were two significant interactions between familiarity of partner and positive versus negative context. The significant interaction with respect to smiles was due to the fact that more smiles were delivered to familiar persons in a positive context than to unfamiliar persons in either context, or to familiar persons in a negative context elicited fewer smiles than familiar persons in a negative context or unfamiliar persons in a positive context.

With respect to loudness, greater volume of speech was directed toward familiar persons in a negative context than to either unfamiliar persons in a negative context or to individuals in a positive context, irrespective of familiarity. Familiarity did not elicit differences in speech volume when the context was positive.

TABLE 3

MEANS, SIGNIFICANT LEVELS, AND INTERACTIONS WITH SITUATIONAL CONTEXTS FOR
HIGH- AND LOW-ASSERTIVE GROUPS

Dependent variable	High $\bar{X}^a$	Low $\bar{X}^a$	F	Expression	Sex	Familiarity
Duration of eye contact	30.2	22.52	<1.00	<1.00	<1.00	<1.00
No. smiles ·	.30	.84	5.24*	<1.00	1.16	<1.00
Affect	13.91	12.25	23.4***	3.02	1.43	1.36
Duration of reply	244.85	120.43	15.8***	4.75	1.08	<1.00
Latency of response	53.52	58.36	<1.00	6.26*	1.10	<1.00
Loudness of speech	12.20	10.33	9.60**	5.15*	<1.00	6.75*
Speech disturbance ratio	.142	.073	6.93*	<1.00	<1.00	<1.00
Compliance content	.89	1.57	9.85***	—	<1.00	<1.00
Requests for new behavior	2.10	.98	31.9***	—	3.41	4.64*
Praise	1.56	1.13	10.80**	—	4.58*	3.70
Appreciation	2.03	1.80	1.40	—	1.00	<1.00
Spontaneous positive behavior	1.66	1.19	14.0**	—	<1.00	<1.00

^{a} $n = 20$.
* $p < .05$.
** $p < .01$.
*** $p < .001$.

Comparisons Between High- and Low-Assertive Subjects

High- and low-assertive subjects were identified from the group used in the previous analysis. Subjects whose mean rating on "overall assertiveness" (across all scenes) fell into the top third of the distribution ($n = 20$) were designated as high assertive. Those subjects whose mean rating fell in the lower third of the distribution ($n = 20$) were designated as low assertive. A t-test performed between the means of these groups indicated a highly significant difference in ratings of assertiveness, $t (38) = 8.95$, $p < .001$. Additionally, subjects in the high-assertive and low-assretive groups differed in the expected direction on the Wolpe-Lazarus Assertiveness Questionnaire, $t (38) = 2.11$, $p < .05$.

Separate four-way analyses of variance with high-assertive and low-assertive subjects as levels of one factor and situational contexts as three separate factors were performed on all dependent measures. Since the effects of situational contexts on measures of interpersonal behavior were previously presented on the full sample of 60 subjects, only the effects of subject differences in assertiveness and their interactions with situational context are presented here.

Table 3 depicts mean ratings and significant differences between high- and low-assertive subjects on all dependent measures. Also shown are interactions between levels of assertiveness and situational contexts. Significant interactions were further analyzed by means of Neuman-Keuls tests.

352   ANNUAL REVIEW OF BEHAVIOR THERAPY

Nonverbal Behavior

The results indicate that over all contexts, high-assertive subjects gave much lengthier replies than low-assertive subjects, $F(1,38) = 15.8$, $p < .001$. However, both high-assertive ($p < .01$) and low-assertive subjects ($p < .01$) responded longer in situations that required negative rather than positive assertions. While there were no differences in latency of response between high- and low-assertive subjects across all contexts ($F < 1.00$), a significant interaction was obtained with type of expression. This resulted from the fact that latency of response was longer for low-assertive subjects than high-assertive subjects when the situation required negative assertion ($p < .05$). There were no differences between groups in the context of positive assertion.

In general, high-assertive subjects spoke significantly louder than low-assertive subjects, $F(1,38) = 9.60$, $p < .01$. This was true irrespective of whether the interpersonal partner was familiar ($p < .01$) or unfamiliar ($p < .01$), or whether the interactional context was negative ($p < .01$) or positive ($p < .01$). However, when the context was negative, high assertive subjects increased their volume of speech compared to when the context was positive ($p < .01$). There was no difference in speech volume for low-assertive subjects irrespective of whether the context was negative or positive. Irrespective of situational context, highly assertive subjects spoke with greater affect more appropriate to the situation than did low-assertive subjects, $F(1,38) = 23.5$, $p < .001$, although frequency of smiles was greater for low-assertive than high-assertive subjects, $F(1,38) = 5.24$, p $< .05$. Finally, with respect to nonverbal expression, high-assertive subjects evidenced a higher ratio of speech disturbances per length of speech than did low-assertive subjects, $F(1,38) = 6.93$, $p < .05$.

Speech Content

With respect to speech content in situations requiring negative assertion, it was found that, as expected, low-assertive subjects were more compliant than high-assertive subjects $F(1,38) = 9.85$, $p < .001$). Additionally high-assertive subjects requested more often that their interpersonal partner change their behavior in all situational contexts, $F(1,38) = 31.9$, $p < .001$. This was true whether their partner was familiar ($p < .01$) or unfamiliar ($p < .01$).

With respect to situational contexts requiring the expression of positive assertion, it was found that subjects in the high-assertive group delivered more praise to their interpersonal partners than did low-assertive subjects, $F(1,38) = 10.8$, $p < .01$. The significant interaction with sex of partner on this variable was due to the fact that low-assertive subjects delivered more praise to females than to males ($p < .01$), whereas high-assertive subjects praised males and females equally. Finally, with respect to content in positive situations, highly assertive subjects offered to spontaneously do a favor for an interpersonal partner more frequently than did less assertive subjects $F(1,38)$ 14.0, $p < .01$.

DISCUSSION

The results of this study substantiated the hypothesis that in situations requiring assertive expression an individual's behavior is functionally related to the social context of the interpersonal interaction. Obviously, content of speech, or *what* one says, will differ in relation to whether the situation requires positive or negative assertion. However, the present results demonstrated significant differences on six of the seven *nonverbal* interactional variables when comparing responses to negative and positive assertive situations. Additionally, males elicited different responses than females across situations on all measures of speech content. In negative situations requiring an individual to "stand up for his rights," male subjects evidenced greater assertion toward women than other men. Similarly, in situations requiring positive assertive expression, subjects were more likely to offer praise and appreciation to female than to male partners. The greater expression of positive assertion to women than men appears to be consistent with sociocultural norms in this country where it is permissible for males to be more effusive toward women than toward other men. Lack of deference on the part of male subjects to women in situations requiring negative assertion was more difficult to explain, and may be specific to the clinical or sociocultural characterists of the present population. Similarly, the finding that unfamiliar individuals, particularly in positive contexts, elicited greater assertiveness than familiar persons may in part be a function of the sociocultural characteristics of these patients.

In general, the results support a stimulus-specific theory of assertiveness. That is, an individual who is assertive in one interpersonal context may not be assertive in a different interpersonal environment. Further, some individuals may have no difficulty responding with negative assertions, but may be unable to respond when the situation requires positive expression. This is consistent with the classic study of Hartshorne and May (1928) who demonstrated that "moral" behaviors in children were not consistent across various situations, and Mischel's (1968) argument against the utility of "trait" theories of personality. While Mischel (1968) did not deny the fact that some stable predispositions to respond in certain ways exist, he concluded:

> While trait and state theories have searched for broad, consistent dispositions, a considerable amount of experimental research has focused, instead, on the determinants of changes in behavior and on the stimulus conditions that seem to control these alterations. The principles that emerge from studies of the variables that control behavior in turn become the bases for developing theory, not about global traits and states, but about the manner in which behavior develops and changes in response to environmental stimulus changes (p. 10).

In addition to showing the stimulus-specific nature of assertive responding, the results of the present study demonstrated the behavioral complexity of what is commonly referred to as "assertiveness." On the majority of verbal and nonverbal measures employed in this study, significant differences emerged between subjects who evidenced high versus low assertion on the global measure of assertiveness. Apparently, assertive responding requires the coordinated delivery of numerous verbal and nonverbal responses.

In general, high-assertive subjects tended to talk longer, with greater affect and speech volume, while smiling less frequently than low-assertive subjects. The fact that there were no significant differences between high- and low-assertive subjects on measures of speech duration and latency of response could, in part, have been a function of the short duration of the experimental interaction. Since subjects were permitted only one response to the role-played partner, who did not respond to the patients' assertions, differences that might have emerged on longer exchanges could have been artificially obscured. The finding that high-assertive subjects evidenced more speech disturbances per unit of time than the lows was an unexpected result. Mahl (1956), in studying the speech disfluencies of patients in psychotherapy, concluded that disruptions were related to judgments of the client's anxiety level although no objective measures of anxiety were used. It may be that assertive individuals take greater "risks" in expressing themselves than unassertive individuals, with concomitant emotional arousal being reflected in increased speech disruptions.

The significant differences obtained in this study between high- and

low-assertive subjects on component behaviors related to negative assertion replicate previous findings by Eisler, Miller, and Hersen (1973).
Additionally, there appear to be numerous behavioral components to
positive assertion as well. In addition to differences in speech content between expression of positive compared with negative assertiveness, differences in nonverbal behaviors were also observed. For example, it was
found that subjects tended to give lengthier replies with greater speech
volume in negative contexts than in positive contexts. Also, when situations require negative assertion, the low-assertive subjects took longer to
reply than the high-assertive subjects.

The generality of the specific effects of context on assertive behavior
found here is, of course, limited to the characteristics of the present
patient population, including their sociocultural background, and the
assertive situations sampled in this study. Additional research is needed
to determine the effects of additional interpersonal context variables
with different populations. For example, further investigations are necessary to determine what constitutes *appropriate* assertive behavior for
women, for individuals in different socioeconomic groups, and for individuals who live in different geographic regions. Nevertheless, this study
has important implications for the treatment of patients who are deemed
to have behavioral deficits in assertion. Positive assertive expression, or
what Wolpe (1969) has termed "commendatory" behavior, appears to
be a real phenomenon that should broaden the scope of assertive training.
To date there appear to be few experimentally validated procedures for
training individuals to increase their expression of affection, appreciation,
satisfaction, etc. In summary, training individuals to be more reinforcing
to others would appear to be indicated in a variety of clinical situations.
Further, it is not likely that therapists can train clients to be "more
assertive" in a general sense. Instead, clinicians should identify classes of
interpersonal situations in which deficits can be identified. Training will
then consist of increasing assertive responding to specific types of interactions with different individuals.

REFERENCES

EDWARDS, N. B. Case conference: Assertive training in a case of homosexual pedo-
philia. *J. Behav. Ther. Exp. Psychiat.,* 1972, 3, 55-63.
EISLER, R. M., HERSEN, M., & AGRAS, W. S. Videotape: A method for the controlled
observation of nonverbal interpersonal behavior. *Behav. Ther.,* 1973, 4, 420-425.
EISLER, R. M., HERSEN, M. & MILLER, P. M., Effects of modeling on components of
assertive behavior. *J. Behav. Ther. Exp. Psychiat.,* 1973, 4, 1-6.

356ANNUAL REVIEW OF BEHAVIOR THERAPY

EISLER, R. M., MIILLER, P. M., & HERSEN, M. Components of assertive behavior. *J. Clin. Psychol.*, 1973, 29, 295-299.

EISLER, R. M., MILLER, P. M., HERSEN, M., & ALFORD, H. Effects of assertive training on marital interaction. *Arch. Gen. Psychiat.*, 1974, 30, 643-649.

FENSTERHEIM, H. Assertive methods of marital problems. In R. D. Rubin, H. Fensterheim, J. D. Henderson, and L. P. Ullmann (Eds.), *Advances in Behavior Therapy*. New York: Academic Press, 1972.

GOLDSTEIN, A. P., MARTENS, J., HUBBEN, J., VAN BELLE, H. A., SHAAF, W., WIERSMA, H., & GOEDHART, A. The use of modeling to increase independent behavior. *Behav. Res. & Ther.*, 1973, 11, 31-42.

HERSEN, M., EISLER, R. M., MILLER, P. M., JOHNSON, M. B., & PINKSTON, S. G. Effects of practice, instructions and modeling on components of assertive behavior. *Behav. Res. & Ther.*, 1973, 11, 443-451.

HARTSHORNE, H. & MAY, M. A. *Studies in the Nature of Character* (Vol. 1). *Studies in Deceit*. New York: Macmillan, 1928.

KAZDIN, A. E. Effect of covert modeling and model reinforcement on assertive behavior. *J. Abnorm. Psychol.*, 1974, 83, 240-252.

LAZARUS, A. A. *Behavior Therapy and Beyond*. New York: McGraw-Hill, 1971.

MAHL, G. F. Disturbances and silences in the patient's speech in psychotherapy. *J. Abnorm. Soc. Psychol.*, 1956, 53, 1-15.

MCFALL, R. M. & LILLESAND, D. B. Behavior rehearsal with modeling and coaching in assertion training. *J. Abnorm. Psychol.*, 1971, 77, 313-323.

MCFALL, R. M. & MARSTON, A. R. An experimental investigation of behavior rehearsal in assertive training. *J. Abnorm. Psychol.*, 1970, 76, 295-303.

PIAGET, G. W. & LAZARUS, A. A. The use of rehearsal-desensitization. *Psychother., Theory Res. Pract.*, 1969, 6, 264-266.

MISCHEL, W. *Personality and Assessment*. New York: Wiley, 1968.

STEVENSON, I. & WOLPE, J. Recovery from sexual deviations through overcoming nonsexual neurotic responses. *Amer. J. Psychiat.*, 1960, 116, 737-742.

WEINMAN, B., GELBART, P., WALLACE, M., & POST, M. Inducing assertive behavior in chronic schizophrenics. A comparison of socioenvironmental, desensitization, and relaxation therapies. *J. Consult. Clin. Psychol.*, 1972, 39, 246-252.

WOLPE, J. *Psychotherapy by Reciprocal Inhibition*. Stanford, Calif.: Stanford University Press, 1958.

WOLPE, J. *The Practice of Behavior Therapy*. New York: Pergamon Press, 1969.

WOLPE, J. & LAZARUS, A. A. *Behavior Therapy Techniques*. New York: Pergamon Press, 1966.

SECTION IV: ASSESSMENT, MEASUREMENT
AND METHODOLOGY

16

AN ASSERTION INVENTORY FOR USE IN ASSESSMENT AND RESEARCH

Eileen D. Gambrill
University of California, Berkeley

and

Cheryl A. Richey
University of Washington, Seattle

The Assertion Inventory is a 40-item self-report inventory
which permits respondents to note for each item their degree
of discomfort, their probability of engaging in the behavior,
and situations they would like to handle more assertively.
Normative data from a college population as well as data
from women taking part in assertion training groups are
included. Comparative distributions of these populations
over four combinations of response probability and discomfort scores are presented as well as reliability and validity
data. The value of the Inventory both in clinical setting and
in research is discussed.

Reprinted with permission from *Behavior Therapy*, 6, 550-561, 1975.

A preliminary report on the Assertion Inventory was presented at the Western
Psychological Association Convention, Anaheim, April, 1973.

Tables of items and their rotated loadings on each factor are available from the
author upon request.

357

Deficits in assertive behavior have been implicated in a wide range of presenting problems (Hersen, Eissler, & Miller, 1973). However only recently have self-report inventories been developed to assess this area of behavior. Galassi, Delo, Galassi, and Bastien (1974) developed a 50-item instrument designed to measure assertiveness in college students across a range of situations. Rathus (1973) developed a 30-item schedule based partly on questions developed by Wolpe and Lazarus (1966). On the Constriction Scale developed by Bates and Zimmerman (1971), respondents indicate in a forced choice format whether they engage in a series of 43 behaviors. McFall and Lillesand (1971) created a 35-item inventory tailored for college students which deals with turning down unfair requests. Respondents select from five options in answering each item. The first four choices are orthogonal dimensions of comfort-discomfort and refusal-acceptance, and a fifth option provides for a lack of refusal because the request is interpreted as reasonable. A multiple choice format was employed in a 112-item inventory developed by Lawrence (1970). Jensen recently constructed a 75-item scale to measure assertiveness in adolescents (Note 1).

The present Inventory is an attempt to develop an instrument which would be useable with a variety of individuals; would include items sampling a range of situations; would be as situationally specific as length reasonably allowed; and which permitted the collection of three types of information regarding assertive behavior: (1) degree of discomfort in relation to specific situations, (2) judged probability of engaging in a behavior, and (3) identification of situations in which a person would like to be more assertive.

The distinction between discomfort and behavior is important since different combinations of these two factors could necessitate different behavior change procedures. For example, a person might experience high discomfort but engage in assertive behaviors in spite of this, or, such discomfort could be coupled with avoidance behavior. If assertion was displayed in spite of high discomfort and was followed by positive consequences, it is likely that a repertoire of appropriate behavior exists. If, however, assertion does not occur, behavior deficits may be involved. In addition, inclusion of discomfort and response probability permits descriptions of possible between group differences, e.g., male vs. female, and treatment vs. nontreatment populations.

METHOD

The Scale

The Assertion Inventory is a 40-item self-report questionnaire (see Table 1). For each item, the respondent is requested to indicate: (1) degree of discomfort or anxiety on a five-point scale which ranges from 1 (none) to 5 (very much); (2) the probability of displaying the behavior if actually presented with the situation on a five-point scale ranging from 1 (always do it) to 5 (never do it); and (3) the situations in which he or she would like to be more assertive. Selected demographic information is collected at the end of the Inventory.

A variety of sources was employed in developing a list of potential items including reports from students and clients as well as a review of the literature to determine frequently occurring assertion difficulties. It was impossible to retain the degree of specificity that would have been desirable due to the length of the instrument that would have been required. The 40 items included fell into the following categories: (1) turning down requests; (2) expressing personal limitations such as admitting ignorance in some areas; (3) initiating social contacts; (4) expressing positive feelings; (5) handling criticism; (6) differing with others; (7) assertion in service situations; and (8) giving negative feedback. It was recognized that assertive behavior may vary according to the relationship between the people involved, i.e., whether they are strangers, acquaintances, or intimates, and this dimension was built into many of the items.

Procedure

Normative data were collected from three samples of undergraduates enrolled in social science classes, two from the University of California at Berkeley and one from the University of Washington in Seattle, as well as from a sample of 19 women participating in assertion training programs. One California sample was collected in 1973 and consisted of 116 men and 197 women (mean age = 22.1 years) and the second was collected in 1974 and consisted of 137 men and 158 women (mean age = 21.6 years). The age range for the California sample was 18-27 years. The Washington sample consisted of 16 men and 33 women (mean age = 23.1 years, range 18 to 53) who completed the inventory at two different time periods five weeks apart. The 19 women taking part in six-week assertion training programs ranged in age from 22 to 48 years

TABLE 1

The Assertion Inventory

Many people experience difficulty in handling interpersonal situations requiring them to assert themselves in some way, for example, turning down a request, asking a favor, giving someone a compliment, expressing disapproval or approval, etc. Please indicate your degree of discomfort or anxiety in the space provided *before* each situation listed below. Utilize the following scale to indicate degree of discomfort:

1 = none
2 = a little
3 = a fair amount
4 = much
5 = very much

Then, go over the list a second time and indicate *after* each item the probability or likelihood of your displaying the behavior if actually presented with the situation.*
For example, if you rarely apologize when you are at fault, you would mark a "4" after that item. Utilize the following scale to indicate response probability:

1 = always do it
2 = usually do it
3 = do it about half the time
4 = rarely do it
5 = never do it

* *Note.* It is important to cover your discomfort ratings (located in front of the items) while indicating response probability. Otherwise, one rating may contaminate the other and a realistic assessment of your behavior is unlikely. To correct for this, place a piece of paper over your discomfort ratings while responding to the situations a second time for response probability.

Degree of discomfort	Situation	Response probability
————————	1. Turn down a request to borrow your car	————————
————————	2. Compliment a friend	————————
————————	3. Ask a favor of someone	————————
————————	4. Resist sales pressure	————————
————————	5. Apologize when you are at fault	————————
————————	6. Turn down a request for a meeting or date	————————
————————	7. Admit fear and request consideration	————————
————————	8. Tell a person you are intimately involved when he/she says or does something that bothers you	————————
————————	9. Ask for a raise	————————
————————	10. Admit ignorance in some area	————————
————————	11. Turn down a request to borrow money	————————
————————	12. Ask personal questions	————————
————————	13. Turn off a talkative friend	————————
————————	14. Ask for constructive criticism	————————
————————	15. Initiate a conversation with a stranger	————————
————————	16. Compliment a person you are romantically involved with or interested in	————————

TABLE 1 (*continued*)

Degree of discomfort		Situation	Response probability
————————	17.	Request a meeting or a date with a person	————————
————————	18.	Your initial request for a meeting is turned down and you ask the person again at a later time	————————
————————	19.	Admit confusion about a point under discussion and ask for clarification	————————
————————	20.	Apply for a job	————————
————————	21.	Ask whether you have offended someone	————————
————————	22.	Tell someone that you like them	————————
————————	23.	Request expected service when such is not forthcoming, e.g., in a restaurant	————————
————————	24.	Discuss openly with the person his/her criticism of your behavior	————————
————————	25.	Return defective items, e.g., store or restaurant	————————
————————	26.	Express an opinion that differs from that of the person you are talking to	————————
————————	27.	Resist sexual overtures when you are not interested	————————
————————	28.	Tell the person when you feel he/she has done something that is unfair to you	————————
————————	29.	Accept a date	————————
————————	30.	Tell someone good news about yourself	————————
————————	31.	Resist pressure to drink	————————
————————	32.	Resist a significant person's unfair demand	————————
————————	33.	Quit a job	————————
————————	34.	Resist pressure to "turn on"	————————
————————	35.	Discuss openly with the person his/her criticism of your work	————————
————————	36.	Request the return of borrowed items	————————
————————	37.	Receive compliments	————————
————————	38.	Continue to converse with someone who disagrees with you	————————
————————	39.	Tell a friend or someone with whom you work when he/she says or does something that bothers you	————————
————————	40.	Ask a person who is annoying you in a public situation to stop	————————

Lastly, please indicate the situations you would like to handle more assertively by placing a circle around the item number.

(mean age = 32.1) and completed the inventory before and after training. Discomfort and response probability scores were computed by adding responses on each dimension and difference scores for each person were determined by subtracting discomfort from response probability. Mean scores and standard deviations for men and women were also determined. A factor analysis of discomfort scores using a principle component solution followed by a varimax rotation was conducted for one sample employing the University of California PICKLE program. A count was made for all samples of the number of times an item was circled by men and women as a situation they would like to handle more assertively.

RESULTS AND DISCUSSION

Reliability and Normative Data

The Pearson correlation between pre- and posttests for the Washington sample were .87 for discomfort and .81 for response probability, indicating high stability of the scores over time.

For all undergraduate samples, the mean discomfort and response probability scores for men and women were fairly similar (Table 2). Men had higher probability scores than did women. That is, in general they reported less likelihood of engaging in the behavior if actually presented with the situation. However, this difference reached significance only for the Washington posttest sample. This raises the question of possible experimenter bias in the Inventory, i.e., are some items representative of assertion only from a woman's perspective? To examine this question, a correlational analysis was conducted for items having a "4" or "5" response probability score in the 1973 California sample. A Spearman's Rank Correlation Coefficient of .88 was found between the items marked by men and women in terms of low probability. That is, items marked as "rarely" or "never" engaged in were very similar for men and women in this sample. Thus, the notion that there were significant sex differences in the probability scores for various items, indicating possible experimenter bias, was not supported.

Although there was a high correlation between items, several reflected sex differences: Men reported that they were less likely than women to resist sexual overtures, turn down a request for a date, or ask whether they have offended someone; women reported less likelihood of discussing someone's criticism of their work, or requesting a date with a person. These differences seem more reflective of the social expectations for men and women than bias within the instrument itself.

The standard deviations for discomfort and response probability reflect a fairly wide range of scores in all undergraduate samples. This indicates that respondents in a normal population are widely distributed along the continuum labeled "assertion." A narrowed distribution might have suggested that the instrument was encouraging stereotypic responses, or that it was inadequate in the variations of situations presented.

All mean difference scores for the undergraduate samples were posi-

TABLE 2

Means and Standard Deviations of Discomfort, Response
Probability and Difference Scores on the
Assertion Inventory

Sample	Sex	N	Mean dis-comfort	S.D.	Mean response prob-ability	S.D.	Mean differ-ence	S.D.
U.C. Berkeley,	Male	116	94.38	19.48	104.85	16.46	10.46	15.77
1973	Female	197	96.34	20.21	103.97	15.27	7.88	17.23
	Both	313	95.61	19.93	104.3	15.70		
U.C. Berkeley,	Male	137	90.28	22.06	103.68	15.5	13.95	23.52
1974	Female	158	94.67	21.97	102.68	17.5	7.92*	17.74
U.W., Seattle	Male	16	95.5	18.82	111.9	13.39	12.87	14.57
Pretest	Female	33	94.8	21.33	106.2	13.73	10.81	12.53
	Both	49	96.0	20.67	108.1	13.88		
U.W., Seattle	Male	16	96.6	20.95	112.7	12.70	16.06	14.18
Posttest	Female	33	94.5	22.29	101.2*	15.49	6.69**	2.52
Assertion training Ss Before	Female	19	107.7	22.37	104.8	22.55	—2.89	12.11
Assertion training Ss After	Female	19	82.0	19.49	87.9	20.09	5.36	7.87

* $p < .02$.
** $p < .002$.

tive indicating that total discomfort scores were typically lower than total response probability scores. A higher mean difference score was consistently found for men and this reached significance for the 1974 California sample, $t(293) = 2.50$, $p < .02$ and for the Washington posttest sample, $t(47) = 3.60$, $p < .002$| Thus, women were more likely to pair a high discomfort score with a high response probability score indicating that they would "rarely" or "never" do it and to pair a low discomfort score with a low probability score indicating that they would "always" or "usually" display a given behavior. The greater discrepancy for men may reflect their underestimation of or hesitation to report anxiety (Mischel, 1970) and/or their higher probability scores.

In contrast to the undergraduate samples, significantly higher discomfort scores were found for women entering assertion training programs, i.e., 107.7 before treatment. This score was significantly higher than both the combined mean discomfort score of 95.6 for the 1973 California sample, $t(330) = 2.55$, $p < .02$ and the combined mean discomfort score of 96 for the Washington pretest sample, $t(66) = 2.02$, $p < .05$.

TABLE 3

Distribution of the 1973 California Sample into Four Profiles

Discomfort	Response probability		Totals
	Low (105+)	High (104—)	
	Unassertive	Anxious-performer	
High (96+)	111 (35%)	35 (11%)	146 (46%)
	Doesn't care	Assertive	
Low (95—)	55 (18%)	112 (36%)	167 (54%)
Totals	166 (53%)	147 (47%)	

TABLE 4

Distribution of the Clinical Sample into Four Profiles
Before and After Training

Discomfort	Response probability				Totals	
	Low (105+)		High (104—)			
	Before	After	Before	After	Before	After
High (96+)	9 (47%)	2 (11%)	5 (26%)	3 (16%)	14 (74%)	5 (26%)
Low (95—)	0	1 (5%)	5 (26%)	13 (68%)	5 (26%)	14 (74%)
Totals	9 (47%)	3 (16%)	10 (53%)	16 (84%)		

The clinical population before training was similar to all undergraduate samples in mean response probability. The pretraining difference score for the clinical group was the only minus score to be recorded indicating that discomfort scores were consistently higher than probability scores for this group prior to training.

The Relationship between Self-Reported Discomfort and Response Probability

As mentioned, the particular mix between discomfort and response probability could have intervention implications in relation to selection of procedures, given that self-report is indicative of actual behavior. Dividing discomfort and response probability into high and low values generates four profiles (Table 3).

Respondents falling into cell one represent the typical person who has an assertion problem, i.e., high discomfort coupled with low assertion whereas those falling into cell two display assertive behavior in spite of high discomfort and might be labeled "anxious-performers." Cell three includes individuals who report low discomfort as well as low response probability. Such people may not be concerned about expressing themselves assertively or may see assertion as futile, i.e., "why bother." Cell four includes individuals who are appropriately assertive, i.e., they have low discomfort and a high response probability.

Thirty-six percent of the 1973 California sample fell into the assertive category whereas the remainder fell into one which could be indicative of a dysfunctional assertion repertoire. Many more people report that they avoid assertion when they experience discomfort (35 percent) than respond in spite of discomfort (11 percent).

Before training, 74 percent of the women in the clinical sample reported high anxiety compared to 46 percent of the undergraduate sample (Table 4). As expected, no subject fell into the category of "doesn't care" before training. If such an attitude were present, it is unlikely that assertion training would be sought. A higher percentage fell in the "anxious performer'" category (26 percent) compared to the normal population (11 percent), and a higher percentage appear in the "unassertive" profile (47 percent compared to 35 percent for the student sample). A surprisingly large percentage of women taking training programs appear in the "assertive" cell prior to training (26 percent). Adjustment of the cutting points for category placement might improve the separation between normal and clinical samples.

After training, the percentage of women in the assertive category was much higher (68 percent) than in the normal population (36 percent) and 74 percent reported lower than average discomfort scores after training compared to 54 percent of the undergraduate sample. Also, 84 percent of the clinical group reported a higher than average probability of engaging in the behaviors after training compared to 47 percent of the normal population.

Situations Respondents Would Like to Handle More Assertively

Over half of all respondents circled at least one item (Table 5). The mean number of items circled in the college samples ranged from 5.0 to 9.1. Women tended to circle more items than did men. However, sex

TABLE 5

Mean Number of Respondents Who Circled Items and Mean
Number of Items Circled for All Samples

Sample	Sex	N	Respondents who circled items Number	Percent	Mean number of items circled
U.C. Berkeley	Male	116	70	60%	8.8
1973	Female	197	147	75%	9.1
U.C. Berkeley	Male	137	83	61%	5.9
1974	Female	158	83	53%	7.96
U.W., Seattle	Male	16	9	56%	6.7
Pretest	Female	33	26	79%	6.8
U.W., Seattle	Male	16	9	56%	5.9
Posttest	Female	33	23	70%	7.1
Assertion training Ss Before	Female	19	17	89%	8.4
Assertion training Ss After	Female	19	12	63%	5.0

differences are unstable, with greater within-sex differences across samples
than between sex differences in any one sample. Even though the undergraduate women expressed lower anxiety and circled fewer items compared to the clinical group, for those women who did circle items, the
mean number was similar to the clinical sample. The number of items
circled is not necessarily related to need or readiness for assertion
training.

A Spearman rank correlation of .72 was found between the items circled by men and women in the 1974 California sample. Thus, it appears
that there is not a sizable sex difference in situations that subjects would
like to handle more assertively. Situations where the ranks were more
divergent included the following: more women circled items related to
admitting personal weakness, such as offering an apology or admitting
confusion; more men circled items having to do with making requests,
e.g., asking a favor, applying for a job, requesting a date.

The Washington pretest sample $(N = 49)$ was used to determine
whether there was a relationship between a respondent's profile and the
number of items circled (Table 6). Subjects falling into the "unassertive"
and "anxious-performer" categories, where higher anxiety is reported,

TABLE 6

Relationship Between Profile and Number of Items
Circled for the Washington Pretest Sample

	Unassertive	Anxious-performer	Doesn't care	Assertive
Percentage who circled items	79%	67%	62%	45%
Mean number of items circled	8.87	9.0	4.5	6.6

circled items more often than subjects in the other two categories. The
low number of items circled by respondents in the "doesn't care" category tends to support the interpretation of this profile.

Factor Analysis of Discomfort Scores

A factor analysis of the discomfort scores for the 1973 California
sample generated 11 factors accounting for 61 percent of the variance.
Each factor accounted for 7 to 3.9 percent. The emergence of a number
of relatively equally weighted factors is supportive of the situational
specificity of unassertive behavior (Alberti & Emmons, 1974; Wolpe,
1969). A factor analysis of the College Self-Expression Scale yielded nine
factors (Galassi & Galassi, Note 2).

An item was included in a factor if it had a loading greater than .40
on that factor as well as loadings of less than .40 on all other factors
(Landy & Gaupp, 1971). Using these criteria, 37 of the 40 items on the
Inventory were included in one of the 11 factors (Table 7).

Validity

An increment of validity is provided by a comparison of the clinical
and undergraduate samples. The mean discomfort score for the 19 women
before training was significantly higher than the mean discomfort scores
for the Washington and 1973 California samples (Table 2). Also, many
more individuals in the clinical population fell into the categories of
"unassertive" and "anxious-performer" compared to respondents in the
normal population. The clinical group decreased significantly in both
discomfort and response probability scores following training whereas

TABLE 7

Factors Within the Assertion Inventory, Their Variance and
Items Loading on Each Factor

Factor	Items	Variance (in percent)
1. Initiating interactions	(9),[a] 15, 17, 18	7
2. Confronting others	26, 32, 35, 36, 38, 39	7
3. Giving negative feedback	(7), 8, 27, 28, (29)	6.7
4. Responding to criticism	5, (12), 14, 21, 24	6.7
5. Turning down requests	1, (3), 6, 11	6.4
6. Handling service situations	4, 23, 25	5.8
7. Resisting pressure to alter one's consciousness	31, 34	4.6
8. Engaging in "happy talk"	30, 37	4.1
9. Complimenting others	2, 16	4
10. Admitting personal deficiencies	10, 19	3.9
11. Handling a bothersome situation	13, 40	3.9

[a] Item numbers in parentheses are situations that do not appear to fit with others falling in a given factor.

no change occurred during a five-week interval in the reliability sample. The mean postdiscomfort score for the clinical sample was 82 and for the reliability sample 95.2, $t(66) = 2.27$, $p < .05$. The postresponse probability scores were even more divergent, 87.9 for the clinical group and 105 for the reliability sample, $t(66) = 3.67$, $p < .002$.

In addition to differentiating between a clinical group and a normal population the Inventory also reflected significant differences within the clinical group itself before and after training. There was a significant reduction in both mean discomfort (107.7 compared to 82.0, $t(36) = 3.67$, $p < .002$) and mean response probability scores (104.8 compared to 87.9, $t(36) = 2.39$, $p < .05$.

In a study assessing the effectiveness of a program designed to increase initiations of social interactions (Gambrill, Note 3), a greater decrease in Inventory discomfort scores was found in the main experimental group (—22.50) as compared to an attention-placebo (—4.67) or waiting list control group (—4.75). Blind observers rated audiotaped role played interactions collected before and after training from the 15 women. A significant correlation was found between changes in observer ratings of discomfort and changes in Inventory scores (Spearman rank correlation = .465, $p < .05$). Additional data are needed regarding the relationship between Inventory scores and independently assessed performance on criterion tasks.

Clinical Implications

A respondent's total anxiety score appears to be a more predictable indicator of potential clinical candidacy than the total response probability score. Yet the probability score is helpful in determining the profile of an individual.

The treatment implications for the "unassertive" person would likely be different than for the "anxious-performer." In the latter case, interfering coverants may cue arousal which may disrupt an otherwise adequate behavioral repertoire. Increased relaxation and coverant control might be more useful in treatment than concentrating on the specific verbal and nonverbal components of assertions. In contrast, for the "unassertive" person, greater emphasis on developing appropriate responses may be necessary to correct behavior deficits.

CONCLUSION

The Assertion Inventory appears to be useful clinically as well as in the investigation of between group differences. It can be used for assessment purposes to scan for areas in which a client may have a dysfunctional assertion repertoire as well as employed as one instrument in determining degree of change following intervention.

REFERENCE NOTES

1. JENSEN, R. E. Personal communication, June, 1974.
2. GALASSI, J. P. & GALASSI, M. D. *A Factor Analysis of a Measure of Assertiveness.* Unpublished manuscript, West Virginia University, June, 1973.
3. GAMBRILL, E. D. *A Behavioral Program for Increasing Social Interaction.* Paper presented at the annual meeting of the Association for Advancement of Behavior Therapy, Miami, December, 1973.

REFERENCES

ALBERTI, R. E. & EMMONS, M. L. *Your Perfect Right* (2nd ed.). San Luis Obispo: Impact, 1974.
BATES, H. & ZIMMERMAN, S. F. Toward the development of a screening scale for assertive training. *Psychological Reports,* 1971, 28, 99-107.
GALASSI, J. P., DELO, J. S., GALASSI, M. D., & BASTIEN, S. The College Self-Expression Scale: A measure of assertiveness. *Behavior Therapy,* 1974, 5, 164-171.
HERSEN, M., EISLER, R. M., & MILLER, R. Development of assertive responses: Clinical, measurement, and research considerations. *Behav. Res. & Ther.,* 1973, 11, 505-522.

370 ANNUAL REVIEW OF BEHAVIOR THERAPY

LANDY, F. J. & GAUPP, L. A. A factor analysis of the Fear Survey Schedule—III. *Behav. Res. & Ther.*, 1971, 9, 89-93.

LAWRENCE, P. S. The assessment and modification of assertive behavior. (Doctoral dissertation, Arizona State University, 1970.) *Diss. Abs. Int.*, 1970, 31, 396B-397B. (University Microfilm No. 70-11, 888.)

McFALL, R. M. & LILLESAND, D. B. Behavior rehearsal with modeling and coaching in assertion training. *J. Abnorm. Psychol.*, 1971, 77, 313-323.

MISCHEL, W. Sex-typing and socialization. In P. Mussen (Ed.), *Manual of Child Psychology* (Vol. II). New York: Wiley, 1970.

RATHUS, S. A. A 30-item schedule for assessing assertive behavior. *Behav. Ther.*, 1973, 4, 398-406.

WOLPE, J. *The Practice of Behavior Therapy.* New York: Pergamon Press, 1969.

WOLPE, J. & LAZARUS, A. A. *Behavior Therapy Techniques: A Guide to the Treatment of Neurosis.* New York: Pergamon Press, 1966.

Section V

ADDICTIVE BEHAVIORS: OBESITY, CIGARETTE SMOKING, ALCOHOLISM, AND DRUG ADDICTION

Commentary

The remarkable growth of literature on the theory and practice of behavior therapy has not left the field of addictive behaviors untouched. On the contrary, it has spawned the fourth new journal referred to in the present volume. In their editorial, Miller and Hersen (1975) describe *Addictive Behaviors* as an interdisciplinary journal "encompassing alcoholism, drug addiction, smoking, and obesity" (p. 3), and devoted to the following emphases: 1) well-designed experimentation using objective assessment methods; 2) research of established relevance to broader clinical issues; 3) study of the interrelationships among the four classes of addictive behaviors; and 4) consideration of the diverse disciplinary conceptions of the nature of addictive behaviors. Although it is not explicitly identified as a behavioral journal, the editorial criteria listed above are more than consistent with a broad behavioral approach to research and therapy. Moreover, the contents of the first few issues, distinctively behavioral in nature, confirm this impression.

Obesity

In last year's volume (Franks & Wilson, 1975, pp. 649-662), we concluded that the clinical efficacy of behavior therapy for obesity remained unproven, as neither long-term success nor weight loss of clinically meaningful proportions had been reliably demonstrated. Unfortunately,

371

the developments of the past year have done nothing to alter this preliminary appraisal of the field.

Comparative Outcome Studies. Hall, Hall, Hanson, and Borden (1974)
evaluated four different conditions in the treatment of overweight university and community people: a) combined self-management, a multifaceted behavioral program of self-control procedures similar to that
used by Wollersheim (1970) and several other investigators; b) simple
self-management, a procedure in which subjects monitored and recorded
their daily number of bites of food, and were instructed to successively
decrease number of bites to achieve a weight loss of 1-2 lbs. per week.
A loss of more than 2 lbs. per week for two successive weeks required
an increase in daily bites to adjust to the target weight loss; c) nonspecific treatment, in which subjects practiced relaxation and developed
hierarchies of stressful situations with the rationale that tension increases
eating. Subjects were told to limit their caloric intake and were given
relaxation homework assignments to practice relaxation, but discussion
of situations directly related to eating was avoided; and d) no-treatment
control. All treatments were conducted on a group basis, although group
participation and interaction were encouraged only in the combined
self-management treatment condition.

Results showed that the two self-management groups produced significantly superior percent of body weight loss than the control groups at
posttreatment and at a three-month follow-up. There was no consistent
difference between the university and community samples.

The implications of these data for the clinical efficacy of behavioral
treatment are particularly negative for the following reasons: 1) The
attrition rates during treatment for the combined and the simple self-
management groups were 16 percent and 20 percent respectively. Since
drop-outs are usually failures, they artifactually inflate treatment success
rates (cf. Franks & Wilson, 1975); 2) There was no difference between
the two self-management programs, despite the fact that the combined
group had more extensive therapist contact, greater group participation,
and considerably more extensive behavioral treatment.

Moreover, the failure to independently assess the credibility of the
nonspecific control condition and its success in mobilizing comparable
subject expectancies of therapeutic improvement (see Commentary, Section II) makes it impossible to attribute the short-term superiority of
the self-management groups to behavioral techniques per se. The most
parsimonious interpretation of Hall et al.'s results is, as the authors
themselves note, in terms of the demand characteristics of the experi-

mental situation. When these were removed at follow-up, inter-group differences disappeared and weight increased.

An evaluation of strategies designed to facilitate maintenance of treatment-produced weight loss was conducted by Hall, Hall, Borden, and Hanson (1975). Following completion of a "typical" 12-week behavioral self-management program (e.g., Wollersheim, 1970), subjects were assigned to one of three maintenance groups: a) a booster condition, in which subjects met every two weeks with the therapist in what was essentially a continuation of the treatment program; b) a self-monitoring condition, in which subjects continued to monitor weight and food and mailed these data to the therapist every two weeks; and c) a no-contact condition. A three-month follow-up assessed the effects of the maintenance strategies.

Eight of the 51 subjects who began therapy terminated prematurely. An additional three subjects in each of the booster and self-monitoring maintenance groups dropped out during follow-up. Weight reduction index analyses showed that the self-monitoring group differed significantly from the no-contact group. The booster group did not differ from either of the other groups. There were no differences between the booster and self-monitoring groups' monitoring performance. Of the 21 subjects who completed both treatment and maintenance, 29 percent lost between 20-40 percent of their initial overweight; 10 percent between 40-60 percent of initial overweight; and 24 percent over 60 percent of initial overweight. The apparent superiority of the self-monitoring over the booster group is puzzling. Hall et al.'s speculation that this was due to half of the booster subjects being switched to a different therapist during follow-up is unconvincing since the self-monitoring subjects similarly lost contact with their original therapist. Despite the attrition rates, this study—one of the first to explicitly investigate maintenance strategies—provides some hope that effective maintenance strategies may produce more long-lasting weight reduction than has hitherto been demonstrated in the behavioral literature.

Horan, Baker, Hoffman, and Shute (1975) found that the use of positive coverants resulted in greater weight loss than negative coverants. During the eight-week treatment program, 75 percent of subjects using positive coverants lost a minimum of 1 lb. per week, compared to only 35 percent of subjects who used negative coverants. Whether high probability eating or noneating behaviors were made contingent on coverants had no effect on weight loss. Treatment carried out on a group basis was more effective than individual intervention. However, this latter finding might simply reflect the superiority of eight weekly group meetings with the therapist as opposed to three longer individual sessions. Horan et al. confounded this difference in number of treatment sessions with the group versus individual factor to equate overall therapist time and caseload.

One of the problems with this study, as with many others in the behavioral literature, is the absence of any meaningful follow-up. Horan et al. attempt to justify the omission of a follow-up on the grounds that previous findings had indicated that subjects' actual use of coverants followed by a high probability behavior declines sharply over the course of an eight-week treatment period. Thus they suggest that "coverant control ought to be considered as a highly reactive, albeit short-range treatment, component of a comprehensive program . . ." (p. 71). But this is a non sequitur. Where is the evidence indicating that coverant control should be used at all? The weight loss achieved in this study is quite unremarkable, and has been consistently matched by several other methods, including the simple strategy of having subjects self-monitor daily caloric intake. Why then use a more complicated technique that subjects apparently begin to abandon even before treatment is over? In short, complicated and often well-controlled comparisons between different behavioral techniques are of limited usefulness unless long-term follow-ups are conducted.

In other studies, Bellack, Schwartz, and Rosensky (1974) found no difference in short-term weight loss between groups in a self-control program that either met weekly with the experimenter or maintained contact only by mail. Both were superior to a no-contact control group. And, not surprisingly, Balch and Ross (1974) showed that a group receiving a broad behavioral program was superior to a group that did not complete the program and a no-treatment control group. Without an adequate follow-up, studies of this latter sort are of little value today.

Bellack (1975) reviewed the behavioral treatment literature on obesity and concluded that "the most effective approach was a combination of antecedent stimulus control procedures supplemented by any of a variety of contingency techniques" (p. 73). In his discussion of covert conditioning procedures, Bellack suggests that they would be most useful as part of a broader treatment battery, reasoning that is very questionable as noted above in connection with the Horan et al. (1975) study. Specifically with respect to covert sensitization, the contention that evaluations "have not been based on optimal evaluation utilization of the technique" is contradicted by more recent evidence. Diament and Wilson (1975) replicated Foreyt and Hagen's (1973) convincing negative findings (discussed in Franks & Wilson, 1974, pp. 169-170) in an investigation of the effects of covert sensitization in an analogue eating situation. Using a counterdemand methodology they failed to find differences between covert sensitization, an attention-placebo condition, and no treatment controls on objective measures of food intake. However, both treatment groups reported significantly greater treatment-produced negative self-report responses to the taste and odor of the target food than the no-treatment control group. Importantly, subjects reported consistently clear imagery, high affective arousal to the aversive scenes, and regular rehearsal of the procedure in homework assignments. And while it is unreasonable to expect differential weight loss over a short treatment period, the absence of any suppression of target food consumption is damaging to the conditioning conceptualization of covert sensitization.

Furthermore, Diament and Wilson point out that uncontrolled clinical reports of the efficacy of covert sensitization (Cautela, 1972) can be explained by factors other than the hypothesized conditioning process. Cautela (1972) emphasizes that the administration of covert sensitization entails instructing the client "to write down everything he eats including the time and place and exact amount. He is also asked to indicate the amount of calories and grams of carbohydrates for each food item" (p. 211). The demonstrable reactivity of self-monitoring could alone account for subsequent weight loss.

Elliot and Denney (1975) similarly demonstrated that covert sensitization was no more effective than an attention-placebo control condition in producing weight loss. The addition of false physiological feedback to the covert sensitization procedure, indicating to the subjects that they were experiencing nausea, failed to influence weight loss. This study differed from Foreyt and Hagen (1973) and Diament and Wilson (1975) in that the covert sensitization group reported significantly decreased ratings of the desirability of the food items included in the treatment as compared to the attention-placebo group. However, the pattern of results on objective behavioral measures was identical. The impressive consistency among these various investigations strongly suggests that covert sensitization is ineffective as a treatment for obesity.

Tondo, Lane, and Gill (1975) reported that systematic implementation and withdrawal of a covert response cost procedure produced corresponding decreases and increases in target food consumption in two subjects. However, as the authors themselves point out, the results can be parsimoniously explained in terms of the uncontrolled demand characteristics or subject expectancies created by the single-subject design.

Virtually all self-control procedures have been administered as a group package in a premature standardization of behavioral treatment that has been appropriately criticized (Mahoney, 1975, 1976). Bellack makes an important point in noting that clients, offered a "smorgasbord" of different techniques, might often select less effective alternatives. He suggests that a restricted list of highly effective techniques should be identified and provided clients to maximize their efforts. Indeed, McReynolds and Paulsen (1976) found that a treatment focusing specifically on stimulus control procedures produced greater weight loss at a three-month follow-up than the "typical" omnibus self-control program. In another context, that of people's adherence to medical regimens they have been placed on, Marston (1970) suggested that single, focal recommendations are better followed than multiple, complicated prescriptions. This may account for the finding that self-monitoring a daily caloric intake alone can result in as much weight loss, at least in the short-term, as more complex, multiple methods (Green, 1976; Romanczyk, Tracey, Wilson, & Thorpe, 1973).

The inability to develop adequate predictor variables in the behavioral treatment of obesity has been a frequently stressed problem. Balch and Ross (1975) presented preliminary evidence that locus of control scores might be a useful predictor of completion and success in a self-control weight reduction program. Bellack (1975) argues against the usual procedure of conducting post hoc correlations between pretreatment variables and successful or unsuccessful outcome, and suggests that "a better strategy would be to determine the characteristics necessary for utilization of specific procedures and then to examine the procedures with people high and low on the characteristic" (p. 81). In this connection, subjects who showed a relatively high base rate of self-reinforcement on a pretreatment experimental task subsequently lost more weight in a self-control program than subjects who had demonstrated a low base rate of self-reinforcement.

In concluding his review of behavior therapy for weight reduction, Bellack states that "the absolute changes achieved in most controlled studies misrepresent the clinical utility of the procedures" (p. 81). He implies that more protracted treatment with individual functional analyses of individuals' problems will be more effective. Although this is an intuitively plausible (not to mention pleasing!) position, it remains speculation, and underscores the pressing need for behavioral researchers to carry out the appropriate investigations.

Methodological Considerations. Although the conspicuous lack of well-controlled, long-term outcome studies is the glaring weakness in the behavioral approach to obesity, it has not been for want of repeated exhortations and necessary methodological prescriptions. Jeffrey (1975) has presented a useful comprehensive analysis of treatment evaluation issues in research on the addictive behaviors considered here. Among the many pertinent issues discussed by Jeffrey are the relative pros and cons of between- and within-subject experimental designs; the necessity of providing detailed statistics and analyses of all treatment drop outs (see Franks & Wilson, 1975, Sections VI, VII, & IX); the importance of therapist and patient variables, hitherto largely ignored in the behavioral literature (see Wilson & Evans, Section X this volume); and the desirability of including multiple measures of treatment outcome. Thus Jeffrey, for example, rightly points out that Stuart's (1967) unprecedented (and unreplicated) success in producing substantial weight loss is plausibly attributed to factors such as client self-selection, motivation, and therapeutic expectancies. With respect to the value of multiple measurement, Stunkard (1976) has reported instances of long-standing clinical lore that some obese patients become depressed and disturbed as they lose weight. This has not been found in behavioral treatment programs where systematic evaluation was undertaken (e.g., Wollersheim, 1970). Nonetheless the issue is far from fully resolved, and thorough clinical assessment of change would contribute meaningfully to the refinement of behavior therapy for obesity.

Jeffrey also stresses the importance of reporting standardized improvement criteria. The use of the weight reduction index (Feinstein, 1959) that is equal to the percent of excess weight loss × relative initial obesity is advocated. A formula for assessing the efficiency of treatment is similarly presented, viz., the mean treatment time per patient divided by the mean weight reduction index. While there is no denying the value of efficiency, it seems a rather distant goal compared to the more critical need to develop any clinically effective methods of weight control.

Theoretical Issues. The typical obese eating style is said to be characterized by rapidity, large bites, brief meal duration, and hypersensitivity to external cues (cf. Schachter, 1971; Stuart & Davis, 1972). The now traditional clinical "stimulus control" and "behavioral management" techniques designed to have obese clients eat more slowly, take smaller bites, lengthen the duration of meals, and restrict or narrow controlling environmental stimuli are obviously consistent with these assumptions about the obese eating style. However, Mahoney (1975, 1976) has recently maintained that the premises underlying these behavioral treatment strategies have been neither systematically examined nor demonstrated.

Mahoney (1975) reported a series of experiments that failed to support the assumption that obese individuals take few bites, less time, and eat more rapidly. In one field study conducted in a restaurant, obese subjects actually took more bites than nonobese subjects (Gaul, Craighead, & Mahoney, 1975). More consistent with behavioral assumptions was Gaul et al.'s finding that obese subjects chewed their food fewer times per bite, and spent less overall time masticating than nonobese subjects. In contrast to the trait-like implications of a generalized distinction between *the* obese and *the* nonobese eating style, Mahoney suggests that these results point to eating style being a "Malleable and situation specific behavior pattern" (p. 52).

These studies are not without some problems, and Mahoney is careful to distinguish between "non-existent and non-supportive data." They do, however, rather forcefully call attention to the absence of empirical support for at least some of the premises on which behavioral methods are based. It is also recognized, of course, that these behavioral methods could be effective for reasons other than those from which they originally derived.

With respect to obese persons being unusually vulnerable to external food-related stimuli, Wooley and Wooley (1975) have contested the externality notion of obesity as elaborated by Schachter (1971). Brown and Williams (1975) showed that obese did not differ from nonobese subjects in terms of their responsiveness to internal cues regulating fluid intake. These data are inconsistent with the view that the obese are generally less responsive to internal cues than their normal weight counterparts. And in a critical analysis of Schachter's externality theory, Milich (1975) discusses the limitations placed on the generalizability of the findings of Schachter and his colleagues by the less than representative nature of the subjects (relatively young, higher socioeconomic level) used in their studies.

Even more importantly, Herman and Polivy (1975) showed that individual differences in eating behavior based on the difference between obese and nonobese subjects, as in Schachter's experiments, could be shown in two groups of normal weight subjects. One group consisted of "restrained" eaters who were constantly dieting and concerned with weight gain. The other comprised "unrestrained" eaters who did not share this concern about the consequences of eating. According to Nisbett's (1972) biological set-point theory of obesity, the former relatively deprived, biologically obese persons are nonobese because of strong social and cultural pressure. Behaviorally, they would be expected to act like obese persons. This is precisely what Herman and Polivy found, replicating the distinction between obese and nonobese eating behavior in the context of a test of the psychosomatic hypothesis of obesity (cf. Schachter, Goldman, & Gordon, 1968). Unrestrained subjects ate significantly less when anxious, while restrained eaters ate more, albeit not significantly more. In addition, the relative hyperemotionality of obese subjects, as demonstrated in previous studies, was paralleled by the relative hyperemotionality of the restrained eaters. Herman and Polivy conclude that these results are inconsistent with Schachter's view that the obese are that way because they are stimulus bound. Rather, they provide support for Nisbett's (1972) theory that the externality that has been shown to characterize the obese is an intervening variable that mediates the effect of the real cause of obesity—biological demand.

Finally, Stunkard (1975) has proposed a revised theory of satiety as a conditioned reflex. Stimulation of the receptor mechanisms in the mouth and the filling of the stomach are hypothesized to act as conditioned stimuli (CS) for terminating eating. The unconditioned stimuli (UCS) could be the signals transmitted through the blood stream to satiety control centers in the brain following food absorption by the gastrointestinal tract. This is a version of the glucostatic theory of food regulation (cf. Stunkard, 1976). The problem with this formulation from a conditioning point of view is that the process of absorption clearly takes time, which means that there would be sizeable delays (anything from 20 minutes to 2 hours) between the CS and UCS. Stunkard (1975), however, proposes that the work of Garcia and his colleagues on biologically appropriate conditioning (cf. Garcia, McGowan, & Green, 1972) removes this objection to a conditioning interpretation of satiety. A critical finding of this research on the conditioning of taste aversions and preferences has been that learning readily occurs despite long delays between CS and UCS— delays long enough perhaps to mediate the process described by Stunkard.

Childhood Obesity. In last year's volume we commented on the surprising dearth of studies on the behavioral treatment of obesity in children, despite the apparent appropriateness of such treatment interventions. Within the past year Aragona, Cassady, and Drabman (1975) reported the treatment of overweight children through parental training and contingency contracting. They compared a response-cost plus reinforcement condition to response-cost alone and a no-treatment control group with overweight girls (ages 5-11 years). The parents in both treatment groups charted their children's caloric intake, kept a daily diary of food intake, and implemented exercise programs. The response-cost involved parents contracting to deposit a certain sum of money with the therapist that they could reclaim in 12 weekly installments as follows: 25 percent weekly for attending sessions; 25 percent weekly for completing weight charts; and 50 percent weekly if their child lost a predetermined amount of weight. The response-cost plus reinforcement group additionally were given copies of *Living with Children* (Patterson & Gullion, 1971), and instructed to reward their children for behavior consistent with the weight control program. Parents were also instructed in the use of stimulus control methods and other behavior management methods.

The two treatment groups showed significantly superior weight loss than the control group at posttreatment. The response-cost plus reinforcement group was still significantly superior to the control group at an eight-week follow-up. A 31-week follow-up, however, indicated no differences among the three groups. As an initial study in this important area these results encourage the further use of behavior principles not only in the treatment of overweight children, but also as an effective form of preventative medicine.

Jordan and Levitz (1975) similarly discussed the possibilities inherent in the application of behavior modification in the treatment of childhood obesity. They cite unpublished data from Rivinus, Drummond, and Combrick-Graham on the treatment of 10 children (ages 7-13 years). The treatment program was based on the type of self-control program typically used with adults. Parents attended sessions with their children, treatment staff had dinner with the children to model appropriate eating behavior, and rewards were made contingent on weight loss. Of the nine children who completed the 10-week program, all lost weight (mean = 6.2 lbs.). The same children had gained an average of 3.5 lbs in the 10 weeks immediately preceding therapy. Perhaps the most important finding was that children's weight loss paralleled that of the parent, strongly indicating the inclusion of parents in future programs.

Cigarette Smoking

Outcome Studies. In summarizing behavioral treatment programs aimed at eliminating or decreasing cigarette smoking, O'Leary and Wilson (1975) concluded that the results had been "uniformly unimpressive" (p. 342). Although a wide variety of techniques had been utilized in often well-designed studies, few treatment-specific effects had been demonstrated. Moreover, placebo treatments appeared to be as effective as explicit behavioral methods (cf. Bernstein, 1969). For example, in an evaluation of eight different behavioral studies, McFall and Hamner (1971) showed that if drop-outs during the course of therapy were included, total abstinence rates "ranged between 7 percent and 40 percent with a mean of 26 percent at the end of treatment, and ranged between 9 percent and 17 percent with a mean of 13 percent at follow-up" (p. 81). McFall and Hammen suggested that "nonspecific" factors such as motivated subjects, structure, and self-monitoring that were common to all studies probably accounted for the similarity in outcome. Indeed, they demonstrated that a "nontreatment" program based on these three "nonspecific" elements produced results that paralleled those obtained in more formal treatment studies.

A promising exception to this otherwise discouraging empirical trend was the research of Lichtenstein and his colleagues on the rapid-smoking method. In two impressively consistent studies (Schmahl, Lichtenstein, & Harris, 1972—reprinted in Franks & Wilson, 1973; Lichtenstein, Harris, Birchler, Wahl, & Schmahl, 1973—reprinted in Franks & Wilson, 1974), substantial and statistically significant reductions in smoking rates were shown at a six-month follow-up. Maintenance of treatment-produced results over this period of time is significant since Hunt and Matarazzo's (1973) review of the treatment literature showed that most reversions to pretreatment smoking occurred by the third month following treatment.

Two recent studies bear on the clinical efficacy of the rapid smoking method. Lando (1975a) compared three modification procedures in the treatment of smokers closely resembling Lichtenstein et al.'s subjects in demographic characteristics. The three groups were as follows: a) rapid smoking, in which subjects were "instructed to smoke each cigarette for a 3-minute period, taking a puff every 6 seconds." There were three such 3-minute trials, separated by two 8-minute breaks, in each of the six treatment sessions. Subjects were warned against "natural" smoking in the natural environment, and provided with portable timers with which to self-administer rapid-smoking trials between sessions; b) excessive smoking, in which subjects were told that the best way to break the habit was to engage in more of it. They were asked to smoke a daily minimum of at least twice their normal number. In each of the six treatment sessions they were instructed to smoke continuously at their own pace for a 25-minute period; and c) a control group, in which subjects were given the same instructions as in the rapid smoking treatment with the single exception that they were required to puff every 30 seconds. All subjects were treated in groups ranging from 5-10 over a one-week period. Subjects were asked to record all cigarettes smoked in booklets that were provided.

Follow-ups one and two weeks after treatment showed that the rapid smoking and excessive smoking treatment groups did not differ, although considered as a single unit, they were smoking significantly less than the control group. No significant differences were obtained at either the one- or two-month follow-ups. Similarly, there were no significant differences among the three groups in terms of total abstinence rates at any posttreatment evaluation. A 12-month follow-up, based on the estimates of 28 of the 45 subjects who had received treatment, showed no inter-group differences. The mean percent reduction in smoking, considering all subjects and counting subjects not contacted as zero reducers, was 23.11 percent.

These negative results are markedly different from the findings of Lichtenstein and his colleagues, a discrepancy that Lando attributes to "methodological weaknesses and/or complications of the earlier studies" (p. 354). Unfortunately, Lando fails to elaborate on what these faults are or how they explain the apparently contradictory findings. For example, he contends that the 100 percent posttreatment abstinence rate of Lichtenstein et al.'s (1973) control group calls into question the role of aversive conditioning per se. But this objection is confused and confusing. What has to be accounted for is the difference between the rapid smoking *procedure* and the control condition *at follow-up* in Lichtenstein et al. (1973) study, a difference not obtained by Lando. The question of what *process* best explains the difference Lichtenstein et al. found is another issue. Certainly it is the case that Lichtenstein and his colleagues maximized certain "nonspecific" social variables whereas Lando attempted to minimize their role. But the most that can be said about this, as Lichtenstein et al. pointed out, is that "nonspecific" variables were not sufficient even if they are necessary (Harris & Lichtenstein, 1971) in producing significant superiority at follow-up. "It appears that some other process, be it a conditioned response or a particular cognitive state, is needed to maintain cessation" (p. 97). Whatever this other process is, it apparently distinguished Lichtenstein et al.'s rapid smoking procedure from that employed by Lando.

Two major procedural differences between the two studies are briefly mentioned by Lando. Unlike Lando, Lichtenstein et al. treated subjects individually, the consequences of which can only be guessed at. Perhaps more importantly, Lando used a fixed number of sessions and standardized aversion trials. Although it is difficult to make precise comparisons between studies, it would seem as if Lichtenstein et al.'s aversion procedure, in which trials continued until subjects could not tolerate another inhalation and trials were continued until subjects could not tolerate another cigarette, was more likely to ensure a strong aversive reaction. It is possible that Lando's failure to replicate the results of previous studies is a product of a procedural departure that produced inadequate or insufficient aversion during treatment itself. A measure of support for this interpretation is provided by the questionnaire data that show that subjects in the rapid smoking and the excessive smoking groups rated treatment as significantly more unpleasant than did the control group. However, there were no differences between the rapid smoking and excessive smoking groups. Contrary to Lando's statement that this is what "might be expected," it could be argued that the rapid smoking group would rate treatment as far more unpleasant than the excessive smoking group. The latter, after all, smoked normally and at their own pace, albeit continuously for 25 minutes. In previous studies, subjects undergoing rapid smoking treatment reported extremely adverse reactions, including nausea, dizziness, and choking. (Indeed, evidence to be discussed below indicates that rapid smoking may be physically hazardous aside from causing profound discomfort.) It may be that Lando's questionnaire measures were insufficiently sensitive to discriminate between the rated reactions of the two treatment groups. A more plausible interpretation, however is that the rapid smoking procedure failed to induce the intensity of aversion that may be necessary if the procedure is to be effective.

Sutherland, Amit, Golden, and Roseberger (1975) compared five procedures in the treatment of smokers: In group 1 (relaxation), subjects were trained in progressive relaxation and instructed how to substitute it as an incompatible response for the smoking habit; group 2 (satiation) subjects smoked two cigarettes, inhaling deeply every four seconds. A 15-minute break separated the two trials that were administered during six sessions held twice a week. Subjects were instructed to treat any cigarettes they might smoke in the natural environment in this fashion; group 3 was a combined relaxation/satiation condition extending for 12 sessions over six weeks. Subjects in groups 1 and 2 maintained contact with the experimenter and handed in records of smoking activity during the additional three weeks group 3 subjects were in treatment; group 4 (motivated self-monitoring) subjects recorded daily cigarette smoking rates and telephoned the experimenter each week to report these frequencies; group 5 (non-motivated self-monitoring) subjects, who had expressed no desire to stop smoking, were asked to record daily smoking rates without any contact with the experimenter. Records were collected at posttreatment. Although Sutherland et al. make no mention of rapid smoking per se or Lichtenstein's clinical research, their satiation procedure bears obvious similarity in purpose and procedure to the rapid smoking method.

The results at posttreatment indicated that groups 1-3 had reduced their smoking in comparison to groups 4 and 5 which showed no change. The combined relaxation/satiation treatment appeared to be most effective, particularly at the three-month follow-up. However, it is clear from the graphs presented by Sutherland et al. that even this combined group showed a steadily increasing relapse rate across the three-month follow-up. The absence of any differences between groups 4 and 5 contrasts with Lipinski et al.'s (1975) data (see commentary, Section III).

In addition to appraising the clinical efficacy of rapid smoking as a treatment for cigarette smoking, therapists and researchers alike will have to consider the degree to which the method is physically dangerous. Lichtenstein (1975) has reported data on the effect of rapid smoking on heart rate and carboxyhemoglobin, showing that both increase during treatment sessions. However, he suggests that the technique involves no undue risk provided adequate screening to ensure healthy subjects without cardiac problems and with their physicians' permission. A less optimistic note is sounded by Horan, Hackett, Nicholas, Linberg, Stone, and Lukaski (1976) who recorded EKGs before and during the use of rapid smoking with six healthy subjects. Not only did they find greater increases in heart rate than those reported by Lichtenstein (1975), but also two of the six subjects developed EKG abnormalities. Further research is necessary to resolve the question of how risky rapid smoking really is. In the meantime it is clear that extreme caution should be exercised in its application to potential subjects or clients. Needless to say, anyone undergoing this procedure should be carefully acquainted with the available evidence—sketchy as it is—suggesting possible hazards.

As in the case with obesity, so too does covert sensitization appear to be relatively ineffective in the modification of smoking behavior. Sipich, Russell, and Tobias (1974) found that covert sensitization was not superior to an attention-placebo treatment, although both produced significantly greater reductions in smoking than monitoring and no contact control conditions. Of interest is the fact that the covert sensitization and placebo groups maintained a smoking rate at a six-month follow-up that was significantly less than pretreatment measures.

Frederiksen, Epstein, and Kosevsky (1975) investigated the reliability and reactivity of self-monitoring of cigarette smoking as a behavior change procedure. In their first experiment, they compared three forms of self-monitoring: a) continuous recording, in which subjects recorded the time they started smoking each cigarette; b) daily recording, in which subjects nightly recorded total number of cigarettes smoked; and c) weekly recording, in which subjects were contacted by telephone and asked to report the average number of cigarettes smoked per day during the preceding week. Continuous recording proved to be the most reliable, and was rated by subjects as being significantly more demanding.

In experiment 2, the effects of three self-monitoring methods on smoking behavior were evaluated. Over a five-week period continuous recording produced the greatest reduction in smoking, but also the highest subject attrition. Those subjects who dropped out cited as their reason the demanding nature of the recording procedure. The superiority of the continuous recording procedure was no longer in evidence at a six-month follow-up.

The most unusual form of treatment of smoking was reported by Suedfeld and Ikard (1974). Using a 2 × 2 factorial design, they compared the following treatment groups: a) sensory deprivation/stop smoking messages (SD/M); b) sensory deprivation/no messages (SD/NM); c) no sensory deprivation/stop smoking messages (NSD/M); and d) no sensory deprivation/no stop smoking messages (NSD/NM). Sensory deprivation involved a 24-hour period in a socially isolated, shielded, completely dark, and sound-proofed chamber. Subjects in the NSD conditions were instructed to remain at home, next to a telephone for a 24-hour period. The messages consisted of reminders of the health hazard cigarette smoking is, in addition to three desensitization-like scenes. In these scenes, subjects were asked to imagine emotional situations that had elicited the urge to smoke. Instead of smoking, subjects were asked to substitute relaxation as a response alternative. Subjects were categorized as either "psychologically addicted" or "preaddictive" smokers. The former were defined as smokers who "are distressed by the awareness of not smoking and who experience a craving for cigarettes whenever they are not in the act of smoking"; the latter as those who are "close to addiction and rely heavily upon smoking as an aid in coping with emotionally arousing experiences" (p. 889).

Sensory deprivation produced significantly greater decreases in smoking throughout 12 months following treatment. Neither the messages factor nor the "type" of subject variable had a significant effect. There were substantial decreases in smoking rate during the first two weeks after treatment for all but the NSD/NM group which remained virtually unchanged. The NSD/M group showed a 60 percent reduction, the SD groups over 80 percent reduction. A 12-month follow-up indicated that the SD groups were, on average, smoking about 48 percent less than at pretreatment, the comparable figure for the NSD groups being only 16 percent. In explaining the role of sensory deprivation, Suedfeld and Ikard suggest that whereas it is very stressful for subjects to abstain from smoking for 24 hours in the normal environment, the unavailability of cigarettes during sensory deprivation is relatively easily tolerable. They attribute this difference, at least in part, to the absence of familiar smoking cues in the deprived environment. Afterwards, the confidence derived from having abstained may serve to bolster resistance when normal smoking cues are once again encountered. They also implicate the cognitive dissonance that would be aroused by relapse after successfully completing and talking about such a remarkable experience. Interestingly, no subject in the SD groups reported any severe discomfort or distress as a result of sensory deprivation.

A Note on Measurement. One of the problems with outcome research on the modification of cigarette smoking has been the lack of an objective measure of smoking behavior. As a result, the dependent measure in these studies has been some sort of self-report of smoking frequencies. Perhaps the best of these involves providing subjects with especially prepared booklets in which they are asked to record systematically all cigarettes smoked. Various procedures have been followed, such as asking subjects to record each cigarette at the time of smoking, to record daily totals, or even weekly estimates. As Frederiksen et al. (1975) have shown, these procedures differ in reliability, even though the lowest reliability index they obtained was no less than 85 percent accuracy. In an improvement on simply collecting subjects' self-reports of smoking, some investigators have included collaborative reports of subjects' behavior from observers in the natural environment (e.g., Schmahl et al., 1972). However, it is not always possible to rule out collusion, unwitting bias, or the error inevitably introduced by the observers' restricted opportunities to witness so ubiquitous a response as smoking.

Against this background we note with interest the reports on the use of measures of carbon monoxide concentration as an objective check on subjects' self-reports (cf. Kopel & Rosen, 1975; Lando, 1975b). A pilot study by Lando (1975b), for example, indicated that breath samples analyzed for carbon monoxide reliably discriminated between subjects who reported abstinence versus those who reported that they continued to smoke. Some of the problems with this technique are the expensive apparatus required and remaining doubts about how robust and finely discriminating it can be. Nonetheless, any progress in this connection will improve outcome research on smoking.

Alcoholism

Outcome Studies. The evidence is now compelling that the drinking of alcoholics is regulated, at least in part, by its reinforcing consequences. Carefully controlled laboratory research has shown that chronic alcoholics were able to control their alcohol consumption provided that moderate drinking was differentially reinforced (Cohen, Liebson, Faillace, & Allen, 1971—reprinted in Franks & Wilson, 1973). And in an extension of this learning-based approach to the large-scale treatment of hospitalized alcoholics, Hunt and Azrin (1973—reprinted in Franks & Wilson, 1974) developed a community-reinforcement therapy program that they demonstrated to be significantly more effective than a control program based on traditional treatment principles.

Miller's article that is reprinted in this Section illustrates the successful use of contingent reinforcement procedures with the most deteriorated of alcoholic populations beyond the controlled and controlling confines of the laboratory setting. Although only the short-term effects of this behavioral intervention procedure are reported, Miller's report is particularly noteworthy in at least two important respects. In the first place, treatment was effective with individuals who are more usually incarcerated rather than treated, and even if they receive treatment their personal, social, and environmental resources are so depleted that they are unlikely to benefit from traditional therapy programs. In the second place, this behavioral approach is eminently practical, such that it could, as Miller points out, be incorporated into existing community rehabilitation programs with minimally increased costs. Although some reorganization would be called for, perhaps the greatest obstacle to the more extensive implementation of this sort of behavioral approach lies in the progressively outmoded treatment philosophy that dominates alcoholism treatment agencies. This issue is discussed below.

Vogler, Compton, and Weisbach (1975) compared treatment groups in an evaluation of the efficacy of a broad-spectrum behavioral approach with chronic hospitalized alcoholics. Group 1 received the following combination of treatment techniques: videotaped self-confrontation of

drunken behavior, blood alcohol discrimination training, electrical aversion conditioning for excessive consumption within the laboratory, alcohol
education, behavioral counseling, and "alternative training." Group 2
received only the latter three techniques. "Behavioral counseling" consisted of a remarkably diverse range of procedures, including the identification and reinforcement of behavior incompatible with drinking,
contingency contracting, "instruction in problem-solving techniques,
role-playing and assertion training often coupled with the use of videotaped feedback, relaxation training, communication skills development,
and role modeling" (p. 237). In addition, all subjects received elements
of the standard hospital treatment program that included large group
therapy meetings, art therapy, and Alcoholics Anonymous (AA) meetings.
The median lengths of treatment were 45 days and 22.5 days for Groups
1 and 2 respectively. Booster sessions were administered to both groups
on a weekly basis during the first month after treatment and then
monthly for the next 11 months. Booster sessions involved an electrical
avoidance conditioning procedure depending on the blood alcohol levels
(BALs) of the subjects. (It is unclear what happened to group 2 subjects). An attempt was made to obtain monthly follow-up evaluations by
an assessor who was unaware of the treatment conditions subjects had
received.

Of the 59 subjects originally selected for treatment, 42 completed the
programs. Seven subjects in group 1 and five in group 2 who attended
more than three sessions dropped out of treatment. A 12-month follow-up
showed that 62 percent of all subjects who completed treatment were
either abstinent or controlled drinkers. (The latter was defined as less
than 50 ozs. of absolute alcohol per month and no more than one
drinking episode in which the BAL exceeded 80 mg/percent.) The two
groups did not differ significantly on the basis of these measures of
treatment outcome. However, group 1 was significantly superior in
terms of decreased alcohol intake. Both groups showed favorable changes
in altering their drinking companions and environment. A useful analysis
of the relation between subject characteristics and treatment outcome
indicated that pretreatment alcohol consumption was the best predictor
variable, correlating from .43 to .52 with outcome measures.

These results are not unambiguous. The overall results indicated that
the two treatments produced similar outcomes across several different
dependent measures, the only significant difference being the amount
of alcohol consumed. Vogler et al. interpret this difference to suggest
the "advantage of the videotaped, discrimination, and aversion pro-

cedures over traditional educational and counseling methods" (p. 242). This is a most extraordinary statement considering that the "traditional counseling methods" as described above encompassed most of the currently practiced behavioral techniques ranging from contingency contracting to assertion training and problem-solving instruction! Moreover, the techniques "isolated" by Vogler et al. would not appear on a prior basis to be critical treatment ingredients. The evidence from numerous studies now shows that electrical aversion conditioning of the sort Vogler et al. employed is ineffective (see below). The little evidence there is on videotaped self-confrontation—the status of which as a "behavioral technique" is seriously open to question—similarly suggests that it too has little independent effect on reducing alcohol consumption in alcoholics (Schaeffer, Sobell, & Mills, 1971). In fact, given the multitude of treatment influences that subjects in both groups 1 and 2 received, it would be extremely difficult to interpret meaningfully even more convincing inter-group differences than those obtained. The data do little to establish the utility of behavioral techniques either singly or in combination in the treatment of alcoholism.

Hedberg and Campbell (1974) compared four behavioral treatments of alcoholism: a) behavioral family counseling, modeled after Patterson (1971) and including assertion training and contingency contracting; b) systematic desensitization; c) covert sensitization; and d) an electrical aversion conditioning procedure based on Feldman and MacCulloch's (1971) anticipatory avoidance training method. A six-month follow-up indicated that behavioral counseling was the most effective, with 74 percent of the patients in this condition reporting that they had attained their treatment goal (either abstinence or controlled drinking). Systematic desensitization resulted in 67 percent of patients reaching their goal. There was a 40 percent goal attainment rate in the covert sensitization group, while only one of the subjects who completed the electrical conditioning treatment reported improvement at follow-up. It is clinically noteworthy that of the 12 alcoholics assigned to this treatment condition, only four remained in the program beyond the third session.

Piorkowski and Mann (1975) compared systematic desensitization, covert sensitization, and a traditional insight-oriented procedure in the treatment of outpatient alcoholics. Of the 40 subjects that entered the program, only 14 completed the 14 sessions of treatment. A six-month follow-up indicated that only three of these 14 subjects were abstinent. The authors comment on the difficulties encountered in using these techniques with alcoholics.

The near total ineffectiveness of Hedberg and Campbell's (1974) electrical aversion conditioning treatment is consistent with other well-controlled clinical research (cf. Miller, Hersen, Eisler, & Hemphill, 1973 —reprinted in Franks & Wilson, 1975; Wilson, in press). In a series of three inpatient studies by Wilson, Leaf, and Nathan (1975), a total of eight chronic alcoholics were variously allowed unrestricted alcohol intake to establish an objective measure of realistic drinking patterns. Following an initial 3-day baseline phase, subjects were administered 30 trials of either escape conditioning or a control treatment procedure (in which the electric shock preceded the alcohol stimulus) on each of the succeeding 3 or 4 days (depending on the experiment). No alcohol was available to subjects during treatment days. The shock parameters and procedure were modeled after Blake (1965) and Vogler, Lunde, Johnson, & Martin (1970). After a second, posttreatment ad lib drinking period, the treatment procedures were reversed in a cross-over design for a second 3 or 4 day treatment phase. A third baseline drinking period was programmed to evaluate the impact of the treatment reversal phase. Neither method had any discernible effects on alcohol consumption except in the case of 1 subject who displayed a substantial reduction in drinking following the escape conditioning treatment. This subject, however, returned to excessive alcohol abuse within a week of being released from the laboratory and was rehospitalized. Subjects' attitudinal responses as measured by the Semantic Differential indicated similar transient placebo effects for both treatments.

It is possible, of course, that the number of aversion conditioning trials administered was insufficient to produce conditioned aversions strong enough to suppress drinking. However, the data show no evidence of any trend that might suggest that an increased number of trials would reduce subsequent drinking. Miller et al. (1973) obtained similarly negative results despite the administration of 500 aversion conditioning trials. Furthermore, the shock intensities employed were comparable to those reportedly used to produce the apparent clinical successes in the treatment literature.

There are important clinical limitations on the extent to which aversion treatment procedures can be employed. All eight subjects reported the procedures to be distinctly unpleasant. The dramatic attrition rate in Hedberg and Campbell's (1974) electrical aversion conditioning treatment underscores this point, as does the fact that using similar frequencies and intensities of shock to the Wilson et al. (1975) study, two subjects voluntarily withdrew from a treatment program described by Wilson and Tracey (1976).

Vogler, Ferstl, Kraemer, and Brengelmann (1975) compared the following treatment groups: (a) a contingent shock group; (b) a random shock group; (c) a "mixed" treatment group including contingent and random shock; and (d) a control group which received standard hospital treatment such as detoxification, improved diet, exercise, and group psychotherapy. A 12-month follow-up of 32 of the 40 subjects (80 percent) in the first three experimental groups indicated abstinence figures of 21 percent, 38 percent, and 40 percent respectively. An estimated 7 percent of the control group subjects were abstinent, legal problems preventing the collection of full follow-up data. Statistical comparisons showed no significant differences among the 3 groups which received shock athough, when combined, they were significantly superior to the control group. The failure of the contingent shock group to produce greater suppression of drinking than the random shock group (indeed, the latter was more effective) suggests that whatever the therapeutic value of these treatments, it cannot be attributed to aversion conditioning.

Unlike classical conditioning procedures that attempt to suppress alcohol intake by reducing the positively valenced properties of alcohol per se, the operant conditioning approach emphasizes the response-contingent consequences of which drinking is a function. Using a modified ABAB single-subject reversal design, Wilson et al. (1975) consecutively introduced and withdrew a punishment procedure (contingent shock delivered immediately after consumption of each one oz. drink) while alcoholics' drinking was continuously recorded. Alcohol consumption ceased almost completely while the punishment contingency was in effect, but recovered to pretreatment baseline levels when punishment was withdrawn. Thereafter a self-administered punishment contingency was introduced, in which subjects were encouraged but not required to self-administer shock contingent on drinking. Furthermore, a variable-ratio schedule was implemented to determine the effect on alcohol consumption of fading out the self-administered contingency. The data indicated that the self-administered method appeared to be almost as effective as experimenter-administered shock. Furthermore, self-administered punishment was gradually withdrawn without alcohol consumption returning to pretreatment baseline levels.

This decreased alcohol consumption could not be unequivocally attributed to the punishment contingency per se as it was confounded with several other potential behavior change influences. Accordingly,

Wilson et al. conducted another experiment in which they compared a contingent shock to a yoked, noncontingent shock procedure. The data clearly showed that the contingent relationship between the shock and alcohol consumption was both necessary and sufficient for most effectively decreasing drinking. The efficacy of these aversive control procedures contrasts sharply with the ineffectiveness of the escape conditioning technique with the same population of alcoholics in the same laboratory. It is unlikely that this difference in results is accounted for by the distinction between classical and operant conditioning techniques. Although the electrical escape conditioning treatment is commonly regarded as a respondent conditioning procedure, it does involve a contingent relationship between response and aversive stimulus. The difference is probably due to the fact that in the punishment procedure, shock was contingent on alcohol consumption during periods when alcohol was available. The electrical escape conditioning failed to endow alcohol with aversive qualities such that consumption was suppressed during the posttreatment assessment periods when subjects could drink with impunity. The efficacy of aversive control was maximal only when the punishment contingencies remained in effect.

In a single-subject design with an alcoholic patient, Ciminero, Doleys, and Davidson (1975) similarly demonstrated that the application of an avoidance conditioning contingency using a strong electric shock effectively reduced alcohol consumption.

Newton and Stein (1974) compared implosion therapy to brief psychotherapy in the treatment of hospitalized alcoholics who also continued to receive a general milieu therapy program. Neither treatment added significantly to the impact of the milieu program alone. No behavioral measure was included in the study, the rationale for which is questionable. The standardized use of implosion therapy was predicated on the tension-reduction theory of alcoholism. However, this theory has been criticized, and it is clear that the determinants of excessive alcohol consumption are far more complex and diverse (see below).

Conceptual Issues. In sharp contrast to the widely held conception of alcoholism as a disease, mediated by an involuntary and irreversible physiological addiction to alcohol, the social learning approach focuses on the relevant learning influences involved in the development and maintenance of drinking behavior. Research within the framework of social learning theory has increasingly emphasized the behavioral assessment and evaluation of drinking problems instead of simply generating and applying new therapeutic techniques as was the custom in the early stage of behavior therapy and alcoholism.

In their creative and informative research program, Marlatt and his colleagues have studied the determinants of alcohol consumption among heavy social drinkers. Recently Higgins and Marlatt (1975) have shown that the anticipation of interpersonal evaluation by women significantly increased alcohol intake in male college students. Whether subjects were internally or externally oriented in terms of the locus of control scale made no difference. The major dependent measure in this, as in the other studies conducted by Marlatt and his associates, was an unobtrusive, analogue measure of actual alcohol consumption. While these results are consistent with the familiar tension reduction explanation of drinking, a previous study by Higgins and Marlatt (1973) found that the physical threat of electric shock did not increase drinking behavior. Although the effectiveness of the tension manipulation in the Higgins and Marlatt (1973) study was questionable, the more probable explanation of the discrepant results is that alcohol reduces specific and possibly different fears in different individuals. As Higgins and Marlatt (1975) state, "drinking will increase only in those situations which the drinker defines as stressful and in which he believes that alcohol will reduce this stress or tension" (p. 649). In addition to personal and situational specificity, the emphasis on the individual's *cognitive appraisal* of the total situation should be noted.

The importance of mediating cognitive factors in the determination of drinking has been largely ignored in some behavioral formulations of alcohol consumption. However, as Carpenter and Armenti (1971) suggested, the circumstances under which alcohol is consumed might be more influential than the pharmacological effects of alcohol per se—at least at low to moderate BALs. And a major factor determining the nature of the circumstances under which drinking occurs is the person's cognitive set. A dramatic illustration of this process is described by Lang, Goeckner, Adesso, and Marlatt (1975). Male social drinkers who had been led to believe that they had consumed alcohol displayed significantly more aggression than subjects who had been led to believe that they had consumed mere tonic water. This finding obtained irrespective of the actual contents of the beverage subjects consumed. Particularly striking is the fact that this example of the overriding importance of subjects' expectancies about alcohol was demonstrated with subjects with BALs of 100 mg/percent—the lower limit of what many authorities define as legally constituting a state of intoxication.

Lang et al. showed the decisive effects of subjects' expectancies about alcohol on subjective and overt behavioral measures. In a replication and extension of this finding, Wilson and Lawson (in press) found that college students showed significantly increased penile tumescence to explicit visual erotic stimuli if they believed that they had consumed alcohol. The actual administration of alcohol (mean BAL = 40 mg/percent) failed to exert a significant effect. These data indicate that autonomic arousal can be significantly modified by cognitions concerning alcohol.

Anger is another antecedent variable that has been shown to influence alcohol consumption (Marlatt, Kosturn, & Lang, 1975). Both male and female social drinkers drank more after being frustrated and angered by a confederate subject. However, if subjects were given the opportunity to retaliate against the person who provoked them prior to drinking they drank significantly less than provoked subjects who were not provided the chance to retaliate.

The role of observational learning in the acquisition of drinking patterns is a major tenet of a social learning analysis of alcoholism (Bandura, 1969; O'Leary & Wilson, 1975). Documenting this influential process, Caudill and Marlatt (1975) showed that male social drinkers showed a significant modeling effect when systematically exposed to a confederate subject who modeled either heavy or light alcohol consumption in the unobtrusive analogue drinking task.

The relative importance of external cues in regulating fluid intake in alcoholics was investigated by Brown and Williams (1975). In results paralleling those of Schachter and his associates with obese subjects, Brown and Williams found that alcoholics were significantly less responsive to internal cues than nonalcoholics. The consumption of different blends of tea on an unobtrusive drinking task (similar to that used by Marlatt) by groups of alcoholics and nonalcoholics was measured under conditions of fluid deprivation and preloading. Whereas the consumption of the nonalcoholics was reduced in the preloading condition, the intake of the alcoholics was similar in both conditions. Moreover, alcoholics consumed significantly more of the tea they rated as most preferred (external cue) and less of their nonpreferred drink than nonalcoholics.

Controlled Drinking as a Treatment Goal. A fundamental implication of the disease theory of alcoholism is an inflexible insistence on total abstinence as the goal of all treatment programs. A social learning analysis, however, suggests that in certain instances controlled drinking may not only be possible but also the preferred treatment goal (O'Leary

& Wilson, 1975). Several of the outcome studies reviewed above reported that some alcoholic patients were drinking in a controlled fashion at follow-up evaluations (e.g., Hedberg & Campbell, 1974; Vogler et al., 1975; Wilson et al., 1975). In a recent review of broad-spectrum behavior therapy with alcoholism, Hamburg (1975) concluded that there is "strong evidence that even alcoholics with long histories of loss of control are capable of drinking moderately, given the appropriate manipulation of environmental contingencies" (p. 78). In a comprehensive evaluative review of the status of controlled social drinking, Lloyd and Salzberg (1975) similarly concluded that the assumption that abstinence is the necessary treatment goal of alcoholics is "not empirically or experimentally substantiated" (p. 815). A significant ramification of this theoretical position is that abuse of alcohol might be prevented by training people (particularly teenagers and young adults) to drink in a moderate/controlled rather than an excessive/uncontrolled fashion. This emphasis on prevention of drinking problems need not necessarily encourage drinking. Rather, as Marlatt (1975) points out, it entails teaching people *how* to drink, *when and if* they choose to drink.

However, the theoretical reasoning and empirical support of the social learning view notwithstanding, this approach has met with such fierce opposition that Sobell and Sobell (1976) have argued that "traditional views, regardless of how lacking in empirical support, present a significant threat to scientific inquiry and treatment innovation in this area" (p. 211). The Sobells' concern may well be warranted if the outcry that greeted the publication of a recent Rand Corporation Report (Armor, Polich, & Stambul, 1976) is any index. The findings of this report were that only 10 percent of alcoholics who had been treated at NIAAA (National Institute for Alcoholism and Alcohol Abuse) treatment centers were abstinent at 6- and 18-month follow-ups. The majority of the 70 percent of improved clients were either drinking moderately or engaging in alternating periods of drinking and abstinence. Armor et al. cautiously concluded that these data were "tentative but nonetheless suggestive that a sizeable group of treated alcoholics can engage in either periodic or regular moderate drinking without relapse during a 1-year interval" (p. 120). Although freely admitting that they had not read it, press reports quoted certain authorities on alcoholism, including a member of the National Council on Alcoholism as excoriating the methodology of the report and denouncing its conclusions as misleading and dangerous to human life.

It is important to stress that the social learning approach is not synonymous with controlled drinking; it merely suggests that this is an alternative to abstinence, which would still be the treatment goal in other circumstances. This confusion was apparent when a boycott of the recent conference on Behavioral Approaches to Alcoholism and Drug Dependencies at the University of Washington, Seattle was threatened by a leading local expert on alcoholism. When the views of the speakers on this issue—cautionary and open-minded—were learned, and both sides of the issue were represented, the conference proceeded harmoniously and productively.

It is clear that the issue of controlled drinking will continue to be something of a hornet's nest in the immediate future.

Finally, in contrast to the rancour surrounding this issue, a constructive attempt by Burt (1975) to compare the behavioral with the AA approach might be noted. He points out several features of the latter that are consistent with behavioral principles, and might be fruitfully researched by behavior therapists to the advantage of both approaches (see also Bassin, 1975).

The Measurement of Treatment Outcome. Laboratory research has been significantly advanced by the development of objective measures of drinking behavior (cf. Briddell & Nathan, 1976). Attempts have been made to obtain objective indices of drinking behavior in the natural environment using portable breath tests (e.g., Sobell & Sobell, 1975a), but these are still of limited utility. As with cigarette smoking, the evaluation of treatment outcome studies is still primarily dependent upon clients' self-reports of drinking. Although these reports are frequently distrusted as having low reliability and validity, recent findings by Sobell and Sobell (1975b) paint a brighter picture.

Thirty-nine alcoholics in a voluntary outpatient setting were interviewed on two separate occasions about their social and drinking histories. The validity of self-reports was determined by checking official records of any hospitalizations or arrests. The self-reports proved to be highly reliable (91.98 percent) and valid (85.98 percent). If anything, the alcoholics were more likely to overestimate than underestimate hospitalizations and arrests. Sobell and Sobell suggest that this double interview technique can help predict whether there is reason to suspect a patient has given an invalid self-report. Although these results are encouraging, care should be exercised in generalizing the findings to different patient populations. Patients who were highly transient were excluded from this study, and those who were finally selected were treatment motivated.

Drug Addiction

The systematic application of behavioral principles to the modification of addictions to narcotic, stimulant, and hallucinogenic drugs has been surprisingly sparse. Moreover, the clinical studies in this area of drug addiction have been very rudimentary in nature. This is clearly evidenced by the fact that the relevant behavioral literature is limited largely to uncontrolled individual clinical case reports. In his evaluative review that is reprinted in this Section, Callner shows that 74 percent of published studies involved the presentation of individual case reports. Of equally great concern is the sole use of self-report data as the measure of outcome in 52 percent of the studies. And the absence of acceptable follow-up assessments—a weakness shared by the behavioral treatment of obesity and cigarette smoking—is particularly pronounced. Only six of the 22 studies summarized in Callner's Table 3 included a discussion of follow-up measures. Callner provides a sound, thorough analysis of the existing inadequacies and many excellent recommendations for future clinical research.

In the developmental history of behavior therapy, much of the initial treatment of antisocial disorders such as sexual deviations and alcoholism centered on the use of a variety of aversion conditioning procedures (cf. Rachman & Teasdale, 1969). Not surprisingly, the same has been true of behavior therapy for drug addictions. Increasingly, however, more multifaceted approaches that emphasize the development of alternative responses and focus on the wider environmental influences affecting an addict's behavior have emerged. Cautela and Rosenstiel (1975) have reviewed the use of covert conditioning techniques in the treatment of drug abuse. In addition to the use of aversive imagery in covert sensitization, Cautela and Rosenstiel summarize the rationale and application of a variety of covert conditioning methods, such as covert reinforcement and extinction. The authors conclude that a comprehensive treatment program is necessary to supplant the reinforcing effects of drug abuse with alternative, more constructive reinforcers. This includes focusing on educational, vocational, social, and recreational aspects of the client's life. Covert conditioning techniques, Cautela and Rosenstiel assert, can be used for this purpose.

Eriksson, Gotestam, Melin, and Ost (1975) described the use of a token economy treatment of drug addiction. A combination of opiate and amphetamine addicts participated in a typical reversal ABABC design in which contingent reinforcers were sequentially introduced and

then withdrawn. The final phase (C) consisted of noncontingent reinforcement. Targeted activity levels increased during reinforced phases
and decreased during reversal to baseline conditions. Since the patients
were free to leave the ward unaccompanied by staff members, illicit
drug abuse could and did occur. During the baseline phases of the study,
patients either refused to give urine samples or the samples were positive
for drugs on 27 percent of measurement occasions. The corresponding
figure during contingent reinforcement phases was 10 percent. Eriksson
et al. discuss the limitations of the inpatient token economy procedure.
They conclude that it is "difficult to improve the token economy as
such, further in the application to drug addicts" (p. 124).

SECTION V: ADDICTIVE BEHAVIORS: OBESITY,
CIGARETTE SMOKING, ALCOHOLISM, AND
DRUG ADDICTION

17

A BEHAVIORAL INTERVENTION PROGRAM FOR CHRONIC PUBLIC DRUNKENNESS OFFENDERS

Peter M. Miller

*Veterans Administration Center and the
Department of Psychiatry and Human Behavior,
University of Mississippi Medical Center, Jackson*

A reinforcement contingency management system for ten chronic public drunkenness offenders was evaluated for short-term effects. Chronic inebriates were provided with required goods and services through skid row community agencies contingent on their sobriety. Intoxication resulted in a five-day suspension of all goods and services. Excessive drinking behavior was assessed by direct observation of intoxication and by randomly administered breath alcohol analyses.

As a result of this intervention, subjects substantially decreased their number of public drunkenness arrests and their alcohol consumption, and increased their number of hours employed. No such changes were observed in a control

Reprinted from the *Archives of General Psychiatry,* July 1975, Vol. 32, 915-918. Copyright 1975, American Medical Association.

This investigation was supported in part by funds provided by the Division of Alcohol Abuse and Alcoholism, State of Mississippi Department of Mental Health.

G. G. Hoffman assisted in the preparation of this report.

group that received services on a noncontingent basis.
Longer-term research studies of one to two years rather than
a few months would be required before any widespread use
of this approach would be warranted.

The chronic public drunkenness offender constitutes a major social,
psychological, financial, and legal problem in society. Although incarceration or monetary fines, or both, have had little positive influence on
the chronic inebriate, alternative rehabilitation programs are few. Unfortunately, this individual is unlikely to benefit from traditional alcoholism treatment services due to his unique and often deteriorated social-
psychological condition. Most typically, the skid row alcoholic lives in
the deteriorated areas of the city, has few stable environmental supports,
and is limited in social and vocational skills (1-3).

New legislative changes, however, are providing an impetus for a search
for viable rehabilitation strategies with this group. Partly due to financial pressures from the federal government (4), many state legislatures
are decriminalizing public drunkenness via the Uniform Alcoholism and
Intoxication Treatment Act. Under this legislation, a public inebriate
must be rehabilitated and not jailed. While halfway house rehabilitation
centers (5, 6) and disulfiram (Antabuse) programs (7) have been used
to cope with public drunkenness in some communities, many of these
programs rely on court-imposed threats of incarceration to sustain the
alcoholic's motivation and cooperation with the program. Under the new
law, such coercion would not be possible. Since the skid row alcoholic
often requires external incentives to motivate him (8), this restriction
seriously limits rehabilitation systems. An alternative method involves
the utilization of a positive motivational system in which incentives are
provided contingent on cooperation or sobriety, or both. Such an approach in which positive reinforcing events (e.g., access to enriched
ward environment and visits to girlfriend) are made contingent on
sobriety or moderate drinking has been demonstrated to reduce alcohol
consumption in alcoholics within controlled laboratory settings (9-12).

Most applications of contingency management in the natural environment (13-15) have focused on less deteriorated alcoholic populations who
still have families, steady employment, and nonalcoholic friends, through
which therapists can administer the program. We (16), however, significantly reduced the drinking behavior of a skid row alcoholic in his
natural environment by providing coupon booklets (exchangeable for
items such as food and clothing) contingent on blood/alcohol concentrations of .00.

In the present study, the short-term effects of a positive contingency management system (administered through skid row social agencies) on chronic public drunkenness offenders was evaluated.

METHODS
Subjects

Twenty chronic alcoholic men were selected from among a group of public drunkenness offenders interviewed in the city jail (Jackson, Miss.) during a period of four months in 1973 (17). These subjects were characterized by the following: 1) a minimum of eight public drunkenness arrests in the previous 12 months; 2) a minimum history of five years of abusive drinking; 3) sporadic work history; 4) residence in a rooming house, hotel, or mission within the central downtown area of the city; and 5) voluntary participation in the study. All subjects were unmarried with the majority having been divorced. No subject had held steady employment in the previous two months. All worked on temporary jobs on a day-to-day basis.

Ten of these subjects were randomly selected for the behavioral intervention program. The remaining ten served as a control group and received routine services from various helping agencies in the city. Mean age, education, length of problem drinking, and number of public drunkenness arrests for both groups are presented in the Table. Using t tests, no statistically significant differences were found between the groups on these variables.

All subjects had been released from jail at the beginning of the study and there were no court-imposed requirements to induce participation in the program. In the city of Jackson, public drunkenness offenders are merely retained in jail until the day following arrest with no court procedures or monetary fines involved.

Apparatus

Alveolar breath samples were collected via small, portable devices consisting of a thin glass tube connected to a balloon-like collection bag. Blowing into the tube fills the bag with a breath sample that is later analyzed via gas chromatography. Analyses of breath samples in this manner are very precise, with an average maximum deviation from actual blood samples of .003 percent (18). Such factors as amount and type of liquor consumed, time since initiation and termination of drinking, and body weight are related to the blood/alcohol concentration obtained.

Behavioral Intervention Group

The intervention program was administered through several service agencies in the community that regularly deal with skid row alcoholics. All agencies were within walking distance of the skid row area of the city.

In exchange for their sobriety, subjects were provided with goods and services that they required. Services were provided continually as long as subjects demonstrated attempts to control their drinking. Sobriety was assessed in two ways. First, direct observations of gross intoxication (i.e., odor of alcohol on breath, staggered gait, and slurred speech) were recorded by personnel of the community agencies and by employers. Second, blood/alcohol concentrations were accumulated by means of breath alcohol analyses on a random basis. This measure was included to provide an indication of alcohol consumption at times when the subject was not accessible to direct observation. These analyses were scheduled on a random basis within five-day intervals. Thus, once in every five-day period of time, the subject was administered a breath analysis. Each new five-day interval began on the day after the previous analysis. At the time when the analysis was scheduled, the subject was contacted through the community agencies, his employer, his living quarters, or his friends. He was instructed to visit one of the agencies or hospitals within the hour for his breath alcohol test. If he were unable to attend, personnel were sent to his whereabouts to administer the test in the natural environment. After the breath sample was accumulated, his blood/alcohol concentration was determined through gas chromatographic analysis at a local university hospital.

Subjects with blood/alcohol concentrations of 10 mg/100 ml of blood volume or less remained eligible for goods and services through the program. Provision of goods and services were immediately discontinued for a period of five days contingent on either 1) observation of gross intoxication by agency personnel or employers, or 2) a blood/alcohol concentration above 10 mg/100 ml of blood volume on any of the breath analyses. Existing services such as housing or employment were also terminated during this time. At the end of the five-day period, the subject was again eligible for goods and services.

Goods and services most desired by this group included housing, employment, medical care, clothing, meals, cigarettes, and counseling. Housing was arranged through an agreement with the Salvation Army.

Normally, this agency will only allow sober individuals to board for two days. Under a special agreement, any of the subjects could be housed or fed, or both, at this agency for the duration of the program. Housing or meals were terminated for five days contingent on evidence of alcohol consumption.

Employment was obtained primarily through Manpower Inc. (a local agency that provides various unskilled jobs on a day-to-day basis) and the Mississippi State Employment Service. An agreement was obtained from these organizations stating that they would place subjects in employment positions that seemed best suited to their needs. Types of jobs included general factory work, assembly line work, road maintenance, building maintenance, and sanitation work. Number of days employed was recorded for each participant. Arrangements were made with these agencies and the employer to terminate any subject for five days who was reported by the experimenter to have failed to remain sober. Subjects would be eligible for that same job at the end of five days.

If a subject were in need of medical assistance, arrangements were made with either the Veterans Administration Hospital or the University Hospital to treat him. Emergency or essential medical care was, of course, not terminated contingent on sobriety. However, nonessential care (such as certain types of dental treatment) could be postponed for the five-day period.

Clothing was obtained via the Salvation Army Store, Goodwill Industry Store, or donations to the program. Subjects eligible for veterans assistance could be provided with canteen booklets exchangeable for cigarettes, meals, or clothing at the Veterans Administration Hospital.

Subjects also received counseling sessions geared toward advising them on numerous practical problems in life, such as money management.

Data on number of public drunkenness arrests and number of hours worked per week were accumulated for two months prior to and two months subsequent to the initiation of the program. Half of the group received random breath alcohol analyses for two months prior to the program to compare these with the analyses obtained during the program.

Control Group

The control group consisted of ten subjects who received the traditional services of the skid row community agencies. Thus, the same goods and services were available to them as the intervention group except these reinforcers were provided on a noncontingent basis. Subjects received services whether they were intoxicated or sober. Mean number of arrests and mean number of days employed per week were recorded two months before and two months after the initiation of the program.

RESULTS

Means and standard deviations for public drunkenness arrests for both groups during the two months before and two months after initiation of the contingencies were calculated. Mean number of arrests for subjects in the behavioral intervention group decreased from 1.70 (SD = 1.15) for the two months before the program to 0.30 (SD = .48) for the two months in which the contingencies were in effect (difference = —1.40). The control group maintained approximately the same number of mean prearrests (M = 1.40; SD = 1.07) as compared with postarrests (M = 1.30; SD = 0.81) (difference = —0.10). Results of an analysis of variance, repeated measures design for these arrests indicated that significant differences were found within prearrests and postarrests ($F = 7.50$, $p < .025$) as a function of experimental conditions ($F = 5.62$; $p < .05$). To analyze these data more thoroughly, a Newman-Keuls test (19) was performed to test the differences between all possible pairs of means for the following conditions: behavioral intervention-pretest; behavioral intervention-posttest; control-pretest; and control-posttest. The results indicated that the groups were comparable on the number of arrests prior to intervention. Also, the mean number of arrests for the control group did not change significantly from pretest to posttest. The behavioral intervention group, however, significantly decreased its mean number of arrests from pretest to posttest ($p < .01$). This group also had significantly fewer arrests during the contingent reinforcement phase than the control group ($p < .01$).

These findings are also evident when differences in the actual number of subjects arrested are examined. While eight out of ten subjects in the behavioral intervention group had been arrested at least once for public drunkenness prior to the initiation of contingencies, only three were arrested during the program. Number of subjects arrested at least once in the control group increased slightly from eight to nine.

Means and standard deviations for number of hours employed per week were also calculated. In the behavioral group, mean number of hours worked per week increased from 3.2 to 12 hours (difference = 8.8 hours) after contingencies were initiated. Mean number of hours worked

Subject Variables

	Intervention, Mean	Control, Mean
Age, yr.	50	47.8
Education, yr.	9.6	8.1
Length of problem drinking	10.4	9.1
No. of public drunkenness arrests in past year	13.0	14.6

per week for the control group decreased slightly from 4.4 to 3.2 hours (difference $= -1.2$ hours). An analysis of variance, repeated measure design was used to calculate the significance of these differences. There was a significant difference within pretest and posttest measures ($F = 4.34$; $p < .05$) and a significant interaction with the experimental condition ($F = 7.50$; $p < .025$). Again, a Newman-Keuls test was performed to evaluate these differences more thoroughly. No significant differences were found between the groups on the measure prior to the initiation of the experimental conditions. The control group did not significantly change in mean number of hours employed per week from pretest to posttest. The behavioral intervention group's employment rate increased significantly as a function of the contingencies ($p < .01$). Also, during the contingency phase, the behavioral intervention group worked significantly more days than the control group ($p < .01$).

Finally, while all subjects in the behavioral intervention group received periodic breath alcohol tests during the contingency phase of the project, five were also administered these tests during the two months prior to initiation of contingent reinforcement. The mean pretest blood/alcohol concentration was 50 mg/100 ml of blood volume, and is the approximate level reached when about 118.3 ml of whiskey are consumed within an hour. The mean blood/alcohol concentration after the intervention was .002 percent, which indicates only a minimal trace of alcohol in the blood. These, of course, are only random probe measures, and drinking by these subjects during other periods of time cannot be ruled out. A t test indicated that during the intervention, blood/alcohol concentrations were significantly lower than prior to contingent reinforcement ($t = 6.95$; $p < .001$).

COMMENT

This study has demonstrated that a behavioral strategy based on principles of contingency management can have a substantial short-term influence on the number of public drunkenness arrests, number of hours employed, and drinking behavior of skid row alcoholics. While it appears that the contingencies placed on drinking behavior constituted the essential therapeutic variable, the role of two other factors cannot be discounted. Both of these factors relate to the fact that the behavioral intervention group was administered breath alcohol tests during the study while the control group was not. First, these administrations necessitated slightly more personal contact with the behavioral group that may have influenced the alterations in their behavior. Second, due to the nature of the contingencies, subjects in the behavioral group were provided with feedback as to their breath/alcohol levels after each analysis. Since performance feedback has been demonstrated to influence behavior patterns, its role in the present study cannot be discounted. It may be noted, however, that the five subjects in the behavioral group who received breath alcohol analyses with feedback during the two months prior to the initiation of contingencies did not significantly decrease their drinking or arrest rate, or both, during that time. Behavior changes occurred only after the contingency program was established. The precise interaction of these variables awaits additional investigation.

Success with some alcoholics may also require shaping successively lower blood/alcohol levels rather than expecting immediate large decreases in habitual alcohol consumption. This approach would necessitate coordination of existing community agencies (i.e., missions and halfway houses) so that the alcoholic is not able to obtain his needs irrespective of his drinking behavior. Present community service agencies are often put in a position of providing more services to alcoholics when they are intoxicated than when they are sober. Such a policy of service, however, is often countertherapeutic and may actually help to maintain the chronic inebriate's drinking pattern.

An advantage of this behavioral intervention system is that it can be implemented with minimal expenditures of time, effort, and money, and incorporated into existing community agencies. Wide-scale use of this procedure on the basis of this report would be premature. Replication of these results in a lower-term evaluative study (perhaps over a one- to two-year period of time) appears warranted.

REFERENCES

1. JACKSON, J. R. & CONNER, R. The skid row alcoholic. *Q.J. Alcohol,* 1953, 14, 468-486.
2. ALFORD, J. A. Medical and psychiatric aspects. In *The Court and the Chronic Inebriate.* Washington, D. C.: U.S. Government Printing Office, 1965, pp. 16-20.
3. BLUMBERG, L. U., SHIPLEY, T. E., & MOOR, J. O. The skid row man and the skid row status community. *Q.J. Stud. Alcohol,* 1971, 32, 909-941.
4. *Special Report:* Alcohol and Drug Problems Association of North America, Washington, D. C., 1974.
5. COFFLER, D. B. & HADLEY, R. G. The residential rehabilitation center as an alternative to jail for chronic drunkenness offenders. *Q.J. Stud. Alcohol,* 1973, 34, 1180-1186.
6. BAKER, T. B. Halfway houses for alcoholics: Shelters or shackles. *Int. J. Soc. Psychiat.,* 1973, 18, 201-211.
7. BOURNE, P. G., ALFORD, J. A., & BOROCOCK, J. Z. Treatment of skid row alcoholics with disulfiram. *Q.J. Stud. Alcohol,* 1966, 28, 42-48.
8. HEILBRUN, A. B. & NORBERT, N. Self-regulatory behavior in skid row alcoholics. *Q.J. Stud. Alcohol,* 1972, 33, 990-998.
9. COHEN, M., LIEBSON, I., & FAILLACE, L. The role of reinforcement contingencies in chronic alcoholism: An experimental analysis of one case. *Behav. Res. Ther.,* 9:375-379, 1971.
10. COHEN, M., LIEBSON, I., FAILLACE, L., ET AL. Alcoholism: Controlled drinking and incentives for abstinence. *Psychol. Rep.,* 1971, 28, 575-580.
11. BIGELOW, G., LIEBSON, I., & GRIFFITHS, R. Experimental analysis of alcoholic drinking. Read before the American Psychological Association, Montreal, 1973.
12. MILLER, P. M., HERSEN, M., & EISLER, R. Relative effectiveness of instructions, agreements, and reinforcement in behavioral contracts with alcoholics. *J. Abnorm. Psychol.,* 1974, 83, 548-553.
13. SULZER, E. S. Behavior modification in adult psychiatric patients. In L. Ullman and L. Krasner (Eds.), *Case Studies in Behavior Modification.* New York: Holt, Rinehart & Winston, Inc., 1965, pp. 196-199.
14. MILLER, P. M. The use of behavioral contracting in the treatment of alcoholism: A case study. *Behav. Ther.,* 1972, 3, 593-596.
15. HUNT, G. M. & AZRIN, N. H. The community reinforcement approach to alcoholism. *Behav. Res. & Ther.,* 1973, 11, 91-104.
16. MILLER, P. M., HERSEN, M., EISLER, R. M., ET AL. Contingent reinforcement of lowered blood/alcohol levels in an outpatient chronic alcoholic. *Behav. Res. & Ther.,* 1974, 12, 261-263.
17. MILLER, P. M. An analysis of chronic drunkenness offenders with implications for behavioral intervention. *Int. J. Addict.,* to be published.
18. HUNTINGTON, J. DWI arrests increase. In *Treasure State Health.* Helena: Montana Department of Health and Environmental Science, 1972.
19. WINER, E. J. *Statistical Principles in Experimental Design.* New York: McGraw-Hill Book Co., Inc., 1971, pp. 191-195.

SECTION V: ADDICTIVE BEHAVIORS: OBESITY,
CIGARETTE SMOKING, ALCOHOLISM, AND
DRUG ADDICTION

18

BEHAVIORAL TREATMENT
APPROACHES TO DRUG ABUSE:
A CRITICAL REVIEW OF
THE RESEARCH

Dale A. Callner

University of Utah

Treatment techniques derived from contemporary theories
of classical and operant learning represent the most recent
attempts to reduce chronic drug use. This review describes
the various behavioral treatment approaches that have been
applied to this problem and critically appraises the research
designed to evaluate the effectiveness of these approaches.
Each study is evaluated on several important design and
measurement variables necessary to ensure adequate control,
representativeness, reliability, and accuracy of inference. Several specific recommendations designed to improve future
research involving behavioral treatment approaches to drug
abuse are made.

Reprinted with permission from *Psychological Bulletin,* Vol. 82, No. 2, March, 1975,
143-164. Copyright 1975, American Psychological Association.

This review includes research completed before January 15, 1974. The author wishes
to thank S. Proctor, D. Hartmann, S. Ross, L. Clark, and N. Cantor for their editorial
comments during the preparation of this review.

In addition to the sizable body of literature devoted to the sociological and pharmacological aspects of drug abuse, there have been many investigations concerning the treatment of drug abusers. The most recent trend in the drug treatment literature has emerged from therapy approaches based upon both classical and operant learning principles, approaches generically referred to as behavior therapies. This review is designed to (a) describe and critically appraise behavior treatments of drug abuse, (b) identify common problems associated with the operation and measurement of these treatments, and (c) propose recommendations for the refinement of future treatment research.

The meaning of *drug abuse* could conceivably apply to a wide variety of chemical compounds consumed in excessive amounts. This review, however, is limited to studies involving the human use of legal and illegal drugs taken in excess amounts without a medical prescription. Common classes of such drugs include opiates (primarily heroin), barbiturates, amphetamines, cocaine, psychedelics, and toxic inhalants. Treatment approaches to other commonly used drugs—such as marijuana, alcohol, nicotine, and caffeine—are not considered in this review. While treatment approaches to caffeine and marijuana abuse are rare, the reader is referred to Bernstein (1969) and Marston and McFall (1971) for reviews of the behavioral approaches to nicotine abuse and to Franks (1958, 1963) and MacCulloch, Feldman, Orford, and MacCulloch (1966) for reviews of the behavioral approaches to alcohol abuse.

BEHAVIORAL THEORIES OF DRUG ABUSE

It is beyond the scope of this review to comprehensively evaluate the many theories and methods that have been introduced to explain and treat drug abuse (see Isbell, 1965, and Siegler & Osmond, 1968, for reviews of theories and treatment approaches to drug abuse). Historically, treatments of drug abuse developed from the philosophy that "enforced abstinence" (prolonged periods either in prisons or sanitariums) would allow the drug user to free himself from his addiction (Brecher et al., 1972). Later treatment approaches developed from psychodynamic concepts such as the "addictive personality," oral cravings, and disrupted psychosexual development (e.g., Fort, 1955; Glover, 1956; Hoffman, 1964; Rado, 1933; Wikler, 1952; Wikler & Rasor, 1953). Social psychological concepts such as social alienation, existential hopelessness, and the need for group acceptance (e.g., Chein, Gerard, Lee, & Rosenfeld, 1964;

Clausen, 1957; Yablonsky, 1967) gave rise to residential halfway house programs employing the "therapeutic community" as their major treatment approach (e.g., Fischmann, 1968; Jones, 1953, 1968; Laskowitz, Wilbur, & Zucker, 1968; Waldorf, 1971; Nash, Note 1). Finally, biochemical theories of drug abuse, suggesting that the structure and action of the drug's chemical organization upon the human nervous system is responsible for drug abuse, have initiated several chemical treatment and maintenance procedures, such as methadone (Dole & Nyswander, 1965, 1966, 1967) and narcotic antagonist drugs (e.g., Chappel, Senay, & Jaffe, 1971; Fink, Zahs, & Freedman, 1973).

With the exception of the recent advances in the biochemical basis of drug abuse, the literature describing nonbehavioral treatment approaches to drug abuse does not appear to be overwhelmingly promising. On the contrary, drug abusers are usually seen as poor candidates for traditional psychotherapy, and treatment attempts have seldom reported long-term success rates (e.g., Glasscote, 1971; Grafton, 1971; Nash, Waldorf, Foster, & Kyllingstad, Note 2).

Theories associated with both classical and operant conditioning represent the most recent attempts to explain and alter drug abuse. In general, conditioning theories suggest that chronic drug use is comprised of many behaviors that are acquired and maintained by a variety of learned internal and environmental stimuli. Although many behavioral theorists suggest that both classical and operant conditioning components occur in the acquisition and maintenance of excessive drug use, the following sections summarize the major principles of each form of conditioning as they have been applied to the explanation of drug abuse.

Classical Conditioning Components of Drug Abuse

Although having stated that both classical and operant processes play a role in the acquisition and maintenance of excessive drug use, Wikler (1965, 1971) suggested that classically conditioned responses are primarily responsible for long-term drug use and posttreatment relapse. The drug user, Wikler stated, initially seeks drugs to relieve tension, which is associated with various emotional states such as guilt, anxiety, anger, and depression. Because tension reduction is repeatedly reinforced by drug ingestion, drug use is maintained while physical dependence quickly develops. In Wikler's theory, initial drug use (prior to physical dependence) is thus explained by the operant principle of negative reinforcement. That is, drugs are originally used to reduce aversive emotional states.

After physical dependence develops, subsequent drug use is primarily aimed at alleviating the aversive symptoms associated with the withdrawal syndrome. With the development of physical dependency, Wikler (1965, 1971) stated that many environmental stimuli in the drug user's life become classically conditioned to the aversive aspects of the withdrawal syndrome. That is, drug use is maintained by repeated temporal contiguity between physical withdrawal symptoms (unconditioned stimulus) and various environmental stimuli (conditioned stimulus) such as peers, familiar neighborhoods, and music. When the drug-induced withdrawal reactions are repeatedly experienced in specific environmental surroundings, the surroundings themselves eventually begin to elicit withdrawal symptoms. Recurrence of withdrawal symptoms, even after detoxification, has also been suggested to occur as a result of internally elicited reactions to the conditioned environmental elements of the addict's life that have never been fully extinguished (Lynch, Fertiziger, Teitelbaum, Cullen, & Gantt, 1973). The effects of this classically conditioned withdrawal syndrome can only be relieved by drug ingestion, thus forcing continued drug use or relapse following detoxification. Wikler used the term *conditioned abstinence* to refer to this recurrence of withdrawal symptoms resulting from classically conditioned environmental stimuli.

In terms of treatment approaches to drug abuse, Wikler suggested that experimental extinction of both the conditioned abstinence syndrome as well as operantly reinforced drug-using behavior must occur. For example, in the case of opiate dependence, narcotic antagonist drugs could be used to block the usual effects produced by heroin or other opioids, both in the treatment setting as well as the addict's natural environment. Wikler (1973a, 1973b) maintained that because the persistence of the conditioned abstinence syndrome depends upon occasional reinforcement by actual withdrawal symptoms, opiate-seeking behavior is extinguished because injections of opiates are blocked by the narcotic antagonists. Although the use of narcotic antagonists to test Wikler's theories of drug abuse and treatment are still in the preliminary stage, these approaches suggest an extremely promising area for future research. As recommended by Krasnegor and Boudin (1973), future research directed toward a more comprehensive understanding of the conditioned abstinence syndrome will add considerably to our knowledge of chronic drug use, the relapse phenomenon, and possible treatment approaches.

Operant Conditioning Components of Drug Abuse

Explanations of drug abuse emphasizing operant conditioning principles have concentrated on several types of reinforcement contingencies in the acquisition and maintenance of drug use (Cahoon & Crosby, 1972; Crowley, 1972; Jaffe, 1970; Wikler, 1965, 1971, 1973a, 1973b). In general, these reinforcement contingencies can be summarized as the following: (a) positive reinforcement associated with the social aspects of drug use (e.g., acceptance by drug-using peer groups, music and language associated with drug use, excitement of hedonistic street life and manipulatory behavior, acting out toward the "establishment"); (b) positive reinforcement associated with the pharmacological properties of the drug (e.g., euphoria, anxiety reduction, "rushes," "flashes," relaxation); (c) negative reinforcement associated with aversive aspects of the environment (e.g., relieving boredom, reduction of aversive aspects of family life and living conditions); (d) negative reinforcement related to nondrug-induced aversive physical states (i.e., relief from chronic or acute pain due to injury or illness); and (e) negative reinforcement related to drug-induced aversive physical states (i.e., relief from physical discomfort of withdrawal symptoms).

Kraft (1968a, 1968b, 1969a, 1969b, 1970a, 1970b) has elaborated upon the operant principle of negative reinforcement by suggesting that social anxiety is the major factor associated with repeated drug use. That is, the drug user can eliminate the anxiety he feels in social situations and deal more appropriately with them by taking drugs. Kraft maintained that reduction of social anxiety will also result in a reduction or elimination of drug use. Treatment procedures are thus aimed at relieving the drug user's anxiety by desensitizing him to the presence of progressively larger numbers of people.

BEHAVIOR THERAPIES FOR DRUG ABUSE

From these notions of classical and operant learning theory have come several treatment approaches to drug abuse. Although the literature involving behavioral treatment approaches to drug abuse includes approximately 25 studies, the various approaches can be summarized in three general treatment categories: counterconditioning, contingent reinforcement, and combined behavioral techniques. These three general categories and the various specific treatment techniques within them are described below.

Counterconditioning

The majority of behavioral treatment approaches to drug abuse to date have been based upon the principle of counterconditioning. In general, counterconditioning involves a variety of techniques designed to condition either incompatible or aversive consequences with specific problem-related stimuli (Bandura, 1969). In the behavior therapy literature, noxious chemical, electrical, and covert stimuli have been used in the presence of problem-related stimuli (aversive counterconditioning), whereas relaxation has been most commonly used as an incompatible response paired with anxiety-provoking stimuli (systematic desensitization). In principle, both aversive counterconditioning and systematic desensitization represent two variations of the same concept. That is, both attempt to reduce the occurrence of specific problem-related stimuli by associating these stimuli with either a negative or incompatible response. Each of these counterconditioning techniques is described more fully below as it has been applied to the treatment of drug abuse.

Chemical aversion therapy (three studies). There have been many applications of aversive conditioning techniques to problem behaviors other than drug abuse (see reviews by Eysenck & Rachman, 1965; Franks, 1958, 1963; Rachman, 1961, 1965; Rachman & Teasdale, 1969). Chemical aversion therapy involves administering to the patient chemical compounds which eventually produce noxious effects such as nausea, vomiting, or temporary paralysis. Once the time for the noxious effects of the chemical to take effect is determined, the patient is instructed to engage in various aspects of his problem behavior, thereby pairing problem-related stimuli with the onset of the aversive experience.

Attempts to reduce drug abuse by chemical aversion techniques closely resemble much of the earlier work done with alcoholic patients (Voegtlin & Lemere, 1942; Wallerstein, 1957). In the treatment of drug abuse, Raymond (1964) and Liberman (1968) paired apomorphine with self-administrations of drugs to produce a conditioned nausea and vomiting response. In a large group study, Thomson and Rathod (1968) used the compound scoline to produce temporary paralysis timed to coincide with self-administrations of heroin. Although all three of these studies sought to reduce subsequent drug use, it was also hoped that the unpleasant responses produced by the chemicals would generalize to other related aspects of the drug user's life, such as thoughts of drug use or watching another person use drugs.

Electrical aversion therapy (four studies). The use of electric shock as the noxious stimulus paired with drug use has the advantage of greater stimulus control, versatility, and safety in comparison to chemically induced noxious stimulation. Electrical shock can be controlled so that it occurs directly after the onset of the behavior to which aversion is to be conditioned. Furthermore, portable shock units permit in vivo counterconditioning, thus enabling the procedure to deal with important environmental stimuli that may be difficult to reproduce in the hospital or clinic setting. Similar to chemical aversion, electrical aversion techniques attempt to link the noxious stimuli with many of the behavioral and subjective components associated with drug taking (e.g., subjective drug urges, preparing the paraphernalia, actual sensations produced by the drugs).

As with chemical aversion therapy, the application of electrical aversion techniques to the problem of drug abuse is similar to the procedures used in earlier studies with alcoholic patients (Blake, 1965; Hsu, 1965; MacCulloch et al., 1966; McGuire & Vallance, 1964). Wolpe (1965) was apparently the first to use electrical shock in an attempt to reduce drug use when he trained a single patient to use a portable shock unit, thus allowing him to deal with the various environmental and internal stimuli that naturally occur in conjunction with drug use. Although electrical shock is used in association with other behavioral techniques, Lesser (1967), O'Brien and Raynes (1972), and Spevack, Pihl, and Rowan (1973) have also used electrical shock as the principal therapeutic intervention in drug abuse. Two other studies (Boudin, 1972; O'Brien, Raynes, & Patch, 1972) have also employed electrical aversion, but not as their principal behavioral intervention. Although not yet tested in a controlled manner, an "electric needle" has been designed by Blachly (1971), which is comprised of an electrically charged syringe that delivers a shock to one or more patients when the plunger is pressed.

Covert sensitization (*three studies*). The counterconditioning technique of covert sensitization (also referred to as verbal aversion or aversive imagery therapy) uses imagined scenes as aversive events. Similarly, the behavior to which the aversion is to be conditioned is often represented in the form of an imaginal scene. This technique of establishing an aversive response to a particular stimulus by imaginally induced noxious scenes has been used in the treatment of many clinical problems such as smoking, obesity, and alcoholism (Cautela, 1966, 1967, 1973).

In the treatment of drug abuse, Anant (1968), Steinfeld (1970), and Steinfeld, Rice, Rautio, and Egan (Note 3) have used covert sensitization in an attempt to produce a covert conditioned avoidance response to many of the behaviors involved with drug seeking and use. In these studies, the patients were asked to imagine a series of scenes in which they first feel like taking a drug, travel to the place where they usually obtain it, prepare to inject it, actually inject it, feel sick, vomit, and then gradually feel better as they move progressively farther away from the place where they took the drug. These studies also used relaxation training techniques initially to enhance the patient's ability to vividly imagine the scenes presented. Covert sensitization has also been used in conjunction with several other behavior therapy techniques by O'Brien et al. (1972) and Wisocki (1973).

Covert sensitization requires no apparatus or drugs, and the patient can be trained so that he can use it in naturalistic settings. Although the validity of a patient's self-reported covert images can never really be known and should always be seriously questioned when drug abuse patients are used, covert sensitization appears to be a particularly applicable counterconditioning technique in training self-control to a variety of drug-related behaviors.

Systematic desensitization (six studies). Like aversion therapies, systematic desensitization involves the pairing of incompatible responses with stimuli that normally elicit anxiety. Rather than developing an aversive response, desensitization procedures involve the conditioning of relaxation responses with anxiety-provoking stimuli which might otherwise lead to drug use. To accomplish this, the patient is first relaxed by verbal training in muscle relaxation, by drugs, or by hypnosis. Situations that elicit anxiety are then rank ordered into a hierarchy depending on the amount of anxiety they elicit. Relaxation is then systematically paired with the various anxiety-eliciting stimuli on the hierarchy by asking the patient to imagine each situation while maintaining a high degree of relaxation.

The use of systematic desensitization for the treatment of many clinical problems is widespread (see reviews by Bandura, 1969; Paul, 1969; Wolpe, 1958; Yates, 1970). As the principal behavioral treatment approach to drug abuse, it has been studied most extensively by Kraft (1968a, 1969a, 1969b, 1970a, 1970b). As described above, Kraft suggested that social anxiety is the major factor associated with drug abuse and that treatment aimed at relieving a patient's anxiety in social situations will also eliminate his drug use. Subsequent procedures are thus aimed at (a) desensitizing the patient to being around progressively larger groups of people, and (b) gradually reducing the patients' dependency on the therapist by having him spend progressively greater periods of time away from the therapist. In each case, the patient actually lives through each step in the hierarchy rather than imagining them.

In a different fashion, Spevack et al. (1973) reported a case study in which several desensitization hierarchies were used to reduce the fears associated with an unpleasant LSD experience. Separate hierarchies were constructed to desensitize the patient to several activities thought to stimulate an aversive LSD "flashback" experience (i.e., rock music produced uncomfortable feelings similar to those experienced while the patient was in the drug state).

Contingent Reinforcement

The second general category of behavioral drug treatment approaches involves techniques designed to reinforce specified prosocial behavior contingent upon a prearranged program. The prearranged contingent reinforcement program outlines the specific behaviors that the patient must perform or reduce in order to obtain desired reinforcers. Contingent reinforcement programs have been applied on both an individual, outpatient basis as well as on a large-scale inpatient basis. When used individually, the technique of contingency contracting outlines a contractual agreement between the patient and the therapist involving the specific behaviors to be reduced or increased and reinforcing or aversive consequences. When there are problem behaviors and reinforcers common to several patients, such as those found within inpatient treatment programs, token economy techniques are often used whereby patients are reinforced for appropriate behaviors with tokens (poker chips or points) which can later be exchanged for desired reinforcers.

Contingency contracting (four studies). The use of contractual agreements to specify appropriate and inappropriate behaviors and corresponding consequences has been used with several populations, such as students (Homme, 1969), delinquents (Stuart, 1971), and married couples (Knox, 1972). In the drug treatment literature, Boudin (1972), Boudin and Valentine (Note 4), Sammons (Note 5), and Ross and Jones (Note 6) have used contingency contracting to connect specific drug-related behaviors to reinforcing and aversive consequences. Although the target of decreasing drug use was included in all of these studies, other targets— such as reducing hospital dress violations, increasing spontaneous group therapy verbalizations, decreasing subjective feelings of frustration, and increasing physical activity—were also included in the contracts. Although more specific and individualized than large-scale token economy programs, high-frequency behaviors such as recreational privileges and money were often used as reinforcers for appropriate behaviors.

Token economy programs (two studies). Although most popularly used for management purposes within hospital inpatient programs, token economy systems have been used in the treatment of several target populations, such as juvenile delinquents (Fineman, 1968; Tyler & Brown, 1968), mentally retarded individuals (Lent, 1968), and chronic psychotic patients (Atthow & Krasner, 1968; Ayllon & Azrin, 1968; Montgomery & McBurney, Note 7). In the treatment of drug abuse, Glicksman, Ottomanelli, and Cutler (1971) and O'Brien, Raynes, and Patch (1971) have used token economies in hospital settings.

Glicksman et al. (1971) developed a system by which a patient could earn his own hospital discharge by accumulating points based upon program performance. In a different manner, O'Brien et al. (1971) developed a system employing the Premack principle (Premack, 1959). Here, narcotic abusing patients were allowed to engage in desired activities or events as reinforcers (e.g., acquiring passes, being allowed visitors, TV and radio privilege) contingent upon increasing the occurrence of various low-frequency behaviors (e.g., punctuality, adherence to program rules, cleanliness).

Although neither study specified drug abstinence as a target, both studies emphasized many of the other problem behaviors commonly found in many inpatient drug programs. In an attempt to individualize large drug programs, the use of token economy systems for the management of general program rules may be supplemented by contingency contracts aimed at dealing with more of the specific problems of each patient.

Combined Behavioral Treatments (Three Studies)

The third general category of behavioral drug treatment approaches involves the combination of several techniques used concurrently or in close temporal sequence. In their treatment programs, Callner (Note 8), O'Brien et al. (1972), and Wisocki (1973) have used several behavioral techniques in an attempt to break down and treat several components of drug abuse. For example, drug abuse has been approached by a combination of relaxation training, electrical aversion, and covert sensitization treatments (O'Brien et al., 1972).

In a different manner, Wisocki (1973) used a combination of covert reinforcement, covert sensitization, and thought-stopping techniques to

TABLE 1

DESCRIPTIVE SUBJECT, PROCEDURAL, AND TREATMENT VARIABLES OF BEHAVIORAL DRUG TREATMENT RESEARCH

Author	Subject				Procedure			Treatment		Follow-up (in mos.)
	N	Sex	Age	Drug history	Setting[a]	Design[b]	Dependent measures[c]	Target: Behavior therapy[d]	Other treatments[e]	
Raymond (1964)	1	F	30	Methadone, 6 yrs.	H	CS	SRDU	↓Drug use: CA (apomorphine)	ECT (3 wks.)	30
Wolpe (1965)	1	M	31	Demerol, 3 yrs.	N	CS	SRDU	↓Drug use: EA	Psychoanalysis	None
Lesser (1967)	1	M	21	Morphine,—	N	CS	SRDU	1. ↓Tension: RT 2. ↑Self-confidence: AT	—	7 and 10
Anant (1968)	1	F	32	"Tranquilizers,"—	N	CS	SRDU	1. ↓Drug use: EA	—	3
Liberman (1968)	2	S1 = M S2 = F	24	Heroin, 8 yrs.	H	CS	SRDU	1. ↓Drug use: CS 2. ↓Anxiety: SD	1. Milieu therapy 2. "Psychotherapy"	—
Thomson & Rathod (1968)	17	15M 2F	$\bar{X}$ = 38 (16–38)	Heroin, 5 yrs. Heroin, 10–104 wks.	H	GD; aversion (N = 13) vs. no aversion (N = 6), posttest only	1. Drug-free weeks in hospital 2. Drug-free weeks out of hospital 3. Negative and positive urine tests	↓Drug use: CA (apomorphine) ↓Drug use: CA (scoline)	1. Individual and group psychotherapy 2. Occupational program 3. Parent therapy program	12
Kraft (1969a)	1	F	50	Pentobarbital, 12 yrs.	H	CS	SRDU	1. ↓Drug use 2. Fear of being alone } SD	1. Group psychotherapy 2. ECT 3. Insulin therapy 4. Antipsychotic medication	None
Kraft (1968b, 1969b, 1970a, 1970b)	2	S1 = M S2 = M	20 18	Drinamyl, 5 yrs. Drinamyl, 4 yrs.	H	CS	1. SRDU (1968b, 1969b, 1970a) 2. Maudsley Personality Inventory, MMPI, Taylor Manifest Anxiety Scale (1970b) SRDU	1. ↓Drug use 2. ↓Social anxiety 3. Dependency on therapist } SD	—	9 mos.
Steinfeld (1970)	2	S1 = M S2 = M	"mid-20s"	Polydrugs,— Heroin,—	H	CS	SRDU	↓Drug use: CS	—	—
Glicksman, Ottomanelli, & Cutler (1971)	32	M	$\bar{X}$ = 20.5 (16–35)	Polydrugs,— Heroin,—	H	GD; token economy group (N = 32) only	Behavioral ratings on: 1. class performance 2. therapy performance 3. program performance	1. ↑Academic perf. 2. ↑Therapy perf. 3. Program perf. } TE	1. Academic classes 2. Group therapy	None

TABLE 1—(Continued)

Author	Subject				Procedure			Treatment		Follow-up (in mos.)
	N	Sex	Age	Drug history	Setting[a]	Design[b]	Dependent measures[c]	Target: Behavior therapy[d]	Other treatments[e]	
O'Brien, Raynes, & Patch (1971)	150	135M 15F	—	"Narcotics," —	H	GD; treatment group ($N = 10$) only	Frequency of "low-frequency" behaviors relating to: 1. cleanliness 2. punctuality 3. program rules 4. personal duties	↑"Low-frequency" behaviors: TE	—	None
Boudin (1972)	1	F	—	"Amphetamines," 3 yrs. "Barbiturates," — Heroin, 10 yrs.	N	CS	Self-ratings of drug urges associated with verbal stimuli SRDU	↓Drug use {CC EA}	—	24
O'Brien & Raynes (1972)	3	—	—	—	—	CS	Self-ratings of drug urges associated with verbal stimuli SRDU	1. ↓Drug use {RT EA SD} 2. ↑Anxiety {CS}	—	None
O'Brien, Raynes, & Patch (1972)	2	S1 = F S2 = M	30 24	Heroin, 8 yrs. Heroin, 6 yrs.	H	CS	1. SRDU 2. Self-ratings of drug urges associated with verbal stimuli	1. ↓Drug use {RT EA CS} 2. ↓Anxiety: SD	—	14 6
Sammons (Note 5)	41	M	—	Narcotics, amphetamines, barbiturates, —	H	CS	1. Urine tests 2. Curfew violations 3. Dress code violations 4. Room inspection	1. ↓Drug use 2. Dress code violations} CC	1. Group therapy 2. Academic classes	None
Boudin & Valentine (Note 4)	1	F	"20s"	Heroin, 2 yrs.	N	GD; contracting ($N = 7$) vs. no contracting ($N = 7$) groups, post-test only CS	Self-ratings on: drug thoughts, drug urges, frustration, marijuana use, hashish use, thoughts of breaking the contract, mental contentment, cigarettes, social discomfort, relaxation, sexual frustrations	↓Drug use: CC	—	None
Callner (Note 8)	8	M	$\bar{X} = 19.5$ (18–25)	5Ss = Heroin, $\bar{X}$ = 4.5 yrs. 2Ss = Methedrine $\bar{X}$ = 3.5 yrs. 1S = LSD, 5 yrs.	H	GD; assertion training ($N = 4$) vs. control group ($N = 4$), pretest and posttest CS	1. Assertion question. 2. Performance on role-playing situations rated for: speech duration, fluency, and general affect	↑Appropriate assertion in drug-related situations} AT	Group therapy	None.

TABLE 1—(Continued)

Author		Subject			Procedure			Treatment		Follow-up (in mos.)
	N	Sex	Age	Drug history	Setting[a]	Design[b]	Dependent measures[c]	Target: Behavior therapy[d]	Other treatments[e]	
Ross & Jones (Note 6)	2	S1 = M	23	Heroin, 2 yrs.	H	MBL	1. Spontaneous group verbalizations 2. Attending recreation 3. Frequency of relaxation sessions 4. Urinalysis and SRDU	1. ↑Rate spontaneous speech 2. ↑Physical activity 3. ↑Relaxation 4. ↓Drug use } CC	Group therapy	None
		S2 = M	26	Methedrine, 5 yrs.	H	RD	1. Frequency of relaxation sessions 2. Marijuana use	↑Frequency of relaxation trials } CC		
Spevack, Pihl, & Rowan (1973)	3	M	—	"Amphetamines," —	H	3N = 1, AB	1. Urinalysis and SRDU 2. Frequency of drug-related thoughts 2. Ratings of drug-related affect 3. SRDU	↓Drug thoughts and use } EA	—	7
	1	M	17	LSD, —	H	N = 1, AB	1. Fear Survey Schedule 2. Self-Rating Symptoms Scale 3. Dance Hierarchy Attitude Scale 4. Sleep Hierarchy Attitude Scale 5. Heart rate	1. ↓Fear associated with unpleasant LSD experience 2. ↑Sleep } SD	—	12
Steinfeld, Rice, Kautio, & Egan (Note 3)	8	M	—	"Narcotics," —	H	GD; treatement group only	1. Ratings of fears 2. Drug Abuse Questionnaire	↓Drug use { RT / CS	1. Encounter groups 2. Group therapy 3. Seminars	None
Wisocki (1973)	1	M	26	Heroin, 5 yrs.	N	CS	1. SRDU 2. Informal observations	1. ↓Drug use { CS / CR / TS 2. Improve self-concept { TS / CR 3. ↑Prosocial behavior { CR / TS / CR		18

Note. A dash indicates unavailable information.
[a] H = hospital; N = natural.
[b] CS = case study; GD = group design; MBL = multiple baseline; RD = reversal design; AB = baseline treatment design.
[c] SRDU = self-reported drug use.
[d] CA = chemical aversion; EA = electrical aversion; CS = covert sensitization; RT = relaxation training; SD = systematic desensitization; TE = token economy; CC = contingency contract; AT = assertion training; CR = covert reinforcement; TS = thought stopping; ↑ = increased; ↓ = decreased.
[e] ECT = electroconvulsive therapy.

treat drug abuse. Here, the technique of covert reinforcement (Cautela, 1970) was used to teach the patient to reinforce himself for refusing drugs by pairing imaginal scenes of refusing a drug offer with another imaginal scene that was pleasurable (e.g., living in a desired area of the country, acceptance by admired people). The technique of thought stopping (Wolpe, 1958) was used in an attempt to interfere with thoughts of heroin use. This combined behavioral treatment approach has particular promise because it can readily be taught to the patient and can be practiced outside the treatment setting.

In the case of other problem behaviors occurring in drug abusers, assertion and communication skills were trained by a combination of role playing, modeling, and videotape feedback (Callner, Note 8). Specific assertion situations likely to occur in the patient's life (e.g., refusing drug offers, applying for a job, asking a "straight" girl for a date) were discussed, modeled, and then role played and videotaped by the members of a small drug-patient group. Subsequent discussion of the videotaped role-playing scenes concentrated upon improving both verbal and non-verbal communication styles. Although the target of drug taking was not specifically addressed by this study, it was hypothesized that many of the situations likely to confront the drug abuser after he returns to nonaddicted society may contribute to his relapse if not handled appropriately (e.g., refusing drug offers, finding a job, meeting nondrug-using friends).

In all of these studies, many of the specific behaviors associated with drug use were isolated, and a combination of several techniques were used to approach them. Although the differential effectiveness of each treatment technique is difficult to measure when used in combination with other treatments, the use of several approaches to specifically defined target problems may prove to increase the probability of success.

A CRITICAL EVALUATION OF THE BEHAVIORAL
DRUG TREATMENT RESEARCH

Having described the three general categories of behavioral approaches to drug treatment and the specific techniques within these general categories, a more detailed analysis of this literature is necessary before recommendations for treatment, and for future research refinements can be made. Table 1 presents the descriptive information relating to the subject, procedural, and treatment variables for each behavioral drug treatment study.

TABLE 2

Summary of Treatment and Follow-up Results for Each Behavioral Treatment Approach to Drug Abuse

Treatment	Author	Duration (period/sessions)	Treatment Results[a]	Assessment[b]	Follow-up Results[a]
Chemical aversion	Raymond (1964)	17 days/17	NDU	1. SRDU 2. Private physician's report	NDU
	Thomson & Rathod (1968)	5 days/5	BTG: N = 8 = NDU N = 2 = relapse	SRDU	BTG: N = 8 = working and NDU N = 3 = relapse
Electrical aversion	Liberman (1968)	5 wks./38	S1 = NDU S2 = NDU	SRDU	S1 = relapse, jail S2 = NDU, job
	Wolpe (1965)	3 mos./7	NDU (8 sessions), then relapse	None	NDU, job, college
	Lesser (1967)	4½ mos./33	RDU	SRDU (letters)	N = 2 = NDU N = 1 = relapse
	O'Brien & Raynes (1972)	—/17	RDU	SRDU	N = 2 = NDU N = 1 = NDU
Covert sensitization	Spevack, Phil, & Rowan (1973)	3½–5 mos./35	1. ↓ Drug thoughts 2. RDU (N = 3)	SRDU	NDU,
	Anant (1968)	—/—	NDU	SRDU	
	Steinfeld (1970)	S1 = —/2 S2 = 3 wks./— —/8	—	None	—
Systematic desensitization	Steinfeld, Rice, Rautio, & Egan (Note 3)		N = 4 = still in treatment N = 4 = discharged	SRDU	N = 3 = NDU N = 1 = relapse
	Kraft (1969a)	8 mos./72	NDU	SRDU	NDU
	Kraft (1968b, 1969b, 1970a, 1970b)	3–5 mos./26-52	1. NDU (1968b, 1969b, 1970a) 2. ↓ Psychometric test scores (1970b)	SRDU	NDU
Contingency contracting	Spevack, Phil, & Rowan (1973)	2 mos./10	1. ↓ LSD "flashbacks" 2. ↓ Psychometric test scores 3. ↑ Sleep 4. ↓ Heart rate	SRDU	No LSD "flashbacks"
	Boudin (1972)	3 mos./—	Negative contract consequence used only once for drug use	SRDU	NDU (12 mos.), then relapse
	Sammons (Note 5)	5 wks./—	BTG < CG: 1. Drug use 2. Dress violations 3. Room inspection violations 4. Curfew violations	None	—

TABLE 2—(Continued)

Treatment	Author	Duration (period/sessions)	Treatment Results[a]	Follow-up Assessment[b]	Follow-up Results[a]
Contingency contracting	Boudin & Valentine (Note 4)	7 mos./—	1. ↑ Ratings of mental contentment; 2. ↓ Drug use; 3. Many functional-related relationships between dependent measures and life events	None	—
	Ross & Jones (Note 6)	S1 = 44 days/—	1. ↑ Spontaneous verbalization; 2. ↑ Recreational activities; 3. ↑ Relaxation; 4. RDU	None	—
		S2 = 43 days/—	1. ↑ Relaxation; 2. RDU	None	—
Token economy	Glicksman, Ottomanelli, & Cutler (1971)	4 mos./—	1. ↑ Academic performance ratings; 2. ↑ Therapy performance ratings; 3. ↑ Program performance ratings	None	—
	O'Brien, Raynes, & Patch (1971)	.9 mos./—	"Low-frequency" program performance behaviors	None	—
	O'Brien, Raynes, & Patch (1972)	S1 = —/27	Relapse once, then NDU	1. SRDU; 2. Needle marks; 3. Employer's report	NDU
		S2 = —/19	NDU	1. SRDU; 2. Family reports; 3. Needle marks	NDU
Combined behavioral treatments	Callner (Note 8)	3 wks./9	BTG > CG: 1. Assertion questionnaire; 2. Verbal performance variables	None	—
	Wisocki (1973)	6-10 wks./6-10	1. RDU; 2. ↑ Self-concept; 3. ↑ Prosocial behavior	SRDU	NDU, job married

Note. A dash indicates unavailable information.
[a] NDU = no drug use; RDU = reduced drug use; ↑ = increased; ↓ = decreased.
[b] SRDU = self-reported drug use.

As seen in Table 1, the majority of studies to date have involved the presentation of individual case reports (74 percent), were typically undertaken in hospital settings (78 percent), and have relied upon self-reported drug use as the only source of treatment and follow-up data (52 percent). Posttreatment follow-up data were reported in only 57 percent of the studies. This information alone suggests the need for more controlled single-subject and group studies using a wider, more reliable and representative variety of dependent measures. Table 2 summarizes the treatment and follow-up results for the studies within each specific behavioral treatment approach.

Several treatment and follow-up trends are apparent. Of those studies reporting the incidence of drug use during treatment, 52 percent reported no drug use and 39 percent reported some degree of drug use before the termination of treatment. Although 29 percent of the studies did not report either increases or decreases in drug use, 35 percent reported reduced drug abuse and 26 percent reported no drug abuse directly following treatment. In terms of follow-up results, only 13 percent of the studies used any other form of data besides self-report, while 43 percent of the studies did not present any follow-up reports whatsoever. Of the studies reporting follow-up data, 43 percent reported no drug use during their respective posttreatment period (follow-up periods ranged from 3 to 24 months), and 22 percent reported that the patient resumed drug use.

Because of both the variability and sparsity of quantifiable data reported, it is difficult to compare the effectiveness of the different specific treatment approaches. Due to the large amount of self-report data and comparatively small numbers of follow-up reports, it is also difficult to compare the effectiveness of individual studies. It may thus be more meaningful to evaluate each study individually on its discussion and treatment of several important variables related to subject, design, procedure, and assessment. Table 3 summarizes a critical evaluation of each of the behavioral drug treatment studies. Each study was given a subjective rating on its discussion, description, and treatment of 11 important criteria relating to subject, procedural, and outcome variables.

To a great extent, the critical ratings in Table 3 speak for themselves. Although the majority of the studies involved individual case reports, there were very few adequate descriptions of sampling procedures and setting variables. Given that 78 percent of the studies were undertaken in hospital drug treatment programs, descriptions of both sampling procedures and settings are particularly important in determining how representative the subjects were and whether or not confounding treat-

TABLE 3

CRITIQUE OF SUBJECT, PROCEDURAL, AND OUTCOME VARIABLES OF BEHAVIORAL DRUG TREATMENT RESEARCH

Author	Subject				Treatment procedure					Outcome			
	Description[a]	Sampling[b]	Representativeness[a]	Setting[b]	Theoretical justification[a]	Description[b]	Baseline assessment[b]	Dependent measures[b]	Concurrent treatments[b]	Data analysis[b]	Follow-ups	Implications[a]	Suggestions for future research[a]
Raymond (1964)	2	0	0	1	2	2	0	1	1	0	1	0	0
Wolpe (1965)	3	0	0	2	2	3	0	1	1	0	0	1	0
Lesser (1967)	1	0	0	1	1	2	1	1	0	0	2	1	0
Anant (1968)	1	0	2	1	3	3	0	0	0	0	1	2	0
Liberman (1968)	3	2	2	1	3	3	3	3	1	1	1	2	0
Thomson & Rathod (1968)	3	0	3	2	2	2	3	3	1	0	1	3	0
Kraft (1969a)	3	0	0	1	2	3	2	1	2	0	1	1	0
Kraft (1969b, 1969b, 1970a)	2	0	0	1	2	3	1	0	0	0	1	1	0
Kraft (1970b)	2	0	1	1	2	3	1	2	0	2	1	1	1
Steinfeld (1970)	1	0	1	1	2	2	0	0	0	0	0	1	0
Glicksman, Ottomanelli, & Cutler (1971)	2	2	2	2	2	2	1	2	0	1	0	3	1
O'Brien, Raynes, & Patch (1971)	1	1	2	1	2	2	3	2	0	2	0	3	0
Boudin (1972)	2	0	0	1	1	2	1	1	0	0	2	1	0
O'Brien & Raynes (1972)	1	0	2	1	2	2	0	1	0	0	0	1	0
O'Brien, Raynes, & Patch (1972)	2	0	2	1	2	2	0	2	0	0	3	3	2
Sammons (Note 5)	1	2	2	2	1	3	3	2	0	3	0	3	0
Boudin & Valentine (Note 4)	2	0	0	1	3	3	3	3	1	3	0	2	0
Callner (Note 8)	2	3	3	3	2	2	3	3	2	3	0	3	2
Ross & Jones (Note 6)	3	2	3	3	3	2	3	3	2	3	0	3	1
Spevack, Pihl, & Rowan (1973)	1	0	1	0	1	2	3	3	0	1	1	1	1
Steinfeld, Rice, Rautio, & Egan (Note 3)	1	1	2	2	1	3	0	1	1	0	1	2	3
Wisocki (1973)	2	1	1	1	2	3	1	1	0	0	2	2	0

[a] Rating system: 0 = no discussion; 1 = brief discussion; 2 = adequate discussion; 3 = comprehensive discussion.
[b] Rating system: 0 = no description; 1 = brief description; 2 = adequate description; 3 = comprehensive description.
[c] Rating system: 0 = no treatment; 1 = brief treatment; 2 = adequate treatment; 3 = comprehensive treatment.

ment variables influenced outcomes. The comprehensive description presented by Ross and Jones (Note 6) illustrates the many subjects and setting variables that must be carefully considered in evaluating treatment outcome.

In Table 3, it is evident from the ratings on variables under the heading *Treatment procedure* that the vast majority of the studies concentrated on presenting detailed treatment descriptions and paid little attention to obtaining data by controlled single-subject and group designs. Many studies virtually ignored the necessity of obtaining baseline data and reliable dependent measures. Furthermore, only a handful of studies made an attempt to discuss the possible confounding variables such as concurrent treatments (see Table 1 under *Other treatments*), maturation, or therapist characteristics.

In terms of *Outcome* variables in Table 3, only 39 percent of the studies made an attempt to present any quantitative treatment of their data. There were only three studies reporting data based upon a single-subject design and only four studies reporting a statistical treatment of their results based upon a group design. Boudin and Valentine (Note 4) illustrated how a sizable amount of data can be obtained from a single subject and then analyzed to provide meaningful inferences. In addition, Sammons (Note 5), and Spevack et al. (1973) also provided good examples of how data can be collected and evaluated with either single-subject or small group studies.

When evaluating the effectiveness of any therapeutic approach, one of the most important variables to consider is the adequacy of follow-up assessment. Considering the long-term nature of drug abuse problems, follow-up assessment is perhaps the most crucial appraisal of treatment effectiveness. Of the studies in Table 3, only six included a discussion of follow-up periods, measures, and outcomes. One of the most impressive and comprehensive follow-up investigations illustrating the use of multiple follow-up measures was made by O'Brien et al. (1972). In general, however, the reluctance to follow patients after treatment and the lack of reliable follow-up measures strongly points to another obvious area for future refinement.

THE FUTURE OF BEHAVIORAL DRUG TREATMENT RESEARCH: SOME RECOMMENDATIONS FOR REFINEMENT

The research evaluating behavioral drug treatment approaches is comparatively new and has not, as yet, included many well-controlled studies.

Like many other clinical areas in which preliminary investigation has begun, efforts are not often made to critically evaluate the early findings. An early critical appraisal of a developing clinical research area can not only identify consistent problem areas but can also suggest ways to solve them. At this stage of development, it is particularly important to assess the existing behavioral drug treatment literature and to recommend changes, refinements, and new directions for future study. The following seven recommendations for future research refinements are made in light of the progress and shortcomings found in the behavioral drug treatment literature to date.

Use Subjects That Are More Representative of the Drug Abusers Seen in Treatment Programs

In an attempt to increase the effectiveness and generalizability of behavioral treatment approaches to more drug patients, future studies should use patients representing the demographic and historical characteristics found most commonly in institutional and private drug abuse programs. For the most part, the behavioral drug treatment research reviewed here did not select subjects that represented good examples of "street addicts" or addicts entering treatment programs under duress from the courts. For example, the subjects selected in the case studies reported by Wolpe (1965; 31-year-old physician), Kraft (1969a; 50-year-old female), and Boudin (1972; female graduate student) represented very few of the characteristics common to the majority of street addicts (e.g., lower socioeconomic status, high school education or less, criminal record). It is thus difficult to evaluate how generalizable the results of these studies would be to other subjects. It may be useful here to reevaluate the sociological literature for descriptions of "street roles," economic status, family characteristics, and other variables found to occur most frequently with drug abusers (e.g., Chein, 1966; Feldman, 1968; Levine & Stephens, 1971; Preble & Casey, 1969; Stephens & Levine, 1971; Sutter, 1966). In addition, the discussion on subject variables presented by Sammons (Note 5) provides a vivid illustration of the various "con games" and other manipulatory behavior commonly found when working with drug abusers.

In the future, it would also be helpful for researchers to speculate about how their treatments and procedures would be altered (if any) for drug patients representing different demographic and behavioral characteristics. It may be demonstrated that some behavioral treatments are most effective with a specific drug patient sample and do not apply equally well to the treatment of all drug users. For example, covert methods, requiring honest reports from the patient on his ability to vividly imagine suggested scenes, may be found to be more effective with middle-class, college drug users than long-term street addicts. Although this recommendation is not designed to stimulate research in "typologies" of drug abusers, it is designed to remind researchers to assess and analyze subject characteristics as to how they relate to treatment procedures and outcomes.

The descriptive subject information presented in Table 1 demonstrates the wide variety of drug abusers investigated. Because the generalizability of treatment results is strongly influenced by a variety of subject variables, it is also recommended that future researchers attempt to estimate the intensity of drug abuse by combining variables such as type of drug used, history of use, typical dose, socioeconomic status, criminal record, and past treatment failures into a system to categorize drug users. For example, one category of drug abuser may include chronic, heavy-dose heroin users of low socioeconomic status having a long history of both drug- and nondrug-related criminal arrests. A different category may include younger, more infrequent users of psychedelics and amphetamines of middle to upper socioeconomic status with few criminal arrests. These descriptive subject variables, when taken in combination, may be helpful in obtaining a relative index of motivation and probability of treatment success. Furthermore, it may enable researchers to determine if specific therapeutic techniques prove to be more effective with one category of drug abusers than with others.

Develop a Larger Variety of Reliable and Representative Dependent Measures

The success of a drug patient's progress should be assessed by verifiable evidence on many important measures related to natural behavior. Tables 1 and 3 clearly demonstrate the need for a greater variety of dependent measures than self-reported drug use. Although 48 percent of the studies included more than one form of measurement, self-reported drug use represented the only form of data in 52 percent of the studies.

One way to generate more dependent measures is to isolate several specific target problems by breaking down *drug abuse* into smaller behavioral components and behaviors surrounding the illicit use of drugs.

Boudin and Valentine (Note 4), for example, identified and measured many variables thought to covary with drug taking (e.g., drug urges, frustration ratings, social discomfort ratings, inability to relax, sexual performance). Data was obtained on each of these behaviors and then analyzed in an attempt to identify any existing trends. In a similar attempt to identify behaviors possibly relating to drug use, Ross and Jones (Note 6) obtained data on such behaviors as marijuana use, spontaneous group therapy verbalizations, physical activity, and subjective urges and intercorrelated these measures to determine what behaviors were most related to drug-intake patterns.

In addition to investigating a greater variety of dependent measures predicted to relate to drug use, it is recommended that future studies in this area work to develop two general measurement techniques. The first technique lies in the development of in vivo measures of natural behavior in a variety of settings. Although in vivo measurement of performance has traditionally been difficult to develop and obtain, it is of particular importance with drug patients to isolate and measure the behaviors that occur in their natural environments that may be related to drug use and posttreatment relapse. Measures of this nature would include assessment of the drug patient in his natural environment on several frequently occurring problems (refusing drug offers, meeting nondrug friends, finding and maintaining a job, etc.).

The second recommended form of measurement might be called "ongoing program performance measures." These measures include a series of assessments of observable and verifiable performance of tasks while the patient is in treatment, designed to assess his ability to deal with the difficult problems likely to occur after treatment termination. For example, the use of prearranged situations involving a patient role playing a difficult situation such as being offered drugs or being asked to sell drugs would probably give the therapist a better assessment of the patient's behavior than self-reports. These performance tasks could be video- or audiotaped, thus enabling the researcher to later reliably rate verbal and nonverbal performance in both group and single-subject treatment designs. Ongoing behavioral measurement prior to treatment termination also has the advantage of allowing the researcher to better assess the possible confounding effects of such variables as maturation and concurrent treatments.

Although seldom used, it is also strongly recommended that urine analysis techniques be employed whenever possible as a reliable measure to verify both treatment and self-report data.

Place Greater Emphasis upon Quantitative Data
Presentation and Analysis

Along with the recommendation to increase the number of dependent variables predicted to relate to drug abuse, there should also be more emphasis on various quantitative treatments of obtained data. It is thus strongly recommended that future researchers in this area work to demonstrate change beyond a rough verbal self-report of drug use. At the simplest level, a graphical analysis of obtained data can be useful in demonstrating that the study assessed some measures of change beyond verbal self-report. Only 13 percent of the studies reviewed here presented a graphical analysis of their data. At a higher level of quantification, a statistical analysis of obtained data not only demonstrates the direction and magnitude of change, but also makes a comparative statement regarding the reliability of whatever differences were found. Table 3 indicates that only 30 percent of the studies reviewed here included a statistical analysis of obtained data.

One graphical way to present comparative change regarding target behaviors is to compare several dependent measures obtained from a representative subject (in group studies) or from the patient himself (in case studies) in several different stimulus conditions. Such a functional analysis, comparing drug use with other behaviors predicted to influence drug use, has three advantages. First, it forces the researcher to consider and, hopefully, to assess many of the antecedent and consequent conditions surrounding the incidence of target behaviors. Second, a functional analysis of the target behaviors clarifies the justification for the particular behavioral treatment approach employed. Finally, a functional analysis provides an organized medium for evaluating a patient's performance due to the effects of a particular treatment approach.

Although rare in the behavioral drug treatment literature, a good example of a functional analysis of drug use and behaviors predicted to influence drug use was done by Boudin and Valentine (Note 4). Here, a graphical analysis of several dependent measures was useful in illustrating many inverse and converse functional relationships between drug use and other important situational and emotional data. A functional analysis of drug use is not only a step toward the quantification of obtained results, but it can also be helpful when making decisions regarding the timing and nature of treatment approaches.

In the case of group research designs, statistical analysis of the obtained data is encouraged, whenever possible, to demonstrate the direction, magnitude, and reliability of whatever changes were found. Because it is recommended that group research in behavioral drug treatment approaches begin on a small scale, statistical techniques that do not depend highly on large sample sizes are suggested.

Use Procedures to Ensure Greater Experimental Control

In the behavioral drug treatment literature, the need for controlled, large-group designs has perhaps not yet surpassed the need for well-controlled single-subject and small-group studies. Tables 1, 2, and 3 demonstrate the strong emphasis placed upon the description of treatment approaches (75 percent were case studies), with comparatively little attention paid to obtaining data and ensuring controlled designs (only 26 percent used single-subject or group designs).

Several recommendations for increasing experimental control in single-subject and small-group drug treatment research can be made. First, accurate and stable baseline data should routinely be obtained from all the dependent measures prior to starting treatment. In terms of baseline drug-use data, an accurate history from the drug user and, if possible, from one or more persons familiar with the user's drug intake should be obtained. For other drug-related behaviors, self-ratings or behavioral observations should be made to ensure stable baseline performance. Stable baseline data are particularly important when research is done in institional or private inpatient drug programs in order to demonstrate that the drug user has adapted to his new environmental settings.

Whenever possible, case studies should employ some form of reversal or multiple baseline design. That is, investigators should attempt to test the strength of their treatment programs by either replicating pretreatment baseline conditions after a suitable treatment period (reversal design) or recording baseline data on several problematic behaviors simultaneously and introducing treatment to one behavior at a time (multiple baseline design). The two case studies reported by Ross and Jones (Note 6) are good examples of the use of reversal and multiple baseline designs in drug treatment research. It should also be noted that in these two particular case studies, several behaviors predicted to relate to drug taking were measured.

In the case of small-group treatment research, future studies should include at least one form of control group comprised of patients matched to the experimental treatment group. The small-group designs used by Callner (Note 8) and O'Brien et al. (1971) exemplify the use of experimental and control groups used to gain a more comparative assessment of the treatment intervention. Because small-group drug treatment research lends itself to subpopulations within large inpatient drug programs, a discussion of the various other treatments existing in that program and speculations as to how they may interact with the experimental treatment approach would be useful in evaluating the possible confounding effects of concurrent treatments.

Finally, all information pertaining to the description, duration, sequence, and timing of the various treatment approaches should be included so that changes in performance can accurately be related to treatment interventions. Again, this is particularly important in the case of inpatient drug treatment programs in order to identify which treatment intervention (if any) was associated with behavioral performance. The descriptions reported by Sammons (Note 5) and Wisocki (1973), for example, provide very useful information on how the treatments, sequencing, duration, and timing affected performance measures.

Develop Better Procedures for Obtaining Accurate and Representative Measures of Posttreatment Follow-Up

With drug-abuse patients, perhaps the most meaningful estimate of treatment effectiveness can be obtained through accurate and reliable follow-up assessment. As demonstrated in Tables 1 and 2, the majority of behavioral drug treatment studies to date have not concentrated on obtaining good follow-up data. In addition, there appear to be no general procedural guidelines indicated in the literature for obtaining follow-up data with drug abusers.

Several recommendations for obtaining better follow-up with drug abusers are suggested. First, future researchers should attempt to obtain more reliable and realistic measures of follow-up than patient self-report data. Reports from people knowledgeable of the patient's behavior should be sought as rigorously as data are sought from the patient himself. For example, if informal reports or behavioral checklist data could be obtained from the patient's employers, family members, and peers, a more representative appraisal of posttreatment success could be made. An agreement of the reliability of the patient's self-reports can also be made by obtaining data from other people. The follow-up data presented by O'Brien et al. (1972) are a good example of obtaining reports from others with a knowledge of the patient's posttreatment progress.

Once again, the validity of the patient's self-reported drug use should routinely be checked by urine analysis.

Measures of posttreatment in vivo performance probably provide the best follow-up assessment. Although more difficult to obtain, it is recommended that future researchers work to develop a technology of measuring the drug abuser in either natural or contrived situations (e.g., confederate offering drugs to the patient), thus enabling a more realistic assessment of the patient's posttreatment performance than self-report.

Attempts should be made to use dependent measures in follow-up assessment similar to those used in the treatment setting. This will enable the researcher to assess the progress of the patient on a time continuum using similar measures of performance from one setting to another. This procedure will also enable the researcher to assess how effective his treatment measures are in predicting posttreatment performance.

Finally, frequent follow-up assessments should be made shortly after treatment termination in an attempt to detect any early relapse trends or problems. Follow-up assessment should be made frequently just after treatment termination and less frequently as the patient becomes more successful in his responses to problems. If early follow-up assessment detects problems or relapse trends, appropriate "booster treatments" should be included in the treatment program to remedy any early posttreatment difficulties. Booster treatments may be particularly important when counterconditioning techniques are used to treat drug abuse in order to minimize extinction to the conditioned aversion.

More Detailed Discussion of Variables Affecting Both Treatment Success as Well as Failure Is Necessary

This recommendation is made in an attempt to identify the important variables associated with both favorable and unfavorable drug treatment outcomes. Because the research in behavioral drug treatment is still within the early developmental stages, it is particularly important to critically assess each variable associated with treatment objectives and outcomes.

Three recommendations can be made to help generate research that lends to our knowledge of the variables affecting drug treatment effectiveness. First, journal editors should encourage researchers to report controlled treatment studies that do not obtain successful results. It may be more important to isolate and discuss the conditions surrounding an ineffective treatment in the context of a well-controlled study than to demonstrate treatment success in a poorly controlled study. Replication research should also be encouraged. Second, researchers should design and later appraise their own studies on variables similar to those presented in Table 3. Although these variables do not exhaust the list of important criteria necessary to critique behavioral drug treatment research, they may provide a list of minimum standards to include and discuss within the study. Finally, researchers should try to suggest future research ideas based upon the refinement, elaboration, or replication of their own work. These ideas for extended study will help to produce a more homogeneous body of literature developing out of past shortcomings and progress rather than a heterogeneous body of literature replicating repeated difficulties (e.g., poor measures, unrepresentative subjects, confounding variables). For example, the ideas suggested by Steinfeld et al. (Note 3) give the reader a good indication of what directions are planned for future study with covert sensitization approaches to drug abuse.

*Greater Awareness of the Biochemical and Pharmacological
Aspects of Drugs Should Be Sought by Behavioral
Drug Treatment Researchers*

Finally, professionals engaged in both the treatment of drug abusers and the evaluation of treatment techniques should remain aware of the current research trends occurring in the biochemical and pharmacological study of drug abuse. At one level of awareness, behavioral drug treatment researchers should consider the usefulness of various pharmacological agents when designing their treatment programs. Drugs such as tranquilizers, narcotic antagonists, and methadone are frequently encountered when treating drug abusers and can often be used to supplement concurrent behavioral approaches (e.g., Liebson & Bigelow, 1972). At another level of awareness, behavioral drug treatment researchers should be cognizant of the various biochemical and physiological processes involved in commonly abused drugs in order to better understand the behavioral pharmacology of their patients. Finally, behavioral drug treatment researchers should remain abreast of the animal research in drug abuse with a watchful eye toward possible human treatment applications. At present, for example, Wikler's theories involving the physiological aspects of conditioned abstinence may prove to have particular importance for the future treatment of human drug abusers.

Although this critical review has primarily addressed itself to the evaluation of treatment research, several brief recommendations regarding the general field of drug treatment can also be made. First, large-scale drug treatment programs should try to include some form of individualized therapy specifically tailored to the individual drug patient. Programs addressed to each individual's particular historical development, problems, and goals may help to augment the general principles taught within the larger drug program. The poor follow-up results commonly found in the drug treatment literature may indicate the inability of treatment contingencies to remain intact in posttreatment settings. It is therefore strongly recommended that treatment programs be designed to utilize the events and occurrences within the patient's natural environment.

Finally, it is recommended that therapists employ a variety of techniques aimed at preparing the drug patient to face the many problem aspects of maintaining a drug-free life. For example, techniques used to prepare the patient for turning down drug offers, to control his own drug urges, to interview for a job, and to interact successfully with nondrug users might prepare the patient more completely for his posttreatment environment.

Although behaviorally oriented treatment programs often represent the most efficient and successful treatment approach to several problem behaviors, only carefully planned treatment research utilizing techniques to ensure control, representativeness, and accuracy of inference will determine the usefulness of behavioral treatment approaches to drug abuse. Only after such steps are taken to ensure more reliable and valid indications of change can the specific behavioral treatment approaches be appraised as to their differential effectiveness.

SUMMARY

This review critically evaluated the behavioral drug treatment literature and discussed several recommendations for future refinements. Because of the consistent deficits in the research to date, large-group studies are not recommended until more reliable and representative data from controlled single-subject and small-group studies are accumulated. However, it was recommended that future studies concentrate on the need for (a) more representative drug subjects, (b) quantitative data analyses, (c) more reliable and varied dependent measures, (d) greater experimental control procedures, (e) better follow-up assessment, (f) more detailed analysis of the variables affecting both treatment success and failure, and (g) more careful consideration of the biochemical and pharmacological aspects of drug abuse and how these variables might be used to supplement behavioral treatments to drug abuse. Once a more reliable and generalizable data base of treatment information can be accumulated through controlled research on a smaller scale, subsequent study can be addressed to testing the effectiveness of treatment approaches with larger and more varied populations of drug abusers.

REFERENCE NOTES

1. NASH, G. The Sociology of Phoenix House—A Therapeutic Community for the Resocialization of Narcotic Addicts. Unpublished paper, Columbia University, 1969.
2. NASH, G., WALDORF, D., FOSTER, K., & KYLLINGSTAD, A. The Phoenix House Program: The Results of a Two-Year Follow-Up. Unpublished manuscript, 1971.
3. STEINFELD, G. J., RICE, A., RAUTIO, E. M., & EGAN, M. *The Use of Covert Sensitization with Narcotic Addicts (Further Comments)*. Danbury, Conn.: Federal Correctional Institution, Narcotic Unit, 1973.
4. BOUDIN, H. M. & VALENTINE, V. E. Behavioral Techniques as an Alternative to Methadone Maintenance. Unpublished manuscript, University of Florida, 1973.
5. SAMMONS, R. A. Contingency Management in a Drug Treatment Program. Paper presented at the 1st annual Rocky Mountain Conference on Behavior Modification, Denver, 1972.
6. ROSS, S. M. & JONES, C. G. Contingency contracting with drug abusers. In D. Cannon (Chair.), *Social Skills Training in a Drug Rehabilitation Program*. Symposium presented at the meeting of the American Psychological Association, Montreal, 1973.
7. MONTGOMERY, J. & McBURNEY, R. D. *Operant Conditioning-Token-Economy*. Camarillo, Calif.: Camarillo State Hospital, 1970. (Mimeo.)
8. CALLNER, D. A. The assessment and training of assertive behavior in a drug addict population. In D. Cannon (Chair.), *Social Skills Training in a Drug Rehabilitation Program*. Symposium presented at the meeting of the American Psychological Association, Montreal, 1973.

REFERENCES

ANANT, S. S. Treatment of alcoholics and drug addicts by verbal aversion techniques. *International Journal of the Addictions*, 3:381-388, 1968.
ATTHOWE, J. M., JR. & KRASNER, L. Preliminary report on the application of contingent reinforcement procedures (token economy) on a "chronic" psychiatric ward. *Journal of Abnormal Psychology*, 73:37-43, 1968.
AYLLON, T. & AZRIN, N. H. *The Token Economy*. New York: Appleton-Century-Crofts, 1968.
BANDURA, A. *Principles of Behavior Modification*. New York: Holt, Rinehart & Winston, 1969.
BERNSTEIN, D. A. Modification of smoking behavior: An evaluative review. *Psychological Bulletin*, 71:418-440, 1969.
BLACHLY, P. H. An "electric needle" for aversive conditioning of the needle ritual. *International Journal of the Addictions*, 6:327-328, 1971.

BLAKE, B. G. The application of behavior therapy to treatment of alcoholism. *Behavior Research and Therapy*, 3:75-85, 1965.

BOUDIN, H. M. Contingency contracting as a therapeutic tool in the deceleration of amphetamine use. *Behavior Therapy*, 3:604-608, 1972.

BRECHER, E. M. & EDITORS of *Consumer Reports. Licit and Illicit Drugs*. Mt. Vernon, N. Y.: Consumers Union, 1972.

CAHOON, D. D., CROSBY, C. C. A learning approach to chronic drug use: Sources of reinforcement. *Behavior Therapy*, 3:64-71, 1972.

CAUTELA, J. R. Treatment of compulsive behavior by covert sensitization. *Psychological Record*, 16:33-41, 1966.

CAUTELA, J. R. Covert sensitization. *Psychological Reports*, 20:459-468, 1967.

CAUTELA, J. R. Covert reinforcement. *Behavior Therapy*, 1:33-50, 1970.

CAUTELA, J. R. Covert processes and behavior modification. *Journal of Nervous and Mental Diseases*, 1973, 157, 27-36.

CHAPPEL, J. N., SENAY, E. C., & JAFFE, J. H. Cyclazocine in a multimodality treatment program: Comparative results. *International Journal of the Addictions*, 6:509-523, 1971.

CHEIN, I. Psychological, social, and epidemiological factors in drug addiction. *Rehabilitating the Narcotic Addict*. Washington, D. C.: Vocational Rehabiiltation Administration, 1966.

CHEIN, I., GERARD, L., LEE, S., & ROSENFELD, E. *The Road to H*. New York: Basic Books, 1964.

CLAUSEN, J. A. Social and psychological factors in narcotic addiction. *Law Contemporary Problems*, 22:34-51, 1957.

CROWLEY, T. J. The reinforcers for drug abuse: Why people take drugs. *Comprehensive Psychiatry*, 13:51-62, 1972.

DOLE, V. P. & NYSWANDER, M. A medical treatment for diacetylmorphine (Heroin) addictions. *Journal of the American Medical Association*, 193:646-650, 1965.

DOLE, V. P. & NYSWANDER, M. Rehabilitation of heroin addicts after blockade with methadone. *New York State Journal of Medicine*, 66:2011-2017, 1966.

DOLE, V. P. & NYSWANDER, M. Heroin addiction: A metabolic disease. *Archives of Internal Medicine*, 120:19-24, -967.

EYSENCK, H. J. & RACHMAN, S. *Causes and Cures of Neurosis*. London: Routledge & Kegan Paul, 1965.

FELDMAN, H. W. Ideological supports to becoming and remaining a heroin addict. *Journal of Health and Social Behavior*, 9:131-139, 1968.

FINEMAN, K. R. An operant conditioning program in a detention facility. *Psychological Reports*, 22:1119-1120, 1968.

FINK, M., ZAHS, A. M., & FREEDMAN, A. M. Clinical trial of Cyclazocine in depression. In *Narcotic Anatagonists* (Rep. Ser. 25, No. 1). Washington, D. C.: National Clearinghouse for Drug Information, 1973.

FISCHMANN, V. S. Drug addicts in a therapeutic community. *International Journal of the Addictions*, 3:351-359, 1968.

FORT, J. P. The psychodynamics of drug addiction and group psychotherapy. *International Journal of Group Psychotherapy*, 5:150-156, 1955.

FRANKS, C. M. Alcohol, alcoholism, and conditioning. *Journal of Mental Sciences*, 104:14-33, 1958.

FRANKS, C. M. Behavior therapy, the principles of conditioning and the treatment of the alcoholic. *Quarterly Journal of Studies in Alcoholism*, 25:511-529, 1963.

GLASSCOTE, R. M. *The Treatment of Drug Abuse*. Washington, D. C.: Joint Information Service of the American Psychiatric Association and the National Association for Mental Health, 1971.

GLICKSMAN, M., OTTOMANELLI, G., & CUTLER, R. The earn-your-way credit system: Use of a token economy in narcotic rehabilitation. *International Journal of the Addictions*, 6:525-531, 1971.

GLOVER, G. *On the Early Development of Mind.* New York: International Universities Press, 1956.

GRAFTON, S. (Ed.). *Addiction and Drug Abuse Report*, 2:2, 1971.

HOFFMAN, M. Drug addiction and "hypersexuality": Related modes of mastery. *Comprehensive Psychiatry*, 5:262-270, 1964.

HOMME, L. *How to Use Contingency Contracting in the Classroom.* Champaign, Ill.: Research Press, 1969.

HSU, J. Electroconditioning therapy of alcoholics: A preliminary report. *Quarterly Journal of Studies on Alcohol*, 26:449-459, 1965.

ISBELL, H. Perspectives in research of opiate addiction. In D. M. Wilner & G. G. Kassenbaum, *Narcotics.* New York: McGraw-Hill, 1965.

JAFFE, J. H. Drug addiction and drug abuse. In L .S. Goodman and A. Gilman (Eds.), *The Pharmacological Basis of Therapeutics* (4th ed.). London: Collier-Macmillan, 1970.

JONES, M. *The Therapeutic Community.* New York: Basic Books, 1953.

JONES, M. *Beyond the Therapeutic Community.* New Haven: Yale University Press, 1968.

KNOX, D. *Marriage Happiness.* Champaign, Ill.: Research Press, 1972.

KRAFT, T. Social anxiety and drug addiction. *British Journal of Social Psychiatry*, 1968, 2, 192-195. (a)

KRAFT, T. Successful treatment of a case of Drinamyl addiction. *British Journal of Psychiatry*, 1968, 114, 1363-1364. (b)

KRAFT, T. Successful treatment of a case of chronic barbiturate addiction. *British Journal of the Addictions*, 1969, 64, 115-120. (a)

KRAFT, T. Treatment of Drinamyl addiction. *International Journal of the Addictions*, 1969, 4, 59-64. (b)

KRAFT, T. Successful treatment of "Drinamyl" addicts and associated personality changes. *Canadian Psychiatric Association Journal*, 1970, 15, 223-227. (a)

KRAFT, T. Treatment of Drinamyl addiction. *Journal of Nervous and Mental Disease*, 1970, 150, 138-144. (b)

KRASNEGOR, N. A. & BOUDIN, H. M. Behavior modification and drug addiction: The state of the art. Proceedings of the 81st Annual Convention of the American Psychological Association, 1973, 8, 913-914. (Summary.)

LASKOWITZ, D., WILBUR, M., & ZUCKER, A. Problems in the group treatment of drug addicts in the community: Observations on the formation of a group. *International Journal of the Addictions*, 1968, 3, 361-379.

LENT, J. R. Mimosa Cottage: Experiment in hope. *Psychology Today*, June 1968, 51-58.

LESSER, E. Behavior therapy with a narcotics user: A case report. *Behavior Research and Therapy*, 1967, 5, 251-252.

LEVINE, S. & STEPHENS, R. Games addicts play. *Psychiatric Quarterly*, 1971, 45, 582-592.

LIBERMAN, R. Aversive conditioning of drug addicts: A pilot study. *Behavior Research and Therapy*, 6, 229-231.

LIEBSON, I. & BIGELOW, G. A behavioral-pharmacological treatment of dually addicted patients. *Behavior Research and Therapy*, 1972, 10, 403-405.

LYNCH, J. J., FERTIZER, A. P., TEITELBAUM, H. A., CULLEN, J. W., & GANTT, W. H. Pavlovian conditioning of drug reactions: Some implications for problems of drug addiction. *Conditioned Reflex*, 1973, 9, 1-18.

MacCULLOCH, M. J., FELDMAN, M. P., ORFORD, J. F., & MacCULLOCH, M. L. Anticipatory avoidance learning in the treatment of alcoholism: A record of therapeutic failure. *Behavior Research and Therapy*, 1966, 4, 187-196.

MARSTON, A. R. & McFALL, R. M. Comparisons of behavior modification approaches to smoking reduction. *Journal of Consulting and Clinical Psychology*, 1971, 36, 153-162.

McGUIRE, R. M. & VALLANCE, M. Aversion therapy by electric shock: A simple technique. *British Medical Journal*, 1964, 1, 151-153.

O'BRIEN, J. S. & RAYNES, A. E. Treatment of heroin addiction with behavioral therapy. In W. Keup (Ed.), *Drug Abuse; Current Concepts and Research*. Springfield, Ill.: Charles C Thomas, 1972.

O'BRIEN, J. S., RAYNES, A. E., & PATCH, V. D. An operant reinforcement system to improve ward behavior in in-patient drug addicts. *Journal of Behavior Therapy and Experimental Psychiatry*, 1971, 2, 239-242.

O'BRIEN, J. S., RAYNES, A. E., & PATCH, V. D. Treatment of heroin addiction with aversion therapy, relaxation training, and systematic desensitization. *Behavior Research and Therapy*, 1972, 10, 77-80.

PAUL, G. Outcome of systematic desensitization I. II. In C. Franks (Ed.), *Behavior Therapy; Appraisal and Status*. New York: McGraw-Hill, 1969.

PREBLE, E. & CASEY, J. J., JR. Taking care of business—The heroin user's life in the streets. *International Journal of the Addictions*, 1969, 4, 1-24.

PREMACK, D. Toward empirical behavior laws: I. Positive reinforcement. *Psychological Review*, 1959, 66, 219-233.

RACHMAN, S. Sexual disorders and behavior therapy. *American Journal of Psychiatry*, 1961, 118, 235-240.

RACHMAN, S. Aversion therapy: Chemical or electrical. *Behavior Research and Therapy*, 1965, 2, 289-300.

RACHMAN, S. & TEASDALE, J. *Aversion Therapy and Behavior Disorders*. Coral Gables: University of Miami Press, 1969.

RADO, S. The psychoanalysis of pharmacothymia (drug addiction). *Psychoanalytic Quarterly*, 1933, 2, 1-23.

RAYMOND, M. J. The treatment of addiction by aversion conditioning with apomorphine. *Behavior Research and Therapy*, 1964, 1, 287-291.

SIEGLER, M. & OSMOND, H. Models of drug addiction. *International Journal of the Addictions*, 1968, 3, 3-24.

SPEVACK, M., PIHL, R., & ROWAN, T. Behavior therapies in the treatment of drug abuse: Some case studies. *Psychological Record*, 1973, 23, 179-184.

STEINFELD, G. J. The use of covert sensitization with institutionalized narcotic addicts. *International Journal of the Addictions*, 1970, 5, 225-232.

STEPHENS, R. & LEVINE, S. The "street addict role": Implications for treatment. *Psychiatry*, 1971, 34, 351-357.

STUART, R. B. Behavioral contracting within the families of delinquents. *Journal of Behavior Therapy and Experimental Psychiatry*, 1971, 2, 1-11.

SUTTER, A. G. The world of the righteous dope fiend. *Issues in Criminology*, 1966, 2, 177-222.

THOMSON, I. G. & RATHOD, N. H. Aversion therapy for heroin dependence. *The Lancet*, 1968, 2, 382-384.

TYLER, V. O., JR., & BROWN, G. D. Token reinforcement of academic performance with institutionalized delinquent boys. *Journal of Educational Psychology*, 1968, 59, 164-168.

VOEGTLIN, W. L. & LEMERE, F. The treatment of alcohol addiction: A review of the literature. *Quarterly Journal of Studies on Alcohol*, 1942, 2, 717-803.

WALDORF, D. Social control in therapeutic communities for the treatment of drug addicts. *International Journal of the Addictions*, 1971, 6, 29-43.

WALLERSTEIN, R. S., ET AL. *Hospital Treatment of Alcoholism*. New York: Imago Press, 1957.

WIKLER, A. A psychodynamic study of a patient during self-regulated re-addiction to morphine. *Psychiatric Quarterly*, 1952, 26, 270-293.

WIKLER, A. Conditioning factors in opiate addiction and relapse. In D. M. Wilner and G. G. Kassenbaum (Eds.), *Narcotics*. New York: McGraw-Hill, 1960.

WIKLER, A. Some implications of conditioning theory for problems of drug abuse. *Behavioral Science*, 1971, 16, 92-97.

WIKLER, A. Dynamics of drug dependence. *Archives of General Psychiatry*, 1973, 28, 611-616. (a)

WIKLER, A. Sources of reinforcement for drug-using behavior—A theoretical formulation. In G. Acheson (Ed.), *Pharmacology and the Future of Man; Proceedings of the 5th International Congress on Pharmacology*. Basel: Karger, 1973. (b)

WIKLER, A. & RASOR, R. W. Psychiatric aspects of drug addiction. *American Journal of Medicine*, 1953, 14, 556-570.

WISOCKI, P. A. The successful treatment of a heroin addict by covert conditioning techniques. *Journal of Behavior Therapy and Experimental Psychiatry*, 1973, 4, 55-61.

WOLPE, J. *Psychotherapy by reciprocal inhibition*. Stanford: Stanford University Press, 1958.

WOLPE, J. Conditioned inhibition of craving in drug addiction: A pilot experiment. *Behavior Research and Therapy*, 1965, 2, 285-287.

YABLONSKY, L. *Synanon: The Tunnel Back*. Baltimore: Penguin Books, 1967. (Originally published by Macmillan, 1965, as *The Tunnel Back: Synanon*.

YATES, A. J. *Behavior Therapy*. New York: Wiley, 1970.

Section VI

BEHAVIOR MODIFICATION IN THE HOME AND CLASSROOM

Commentary

Although this section is devoted exclusively to children, the application of behavioral principles and procedures to a variety of children's problems is featured in both reprinted articles and the Commentaries in other Sections of this volume, e.g., the use of modeling and other techniques in fears and phobias (Section II), self-control strategies with disruptive behavior in the classroom (Section III), and clinical case reports of diverse children's disorders (Section X). In the present Section we have focused on the following topics in behavior modification with children: special problems such as hyperactivity, learning disabilities, and seizure disorders; language training in nonverbal psychotic and retarded children; the generalization and maintenance of classroom treatment effects; the theoretical and ethical issues involved in the use of behavioral methods in the schools; the role of mediators in behavior change programs; and behavioral interventions with families of predelinquent and delinquent children.

Hyperactivity (hyperkinesis) is a childhood disorder characterized by overactivity, restlessness, distractibility, and short attention span. A problem that can seriously interfere with a child's academic and social development, the prevalence of hyperactivity in the general population has been estimated as high as 5-10 percent (Wender, 1971). Probably the most common form of treatment for hyperactivity is the use of central stimulant drugs, particularly Ritalin. Although this treatment has been effective in many instances, negative side-effects have also been reported. For example, reduction in both height and weight gain is a possibility.

441

Furthermore, not all children are responsive to the drugs, and some long-term follow-up studies have indicated a poor prognosis for hyperactive children despite drug treatment (Huessey et al., 1973, cited in Rosenbaum, O'Leary, & Jacob, 1975). The conflicting evidence, allied to the increasing ethical concern about chemotherapy with children, has resulted in the critical scrutiny of drug treatment and the search for more acceptable alternative treatments.

Ayllon, Layman, and Kandel's article that is reprinted here describes a behavioral-educational alternative to drug control of hyperactive children. Although their data demonstrate that Ritalin was indeed effective in suppressing hyperactive behavior in the classroom, reading and math performance were not improved and might even have been hindered by the drug administration. The reinforcement program not only controlled hyperactive behavior at a level comparable to that produced by Ritalin, but also enhanced academic performance significantly. A particularly important finding of this study, replicating that of Ayllon and Roberts' (1974) with a less disturbed population, is that deviant behavior can be suppressed and academic growth promoted when academic behaviors are targeted for reinforcement (see below). Ayllon et al.'s results demonstrate that behavioral programs constitute a feasible alternative to drug treatment for hyperactive children. A more definitive statement must await long-term follow-ups of the sort of drug-free intervention developed by Ayllon et al.

An encouraging step in this direction was reported by Rosenbaum et al. (1975), who found that significant treatment-produced decreases in hyperactive behavior in the classroom were maintained at a four week follow-up. Two behavioral programs, each lasting four weeks, were compared: an individual reward condition, which involved a private contract between the teacher and a single child; and a group reward condition, that emphasized participation of the whole class, and in which reward for the class was based on the performance of the single child. Standardized teacher ratings of hyperactivity and weekly ratings of problem behaviors both evidenced a significant treatment effect although the two reinforcement conditions did not differ. Noteworthy is the fact that a posttreatment questionnaire indicated that the teachers significantly preferred the program based on a group reward than the program involving individual reward. Interestingly, this finding was obtained despite the fact that the group reward program required more teacher time. (The pros and cons of group reward programs are discussed below.) The significance of teachers' liking for different interventions is remarked upon by Rosenbaum et al., who point out that popular programs not only have a better chance of being implemented in the first place, but also have a higher probability of success and of being maintained subsequently.

Rosenbaum et al. note that hyperactivity is often poorly defined, with parent and/or teacher reports often considered sufficient criteria for the diagnosis to be made. Accordingly, it should be noted that they were unsuccessful in their attempt to develop an observation code of hyperactivity. They found that it only discriminated between hyperactive and nonhyperactive children "in a classroom involving lack of choice and high demand requirements, unlike the regular classroom of these children" (p 317). On the other hand, Ayllon et al. state that the differences between disruptive and hyperactive behaviors, although similar in response typography, "are well documented." Given the profoundly important consequences that attach to the application of the labels of "hyperactive" and "minimal brain dysfunction," further controlled investigation of this issue appears warranted.

Providing further support for the applicability of reinforcement procedures to the problem of hyperactivity, Alabiso (1975) demonstrated that attention span, focus of attention, and selective attention could be brought under operant control. Alabiso also suggested an eminently sound and constructive means of increasing the generalizability of behavioral improvement in hyperactive children: gradually introduce distracting stimuli during behavioral training to reinforce inhibitory responses to distracting cues. Such a procedure could be thought of as conceptually similar to "stress inoculation" training (cf. Meichenbaum, 1973—in Franks & Wilson, 1973) in which subjects are deliberately prepared to cope successfully with difficult situations in their environment.

Children with learning disabilities have been the subject of much productive behavioral research and practice. In this connection, Lovitt (1975) has provided a detailed but concise review of specific research recommendations and suggestions for practitioners. Among his many valuable pointers for the practitioner, Lovitt emphasizes two factors that he claims should be considered in order to select the best teaching technique for a particular problem. The first is whether the child is unable or reluctant to perform. The second is the difference between the process of acquiring a behavior as opposed to becoming more proficient with a behavior that has already been acquired. With respect to the child who is unable to perform, or who is in the developmental process of acquiring a behavior, Lovitt recommends the use of "noncontingent" techniques. These include "modeling (showing the pupil how to do something); cueing or prompting (showing or telling the pupil a part of what he should do); using mnemonic devices (e.g., the ABC song to remember the alphabet); or using aids (e.g., the abacus)" (p. 48). In the case of the child who is not motivated to perform, Lovitt suggests the use of contingent events that are differentially scheduled to follow the appropriate behavior.

Moreover, in addition to describing the technology of behavior change, Lovitt points to the importance of developmental research in indicating what the relationships are among different academic behaviors. This knowledge could then help to insure that behavioral techniques will be used to teach the appropriate skill at the right developmental time. This interest in the content of behavioral programs is discussed more fully in Section VII below.

The second paper reprinted in this Section, by Zlutnick, Mayville, and Moffat, describes the modification of a clinically significant but relatively novel target behavior in children—seizure disorders. The authors are appropriately cautious about generalizing on the basis of their modest but nonetheless promising results.

This innovative application of behavioral principles is yet another example of the growing role of behavioral science in medicine—an interdisciplinary effort that is being hailed as "behavioral medicine" (cf. Katz & Zlutnick, 1975).

The consistent conceptualization of behaviors such as seizures as the terminal links in a complex behavioral chain would appear to be a particularly productive endeavor. As Zlutnick et al. point out, the predictability they discovered in the antecedent events to a seizure "is as important to its subsequent control as the development of a technology needed to eliminate it." We might also re-emphasize the enduring wisdom that forewarned is forearmed. Children and adults might be equipped with self-regulatory skills that would allow them to control the development of seizures once they have identified the early indicators in the chain that are more amenable to behavior modification. Clinically speaking, we might also note that the knowledge that previously frightening and unpredictable events are now more predictable could significantly reduce the stress secondarily associated with disorders of this nature (cf. Seligman, 1975).

Parenthetically, Zlutnick et al.'s study highlights some of the difficulties inherent in the use of single-subject methodology. Firstly, the authors indicate their sensitivity to the ethical issues involved in the use of a traditional reversal design with a behavior as severe as seizures.

It can well be argued that this is a questionable procedure even if the reversal was a brief probe. The desirability of demonstrating the efficacy of a particular technique must be weighed against any subject risk and/or discomfort, and alternative designs, such as a multiple baseline across subjects might offer some advantage.

A second problem with the reversal design is also illustrated by subject #1 in this study. Number of seizures decreased during the first treatment phase, recovered during the reversal phase, and were eliminated during the second treatment phase. Thus far this is a classic demonstration of the control of seizure behavior by the independent variable—interruptions. But why then did the seizures not reoccur at follow-up, after the removal of the explicit experimental manipulation? This happy combination of the demonstration of a functional relationship between classes of variables during treatment and subsequent disappearance of the problem behavior thereafter has been referred to by Hartmann and Atkinson (1973) as "having your cake and eating it." They discuss the logical and methodological difficulties presented by this sort of outcome—regrettably rare in most applied settings, practitioners insist (see also Franks & Wilson, 1974, pp. 369-371).

The application of reinforcement principles to language training in nonverbal children and adults has been a major area of interest in behavior modification ever since its emergence towards the end of the 1950s as a distinctive model of the etiology and treatment of behavior problems. In her evaluative review article reprinted here, Harris provides a valuable summary of the contemporary status of this aspect of behavior modification. Of special significance is her identification of the main problem areas in this research.

Much of the progress in this field can be directly attributed to the creative use of single-subject methodology. However, the use of a relatively small number of subjects as their own control raises problems for the practitioner about how widely the data can be generalized to the general population of nonverbal children. As Harris points out, the category of "nonverbal" has included very heterogeneous sampling of children with a diverse array of diagnostic labels. Indeed, this was one of the basic reasons for employing own-control designs. Dwarfing all other problems, however, has been the difficulty of producing adequate generalization, a familiar refrain throughout this entire volume. Although there are many facets to this problem, one of the most important strategies will undoubtedly involve the more effective use of reinforcing agents in the children's natural environment to sustain and further develop rudimentary language skills acquired in limited laboratory or institutional settings.

Another informative analysis of language training with severely retarded persons is presented by Snyder, Lovitt, and Smith (1975). They focused on the 23 applied behavior analysis studies published from 1968 to 1973 and which met the fundamental methodological criteria of this approach. They concluded that "it is definitely possible to improve the language skills of severely retarded children and adults through the application of systematic instructional techniques and reinforcement contingencies" (p. 13). The measured caution in this statement contrasts favorably with once overly optimistic pronouncements about the power of operant technology to rehabilitate psychotic and retarded children. In view of Harris' reservations about the generalizability of findings on the basis of a small sample of children, Snyder et al.'s review statistics are of some interest. The 23 studies they covered involved a total of only 64 subjects. Four of the studies of children under eight years of age involved only 9 subjects.

Two other observations should be noted. Firstly, Snyder et al. expressed their surprise that every one of the studies they reviewed used tangible reinforcers. As we discuss below, behavior modification has been criticized for an undue and unfortunate reliance on tangible reinforcers. As in other areas, the skillful selection of social reinforcement or some natural reward might be more effective on several counts, not the least being the significance it might have for improving generalization. Secondly, in line with a broader social learning approach, Snyder et al. recommend the investigation of the effects of different antecedent events on language behavior. "Certainly, in studies of language acquisition, the efficiency of waiting for the subject to emit a desired response, which has not yet been mastered, and reinforcing it, may be questioned. Although most studies have employed antecedent strategies as a 'last resort,' it is hoped that future investigators will focus more direct attention on these antecedent instructional interventions" (p. 14).

The question of the generalization and maintenance of behavior change when token reinforcement is discontinued has been a major topic of discussion in this series, e.g., O'Leary and Drabman (1971—reprinted in Franks & Wilson, 1973) and Drabman, Spitalnik, and O'Leary (1973—reprinted in Franks & Wilson, 1974). It remains the single most important issue in the evaluation of the usefulness of token economy programs in the classroom.

Happily, three well-controlled investigations addressed this issue with different strategies but all with some gratifying success. First, the Turke-witz et al. study that is reprinted in Section III of this volume is a demonstration of the use of self-regulatory procedures for enhancing maintenance. Behavioral improvement was maintained after all back-up reinforcers had been completely withdrawn, albeit for the relatively short period of five days. Second, the paper by Walker, Hops, and John-son that is reprinted here shows how an alternative maintenance strategy produced maintenance of treatment-produced improvement over a four-month period. While Walker et al. are careful to point out that their results cannot be unequivocally attributed to the use of the maintenance strategy per se—it may simply have been the greater duration of inter-vention that Group 1 subjects received—the important finding is that long-term maintenance was produced at all. The tentative nature of the results in experiment 2 limits significant discussion. However, the data strongly suggest the value of assessing behavior broadly across different situations to evaluate the consequences of an intervention program. More broadly, the covariation within behavioral repertoires of children is considered in more detail by Wahler (1975).

Jones and Kazdin (1975) provided the third example of effectively programming response maintenance after eliminating token reinforce-ment in a special classroom for educable retarded children. Following a five-day token program for attentive behavior, tokens were faded out by introducing delayed back-up reinforcement, peer and teacher praise, and a group contingency in which everyone in the class received a reward provided the four target children had been well-behaved. A three-month follow-up after all explicit token, teacher, and peer rein-forcement contingencies had been removed indicated that inattentive behavior remained at an acceptably low level. As the authors remarked in decidedly restrained fashion, "12-week follow-up information on token reinforcement programs after the contingencies have been completely withdrawn is not frequent in the literature" (p. 161). Few would disagree.

In one of the most controversial papers published in the field of behavior modification over the past several years—provocatively entitled *Token Rewards May Lead to Token Learning*—Levine and Fasnacht (1974) emphasized the lack of evidence on generalization and main-tenance of the effects of token reinforcement programs. Moreover, they asserted that specific maintnance strategies merely temporarily prolong the effects of token programs (resistance to extinction), and make be-havioral intervention more complicated and less practical.

In a spirited reply, Ford and Foster (1976) charge that Levine and Fasnacht's consideration of the token economy literature is "oversimplified and inaccurate." They cited the Drabman et al. (1973), Turkewitz et al. (see Section III), and Walker and Buckley (1972—reprinted in Franks & Wilson, 1974) studies to demonstrate that maintenance can be achieved. Disputing the notion that explicit maintenance strategies make behavioral programs too impractical, they acknowledge that "extensive involvement may be required on the part of the change agents." In a rejoinder to Ford and Foster, Levine and Fasnacht (1976) "state flatly that the studies cited as evidence for generalization support no such conclusion." They claim that the Drabman et al. (1973) and Turkewitz et al. (Section III) studies were too short (12 and 5 days respectively) to allow meaningful conclusions to be drawn, and suggest that Cone's (1973) reanalysis of the Walker and Buckley (1972) findings (see Franks & Wilson, 1974, pp. 215-216) limits their significance.

Certainly Levine and Fasnacht (1974) are correct in emphasizing the brief follow-ups in the Drabman et al. and Turkewitz et al. studies, although Cone's (1973) reanalysis does not necessarily mean that Walker and Buckley (1972) failed to demonstrate effective maintenance over a three-month period. And, subsequent to this debate, the Walker et al. study reprinted here and Jones and Kazdin (1975) have provided additional, more compelling evidence that generalization and maintenance can be effected following the withdrawal of reinforcement programs.

Most fiercely contested has been Levine and Fasnacht's (1974) thesis that "because of the danger that use of tokens will decrease the intrinsic satisfaction of activities, they should be avoided unless there is a real danger to the person or there is no alternative" (p. 820). This statement was based on a series of studies (cf. Lepper, Greene, & Nisbett, 1973) purportedly demonstrating that external rewards can undermine intrinsic interest in the rewarded activity. Lepper et al. (1973) interpreted these findings as supporting one implication of attribution theory—the overjustification hypothesis. This hypothesis predicts that if a person engages in a behavior to obtain a reward, he/she will infer that the behavior is determined by the reward and his/her interest in that behavior will decrease when external reward is no longer available. There are two major issues here: firstly, the validity of the overjustification hypothesis; and secondly, the implications for token economy programs of the studies on this issue. Both have been the focus of lively debates in two prominent journals, *American Psychologist* (Bornstein & Hamilton, 1975; Ford & Foster, 1976; Levine & Fasnacht, 1976; Reiss & Sushinsky, 1975a) and

Journal of Personality and Social Psychology (Lepper & Greene, 1976; Reiss & Sushinsky, 1975b, 1976).

With respect to the overjustification hypothesis per se, Feingold and Mahoney (1975) have criticized the internal validity of some of the studies supporting the overjustification hypothesis. They point out problems with reliability assessment in Lepper et al. (1973) and unmatched control groups in Deci (1971). Reiss and Sushinsky (1975a, 1975b, 1976) have offered an alternative interpretation to Lepper et al.'s (1973) attribution analysis. They have argued that decreased intrinsic motivation following extrinsic reward can be easily explained in terms of competing responses elicited by distraction and/or frustration. Feingold and Mahoney (1975) also suggest that Lepper et al.'s (1973) procedure can be reinterpreted as a successive discrimination between reinforcement schedules. This would account for Lepper et al.'s (1973) finding that only the subjects in the Expected Reward condition showed the post-treatment performance decrement below pretreatment level when reward was withdrawn (i.e., the operational definition of intrinsic interest in these studies). Subjects in the Unexpected Reward condition did not show this effect; if anything they showed a slight increase in pre-post performance. As Feingold and Mahoney (1975) point out, the overjustification hypothesis would have predicted decrements in both Expected and Unexpected Reward conditions.

In trying to summarize the conflicting data and theoretical disputes in this continuing controversy—the final word is far from in—it appears that a negative effect of extrinsic reward on subsequent intrinsic interest can be demonstrated, although no theory can as yet adequately account for all results, or, more importantly, reliably predict the conditions under which this effect will occur. Specific characteristics of the nature of the reward employed (e.g., expected or not expected; salient versus non-salient rewards, Ross [1975]; social versus tangible rewards, Deci [1971]; Smith [1974]); of the subjects; and of the task might all play a role in determining the effect.

It is in reference to the implications of the laboratory studies on the overjustification hypothesis for token reinforcement programs in the classroom that the criticism of Levine and Fasnacht's (1974) position is compelling. As all the critics have stressed, the procedures employed in these studies differ significantly from conditions involved in token economies. As summarized by Reiss and Sushinsky (1975a) the overjustification studies elicited a behavior and provided only one trial or one session reward that was *noncontingent* on quality of performance.

"By contrast, token economies provide *multiple trials of both reward and nonreward,* dispense *reward contingent on quality performances,* and *are designed to explicitly teach behaviors*" (p. 783). In a study explicitly designed to represent more accurately conditions that hold in token reinforcement programs in the classroom, Feingold and Mahoney (1975) found no evidence of a decrease in intrinsic motivation. On the contrary, they showed an increase in performance from pretreatment to posttreatment baseline (operant level) performance. This outcome is consistent with the fact that token economies that have included follow-up data typically report that when treatment-produced behavioral improvement decreased after the abrupt withdrawal of tokens, behavior did *not* deteriorate to a level worse than pretreatment baseline as Levine and Fasnacht's (1974) argument would imply.

A little common sense helps to put the limits of the overjustification hypothesis in perspective. As we write our books for the pure enjoyment of it ("intrinsic interest") we simultaneously look forward to the social and financial fruits ("extrinsic reward")—regrettably not always to be relied upon!—that they may bring. Speaking for all academics that we know, at least in New Jersey, Reiss and Sushinsky (1975a) state that "We reject the position of some of our state legislators that because our jobs are so enjoyable we should not expect higher pay, and we consider a pay raise appropriate and more likely to bring us good than harm" (p. 783).

In the ultimate analysis, however, the fundamental limitation of the Levine and Fasnacht (1974) position is that it is predicated on external reward of high frequency behaviors that are intrinsically reinforcing. Ideally, of course, token reinforcement would not be used in such instances. As the general behavioral literature and both O'Leary, Poulos, and Devine (1972—reprinted in Franks & Wilson, 1973) and May, Risley, Twardosz, Friedman, Bijou, Wexler, et al. (1975) in particular make clear, token reinforcement should be used only when necessary and there are no better alternatives. Token economies should be employed only after simpler strategies such as "praise and ignore" practices have failed to change behavior. When token reinforcement is used to strengthen behavior, the system should be gradually eliminated as social reinforcement and various forms of intrinsic reinforcement become effective consequences so that behavior change generalizes to the natural environment. (There is little doubt that Levine and Fasnacht would agree with this position; the earlier quote from their 1974 article confirms this, and validates Borstein and Hamilton's [1975] complaint about straw men.)

Although they appear to have chosen a partly inaccurate and unnecessarily provocative means of doing so, Levine and Fasnacht (1974)—as their critics concede—are correct in cautioning against the "promiscuous use" of token reinforcement. Undoubtedly abuses have occurred. For example, despite the theoretical and practical importance of fading out tangible reinforcers as quickly as possible, it is clear that this has not always been the case in behavioral programs. In their most recent review of the token reinforcement literature, O'Leary and O'Leary (1976) note the trend towards more frequent use of natural reinforcers and less frequent use of tangible rewards since 1970. Specifically, twice as many programs employed natural rather than tangible rewards regardless of whether the target behavior was academic or social. These findings are consistent with Wexler's (1973) observation that the earlier token economies often unnecessarily resorted to the use of more severe, artifical reinforcers where more desirable methods might have sufficed.

In sum, criticisms of Levine and Fasnacht's (1974) paper have not argued that token economies cannot produce adverse consequences, but that negative effects are improbable in a well-conceived, well-executed program that receives quality-control monitoring. The real issue is whether one makes hyperbolic pronouncements about potential dangers or acts constructively to reduce the probability of their occurrence.

Two other potential disadvantages of using tangible reinforcers in behavior modification in the classroom have been addressed this past year. The concern has been expressed that token reinforcement applied selectively to a few target children in a class might have negative effects on other, nontarget children. More specifically, will the latter children feel deprived, or perhaps behave badly themselves to obtain reinforcers? O'Leary et al. (1972) suggested strategies for coping with this problem should it arise. Perhaps more importantly, Christy (1975) has recently demonstrated that the use of tangible reinforcers with target children in a preschool setting resulted in behavioral improvement in unrewarded peer observers.

Another concern has involved the use of group contingencies in the classroom. Different procedures have been included under this rubric, and evaluative reviews by Litow and Pumroy (1975), McLaughlin (1974), and O'Leary and O'Leary (1976) are extremely timely in drawing distinctions between various procedures and analyzing their positive and negative features. Basically there appear to be two types: one in which reward for everyone is made contingent upon the performance of the entire class, or whole group; the other in which group reward depends on the behavior of one or two target children. As a whole, group reward contingencies have been shown to be as effective—in some instances more effective—than individual reward contingent on individual performance. However, ethical concern over the use of group contingencies is warranted.

One of the questions the behavioral psychologist must consider is whether serving the individual child's (or a minority of children's) interests will be contrary to the interests of others (often the majority) in the classroom. Group contingency problems have been criticized for improperly and unfairly using non-problem children to influence the behavior of problem children. There is a very real possibility that group contingencies may be detrimental to positive interpersonal relations among the children. Axelrod (1973), for example, found that a group contingency resulted in peer group pressure (in the form of verbal threats) which itself was a source of classroom disruption. Similarly, both Harris and Sherman (1973), and Packard (1970—cited in McLaughlin, 1974) reported pupil harassment in group contingency programs. O'Leary and Drabman (1971), in cautioning about the use of group-oriented contingencies, rightly point out the danger that one or two children might find it reinforcing to "subvert the program or 'beat the system'" (p. 390). And if the target child is unable to perform the requisite criterion behavior, that child will be placed under unfair and potentially damaging self and social pressure.

Another reason for concern is that Drabman, Spitalnik, and Spitalnik (1974) demonstrated that a group contingency token program in which group reward was determined by the behavior of a single, randomly chosen child required least teacher time and was the teacher's preferred method over individual contingencies and other group-oriented programs. As token programs can be abused in the interests of making the teacher's or the school's task easier (rather than the child's experience more productive), the use of group contingency procedures merits close supervision and evaluation. However, Rosenbaum et al.'s (1975) data discussed earlier in this Section showed that their teachers preferred the group contingency program even though it required more time and effort. On the other hand, practical considerations are important, and the behavioral literature has emphasized that individually scheduled contingencies for different children are often impractical if not impossible (e.g., Bushnell, Wrobel, & Michaelis, 1968). It may be possible to use group contingency procedures to achieve worthy goals without adverse side-effects. At the very least, however, their use must be explicitly monitored with a view to these potential side-effects.

In addition, Martin (1972) has questioned the legality of group contingency programs. Contending that group pressure might interfere with the "psychological well-being" of a student, Martin suggests that the fifth and fourteenth amendment clauses about the right to *life, liberty,* and *property* can be construed to imply the right to "psychological integrity." He makes the point that while the behavioral psychologist is responsible for the consequences of a group contingency program, he/she cannot control precisely the level of pressure exerted by other children in the class. Martin (1972) recommends that this procedure be used only in "severe situations where traditional methods fail and where the teacher makes special efforts to control the severity of the pressure" (p. 57).

With increasingly publicized reports of abuses of behavior modification in institutional settings, there has been a serious attempt to delineate some set of guidelines for the selection and application of behavioral procedures that would safeguard the human rights of patients and protect the integrity of the practitioner. One such set of guidelines for the use of behavioral procedures with retarded persons in institutions in Florida was prepared by May et al. (1975).

Categorizing different techniques according to whether they strengthen or weaken behavior, these guidelines embody the hierarchical principle in which initial treatment procedures are those which are the least intrusive and restrictive, the most benign, practical and economical (in the long run) in implementation, but yet optimally effective. According to May et al. (1975), progressing to more intrusive and restrictive techniques is justified only when simpler methods have been shown to be ineffective (e.g., supplementing "praise and ignore" actions with token programs involving tangible reinforcers). Similarly, May et al. advocate recourse to procedures designed to weaken behavior only where necessary, i.e., in those cases where reinforcement of positive alternative behaviors have failed to overcome a problem which interferes with the child's (or other children's) educational progress. Again, with procedures aimed at weakening behavior, as with those used to strengthen behavior, there is a definite hierarchy of interventions (e.g., soft reprimands would be used before overcorrection, which in turn might precede seclusion timeout).

This is an ethical position consistent with the "least restrictive conditions" rationale which has been upheld legally (see Wexler, 1973). There is, however, little empirical evidence on the subject. The point has been

made that sequencing intervention strategies in the manner suggested
by May et al. might, under some circumstances, undermine the ultimate
efficacy of the program. For example, O'Leary, Becker, Evans, and Saudargas (1969) introduced rules, structure, and praise and ignore as treatment components prior to instituting a token economy. Disruptive
behavior was reduced only during the token economy. The question
is whether an earlier introduction of the token program might not
have produced more efficient and effective behavior change. Although
controlled comparisons were not made, O'Leary anecdotally reports
his impression that the token economy which was eventually introduced
in the O'Leary et al. (1969) study resulted in less behavior change than
previous studies with similar populations in which token programs were
introduced earlier in the treatment. Irrespective of the accuracy of this
speculation, this example serves to point out the potential adverse
effects of inflexibly sequencing intervention strategies from the least
severe to the most severe. Future research might clarify the question
about the possibility of diminished effectiveness of behavioral treatment
techniques applied in this fashion, but the ethical issue remains. Possibly
the most realistic alternative is that the behavioral psychologist be
mindful of the May et al. guidelines but retain the flexibility to introduce some of the more restrictive methods without first determining the
effects of less restrictive as competent professional judgment dictates.

Training non-professionals to apply behavioral principles in real
world settings beyond the therapist's office and the laboratory has become an integral feature of behavior therapy. This recognition that
parents, for example, are not only useful but also the preferred behavior
change agents for their children ranks as one of the most significant
developments in the field. The use of non-professionals is best understood in terms of Tharp and Wetzel's (1969) triadic model—the professional consultant acting through a natural mediator to produce changes
in the behavior of a third person. Mediators are important because they
have the most contact with the individual for whom they also control
powerful natural reinforcers.

Parents have been widely used as behavioral mediators. However,
behavior therapy is not the only approach that has attempted to involve
parents in the therapeutic process. Tavormina (1974) has reviewed the
behavioral model and what he calls the reflective model of parental
intervention. An example of the latter would be Guerney's (1964) filial
therapy in which parents are taught to conduct client-centered play
therapy with their own children. The goal of this operation is the

traditional one, viz., to allow the child to "work through" underlying problems via the parents' empathic and accepting understanding. Although controlled outcome evaluations are lacking, there are several positive clinical reports of the use of methods based on the reflective model of parental counseling. Tavormina found only one comparative outcome study between the behavioral and reflective models, which indicated roughly equivalent results. He calls for further comparative and cost efficiency studies.

There are now numerous reports of training parents as therapists, and research has documented behavior change following these interventions. Gordon and Kogan (1975) have concentrated on the interactional process between the mother-child dyad during behavioral training using the bug-in-the-ear device. They concluded that the critical component of the intervention procedure has not yet been specified. For example, they state that suggestions made to mothers prior to the specific training may have been more important than the instructions they were given during the bug-in-the-ear practice sessions.

Aside from parents, teachers, psychiatric nurses, elementary school children, and even learning-disabled children have been employed as behavioral mediators. For example, McLaughlin and Malaby (1975) reported how elementary school children served as self-observers, as proctors in Keller-type programs, and even as experimenters in simple behavioral experiments. Yet another addition to these ranks has been described by Cash and Evans (1975) who trained pre-school children to modify their retarded siblings' behavior. A brief modeling film was used to establish instructional skills such as prompting, modeling, and appropriate use of reward, although no attempt was made to demonstrate that the acquisition of these skills by the preschoolers significantly benefitted their retarded siblings.

The use of children to modify the behavior of other children is theoretically consistent with the social learning approach to behavior change. The modeling literature, for example, shows that certain models are more influential than others, and one of the factors that determines differential efficacy may be model similarity. For instance Kornhaber and Schroeder (1975) found that peer group models were significantly more effective than adult models in reducing behavioral inhibitions in snake fearful children (see Commentary to Section II). In view of these findings, the findings of Coates and Pusser's (1975) social learning analysis of the contents of two of the most popular television programs for children in the U.S.A. are surprising. The data showed that most of the reinforcing consequences in "Sesame Street" and "Mister Rogers" were delivered by adults rather than children. The authors comment on this departure from social learning principles and suggest how similar programs could be improved by closer adherence to empirical findings.

One of the presumed advantages of training parents to treat a problem child is that this facilitates generalization. This would suggest that the actions of the siblings of the treated child might also be influenced by parent-training programs. The fifth paper reprinted in this Section, by Arnold, Levine, and Patterson, is an analysis of changes in the behavior of the siblings of 27 predelinquents who were treated at the Oregon Research Institute. Patterson (1974) has previously described a 12-month follow-up of the results obtained with the treated youngsters, concluding that the treatment program had produced significantly reduced deviant behavior in both the home and classroom. As we discussed in last year's volume (Franks & Wilson, 1975, pp. 435-437), Kent (1976), in a methodological critique of this study, took issue with Patterson's (1974) claim that maintenance of treatment effects at 12 months had been demonstrated. In a rejoinder to Kent (1976), Reid and Patterson (1976) provided additional reanalyses of the original results, contending that Kent's analysis of the data was highly selective. Although the methodological issues raised in this dialogue should be taken into consideration in appraising Arnold et al.'s paper, their emphasis on the first six months of the follow-up period makes the discussion of persistence of their long-term data less pertinent to the present study.

Of major importance is the finding that the child who was referred for treatment was not significantly more deviant than his siblings. For the several reasons Arnold et al. discuss, this strongly indicates that the family and not just the individual predelinquent child should be the focus of behavioral intervention. An analysis of the process whereby one particular family member is labeled deviant would also be important. This process may not be as "capricious" as Arnold et al. presume.

The final paper in this Section is an analysis of the efficacy of contingency contracting with families of delinquent adolescents by Weathers and Liberman. Their conclusion, that contingency contracting is ineffective in the short-term treatment of delinquents, is sobering. Although Alexander and Parsons (1973—reprinted in Franks & Wilson, 1974) reported favorable results using a multifaceted behavior intervention program, Weathers and Liberman argue that the study was methodologically flawed, and cite other research that is less favorable to behavior therapy. The factor of overriding importance seems to be the resources within the family, and beyond that, the community with which the therapist can work. In the absence of at least some still undetermined resources of this nature, Weathers and Liberman point out that "the introduction of a contingency contract is worth about as much as the paper it's written on." They pessimistically observe that progress in helping families of the sort they describe will hinge on "massive intervention that is currently not ethically acceptable or financially supportable by society." This emphasis on community reorganization for dealing with problems such as delinquency is reiterated in Sections VII, VIII, and IX in this volume.

The Weathers and Liberman study has already begun to have a practical impact upon the design and implementation of community intervention programs, especially with less involved families. However, Blechman-Beck (in press, 1976) sounds a note of caution against both broad and overly hasty generalization from this study and premature rejection or even disparagement of the contractual approach to family intervention. Her point, open to debate, is that Weathers and Liberman neglect four crucial conditions necessary to maximizing success with the contractual approach. Therapeutic praise for successful compliance is valued by family members; in the Weather and Liberman study the family had little chance to value the therapists' opinions. Adolescents regard contracting as a method of increasing their power in parent-adolescent interactions; in the Weathers and Liberman study, contracts were written to change adolescents' but not parents' undesirable behavior. Family members feel pride when contracts succeed; in the Weathers and Liberman study, no such reinforcer was built in. Family members learn strategies which they apply to new family problems; Weather and Liberman's brief focused procedures made no attempt to shape such skills. When contractual approaches to family intervention do take cognizance of these conditions, results—at least short-term—appear to be highly favorable (e.g., Alexander & Parsons, 1973; Blechman, Olson & Hellman, 1976) see also, Commentary, Section VIII).

19

A BEHAVIORAL-EDUCATIONAL ALTERNATIVE TO DRUG CONTROL OF HYPER-ACTIVE CHILDREN

Teodoro Ayllon, Dale Layman

and Henry J. Kandel

Georgia State University
and
University of Illinois at Chicago Circle

A behavioral procedure for controlling hyperactivity without inhibiting academic performance is described. Using a time-sample observational method, the hyperactivity displayed by three school children was recorded during math and reading classes. Concurrently, math and reading performances were measured. The study consisted of two baselines, one while the children were on medication and the second while they were off medication. A multiple-baseline design across the two academic subject matters was used to assess the behavioral intervention, which consisted of token reinforcement for correct academic responses in math and

Reprinted from the *Journal of Applied Behavior Analysis*, 1975, 8, 137-146. Copyright 1975, the Society for the Experimental Analysis of Behavior, Inc.

The cooperative spirit of the parents and teachers of the children in this study is gratefully acknowledged. Special thanks go to Dr. E. Ensminger for his unflagging interest and encouragement.

subsequently math and reading. Discontinuation of medication resulted in a gross increase in hyperactivity from 20 percent to about 80 percent, and a slight increase in math and reading performance. Introduction of a behavioral program for academic performance, during no medication, controlled the children's hyperactivity at a level comparable to that when they were on drugs (about 20 percent). At the same time, math and reading performance for the group jumped from about 12 percent during baseline to a level of over 85 percent correct. Each child performed behaviorally and academically in an optimal manner without medication. Contingency management techniques provided a feasible alternative to medication for controlling hyperactivity in the classroom while enabling the children to grow academically.

Descriptors: drug therapy, hyperactivity, classroom behavior, academic behavior, emotionally disturbed, multiple baseline, token economy

Hyperactivity or hyperkinesis in the classroom is a clinical condition characterized by excessive movement, unpredictable behaviors, unawareness of consequences, inability to focus on and concentrate on a particular task, and poor academic performance (Stewart, Pitts, Craig, & Dieruf, 1966). It is estimated that about 200,000 children in the United States are currently receiving amphetamines to control their hyperactivity (Krippner, Silverman, Cavallo, & Healy, 1973).

Drugs such as methylphenidate (Ritalin) and chlorpromazine have been shown to control hyperactivity in the laboratory and applied settings. The evidence from the laboratory is based on recording devices actuated by the child's movements (Hollis & St. Omer, 1972; Sprague, Barnes, & Werry, 1970; Sykes, Douglas, Weiss, & Minde, 1971). In the classroom, children have been rated by their teachers along various dimensions to determine the effectiveness of stimulants on their behavior. Comly (1971) found that of 40 hyperactive children, whose behavior was rated twice weekly by teachers, those children receiving stimulants were rated as having better listening ability, less excitability, less forgetfulness, and better peer relationships. In a similar study, Denhoff, Davis, and Hawkins (1971) showed that teachers rated hyperactive children on dextro-amphetamine (Dexedrine) as improved on measures of hyperactivity, short attention span, and impulsivity. In addition, global ratings by parents, teachers, and clinicians have shown that drugs such as methylphenidate (Ritalin) and dextro-amphetamine decreased children's hyperactivity in school and at home (Conners, 1971).

While there is still some conflicting evidence on drug effectiveness (Krippner et al., 1973), as well as a growing ethical concern for the morality and wisdom implied in administering medication to children (Fish, 1971; Hentoff, 1970; Koegh, 1971; Ladd, 1970) drugs are commonly used to control hyperactivity in the classroom.

Because the often-implied objective behind the use of drugs for the hyperactive child is that of enabling him to profit academically, it is surprising that few data directly support this belief. Most studies have measured the effect of medication on component skills of learning, e.g., attention, concentration, and discrimination. For example, Conners and Rothschild (1968), Epstein, Lasagna, Conners, Rodriquez (1968), Knights and Hinton (1968) tested drug effects on general intelligence test performance. Sprague et al. (1970) studied children's responses of "same" or "different" to pairs of visual stimuli presented on a screen. Conners, Eisenberg, and Sharpe (1964) studied the effects of methylphenidate (Ritalin) on paired-associate learning and Porteus Maze performance in children with hyperactive symptoms. Others (Conners, Eisenberg, & Barcai, 1967; Sprague & Toppe, 1966), concentrated their efforts on the effects of drugs on the attention of hyperactive children to various tasks. These laboratory studies investigated the effects of drugs on component skills related to learning, but they did not measure academic performance per se (e.g., math and reading) in the classroom.

Sulzbacher (1972) experimentally analyzed the effects of drugs on academic behaviors of hyperactive children in the classroom. Measures of correct solutions and error rates were taken in arithmetic, writing, and reading in three hyperactive children. In addition, measures were taken of the children's rates of talk-outs in class and their rates of out-of-seat behavior during class. The children were successively given a placebo, then 5 mg. of dextro-amphetamine (Dexedrine), and finally 10 mg. of dextro-amphetamine. The results showed that medication of 5 mg. improved the children's academic responses; however, there was wide variance in academic performance when the children were administered 10 mg. The results for social behavior also varied. Of two children, one showed less hyperactive classroom behavior (talk-outs and out-of-seat behavior) at a dosage level different than the second child. However, the placebo had more effect on controlling the third child's behavior than did medication. The author's conclusion was that stimulant drugs "can effectively modify disruptive behaviors without adversely affecting academic performance in the classroom." Drug effects on academic performance, however, were highly variable.

Since Sulzbacher's major interest was in determining the role of drugs on hyperactivity and academic performance, he did not pursue behavioral alternatives to the control of hyperactivity. Yet, there is at present, a body of established findings indicating that such alternatives may be available. For example, O'Leary and Becker (1967) found that when children were rewarded for sitting, making eye contact with the teacher, and engaging in academically related activities, their misbehavior was virtually eliminated. Ayllon, Layman, and Burke (1972) showed that misbehavior may be also reduced, not by rewarding the child for good conduct, but by imposing academic structure in the classroom. This structure involved giving academic assignments with a short time limit for their completion. Ayllon and Roberts (1974) found that another behavioral technique to eliminate classroom misbehavior is to reward children for academic performance only. These findings suggest that disruptive behavior can be weakened by reinforcing incompatible academic performance. Using this method, the child performs well both academically and socially without treating the disruptive behavior directly.

The children in the above studies were disruptive, not hyperactive. Although the topography of the response is similar, hyperactivity differs from disruption in its magnitude, duration, and frequency. Illustrations of this difference are well documented, indicating that hyperactive children are in constant motion, fidget excessively, frequently enter and leave the classroom, move from one class activity to another and rarely complete their projects or stay with one particular game or activity. Their academic performance is typically poor (Campbell, Douglas, Morgenstern, 1971; Freibergs & Douglas, 1969; Stewart, Pitts, Craig, & Dieruf, 1966; Sykes, Douglas, Weiss, & Minde, 1971).

Two questions arise:

Can behavioral techniques used to decrease disruptive behavior be at least as effective as drugs in controlling an extreme form of classroom misbehavior such as hyperactivity? At the same time, can such techniques help the hyperactive child to grow educationally? The present study attempted to answer these questions.

METHOD

Subjects and Setting

Three school children (Crystal, Paul, and Dudley) clinically diagnosed as chronically hyperactive, were all receiving drugs to control their hyperactivity.

Crystal was an 8-year-old girl. She was 47 inches (118 cm) tall and weighed 76 lb (34.2 kg). She had an I.Q. of 118 as measured on the WISC. She was enrolled in a learning-disability class because of the hyperactive behavior she displayed before taking medication and because of her poor academic work. She had been on drugs since she was 5 years old, when her doctor felt that her behavior was so unpredictable that he prescribed 5 mg of Methylphenidate q.i.d. to calm her down.

Paul was a 9-year-old boy. He was 53 in. (133 cm) tall and weighed 65 lb (29.2 kg). He had an I.Q. of 94 as measured on the WISC. He had been enrolled in the learning-disabilities class for 2 years before the study and had been taking 5 mg of methylphenidate b.i.d. for 1 year to control his hyperactive behavior.

Dudley was a 10-year-old boy. He was 55 inches (138 cm) tall and weighed 76 lb (34.2 kg). He had an I.Q. of 103 as measured on the WISC. He was enrolled in a learning-disabilities class for 2 years before the study and on the advice of his doctor had been taking 5 mg of methylphenidate t.i.d. for 4 years.

In addition to their drug treatment, Crystal and Dudley were under the care of a child psychiatrist and a pediatrician during the study.

The three children attended a private elementary school. They were enrolled in a self-contained learning disability class of 10 children and one teacher. The children and the teacher remained together throughout the school day in the same room. Other personnel during the study consisted of two observer-recorders: one of the authors and an undergraduate student.

Response Definition

Hyperactivity and academic performance across two academic periods, math and reading, were measured.

Math. Math was defined as addition of whole numbers under 10. The teacher wrote 10 problems on the board at the beginning of each class. The children were given 10 minutes to complete the problems. Problems were taken from Laidlaw Series Workbooks, Levels P and 1.

Reading. Reading was defined as comprehension and was measured by workbook responses to previously read stories in a basal reader. Each child had 20 minutes to complete a 10-question workbook page per day. The books were Merril-Linguistic Readers—3. In both math and reading, the written response served as a permanent product from which the percentage of correct answers could be determined.

The academic assignments in both math and reading increased slightly in difficulty as the child progressed through the work.

Hyperactivity. Since hyperactive behavior has overlapping topographical properties with other deviant behaviors, hyperactive behavior was defined using the same response definition as presented by Becker, Madsen, Arnold, and Thomas for deviant behavior in the classroom (1967). To define and record deviant behavior, Becker and his colleagues used seven general categories of behavior incompatible with learning. These included gross motor behaviors, disruptive noise with objects, disturbing others, orienting responses, blurting out, talking, and other miscellaneous behaviors incompatible with learning. In the present experiment, the behaviors of the hyperactive children most often fell into the following four categories: gross motor behaviors, disruptive noise, disturbing others, and blurting out. The most frequently recorded category for these hyperactive children was gross motor behaviors, which included running around the room, rocking in chairs, and jumping on one or both feet. Disruptive noise with objects included the constant turning of book pages and the excessive flipping of notebook paper. Disturbing others and blurting out included the constant movement of arms, resulting in the destruction of objects and hitting others, screaming, and high-pitched and rapid speech. Categories that were not recorded with any consistency included orienting responses and talking, as in a conversation with another person. Thus, although the response definition for deviant behavior was used, the actual recording was heavily weighted on those behaviors described by Stewart et al. (1966) as being typical of hyperactive children.

Observational and recording procedure for hyperactivity. Initially, six children were identified by the school director as being hyperactive and receiving medication for it. These children were observed across two class periods: math and reading. The duration of each class period was 45 minutes. Each child was observed in successive order on a time-sample of 25 seconds. At the end of each 25-second interval, the behavior of the child under observation was coded as showing hyperactivity or its absence. At that time, the observer marked a single slash in the appropriate interval, on a recording sheet, if one or more hyperactive behaviors occurred. If no hyperactive behaviors were observed at that time, the appropriate interval was marked with an "O". The number of intervals of hyperactivity over the total number of intervals for each child gave the observer the percent of intervals in which each child was hyperactive. Each of the six children was observed a total of 17 times per 45-minute class period. Using this recording procedure, it was possible to determine, during baseline, that the most chronically hyperactive children were Crystal, Paul, and Dudley. By dropping observations on the less-severely hyperactive children it was possible to increase the number of observations for the chronically hyperactive ones. Recording hyperactivity from one child to the next was now sampled about every 18 seconds in the manner described above. Each child was now observed approximately 50 times each class period throughout the remaining phases of the experiment.

Observer agreement on academic performance and hyperactivity. The percentage of correct math and reading problems was checked by the teacher and one of the authors each day and the obtained agreement score was 100 percent on each occasion for each child.

Reliability checks for hyperactivity were taken by one of the authors and one of three undergraduate students in Special Education. The student was given the list of deviant behaviors described by Becker et al. (1967) one day before the reliability check to become familiar with the responses. The students were not told of the purpose of the study or of the changes in experimental conditions. Each observer during the reliability check used a watch with a sweep second hand. In addition, a prepared sheet showed the observers the sequence in which the children were being sampled and the intervals at the end of which each observer was to look at the subject and record whether or not the behavior was occurring at that instant. Each observer sat on opposite sides of the room to ensure unbiased observations.

The percentage of agreement for hyperactive as well as nonhyperactive behavior was calculated by comparing each interval and dividing agreements in each by the total number of observations and multiplying by 100. Reliability checks were taken to include the baseline period under medication (Blocks 2, 3, 5, and 6; in Figures 1, 2, and 3), the period when medication was discontinued and no reinforcement was available (Blocks 7 and 9), and the final period when reinforcement was introduced in both math and reading (Block 11). Reliability scores for hyperactivity for each child were always more than 85 percent, with the scores ranging from a low of 87 percent to a high of 100 percent. The average reliability score was 97 percent.

Check-point system and back-up reinforcers. A token reinforcement system similar to that used by O'Leary and Becker (1957) in a classroom setting was used. Children were awarded checks by the teacher on an index card. One check was recorded for each correct academic response. The checks could be exchanged for a large array of back-up reinforcers later in the day. The back-up reinforcers ranged in price from one check to 75 checks, and included such items and activities as candy, school supplies, free time, lunch in the teacher's room, and picnics in the park.

Procedure

Each subject's daily level of hyperactivity and academic achievement, on and off medication, were directly observed and recorded before the behavioral program. In addition, using a multiple-baseline design, the relative effectiveness of the motivational system on (a) hyperactivity and (b) academic performance, in math and reading was evaluated. This type of design allowed each child to serve as his own control, thereby minimizing the idiosyncratic drug-behavior interactions that have the potential for confounding the interpretations and even the results when comparing one subject with another. This design is particularly useful in the study of the effects of discounting drugs on behavior, since as Sprague et al. (1970) and Sulzbacher (1972) have pointed out, the inherent problems in assessing effects of medication lies in the fact that each child reacts to the presence or absence of medication on an individual basis.

The design of the study included the following four phases:

Phase 1: *on medication.* Crystal, Paul, and Dudley were observed for 17 days to evaluate hyperactive behavior when they were taking drugs. Academic performance in math and reading was also measured.

With the full cooperation of the children's doctors and their parents, medication was discontinued on the eighteenth day, a Saturday. An additional two days, Sunday and Monday (a school holiday) allowed a three-day "wash-out" period for the effect of medication to disappear. It is known that these stimulant drugs are almost completely metabolized within one day. No measures of hyperactivity or academic performance were obtained during this weekend period.

Phase 2: *off medication.* Following the three-day "wash-out" period, a three-day baseline when the children were off medication was obtained. Time-sampling observations of hyperactivity were continued, as well as measures of academic performance. This phase served as the basis against which the effects of reinforcement on hyperactivity and academic performance could later be compared.

Phase 3: *no medication; reinforcement of math.* During this six-day period, the children remained off drugs while the teacher introduced a reinforcement system for math performance only. Observations of hyperactivity continued and academic performance was measured.

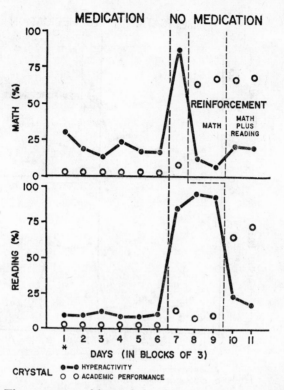

Fig. 1. Crystal. The percentage of intervals in which hyperactivity took place and the percent of correct math and reading performance. The first and second segments respectively show the effects of medication, and its subsequent withdrawal, on hyperactivity and academic performance. A multiple-baseline analysis of the effects of reinforcement across math and reading and concurrent hyperactivity is shown starting on the third top segment. The last segment shows the effects of reinforcement on math plus reading and its concurrent effect on hyperactivity. (The asterisk indicates one data point averaged over two rather than three days.)

Phase 4: *no medication; reinforcement of math plus reading.* During this six-day phase, the children remained off drugs while reinforcement was added for reading and reinforcement of math was maintained. Observations of hyperactivity and measures of academic performance were continued.

RESULTS

When Ritalin was discontinued, the level of hyperactivity doubled or tripled its initial level. However, when reinforcement was systematically

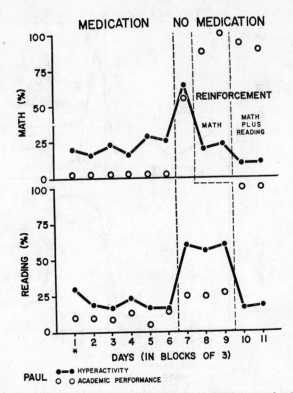

Fig. 2. Paul. The percentage of intervals in which hyperactivity took place and the percent of correct math and reading performance. The first and second segments respectively show the effects of medication, and its subsequent withdrawal, on hyperactivity and academic performance. A multiple-baseline analysis of the effects of reinforcement across math and reading and concurrent hyperactivity is shown starting on the third top segment. The last segment shows the effects of reinforcement on math plus reading and its concurrent effect on hyperactivity. (The asterisk indicates one data point averaged over two rather than three days).

administered for academic performance, hyperactivity for all three children decreased to a level comparable to the initial period when Ritalin chemically controlled it.

Figure 1 shows that hyperactivity for Crystal during the drug phase in math averaged about 20 percent, while academic performance in math was zero. When Ritalin was discontinued, hyperactivity rose to an average of 87 percent and math performance remained low at an average of 8 percent. When math was reinforced, and Crystal continued to stay off drugs, hyperactivity dropped significantly from 87 percent to about

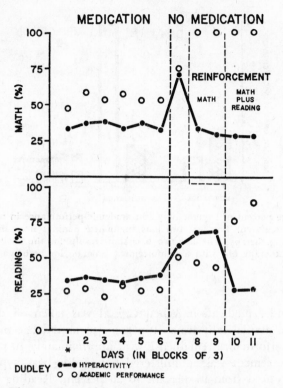

FIG. 3. Dudley. The percentage of intervals in which hyperactivity took place and the percent of correct math and reading performance. The first and second segments respectively show the effects of medication, and its subsequent withdrawal, on hyperactivity and academic performance. A multiple-baseline analysis of the effects of reinforcement across math and reading and concurrent hyperactivity is shown starting on the third top segment. The last segment shows the effects of reinforcement on math plus reading and its concurrent effect on hyperactivity. (The asterisk indicates one data point averaged over two rather than three days).

9 percent. Math performance increased to 65 percent. Hyperactivity in math was effectively controlled through reinforcement of math performance. However, the multiple-baseline design shows that concurrently Crystal's hyperactivity during reading class remained at 90 percent before reinforcement was introduced for correct reading responses.

At the same time measures were taken in the area of math, hyperactivity and academic performance were also measured in the area of reading. Crystal's hyperactivity during reading class averaged approximately 10 percent under medication. Academic performance in reading

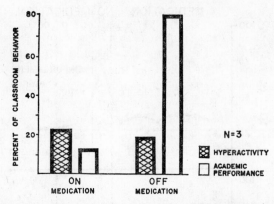

FIG. 4. Average percent of hyperactivity and academic performance in math and reading for three children. The first two bars summarize findings from the 17-day baseline under drug therapy. The last two bars show results for the final six-day period without drug therapy but with a reinforcement program for both math and reading performance.

was zero under medication. When Crystal was taken off drugs, hyperactivity rose dramatically from 10 percent to an average of 91 percent. Academic performance remained low at approximately 10 percent. Only when reinforcement was administered for reading was hyperactivity in this area reduced from 91 percent to 20 percent. Reading performance increased from 10 percent to an average of 69 percent.

Similar results were found for Paul and Dudley, as can be seen in Figures 2 and 3.

Figure 4 shows the pre and post measures of hyperactivity and academic performance for Dudley, Crystal, and Paul as a group. It can be seen that when the children were taking drugs, hyperactivity was well controlled and averaged about 24 percent during math and reading. When medication was discontinued and a reinforcement program was established to strengthen academic performance, the combined level of hyperactivity was about 20 percent during math and reading for the three children. This level (20 percent) of hyperactivity matched that obtained under medication (24 percent).

During the period when the children were taking drugs, their percent correct in math and reading combined, averaged 12 percent. When medication was discontinued and a reinforcement program was established, their average percent correct in both academic subjects increased from 12 percent to 85 percent.

DISCUSSION

These findings show that reinforcement of academic performance suppresses hyperactivity, and they thus support and extend the findings of Ayllon and Roberts (1974). Further, the academic gains produced by the behavioral program contrast dramatically with the lack of academic progress shown by these children under medication.*

The multiple-baseline design demonstrates that token reinforcement for academic achievement was responsible for the concurrent suppression of hyperactivity. Indeed, while this control was demonstrated during math periods, the children's concurrent hyperactivity during reading remained at a high level, so long as the reinforcement procedure for reading was withheld. Only when reinforcement was introduced for both math and reading performance did the hyperactivity for all three children drop to levels comparable to those controlled by the drug.

The control over hyperactivity by the enhancement of academic performance was quick, stable, and independent of the duration and dosage of the medication received by each child before the program. One child had been under medication for as long as 4 years, another child for 1 year. Despite this extreme difference in history of medication, the behavioral effects were not differential to that history.

When medication was discontinued, hyperactivity increased immediately and to a high level in all three children. The effectiveness of medication in controlling hyperactivity, evaluated through direct observations of behavior, supports the data of earlier studies using recordings based on instrumentation (Hollis et al., 1972; Sprague et al., 1970; Sykes et al., 1971).

During the few days of no medication, hyperactivity became so severe that the teacher and parents freely commented on the gross difference in the children's behavior in school and at home. Their reports centered around such descriptions as "He's just like a whirlwind," "She is climbing the walls, it's awful," "Just can't do a thing with her . . ." "He's not attending, doesn't listen to anything I tell him," and others. It was only with a great deal of support and counselling that the teacher and parents were able to tolerate this stressful period. It was this high level of hyperactivity shown by all three children that allowed the opportunity to test the effectiveness of a reinforcement program for academic performance in controlling hyperactivity.

---

* For a systematic replication of this study see Layman, *unpublished*.

Since both hyperactivity and academic performance increased con-currently, as soon as medication was discontinued, it might be construed that these two dimensions are compatible. This may be an unwarranted conclusion, however, because the slight increments in academic perform-ance concurrent with increments in hyperactivity may also reflect the type of recording method used in this study. For example, measures of the behavior of the children show that once they had finished their academic assignments, they became hyperactive. Thus, academic per-formance and hyperactivity could take place sequentially. When the time limit for academic performance had expired (e.g., after 10 or 20 minutes, depending on the subject matter) the child could engage in hyperactivity for the rest of the class period.

It usually took only one session for each child to learn that academic performance was associated with reinforcement while hyperactivity was not, suggesting that in the absence of medication these children react to reinforcement as normal children do. The classroom with reinforcement procedures now set the occasion for academic performance, rather than hyperactivity.

The present results suggest that the continued use of Ritalin and possibly other drugs to control hyperactivity may result in compliant but academically incompetent students. Surely, the goal of school is not to make children into docile robots either by behavioral techniques or by medication. Rather, the goal should be one of providing children with the social and academic tools required to become successful in their social interactions and competent in their academic performance. Judging from the reactions and comments of both parents and teacher, this goal was achieved during the reinforcement period of the study. The parents were particularly relieved that their children, who had been dependent on Ritalin for years, could now function normally in school without the drug. Similarly, the teacher was excited over the fact that she could now build the social and academic skills of the children be-cause they were more attentive and responsive to her than when they were under medication.

On the basis of these findings, it would seem appropriate to recom-mend that hyperactive children under medication periodically be given the opportunity to be drug-free, to minimize drug dependence and to facilitate change through alternative behavioral techniques. While this study focused on behavioral alternatives to Ritalin for the control of hyperactivity, it is possible that another drug or a combination of medication and a behavioral program may also be helpful.

This study offers a behavioral and educationally justifiable alternative to the use of medication for hyperactive children. The control of hyperactivity by medication, while effective, may be too costly to the child, in that it may retard his academic and social growth, a human cost that schools and society can ill afford.

REFERENCES

AYLLON, T. & KELLY, K. Effects of reinforcement on standardized test performance. *J. Appl. Behav. Anal.*, 1972, 5, 477-484.

AYLLON, T., LAYMAN, D., & BURKE, S. Disruptive behavior and reinforcement of academic performance. *Psychol. Rec.*, 1972, 22, 315-323.

AYLLON, T. & ROBERTS, M. Eliminating discipline problems by strengthening academic performance. *J. Appl. Behav. Anal.*, 1974, 7, 71-76.

BECKER, W., MADSEN, C., ARNOLD, C., & THOMAS, D. The contingent use of teacher attention and praise in reducing classroom problems. *J. Spec. Educ.*, 1967, 1, 287-307.

CAMPBELL, S., DOUGLAS, U., & MORGENSTERN, G. Cognitive styles in hyperactive children and the effect of methylphenidate. *J. Child Psychol. Psychiat.*, 1971, 12, 55-67.

COMLY, H. Cerebral stimulants for children with learning disorders. *J. Learn. Dis.*, 1971, 4, 484-490.

CONNERS, C., EISENBERG, L., & BARCAI, A. Effect of dextro-amphetamine in children: Studies on subjects with learning disabilities and school behavior problems. *Arch. Gen. Psychiat.*, 1967, 17, 478-485.

CONNERS, C., EISENBERG, L., & SHARPE, L. Effects of methylphenidate (Ritalin) on paired-associate learning and Porteus performance in emotionally disturbed children. *J. Cons. Psychol.*, 1964, 28, 14-22.

CONNERS, C. & ROTHSCHILD, G. Drugs and learning in children. In J. Hellmuth (Ed.), *Learning Disorders*, Vol. 3. Seattle: Special Publications, 1968.

CONNERS, K. Recent drug studies with hyperkinetic children. *J. Learn. Dis.*, 1971, 4, 476-483.

DENHOFF, E., DAVIS, A., & HAWKINS, A. Effects of dextro-amphetamine on hyperkinetic children: A controlled double blind study. *J. Learn. Dis.*, 1971, 4, 491-499.

EPSTEIN, L., LASAGNA, L., CONNERS, K., and RODRIGUEZ, A. Correlation of dextro-amphetamine excretion and drug response in hyperkinetic children. *J. Nerv. Ment. Dis.*, 1968, 146, 136-146.

FISH, B. The "one child, one drug" myth of stimulants in hyperkinesis: importance of diagnostic categories in evaluating treatment. *Arch. Gen. Psychiat.*, 1971, 25, 193-203.

FREIBERGS, V. & DOUGLAS, V. Concept learning in hyperactive and normal children. *J. Abnorm. Psychol.*, 1969, 74, 388-395.

HENTOFF, N. The drugged classroom. *Evergreen Review*, December, 1970, 6-11.

HOLLIS, J. & S9. OMER, V. Direct measurement of psychopharmacologic response: Effects of chlorpromazine on motor behavior of retarded children. *Amer. J. Ment. Defic.*, 1972, 76, 397-407.

KEOGH, B. Hyperactivity and learning disorders: Review and speculation. *Except. Child.*, 1971, 38, 101-109.

KNIGHTS, R. & HINTON, G. Minimal brain dysfunction: Clinical and psychological test characteristics. *Acad. Ther.*, 1968, 4, 265-273.

KRIPPNER, S., SILVERMAN, R., CAVALLO, M., & HEALEY, M. A study of hyperkinetic children receiving stimulant drugs. *Acad. Ther.*, 1973, 8, 261-269.

LAYMAN, D. A Behavioral Investigation: The Effects of Medication on Disruptive

Classroom Behavior and Academic Performance. Unpublished doctoral dissertation, Georgia State University, 1974.

O'LEARY, K. D. & BECKER, W. C. Behavior modification of an adjustment class: A token reinforcement program. *Except. Child.,* 1967, 33, 637-642.

SPRAGUE, R., BARNES, B., & WERRY, J. Methylphenidate and thoridazine: Learning, reaction time, activity, and classroom behavior in disturbed children. *Amer. J. Orthopsychiat.,* 1970, 40, 615-628.

SPRAGUE, R. & TOPPE, L. Relationship between activity level and delay of reinforcement. *Exp. Child Psychol.,* 1966, 3, 390-397.

STEWART, M., PITTS, F., CRAIG, A., & DIERUF, W. The hyperactive child syndrome. *Amer. J. Orthopsychiat.,* 1966, 36, 861-867.

SULZBACHER, S. Behavior analysis of drug effects in the classroom. In G. Semb (Ed.), *Behavior Analysis and Education.* University of Kansas, 1972.

SYKES, D., DOUGLAS, V., WEISS, G., & MINDE, K. Attention in hyperactive children and the effect of methylphenidate (Ritalin). *J. Child Psychol. Psychiat.,* 1971, 12, 129-139.

20

MODIFICATION OF SEIZURE DISORDERS: THE INTERRUPTION OF BEHAVIORAL CHAINS

Steven Zlutnick, William J. Mayville

and Scott Moffat

*University of Utah College of Medicine, Rural Clinics—Reno,
Nevada, and Garfield School, Salt Lake City, Utah*

This study investigated the effects of interruption and differential reinforcement on seizures in children. Seizures were conceptualized as the terminal link in a behavioral chain, resulting in a strategy aimed at identifying and modifying behaviors that reliably preceded the seizure climax. Seizure frequency was reduced in four of five subjects, whereas the frequency of preseizure behavior was reduced in only three subjects. Parents and school personnel were successfully used as change agents.

Descriptors: chaining, seizures, epilepsy, children, DRO, interruption of seizure chains, parent (s) as therapist.

Reprinted from the *Journal of Applied Behavior Analysis,* 1975, 8,1-12. Copyright 1975, the Society for the Experimental Analysis of Behavior, Inc.

Portions of this research were supported by the University of Utah Biomedical Research Grant 6139-365. The authors thank Drs. David Born, Donald P. Hartmann, and Roger Katz for their comments and suggestions, as well as Drs. Jack Madsen and Patrick Bray, Department of Neurology, University of Utah College of Medicine and Dr. Garth Myers, Department of Neurology, Primary Children's Hospital, Salt Lake City, Utah, for their referrals and consultation.

Recent laboratory advances in the operant control of autonomic functioning (Kimmel, 1967; Miller, 1969), lend credence to anecdotal clinical reports on the success of environmental manipulations in modifying behaviors previously thought to be beyond voluntary control. One example of this strategy has been the control of seizure disorders by conditioning techniques. Forster (1969), for example, treated reflex epilepsies by repeatedly presenting the eliciting stimulus until extinction occurred, or gradually shifting the stimulus from noneliciting to eliciting values. In a similar conditioning paradigm, Parrino (1971) eliminated grand mal seizures in a 36-year-old male using systematic desensitization.

Gardner (1967) reported one of the first explicit applications of operant-conditioning techniques to the control of seizures. He eliminated psychogenic seizures of a 10-year-old girl by using differential reinforcement, i.e., extinction contingent upon seizure occurrence, and reinforcement for incompatible behaviors, such as appropriate play with siblings.

The fact that seizures can be interrupted before the seizure "climax" has been frequently noted anecdotally in neurological practice. Such a phenomenon has been observed most commonly in Jacksonian seizures, with methods as diverse as mustard applications and stimulation being employed (Lennox, 1960).

The cases described below represent a further attempt at controlling seizures of both organic and nonorganic etiology with operant-conditioning techniques by applying consequences to behaviors that reliably *precede* the seizure itself. Reliably occurring preseizure behaviors (prodromal behavior, or premonitory symptoms) such as headaches, tinnitus, polydipsia, and localized spasms have been described by Henner (1962). In some cases, these behaviors precede the seizure by as long as 10 days.

Basic research has shown that chained behavior can be disrupted, particularly if earlier components are involved (Findley, 1962; Kelleher & Fry, 1962; Skinner, 1934; Thomas, 1964). If seizures are viewed as the terminal link in a chain of behaviors, these data suggest that seizures can be prevented by interfering with preseizure behaviors.

Clinical-experimental applications of this chain-disruption strategy are rare. Efron (1957a, 1957b) was able to abort grand mal seizures in a 46-year-old woman by presentation of what might be described as an aversive stimulus (odor of hydrogen sulfide) contingent upon behaviors that she reported occurring before the grand mal climax. Similarly, Kohlenberg (1970) successfully eliminated vomiting in a 21-year-old retarded girl by applying electric shock contingent upon stomach contractions that reliably preceded vomiting episodes.

The present study sought to eliminate or decrease the rate of seizures in children by identifying and modifying reliable preseizure behaviors. Effects of two operant procedures were examined: contingent interruption and reinforcement of behavior incompatible with seizures. Concomitantly, an effort was made to investigate predictability of seizures and to confirm feasibility of employing nonprofessionals in the environment of seizure-prone children as primary change agents. That parents can be employed successfully as therapists for their children has been amply demonstrated (Johnson & Katz, 1973).

GENERAL METHOD

The pool of 18 subjects, from which five were selected for this study, was obtained from a variety of sources, including referrals from local neurologists, public schools, physicians, and psychologists. The criteria for selection were that subjects show: 1) a behaviorally observable seizure, such that at least a 90 percent agreement could be established between two independent observers; 2) a minimum seizure frequency of at least one per day, to facilitate data collection and more easily assess the effects of experimental manipulations; and, when possible, 3) a formal diagnosis of epilepsy based upon EEG and/or clinical observation by a certified neurologist. With the exception of Subject 1, all subjects in this investigation met these criteria. Subjects were eliminated before treatment when either reliable data could not be acquired (eight children) or the seizure could not be operationalized for accurate measurement (five children).

Reliability checks were obtained for all dependent measures and consisted of two trained observers (or one observer and a parent) watching the subject for 1 hour or more from opposite sides of the room, noting the time and occurrence of each seizure. Reliability was computed as percent agreement by dividing the number of intervals scored identically by the total number of intervals. Because perfect reliability could be obtained even though no seizure had occurred, reliability checks were not concluded until at least six seizures had been noted. The same procedure was employed for determining reliability figures on preseizure behaviors. Absolute frequencies were used due to the relatively low frequency of the behaviors in question. Once satisfactory reliability was established, subsequent reliability checks were made once in each experimental phase.*

---

* See General Discussion for an elaboration of the reliability issue.

Based on anecdotal reports mentioned earlier, an interruption procedure for preseizure behavior was implemented for Subjects 1 to 4.
Essentially, it consisted of the following, implemented by the change
agent: 1) shout, "No!" loudly and sharply, and 2) grasp the subject by
the shoulders and shake him once, vigorously.

For Subject 5, a differential-reinforcement procedure was implemented
contingent upon the preseizure behavior of arm raising. It consisted of:
1) placing the subject's hands down to her side (or lap if she were
sitting), 2) waiting approximately 5 seconds, and 3) delivering a combination of primary and social reinforcement contingent upon "arms
down."

SUBJECT 1

This subject was a 7-year-old male Caucasian enrolled in a behavior
modification program for emotionally disturbed children. He had been
alternately diagnosed as autistic, brain damaged, and as having a learning disability. He had a history of seizures from the time that he was
2 years old. No recent EEG testing results were available, and earlier
testing had evidently revealed no abnormalities. Although these seizures
were not at any time described as functional, a formal diagnosis of
epilepsy was never specifically made.* Medication notwithstanding (8¼
grain tablets of Dilantin per day), seizures averaged 12 per day.

The seizure itself consisted of three distinguishable component behaviors: 1) fixed gaze at a flat surface (either a table top or wall), followed by 2) the body becoming rigid, followed by 3) myoclonic spasms
(violent shaking), and 4) terminating with a fall to the floor. Corresponding seizure symptoms such as confusion, incontinence, etc., were not
observed. No seizures were ever observed that were not preceded by the
fixed stare. As a result, the staring behavior was chosen as the target
for modification.

With the discrete nature of these behavioral components, interobserver
reliabilities on the seizure and preseizure responses were 100 percent.

Subject 1 was treated within a local public school behavior modification unit. With few exceptions, all procedures were carried out in the
regular classroom, which consisted of a group of 10 to 12 children who
were involved in a developmental curriculum.

---

* This subject was treated before formalization of an experimental design and was
essentially considered to be a pilot study. The more stringent criteria for subject
selection began with Subjects 2 through 5.

Procedure

Baseline. The child was observed continuously from 9:00 A.M. until 3:00 P.M. for a period of three weeks by an assigned staff member who worked in his classroom and recorded the total number of seizures per day. Further data were also obtained to determine whether the seizures were discriminated as a function of time, activity, or person (s). Once a seizure occurred, the typical reaction of the school staff was that of general inattention, which approximated the conditions in effect before baseline.

Interruption phase. When baseline data had stabilized, the staff were instructed to implement the interruption procedure described above contingent upon the occurrence of visual fixation. No consequences were applied once the seizure itself had commenced.

Reversal phase. During this condition, a multiple-schedule strategy was instituted to determine if the reduction in seizure rate was a function of the independent variables. From 9:00 A.M. to 12:00 P.M., the interruption contingency was removed, and fixated staring was no longer followed by any interruptions. From 12:00 P.M. until 3:00 P.M., however, the interruption contingency remained in effect. The reversal was implemented for one day only, due to the reluctance of the investigators to re-instate a behavior as severe as seizures.* Parental permission was obtained before this phase was implemented.

Interruption phase. The interruption procedure was reinstated in all conditions.

RESULTS AND DISCUSSION

Figure 1 shows the number of seizures plotted per week. During baseline, seizures occurred with a frequency of just under 60 per five-day school week, or about 12 per day. Data from prebaseline conditions revealed no apparent discrimination of these seizures on person, place, time, or activity. With introduction of the interruption procedure, the frequency quickly fell to five to 10 per week, or about one or two per day. Seizures were eliminated by the seventh week of treatment. During reversal, when the interruption procedure was removed in the morning, six seizures occurred during the 3-hour period when it was not in effect.

---

* It should be remembered that this case was treated before neurological consultation and the senior author was less than enthusiastic about implementing a reversal. Problems associated with a 3-hour reversal are acknowledged.

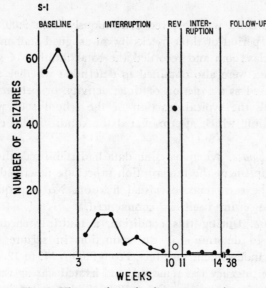

Fig. 1. The number of minor motor seizures per
week for Subject 1. The reversal is prorated for a five-
day week. During reversal, ● = A.M. and ○ = P.M.
Follow-up data represent the absolute number of
seizures for the next six months.

Before this time, seizures had been distributed systematically throughout the day. With the re-introduction of interruptions, seizure frequency
quickly dropped to zero, where it remained.

Two additional points merit discussion. First, the preseizure behavior
of fixed staring decreased in direct proportion to the decline in rate of
the seizures themselves (since this was the case for all subjects, only the
seizure data are presented in the figures). Second, after introducing interruptions, seizures occurred only when staff members were unable to
apply the contingency in time, i.e., within 10 to 15 seconds after the
onset of staring.

Further, the subject's anticonvulsant medication was systematically
reduced by one tablet every two weeks. At termination of treatment,
seizure frequency was zero and no medication was administered.

Although therapy plans originally called for parental involvement,
almost complete and spontaneous generalization from school to home
eliminated the need to do so. Although no data were formally collected

in the home, the parents reported a gradual reduction in both staring and seizures, which coincided with introduction of the interruption procedure at school.

At the end of the first six-month follow-up, only one seizure had been observed, which occurred while the subject was on the playground. However, the child was reported only to have fallen; whether a seizure in fact occurred is unclear. No interruption procedures were applied after termination of treatment.

SUBJECT 2

Subject 2 was a 4-year-old male Caucasian, diagnosed as moderately retarded with undetermined brain damage. Seizures began at the age of 18 months. A diagnosis of epilepsy, minor motor type, had been made by a neurologist on the basis of seizure pattern, history, and corroborative abnormal EEG findings. A wide spectrum of anticonvulsant medications had been tried with slight or no success.

Behaviorally, the most prominent seizure pattern consisted of 1) a lowered activity level, followed by 2) the minor motor seizure, which was characterized by a sudden flexion of the arms and head. A second, less serious form of seizure, referred to neurologically as an "absence," was characterized by 20 to 30 seconds of vacant staring, which terminated with brief vomiting.

Reliabilities of 100 percent agreement between observers were obtained on both variants of seizures, and reliabilities of 92 percent were obtained between two observers and the subject's mother for the lowered activity level. The predictability of this response ranged between 50 and 80 percent (i.e., the lowered activity level preceded an average of 60 percent of the seizures). No preseizure behaviors were observed for the absence seizure.

Since this study was initiated during the summer months before the subject's enrollment in a behavior modification school program, the minor motor seizures were treated in the home environment. The absence-seizure pattern commenced in the fall and was treated at school.

Procedure

Baseline—minor motor seizures. The child's parents were interviewed to determine the approximate number of seizures per day, relevant stimulus conditions, possible consequences, and the existence of preseizure behaviors (i.e., predictability). Next, a running description of the child's behavior (Bijou, Peterson, & Ault, 1968) was collected in his home. Finally, the parents were instructed to record the total seizure frequency per day, and the percent of seizures per day that were predictable.

Interruption—minor motor seizures. Once baseline data had stabilized, the same interruption procedure that was employed for Subject 1 was instituted, except in this case it was contingent upon the occurrence of the lowered activity level. The subject's mother was successfully utilized as the therapeutic agent and no difficulties were encountered.

Baseline—absence seizures. In the fall, the "absences" with vomiting began. In this absence, periods of "absences" as well as episodes of vomiting were recorded each day, along with relevant information regarding the stimulus conditions under which they occurred. Parents and staff were instructed not to exceed attention previously given to these behaviors in order to get accurate baseline data and to reduce the chance of reinforcing seizures.

Interruption—absence seizures. During this phase, the standard procedure was instituted as close to the onset of the absence (and before vomiting) as possible. No consequences were delivered contingent upon the vomiting. Consequences were delivered according to a multiple-schedule design, i.e., absence seizuers were interrupted at school but not at home.

Reversal—absence seizures. At this point, the interruption procedure was removed for a four-week period to determine the effectiveness of the procedures. Thus, when the absence began, no consequences were scheduled at any time in either stimulus condition.

Interruption—absence seizures. The interruption was reinstated for the absence seizures during school hours (9:00 A.M. to 3:00 P.M. only).

RESULTS AND DISCUSSION

Figure 2 shows the number of minor motor seizures plotted daily for Subject 2. During baseline, minor motor seizures averaged six per day. With introduction of the interruption component, the number dropped to an average of three per day. The effect proved transitory, however, and eventually seizure frequency recovered to approximately five per day. Eight months later, frequency had reduced gradually to an average of two per day. This effect was independent of experimental operations. Although approximately 60 percent of the minor motor seizures were predictable, they were only immediately reducible by 50 percent, and terminally by 17 percent.

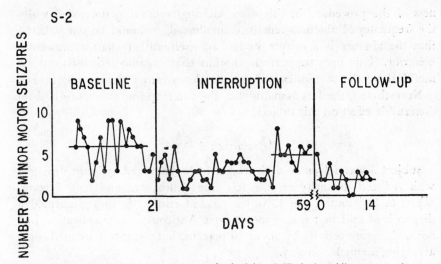

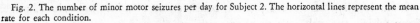

Fig. 2. The number of minor motor seizures per day for Subject 2. The horizontal lines represent the mean rate for each condition.

Figure 3 shows the frequency of absence and vomiting episodes for Subject 2 plotted daily. During baseline conditions (Part B), the frequency of absences and subsequent vomiting covaried exactly and continued to increase. Because the vomiting caused the subject's family a great deal of discomfort, baseline conditions were terminated before stability was achieved. Part B of Figure 3 shows the total number of vomiting episodes (open circles). With introduction of the interruption procedure, the vomiting was reduced to a near-zero frequency. However, the number of absences increased over baseline.

The effects of the reversal are not immediately apparent until the data are scrutinized carefully. Although vomiting did not recur during this phase, on the third day of the reversal, Subject 2 began hyperventilating both at home and school (Part A of Figure 3). Further, when the absences are viewed separately by stimulus conditions (i.e., home and school as in Part C of Figure 3), it can be seen that relative to the number during interruption, the frequency of absences during reversal increased temporarily at school (closed circles) where the interruptions were originally introduced, and declined further with re-introduction of the interruption procedure.

Absence seizures differ markedly from those of the minor motor variant, however, and these differences might account for the relative ineffectiveness of the procedure in this case. Although vomiting decreased while the frequency of absences remained unaffected, it should be remembered that the absence is a seizure in and of itself, rather than a preseizure behavior. This may support the notion that organic seizures must be modified by the manipulation of antecedents rather than consequences.

Nevertheless, the fact remains that the interruption procedure had no discernible effect on this subject.

SUBJECT 3

Subject 3 was a 4-year-old Caucasian male diagnosed as brain damaged with reduced dexterity on the left side (both arm and leg). Seizures began at 20 months and EEG testing and clinical history confirmed a diagnosis of epilepsy: minor motor type. Anticonvulsant medication had reduced seizure activity by about 10 percent, but the rate remained high, averaging about 12 per day.

Behaviorally, the seizure pattern consisted of 1) subtle behavior change from which the subject's mother could predict 45 to 50 percent of his seizures, yet which proved impossible to define clearly and yielded an interobserver reliability of only 15 percent, and 2) the seizure, characterized by a sudden flexion of arms and head.

Reliabilities of 100 percent were obtained between two observers and the subject's mother for seizures. Subject 3 was treated at home during the summer months before his enrollment in a formal special education program.

Procedure

The procedure for Subject 3 was identical to that described for Subjects 1 and 2, with the interruption implemented contingent upon periods of "lowered activity." Data were collected by the subject's mother. As with the two previous subjects, one of the child's parents served as the therapeutic agent.

RESULTS AND DISCUSSION

Figure 4 shows the number of minor motor seizures for Subject 3 plotted weekly. During baseline, the rate averaged about 75 seizures per week, or 10 to 12 per day. Prebaseline and baseline observations revealed no predictable pattern of seizure occurrence. With introduction of the interruption procedure, the frequency quickly decreased and stabilized at

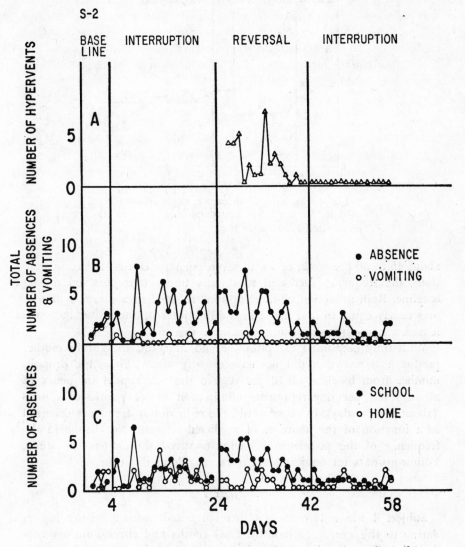

Fig. 3. The number of absence seizures, hyperventilations, and vomiting episodes per day for Subject 2.

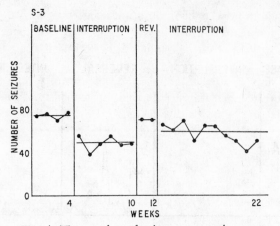

Fig. 4. The number of minor motor seizures per week for Subject 3. The horizontal lines represent the mean rate for each condition.

about 45 to 50 per week, or six to seven per day. During reversal conditions, the frequency increased to slightly under that observed during baseline. Reintroduction of interruptions resulted in a decrease of seizures nearly equal to that noted in the first interruption phase, although it took a longer period of time to achieve this effect.

With only occasional exceptions, at no time did the child's mother predict a seizure that did not subsequently occur. Thus, the drop in number from baseline of 12 per day to the interrupted frequency of about seven per day represents elimination of all predicted seizures (about five per day). In other words, the reduction of frequency occurred as a function of the abortion of predicted seizures. No change in the frequency of the preseizure behavior occurred throughout the study. Follow-up data for Subject 3 are not available at this time.

SUBJECT 4

Subject 4 was a 14-year-old Caucasian female with a seizure history dating to the age of 18 months. EEG results and clinical history confirmed a diagnosis of epilepsy, minor motor and focal types. Even with anticonvulsant medication, seizure activity remained relatively high, averaging about two per day.

Behaviorally, this subject's seizure pattern was characterized by 1) the right arm slowly raised to a position parallel to the head, followed by 2) the seizure (about 60 seconds in duration) consisting of myoclonic jerking and vacant staring. Predictability of the seizure from arm-raising was 100 percent, with interobserver reliabilities of 100 percent on the seizure itself.

Subject 4 was treated at home, since the severity and regularity of seizures prohibited her attending school. A teacher from the local school district visited the house twice weekly. The girl's mother was used as the therapist and other siblings were frequently employed as ancillary data collectors.

Procedure

The procedure was identical to that described previously for Subjects 1, 2, and 3. Data were collected throughout the study by the subject's mother, who was instructed to note each seizure occurrence, when it occurred, who was present, and the activity in which the child was engaged. She was further instructed to respond to any seizure occurrence as she had in the past, that is to ignore it.

RESULTS AND DISCUSSION

Figure 5 shows the number of minor motor seizures plotted weekly for Subject 4. During baseline, seizures occurred on an average of 11 per week, or one to two per day. Prebaseline and baseline observations did not show that seizures were discriminated on people, location, time, or activity. With introduction of the interruption procedure, the frequency was quickly reduced and eventually stabilized, averaging two and one-half per week, or one every three days. With introduction of reversal procedures, the frequency gradually increased to a peak of eight per week, at which time interruptions were reintroduced. With this change in procedure, the number decreased to approximately three per week, or one seizure every two days. The occurrence of the preseizure behavior (arm-raising) covaried exactly with seizure occurrence, and decreased in direct proportion to seizure activity.

The only deviation from the downward trend of the data during punishment was the one near-recovery of baseline frequency (arrow in Figure 5). During this week, the subject began her menstrual period and this may have contributed to the unusually high number of seizures. As reported by her mother, the subject's menstrual periods were irregular and occasionally accompanied by an abnormally high number of seizures.

The subject's mother reported that a further reduction in seizures

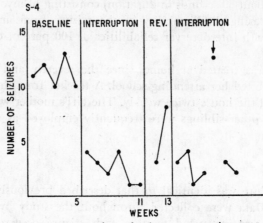

Fig. 5. The number of minor motor seizures per
week for Subject 4.

might have been possible, but the other children were too young to
employ the procedure, and the father was reluctant to become involved
in the treatment.

At the end of six months, follow-up data indicated that in spite of
continued use of interruption procedure, the seizure frequency had increased by one or two per week, though remaining far below the initial
baseline level. A 1-year follow-up indicated that the interruption procedure had been used sporadically during the second six months after
treatment terminated, with a reported (no reliability) gradual loss of
effectiveness. Seizure frequency at this time is about equal to that observed
during baseline.

SUBJECT 5

Subject 5 was a 17-year-old Caucasian female diagnosed as mentally
retarded with major motor epilepsy. She had a life-long seizure history,
and at the time of this research was exhibiting multiple seizures daily,
despite large doses of dilantin and phenobarbitol.

Behaviorally, her seizures consisted of the following chain of behaviors:
1) her body became tense and rigid, 2) she clenched her fists and raised
her arms at a 90-degree angle from her body, 3) her head snapped back
and a grimace appeared on her face, and 4) the major motor seizure
ensued. Reliabilities of 100 percent were obtained on the seizure and
preseizure target behavior of arm-raising.

Subject 5 was treated at a training center for adolescent retarded children. This experiment was conducted by the second author concurrent to, but not in conjunction with the treatment of Subject 1.

Procedure

Data collection, observation, and reliability measures were identical to those described earlier. However, in place of the interruption procedures used with Subjects 1 to 4, a differential-reinforcement procedure (DRO) was implemented in an attempt to suppress seizure frequency. Essentially, this procedure consisted of the following steps: 1) as soon as the subject raised her arms into the air (component 2 described above) they were placed back down to her side, or in her lap if she were sitting, 2) a delay of 5 seconds was interposed, 3) she was praised effusively for having her arms lowered, and 4) she was given a piece of M & M candy. The time delay was used to ensure that reinforcement was not contingent upon an undesired chain of behaviors, e.g., hands up, followed by hands down.

This procedure was initially implemented by the second author and other teaching staff. Eventually, however, control was faded to other students at the training center.

RESULTS AND DISCUSSION

Figure 6 shows the number of major motor seizures plotted daily for Subject 5. During baseline, seizures occurred on the average of 16 per day. With introduction of the differential-reinforcement procedure, the frequency of seizures diminished rapidly to a near-zero frequency. During the reversal phase, this contingency was removed and seizure frequency increased to about six per day. When the differential-reinforcement procedure was re-introduced, seizure frequency again dropped to a near-zero level.

The occurrence of arm-raising was observed consistently before the seizure climax. As with Subjects 1 and 4, the frequency of the preseizure target behavior decreased as a function of the experimental manipulation, in this case differential reinforcement. No seizures were observed that were not preceded by this behavior. Only when staff were unable to reach the subject in time to lower her arms did seizures occur during the DRO phase.

A nine-month follow-up indicated that the subject's seizures frequency remained at a near-zero level without treatment procedures being re-

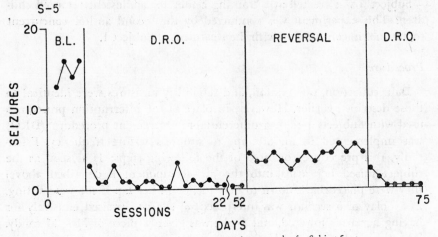

Fig. 6. The number of minor motor seizures per day for Subject 5.

quired. One instance of marked seizure increase occurred during a three- or four-day period about six months after treatment terminated. The DRO procedure was again introduced and seizures were rapidly eliminated.

GENERAL DISCUSSION

The present data support a number of conclusions concerning the control of seizures with conditioning techniques. First, it seems clear that some variants of seizures, particularly those involving gross motor movements, are modifiable by systematic environmental manipulations introduced before the seizure climax. With the exception of Subject 2, some degree of control was exerted over the remaining four subjects. Further, contrary to traditional clinical impressions (Gibbs & Stamp, 1958), identifiable behaviors frequently occur reliably before a minor motor seizure climax, thus allowing for a degree of predictability heretofore nonexistent. In one sense, the degree of predictability of a behavior is as important to its subsequent control as the development of a technology needed to eliminate it.

The notion of chaining as a conceptual framework within which to develop treatment methods for seizure control appears to be both practical and efficacious. Furthermore, the data presented here are generally consistent with outcomes of similar treatment strategies described by

Efron (1957a, 1957b) and Kohlenberg (1970). Theoretically, any component could be selected as the target behavior. Further research and observation are needed to determine if multiple behaviors occur before the seizure that could increase the number of therapeutic options.

Although the interruption of preseizure components reliably altered seizure frequency in most areas, the specific behavioral effects of this procedure are unclear. Azrin and Holz (1966) defined punishment as a decrease in the occurrence of a response following the contingent application of an aversive stimulus. In some instances described earlier, the frequency of preseizure behavior decreased (Subjects 1 and 4), while in others it remained unaffected (Subjects 2 and 3). Precise data on the number of times the interruption procedure was used and changes in preseizure behavior are not available. In general, however, the number of interruptions remained constant in cases where the overall frequency of the preseizure behavior was unaffected, and decreased proportionally in those where the preseizure rate declined.

Two additional parameters of punishment are relevant to this discussion: 1) the intensity of the aversive stimulus, and 2) the schedule with which it is delivered. Numerous studies on the intensity of punishment have shown that the greater the intensity of the aversive stimulus, the greater the magnitude of suppression (Appel, 1963; Azrin, Holz, & Hake, 1963). These data suggest that a stimulus more intense than the one employed here might have produced greater suppression of preseizure behaviors. Further, the degree of sezure predictability may also affect seizure suppression. With only 42 percent of Subject 3's seizures predicted, the schedule of punishment to preseizure response would be an intermittent one, i.e., about 2.5 to 1. Intermittent punishment schedules have been consistently less successful in suppressing behavior than continuous schedules of punishment (Azrin et al., 1963; Estes, 1944).

The partial effectiveness of the startle-and-shake procedure, if due to punishment, is in some ways consistent with findings reported by other investigators (Azrin, 1968; Hollenberg & Sperry, 1951; Karsh & Williams, 1964) who have shown that loud noise and verbal punishment can suppress behavior. One limitation of this procedure is that it may vary in intensity and duration and cannot be applied as uniformly as other stimuli, such as electric shock. In this respect, other forms of aversive control such as timeout or shock might prove to be more effective and should be investigated. Conversely, the effective use of differential reinforcement also suggests the feasibility of more innocuous approaches.

A brief note on reliability is appropriate. The dangers inherent in data reported by parents are obvious. In most cases, trained observers can be easily implemented to solve this dilemma. Behaviors of such reduced frequency as seizures, however, produce two problems, whose solution remains elusive. On the one hand, it is extremely difficult to obtain accurate reliability because a frequency of two per day would require approximately 40 hours of total observer time. In addition, if punishment is the phenomenon producing seizure suppression, the question arises as to whether the child is simply avoiding the change agent; i.e., the frequency is not reduced, seizures simply occur out of sight of the observer. The first problem was dealt with by requiring the observance of at least six seizures, and agreement on occurrence only; the latter problem is difficult to evaluate. While it is likely that a child could discriminate seizures on the absence of an observer, it seems implausible to assure that he could accomplish this on all or even a majority of occasions.

The focus of this study has been placed on preseizure behavior and its relationship to seizure occurrence. Nevertheless, the importance of the consequences of seizures *per se* should not be overlooked. If reinforcing consequences could be identified, treatment strategies might be enhanced by straightforward extinction operations.

A decided advantage of the present procedure is that it can be carried out by appropriately trained parents and other nonprofessionals in the child's natural environment. In this respect, the investment of time for training parents and staff in the intervention techniques was minimal. Each parent was seen for a total of 4 to 6 hours, which included the initial history-taking and assessment, preliminary observations, and the explanation and initial implementation of the interruption procedure. Beyond this, the investigator made one to three phone calls per week to each parent to collect data and monitor progress.

In summary, the present procedures may hold promise in the treatment of some types of epilepsy. Precisely which phenomenon accounts for the observed reduction after interruption remains unclear; hopefully, further replication will answer this question. Nevertheless, interruption and differential reinforcement do seem to be potentially useful and practical techniques.

A final point concerns the fact that environmental events may effect seizures of organic etiology. The present data suggest the possibility of promising behavioral interventions for this and other disorders, and highlight the importance of improved communication between the medical and behavioral sciences.

REFERENCES

APPEL, J. Punishment and shock intensity. *Science*, 1963, 141, 528-529.

AZRIN, N. Some effects of noise on human behavior. *J. Exp. Anal. Behav.*, 1968, 1, 183-200.

AZRIN, N. & HOLZ, W. Punishment. In W. K. Honig (Ed.), *Operant Behavior: Areas of Research and Application.* New York: Appleton-Century-Crofts, 1966, pp. 380-447.

AZRIN, N., HOLZ, W., & HAKE, D. Fixed-ratio punishment. *J. Exp. Anal. Beh.*, 1963, 6, 141-148.

BIJOU, S., PETERSON, R., & AULT, M. A method to integrate descriptive and experimental field studies at the level of data and empirical concepts. *J. Appl. Behav. Anal.*, 1968, 1, 175-191.

EFRON, R. The effect of olfactory stimuli in arresting uncinate fits. *Brain*, 1957, 79, 267-281. (a)

EFRON, R. The conditioned inhibition of uncinate fits. *Brain*, 1957, 80, 251-262. (b)

ESTES, W. An experimental study of punishment. *Psychological Monographs*, 1944, 57, (3, Whole No. 263).

FINDLEY, J. An experimental outline for building and exploring multioperant behavior repertoire. *J. Exp. Anal. Behav.*, 1962, 6, 113-166.

FORSTER, F. Clinical therapeutic conditioning in epilepsy. *Wisconsin Med. J.*, 1969, 68, 289-291.

GARDNER, J. Behavior therapy treatment approach to a psychogenic seizure case. *J. Consult. Psychol.*, 1967, 31, 209-212.

GIBBS, F & STAMP, F. *Epilepsy Handbook.* Springfield, Ill.: Charles C Thomas, 1958.

HENNER, K. Aurae and their role in reflex mechanisms of epileptic seizures. *Epilepsia*, 1962, 3, 391-401.

HOLLENBERG, E. & SPERRY, M. Some antecedents of aggression and the effects of frustration in doll play. *Personality*, 1951, 1, 31-42.

JOHNSON, C. & KATZ, R. Using parents as change agents for their children: A review *J. Child Psychol. Psychiat.*, 1973, 14, 181-200.

KARSH, E. & WILLIAMS, J. Punishment and reward in instrumental learning. *Psychonomic Science*, 1964, 1, 359-360.

KELLEHER, R. and FRY, W. Stimulus functions in chained fixed-interval schedules. *J. Exp. Anal. Behav.*, 1962, 5, 167-173.

KIMMEL, H. Instrumental conditioning of autonomically mediated behavior. *Psychol. Bull.*, 1967, 5, 337-345.

KOHLENBERG, R. The punishment of persistent vomiting: A case study. *J. Appl. Beh. Anal.*, 1970, 3, 241-246.

LENNOX, W. *Epilepsy and Related Disorders.* Boston: Little, Brown, 1960.

MILLER, N. Learning of visceral and glandular responses. *Science*, 1969, 163, 434-445.

PARRINO, J. Reduction of seizures by desensitization. *Beh. Ther. Exp. Psychiat.*, 1971, 2, 215-218.

SKINNER, B. F. The extinction of chained reflexes. *Proc. Natl. Acad. Sci.*, 1934, 20, 234-237. Cited by A. C. Catania (Ed.), *Contemporary Research in Operant Behavior.* Glenview, Ill.: Scott, Foresman, 1968.

THOMAS, J. Multiple baseline of stimulus functions in an FR chained schedule. *J. Exp. Anal. Behav.*, 1964, 7, 241-245.

21

TEACHING LANGUAGE TO NON-VERBAL CHILDREN—WITH EMPHASIS ON PROBLEMS OF GENERALIZATION

Sandra L. Harris

Rutgers University, New Brunswick, New Jersey

Operant conditioning techniques have been successfully used to teach nonverbal children the skills necessary for functional language. A typical sequence of training is: attention, nonverbal imitation, verbal imitation, and functional speech. The basic components of these procedures have been well documented. However, research showing means of facilitating the extension of functional speech beyond the therapy room into the natural environment (i.e., generalizing therapeutic gains) is limited in scope and adequacy. The heterogeneous population included under the umbrella *nonverbal* makes research in this area especially difficult.

The past decade has witnessed the emergence of powerful new operant conditioning procedures to establish speech in the repertoire of subjects previously consigned to muteness. The present review summarizes the

Reprinted with permission from *Journal of Consulting and Clinical Psychology*, Vol. 82, No. 4, 1975, 565-580. Copyright 1975, American Psychological Association.

This work was supported in part by a grant from the Charles and Johanna Busch Fund of Rutgers, The State University of New Jersey. Peter E. Nathan made helpful suggestions on the manuscript.

operant research relevant to teaching language to nonverbal subjects; it also attempts to identify problem areas in the research. In particular it raises the question of the extent to which operantly trained speech generalizes to the natural environment. While much of the cited literature is related to the theoretical analysis of language acquisition, the present discussion focuses more on the pragmatic issue of teaching speech rather than on the theoretical questions regarding learned versus innate language functions.

Few reviews are complete. The present article excludes unpublished dissertations as well as papers read at meetings. The term *nonverbal* has generally been limited to intellectually retarded subjects who are mute or have minimal functional speech, although a few critical studies of somewhat more verbal subjects have been included. As a result, studies of normally developing or "culturally deprived" children are excluded here, as are those with "electively mute" subjects, since these subjects have a full repertoire of responses but have difficulty identifying the discriminative stimuli of speech (Isaacs, Thomas, & Goldiamond, 1965; Sherman, 1963, 1965).

This review has been divided into four sections: attention, nonverbal imitation, verbal imitation, and functional language, which correspond to the stages of training typically used to teach nonverbal subjects.

ATTENTION

The first prerequisite for teaching speech is a child who attends to his teacher. There are two basic settings for establishing attending behavior. In one, the child and adult are seated facing each other in an open space. In the other, the child is enclosed in an isolation booth. Using the first procedure, Lovaas, Berberich, Perloff, and Schaeffer (1966) seated their child and model with their heads approximately 30 cm apart, and the adult used his legs to restrain the child from leaving. The booth procedure was pioneered by Hewett (1965) and later used by Blake and Moss (1967) and Fineman and Ferjo (1969). All researchers placed their subjects in booths in order to maximize the probability that they would be facing the experimenter when the stimuli were presented. The direct contact procedure between experimenter and subject is more popular than the booth, probably because of simplicity, as well as the concern that the booth creates specific stimulus conditions that might hamper later generalization. While Hewett reported no such difficulty, the direct contact method still appears intuitively more parsimonious.

The general pattern in establishing eye contact is to: (a) reinforce spontaneous eye contact if it occurs or prompt eye contact with food held near the model's face and the verbal command, "Look at me" and then (b) reinforce on a continuous basis responses occurring within 5 seconds of the command. The reward schedule is gradually reduced to an intermittent one (e.g., Brooks, Morrow, & Gray, 1968; Kozloff, 1973). The primary variations around this pattern depend upon whether: (a) the subject is given a command, (b) training is done individually or in a group, (c) the eyes or the mouth are the focus of gaze behavior, and (d) primary or secondary reinforcement is used.

Lovaas et al. (1966) rewarded their subjects with food for visually fixing, without command, upon the model's mouth to a criterion of 50 percent of each session. Hewett (1965) and Martin, England, Kaprowy, Kilgour, and Pilek (1968) likewise waited for the child to attend and then rewarded the behavior. This strategy appears well suited in the group setting employed by Martin et al. While Gardner, Pearson, Bercovici, and Bricker (1968) relied exclusively upon praise and physical contact to increase attending behavior in their subject, food is generally heavily used in the early stages of training. Although most researchers describe rapid establishment of eye contact, Kent, Klein, Falk, and Guenther (1972) reported difficulty with their subjects.

Less formal strategies for establishing attention include holding the child in one's lap (Kerr, Meyerson, & Michael, 1965) and using a mirror and glasses to induce the subject to look at the experimenter (Colligan & Bellamy, 1968). Ney (1973) examined the effects of noncontingent, as contrasted with contingent, reward upon eye contact. His observation of increased eye contact during noncontingent reward, as compared to baseline, can best be explained as an experimental artifact (Harris, 1974). Risley (1968), in a widely cited study of the use of shock to eliminate dangerous climbing behavior, reported increased sitting and eye contact as positive side effects of the aversive conditioning procedures.

McConnell's (1967) study suggests the extent to which eye contact may be under stimulus control. Having established eye contact with smiles and praise, he went on to show that the nature of specific toys in the room influenced the degree of eye contact emitted by the subject. His data point to the pervasive problem of teaching generalization of response to the child with autistic behavior.

NONVERBAL IMITATION

Once attending behaviors are established, the next step in language training is teaching nonverbal imitative behaviors (e.g., Bricker &

Bricker, 1970; Buddenhagen, 1971; Kozloff, 1973), although not all researchers report this phase (e.g., Lovaas et al., 1966). Typically the child is taught a series of gross motor imitations such as clapping, standing, or touching his toes. These gross movements then progress to more refined movements around the mouth (e.g., Marshall & Hegrenes, 1970; Sloane, Johnston, & Harris, 1968; Stark, Giddan, & Meisel, 1968). Nonverbal imitation training may be done individually or in a group (e.g., Borus, Greenfield, Spiegel, & Daniels, 1973; Koegel & Rincover, 1974).

Interestingly there are few data documenting the extent to which nonverbal training facilitates later verbal imitative training nor the quantity of training necessary to enhance generalizations from nonverbal to verbal imitation. The value of nonverbal imitation training has been more a clinical assumption than an empirical fact. When Garcia, Baer, and Firestone (1971), using four retarded subjects in a multiple-baseline design, explored the degree of generalization across four topographically different classes of imitative behavior (small motor, large motor, short vocal, and long vocal) they found a lack of generalization across classes. Probe responses were imitated only when they were of the type previously trained or currently being trained. Buddenhagen (1971) likewise reported that the transition from nonverbal to verbal imitation was extremely difficult.

In a related vein, Churchill, Hingtgen, and their colleagues looked at the generalization of various forms of imitative behavior (Churchill, 1969; Hingtgen & Churchill, 1970; Hingtgen, Coulter, & Churchill, 1967). Their results point to the variability existing among subjects and the need for caution in assuming that skills acquired in one modality will generalize to another. Some subjects acquired perceptual skills in 10 hours that other subjects had not acquired after 600 hours (Hingtgen & Churchill, 1969).

In an early study of nonverbal imitation in autistic chlidren, Metz (1965) established generalized imitation of nonverbal behavior using praise and food as reinforcement. However, as Baer, Peterson, and Sherman (1967) pointed out, verbal praise was also delivered for new imitations, thus making it difficult to separate the effects of generalization from the reinforcing properties of praise. This study also failed to include a reversal or a similar experimental manipulation, making it impossible to attribute the increase in imitative behavior to training. Nevertheless, the demonstration that imitative behavior could be trained in subjects with little initial inclination to imitate provided an impetus for further research.

In a study focused upon using imitation to build complex behaviors in schizophrenic children, Lovaas, Freitas, Nelson, and Whalen (1967) successfully established such activities as drawing, printing, self-care skills, and preschool games by these means. The degree of generalization and the use of shaping to develop simple imitative acts into complex skills that were maintained without immediate external reinforcement suggests how useful generalized imitative behavior can be in training nonverbal behavior. Nevertheless, as Lovaas et al. (1967) indicated, even after a year of intensive training there were limits to the extent of generalized imitation observed. The gap between the imitative behavior of their subjects to the wide-ranging imitation of the normal child remains formidable.

The maintenance of nonreinforced imitation is a critical issue in the generalization of appropriate verbal behavior. The goal of language training is verbal behavior that is maintained on the intermittent basis that characterizes reinforcement in the natural environment. The normal child must emit familiar responses again and again with minimal reinforcement and must generate novel responses that may or may not be reinforced. These requirements make language training difficult and enhance the importance of that literature which has dealt with the question of generalized imitation, both verbal and nonverbal. The identification of variables central to this process would certainly aid in the programmed development of generalized verbal imitation.

An important study by Baer et al. (1967) systematically evaluated the learning of generalized imitation in three retarded youngsters showing no preliminary evidence of imitation. The authors trained a variety of imitative behaviors with shaping, fading, and physically moving the subject's body through the act. They used probes to test for generalization, a differential-reinforcement-of-the phase in which activities other than imitation were reinforced to demonstrate the importance of reinforcement in maintaining imitation, and new experimenters to show generalization from the original trainer to others. Generalized imitative behavior was established in all three subjects, who learned new responses in shorter periods of time and became increasingly likely to imitate new responses upon their initial introduction. In explaining their results Baer et al. suggested that generalized imitation occurs because similarity to the model takes on a reinforcing function as well as a discriminative one. Similarity in and of itself could then serve to reinforce imitative behavior.

Peterson (1968) pursued the studies of Baer et al. (1967) using one of the subjects from that earlier research. In his first experiment, he attempted to free one of the previously learned imitative responses from the general response class of imitative behavior. Although it was possible to extinguish a single response under conditions of massed evocation without reinforcement, this same response continued to be emitted when the evoking stimulus was interspersed among a series of imitative stimuli. Thus, the discrimination of this nonreinforced response proved difficult to establish. Investigating the idea that similarity between model and subject might be a factor reinforcing continued imitative behavior during extinction, Peterson hypothesized that if similarity per se were reinforcing, then non imitative behavior, unlike imitative behavior, would extinguish under both massed and interspersed presentations. Contrary to prediction, the nonimitative responses resembled imitative responses under both massed and interspersed conditions, suggesting that similarity per se was not the crucial variable maintaining responding under interspersed conditions. In his discussion, Peterson referred to Bandura's (1968) notion that difficulty in discrimination may account for the maintenance of nonreinforced imitative behavior. Massed evocation makes this discrimination easier than does interspersed evocation.

Demonstration of generalized imitation has been easier than its explanation. Studies with normal children point to a number of variables that may influence the performance of nonreinforced imitative behavior. Burgess, Burgess, and Esveldt (1970) suggested that nonreinforced imitation occurs as a function of one (or a combination) of four variables: (a) the similarity between experimenter and subject takes on reinforcing value, (b) the subject imitates because of his interpretation of the experimenter's instructions, (c) subtle cues from the experimenter reinforce behavior, or (d) the subject discriminates (or fails to discriminate) situations in which he is reinforced from those in which he is not. Peterson and Whitehurst (1971) found, for example, that the presence or absence of the experimenter influenced the likelihood that their young subjects would imitate.

Subject characteristics such as intelligence may influence which of these factors is most important in a given instance. Bright children, for example, may discriminate reinforced from nonreinforced behavior and then respond on the basis of what they believe the experimenter expects. In the case of the nonverbal child, many of whom are below average intellectually and who lack the language for complicated conceptualizations, a parsimonious explanation may lie in their failure to discriminate reinforced from nonreinforced behavior. The task of discrimination may actually be too complex for some of these children.

It might be instructive to create a situation in which added stimulus cues would make it easier for the retarded nonverbal child to discriminate reinforced and nonreinforced behavior. If, for example, nonreinforced imitations were always done in a dim light or were accompanied by a buzzer, this cue might reduce task complexity. Peterson's (1968) massed extinction procedure might have served primarily to aid the child in her discrimination of the nonreinforced task. The observation that the extinguished response reoccurred when interspersed among imitative stimuli might be interpreted to mean that the discrimination broke down in a more complex environment.

Although the roles of task complexity and similarity between model and subject remain somewhat obscure, the importance of reinforcement is clearer (Bry & Nawas, 1972). As Baer et al. (1967) and Peterson (1968) have shown, reinforcement of some imitative behavior serves to maintain the general class of imitative behavior, and withdrawal of reinforcement leads to the extinction of previously reinforced, as well as nonreinforced, imitative behavior.

The small number of well-executed studies using atypical children and the limited number of subjects employed in these studies make general statements about learning nonverbal imitation difficult. Although subjects do learn generalized imitation, at least within topographically similar categories, the amount of time required and the degree of generalization to dissimilar categories vary. Parametric studies examining variables that influence the speed of generalization and the limits of transfer would have pragmatic value for the clinician.

Related to training of imitative behavior is training to follow commands. While most imitative training consists of a sequence in which the experimenter says to the subject, "Do this," and then models a nonverbal behavior, in teaching obedience to commands the subject is told, "Clap your hands," Stand up," and so forth. The subject must make a vocal-motor association involved in nonverbal imitation. While developmentally normal children acquire the ability to imitate before they can follow commands, it is not clear what implications this holds for teaching language to the nonverbal child, since the developmental model has not been shown to be superior for the training of these chlidren. The value of teaching the following of commands, as compared to nonverbal imitation, has not been fully explored nor has it been shown in what sequence to place these two behaviors. Clinically, various approaches have been taken to the problem. Thus, Hewett (1965) mixed both imitation and command training during the same phase, Blake and Moss (1967) appear to have relied exclusively upon command training as their precursor to verbal imitation, and the bulk of the studies, as cited above, used imitation training but also included a few simple commands, such as, "Look at me" or "Sit down." While it is not clear which approach is most efficient, the data suggest that generalized obedience to commands follows later than generalized nonverbal imitation. This conclusion is based upon a few, but very consistent, studies.

Studies of following commands have generally not been oriented toward eventual development of verbal behavior but have focused instead upon the kind of nonverbal obedience that is adaptive within an institutional setting. Whitman, Zakaras, and Chardos (1971) trained two retarded subjects to obey instructions and to generalize this obedience to new instructions—although generalization was less likely to occur with more complex commands or when the instructions contained unfamiliar words. Two other important studies show the serious limits encountered during the generalization of compliance to commands by nonverbal subjects. Striefel and Wetherby (1973) found that although their subject learned to obey commands, this behavior failed to generalize to untrained probes. Their data suggest that the number of words in the command, the position of the verb, and previous training with the noun and verb all influenced the subject's ability to respond to a new command. In a later study, Striefel, Bryan, and Aikens (1974) transferred control of behavior from nonverbal imitation to verbal instruction. Like Striefel and Wetherby they reported a lack of generalization to responses that had not been specifically trained. The need for procedures to enhance generalization of auditory-motor training is clear. It seems that on an intuitive basis visual-motor generalization may be simpler than auditory-motor because in the first case, once the subject has learned to relate his body to that of the model, he can *see* what he has to do, while in the second case he must understand all of the words involved and make discriminations about the sequence of words before he responds. Thus, while a few simple commands such as "Look at me" or "Sit down" may be quickly taught as specific instances, the general training of commands may follow more readily at a later stage of language training than nonverbal imitation.

VERBAL IMITATION

Most researchers adopt some variation of the four steps established by Lovaas et al. (1966) in training verbal imitation: (a) Reward all vocalization, (b) reward vocalization occurring within 6 seconds of the model's vocalization, (c) reward vocalization within 6 seconds of the model's vocalization that approximates the vocalization of the model, and (d) introduce a new sound randomly interspersed with the sound from Step c. Beyond this point the process is one of increasing the number of discriminated sounds.

Since the initial research of the mid-1960s (Hewett, 1965; Lovaas et al., 1966; Salzinger, Feldman, Cowan, & Salzinger, 1965; Wolf, Risley, & Mees, 1964; Risley & Wolf, Note 1), there have been a variety of case reports describing operant procedures for teaching speech to mute or echolalic children (e.g., Blake & Moss, 1967; Chapel, 1970; Colligan & Bellamy, 1968; Cook & Adams, 1966; Goldstein & Lanyon, 1971; Guess, Rotherford, & Twichell' 1969; Kerr et al., 1965; Marshall & Hegrenes, 1970, 1972; Picaizen, Berger, Baronofsky, Nichols, & Karen, 1969; Risley & Wolf, 1967; Schell, Stark, & Giddan, 1967; Sloane et al., 1968; Stark et al., 1968; Sulzbacher & Costello, 1970). These procedures have been applied in group as well as individual settings (e.g., Borus et al., 1973; Koegel & Rincover, 1974). Reports on this work vary widely in sophistication and innovation. Nevertheless, replicating basic procedures in a variety of laboratories increases the confidence one can place in the techniques. Since these procedures are now well established, new case studies should involve exploration of novel procedures and should incorporate appropriate controls. The need for continual evaluation is highlighted by the suggestion of the preceding section that the value of nonverbal imitation training may be largely "superstitious" in relation to training verbal imitation.

As Jacobson, Bernal, and Lopez (1973) have shown, this insistence upon experimental control is not an academic exercise. These authors trained a retarded youth who had no intelligible speech to make a nonverbal two-choice discrimination. Their subject learned the discrimination, but of greater interest in the present context, he also started speaking intelligible words. The skill was acquired without direct verbal training. This finding suggests how essential it is that studies be designed to allow precise identification of those factors that are in fact responsible for the establishment of speech behavior.

A wide range of reinforcing agents have been used to establish verbal behavior in nonverbal subjects. Although the most common of these is food coupled with praise, others have included colored lights (Blake & Moss, 1967; Fineman, 1968a, 1968b), tokens (e.g., Borus et al., 1967; Guess et al., 1969; McReynolds & Huston, 1971; Steeves, Martin, & Pear,

1970), music (Buddenhagen, 1971), physical contact (e.g., Kerr et al., 1965; Lovaas et al., 1966), games (Hewett, 1965; Sloane et al., 1968), and play with a tape recorder (Buddenhagen, 1971). Following initial training on a continuous reinforcement schedule, reinforcement is typically shifted to an intermittent schedule although praise may remain on the continuous reinforcement schedule (e.g., Drash, Caldwell, & Leibowitz, 1970; Salzinger et al., 1965; Schroeder & Baer, 1972; Steeves et al., 1970). This shift is critical because maintenance in the natural environment is almost always on an intermittent basis. The importance of using different kinds of reinforcement in different phases of training was suggested by McReynolds (1970), who demonstrated that primary reinforcers were more effective than social reinforcers during the initial phases of learning a verbal behavior but that once the behavior was established, social reinforcement was sufficient to maintain the response.

The forms of punishment used to suppress unwanted behaviors during language training are quite variable and include isolation and darkness (Hewett, 1965), time-out (e.g., Borus et al., 1973; McReynolds, 1969), response cost (McReynolds & Huston, 1971), increased task complexity (Sailor, Guess, Rutherford, & Baer, 1968), and shouts and slaps (Koegel & Rincover, 1974; Lovaas et al., 1966). The report by Steeves et al. (1970) that under certain conditions a self-imposed time-out may be reinforcing, illustrates once again the importance of careful observation of each subject as well as definition of reinforcement and punishment on the basis of behavior change. While the majority of studies ignored errors and used punishment only to reduce disruptive behavior, McReynolds and Huston (1971) punished imitative errors by response cost. Their finding of decreased performance with response cost, as compared to reinforcement only, suggests that their subjects may have had difficulty forming a discrimination between punishment for speech errors and speech per se.

Generally in teaching verbal behavior, the model provides help for the subject in the form of prompting, fading, and other cues to responding. The form and extent of these cues has been variable. In a study designed to develop vocalization in the presence of another child, Hingtgen and Trost (1966) increased the rate of vocalization between their subjects without any modeling or instructions by the experimenter, but simply by shaping successive approximations of the desired response. However, the level of vocalization that emerged was not as complex as that achieved in studies using more direct procedures. Sounds that permit manual prompting and those that offer visual cues are often selected for early training to maximize available cues (e.g., Lovaas et al., 1966; Sloane et al., 1968). Those studies using fading and prompting generally describe a procedure of forwarding chaining and fading (e.g., Yellow, Yell, Ye). However, McReynolds (1967, 1970) and MacCubrey (1971) used backward chaining to teach complex sounds (e.g., m, im, rim, cream). There are no data comparing the differential effectiveness of these two strategies. More importantly, there are no data indicating the long-term desirability of providing prompts in language training, nor that it is appropriate to reinforce prompted behavior. Lovaas, Koegel, Simmons, and Long (1973) and Lovaas, Schreibman, and Kogel (1974) indicated that experience with their subject population led to serious reconsiderations of the use of prompts and prompt-fading procedures. They suggested that stimulus overselectivity in autistic children slows the acquisition of responses where a shift in stimulus control is required. Regardless of the theoretical explanation, the pragmatic question of the use of prompts and the rewarding of prompted behavior remains of critical clinical importance. Research in this area must examine both short-term effects of learning on individual trials and long-term effects in terms of retention and generalization.

Hewett (1965), commenting on the difficulty of teaching his subject to form the discrimination between the first two sounds he learned to imitate, noted that the use of two different reinforcers may have aided in the discrimination. Data from Schroeder and Baer (1972) suggest that verbal imitation training is facilitated when the subject is trained on a set of words concurrently, as opposed to a serial procedure, in which the words are trained one at a time and discrimination must then be established. These data are compatible with Sailor and Taman's (1972) demonstration that language-deficient autistic children had difficulty forming a discrimination between two prepositions taught with the same stimulus object.

Bricker and Bricker (1972), in evaluating imitation errors made by retarded subjects, found that these errors were not random but instead contained parts of the correct responses. Finding that the most common errors were labial-dental and lingua-dental placements, they attempted to train one group in these deficiencies, while a second group was trained on each sound directly. Contrary to expectation, there were no posttest differences between the two groups. Nelson and Evans (1968) used many physical prompts in articulation training.

While most published articles describe successful attempts to establish verbal imitative behavior, one occasionally comes upon an observation of failure (e.g., Garcia et al., 1971; Marshall & Hegrenes, 1972). One has to wonder about the rate of other failures, which are unpublished. While it is possible to raise methodological questions about these studies, in both cases cited the authors were established researchers who reported success with other subjects. Thus, it does not seem likely that they did not know how to implement the procedures. Possibly there are subjects in whom biological damage prohibits the learning of speech (although they are doubtless rare). More likely, we still have a good deal to learn about creating the proper conditions for teaching speech. Reports of failure might be very instructive for this purpose.

FUNCTIONAL LANGUAGE

Following the establishment of verbal imitation, the main thrust of language training is aimed at functional language. Generally the subject is first taught noun labels and then other forms of grammar. There are, however, no data to aid in deciding the proper temporal sequence for introducing various grammatical forms. The only guidelines thus far are convenience and developmental norms. Neither of these criteria has been demonstrated to bear any direct relationship to the learning needs of the nonverbal youngster. It is this stage that transforms the previous training into a useful skill—imitative speech per se has no communication value.

Many case studies have reported attempts to teach functional language to nonverbal subjects. Some of these involved children who were initially mute (e.g., Brawley, Harris, Allen, Fleming, & Peterson, 1969; Colligan & Bellamy, 1968; Hewett, 1965; Stark et al., 1968), while others had limited or echolalic speech (e.g., Goldstein & Lanyon, 1971; Jensen & Womack, 1967; Matheny, 1968; McClure, 1968; Ney, 1967; Ney, Palvesky, & Markely, 1971; Shaw, 1969; Sulzbacher & Costello, 1970; Tramontana & Shivers, 1971; Tramontana & Stimbert, 1970; Weiss & Born, 1967; Wetzel, Baker, Roney, & Martin, 1966; Wolf, Risley, & Mees, 1964). Although all researchers reported some success in establishing functional speech, the degree of experimental control was highly variable; consequently, it is difficult to identify the active treatment ingredients. Of particular interest, there is often little information about the degree of support for verbal behavior available from the environment.

In addition to case reports, a series of empirical studies during the past few years have explored the teaching of various grammatical forms and the procedures for establishing generalization of language. In one of the first of these studies, Guess, Sailor, Rutherford, and Baer (1968), using imitation and differential reinforcement, taught expressive plural nouns to a subject who had never used plural forms. The following year, Guess (1969) used similar procedures to establish receptive auditory plurals in two retarded subjects. He demonstrated once again the relative ease of building the response class of plurals but found that in spite of their receptive skill, the subjects were unable to generalize the knowledge to an expressive plural response class until specifically trained in that class. It appears that for some subjects expressive and receptive language may be functionally independent. Sailor (1971) explored the extent to which differential reinforcement influenced a subject's acquisition of various plural endings. The /-s/ and /-z/ endings were both acquired with similar ease, supporting the notion that differential reinforcement rather than a physiological factor is the crucial element in this learning. Guess and Baer (1973a) attempted to remedy some of the faults of earlier research on the plural response class with a study in which generative plural formation rules were taught concurrently for both expressive and receptive language. Their study merits additional description. Four severely retarded subjects able to articulate the /-s/ and /-es/ sounds necessary to form plurals, but displaying neither expressive nor receptive plural usage on pretest, were trained for 30 minutes a day using tokens and praise on an intermittent schedule. Two subjects were taught to use the /-s/ ending receptively and the /-es/ ending expressively, while the other two subjects received the opposite training. The words used were appropriate to the ending being trained (e.g., hat/hats versus bus/busses). Generalization to the other modality (receptive or expressive) using the same plural ending (/-s/ or /-es/) was tested by nonreinforced probes. Thus, a subject trained on expressive use of /-s/ endings was periodically probed for his receptive use of /-s/ endings. Consistent with previous research, Guess and Baer (1973a) found that teaching subjects to respond to novel instances within the same response class was relatively easy but that generalization across response classes remained more difficult to establish. Interestingly, however, one of the four subjects did show this generalization without any additional training. The remaining three subjects were trained in the opposite response classes by reinforcement of probe responses. In their discussion, Guess and Baer (1973a) emphasized,

> it is apparent that generalization between two modalities can occur, but by no means is an "automatic" phenomenon, even in condi-

tions . . . strongly emphasizing the functional similarity of both modalities (p. 328).

A more detailed description and a discussion of the theoretical importance of these studies for language acquisition may be found in a recent chapter by Guess and Baer (1973b).

Other studies that have built expressive or receptive response classes into the language of subjects of limited verbal ability include the training of receptive prepositions (Frisch & Schumaker, 1974), singular and plural declarative sentences (Garcia, Guess, & Byrnes, 1973), verb tenses (Lutzker & Sherman, 1974; Schumaker & Sherman, 1970) adjectival inflections (Baer & Guess, 1971), compound sentences (Stevens-Long & Rasmussen, 1974), complex sentences (Odom, Liebert, & Fernandez, 1969; Wheeler & Sulzer, 1970), and interrogative sentences (Twardosz & Baer, 1973). Many of these studies point toward the difficulty of teaching retarded or autistic subjects to generalize from expressive to receptive language or vice versa, an important finding whose implications extend beyond the training of any particular grammatical form. While it has been theorized that receptive language precedes expressive language (Chomsky, 1967; Lennenberg, 1962; Mykelbust, 1957) and even demonstrated with normal subjects (Fraser, Bellugi, & Brown, 1963; Mann & Baer, 1971; Winitz & Preisler, 1965), this developmental model may not hold true for the nonverbal child. The risk inherent in attempting to generalize from the normal speaker to the nonverbal child thus becomes evident.

Although the subjects in the studies by Guess (1969) and Guess and Baer (1973a) failed to show "spontaneous" generalization to probes in the untrained (expressive or receptive) modality, both studies suggest that training in one modality may facilitate learning in the other. Thus, Guess (1969) observed that the expressive acquisition of singulars and plurals was more rapid than the earlier receptive training. Likewise, Guess and Baer (1973a) noted that reinforcement of probe responses in the untrained modality lead to the fairly rapid acquisition of the correct response in that modality. These data are encouraging because they suggest that while responses across modalities are not automatic for all subjects, many show a savings with previous training in another modality. For some subjects it appears that the task is to learn not the content of the response but the discriminative stimuli setting the occasion for the response. For example, once learning that plural responses are called for in both expressive and receptive conditions, they have available the knowledge learned from one modality for use in the other.

Once language has been established within the training situation, the next step is the extension of functional speech to other people in addition to the trainer and to other settings beyond the therapy room. Many of the best-designed studies have failed to attempt this level of generalization. One exception is the recent study by Garcia (1974), who first trained his subjects in a simple conversational sequence and then probed for generalization to other persons and settings. His data point to the importance of using more than one person to train subjects from the onset of training.

The desirability of training subjects to respond in a variety of settings is also illustrated by the work of Koegel and Rincover (1974), who found that behaviors learned in a one-to-one setting did not systematically transfer to a one-to-eight classroom. Since a number of studies (Borus et al., 1973; Gray & Ryan, 1973; MacCubrey, 1971; Martin et al., 1968) have demonstrated the feasibility of group training, it appears desirable to ensure that at least part of a nonspeaker's training be done within a group to facilitate generalization.

One outgrowth of the research on teaching functional language has been the publication of systematic training programs (e.g., Blindert, 1971; Bricker, 1972; Bricker & Bricker, 1970; Gray & Ryan, 1973; Hartung, 1970; Kent, 1974; Kent et al., 1972 Lovaas, 1971 Marshal;l & Hegrenes, 1970; McKenna-Hartung & Hartung, 1973; McLean & McLean, 1974; Miller & Yoder, 1972; Rosen, Wesner, & Zisfein, 1972; Sailor, Guess, & Baer, 1973, Stark, Rosenbaum, Schwartz, & Wilson, 1973; Stremel, 1972). These programs vary widely in the empirical support they provide for the assumptions upon which they are based, the extent to which they have been tested on clinical populations, prerequisite language for entrance to the program, guidance in selecting criteria for advancing from step to step in the program, and the amount of detail provided. For example, Sailor et al. (1973) observed that if Bricker's (1972) model were fully carried out, it would surely produce functional language, but it would be so lengthy to execute that it would rarely be applied.

Two language training programs built upon a developmental model are Stremel's (1972) and Miller and Yoder's (1972), both of which cite the developmental data of Bloom (1970). The Gray and Ryan (1973) program, not built exclusively upon developmental assumptions, is highly elaborate in detail and logical in construction but has been tested primarily with dysphasic children of normal intelligence (Fygetakis & Gray, 1970; Gray & Fygetakis, 1968a, 1968b). The program of

Kent et al. (1972) focuses upon the early stages of language training including nonverbal precursors, while that of Gray and Ryan (1973) focuses more upon higher levels of functioning and assumes some initial competence. In general these programs all require continued testing with a diversity of subjects. There should be an emphasis in all of them upon generalization to the natural environment.

The transition from a formal training setting, be it individual or group, to the natural environment has received almost no systematic evaluation although this is the end goal of language training. Most of our data in this area come from case reports. Weiss and Born (1967), in an early report, observed that the generalization of functional language shown by their subject was disappointingly small in spite of encouragement by the ward staff. In general, studies that set out to train parents as therapists have reported good results in achieving generalization to the home and school (e.g., Brawley et al., 1969; Hewett, 1965; Kozloff, 1973).

The data pointing most dramatically to the importance of the environment in maintaining languaeg behavior taught within the clinical setting are those in the follow-up report of Lovaas et al. (1973), which clearly show the reversibility of treatment effects when the environment fails to make appropriate demands and reward desirable behavior.

DISCUSSION

Among the most important issues to emerge from this review are questions of prognosis, experimental design, and generalization to the natural environment.

Prognosis

Data suggest that children who fail to develop speech by 5 years of age have a poorer prognosis than do those who have language by that time (DeMyer, Barton, DeMyer, Norton, Allen, & Steele, 1973; Eisenberg, 1956; Rutter & Lockyer, 1967a, 1967b). What influence will the use of operant procedures for teaching speech have upon that prognostic factor? There is agreement among researchers that it is easier to teach language to a child who is echolalic or has had previous language than it is to teach a child who has never spoken. Wolf, Risley, and Mees (1964) discussed the greater ease with which their echolalic subjects learned to speak. Evans (1971) noted that for the child who has had at least a limited amount of language prior to training, "once some speech begins to emerge in the presence of an audience, a great deal more that has not been specifically taught will emerge as well" (p. 239). Lovaas et al. (1973) reported that their mute subjects were more behaviorally retarded than their echolalic subjects at intake, and while the mute subjects made proportionally greater gains, the echolalic subjects still appeared qualitatively superior at follow-up. Although these data do not negate the value of speech to a child who would have been mute without training, they do suggest that the existence of language prior to training may remain an important prognostic index.

Experimental Design

Although difficulties inherent in this area demand that a systematic view be taken of the problems confronting the researcher, much of the research regarding teaching language to the nonverbal subject is open to criticism. First, a number of different populations have been subsumed under the umbrella term *nonverbal*. Some subjects are echolalic, others have limited functional speech, some are mute and have never talked, others are presently mute but have a history of some language. The subjects likewise vary in IQ estimates—from "untestable" to normal intellectual potential. The diagnostic labels include *autism, childhood schizophrenia, dysphasia, mental retardation,* and *brain damage.* For some, environmental trauma may be identified; for others there are no obvious precursors of deficient language. These factors produce a highly heterogeneous population under the rubric of *nonverbal* and thereby compound the researcher's job by making it hard to find matched groups of subjects.

One response to this heterogeneity of subject population has been to design most research using single subjects. This strategy, using both reversal and multiple-baseline designs to employ each subject as his own control, answers some of the methodological problems presented by a mixed population. Nevertheless, it raises another question—the extent to which data based on one or two subjects can be safely generalized to a wider group. The need for larger studies with randomly selected subjects (Bricker, 1972) or for replications of single-subject studies is obvious. If the $n = 1$ study is repeated several times, this permits the identification of those variables that may influence behavior in different subjects. Hence, it is not the use of single-subject studies that is objectionable, but the use of only one or two subjects to draw conclusions that are applied to a heterogeneous population. Even within many of the operant studies using two or three subjects, the authors described one subject who failed to follow the pattern of the others. These varia· tions make it clear that we have not identified all of the parameters involved in language training; they make broader sampling and repli- cation imperative.

One fact that emerges from the examination of the case studies re- viewed here is that in many instances the authors excused their research on clinical grounds for failing to provide even minimal controls, to collect systematic data, or to determine the reliability of their observa- tions. The use of reversals, even for a brief time, or of a multiple- baseline design would strengthen many a clinical report beyond the state of being simply an anecdotal description.

Many psychologists have understandable reservations about using the reversal design in a clinical setting. Nevertheless, to the best of the pres- ent author's knowledge there are no reports of studies in which a return to baseline, once instituted, could not be readily undone, with a rapid return to treatment levels of responding. To the contrary, the more typical problem is to show the decrement in performance that ideally accompanies the reversal. It is often important to execute the reversal early enough in training to ensure that responding has not become so generalized that extinction is difficult. In addition, an experimental necessity may be turned into a therapeutic asset by using the reversal de- sign to show parents or other caretakers precisely how important the training procedures are for the maintenance of behavior. An effective reversal can illustrate for the lay person in a concrete and dramatic fashion the importance of maintaining appropriate environmental de- mands in the training of the nonverbal child.

In situations in which the reversal design is ethically questionable or esthetically unattractive, the multiple-baseline design provides valuable experimental control. Here again, parents or staff can be involved in the learning experience and sensitized to the importance of maintain- ing proper demands upon the child. Generally, people are responsive to the notion that a given behavior, having existed for n amount of time, can be allowed to go on for $n + 2$ weeks (say) until other behaviors have been trained. Obviously the span of time is a critical variable. Just as the duration of a reversal must be as brief as possible, so too must be the amount of time that treatment is withheld in a multiple baseline. Few people would object to withholding some aspect of training for a few weeks, while many would be appropriately distressed if training were withheld for months simply to satisfy experimental demands. The nature of the behavior must likewise be considered. The withholding of treatment for a life-threatening behavior has different implications than not training the preposition *on*, while the preposition *in* is trained.

Generalization

One issue emerged again and again throughout this review: the problem of teaching subjects to generalize their responses to novel stimuli within the same response class and to respond in a variety of settings and to a variety of people. The work of Lovaas, Schreibman, Koegel, and Rehm (1971) regarding the responses of autistic, retarded, and normal children to multiple-stimulus input may be relevant to this problem. In their study multiple stimuli (auditory, visual, and tactile) were presented simultaneously as signals that bar pressing would be reinforced. After responding was established, the subjects were tested by the presentation of the various components of the multiple-stimulus complex. Lovaas et al. found that autistic subjects responded to only one of the stimuli, retarded subjects to two, and normal subjects to all three. What stands out, in the context of the present discussion, is that neither autistic nor retarded subjects were able to use all of the cues available in the environment to mark the time for correct responding. A similar phenomenon may be noted in the language behavior of both groups. Having learned language under highly controlled conditions, they often failed to generalize to conditions that contained some, but not all, of the cues present during initial training. Since the autistic children in the Lovaas et al. research were also the most intellectually deficient, it may be that the important dimension was IQ rather than the phenomenon of stimulus overselectivity that is linked with autism. This more parsimonious explanation would cut across diagnostic groups and account for generalization difficulties in heterogeneous subjects.

If intellectually retarded nonverbal people have particular difficulty forming necessary discriminations and identifying the cues that set the occasion for different responses, one of the important factors in facilitating generalization is repeated training in a wide number of settings. This means that language training must focus upon the natural environment rather than the classroom.

This review has shown that it is relatively easy to establish generalized responding within a given response class, be it gross motor imitation, verbal imitation, or a given grammatical construct. However, the transition from this stage to performance under wide-ranging conditions has received far less attention than it deserves. This doubtless reflects, at least in part, the greater difficulty that gathering data within the natural environment presents, as compared to the laboratory. Nevertheless, the technology for doing such research exists. It appears that this is the critical direction our attention must now take. The training of parents as therapists is doubtless especially important in this respect (e.g., Goldstein & Lanyon, 1971; Hewett, 1965; Kozloff, 1973). Lovaas et al. (1973), in their follow-up study, made it clear that we must facilitate the transfer of the child's skills to the natural environment and ensure that there is sufficient reinforcement to sustain these behaviors beyond the therapy room.

REFERENCE NOTE

1. RISLEY, T. R. & WOLF, M. M. Experimental manipulation of autistic behaviors and generalization into the home. In H. Work (Chair), *Experimental Studies in Childhood Schizophrenia.* Symposium presented at the meeting of the American Psychological Association, Los Angeles, September 1964.

REFERENCES

BAER, D. M. & GUESS, D. Receptive training of adjectival inflection in mental retardates. *J. Appl. Behav. Anal.,* 1971, 4, 129-139.

BAER, D. M., PETERSON, R., & SHERMAN, J. The development of imitation by reinforcing behavioral similarity to the model. *J. Exp. Anal Behav.,* 1967, 10, 405-416.

BANDURA, A. Social-learning theory of identifacatory processes. In D. A. Goslin & D. D. Glass (Eds.), *Handbook of Socialization Theory and Research.* Chicago: Rand McNally, 1968.

BLAKE, P. & MOSS, T. The development of socialization skills in an electively mute child. *Behav. Res. & Ther.,* 1967, 5, 349-356.

BLINDERT, H. D. The science of behavior, behavior modification, and verbal behavior. *IRAL,* 1971, 9, 53-62.

BLOOM, L. *Language Development: Form and Function in Emerging Grammars.* Cambridge, Mass.: MIT Press, ,1970.

BORUS, J. F., GREENFIELD, S., SIEGEL, B., & DANIELS, G. Establishing imitative speech employing operant techniques in a group setting. *J. Speech Hear. Dis.,* 1973, 38, 533-541.

BRAWLEY, E. R., HARRIS, F. R., ALLEN, K. E., FLEMING, R. S., & PETERSON, R. F. Behavior modification of an autistic child. *Behav. Sci.,* 1969, 14, 87-97.

BRICKER, W. A. A systematic approach to language training. In R. L. Schiefelbusch (Ed.), *Language of the Mentally Retarded.* Baltimore, Md.: University Park Press, 1972.

BRICKER, W. A. & BRICKER, D. D. A program of language training for the severely handicapped child. *Except. Child.,* 1970, 37, 101-111.

BRICKER, W. A. & BRICKER, D. D. Assessment and modification of verbal imitation with low-functioning retarded children. *J. Speech Hear. Res.,* 1972, 15, 690-698.

BROOKS, B. D., MORROW, J. E., & GRAY, W. F. Reduction of autistic gaze aversion by reinforcement of visual attention responses. *J. Spec. Educ.,* 1968, 2, 307-309.

BRY, P. M. & NAWAS, M. M. Is reinforcement necessary for the development of a generalized imitation operant in severely and profoundly retarded children? *Amer. J. Ment. Defic.,* 1972, 76, 658-667.

BUDDENHAGEN, R. *Establishing Vocalizations in Mute Mongoloid Children.* Champaign, Ill.: Research Press, 1971.

BURGESS, R. L., BURGESS, J. M., & ESVELDT, K. C. An analysis of generalized imitation. *J. Appl. Behav. Anal.,* 1970, 3, 39-46.

CHAPEL, J. L. Behavior modification techniques with children and adolescents. *Can. Psychiat. Assn. J.,* 1970, 15, 315-318.

CHOMSKY, N. The general properties of language. In C. Millikan and F. Darley (Eds.), *Brain Mechanisms Underlying Speech and Language.* New York: Grune & Stratton, 1967.

CHURCHILL, D. W. Psychotic children and behavior modification. *Amer. J. Psychiat.,* 1969, 125, 1585-1590.

COLLIGAN, R. C. & BELLAMY, C. M. Effects of a two-year treatment program for a young autistic child. *Psychother., Theory, Res. Pract.,* 1968, 5, 214-219.

COOK, C. & ADAMS, H. E. Modification of verbal behavior in speech deficient children. *Behav. Res. & Ther.,* 1966, 4, 265-271.

DeMYER, M. K., BARTON, S., DeMYER, W. E., NORTON, J. A., ALLEN, J., & STEELE, R. Prognosis in autism: A follow-up study. *J. Aut. Child. Schiz.,* 1973, 3, 199-246.

DRASH, P. W., CALDWELL, L. R., & LEIBOWITZ, J. M. Correct and incorrect response rates as basic dependent variables in the operant conditioning of speech in nonverbal subjects. *Psychol. Aspects Dis.,* 1970, 17, 16-23.

EISENBERG, L. The autistic child in adolescence. *Amer. J. Psychiat.,* 1956, 112, 607-613.

EVANS, I. M. Theoretical and experimental aspects of the behavior modification approach to autistic children. In M. Rutter (Ed.), *Infantile Autism: Concepts, Characteristics and Treatment.* Baltimore, Md.: Williams & Wilkins, 1971.

FINEMAN, K. R. Shaping and increasing verbalizations in an autistic child in response to visual-color stimulation. *Percept. Motor Skills,* 1968, 27, 1071-1074. (a)

FINEMAN, K. R. Visual-color reinforcement in establishment of speech by an autistic child. *Percept. Motor Skills,* 1968, 26, 761-762. (b)

FINEMAN, K. R. & FERJO, J. Establishing and increasing verbalizations in a deaf schizophrenic child through the use of contingent visual-color reinforcement. *Percept. Motor Skills,* 1969, 29, 647-652.

FRASER, C., BELLUGI, U., & BROWN, R. Control of grammar in imitation, comprehension, and production. *J. Verbal Learn. Verbal Behav.,* 1963, 2, 121-135.

FRISCH, S. A. & SCHUMAKER, J. B. Training generalized receptive prepositions in retarded children. *J. Appl. Behav. Anal.,* 1974, 7, 611-621.

FYGETAKIS, L. & GRAY, B. Programmed conditioning of linguistic competence. *Behav. Res. & Ther.,* 1970, 8, 153-163.

GARCIA, E. The training and generalization of a conversational speech form in nonverbal retardates. *J. Appl. Behav. Anal.,* 1974, 7, 137-149.

GARCIA, E., BAER, D. M., & FIRESTONE, I. The development of generalized imitation within topographically determined boundaries. *J. Appl. Behav. Anal.,* 1971, 4, 101-112.

GARCIA, E., GUESS, D., & BYRNES, J. Development of syntax in a retarded girl using procedures of imitation, reinforcement, and modeling. *J. Appl. Behav. Anal.,* 1973, 6, 299-310.

GARDNER, J. E., PEARSON, D. T., BERCOVICI, A. N., & BRICKER, D. E. Measurement, evaluation, and modification of selected social interactions between a schizophrenic child, his parents, and his therapist. *J. Consult. Clin. Psychol.,* 1968, 32, 537-542.

GOLDSTEIN, S. B. & LANYON, R. I. Parent-clinicians in the language training of an autistic child. *J. Speech Hear. Dis.,* 1971, 36, 552-560.

GRAY, B. B. & FYGETAKIS, L. The development of language as a function of programmed conditioning. *Behav. Res. & Ther.*, 1968, 6, 455-460. (a)

GRAY, B. B. & FYGETAKIS, L. Mediated language acquisition for dysphasic children. *Behav. Res. & Ther.*, 1968, 6, 263-280. (b)

GRAY, B. B. & RYAN, B. *A Language Training Program for the Non-Language Child.* Champaign, Ill.: Research Press, 1973.

GUESS, D. A functional analysis of receptive language and productive speech: Acquisition of the plural morpheme. *J. Appl. Behav. Anal.*, 1969, 2, 55-64.

GUESS, D. & BAER, D. M. An analysis of individual differences in generalization between receptive and productive language in retarded children. *J. Appl. Behav. Anal.*, 1973, 6, 311-329. (a)

GUESS, D. & BAER, D. M. Some experimental analyses of linguistic development in institutionalized retarded. In B. B. Lahey (Ed.), *The Modification of Language Behavior.* Springfield, Ill.: Charles C Thomas, 1973. (b)

GUESS, D., RUTHERFORD, G., & TWITCHELL, A. Speech acquisition in a mute, visually impaired adolescent. *New Outlook for the Blind*, 1969, 63, 8-13.

GUESS, D., SAILOR, W., RUTHERFORD, G., & BAER, D. M. An experimental analysis of linguistic development: The productive use of the plural morpheme. *J. Appl. Behav. Anal.*, 1968, 1, 297-306.

HARRIS, S. L. On the importance of being contingent—A reply to Ney. *J. Aut. Child. Schiz.*, 1974, 4, 94-97.

HARTUNG, J. R. A review of procedures to increase verbal imitation skills and increase functional speech in autistic children. *J. Speech Hear. Dis.*, 1970, 35, 203-217.

HEWETT, F. M. Teaching speech to an autistic child through operant conditioning. *Amer. J. Orthopsychiat.*, 1965, 35, 927-936.

HINGTGEN, J. N. & CHURCHILL, D. W. Identification of perceptual limitations in mute autistic children: Identification by the use of behavior modification. *Arch. Gen. Psychiat.*, 1969, 21, 68-71.

HINGTGEN, J. N. & CHURCHILL, D. W. Differential effects of behavior modification in four mute autistic boys. In D. W. Churchill, G. D. Alpern, & M. K. DeMyer (Eds.), *Infantile Autism.* Springfield, Ill.: Charles C Thomas, 1970.

HINGTGEN, J. N., COULTER, S. K., & CHURCHILL, D. W. Intensive reinforcement of imitative behavior in mute autistic children. *Arch. Gen. Psychiat.*, 1967, 17, 36-43.

HINGTGEN, J. N. & TROST, F. C. Shaping cooperative responses in early childhood schizophrenics: II. Reinforcement of mutual physical contact and vocal responses. In R. Ulrich, T. Stachnick, and J. Mabry (Eds.), *Control of Human Behavior* (Vol. 1). Glenview, Ill.: Scott, Foresman, 1966.

ISAACS, W., THOMAS, J., & GOLDIAMOND, I. Application of operant conditioning to reinstate verbal behavior in mute psychotics. *J. Speech Hear. Dis.*, 1960, 25, 8-12.

JACOBSON, L. I., BERNAL, G., & LOPEZ, G. W. Effects of behavioral training on the functioning of a profoundly retarded microcephalic teenager with cerebral palsy and without language or verbal comprehension. *Behav. Res. & Ther.*, 1973, 11, 143-145.

JENSEN, G. D. & WOMACK, M. Operant conditioning techniques in the treatment of an autistic child. *Amer. J. Orthopsychiat.*, 1967, 37, 30-34.

KENT, L. R. *Language Acquisition Program for the Severely Retarded.* Champaign, Ill.: Research Press, 1974.

KENT, L. R., KLEIN, D., FALK, A., & GENTHER, H. A language acquisition program for the retarded. In J. E. McLean, D. E. Yoder, & R. L. Schiefelbush (Eds.), *Language Intervention with the Retarded.* Baltimore, Md.: University Park Press, 1972.

KERR, N., MEYERSON, L., & MICHAEL, J. A procedure for shaping vocalizations in a mute child. In L. P. Ullman and L. Krasner (Eds.), *Case Studies in Behavior Modification.* New York: Holt, Rinehart & Winston, 1965.

KOEGEL, R. L. & RINCOVER, A. Treatment of psychotic children in a classroom environment. I. Learning in a large group. *J. Appl. Behav. Anal.*, 1974, 7, 45-60.

KOZLOFF, M. *Reaching the Autistic Child. A Parent Training Program.* Champaign, Ill.: Research Press, 1973.

LENNENBERG, E. H. Understanding language without ability to speak: A case report. *J. Abnorm. Soc. Psychol.*, 1962, 65, 419-425.

LOVAAS, O. I. Considerations in the development of a behavioral treatment program for psychotic children. In D. W. Churchill, G. D. Alpern, and M. K. DeMyer (Eds.), *Infantile Autism.* Springfield, Ill.: Charles C Thomas, 1971.

LOVAAS, O. I., BERBERICH, J. P., PERLOFF, B. F., & SCHAEFFER, B. Acquisition of imitative speech by schizophrenic children. *Science*, 1966, 151, 705-707.

LOVAAS, O. I., FREITAS, L., NELSON, K., & WHALEN, C. The establishment of imitation and its use for the development of complex behavior in schizophrenic children. *Behav. Res. & Ther.*, 1967, 5, 171-182.

LOVAAS, O. I., KOEGEL, R., SIMMONS, J. Q., & LONG, J. S. Some generalization and follow-up measures on autistic children in behavior therapy. *J. Appl. Behav. Anal.*, 1973, 6, 131-166.

LOVAAS, O. I., SCHREIBMAN, L., & KOEGEL, R. L. A behavior modification approach to the treatment of autistic children. *J. Aut. Child. Schiz.*, 1974, 4, 111-129.

LOVAAS, O. I., SCHREIBMAN, L., KOEGEL, R., & REHM, R. Selective responding by autistic children to multiple sensory input. *J. Abnorm. Psychol.*, 1971, 77, 211-222.

LUTZKER, J. R. & SHERMAN, J. A. Producing generative sentence usage by imitation and reinforcement. *J. Appl. Behav. Anal.*, 1974, 7, 447-460.

MACCUBREY, J. Verbal operant conditioning with young institutionalized Down's syndrome children. *Amer. J. Ment. Defic.*, 1971, 75, 696-701.

MANN, R. A. & BAER, D. M. The effects of receptive language training on articulation. *J. Appl. Behav. Anal.*, 1971, 4, 291-298.

MARSHALL, N. R. & HEGRENES, J. R. Programmed communication therapy for autistic mentally retarded children. *J. Speech Hear. Dis.*, 1970, 35, 70-83.

MARSHALL, N. R. & HEGRENES, J. The use of written language as a communication system for an autistic child. *J. Speech Hear. Dis.*, 1972, 37, 258-261.

MARTIN, G. L., ENGLAND, G., KAPROWY, E., KILGOUR, K., & PILEK, V. Operant conditioning of kindergarten class behavior in autistic children. *Behav. Res. & Ther.*, 1968, 6, 281-294.

MATHENY, A. B. Pathological echoic responses in a child: Effect of environmental mand and tact control. *J. Exp. Child Psychol.*, 1968, 6, 624-631.

McCLURE, R. Reinforcement of verbal social behavior in moderately retarded children. *Psychol. Reports*, 1968, 23, 371-376.

McCONNELL, O. L. Control of eye contact in an autistic child. *J. Child Psychol. Psychiat. All. Disci.*, 1967, 8, 249-255.

McKENNA-HARTUNG, S. & HARTUNG, J. R. Establishing verbal imitation skills and functional speech in autistic children. In B. B. Lahey (Ed.), *The Modification of Language Behavior.* Springfield, Ill.: Charles C Thomas, 1973.

McLEAN, L. P. & McLEAN, J. E. A language training program for nonverbal autistic children. *J. Speech Hear. Dis.*, 1974, 39, 186-193.

McREYNOLDS, L. V. Application of time-out from positive reinforcement for increasing the efficiency of speech training. *J. Appl. Behav. Anal.*, 1969, 2, 199-205.

McREYNOLDS, L. V. Reinforcement procedures for establishing and maintaining echoic speech by a nonverbal child. Applications of a functional approach to speech and hearing. In F. Giradeau and J. Spradlin (Eds.), *ASHA Monographs*, 1970, 14, 60-66.

McREYNOLDS, L. V. & HUSTON, K. Token loss in speech imitation training. *J. Speech Hear. Dis.*, 1971, 36, 486-495.

METZ, J. R. Conditioning generalized imitation in autistic children. *J. Exp. Child Psychol.*, 1965, 2, 389-399.

MILLER, J. F. & YODER, D. E. A language acquisition program for the retarded. In J. E. McLean, D. E. Yoder, and R. L. Schiefelbusch (Eds.), *Language Intervention with the Retarded.* Baltimore, Md.: University Park Press, 1972.

MYKELBUST, H. R. *Auditory Disorders in Children.* New York: Grune & Stratton, 1957.

NELSON, R. O. & EVANS, I. M. The combination of learning principles and speech therapy techniques in the treatment of non-communicating children. *J. Child Psychol. Psychiat All. Disci.,* 1968, 9, 111-124.

NEY, P. Operant conditioning of schizophrenic children. *Can. Psychiat. Assn. J.,* 1967, 12, 9-15.

NEY, P. G. Effects of contingent and non-contingent reinforcement on the behavior of an autistic child. *J. Aut. Child. Schiz.,* 1973, 3, 115-127.

NEY, P. G., PALVESKY, A. E., & MARKLEY, J. Relative effectiveness of operant conditioning and play therapy in childhood schizophrenia. *J. Aut. Child. Schiz.,* 1971, 1, 337-349.

ODOM, R. D., LIEBERT, R. M., & FERNANDEZ, L. Effects of symbolic modeling on the syntactical productions of retardates. *Psychonomic Science,* 1969, 17, 104-105.

PETERSON, R. F. Some experiments on the organization of a class of imitative behaviors. *J. Appl. Behav. Anal.,* 1968, 1, 225-235.

PETERSON, R. F. & WHITEHURST, G. J. A variable influencing the performance of generalized imitative behaviors. *J. Appl. Behav. Anal.,* 1971, 4, 1-9.

PICAIZEN, G., BERGER, A. A., BARONOFSKY, D., NICHOLS, A. C., & KAREN, R. Applications of operant techniques to speech therapy with nonverbal children. *J. Com. Dis.,* 1969, 2, 203-211.

RISLEY, T. R. The effects and side effects of punishing the autistic behaviors of a deviant child. *J. Appl. Behav. Anal.,* 1968, 1, 21-34.

RISLEY, T. R. & WOLF, M. M. Establishing functional speech in echolalic children. *Behav. Res. & Ther.,* 1967, 5, 73-88.

ROSEN, M., WESNER, C., & ZISFEIN, L. *Your Child Can Talk Too.* Elwyn, Pa.: Elwyn Institute, 1972.

RUTTER, M. & LOCKYER, L. A five to fifteen year follow-up study of infantile psychosis: I. Description of the sample. *Brit. J. Psychiat.,* 1967, 113, 1169-1182. (a)

RUTTER, M. & LOCKYER, L. A five to fifteen year follow-up study of infantile psychosis: II. Social and behavioral outcome. *Brit. J. Psychiat.,* 1967, 113, 1183-1199. (b)

SAILOR, W. Reinforcement and generalization of productive plural allomorphs in two retarded children. *J. Appl. Behav. Anal.,* 1971, 4, 305-310.

SAILOR, W., GUESS, D., & BAER, D. M. Functional language for verbally deficient children. *Ment. Retard.,* 1973, 11, 27-35.

SAILOR, W., GUESS, D., RUTHERFORD, G., & BAER, D. M. Control of tantrum behavior by operant techniques during experimental verbal training. *J. Appl. Behav. Anal.,* 1968, 1, 237-243.

SAILOR, W. & TAMAN, T. Stimulus factors in the training of prepositional usage in three autistic children. *J. Appl. Behav. Anal.,* 1972, 5, 183-190.

SALZINGER. K., FELDMAN, R. S., COWAN, J. E., & SALZINGER, S. Operant conditioning of verbal behavior of two young speech-deficient boys. In L. Krasner and L. P. Ullmann (Eds.), *Research in Behavior Modification.* New York: Holt, Rinehart & Winston, 1965.

SCHELL, R. E., STARK, J., & GIDDAN, J. G. Development of language behavior in an autistic child. *J. Speech Hear. Dis.,* 1967, 32, 51-64.

SCHROEDER, G. & BAER, D. M. Effects of concurrent and serial training no generalized vocal imitation in retarded children. *Devel. Psychol.,* 1972, 6, 293-301.

SCHUMAKER, J. & SHERMAN, J. A. Training generative verb usage by imitation and reinforcement procedures. *J. Appl. Behav. Anal.*, 1970, 3, 273-287.
SHAW, W. H. Treatment of schizophrenic speech disorder by operant conditioning in
play therapy. *Can. Psychiat. Assn. J.*, 1969, 14, 631-634.
SHERMAN, J. A. Reinstatement of verbal behavior in a psychotic by reinforcement
methods. *J. Speech Hear. Dis.*, 1963, 28, 398-401.
SHERMAN, J. A. Use of reinforcement and imitation to reinstate verbal behavior in
mute psychotics. *J. Abnorm. Psychol.*, 1969, 70, 155-164.
SLOANE, H. N., JOHNSTON, M. K., & HARRIS, F. R. Remedial procedures for teaching
verbal behavior to speech deficient or defective young children. In H. N. Sloane
and B. D. MacAulay (Eds.), *Operant Procedures in Remedial Speech and Language Training*. Boston: Houghton Mifflin, 1968.
STARK, J., GIDDAN, J. J., & MEISEL, J. Increasing verbal behavior in an autistic child.
J. Speech Hear. Dis., 1968, 33, 42-48.
STARK, J., ROSENBAUM, R. L., SCHWARTZ, D. & WILSON, A. The nonverbal child: Some
clinical guidelines. *J. Speech Hear. Dis.*, 1973, 38, 59-71.
STEEVES, J. M., MARTIN, G. L., & PEAR, J. J. Self-imposed time-out by autistic children
during an operant training program. *Behav. Ther.*, 1970, 1, 371-381.
STEVENS-LONG, J. & RASMUSSEN, M. The acquisition of simple and compound sentence
structure in an autistic child. *J. Appl. Behav. Anal.*, 1974, 7, 473-479.
STREMEL, K. Language training: A program for retarded children. *Ment. Retard.*, 1972,
10, 47-49.
STRIEFEL, S., BRYAN, K. S., & AIKENS, D. A. Transfer of stimulus control from motor to
verbal stimuli. *J. Appl. Behav. Anal.*, 1974, 7, 123-136.
STRIEFEL, S. & WETHERBY, B. Instruction-following behavior of a retarded child and
its controlling stimuli. *J. Appl. Behav. Anal.*, 1973, 6, 663-670.
SULZBACHER, S. I. & COSTELLO, J. M. A behavioral strategy for language training of a
child with autistic behavior. *J. Speech Hear. Dis.*, 1970, 35, 256-276.
TRAMONTANA, J. & SHIVERS, O. Behavior modification with an echolalic child: A case
note. *Psychol. Reports*, 1971, 29, 1034.
TRAMONTANA, J. & STIMBERT, V. E. Some techniques of behavior modification with an
autistic child. *Psychol. Reports*, 1970, 27, 498.
TWARDOSZ, S. & BAER, D. M. Training two severely retarded adolescents to ask ques-
tions. *J. Appl. Behav. Anal.*, 1973, 6, 655-661.
WEISS, H. H. & BORN, B. Speech training or language acquisition? A distinction
when speech training is taught by operant conditioning procedures. *Amer. J.
Orthopsychiat.*, 1967, 37, 49-55.
WETZEL, R. J., BAKER, J., RONEY, M., & MARTIN, M. Outpatient treatment and autistic
behavior. *Behav. Res. & Ther.*, 1966, 4, 169-177.
WHEELER, A. J. & SULZER, B. Operant training and generalization of a verbal response
form in a speech-deficient child. *J. Appl. Behav. Anal.*, 1970, 3, 139-147.
WHITMAN, T. L., ZAKARAS, M., & CHARDOS, S. Effects of reinforcement and guidance
procedures on instruction-following behavior of severely retarded children. *J.
Appl. Behav. Anal.*, 1971, 4, 283-290.
WINITZ, H. & PREISLER, L. Discrimination pretraining and sound learning. *Percept.
Mot. Skills*, 1965, 20, 905-916.
WOLF, M. M., RISLEY, T. R., & MEES, H. Application of operant conditioning pro-
cedures to the behavior problems of an autistic child. *Behav. Res. & Ther.*, 1964,
1, 305-312.

22

GENERALIZATION AND MAINTENANCE OF CLASSROOM TREATMENT EFFECTS

Hill M. Walker, Hyman Hops

and Stephen M. Johnson

University of Oregon

Two experiments involving children with behavior problems investigated, respectively, 1) the maintenance of appropriate classroom behavior following treatment in an experimental classroom, and 2) cross-situational consistency and generalization of treatment effects. In Experiment 1, two groups of four subjects were observed after treatment in a token economy operated classroom. Procedures to facilitate maintenance of treatment-produced behavior changes were successfully implemented for one group of subjects in their respective regular classrooms. The effects of the combined treatment generalized to a significantly greater degree in the subsequent academic year than did the treatment effects for subjects who were involved in only experimental classroom procedures. The results were discussed comparing process variables with duration of treatment. In Experiment

Reprinted with permission from *Behavior Therapy*, 6, 188-200, 1975.

The preparation of this manuscript and the research reported herein was supported by grants from the Bureau of the Handicapped, U.S. Office of Education, and from the National Institute of Mental Health. The authors thank Roberta Taussig for editing the manuscript.

2, children from the first study were observed in family interactions to determine whether they were also behavior
problems at home. Results indicated that only one of the five
subjects studied was deviant in the home setting. Further
observations following experimental classroom treatment
showed more child deviancy and parental negativeness than
before school intervention. A "behavioral contrast" interpretation of the results was discussed.

Countless studies have demonstrated that behavor modification procedures can be applied successfully in varied settings. However, there
has been an increasing recognition that such treatment effects tend to be
specific to the settings in which they are produced (O'Leary & Drabman, 1971; Kazdin & Bootzin, 1972). Researchers and other change
agents have experienced considerable difficulty in getting behavior
changes to generalize to settings in which the intervention procedures
have not been implemented. A number of studies have demonstrated
that "unprogrammed" generalization of treatment effects to nontreatment settings is the exception rather than the rule (Wahler, 1969;
Kuypers, Becker & O'Leary, 1968; Walker, Mattson & Buckley, 1971).

A problem closely related to setting generality is the persistence of
treatment effects over time, after formal treatment procedures have been
withdrawn. The available data indicate that treatment effects do not
automatically maintain when treatment procedures are abruptly withdrawn (Walker, Mattson & Buckley, 1971; Walker & Buckley, 1968;
Birnbrauer, Wolf, Kidder & Tague, 1965; and Kuypers, Backer & O'Leary,
1968). Unless gradual fading procedures or other scheduling techniques
are employed in the treatment process, it seems unlikely that the level
of behavior change achieved during treatment would be maintained
following intervention.

The present study investigated four questions related to generalization
and maintenance of treatment effects across both time and settings, and
to behavioral consistency across settings:

1. To what extent does behavior change produced in a highly
structured environment such as an experimental classroom generalize and maintain in a regular classroom setting under programmed
maintenance conditions?
2. Will maintenance of classroom treatment effects be greater,
over the long term, for a group of subjects who are involved in a
maintenance program in their regular classrooms after treatment in
an experimental classroom than for an equivalent group of subjects
who receive treatment in the experimental classroom only?

3. To what extent do deviant children exhibit disruptive behavior across settings? That is, to what extent does a child who is deviant in one setting, such as the school, exhibit deviant behavior in another setting, such as the home?

4. To what extent will intervention procedures implemented in one setting be reflected in changed behavior in a second setting where there has been no intervention?

Two separate experiments were conducted: Experiment 1 to investigate questions 1 and 2 and Experiment 2 to investigate questions 3 and 4.

EXPERIMENT 1: MAINTENANCE OF APPROPRIATE CLASSROOM BEHAVIOR FOLLOWING TREATMENT IN AN EXPERIMENTAL CLASSROOM

The purpose of Experiment 1 was to compare the performance of two groups of subjects after treatment in a token economy. Both groups were involved in approximately 4 months of intensive treatment in a special classroom setting. Following treatment, all subjects were returned to their regular classrooms.

For Group I subjects, additional procedures were implemented in the regular classroom to facilitate maintenance of their treatment-produced high rates of appropriate behavior. No such procedures were implemented for Group II subjects. Long-term follow-up data were collected for both groups.

METHOD

Subjects

Two groups were referred to the experimental classroom. The first consisted of four boys and one girl; the second of five boys. The children, ranging in age from 6 to 9 years, were enrolled in grades one, two, and three. One subject from each group moved away from the area before the present study was concluded. None of the eight remaining subjects came from the same elementary school.

Children in the two samples were referred for treatment because 1) school personnel reported extreme difficulty in managing their disruptive behavior in the regular classroom setting, 2) their behavior was characterized as acting-out and 3) they were regarded by the referring schools as highly deviant (Table 1). The comparative peer data provided for group I indicate the relatively high rates of inappropriate behavior emitted by the subjects.

TABLE 1

Percent of Total Time During Baseline Spent in Selected
Inappropriate Classroom Behaviors for Group 1 (and
Respective Peers) and Group II Subjects

		Non-attending	Noisy	Inappropriate vocal	Inappropriate physical	Inappropriate movement
Group I	S1	25.46%	7.38%	6.73%	0.48%	13.21%
	Peers	15.16%	1.69%	5.70%	0.24%	1.69%
	S2	27.94%	2.99%	12.90%	0.85%	5.21%
	Peers	15.16%	1.69%	5.70%	0.24%	1.69%
	S3	25.66%	10.78%	11.03%	0.83%	12.45%
	Peers	15.91%	2.71%	3.30%	0.00%	5.54%
	S4	17.78%	8.24%	14.24%	0.65%	12.65%
	Peers	16.01%	4.00%	2.70%	0.00%	4.00%
Group II[a]	S1	10.62%	9.32%	9.84%	0.52%	11.67%
	S2	6.38%	4.23%	16.66%	2.79%	14.97%
	S3	19.25%	6.10%	14.69%	0.05%	9.65%
	S4	11.75%	4.85%	14.09%	0.11%	6.05%

a Comparative peer data were not collected on Group II subjects.

The subjects met the following additional criteria: 1) high scores on the acting-out subscale of the Walker Problem Behavior Identification Checklist (Walker, 1970); 2) at least average IQ scores; 3) inadequate academic performance (educational deficit in the basic skills areas, for the two groups, ranged from 3 months to 1.5+ years); and 4) no gross physical or sensory deficit.

Settings

The experimental classroom facilities were adjoining and affiliated with a public elementary school in the Eugene School District. There were 32 elementary schools in the district with an average teacher-child ratio of 1:24.

The primary area for academic activities contained 6 double desks (approximately 20 × 45 in work surface), the teacher's desk, shelves and tables for the display of high interest materials for science and art projects and a carpentry room with a variety of tools and wood. Adjacent rooms provided sink and table facilities and an observation area with a one-way mirror. Space was also available for individual testing, tutoring, and remedial instruction. A small isolation (time-out) room containing a chair and desk adjoined the classroom.

Observation Recording System

A 17-category behavioral coding system was used to record the classroom behavior of the subjects and the social consequences provided by their teachers and/or peers. Eleven precisely defined subject behavior codes were designated *a priori* as appropriate (5) or inappropriate (6). The former consisted of Appropriate Work, Group Activity, Appropriate Vocalization, Positive Physical Contact, and Appropriate Movement. The inappropriate response classes were Inappropriate Work, Non-Attending, Noisy, Inappropriate Vocalization, Negative Physical Contact, and Inappropriate Movement. The codes Attention, Praise, Disapproval, Ignore, Positive Physical, and Negative Physical comprised the six social consequences.

Each subject's behaviors and consequences were recorded in 15-second intervals for 6-minute blocks. After recording the target child's behavior, the observer recorded the behavor of a peer for the next 6 minutes and then returned to record the behavior of the subject again. Thus, the observer alternated between the subject and his peers in each observation session.

Observations of the subjects were made in the regular classroom prior to enrollment in the experimental classroom; during treatment in the experimental classroom; and after treatment following their return to the regular classroom. Baseline data for each subject consisted of a minimum of 120 minutes of observation in the regular classroom over a 2-week period. Daily observations were recorded during the treatment phase and weekly observations during follow-up.

Observer Training

Eleven graduate and undergraduate students in education and psychology, interested in working with handicapped children, served as observers during the treatment and maintenance phases in the first year of the study. Second year follow-up data were collected by a graduate research assistant.

Observer training required approximately 1 week of daily 1-hour sessions. Training occurred in the experimental classroom observation facilities and in the regular classroom setting with the trainer, until specified criteria were reached.

Observer Reliability

Obeserver reliability was calculated using the percent agreement method. Each 15-second interval was scored for the number of agree-

ments and disagreements between pairs of observers. The total number
of agreements was divided by the total number of behaviors recorded
(agreements plus disagreements) to obtain the reliability coefficient. For
an agreement to be scored in any interval, observers were required to
agree not only on the behavior being coded, but also on the type of
agent response that followed the behavior.

All observers were required to meet the criterion of .90 for 5 consecutive 6-minute observations before their data were acceptable. In addition,
weekly reliability checks were required to maintain acceptable interobserver agreement. The mean reliability checks for the maintenance
period was .93, with individual reliabilities ranging from .90 to .97. For
the follow-up observer, the mean reliability was .90 with a range of
.70-.98.

Procedures

Group I subjects were enrolled in the experimental classroom from
October through January of the 1970-1971 school year. From February
through June of the same school year, Group II subjects were brought
into the experimental classroom and subjected to the same treatment,
while the maintenance procedures were simultaneously established for
Group I subjects in their regular classrooms.

Experimental classroom treatment. Both groups of subjects received
identical treatment in the experimental classroom. A complete description of the procedures is contained in Walker, Hops, and Fiegenbaum
(1971). Briefly, the treatment consisted of a token economy combined
with an intensive remedial instruction program in the basic skill areas
of reading, mathematics, spelling, and vocabulary. The three primary
non-academic treatment variables manipulated were token reinforcement,
social reinforcement, and response cost (subtracting earned points).

Regular classroom maintenance. Four major components were contained in the procedures designed to maintain the child's appropriate
behavior following his return to the regular classroom. A contract was
established between each teacher and the research project which specified the roles each would play in programming behavior maintenance.
The contract provided for: 1) training the teacher in behavior maintenance techniques; 2) weekly feedback on the child's performance; 3)
weekly meetings between the teacher and a project consultant; 4) positive
teacher consequences contingent upon the teacher's performance; and 5)
the child's performance. The purpose of the training was to acquaint

the teacher with principles and practice of behavior modification so that she could knowingly reinforce and thereby maintain the child's appropriate behavior in her classroom. Feedback was provided to help the teacher monitor the child's performance while a consultant provided support and guidance in establishing behavior modification procedures. In addition, the child's two reinforcement contingencies were introduced in an effort to maintain the teacher's newly acquired skills.

1. *Teacher training.* About a month before each child was to return to his regular classroom, his teacher was contacted to help her plan ways to make the child's re-entry as smooth as possible. Problems involved in maintaining behavioral gains made in the experimental classroom were also discussed. Considerable emphasis was placed on the importance of the teacher's role in maintaining the child's new behavior pattern.

The teacher agreed to read and master a semi-programmed basic text entitled *Modifying Classroom Behavior* (Buckley & Walker, 1970). Each teacher agreed to take a review test and to achieve a passing score of 90 percent. The test could be retaken until the teacher achieved the criterion.

2. *Feedback on student's performance.* An observer met weekly with each teacher to provide graphic records of the child's level of appropriate behavior during each observation session. These data indicated both how well the child was maintaining his new behavior pattern, and, indirectly, how well the teacher was succeeding in reinforcing that pattern.

3. *Teacher consultation.* Once a week, a project staff member who acted as a consultant met with each teacher. The consultant, a resource teacher, provided the regular classroom teacher with back-up support, consultation, feedback, and additional training and supervision in the application of specific behavior modification techniques. At these meetings, considerable attention was placed on the child's performance level as indicated by observer collected data.

The consultant did not dictate specific techniques which the teacher would have to use to achieve the desired level of maintenance. It was the teacher's responsibility to select which procedures would be most feasible in her classroom, following which the supervisor provided support, encouragement and guidance in implementing the teacher's decisions.

4. *Maintenance of teacher behavior.* Prior research (Walker, Mattson & Buckley, 1971; Walker & Buckley, 1972) suggests that appropriate behavior achieved in a token economy shows a considerable decline following simple reintegration into the regular classroom. This may be due,

in part, to the response cost involved in the extra effort required by the teacher to achieve maintenance. In the present study, the authors introduced two reinforcement contingencies to motivate the teacher to emit the necessary behaviors. The first involved reinforcement for fulfilling the terms of the contract between the project and the teachers. This required the teachers to read and master the text, and to meet weekly with the observer and the consultant. Reinforcement was given in the form of credit for a 6-hour course. Tuition for the course was paid by the project for each participating teacher. However, this contingency ensured only that the teacher had learned the skills and would accept feedback from project personnel. Thus, another reinforcer was made contingent upon the child's behavior, and, indirectly, the teacher's. The teacher's course grade was made dependent upon how well the child's behavior maintained during the 4-month period which constituted the remainder of the school year. The contingency was structured so that higher levels of posttreatment behavior maintenance resulted in higher grades. Criteria for grades ranging from A to C were based upon ratios computed between the child's appropriate behavior rates during the maintenance period and during treatment in the experimental classroom. The child's level of appropriate behavior averaged across all conditions in the experimental classroom constituted the baseline component for this ratio. For example, if the child maintained at 85 percent or better of this figure over the 4-month maintenance period, his teacher received a grade of A; if he maintained between 75 and 85 percent, she received a B; and if his behavior was maintained at less than 75 percent, a C grade was given. It was hoped that the ratio requirements coupled with appropriate reinforcement consequences would be instrumental in helping the teacher learn to shape adequate behavior maintenance.

Follow-up Procedures

Both groups were followed up for the first 4 months of the next school year (1971-1972). No maintenance procedure was implemented for either group during this period. Thus, it was possible to compare the follow-up performance of Group I subjects who received experimental classroom treatment plus maintenance with Group II subjects who received experimental classroom treatment only.

RESULTS

Treatment in the experimental classroom produced a dramatic increase in the appropriate behavior of subjects on both groups (Table 2).

TABLE 2

Means and Standard Deviations of Percent Appropriate Behavior
for Experimental Subjects During Baseline, Intervention,
Maintenance, and Follow-Up Conditions

	Baseline		Last 2 wk		Maintenance[a]		Follow-up	
Group I								
	X̄	SD	X̄	SD	X̄	SD	X̄	SD
S1	33.90%	15.22%	95.48%	5.81%	86.35%	19.25%	74.00%	15.05%
S2	24.05%	21.32%	92.36%	8.39%	86.41%	12.88%	89.00%	10.36%
S3	39.15%	16.44%	89.91%	14.18%	84.56%	19.84%	75.00%	15.91%
S4	38.23%	16.53%	98.69%	1.84%	91.66%	8.63%	83.00%	20.29%
X̄	33.83%	17.38%	94.11%	7.56%	87.25%	15.15%	80.25%	15.40%
Group II								
S1	42.00%	14.89%	98.88%	1.52%			57.00%	15.05%
S2	45.86%	17.60%	97.54%	3.43%			80.00%	10.36%
S3	35.23%	20.01%	97.23%	2.61%			67.00%	15.91%
S4	36.90%	11.69%	96.94%	2.26%			55.00%	20.29%
X̄	40.00%	16.05%	97.65%	2.46%			64.75%	15.40%

[a] Group II subjects did not receive the maintenance program.

No significant difference was found between the groups during baseline
($t(6) = 1.47$, $p =$ n.s.) or during the final weeks of intervention ($t(6)$
$= 1.69$, $p =$ n.s.) using arcsin transformations of the raw data.

To answer the question regarding the effects of establishing a maintenance program in the regular classroom following treatment in a token
economy, a repeated measures ANOVA was carried out on the baseline,
intervention, and maintenance scores of Group I. The means during
these periods were 33.83 percent, 94.11 percent, and 87.25 percent, respectively. The F ratio computed on the arcsin transformed scores was
statistically significant ($F(2,6) = 195.67$, $p < .001$). A Tukey *post-hoc* test
for the difference between the means showed the baseline level to be
significantly lower than either the means at the end of the treatment
phase ($p < .01$) and the maintenance phase ($p < .01$). However, a significant difference was found between the means for the last 2 weeks of
intervention and the maintenance period ($p < .01$). These data indicate
there was a significant drop in the level of appropriate behavior for
Group I subjects following reintegration into the regular classroom. However, the data indicate a superior maintenance effect for Group I subjects
in the next academic year under different stimulus conditions; Group I
subjects averaged 80.25 percent compared to the 64.75 percent mean for

Group II subjects. This difference was statistically significant $(t\,(6) =$ 2.27, $p < .05)$. Thus, appropriate behavior was maintained to a significantly greater degree for Group I than Group II subjects in long-term follow-up.

During the 4-month follow-up period, 12 minutes (two 6-minute periods) of observation data were collected on every peer in each subject's regular classroom. The peer group for Group I subjects averaged 80 percent appropriate behavior; for Group II, the peer group mean was 78 percent. A t-test of the difference between the means of the transformed scores was not statistically significant $(t\,(6) = 1.72, p =$ n.s.). These data indicate that there were no significant differences in the general level of appropriate behavior in the classroom environments of the two experimental groups during long-term follow-up.

DISCUSSION

The results of Experiment 1 suggest that superior long-term maintenance of treatment-produced behavior change may be achieved if experimental classroom treatment is immediately followed by an effective short-term maintenance program implemented in the regular classroom setting. The existence of the long-term effect is shown by the significantly greater generalization over time of behavior changes for Group I, which received both treatment and short-term maintenance procedures, when compared with Group II, which received only treatment.

The effectiveness of the regular classroom maintenance program used in this study can be shown by comparing it with two similar studies, Walker and Buckley (1972), and Walker, Mattson and Buckley (1971). All three studies reported using short-term maintenance procedures following experimental classroom treatment. Under these conditions, all found decreases in levels of appropriate behavior following return of subjects to the regular classroom. The 1972 and 1971 studies both found a decrease of 24 percentage points in level of appropriate behavior from treatment to maintenance conditions. The 1972 level decreased from 90 percent in treatment to 66 percent in maintenance; the 1971 level from 91 percent to 67 percent. By comparison, the present experiment resulted in a decrease of only 7 percentage points in appropriate behavior when subjects returned to the regular classroom. Presumably, this result can be attributed to differences in the efficacy of the short-term maintenance procedures used in the three studies.

The specific process (es) accounting for the superior long-term maintenance effect for Group I subjects were not evident from data collected in Experiment 1. Group I subjects were exposed to some type of behavioral intervention, in either an experimental or a regular classroom setting, for an entire academic year. Group II subjects were exposed to only 4 months of treatment. Therefore, the superior maintenance effect for Group I subjects in the following year could have been due simply to an increased length of exposure to behavioral intervention procedures and not to the regular classroom maintenance procedures *per se*. Presumably, a longer treatment period would provide for the acquisition of social and academic skills that would be more resistant to extinction than those acquired within a brief treatment period. Consequently, the same long-term persistence of treatment effects might have been achieved if Group I subjects had remained in the experimental classroom for the entire academic year. This, however, is an empirical question that cannot be answered within the context of the present experiment.

A limitation of the present study consists of the small number of subjects in both groups, thereby restricting generalization of the results beyond the experimental subjects. Replication using a larger number of subjects in both groups would be required to document thoroughly the effect of either an increased treatment period or a post-treatment maintenance procedure in accounting for superior long-term maintenance of appropriate behavior.

Additional research is needed to evaluate the effectiveness of different treatments in producing behavior maintenance over the long term. Moreover, very little data are available on the question of how long a given treatment has to be in effect before long-term maintenance can be achieved. Intervention procedures have traditionally been evaluated in terms of the magnitude and efficiency of behavior changes attributable to them. However, this may be an inappropriate criterion. It could be argued that the most effective treatment is the one that produces the most durable maintenance of appropriate behavior across settings and situations, across behaviors, and across time.

EXPERIMENT 2: CROSS-SITUATIONAL CONSISTENCY AND GENERALIZATION OF TREATMENT EFFECTS

The purpose of Experiment 2 was to examine the related questions of cross-situational consistency in behavior and generalization of behavioral treatment effects. More specifically, were children in Experiment 1, who were clearly deviant at school, also behavior problems at home? And did the successful classroom treatment program have any systematic effect on the children's behavior in the home?

Subjects

The subjects for this experiment were the five children who made up Group II in Experiment 1. As indicated earlier, post-treatment data could be gathered on only 4 of these 5 subjects.

Settings

The children were observed in their homes under the same conditions employed in earlier normative research on child behavior and family interaction (e.g., see Johnson, Wahl, Martin & Johansson, 1973):* Each child and his family were observed for 3 consecutive days prior to and after experimental classroom treatment. The 45-minute daily observation periods occurred during the hour prior to the family's regular dinner time when all family members were usually present.

A revision of the observational coding system developed by Patterson, Ray, Shaw, and Cobb (1969) was employed. The revised system utilizes 35 distinct behavior categories to record all the behaviors of the target child and family members who interact with him. The system is designed for rapid sequential recording of the child's behavior, the responses of family members, the child's ensuing response, etc. As in previous home observation studies, 15 of the 35 behaviors were designated as "deviant" for young children; the sum of the rates of these behaviors comprise the child's deviant behavior scores.

The two dependent variables for Experiment 2 were the proportion of child deviant behavior and the proportion of parental negative consequences. Seven observer agreement checks were made in this study with at least one check per family. Observer agreement for individual child behaviors and for parental negativeness was .91 and .95, respectively, using the Spearman-Brown correction procedures.

The availability of normative behavioral data on children of the same age in the classroom and home now makes it possible to determine

---

* A more detailed presentation of these procedures may be found in Johnson et al., 1973. The coding manual may be obtained from the third author on request.

TABLE 3

Child Deviant Behavior and Parental Negativeness Scores Before
and After School Treatment for Group II Subjects

Family	Proportion: Child deviant behavior			Proportion: Parental negativeness		
	Pre	Post	Difference	Pre	Post	Difference
1	1.5%	4.1%	+2.6%	0.4%	1.9%	+1.5%
2	2.0%	4.5%	+2.5%	2.1%	3.3%	+1.2%
3	0.7%	1.1%	+0.4%	1.3%	1.8%	+0.5%
4	1.2%	1.7%	+0.5%	2.0%	7.6%	+5.6%
5	14.1%			2.5%		

whether children who have abnormal difficulties in the school also exhibit high levels of problematic behavior in the home (Johnson et al.,
1973). Of the five children in the present study who were clearly deviant
in the school setting, all but one appeared to be within normal limits in
their rates of deviant behavior in the home. The average deviant behavior score for a sample of 40 same-aged normal children was 14.08 per
day (SD = 13.60), comprising 3.09 percent (SD = 2.60 percent) of the
total observed behavior. The overall proportions of deviant behavior
observed in the present cases, prior to treatment, are presented in the
first column of Table 3. Only one child exceeded the normal mean (3.09
percent) in the deviant direction by more than one standard deviation.
Furthermore, the normal sample and the present "school deviant" sample
were statistically equivalent ($t < 1$). In addition, no noticeable or systematic difference between the samples was apparent in the analysis of
the 15 individual deviant behavior codes.

Similarly, no apparent or significant difference between the samples
appeared in the overall parental summary scores. The pre-treatment
parental negativeness scores are presented in column 4 of Table 3. No
family in the sample exceeded the same age normative average of 3.09
percent parental negative behavior (SD = 2.05 percent).

The second question of interest concerns the behavior changes from
pre- to posttreatment observed in the home. The total deviant behavior
percents for the second assessment are presented in column 2 tof Table
3. In all 4 cases where data could be obtained, there was some increase
in the proportion of deviant behavior on the second assessment. After
arcsin transformations of these proportion scores, a t-test for paired observations indicated that this trend was not significant ($t (3) = 3.04$, $p <$

.06). The same nonsignificant trend was observed for the proportion of parent negative responding in that all parents exhibited more negativeness on the second assessment ($t\,(3) = 2.50$, $p < .10$). The child deviancy proportions remained within "normal limits" as defined by the normative sample data as did all but one of the parental negativeness scores (i.e., family four). Thus, the scores of child deviancy and parental negativeness were consistently higher after treatment.

DISCUSSION

The first and most obvious implication of this research is that children who exhibit high rates of deviant behavior in school do *not necessarily* show similar difficulties at home. Neither do the parents in this sample deliver higher than average rates of negative consequences for their behavior.

Subsequent research (Johnson, Bolstad & Lobitz, 1974) on a total of 18 school cases has yielded a somewhat higher estimate of the proportion of school deviant children who would be considered deviant at home (45 percent vs. the 20 percent observed in the present sample). Nevertheless, these findings taken together would seem at least to call into question the not infrequent practice of referring parents for counseling because of their child's behavior problems in school. Furthermore, based on the meager available data on generalization of treatment effects (e.g., O'Leary & Drabman, 1971; Meichenbaum, Bowers & Ross, 1968; Skindrud, 1972; and Wahler, 1969), it would not appear likely that improved behavior in relation to the family would have any necessary impact on the child's behavior in the classroom.

The consistent, although nonsignificant, finding that all four families showed more child deviancy and parental negativeness after school treatment may suggest a "behavioral contrast" effect. As has been noted in animal reseach, when certain forms of behavior are suppressed in one setting, they may tend to increase in another setting where similar controls are not operative (e.g., Freeman, 1971; Terrace, 1966). It is possible that the high level of deviancy reduction in the classroom may have caused increases in deviancy at home where behavioral controls were looser. This behavioral contrast interpretation should, however, be viewed tentatively for the following reasons: (a) small sample, (b) lack of significance, (c) the present research is only descriptive, and (d) subsequent controlled investigations of behavior modification programs in regular classrooms reveal no significant changes in deviancy in the home (Johnson, Bolstad & Lobitz, 1974).

Despite the absence of a control group, the present results and those of subsequent cases clearly replicate the Wahler (1969) descriptive study and are consistent with Skindrud's (1972) findings of no positive generalization of improved behavior at home to similar improvements at school. Positive generalization from school to home remains to be demonstrated.

REFERENCES

BIRNBRAUER, J. S., WOLF, M. M., KIDDER, J., & TAGUE, C. E. Classroom behavior of retarded pupils with token reinforcement. *J. Exp. Child Psychol.,* 1965, 2, 219-235.

BUCKLEY, N. K. & WALKER. H. M. *Modifying Classroom Behavior: A Manual of Procedures for Classroom Teachers.* Champaign, Ill.: Research Press, 1970.

FREEMAN, B. J. Behavior contrast: Reinforcement frequency or response suppression? *Psychol. Bull.,* 1971, 75, 347-356.

JOHNSON, S. M. & BOLSTAD, O. D. Methodological issues in naturalistic observation: Some problems and solutions for field research. In L. A. Hamerlynck, L. C. Handy and E. J. Mash (Eds.), *Behavior Change: Methodology, Concepts and Practice.* Champaign, Ill.: Research Press, 1973, pp. 7-67.

JOHNSON, S. M., BOLSTAD, O. D., & LOBITZ, G. K. Generalization and contrast phenomena in behavior modification with children. Paper presented at the Sixth Annual Banff International Conference on Behavior Modification, 1974.

JOHNSON, S. M. & LOBITZ, G. K. Parental manipulation of child behavior in home observations. *J. Appl. Behav. Anal.,* 1974, 7, 23-31.

JOHNSON, S. M., WAHL, G., MARTIN, S., & JOHANSSON, S. How deviant is the normal child: A behavioral analysis of the preschool child and his family. In R. D. Rubin, J. P. Brady, and J. D. Henderson (Eds.), *Advances in Behavior Therapy.* Volume 4. New York: Academic Press, 1973, pp. 37-54.

KAZDIN, A. E. & BOOTZIN, R. R. The token economy: An evaluative review. *J. Appl. Behav. Anal.,* 1972, 5, 343-372.

KUYPERS, D. S., BECKER, W. C., & O'LEARY, K. D. How to make a token system fail. *Exceptional Children,* 1968, 35, 101-109.

MEICHENBAUM, D. H., BOWERS, K. S., & ROSS, R. R. Modification of classroom behavior of institutionalized female adolescent offenders. *Behav. Res. & Ther.,* 1968, 6, 343-353.

O'LEARY, K. D., BECKER, W. C., EVANS, M., & SAUDARGAS, R. A. A token reinforcement program in a public school: A replication and systematic analysis. *J. Appl. Behav. Anal.,* 1968, 2, 3-13.

O'LEARY, K. D. & DRABMAN, R. Token reinforcement programs in the classroom. *Psychol. Bull.,* 1971, 75, 379-398.

PATTERSON, G. R., RAY, R. S., SHAW, D. A., & COBB, J. A. *Manual for Coding Family Interactions,* Sixth Revision, 1969. Available from ASIS National Auxiliary Publications Service, in care of CCM Information Service, Inc., 90 Third Avenue, New York, N. Y. 10022. Document #01234.

SKINDRUD, K. Generalization of treatment effects from home to school settings. Unpublished manuscript, Oregon Research Institute, Eugene, Oregon, 1972.

TERRACE, H. S. Stimulus control. In W. K. Honig (Ed.), *Operant Behavior: Areas of Research and Application.* New York: Appleton-Century-Crofts, 1966, pp. 299-301, 317, 323.

WAHLER, R. G. Setting generality: Some specific and general effects of child behavior therapy. *J. Appl. Behav. Anal.,* 1969, 2, 239-246.

WALKER, H. M. The Walker problem behavior identification checklist. Western Psychological Services, 1970. 12031 Wilshire Blvd., Los Angeles, Cal.
WALKER, H. M. Early identification and assessment of behaviorally handicapped children in the primary grades. Report No. 2, Center at Oregon for Research in the
Behavioral Education of the Handicapped, 1971.
WALKER, H. M. & BUCKLEY, N. K. The use of positive reinforcement in conditioning
attending behavior. *J. Appl. Behav. Anal.*, 1968, 1, 245-250.
WALKER, H. M. & BUCKLEY, N. K. Programming generalization and maintenance of
treatment effects across time and across settings. *J. Appl. Behav. Anal.*, 1972, 5,
209-224.
WALKER, H. M., HOPS, H., & FIEGENBAUM, W. E. Deviant classroom behavior as a func-
tion of change in setting, social and token reinforcement, and cost contingency.
Report No. 3, Center at Oregon for Research in the Behavioral Education of the
Handicapped, Eugene, Oregon, 1971.
WALKER, H. M., MATTSON, R. H., & BUCKLEY, N. K. The functional analysis of behavior within an experimental classroom setting. In W. C. Becker (Ed.), *An
Empirical Basis for Change in Education.* Chicago: Science Research Associates,
1971, pp. 236-263.

23

CHANGES IN SIBLING BEHAVIOR FOLLOWING FAMILY INTERVENTION

J. E. Arnold, A. G. Levine and G. R. Patterson

Oregon Research Institute, Eugene, Oregon

Changes in the behavior of the siblings of 27 treated pre-delinquents are reported. The parents of the referred pre-delinquents had been trained in social learning techniques of child management. Prior analysis of home observation data showed significantly reduced rates of deviant behaviors for the identified problem children. These reductions were maintained over a 12-month follow-up. The child management procedures taught to the parents were presumably applied to siblings as well as to the identified problem child. Analyses were conducted for the data from the 55 siblings of these families. The baseline data showed no significant differences between siblings and identified problem children. At termination of treatment, there were significant reductions in rates of deviant behavior for the siblings. The follow-up results showed the effects were maintained over a

Reprinted with permission from *Journal of Consulting and Clinical Psychology*, Vol. 43, No. 5, 1975, 683-688. Copyright 1975, American Psychological Association.

This study was supported by ROI MH 15985 from the National Institute of Mental Health section on Crime and Delinquency. Computing assistance was obtained from the Health Sciences Computing Facility, University of California, Los Angeles, sponsored by National Institutes of Health Grant FR-3.

The first author is now at the University of California, Santa Barbara.

Order of authorship for the first two authors was randomly determined.

6-month period. Some clinical implications of home intervention programs for socially aggressive boys and their siblings are discussed.

Social learning approaches to family intervention emphasize the assumption that parents control many of the contingencies presumed influential in the acquisition and maintenance of child behaviors. In keeping with this assumption, parents are regarded as logical, even preferred, therapists for their own child's problem behavior. During the past decade, numerous attempts by behavior modifiers have been made to help parents manage their children's behavior more effectively (see reviews by Berkowitz & Graziano, 1972; Patterson, 1971). One as yet unsubstantiated advantage of having the parent treat the child is that the effects should maximally generalize and persist. In the present context, this would imply that the behavior of siblings as well as that of the identified problem child would be altered by such parent-training programs. This would seem particularly desirable since prior studies have shown that siblings of aggressive boys also perform aggressive behaviors at high rates (Patterson, 1976; Patterson, Cobb, & Ray, 1973) and often provide the stimuli that "trigger" the problem child's deviant responses (Patterson, 1973; Patterson & Cobb, 1973).

The data summarized in Patterson (1975) strongly suggest that aggressive boys are raised in families comprised of aggressive family members. Of these family members, the siblings were the most aggressive. Effective treatment therefore requires changes in the family system particularly in the behavior of the siblings.

Undoubtedly the safest means of assuring maximal generalization and persistence of treatment effects would be to program them (Baer, Wolf, & Risley, 1968; Kazdin & Bootzin, 1972; Wahler, 1969). This implies that the parents should be supervised while applying the child management procedures to the sibling. In the present study, two-thirds of the families did in fact receive this type of supervision in sibling management. Siblings so treated are referred to as "involved" to distinguish them from the "uninvolved" siblings who were not intentionally supervised by their parents.

The present study assessed rates of deviant behavior of the siblings of 27 socially aggressive boys whose parents were trained in social learning techniques of child management in the Social Learning Project at the Oregon Research Institute. Previous analyses of the training program's effect on the problem children (Patterson, 1974; Patterson et al., 1973;

TABLE 1

Demographic Information for the Families and Siblings

Variable	n	M age, years	Range	M socio-economic level*
Families	27	—	—	4.3
Father absent	8	—	—	—
Referred child	27	8.7	5-13	—
Siblings	55	8.4	2-16	—
Male	21	9.4	3-16	—
Female	34	8.1	2-16	—
Older	28	11.8	6-16	—
Younger	27	5.3	2-11	—

* Based on a system developed by Hollingshead and Redlich (1958).

Patterson & Reid, 1973) have detailed the nature of the parent-training procedures and have shown that the problem children's rates of deviant behavior were significantly reduced over intervention and maintained over a 12-month follow-up period. Observation data were collected in the homes prior to, during, and following treatment. These data constituted the primary criteria for evaluating treatment outcome.

The baseline observation data were used to test the hypothesis that the identified problem children differ significantly from their siblings. Prior analyses for small samples have shown no significant differences in rates of deviant child behaviors (Patterson, Ray, & Shaw, 1968; Patterson et al., 1973). The observation data collected throughout intervention and follow-up were used to test the hypothesis that at termination there would be significant reductions from baseline levels for the siblings and that these changes would be maintained through follow-up.

METHOD

Sample

This study's data came from 27 families that had been referred to the Social Learning Project at the Oregon Research Institute by community agencies because one or more of the children within each family had been identified as having a severe conduct disorder. The majority were aggressive boys; others engaged in stealing, truancy, or fire setting. The majority of the families were from the lower socioeconomic class; 8 were mother-only families. The treatment that the families received is described in Patterson et al. (1973). The effects of treatment on the behavior of the referred children are summarized in Patterson (1976).

The sample for the present study consisted of the 55 siblings of the 27 referred children who were 3 years of age or older. The families had been screened at intake to include at least 1 sibling. The mean number of siblings averaged 2.44 per family, with a range of 1-5. Additional demographic information can be found in Table 1.

Therapists

Five staff members, each having spent 2 or more years on the project, carried the bulk of the treatment load. During that time, five trainees, supervised by the staff, also worked with one or more families. The families received an average of 31.5 hours of professional time during intervention and an additional 1.9 hours during follow-up.

Observational Procedures

The time sampling observation procedures described in Patterson, Ray, Shaw, and Cobb* were used in this study and were designed to describe 14 noxious and 15 prosocial behaviors displayed among family members. An earlier series of methodological studies on the problem associated with use of the code was summarized in Patterson et al. (1973, pp. 156-165). A more complete discussion of observer reliability, observer bias, reactivity to observer presence, observer drift, code complexity, and stability of event estimation can be found in Jones, Reid, and Patterson (1975). To conserve space, no attempt was made to summarize these materials here.

Six to 10 baseline observations were made in each home prior to intervention. For each session the observer went to the home at about dinner time and made two 5-minute observations on each family member in a prearranged random order. This produced a sequential account of each target subject's behavior and the reaction of other family members to him. A portable interval timing device signaled the observer every 30 seconds, at which time she shifted to the next line on the protocol sheet. A trained observer could record five reactions of the target subject

---

* G. R. Patterson, R. S. Ray, D. A. Shaw, and J. A. Cobb. *Manual for Coding of Family Interactions,* 1969 revision. See NAPS Document #01234. Order from ASIS/NAPS, c/o Microfiche Publications, 305 E. 46th Street, New York, New York 10017. Remit in advance $5.45 for photocopies and $1.50 for microfiche. Make checks payable to Microfiche Publications.

and five reactions of the family members on each line. In the discussion to follow, many of the variables are expressed as a "rate per minute." It should be understood that the upper limit for such rates is approximately 10 responses per minute for any given subject.

Periodic observation probes were conducted at 4-week intervals throughout intervention. Each probe consisted of two consecutive observation sessions during which the referred child was observed for 20 minutes and each of the other family members for 5 minutes. Probes were introduced immediately following the parents' reading of the programmed text, after 4 and 8 weeks of intervention, and at termination. During follow-up, two probe sessions were carried out monthly for the first 6 months. Additional probe sessions were conducted in the 8th, 10th, and 12th months.

Reliability

The same five observers collected the data for the entire study. Biweekly observer training sessions were conducted, and biweekly reliability checks were carried out in the homes in order to guard against decay in observer reliability (Reid, 1970). Agreement between pairs of observers was calculated by dividing total agreement by total agreements plus disagreements for each 30-second segment. The event-by-event analysis required agreement on behavior, family member, and sequence. The analysis for the data in the present article showed an average agreement of 74.2 percent.

Dependent Variable

The observation data provide average rates per minute for 14 noxious responses. Their sum is labeled total deviant and consists of the following behaviors: command negative, cry, destructive, dependency, disapproval, high rate, humiliate, ignore, noncomply, negativism, tease, whine, yell, and physical negative. Definitions for all behavior categories can be found in Patterson et al. (see footnote, p. 538). Data reviewed by Patterson (1974) suggest a rate of .450 responses per minute as the most efficient cutting score for differentiating between samples of aggressive and nonaggressive boys.

Estimates of the total deviant score based on 3-5 observation sessions were correlated with estimates made a week later using a comparative number of sessions. The test-retest reliability correlation (uncorrected) was .78 ($df = 26$, $p < .01$). The validity data summarized in Jones et al.

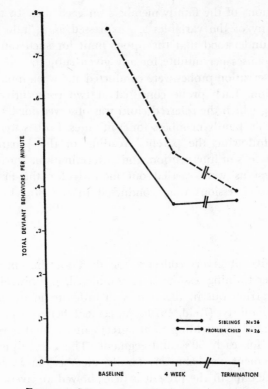

FIGURE 1. Mean rates of total deviant behaviors
for the problem child and his siblings. (*N* refers to
the number of families contributing to the mean
rates.)

(1975) showed that the total deviant score correlated significantly with
parents' ratings of aggressiveness for their boys.

RESULTS

Comparison of Siblings and Identified
Problem Children at Baseline

As can be seen in Figure 1, sizeable baseline rate differences existed
between siblings and the identified problem children. The mean total
deviant scores were .563 and .759, respectively. A *t*-test for related measures compared the baseline scores for these two samples. Expecting that
the deviancy rates of referred children would exceed that of their

TABLE 2

WITHIN-FAMILY MEAN SIBLING RATES OF TOTAL DEVIANT BEHAVIOR (RESPONSES PER MINUTE) FOR INTERVENTION AND FOLLOW-UP

Case no.	Status	Baseline	4th week	Termi- nation	% change from baseline	M follow-up, months 1–6	% change from baseline	M follow-up, months 8–12	% change from baseline
				Intervention			Follow-up		
11	B	.492		1.089	+121.3	.294	−40.2	.383	−22.2
12	B	.277	.125	.100	−63.9	.129	−53.4	.108	−61.0
14	A	1.150	.650	.325	−71.7	.635	−44.8	.329	−71.4
15	A	.345	.450	.275	−20.3	.475	+37.7	.450	+30.4
16	A	.540	.100	.034	−93.7	.367	−32.0	.217	−59.8
17	A	.073	.000	.000	−100.0				
18	A	.790	.850	.250	−68.4				
21	A	.980	.200	.900	−8.2	.350	−64.3		
22	B	.360	.000	.000	−100.0	.050	−86.1	.450	+25.0
24	A	.280	.267	.733	+161.8	.456	+62.9	.745	+166.1
25	A	1.450	.200	.200	−86.2	.592	−59.2		
26	A	.460	.125	.500	+8.7				
27	A	.900	1.400	.200	−77.8	1.000	+11.1	1.450	+61.1
28	B	.280	.700	.200	−28.6	.550	+96.4	.400	+42.9
29	A	.105	.350	.100	−4.8				
31	B	.561	.400	.100	−82.2	.470	−16.2	.306	−45.5
32	B	.375	.250	.350	−6.7				
33	B	.267	.250	.625	+134.1	.373	+39.7	.258	−3.4
35	B	.529	.375	.325	−38.6	.521	−1.5	.692	+30.8
36	B	.133	.000	.200	+50.4	.275	+106.8	.267	+100.8
38	A	.167	.100	.500	+199.4	.362	+116.8	.317	+89.8
39	A	.367	.600	.400	+9.0	.288	−21.5	.475	+29.4
40	A	.133	.000	.100	−24.8	.058	−56.4	.133	0
42	A	.284	.700	.450	+58.5	.125	−56.0		
43	A	.750	.100	.900	+20.0				
44	A	1.625	.550	1.200	−26.2	.471	−71.0		
45	A	1.411	.600	.400	−71.7				
Mean		.559	.359	.387	−30.8	.392	−29.9	.436	−22.0

Note. "A" status signifies "involved"; "B" status signifies "uninvolved."

siblings, a one-tailed test seemed appropriate; $t(26) = 1.678$, $p > .10$. The problem child/sibling correlation for these scores was .74 ($df = 26$, $p < .001$).

Changes in sibling behavior at termination. Table 2 presents the mean sibling values at baseline, the fourth week of intervention, and at termination for each family. Complete intervention data were available for 26 of the 27 treated families.

The one-way repeated-measures analysis of variance produced a significant F value of 3.785 ($df = 2,50$, $p < .029$). Across the 26 families the average sibling showed an average reduction of 36 percent from baseline level. In 11 families the average sibling's rate of deviant behavior had dropped by more than 30 percent by termination. Twenty-seven of the 55 siblings in the study (or 40 percent) evidenced a reduction of at least 30 percent in deviant behavior rates over intervention. Across-family means of sibling and identified problem-child deviant behavior rates during intervention are presented in Figure 1. In general, the magnitude of the treatment was less for the siblings than it had been for the identified problem child (Patterson, 1974).

Maintenance of Changes in Sibling Behavior through Follow-Up

Whereas relatively complete data (at least 3 months) were collected for 74 percent of the families in the first 6 months of follow-up, home observation data were available for only 59 percent of the families during months 8-12 of follow-up. The 16 families for whom relatively complete, 1-year sibling follow-up data were obtained appear, as a group, to be unrepresentative of the sample as a whole. That is, the average sibling in the subsample that completed follow-up was less deviant at baseline than the subsample that failed to participate in or finish follow-up. The mean rates were .478 and .755, respectively. Additionally, the average sibling who completed follow-up evidenced less reduction in deviant behavior during intervention than did the average sibling who dropped out of follow-up (mean percentage of reduction during intervention of siblings *not* completing follow-up was 36.8 percent $(N = 11)$ as compared to a percentage reduction of 23.3 percent $(N = 16)$ for those families for whom relatively complete 1-year follow-up was available). Therefore, emphasis is placed on observation data collected in the first 6 months of follow-up.

From Table 2 the mean deviancy rate for the average siblings in the 20 families who participated in the first 6 months of follow-up was .392. Comparing this to the termination mean of .398 for this group indicates that, on the whole, the siblings' treatment effects were maintained over the first 6 months following intervention. This conclusion is supported by the t-test for related measures that compared rate changes between termination and the average of Months 1-6 of the follow-up, $t (19) = .067$, *ns.* There were 42 siblings in the 20 families that completed the first 6 months of follow-up. For 21 of them, their mean follow-up rate was at least 30 percent below their base rate level.

In 18 of the 27 families, one or more of the siblings were actively included in the parents' treatment program. The mean baseline rates for the involved subset of siblings were higher than those for the remainder of the sample (.658 vs. .365), thus indirectly supporting the clinical judgment to include those siblings in treatment. However, a two-tailed t-test comparing baseline rates for the involved and non-involved groups yielded nonsignificant results, $t\,(25) = 1.718$, $p < .10$, two-tailed. This magnitude of the treatment effect also appeared larger for the involved subset of siblings; however, the appropriate two-way repeated-measures analysis of variance comparing involved and uninvolved sibling rates from baseline to termination yielded a nonsignificant F value. Similar nonsignificant results were obtained when male/female sibling behavior was examined using a two-way repeated-measures analysis of variance.

DISCUSSION

The initial hypothesis of this study was that the children referred for treatment to the Oregon Research Institute were not significantly more deviant than their siblings. Analyses performed on the baseline home observation data supported this hypothesis; nonsignificant results were found when comparing the rates of total deviant behavior of the referred child to the total deviant behavior of his siblings. This tends to support the results from earlier analyses for small samples (Patterson et al., 1968, 1973).

The fact that there were no significant differences between siblings and problem children in their rates of deviant behavior at baseline raises a question about the process by which a family comes to label one of its members as deviant. The data presented here emphasize the often capricious quality of the deviancy labeling process.

The high baseline deviant behavior rates of siblings also raise a question about the appropriateness of solely treating the referred child in home intervention programs. In many instances a family may contain more than one "deviant" child, although only one child may be so *labeled* by the parents. In such cases, failure to treat all deviant children within the family may portend ill for the long-term treatment outcome of the referred child, since as has already been mentioned, there is some evidence to implicate siblings as "triggers" for considerable portions of the "problem child's" deviant behavior (Patterson, 1973; Patterson & Cobb, 1973). Thus, effective treatment seems to require changes in the family system, particularly in the behavior of the siblings.

In addressing the generalization issue of whether intervention did have an impact on the observed rates of deviant behavior of the siblings of the referred children, we hypothesized that the repeated-measures analysis of variance on the observation data from baseline to termination would demonstrate a significant decrease in the siblings' rates of deviant behavior and that the treatment effects would maintain through follow-up. The results clearly support the hypothesis that the family intervention aimed primarily at the referred child did, in fact, generalize to the siblings as well. Whether the sibling data are looked at across families, within families, or individually without reference to family, the data analyses consistently reveal that sibling rates of deviant behavior were greatly reduced by the end of treatment and that, as a group, these reductions were maintained during the first 6 months of follow-up.

It would appear that the parents are learning a set of skills that they are then applying to the siblings as well as the referred children. This is in keeping with the findings of Taplin (1974), who showed changes in the consequences provided by the parents for deviant child behaviors. Even though some of the changes in sibling deviant behavior may be attributable directly to the changes in the behavior of the referred child (it would be logical to assume that referred children act as triggers for their siblings' deviant behavior), the series of studies suggests that changes may occur within the entire family system, lending further support to the growing body of evidence that families function as an interactive system (Patterson & Reid, 1970; Patterson & Cobb, 1973) and also suggests that in home intervention programs closer attention should be paid to sibling behavior during and following treatment of the referred child. It is interesting to note, however, that while the magnitude of the treatment effect appeared larger for those siblings who were actively involved in treatment, the appropriate analysis comparing involved and uninvolved siblings from baseline to termination yielded nonsignificant results. Apparently, treatment generalized to the siblings of the referred children whether or not the siblings were specifically involved in the intervention, yielding further credence to the notion that the parents have learned a general set of child management skills rather than a specific method of dealing with a child. Additional studies involving more random assignment of siblings to involved and uninvolved groups are indicated to further test this notion.

REFERENCES

BAER, D. M., WOLF, M. M., & RISLEY, T. R. Some current dimensions of applied behavior analysis. *J. Appl. Behav. Anal.*, 1968, 1, 91-97.
BERKOWITZ, B. P. & GRAZIANO, A. M. Training parents as behavior therapists: A review. *Behav. Res. & Ther.*, 1972, 10, 297-317.

HOLLINGSHEAD, A. B. & REDLICH, F. C. *Social Class and Mental Illness.* New York: Wiley, 1958.

JONES, R. R., REID, J. B., & PATTERSON, G. R. Naturalistic observations in clinical assessment. In P. McReynolds (Ed.), *Advances in Psychological Assessment* (Vol. 3). San Francisco: Jossey-Bass, 1975.

KAZDIN, A. E. & BOOTZIN, R. R. The token economy: An evaluative review. *J. Appl. Behav. Anal.,* 1972, 5, 343-372.

McCALL, R. B. & APPELBAUM, M. I. Bias in the analysis of repeated-measures designs: Some alternative approaches. *Child Devel.,* 1973, 44. 401-415.

PATTERSON, G. R. Behavioral intervention procedures in the classroom and in the home. In A. E. Bergin and S. L. Garfield (Eds.), *Handbook of Psychotherapy and Behavior Change.* New York: Wiley, 1971.

PATTERSON, G. R. Changes in the status of family members as controlling stimuli: A basis for describing treatment process. In L. A. Hamerlynck, L. C. Handy, and E. J. Mash (Eds.), *Behavior Change: Methodology, Concepts and Practice.* Champaign, Ill.: Research Press, 1973.

PATTERSON, G. R. Intervention for boys with conduct problems: Multiple settings, treatments and criteria. *J. Consult. Clin. Psychol.,* 1974, 42, 471-481.

PATTERSON, G. R. The aggressive child: Victim or architect of a coercive system. In L. A. Hamerlynck, L. C. Handy, and E. J. Mash (Eds.), *Behavior Modification and Families.* New York: Brunner/Mazel, 1976.

PATTERSON, G. R. & COBB, J. A. Stimulus control for classes of noxious behavior. In J. F. Knutson (Ed.), *The Control of Aggression: Implications from Basic Research.* Chicago: Aldine, 1973.

PATTERSON, G. R., COBB, J. A., & RAY, R. S. A social engineering technology for retraining the families of aggressive boys. In H. Adams & I. Unikel (Eds.), *Issues and Trends in Behavior Therapy.* Springfield, Ill.: Charles C Thomas, 1973.

PATTERSON, G. R., RAY, R. S., & SHAW, D. A. Direct intervention in families of deviant children. *Oregon Res. Inst. Res. Bull.,* 1968, 8, No. 9.

PATTERSON, G. R. & REID, J. B. Reciprocity and coercion: Two facets of social systems. In C. Neuringer & J. Michael (Eds.), *Behavior Modification in Clinical Psychology.* New York: Appleton-Century-Crofts, 1970.

PATTERSON, G. R. & REID, J. B. Intervention for families of aggressive boys: A replication study. *Behav. Res. & Ther.,* 1973, 11, 383-394.

REID, J. B. Reliability assessment of observation data: A possible methodological problem. *Child Devel.,* 1970, 41, 1143-1150.

TAPLIN, P. S. Changes in parent consequating behavior as an outcome measure in the evaluation of a social programming approach to the treatment of aggressive boys. Unpublished doctoral dissertation, University of Wisconsin-Madison, 1974.

WAHLER, R. G. Setting generality: Some specific and general effects of child behavior therapy. *J. Appl. Behav. Anal.,* 1969, 2, 239-246.

24

CONTINGENCY CONTRACTING WITH FAMILIES OF DELINQUENT ADOLESCENTS

Lawrence Weathers and Robert Paul Liberman

*Camarillo-Neuropsychiatric Institute Research Center,
California*

A program of intensive, brief behavioral treatment was
implemented with 28 recidivistic delinquent adolescents and
their parents. Treatment, carried out in the home by a master's degree psychologist, consisted of three interventions
spaced at weekly intervals. Contingency contracting, communication skills training, and videotape feedback were used
with the six families who did not drop out of the program.
A within-subject, multiple baseline design for these six
families was used to assess the impact of the interventions
on school attendance, compliance with curfew and chores,
and verbal abusiveness to parents. Reliability of parental
report was established for curfew compliance by random

Reprinted with permission from *Behavior Therapy*, 6, 1975, 356-366.
This work was supported by Grant No. 0566 from the California Council on Criminal Justice to the Camarillo Resocialization Program for Drug Abusers, Robert H.
Coombs (Project Director). The opinions stated here are those of the authors and are
not to be construed as official policy of the Regents of the University of California,
the California Department of Health, or the California Council on Criminal Justice.
The authors are indebted to Lloyd Homme and Richard B. Stuart for their pioneering work describing the theoretical and practical aspects of contingency contracts.
The first author is now working at the Miami, Florida Mental Health Center.

calls by a telephone answering service. The experimental group of six adolescents was compared with 16 adolescents who had an initial home visit before dropping out of the study on such measures as school grades, anti-social probationary incidents, and the Jesness Behavior Checklist.

Results failed to show any systematic impact of the behavioral interventions on any of the response measures employed except for a possible beneficial effect of contracting on verbal abusiveness. Together with other studies showing a lack of effect of direct, behavioral intervention with families containing delinquent adolescents, the findings from this research should lead behavior therapists to be cautious in their applying contingency contracting in the short-term family treatment of delinquents.

Contingency contracting with families has become a popular, community-based intervention strategy because it seems to be a simple and expedient way to harness natural reinforcers present in the family milieu. Behavioral contracts specifically structure interpersonal exchanges in terms of *who* does *what* to *whom*, and *when.* Target behaviors and their positive and negative consequences can be clearly delineated.

Contingency contracting, as a therapeutic procedure for families, derives from three conceptual models. The first, called the exchange model, describes the principles of social interaction essential for effective interpersonal exchanges. Stuart (1971) outlines the assumptions of the exchange model of contracting:

1. "Receipt of positive reinforcers in interpersonal exchanges is a privilege to be earned rather than a right."

2. "Effective interpersonal agreements are governed by the norm of reciprocity." Receiving rewards for self depends upon giving rewards to others.

3. "The value of an interpersonal exchange is a direct function of the range, rate, and magnitude of the positive reinforcement mediated by that exchange."

4. "Rules create freedom in interpersonal exchanges." Making reinforcement contingencies predictable allows opportunities for choice.

In the second model underlying contracting procedure, a hierarchy of roles is prescribed for the individuals who will be intervening with the family. Tharp and Wetzel (1969) describe the triadic model as consisting of a therapist who acts as a consultant to a mediator who has control over natural, powerful, and immediate reinforcers in the life of the targeted "problem person." Individuals such as parents and teachers who naturally control and dispense reinforcers should occupy an intermediate mediator role between consultant and the designated patient, who is the ultimate target of behavioral intervention. The triadic model is diagrammed as follows:

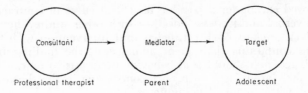

The third model for contracting is based upon negotiation and interpersonal skills training. In troubled families, compromise and negotiation skills are rarely apparent. Negotiation, bargaining, empathizing, and compromising are taught during the contracting procedure. These skills are modeled and reinforced by the therapist during the process of negotiating a contract. The ultimate effectiveness of a contracting intervention is directly related to the extent to which these interpersonal skills generalize beyond the duration of the contract and to noncontract problem-solving. Alexander and Parsons (1973) present data which indicate that families that show active verbal skills while discussing problems experience less recidivism in the juvenile court records of their delinquent offspring.

Even though contracting is becoming a popular intervention, there are only a small number of published reports of success with contingency contracts (Cantrill, Cantrill, Huddleston & Woolridge, 1969; Mann, 1972; Stuart, 1971; Tharp & Wetzel, 1969; Alexander & Parsons, 1973). Four studies (Cantrill et al., 1969; Mann, 1972; Jayaratne, Stuart & Tripodi, 1974; Alexander & Parsons, 1973) used controlled, experimental designs. The studies by Cantrill et al. (1969) and Mann (1972) were for limited target behaviors—school attendance and obesity, respectively. Stuart and his colleagues mounted a large scale, 3-year investigation with over 100 families. Evaluating the differential effectiveness of (a) three treatment durations, (b) standard versus negotiated contracts, (c) fading versus sudden termination of contracts, and (d) contract versus activity group interventions, the authors found no significant differences among the various forms of intervention. The lack of statistically significant differences could have been a result of the myriad of methodological problems which plagued the study. Alexander and Parsons (1973) reported that 46 families referred by a juvenile court receiving short-term behavioral interventions, including contracting, had one-half the recidivism of 30 families who received client-centered or eclectic psychodynamic family treatment. However, these authors did not describe how much time and effort was invested on each case by the behavior therapists in contrast with the two groups of comparison therapists. No clear description was made of what criteria were used in determining "recidivism" from the juvenile court records at the time of follow-up. A more damaging flaw in the study by Alexander and Parsons was their use of a variable follow-up interval of 6-18 months with the obvious possibility for biasing results by conducting follow-ups when recidivism had not yet appeared in the families treated behaviorally.

The current study was undertaken to provide another controlled evaluation of short-term behavioral interventions, including contingency contracting, with delinquent adolescents and their parents. Both within-subject and comparison group designs were used.

METHODS

Subjects

Male and female probationers, between 14 and 17 years of age, were referred to the therapist (senior author) by the Ventura County Probation Department. Of 28 families referred, 16 completed the first home visit, eight finished the baseline period, and six completed the three home interventions and follow-up. The drop-out rate is depicted in Figure 1. Of the 28 families referred, 20 were one-parent households. The probationers had multiple offenses, had all spent time in Juvenile Hall, and were considered ready for disposition to a youth authority institution by their probation officers.

Baseline

A home visit was arranged after an initial phone contact and the family was offered a series of three home interventions which were described as of potential benefit to the family in dealing with their problems. Participation was voluntary and there were no conditions placed on involvement by the Probation Department.

Parents gathered baseline data on four behaviors of their adolescent offspring that a pilot study uncovered as important targets in families

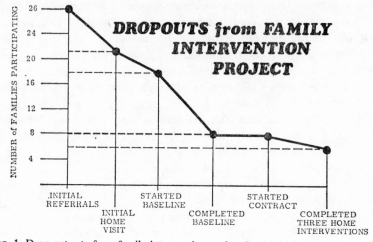

FIG. 1. Drop-out rate from family intervention project from initial referrals from Probation Department to completion of three home interventions.

with delinquents. These behaviors were verbal abusiveness, curfew compliance, school attendance, and performance of chores. Exact definitions of verbal abusiveness, curfew compliance, and performance of chores were negotiated with each individual family. Verbal abusiveness encompassed talking back, arguing, caustic remarks, and derogatory and obscene comments as subjectively determined by the parents. Chores included cleaning own room, taking out the trash, yard work, and doing dishes. The family was requested to make no changes in their behavior during the baseline period. Data were reported by parents on specially printed postcards which were mailed to the therapist each week.

Other dependent measures collected before and three months after the home interventions were the Jesness Behavior Checklist (Jesness, 1970) filled out by parents and adolescents, probation incident records, and school grades. Any incident which was considered by the probation officer to represent a violation of probation (e.g., drug abuse, alcohol intoxication, truancy, running away) was counted.

Experimental Design

To assess the influence of contingency contracting on the behaviors of delinquent adolescents, a multiple baseline design was used. Various lengths of pre-contracting baselines, ranging between 11 and 32 days,

CONTINGENCY CONTRACTING EXERCISE

FIG. 2. Schema for the Family Contracting Exercise which was conducted during the first home visit. The sequence of steps in the Exercise are outlined for the parent(s) in circles and for the adolescent in squares.

were randomly assigned to the participating families. Each family reported baseline data on the four adolescent behaviors noted above. Contingency contracting and two other home interventions, remote-control prompting and videotape feedback, were introduced to each family after differing durations of baseline periods.

The experimental group of six families also were compared with the 16 families who consented to an initial home visit but dropped out before completing the home interventions. Comparisons were made for school attendance, school grades, and probation incidents during the three months prior to and the 3 months following the first home intervention.

Interventions

The first intervention was a contingency contract negotiated between parents and adolescent by means of a structured exercise (Weathers & Liberman 1974). The exercise consisted of identification of potential reinforcers for self and others, and bargaining for contingencies that were arranged between responsibilities and rewards. The schema for the contracting exercise is outlined in Figure 2. The therapist set the rules for the exercise and guided the family's participation by using prompts and verbal reinforcements. A videotape which demonstrates the structured exercise leading to a family contract is available from the second author (Liberman & Weathers, 1972).

By means of the structured exercise five to seven contingencies were negotiated on a quid pro quo basis. Provision was made for continued data collection on the baseline behaviors if any of them were not explicitly placed in the contract. The exercise leading to a contract was accomplished in less than two hours. A copy of the contract was left with the family for their immediate use. The primary source of data for compliance on terms of the contract was a weekly check-strip postcard located in the contract form. Parental report provided most of the data. Although the adolescent was instructed to make checkmarks on his parents' compliance with contract clauses, few actually did this.

The second and third home interventions were attempts to teach the family members effective negotiation skills. The family as a group was asked to discuss some topic of mutual interest or disagreement and to bargain for a verbal agreement with one another. During the second home intervention (which was the third actual home visit), a portable, four channel, electronic, bug-in-the-ear unit was used to prompt and acknowledge effective interpersonal negotiation behaviors. This *Porta-Prompter* is described in another publication (Weathers & Liberman, 1973).

Effective communication behaviors were considered to be the following:

1. eye contact;
2. open body postures frontally facing each other;
3. face unsupported and uncovered;

4. firm, assertive voice that did not convey intimidation, mockery, or a request for sympathy;

5. use of specific, concrete descriptions of what was wanted for self and expected from others;

6. clear statements of needs and feelings using the first person pronoun as the syntactic subject;

7. posing and accepting compromises.

The session lasted about 40 minutes during which time the therapist gradually faded his prompts and feedback.

The third home intervention was similar to the second with the addition of videotape feedback using a Sony Video-Rover II. Every 5-7 minutes, the family was stopped in their discussion and viewed a brief, 2-3 minute sample of their interaction. During the feedback the therapist directed their attention to verbal and nonverbal aspects of their communicating that facilitated effective negotiation. Total time invested in each family, including phone calls and home visits, averaged 5.6 hours.

Reliability

Reliability checks on the parental report of the adolescent's compliance with curfew was obtained by having a telephone answering service place three calls per week to the adolescent just after the agreed upon curfew. The chosen days for the calls were randomly assigned without prior notification of the family. The family members agreed to this procedure during the initial home visit when the project was explained to them.

The reliability of parental report on school attendance was checked by reviewing the adolescent's attendance record at school. This means of assessing reliability is an approximation since the parents and the school are measuring somewhat different events. The parents are reporting the adolescent's *leaving the home* for school while the school is recording the teenager's actual *presence* in school.

In Figure 3, the procedures for the entire project are graphically represented.

RESULTS

Reliability

Parental and answering service reports on the adolescent's compliance with curfew agreed 76 percent of the sampled evenings. Of the 24 percent disagreements, 19 percent consisted of the parent reporting com-

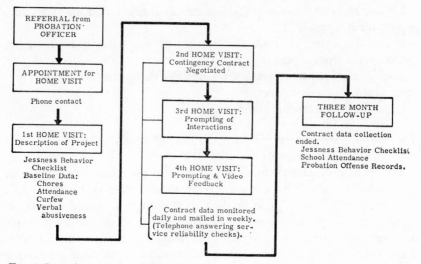

FIG. 3. Procedures employed in the family intervention project diagrammed in temporal order with the independent variables (interventions) placed in boxes and the dependent variables (response measure) noted below the boxes.

pliance with curfew when the teenager was not present to receive the answering service's calls.

Parent's report of school attendance agreed with school records 79 percent of the time. Of the 21 percent disagreements, 13 percent consisted of parents indicating that the child had left for school and the school records showing absence.

Multiple Baseline Measures

Of the four measures monitored during baseline and intervention periods, performance of chores was confounded by the contracting procedure and could not be used in the analysis. Parents and their children contracted for considerably fewer chores to be completed than had been expected and monitored during the baseline period. The data is shown in Figure 4. While 64 percent of assigned chores were completed after the contract in contrast to only 27 percent during the baseline period, the average *number* of chores actually performed each week was approximately the same for baseline and post-contract periods.

The effect of the contracting intervention on curfew compliance is shown on the multiple baseline of the six participating families in Fig-

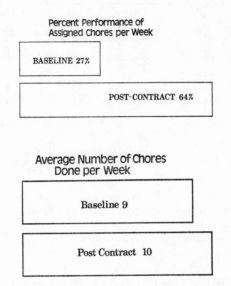

Percent Performance of
Assigned Chores per Week

BASELINE 27%

POST-CONTRACT 64%

Average Number of Chores
Done per Week

Baseline 9

Post Contract 10

FIG. 4. Compliance with assigned chores each week by the group of six adolescents before (baseline) and after completing contingency contracts.

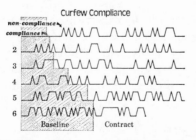

Curfew Compliance

non-compliance
compliance

2

3

4

5

6

Baseline   Contract

FIG. 5. Compliance with curfew times by six adolescents before and after completing a contingency contract with their parent(s). After contracting, curfew times were mutually agreed upon. Data points represent each evening's report by the parent(s).

556   ANNUAL REVIEW OF BEHAVIOR THERAPY

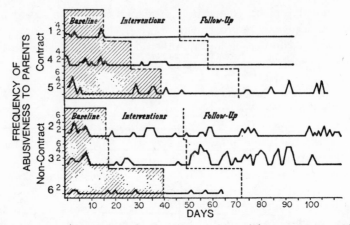

FIG. 6. Frequency of verbal abusiveness expressed by adolescents to parent(s) before and after completing contingency contracts. Note that only in cases 1, 4, and 5 did the contract include a clause dealing with reductions in verbal abusiveness. The data derived from daily counts made by parent(s) and reported to the research project by weekly postcards.

ure 5. Onset of the contract period had no impact on the baseline rate of compliance to curfew. Only verbal abusiveness, as reported by the parents, showed any systematic impact by the contracts. In the three families where a decrease in verbal abusiveness was specifically contracted for, the adolescents indeed showed a marked decrease or cessation of verbal abuse with the onset of contracting. One of these three adolescents resumed his baseline level of abusiveness four weeks after the signing of the contract and two weeks after the final home intervention. None of the three adolescents who did not contract for a decrease in their abusiveness showed any systematic change in this behavior at the point of contracting. These data are shown in Figure 6. There was no systematic effect on school attendance by the introduction of the home interventions and contingency contract.

Three Month Follow-Up

The Jesness Behavior Checklist revealed no significant differences between administrations prior to and three months after the contracting procedure. While there was a decrease in the average number of antisocial incidents recorded by the Probation Department from one to one-half per adolescent in the contract group, this was not a statistically significant difference from the *smaller* decrease in the average number of incidents noted for the comparison group. A review of school grades revealed no academic improvement between the three month periods before and after contracting and no differences between the contract and comparison groups.

DISCUSSION

Contingency contracting, as applied in this study, cannot be considered an effective intervention strategy. The only behaviors which systematically responded to negotiated contingencies were verbal abusiveness by adolescents to parents. Since these data came solely from the subjective reports of parents without any reliability assessment, it is not possible to place much confidence in them. The lack of demonstrable efficacy for contingency contracting with delinquent adolescents and their parents is consonant with the reports of other investigators. Tharp and Wetzel (1969) and Stuart and Tripodi (1972) report uncontrolled data that are not impressive in showing the effectiveness of contracting. Studies by Cantrill et al. (1969) and Mann (1972) showing experimental control over school attendance and weight respectively through contingency contracting differ from the current study by their focus on single, discrete, reliably measurable behaviors and by their gaining control over the dispensing of reinforcers to their subjects. The study of Alexander and Parson (1973) is flawed by possible methodological bias. While it is inviting to speculate that the type of interventions, the frequency and duration of contact, and the therapeutic support with the subjects in this study were insufficient to produce significant change, previous research by Stuart and Tripodi (1972) and Jayaratne, Stuart and Tripodi (1974) indicates that duration of therapist-client contact is not an important variable in the outcome of contingency contracting. In working with families that are decimated by divorce, crime, drug abuse and woefully inadequate communication and negotiation skills, the introduction of a contingency contract is worth about as much as the paper it's printed on. Consistent use of contingencies of reinforcement directed toward positive behavioral goals may be impossible to achieve in such families without some massive intervention that is currently not ethically acceptable or financially supportable by society. In the case of families with adolescents, the parents have lost much of their reinforcement control over their offspring; thus, without engaging the peer group in an intervention strategy little can be gained by family therapy alone.

With less deviant and disorganized families, contingency contracting may be shown to be effective in producing desirable behavioral change. As experience with behavior modification techniques grows, cost-benefit concerns will be tested and the cost and extensiveness of interventions can be titrated against outcomes. For the present, contingency contracting should be used with caution and with limited objectives. Contracting should not be viewed as an effective intervention strategy or "treatment package" in itself, but rather as a supplementary aid in a wider range of interventions.

REFERENCES

CANTRILL, H., CANTRILL, C., HUDDLESTON, B., & WOOLRIDGE, R. Contingency contracting with school problems. *J. Appl. Behav. Anal.*, 1969, 2, 215-220.
HOMME, L. *Contingency Contracting in the Classroom.* Champaign, Ill.: Research Press, 1969.
JAYARATNE, S., STUART, R. B., & TRIPODI, T. Methodological issues and problems in evaluating treatment outcomes in the family and school consultation project 1970-1973. In *Evaluating Social Programs in Community, Residential and Social Settings: Proceedings of the 5th Banff International Conference on Behavior Modification.* Champaign, Ill.: Research Press. Pp. 141-174.
JESNESS, C. *Manual for Jesness Behavior Checklist.* Palo Alto, Cal.: Consulting Psychologists Press, 1970.
LIBERMAN, R. P. & WEATHERS, L. Contingency contracting: A Family Therapy ½ inch Sony videotape available from senior author at Camarillo-Neuropsychiatric Institute Research Program, Camarillo State Hospital, Camarillo, Cal. 93010.
MANN, R. A. The behavioral therapeutic use of contingency contracting to control an adult behavior problem-weight control. *J. Appl. Anal.*, 1972, 5, 99-109.
STUART, R. B. Behavioral contracting within the families of delinquents. *J. Behav. Ther. Exp. Psychiat.*, 1971,2, 1-11.
STUART, R. B. & LOTT, L. A. Behavioral contracting with delinquents: A cautionary note. *J. Behav. Ther. Exp. Psychiat.*, 1972, 3, 161-169.
STUART, R. B. & TRIPODI, T. Experimental evaluation of three time-constrained behavioral treatments of predelinquents and delinquents. In R. D. Rubin, J. P. Brady, and J. D. Henderson (Eds.), *Advances in Behavior Therapy*, Vol. 4. New York: Academic Press, 1973, pp. 1-12.
THARP, R. G. & WETZEL, R. J. *Behavior Modification in the Natural Environment.* New York: Academic Press, 1969.
WEATHERS, L., & LIBERMAN, R. P. The Porta-Prompter—A new electronic prompting and feedback device: A technical note. *Behav. Ther.*, 1973, 4, 703-705.
WEATHERS, L. & LIBERMAN, R. P. The Family Contracting Exercise. Submitted to *J. Behav. Ther. Exp. Psychiat.*, 1974.

Section VII

BEHAVIOR MODIFICATION IN INSTITUTIONAL SETTINGS

Commentary

There is perhaps no more important issue on the contemporary behavioral scene than the continuing discussion of the ethical and legal implications of the use of behavior modification procedures. As Friedman's paper and our Commentary in Section I of this volume make clear, the concern about ethical and legal issues has centered around the role of behavior modification in institutional settings, particularly schools, psychiatric hospitals, and prisons. And, with very few exceptions, behavior modification in institutional settings has meant the use of some sort of token economy program.

In describing the experimental and clinical advances of the token economy two years ago (Franks & Wilson, 1974, pp. 211-222), we cited Atthowe's (1973) conclusion that token economies had come of age, that they had proliferated to the point where countless treatment, rehabilitative, correctional, and educational institutions used some form of contingency contracting procedure. If the token economy has come of age, so too have its limitations become more apparent. During the 1960s the major questions about token economies were whether they did in fact change the behavior of entire groups of people and if this change could be attributed to specific reinforcement contingencies rather than some uncontrolled "nonspecific" influence. The questions are different now. Who sets the goals of token reinforcement programs, particularly in the case of children who are too young and mental hospital patients who are presumably too disturbed to participate meaningfully in this negotiation process? What are the goals of these programs? What behaviors are reinforced? And of the diverse range of methods available to them, what techniques should behavior modifiers employ? What constitutes an individual's absolute right and what can be used as a contingent reinforcer? The Commentary in Section VI discusses the use of token reinforcement procedures in the classroom in the light of these various questions. The present Section is concerned primarily with behavior modification in institutions such as mental hospitals, residential homes for the severely retarded and for the elderly, and correctional facilities.

Patients in Psychiatric Hospitals

More than anyone else, Wexler (1973), an attorney, was responsible for initiating the systematic evaluation of token economies in mental hospitals in the context of pertinent legal statutes (see also Friedman's [1975] excellent summary of legal regulation). More specifically, Wexler queried the selection of reinforcers and the nature of the behavior on which they were made contingent. More recently, Page, Caron, and Yates (1975) have vigorously asserted that most behavioral programs in mental hospitals have failed to accomplish what might be assumed to be their main objective of producing beneficial changes in individual patients that would hasten and sustain the return of patients to the natural environment. Instead, Page et al. conclude, behavior modification methods have been prostituted as a convenient means of enforcing nursing routine.

Making the now all too familiar case, Page et al. argue that in understaffed and overcrowded hospitals, a mindless conformity to a standardized hospital routine is reinforced in the interests (of the staff) of efficient patient management and to the detriment of individual behaviors such as initiative, assertion, and self-reliance that are vital to a successful return to society at large. Persuasively, they point out that the target behaviors of token reinforcement programs have "shown a monotonous repetition from one hospital to another. The programs continue to stress, with few exceptions, the traditional institutional values of cleanliness, order, punctuality, deference, and demeanor. These sorts of behaviors are of importance to program supervisors; but as a range of behaviors officially deemed worthy of receiving reinforcement, they are extremely narrow" (p. 176).

Of special interest is Page et al.'s analysis of the causes of this state of affairs, which they attribute neither to coincidence nor scientific planning. They suggest that mental hospitals—even those that may utilize behavioral principles on some wards—are still dominated by traditional notions of "mental illness" and that they are operated on the basis of "curing" medical problems. In this context the hospital policy must be enforced and since behavior modification programs appeared to do this, they were accordingly tolerated. This argument emphasizes that behavior modification was tolerated; its basic premises about the maintenance and modification of abnormal behavior were not—have not been—embraced. The fundamental treatment philosophy remains that of the quasi-disease, pathology model.

It is this departure from the basic tenets of Skinnerian principles, Page et al. continue, that accounts for programs in which ward staff "penalize patients for minor rule transgressions and reward them for equally uninspiring achievement" (p. 177). It is this distortion that creates a mechanistic climate in which the administration of tokens per se becomes the object of the exercise. Following Krasner and Krasner (1973), Page et al. correctly note that if token programs in institutions are to remain true to the basic concept of positive reinforcement (Skinner, 1971), it must be recognized that "a large part of what makes a reinforcer reinforcing is the social and interpersonal context in which it is given" (p. 178). We concur. There is simply no substitute for the expression of genuine care in therapeutic programs of any ilk.

The issues of politics and the token economy are also the subject of an article by Richards (1975b). Describing his experience—and frustration—in developing token programs in state hospitals, Richards urges that the behavior therapist receive training in dealing with the interpersonal and institutional politics of such hospitals, and suggests some examples of "power tactics"—including the ability of "Machiavellianism" —that could be used in "shaping the shapers." One is left with a rather uncomfortable feeling upon reading this analysis. In the first place, such an attempt to manipulate others, even if it is, as we can assume, well-intentioned, would be a clear example of Argyris' (1975) Model 1 of applied social psychology. It implicitly sanctions the right of some to control others, either overtly or, perhaps worse still, covertly; it is one-sided influence. As an alternative, Argyris offers his Model 2 of social influence which involves sharing of power and "couples articulateness and advocacy with an invitation to others to confront one's views, to alter them, in order to produce the position that is based on the most complete, valid information possible, to which people can be internally committed" (p. 482).

In the second place, ethical/philosophical objections notwithstanding, would this attempt to play politics ever be effective? We strongly doubt it. Richards himself cogently points out the alternative—developing and implementing entirely new approaches to the problem. Echoing Winett and Winkler (1972), he makes the provocative observation that token economies in state mental hospitals "are in the ironic position of being 'dangerous'—dangerous in the sense that, if they counteract the effects of institutionalization, they serve to support and justify a bad system when it would be preferable to adopt a new one" (p. 619).

Another limitation of token reinforcement programs is that there are few well-controlled comparative outcome studies in which their efficacy has been assessed. As Carlson, Hersen, and Eisler (1972) observed, token programs have been shown to be superior to the routine custodial-type of program, but have not been adequately compared with active alternative treatments. A recent article by Greenberg, Scott, Pisa, and Friesen (1975) addressed this very issue. They concluded that a combined social learning/milieu program was more effective than a token program alone because patients who had received the former treatment spent significantly more days in the community after discharge. However, statistical and substantive significance are not always commensurate. Thus the combined social learning/milieu patients spent 140 days in the community compared to 100 days for the token economy program patients. Although Greenberg et al. provide a detailed discussion of the possible reasons for the greater efficacy of the combined program, our emphasis in interpreting these results is slightly different.

The apparently similar hospital readmission rates for patients who received two very different programs strikes us as the most salient datum. One is reminded of Fairweather's (1964) results that showed that two different forms of therapy produced strikingly different behavioral outcomes in the hospital, but eventuated in similar rehospitalization rates at follow-up. Certainly the various features of Greenberg et al.'s combined treatment program—developing patient decision-making and fostering self-determination—seem eminently more constructive and therapeutic than the relatively trivial responses Page et al. (1975) rightly objected to. However, the upshot of these findings is that even the best of institutional programs cannot be relied upon to re-integrate a patient, the marginal man described by Atthowe (1973—reprinted in Franks & Wilson, 1974), into society. The generalization of treatment-produced improvement to the real world, and its maintenance there over time, are governed primarily by factors that cannot by definition be fully dealt with in the institutional environment. Emphasis has to be placed squarely on the real world environment to which the patient returns. When this is effectively accomplished, significant generalization and maintenance can be obtained (e.g., Atthowe, 1973; Fairweather, Sanders, Maynard, & Cressler, 1969).

As a final point about Greenberg et al.'s study, it must be pointed out that its procedures violate Wexler's (1973) well-reasoned proposals. The patients' absolute rights became their contingent rights when "the necessities of life, such as meals or a bed" had to be purchased with tokens. Greenberg et al.'s failure to even mention these issues is unfortunate. Hopefully we may anticipate the discontinuation of these procedures except under very special, ethically appropriate circumstances.

Several other studies of the efficacy of token economies indicate what we have known before—that they do change the behavior of inpatients —but have not satisfactorily met Carlson et al.'s methodological criticisms. Schwartz and Bellack (1975) found that a 15-week token program was more effective than a traditional psychiatric treatment that the "average non-private hospital inpatient . . . can expect" (p. 108). Rybolt (1975) reported a three-year follow-up of a token economy program which was initiated without the addition of new staff or different facilities under the aegis of outside funding. Patients showed significant improvement on five of the seven scales of the NOSIE-30 (Nurses' Observation Scale for In-Patient Evaluation) after participation in the program. Readmission rates for patients discharged from the hospital appeared to be low. For 30 patients who had not been readmitted the mean number of months since discharge was 9.33, while the six patients who had been readmitted had spent an average of almost five months in the community. In the absence of a control group these results are difficult to interpret. An investigation of staff and patient attitudes towards a token economy with adult psychiatric inpatients was conducted by Milby, Pendergrass, and Clarke (1975). A comparison of a token program and a control ward with similar environments, staff, and staff/patient ratios showed that the token economy staff and patients had consistently more positive attitudes than their respective counterparts on the control ward. As the authors point out, it is impossible to account for the reasons for this attitudinal difference from their study.

Lastly, Mumford, Patch, Andrews and Wyner (1975) described the development and implementation of one of the relatively few token reinforcement systems for the management of a ward of schizophrenic patients in England. While both qualitative and quantitative evidence of behavior change was obtained, Mumford et al. emphasized the practical problems involved in maintaining a token program. Not surprisingly their findings parallel those of investigators elsewhere. On the basis of their clinical experience they stress the "strong danger that operant ward procedures . . . may serve to increase rather than decrease authoritarian attitudes on the part of the staff" (p. 61). Other factors singled out by Mumford et al. as important include the continuity of nursing staff, the conceptualization of the token economy as a hospital rather than a ward program, and the necessity of establishing an environment geared to maintaining progress produced by the token program. Despite the various difficulties these investigators encountered, they concluded that behavior modification procedures using ward personnel as therapists "have a valuable contribution to make towards the rehabilitation problems that confront us on our chronic wards" (p. 71).

On a more theoretical level, research on the basic process of the reinforcement of chronic psychiatric patients has also continued. Using single-subject methodology, Stahl, Thomson, Leitenberg, and Hasazi (1974) demonstrated that social praise could be established as a reinforcer for socially unresponsive psychiatric patients by repeated pairings with token reinforcement. Praise was then used to directly modify behaviors of clinical relevance. The fact that token reinforcement—itself a generalized, conditioned reinforcer—was used to create another conditioned reinforcer has both theoretical and practical significance, as the authors point out. Mitchell, Mowat, and Stoffelmayr (1975) explored the effects of social deprivation and satiation on the reinforcing properties of social stimulation in chronic male hospitalized schizophrenics. Their results showed that prior social deprivation increased the patients' responsiveness to social stimulation whereas a prior conversation with the experimenter decreased subsequent social responsiveness.

The studies discussed above involved chronic psychiatric patients who were almost exclusively schizophrenics. Wooley and Blackwell (1975) have briefly reported an analysis of the social reinforcement contingencies in a psychosomatic ward for patients exhibiting "chronic illness behavior." This disorder is characterized by distress disproportionate to known physical problems, enactment of the role of a severely ill person, and constant demands for care and attention from hospital staff, family and friends. Wooley and Blackwell's behavioral probe not only confirmed these patients' high motivation to be cared for, but also indicated that they consistently rewarded staff and other patients for attending to them. The authors suggest how contingencies can be rearranged to produce less passivity and greater independence and self-reliance.

A basic objective of the social learning approach to psychiatric patients is to develop their social and interpersonal skills so that they can function more competently in the natural environment. In some cases—assuredly the most difficult and complex—patients never possessed the skills; in others, they once had them but subsequently lost them. Regardless of this distinction, and whatever the origins of the lacunae, the therapeutic process must assist the patient to acquire or reacquire some level of social skills if return to the real world is to be a realistic goal. As we have noted, the majority of token economy programs with chronic hospitalized patients have focused on narrowly limited—at times trivial—responses. And even in the few comprehensive programs that have targeted crucial behaviors such as problem-solving and self-determination, the utility and validity of the specific skills that are reinforced have never been systematically analyzed.

The major thesis of the first article in this Section, by Goldsmith and McFall, is that "content validity and treatment efficacy are inseparable concerns in therapy research." Yet it is clear that not only in the treatment of psychiatric patients, but also in the use of social skills training with such problems as heterosexual anxiety and lack of assertiveness (see Commentary in Section II), behavior therapy has emphasized the development of different techniques and their outcome evaluation to the virtual exclusion of content analyses. Indeed, Evans (1971) earlier voiced his concern about the relative neglect of the nature of specific response skills that are reinforced in behavioral programs with autistic children. Accordingly, this thoughtful, well-controlled study of Goldsmith and McFall's is very timely, illustrating a workable methodology for constructing relevant, empirically-based skill-training programs. Of particular clinical interest is the responsiveness of the psychotic patients to the training procedure. These results clearly show that it is time that behavioral treatment programs for psychotic patients—hitherto almost exclusively limited to simple applications of operant conditioning principles—be broadened by incorporating methods such as modeling, role playing, and guided participation.

Geriatric Patients in Residential Nursing Homes

Behavior modification in institutional settings has concentrated on the treatment of psychotic patients, juvenile delinquents, retarded and autistic children. Little attention has been paid to geriatric patients, in or out of an institution. It is therefore encouraging to note the publication during the past year of a number of papers describing the application of behavioral principles to one of the least publicized but nonetheless deserving of our many "minority" groups.

Sometimes institutionalization is both unavoidable and even desirable, and much can be accomplished to make this process more healthy and humane. Yet McClannahan and Risley (1975) point out the depressing facts that selected surveys of nursing homes indicate that only a small proportion offered recreational programs for their residents. And although the need for recreational activities has been emphasized in the nursing home literature, and specific recommendations have been made, scant empirical research has evaluated the efficacy of these recommendations. In an investigation of ways in which to increase participation by nursing home residents in recreation activities, McClannahan and Risley (1975) compared levels of participation in an activity area in the lounge under three conditions: a) when equipment and materials were provided residents and they were prompted to participate; b) when equipment and materials were available only upon request; and c) when they were not available. Subjects were residents of a 100-bed, skilled-care nursing home located in a middle-income neighborhood. Their ages ranged from 25-100 (76-80 years the modal age group). Residents under 50 years of age were either retarded or severely physically disabled.

Level of participation on days when the materials were unavailable averaged 20 percent; this increased to 74 percent when materials were present and residents were prompted to participate. Simply providing materials without prompting participation was ineffective. McClannahan and Risley contrast the latter finding with data from younger populations in which mere availability of materials and activities sufficed to engage people's participation.

Very similar results were reported by a group of British investigators. Working with geriatric patients suffering from dementia, Brook, Degun, and Mather (1975) studied the effects of systematically exposing patients to a "reality orientation" room. The purpose of this room was to remove patients from their isolation on the ward and provide them with a stimulating environment in which they could converse and interact with staff and other patients. Ratings of intellectual and social functioning showed that simply removing patients to a stimulating environment did not in itself produce much improvement. Rather, it appeared that active participation of therapists and their reinforcement of increased patient behavior were critical in maintaining improvement.

The application of operant conditioning procedures in the modification of walking, social interaction, and oral hygiene in residential geriatric patients was investigated by Sachs (1975). Although the majority of the applications reported represent systematic case studies of the A-B variety, one study with a socially inactive patient used an ABAB design in which reinforcement for social contact was briefly withdrawn and then reinstated. The results indicate that the target behaviors in this investigation are within the repertoire of at least many geriatric residents, and show that they can be modified. To avoid the adverse labeling effect and the "sick role" it often confers, Sachs advocates abandoning the term "patient" in favor of "resident" to describe these people.

Among the many difficulties presented by a residential geriatric population, urinary incontinence is one of the more time-consuming and chronic problems. Moreover, as Atthowe (1972—reprinted in Franks & Wilson, 1973) noted, incontinence in the elderly increases the probability that they will be placed in extended care, residential facilities.

Collins and Plaska (1975) compared three groups of geriatric residents in a nursing home in the treatment of enuresis: group 1 received the standard bell-and-pad conditioning treatment; group 2 received the same treatment with the exception that the buzzer (UCS) was delayed up to 15 seconds; and group 3 was a no-treatment control group. The 29 subjects' mean age was 81 years; they wet their beds four or more times during a baseline assessment week, and over half were incontinent during the day; two-thirds were bedridden or confined to wheelchairs; and about two-thirds were judged to have an impaired awareness of their surroundings.

Only one subject in each of the three groups remained dry for 10 consecutive nights during the eight-week treatment program. However, there was a significant decrease in frequency of bedwetting for the standard conditioning group but not for the delayed or control group over the course of treatment. Although a slight but reliable treatment effect was demonstrated, the relative ineffectiveness of the bell-and-pad procedure with this population, as compared to its use with normal children, is striking (cf. O'Leary & Wilson, 1975). Collins and Plaska discount the notion that hearing difficulties in their patients might have attenuated the efficacy of the method, and attribute the largely negative findings to impaired conditionability in old age (cf. Yates, 1970). However, given the fact that sphincter contraction was demonstrated at least to some degree in these geriatric subjects, the authors advocate further exploration into ways of enhancing the usefulness of the bell-and-pad method with this population. Biofeedback is one such possibility.

Pollock and Liberman (1974) described the use of behavior therapy in treating urinary incontinence in demented geriatric patients. Five patients completed a study consisting of three stages: a) a one-week baseline in which customary residential procedures were followed, i.e., frequent checking and changing of patients' pants by staff; b) one week during which patients had to mop up their incontinence and were not changed unless they requested it; and c) the addition to phase 2 conditions of contingent reinforcement if patients were dry at check points during the day. The results were almost totally negative. No patient showed significant improvement during phase 2 or 3 of treatment, and two actually displayed greater incontinence at the end of treatment than during baseline. Pollock and Liberman considered several explanations for these results, including the low frequency of reinforcement patients actually received. (This suggests that a more gradual shaping procedure might have been appropriate.) However, they concluded that operant procedures may be of help only to those few patients where the primary incontinence is maintained by the differential reinforcement provided by the staff.

Retarded Persons in Institutions

Azrin, Gottlieb, Hughart, Wesolowski, and Rahn's article that is reprinted in this Section describes yet another creative application of learning principles to the modification of severely disturbed behavior by Azrin and his colleagues. The results are quite remarkable. Rarely is it the case that any treatment of any severe behavior disorder can claim a 99 percent reduction in frequency of occurrence of the target problem. Moreover, self-injurious behavior was almost entirely eliminated in four of the subjects. The development of an alternative, seemingly more robust and effective procedure to the use of faradic shock in the treatment of self-injurious behavior is especially welcome.

As in the case of geriatric residents, incontinence among institutionalized retarded persons is a pressing and prevalent problem. Smith, Britton, Johnson, and Thomas (1975) report that a survey of hospitalized mentally handicapped people in England and Wales described 20 percent of these as "severely incontinent" during the day. Moreover, incontinence was a major reason for admission to institutions in the first place. In what they describe as a cross-validation of the work of Azrin and Foxx (1971; Foxx and Azrin, 1973) in the United States, Smith et al. used a slightly modified version of the Azrin and Foxx procedure in toilet training five profoundly retarded males. Independent toileting was produced in all patients, none of whom had ever shown this behavior previously. In a usefully detailed comparison of their treatment procedures and outcome with those of Azrin and Foxx, Smith et al. discuss their difficulties in maintaining initial success and the problems posed by unreliable nursing reports of what at first blush appears to be an easily definable clear-cut phenomenon.

Positive practice, that requires an individual to practice the correct manner of performing an action that is either deviant or deficient, has been successfully used in the treatment of a variety of problem behaviors, including toilet training. Most recently, Azrin and Weslowski (1975) have reported its application in eliminating persistent sprawling on the floor by profoundly retarded adults. Whenever a resident sat on the floor he was informed that he must not do so, was asked to get up, walk to a nearby chair, and seat himself for one minute. He was then told to repeat the process in other chairs until he had sat in 10 chairs. Physical guidance was used only if residents failed to respond to the verbal instructions, and then only the minimum necessary. Sprawling was eliminated after eight days of treatment, with verbal prompts being all that was necessary to obtain alternative behavior (i.e., sitting on chairs or sofas) after the fourth treatment day.

Another reeducative method devised by Azrin is overcorrection. The use of overcorrection for eliminating stealing by retarded residents of an institution ("theft reversal") was compared to a simpler correction procedure (restitution). In the former, the thief is required to return the stolen item and additionally give the victim an item identical to the one which had been stolen. The latter involves only the return of the stolen item. Theft reversal was significantly more effective, totally eliminating stealing after the fourth day of its introduction. Aside from this almost stunning success rate, the extra compensation of the victim is both appealing and in line with some contemporary thinking on criminal acts.

If there is any one common observation that the majority of investigators of the above-mentioned behavioral programs in institutional settings have emphasized it is the make-or-break role played by the institutional staff. As the practitioner has complained on more than one occasion, it is one thing to obtain positive results in a well-coordinated demonstration project, it is another to implement behavioral procedures effectively on a routine basis. Addressing himself to this crucial administrative problem, Quilitch (1975) compared the efficacy of three different types of staff-management procedures. The administrator of an institution for the retarded either a) sent a memo instructing all staff to lead daily recreational activities; b) sponsored a workshop to teach the implementation of these activities; or c) assigned staff activity leaders and provided public performance feedback by posting the daily average number of active residents in each ward. Only the latter procedure was effective, producing more than a fourfold increase in number of residents who participated in activities. Devising procedures such as the public posting of performance to promote accountability by specific individuals may be necessary if frequently complex and effortful behavioral procedures are to be systematically employed by institutional staff.

Children in Residential Treatment

Davids (1975) has provided an informative and engaging analysis of the progression from older therapeutic approaches to more innovative methods currently in use with children in a residential treatment center. According to Davids, psychodynamic psychotherapy was the only acceptable approach from the mid-1950s until the mid-1960s. The de-emphasis on, or even prohibition against, the child's therapist involving the parents in treatment that is inherent in this approach is contrasted with the active use of family and diverse staff members in the therapeutic influence process. Since then the development of behavior therapy and family therapy approaches have resulted in the recognition that "therapy" goes on around the clock in a residential treatment center. As Davids puts it, "Individual psychotherapy conducted by a professional staff member in the play therapy room is no longer viewed as having magical powers" (p. 814). Davids concludes that future advances in the understanding and treatment of psychotic children are most likely to come from biological and behavioral approaches.

Dramatically illustrating the sort of innovative thinking that has replaced the out-dated notions of one-to-one therapy behind closed doors, Twardosz, Cataldo, and Risley (1974) have described an open environment design for infant and toddler day care. The open environment they studied decreased the amount of time the child could not be seen by any adult and greatly facilitated supervision of staff members' activities. The sleep of the infants was not impaired, and the open environment seemed conducive to small group pre-academic activities despite the presumed distractions in the situation. A survey of the staff indicated that they liked working in this environment, which, Twardosz et al. suggest, can and should be used for infant day care.

Behavior Modification in Prisons

We began this Section by commenting on the public and professional controversy that marks the use of behavior modification methods in institutions. In many ways, behavioral programs in prisons have received the greatest publicity and aroused the most condemnation. Among other consequences for the field, the public announcement on February 14, 1974 by the Law Enforcement Assistance Administration that it was banning further use of anti-crime funds for behavior modification in prisons led to the creation by the American Psychological Association of a special Commission on Behavior Modification. This Commission was asked to make an analysis of the ethical and legal issues involved in the use and misuse of behavioral programs, and has yet to make final the report of its deliberations.

The charge that token reinforcement programs basically are predicated on serving the institution's purpose (easier, efficient management) rather than the inmate's once he/she is discharged has been made repeatedly and vigorously with respect to the prisons. Although specific abuses can and have been documented, and while some safeguards of prisoners' human rights can be built into the penal system, it is, as Bandura (1975—see Franks & Wilson, 1975) has argued, "the development of alternatives to prisons rather than guidelines for behavioral treatment in prisons that should command our attention" (pp. 16-17). In the meantime, however, behavioral programs are being utilized in prisons, and must be subjected to critical scrutiny in terms of their observance of ethical considerations.

An exception to programs that target behaviors designed to reduce individualism and self-assertion on the part of inmates is a recent study by Bassett, Blanchard, and Koshland that is reprinted here. They examined the effectiveness of reinforcing behaviors of potential adaptive value in the "free world." Unfortunately, as the authors themselves note, the absence of a follow-up upon release really limits the interpretation that can be placed on the outcome.

25

DEVELOPMENT AND EVALUATION OF AN INTERPERSONAL SKILL-TRAINING PROGRAM FOR PSYCHIATRIC INPATIENTS

Jean B. Goldsmith

Illinois State Psychiatric Institute

and

Richard M. McFall

University of Wisconsin—Madison

An interpersonal-skill-training program for male psychiatric inpatients was empirically developed and experimentally evaluated. The program development phase involved iden-

Reprinted with permission from *Journal of Abnormal Psychology,* Vol. 84, No. 1, 1975, 51-58. Copyright 1975, American Psychological Association.

This paper is based, in part, on the first author's doctoral dissertation. A brief summary of the research was presented in a symposium at the American Psychological Association meetings in Montreal, 1973. The authors thank George Meschel, Leila Foster, Richard Issel, Richard Cook, John Hamilton, Vida Dawson, Don Kraybill, June Williams, Oberta Roberts, and the staffs at the Chicago West Side Veterans Administration Hospital and the Illinois State Psychiatric Institute for their assistance in the Research.

The first author administered all assessment and treatment procedures. She was not on the VA staff and thus had no influence or contact outside the experimental context.

573

tifying patient-relevant problem situations, analyzing effective responses for these situations, deriving principles governing such effective behavior, and developing explicit scoring criteria for such behavior. In the evaluation phase, 36 male psychiatric inpatients received three individual sessions of either interpersonal skill training or pseudotherapy, or they were in an assessment-only control group. Skill training was found to be superior to the other two conditions on a number of behavioral and self-report measures, both in the training context and in a more real-life context.

Social skill training is a general therapy approach aimed at increasing performance competence in critical life situations. In contrast to therapies aimed primarily at the elimination of maladaptive behaviors, skill training emphasizes the positive, educational aspects of treatment. It assumes that each individual always does the best he can, given his physical limitations and unique learning history, to respond as effectively as possible in every situation. Thus, when an individual's "best effort" behavior is judged to be maladaptive, this indicates the presence of a situation-specific skill deficit in that individual's repertoire (Mager & Pipe, 1970). Whatever the origins of this deficit (e.g., lack of experience, faulty learning, biological dysfunction) it often may be overcome or partially compensated for through appropriate training in more skillful response alternatives. Presumably, once these new skills have been acquired and reinforced, they will displace any competing, less reinforcing maladaptive behaviors.

Research on the skill-training approach has been fairly limited to date, but encouraging results have been obtained in several treatment studies. These studies have involved such behavioral problems and populations as nonassertive college students (McFall & Twentyman, 1973), nondating college males (Melnick, 1973), college students hesitant about participating in class discussions (Wright, 1972), juvenile delinquents (Sarason & Ganzer, 1971), nonassertive psychiatric patients (Herson, Eisler, Miller, Johnson, & Pinkston, 1973), and interpersonally inadequate psychiatric patients (Goldstein, 1973).

The content of a skill-training program is at least as critical to its ultimate success as the training methods it employs. Of course, if the training methods fail to teach, then the patient cannot possibly benefit from the program, no matter how helpful the unlearned skills might have been. At the same time, however, if the response skills being taught do not offer valid solutions to the patient's life problems, then the program will fail regardless of the particular training methods used.

Clearly, the efficacy of a training program's methods can never be assessed apart from an evaluation of the program's content; both of these, in turn, will depend upon the particular patients and target problems being treated.

Goldfried and D'Zurilla (1969) have set forth basic methodological guidelines for systematically and empirically developing valid skill-training programs for specific behavioral problems and patient populations. Unfortunately, these guidelines have been virtually ignored in the skill-training research to date. Investigators have concentrated on evaluating the relative efficacy of various training methods, relying almost entirely on their clinical intuition for selecting the specific performance deficits and response skills to be trained. For this reason, the available studies provide only a tantalizing hint of what might be achieved if proper care were taken to construct skill-training programs empirically for specific populations with well-defined problems.

The present research was an effort to extend the laboratory work of McFall and his associates (McFall & Lillesand, 1971; McFall & Marston, 1970; McFall & Twentyman, 1973) into the treatment of behavioral problems among actual clinical patients in an applied clinical setting. The research was conducted in two phases. The first phase, which required by far the greater effort, was devoted to the systematic development of an interpersonal-skill-training program for male psychiatric inpatients following the methodological guidelines proposed by Goldfried and D'Zurilla (1969). The second phase was a treatment outcome study experimentally evaluating the skill-training program developed in the first phase.

PROGRAM DEVELOPMENT

Eliciting Problem Situations

The first developmental step involved obtaining a sample of problematic interpersonal situations common to psychiatric patients. Seventy-four outpatients at the Illinois State Psychiatric Institute were administered three 9-point rating scales to assess: (a) how much of a problem they have in meeting and talking to people for the first time, (b) how able they were to handle such situations, and (c) how comfortable they feel in such situations. Based on their responses, 16 patients (8 men, 8 women) subsequently were seen for 1-hour individual interviews. They were asked to give specific examples of difficult interpersonal situations they had experienced, including detailed descriptions of the contexts, participants, and purposes of each interaction. Also, details about the flow of each interaction (i.e., who said what to whom) and the most critical moments within the interactional flow were solicited.

Interview protocols revealed the extensive intersubject redundancy, with virtually no new situations being elicited by the last several interviews. The general situational contexts most frequently reported were: dating, making friends, having job interviews, relating to authorities, relating to service personnel, and interacting with people perceived as more intelligent or attractive or people whose appearance was somehow different (e.g., length of hair, race). The most frequently mentioned critical moments within these interactions were: initiating or terminating interactions, making personal disclosures, handling conversational silences, responding to rejection, and being assertive.

The 16 interview protocols were condensed to a list of 55 common problematic interpersonal situations. Where possible, the exact language, situational contexts, the critical moments obtained in the interviews were retained. Although some items involved isolated contexts and critical moments, other items involved an interrelated sequence of critical moments within the same situational context.

Selection of Relevant Situations

To select those problem situations most relevant to male psychiatric inpatients, the 55 problem situations were presented to 20 male inpatients from the psychiatric unit of the Westside Veterans Administration Hospital in Chicago. Patients' ages ranged from 19 to 49 years; there were approximately equal numbers of white and nonwhite patients. Diagnostic classifications included character disorders, neurotics, and schizophrenics.

Patients listened in groups of four to audiotaped presentations of the situations (to control for reading ability) and indicated which of five alternatives best described the way they would respond in each situation. The first four alternatives ranged from feeling comfortable and being able to handle the situation satisfactorily to feeling uncomfortable and being unable to handle it; the fifth alternative allowed them to exclude a situation if it probably would never occur to them.

Item relevance was judged on the basis of the following criteria: (a) More than 80 percent of the subjects reported some difficulty in the situation; (b) more than 20 percent reported being both uncomfortable in the situation and unable to handle it; and (c) less than 25 percent rated the situation as personally irrelevant. Twenty of the original 55 items met all three criteria; another 12 items met two of the criteria.

Eliciting Responses to Problem Situations

Next, eight male staff members at the Illinois State Psychiatric Institute (four white, four black; psychiatrist, social worker, child care worker, nurse, nurses' aide, and three psychologists) were individually administered the 55 tape-recorded interpersonal situations. They were instructed to role play each situation, responding out loud as if it were actually happening to them. This generated a sample of eight responses for each item.

Evaluating Response Competence

In 2-hour individual sessions, additional staff members from the Illinois State Psychiatric Institute evaluated the competence of the eight response alternatives for each of the 55 problem situations. Raters indicated which were effective ways of dealing with each situation, which were ineffective ways, and which were neither especially effective nor ineffective. Responses to situations involving interactions with women were judged by three males and two females; responses to situations involving interactions with men were judged by five males. In all, there were five white and five black raters; they were a psychiatrist, a child care worker, an occupational therapist, three psychologists, and four nurses' aides.

For a particular response alternative to be classified as "competent," at least four of the five judges must have rated it as such, with no judge rating it as incompetent. In 44 out of the 55 situations, at least one of the eight response alternatives met these criteria. Whenever judges classified a particular response alternative as either competent or incompetent, they were asked to explain what it was about the response that led them to make their evaluation. From these rationales, a set of principles governing effective behavior was derived. Any principle stated by more than one judge was retained and its wording refined. For some items more than one principle was developed. These were stated both positively (what the behavior should include) and negatively (what it should not include). The written principles subsequently became the coaching content employed in training. The same principles were also enumerated in a manual as explicit criteria for scoring subjects' responses.

Results

Out of the above four steps of program development emerged a list of problematic interpersonal situations, a list of competent responses for these situations, specific principles governing effective behaviors in these situations, and a manual for scoring responses in these situations. These materials provided the basis for the assessment procedures and training program content in the subsequent treatment study.

PROGRAM EVALUATION—METHOD

Subjects

The 41 male inpatients on the psychiatric ward at Chicago's West Side Veterans Administration Hospital were invited to participate as subjects. One refused and four were unable or unwilling to complete the initial assessment procedures, leaving a final sample of 36 patients. These subjects were randomly assigned to one of three experimental treatment conditions: interpersonal skill training, pseudotherapy control, or assessment-only control ($n = 12$ per group). The resulting groups were roughly equivalent in age (range: 18-49 years; $\bar{x} = 35.2$), racial composition (overall: 18 white, 18 black), diagnostic category (overall: 18 schizophrenics, 18 neurotics or character disorders), and marital status (overall: 6 married, 11 divorced, 19 single).

Procedure

The pretreatment assessment instructions and stimuli were presented entirely via audiotape, and subjects' responses were recorded for subsequent analysis. The first two measures were administered to subjects in groups of four: First, using 9-point scales, subjects rated (a) their difficulty meeting and talking to people, (b) their expected future ability to handle social interactions outside the hospital, and (c) their feeling of self-worth. Next, they were given the Interpersonal Situation Inventory (ISI), which consisted of the 55 problematic interpersonal situations developed in the preceding study. Subjects responded by choosing which of five options best reflected their probable response in each situation. The choices, in essence, were: 1—comfortable and competent; 2—uncomfortable but competent; 3—comfortable but incompetent; 4—uncomfortable and incompetent; and 5—situation not personally relevant. Subsequently, the Interpersonal Behavior Role-Playing Test (IBRT) was administered to subjects individually. For each of 25 tape-recorded simulated interpersonal situations, the subject role played his response, using the words he might use if he were in the actual situation. The situations, taken from the 55-item ISI, were selected from those previously identified as most relevant to the subject population and for which scoring criteria had been developed. Immediately following the IBRT, the subject began his assigned experimental treatment.

Assessment-only control. These subjects received only the pretreatment and posttreatment assessments. However, they were told that the IBRT was a new form of treatment involving "response practice." They were praised for their efforts, were told that within a week they would have another practice session, and were dismissed.

Interpersonal skill training. Subjects in this condition were individually administered three 1-hour training sessions within a 5-day period; 15 minutes were devoted to covering each of 11 problem situations (a subset of the 25-item IBRT) with an additional 15 minutes of review at the end of training. Training covered such interpersonal tasks as initiating and terminating conversations, dealing with rejection, and being more assertive and self-disclosing. The training procedures, which were adapted directly from the experimental procedures of McFall and his associates (1970, 1971, 1973), employed the components of behavior rehearsal, modeling, coaching, recorded response playback, and corrective feedback. Training instructions and stimuli were prerecorded on audiotape.

The training sequence for each situation was as follows: (a) The subject listened to a narrative description of the problem situation; (b) he was coached about the principles of effective behavior in that situation (as determined in the preceding study); (c) he heard a competent response by a male model (selected in the preceding study); (d) he heard a review and summary of the training material, along with a description of the likely consequences of various response alternatives; (e) the experimenter stopped the recorder and ascertained through discussion that the subject understood and accepted the training material and was willing to attempt the proposed behavioral solution; (f) the recorded situation was replayed; (g) the subject rehearsed responding and his response was tape recorded; (h) his response was played back and evaluated, first by the subject and then by the experimenter, who provided corrective feedback; (i) rehearsal was repeated until both the subject and experimenter agreed that the criteria for effective behavior had been advanced either to the presentation of a new coaching segment for the same situation or to the next situation. (Some situations had been broken down into small subunits to facilitate acquisition.)

Pseudotherapy control. This treatment condition closely paralleled the skill-training condition. There were three individual sessions, each lasting 1 hour, over a 5-day period. The same 11 situations were covered on the same time schedule. However, no training was given in specific response alternatives. Instead, after hearing each audiotaped problem situation, the subject was encouraged to explore his feelings about it and to seek insight into the psychological and historical reasons for these feelings. The experimenter was supportive and participated in the search for insight, but always avoided suggesting specific behavioral changes or solutions.

Posttreatment assessment. One day after his last treatment session, each subject was readministered the Interpersonal Behavior Roleplaying Test (IBRT). Scheduling for assessment-only subjects was determined by a yoking procedure. Following the IBRT, a simulated real-life behavior test was given. The subject was asked via prerecorded instructions to meet and carry on a general conversation with a male stranger (a "blind" confederate). He was given specific instructions to initiate the conversation, to ask the stranger to lunch, and to terminate the conversation after 10 minutes (a clock was visible). Unbeknown to the subject, the confederate was programmed to confront him with three "critical moments": not hearing the subject's name when introduced, responding to the lunch invitation with an excuse, and saying "Tell me about yourself" at the first convenient pause. The interaction was tape-recorded for subsequent analysis. Afterwards the subject rated his own skill and comfort in the interaction on a 5-point scale. The confederate, meanwhile, recorded whether the subject successfully dealt with the planned interactional tasks and also used 9-point scales to rate the subject's apparent comfort, general ability, and pleasantness in the interaction. On the following day, the subjects were seen in groups of four and were readministered the battery of global self-report measures—three 9-point scales assessing general comfort and ability in social situations and the 55-item ISI.*

RESULTS

There were no significant pretreatment differences among groups on any of the dependent measures; therefore, except as noted, treatment effects were analyzed with one-way analyses of variance for pretreatment to posttreatment change scores,** and subsequent comparisons were performed using the Scheffé test.

---

* Nurses' aides also were enlisted to provide "blind" ratings of general social skill and comfort of subjects' ward behavior both before and after treatment. Interrater reliability was so unsatisfactory ($r = .04$ or less) that these ratings were not analyzed further.

** Whenever the variance of one group was seven times that of another group, a log-10 transformation of raw scores was performed to achieve greater homogeneity.

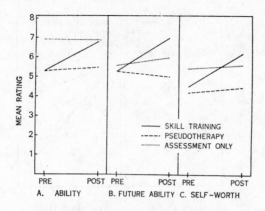

FIGURE 1. Group means for ratings on Global Self-Perception Questionnaire items (scores transformed so that higher values reflect more positive ratings).

Self-Report Measures

Figure 1 shows group means on the three global self-rating questions assessing (a) difficulty in meeting strangers, (b) projected future ability to interact socially, and (c) self-worth. Significant change-score differences were obtained on the dimensions of difficulty ($F = 4.32$, $df = 2/33$, $p < .05$) and self-worth ($F = 5.95$, $df = 2/33$, $p < .01$), but the difference on future ability only approached significance ($F = 2.94$, $df = 2/33$, $p < .10$). Subsequent comparisons revealed that the skill-training group reported more improvement than the assessment-control group on the difficulty question ($p < .05$) and more than either control group on the self-worth question (both $ps < .05$). It also was the only group to show positive change on the future ability question, although this contrast was not significant.

The ISI was scored for the number of items, out of 55, on which the subject reported that his response would be both uncomfortable and incompetent. Change scores revealed significant overall treatment effects ($F = 3.61$, $df = 2/33$, $p < .05$). The only significant individual contrast was between the skill-training and assessment-only control group ($p < .05$).

To assess for generalization of treatment effects, the 44 ISI items on which subjects received no specific training were analyzed separately from the 11 items on which training was given. This breakdown is summarized in Figure 2. The overall difference among groups on the attenuated number of trained items was only marginally significant ($F =$

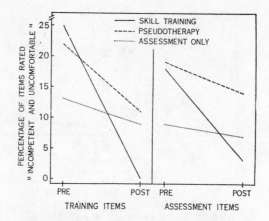

FIGURE 2. Group means for percentage of Interpersonal Situation Inventory items in which subjects indicated they would be both incompetent and uncomfortable (training items, $n = 11$; assessment items, $n = 14$).

2.67, $df = 2/33$, $p < .10$). However, the difference on untrained items was significant ($F = 3.98$, $df = 2/33$, $p < .05$), with skill-training subjects improving more than assessment-only controls ($p < .05$).

Interpersonal Behavior Role-Playing Test

Subjects' tape-recorded responses on this measure were transcribed, scrambled, and rated by two "blind" male raters using the scoring manual developed in the preceding study. A response was given two points if it met all the criteria for that situation, one point if it met only some, and zero points if it met none. Overall, there was 95 percent agreement as to the exact scoring of all responses.

Analysis of change scores revealed highly significant group differences ($F = 49.78$, $df = 2/33$, $p < .001$). Subsequent comparisons indicated that the skill-training group improved more than either of the two control groups ($p < .05$), and the two control groups neither changed appreciably nor differed from each other. The change in frequency of "no answer" responses on the behavior test also was related to treatment ($F = 5.18$, $df = 2/33$, $p < .05$), with skill-training subjects showing a greater decrease than subjects in either control condition (both $ps < .05$).

Figure 3 presents group means for trained items ($n = 11$) and untrained items ($n = 14$) on the behavior test. Significant treatment effects were found on both types of items (trained: $F = 56.57$, $df = 2/33$, $p <$

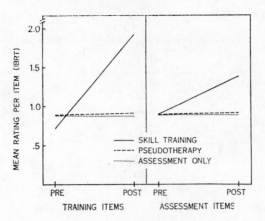

FIGURE 3. Group means for performance ratings on Interpersonal Behavior Role-playing Test training items and assessment items.

.001; untrained: $F = 15.41$, $df = 2/33$, $p < .001$). Subsequent comparisons revealed that skill-trained subjects improved significantly more on both types of items than subjects in either of the control groups (both $ps < .05$).

Simulated Real-Life Behavior Test

This measure, which provided a partial assessment of the transfer of training (see Table 1) yielded evidence of overall treatment effects when analyzed in terms of the number of interaction tasks (out of seven) satisfactorily completed by subjects ($F = 15.11$, $df = 2/33$, $p < .001$). Skill-training subjects completed significantly more tasks than subjects in either of the control conditions (both $ps < .05$). The confederate's ratings of subjects' performance also provided evidence of transfer, with skill-training subjects perceived as more able, or skillful, than control subjects (both $ps < .05$). In addition, significant differences were found for subjects' self-appraisals of their performance in the interaction: skill-training subjects rated their performance as more comfortable and more competent than did subjects in either of the control groups (both $ps < .05$).

Follow-Up

Eight months following treatment, recidivism rates for the three experimental groups were compared. Unfortunately, it was possible to

TABLE 1
Summary of Simulated Real-Life Behavior Test Means

Variable	Group means			F	p
	Interpersonal skill training	Pseudotherapy control	Assessment control		
Number of performance tasks completed	6.33	3.50	3.17	15.113	<.001
Rating of Subject's ability to handle the situation	7.00	4.33	4.33	7.610	<.01
Rating of Subject's comfort	7.33	6.00	6.42	1.283	ns
Rating of how pleasant it was to talk with Subject	7.42	5.75	5.92	3.623	<.05
Subject's self-rating of comfort and competence	1.27	2.44	2.33	7.042	<.01

obtain follow-up data for only 72 percent of the original sample (10 skill-training subjects, 8 pseudotherapy subjects, 8 assessment-only subjects). Based on the available data, however, the readmission rates were: skill training, 20 percent; pseudotherapy, 25 percent; assessment-only, 31 percent. This pattern is in the expected direction, but because of the small and incomplete sample, it provides only suggestive evidence that cannot be interpreted with much confidence.

DISCUSSION

Content validity and treatment efficacy are inseparable concerns in therapy research. The ultimate measure of a program's content validity is its therapeutic utility; conversely, therapy outcome inevitably depends on the validity of the intervention program's content. The present research attempted to deal with these interdependent concerns in an integrated and systematic manner. As a result, the research not only demonstrated that skill training is a feasible and potentially effective treatment approach for use with severely disturbed patients, but it also illustrated a viable methodology for empirically constructing the training content for a specific population and target problem. When male psychiatric inpatients were given only 3 hours of interpersonal skill training, they demonstrated significantly greater improvement in their ability to handle difficult interpersonal situations than did patients receiving either 3 hours of pseudotherapy or the experimental assessment procedures alone. The superiority of the skill-training condition over the two control conditions was evident on virtually every experimental measure, including global self-rating scales, self-report measures of specific interpersonal comfort and competence, behavioral measures of performance in specific problem situations, and a simulated interaction approximating a real-life encounter. However, the margin of the training program's superiority became more evident and convincing as one moved from the results on the more subjective, global self-report measures to the results on the more objective behavioral measures, which tapped actual performance in simulated interpersonal situations. This tendency for the greatest changes to occur in subjects' overt behavior is consistent with the underlying assumptions of the treatment model.

There also was evidence of treatment generalization. Treatment effects were evident not only in situations for which subjects had received specific training, as one would expect, but also in situations for which no training was given. This was the pattern for both the situation-specific self-report measure and the behavior test. Equally important, the simulated interaction test showed that treatment effects transferred to a novel task involving a lifelike conversation with a stranger. In addition, a follow-up measure—readmission rate—yielded suggestive evidence of positive transfer to real life.

Finally, there was anecdotal evidence of positive treatment effects. For example, six skill-training subjects spontaneously requested more of the same treatment, whereas only two pseudotherapy subjects and no assessment-only subjects did so. Three unsolicited reports from "blind" hospital staff members also supported the impression that training had positive extraexperimental effects; all three reports involved subjects in the training condition. Such anecdotal reports highlight the problem of designing standardized and controlled follow-up measures capable of detecting idiographically manifested treatment effects. This problem requires concerted attention in future research.

One of the most encouraging findings of the research was that the skill-training program was as beneficial for the psychotic patients as for the neurotic and character disorder patients. Psychotic patients, who generally are regarded as resistant to most forms of treatment, were able to participate satisfactorily in all of the assessment and training procedures and clearly benefited from them. Perhaps this was because the training procedures were broken down into small units, were paced according to the patient's individual progress, and were highly repetitive, permitting the patient to "tune out" periodically without serious loss.

This study's treatment and assessment procedures were necessarily limited. The interpersonal-skill-training program, as a whole, led to improved performance; however, the specific contributions of individual program components were not assessed. Future research must make this assessment and then refine and extend the program to make it even more effective. Logical directions for expanding the procedures in the future would be (a) to give patients more time to practice each new behavior, (b) to provide more training sessions covering more problem situations, (c) to allow patients greater flexibility to focus on those problems most pertinent in their own lives, and (d) to develop better methods of assessing long-term, real-life therapeutic change. Also, since the present study was limited to male patients, similar skill-training programs for female patients should be developed and evaluated.

Although the present study focused on interactions with relative strangers, it demonstrated a useful methodology for the definition and assessment of behavioral competence in other problem areas (e.g., problems involving interactions with family members, children, employers, or friends). Future skill-training research could use this methodology to develop a taxonomy of prevalent behavioral problems encountered in clinical patients, to analyze the situations in which these problems occur, to define what constitutes competent behavior in these situations, and to generate the content of problem-specific skill-training programs.

REFERENCES

GOLDFRIED, M. R. & D'ZURILLA, T. J. A behavior-analytic model for assessing competence. In C. D. Spielberger (Ed.), *Current Topics in Clinical and Community Psychology.* Vol. 1. New York: Academic Press, 1969.

GOLDSTEIN, A. P. *Structural Learning Therapy.* New York: Academic Press, 1973.

HERSON, M., EISLER, R. M., MILLER, P. M., JOHNSON, M. B., & PINKSTON, S. G. Effects of practice, instructions, and modeling on components of assertive behavior. *Behav. Res. & Ther.* 1973, 11, 443-451.

MAGER, R. F. & PIPE, P. *Analyzing Performance Problems.* Belmont, Calif.: Fearson, 1970.

McFALL, R. M. & LILLESAND, D. B. Behavior rehearsal with modeling and coaching in assertion training. *J. Abnorm. Psychol.,* 1971, 77, 313-323.

McFALL, R. M. & MARSTON, A. R. An experimental investigation of behavior rehearsal in assertive training. *J. Abnorm. Psychol.,* 1970, 76, 295-303.

McFALL, R. M. & TWENTYMAN, C. T. Four experiments on the relative contributions of rehearsal, modeling and coaching to assertion training. *J. Abnorm. Psychol.,* 1973, 81, 199-218.

MELNICK, J. A. Comparison of replication techniques in the modification of minimal dating behavior. *J. Abnorm. Psychol.,* 1973, 81, 51-59.

SARASON, I. G. & GANZER, V. J. *Modeling: An Approach to the Rehabilitation of Juvenile Offenders.* (Final report on Grant No. 15-P-55303 from the Division of Research and Demonstration Grants, Social and Rehabilitation Service.) Washington, D. C.: U.S. Department of Health, Education, & Welfare, 1971.

WRIGHT, J. C. The relative efficacy of systematic desensitization and behavior training in the modification of university quiz section participation difficulties. Unpublished doctoral dissertation, University of Wisconsin—Madison, 1972.

26

ELIMINATING SELF-INJURIOUS BEHAVIOR BY EDUCATIVE PROCEDURES

N. H. Azrin, L. Gottlieb, L. Hughart, M. D. Wesolowski

Anna State Hospital, Illinois

and T. Rahn

St. Lawrence State Hospital, Ogdensburg, N. Y.

Summary—Self-injury is a common problem among autistic and severely retarded persons. The most effective treatment has been pain-shock punishment. To provide a possible alternative treatment, modifications were made in previously developed treatments for autistic behavior. The revised method included positive reinforcement for non-self-injurious behavior, a period of required relaxation or incompatible postures upon each occurrence of a self-injurious episode, and a hand-awareness training procedure. The treatment procedure was used with 11 clients, ten of whom were very severely retarded. No clients were excluded. The mean number of self-injurious episodes was reduced by 90 percent on the first day, by 96 percent at the end of one week and

Reprinted with permission from *Behaviour Research and Therapy*, 1975, Vol. 13, 101-111.

This research was supported by the Illinois Department of Mental Health. Grateful acknowledgement is given to the many staff members of the several institutions in the State of Illinois who participated in this project.

by 99 percent by the end of three months. For four of the clients self-injury was eliminated almost entirely. The new procedure appears to be an effective method of treating self-injurious behavior and avoids the general reluctance to use pain-shock.

Self-injurious behavior by the profoundly retarded or mentally ill is one of the most severe psychological disorders since physical injury always results and sometimes, even death, if ignored. Yet, this problem persists in spite of a large number of recent reports of effective treatment by learning therapy procedures. One frequently used method is pain-shock punishment which has been effectively used by Risley (1968), Tate and Baroff (1966), Yeakel et al. (1970), Corte, Wolf and Locke (1971), and see review by Bucher and Lovaas (1968). A second method of treating self-injury is timeout from positive reinforcement which has been used effectively by Wolf, Risley and Mees (1964), Hamilton, Stephens and Allen (1967), Myers and Deibert (1971), Risley (1968) and Tate and Baroff (1966). In a few instances, effective treatment has resulted from a third method, that of reinforcement for non-injurious behavior (Lovaas et al., 1965; Lane & Domrath, 1970; Peterson & Peterson, 1968).

Unfortunately, the general applicability of the above treatments is an open question since all of the above reported applications have been case studies in which one selected client was used, except for two reports where the same method was used with three clients (Bucher & Lovaas, 1968) and four clients (Corte et al., 1971). Also, most of the studies have eliminated the self-injurious behavior during restricted time periods of an hour or less per day. Exceptions are the all-day elimination obtained by Tate and Baroff (1966), Hamilton et al. (1967), Wolf et al. (1964).

Of the three methods, shock seems to have the extreme advantage of extreme rapidity in eliminating self-injury, often within 1 hour. Perhaps the greatest restraint on the use of shock has been the reluctance of therapists to resort to this physical punishment (see discussion by Bucher & Lovaas, 1968, and Risley, 1968). As Lovaas and Bucher have stated, regarding the use of shock-punishment by the ward staff members, "all have approached the task with extreme reluctance and anxiety" (p. 140). In addition, the spectre of a ward attendant carrying an electric prod discourages the widespread use of this demonstrably effective and rapid treatment.

The alternatives to shock have been less satisfactory. Physical restraint by tying the client to a chair (Lane & Domrath, 1970) is not as rapid a treatment as shock and also suffers from the characteristic of being excessively aversive. Timeout from positive reinforcement has not been as rapid or as effective as shock and seems to suffer from the disadvantage that the client can continue to injure himself during the timeout, thereby precluding its use with severe self-injury (Corte et al., 1971). Reinforcement of incompatible behavior has the advantage of being totally non-aversive but has not been used effectively alone, only in combination with other methods (Lane et al., 1970, and Lovaas et al., 1965).

The present study devised a new treatment program based largely on three recently developed procedures that appear to hold promise as a relatively non-aversive treatment for self-injury. The first method is that of Autism Reversal (Azrin, Kaplan & Foxx, 1973; Foxx & Azrin, 1972) which has been found to be effective as a general treatment for autistic behavior, of which self-injury may be considered a sub-class and is based on the Overcorrection principle (Foxx & Azrin, 1972; Foxx & Azrin, 1973). In the Autism Reversal procedure, the client is required by instruction and manual guidance to engage in several different fixed postures which are non-self-stimulatory. This required practice is given upon each self-stimulatory episode on a response contingent basis. When the client is not self-stimulating, he is given positive reinforcement for alternative, incompatible activities. The second promising method, the Required Relaxation procedure, is also derived from the Overcorrection principle, and has been effectively used to eliminate a variety of agitative-disruptive behavior, including one client who injured himself (Webster & Azrin, 1973). This Required Relaxation procedure was found to be especially favored by hospital ward staff as a humane and meaningful type of treatment. The third promising procedure was Hand-Awareness Training. In a recent treatment developed for eliminating nervous habits of normal clients (Azrin & Nunn, 1973), the lack of awareness by the client of the location of his hands seemed to be contributing toward nervous habits involving the hands. Consequently the normal clients were given training in being continually aware of the position of their hands as part of the treatment. Since self-injury almost always includes striking oneself with the hands, the Hand-Awareness Training might be expected to help the self-injurious client to control this problem.

The present study modified these three promising procedures of Required Relaxation, Autism Reversal, and Hand-Awareness Training for use with a larger number of self-injurious clients in an attempt to eliminate self-injury on an all-day basis.

METHOD

Clients

Eleven clients were obtained in response to an offer to several institutions to provide assistance in treating clients who repeatedly inflicted injury on themselves that resulted in evident tissue damage. No clients were excluded. Five were from the same institution, the remaining six from four other institutions. Treatment was given in the client's institution. Table 1 shows the age, sex, diagnosis, IQ, years of institutionalization, years of exhibiting self-injury, the type of self-injury and the frequency of the behavior. Ten clients were diagnosed as severely or profoundly retarded, having an average IQ of 13, the highest IQ being 26 and the lowest 6. The eleventh client was diagnosed as schizophrenia, childhood type with an IQ of 89; he exhibited many of the diagnostic signs of autism. The retarded clients had an average age of 30 years with an average duration of institutionalization of 18 years, all having been institutionalized before the age of 15. Self-injury was reported to have been a problem for an average of 12 years except for the schizophrenic boy who developed the problem only a year earlier. One noteworthy instance was the 18-year-old female who was reported in her records to have started hitting her head against the sides of her crib at 2 years of age and had evidently self-inflicted scratches on her cheeks and ears during her first year of life. All clients had visible swelling and most also had scratches, scabs, bruises, or open wounds. All clients struck themselves on the face or head or on one part of their head such as the ears, side of the face, or eyes, usually with their fist or open hand. In addition, 2 clients banged their head on a floor or wall (listed as headbanging in Table 1), one of them as his predominant method of self-injury. Five of the clients had been given protective clothing such as a helmet or gloves or put in physical restraints such as special jacket or wrist restraints. Ten of the 11 clients were receiving tranquilizing or sedative medication. For 4 of the clients, treatment has also been given previously in the form of Electro Convulsive Shock therapy or timeout seclusion, or manually holding the client's hands behind the back. For 2 of the clients, the ward staff was only mildly interested in treating the problem. For one of these clients they felt that the protective helmet was adequately preventing self-injury; for the other client, the problem of eye-gouging usually was subordinated to other pressing ward problems.

Recording

The extent of self-injurious behavior prior to treatment was directly recorded by observing the client for as long as was feasible. For 2 clients who were in restraints or protective clothing, the restraint clothing was removed and the client observed until the self-injury responses appeared to be causing damage. For one of these clients, only 10 minutes of observation was feasible; for the other, 38 minutes. For the other 9 clients, the duration of observation was adjusted to the frequency of the behavior. One client who hit himself continuously was observed for 30 minutes, whereas another client who had a few episodes per day was observed for 8 hours per day for 12 days, by a time-sample procedure. A response was considered self-injurious if the client struck, bit or scratched himself. The nature of the behavior was so unusual that the observers felt little difficulty in differentiating these self-injurious actions from normal ongoing activities. In every instance, the ward staff reported that the recorded frequency was representative of the client's usual frequency. For one client, the self-injurious response was static, namely pressing her hand hard against her eyeball; this response was recorded in terms of duration. When the self-injury consisted of spaced blows, the measure was number of blows. If the self-injury consisted of a rapid flurry of blows the measure was the number of such episodes (see last column of Table 1).

Response Detection

After treatment was initiated, two instructors continually observed the client for about 12 hours/day for the first 2 or 3 days, always keeping the client in full view, and within arms' length since the instructors were required to give continuing positive reinforcement for appropriate non-injurious behavior. Members of the ward staff assisted the instructors in recording and carrying out the treatment during these first few days and were encouraged to assume this responsibility when the instructors were absent. For 5 of the clients, the special instructors were present for at least 2 weeks. For the other 6 clients who were at remote institutions, the instructors returned periodically for direct confirmatory observation of reported benefits.

Duration of Treatment

On each ward, the special instructor taught those employees who were interested how to conduct the procedure and supervised their performance. The instructors role-played the procedure with the staff members prior to application of the procedure to a client. The staff was advised of the importance of using the procedure immediately upon detection of a self-injurious response and upon every self-injurious response. One ward employee was typically designated as the coordinator but all were instructed to record the self-injurious behavior and to initiate the treatment procedure. The ward staff was advised to continue the treatment for several weeks after the special instructor departed but his role was advisory only. Telephone contact was made daily with the employees to encourage their continuation of the treatment. For all clients, the treatment lasted for at least 12 days. For 4 clients, the ward employees were not motivated to continue the procedure after the special instructors were absent. The ward employees discontinued treatment for 1 client after 12 days, another after 1 month, and the third and fourth clients after 2 months.

Positive Reinforcement for Outward-Directed Activities

The client was given positive reinforcers for engaging in a variety of outward-directed and incompatible responses. For the clients whose behavior was most "inner-directed" these activities included eye contact with the instructor, looking at specific objects when instructed, sitting down or arising from a chair when instructed, walking, banging drumsticks together, grasping the armrests of their chair, catching and throwing a ball, or even simply sitting still without injuring themselves. For the clients who were more "outward-directed," the responses included playing with a jig-saw puzzle, educational games, toileting, dressing, grooming, washing oneself, word recognition, ward cleaning chores, making beds, trips to the ward commissary, playing with simple music-making instruments, group recreational activities, swimming at a local pool, and bus rides. The guiding principle was to select those responses that involved active interaction with the physical and social environment, especially responses that were functional and could be expected to be maintained later because of their potential enjoyment or utility in their own right. If the ward program included regular supervised activities or classes, every attempt was made to enroll the client in these activities or classes. The reinforcers selected for use included verbal

TABLE 1

Description and Frequency of Occurrence of the Self-Injurious
Behaviors for Each of 11 Clients

Client age and sex	Diagnosis	IQ	Years inst'd	Years exhibit- ing self- injury	Nature of injury	Pre-treat- ment frequency of behavior
28-yr-old male	Mentally retarded profound	11	22	14	face hitting, self-choking, biting, kicking	32/day
44-yr-old female	Mentally retarded profound	8	31	6	face slapping	6/day
26-yr-old female	Mentally retarded severe	26	19	6	scratching, face slapping	9/day
25-yr-old male	Mentally retarded profound	14	20	20	face and head slapping, punching	748/day
32-yr-old female	Mentally retarded profound	6	19	8	eye gouging	86% of the day
46-yr-old female	Mentally retarded profound	11	31	31	face, arm, leg slapping, finger biting	200/day
24-yr-old male	Mentally retarded profound	12	14	20	hand biting, head hitting and banging	25/day
10-yr-old male	Mentally retarded profound	9	9	7	ear punching	3528/day
18-yr-old female	Mentally retarded profound	6	18	18	face, ear, and head slapping	3500/day
15-yr-old male	Schizo- phrenia, childhood type	89	3	0.65	face punching	48/day
17-yr-old male	Mentally retarded profound	8	8	7	head banging	41/day

praise, back-stroking, and desired snack items such as candy, pudding, coffee, and juice. The ward staff usually knew what was reinforcing for a given client. In general, the snack items proved to be the best reinforcers for the more inward-directed clients. Reinforcers were delivered very frequently at first; the verbal praise was almost continuous. Once the client began spending extended periods without self-injury, the reinforcers were made more intermittent by reinforcing for longer response sequences.

Required Relaxation

The Required Relaxation was essentially the same as described elsewhere as a treatment for agitative-disruptive conduct (Webster & Azrin, 1973). When the client injured himself, he was told that he was overexcited and agitated and was required to go relax in his bed. He was assisted in putting on a hospital gown and directed to his own bed where he remained for 2 hours. The instructor stood behind the head of the bed and assured that the client did not leave the bed.

A modification in the previously described procedure was made because of the severe nature of the self-injurious conduct. The client was required not only to remain in bed but to maintain his arms in an extended downward position with the hands alongside his legs away from his head, a position that was incompatible with striking one's head. The instructor used verbal instruction and gentle manual guidance, according to the Graduated Guidance Method which provides no more manual contact than is minimally necessary to obtain the required posture. This gentleness of contact as prescribed by the Graduated Guidance procedure was essential; otherwise great resistance resulted. His fixed posture was required for an uninterrupted 10 minutes in this arms-extended position. If he moved his hands toward his head or hit himself, 10 more minutes were required. All clients required considerable manual guidance initially, but after 1 or 2 days they usually performed the Required Relaxation Procedure upon verbal direction and with minimal manual contact. After the client began spending several hours on the ward without injuring himself, the Required Relaxation was given for any emotional or agitated conduct that was found to be a usual precursor of self-injury, such as excitedly pacing or rocking, muttering, screaming, or cursing in which case the Required Relaxation was given only for 10 minutes, again explaining to the client that he was overexcited and had to calm himself. The instructor's presence at bedside was usually required only during the first 1 or 2 days until the client learned to lay fairly still with the arms extended. Thereafter, the instructor usually remained with the client for only about 5 minutes until he was assured that the client was resting in the correct posture. The instructor, or any other staff member passing by the open door, could determine whether the client was resting as required. The pressure-sensitive device attached to the leg of the bed, and described previously (Webster & Azrin, 1973) sounded a signal to the staff if the client left the bed.

Hand Control

The Hand Control Procedure was very similar to the arm exercises described in the previous report (Azrin et al., 1973) for eliminating hand autisms. In the previous report, when the client exhibited an autism he was immediately reprimanded and told that he must now practice holding his hands away from his body. The instructor stood behind him and guided him. The client was required to hold his arms extended at his sides, then outstretched horizontally to the front, then to the side, then extended over his head. Thirty seconds was required in each position preceded by a verbal instruction prior to each change in position. This cycle was repeated for 20 seconds in the standing posture. No conversation occurred between the instructor and the client, except the instruction every 30 seconds as to the change in hand posture. The client received no praise or cajoling from the instructor during the exercises.

Several modifications were made in the above procedure to make it suitable for use with self-injurious clients. The arms-forward position was eliminated since a head-striking movement could be made easily from that position leaving only the arms down, side, and up position. Secondly, the arm-down position was modified to include clasping of the hands together behind one's back in order to make the response more incompatible with striking oneself than was the hands-by-side position. This clasping of the hands also seemed easier to teach and seemed to be used spontaneously after training by the clients as a method of self control. Another modification was to require a position change every 10 seconds rather than every 30 seconds in order to have the client more active and to give more opportunity to react to the instructions. A fourth modification was to conduct the exercises in the sitting posture rather than standing for those clients who were physically unable to stand easily or who became too fatigued or emotionally upset by having to stand. A fifth modification was omission of the head-orientation exercises at the start of the practice period since the self-injurious clients could easily hit themselves while the instructor was manually guiding their head. A sixth modification was to terminate the arm exercise period while the client was in the arms-down position since this posture merged more naturally with his usual posture. This last posture was maintained for a longer period, 30 seconds to 1 minute, until the client was standing calmly with his arms down with no need for the instructor to hold his arms there. As in the previous report, the clients usually learned after 1 or 2 days to move their arms to the new position upon hearing the verbal instruction with a need for only minimal manual guidance.

In the event that the client became very upset during the Hand Control exercises, the instructor attempted to continue while paying special note to the need for gentleness of contact during the Graduated Guidance. If the agitation still persisted, the client was seated in a chair and the practice continued. In the event the agitation still persisted, the client was given the Required Relaxation procedure in his bed for a few minutes, until he was calm, at which time he completed the remainder of the 20-minute practice period. The general rule was that the client should learn that the full 20 minutes of practice would be required whenever he injured himself.

Hand-Awareness Training

The Hand-Awareness Training procedure of Azrin and Nunn (1973) was modified for use with the present type of clients. At the start of treatment the instructor continually made comments to the client regarding the need to position his hands away from his head. The instructor used gestures, pointing, and touching as well as verbal statements. When the hands were away from the client's head, the instructor praised him for keeping them there. Conversely, when his hands moved upward for any reason, the instructor directed him to lower them. To maintain awareness of their hands, the clients were instructed to walk with their hands clasped behind their back and to clasp the armrests of their chairs while seated. As in the other procedures, the reinforcers were snack treats, praise, and stroking. As the client learned to maintain his hands away from his head, the instructor commented on the client's hand position progressively less often, but after having commented almost continuously for the first 2 days. This awareness was also being taught indirectly as an integral part of the Hand Control procedure when the client changed his hand position every 10 seconds in response to the direct instruction regarding his hands. Similarly, in the Positive Reinforcement procedure, the client was being reinforced for using his hands in a functional manner.

Sequence

At the start of treatment, the protective helmet or mittens were removed and the client was given the Hand-Awareness training, and the Positive Reinforcement for outward-directed activities. When the client injured himself, the instructor immediately reprimanded him in a stern tone of voice that conveyed his displeasure and gave the Hand Control Procedure for 20 minutes or the Required Relaxation procedure for 2 hours. (See Results section as to which clients received which procedure.) The Positive Reinforcement for outgoing behaviors and the hand-awareness training were then reinstated after indicating to the client that he should not injure himself and that the Hand Control or Required Relaxation would be needed if he did injure himself. Initially, all instruction was conducted in special locations on the ward to obtain a more distraction-free atmosphere. After a few trials the locations were varied so that the client would learn that the procedure would eventually be applied in any locations in which he might self-injure.

Fading Out of Treatment

In both the Required Relaxation and Hand Control procedures, the instructor "faded out" the need for his guidance or even his presence. In the Required Relaxation procedure, once the client attained the fixed-posture, and his behavior was agitation-free while in bed, the instructor moved himself gradually to the rear of the client, and eventually completely out of the client's view. In the Hand Control procedure, once the client was responding to the postural instructions and maintaining the positions unassisted, the instructor reduced his guidance of the client's arms to merely a touch and then to just "shadowing" the client's movements.

When the client had spent one day without self-injury, the duration of the scheduled Required Relaxation or Hand Control was reduced to about 5 minutes on the next day, then to 2 minutes, and then to a simple warning on successive days, providing no self-injurious responses had occurred on the preceding day. Even in the final stage, a warning or reminder was given to the client for any attempt at self-injury.

Figure 1 shows the change in self-injurious conduct averaged for the 11 clients. Each data point is expressed as a percentage of the baseline level. On the first day of training the self-injurious responses decreased by 90 percent from the pre-treatment level and decreased further by about 96 percent by the end of the first week. By the fourth week of training, the self-injurious responses had decreased by 98 percent and by 99 percent by the third month. A t-test of differences showed that all of the data points were significantly less than the baseline level ($p < 0.001$). (Four clients received no treatment by the ward staff after the special instructors were absent. The data for these 4 clients are therefore included only up to the date that treatment was terminated.)

The Relaxation Procedure was used as the treatment for the first 6 clients. For 3 of these clients, the Relaxation Procedure was very effective, but none of the other 3 clients was benefited substantially and 2 of them began injuring themselves in a seemingly deliberate fashion in order to obtain the bed-rest indicating that the bed-rest involved in the procedure was serving as a reinforcer for self-injury. In addition, these 3 clients continued to attempt to injure themselves while in bed unless very closely supervised. Consequently, the Relaxation Procedure was discontinued for these 3 clients and the Hand Control procedure substituted for it. The last 5 clients were given only the Hand Control procedure and no Relaxation Training. The data treatment points in Figure 1 are for the Hand Control procedure for all but the first three clients whose data points are for the Relaxation Procedure.

Analysis of the individual benefits showed that 4 of the 11 clients were almost totally free of the self-injurious responses, either having no further self-injurious responses or less than one per week. One of these was discharged to a shelter-care facility where the operators reported he has not exhibited any self-injury. Each of the other 7 clients averaged less than 4 self-injurious responses per day by the second week of treatment. The client who had exhibited self-injurious behavior for the longest period, 31 years, had the highest level of self-injury after 2 weeks, an average of four self-injurious responses per day. The client who had exhibited self-injurious responses shortly after birth, and a high pre-treatment rate of 3500 responses per day, exhibited an average of only one self-injurious response per week after 2 months of treatment.

Three of the clients often physically aggressed against other residents or staff members at the same time that they exhibited self-injury. The

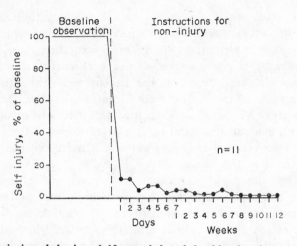

FIG. 1. Self-injurious behavior of 10 retarded and 1 schizophrenic persons. The frequency of self-injury is expressed as a percentage of the frequency recorded prior to treatment. The self-injury prior to treatment (Baseline Observation) was recorded for varying durations dictated by the safety of the client and the frequency of the behavior. The data points are for the average number per day for the first 7 days and weekly thereafter. Each data point is for 11 clients for the first 2 weeks, 9 clients for the 3rd week, 8 for the 4th to 7th weeks and 7 clients thereafter. During the "Baseline Observation," the self-injury was simply recorded; during the "Interruptions for Non-Injury," the instructors used positive reinforcement for non-injurious behavior, a Required Relaxation procedure for agitated states, a Hand Control procedure for self-injury and a Hand-Awareness procedure. The vertical dashed line designates the time that the treatment procedure started.

physical aggression by all 3 clients decreased substantially once treatment was initiated for the self-injury.

General improvements in the clients' overall manner were evident when the self-injurious behavior was decreased. Ten of the 11 clients seemed to greatly increase their social interactions and social responsiveness. The notable exception was one client located on a ward with virtually no programmed activities and whose pre-treatment routine was to sit limply in a chair or to lie in a corner asleep wearing his protective helmet. He exhibited little muscle tone when the instructor manually guided him during attempts at reinforcement during the treatment phase.

DISCUSSION

The new procedure was effective in eliminating, or greatly reducing, the self-injurious behavior of the mentally ill and retarded clients. The treatment was fairly rapid as seen by the average reduction of about 90 percent on the first day and about 96 percent by the seventh day. The treatment appears applicable to the general population of self-injurious clients as seen by its effectiveness with all 11 clients in the present unselected sample. The extent of the benefit was substantial in that after three months of treatment, the self-injurious behavior was reduced by an average of 99 percent. Self-injury was virtually eliminated for 4 clients. The general acceptability of the treatment was evidenced by the positive reaction of the clinical personnel in all five institutions in which the clients were treated.

Speculatively, the degree of benefit for a given client seemed to be greater if he had a pre-existing high level of outward-directed behavior, or if the ward environment strongly encouraged outward-directed activity. All 4 of the clients who were virtually "cured" had considerable social and attention-getting behavior, including aggression toward others by three of them, whereas the clients who benefited less were seemingly oblivious to the presence or actions of others. The "custodial" type of wards in which little attention was paid to residents often abandoned the treatment effort, whereas the clients in the treatment-oriented ward situations continued to receive the instruction and continued to benefit. The Required Relaxation procedure seemed most appropriate for the outward-directed client whereas the Hand Control procedure seemed more appropriate with the inward-directed client. The 3 clients with whom the Required Relaxation was successful were all of the outward-directed type, whereas the 3 clients with whom it was unsuccessful were inward-directed.

Comparison of the present procedure with alternative procedures must be somewhat tentative since the clients treated in the previous reports are of unknown comparability. Nevertheless, the present method appears to be more acceptable as a treatment than either shock or timeout seclusion, in that no physical punishment is used and the emphasis is on instruction and adding reinforcers. In all of the institutions included in this study, shock was viewed as a last resort and the staff were apprehensive about its abuse. They were eager to use this procedure before considering shock punishment. With respect to the speed of treatment, the present method appears at least as rapid as has been reported for the alternative methods but far less rapid than the almost instantaneous benefit obtained in most reports of shock (Bucher & Lovaas, 1968; Corte et al., 1971; Tate & Baroff, 1966; Risley, 1968). With respect to general applicability to a variety of clients, the present method would be considered superior at this time if only because the previous reports have been case studies that have not as yet reported results for a large number of unselected clients. In general, the present method seems to provide many advantages over the alternative methods.

REFERENCES

AZRIN, N. H., KAPLAN, S. J., & FOXX, R. M. Autism reversal: Eliminating stereotyped self-stimulation of retarded individuals. *Amer. J. Ment. Defic.*, 1973, 78, 241-248.

AZRIN, N. H. & NUNN, R. G. Habit-reversal: A method of eliminating nervous habits and tics. *Behav. Res. & Ther.*, 1973, 11, 619-628.

BUCHER, B. & LOVAAS, O. I. Use of aversive stimulation in behavior modification. In M. R. Jones (Ed.), *Miami Symposium on the Prediction of Behavior, 1967: Aversive Stimulation.* Florida: University of Miami Press, 1968, pp. 77-145.

CORTE, H. E., WOLF, M. M., & LOCKE, B. J. A comparison of procedures for eliminating self-injurious behavior of retarded adolescents. *J. Appl. Behav. Anal.*, 1971, 4, 201-213.

FOXX, R. M. & AZRIN, N. H. Restitution: A method of eliminating aggressive-disruptive behavior of retarded and brain damaged patients. *Behav. Res. & Ther.*, 1972, 10, 15-27.

FOXX, R. M. & AZRIN, N. H. The elimination of autistic self-stimulatory behavior by overcorrection. *J. Appl. Behav. Anal.*, 1973, 6, 1-14.

HAMILTON, J., STEPHENS, L., & ALLEN, P. Controlling aggressive and destructive behavior in severely retarded institutionalized residents. *Amer. J. Ment. Defic.*, 1967, 71, 852-856.

LANE, R. G. & DOMRATH, R. P. Behavior Therapy: A case history. *Hosp. Comm. Psychiat.*, 1970, 21, 150-153.

LOVAAS, O. I., FREITAG, G., GOLD, V. J., & KASSORLA, I. C. Experimental studies in childhood schizophrenia: Analysis of self-destructive behavior. *Behav. Res. & Ther.*, 1965, 2, 67-84.

MYERS, J. J. & DEIBERT, A. N. Reduction of self-abusive behavior in a blind child by using a feeding response. *J. Behav. Ther. & Exp. Psychiat.*, 1971, 2, 141-144.

PETERSON, R. F. & PETERSON, L. R. The use of positive reinforcement in the control of self-destructive behavior in a retarded boy. *J. Exp. Child Psychol.*, 1968, 6, 351-360.

RISLEY, T. The effects of punishing the autistic behaviors of a deviant child. *J. Appl. Behav. Anal.*, 1968, 1, 21-34.

TATE, B. G. & BAROFF, G. S. Aversive control of self-injurious behavior in a psychotic boy. *Behav. Res. & Ther.*, 1966, 4, 281-287.

WEBSTER, D. R. & AZRIN, N. H. Required relaxation: A method of inhibiting agitative-disruptive behavior of retardates. *Behav. Res. & Ther.*, 1973, 11, 67-78.

WOLF, M., RISLEY, T., JOHNSON, M., HARRIS, F., & ALLEN, E. Application of operant conditioning procedures to the behavior problems of an autistic child: A follow-up and extension. *Behav. Res. & Ther.*, 1967, 5, 103-111.

WOLF, M., RISLEY, T., & MEES, H. Application of operant conditioning procedures to the behavior problems of an autistic child. *Behav. Res. & Ther.*, 1964, 1, 305-312.

YEAKEL, M. H., SALISBURY, L. L., GREER, S. L., & MARCUS, L. F. An appliance for auto-induced adverse control of self-injurious behavior. *J. Exp. Child. Psychol.*, 1970, 10, 159-169.

27

APPLIED BEHAVIOR ANALYSIS IN A PENAL SETTING: TARGETING "FREE WORLD" BEHAVIORS

John E. Bassett, Edward B. Blanchard

and Edwin Koshland

Shelby County Penal Farm,
Memphis, Tennessee

Two studies are presented in which potentially adaptive "free world" behaviors were increased among a group of male prisoners participating in a token economy on a county penal farm. In the first, percentage of time watching television news and comprehension of the content of the news were targeted behaviors which were experimentally analyzed using instructions, noncontingent quizzes, and quizzes on which correct answers earned points in the token economy. The last condition proved to be the most effective over a prolonged period. In the second, attending a remedial education center during evening free time was the targeted response. Manipulation of the token economy, primarily through awarding additional points for attendance, was ex-

Reprinted with permission from *Behavior Therapy*, 6, 639-648, 1975.

This research was sponsored in part by a grant from the Department of Justice, Law Enforcement Assistance Administration, 209A 74-1.11-H-2. However, the views expressed in this paper are those of the authors and in no way reflect the official position of the Department of Justice. Thanks are expressed to Commissioner Lee Hyden, Superintendent James G. Harbour, and Robert W. Wood for their administrative assistance with this project.

perimentally analyzed and shown to be effective in increasing this target behavior.

Behavior modification programs have been used on a round-the-clock basis in settings housing adult psychiatric patients (Ayllon & Azrin, 1968), mental retardates (Fielding, 1972), and adolescent offenders (Cohen & Filipczak, 1971). One of the last bastions of resistance to the widespread application of learning principles in rehabilitation is the adult penal institution, as evidenced by the relative lack of reports in the professional literature. Bishop and Blanchard's review (1971) yielded only three pertinent publications (Boren & Coleman, 1970; Clements & McKee, 1968; Lawson, Greene, Richardson, McClure & Padina, 1971). Since then only a few more have appeared (e.g., Bassett, Blanchard, Harrison & Wood, 1973; Schnelle & Lee, 1974; Milan & McKee, 1974). Moreover, two of the above mentioned reports took place in a psychiatric facility for prisoners (Boren & Coleman, 1970; Lawson et al., 1971).

Furthermore, these projects have typically involved small scale programs directed toward circumscribed behavioral domains (e.g., academic performances (Clements & McKee, 1968), or attendance at a remedial education center (Bassett et al., 1973)). While it is difficult to estimate accurately the number of behavioral programs in existence in adult penal settings, personal communications indicate similar nonpublished efforts are being conducted (Geller, Note 1). Certainly some programs have received widespread publicity as they come under legal attack (Trotter & Warren, 1974a; Trotter, 1974).

Applied behavioral programs dealing with nonprison populations have occasionally been criticized on the grounds that they often target behaviors for change which serve the purpose of maintaining institutional tranquility, but bear little, if any, relationship to the subject's daily behavioral repertoire once he is discharged (Winett & Winkler, 1972). More recently this same criticism has been leveled at behavior modification programs in penal settings (Bandura, in Trotter & Warren, 1974b).

The purpose of the present study was to examine the effectiveness of targeting behaviors not subservient to the maintenance of institutional harmony, but which, instead, had potentially adaptive value for the inmates once they returned to the free world. Two studies are reported: In the first we sought to increase television news watching and also to increase attending to and understanding of the content of the news. In the second, we sought to increase voluntary attendance at a remedial education center during free time.

Both of these target behaviors should be available to the inmates in the free world and should have some adaptive value if carried over in the free world. Thus, being informed of current events from having watched the news would seem to lead to being a better citizen, more in tune with society's values. Furthermore, spending free time in educational or other self improvement pursuits would also seem to lead to being a better and potentially more productive citizen.

EXPERIMENT 1—TELEVISION NEWS WATCHING

Method

Both this experiment and the one to be described later were conducted in the same setting and over approximately the same time interval with the same subject population.

Setting

Shelby County Penal Farm. The Shelby County Penal Farm, a minimum security correctional institution located near the city limits of Memphis, Tennessee, houses approximately 600 men serving sentences for a variety of misdemeanors and felonies. The inmates are regularly scheduled to work 8 hour/day on either farm-related tasks, highway maintenance, or prison operations (such as serving as kitchen cooks). Several rehabilitative programs are operated within the prison which altogether engage approximately 58 percent of the inmates.

Behavioral Management Program. The two experiments were conducted with the inmates enrolled in the rehabilitative Behavior Management Program. It consists of a contingent point economy (see Bassett, Note 2) for the men housed in one dormitory. The system provides a supervised contingency environment in which activities are scheduled for approximately 16 hours/day, 6:00 A.M. to 10:00 P.M., 7 days a week. Points could be earned for such categories of behavior as personal hygiene and grooming, participation in Penal Farm work assignments, and Behavior Management Program rehabilitative activities. Points could be spent on such things as extra telephone calls; special food treats such as cokes, coffee, and popcorn; additional visiting hours over the minimum granted all men; participation in special outings, such as basketball games; and access to a Reinforcement Center containing a television set, magazines, games, and a stereo.

All behaviors, both earning opportunities and reinforcers, were behaviorally defined; the contingent point economy was mediated by staff and inmate coordinators.

Subjects

The subjects were the inmates enrolled in the Program from November 1, 1973 through August 30, 1974. The number of subjects enrolled in the program varied from day to day, as men were admitted to the program or released, either because of completing their sentence or failing to adhere to the program. Because of the variable enrollment, the composition of the group by age, race, and length of sentence also varied.

The number of participants varied from 7 to 19 with a mean of 13; 39 men took part in the study. The age range was 18 to 34 years with a mean of 22.5. The racial composition varied from 23 to 50 percent white with a mean of 33 percent. Length of sentences ranged from 9 to 60 months with a mean of 14.2 and represented a fairly typical cross section of the offenses for which men were incarcerated at the Shelby County Penal Farm.

Procedure for Experiment 1

This experiment sought to increase initially the watching of televised news and later the comprehension and attending to the content of the news. All men in the program were taken to the Reinforcement Center shortly before the evening news began. At the conclusion of the news the men were escorted to the next activity. Ordinarily points were charged for admission to the Reinforcement Center, but during news time no admission was charged.

Observation procedures. Three times during the half hour news program, at approximately equal time intervals, a counselor observed whether each man was apparently watching the news or not. A man was scored as watching the news if his eyes were oriented toward the television set and were open.

Reliability checks. A second counselor also observed, at the same time, whether the men were watching the news or not. In all, 15 reliability checks were obtained, with at least one being conducted during each condition of the experiment.

Reliability was determined by counting the number of agreements between the two observers as to whether a man was watching or was not watching, and dividing that number by the total number of observations.

Percentage of agreement ranged from 73 to 98 percent, and averaged 89 percent over the 15 checks.

Experimental Conditions

Baseline. During this condition, no instruction was given regarding watching the news. However, in this condition, as in all others, the TV set was on and tuned to the news. This continued for 6 weeks until the data seemed (by visual inspection) relatively stable.

Instructions. During the next condition, the men were told that they should watch and attend to the news, that it was good to be informed of current events in the outside world, and that being informed would help them. These instructions were repeated every other day during the 6 weeks of this condition.

Instructions and noncontingent quiz. In this condition, men were given a brief five question quiz related to items on that night's news at the conclusion of the broadcast. The counselor present was responsible for making up the questions for that session.

Prior to the beginning of this condition, the counselors were given practice in making up questions which related to major news stories and which could be answered by true-false responses or a few words. When all of the counselors were able to make up quizzes of this nature to the satisfaction of the experimenters, the condition was initiated.

This condition was introduced with the announcement that it was important not only to watch the news, but to learn and retain some facts from it. The men were then told there would be a short quiz at the end of each news broadcast and were urged to do well on it.

The men were given paper and pencils at the end of the news, and the counselor read the questions while the men recorded their answers. For six of the sessions, a second person, one of the experimenters, also answered the questions and checked the men's answers to the quizzes for that session. This yielded 100 percent agreement on scoring of the quizzes.

During this condition the instructions about the importance of watching the news were repeated once/week. This condition also was continued for 6 weeks.

Instructions and contingent quiz. In this condition, it was announced that the men could start earning points by correctly answering the quiz questions. Points were awarded at the rate of 20 percent response for a maximum total of 100. The 100 points represented about 5 to 10 percent of the average inmate's daily earnings on the token economy.

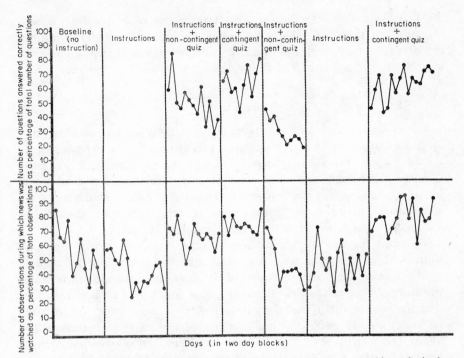

FIG. 1. Percentage of total observations during which men were watching televised news, and percentage of correct responses to news quiz as a function of experimental condition.

Other than the awarding of contingent points at the end of each session, this condition was the same as the preceding one. This condition continued for 4 weeks.

Instructions and noncontingent quiz. For the next 4 weeks we returned to the conditions previously described for this phase. This change was initiated by announcing that points would no longer be given for quiz scores, but that the men should continue to try to answer the questions correctly.

Instructions. Next, the quizzes were discontinued altogether. During this phase, the men were again reminded to watch the news and that paying attention to current events was good for them. These instructions were repeated at least two times/week for the 8 weeks of this phase.

Instructions and contingent quiz. The final phase of this experiment was return to the administration of the five-question quiz at the end of the news each day and the contingent awarding of points for correct responses on the quiz. This condition was continued for the duration of the experiment, and continues in effect as it was shown to be the most effective means of obtaining the desired "free world" behavior.

RESULTS

The desired "free world" behavior targeted by this study was keeping up with current events. A necessary precursor of this behavior was watching the televised news. In all phases of the experiment, it was possible to determine whether men were watching the news or not. In some phases, those in which quizzes were given on the content of the news, it was possible to determine if the ultimate target response, showing a knowledge of current events, was being emitted (Figure 1).

To allow for the varying number of men enrolled in the program from week to week, the data were converted to percentages: for actual news watching, the total number of observations on which men were watching television was divided by the total number of observations for that day (three/man) and then converted to a percentage; for correct responses on the quiz, the total number of correct responses made by all of the men was divided by the total number of possible correct answers for that day (five/man) and then converted into a percentage.

Initial high watching of television news during baseline gradually declined (Figure 1). Instructions alone caused a slight initial increase, but watching again decreased. (This Instruction condition was introduced, and probably serves, as the true baseline against which other effects should be compared. There were implicit instructions in all of the other phases of the experiment that the Experimenters wanted the men to watch the news.) Introduction of the noncontingent quiz led to an increase in watching. The scores on the quizzes averaged about 60 percent correct responses initially, but dropped off to about 40 percent.

The addition of points, exchangeable for other reinforcers and contingent on correct responses led to a slight increase in the news watching behavior. The average value for this condition was 70 percent. Moreover the percentage of correct responses on the quizzes increased to about 70 percent.

Removal of the contingent points has dramatic effects: News watching dropped to about 40 percent, and correct responding on the quiz dropped to about 25 percent. It appeared that the contingent points were maintaining news watching behavior which otherwise would have dropped out. Discontinuance of the quizzes altogether led to no further decrease in news watching; however, the response became more variable.

Reinstatement of the Contingent Quiz to complete the experimental analysis led to dramatic increases in both news watching and correct responding. The news watching stabilized at about 80 percent, and correct responding, with rare exception, stabilized at about 70 percent.

EXPERIMENT 2—VOLUNTARY ATTENDANCE AT A REMEDIAL EDUCATION CENTER

Method

The same subjects were used in both experiments; hence the overall setting and program are the same as described above.

Learning Center

The Learning Center was a facility devoted to remedial adult education housed within the prison itself. Instruction was through programmed material and was completely individualized. The facility consisted of 35 individual carrels equipped with a variety of audiovisual gear and was housed in a large, cheery, well-lighted room.

The Learning Center was open in the evening for 3 hours/night, 6-9 P.M., for four nights a week. Inmates attending the Learning Center were assessed initially as to grade level in various areas and then reassessed every 4 to 5 weeks. Detailed attendance and performance records were kept on each man on a routine basis and consisted of the number of hours each man spent at the facility each night as well as his monthly achievement test scores.

Men enrolled in the Behavior Management Program were routinely scheduled to attend the Learning Center for 2 hours/day, 5 days/week, during the regular work day. They earned 50 points/hour for this attendance. In addition, during the evening free time, they could earn additional points, at the rate of 50/hour, for additional attendance at the Learning Center.

Procedure

The desired target behavior was increased extra attendance at the Learning Center. Such behavior would represent efforts at self-improvement during leisure time, a "free-world" behavior which seemed highly adaptive.

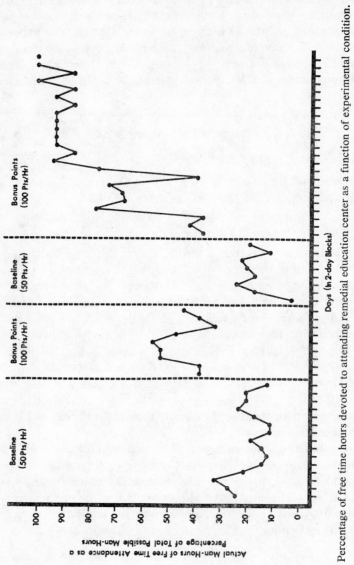

FIG. 2.   Percentage of free time hours devoted to attending remedial education center as a function of experimental condition.

During their unscheduled time, from approximately 6-9 P.M. each evening, the men of the Behavior Management Program had several options as to activities. They could attend the Reinforcement Center (described in Experiment 1), attend other activities, loaf and hold "bull sessions," or earn additional points. One of the ways of earning additional points, as mentioned above, was through additional attendance at the Learning Center.

This experiment was conducted without the use of explicit instructions regarding the desired target behavior as was used in Experiment 1. Instead, changes in conditions were made known to the men in the form of announcement of changes in the point system.

Data Sources and Reliability

Since the subjects were living under a 24-hour point system and were regularly rewarded for attendance at the Learning Center during free time, attendance data were regularly recorded on the men's points cards and in the records kept on the Behavior Management Program. Furthermore, the teachers at the Learning Center routinely recorded a man's attendance and progress on a day to day basis. Thus, it was possible to cross validate the attendance data from an independent source.

A comparison of daily data from the two sets of records (one man for 1 day) during the study revealed 96 percent agreement on attendance and nonattendance.

Conditions

Baseline attendance data, during which men earned 50 points/hour for attendance during free time, were recorded for 2 months. Next, the announcement was made that *bonus points* would be paid for attendance and an additional 50 points/hour was instituted for 1 month. Then it was announced that the bonus points would be discontinued, returning to baseline conditions for about 1 month. Finally, to complete the ABAB design, the bonus points were reinstated and left in effect in line with the goal of continuing to strengthen "free world" behavior. Data were collected for 3.5 more months.

RESULTS

To correct for variation in enrollment in the Behavior Management Program on a week to week basis, and to correct for variations in the day to day schedule with regards to free time available, the total number of man-hours of attendance at the Learning Center during free time for each day was divided by the total possible number of man-hours of attendance permitted by the day to day schedule (Figure 2).

During Baseline, attendance varied from 10 to 35 percent and averaged about 20 percent. The addition of Bonus Points increased attendance during free time to an average level of 45 percent. The return to Baseline for 4 weeks led to a decrease in attendance to 20 percent. Reinstatement of the Bonus Points led eventually to an increase in attendance to about 90 percent of that theoretically possible. This high level held up over the 3.5 months in which this condition was maintained.

DISCUSSION

In the television news watching study, there was initially a very high level of watching, probably due to the novelty of the situation. This high level of attention gradually decreased, probably as a function of adaptation. Instructions alone about the value and importance of watching the news led to some increase in watching, which also dropped off to some degree after the initial surge. Introduction of the quizzes led to a sizeable increase in watching. The latter may well be due to the men's knowing they were being evaluated and seeking to do well, either to win approval or because they expected to be rewarded for the task.

The addition of contingent reinforcement for correct answers on the quizzes led to improved scores on these quizzes, but only slight overall increase in news watching behavior. The latter is not too surprising: the behavior targeted, knowledge of events, increased while a possible precursor to that targeted behavior, watching television, did not. However, one must remember that one can gain information from listening as well as by observing.

Removal of the contingent reinforcement led to a large decrease in both quiz scores and news watching. It may have been that the contingent reinforcement was maintaining these two behaviors at their relatively high levels and that without it, they both would have gradually decreased. Removal of the noncontingent quizzes led to no further decrease in watching, but to increased variability.

Reinstatement of the quizzes and points contingent on correct answers led to a marked increase in television watching and to a fairly high level of learning as shown by the quiz scores. The latter effects held up well throughout the 2.5 months of this condition.

For the second experiment, voluntary attendance at the Learning Center, the results speak for themselves. There was a marked increase in attendance with the addition of Bonus Points, and a subsequent sharp decrease with their removal. Reintroduction of the Bonus Points led to a very high level of attendance, about 90 percent, with some days seeing the men using 100 percent of the available free time to attend the Center. This effect held up well over the 3.5 months of the final condition.

Considering the two studies together, there are several points which might be made. First both studies are demonstrations that reinforcement works. This is hardly novel or surprising. Second, the studies demonstrate that reinforcement works in penal settings. Again, this is not surprising, but reports of demonstrations of it have been relatively rare so it is somewhat novel.

Finally, what these two studies show, and the relatively novel contribution they make, is that it is possible to target and to increase the rates of behavior which have potential benefits to prisoners once they return to the "free world" *while they are still incarcerated.* This last point is a large part of what rehabilitation should be about, in our opinion. This study has shown that it is possible, and we believe it is highly desirable, to maintain adaptive "free world" behaviors at high rates while a man is in prison through the use of contingent reinforcement.

The ultimate goal of such a program would be for the subjects to continue to emit these behaviors at high rates without explicit external reinforcement. For such a goal to be obtained, the reinforcing properties of the behavior, or the naturally occurring consequences of the behavior, would have to take over in a manner analogous to what occurs in the process of natural socialization.

Although this last point was not tested, or demonstrated, in this study, we believe a first step must be emitting the behavior at high rates which was demonstrated. This was important because many of the men emitted little or none of these behaviors at the beginning of the study.

Ideally one would want to follow the men back to the free world after discharge to see what carry-over there was. This was not done in this study, and thus makes this work an analogous study. However, this experimental socialization experience of engaging in "adaptive free world" behavior may have long range benefits, if continued for a long enough interval or if programmed through the use of fading or attenuating the extrinsic reinforcement schedule, because of the eventual resocialization of the inmate, the ultimate goal of correctional institutions.

REFERENCE NOTES

1. GELLER, E. S. Personal communication, September, 1974.
2. BASSETT, J. E. *Behavior Management Program: Applied Behavior Analysis in an Adult Male Correctional Facility.* Unpublished LEAA Grant Report, Shelby County Penal Farm, Memphis, Tennessee, 1974.

REFERENCES

BASSETT, J. E., BLANCHARD, E. B., HARRISON, H., & WOOD, R. Applied behavior analysis on a county penal farm: A method of increasing attendance at a remedial education center. *Proceedings, 81st Annual Convention, APA,* 1973, pp. 907-908.
BISHOP, C. H. & BLANCHARD, E. B. *Behavior Modification and Corrections.* Athens, Ga.: Institute of Government, University of Georgia, 1971.
BOREN, J. J. & COLEMAN, A. D. Some experiments on reinforcement principles within a psychiatric ward for delinquent soldiers. *J. Appl. Behav. Anal.,* 1970, 3, 29-37.
COHEN, H. L. & FILIPCZAK, J. *A New Learning Environment.* San Francisco: Jossey Bass, 1971.
CLEMENTS, C. B. & McKEE, J. M. Programmed instruction for institutionalized offenders: Contingency management and performance contracts. *Psychol. Reports,* 1968, 22, 957-964.
FIELDING, L. Initial ward-wide behavior modification programs for retarded children. In T. Thompson & J. Grabrowski (Eds.), *Behavior Modification of the Mentally Retarded.* New York: Oxford University Press, 1972.
LAWSON, R. B., GREENE, R. T., RICHARDSON, J. S., McCLURE, G., & PADINA, R. J. Token economy program in a maximum security correctional hospital. *J. Nerv. Ment. Dis.,* 1971, 152, 199-205.
MILAN, M. A. & McKEE, J. M. Behavior Modification: Principles and applications in corrections. In D. Glaser (Ed.), *Handbook of Criminology.* Chicago: Rand McNally, 1974.
SCHNELLE, J. F. & LEE, J. Frank A quasi-experimental retrospective evaluation of a prison policy change. *J. Appl. Behav. Anal.,* 1974, 7, 483-496.
TROTTER, S. ACLU scores token economy. *APA Monitor,* 1974, 5, 7.
TROTTER, S. & WARREN, J. Behavior modification under fire. *APA Monitor,* 1974, 5, 1, 4, (a)
TROTTER, S. & WARREN, J. The carrot, the stick and the prisoner. *Science News,* 1974, 105, 180-181. (b)
WINETT, R. A. & WINKLER, R. C. Current behavior modification in the classroom: Be still, be quiet, be docile. *J. Appl. Behav. Anal.,* 1972, 5, 449-504.

Section VIII

BEHAVIOR MODIFICATION AND THE EXTENDED SOCIETY: INDUSTRY AND COMMUNITY

Commentary

It is no accident that industry has not featured prominently in past Annual Reviews. With a few notable exceptions, scholarly publications in this sector have been limited in quantity and, more importantly, quality and it is only very recently that this has begun to change. Both productivity and work satisfaction are still low in many highly developed organizational facilities throughout much of the world and management-labor relations are often strained. There is thus considerable scope for sophisticated analysis and intervention—not necessarily exclusively behavioral—across all strata of the industrial scene.

The applicability of a behavioral approach to the contemporary industrial complex is but one issue in the seemingly endless debate about the nature of the organizational process. In perhaps what will turn out to be one of the most important books of the year, Moos (1976) has neatly and critically outlined the evolution of some of the major perspectives in organizational theory. First came scientific management, a thoroughly economic stand focused on a vertical chain of command, a sharp division of labor and the assumption that motivation is accomplished primarily by material rewards. Gradually, as informal social networks were found to be operative in industry, a new approach designated as human relations developed. Here social norms sanctions and group values became paramount. But it is as limited to focus primarily on social concerns to the exclusion of all others factors as it is to empha-

615

size only the economic stance of scientific management. Structuralism, the new perspective that emerged in reaction to the one-sidedness of the human relations model, is a synthesis of classical organization theory, human relations and the concepts of Max Weber and Karl Marx. Finally, there is what Moos refers to as the open systems approach which sees an organization as a dynamic interrelation of many subsystems, each interacting with the external environment and with each other and constantly in a state of adaptation and change. It is within this setting that attempts to apply behavior modification principles to industry must be evaluated. Clearly, then, there will be a place, but only a limited place, for the concepts of conventional behavior therapy.

Management researchers and practitioners have depended primarily upon theories of motivation in their attempts to unravel the determinants of organizational behavior in industry, focusing upon mysterious internal entities such as attitudes, desires, drives and so forth. Luthans and Kreitner (1975), two of the notable exceptions to this tradition, hopefully herald the surfacing of a new trend in industrial psychology. Organizational Behavior Modification (OBM) pertains to the integration of operant learning theory and the principles of behavior modification with the management field of organizational behavior. As yet, the emphasis is on external determinants of behavior, and recent developments in cognitive behavior modification, self-control and covert internal processes do not seem to have percolated through. In rightly rejecting the vague and unanchored internal data of the traditional industrial psychologist, it is not necessary to disregard the probability that covert events can be manipulated in terms of a behavioral framework if appropriately defined and conceptualized. This applies both to OBM and related strategies such as Management by Objectives and Job Enrichment. Doubtless, future editions of Luthans and Kreitner's book will consider these developments. Meanwhile, their commendable emphasis upon the transition to positive control and their attention to ethical issues within an industrial setting are very much in tune with the spirit of both the times and modern behavior therapy. The next step could be the integration of these developments within the open system of Moos.

Jablonsky and DeVries' (1972) model of organizational behavior, based upon a combination of instrumentality theory and the principles of operant conditioning, represents the beginnings of an attempt to apply an integration of operant and cognitive principles to work motivation. However, the cognitive frameworks that are utilized are not those of contemporary behavior therapy so much as the more motivation oriented systems of an earlier era (e.g., Vroom, 1964; Porter & Lawler, 1968; Green, 1969). Heiman (1975) has pointed correctly to a number of conceptual errors in their application of reinforcement principles, but still does not come to grips with what modern behavior therapists mean by cognitive processes.

Clinical behavior therapy is moving with dramatic speed into the area of cognition and the behavioral "inner man" (see Commentary, Section I). In industrial psychology, an equivalent advance, albeit at a more limited and perhaps more cautious pace, may be evidenced in the current intrinsic-extrinsic controversy about the parameters of motivation, reinforcers and feedback. Rewards such as pay, fringe benefits and promotion are extrinsic to the extent that they provide reinforcements that are not directly dependent upon the activity itself and that they are direcly controlled by someone other than the employee. By contrast, intrinsic rewards stem from within the individual, are an integral part of the work activity itself and the employee perceives himself as exerting a high degree of self-control. According to deCharms (1968), if an individual sees his own behavior as stemming from his own choice, he is more likely to cherish that behavior and its consequences than when he sees his behavior as stemming from external sources not of his choosing, even though the end results are identical.

Most theorists, e.g., Porter and Lawler (1968), assume that the effects of intrinsic and extrinsic rewards are independent and additive. This would seem to be a not unreasonable assumption and it was therefore somewhat surprising when a series of well-designed studies by Deci (1971, 1972a, 1972b) reported that a person's intrinsic motivation to perform an activity actually decreases when he receives contingent monetary payment for performing a task which is of interest to him. He attempted to account for this seemingly anomalous finding in terms of what he calls a *cognitive evaluation theory* which states that a person's perception of why he is doing the task determines his level of intrinsic motivation. Deci's recommendation that workers be paid on a noncontingent basis would seem difficult to implement within our present societal structure system.

Hamner and Foster (1975) have now re-examined Deci's findings and tested his prediction experimentally. Apart from highlighting certain inconsistencies within his logical system, Hamner and Foster conclude from their equally well-designed study that intrinsic and extrinsic rewards do indeed have an additive effective on task motivation. They also conclude from their data that, although quantity of performance initially decreases as individuals are required to attend to stimulation of greater variety and complexity, quality of performance is enhanced. In this somewhat artificial laboratory study conducted with students—a limitation acknowledged by the authors concerned—Hamner and Foster found that the best performers in the contingent-pay conditions were more satisfied than the poorer performers, but that there was no relationship between performance and satisfaction in the noncontingent-pay conditions. If the recommendation by Deci that workers be paid on a noncontingent basis had been followed, then—at least relatively—the poor performers would actually be rewarded and the good performers punished.

There is a need to extend this laboratory study to the more natural environment. If confirmed, it could mean that work settings should emphasize both intrinsically interesting and extrinsically rewarding situations. Notz (1975) concludes his scholarly review and analysis of the available data that intrinsic and external motivations can well be non-additive and that the arousal of extrinsic motivation may occur at the expense of intrinsic motivation. Similarly, under certain conditions, the withdrawal of an extrinsic reward can actually enhance intrinsic motivation. What is far less certain seems to be the circumstances under which these seemingly paradoxical effects emerge. As Notz points out, theoretical formulations of work motivation cannot account for the complexities of human behavior even in the laboratory setting. To manipulate simultaneously intrinsic and extrinsic motivational variables coupled with innovations such as job enrichment, participative management and sociotechnical systems seems, at the very least, to be premature.

Greller (1975a) is interested in the concept of performance feedback as it relates to internal and external sources of reinforcement. Behavior modification in the classroom, correctional facility or mental hospital occurs within a relatively total institution and can tolerate a certain amount of exploration to find the ideal reinforcers. Opportunity for disturbances of the subject's environment (potential unauthorized feedback) can be minimized. In most industrial organizations, the situation is quite different. Most of the individual's day, including his time at work, is not highly controlled by the organization. Even routine factory work offers considerable opportunity for peer conversation and feedback about performance, pertinent employee issues and expectations, often at variance with the more formal information and feedback provided by the organization.

The parameters of feedback are thus complex and unresolved. Different circumstances can heighten or reduce the importance of different potential sources of feedback. Feedback can come from others or from the task itself (Hackman & Oldham, 1975). Extrinsic feedback can occur either through comments from others or by others providing such consequences to the individual as salary increments or task assignments. Similarly, says Greller (1975b), intrinsic feedback can be of two types: Comparisons the individual makes of his or her own performance to that of others and comparison he makes with his own internalized standards. Each of the different types of feedback is used differently and each has implications for the management role.

Greller and Herold (1975) compared five sources of feedback, cutting across a wide variety of jobs: the formal organization, supervisor, co-workers, the task, one's own self. Their results strongly indicate that sources identified as intrinsic (psychologically "close" to the individual) are relied upon more than external referents. In no case did variation in extrinsic job characteristics affect the absolute importance of an intrinsic source. The converse is also true. The value of intrinsic information can be enhanced without damaging the importance of extrinsic feedback, and vice versa. However, these complex, subtle and inadequately understood variations are related to specific job and individual characteristics, and much further unraveling is indicated.

Instrumentality theory, which attempts to predict worker performance by means of a cognitive decision model, is receiving increasingly less support from the findings of such leading investigators as Yukl and his associates (e.g., Yukl, Latham, & Pursell, 1976). Operant conditioning theory would seem to predict that response rates are greater with a variable ratio schedule of reinforcement (in which a response is reinforced after a specific number of occurrences, the number varying from reinforcement to reinforcement) than with a continuous schedule of reinforcement (in which a reinforcer is administered every time an employee admits specific behavior). Instrumentality theory seems to arrive at an opposite conclusion. In 1972, Yukl, Wexley and Seymore demonstrated that a variable ratio schedule of reinforcement is a more efficient way of using pay incentive than a continuous reinforcement schedule. However, as Yukl et al. point out, apart from the hazard of generalizing from temporary, part-time employees to full-time employees, there are some obvious practical limitations to the adoption of this suggestion by either management or labor.

Much of the research in support of Ferster and Skinner's (1957) finding that the schedule of reinforcement may have a greater effect on response rate than the size or magnitude of the reinforcer, has been conducted in laboratory, hospital or school settings. Virtually no study has been attempted to investigate this important finding within the industrial environment. The nearest approximation to such a setting is the job simulation study by Yukl, Wexley and Seymore described above, conducted with female college students. Students paid 50 cents on a random half of the occasions they completed a unit of output (50¢-VR2) increased their performance significantly more than students paid 25 cents for each unit of output (25¢-CRF). Workers who were paid 25 cents on a random half of the occasions they completed a unit of output (25¢-VR2) performed at the same level as the workers on a continuous schedule of reinforcement. However, when Yukl and Latham (1975) later compared the results of continuous and variable ratio schedules of reinforcement in tree-planters in the rural South, productivity was highest for the workers on the continuous schedule of reinforcement.

This was the first study to compare the relative effects of pay incentive and productivity in industry using different reinforcement schedules. Unfortunately, the drawing of firm conclusions is limited by a variety of partly unavoidable methodological factors. Recognizing this restriction, Yukl, Latham and Pursell (1976) conducted a similar study to see if the earlier results would be supported and also to investigate worker preferences for different incentive plans. The subjects, 16 males and 12 female employees planting pine seedlings in North Carolina, were semi-literate whites as well as blacks. Their productivity was considered adequate by management. Despite larger average earnings in the variable ratio conditions, the planters preferred the continuous schedule of reinforcement and performed as well or better under this condition. These results are consistent with the results from the previous study (Yukl & Latham, 1975). Thus, the latest conclusion seems to be that, at least for the type of workers studied, a variable ratio schedule is less effective for improving performance than a continuous reinforcement schedule. The conflicting findings in their various studies are very likely related to such factors as the differences between simulated and real work situations, the differences between tree-planters and college students in educational and cultural background and perhaps changes in economic conditions in our society at large over time.

Positive reinforcement procedures and goal setting have been used with considerable success to improve the performance of employees. Variables such as tardiness (Hermann, deMontes, Dominguez, Montes, & Hopkins, 1973), and productivity (Latham & Baldes, 1975; Yukl & Latham, 1975). In the first paper reprinted in this Section, Pedalino and

Gamboa address themselves to the problem of absenteeism (see also Latham & Kinne, 1974). There is some evidence, reviewed by Moos (1976) to suggest that, at least among blue-collar workers, absenteeism increases as the size of the organization grows. What is most impressive is the consistency of these findings across a variety of industrial settings. Unfortunately, white-collar workers and managers seem to have been excluded from the study to a large extent (in itself an interesting observation) and there is no evidence with respect to these individuals. Similar findings seem to apply to turnover rates with respect to setting size, but here again there has been, as yet, no attempt to link size with other organizational outcomes, such as proximity, labor disputes, untoward incidents and so forth.

Pedalino and Gamboa show behavior modification can be successfully used to decrease absenteeism in a selected industrial facility. Unfortunately, their incentive system had to be terminated after four months for reasons beyond the control of the investigators. Thus, as Pedalino and Gamboa point out, further work is necessary with respect to the maintenance over the long-term of their system. It is also important to stress the sensitive nature of the application of behavior modification to the reduction of absenteeism and the need for stringent ethical deliberations in both the conception of these principles and their application within the industrial setting. Pedalino and Gamboa suggest a possible device for the integration of the employees themselves in direct and active involvement in the reduction of absenteeism in such a manner as to maximize the benefit to all concerned. Their concluding two paragraphs are significant both in the light of ethical issues and the ongoing discussion of the limitations or general efficacy of behavior modification principles in the understanding of the entire industrial complex.

As Mawhinney (1975) implies in a thoughtful and thought provoking article, industrial psychologists tend to think of contingencies of reinforcement primarily by reference to two terms, a response and a schedule of reinforcement. Important antecedents of behavior, such as the previous reinforcement history of the individual, tend to be omitted when contingencies are being described. Errors of technical interpretation (e.g., grouping together variable ratio and variable interval schedules) and conceptual fallacies (e.g., presupposition about behavioral denial of cognitions) abound. Even the more sophisticated and experienced investigators neglect behavioral antecedents in the descriptions and application of operant procedures and this can have unfortunate consequences. Mawhinney points to the Pedalino and Gamboa study as offering just such an instance. There was a significant reduction in absence rates before anyone received a $20 prize and only one worker per department per week received a prize. Thus, argues Mawhinney, antecedents in the form of SDs were involved (e.g., past histories with lotteries) or something other than the $20 prize reinforced on time behavior. Numerous alternative processes could have been in operation in terms of reinforcement schedules depending on what is considered to be the reinforcer. Luthans and Kreitner (1975) attempt to avoid the problem of reinforcer identification by using a feedback-control-system paradigm.

It is of interest to note that positive reinforcement procedures and goal setting (Locke, 1968; Latham & Baldes, 1975) have been applied virtually exclusively to labor and never to management. For reasons at which we may only guess, the strategies of choice for the improvement of managerial effectiveness seem to consist of apparently more "fitting" procedures such as sensitivity training, managerial games and the conference method. Working with managers in nine different departments in a large urban medical center, Wexley and Nemeroff (1975) demonstrated convincingly that a combination of positive reinforcement and goal-setting procedures could be as effective with management as with labor, improving not only direct managerial processes but the absenteeism of their subordinates. Hopefully, this will trigger a series of more extensive projects along related lines.

The second paper reprinted in this Section, by Azrin, Flores and Kaplan, deals with absenteeism of a different sort—unemployment. Azrin et al. employ an extensive array of by now more or less traditional behavioral strategies in their determined and, in the main, successful endeavors to help the jobless cast off this unfortunate mantle. While the individual strategies are conventional ones for behavior therapy, their massed deployment in the present context is impressive and the many-faceted application of these procedures to some partial resolution of the problem of joblessness is unquestionably innovative. It is for this reason that it is reprinted here, in the hope that it will stimulate further controlled research into the various ingredients of their program and the relative contributions of each.

Our only note of concern—and this may be doing less than justice to Azrin himself—stems from a recent *New York Times Magazine* article (June 20, 1976) which—perhaps unwittingly—gives the impression that "con artist" techniques rather than expert but honest presentations of assets and skills are being shaped up. To quote the article in question: "One prospective employer become so intrigued by Joy's lively account that he offered a job without meeting her—or noticing that she didn't have the skills he'd specified." In another example, the prospective young married female job applicant is trained to say "I'm not going to have children." Encouraging this kind of response may be neither behaviorally sound, honest, ethical or legal, nor in tune with the times in regions where civil and feminine rights are taken seriously. The solution to the question could lie in a lawsuit rather than a ploy. No wonder the hapless candidate complained privately that "they shouldn't be allowed to ask you that." It surely must be possible to develop a viable program which trains the applicants to present themselves in the best possible light without any loss of integrity—or so it seems to us.

Recent developments in organizational theory apply beyond the confines of the industrial setting, and implicate a variety of systems and disciplines beyond those of behavior modification or even the mental health professions. Moos (1976) calls his system a social ecological approach. By this he means not so much the development of a new field of inquiry as an integration of environmental psychology, ecological psychology and broad behavioral principles (see Commentary, Section IV). A closely related concept in man-environment relations is that of the *behavior setting*, as developed by Barker and his associates over the past two decades at the Midwest Psychological Field Station and the University of Kansas (Barker, 1968). It refers to groups of individuals behaving together rather than to the behavior of the particular individuals, with an emphasis on naturalistic methods of observation rather than manipulative experimental designs (e.g., see Willems, 1969). The methodology is demonstrably applicable to a wide variety of settings, including the behavior of young children in their homes, rehabilitation facilities, industry, the mental health community center and the college campus. Willems (1972) and LeCompte (1972) have engaged in such activities as intensive behavioral setting surveys of rehabilitation hospitals for spinal cord injury patients. By making a detailed analysis of the behavior of the various performers in each setting, e.g., the physician, the social service personnel, and the patient himself, it is possible to measure in operationally defined terms patient progress and what the facility is actually accomplishing. It is then possible to modify any particular facets of these behaviors within the desired direction in terms of the setting in which they occur.

Eddy and Sinett (1973) incorporated individual personality differences into this approach in their study of emotionally disturbed college students. The relationship of personality and behavior to the utilization of space is one of the more focal areas towards which contemporary organizational theory and practice now seem to be developing. The Eddy and Sinett study highlights not only the importance of these relationships, but that the individual choice of the manner in which people select settings and select people is paramount to the operation of the resulting system.

Laboratory analogue strategies can be extended to and adapted for the more natural setting. We have noted the projection of the behavioral setting approach of Barker to industrial and other applied settings. Recent developments in ethological psychology, behavioral decision theory and systems theory also offer promise of new approaches to cultural behavioral analysis. We are referring here in particular to the work of such individuals as Barron (1974), Jones (1972), Willems (1965), Ray and Brown (1975), Ray and Ray (1976) and Wahler (1975).

One difficulty in making a naturalistic study of the total environment is the restrictions this places upon the instigation of adequate controls. Many procedures have been developed to achieve what is an acceptable compromise or balance between naturalism and control, the definition of the word "acceptable" varying from investigator to investigator. One procedure of promise is that of the micro-economy, as developed by Miles and his associates as an assessment device (Miles, 1975). A relatively value-free organization, it can, at least in theory, be adapted to simulate virtually any feature of the natural economy—private ownership, inflation, unemployment—at will. The emphasis can be upon behavior modification, economic theory, social policy making or any desired admixture of the three. As Miles suggests, what we are witnessing is the creation of a new interdisciplinary approach which could be called behavioral economics, a collaboration of specialists in various disciplines rather than the development of a new field, per se.

Micro-economies and token economies could provide data relevant to economics and epidemiology as well as operant conditioning. To date, such procedures have been most extensively applied to the study of alcohol and drug abuse. But perhaps one of the more intriguing aspects of this cooperation between economists and psychologists pertains to the investigations of Winkler and his group into the relationships between income, consumption and savings behavior in token systems and their application in the making of complex economic analyses (e.g., see Kagel, Battalio, Winkler, Fisher, Miles, Basmann, & Krasner, 1975). It is the contention of such individuals as Winkler that the concepts employed by economists can add to the understanding of individual behavior achieved by behavioral psychologists and, as such, complement rather than substitute for traditional behavioral psychology. Controlled economic systems can provide elegant laboratories for observation and experimental analysis of those aspects of economic behavior which are of importance to understanding of national economic systems. But, as already noted, they can also be effective in the study of economic and reinforcer variables as they apply to specific groups such as alcoholics or drug abusers.

As yet, the systematic integration of economic and behavioral theory in the study of planned environments is still in its early stages and we look forward with confidence to expanding developments in this area. Apart from technical difficulties awaiting resolution, considerable difficulties arise in empirical investigation from the fact that the conceptions and methodological orientations of economists and applied behavioral analysts are so very different. Winkler and his group have striven to highlight some of the differences and similarities in an attempt to formulate an integrative working relationship between the two disciplines. Krasner (1975) has addressed himself to the variables necessary for the training of current workers in environmental design.

Community-based intervention seems to be shifting away from the more formal type of center towards more "natural environment" situations and the self-controlling community (Gambrill, 1975; Meyers, Craighead & Meyers, 1974). Such strategies are likely to be more successful in the treatment, for example, of delinquent and antisocial behavior than traditional methods of incarceration (Braukmann & Fixsen, 1975; Braukmann, Fixsen, Phillips & Wolf, 1975; Davidson & Robinson, 1975; Stumphauzer, 1976). The demonstrable success of such noteworthy facilities as Achievement Place notwithstanding, it would still seem to be essential to program direct intervention within the youth's natural environment and it is to an impetus in such areas that we must look in the future (e.g., Burchard, Harig, Miller & Amour, 1976).

The traditional custodial approach to the emotionally disturbed individual is fraught with danger. On the one hand, we have the need to emancipate the mental hospital patient from his incarceration within a residential hospital setting. On the other hand, as Slovenko and Luby (1975) document in compelling fashion, it is a cruel joke of fate to send an unfortunate mental hospital resident who has already received more than his allocated share of nature's blows back to the inner city at a time when such areas are being all but abandoned by anybody who can get away. Very often, this return is justified in terms of some high-sounding doctrine of community involvement, but all too often the term "community" is little more than a pious euphemism and patients discharged into this so-called community are often worse off than they were in the original mental hospital. In the words of Tannay, cited by Slovenko and Luby, this is little more than a pseudo-freedom. Other observers call the liberation "from back wards to back alleys." Thus, return to the community could well be a project which backfires unless due precautions are undertaken.

Kirk and Therrien (1975) address themselves to the myths that are building up about the inevitable advantages and desirability in making the transition from state hospital based mental health services to community facilities. In his widely cited book, *Asylums,* Goffman (1961) suggested that mental hospitals were as much the cause of chronic mental illness as the places to cure it. Perhaps this contributed, despite its intrinsic truth, to the mythology about the advantages of a return to the community. According to Kirk and Therrien, there is the myth of rehabilitation, that inevitably and come what may, the patient will be rehabilitated and better off back in the community. Then there is the myth of reintegration, that somehow the mere fact of returning to the community setting will ensure the ex-patient's integration into this community. If anything, the evidence suggests that placing the hospitalized patient back in the community runs the risk of his subjection to the negative attitudes about such individuals that many members of the public still hold. Then there is the myth of monetary savings and the assumption that it is, of necessity, cheaper in the short- and the long-run to remove the patient from the mental hospital. Finally, there is the myth that it is only within the community that there are the necessary diverse resources for continuity of care over a broad front. So far, we are witnessing the intentions and, often naive hopes of community mental health thinkers rather than any demonstrably viable programs for such individuals.

A decade ago, the Children's Bureau arrived at the alarming statistic that one out of every six youths will be referred to juvenile courts for delinquent acts before reaching 18 years of age (U.S. Dept. of Health, Education & Welfare, 1966). The situation is probably even more acute now. For a variety of reasons, institutionalization does not seem to be the solution and alternate solutions are being sought (Marholin, Plienis, Harris & Marholin, 1975). Adult-delivered contingent reinforcement schedules have been shown to increase the frequency of desired behaviors and punishment is effective in decreasing the frequency of undesired behaviors (see Braukmann and Fixsen, 1975; Davidson and Seidmen, 1974 for reviews). Peer groups have been shown to be important sources of social contingencies, and often not in the direction desired in the interests of rehabilitation. Systematic peer approval is likely to follow antisocial behavior of institutionalized delinquent children, and pro-social responses end up being punished by the peer group. Several strategies have been developed to direct peer reinforcement towards desired rather than deviant behavior. One such technique involves making reinforcement for the group contingent upon the performance of a single child in the group. Davidson and Seidman (1974) report that only 18 percent of the studies reviewed offer any follow-up data or attempts to program generalization to the natural environment. The thrust must be towards the teaching of relevant behaviors that can be constructively maintained within the natural environment.

Resolving delinquent child problems in the artificial and controlled setting of an institution, no matter how forward-looking, is not likely to contribute drastically towards later resolution of his or her problems within a complex community involving school, home, peer and other groups. And any attempt to intervene directly within the community has to implicate directly these many sources of reinforcement, including parents, guardians, school teachers, peers and local law enforcement agencies.

In last year's Annual Review we reprinted a paper by Fo and O'Donnell (1974) reporting upon their now well-known Buddy System for delinquent youths. This is a community-based program which deploys indigenous nonprofessionals as behavior change agents. Their findings clearly indicate that school attendance increased when the youngsters were placed on social or social-material contingencies, whereas no change occurred in non-contingent relationships or under control conditions. Social-material contingency was also effective in decreasing such problem behaviors as fighting, returning home late and not doing home chores. More recently, Fo and O'Donnell (1975) further compared 264 participating youths with 178 matched youngsters in a no-treatment control group. These latest results suggest that the Buddy System is most effective for youngsters with major offense records in the preceding year offering empirical support for the assumption that the commitment of delinquent acts can be modified by the targeting of other behavior problems. On the other hand, for those with no major offense in the preceding year, participation in the project resulted in a greater number of youths committing serious offenses as compared with nonparticipating

matched youngsters. As Fo and O'Donnell suggest, this raises the possibility of iatrogenic treatment effects when the Buddy System is applied
to youngsters with no record of prior major offenses. It is thus conceivable that current efforts aimed at preventive and early identification
of potential youth offenders could result in more harm than good for
those youngsters with no serious history of delinquent acts.

In somewhat different vein, Marholin et al. (1975) describe the methods
whereby they are systematically mobilizing the various components of a
community of therapeutic potential, a strategy outlined as essential as
long ago as 1969 by Tharp and Wetzel. Webster Hall in Decatur, Illinois
is a community-based residential treatment facility for pre-delinquent
females ranging in age from 12 to 19 years of age. Similar in some
respects to Achievement Place, founded in Lawrence, Kansas in 1967
(for an up-to-date evaluative review, see Hoefler and Bornstein, 1975),
the emphasis is even more directly upon community involvement. But
again, few long-term data are offered with respect to maintenance of
these changes over time and beyond the residential setting.

The last two papers in this Section address themselves to somewhat
different aspects of the community scene. The term behavioral community psychology is somewhat of a grab-bag which can mean many
things to many people and it is difficult at times to allocate any unique
identity to this term. It always seems to be the individuals who are
already "community and psychologically aware" who are most likely to
cooperate, respond to, and be available for such intervention. Attempts
to develop strategies of involvement for the uninvolved are relatively
rare and rarely successful when they are attempted. Given the difficulties
of successful contingency contracting (see Commentary, Section VI), it is
gratifying to see any successful endeavor, no matter how uncontrolled
or specific, to establish programs for increasing the effective participation of low income and culturally minimal individuals in community
programs. At present, a technology for teaching low-income participants
the necessary problem solving skills to be effective does not exist, and it
is primarily for this reason that the reprinted report by Briscoe, Hoffman
and Bailey is encouraging despite its obvious limitations. Their concern
is with the development of a behaviorally based program for teaching
low-income members of a community board specific problem-solving skills.
It is too bad that they restricted major evaluation of their program to
the measurement of changes in the board members' behavior during
the weekly meetings rather than waiting to assess the long-range results of
their training in problem-solving.

Finally, we reprint a paper by Rinn and Vernon on the development of a system for evaluating treatment process in a behaviorally oriented community mental health center which could as well appear in Section IV on Assessment and Measurement as here. One strength of the Huntsville-Madison County Mental Health Center behavioral intervention program is that, by the stressing of identifiable techniques and procedures, it readily permits the evaluation of both process and outcome. Rinn and Vernon report the evaluation of ongoing in-service training programs, therapeutic treatment skills, and whether or not behavioral techniques were administered consistently. While far from complete and, as all too often is the case, awaiting long-term evaluation, it is a step towards comprehensive process evaluation. Hopefully, coming years will see more elaborate, systematic and thoroughgoing evaluation programs for both process and outcome in a variety of behavioral community settings.

28

BEHAVIOR MODIFICATION AND ABSENTEEISM: INTERVENTION IN ONE INDUSTRIAL SETTING

Ed Pedalino

*Pedalino and Associates, Inc.,
Ann Arbor, Michigan*

and

Victor U. Gamboa

*School of Business Administration,
University of Michigan*

Behavior modification was used in an attempt to decrease absenteeism in a sample of 215 hourly employees at a manufacturing/distribution facility. Employees in four adjoining plants served as comparison groups. An ABA (baseline, intervention, return to baseline) intervention using a lottery incentive system constituted the experimental design. Absenteeism decreased significantly following the experimental group intervention but did not decrease in any of the four comparison groups. Further, stretching the schedule of rein-

Reprinted with permission from *Journal of Applied Psychology*, 1974, Vol. 59, No. 6, 694-698. Copyright 1974, American Psychological Association.

This paper was originally presented at the Academy of Management Convention at Seattle, Washington, August 1974.

forcement did not increase the rate of absenteeism. Findings
are discussed in light of Lawler and Hackman's 1969 study
which indicated participation, not the incentive system,
decreased absenteeism.

There is a growing interest in the application of behavior modification in industrial organizations. One area of potential application has
been the absenteeism of the marginal worker (Porter, 1973). Interest in
the use of behavior modification is on two levels—theoretical and applied. On a theoretical level, two landmark articles have been written,
Porter (1973, pp. 113-133) and Nord (1972). Also Gamboa (1974) addressed the issue of compatibility between behavior modification and
current organizational theories of motivation, and came to the conclusion
that the two can be synthesized along content and process dimensions.
Jablonsky and DeVries (1972) critically evaluated Nord's article and
developed an "interactive" model of behavior which accounts for multiple reinforcement on employee behavior.

On the applied level, the laboratory experiments of Yukl, Wexley,
and Seymore (1972), Cherrington, Reitz, and Scott (1971), and Adam
(1972) attempted to measure the efficacy of behavior modification in
addressing organizational issues (i.e., pay incentives, satisfaction, productivity quagmire, increasing performance quality and quantity). Popular literature citing successful application of behavior modification in
industry has largely revolved around the Emery Air Freight experience
("New Tool," 1971; "Where Skinner's Theories Work," 1972). Nord
(1972) described a case study of a hardware company which used a lottery
system to decrease absenteeism and tardiness. Brethower (1973), in a field
study, focused on the use of feedback as a behavioral technique to intervene in two industrial settings. With the exception of Brethower, there
is a dearth of field experiments evaluating the applicability of behavior
modification in industrial organizations.

The article written by Porter (1973) provided the theoretical and
applied framework on which to base this study. Porter's focus is on the
marginal worker, defined as an individual who has failed to demonstrate
consistent work attendance and/or has failed to meet organizationally
defined standards of adequate performance (Porter, 1973). According to
Porter, acquisition of behavior via shaping, and maintenance of acquired
behavior via schedules of reinforcement are the key tools for improving
attendance and performance on the part of the marginal worker.

The basic hypothesis of this study is that behavior modification can
be utilized in an industrial organization to reduce absenteeism. Gamboa

(1974) reviewed the literature on absenteeism and concluded that the bulk of studies reported were either surveys or anecdotal reports of what companies did to decrease absenteeism. Three studies, Mann and Baumgartel (1952), Mann and Sperling (1956), and Lawler and Hackman (1969) were exceptions. All were interventions in industrial settings and attempted to evaluate the effects of their intervention on absenteeism.

The study by Lawler and Hackman (1969) is related to the present study in two important aspects: (a) the use of a pay incentive plan to decrease absenteeism and (b) the use of a field experiment to evaluate the effect of experimental intervention. Lawler and Hackman (1969), however, focused on participation of employees as the explanatory variable leading to decreased absenteeism. The present study focused on the use of behavior modification and attempts to test its efficacy in decreasing absenteeism.

B. F. Skinner, in an interview, has only recently stated his ideas on how behavior modification can be applied in industrial organizations (see Conversation with Skinner, 1973). For example, Skinner suggests that a lottery (such as a door prize) may well solve the problem of absenteeism. Formally stated, therefore, the basic hypothesis of the study is: intermittent reinforcement using financial rewards will lead to a significant decrease in absenteeism.

METHOD

Research Strategy

The basic hypothesis of the study was tested in a field experiment. The experimental approach chosen followed a two-pronged design: (a) the ABA design whereby baseline measures are taken (A), intervention takes place (B), and the intervention strategy is removed (A) with measures systematically monitored in all three phases, and (b) the "controlled" design whereby the experimental group is compared with four other groups in the same research site; the "control" feature uses comparison groups to assess the impact of trend as an alternative hypothesis for any change in absenteeism rate.

Research Site and Subjects

The research was conducted at a manufacturing/distribution center that handles numerous products, with each product housed in a separate plant. Each plant operation was, for all practical purposes, independent of the others. Experimental intervention took place in one plant with the other plants serving as comparison groups.

The plants were made up of a four-level reporting hierarchy with a plant manager at the top, then superintendents, followed by foremen, with unionized employees at the lowest level. Each foreman was responsible for a group of employees ranging in size from 14 to 26.

The average employee had an eleventh grade education. Only full-time employees (95 percent of total) were included in the study. All were blue-collar unionized employees. The average amount of time an employee worked in the experimental plan was approximately one year and six months. All were hired through the division personnel office, where applicants were required to be at least 18 years or older, with no felony or narcotics record, and in acceptable physical health. The average wage received was $4.86 per hour paid on a weekly basis. Four of the five groups followed the same sick day policy (allowed six days a year of paid sick leave); the only exception was Group 4.

The experimental group and Group 1 were assembly line operations, while Groups 2 and 3 were order picking and unloading operations, and Group 4 involved unloading and meat processing. Groups 1 to 4 had more than one shift. Size of the groups ranged from 215 (experimental) and 370 (Group 2) to 65 (Group 3), 43 (Group 4) and 30 (Group 1).

Prior to the intervention, the plant chosen to be the experimental group had a significantly lower absenteeism rate compared to the other plants. This plant was chosen as the experimental group since the plant manager initiated the request to reduce absenteeism, thus reducing usual entry and resistance difficulties. However, matching or random assignment of subjects did not take place. Thus, rather than being "control" groups in the strict sense, the other four groups would be more accurately described as "comparison" groups.

Procedure

The behavior modification procedure utilized to reduce absenteeism consisted of four phases:

1. Baseline 1—where the problem was identified in measurable terms.
2. Phase 1—where the program was operational *each* week for six weeks.
3. Phase 2—where the program was operational *every other* week for ten weeks.
4. Baseline 2—where the program was removed.

Baseline 1. Absenteeism records for the five groups in the company were obtained in order to determine baseline attendance measures. Other than for vacation, bereavement, jury duty, and paid holidays, any employee not present for work was considered absent. An absenteeism rate was computed weekly by determining the number of man-days lost and comparing this to total number of man-days possible. Such baseline data was obtained for 32 weeks for all groups prior to installing the intervention program.

Phases 1 and 2. A lottery incentive system was developed in line with two basic principles of behavior modification—shaping and stretching the schedules of reinforcement. From the lottery notion, the idea of using a poker game intervention strategy occurred. The poker game idea was checked with management and their reaction was positive. Thus, a poker game incentive plan was chosen as the intervention strategy. The plan was to work as follows:

> Each day an employee comes to work and is on time, he is allowed to choose a card from a deck of playing cards. At the end of the five-day week, he will have five cards or a normal poker hand. The highest hand wins $20. There will be eight winners, one for approximately each department.

The implementation of such a strategy constituted Phases 1 and 2 of the program. Basically the program provided an added incentive for entering the work environment each day.

Since the number of men in each department ranged from 14 to 26, the chances of winning were greater in certain departments than in others. However, since each department was a naturally existing functional unit, it was decided to preserve the current divisions for the program.

Each time an employee came to work on time, he received a card from a poker deck from his foreman. The foreman recorded the card chosen by the employee on a score sheet. The foreman also recorded the card on a poker game chart. The chart was a larger version of the score sheet and was posted where men of the same department could see how everyone else was doing.

It is one thing to introduce a program to reduce absenteeism, and it is another thing to maintain such reduced absenteeism over a period of time. A fading procedure, therefore, was designed to stretch the interval of reinforcement. In Phase 1, the first 6 weeks, the program was run each week (fixed interval—1 week). In Phase 2, the last 10 weeks, the program was run every other week—fixed interval—2 weeks).

Baseline 2. After 16 weeks the program was discontinued. Absenteeism measures over 22 weeks continued to be monitored for the experimental group to determine long-run effectiveness of the program. The procedure employed provides two ways of evaluating the effectiveness of the experimental intervention: (a) the ABA design uses the experimental group as its own control in determining the differential impact of introducing and removing the intervention, and (b) the comparison groups enable us to "control" for *trend* as an alternative hypothesis to explain the effect of experimental intervention.

RESULTS

Results of the experiment are shown in Figure 1. The baseline measure of 32 weeks showed the overall weekly absenteeism rate of the experimental group to be 3.01 percent. The goal aimed for was an absenteeism rate of 2.31 percent. This was determined by computing what the absenteeism rate would be if all employees took just their six days sick leave each year. It should be noted that absenteeism rates for some weeks had been as low as, if not lower than, the 2.31 percent goal line. In effect, with existing personnel, technology, and structure, the goal of 2.31 percent had already been achieved and was thus realistic.

Figure 1 shows that the overall absenteeism rate actually achieved as a result of the intervention was 2.46 percent. Compared to the baseline of 3.01 percent this represented an 18.27 percent decrease in absenteeism. This baseline-intervention decrease in absenteeism was tested for statistical significance by a one-tailed t test ($t = 1.98$, $p < .05$). A one-tailed test was chosen since a directional decrease in absenteeism from baseline to intervention period was hypothesized for the experimental group. A 22-week follow-up after the incentive system intervention was phased out showed the absenteeism rate to have climbed to 3.02 percent. This represented an increase of 30.08 percent over the intervention rate. This intervention-follow-up increase was tested for statistical significance by a two-tailed t-test ($t = 3.34$, $p < .01$). A two-tailed test was chosen since there was no a priori basis for hypothesizing a change in absenteeism in a specific direction for this intervention-follow-up period.

An unplanned manipulation occurred in the eighth week of the experimental period. In Phase 1, the incentive program was structured to reward good attendance (five work days present on time) on a weekly basis; in Phase 2, the incentive program was to be operational on a biweekly basis. Thus, while the bonus for the poker game was awarded on the week of September 24, no poker game was to take place on the week following. The next poker game was to take place on October 15, and so on.

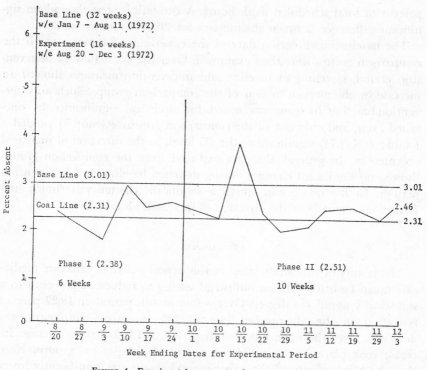

FIGURE 1. Experimental group attendance program results.

Unanticipated circumstances resulted in no incentive program being put into operation on the weeks of October 1, 8, and 15, three weeks in a row. Absenteeism, as can be shown in Figure 1, immediately increased from 2.3 percent to 3.9 percent. The interval for reinforcement had been stretched beyond the point which could maintain good attendance. When the incentive was again reinstituted, absenteeism immediately dropped to 2.4 percent and stayed at about that level for the next six weeks. In effect, an accidental manipulation within the ABA design provided further evidence for the efficacy of the intervention.

To test the effectiveness of "stretching the schedule of reinforcement," the average absenteeism rate of the employees in the experimental group during Phase 1 (weekly schedule of reinforcement) and Phase 2 (bi-weekly schedule of reinforcement) were compared. During Phase 1, the average employee in the experimental group was absent 2.38 percent of total scheduled work hours. During Phase 2 the employee was absent 2.51

percent of total scheduled work hours. A two-tailed t-test showed no significant difference between absenteeism for Phase 1 and Phase 2.

The baseline-intervention data of the experimental group vis-à-vis the comparison groups were then examined. Over the same 16-week intervention period, matching of baseline and intervention measures showed an increase in absenteeism in four of the comparison groups. Such an intervention-baseline increase was tested for statistical significance by one-tailed t-test, and only one of the comparison groups (Group 1) yielded a t value $(t = 1.71)$ significant at the .05 level, in the direction of increased absenteeism. In general, the data gathered from the comparison groups showed no significant changes during matched baseline and intervention periods. In the one group where a significant change was shown, the change was actually in the direction of increased absenteeism.

DISCUSSION

The results of this study support the hypothesis that behavior modification can be utilized in an industrial setting to reduce absenteeism to a statistically significant degree. Over a four-month period an 18.27 percent reduction in the absenteeism rate of 215 unionized employees was achieved. Over the same four-month period, a 13.79 percent average increase took place in the absenteeism rate of comparison groups. Note that the baseline rate of the experimental group was significantly lower than any of the comparison groups to start with. Further, the results showed that stretching the schedule of reinforcement from weekly to biweekly could be achieved without bringing about a significant increase in the rate of absenteeism. Also, since the program was designed so that an employee had to be on time before an incentive was given, a decrease in tardiness was also observed.

The incentive system was terminated after 16 weeks. The reason for doing so was that a bargaining date for a new union contract was approaching and the company did not want to find itself negotiating this incentive system into the contract. Thus, while the results of this study are encouraging, further work is necessary relative to the long-range maintenance of such behavior.

It would be interesting to compare the present study with a previous study by Lawler and Hackman (1969). They also decreased absenteeism by using an incentive system. However, Lawler and Hackman (1969) emphasized participation as the explanatory variable. In this study, emphasis was placed on behavioral principles as bringing about the decrease in absenteeism. Does this suggest two ways of decreasing absenteeism in industrial organizations—participation and behavior modification?

Gamboa (1974) suggested that processes given the label "participation" can simply be much better understood and operationalized using behavior modification principles. Thus, participation and behavior modification are not two ways of decreasing absenteeism (or improving any other behavior). Rather, behavior modification simply helps to make the concept of participation operative and effective. It is the consideration of these issues, both theoretically and empirically, which promises a continued growing interest in the application of behavior modification in industrial settings in the years to come.

REFERENCES

ADAM, E. E. An analysis of changes in performance quality with operant conditioning procedures. *Journal of Applied Psychology*, 1972, 56, 480-486.

BRETHOWER, K. S. Performance indicators as feedback in business settings. Unpublished doctoral dissertation, University of Michigan, 1973.

CHERRINGTON, D. J., REITZ, H. J., & SCOTT, W. E. Effects of contingent and noncontingent reward on the relationship between satisfaction and task performance. *Journal of Applied Psychology*, 1971, 55, 531-536.

Conversation with B. F. Skinner. *Organizational Dynamics*, 1973, 1 (3), 31-40.

GAMBOA, V. Beyond Skinner with dignity: An investigation of the application of behavior modification in industrial settings. Unpublished doctoral dissertation, University of Michigan, 1974.

JABLONSKY, S. F. & DEVRIES, D. L. Operant conditioning principles extrapolated to the theory of management. *Organizational Behavior and Human Performance*, 1972, 7, 340-358.

LAWLER, E. F. & HACKMAN, J. R. Impact of employee participation in the development of pay incentive plans: A field experiment. *Journal of Applied Psychology*, 1969, 53, 467-471.

MANN, F. & BAUMGARTEL, H. *Absences and Employee Attitude in an Electric Power Company*. Ann Arbor, Mich.: University of Michigan, Institute for Social Research, 1952.

MANN, F. C. & SPARLING, J. E. Changing absence rates: An application of research findings. *Personnel*, 1956, 32, 392-408.

New tool: "Reinforcement" for good work. *Business Week*, December 18, 1971, p. 76.

NORD, W. R. Beyond the teaching machine: The neglected area of operant conditioning in the theory and practice of management. In W. R. Nord (Ed.), *Concepts and Controversy in Organizational Behavior*. Pacific Palisades, Calif.: Goodyear, 1972, 145-168.

PORTER, L. W. Turning work into non-work: The rewarding environment. In M. D. Dunnette (Ed.), *Work and Non-Work in the Year 2001*. Monterey, Calif.: Brooks/Cole, 1973.

Where Skinner's theories work. *Business Week*, December 2, 1972, p. 64.

YUKL, G., WEXLEY, K. N., & SEYMORE, J. E. Effectiveness of pay incentives under variable ratio and continuous reinforcement schedules. *Journal of Applied Psychology*, 1972, 56, 19-23.

29

JOB-FINDING CLUB: A GROUP-ASSISTED PROGRAM FOR OBTAINING EMPLOYMENT

N. H. Azrin, T. Flores

and S. J. Kaplan

Behavior Research Laboratory,
Anna State Hospital, Anna, Ill.

Summary—Although joblessness is a major problem, no method of job-counseling has been demonstrated to be superior to usual job-finding practices. The present study describes a new type of program, which has now been evaluated experimentally in a matched-control design. The new program was conducted in a group and stressed such distinctive techniques as mutual-assistance among job-seekers, a "buddy" system, family support, and sharing of job leads. In addition, the program arranged special ways of using such common practices as searching want-ads, role-playing, telephoning, motivating the job-seeker, constructing a resumé and contacting friends. Within 2 months 90 percent of the counseled job-seekers had obtained employment vs. 55 per-

Reprinted with permission from *Behaviour Research and Therapy*, 1975, Vol. 13, 17-27.

This research was supported by the State of Illinois Department of Mental Health. Grateful acknowledgment is made to R. Philip and J. Ulman for their advice and assistance in conducting part of this study.

cent of the non-counseled job-seekers. All clients who attended the program regularly obtained employment. After 3 months, 40 percent of the non-counseled job-seekers were still unemployed. The average salary was about a third higher for the counseled job-seekers. The present procedure appears to be an effective method of assisting a greater proportion of the unemployed to obtain jobs and more quickly, and at a higher salary than they could obtain when they used the usual job finding procedures.

Unemployment has been correlated with higher crime rates (Johnson, 1964), alcoholism (Plaut, 1967), and mental hospital institutionalization (Hollingshead and Redlich, 1958) and is generally acknowledged as a major problem for an individual as well as for society. Yet, the typical job-seeker is usually left to his own initiative. He is likely to use generally known procedures such as help-wanted advertisements and to ask some of his friends (Jones & Azrin, 1973; Sheppard & Belitsky, 1966) in an unstructured manner. Job counseling programs and job-seeking manuals (Jameson, 1973; Marshall, 1964; Lyons & Martin, 1940) have been devised to meet this urgent need, but none seem to have been experimentally evaluated to determine whether they succeed in obtaining employment more efficiently than the job-seeker could have by his own efforts. The need exists for a job-counseling program which has been shown experimentally to be superior to the efforts of the individual job-seeker. To meet this need, the present study devised a counseling program which consisted of many different procedures, some of which have been used relatively infrequently, such as group counseling as well as other procedures which have been used commonly but in different ways than in this program. The effect of the program was experimentally compared with the results of the efforts of non-counseled job seekers.

The hiring process was conceptualized in a previous report (Jones & Azrin, 1973) as a social reinforcement process in which skill-irrelevant factors played a substantial role. The present study extended that view to the job-counseling situation. Job-finding was viewed as requiring a number of complex skills which should be learned best in a structured learning situation that emphasized such learning factors as motivation, maintenance of behavior, feedback, imitation, and practice. Job counseling was considered as a learning experience which should be taught in a structured and continuing manner until the job was obtained. In addition, the present program was a "systems" approach oriented to the perspective of the job-seeker: the program assisted the job seeker in every area that was believed to be influential in obtaining a job. Assistance was provided for such diverse problems as discouragement in job-seeking, need for family understanding, transportation, peer assistance, professional advice, job leads, preparation of a resumé, interview skills, techniques for approaching friends, practice in obtaining interviews, scheduling of one's time, and expanding one's vocational choices.

METHOD

Setting

The program took place in a small college town located in a sparsely populated community with no public transportation and a long history of above-average unemployment. Many of the 30,000 population of the town were students.

Clients

The clients were referred from several sources, including a newspaper advertisement, a State of Illinois Employment Service Agency, the personnel departments of several large businesses, and word-of-mouth information. The only criteria for selection were that the individual desired permanent full-time employment and was not currently employed full-time. An initial orientation meeting described the overall counseling procedure and the need for daily attendance. All clients who agreed to that participation were considered. The only individuals excluded were those receiving unemployment compensation since preliminary study indicated that some of these individuals made little effort in the program until their payments terminated.

Experimental Design

All clients who indicated a desire to participate were matched in pairs each week after they were given a description of the program. An overall criterion of probable employability was used as the general matching criterion and was based on the more specific criteria of age, sex, race, education, marital status, desired type of position and salary level, number of dependents, and current financial resources to the closest extent that such matching was possible. The individuals were divided into pairs and a coin toss determined which individual in a pair received the counseling. The other member (control client) received no counseling. Clients who attended four sessions or less were omitted from the study and their matched controls also were not considered. Of the

INTERVIEW—BUDDY SYSTEM—MOTIVATION
GROUP COUNSELING- SYSTEMS APPROACH
RECORDING—TRANSPORTATION—RESUME
REFERENCES—ROLE PLAYING—FAMILY SUPPORT

Fig. 1. Pictorial representation of the job-seekers in the Job-finding Çlub.

resulting 60 clients who received counseling for at least 5 sessions, 28 were male and 32 female. They had an average age of 25 years, had 14 years of education, and had been employed an average of 6 months during the past year. The 60 persons in the control group differed only slightly: 27 were male and 33 female, they had an average age of 26 years, also 14 years of education, and had been employed an average of 5 months during the past year. There were 9 blacks in the counseled group and 8 in the control.

Session Scheduling

The clients were given group counseling, the size of the group being determined each week by the number available for starting that week and varied from two to eight clients. The first two sessions were about 3 hours in duration, whereas the subsequent sessions were 1-2 hours. A new group was started about every 2 weeks. After the first two lectures, the new clients met with the clients who had started in earlier weeks. The sessions were scheduled daily and the client was urged to attend each day until he obtained a job.

Group Meeting

Job-seeking is usually considered to be a solitary concern. The present program made job-seeking part of a group effort by having clients meet in a small group as pictorially illustrated in Figure 1. The group meeting allowed the use of the buddy procedure, mutual auto transportation to employers, role-playing, supervision of their manner of telephone inquiry, mutual review of their resumés, sharing job leads and mutual encouragement by a peer group.

Buddy System

To provide strong social support from their peers, the clients were paired off with each other during each session. They could thereby give individualized as well as group assistance, advice and encouragement to each other.

Motivation

Job-seekers frequently became so discouraged by their failure to obtain a job that they abandoned all efforts. To overcome this discouragement, the present program 1) enlisted support from the applicant's family, 2) provided statistics and played tape commentaries of former job-seekers in this program who were successful in obtaining employment, 3) enlisted encouragement and support from other group members, and 4) provided encouragement from the counselor.

Family Support

Job-seekers often receive no psychological support from their family and indeed are sometimes hindered by the new duties that their family imposes on them because of their unemployed status. To reverse this attitude, the family was viewed as a strong potential source of encouragement and assistance. The counselor sent a letter to a family member (spouse, sibling or parent) or friend with whom the job-seeker was living, and explained how that person could help the job-seeker obtain employment. The assistance suggested was: 1) limiting use of the family phone by other family members, 2) providing arrangements for transportation of the job-seeker, 3) emotional support and encouragement, 4) offering of job leads and making suggestions for his job search, 5) making allowances for the great amount of time spent job-hunting.

Full-Time Job Search

The job search is usually considered a part-time incidental effort, but as other programs have emphasized, the job search deserves full-time concentration. The present program required the applicant to be occupied full-time in such activities as phoning, being interviewed, writing letters, and contacting friends and relatives. Counseling sessions were arranged daily to provide a structured setting for these activities and to review the job-search activities he performed outside of the session.

Widening Variety of Positions Considered

Applicants often limit themselves to considering only one type of job, such as waitress or factory worker, and by so doing have few positions to choose from. The applicants were, therefore, encouraged to consider many other types of positions. They were given examples of other positions for which they would qualify and were made to realize that many employers will provide on-the-job training, especially if they like the person. Examples were given of previous clients who obtained better positions by considering many types of jobs.

Self-Help

Having obtained previous jobs by the direct intervention of another party (employment agency, relative), the job-seeker may later be at a loss regarding job finding when such direct assistance is not available. The present program taught the job-seeker the various techniques of job seeking such that he would be in a better position to obtain employment in the future. This instruction was accomplished by providing no more assistance than was needed and by requiring the client to explain the procedures to the other clients, especially his "buddy," in the group. The counselor never arranged the interview; the client learned to do so himself.

Dress and Grooming

The initial impression that a client makes on an interviewer is probably influenced greatly by the manner of dress. Consequently, written instructions as to the need for dressing appropriately for the position were given to the clients and discussed. Yet, some younger clients considered such advice as unimportant, especially regarding length of hair. To influence them more meaningfully, the "buddy" was required to comment on the suitability of the clothing and grooming of the client during a role-playing interview, thereby bringing peer standards to bear, rather than those of the counselor.

Personal Attributes

As noted previously, employers seem to hire in large part on the basis of personal-social attractiveness of the applicant. Therefore, the program emphasized these personal-social characteristics by such procedures as including on the resumé a photograph and a list of hobbies and interests, use of friends and relatives as referral sources, and attempting face-to-face interviews, or at least phone contact, rather than merely submitting an impersonal application form.

OBTAINING JOB LEADS

Procedures

Job leads from other job-seekers. Each job-seeker must discover anew by his own efforts the existence of job openings that are not widely publicized. As found by Jones and Azrin (1973) most jobs were not publicly advertised. To minimize the need for this continued re-discovery of the same job leads, each new job-seeker was provided with the job leads obtained by the other job-seekers in the program. The counselor arranged for the job-seekers to inform each other 1) of job offers that they did not wish to accept, especially after having accepted an alternative position, 2) of job openings they had discovered incidentally but for which they were not qualified or interested, and 3) after they were hired, of openings available in their new place of employment as well as a list of all previous potential employers that had expressed interest or granted an interview. This communication was facilitated by the group meetings, by having each job-seeker keep a record of his job contacts, and by mailed inquiries to job-seekers after their employment.

Friends and Relatives

Friends and relatives are the single most important source of job leads (Jones & Azrin, 1973; Sheppard & Belitsky, 1966), yet this source is typically pursued in a happenstance manner. The present program structured the use of friends and relatives by having the client list all close friends and relatives, then contacting several of them in the following manner: 1) asking them for use of their name as a reference on application forms, 2) asking them for incidental job leads or openings at their place of employment, and 3) asking them for an open letter of recommendation.

Situation Wanted Advertisement

Very few job-seekers advertise their need for a position, perhaps because so few jobs are obtained by this method (Jones & Azrin, 1973; Sheppard & Belitsky, 1966). When such advertisements are used, the usual practice is to list only one's formal qualifications. The present program used these "Situations Wanted" newspaper advertisements for all clients and, in contrast, emphasized attractive personal attributes by such phrases as "likes to meet people" in the advertisement.

Help-Wanted Advertisement

Help-wanted ads are the most often used source of job leads by job-seekers and of public notices of position availability by employers. Yet, job-seekers did not seem sufficiently exhaustive of their examination of the advertisements, often dismissing a position from consideration because of slight preferences regarding geographic location, the type of job, presumed lack of training, or simply because of incomplete information in the ad. The present rationale was that job prerequisites are flexible, that apparent deficits might be outweighed by other unknown attractions and that the personal factors would weigh heavily. Consequently, the job-seeker was encouraged to explore every reasonable lead. By meeting the employer in a personal interview, the job-seeker could obtain the additional information and allow the personal factors to operate. The help-wanted section of the local newspapers were closely scrutinized during each session. The counselor, the group members and, especially, the client's "buddy" pointed out every possible job of interest for each client.

Former Employers

Former employers have the unique status of having first-hand knowledge and appreciation of a former employee's productivity and reliability, especially if the employment was terminated under pleasant circumstances. The job-seeker was instructed to follow up several possible options. He could ask his former employer for: 1) his previous position or any openings in the near future, 2) other positions he might be qualified for because of increased experience or education, or openings in a branch of the company, 3) incidental job leads that the employer knew about, 4) an open letter of recommendation, or 5) a personal referral to other employers. The job-seekers engaged in supervised practice of what to say to previous employers.

Telephone

Telephone contact with potential employers appears to be used as a minor procedure by job-seekers. The present program made extensive use of phone contacts since this medium was far more efficient than traveling to the job location. Telephone conversation with the employer was usually obtained more easily than was face-to-face interviews, yet the face-to-face interviews could then be arranged more readily once phone contact was made, even more so than by a written request alone. The client was given a prepared outline of what to say over the phone. The counselor, the other clients and the client's "buddy" advised him on his telephone manner of inquiry. Especially suitable for phone contact was the listing of the telephone classified directory (yellow pages) of companies that were especially likely to be interested in the client's skills. In the phone contact, the client attempted to speak directly to the person who did the hiring, to arrange an interview, and, if not, to obtain suggestions for other potential employers (see Personal Referral Procedure below).

Personal Referral Procedure

When a potential employer states that no positions are available, the usual practice is to terminate the discussion. The present program taught the applicants to obtain suggestions from the employer regarding other possible employers, and, further, to request permission to use the referral source's name in making the future inquiry. This personal referral resulted in a continual source of job leads and made the subsequent initial contact more personalized and comfortable for the applicant.

PURSUING LEADS

Resumé

A convenient method of presenting one's distinctive and positive attributes is the personal resumé. Yet, job-seekers often omit this submission, especially in the non-professional types of positions, or do not furnish it until after the initial screening, or omit highly relevant personal-social characteristics, or organize it such that the employer will not easily discern the positive attributes. The present approach was to view the resumé as a tool for impressing the employer with one's strongest assets. The resumé was submitted at the time of initial contact, was organized into easily distinguishable topics, and emphasized the positive personal-social attributes as well as the distinctive vocational skills, and included a photograph for distinctive personal identification. The resumé was given for every job contact including (a) before an interview, (b) as an attachment to application forms if an interview was unobtainable, (c) with letters of inquiry about openings, or (d) when applying to a help-wanted advertisement or a telephone interview.

Open Letter of Recommendation

A recommendation from a friend is a method of providing a favorable portrayal of one's assets. Yet, the inconvenience of obtaining a letter of recommendation is so great that employers seem to obtain a letter from possible references only in the final stage of hiring, if at all. In order to obtain an initial advantage by the present program, the client obtained "open" letters of recommendation and presented them at the time of initial application. In addition, this request for a recommendation seemed to serve as a subtle but acceptable method of notifying friends of the desire for a position without appearing to impose on the friendship.

Interview Instruction and Role-Playing

Many job-seekers have had little experience with interviews, do not know what to anticipate, and fear the confrontation with potential employers. Intensive instruction and supervised practice was given by role-playing between buddies, and by comments on the telephone contacts made during the sessions. Barbee and Kiel (1973) have demonstrated the value of such instruction in a simulated job-seeking situation.

Call-Back

Job applicants usually do not inquire further from a potential employer who has no positions available at the time of the initial inquiry. In the present procedure, the clients requested permission to call again. They called back one or more times in order to obtain an interview. After an interview had been obtained, they called back rather than waiting for the employer's decision. The clients were again given printed forms to simplify their scheduling and timing of these calls.

Recording

In order to keep one's job search adequately organized, one must maintain records. The job-seekers recorded information about job leads, such as the name of the personnel manager, his address, phone number, and the overall results of the first contact. The recording assisted the job-seeker in making the future call-backs and in providing leads to other clients.

Transportation

Lack of transportation to potential employers often prevents job-seeking in a wider geographical area, especially in rural areas where public transportation is unavailable and the client has no auto. The program reduced this problem by encouraging mutual auto usage between clients in the group, by encouraging their family members to provide transportation, and instructing clients to seek out a "car pool" from their fellow employees if the job was obtained.

Job-Finding Materials and Aids

In order to assist the job-seekers with tangible items that some of them could not afford, various aids were made available to the clients, free of charge. Clerical staff assisted in typing resumés, letters of recommendation, letters of inquiry, and employment application forms. The postage for letters and applications was also supplied. Photocopies of resumés, letters of recommendation, and important papers such as transcripts and teaching certificates were supplied when required for the client's job application. Local and area telephone directories were made available and also specialized listings of industries such as members of the local Chamber of Commerce, a list of social service agencies, and a list of day care centers. Telephones with extension lines for monitoring were also available for use by the job-seekers. Instant-developing photographs were given to the clients to give to employers.

RESULTS

The average job-seekers who were counseled started work in 14 days (median time), whereas the average non-counseled job-seeker started work in 53 days. (The median, rather than the mean, time was necessary since some persons did not obtain a job and no specific time could be assigned to them.) This superiority of the Job-Finding Club was statistically significant ($p < 0.001$) by the Wilcoxin Test (Siegel, 1956). Part-time jobs of 20 hours or less per week were not included in this calculation. Very intensive efforts were made to obtain the necessary follow-up in-

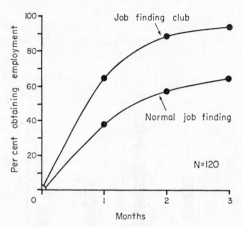

Fig. 2. The percentage of clients who obtained full-time employment. The upper curve is for the job-seekers in the counseled Job-finding Club. The lower curve is for the matched control clients who were not enrolled in the Job-finding Club. Each data point is the cumulative percentage of clients who had obtained employment by the time specified on the abscissa.

formation, but six of the non-counseled clients could not be located; therefore, their data were not included in the calculations, nor were the data of their six matched clients who were counseled.

Figure 2 shows the progress of the counseled and the non-counseled job seekers during the first 3 months. One month after counseling began, about two-thirds of the counseled persons, but only about one-third of the non-counseled persons, had obtained employment. Two months after counseling began, 90 percent of the counseled clients had obtained a job, compared with 55 percent of those who were not counseled. After 3 months, the status of the job-seekers was little changed. Ninety-two percent of the counseled group had found a job, but 40 percent of the non-counseled persons had not found full-time employment. Interpretation of the status of the job-seekers after 3 months became ambiguous since some individuals were no longer seeking employment because of such factors as enrollment in college, marriage, or a return to parental support.

The mean starting salary for the jobs obtained by the counseled clients was $2.73 per hour vs. $2.01 per hour for the jobs obtained by the non-counseled job-seekers. This 36 percent greater salary was statistically different by the t-test ($p < 0.05$).

The speed of finding a job was greater for those clients who attended regularly than for those who attended irregularly. The Pearson r corre-

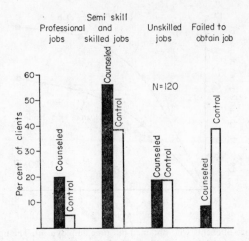

Fig. 3. Type of job obtained by 60 clients in the Job-finding Club and 60 clients in the control condition (non-counseled). The ordinate is expressed in terms of the percentage of clients. The solid line bar designates the percentage of clients in the Job-finding Club whereas the white bar designates the percentage of non-counseled clients (control condition). The time period was 3 months.

lation coefficient between the proportion of sessions attended and the number of days unemployed was —0.80 and shows that regular attendance was highly correlated with early success in finding a job. The five clients in the Job-Finding Club who did not obtain a job attended very irregularly or attended the club for no more than three weeks at the longest. All the clients found jobs who attended the sessions regularly and continuously.

Figure 3 shows the type of job obtained by the end of 3 months. The same proportion of the job-seekers (17 percent) in each condition obtained unskilled jobs, but a higher proportion of the counseled members obtained professional employment (20 percent) than did the control group clients (5 percent). Also the proportion of counseled groups who obtained skilled types of jobs was greater than for the control clients, 55 vs. 38 percent. As noted also in Figure 2, 45 percent of the non-counseled clients did not obtain a job vs. only 8 percent of the clients in the Job-Finding Club.

DISCUSSION

The present program was more effective than the individual efforts of the job-seekers. Under the program, virtually all (90 percent) job-seekers obtained full-time employment within two months in comparison with only half of the non-counseled seekers. The average counseled person obtained his job within 2 weeks compared to about 8 weeks required by the average job-seeker who was not counseled. The average starting salary was about a third higher for the counseled job-seekers than the non-counseled. All clients who attended the classes regularly and consistently obtained a job. These findings appear to provide the first controlled demonstration that a job counseling program is more effective than the usual unstructured job-seeking.

From the perspective of the job-seeker, the program provided assistance, as well as abstract advice. He received this assistance for as long as he required. He was assisted not only in such obvious matters as manner of dress and his interview conduct, but in areas that are ordinarily neglected, such as discouragement in job-seeking, transportation, telephone availability and usage, maximum use of friends, resumé preparation, and peer assistance.

From the perspective of the counseling agency, the present program appears to be practicable. Because of the "buddy" procedure, each client receives continuing individual attention. The cost was fairly moderate, about $20 per client for the unusual, tangible commodities and services such as photocopying, resumé photographs, postage, and telephone.

The present program appears to be applicable to unemployment situations that offer special problems. Since job opportunities are less available in rural than urban areas, the success of the program in the rural environment of the present study suggests that an urban locale would be an even more favorable environment for this type of program. Some subpopulations suffer especially from joblessness, such as the ex-alcoholic, ex-mental patients, the teenagers, the elderly, females, and blacks. Although the present sample was insufficiently large to include representation of all such "disenfranchised" clientele, the program seems well suited to their common need for continued assistance, especially their common problems such as job discouragement, transportation and telephone usage, and relative lack of financial resources. The successful application of this type of program to alcoholics (Hunt & Azrin, 1972) demonstrates this applicability to one of these special populations of marginal employability.

In the selection of clients for this study, clients were deliberately excluded who were currently receiving unemployment payments since their motivation was often low. This exclusion was dictated primarily by research consideration to avoid drop-outs from the counseling program. If participation in the present program was a requirement for obtaining unemployment payments, the time and effort required by this participation in the program would reduce the opportunity for competing leisure activities and would be expected to motivate the client to obtain employment.

REFERENCES

BARBEE, J. R. & KEIL, E. C. Behavior modification and training the disadvantaged job interviewee. *Vocational Guidance Quarterly*, September, 1973.

HOLLINGSHEAD, A. B. & REDLICH, F. C. *Social Class and Mental Illness.* New York: Wiley, 1958.

JAMESON, R. *The Professional Job Hunting System.* New Jersey, Performance Dynamics, Inc., 1972.

JOHNSON, E. H. *Crime, Correction, and Society.* Illinois: Dorsey Press, 1964.

JONES, R. J. & AZRIN, N. H. An experimental application of a social reinforcement approach to the problem of job-finding. *Journal of Applied Behavior Analysis,* 6: 345-353, 1973.

LYONS, G. J. & MARTIN, H. C. *The Strategy of Job Finding.* New Jersey: Prentice-Hall, 1940.

MARSHALL, A. *How to Get a Better Job.* New York: Appleton-Century-Crofts, 1964.

PLAUT, T. F. A. *Alcohol Problems. A Report to the Nation by the Cooperative Commission on the Study of Alcoholism.* New York: Oxford University Press, 1967.

SHEPPARD, H. L. & BELITSKY, A. H. *The Job Hunt.* Maryland: Johns Hopkins, 1966.

30

BEHAVIORAL COMMUNITY PSYCHOLOGY: TRAINING A COMMUNITY BOARD TO PROBLEM SOLVE

Richard V. Briscoe, David B. Hoffman,

and Jon S. Bailey

The Florida State University

This study demonstrated the effect of training nine lower socio-economic adults participating as policy board members in a federally funded rural community project to make behaviorally defined statements to increase problem-solving behaviors in board meetings. A multiple-baseline design across subjects and skills was used to analyze the behavioral categories of: 1) stating the *problem;* 2) finding *solutions* to the problem; and 3) implementing the *action* to the

Reprinted from the *Journal of Applied Behavior Analysis*, 1975, 8, 157-168. Copyright 1975, the Society for the Experimental Analysis of Behavior, Inc.

This research is based upon a thesis submitted in partial fulfillment of the M.S. degree of the first author under the chairmanship of the second author. This research was supported by the U.S. Office of Education under Title I, Higher Education Act, through the Florida Board of Regents, Grant No. 72-125-001, D. Hoffman, Principal Investigator. The authors wish to express their appreciation to A. Footman, chairman of the Wadesboro Policy Board, and other members of the organization whose cooperation made the study possible.

656 ANNUAL REVIEW OF BEHAVIOR THERAPY

solution. Problem-solving responses during board meetings increased for subjects following training and remained higher than baseline during follow-up.
Descriptors: training problem solving, adults, rural poor, board training, behavioral community psychology, group problem solving, multiple baseline.

Applied behavior analysis, which began as an experimental-therapeutic endeavor with individual subjects exhibiting deviant or undesirable behavior (Ullmann & Krasner, 1965) has broadened in scope and application such that the principles may now be applied to solve social problems. The term *Behavioral Community Psychology* seems appropriate to denote applications to socially significant problems in unstructured community settings where the behavior of individuals is not considered deviant in the traditional sense. Encouraging welfare recipients to attend self-help meetings (Miller & Miller, 1970), reinforcing the picking up of litter (Burgess, Clark, & Hendee, 1971; Chapman & Risley, 1974; Clark, Burgess, & Hendee, 1972; Kohlenberg & Phillips, 1973; Powers, Osborne, & Anderson, 1973), prompting the purchase of soft drinks in returnable bottles (Geller, Farris, & Post, 1973), and increasing bus ridership through token reinforcement (Everett, Hayward, & Myers, 1974) are all applications of behavior principles to solve community problems. Motivating delinquents to participate in self-government (Fixen, Phillips, & Wolf, 1973), and using access to a recreation center as a reinforcer for increasing membership and reducing disruptions (Pierce & Risley, 1974) also represent promising new applications to longstanding community problems. Another area to which the principles may be relevant is in analyzing behaviors in the poor which, if strengthened or developed, might provide greater effectiveness and self-sufficiency on their part. Relevant to this approach is a study by Kifer, Lewis, Green, and Phillips (1974), which showed that conflict-resolution behavior could be analyzed and modified in parent-child pairs.

In recent years, many federally funded programs designed to help the poor (Head Start, Community Action, Model Cities, Elementary and Secondary Education Act Title I, etc.) have required the participation of low-income parents, clients, and residents in decision-making roles. This has usually taken the form of service on advisory or policy boards, often with low-income parents and community representatives constituting over 50 percent of those decision-making bodies (Hoffman, Jordon, & McCormick, 1971). More often than not, such participation has been ineffective. Marshall, for example (1971), reached that conclusion after interviewing every member of the greater Los Angeles community action board and analyzing board meetings. Moreover, she found that representatives of the poor saw themselves as ineffective, as did other (non-poor) board members. Many resigned in frustration and bitterness.

One reason for the ineffectiveness of low-income representatives on a policy board is their lack of familiarity with formal group decision-making procedures. Few programs have provided the necessary training for their boards. While Head Start programs all have parents on advisory or policy boards, less than 10 percent provide formal training, and fewer than 20 percent provide informal training (Hoffman, 1974). When used at all, training has usually involved lectures and readings on procedures (e.g., Robert's Rules of Order), discussion of the roles and responsibilities of board members, and review of ongoing programs, usually provided by program directors. These approaches may be supplemented by human relations training designed to increase "trust" and "communication" between board members. A review of all training programs being used by or with Office of Education and Office of Child Development programs in 1970 (Hoffman, 1970) revealed few that dealt specifically with training problem-solving behaviors of board members. Thus, a technology to teach low-income participants the necessary problem-solving skills to be effective does not exist at present. The present research sought to develop a behaviorally based program for teaching low-income members of a community board specific problem-solving skills; the program was evaluated by measuring changes in the board member's behavior during the weekly meetings.

METHOD

Subjects

Three men and six women comprising the policy board of a university sponsored but community controlled self-help education project were subjects (ages 15 to 69, $\bar{x} = 37$). The two youngest were 15-year-old junior high-school girls. The median education level for the subjects was eighth grade in segregated rural schools. Only one board member completed the twelfth grade, two stopped during the eleventh grade, two dropped out in the eighth grade, two subjects never completed the fourth grade and two teenagers were enrolled in the eighth grade.

The socio-economic level of the subjects can best be characterized by their incomes and type of employment: only three board members earned an annual income of $5000; the rest earned $2000 or less per year.

The jobs held by the subjects included service as plumbers, bus drivers, carpenters, maids, cooks, and farmers.

The nine board members were elected by area residents during community meetings and included representation of different social groups, age groups, occupations, and interests within the community. The major decision-making part of the project took place during weekly board meetings. At these meetings, the board emphasized identifying and solving community problems, such as arranging to have repairs made to the community center, organizing social and educational events, discovering and distributing social welfare resources to the community, finding and providing medical care, and administering a $20,000 budget to fund these projects.

To maintain attendance, each member was paid $4.00 for attending each of the 18 meetings scheduled during the study. Total cost for payment of subjects was $648.00. Board meetings were generally held once or twice a week.

Setting

The study was conducted in a single-story, four-room frame school house built in the early 1900s in an isolated rural black community in northwestern Florida, 15 miles east of Tallahassee. The meetings were held in the largest room, also used for other group activities of the project. A microphone was suspended from the ceiling in a central location to record the voices of members of the policy board. A Sony video camera, model AVC 3200 was positioned in the back of the room to record the meetings. Both were installed with the full consent of the board. Other equipment included: Sony V32 0.5 in. (1.3 cm) videotapes, Sony monitor CVM 920 U, and Sony tape video recorder model AV-3600. Figure 1 shows schematically where board members were located relative to the video recording equipment and the area where training was carried out.

Rationale

In extensive contact with the board for 1 year before starting the study, it was noted that discussion of one topic blended into another, board members talked about different problems simultaneously, the meetings lasted for long periods of time without clear decisions being reached, and when decisions were made, it was not clear who would carry them out.

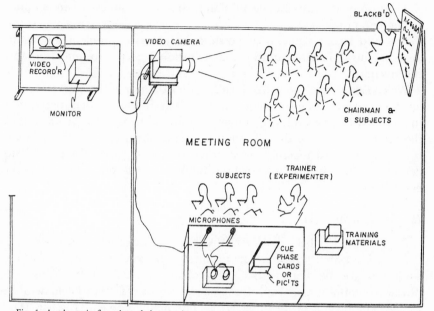

Fig. 1. A schematic floorplan of the meeting room where the experimenter carried out the training program and the board members held their meetings. The training program was held before the actual board meetings by the experimenter with one or two subjects. During the meetings, all board members were videotaped with the video camera located so as to have all board members on the screen at the same time.

Early unsystematic attempts to increase the effectiveness of the policy board consisted of assigning graduate students in community psychology to work with individual board members to help them plan and prepare for meetings. Several project staff members and university graduate students and faculty met with board members during meetings to serve as models for problem-solving. An analysis of videotapes of several board meetings without these aides indicated little improvement in their skills.

Our analysis suggested three minimum, necessary, and sufficient steps for effective problem-solving: 1) identifying and isolating the problem under discussion, 2) stating and evaluating alternative solutions, and 3) selecting a solution and making explicit decisions for implementation (what would be done, by whom, when, and how). In practice, this involved training subjects to make key statements that led to problem-solving behavior. Thus, board members were taught to identify the cause of the problem, to label it with a key statement, and to use the key statement as a lead-in to a possible solution of the problem.

These steps constituted the minimum behaviors necessary to produce a complete problem-solving cycle. A decision was made to use a procedure that would lead as quickly as possible to increased problem solving in the meetings, leaving until later additional steps to enhance this effectiveness.

We chose to train the entire board, rather than only the chairman or a few members, because one objective was to facilitate active participation in problem-solving and decision-making by as many representatives of the community as possible. In addition, some absenteeism and a gradual turnover in board members was anticipated, and there was no way to determine in advance who would be the better problem solvers or emerging leaders.

Response Definitions

Problem-solving behaviors were divided into three major categories:

1. *Problem identification.* The problem behavior was scored when any subject made the statement, "The problem is . . ." or an equivalent phrase containing the word "problem," such as "The problem will be . . ."; "The biggest problem is . . ."; "The main problem is . . ."; "The problem seems to be . . ."; etc.

2. *Solving problems.* The solution behavior was scored when subjects made the statement, "One solution is . . ."; "Another solution is . . ."; or an equivalent phrase containing the word "solution," such as, "There is another solution . . ."; "The best way to solve this problem is by . . ."; "Could you solve that by. . . ?"

3. *Deciding on action to be taken.* The action behavior was scored only when subjects directed the following question(s) directly towards another member: "What action are we going to take?" "Who will do it?" "Where will it be done?" "When will it be done?" and, "How will it be done?" No equivalent phrases were accepted for this behavior.

Observational System

Each board meeting was videotaped in its entirety (the board agreed to standardize the meetings to 1 hour) and viewed later by observers to collect data. The observers recorded only responses that specifically met the criterion specified above for each problem-solving behavior. The specific behavioral response statements (e.g., "The problem is . . .") were used as measures of problem-solving skills for two primary reasons. First, the use of these particular responses (or equivalents) could be easily and reliably measured. That is, it was not necessary for observers to make subjective judgments of the "intent" of the subjects' statements. Second, these statements would provide the subjects with clear, direct information during the meeting. Informal observations showed that these statements helped subjects to recognize types of information being communicated. Before using the behavioral statements, board members did not know whether others were stating a problem, suggesting a solution, or discussing irrelevant information.

The observational form, shown in Figure 2, was divided into separate agenda items that were further divided by having subjects' names contained within each topic in order to collect individual data. Board members decided upon agenda items one week in advance and the chairman wrote the topics on a chalk board placed in front of the group at the beginning of each meeting. Observers were able to follow the sequence of the meetings because the videotape of each meeting began with the camera focused on the agenda written on the chalk board. Having agenda items thus labeled helped subjects to prepare for their meetings and observers to differentiate the topics under discussion. When a subject made a problem-solving statement, his (or her) response was recorded for that particular topic. Problem-solving responses were scored as follows: "P" for the problem category, "S" for the solution category, and "W" for the action category.

Reliability

Reliability checks were taken during nine of the 18 meetings by having a second observer view the tapes and independently record the three categories of responses. An agreement was scored only if both observers recorded the same behavior for the same person for the same topic. Any difference was scored as a disagreement. Agreement was also scored if both observers agreed that for a given topic and board member no correct response was made. The formula, agreements divided by agreements plus disagreements multiplied by 100, was used to calculate percentage agreement.

EXPERIMENTAL CONDITIONS
Baseline

During baseline, board meetings were conducted much as they had been for the previous six months by the chairman. The members agreed

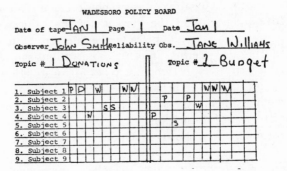

Fig. 2. Sample of observational form used to record the problem-solving statements made by the subjects during the meetings. The form was divided into separate agenda topics with the subjects listed with each one. The observers scored the behaviors as "P" for stating the problem, "S" for stating a solution, and "W" for initiating some action to be taken. The responses were recorded for individual subjects, during the particular topic and in the order in which the responses were made.

to have the meetings recorded and the camera was positioned so that all eight members plus the chairman were on-camera at the same time.

Pilot Training

A pilot training procedure preceded the training phase, during which the first author attempted to train the entire board as a group to make the first problem-solving statement, "The problem is. . . ." This pilot training session preceded the regular board meeting and included a combination of written definitions and instructions on problem-solving behavior, a lecture on proper methods of solving problems, a demonstration of the correct behaviors, and verbal and written responses required by each board member. Following this session, the data show an increase of responding for only the chairman, even though the procedure was to increase responding of all subjects. Informal observations of a videotape of the training session showed several critical faults of the group instructions: 1) subjects were engaging in off-task behaviors (talking to each other, passing papers and pencils, reading) during the training session; 2) the training program was more appropriate for subjects with a stronger educational background (i.e., the major emphasis on the lecture method and the requirement that subjects read many printed materials); 3) subjects were required to perform several different behaviors during the training session, such as, writing out problem-solving responses, comprehending the printed materials, and following the lecture. They also had extraneous information presented to them including the various purposes of a training program, the responsibilities of board members, theories of problem-solving, and so on. In short, the authors misjudged the appropriateness of a traditional university style instructional model for use in this community.

Since the procedure involving the whole board was ineffective, the following week the board chairman alone was trained during the 30 minutes preceding the regular board meeting, using an approach similar to that used with the group.

Training

Individual training on problem-solving behaviors occurred 30 minutes before board meetings. When the training session finished, the board member went to the meeting to incorporate the learned skills into the discussion of the different topics. The subjects' acquisition of problem-solving skills from the training program was measured in the board meetings. Board meetings were otherwise carried out in the normal fashion, i.e., no contingencies were in effect during the meetings and the members followed their own agenda.

The research was initially designed to train two board members on each of the problem-solving skills; that is, two subjects were to be trained to identify the problem, two subjects trained to find solutions, and two subjects to decide on the action to be taken. In order for the group to follow the problem-solving sequence during the meetings, the chairman needed to have a knowledge of all three skills, and thus was to receive training in all three behaviors. However, the chairman was absent from three meetings and to correct for this unanticipated problem, the scheduling of subjects was altered. Thus, seven subjects in all were trained on various aspects of problem solving. The remaining two subjects received no training and served as controls. Individual subjects were aware that others were receiving training but not of the type of training and skills being learned.

The training of an individual board member was graduated from simple to difficult tasks and employed the use of fading, shaping, prompting, and differential social reinforcement of correct responding. Training for each skill began by teaching the member to say the key phrase (e.g., "One solution is . . ."), then apply it to a simple problematic situation shown pictorially on a card, and finally to apply it to more and more complex situations described verbally to the subject. Modeling and role playing were used throughout the 30-minute training session. Training of each of the three skills was carried out in a similar fashion. Table 1 shows the steps for a particular program in detail.

Follow-Up

Follow-up consisted of recording the problem-solving behaviors of the subjects from a minimum of one week up to two months after the training phase for each problem-solving skill had ended, under conditions similar to the baseline phase.

Professional Evaluation

To determine if training in problem solving was discriminable by an outside observer, a composite videotape of one baseline and one post-training meeting was made. The first, middle, and last topic of the last meeting in baseline (meeting 5), and the last meeting following training (meeting 16) were randomly matched in pairs for comparison. Two university professors who taught courses in group problem-solving and two community leaders active in local policy boards were shown the composite tape independently. They were asked to view two topic discussions (one from baseline and one from training) and to judge which showed greater problem-solving ability. The three pairs of topics were judged in this manner.

RESULTS

Reliability

The overall mean reliability on the occurrences of all problem-solving categories for the meetings was 79 percent. Reliability for the individual problem-solving skills were 88 percent for stating the problem, 85 percent for stating the solution, and 63 percent for stating the appropriate action.

Group Data

Baseline and pilot training. Baseline was carried out for five meetings, as shown in Figure 3. No statements involving the problem or solution were made during this time; one action statement was made. Just before meeting 6, the pilot training procedure involving the whole board on "stating the problem" was carried out. As shown in Figure 3, this had

TABLE 1

The Model for the Instructional Program
for the Board Training Sessions

Step I. The trainer introduced the subject to the problem-solving skill that was to be learned. The trainer showed the subject a card with the cue phrase painted on it, e.g., "The problem is . . ."

A. Trainer and subject read the cue phrase together.
B. Subject read the cue phrase alone.
C. After removing the cue card, subject repeated the cue phrase.
D. Trainer reinforced the subject's correct response.

Step II. The subject practiced making statements using the cue phrase. The trainer explained to the subject that the cue phrase was to be used during the board meeting and he (she) should practice it by making statements using the phrase during the training session.

A. Subject was shown a picture of a problematic situation and asked to make a statement describing the picture using the cue phrase (e.g., picture of girl in dentist's chair; dentist is examining her teeth. The subject's statement of the problem was "The problem is something wrong with the little girl's teeth"). Praise was given for correct responses.
B. Subject had problematic situations read to him and made a statement using the cue phrase (e.g., "There is a discussion of the Adult Education class. Fifteen adults are in the reading class. Everyone is to use a book to practice their reading, but there are only seven books. What is the problem?" The subject responded by saying, "The problem is the reading class does not have enough books"). Praise was given for correct responding.

Step III. The subject explained what was to be performed during the board meetings.

A. Subject verbalized the response to be made during the board meeting (e.g., the trainer asked the subject, "What are you going to say during the meeting?" The subject responded by saying, "The problem is . . ."). Praise was given for correct response.
B. Subject responded with a complete sentence telling what he was to perform during the meeting (e.g., trainer asked the subject, "Tell me with a complete sentence what you will say during the meeting." Subject responded by saying, "I will state the problem for each topic during the meeting by saying, the problem is . . ."). Praise was given for correct response.

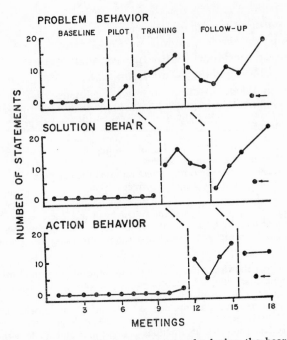

Fig. 3. Number of problem-solving statements made during the board meetings by all nine subjects. In the pilot condition, the training program utilized a lecture and discussion approach. This approach was attempted during one training session with all subjects and the next session with only the chairman. In the training condition, the programmed instructional model was utilized as the training procedure with the chairman and individual subjects. In the follow-up condition, the subjects no longer received training but were observed during the meetings. The arrow at meeting 17 indicates that during this meeting several outsiders and the first two authors attended the meeting and participated extensively. The participation of the subjects appeared to decrease greatly as a result.

almost no effect. Before the seventh meeting, a similar procedure was used with the chairman only. As can be seen, the rate of problem statements rose to five (all made by the chairman).

Training. Before meetings 8 through 11, three board members (including the chairman) were trained to state the problem. As shown in Figure 3, problem statements quickly climbed to 15 in the next four meetings (an average of 12). No increases in solution or action statements were seen. Using similar instructional methods, three board members (including the chairman) were trained to pick out and describe potential solutions to problems that had been stated. This training took place just before each of meetings 10 through 13. Again as shown in Figure 3, solution statements increased from zero to approximately 10 per meeting for the next four meetings; action statements increased slightly during this time. Before meetings 12 through 15, four board members (including the chairman) were trained to decide upon action that should be taken on the solutions to problems that had been stated; action statements jumped immediately to 10 in the first meeting, and over the next four meetings rose to 15.

Follow-up. Once training was completed for a subject, he (she) received no prompting or feedback and they were considered to be in a follow-up phase for the remainder of the experiment. Figure 3 shows a slow decline in problem statements for six meetings following this training and a large jump during the last meeting that data were taken (one month after training had commenced). The number of solution statements made following training also dropped, but a trend toward even higher levels than had been achieved during training was seen by the end of the follow-up period. Action statements remained fairly high in the follow-up phase, an average of about eight per meeting.

Individual Data

The data for individual subjects are shown in Figures 4 and 5. The data are broken down by number of statements in each of the three categories for each subject. Where a subject was given training on one of the skills, vertical dashed lines marked with a capital T show the meetings preceded by training.

Subject 1 (chairman). The chairman's baseline of problem, solution, and action statements was almost zero during baseline. In the meetings following training for each of the skills, his frequency of making the appropriate problem, solution, and action statements immediately increased.

Subject 2. This board member was trained on two skills, problem and action statements. Figure 4 shows that her frequency of making these statements increased immediately after the training. She showed some small increases in solution statements in which she did not receive any training.

Subject 3. This member was trained only on the problem statements and, as shown in Figure 4, training resulted in large increases from her zero rate of problem statements. Her performance fell when training was completed and in the follow-up she showed some small gains in solution and action statements.

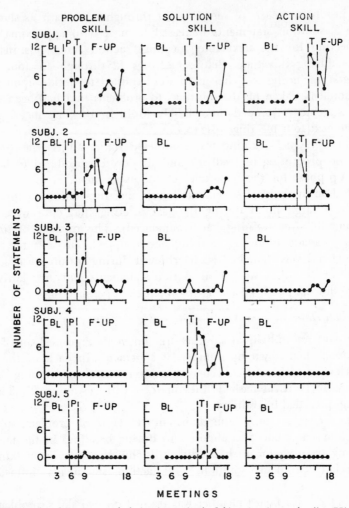

Fig. 4. The number of statements made during the meeting by Subjects 1 to 5 across baseline (BL), pilot (P), training (T), and follow-up (F-up).

Subject 4. This member was trained only on the solution skill and, as shown in Figure 4, his rate of solution statements increased only after the training; his rate did not maintain throughout the follow-up period.

Subject 5. This member was also trained to find solutions to problems and showed a small increase in such statements during and shortly after training. Her rate also fell to zero during the subsequent follow-up phase.

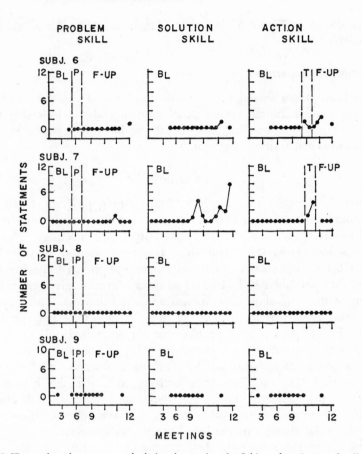

Fig. 5. The number of statements made during the meetings by Subjects 6 to 9 across baseline (B$_L$), pilot (P), training (T), and follow-up (F-up).

Subject 6. Training on action statements was given to this subject and he showed a small increase in such statements. This repertoire held up for three meetings in the follow-up but did not maintain.

Subject 7. Although given no training on solution statements, this subject showed a high frequency of such statements when Subjects 1, 4, and 5 received their training. Her rate was lower for three meetings and then again rose to a high level at the end of follow-up. This member was trained on action statements and showed an increase during training, but the repertoire did not maintain.

Subjects 8 and 9. These subjects were not trained on any of the skills and, as shown in Figure 5, their rates remained at zero for all skills for all sessions.

Professional Evaluation

The four judges agreed unanimously that two of the three segments that they viewed showed greater problem-solving ability following training as compared to baseline; they rated one baseline segment as better than its matched training segment.

DISCUSSION

These data suggest that the individual training program, based on a behavioral model, was effective in teaching low-income individuals problem-solving skills usable in community board meetings. The multiple-baseline across skills and subjects design showed that problem-solving behavior occurred (with only three exceptions) following training on that particular skill; control subjects who were given no training on any of the skills showed no increases in the behaviors. Three subjects (2, 3, and 7) showed some increases in skills they were not specifically trained in, and this poses a problem for the analysis. In all cases, these increases in responding were correlated with increases shown by other subjects being trained on the skill. Informal observation of the tapes suggests that these subjects were actively imitating the behavior of trained board members (e.g., using the same phrases to talk about a problem). It would be impossible to eliminate such effects without making substantial changes in the board meetings themselves.

This study represents our first attempt to modify complex group problem-solving in a natural unstructured setting. The particular skills taught may appear unimportant or trivial; however, as described in the introduction, a thorough review of relevant research revealed no programs, with an ongoing evaluation component, that approximate the setting and behavior dealt with here. Thus, although the research design was not complicated, the methodological contribution is unique.

"Real world" problem-solving does not always consist of the three simple steps of stating the problem, finding solutions, and deciding on action to be taken. Other authors consider more steps to be involved. Perlman and Gurin (1972) for example, argued that problem-solving consists of: 1) defining the problem, 2) building a structure, 3) examining alternatives, 4) taking action, and 5) evaluating outcomes. They presented no data showing how one teaches these skills and did not suggest how one could evaluate their use. Theirs is a theoretical model for social problem-solving; the present study presents an experimental approach to the same problem.

The present experiment has much in common with a recent analysis of conflict-resolution behavior between adolescents and their parents (Kifer et al., 1974). In that study, the components of successful conflict resolution were determined and then taught in individual role-playing situations to parent-child pairs. A multiple-baseline design across subjects showed that training generated negotiation skills. Data taken in the subjects' homes revealed good generalization to actual conflicts. Thus, while completely different subject populations were dealt with, and considerably different target behaviors taught, the findings were similar to those of the present study.

The present research represents the formative stages in the development of a new field of application, namely behavioral community psychology. The present results are tentative in several respects. First, although the training program was effective in teaching the skill, those skills were not maintained at high levels in all subjects.

This was due, in part, to subjects' drifting away from the particular terms learned in training toward words and phrases with which they were more comfortable. Nonetheless, the maintenance of problem-solving skills over time may present major problems A preliminary analysis suggests several alternatives: 1) the actual behaviors taught could be different, i.e., perhaps the behaviors taught did not maintain because they were not followed immediately by natural reinforcers; 2) the training itself needs to be more intensive, i.e., training in the present study took place in half-hour sessions on two separate days. Perhaps 5 or 6 hours of training over a two-day period would be more effective; 3) monitoring during the meetings and extrinsic reinforcers could be provided for those using problem-solving skills during the meeting. This last proposal is based on the notion that problem-solving behavior is too far removed in time for the natural consequences to maintain by itself, at least at first.

The results are tentative in another respect. No information is available on whether the board more successfully accomplished its objectives as a result of the training. A preliminary and informal assessment of this area suggests that measurement will be difficult. The board has many goals and objectives, some short- and others long-range (e.g., having a window repaired in the center *versus* obtaining a grant for a farm cooperative), some involve an observable product (e.g., was a piece of equipment actually purchased, or was an item repaired, etc.), while others are more "process" oriented (e.g., a person is to be contacted, a meeting held, or a form sent in) where the actual product of the behavior may be far removed in time. In addition, the specified action can be carried out but the result may still be negative (e.g., the visiting nurse is contacted about a visit but does not show up). In short, there are many complexities involved in assessing the long-range result of training in problem-solving. Research is underway to address this issue.

A behavioral approach to community psychology may represent a useful departure from the traditional mental health orientation of that field. In this poor, black community, for example, some very real behavioral problems exist, such as failure of members to participate in preventive health care programs, or adult education programs. Other problems involve high unemployment and school drop-out rates, and failure to receive the dental, medical, and social services to which they are entitled. We anticipate that applied behavior analysis will provide new and successful remedies to these longstanding community problems.

REFERENCES

BURGESS, R., CLARK, R., & HENDEE, J. An experimental analysis of anti-litter procedures. *J. Appl. Behav. Anal.*, 1971, 4, 71-75.

CHAPMAN, C. & RISLEY, T. R. Anti-litter procedures in an urban high-density area. *J. Appl. Behav. Anal.*, 1974, 7, 377-383.

CLARK, R. N., BURGESS, R. L., & HENDEE, J. C. The development of anti-litter behavior in a forest campground. *J. Appl. Behavior Analysis*, 1972, 5, 1-5.

EVERETT, P. B., HAYWARD, S. C., & MEYERS, A. W. The effects of a token reinforcement procedure on bus ridership. *J. Appl. Behav. Anal.*, 1974, 7, 1-9.

FIXSEN, D. L., PHILLIPS, E. L., & WOLF, M. Achievement Place: Experiments in self government with pre-delinquents. *J. Appl. Behav. Anal.*, 1973, 6, 31-47.

GELLER, E. S., FARRIS, J. C., & POST, D. S. Prompting a consumer behavior for pollution control. *J. Appl. Behav. Anal.*, 1973, 6, 367-376.

HOFFMAN, D. Final Report, *An Analysis of Parent Involvement in Daycare and Early Childhood Education in the United States, 1970*. Child Development/Daycare Workshop and Office of Child Development, October, 1970.

HOFFMAN, D. B., JORDAN, J. S., & MCCORMICK, F. *Parent Participation in Preschool Daycare*. Monograph No. 5, Atlanta, Georgia: Southeastern Educational Laboratory, 1971.

HOFFMAN, D. A study of parent roles in daycare programs for five types of sponsorship. *Child Care Quart.*, 1974.

KIFER, R. E., LEWIS, M. A., GREEN, D. R., & PHILLIPS, E. L. Training predelinquent youths and their parents to negotiate conflict situations. *J. Appl. Behav. Anal.*, 1974, 7, 357-364.

KOHLENBERG, R. & PHILLIPS, T. Reinforcement and rate of litter depositing. *J. Appl. Behav. Anal.*, 1973, 6, 391-396.

MARSHALL, D. B. *The Politics of Participation in Poverty: A Case Study of the Board of Economic and Youth Opportunities Agency of Greater Los Angeles.* Berkeley: University of California Press, 1971.

MILLER, L. K. & MILLER, O. Reinforcing self-help group activities of welfare recipients. *J. Appl. Behav. Anal.,* 1970, 3, 57-64.

PERLMAN, R. & GURIN, A. *Community Organization and Social Planning.* New York: John Wiley and Sons, Inc., 1972.

POWERS, R. B., OSBORNE, J. G., & ANDERSON, E. G. Positive reinforcement of litter removal in the natural environment. *J. Appl. Behav. Anal.,* 1973, 6, 559-586.

PIERCE, C. H. & RISLEY, T. R. Recreation as a reinforcer: Increasing membership and decreasing disruptions in an urban recreation center. *J. Appl. Behav. Anal.,* 1974, 7, 403-411.

ULLMANN, L. P. & KRASNER, L. (Eds.). *Case Studies in Behavior Modification.* New York: Holt, Rinehart and Winston, 1965.

31

PROCESS EVALUATION OF OUT-PATIENT TREATMENT IN A COMMUNITY MENTAL HEALTH CENTER

R. C. Rinn and J. C. Vernon

*Huntsville-Madison County Mental Health Center,
Huntsville, Alabama*

Summary—A system for evaluating treatment process at a behaviorally-oriented community mental health center is described. Three separate evaluation procedures were employed. First, ongoing inservice training programs were evaluated routinely to establish and maintain therapists' cognitive-verbal skills in behavior therapy. Second, therapists were supervised by audiotaping or the co-therapist approach in order to assess their treatment skills, *in vivo*. Finally, a system was devised which measured whether or not behavioral techniques were administered consistently as determined by recordkeeping competencies (such as specifying goals in behavioral terms, maintaining data, graphing, etc.). Basing salary increments upon recordkeeping skills markedly improved performance. As interest in outcome evaluation has risen (e.g., Eysenck, 1952, 1966; Baer, Wolf &

Reprinted with permission from the *Journal of Behaviour Therapy and Experimental Psychiatry*, Vol. 6, 5-11, 1975.

Risley, 1968; Bergin, 1971; Fox & Rappaport, 1972) the necessity for process evaluation has become apparent.

The Huntsville-Madison County Mental Health Center employs behavior therapy as its primary intervention technique (Rinn, Tapp, & Petrella, 1973). Among other assets, the behavioral approach facilitates both process and outcome evaluation due to the emphasis in behavior therapy on identifiable techniques for measurable problems. The following sections describe the general outline of therapeutic transactions in the Outpatient Service of the Center and then present the Center's method of process evaluation.

AN OUTLINE OF THERAPEUTIC INTERVENTIONS

After a client has been screened for admission into treatment by the Intake Service, an initial therapy visit is scheduled. This session is the most important since the "ground rules" and behavioral limits of the intervention are established. The therapist presents the client with a short contract (Figure 1) which states the client's general responsibilities during treatment (e.g., "keep records of behavior," "allow a Mental Health Center representative to contact me in the future, by mail or by phone, for follow-up") and the therapist's responsibilities (e.g., "respect confidentiality of the client's communication," "assist the client in defining the problem as specifically as possible, so that measurement of effectiveness can be achieved"). After each item in the contract is explained and discussed, client and therapist sign the document. The original is placed in the client's file and a copy is given to the client. If he refuses to sign, the contract (with the reason for refusal noted on the back) is placed in the client's file.

The next step during this session is identifying the problem behavior(s). The therapist assists the client in pinpointing behavioral excesses and/or deficits. The client is instructed in behavioral measurement and is presented with the Baserate Data Sheet (Figure 2). This form helps the client compile information about the pinpointed behaviors, such as frequency, antecedent and consequent events, time of day, and date. The client's assignment is to record baserates on one, two, or three behaviors (depending upon the number of problematic behaviors*) and present the data to the therapist during the second session.

---

* No more than three problematic behaviors are treated at one time. Additional behaviors are treated when goals for the initial three behaviors are reached or abandoned.

CONTRACT BETWEEN CLIENT AND THERAPIST

Outpatient Service

Huntsville-Madison County Mental Health Center

1. The client (and/or family) agrees:
   (a) to keep scheduled appointments unless illness or emergency prohibits.
   (b) to inform the therapist if unable to keep appointment.
   (c) to pay fees according to the Mental Health Center's fee scale.
   (d) to communicate openly and honestly with the therapist.
   (e) to keep records of behavior as requested by the therapist.
   (f) to allow data accumulated during the therapy to be used for research pur-
       poses, with protection of confidentiality assured.
   (g) to allow a Mental Health Center representative to contact me in the future,
       by mail or by phone, for follow up.

2. The therapist agrees:
   (a) to keep appointments as scheduled unless illness or emergency prohibits.
   (b) to inform the client if appointment has been cancelled.
   (c) to use the techniques of therapy which offer the best chance of an effective and
       efficient resolution of the problem.
   (d) to respect confidentiality of the client's communication and to divulge infor-
       mation to other parties only with the client's consent. (Unless an emergency
       dictates that the therapist use his or her judgment in doing so when there is a
       need to know by other parties.)
   (e) to assist the client in defining the problem as specifically as possible, so that
       measurement of effectiveness can be achieved.

_____   _____
        Therapist   Client

                    _____
                             Date

                    FIG. 1. Client-therapist contract.

BASERATE DATA SHEET

Outpatient Service

Huntsville-Madison County Mental Health Center

Name

Behavior to be counted

Sampling interval

Therapy session No.

Date	Hour	Number of times occurred	Antecedent and consequent events

FIG. 2. Baserate data sheet.

The second session begins with the client presenting the baserate data to the therapist. If no data are forthcoming, the client is again instructed in measurement and invited to return with the data at a later date (usually 1 week). If he has maintained records of the pinpointed behaviors, quantified goals are set by him and his therapist, founded upon the baserates, and entered by the therapist on the Goal Setting Form (Figure 3). Also, the data are transferred from the Baserate Data Sheet to the Multiple Baseline Data Graph (Figure 4). The use of a multiple baseline technique to demonstrate functional control of behavior is well known (e.g., Baer, Wolf & Risley, 1968). Essentially, the client consistently gathers data on two or more behaviors while each individual behavior is altered in sequence rather than simultaneously.*

During the second session, the therapist presents his plans for altering the pinpointed behavior (see Figure 3) and explains them to the client. An intervention is begun on a single mutually-agreed upon problem behavior. The therapist gives the client an intervention assignment and reminds him to continue collecting data on the same behaviors as before.

Subsequent sessions involve continued data collection, graphing, intervention, and evaluation of goal attainment. The therapist dictates the proceedings of each session and places them in the client's file. After treatment has been terminated, the therapist dictates a note concerning his overall impression of treatment and any ideas he may have concerning innovations, observations, etc.

Two procedures of ancillary interest are: 1) communications with the referring professional (if any) and 2) diagnosis of the client's problem. It is the practice of the Center to notify, in writing, the referring professional before treatment begins (immediately after the first session) and after treatment has ended. For easier communication, two form letters (Figures 5 and 6) have been developed in order to inform the referral source about goals, plans, and progress of the client. Although labeling of clients with diagnostic jargon is particularly noxious to most behavior therapists, it is required at the Center because of state regulations. Therefore, a diagnosis is given during the initial session and recorded on the Goal Setting Form (Figure 3). The following sections will describe the process evaluation in use at the Center.

---

* If only one behavior is to be altered, a multiple baserate is not possible, of course.

GOAL SETTING FORM
Outpatient Service
Huntsville-Madison County Mental Health Center

Goals	Duration of problem behavior	Plans type of therapy	%Success termination
1.			
2.			
9.			
10.			

Note: Goals are set as to importance—most important first, etc.

Diagnosis_____

DSM-II No. _____

Name_____ Date_____

FIG. 3. Goal setting form.

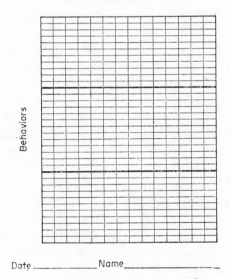

FIG. 4. Multiple baseline data graph.

Dear_____:

    This report concerns_____who was
referred by you for evaluation and was seen by me on_____

    A. *Goals*   B. *Plans*
        1.   1.
        2.   2.
        3.   3.
        4.   4.

    C. *Treatment mode*
        ☐ Inpatient   ☐ Day treatment
        ☐ Outpatient   ☐ Positive parents training
        ☐ Other

    D. Diagnostic impressions:
    If you require further information concerning this client, please contact my office. Thank
you for this referral.

                                  Sincerely,

                                  Roger C. Rinn, Ph.D.
                                  Coordinator
                                  Consultation and Education Service
RCR:mej

FIG. 5. The form letter to the referring professional, completed and mailed immediately following
the first therapy session.

Dear_____:

    This report concerns_____who was
referred by you for evaluation and treatment and who has now been terminated as a client of the
Center.

    A. *Goals*   B. *Progress*
        1.   1.
        2.   2.
        3.   3.
        4.   4.

    C. *Treatment mode*
        ☐ Inpatient   ☐ Day treatment
        ☐ Outpatient   ☐ Positive parents training
        ☐ Other

    D. *Condition at termination*
        ☐ Much improved   ☐ Not improved
        ☐ Moderately improved

    If you require further information concerning this client, please contact my office.

                                  Sincerely,

                                  Roger C. Rinn, Ph.D.
                                  Coordinator
                                  Consultation and Education Service

RCR:mej

FIG. 6. The form letter to the referring professional, completed and mailed immediately following
the last therapy session.

PROCESS EVALUATION

Inservice Training

The Training Service of the Center provides an ongoing educational program for therapists which is routinely evaluated by objectively scored pre- and post-tests. For example, if the topic of training is systematic desensitization, multiple choice and/or true-false questions are administered, before and after training, in order to test the therapist's ability to conduct 1) progressive relaxation, 2) fear hierarchy construction, and 3) desensitization. Treatment procedures are reduced to simple components and therapists are examined for their competence (at least, verbal competence) in each.

Another evaluation procedure is presenting a contrived case study to therapists, before and after training. The therapist is required to show, step-by-step, how he/she would conduct treatment including pinpointing, measuring, intervening, trouble-shooting, etc. Again, the responses are objectively scored. In both these approaches, the ability (or inability) of the therapist to "write" or "verbalize" his/her expertise in behavior therapy is demonstrated. The next section will mention the method used to indicate a therapist's ability to apply the techniques *in vivo*.

Therapy Supervision

A most important aspect of process evaluation is measurement of the therapist's actual abilities "on the job." In order to observe the therapist *in vivo,* the Coordinator of the Service monthly monitors his performance by acting as a co-therapist or by listening to an audio tape of a therapy session. To date, this evaluation approach has not been quantified. However, an evaluation scheme is being developed in which the Coordinator will 1) pinpoint the therapist's behaviors to be altered, 2) measure the frequency of such behaviors, 3) develop a program to alter the therapist's behaviors, and 4) provide the therapist with behavioral feedback. In the future, video cameras will be mounted permanently in each therapist's office and will provide data more comprehensive than audio recordings about his skills without the reactive components present in co-therapy. As in all procedures involving recording, clients are informed about them, and the Center obtains written permission from the client before making any recording. The two aforementioned approaches to process evaluation test the ability of the therapist to 1) conceptualize behavior therapy and 2) perform the treatment in the presence of a supervisor. The following approach has been developed to indicate, at least partially, whether or not the therapist applies behavior therapy to cases when not being supervised directly.

Record-Keeping Assessment

In order to determine the consistency (or lack thereof) with which a therapist administers behavioral techniques, the Therapist Evaluation Data Sheet (TEDS) was developed (Figure 7). The underlying assumption for employing the form is that a therapist who sets behavioral goals, collects behavioral data, etc., also employs behavior therapy. This assumption is warranted, it seems, since the staff training and therapy supervision at the Center are both behaviorally oriented. The TEDS specifically monitors the therapist's record-keeping. The forms described in the preceding section on therapeutic interventions are used to monitor various aspects of treatment regimen. The TEDS measures, indirectly, eight specific aspects of treatment. It determines whether the therapist has: 1) enacted the client-therapist contract (Figure 1), 2) set behavioral goals and made plans based upon behavioral techniques (Figure 3) 3) maintained a multiple baseline data graph (Figure 4), 4) dictated an initial therapy note concerning the therapist's clinical impression of the client and a diagnosis (in compliance with state regulations), 5) described each therapy session, including the presence or absence of client data, 6) informed the referring professional concerning the client's goals and plans before therapy (Figure 5), 7) informed the referring professional concerning the client's progress after therapy (Figure 6), and 8) entered a termination note including innovations, problems in treatment, etc. The first six steps earn the therapist 5, 5, 5, 5, 10, and 4 points per client, respectively. If either of the last two steps is not completed, 3 and 5 points, respectively, are subtracted from the therapist's total score for the particular client.

In practice, each therapist is evaluated monthly on five client files, drawn randomly from his/her case load. The therapist can earn from zero to 34 points per file. A mean score for all five files is computed.

Of additional interest is the fact that therapists' annual salary increments are determined, in part, by their TEDS scores. In order to show the effectiveness of basing salary increments upon TEDS scores, the monthly medians on the TEDS are shown in Figure 8. As the chart suggests, the salary-contingent condition resulted in a marked increment in the median scores on the TEDS.

There are several additional sources of data available for process

THERAPIST EVALUATION DATA SHEET
Outpatient Service
Huntsville-Madison County Mental Health Center

Name of therapist _____   Month _____

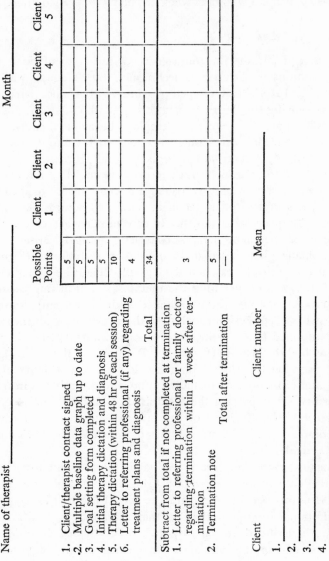

	Possible Points	Client 1	Client 2	Client 3	Client 4	Client 5
1. Client/therapist contract signed	5					
2. Multiple baseline data graph up to date	5					
3. Goal setting form completed	5					
4. Initial therapy dictation and diagnosis	5					
5. Therapy dictation (within 48 hr of each session)	10					
6. Letter to referring professional (if any) regarding treatment plans and diagnosis	4					
Total	34					
Subtract from total if not completed at termination						
1. Letter to referring professional or family doctor regarding termination within 1 week after termination	3					
2. Termination note	5					
Total after termination	—					

Client number _____   Mean _____

Client

1. _____
2. _____
3. _____
4. _____
5. _____

FIG. 7. Therapist evaluation data sheet.

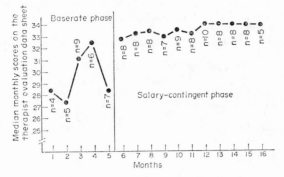

FIG. 8. The effects of a salary-contingent program upon
TEDS scores.

evaluation. For example, the Service purportedly is oriented toward short term intervention. Thus, the average number of treatment sessions indicates whether or not, overall, the Service provides short-term treatment. Also, the Service is vitally interested in the quality of its referrals to other agencies. In order to establish the appropriateness and effectiveness of referrals, all referrals to other agencies are followed-up routinely. Finally, demographic data on all clients are collected and analyzed in order to determine which sectors of the community utilize the outpatient facilities of the Center.

CONCLUSION

This paper has outlined the system employed for the evaluation of treatment process at the Huntsville-Madison County Mental Health Center. Although the approach is not complete, it is a step toward comprehensive process evaluation. Outcome measures generally are not useful for further planning *unless* the intervention technique is quantifiable and its consistent application insured. Thus, the inclusion of process evaluation is mandatory for interpretation of outcome data. As studies concerning the efficacy of psychotherapy approximate more closely the experimental model by carefully specifying both dependent and independent variables, their value and numbers will increase.

REFERENCES

BAER, D. M., WOLF, M. M., & RISLEY, T. R. Some current dimensions of applied behavioral analysis. *J. Appl. Behav. Anal.,* 1968, 1, 91-97.

BERGIN, A. E. The evaluation of therapeutic outcome. In A. E. Bergin and L. Garfield (Eds.), *Handbook of Psychotherapy and Behavior Change: An Empirical Analysis.* New York: Wiley, 1971.

EYSENCK, H. J. The effects of psychotherapy: An evaluation. *J. Consult. Psychol.,* 1952, 16, 319-324.

EYSENCK, H. J. *The Effects of Psychotherapy.* New York: International Science Press, 1966.

FOX, P. D. & RAPPAPORT, M. Some approaches to evaluating community mental health services. *Arch. Gen. Psychiat.,* 1972, 26, 172-178.

RINN, R. C., TAPP, L., & PETRELLA, R. Behavior modification with outpatients in a community mental health center. *J. Behav. Ther. & Exp. Psychiat.,* 1973, 4, 243-247.

Section IX

BEHAVIOR THERAPY AND ITS RIVALS

Commentary

Ever since Eysenck's (1952) classic paper in which he argued that there was no scientifically acceptable evidence that psychotherapy was effective, the issue of therapeutic outcome has been the continuing subject of heated—and often bitter—controversy. A great deal has been written on this topic, ranging from irrational, ad hominem denunciations of Eysenck's position to equally vigorous reaffirmations of his thesis (e.g., Eysenck, 1961; Rachman, 1971; Rosenzweig, 1954; Strupp, 1964). In the introduction to his own balanced and comprehensive evaluation of therapeutic outcome, Bergin (1971) notes that "It is slightly amazing to find that 18 years after his original critique of therapeutic effects, Professor Hans Eysenck is still agreed and disagreed with more than any single critic on the psychotherapy scene" (p. 217). Bergin attributes the subjective and emotional nature of this debate to two main reasons: a) the fact that the efficacy of traditional psychotherapy is an absolutely vital question; and b) the ambiguity of the evidence that bears on the question.

A consuming aspect of the debate has concerned the methodological adequacy of the different outcome studies. Among the issues that have been contested are the very definition of psychotherapy itself; the nature of psychotherapeutic change and how best to measure it; and the comparability of various control groups. In view of the enormously complex issues involved in evaluating therapeutic outcome, it is not surprising that acrimonious discussion and not well-controlled comparative outcome studies have been the order of the day. The methodological requirements for the controlled investigation of psychotherapy outcome have been spelled out (e.g., Paul, 1969a), but few attempts have been made to incorporate these prescriptions in studies of the general patient population. It is in this context that the careful comparison of behavior therapy with short-term analytically oriented psychotherapy by Sloane, Staples, Cristol, Yorkston, and Whipple is so refreshingly impressive. The paper reprinted in this Section is the first publication in journal form of the results of their study that is more fully reported in the book *Psychotherapy versus Behavior Therapy* (Sloane et al., 1975).

In his Foreword to the book, Wolpe passes the following verdict: "In the perceptiveness of its planning, the variety and vigor of its comparisons, and the care of its execution, it is unmatched by any other clinical study in the history of psychotherapy" (p. xix). Well may one inquire into the distinguishing characteristics of this study that drew such plaudits from an erstwhile critic of psychotherapy outcome research. The following are the methodological highlights: 1. The therapists were experienced practitioners of the respective treatments. The use of inexperienced therapists (often graduate students in training) who are not representative of more common clinical situations in behavior therapy outcome studies (usually analogue research) has frequently drawn criticism (e.g., Bernstein & Paul, 1971; Wolpe & Lazarus, 1966). Although it cannot be known how representative the six therapists Sloane et al. used were of therapists as a whole, the participation of Wolpe and Lazarus as two of the three behavior therapists would seem particularly appropriate given the fact that they pioneered the clinical practice of behavior therapy, wrote the first practical therapeutic guide (Wolpe & Lazarus, 1966), and have, each in his own way, continued to exercise a profound influence on the field. 2. A large number of motivated patients from the general patient population rather than recruited volunteers served as subjects. 3. Patients were randomly assigned to groups. 4. The inclusion of a no-treatment control group that underwent all assessment procedures and the promise of treatment provided a base-rate of improvement against which treatment-produced change could be assessed. 5. The length of treatment (four months) was sufficient to presume that reasonable improvement could be effected. 6. The dependent measures consisted of multiple criteria including *specific* target behaviors ("symptoms") and independent assessment ratings by objective judges. 7. Process measures sampled during treatment provided an independent check on the adequacy of the independent variable manipulated, i.e., psychotherapy that was discriminably different from behavior therapy. 8.

Long-term follow-ups—the greatest inadequacy of the behavioral literature—of one and two years were conducted (eight and 16 months respectively if measured from posttreatment). 9. Virtually no subject attrition occurred over the course of the study, thereby avoiding complicated interpretive problems.

Unquestionably, this is the best study of its kind that has ever been conducted. If there is any weakness, it is in the omission of actual behavioral measures of improvement in the target "symptoms." The practical difficulties entailed in such measurement are legion, and in some instances simply not feasible. Nonetheless, a conservative appraisal of the results of this study would have to consider Bandura's (1969) caution that "one would expect diminishing correspondence between actual behavior and subjective ratings as one moves from objective measures of clients' behavior to their own self-assessments, from clients' verbal reports of performance changes to therapists' judgments of improvement, (to) therapists' inferences based on clients' self-reports . . ." (p. 458). To Sloane et al.'s credit it must be pointed out that the ratings of blind, independent assessors of specific dimensions of behavior are the most rigorous means of measurement in lieu of actual behavioral measurement. Moreover, in addition to the clients', the therapists', and the assessors' ratings, those of informants were included. ("Informants" were close friends or relatives of the patients.) Unlike the assessors and the therapists whose ratings were judgments of clients' self-reports, the informants presumably based their ratings on firsthand observation of clients' functioning in the natural environment.

Taken in their entirety, the results indicate that behavior therapy and psychotherapy were about equally effective. However, without being unduly partisan, we can point to behavior therapy's having had a consistently superior edge. On all three major dependent measures behavior therapy was either equal or superior to psychotherapy at posttreatment. In terms of target behaviors, approximately 50 percent of the waiting list patients, and 80 percent of the behavior therapy and psychotherapy patients were considered improved or recovered. Patients treated by behavior therapy showed significant improvement in both work and social adjustment, whereas the psychotherapy patients showed only marginal improvement in work and no change in social adjustment. Finally, behavior therapy was significantly superior to both psychotherapy and the control group on the global rating of improvement. The global ratings were, as Sloane et al. note, "a very subjective measure." Yet it is interesting that behavior therapy showed more prominently. If anything, one would have expected behavior therapy to have produced differences on specific target behaviors, not global measures.

At the one-year follow-up there was no overall difference among the three groups on any of the dependent measures. However, when differences between treatments were tested by individual t-tests, behavior therapy showed significantly greater improvement on target behaviors than the control group. There was no difference between psychotherapy and the control group. Sloane et al. properly point out that differing amounts of treatment were given the three groups after the four-month treatment phase, and that this makes it difficult to attribute differences observed at one year to the respective treatments. However, a closer look at who received what treatment following the four-month therapy period is revealing.

Fifteen of the patients in the behavior therapy group subsequently received more treatment. However, only three of these patients saw new therapists, who were psychoanalytically-oriented and hence complicated analysis of the outcome for these three patients at the one-year follow-up. Nine patients in the psychotherapy group subsequently received additional treatment. These latter patients received substantially more treatment (a mean of 19.3 sessions) than the 15 patients who had originally received behavior therapy (a mean of 10.1 sessions). What this means is that except for three patients in the behavior therapy condition, the extra treatment subjects in both the behavior therapy and psychotherapy conditions received after the four months period was consistent with their original group assessment. It is unlikely that these three patients significantly affected the overall performance of the large behavior therapy group.

More importantly, Sloane et al. do not emphasize that the one-year superiority of behavior therapy over the control group takes into account the fact that 19 of the former waiting list control patients received psychotherapy between the four- and 12-month evaluations. Moreover, the amount of treatment these patients received was substantial. Nine subjects had between 11-25 sessions, six more than 26 sessions of psychotherapy. In other words, the comparison between behavior therapy and the original waiting list control group at the one-year follow-up really could be interpreted as a comparison between behavior therapy and psychotherapy. (Of course, this comparison is confounded by the presumably different levels of experience between the therapists in the study and the psychiatric residents who conducted most of the therapy given after four months.)

A finding that will come as no surprise to most behavior therapists is that questionnaire measures of personality trait characteristics did not predict which patients respond better to which sort of treatment. What may be surprising was the agreement among the different raters of the psychotherapy and waiting list patients as opposed to the variability among the raters of the behavior therapy patients. The latter was due to the disconcerting fact that behavior therapists rated their patients as showing greater improvement than did the assessors, patients, or informants. Summing the ratings for work, social, and sexual improvement for each patient, Sloane et al. examined the intercorrelations among the different raters. Correlations of all therapists' ratings with those of assessors, patients, and informants were .13, .21, and —.04, respectively. These figures show little relationship, and underscore the limitations involved in relying on therapists' judgments of their patients' progress. Assessors' ratings correlated highly with those of the patients themselves $(r = .65, p < .001)$, and, to a lesser degree, with those of the informants $(r = .40, p < .01)$. The agreement between patients' and informants' ratings was not significant $(r = .25)$. We have previously alluded to the difficulties involved in obtaining valid corroborative reports of specific behavior patterns from close associates of patients (see Section V). Sloane et al. (1975) elaborate on the limitations imposed on their informants' ratings. For example, the mother of a male patient might not have adequate knowledge of his sex life. In such a case the informant did not complete a rating on this subject. They note that this sort of restriction, plus the failure of several informants to return for the four-month post-treatment structured interview, "severely limited the number of patients for whom complete ratings were available" (p. 109). In commenting upon these relatively low correlations, Sloane et al. (1975) observe that they "support the hypothesis that different raters may have different goals for treatment or use different criteria for improvement. Even though the average degree of improvement for a group may be similar for two raters, the low intercorrelations indicate that a patient considered improved by one rater may not be the same patient considered improved by the second rater. This further underscores the hazard of interpreting similar group means as reflecting similar perception of individuals" (p. 112). These low correlations, particularly the lack of a significant relationship between informants' and patients' ratings, highlight the relevance of Bandura's cautionary comments on basing estimates of therapeutic outcome on the judgments of therapists (or even blind assessors) of patients' self-reports. Objective behavioral measures are necessary to establish the reliability and validity of these ratings.

The results help shatter several erroneous stereotypes that are still held about behavior therapy. There was absolutely no evidence of symptom substitution. Sloane et al. (1975) state that "there was not a single patient in any group whose original problems had substantially improved but who reported new symptoms cropping up. On the contrary, assessors had the informal impression that when a patient's primary symptoms improved, he often spontaneously reported improvement of other minor difficulties" (p. 100). This reaffirms what previous behavioral studies have repeatedly shown.

While the overwhelming weight of experimental evidence and a more accurate understanding of the social learning conceptualization of behavior therapy have diminished objections about the alleged danger of symptom substitution, the notion that behavior therapy is suitable for circumscribed, monosymptomatic phobias but not for more complex psychiatric disorders, persists. The finding that behavior therapy was as effective as psychotherapy, if not more so, with a wide range of moderately severe neurotic and personality disorders drawn from the general patient population, directly contradicts this illusion. Indeed, behavior therapy proved to be more effective with a broader range of patients than psychotherapy. On the basis of MMPI scores of patient characteristics, psychotherapy was more effective with patients who initially scored low on the scales. In addition, psychotherapy was relatively ineffective with patients who scored high on the Hysteria and Psychopathic Deviate scales that are generally interpreted to reflect antisocial, acting out behavior. In contrast, behavior therapy was equally effective whether patients had high or low scores. Moreover, behavior therapy patients with high initial scores on the Hysteria and Mania scales improved more than those with low initial scores. Overall, behavior therapy produced more improvement than psychotherapy in the treatment of patients characterized by high initial scores on the Hysteria, Psychopathic Deviate, and Mania scales, although the only statistically significant difference was in the case of Hysteria.

The indications that behavior therapy was more effective than psychotherapy with the more severely disturbed patients are noteworthy. Two of the patient selection criteria in the study involved excluding patients who were a) extremely disturbed, and b) whom the assessor under normal circumstances would have accepted or referred for psychotherapy. Although speculative, it may be that behavior therapy would have been relatively more effective had certain types of problems been included in the patient sample, e.g., alcoholism and sexual deviation. Wolpe may well be correct in likening these results to those obtained in analogue research with systematic dsesnsitization in which mild but not high intensity fears can be modified by the demand characteristics of the situation (see Section II). In generalizing the results of this study to other settings, the distinctive nature of Sloane et al.'s patients must be borne in mind. Well-educated, young, predominantly white, and not too severely disturbed, these patients typified the YAVIS patient-type (cf. Goldstein, 1971). As several studies have shown, these patients tend to have a more favorable prognosis than their non-YAVIS counterparts regardless of the sort of treatment they receive.

Critics of behavior therapy frequently allege that it might modify specific symptoms but fail to affect "more important" processes related to general adjustment (e.g., Luborsky et al., 1975). The Sloane et al. data effectively reinforce previous clinical and experimental research in discrediting this widely held misinterpretation. The patients treated by behavior therapy showed significant improvement on general adjustment measures such as work, social, and sexual adjustment. In fact, behavior therapy tended to be more effective than psychotherapy on these measures which, if the critics were correct, should have favored psychotherapy. As Sloane et al. (1975) concluded, "Behavior therapy is clearly a *generally* useful treatment" (p. 224).

Finally, the results should help dispel the unfortunate public and professional image of behavior therapists necessarily being mechanistic and impersonal. This important issue is considered in detail in the Wilson and Evans paper in Section X of the present volume. Suffice it to note here that process measures of therapy indicated that the three behavior therapists showed higher levels of accurate empathy, interpersonal contact, and therapist self-congruence than the three psychotherapists. However, in contrast to the predictions from client-centered therapy, none of these process measures were differentially related to therapeutic outcome.

Any explanation of the apparently equal efficacy of behavior therapy and psychotherapy in this study must take into account the fact that process measures clearly established that two distinctive forms of treatment, eminently consistent with their theoretical rationales, were provided (cf. Staples, Sloane, Whipple, Cristol, & Yorkston, 1975). In addition to the differences summarized in Appendix 1 of the article reprinted in this Section, the behavior therapists were more directive, more active,

and more personally involved with their patients. Although both groups
of therapists made virtually the same number of interpretive statements,
the quality of the interpretations differed, the one focusing psychoanalytically on feelings, the other on behavior.

Despite these differences, Staples et al. (1975) suggest that the similarities were more important—that "fundamentally they may have been
saying the same thing" (p. 1522). Marmor, in his Foreword to the Sloane
et al. (1975) book, similarly suggests that basic ingredients common to
both treatments were responsible for comparable therapeutic outcome.
Some idea of what these common elements may have been is provided
by a retrospective questionnaire answered by successful patients one to
two years after completing therapy. Encouragement, advice, reassurance,
the therapists' understanding and acceptance, and the prompting of
patients to face their difficulties were all emphasized. Staples et al.
(1975) properly caution that while patients may know what they like,
they are not necessarily accurate judges of what factors were responsible
for their improvement. Also, as Wilson and Evans (in press) point out,
correlation must not be confused with causation. A therapist who successfully helps a client improve will almost inevitably be described in
positive terms.

The behavioral interpretation of the similar therapeutic outcomes
would acknowledge the importance of these common treatment factors
in producing improvement, and suggest that the way in which patients
were selected as subjects maximized their influence. As discussed above,
the behavior therapist would predict that the incremental efficacy of
specific learning-based behavioral techniques would become more apparent
with more severe problems.

Regardless of the merit of any individual study, the question of therapeutic outcome will be decided eventually by the general consensus of a
variety of studies. Luborsky et al. (1975) reviewed all comparative outcome studies in which they claimed that "some attention was paid to the
main criteria of controlled comparative research" (p. 995). More specifically, they graded studies in terms of 13 methodological criteria. Patients
in the studies included in their review were adult, mostly nonpsychotic,
and "bona fide patients." They explicitly excluded "the huge literature
specifically on habit disorders (e.g., addiction and bed wetting) and . . .
many studies with student volunteers" (p. 1006).

Although they attempted to compare various forms of psychological
therapy and chemotherapy, it is their comparison of behavior therapy
versus psychotherapy that is of interest here. Luborsky et al. analyzed 19

controlled comparisons in 12 studies. In terms of their "base score" of treatment successes, six of these comparisons favored behavior therapy, the remaining 13 indicating no difference. Virtually all these studies involved the application of systematic desensitization; the average date of publication of the 12 studies was 1966-1967. Only two studies published in the 1970s were included, one of which was the Sloane et al. (1975) study we have already discussed in detail.

Luborsky et al.'s major conclusion was that "everybody has won and all must have prizes"—the verdict of the dodo bird in *Alice in Wonderland*. According to their review, there were insignificant differences between the various forms of therapy, although most patients purportedly benefitted irrespective of the specific type of therapy employed. Another major conclusion was that only two "especially beneficial matches between type of treatment and type of patient" were reportedly identified. One of these was that "Behavior therapy may be especially suited for treatment of circumscribed phobias" (p. 1004).

As we have discussed in the preceding pages, the latter is a prime example of one of the more prevalent misconceptions about behavior therapy. What is quite incredible is that Luborsky et al. somehow managed to arrive at this conclusion despite the fact that the Sloane et al. study—which flatly debunks the notion—was included among the comparisons they reviewed! The rest of the 12 studies reviewed by Luborsky et al. received relatively poor methodological grades—and with good reason. Four of these studies (33 percent) are some of the early outcome studies on systematic desensitization by Marks and Gelder at the Maudsley Hospital in London, research that has not gone without criticism (cf., Bandura, 1969; Paul, 1969b, Sloane et al., 1975). Some of their results indicating that desensitization was less effective with complex phobias (agoraphobia) than simple phobias has been disputed in more recent, better controlled research (Gelder, Bancroft, Gath, Johnston, Mathews, & Shaw, 1973—reprinted in Franks & Wilson, 1975). Furthermore, there is more to behavior therapy than systematic desensitization studies, outdated or not. The availability of procedures still more effective than imaginal desensitization is made clear in Section II.

It is easy to find fault with Luborsky et al.'s sloppy reasoning from ill-chosen studies. But there is a more fundamental problem. The fascination with "box scores" and "tie scores" of something called "behavior therapy" versus something else called "psychotherapy" is better suited to fanning the flames of controversy between rival schools than elucidating the processes of therapeutic change. The fundamental outcome question remains: What technique should be applied to what problem in which patient by which therapist (Paul, 1969a)? Research directed towards answering this question involves objective behavioral assessment of the effects of well-defined treatment variables on specific problems. The use of single-subject methodology to establish cause-effect relationships between treatment variables and designated behavioral outcomes provides an excellent example of this means of evaluating treatment outcome (cf. Leitenberg, 1973—reprinted in Franks & Wilson, 1974).

This approach does not mean that behavioral outcome research focuses only on narrowly conceived, single treatment manipulations to the exclusion of more complex clinical interventions. Numerous studies have assessed the efficacy of broad treatment packages that seem necessary for modifying severe disorders with multiple determinants. In these cases the strategy has been to demonstrate that the treatment package is effective and then to conduct component analyses of the different elements to identify the key behavior influence processes involved and ultimately to refine the treatment program. If this strategy is to be successful, the various procedures must be clearly specified and operationally defined. Global treatment approaches that are vague and inadequately described cannot be subjected to the critical testing designed to demonstrate effective procedures.

Both Sloane et al. (1975) and Luborsky et al. (1975) downgraded the significance of behavioral outcome studies not employing "bona fide patients"—motivated patients typical of the general patient population seen in clinical practice. However, it would be unwise to dismiss summarily the relevance of many well-controlled analogue studies to more common clinical situations. Contrary to Luborsky et al., not all analogue research has involved "student volunteers." It is true that many studies have, and these have been appropriately criticized (see Section II). Others, however, have drawn subject samples from the general community. The distinction between people who respond to public announcements of an available treatment program instead of seeking therapy at some other initiative is often blurred. The presenting problems of these subjects are very real, generating subjective distress and interfering with daily life functions. The motivation of these subjects can hardly be doubted and is perhaps no less real than the majority of patients in therapy. Care is urged in generalizing the results of these studies to other situations, but it seems very arbitrary to dismiss the finding implications of these studies for clinical practice.

The Sloane et al. (1975) outcome study and the Luborsky et al. (1975)

review focused on the treatment of adults. The second paper reprinted in this Section, by Jesness, describes a comparative outcome study with a teenage delinquent population. The importance of the target problem, the detailed reporting of multiple outcome measures, explicit descriptions of the treatment programs, and the inclusion of follow-up measures are among the important features of Jesness' paper.

Of more than a little concern is the finding that behavior modification treatment met with significantly greater student dissatisfaction. Unfortunately, it appears that goals were arbitrarily imposed without sufficient consultation or explanation by the Holton staff. As Jesness himself observes, there is no good reason why this should have been the case. Clients participating in behavior modification programs should be accorded the respect and understanding that characterize any basically humanistic form of treatment. Enlisting the cooperation of clients, including children and adolescents, in the setting of goals, and the negotiation of mutually agreed upon contracts is ethically desirable. It is also often necessary if the treatment program is to be effective. Counter control behavior is a reality, and distrustful or resentful clients who feel that they are being manipulated or treated unfairly can readily disrupt otherwise technically sound reinforcement procedures (Mahoney, 1974; Wilson & Evans, in press).

Finally, while the superiority of the behavior modification in terms of the objective behavioral ratings is what would be expected, the dismal results at the two-year follow-up are discouraging. Only 23 percent of subjects released on parole showed no record of arrest during this period. As Jesness notes, the institution's impact appeared to be "transitory." These results are consistent with previous findings that the continuing adverse influence of the natural environment to which parolees and ex-mental hospital patients return is decisive in determining their adjustment in the long run (e.g., Atthowe, 1973—reprinted in Franks & Wilson, 1974). Of course this is exactly what behavior modification with its emphasis on reinforcement contingencies in the environment predicts. Special institutional environments can contribute to enduring changes. But the persistent problem of high recidivism rates highlights the need to restructure the nature of the post-institution environment so as to support pro-social as opposed to antisocial behavior.

SECTION IX: BEHAVIOR THERAPY
AND ITS RIVALS

32

SHORT-TERM ANALYTICALLY ORIENTED PSYCHOTHERAPY VERSUS BEHAVIOR THERAPY

R. Bruce Sloane, Fred R. Staples,
University of Southern California Medical School

Allan H. Cristol,
Temple University Medical School, Philadelphia

Neil J. Yorkston
Friern Hospital, New Southgate, England

and

Katherine Whipple
University of Southern California Medical School

Ninety-four outpatients with anxiety neurosis or personality disorder were randomly assigned for four months to a waiting list, behavior therapy, or psychoanalytically oriented

Reprinted with permission from the *American Journal of Psychiatry*, 132:4, April, 1975. Copyright 1975, American Psychiatric Association.

Based on a paper read at a New Research session at the 125th annual meeting of the American Psychiatric Association, Dallas, Tex., May 1-5, 1972.

This work was supported by grant MH-15493 from the National Institute of Mental Health.

The authors would like to thank Drs. Herbert Freed, Arnold A. Lazarus, Michael Serber, Jay Urban, Raul H. Vispo, and Joseph Wolpe for their help in the completion of this study. They would also like to thank Ms. Olga Aigner and Ms. Diana Horvitz for their help as research assistants.

697

therapy. The target symptoms of all three groups improved
significantly, but the two treated groups improved equally
well and significantly more than those on the waiting list.
There were no significant differences among the groups in
work or social adjustment; however, the patients who received behavior therapy had a significant overall improvement at four months. One year and two years after the
initial assessment, all groups were found to be equally and
significantly improved.

Behavioral techniques are coming to be widely accepted in the treatment of monophobias, sexual impotence, and other "unitary" psychiatric
problems; this acceptance is supported by a good deal of research. Gelder
and associates (1, 2) showed that patients suffering from severe phobias
tend to improve more quickly with behavioral than with psychoanalytically oriented or group therapy. However, in their studies this initial
advantage was not maintained over time. Moreover, this research and
that of others (3) have been criticized for failing to use experienced
therapists for either modality.

Paul's study (4), which is often cited in support of behavior therapy,
showed one technique, desensitization, to be clearly superior in treating
unitary phobias among college students recruited as subjects; this superiority was maintained at follow-up (5). However, it is unlikely that the
nature of these subjects' problems and their motivation for improvement
are comparable to those of patients who spontaneously seek treatment.
Similar criticisms as well as the use of inexperienced therapists apply in
Di Loreto's comparative study of students with anxiety (3). In this
study, desensitization clearly worked best, but this was because it was
applicable to both introverts and extroverts.

Phobic patients, especially monophobic patients, are much rarer than
patients with anxiety neuroses and personality disorders. There have
been very few controlled evaluations of behavior therapy with patients
with anxiety neuroses and personality disorders. The tendency has been
to assume that only a "deeper" therapy could produce a lasting effect
for these patients by attacking the underlying causes of general psychiatric problems.

Our aim in this study was to compare the relative effectiveness of
behavior therapy and more traditional analytically oriented therapy
conducted by experienced therapists with patients with anxiety neuroses
and personality disorders. We also compared both therapies with the
effect of an initial assessment interview plus the mere promise and
expectation of help.

METHOD

Patients

Patients who applied for treatment at a university psychiatric out-patient clinic were initially seen by one of three experienced psychiatric interviewers (assessors). Patients who were below the age of 18 or over the age of 45, who seemed too mildly ill, or who were too seriously disturbed to risk waiting four months were excluded from the study. Also excluded were those who were psychotic, mentally retarded, organically brain damaged, or primarily in need of drug therapy. All others who wanted to have psychotherapy rather than drugs or some other treatment and for whom the assessor considered this to be the treatment of choice were accepted into the study. Twenty-nine applicants did not meet the criteria and were referred elsewhere or treated outside the study.

The 94 patients who were accepted were predominantly in their early 20s, women (60 percent) and white (only 7 were black). They had completed an average of 14 years of education (about 2 years of college or other post-secondary-school training). Over half of the patients were students, and about half were self-supporting. Roughly two-thirds suffered from psychoneuroses (usually anxiety) and one-third from personality disorders. The most frequent specific symptoms were, in decreasing order, generalized anxiety; interpersonal difficulties, especially with the opposite sex; low self-esteem; generalized worry; and bodily complaints.

Psychological Tests

Mill Hill Vocabulary Scale: The mean intelligence quotient of the whole sample on this scale was 99.

MMPI. The overall means on this test showed a considerable degree of pathology in these patients. Four of the nine subscale mean scores (for depression, psychopathic deviate, psychasthenia, and schizophrenia) were within the abnormal range (above 70). The overall mean of the eight clinical scales was also in the abnormal range. Only 8 patients scored normally on all scales.

Eysenck Personality Inventory. The mean scores of the patients on this scale showed them to be introverted and neurotic at the 86th percentile of neuroticism.

California Psychological Inventory. The patients as a group showed lowered but not abnormal self-control, sociability, and socialization on this scale.

Assessment

One of three experienced psychiatrists saw each patient at the initial interview. These psychiatrists were not connected with the treatment. The patient and interviewer together drew up a list of three target symptoms —the major specific symptoms that had led the patient to seek treatment. Both the psychiatrist and the patient rated each target symptom on a 5-point scale of severity (6, 7). To judge the patient's general level of functioning, the Structured and Scaled Interview to Assess Maladjustment (SSIAM) (8, 9) was used. The SSIAM rates the patient's level of adjustment on 11-point scales for 10 items in each of the following five areas: work; social and leisure; sexual; and relationships with spouse, children, and family of origin.

These two measures, the list of target symptoms and the SSIAM, provided the main indices of change. In addition, a global impressionistic rating of overall improvement was made. Other measures taken will be reported separately.

Treatment

After interviewing and testing, the patients were randomly assigned in the following manner: 31 were assigned to behavior therapy, 30 to psychotherapy, and 33 to the waiting list. Within this random assignment, patients were matched within the three groups in terms of sex and severity of neurosis as assessed by the Eysenck Personality Inventory.

The Therapists

Of the three therapists in each group, one had more than 20 years of experience, one had 10 to 12 years of experience, and one had 6 or more years of experience. One was a Ph.D. psychologist and the other five were M.Ds. Two of the psychotherapists were psychoanalysts and a third was in personal analysis with a training analyst. All of the behavior therapists were formally trained. By using experienced therapists, we hoped to avoid the twin pitfalls of exposing a patient to an ineffective treatment (because a technique probably does not attain its full potential in the hands of a beginning therapist) and of biasing our results in favor of behavior therapy (where it is possible that less experience is required to attain a minimal level of competence than in psychotherapy) (10, 11). Each therapist treated at least 10 patients.

A list of stipulative definitions of each therapy was drawn up. This is presented in abbreviated form in appendix 1. This list outlined which procedures were common to both therapies and which were allowable only within one or the other modality. The therapists approved these definitions and felt that they would not restrict them in their respective treatments. Tranquilizers were discouraged; they were used very rarely in either treatment group.

Each behavior therapist used a variety of behavioral techniques, including systematic desensitization, assertive training, and avoidance conditioning, which he tailored to the needs of each individual patient. Similarly, the psychotherapists used various analytically oriented techniques of short-term insight therapy.

Analyses of the two therapies using a variety of rating scales and other questionnaire measures will be reported in detail elsewhere (12). These data verify that the two groups of therapists were using quite different techniques, had formed different types of relationships with their patients, and were in fact doing in therapy very much what they said they did.

Behavior therapy and psychotherapy patients received four months of usually weekly hour-long therapy (an average of 13.2 and 14.2 sessions, respectively). Fees were paid through the outpatient clinic according to its usual sliding scale.

Waiting List

The control patients were told that they would be placed in treatment but that because there were currently no openings in the clinic there would be a waiting period of no more than four months. During this waiting period they were contacted by telephone every few weeks by a research assistant, who asked how they were getting along and assured them that they had not been forgotten and would be placed in treatment as soon as there was a vacancy. They were also told that if there was a crisis they could call on the psychiatrist who interviewed them initially or the emergency unit of the department at any time. They thus received a moderate amount of nonspecific therapy that aroused hope, expectation of help, and the relief afforded by an initial interview.

Follow-Up

The patients were reinterviewed and reassessed by the original interviewers after four months and after one year. These assessors were blind

TABLE 1

Interviewer Ratings of Severity of Three Target Symptoms for 92 Patients at Initial Interview and Follow-Up*

Group	Rating at Initial Interview Mean	SD	Rating at Four Months Mean	SD	Significance**	Rating at One Year Mean	SD	Significance**
Behavior therapy*								
Total group (N = 29)	8.79	1.36	4.52	1.89	p<.001	3.83	2.59	p<.001
Patients who obtained no further therapy after four months (N = 14)	8.85	1.66	4.85	1.99	p<.001	4.14	2.30	p<.001
Psychotherapy								
Total group (N = 30)	9.13	1.65	5.27	2.70	p<.001	4.90	3.54	p<.001
Patients who obtained no further therapy after four months (N = 21)	9.14	1.71	4.90	2.32	p<.001	4.24	3.18	p<.001
Waiting list								
total group (N = 33)	8.82	2.01	6.45	2.84	p<.001	5.45	2.95	p<.001
Patients who obtained no therapy after four months (N = 14)	8.43	1.76	5.57	2.38	p<.001	5.29	2.77	p<.01

* The scores represent the sum of the severities of the three target symptoms, each rated on a 5-point scale (4 = severe, 3 = moderate, 2 = mild, 1 = doubtful or trivial, and 0 = absent).

** Represents change from initial interview (by two-tailed t-tests).

*** The numbers represent the number of patients who had complete ratings on all three assessments.

as to type of therapy in most cases, but a few patients inadvertently gave clues to their therapist's identity.

The assessor rated the target symptoms as before on an absolute severity scale and on a comparative rating scale. He also made a rating of overall improvement. Both patient and assessor rated work, social, sexual, and overall adjustment. The SSIAM was administered again.

A comparison of outcome ratings did not reveal bias by an assessor toward any group. Symptomatic self-assessments by the patient correlated well with the assessor ratings ($r = .66$ by Pearson product-moment correlation).

Two years after the initial assessment, a research assistant contacted as many patients as possible to rate target symptom severity and take SSIAM measures.

RESULTS

Four-Month Follow-Up

At four months all three groups had significantly improved on their three target symptoms (see Table 1), but the psychotherapy and behavior therapy groups improved equally well and significantly more than those on the waiting list (see Table 2).

Patients treated by behavior therapy improved significantly on both work adjustment and social adjustment (see Table 3). Psychotherapy patients showed marginally significant improvement in social functioning. Patients placed on the waiting list had significantly improved in social adjustment and marginally in work adjustment. However, analyses of variance indicated that the amount of improvement shown by the three groups was not significantly different either for work ($F = 1.46$, $p > .10$) or social adjustment ($F = .55$, $p > .10$).

On a rating scale of overall improvement, 93 percent of the behavior therapy patients in contrast to 77 percent of the psychotherapy and waiting list patients were considered either improved or recovered $\chi^2 = 3.93$, $p < .05$). Thus all treatments (including placement on the waiting list) were highly successful, but behavior therapy was significantly more successful in terms of the traditional global measure of improvement.

The amount of improvement was independent of the sex of the patient, the amount of experience of the therapist, and the severity of the neurosis, except that the anxiety of women, especially those with high neuroticism scores, improved more than that of men.

A few patients whose initially reported symptoms had not improved

TABLE 2

Univariate and Multivariate F Values for Comparisons Among
Treatment Groups and Control Group of Changes in
Target Symptoms at Four-Month Follow-Up

	Univariate F Values			Multi-
Groups Compared	Symp- tom 1	Symp- tom 2	Symp- tom 3	variate F Value
Behavior therapy versus waiting list	9.0148*	8.0513*	9.5708*	4.9292*
Psychotherapy versus waiting list	12.1725*	6.7628**	4.6018***	4.5742**
Behavior therapy versus psychotherapy	.2374	.0563	.9027	.5184

* $p < .005$.
** $p < .01$.
*** $p < .05$.

in four months reported additional symptoms that were either new or had been too trivial to report at the initial interview. However, no patient in any group whose original problems had substantially improved reported new symptoms. Thus there was no evidence of symptom substitution.

One-Year Follow-Up

One year after the initial interview all three groups of patients had significantly improved symptomatically since their initial assessment (see Table 1). The behavior therapy patients had improved significantly more on their target symptoms ($p < .05$) than the waiting list patients ($t = 2.18$, $p < .05$), but the psychotherapy patients had not. These data excluded two behavior therapy patients whom it was impossible to interview. (They were informally known to have improved.)

Both treated groups were significantly improved on work and social adjustment at the end of one year, but the control group was no longer significantly improved on work adjustment (see Table 3); there were no significant intergroup differences in amount of adjustment improvement.

However, after four months on the waiting list, 14 of the control patients no longer felt that they required therapy; those who did were assigned to senior residents, most of whom practiced analytically oriented insight therapy. In addition, many of those who had received treatment wanted and received small amounts of additional therapy, in most cases

TABLE 3

Mean Scores on SSIAM Factors for Treatment Groups and Control Group at Initial Interview and Follow-Up

Group	Score at Initial Interview		Score at Four Months				Score at One Year			
	Work	Social Adjustment	Work	Significance	Social Adjustment	Significance	Work	Significance	Social Adjustment	Significance
Behavior therapy*										
Total group (N = 29)	4.02	3.31	2.98	p<.001**	2.71	p<.05**	2.59	p<.001**	2.27	p<.001**
Patients who obtained no further therapy after four months (N = 14)	3.98	3.56	2.79	p<.05**	2.64	p<.05**	2.54	p<.05**	2.73	p<.05***
Psychotherapy										
Total group (N = 30)	3.42	3.10	2.85	p<.05***	2.72	n.s.	2.15	p<.001**	2.12	p<.001**
Patients who obtained no further therapy after four months (N = 21)	3.07	3.15	2.67	n.s.	2.48	p<.05**	2.14	p<.05**	1.92	p<.001**
Waiting list*										
Total group (N = 30)	3.49	3.52	2.81	p<.05***	2.78	p<.01**	2.85	n.s.	2.77	p<.05**
Patients who obtained no therapy after four months (N=11)	4.04	3.78	2.57	p<.05**	2.64	p<.05**	2.80	p<.05***	2.38	p<.05***

* The numbers represent the number of patients who had complete ratings on all three assessments.
** By two-tailed t-tests.
*** By one-tailed t-test only.

with their original therapists, between the four-month and one-year interviews. Thus 15 behavior therapy patients averaged a further 10.1 sessions and 9 psychotherapy patients averaged 19.3 sessions.

The varying amount and type of therapy between four months and one year tended to make comparisons between the original groups less valid than comparisons with those who received no treatment after four months. These latter patients, who did not differ from their total groups in any pretreatment or change measures, showed significant and equal symptomatic, social, and work improvement at one year (see Tables 1 and 3).

Two-Year Follow-Up

Two years after the initial interview, 61 patients were interviewed by a research assistant. All groups had either maintained their status or continued to improve in all areas. Unfortunately, the psychotherapy patients who could be reassessed at two years proved to be those who had already shown the most improvement at one year. Because of this sample bias, a between-group comparison with the behavior therapy and waiting list patients, who were representative of their original samples, was not feasible.

DISCUSSION

There was very little difference between the two active treatment groups in amount of improvement, although it is tempting to argue that behavior therapy was somewhat more effective than psychotherapy. On a global measure of improvement, behavior therapy proved significantly better at four months than either psychotherapy or being on a waiting list. Moreover, behavior therapy patients had significantly improved on all three specific measures at four months, while psychotherapy patients had not improved in social adjustment.

At one year, patients originally treated by behavior therapy but not those originally treated by psychotherapy showed greater improvement than waiting list patients in reduction of the severity of target symptoms. The conclusion that behavior therapy is therefore more effective is tempered by the finding of no significant difference between groups in the amount of improvement in social adjustment and the fact that the one-year comparison of the two groups was confounded by treatment after four months. We conclude that there is no clear evidence for the superiority of behavior therapy over psychotherapy.

However, behavior therapy is clearly a generally useful treatment. Both active treatments were found effective in treating specific symptoms and in improving the patient's reported ability to cope with life. Our data do not support the view that although behavior therapy may have a short-term or limited value in dealing with specific symptoms, only deeper and more analytic treatment can produce general change in the patient by treating the underlying causes of symptoms as well as the symptoms themselves.

CONCLUSIONS

Behavior therapy produced significantly more overall improvement at four months than psychotherapy. However, this is a very general subjective measure and there was no significant difference between psychotherapy and behavior therapy on any other measure at any other time.

At four months both treated groups had improved significantly more than the waiting list group on target symptoms but not in general adjustment. This is impressive in view of the great improvement shown by patients receiving the minimal treatment of placement on a waiting list.

All groups improved in general adjustment, but at four months this improvement was clearly significant only for the behavior therapy and control groups.

At one year, behavior therapy patients but not psychotherapy patients showed significantly more symptomatic improvement than did control patients. However, this result may be confounded by the fact that differing amounts of further treatment were given after the four-month study period. There were no differences between those who received no further treatment after four months.

All groups maintained or continued their improvement between four months, one year, and two years regardless of whether or not further treatment was received during this period.

REFERENCES

1. GELDER, M. G. & MARKS, I. M. Severe agoraphobia: A controlled prospective trial of behavior therapy. *Brit. J. Psychiat.*, 1966, 112, 309-319.
2. GELDER, M. G., MARKS, I. M., & WOLFF, H. H.: Desensitization and psychotherapy in the treatment of phobic states: A controlled inquiry. *Brit. J. Psychiat.*, 1967, 113, 53-73.
3. DI LORETO, A. O. *Comparative Psychotherapy: An Experimental Analysis.* Chicago: Aldine-Atherton, 1971.

4. PAUL, G. L. Insight vs. desensitization in psychotherapy two years after termination. *J. Consult. Psychol.*, 1967, 31, 333-348.
6. SLOANE, R. B., CRISTOL, A. H., PEPERNIK, M. C., ET AL.: Role preparation and expectation of improvement in psychotherapy. *J. Nerv. Ment. Dis.*, 1970, 150, 18-26.
7. HOEHN-SARIC, R., FRANK, J. D., IMBER, S. D., ET AL. Systematic preparation of patients for psychotherapy: I. Effects on therapy behavior and outcome. *J. Psychiat. Res.*, 1964, 2, 267-281.
8. GURLAND, B. J., YORKSTON, N. J., STONE, A. R., ET AL. The structured and scaled interview to assess maladjustment (SSIAM): I. Description, rationale, and development. *Arch. Gen. Psychiat.*, 1972, 27, 259-263.
9. GURLAND, B. J., YORKSTON, N. J., GOLDBERG, K., ET AL. The structured and scaled interview to assess maladjustment (SSIAM): II. Factor analysis, reliability, and validity. *Arch. Gen. Psychiat.*, 1972, 27, 264-269.
10. HARTLAGE, L. C. Subprofessional therapists' use of reinforcement versus traditional psychotherapeutic techniques with schizophrenics. *J. Consult. Clin. Psychol.*, 1970, 34, 181-183.
11. PATTERSON, V., LEVENE, H., & BREGER, L. Treatment and training outcomes with two time-limited therapies. *Arch. Gen. Psychiat.*, 1971, 25, 161-167.
12. SLOANE, R. B., STAPLES, F. R., CRISTOL, A. H., ET AL. *Psychotherapy vs. Behavior Therapy. Commonwealth Fund Publication.* Cambridge, Mass.: Harvard University Press (in press).

APPENDIX 1

TECHNIQUES CHARACTERISTIC OF BEHAVIOR THERAPY AND PSYCHOTHERAPY

CONTRASTING ELEMENTS

Specific advice is given frequently by behavior therapist; given infrequently by psychotherapist.

Transference interpretation is avoided by behavior therapist; may be given by psychotherapist.

Interpretation of resistance is not used by behavior therapist; used by psychotherapist.

Report of dreams: behavior therapist shows polite lack of interest; psychotherapist may use in treatment.

Relaxation training is directly undertaken by behavior therapist; occurs only as an indirect consequence of a relaxed atmosphere in psychotherapy.

Desensitization is directly undertaken by behavior therapist; occurs only as an indirect consequence of discussing problems in a relaxed atmosphere in psychotherapy.

Practical retraining is directly undertaken by behavior therapist; not emphasized by psychotherapist.

Assertive training is directly undertaken and encouraged in everyday life by behavior therapist; only indirectly encouraged in everyday life by psychotherapist, but assertive or aggressive speech permitted in psychotherapy session.

Report of symptoms: interest is shown by behavior therapist, who may explain them biologically; discouraged by psychotherapist, who may explain them symbolically.

Childhood memories: behavior therapist usually takes history as such; psychotherapist usually looks for further memories.

Aversion (e.g., electric shock) may be used by behavior therapist; not used by psychotherapist.

Role training may be used by beavior therapist; not used by psychotherapist.

Repetition of motor habits may be used by behavior therapist; not used by psychotherapist.

ELEMENTS IN COMMON

Both therapists may take a biographical psychiatric history, formulate the patient's problems; attempt to reconstruct possible original causes of the disorder, look for continuing causes of the difficulty; aim to produce a change that benefits the patient, such as reducing subjective complaints or behavior that disturbs the patient or others; correct misconceptions; elucidate objectives; and attempt to change others, e.g., family, employer, doctor.

33

COMPARATIVE EFFECTIVENESS OF BEHAVIOR MODIFICATION AND TRANSACTIONAL ANALYSIS PROGRAMS FOR DELINQUENTS

Carl F. Jesness

California Youth Authority, Sacramento, California

The Youth Center Research Project studied the effectiveness of two different treatment programs with 983 adjudicated delinquents assigned by random procedures to two institutions, one of whose programs was based on transactional analysis (O. H. Close School) and the other on the principles of behavior modification (Karl Holton School). The results summarized here suggest that institutions can be run so that most residents change for the better. Improvement on psychological measures favored the transactional analysis program; the behavior ratings slightly favored the behavioral program. Parole follow-up showed no differences in the revocation rates of the two programs, but subjects from both were doing significantly better than comparison groups of the same age assigned to other institutions.

Reprinted with permission from *Journal of Consulting and Clinical Psychology,* Vol. 43, No. 6, 1975, 758-779. Copyright 1975, American Psychological Association.

The Youth Center Research Project was supported by U.S. Public Health Service Grant MH 14411 NIMH (Center for Studies of Crime and Delinquency). The grant was made to the American Justice Institute, which worked closely with the California Youth Authority in the development and implementation of the project. The substance of the article was presented as an invited address at the Western Psychological Association, Sacramento, California, April 1975.

Do juvenile rehabilitation institutions rehabilitate? In the absence of evidence to the contrary, there is a growing consensus that they do not. Many believe that the worst of them are breeding grounds for career criminals (Ohmart, 1968; Wheeler & Cottrell, 1966). Over the years the expectation has come and gone that vocational training, group counseling, psychiatric treatment, the "therapeutic community," or other tactics might prove to be the panacea. Research by the California Youth Authority has reflected this expectation, and the effects of several different kinds of program elements have been evaluated without impressive positive results. In one of the better controlled large-scale studies of "psychiatric treatment" in an institution for delinquents, the inmates who received psychotherapy did no better on parole than the subjects in the randomly selected control groups (Guttman, 1963). Overall, 99 of 168 experimental subjects who received psychotherapy (59 percent) violated parole within 18 months of release, compared with 97 of 170 (57 percent) of the controls. The results are consistent with other evaluative studies of traditional psychotherapy, most of which have not demonstrated positive treatment effects (Eysenck, 1954, 1961). The much quoted Cambridge-Somerville Youth Study, for example, offered guidance and counseling to an experimental group of 325 subjects. A follow-up of the treated subjects and matched controls failed to show that treatment reduced the incidence of delinquency (McCord & McCord, 1959). Even though many of these studies have been rightfully criticized for a variety of reasons (e.g., they did not take account of possible differential program effectiveness with different types of offenders, did not offer sufficiently intensive in-depth treatment, did not provide aftercare services, or did not provide clearly defined treatment programs), the repeated failure of counseling or psychotherapy to show measurable effects has led to deep skepticism about the potential effectiveness of rehabilitative programs. This article summarizes data from a large-scale action research project pointing to a more optimistic possibility—that improved institutional programs can lead to positive changes in the behavior and attitudes of inmates and increase their chances for success in the community.

The Youth Center Research Project was a 4-year research demonstration project that compared the effectiveness of behavior modification and transactional analysis in the rehabilitation of institutionalized delinquents (Jesness, DeRisi, McCormick, & Wedge, 1972). The study was designed to provide data regarding the feasibility of applying these two approaches to the treatment of an institution's entire population and to evaluate the relative effectiveness of the treatment strategies in modifying the behavior of different types of delinquents.

The two treatment approaches implemented during the Youth Center Project were widely accepted as tenable. At the O. H. Close School the treatment strategies were based on the psychodynamic principles and group therapy methods of transactional analysis. The primary sources on transactional analysis are the writings of Eric Berne (1961, 1966, 1967). At the Karl Holton School the treatment program was based on the principles of behavior modification. Extensive descriptions and bibliographies concerning the principles of behavior modification and the application of operant conditioning principles can be found in a variety of sources (Bandura, 1969; Krasner & Ullmann, 1967; Ullmann & Krasner, 1969).

The study's primary objective was to develop new programs and explore their effectiveness. A secondary objective of the study was to evaluate the relative contribution to treatment outcomes of client characteristics, treatment variables, and measurable, more subjective, therapist and milieu variables. Among others, Bergin and Strupp (1972) and Russell (1974) have stressed the importance of nonspecific factors in all forms of psychotherapy, including the various forms of behavior modification. In the present study, the residents' perceived relationship with staff, labeled *positive regard,* was measured by their responses to three questionnaire items. The hypotheses to be explored were whether the nonspecific relationship dimension of positive regard was as important in the behavior modification program as in the transactional analysis program and whether its influence was as great or greater than either treatment modality.

METHOD

Study Setting

The Youth Center Research Project was located at two newly opened California Youth Authority institutions for boys, the O. H. Close School and the Karl Holton School, adjacent to the Northern California Youth Center in Stockton, California. These two institutions provided an ideal setting for this comparative research project. They were alike in their organizational structure, staffing patterns, and physical layout. Each was designed to house approximately 400 youths in eight 50-bed living halls. When the project began, boys of nearly the same age were being assigned to the institutions, so that random assignment to either institution was immediately feasible.

The organizational structure and the number and type of personnel at the two schools were almost identical throughout the period of the study. Four treatment team supervisors headed the eight treatment teams, with each treatment team supervisor overseeing the operations of two living units. Each treatment team had one senior youth counselor, four youth counselors, one night supervisor, academic and vocational teachers (usually three for each team), and a social worker, responsible for 50 boys. Selection of O. H. Close for the transactional analysis program, and of Karl Holton for the behavior modification program resulted from the mutual agreement of the superintendents of the two institutions, neither of whom knew much about the two treatment models at that time and both of whom would have accepted either one.

Subjects

Experimental subjects in the research project included all boys from 15 to 17 years of age assigned to the two institutions for the 18-month period from August 1969 through March 1971. Random assignment procedures were instituted earlier (on September 1, 1968) in order to ensure that by the project's start most of the confounding variables due to possible population differences would have been minimized. By the time the operational phase of the project began almost all boys in the institutions had been assigned through randomization procedures that had been established at the central reception center.

Only boys from 15 to 17 years of age designated by the California Youth Authority board for placement at either Close or Holton were assigned to the common pool. Because the academic program and facilities at Close had originally been intended for a junior high curriculum, and Holton had been equipped to place more emphasis on the vocational training of slightly older boys, those 14 years of age and under were not included as experimental subjects and were all assigned to Close. Those 18 and older were also excluded as experimental subjects and were assigned to Holton. (During the operational period of the study, approximately 30 percent of the Holton residents and 20 percent of the Close residents were not considered by the researchers as part of the study, but they participated fully in the treatment programs.) No other criteria were imposed. First offenders, those with prior institutionalization, and those transferred from other institutions for disciplinary purposes were all included, provided they remained in the program at least 3 months and spent more than half their stay in the institution after the experimental programs were fully operational. Attrition on the potentially eligible 1,130 subjects was as follows: (a) Forty-nine from Close and 54 from Holton were transferred to other institutions during the project (about half for breaches of discipline); (b) 15 escaped and were not returned; (c) 24 did not remain in the program for at least 90 days. Thus, from an original pool of 1,130 prospective cases, 983 remained as subjects for parole follow-up. Complete test data were available for 904. However, all subjects except for those transferred out were included in the parole follow-up, including, of course, those transferred in.

Pretesting of subjects continued for 18 months. The final posttesting was done in October 1971, approximately 7 months after pretesting was discontinued. Those still in the institution at that time but not ready to be paroled ($n = 125$) were also posttested to enlarge the sample size and ensure a representative sample. A few of these boys had been in the program as long as 2 years, and all had been in for at least 7 months.

The median age of the subjects were 16.6 years. They had been committed to the California Youth Authority for offenses ranging from murder to incorrigibility; burglary and auto theft were the most common. Thirty-three percent had been in the California Youth Authority previously, and almost all had fairly extensive prior records. Only 5 percent were committed for offenses associated with drugs, although 60 percent had some narcotic or drug use history. The sample was 56 percent white, 13 percent Mexican-American, 28 percent black, and 2 percent other.

The fact that the subjects had experienced serious difficulty in school was shown by their reading ability scores, which were at the 8th grade level (Gates & MacGinitie, 1965), and by their arithmetic scores, which were at the 6th grade level according to the Comprehensive Test of Basic Skills (CTBS). Seventy-two percent had been suspended from school on at least two occasions, and 40 percent had been sent to the principal's office for misbehavior 10 or more times.

Research Design

The essential purpose of the Youth Center Research Project was to provide knowledge about the extent to which two specific forms of treatment contributed to immediate changes in behavior predictive of reduced rates of delinquent acts among delinquents of different types. To do so it was necessary to classify subjects according to I-level types (described below) and to control for irrelevant variables that might have an effect on outcomes including (a) individual differences among subjects, (b) differences in physical and social environments, and (c) differences in the delivery of treatment. Subject differences included background data (such as age, race, drug involvement), personality type, and pretest personality and behavioral characteristics as measured by the Jesness Behavior Inventory (Jesness, 1966), the Jesness Behavior Checklist (Jesness, 1971), and a questionnaire (the Youth Opinion Poll). Differences in initial environments were evaluated by the Correctional Institutions Environment Scale (Moos, 1970). Differences in the extent and quality of treatment delivered were estimated from several sources. Direct observation and counting of behaviors by trained observers would have been the preferred way of evaluating and measuring staff performance and the extent of program implementation, but such procedures would have required more time than was available. Consequently, variation in quality and quantity of treatment was evaluated through ratings of staff effectiveness made by their supervisors and ratings made by the wards. At Close, the number of transactional analysis group sessions held was recorded throughout the entire period of the study. Following each session, the youth counselor or social worker turned in a standard form on which he had listed the names of wards in his group and had rated their active participation, their "work," in that meeting. At Holton similar data were collected. The staff counted the contracts completed by each subject, and research staff rated the quality of the contracts. With a smaller sample of Holton wards, records were kept of the number and rate of earnings of convenience behavior points, critical behavior points, and academic points.

I-Level Classification

Because the I-level classification system used to evaluate differential outcomes is relatively new, a brief description is in order. The theory on which the interpersonal maturity level classification system (I level) is based was first presented in an article written by Sullivan, Grant, and Grant in 1957. The authors postulated a "basic core structure of personality" comprised of a relatively consistent set of expectations in regard to the external world. Seven successive levels of integration (I levels) were described, each stage of which is defined by crucial interpersonal problems that must be resolved before further maturity can occur. The level of integration is manifested primarily through the

ANNUAL REVIEW OF BEHAVIOR THERAPY

person's perceptions of self and others, that is, his ability to understand intrapersonal and interpersonal events. Most recent research has concentrated on levels 2, 3, and 4, which include the great majority of delinquent subjects. Within each of these three maturity levels, subtypes are distinguished according to the characteristic manner in which the individual responds to interpersonal events. Names of the nine delinquent subtypes and the proportions found in the total sample are as follows:

Code	Delinquent subtype	Percentage in Study
I-2	Unsocialized, aggressive	1
I-2	Unsocialized, passive	5
I-3	Immature conformist	17
I-3	Cultural conformist	14
I-3	Manipulator	21
I-4	Acting-out neurotic	23
I-4	Anxious neurotic	17
I-4	Situational emotional reaction	2
I-4	Cultural identifier	1

All subjects were classified into one of the nine I-level subtypes by use of the Sequential I-level Classification System (provisional), a semiobjective approach to classification that used data from three independent sources: the Jesness Inventory, a sentence completion test, and a brief interview. This method has now been superseded by a more objective system (Jesness, 1975).

Positive Regard

Positive regard, the nonspecific (subjective) measure of client-therapist relationship, was defined by each subject's response to three items on the Postopinion Poll Questionnaire: (a) "My counselor (caseworker) almost always found something good (positive) rather than bad to say to me." (b) "The youth counselors in my hall treated everyone the same and were fair to me." (c) "The youth counselors in my hall did not show respect. They put me down, made me feel like nobody, and insulted me" (reverse scoring). Although it might have been preferable to obtain a measure of this relationship earlier in treatment (late enough for the client to have decided how he felt about his caseworker but too early for significant behavioral changes to have occurred), the posttest responses were the only data available. Positive regard was used in one analysis as an indicator of the quality of the contingency relationship that existed between staff and client throughout most of the resident's stay.

Statistical Methodology

Significance of change in scores from pretest to posttest and differences in adjusted posttest means were both tested. In some instances, such as evaluating the extent to which both programs led to behavioral improvement, it was important to understand the extent or degree to which change occurred. However, in comparing the effectiveness of the two treatment programs on variables that measured both preexperimental and postexperimental intervention, the use of change (gain) scores may lead to erroneous conclusions, primarily because such scores are systematically related to random errors of measurement. According to Cronbach and Furby (1970), if one is testing the null hypothesis that two treatments have the same effects, the essential question is whether posttest scores vary from group to group. Because posttest scores are partly dependent on initial status, the posttests were adjusted to account for initial status by use of an analysis of covariance program in which the pretest scores were the covariate. The adjustment was made in all instances in which pretest and posttest scores were obtained. After evaluating the effects of the two treatment programs, the influence of other variables singly and in combination was evaluated by use of a complex analysis of variance. The analysis of variance program was designed to analyze data according to the rationale of a fixed-model design using computation formulas taken from Winer (1971). The program adjusts for unequal groups by an unweighted- (harmonic) means method. However, because few interaction effects were found, most of the data presented here were from multiple covariance analyses (Cooley & Lohnes, 1971). Multiple covariance analysis is a procedure that makes it possible to explore the effects of one independent variable on a variety of dependent variables when the influences of a set of related measures are parceled out.

Training of Staff

Training and supervision of staff in their respective treatment methods were given high priority throughout the first 3 years of the project. After the initial training period, the goals for continuing inservice training of staff in the institutions were (a) to increase sophistication of staff in their respective treatment models, (b) to take care of turnover by offering new staff the basic training course, and (c) to help staff thing creatively in applying the treatment theories to the institutional programs.

Training in transactional analysis. At the start of the Youth Center Research Project, Close staff had virtually no knowledge of transactional analysis. The project's transactional analysis specialist began by scheduling a 16-hour introductory course in transactional analysis for each of the hall's treatment teams, teachers, administrative staff (including the superintendent), special treatment sections, security staff, the two chaplains, the food service workers, and some clerical staff. A unique feature of the ongoing training was the participation of treatment staff as clients themselves. Over a period of several months following the introductory course, almost all management and treatment staff voluntarily attended, by twos and threes, a 3-day transactional analysis treatment marathon held away from the institution at an institute for transactional analysis therapy. Throughout the action phase of the study, each of the seven treatment teams, after their introductory course in transactional analysis, scheduled periodic minithons and weekly training seminars for more advanced instruction. The four staff trainers and the school's eight social workers met weekly for their own 3-hour transactional analysis workshops. Most youth counselors and teachers participated in approximately 100 hours of training each year of the project, and most social workers spent much more time in training.

Training in behavior modification. During the project's first year, and in the training of new management and treatment staff, the training at Holton emphasized the basic principles and terminology of behavior modification. Management completed an 80-hour basic course; and all treatment staff, including youth counselors, social workers, and teachers, completed a 40-hour course that required mastering the content of the programmed text *The Analysis of Behavior* (Holland & Skinner, 1961). The 80 hours a year of training for treatment staff was mostly accounted for by 2 hours a week of on-the-job consultation. The project behavioral specialist, the supervisor of special treatment, and the head social worker were designated as consultants to certain living units. They consulted weekly with counselors and social workers in the management of cases and the writing of contingency contracts in case conferences and in meetings with middle management and social workers. Special management committees were largely responsible for establishing and modifying the overall program. Advanced training was held during the third year, with the development and presentation to hall staff of newly developed materials covering various aspects of contingency contracting. For the first time in the school's history, new employees had to demonstrate basic knowledge of a treatment theory in order to pass their probationary period of employment, and an attempt was made to ensure that passing the advanced training course became one of the criteria for meriting incentive pay increases.

Treatment Programs

The programs have been described in detail elsewhere (Jesness & DeRisi, 1973; Jesness et al., 1972). Only a brief sketch is presented here.

Holton (behavior modification). All eight living units and all classrooms in the Karl Holton School operated under a microeconomy and a parallel parole-contingent point system. To be recommended to the Youth Authority Board for release, each boy had to accumulate a predetermined number of behavior-change units. Boys were required to earn Karl Holton dollars (scrip) to buy more immediately desired comforts, materials, services, and recreational opportunities. For each behavior change unit earned toward release, each boy also got $1 in scrip for his more immediate needs. Reinforcer menus posted in each hall indicated the cost of all goods and services available to the youth in the economy. Conspicuously placed charts, updated weekly, showed the progress each boy was making toward his criterion number of parole release points.

Three different kinds of point systems and microbehaviors were identified for contingency management in the Holton economy. The first category consisted of convenience behaviors, not always crucial to the subject's becoming a nondelinquent but important to the efficient, orderly function of the institution (such as not talking loud at bedtime). Academic behaviors consisted of units of educational subject matter and skills. Critical behavior deficiencies were those behaviors seen as most likely to affect the probability of a subject's failing or succeeding on parole. For example, chronic fighting behavior was dealt with through a series of individual contracts that suppressed and replaced the behavior. Forty-five percent of the boy's points had to be earned by convenience behaviors, 28 percent by academic behaviors, and 27 percent by the correction of critical behavior deficiencies. Each of these program elements was described in detail in the Holton program manual, which served as a guideline for the youth counselors in the Karl Holton School.

Close (transactional analysis). Upon arrival at the school, each boy met with an intake worker who interviewed him briefly, gave him a primer in transactional analysis (McCormick & Campos, 1969) written specifically for this purpose, and assigned him to one of the seven residence halls. (The eighth hall served as a temporary restraining facility.) After assignment to one of the residences, a new boy was placed in the caseload of one of the youth counselors or the social worker on the hall. The counselor held a life-script interview with him that ended with questions useful in negotiating a mutually agreeable verbal treatment contract. The counselor encouraged the boy to describe aloud, for himself and for the record, ways in which he wanted to be different. As therapists, staff tried not to impose any expectations on a boy except those that he set for himself. They agreed, however, to work with him only toward self-enhancing and socially desirable goals, including converting from an offender to a nonoffender.

Counselors were expected to meet with their caseloads (which averaged eight boys) twice weekly for group treatment. Each counselor was expected to negotiate verbal treatment contracts of three kinds: (a) academic, (b) small group, and (c) overall social behavior. The most important of these were the contracts made in the small-group treatment sessions aimed at changes in broad life patterns (the life script).

In addition to the twice weekly small-group therapy sessions, transactional analysis principles were applied to varying degrees in everyday management, in classrooms, and in the large group community meetings held two or three times each week.

Outcome Measures

The Postopinion Poll. Project subjects completed a specially devised questionnaire (the Postopinion Poll) along with the other posttest measures just prior to their departure on parole. The majority of the poll's 45 items called for the boys' evaluations of their experience in the treatment program and solicited their opinions of institution staff.

Achievement tests. Achievement tests (Gates-MacGinitie Reading Survey and the arithmetic subtest of the Comprehensive Test of Basic Skills) were administered at admission and again shortly before each subject's departure on parole. For all subjects having valid tests, pretest scores were subtracted from posttest scores to determine the amount of change in achievement level. To compare scores for project subjects against average gains of same-age nondelinquent groups (the expected gain), the mean-gain scores were divided by average number of months spent in the program. The resulting figures represented the mean gains in achievement level per month of stay.

The Jesness Inventory. The Jesness Inventory is a personality test designed to distinguish delinquents from nondelinquents, to classify children and adolescents into personality types, and to provide scales useful in evaluating change (Jesness, 1966). The 155 true-false items yield scores on the following 11 scales: Social Maladjustment, Value Orientation, Immaturity, Autism, Alienation, Manifest Aggression, Withdrawal-Depression, Social Anxiety, Repression, Denial, and Asocial Index.

In addition to the original Jesness Inventory scales, a new scale was recently developed specifically to measure the psychological-attitudinal correlates of drug use as measured by inventory items (Haney, 1971).

Jesness Behavior Checklist. The Jesness Behavior Checklist was designed to provide a systematic way of recording data about behavior (Jesness, 1971). The instrument contains 80 statements (items) describing behavioral units that encompass a broad spectrum of observable, noncognitive, social acts. The observer rates a person on each item by marking a score of from 1 to 5, depending on the observer's judgment of how frequently the person does what is described in the item. Factor analysis was used to define the following 14 scales: Unobtrusiveness versus Obtrusiveness, Friendliness versus Hostility, Responsibility verus Irresponsibility, Considerateness versus Inconsiderateness, Independence versus Dependence, Rapport versus Alienation, Enthusiasm versus Depression, Sociability versus Poor Peer Relations, Conformity versus Nonconformity, Calmness versus Anxiousness, Effective Communication versus Inarticulateness, Insight versus Unawareness and Indecisiveness, Social Control versus Attention Seeking, and Anger Control versus Hypersensitivity.

There are two forms of the instrument, a self-appraisal form and an observer form, with equivalent items on each, but differently phrased. Soon after the subject's arrival at the institution he completed the self-appraisal form, written in language appropriate for elementary-level readers. Approximately 4 weeks later, three staff members rated each subject on the observer form. The items were keypunched for a computer program that produced profiles showing both the composite (averaged) staff ratings and the subject's self-ratings. In addition to the print-out profile of 14 factor scores, the computer also listed any behavior item rated by either the subject or staff at the extreme 20 percent of the distribution. These profiles and item printouts were useful in negotiating treatment contracts, as well as in evaluating change.

Other variables derived from scores on the Behavior Checklist included a measure of self-appraisal and observer-rating agreement, based on the distance between factor scores, and a measure of profile congruence based on the correlation between self and observer scores.

Ego level. Loevinger postulated that ego development follows a continuum, and identified and described several levels within the continuum (Loevinger, 1966). The abstraction *ego development* is a term applied to a developmental sequence in which each successive stage becomes more complex in that it incorporates and transcends the previous one. The scoring system for measuring the level of ego development is based on written responses to 36 open-ended sentences (Loevinger & Wessler, 1970). In order to reduce the time needed to score the large number of protocols anticipated in this study, a shorter 15-item form was developed. Short and long forms administered 1 week apart to 36 subjects correlated .77. Test protocols were scored blind, without identification of school, subject, or knowledge of its being a pretest or a posttest.

Parole Follow-Up

Reconviction data obtained from the California Youth Authority's data information system were used in most of the analyses for comparisons with other groups and other years. However, since all legal actions that may occur during a subject's period of parole in the community were not systematically reported to the youth authority, additional data were needed to evaluate accurately the behavior of some parolees. In about 50 percent of the cases in which doubt existed about subjects' activities while on parole, "rap sheets" (records of arrests, convictions, and dispositions) were obtained from the California Bureau of Criminal Statistics. These data made it possible to determine the length of time spent on parole before being returned to an institution and the amount of time spent in the community (as opposed to time in confinement) over the 24-month follow-up period. The proportion of subjects in confinement 6, 12, 18, and 24 months after release on parole was also calculated.

RESULTS

Implementation Data

The effects of the experimental programs on management problems within the institutions were examined by tallying all written reports of serious behavior incidents that occurred over a period of 30 months. Over the 30-month period the number of incident reports did not change appreciably, but the disposition of them did. The number of residents placed in special security quarters for misconduct was reduced by 61 percent at Close and 69 percent at Holton. Staff in the institutions also reported that when special security procedures were used, they were used differently, that is, for briefer periods and for promoting change in behavior rather than for retribution. Significantly fewer incident reports were written at Holton, but this may have been more highly related to differences in procedures and practices than to differences in the effectiveness of the behavior program in reducing management problems.

There was, of course, room for improvement in both programs, even after 3 years of training. Counselors at Close were expected to conduct at least two transactional analysis sessions with their clients each week. In addition to the academic contracting, Holton counselors were expected to negotiate at least one behavioral contingency contract each week with their clients. Staff at Close fulfilled two-thirds of their expected quota, Holton staff one-half of theirs. Boys at Close, averaging a 30-week stay, participated in an average of 40 transactional analysis group sessions. Boys at Holton, averaging a 35-week stay, negotiated an average of 19 written treatment contracts covering critical behavior deficiencies.

After each transactional analysis group meeting, the counselor rated each subject's degree of participation in fulfilling his treatment contract. Six-month and 12-month parole recidivism data indicated that the boys who had done the most intensive work in their transactional analysis groups were least subject to parole revocation ($p < .05$). Based on a sample of 152 subjects, ratings made by project staff of the quality and quantity of written, completed critical behavior deficiency contracts at Holton were not significantly related to parole outcome. It is quite evident, however, that this analysis was confounded by the acknowledged tendency for staff to write more contracts with subjects showing more behavior problems.

Supervisor ratings of staff competency showed a significant but small relationship with the success on parole of all subjects assigned to the two schools (at 12 months, $r = .16$, $n = 610$, $p < .01$) but the relationship was clearer at Close. After 6 months, 12 percent of the transactional analysis subjects in the high-, 22 percent in the medium-, and 27 percent in the low-staff-competency groups had been reconvicted ($p < .05$). At 12 months the failure rates were 20 percent, 35 percent, and 37 percent ($p < .05$).

At Karl Holton the same trend prevailed at 6 months but the difference in reconviction rates was not significant. For both schools, differences in recidivism rates were nonsignificant by 15 months, no matter what the rated competence of the counselor had been. The boys' consensual ratings of staff competency showed no relationship with either parole success or supervisor's competency ratings, a finding that detracts from the suspicion that clients are better judges of staff competence than are supervisors.

Social Climate Change

The Correctional Institutional Environment Scale provides measures on 10 subscales that can be combined into four major dimensions—relationship, treatment, systems maintenance, and aggression (Moos, 1970). The scale was administered to staff and residents early in the study and then a second time more than 2 years later. These data indicate that the new treatment programs had measurably changed the staff's and residents' perceptions of the social climates of the institutions. During this period scores of Close staff increased slightly (but not significantly) on the relationship and treatment dimensions, whereas scores of Holton staff decreased significantly on these two dimensions ($p < .01$). Examination of the change in subscale scores suggests that Holton staff saw less emphasis being placed on client-staff relationships, expressions of feelings, and discussions of personal problems leading to insight. The difference between posttest scores of Close and Holton staff on the relationship and treatment dimensions were significant beyond the .01 level. For staff of both schools, the greatest change was on the aggression scale, where scores decreased dramatically—more than 1 standard deviation ($p < .001$). This suggests that staff of both schools perceived much less argumentative and aggressive behavior among residents 2 years after the project began.

Even greater shifts were apparent in the perceptions of the residents. On the pretest, average scores of the residents were almost identical on all four scales. On the posttests, scores of Close residents had not changed significantly, whereas scores of Holton residents had decreased significantly on the relationship, treatment, and systems maintenance dimensions (all ps $< .001$). Residents' posttest scores for the two schools were significantly different on all four scales ($p < .01$). On the treatment and relationship scales the means differed by more than 1 standard deviation, with the residents at Holton being much more negative in their evaluation of their school's emphasis on these program elements.

Achievement Test Gains

All academic classes at Holton were based on a contingency management model. It was expected that the behavioral academic programs would be especially effective with the lower and middle maturity I-level subjects. The outcomes on the achievement tests were, therefore, completely unexpected. For all subjects at Holton, the monthly gain in reading comprehension was twice the expected—50 percent greater for lower and middle maturity subjects, and more than three times greater than expected for higher maturity subjects. The amount of gain for Holton subjects was near the expected in vocabulary and somewhat less than the expected in arithmetic. For subjects at Close, the monthly gain was twice the expected in reading comprehension (even more for middle maturity I-3s) and 50 percent greater in vocabulary and arithmetic (again, greatest for I-3s). The gains per month achieved by Close middle maturity (I-3) subjects on comprehension were statistically greater than those of Holton I-3 subjects ($p < .05$), whereas the Karl Holton higher maturity (I-4) subjects achieved at a faster rate ($p < .05$) than the I-4 subjects at Close. In summary, the Close academic program was more successful with middle maturity (I-3) boys, and the contingency-managed classrooms at Holton had greater effect with higher maturity (I-4) subjects.

The Jesness Inventory

On most Jesness Inventory scales, evidence of positive change is assumed when the posttest score is lower than the pretest score. However, the Denial scale has been shown to be correlated with other indicators of optimism and ego strength, particularly in the upper-middle range of scores (i.e., T scores of 55-60). It is the only scale on which nondelinquents consistently score higher than delinquents. Similarly, moderately high scores on the Repression and Immaturity scales (i.e., between 55 and 60) are generally more indicative of self-reports of well-being and positive feelings toward self and others than they are of negative feelings. Very low scores are indicative of pessimism and cynicism; very high scores, such as those obtained by I-2 subjects, point to naivete and rigidity.

Close subjects showed a significantly greater decrease ($p < .05$ or better) than Holton subjects on Social Maladjustment, Value Orientation, Alienation, Withdrawal, and Social Anxiety, and significantly higher posttest scores on Repression and Denial. Covariance analysis with pretest scores used as covariates confirmed the results of t-tests of change scores and showed one additional difference—the mean Asocial Index posttest score of Close subjects was significantly lower than that of Holton subjects.

The most marked differential improvement on the inventory scales was shown by the Close I-3 manipulators. Compared with the I-3 manipulators at Holton, those who completed the Close program earned significantly lower scores on Social Maladjustment, Value Orientation,

Alienation, Withdrawal, Social Anxiety, and the Asocial Index. Their posttest score on the Denial scale was also significantly higher, a direction of change indicative of improvement. Holton I-2 unsocialized passive subjects and I-3 cultural conformists showed significantly greater improvements than Close subjects in these classifications. The Holton I-2s obtained lower scores on Immaturity and Repression ($p < .05$) and the I-3 cultural conformists on Autism ($p < .05$). Close I-3 immature conformists had lower posttest scores on Alienation, Social Maladjustment, Value Orientation, Manifest Aggression, and Withdrawal. They also scored significantly higher than Holton immature conformists on the Denial scale. Changes shown by the I-4 neurotic-anxious subjects and I-4 acting-out neurotics were consistently in the direction of improvement for subjects in both schools. However, on Withdrawal and Social Anxiety, the I-4 acting-out neurotics at Close showed significantly greater improvement than did the Holton acting-out neurotics, and the I-4 neurotic-anxious subjects at Close scored significantly higher on Repression, a direction of change that can be considered as indicative of improvement for subjects of this subtype.

Haney Drug Scale

Only the posttest scores on the Haney Drug Scale were available for analysis. Other pretest inventory scores of subjects from both institutions, however, were similar enough to suggest that their pretest scores would not have differed on the Haney scale.

Results of a one-way analysis of variance of the unadjusted posttest scores for a large sample of subjects showed that on the average Close subjects achieved lower (more desirable) posttest scores, $F(1,511) = 11.58$, $p < .001$.

Behavior Checklist, Self-Appraisal Form

Scores for most subjects on the self-appraisal form of the Behavior Checklist improved from pretest to posttest. Covariance analysis showed significant posttest differences on Enthusiasm ($p < .001$) and Sociability ($p < .05$), both favoring Close. The greatest differential gains for a subtype were shown by Close manipulators.

Behavior Checklist, Observer Form

The scores used to evaluate observed behavior change were based on combined ratings of the subject's assigned caseworker, a member of the teaching team, and another staff member on the living hall. They completed the pretest ratings 30-45 days after each subject arrived at the institution, a period of time that appeared to be the minimum needed for a reliable appraisal. Analysis of covariance of the adjusted posttest scores (with pretest scores as covariates) showed significant differences ($p < .05$) between populations of the two schools on Independence, Calmness, Communication, and Insight. Holton subjects showed greater independence, ability to communicate, and calmness; Close subjects showed more insight.

When analyzed by I-level subtype, the clearest differential behavioral responses were shown by the two I-4 subtypes (acting-out neurotics and neurotic-anxious subjects) and by the I-3 cultural conformists. Covariance analyses indicated that neurotic-anxious subjects at Holton showed significantly ($p < .05$) less alienation, depression, anxiety, and more social control. The acting-out neurotics' ratings also suggested greater gains from the behavior modification program. Acting-out neurotics at Holton were rated as showing greater independence and as being more calm and more articulate at release than the acting-out neurotics who completed the transactional analysis program at Close.

The cultural conformists at Close were rated as being less obtrusive, more conforming, more insightful, more socially controlled, and less hypersensitive (greater control over feelings of anger) than Holton subjects. No differential outcomes were shown for unsocialized passive, immature conformist, and manipulator subjects.

Measures of Behavior Checklist Congruence

Self-observer distance was defined as the square root of the sum of the squares of the differences between an individual's self-ratings and observer ratings on each corresponding Behavior Checklist factor scale. *Self-observer correlation* was the correlation between an individual's self-appraisal and observer scores on the 14 factors. Analysis of self-observer distance scores showed no difference between the adjusted posttest means for Close (52.6) and Holton (54.4). On the second measure of congruence, the correlation between self-appraisal and observer ratings, there was marked (and significant) improvement from pretest to posttest for both schools. The difference between the adjusted posttest means (of the z-score equivalent) for subjects from the two institutions was also significant. The average adjusted posttest correlation between self- and observer-ratings was .55 at Close and .46 at Holton. The significant F

ratio, $F(1,843) = 26.3$, $p < .001$, indicates that there was closer correspondence between the posttest Behavior Checklist profile configurations of Close staff and residents.

It is probable that the closer agreement between boys and staff at Close was, in part, a consequence of the group therapy sessions, which enabled the staff to learn quickly about the boys' self-perceptions, and the boys, in turn, to learn how others perceived them.

Loevinger Ego Development Scale

Nearly the same percentage of subjects in each institution showed self-reported growth in ego level: At Close the increase was 39.9 percent, and at Holton, 40.3 percent. At Close 29.8 percent of the scores decreased, and at Holton 25.1 percent decreased. Scores of 30.3 percent of Close and 34.6 percent of Holton subjects remained unchanged. The difference between the proportions of those who changed ego level in the two schools was not significant.

Analysis of mean pretest to posttest change in ego level by I-level subtype showed only one significantly different outcome—the I-2 unsocialized passives' scores at Holton rose significantly more than those of the I-2s at Close ($p < .05$). This finding was the first of several pointing to the probability that the I-2s in the behavioral program gained more on self-report scores and behavioral change measures than those involved in transactional analysis.

Postopinion Poll Questionnaire

Positive regard. Staff in the transactional analysis program were expected to freely provide verbal "strokes" for their clients. They apparently did so, because 70 percent of Close subjects agreed that the staff almost always said positive rather than negative things about them, whereas only 50 percent felt so at Holton (p $< .001$). Fifty-three percent at Close thought the staff treated everyone fairly and equally; only 36 percent thought so at Holton ($p < .001$). When asked if the staff treated them without respect, insulted them, or implied they were inferior, 31 percent of the subjects at Holton and 15 percent at Close said that staff did ($p < .001$).

Staff involvement and understanding. Nearly three-fourths of the subjects at Close answered that they had spent at least "quite a lot" of time talking with their counselors, while at Holton just over half said so (p $< .001$). In both schools, the subjects who perceived themselves as spending the most time conversing with staff were the neurotic-anxious subjects, and those reporting the least time spent talking with staff were the cultural conformists. More Close subjects also said they had been able to discuss their problems fully (72 percent at Close and 50 percent at Holton, p < .001). Close subjects of all subtypes (except I-2 unsocialized passives) believed that their counselors understood them and their feeling more often (73 percent at Close and 53 percent at Holton, $p <$ .001). Close subjects were also more likely to report that counselors had helped them to understand themselves.

Performance demands. On items related to the Perceived Performance Demands factor, a significantly greater percentage of subjects (64 percent at Holton and 54 percent at Close) said they were required to work hard to earn grades or points in the classroom ($p < .05$). Consistent but not significant was the finding that Holton subjects also said they had to work harder for good reports on the hall. Significantly more subjects at Holton also believed that their counselors had been too strict, an opinion that was more pronounced among the lower maturity subjects. More subjects at Close said they had been allowed to participate in making rules and plans ($p < .001$).

The finding that Holton subjects tended to perceive their counselors as more strict, less willing to allow them to participate in rule making, and their teachers as more demanding of performance in the classroom is important. It provides support for the hypothesis that, at least in part, the less positive reaction of Holton subjects to their program and staff may have been related to a perception of greater pressure being placed on them to perform in accordance with preestablished criteria.

Liking for school. Significantly more subjects at Close made positive evaluations of their academic teachers. Sixty-three percent at Close agreed that most or all of their teachers were "really good," while 41 percent at Holton thought so (p < .001). This was true for all subtypes except the I-2 unsocialized passives, more of whom in the Holton program rated their teachers positively.

Again with the single exception of the I-2 unsocialized passives, significantly more subjects at Close said they had liked their teachers. The greatest subtype differences on this item occurred among I-4 acting-out neurotics and I-4 neurotic-anxious subjects, considerably fewer of whom at Holton responded favorably regarding their teachers even though their academic gains were greater.

Inmate code. Five questions were designed to determine the extent to which antiinstitutional "delinquent" subcultures existed. The majority

TABLE 1

Parole Violation Rates for Close and Holton Project Subjects
After 3, 6, 12, 15, and 24 Months of Parole Exposure

Parole exposure period	Close			Holton		
	R*	V	%V	R	V	%V
3 months	500	31	6.2	459	31	6.8
6 months	499	102	20.4	451	84	18.6
12 months	479	154	32.2	415	133	32.0
15 months	437	167	38.2	370	140	37.8
24 months	487	232	47.6	426	205	48.1

Note. R = number of releases on parole; V = number of violators; %V = percentage of violators.
* Twenty-four-month data were collected at a later point in the project, thus the larger sample.

of subjects at both schools reported that they would warn an adult if they became aware of a plot to assault a boy or a staff member (85 percent at Close, 69 percent at Holton, $p < .001$). When asked if they would warn staff if they knew another boy intended to escape, 68 percent at Close and 39 percent at Holton said they would ($p < .001$). Of the I-4 acting-out neurotics, only 23 percent of those at Holton agreed they would inform; 60 percent at Close said they would. Responses to three other items relating to the existence of an inmate code that would presumably impede effective treatment also indicated that the transactional analysis program was more effective than the behavior modification program in developing proinstitutional attitudes among residents.

Other items. Chi-square analyses of other attitudinal items and factors suggested that the Close program had been more effective in (a) improving the subjects' self-concepts; (b) increasing the subjects' certainty that they would not again break the law; and (c) convincing the subjects that they, not circumstances, controlled their lives. At release, 70 percent of Close subjects strongly agreed that their lives were in their own hands; only 55 percent at Holton so agreed. There was, however, no significant difference between the proportion of subjects in each school who (a) had been involved in illegal activities in the institutions, (b) believed they had made an effort to work through their problems, and (c) had made changes in their lives during their institutional stay (about 74 percent at both institutions). There was no indication that being in the behavior modification program had led these subjects to believe that they should receive a tangible reward for tasks accomplished. (Only 14 percent at Holton and 10 percent at Close thought that they should.)

Parole Follow-Up

Parole violation rates. Table 1 shows the parole violation rates for experimental subjects at 3, 6, 12, 15, and 24 months after their release on parole.* There were no significant differences between the revocation rates of subjects from the two schools at any parole exposure period. As shown, 32.2 percent of Close subjects and 32.0 of Holton subjects had been returned to an institution after 12 months. At 24 months, 47.6 percent of Close and 48.1 percent of Holton subjects had violated parole and been returned to an institution.

Table 2 shows the parole violation rates of Close and Holton parole release cohorts for the 2-year baseline period (1968-1969) prior to the full implementation of the experimental programs and the rates for the project subjects (1970-1971). The differences from baseline to experimental period were statistically significant for both Close and Holton; for Holton, $\chi^2 (1) = 8.09$, $p < .01$; for Close, $\chi^2 (1) = 23.32$, $p < .001$. The parole performance of project parolees was clearly superior to that shown by preexperimental subjects.

Prorated failure rates. It has been repeatedly shown that age at release is highly correlated with success on parole, with younger subjects being more likely to fail. To make certain that differences in age did not account for the observed differences in failure rates from baseline to experimental period, an analysis was run in which age was controlled. The 1968, 1969, 1970, and 1971 release cohorts from each of the two schools were prorated on the basis of the proportion of subjects at each age in the Close-Holton project sample, and expected violation rates were recalculated for all 4 years. Chi-square analyses of these prorated data revealed no significant differences between the Close and Holton rates, but significant differences were found between baseline and experimental rates favoring the experimental period for both schools (42.6 percent vs. 31.4 percent violation rates for Close and 44.9 percent vs. 35.1 percent violation rate for Holton). Recidivism rates were also obtained for releases from two other California Youth Authority institutions

---

* Included in the analyses were 51 subjects transferred into Close-Holton from other institutions. The recidivism rate for these subjects was 47.0 percent at 12 months. During the project, 103 subjects were transferred out and 11 escaped. The 12-month recidivism rate for these subjects was 45.6 percent. If the subjects who transferred out and escaped were included in the analysis and those transferred in were excluded, there would be little effect on the recidivism data. If anything, the number transferred out during the project was fewer than in previous years because an effort was made by both schools to avoid passing along their difficult cases to someone else.

TABLE 2

Parole Violation Rates for Holton and Close
Release Cohorts 1968, 1969, 1970, and 1971
at 12-Months' Parole Exposure

Year of release	Close			Holton		
	R	V	%V	R	V	%V
1968	253	124	49.0	232	99	42.7
1969	407	189	46.4	267	109	40.8
1970	233	80	34.3	187	58	31.0
1971	220	69	31.4	211	71	33.6

Note. The years 1968 and 1969 include only boys who were 15, 16, or 17
at entry; 1970 and 1971 include project cases only. R = number of releases
on parole; V = number of violators; %V = percentage of violators.

(Nelles in Whittier and Paso Robles in Paso Robles) to which boys of
approximately the same age were assigned. The violation rates for these
release cohorts were also prorated according to the distribution of ages
in the project sample. All four schools showed a significant decrease in
violation rates over the 4 years from 1968 to 1971 ($p < .01$). The decrease in rates, however, between 1969 (the year prior to the project)
and 1970 (the first year of the project) was significant for Close, $\chi^2(1) =$
6.71, $p < .01$, and Holton, $\chi^2(1) = 4.40$, $p < .05$, but not for Paso
Robles or Nelles.

Table 3 shows the prorated failure rates for the project period (1970-
1971) for the combined sample of experimental subjects at Close and
Holton and for subjects from Nelles and Paso Robles. The 1970-1971
prorated failure rates for project subjects released from Close and Holton
(33.1 percent) was significantly lower ($p < .001$) than failure rates at
either Nelles (42.5 percent) or Paso Robles (42.8 percent).

Base expectancy. In addition to age, other characteristics have been
shown to be related to probability of parole failure. The Youth Authority
Research Division has devised a formula that combines these variables
into a base expectancy score that allows the researcher to place each
subject into a risk category. Variables included in the base expectancy
formula used here were age at release, number of admissions to the Youth
Authority, number of commitments prior to coming to the California
Youth Authority, and race. The 12-month parole failure rates for Close
and Holton subjects grouped in low- (poor risk), medium-, and high-
base-expectancy categories showed that the good risk subjects failed
parole less often (20.5 percent) than those subjects in the medium- (35.2

TABLE 3

Prorated 12-Month Violation Rates Comparing
Close-Holton with Nelles and Paso Robles:
Combined 1970-1971 Release Cohort

Combined 1970-1971 release cohort	R	V	%V
Close-Holton	842	279	33.1
Nelles	835	355	42.5
Paso Robles	710	304	42.8

Note. For Close-Holton versus Nelles χ^2 (1) = 15.42, $p <$
.001; for Close-Holton versus Paso Robles χ^2 (1) = 15.15, p
$<$ .001. R = number of releases on parole; V = number of
violators; %V = percentage of violators.

TABLE 4

Differential 12-Month Parole Violation Rates by I-Level Subtype

Subtype	R	Close V	%V	R	Holton V	%V
Unsocialized aggressive	5	2	40.0	3	2	66.7
Unsocialized passive	18	9	50.0	18	5	27.8
Immature conformist	96	31	32.3	73	23	31.5
Cultural conformist	72	27	37.5	60	21	35.0
Manipulator	88	23	26.1	90	36	40.0*
Acting-out neurotic	89	27	30.3	92	25	27.2
Anxious neurotic	99	33	33.3	68	17	25.0
Situational emotional reaction	10	2	20.0	7	3	42.9
Cultural identifier	2	0	0.0	4	1	25.0
Total	479	154	32.2	415	133	32.0

*$p <$ .05 ($\chi^2 = 3.86$).

percent) or low- (38.8 percent) score groups. However, failure rates for
Close and Holton did not differ significantly in any risk category.

I-level subtype. One of the major hypotheses of the study was that
subjects of the several I-level personality types would respond differently
to the two treatment programs. Differential outcomes were noted on
several personality and behavioral measures, and revocation data for
subjects grouped according to their I-level subtypes were consistent with
these data. As shown in Table 4, the lowest violation rates for Close
subjects were for the I-4 situational emotional reaction subjects (20
percent) and I-3 manipulator (26.1 percent) subjects; the highest (worst)

rates were for the I-2 unsocialized passive (50 percent) group. At Holton the lowest failure rates were for neurotic-anxious subjects (25 percent), acting-out neurotics (27.2 percent), and I-2 unsocialized passives (27.8 percent), whereas the highest rate was found for manipulators (40 percent). The only significant difference between the institutions was in the violation rates for the manipulators ($p < .05$). Because of the few subjects involved (18 at each school), the difference in rates for I-2 unsocialized passives was not significant.

Other parole outcome criteria. It has been pointed out by Glaser (1973) that success is "too often measured as though it were an all-or-nothing matter" (p. 22). A modest refinement in the parole performance criterion was achieved by going to the rap sheets from which additional criteria were defined as follows: (a) score on a 4-point scale according to degree of delinquent involvement, (b) number of months to failure, (c) total months not in custody, and (d) custody status at specific times (6, 12, 18, and 24 months after release). Analysis of these data showed that the I-3 manipulators at Close achieved significantly lower scores on the 4-point code at 24 months ($p < .05$), were in the community significantly longer (3.7 months) before committing an offense that led to parole failure ($p < .01$), and significantly fewer were in custody 24 months after release (p < .01). Although there was a consistent trend favoring the I-2s from Holton, the difference was significant on only one criterion—6.3 percent of the Holton unsocialized passive subjects were in custody 6 months after release, compared to 43.8 percent of those from Close ($p < .05$).

MULTIPLE COVARIANCE ANALYSIS

Treatment

Treatment was the independent (predictor) variable. Ten covariates were entered to eliminate as much as possible any linear effect of pre-existing random differences in the groups. The covariates were (a) age at admission; (b) race (white vs. other); (c) length of institutional stay; (d) maturity level (I-level); (e) ego level; (f) pretest Behavior Checklist self-appraisal form, rapport scale; (g) pretest Behavior Checklist observer form, mean score; (h) pre-Youth Opinion Poll item, "expects future trouble"; (i) pre-Youth Opinion Poll factor, Expects Good Relations with Staff; and (j) pre-Youth Opinion Poll factor, Perceived Need for Change.

The dependent variables were grouped into five classes of outcome measures: (a) process measures, consisting of eight Postopinion Poll factors; (b) attitudinal (self-report) measures, consisting of 11 Jesness Inventory scales, 14 Behavior Checklist self-appraisal factors, ego level score, and three Postopinion Poll factors; (c) behavioral measures, consisting of the 14 factors of the Behavioral Checklist observer form; (d) six parole measures; and (e) a combined set of 28 measures selected to assess the overall impact of the independent variable. Although the main focus of the analysis was on the combined set of measures, brief mention is made of the multiple covariance analysis results with the other measures.

Process and attitudinal measures. Analysis of the adjusted scores on the process measures showed significant differences beyond the .001 level on six of the seven factors. Consistent with the chi-square analysis presented in the previous section, subjects from the Close transactional analysis program emphatically expressed more positive opinions about staff and program. Multiple covariance analysis of the attitudinal measures consistently supported the conclusions that the transactional analysis program at Close resulted in greater attitudinal improvement, especially on the affective or mood scales related to perceived anxiety, withdrawal, and depression.

Behavioral measures. Differential effects were more apparent on the behavioral scores. Close subjects achieved significantly higher adjusted posttest scores on Considerateness and Insight, whereas Holton subjects were higher on Independence, Calmness, Effective Communications, and Anger Control. The fact that the average observer pretest rating over all 14 Behavior Checklist factors was included as one of the 10 covariates decreases the possibility that these results were an artifact of rater halo or bias.

Parole measures. Multiple covariance analysis showed no significant differences in parole outcome for subjects from the two programs. The multivariate analysis of variance (done prior to the covariance adjustment) also showed no significant differences in parole outcomes for graduates of the two schools.

Combined measures. In order to enable comparisons to be made of the relative influence of different program and individual difference variables, a set of measures was selected that appeared to best serve as a criterion of overall program impact. Inclusion of these particular variables was in part guided by previous factor analyses and by their a priori importance and relevance as treatment objectives.

Data from the multiple covariance analysis shown in Table 5 indicate that the treatment groups differed significantly on 8 of the 28 variables. Overall, 19 percent of the variables was accounted for by type of treatment. (The multivariate analysis of variance run prior to controlling for the influence of the covariates accounted for 23 percent of the variance.)

It is worth emphasizing that the amount of variance accounted for by the independent variable is in large part dependent upon the number and type of dependent variables included. Due to the fact that the dependent variables were reasonably comprehensive, and the number of subjects was large in relation to the number of dependent variables, the analyses enable valid comparisons to be made of the relative influence of various independent variables, such as positive regard.

Positive Regard

The effect on outcome of client-reported relationship with staff was evaluated in a series of multivariate analysis of variance and multiple covariance analysis problems with positive regard as the independent variable or group determinant. The hypothetical assumption was made that each program generated the same degree of client positive regard for staff. In those solutions in which assignment to groups was not random, the statistic of covariance was used in the observational and hypothetical sense, rather than the experimental sense, and the data are open to the difficulties of interpretation "which becloud any contrafactual conditional statement" (Hope, 1968, p. 154).

The average positive regard scores for Close and Holton were 12.5 and 10.3, respectively (for Close, $SD = 2.7$; for Holton, $SD = 3.1$). The overall mean for all Close and Holton subjects was used to divide the subjects into high and low positive regard groups, with the result that the high positive regard group was comprised of more Close subjects, and concomitantly, the low positive regard group contained more Holton subjects. Although the exact proportions varied depending on the variables included in the analysis, approximately 62 percent of the high positive regard groups consisted of subjects from Close, and 63 percent of subjects in the low positive regard groups were from Holton.

The covariates were the same set used in the multiple covariance analysis problem with treatment as the independent variable. With treatment as the designed comparison variable, significant differences between the group means were found on only two covariates—length of stay and need for change (with Holton subjects having a longer average length of stay and Close subjects expressing a greater need for change). The groups defined by high and low positive regard scores differed significantly on 9 of the 10 covariates, the exception being expectation of good relations with staff as expressed on the pretest opinion poll.

TABLE 5

Adjusted Posttest Means and F Ratios for Close
and Holton Subjects on Selected Outcome
Variables with 10 Covariates

Variable	Close	Holton	F ratio
Post opinion poll			
Decision not to use drugs (low)	2.0	2.2	2.79
Perceived change in self (low)	1.9	1.8	.03
Fate control (low)	1.7	2.0	5.91*
Self-concept	4.1	3.9	2.35
Jesness Inventory			
Manifest Aggression	48.6	50.0	2.31
Withdrawal-Depression	48.7	50.6	5.07*
Social Anxiety	41.3	44.1	8.09**
Repression	55.9	53.5	7.69***
Self-appraisal Behavior Checklist			
Unobtrusiveness	51.9	52.4	.28
Responsibility	66.6	66.6	.00
Independence	60.7	59.4	1.27
Rapport	59.3	57.2	3.52
Conformity	55.3	55.5	.05
Calmness	59.1	56.8	3.83*
Anger Control	55.4	54.1	1.22
Observer Behavior Checklist			
Unobtrusiveness	45.3	46.4	2.64
Responsibility	57.8	57.4	.20
Independence	52.9	54.5	3.48
Rapport	53.5	53.4	.01
Enthusiasm	52.5	53.7	2.10
Calmness	49.1	51.8	11.24**
Communication	55.6	57.3	3.39
Insight	61.5	58.6	19.27***
Anger Control	47.6	48.7	2.0
Parole outcome			
4-point evaluation (12 mo.)	2.1	2.1	.11
4-point evaluation (24 mo.)	2.5	2.5	.01
Mean months to parole failure	16.0	15.4	.65
Total months not in custody (24 mo.)	18.1	18.4	.36

Note. The covariates were (a) age at admission, (b) race (white vs. other), (c) length of institutional stay, (d) maturity level, (e) ego level, (f) pretest self-appraisal Behavioral Checklist Rapport factor, (g) pretest Behavioral Checklist observer mean factor score, (h) pre-Youth Opinion Poll Item 10—"expects trouble," (i) pre-Youth Opinion factor—Expects Good Relations with Staff, (j) pre-Youth Opinion Poll factor—Perceived Need for Change in Self.
* $p \leq .05$.
** $p \leq .01$.
*** $p \leq .001$.

Process and attitudinal measures. Because positive regard was defined by responses to items on the Postopinion Poll, the common measurement method shared with other Postopinion Poll items is a source of a considerable amount of the variance in the process variables. Therefore, the higher scores obtained by the high positive regard group on process variables, indicating they perceived staff as more competent, involved, and non-demanding, were not unexpected. The high positive regard group also obtained more desirable scores on all but 1 of the 11 inventory scales (Social Anxiety). The differences in scores on most of the scales were highly significant, approximately ½ standard deviation. On the Haney Drug Scale, which is comprised of inventory items, high positive regard subjects also had lower scores, suggesting less likelihood of future drug use. On the Self-Appraisal Behavior Checklist, those in the high positive regard group had significantly higher (i.e., more positive) scores on 10 of 14 factors. Differences between scores of the high and low positive regard groups were also significant for ego level, self-concept, and two items from the Postopinion Poll.

The data indicate that expressed positive regard for staff was related to, and on the basis of our best judgment probably contributed to, improved attitudes and self-reported well-being of the subjects.

Behavior measures. More convincing evidence for the importance of client positive regard was that from the behavioral ratings for these data, which, although obtained at about the same time, were collected by a totally different method. Multiple covariance analysis showed that the groups' adjusted posttest scores were significantly different on 9 of the 14 factors of the Behavior Checklist, observer form—all favoring the high positive regard group. The data were remarkably consistent with those obtained from the Behavior Checklist self-appraisal scales, with the high and low groups showing significant differences in the same direction on 9 of the 10 same scales. Although generalized halo effects no doubt influenced the raters' evaluations, this convergence of data and the fact that outcomes from the two programs were different increase our confidence in the likelihood that positive client-staff relationships contributed to improved client behavior in several specific areas.

Parole measures. Subjects in the high positive regard group achieved better scores on all six parole measures; the differences were significant on two measures—total months not in custody ($p < .001$) and 4-point evaluation ($p < .05$). If it is assumed that subjects in the high positive regard group might be expected to do better on parole, the significance of the differences in outcomes may be evaluated using a one-tailed test.

Using a directional one-tailed test, significant differences at the .05 level were shown on two additional parole outcome measures: Those expressing higher positive regard for staff remained on parole longer before getting into trouble and were involved in fewer infractions while on parole.

Combined measures. The adjusted posttest scores and parole data on the combined criterion variables are shown in Table 6. Some idea of the relative importance of the different independent variables can be gained by contrasting the variance accounted for.

The covariance analysis showed that groups defined by high and low scores on positive regard accounted for 14 percent of the variance in the dependent variables (multivariate analysis of variance accounted for 21 percent). The 14 percent compares favorably with the 19 percent accounted for by treatment. Further analysis of these data suggests that treatment and positive regard accounted for quite different effects.

Treatment Versus Positive Regard

It has been shown that treatment and positive regard were related to outcomes. It has also been shown that subjects in the Close program expressed greater regard for staff than did subjects at Holton. Assuming that positive evaluation of staff is not a unique accompaniment of a transactional analysis program and if attended to could be generated with equal intensity in a behavior modification program, what then would the differential treatment effects be? Some information about the specific effects of the two treatment programs under the hypothetical condition of equal positive regard can be gained by including positive regard as a covariate, with treatment as the predictor variable.

In a multiple covariance analysis on the combined set of outcome variables with positive regard included as a covariate, differences were evident on 9 of the 28 variables. Treatment accounted for 19 percent of the variance in the outcome variables, exactly the same amount accounted for when positive regard was not included as a covariate. However, some interesting changes occurred in the adjusted posttest means of several variables. Using positive regard as a covariate, thus parceling out or equalizing its effects for the two treatment groups, decreased the superiority of the Close program on the attitudinal outcome measures and further increased the impact of the Holton behavior modification program on the behavior factors. From the fact that some scores were only slightly affected by the introduction of positive regard as a covariate, it can be

TABLE 6

Posttest Means and F Ratios for Subjects in High and Low
Positive Regard (PR) Groups on Selected Outcome
Variables with 10 Control Variables (Covariates)

Variable	High PR (n = 320)	Low PR (n = 278)	F ratio
Post opinion poll			
Decision not to use drugs (low)	1.9	2.2	5.19*
Perceived change in self (low)	1.7	2.0	7.69**
Fate control (low)	1.6	2.1	13.31***
Self-concept	4.2	3.8	10.24**
Jesness Inventory			
Manifest Aggression	47.8	51.0	12.01***
Withdrawal-Depression	49.0	50.4	2.47
Social Anxiety	42.5	42.9	.23
Repression	56.1	53.0	12.57***
Self-appraisal Behavior Checklist			
Unobtrusiveness	53.2	51.0	6.65**
Responsibility	68.5	64.5	18.47***
Independence	59.9	60.2	.04
Rapport	61.6	54.6	39.73***
Conformity	57.0	53.7	9.03**
Calmness	58.7	57.1	1.80
Anger Control	56.8	52.6	11.87***
Observer Behavior Checklist			
Unobtrusiveness	46.5	45.2	3.65
Responsibility	58.5	56.6	5.80*
Independence	54.0	53.3	.76
Rapport	54.7	52.2	9.54**
Enthusiasm	53.7	52.3	2.87
Calmness	50.8	50.1	.72
Communication	57.1	55.8	2.13
Insight	61.4	58.6	16.87***
Anger Control	48.9	47.4	3.23
Parole outcome			
4-point evaluation (12 mo.)	2.1	2.2	1.54
4-point evaluation (24 mo.)	2.5	2.6	2.92
Mean months to parole failure	16.1	15.3	1.31
Total months not in custody (24 mo.)	18.9	17.4	9.34**

Note. The covariates were (a) age at admission, (b) race (white vs. other),
(c) length of institutional stay, (d) maturity level, (e) ego level, (f) pretest
self-appraisal Behavioral Checklist Rapport factor, (g) pretest Behavioral
Checklist observer mean factor score, (h) pre-Youth Opinion Poll Item 10—
"expects trouble," (i) pre-Youth Opinion factor—Expects Good Relations
with Staff, (j) pre-Youth Opinion Poll factor—Perceived Need for Change
in Self.
   * $p < .05$.
  ** $p < .01$.
 *** $p < .001$.

inferred that lower posttest scores on inventory scales Withdrawal-Depression and Social Anxiety, higher scores on Behavior Checklist observer form factors Rapport and Insight, and higher scores on the Calmness factor of the Behavior Checklist self-appraisal form were to a large degree specific treatment effects of the transactional analysis program.

The same type of analysis was made with positive regard as the independent variable. For the combined set of outcome variables with 10 covariates, including type of treatment, 13 percent of the variance was accounted for, compared with 14 percent in the solution that did not include treatment as a covariate. Here again, although the amount of variance accounted for has remained much the same, shifts in the adjusted posttest means provide a source of information about the effects of positive regard. Inspection of posttest scores with and without treatment as a covariate showed that the effects of positive regard were most evident on self-appraisal Behavior Checklist factors Responsibility, Rapport, and Conformity; inventory scales Manifest Aggression and Repression; Behavior Checklist observer form factors Unobtrusiveness, Responsibility, and Anger Control; and on the parole follow-up criteria. In other words, regardless of type of treatment, whether behavior modification or transactional analysis, the fostering of positive regard correlated with, and probably can be considered an antecedent of, improvement on these variables.

Perhaps the clearest comparison of the effects of treatment and positive regard can be gained from the data presented in Table 7. Four groups were defined as follows: (a) Close, high positive regard, (b) Close, low positive regard, (c) Holton, high positive regard, and (d) Holton, low positive regard.

Results of the multiple covariance analysis shown in Table 7 indicate that in general, and consistent with the relatively few interactions found in several analysis of variance problems, the high positive regard groups in both programs obtained more desirable scores, with the transactional analysis/high positive regard group having significantly better scores on eight variables and the behavior modification/high positive regard group on eight variables. The transactional analysis/high positive regard group had the highest scores on Postopinion Poll factors Perceived Change in Self, Fate Control, and Self-Concept; inventory scale Manifest Aggression; self-appraisal Behavior Checklist factors Responsibility, Rapport, and Anger Control; and observer Behavior Checklist factor Insight. The behavior modification/high positive regard group had best scores on self-

TABLE 7

Posttest Means and F Ratios for Close and Holton Subjects in
High and Low Positive Regard (PR) Groups on Selected
Outcome Variables with 10 Control Variables (Covariates)

Variable	TA/ high PR ($n=202$)	TA/ low PR ($n=99$)	BM/ high PR ($n=118$)	BM/ low PR ($n=179$)	F ratio
Postopinion poll					
Decision Not to Use Drugs (low)	1.8	2.2	2.1	2.2	2.31
Perceived Change in Self (low)	1.7	2.2	1.8	1.9	3.91**
Fate Control (low)	1.6	1.8	1.7	2.2	6.14***
Self-Concept	4.2	3.8	4.0	3.8	3.90**
Jesness Inventory					
Manifest Aggression	47.8	50.2	47.9	51.5	4.31**
Withdrawal-Depression	48.1	49.8	50.6	50.7	2.44
Social Anxiety	41.6	40.8	43.9	44.1	2.80*
Repression	56.6	54.4	55.3	52.3	5.43**
Self-Appraisal Behavior Checklist					
Unobtrusiveness	53.1	49.8	53.4	51.7	3.03*
Responsbility	68.7	62.5	68.1	65.7	8.15***
Independence	60.5	61.1	58.9	59.7	.59
Rapport	61.7	54.9	61.4	54.5	13.23***
Conformity	56.8	52.4	57.4	54.3	3.49*
Calmness	59.7	58.0	57.0	56.6	1.70
Anger Control	56.9	52.8	56.5	52.5	3.97**
Observer Behavior Checklist					
Unobtrusiveness	46.2	43.6	47.0	46.1	3.52*
Responsibility	58.7	56.0	58.1	57.0	2.38
Independence	53.6	51.6	54.8	54.2	2.07
Rapport	54.6	51.4	54.7	52.6	3.52*
Enthusiasm	53.4	50.7	54.4	53.2	2.62***
Calmness	49.8	47.7	52.4	51.4	5.13**
Communication	56.5	53.9	58.1	56.8	2.61*
Insight	62.4	59.9	55.7	57.9	9.77***
Anger Control	48.7	45.5	49.3	48.5	3.06*
Parole outcome					
4-point evaluation—12 mo.	2.1	2.2	2.0	2.2	.54
4-point evaluation—24 mo.	2.5	2.7	2.4	2.6	1.09
M mo. to parole failure	16.1	15.7	16.1	15.0	.58
Total mo. not in custody—24 mo.	18.8	16.8	19.2	17.8	3.83*

Note. The covariates were (a) age at admission, (b) race (white vs. other), (c) length of institutional stay, (d) maturity level, (e) ego level, (f) pretest self-appraisal Behavior Checklist Rapport factor, (g) pretest Behavior Checklist observer mean factor score, (h) Pre-Youth Opinion Poll Item 10—expects Trouble, (i) Pre-Youth Opinion Poll factor—Expects Good Relations with Staff, (j) Pre-Youth Opinion Poll factor—Perceived Need for Change in Self. TA = transactional analysis; BM = behavior modification.
* $p < .05$.
** $p < .01$.
*** $p < .001$.

appraisal Behavior Checklist factors Unobtrusiveness and Conformity, and on observer Behavior Checklist factors Unobtrusivenes, Rapport, Enthusiasm, Communication, and Anger Control. They also showed the least time spent in custody over the 24-month parole follow-up period.

Perusal of the table clarifies earlier findings. It can be seen that (a) subjects with higher positive regard did better than those with lower positive regard scores in both programs. Interaction effects appear to be inconsequential. (b) Specific transactional analysis effects were most clearly evident on inventory scales Social Anxiety, Withdrawal-Depression, Behavior Checklist self-appraisal scale Independence, and observer Behavior Checklist factor Insight. (c) Behavior modification effects were most clearly evident on observer Behavior Checklist factors Independence, Calmness, and Effective Communication.

Overall, after the contribution of the covariates were parceled out, 32.4 percent of the variance was accounted for by treatment and positive regard. This approximates the total contributed by each with the other parceled out, 13.3 percent for positive regard with treatment included as a covariate and 18.5 percent for treatment with positive regard included as a covariate.

DISCUSSION

At the time this study began on April 1, 1968 few comprehensive institutional treatment programs based on the behavioral principles of operant psychology existed. Cohen (Cohen & Filipczak, 1971) designed one of the first behaviorally engineered educational classrooms as part of the CASE II project (Contingencies Applicable to Special Education) at the National Training School for Boys. Homme (1966) and McKee (1964) had both begun implementation of contingency-managed programs, and a token economy in a mental institution was being refined at about the same time (Ayllon & Azrin, 1968). Most of the applications of learning theory, however, were made with single subjects, and the studies were administered by experimental psychologists or specially trained personnel. Consequently, to implement an institutionwide behavioral program, it was necessary for the staff of Karl Holton to learn the basic principles of operant psychology to the point where they could participate actively in designing their own program.

Similarly, transactional analysis had not been implemented in an institutional setting to the extent that it was at Close. Although the initial training was concentrated on the transactional analysis therapy groups, its application was eventually extended to virtually all phases of the program. Perhaps most novel was the notion that a correctional staff should experience the same type of therapy they would use with their clients. Administrators and project staff at Close approached the idea with a great deal of caution. That we have come a long way since then can be judged by the fact that such therapeutic involvement by staff in the California Youth Authority is now almost taken for granted. At several institutions management expects staff to involve themselves with such experiences, even though they do not (and cannot) demand such participation.

Because the programs were innovative, there were many implementation problems, some of which were never fully solved (e.g., how to record and reinforce positive behaviors rather than attend to the more conspicuous, infrequently occurring, and easily recorded negative behaviors). Nevertheless, model treatment programs did evolve. The data presented here provide evidence that subjects at both institutions experienced positive attitudinal and behavior changes. These were not trivial changes. Subjects from both programs showed behavioral improvement of more than $\frac{1}{2}$ standard deviation (5 T-score points) on 8 of the 14 factors of observer form on the Behavior Checklist. The subjects also averaged more than $\frac{1}{2}$ standard deviation improvement on inventory scales Social Anxiety, Withdrawal, and Denial, indicating that they left the institutions feeling less anxious, aggressive, hostile, and withdrawn, and more optimistic and confident. That these were not simply "hello-goodbye" or "Hawthorne" effects could be inferred from the fact that the subjects improved in areas directly related to the two types of treatment in which they were involved and from the presence of differential outcomes for subjects of different I-level subtypes.

Both programs seemed equally effective as measured by parole criteria. Although the lowest maturity (I-2) subjects appeared to profit more from the Holton behavioral program, the difference on most measures was not statistically significant. I-4 subjects appeared to profit about the same from both programs. The clearest differential response was made by the I-3 manipulator subjects. The manipulators in transactional analysis showed greater attitudinal and behavioral gains and achieved significantly lower recidivism rates in contrast with those at Holton.

Perhaps the most important finding of the study was that each program generated specific treatment effects. That the behavioral program resulted in greater gains on the observer ratings and the transactional analysis program in greater gains on attitudinal and self-report dimensions should not come as a surprise. At present, it is nonetheless reassuring to actually find what one would logically expect to find. That both the attitudinal and the behavioral gains were relevant intermediate objectives can be surmised from the fact that both the Behavior Checklist posttest ratings and the posttest attiudinal variables correlated with parole performance criteria. The correlation between the first five variables selected by a stepwise regression program run with the 14 Behavior Checklist posttest observer ratings showed a multiple correlation with parole failure at or before 12 months of —.24 $(n = 385, p < .01)$ for Holton subjects and —.12 $(n = 419, p < .05)$ for Close subjects. The first five attitudinal variables selected from self-report measures showed a multiple correlation with parole failure at or before 12 months of —.26 $(n = 276, p < .01)$ for Holton subjects and —.25 $(n = 316, p < .01)$ for Close subjects.

The data show that both schools' recidivism rates for the experimental period were significantly lower than the base rate for the year prior to the start of the project. Violation rates for project subjects were also significantly lower than boys of the same age released from two other youth authority institutions.

To label the Close-Holton programs as successful is, however, to use the term loosely and strictly in a relative sense since a perusal of the subjects' postrelease arrest records paints a less sanguine picture. Out of 929 subjects released on parole from both schools, only 215, or 23 percent, had records clear of arrest after 2 years, and it can be assumed that many of those with clear records would later be involved in some illegal behaviors (Davis, 1974; Jesness, 1971). This suggests that the criterion of recidivism can more accurately be conceptualized as distinguishing early (or frequent) from late (or less frequent) offenders rather than as differentiating violators from nonviolators. Of course, these high parole failure rates should not necessarily be attributed to the inadequacy of institutional programs. Although institutional staff may want to take responsibility for their clients' successes, they may be equally prone, and equally erroneous, in blaming their failures on the absence of effective aftercare services. In the long run, both institution programs and parole or probation services, in comparison with the offenders' entrenched behavior patterns, and the continuing influence of home, friends, and neighborhood, may be relatively unimportant in affecting offenders' lives. The data in this study demonstrate quite clearly, however, that institutional programs do effect behavioral changes—changes that are related to the quality of the service provided. That the institution's impact appeared transitory rather than enduring should not obscure the potential impact of the special learning environments that institutional settings can provide.

An important finding was that the nonspecific factor of client positive regard for staff potentiated whatever specific treatment effects were present and contributed about as much to outcome as did type of treatment. The data suggest that where specific overt behaviors are targeted in a behavioral program, greater changes can be made when the client feels positively toward staff; similarly in a transactional analysis program, greater changes on attitudinal and self-report measures can be obtained where good relationships exist. At least one explanation for these findings is that increased positive regard enhances the youth counselors' social reinforcing value. The data are consistent with those from other studies (see those reviewed by Russell, 1974, and McCardel and Murray, 1974). Although his data do not lead one inevitably to the same conclusion, Russell (1974) felt that his examination of the literature on the power of behavior therapy "pointed rather definitely to nonspecific suggestion or placebo as the major source of this therapy's power" (p. 131). McCardel and Murray (1974) evaluated outcomes of three encounter groups that differed markedly in procedures and techniques. After noting that the groups achieved nearly identical outcomes on all personality and behavioral measures, they concluded that their results would seem to place the burden of proof on those who hypothesize "a specific effect for a specific technique" (p. 344). Marks, Sonada, and Schalock (1968) found nearly identical positive outcomes both in kind and quality with relationship therapy and a reinforcement program (token economy) but found the reinforcement program more economical of extra staff time. No conclusions can be drawn concerning which treatment program was most economical of staff time in the present study. More hours were spent in training by the Close staff, and more hours appear to have been spent in direct contact with wards in group and individual counseling at Close. Ideally, each 50-bed unit at Holton could have used a full-time behavioral consultant and paraprofessional assistance with data collection. In some instances, residents served successfully in this capacity. Implementation of a systematic data collection system at Close would probably have increased the program's effectiveness and undoubtedly increased the number of hours needed to administer this program. That specific differential outcomes were found in the present project may be attributed to the duration and intensity of the treatment programs, the large number of

subjects involved (which increased the sensitivity of the tests of significance), and the fairly comprehensive types of outcome measures used.
Why did the transactional analysis program generate so much more positive regard for staff? More dissatisfaction from recalcitrant, non-volunteer clients would be expected in a program in which present performance criteria are established and adhered to. If in addition the criteria are established without consulting with the client, and contracts are imposed rather than negotiated, as was sometimes probably the case at Holton, positive regard for staff would be expected to be low.

Recognition of the fact that the goal of treatment must be toward client self-management reinforces the requirement that the client's own stated goals should serve as the focal point for negotiating and implementing contracts. The client needs to understand the relevance of the specified behavioral goals in helping him achieve his own goals. The program at Holton would probably have generated more positive regard for staff if these two issues had been stressed more heavily in the training of the Holton staff.

At Close, emphasis was placed on initial goal setting in conjunction with the client, and in theory, all contracts required staff-client negotiations. Transactional analysis, on the other hand, might profit by more clearly specifying overt behavioral goals and establishing performance criteria. Doing so might increase the impact of transactional analysis on some of the behavioral measures without decreasing positive regard or attitudinal scores. An integration of these two types of therapy is not inconceivable, and experimental efforts in this direction are already underway.

REFERENCES

AYLLON, T. & AZRIN, N. *The Token Economy: A Motivational System for Therapy and Rehabilitation.* New York: Appleton-Century-Crofts, 1968.
BANDURA, A. *Principles of Behavior Modification.* New York: Holt, Rinehart & Winston, 1969.
BERGIN, A. & STRUPP, H. *Changing Frontiers in the Science of Psychotherapy.* Chicago: Aldine/Atherton, 1972.
BERNE, E. *Transactional Analysis in Psychotherapy.* New York: Grove Press, 1961.
BERNE, E. *Principles of Group Treatment.* New York: Grove Press, 1966.
BERNE, E. *Games People Play.* New York: Grove Press, 1967.
COHEN, H. L. & FILIPCZAK, J. *A New Learning Environment.* San Francisco: Jossey-Bass, 1971.
COOLEY, W. W. & LOHNES, P. R. *Multivariate Data Analysis.* New York: Wiley, 1971.
CRONBACH, L. J. & FURBY, L. How should we measure change—or should we? *Psychol. Bull.,* 1970, 74, 68-80.
DAVIS, G. Post-discharge studies. In K. Griffiths and G. Ferdun (Eds.), *A Review of*

Accumulated Research in the California Youth Authority. Sacramento: California Youth Authority, 1974.

EYSENCK, H. J. The effects of psychotherapy: An evaluation. *J. Consult. Psychol.,* 1954, 45, 319-324.

EYSENCK, H. J. The effects of psychotherapy. In H. J. Eysenck (Ed.), *Handbook of Abnormal Psychology.* New York: Basic Books, 1961.

GATES, A. I. & MACGINITIE, W. H. *Teachers' Manual for the Gates-MacGinitie Reading Test.* New York: Teachers College Press, Teachers College, Columbia University, 1965.

GLASER, D. *Routinizing Evaluation: Getting Feedback on Effectiveness of Crime and Delinquency Programs.* Rockville, Md.: NIMH Center for Studies of Crime and Delinquency, 1973.

GUTTMAN, E. S. *Effects of Short-Term Psychiatric Treatment* (Research Report No. 36). Sacramento: California Youth Authority, 1963.

HANEY, R. E. Research design and preliminary results of a treatment and education program for adolescent early drug offenders. Paper presented at the meeting of the Southern California Regioial Research and Evaluation, sponsored by the California Department of Mental Hygiene, May 1971.

HOPE, K. *Methods of Multivariate Analysis.* London: University of London Press, 1968.

HOLLAND, J. G. & SKINNER, B. F. *The Analysis of Behavior.* New York: McGraw-Hill, 1961.

HOMME, L. E. Contiguity theory and contingency management. *Psychol. Record,* 1966, 16, 233-241.

JESNESS, C. F. *The Jesness Inventory.* Palo Alto, Calif.: Consulting Psychologists Press, 1966.

JESNESS, C. F. Comparative effectiveness of two institutional treatment programs for delinquents. *Child Care Quart.,* 1971, 1, 119-130.

JESNESS, C. F. The Preston Typology Study: An experiment with differential treatment in an institution. *J. Res. Crime Delin.,* 1971, 8, 38-52.

JESNESS, C. F. *The Jesness Behavior Checklist.* Palo Alto, Calif.: Consulting Psychologists Press, 1971.

JESNESS, C. F. *Classifying Juvenile Offenders: The Sequential I-Level Classification Manual.* Palo Alto, Calif.: Consulting Psychologists Press, 1975.

JESNESS, C. F. & DERISI, W. Some variations in techniques of contingency management in a school for delinquents. In J. S. Stumphauzer (Ed.), *Behavior Therapy with Delinquents.* Springfield, Ill.: Charles C Thomas, 1973.

JESNESS, C. F., DERISI, W., McCORMICK, P. M., & WEDGE, R. F. *The Youth Center Research Project.* Sacramento, Calif.: American Justice Institute, July 1972.

KRASNER, L. & ULLMANN, L. P. *Research in Behavior Modification: New Developments and Implications.* New York: Holt, Rinehart & Winston, 1967.

LOEVINGER, J. The meaning and measurement of ego development. *Amer. Psychol.,* 1966, 21, 195-206.

LOEVINGER, J. & WESSLER, R. *Measuring Ego Development I & II.* San Francisco: Jossey-Bass, 1970.

MARKS, J., SONODA, B., & SCHALOCK, R. Reinforcement versus relationship therapy for schizophrenia. *J. Abnorm. Psychol.,* 1968, 73, 397-402.

McCARDEL, J. & MURRAY, E. J. Nonspecific factors in weekend encounter groups. *J. Consult. Clin. Psychol.,* 1974, 42, 337-345.

McCORD, W. & McCORD, J. *Origins of Crime: A New Evaluation of the Cambridge-Somerville Youth Study.* New York: Columbia University Press, 1959.

McCORMICK, P. & CAMPOS, L. *Introduce Yourself to Transactional Analysis.* Berkeley, Calif.: Transactional Publications, 1969.

McKee, J. M. The Draper experiment: A programmed learning project. In G. Ofiesh & W. Meierhenry (Eds.), *Trends in Programmed Instruction.* Washington, D. C.: National Education Association, 1964.

Moos, R. Differential effects of the social climates of correctional institutions. *J. Res. Crime & Delin.,* 1970, 7, 71-82.

Ohmart, H. The challenge of crime in a free society. *Youth Authority Quart.,* 21, Fall, 1968, 2-11.

Russell, E. The power of behavior control: A critique of behavior modification methods. *J. Clin. Psychol.,* 1974, 30, 111-136.

Sullivan, C. E., Grant, M. Q., & Grant, J. D. The development of interpersonal maturity: Applications to delinquency. *Psychiat.,* 1957, 20, 373-385.

Ullmann, P. & Krasner, L. A *Psychological Approach to Abnormal Behavior.* Englewood Cliffs, N. J.: Prentice-Hall, 1969.

Wheeler, S. & Cottrell, L. S. *Juvenile Delinquency, Its Prevention and Control.* Hartford, Conn.: Connecticut Printers, 1966.

Winer, B. J. *Statistical Principles in Experimental Design* (2nd ed.). New York: McGraw-Hill, 1971.

Section X

CLINICAL ISSUES, INNOVATIONS
AND CASE STUDIES

Commentary

Strategies of clinical intervention have evolved radically since those early days of the anecdotal case study, when even an uncontrolled demonstration that conditioning techniques could be successfully deployed on a one-to-one basis with patients traditionally treated by psychotherapy was a cause of celebration. But contemporary sophistication brings with it certain disadvantages as well as advantages and we shall attempt to place these developments in perspective. This year we will focus primarily on marital problems, orgasmic dysfunction, self-control and biofeedback, functional speech disorders and the management of the suicidal patient. Key areas such as depression and insomnia—topics apparently held in high regard by the "audiotapophiles"—will be left for future coverage in view of the dearth of outstanding case studies to appear during 1975. Probably the most popular behavioral topic—especially for those who prefer to offer intervention without going through the necessary stage of data collection—is that of "assertive training" or, as we would prefer, "assertion training." All too often, the term assertive training is unfortunately a more appropriate one since many of the individuals who offer such training programs for the layperson or the specialist have little else to fall back upon but their ability to offer training in an assertive manner. Since we have commented at length upon the assertion scene in other Sections of the Annual Review (especially Sections II and IV) we will not dwell further upon this current fad in behavior therapy.

We have advanced to the stage where it is possible to present a

751

752 ANNUAL REVIEW OF BEHAVIOR THERAPY

precise description and analysis of the entire course of the behavior therapy process with the individual patient (see Cautela & Upper, 1975). An exact procedure for developing individualized therapy goals has been described by Weigel and Uhlemann (1975), based upon a strategy developed and tested out over the last three years at Colorado State University. Ten specific and sequential steps emerge as being particularly effective for assisting clients in developing individual behavior change goals, ranging from the more general to the highly specific, with a built-in facility for constant re-evaluation and renegotiation as experience dictates.

Considerable attention has also been given of late to study of the effects of nonspecific therapeutic factors in the development of outcome research designs. Sophisticated studies have explored the intricacies of demand characteristics and client expectancies in a variety of research situations (e.g., see Borkovec & Nau, 1972). However, few investigators have focused in detail upon these loosely defined nonspecific factors as they apply within the one-to-one therapeutic relationship.

Behavior therapy is technique oriented and there is little doubt that most of these techniques do have an intrinsic validity which is independent of the therapist who applies them. Given this fact, together with the current emphasis on self-administered methods, packaged materials, automation and tape-recorded programs, it is not surprising that the widely held image of behavior therapy as being mechanistic, simplistic and impersonal prevails. If this is untrue—as we certainly believe —much of the responsibility for this state of affairs may well lie with behavior therapists themselves. Apart from the mechanistic metaphors behavior therapists sometimes employ (e.g., behavioral analyst, behavioral engineer, social reinforcement machine) insufficient attention has been given to the conceptualization and study of situational variables as they apply within the individual therapy setting.

We disagree sharply with those who would have it that behavior therapists are really little more than skilled technicians and that it is procedures rather than people who should be evaluated (e.g., London, 1972). In our opinion, such views reflect a limited understanding of what behavior therapy is all about. Consistently, throughout the Annual Reviews, we try to reaffirm and demonstrate the philosophy that behavior therapy is an approach rather than a series of techniques. It is our contention that, almost by definition, the skilled behavior therapist is well-versed in the scientific foundations of behavior therapy, familiar with techniques and also possessed of the clinical and interpersonal skills that are essential to the development of an adequate therapeutic relationship.

Behavior therapy has now reached the stage where it is possible to conceptualize the vast array of nonspecific factors—such as placebo, suggestion, demand characteristics, empathy and rapport—in terms of a broad social learning framework. It is to these issues which Wilson and Evans address themselves in the first paper, specially written for this year's Annual Review.

The second paper, by Greer and D'Zurilla, reviews empirical research findings with respect to behavioral approaches to marriage and marital therapy. Marital behavior therapy has now reached the letter stage and is known to the initiated simply as MBT but this alone cannot compensate for the inadequacies that prevail in this field. Gurman's (1973, 1975) optimism notwithstanding, case studies tend to be anecdotal, outcome studies poorly designed, adequate measures limited, follow-ups inadequate and generalization effects rarely demonstrated.

Although MBT's hybrid origins stem from diverse disciplines, in particular psychiatry, clinical psychology, sociology and social work, its theoretical bases are few: the reciprocity hypothesis, social exchange theory and the coercion hypothesis. According to the reciprocity hypothesis, the mutual exchange of positive reinforcement is the major factor which distinguishes distressed from nondistressed couples; social exchange theory views all relationships as bargaining situations in which an individual enters a stage of marriage only as long as it is satisfying to him or her in terms of his or her rewards and costs. The coercion hypothesis acknowledges the needs of two people to request changes in each other's behavior in any intimate relationship such as marriage. These requests are not always immediately heeded, the request becomes a demand, eventually one partner gives in to the other's demands, one party is reinforced by using aversive means of control and the other is reinforced by complying. Thus, aversion generates aversion and the conflict escalates.

Stuart (1969) views marital distress as a breakdown in mutual reinforcement, to be corrected by an operant approach stressing reinforcement principles and behavioral contracts as vehicles for the correction of the imbalance. The emphasis in the dyadic relationship is mostly upon the individual, with treatment focusing upon specific interventions aimed at increasing the frequency of reinforcing behaviors. More cautious investigators, such as Vincent, Weiss and Birchler (1975), urge us to avoid the premature crystallization of concepts until we have obtained more adequate data and examined the complex phenomena of marriage with methodologically sound principles. Marital behaviors are but one class of interpersonal behaviors and the complexities of social exchange may call for as yet unknown or modified concepts which are rather different from those currently employed. For example, nowhere in MBT is any attention given, as yet, to the concept of sex-role stereotypes and how this influences interactions between couples. Consideration of this emerging new facet of heterosexual relationships could well influence future directions for MBT (see V. Franks, in press).

Both Stuart and the Oregon Research Institute programs (probably the two most thorough and systematic programs in existence to date) delineate hierarchically ordered phases of intervention in their respective treatment packages. For Stuart, intervention proceeds through the following five phases: shaping of a behaviorally specific interpersonal vocabulary; acquiring behavior change skills based upon shaping and positive controls; increasing skills in giving and neutralizing feedback; the reallocation of power to avoid coercion as a means of decision-making; and the development of natural and efficient procedures for cueing and maintaining interaction changes. These goals are effected by such techniques as contracting, cueing devices and token exchanges.

The Oregon treatment package also has contracting as its end goal but the following modules are covered to insure smooth contracting: pinpointing of contingencies; communication skills training; positive and negative contingency options; negotiation and contracting. The specific techniques employed generally include modeling, video-tape feedback and role-playing.

Assessment and intervention are closely interwoven facets of MBT at all stages, from the study of initial maintaining relationships prior to intervention to evaluation of outcome. All too often, global ratings, characterized by unreliability and reactivity, are employed rather than a range of specific measures. It is also difficult to compare studies because of the large differences in populations studied. Much of the evidence for the efficacy of MBT comes from case studies but these studies rarely utilize baseline periods or other methods of control. The difficulties of using ABA designs are obvious, since most couples would probably be unwilling to go back to their aversive ways even if a therapist could ethically recommend that they do.

The best outcome studies to date unquestionably come from the Oregon Research Institute, with its emphasis on multiple assessment, controlled data, adequate baseline and follow-up and some concern with problems of generalization. However, we still need to see multiple measures employed throughout intervention and follow-up, and the definition of marital satisfaction clarified. Populations studied need to be better described and more attention given to the use of adequate control groups. The subtle and exquisitely complex nature of most marital relationships presents a challenge to the clinician and researcher at all stages. The clinician must be prepared to design a variety of programs to be monitored simultaneously and usually in an atmosphere of tension and mistrust by the subjects of his investigation (Patterson, Weiss & Hops, 1976).

Many of the devices currently in use, such as SAM (Carter & Thomas, 1973), remain to be tested. Group behavioral marital therapy (Turner, 1972) has been proposed but rarely investigated. Systematic study of the many parameters involved will depend in large part upon the use of more sophisticated designs. To establish specific treatment effects, multiple baseline designs in which problem areas are treated one at a time and changes in functioning monitored in many areas are highly desirable. Attention placebo groups, control periods and baseline periods are minimal requirements.

In line with the prevailing *Zeitgeist,* cognitive factors are becoming prominent in MBT. Increasingly, the marital studies program at the University of Oregon is stressing cognition in all facets of the therapeutic intervention (see Margolin, Christensen & Weiss, 1975). The assessment-intervention package originally described by Weiss, Hops and Patterson (1973) has been modified to incorporate recent developments in the areas of cognition and contingency management. Couples are given an opportunity to acquire behavior change skills based upon positive control, shaping and extinction procedures, contingency management, contracting and negotiation training, and development of cognitive awareness.

One of the most well-known marital pre-counseling questionnaires employed in MBT is that of Stuart and Stuart (1972). Another popular questionnaire is the Locke and Wallace Marital-Adjustment Test (1959). While not strictly behavioral, it does offer a very convenient gross evaluation of the marriage in 15 global areas. Yet another set of pre-counseling questionnaires has been developed and used by the investigators at Oregon.

All of these measures suffer from some of the deficiencies outlined above, and the search for improvement continues. To overcome the limitations of self-reports, a variety of analogue tests or simulation situations are being developed. For example, couples can be asked to discuss a conflict area for a fixed time, while being recorded by video or audio tape. Informational feedback can then be used to provide a structure for therapeutic behavior change.

With the notable exception of the Oregon group, multiple assessment during training or follow-up has been neglected. Birchler, Weiss and Vincent (1975) combined home and laboratory based measures to compare distressed and nondistressed marital interactions. Quite apart from their contribution to the study of parameters of marital distress, their findings lend considerable support to the situation-specific point of view of marital distress, namely that the distress is a function of a particular dyadic interaction rather than being a generalized trait (see also Vincent, Weiss & Birchler, 1975).

Among the contributions of the Oregon School may be singled out the demonstration by Wills, Weiss and Patterson (1974) that global ratings of satisfaction can be separated successfully into different components. For example, pleasurable and displeasurable dimensions of marital interactions are independent. Changing a spouse's behavior along one dimension may have little effect on the partner's behavior along another. Thus, for maximum efficacy and maintenance, marital therapies should develop separate and specific programs for both pleasure and displeasure behaviors.

Finally, we might mention the behavioral interaction model of Lickorish (1975), based upon a perhaps idiosyncratic interpretation of Von Bertalanffy's (1971) definition of a "system." Marital therapy cannot really be differentiated from family therapy and, to be fully effective, any marital system has to focus upon total family relationships. While the model proposed by Lickorish breaks new ground in its integration of linguistic and behavioral concepts, as yet it lacks empirical confirmation. Nevertheless, Lickorish's coding system, in which the family is described in discrete attitudes of behavior linked together in a phenomenological system, is of particular interest. As Greer and D'Zurilla point out, if family therapy is defined not by the number of family members in the room during a session, but by the interest and allegiance of the therapist towards the whole family, then MBT may be called family therapy in both theory and practice.

With the exception of the first two papers and Kelman's commentary on the Levendusky and Pankratz study, all of the articles in this Section are case studies of one sort or another. In recent years, the use of single subjects in experimental methodology has been expanded and refined to the point where at least one influential behavior therapist (Yates, 1975) maintains that the controlled investigation of a single case is virtually the only uniquely distinguishing feature of behavior therapy and that the validity of behavior therapy rests squarely on its ability to demonstrate that changes in individual behavior are functionally related to the experimental procedures intended to produce them. However, if the contents of the leading behavior therapy journals are any indication— the probable exception being the *Journal of Applied Behavioral Analysis* —such a position is by no means unequivocally accepted. Indeed, such informed sources as Bandura (1976), Kazdin (1973—reprinted in the 1975 Annual Review) and Leitenberg (1973—reprinted in the 1974 Annual Review) have all explicitly expressed the conviction that between-group designs are often necessary. Nevertheless, there is a growing disenchantment among researchers and clinical investigators alike with the use of traditional intergroup experimental methodology in behavior therapy. A more detailed discussion of the advantages and disadvantages of single subject and between-group designs is presented in Section IV of this year's Annual Review, and it is in the light of this discussion that we turn now to the case studies which constitute the bulk of Section X.

The first case study to be reprinted, by Snyder, LoPiccolo and Lo-Piccolo, deals with the treatment of secondary orgasmic dysfunction. The initial step in the management of failed sexual function is adequate delineation of the difficulty, whether this be psychological or otherwise (Marks, 1976). Current thinking divides female orgasmic dysfunction, with which we are concerned here, into two major categories. Primary organic dysfunction is a condition of the female who has never experienced an orgasm through any mode of physical stimulation. By contrast, a woman with secondary orgasmic dysfunction has experienced at least one orgasm through some mode of sexual stimulation but is dissatisfied either because of a low frequency of orgasmic response or with the type of sexual stimulation required for orgasm or with the stimulus conditions under which the orgasm occurs (McGovern, Stewart & Lo-Piccolo, 1975).

The largest series of cases treating orgasmic dysfunction by far, that of Masters and Johnson (1970), relies essentially on uncontrolled studies. Variations of their methods have been described by Bancroft (1974) and Brown (1972). The work of Masters and Johnson, now part of our general culture, requires no elaboration here. In any event, it is discussed in detail in various sections of this and earlier Annual Reviews. What is of more interest is the variety of specific off-shoot techniques which have been developed and await further study. There is, for example, the feedback strategy of Serber (1974), in which the couples engage in sexual relations in their rooms with a videotape recorder which automatically switches on upon entering. The videotapes are subsequently viewed with the therapist and problems and solutions discussed.

The use of orgasmic reconditioning (Wilson, 1973) has been reported. Faulk (1973) reviews a number of investigators who treat orgasmic dysfunction by graded exposure in one form or another. Here, however, we are primarily concerned with the work of LoPiccolo and his group. Over the last half a decade, these investigators have developed a successful and significant behavioral treatment program for clients with a variety of sexual dysfunctions (see McGovern, Stewart & LoPiccolo, 1975; Lobitz & LoPiccolo, 1972). Clients also complete an extensive assessment battery before treatment (LoPiccolo & Steger, 1974).

Female orgasmic dysfunction is a common complaint, according to the experiences of LoPiccolo and his group. In a series of six primary and six secondary orgasmic dysfunctional women and their spouses, it was found that women with primary and women with secondary orgasmic dysfunction both reported increased satisfaction with their sexual and marital relationships following treatment. However, all of the primary orgasmic women became orgasmic in coitus whereas the majority of the secondary orgasmic women did not (McGovern, Stewart & LoPiccolo, 1975). In contrast, the Marriage Council of Philadelphia reports a higher rate of success with secondary than with primary dysfunction (Brenton, 1972). McGovern et al. speculate that the reversal in treatment success rates with primary and secondary cases between their results and those of the Philadelphia Marriage Council possibly reflects a difference in the percentage of time devoted to sexual versus marital intervention. Their conclusion is that primary inorgasmic women may respond best to therapy which focuses specifically on sexual matters, whereas secondary inorgasmic women may respond better when the sex treatment is combined with traditional marital therapy. Their recommendation is that either most secondary dysfunctional couples be referred to another agency for short-term marital therapy prior to beginning a sexual treatment program, or that the therapist extend the number of therapy hours to allow sufficient time for full treatment of all marital problems involved.

McGovern et al. point to another factor which may be relevant to the differential results obtained in treating these two client groups. The primary dysfunctional woman has never experienced an orgasm whereas the secondary dysfunctional woman has already established a pattern of orgasmic release which often seems to interfere with her ability to experience orgasm during intercourse. In their experience, what occurs is that a majority of secondary dysfunctional women have long been accustomed to masturbating in some very constricted fashion. For example, they describe one of their clients who was orgasmic only when lying on her stomach with her legs pressed together, a bedsheet between her genitals and her hands, stimulating herself by cupping her hands over her genital area. This excessive reliance on one particular technique tended to bring orgasm under very tight stimulus control. In such cases, it is recommended that the therapist teach the secondary orgasmic client how to extinguish these narrow stimulus response links and learn new techniques which can be generalized into intercourse.

They advocate two therapy approaches for helping a woman with a constrained masturbation pattern extinguish her previous pattern and transfer orgasmic responses from masturbation to sexual intercourse. The first involved the prohibition of the previous method of obtaining orgasmic release, allowing sexual tension to build up over a few weeks and then having her learn a new way of masturbation to orgasm in accordance with their nine-step program of directive masturbation (Lo-Piccolo & Lobitz, 1972). The second approach is an adaptation of Annon's (1971, 1975, 1976) method of successive approximation. This involves instructing the woman gradually to shift the locus of her self-stimulation from the clitoris downward to the vulva and eventually to the vaginal opening. In contrast to the first approach, this does not rely on a high level of sexual attention and the learning of entirely new methods of self-stimulation. However, there are no data at this point to indicate which of these two approaches is more effective.

The importance of the paper reprinted by LoPiccolo is that it reports a direct behavioral re-training program to increase a couple's repertoire of effective sexual behaviors. Since nonsexual marriage problems contribute to the makings of secondary orgasmic dysfunction, a direct, confrontive intervention in the marital relationship is made concurrent with the sexual re-training program. Most importantly, they present outcome data to illustrate the effectiveness of the treatment procedure.

The next group of papers focuses upon self-control in a variety of areas: the treatment of an obsessive-compulsive ritual; self-control over intrusive experiences; and self-control as an alternative to pain medication. Thoresen and Coates (1976) have outlined recent developments in the concept of self-control. Pointing to the restrictive limitations of operational definitions, they offer a conceptual definition of self-control as "learnable cognitive processes used in generating controlling responses, which, in turn, alter factors modifying behavior over time." A distinction is made between self-control and self-regulation. Countless human processes are monitored and altered by cognitively mediated self-regulatory mechanisms, but these do not require direct attention and ongoing effort (see also our Commentary to Section III).

In operational terms, according to Thoresen and Coates, self-control is demonstrated when a person "in the relative absence of immediate external constraints, engages in behavior whose previous probability has been less than that of alternatively available behaviors" (e.g., involving lesser or delayed reward, greater exertion or aversive properties). As they point out, such a definition carries with it three key features: there must be two or more alternative behaviors available; the consequences of these behaviors are usually conflicting; and the behaviors are usually prompted and maintained by external factors such as environmental cues and long-term consequences. Finally, it should be noted that the above definition emphasizes that a person is "self-controlling" when he engages in an action that is relatively less likely, given particular situations, than other behaviors.

Thoresen and Coates conclude that self-control is "clearly in its infancy with further development warranted on many fronts." We concur with the conclusion that at present there is no sufficiently comprehensive theory or rationale available to encompass the broad range of phenomena involved in self-control. Modern learning theory is simply not adequate in its explanatory power. Or, as they put it, our clients' problems are more complex than either our theories or our techniques.

Despite these limitations, self-control has already arrived at the stage where it can be successfully applied to problems in preventive medicine (Pomerleau, Bass & Crown, 1975). For example, Youell and McCullough (1975) report the case of a 22-year-old female graduate student who suffered daily attacks of mucus colitis and was apparently successfully treated by a procedure in which the therapist taught the client the necessary behavioral strategy to counter the stress events.

The fourth paper in this grouping, by Melamed and Siegel, deals with a self-directed in vivo treatment of an obsessive-compulsive checking ritual. Of all forms of psychological disturbances, obsessional states must surely constitute one of the most puzzling (Beech, 1974). The key role that anxiety plays in obsessional states remains unresolved despite the demonstrable stress-reducing nature of most rituals (Hodgson & Rachman, 1972). What is of interest is the intriguing parallel that exists between the development of behavioral strategies for the treatment of obsessive-compulsive neuroses and other phobias (Leitenberg, 1976). Both have shifted away from systematic desensitization in the imagination to direct attacks on overt behavior.

If the emphasis is to be on overt response prevention, then the development of self-control mechanisms is important, preferably in an inpatient setting with its opportunities for continual surveillance and objective recording. But here, again, as Leitenberg points out, treatment in the hospital alone is probably not sufficient. The strategy employed by Leitenberg and his associates at Vermont is to try to bring rituals under control in the home following hospitalization, by combining features of simple scheduling and paradoxical intention (Frankl, 1960; Gertz, 1966). Patients are instructed to engage in their rituals only at prescribed periods of the day regardless of whether they have an urge to do so during these times or not.

The interesting feature about the case study reported by Melamed and Seigel is that it was conducted in vivo by the client and his wife, rather than under the closer supervision of trained personnel in an institutional setting. While the fact that the patient remained symptom-free is encouraging, the inability to determine the relative contributions of their numerous procedures limits the usefulness of the report. From the point of view of self-control strategy, this study is of particular importance in that, as the client learned to gain a sense of control over his own behavior, there was a concomitant improvement in his self-concepts.

The fifth paper in this Section, by Fisher and Winkler, focuses upon the self-control of a variety of experiences of depersonalization and unreality, including possible visual sensations. There is little doubt that private events such as depressive feelings may yield to self-control (e.g., Tharp, Watson & Kaya, 1974). However, the notion that hallucinations may yield to self-control procedures is bold but questionable. Both data and rationale are intriguing, but considerable replication and long-term follow-up are required before we elect to believe that Fisher and Winkler's strategy is of lasting and significant value in the treatment of what seems to us to be some form of more insidious disorder.

The last major paper in this group, by Levendusky and Pankratz, deals with self-control techniques as an alternative to pain medication. It is of particular importance on two accounts. First, in its own right, as a potentially viable method of coping with pain, and second, because of the ethical issues raised. To appreciate contemporary behavioral ap-

proaches to the management of pain, it is necessary to make a reformulation of what is traditionally known as psychosomatic medicine
in terms of current learning theory principles. The psychosomatic approach to disease is essentially a psychodynamic one and can be
criticized in such terms. It evokes unnecessary hypothetical constructs
between the stimuli confronting the patient and the behavior in question,
resulting in a treatment plan aimed more at hypothetical causes rather
than the presenting problem itself. Therefore, therapy tends to be slow
and to neglect the presenting symptoms (Shapiro & Surwit, 1976). In
sharp contrast, the behavioral model employs learning techniques and
sees as its primary target for therapy the environment of the individual
rather than his or her personality.

Pain is extremely complex and variable in its manifestations. It can
occur in the absence of apparent stimulation; it can fail to occur even
after extensive tissue damage (Shapiro & Surwit, 1976; Melzack, 1973).
One of the leading figures in its study from a behavioral rather than a
medical or disease perspective is Fordyce (1976). The traditional medical
inference is that pain is a symptom of some underlying pathology, that
the strategy and treatment lie in the modification of this pathology for
the symptom to disappear or be reduced. When this is not effective,
medical management tends to focus on symptomatic relief by way of
medication or surgery (Fordyce, Fowler, Lehmann & Delateur, 1968).
While, in the obviously correct opinion of Fordyce and his associates, this
model cannot be dismissed in all circumstances, there does not seem
to be sufficient justification for its universal application. Fordyce's basic
alternative premise is that pain behavior is subject to the same laws as
other kinds of behaviors and that the principles of behavior modification
can be applied accordingly. In his challenging new book, Fordyce (1976)
outlines in relatively nontechnical language the rationale and principles
of application for all health-care professionals who have to cope with
the problem of pain. Throughout, a basic axiom is that the patient and
his or her family must be presented in specific detail, with a clear explanation of evaluation findings and all treatment proposals, carefully
spelling out that an operant approach in no way implies, in any shape
or form, that the pain is unreal. The essence of Fordyce's treatment
model is that openness, informed consent and explicit statement of
objectives are paramount.

Fordyce sets forth a clear strategy for the transfer of a patient from a
pain-medication to a self-control model. The aim, preferably in an inpatient setting, is to break the pain-behavior medication consequence

relationship through extinction. The patient is systematically instructed in a procedure calculated to reduce the amount of pain medication needed and this is accomplished with no deception whatsoever. The notion of the pain-cocktail, a procedure in which all the medications are incorporated into a single dose, is carefully explained to the patient, together with the phasing-out procedure to be employed. A cocktail is given at fixed time-intervals, around the clock, and is *not* pain-contingent. It is always taken when scheduled, whether pain is experienced or not or whether a need for medication is expressed or not expressed. It is never taken between intervals, even if it should be requested. The object of the fading process is not simply to eliminate the potentially toxic or addictive agents from the patient's regimen as rapidly as possible, but for the patient to learn that the pain behaviors making up the signal for medication or the act of taking it are no longer to be systematically reinforced by immediate medication.

In the case report of Levendusky and Pankratz, the patient was taught self-control of his pain through a program of relaxation, covert imagery and cognitive re-labeling. He was then withdrawn from medication by diluting the drug with increasing proportions of normal saline. However, deception was employed in that withdrawal was carried out without the patient's knowledge. It was this feature of an apparently successful treatment program that motivated the editor of the *Journal of Abnormal Psychology* to invite four discussants to comment upon the case. The first discussant, Cook (1975), served as Chairman of the committee that drafted *Ethical Principles in the Conduct of Research with Human Participants*, now part of the ethics code of the American Psychological Association (1973). Kelman, whose contribution is the only one of the four to be reprinted here in full, also served on that committee, and is well-known for his fortright comments upon the use of deception in social-psychological experiments.

Cook examines the ethical issues confronted by the therapist in situations such as Levendusky and Pankratz describe from the perspective of the code of ethics of the American Psychological Association. Pointing out that it was precisely the information held back by the therapist that would have led their client to refuse his consent, the suggestion is made that a closer approximation to informed consent might have been obtained. He advocates the consideration of an approach used in drug research, mainly to obtain consent for the administration of each of several drugs, including a placebo, without specifying the particular one that any given individual will receive. But, as Cook points out, from

Levendusky and Pankratz's description, their client would probably not have included interference with the drug regime in his list of acceptable possibilities. With this, we concur.

Kelman's discussion focuses on the patient's right to informed consent, on the quality of the patient-therapist relationship, and on potential damages to the patient's self-concept. As he points out, it is precisely the role of the outsider to consider the kinds of questions that may not emerge from the perspective of the investigators. His concluding sentence, that deception might have been more likely to retard than advance the treatment process, is a thought-provoking one.

Karoly's (1975) commentary urges readers to consider the legality of withholding information relevant to a client's decision to remain in treatment. He also takes up the subtle nature of contract negotiation in therapy and the need to pursue alternatives to deceptions in such settings. Skinner (1974) has pointed out that morality is a condition not solely of persons but of persons-in-environments. Therefore, says Karoly, behavior therapists are constrained to observe the rules and best interests of the behavior systems with which they make contact in the course of treatment. And in addition, of course, the psychologist is accountable to his profession. As Karoly notes, a scanning of the literature reveals numerous cautions against deception and diverse alternatives are often available.

Goodstein (1975) sums up the whole issue, including the positions espoused by the various protagonists. Cook, Kelman and Karoly all raise the issue of the degree to which the specific consent inferred by Levendusky and Pankratz meets ethical requirements for informed consent. He points to one issue not directly addressed by Cook, namely the need for professional associations to take into more account the rights of patients, sometimes overlooked in behaviorally based treatments. (See also, criticisms by such legal authorities as Milford, 1973 and Wexler, 1973.) All commentators note that the contract between therapists and patient was made neither clear nor explicit, and Goodstein comes to the core of the dilemma when he affirms that the central question is not what is or is not in the patient's best interest, but whether or not the patient has to be directly included in the assessment of his or her best interest. Patients and others may well have the right to irrational fears, and even more important, who is to decide which fears should be viewed as irrational. Finally, Goodstein makes the questionable point that, despite the adherence of Levendusky and Pankratz to a behaviorally based treatment regime, they seem to have implicitly adopted the traditional medical stance: The doctor knows best! But of course, it is not necessarily true that a behavioral approach is inconsistent, as Goodstein seems to imply, with a "doctor knows best" position.

In a rejoinder, Levendusky and Pankratz (1976) point out that they did attend to the well-being of the whole person and that the philosophy of the ward program did indeed emphasize cognitive therapy together with a large array of ongoing techniques. These included relaxational and visualization training, cognitive re-labeling and participation in a wide variety of ward activities such as individual counseling, ward government, biofeedback, family therapy and post-hospital planning. Stressing the need for a Bill of Rights for Patients (Noll, 1974) they reaffirm that the mere fact of the recognition of the rights of a patient does not make the staff less responsible for making a responsible decision. As they indicate, they could have refused to help their patient because of his rigidity or they could have provided him with the details of withdrawal procedures for better informed consent. But in their opinion, either of these options would have deprived him of the right to obtain the relief which he sought at their hospital. And they make it clear that the decision to withdraw the patient from his Talwin was made in open arena by all of the staff involved after much agonized discussion of the pros and cons. As Levendusky and Pankratz note, such dilemmas are not likely to arise in a closed and repressive environment. The ethical dilemma only surfaced because they had established an open atmosphere. Withholding some information for a time was contradictory to the milieu that they had worked so hard to establish. There is no doubt that the issues raised are complex and difficult ones to resolve and that there is probably no final answer to their resolutions.

The next paper reprinted in this section, by Blanchard and Haynes, deals with the application of biofeedback to Raynaud's disease. In their review of biofeedback and related mechanisms for the control of the physiological activities of the body and various disease processes, Shapiro and Surwit (1976) take a somewhat conservative approach. While accepting "tentative evidence" that direct biofeedback can help in the remediation of physical problems once treatable only by somatic therapy, they conclude that "much research needs to be done before biofeedback can be advocated as a viable treatment for any disorder. In addition to the question of efficacy there are a host of practical issues which need to be dealt with in evaluating the possible place of biofeedback in the treatment of disease." For the most part, biofeedback procedures may be too costly with respect to the time and effort involved by either patient or practitioner or it to be very effective. In many cases, medication may be a simple, effective and painless way to cope with the difficulty, and biofeedback is not the treatment of choice (see also Commentary, Section III).

There is also the related issue of patient motivation to consider. It cannot be assumed that feedback about improvement will, in and of itself, serve as a reinforcer and maintain the persistent practice necessary to gain therapeutic benefit. Sometimes, as Shapiro and Surwit point out, the symptom itself may be reinforcing and the disorder may have secondary gains. Surwit (1973) reports the case of a patient involved in intensive biofeedback for Raynaud's disease who spontaneously expressed her ambivalence to giving up her illness because she did not know how to relate to people without it. She was explicitly aware of using her disease as an excuse for her poor social life and dependent relationship with her mother. Behaviors strongly entrenched in the patient's repertoire may be in conflict with the aim of therapy (Schwartz, 1973).

Then there is the question of transfer of training, and the difficulties of generalizing beyond the therapy situation. As Shapiro and Surwit note, in most cases biofeedback procedures are applied in resting, non-stimulating laboratory settings. It may be that the patient is not able to transfer this training to relevant situations in everyday life. Also unknown is the effectiveness of biofeedback with less well-educated or less well-adjusted individuals than those who have up to now been the subject of most studies in this area. Finally, attention is drawn to the possibility that the symptoms may indeed be symptoms and that there may well be a profound physiological dysfunction requiring medical attention.

It is for such reasons that Shapiro and Surwit urge that biofeedback be used clinically only after a competent medical diagnosis has been made and the examining physician satisfied that biofeedback could be of value. The need for medical participation is both an ethical and a legal responsibility. By the same token, it is also the ethical responsibility of the physician who wishes to employ biofeedback in treatment to consult with a psychologist on the behavioral aspects of his proposed therapy. In this context, it is encouraging to see a whole article in a recent issue of *Patient Care* (Biofeedback, 1975) devoted primarily not to the promotion of biofeedback as an office technique for the physician but to a clarification of general concepts and the offering of suggestions as to when to refer patients and when not to refer patients for possible biofeedback therapy. The difficulty stems from the fact that we do not have adequate data for arriving at informed decisions. There is a need for considerable research into individual differences (e.g., Haynes, Griffin, Mooney & Praise, 1975).

Too often, biofeedback is included as part of a package program and it is difficult to unravel the effective ingredients. This is especially true when a number of techniques are applied to a single patient with no attempt at control whatsoever. Reavley (1975), for example, reports the successful treatment of writer's cramp in which—all with one patient and no design of any sort—the following techniques were used, sometimes singly and sometimes in combination: relaxation training, EMG feedback, GSR feedback, writing retraining. And the seventeen treatment sessions were spread over seven months, many of them unsupervised and carried out by the patient at home following discussion and demonstration in the clinic.

Raynaud's disease is an essentially functional disorder of the cardiovascular system involving—at least in its early stages—no observable organic pathology. Roberts, Schuler, Bacon and Zimmerman (1974) were able to train subjects differentially to raise and lower the skin temperature of their hands. However, subsequent attempts to replicate this finding were less than successful and the exact conditions necessary to reproduce this phenomenon do not seem to be known (Surwit & Shapiro, 1974; Lynch, Hama, Kohn & Miller, 1974). On the other hand, Surwit (1973) is somewhat more encouraging and concludes from his review of four cases that, in each instance, the patients reported achieving control of a Raynaud symptom (not necessarily synonymous with Raynaud's *disease*) which had been previously thought to be involuntary. Likewise, Jacobson, Hackett, Surman and Silverberg (1973) reported success in the alleviation of Raynaud-like symptoms in a 31-year-old man.

Despite these limited successes, Shapiro and Surwit feel that it is premature to conclude that biofeedback is characteristically the sole therapeutic agent responsible for improvement. In evaluating the place of biofeedback in the treatment of Raynaud's disease, they urge consideration of the record of conventional treatments now available. Neither medical-pharmacological remedies, nor sympathectomy seem to be reliable as therapeutic agents. It is therefore suggested that biofeedback be attempted in lieu of surgery, at any rate, only when more conservative techniques have failed.

In our opinion, the case report described by Blanchard and Haynes represents a definite advancement in technique. It is one of the few case studies to present systematic data, and baseline and control phases are included as well as the training phase to assess the ability of the patient to control the response in the absence of feedback. Equally important, no other form of psychological intervention was given concurrently, thus making it possible to attach meaning to the findings.

The next paper in this section, by Marshall and Watts, deals with the behavioral treatment of functional aphonia. Functional speech disturbances—as contrasted with physical disorders such as the aphasias (Ayers, Potter, & McDearmon, 1975)—have been somewhat neglected by behavioral clinicians and researchers. A recent exception is the report of Van Der Kooy and Webster (1975) of a behavior modification program for a six-year-old electively mute boy. Elective mutism is the term used to describe children who do not respond verbally in some situations, although they may often speak fluently in others, such as the home. This boy had not spoken in most social situations outside the home for nearly two years, even though he spoke fluently at home to his family. The one-week program involved initial avoidance conditioning, positive social reinforcement, generalization procedures and the fading of extra attention. Speech was maintained outside the home six months later. The study reported here of the vocal rehabilitation of a 48-year-old man with a three-year history of functional aphonia points to the useful collaboration of speech pathologist and medical practitioner. Without the active cooperation of the attending physician, who agreed to ignore whenever possible the patient's somatic complaints during the one-month period of speech therapy, this program of rehabilitation would not have been possible.

The final paper in this section deals with an area of clinical investigation which has been virtually entirely neglected, namely the problem of suicidal behavior. Bachman (1972) offers a behavioral analysis of self-injurious behavior and Lester (1972) has remarked upon the relationship between the consequent events of self-mutilating behavior and suicidal behavior, pointing to the close similarities between the controlling aspects and the manipulation of situations and people by these two classes of behavior. Bachman considers that self-injurious behavior occurs in many cases only in the presence or absence of specific determining stimuli and that it is maintained by the social reinforcement that often follows. Furthermore, self-injurious behavior can be modified by manipulating its environmental consequences, indicating that the specific stimuli that set the occasion for its occurrence are learned, operant, discriminative stimuli.

The remarkable case of Peter, referred to the Psychological Clinic at

Rutgers University, written up in detail by Romanczyk and Goren (1975) and made the basis of the appendix to Friedman's article, reproduced in Section I of this year's Annual Review, is very much a case in point of the limitations of making any generalization about the treatment of self-injurious behavior. While total suppression was eventually achieved in the laboratory setting, success was only moderate in extending this control to the natural environment. Generalization from the laboratory to the natural setting is still very much in question with respect to the treatment of self-injurious behavior.

Elsewhere, Bostock and Williams (1975) make a somewhat similar analysis of suicidal behavior within the context of social learning theory. The term manipulative suicide refers to suicidal behavior aimed at controlling the actions of significant others. Those patients who manipulate by means of suicidal behavior are prone to make future attempts once they discover that this class of behavior commands attention and it is just such contingent consequent interpersonal manipulations following suicidal behavior that can reinforce and maintain this particular behavior. In the study reprinted here, Bostock and Williams report a single-case demonstration of an operant paradigm which employs shaping within a ward program in a general hospital setting using extinction of the suicidal behavior and introducing response contingent rewards for adaptive and coping behavior.

Implementation of such programs requires appropriately trained staff, precise communication and adequate control. The crucial issue in such a program is the gaining of adequate control over the reinforcers operating within the involved environment. Certainly, suicidal behavior is a powerful operant and almost invariably evokes a response from the environment. As yet, however, it is not possible, especially in the study reported by Bostock and Williams, to separate out the effects of contingency reinforcement from other concomitant traditional procedures. However, despite this limitation, the fact that an 18-month follow-up revealed no form of suicidal behavior, and that the patient was no longer receiving any active treatment, is encouraging. The limitations of the study, as the authors are well aware, is that it was expensive with respect both to staff and therapist time.

Crisis intervention procedures are traditionally concerned with the prevention of suicide. It may be helpful to differentiate successful suicides, which for obvious reasons are difficult to study, from the attempted suicides referred to by Henderson and Williams (1974) as parasuicides. It is suggested that traditional crisis intervention procedures may actually increase the incidence of parasuicidal behavior. There are powerful institutional rewards or reinforcers for those who engage in such self-injurious activities in terms of the attention they receive and the easy-access routes to therapeutic help. It is for such reasons that Henderson and Williams take the viewpoint, quite heretical to the best of modern medicine, that parasuicide is a "circuitous, wasteful and often dangerous path to help." They question the currently promoted view of parasuicide patients as persons who have been driven to desperate means and who deserve the understanding and compassion of relatives and medical personnel.

34

ADULT BEHAVIOR THERAPY
AND THE THERAPIST-CLIENT
RELATIONSHIP

G. Terence Wilson

Rutgers University

and

Ian M. Evans

University of Hawaii

Elsewhere, in a discussion of conceptual trends in behavior therapy, we described in some detail how the therapeutic relationship, although recognized as significant, was originally relegated to the position of a "nonspecific" influence in behavior therapy (Wilson & Evans, in press). Traditionally, these supposedly nonspecific factors—including loosely defined concepts of placebo, suggestion, demand characteristics, empathy, and rapport—have been de-emphasized and held in sharp contrast to specific behavioral techniques derived from learning theory. However, by conceptualizing behavior therapy within a broader social learning

Sections of this paper are based on a longer and more complete account of relationship variables which appears in A. Gurman and A. Razin (Eds.), *The Therapist's Contribution to Effective Psychotherapy: An Empirical Approach*. New York: Pergamon Press, in press.

The authors are most grateful to Frances Wilson, University of Hawaii, for numerous valuable suggestions and for her careful critique of an earlier draft of this paper.

framework, the interpersonal influence factors which characterize the therapeutic relationship can be seen as an integral part of behavior therapy (Wilson, Hannon, & Evans, 1968). It would be realistic, therefore, to propose that, although many "nonspecific" influences still remain to be specified, they are neither intrinsically unspecifiable nor qualitatively very different from other independent variables involved in planned behavior change (Wilson, 1975).

Our purpose here is to foster this integration by considering those aspects of the therapeutic relationship that could be more directly addressed in behavior therapy. By describing the relationship in behavioral terms, it may be possible to halt the unfortunate distinction that is developing between practice and research paradigms in behavior therapy (Meyer, 1975). By recognizing the therapist's interpersonal behavior as a legitimate and essential part of the influence process, behavior therapy can be seen as a more human endeavor than some critics acknowledge. Therapeutic relationships can then be more explicitly tailored to accomplish treatment goals. At the same time, recognition of the importance of the therapeutic relationship justifies combing the social psychology literature for suggestions as to how the therapist's personal influence might be still more effectively employed (e.g., Goldstein, Heller, & Sechrest, 1966; Johnson & Matross, in press).

In one sense, every "technique" of behavior therapy can be described in terms of the therapist's behavior. One reason why systematic desensitization, for instance, has received such concerned research attention is because the procedure is so clearly specified that the appropriate therapist behaviors can be reproduced by almost anyone—although this is not true for such aspects as the construction of the hierarchy. Nevertheless, the reason that systematic desensitization is seen as a technique, and not simply as a refined personal skill of the therapist, is that in arranging the systematic relearning experiences for the client (imagining anxious situations while relaxing) which are generally considered to be the active ingredients of the therapy, the therapist's behavior is only indirectly effective. However, while the normal social context of systematic desensitization may not always be necessary (Lang, Melamed, & Hart, 1970), there are many other clinical situations in which it is the therapist's behavior that has a direct effect in modifying the client's behavior, through both the emotional and verbal qualities of the personal interactions the client experiences. This we call a direct influence. Although the direct-indirect dichotomy may be somewhat artificial in the long run, the way behavior therapy is commonly described and studied justifies this distinction. The two categories also encompass Kanfer and Phillips' (1966) quadripartite classification of behavior therapy: in what they called *instigation* therapy and *intervention* therapy, the personal relationship has an indirect influence in determining therapeutic outcome; in what they called *interactive* therapy and *replication* therapy, the active variables are contained in the direct influence of the social relationship.

We will begin by looking at some interpersonal skills that are important and influential in clinical behavior therapy—important in the sense that they maintain the therapeutic relationship and influential in the sense that they determine the nature of the treatment planned. Then we will describe some ways in which the therapist's social behavior modifies the client directly during their therapeutic interactions. Finally, we will consider the effects of the therapeutic relationship on the therapist's ability to instigate those client activities considered beneficial.

INTERPERSONAL SKILL IN CLINICAL BEHAVIOR THERAPY

All forms of psychotherapy, particularly client-centered approaches (Truax & Mitchell, 1971), stress the importance of the therapist's personal qualities. In behavior therapy, the interpersonal skills required over and above "technical" virtuosity have been acknowledged, albeit begrudgingly so and with little specification of the desirable behavior. According to Eysenck (1965), the behavior therapist requires "a very special ability to understand the difficulties and troubles of the neurotic" (p. 157). Kanfer and Phillips (1966) recommend "the qualities of a *menschenkenner* who is sensitive to human behavior beyond his academic knowledge" (p. 126); Agras (1973) lists a number of "general clinical skills," including an awareness of the "total needs of the patient" and "an ability to deal with ambiguous and uncertain situations" (p. 169). Somewhat more specific therapist qualities are advocated in Lazarus and Fay's (1975) 17-item Therapist Selection Questionnaire; yet really significant progress in this area hinges on being able to describe therapist behaviors as systematically as the better-known technical procedures and within a consistent theoretical framework.

One possible strategy for isolating such therapist behaviors is direct observation of behavior therapists in therapy. In a recent attempt to do this, Staples, Sloane, Whipple, Cristol, and Yorkston (1975) found basic differences in the relationships formed by behavior and psychodynamic therapists. The behavior therapists showed higher levels of the Truax-

triad of facilitative conditions, being more open and natural, and becoming more personally involved with their clients. They exercised more
control over the content of the interaction by frequently eliciting information from the clients, giving explicit advice, providing information,
and presenting their own value judgments. Clients viewed the behavior
therapists as more authoritarian and reported that the psychoanalysts
encouraged greater independence. As Staples et al. concluded, "Behavior
therapy is not psychotherapy with special 'scientific techniques' super-
imposed on the traditional therapeutic paradigm; rather, the two appear
to represent quite different styles of treatment although they share some
common elements" (p. 1521).

It is not, of course, known how representative the three experienced
behavior therapists observed by Staples et al. really were. Nor is it
known to what extent behavior therapists' personal styles are a direct
function of training in the general principles and theoretical models of
behavior therapy. How a scientific model affects interpersonal therapeutic behavior is an underlying theme of this section, which will speculate upon some of the general interpersonal skills thought to be important
in setting up the conditions of effective therapy, such as goal selection
and assessment.

Therapist's Influence on Selection of Treatment Goals

It is fundamental to the behavioral approach that the client should
have the major say in setting the goals of treatment. Accordingly, it is
important that the fully informed client consents to, and participates
in the setting of goals. While ideally the client has decision-making
primacy, it would be naive to imagine that in practice the therapist
plays no part in determining treatment goals. The manner in which
this occurs is one of the ways in which the therapist influences the
client.

One very common influence, as Evans and Nelson (in press) have
argued with respect to child behavior assessment, occurs when general
therapeutic goals are approached indirectly via the strategy of modifying
some other, more fundamental or mediating behavior pattern (the *target*
response) to effect, in turn, more general changes in the desired behavior
(the *treatment* goal). Marital disharmony, for example, might be resolved
by teaching more effective communication skills, or a pattern of depression most readily changed by assertion training. Selecting these critical
mediating responses is one of the most difficult tasks in behavior therapy

(Meyer & Crisp, 1966) for which there are few guiding principles from learning theory.

Sometimes treatment goals have to be set at less ambitious levels—the nonorgasmic client who wishes to become multiply orgasmic, during intercourse, for instance, might be persuaded to settle for the more realistic outcome of achieving orgasms by any method of stimulation. Alternatively, the therapist might suggest or encourage goals which the client did not know were possible. An example of this would be suggesting to clients with problems of alcohol abuse that they consider controlled drinking rather than total abstinence as the therapeutic objective (e.g., Sobell & Sobell, 1973).

It is when the client has no clear goal, and has sought treatment out of diffuse personal unhappiness, that the influence of the therapist is likely to be most marked; ideally, the therapist's contribution might be to help clients develop appropriate problem-solving strategies for establishing realistic and personally satisfying goals for themselves. If the unhappiness stems from a current behavior that is generally condemned socially, specific influence becomes still harder to avoid. The modification of sexual orientation is a case in point (e.g., Begelman, 1976; Davison, 1976). Bias in this particular area seems difficult to avoid; Davison and Wilson (1973) found that behavior therapists acknowledging that homosexuality is not a form of mental illness, nevertheless rated it as less good, less moral, and less rational than heterosexuality. In addition, therapists must not abrogate their societal responsibilities and automatically acquiesce to every client goal. Behavior therapists are governed by personal as well as professional values and are not under obligation to work towards client-determined goals considered ill-advised.

In principle, therefore, behavior therapists are encouraged to assist the client by generating alternative courses of action and attempting to analyze their likely consequences. In doing so, it is crucial that the therapist's personal biases be recognized and honestly declared. Particular care should be exercised in helping the client differentiate between advice and information having some empirical basis (see the information-giving described by Annon, 1974) and that which largely reflects the therapist's own values. Performing this delicate task obviously demands self-knowledge and self-understanding on the part of the therapist, some of which doubtless emerges from a sound scientific training in psychology. For example, a background in behavioral science should reveal to student therapists that their behaviors are as much a function of learning histories as those of their clients. And sound academic knowledge can give insight into the alternative life-styles that are available to married couples (O'Neill & O'Neill, 1972), women (Franks & Burtle, 1974; Rice & Rice, 1973) or even people from different cultures even though the therapist lacks direct experience in these areas. Conversely, it has been suggested that, as a result of their experimental training, behavior therapists are prone to subtle biases which cause too narrow a focus upon overt, measurable behaviors—powerful values in graduate settings emphasizing applied research. This may result in the premature selection of an observable target behavior that is only peripherally related to the client's subjective concerns and sometimes even clinically irrelevant.

Interpersonal Skills and Problem Analysis

Although periodically typecast as simple, clinical behavior therapy is highly intricate, particularly when it comes to such tasks as identifying the factors responsible for the development and maintenance of the client's problem (e.g., Evans & Nelson, 1974; Mischel, 1968). In addition to knowing the formal technology of behavioral observation, the behavior therapist should be an astute observer in social situations, able to read between the lines, pick up fleeting perceptual cues, and recognize sources of stress in a client's life. Behavior therapy does not assume that the client's "real" behavior is inevitably filtered through so-called defense mechanisms or transference reactions. Yet the probability of unrevealed emotional experiences should not be ignored. The client's self-descriptions are not necessarily taken at face value, and inconsistent, evasive, or ambiguous responses are noted and thoroughly explored to elucidate either unexpressed or unrecognized thoughts and feelings. Behavior is highly situation specific and one should be able to observe and utilize subtleties of the client's interpersonal responses without assuming that they are typical in situations other than the therapeutic interview.

As interviewing is the major vehicle for obtaining information about controlling variables, the behavior therapist's ability to make the client feel trustful—able to disclose personally distressing material without fear of being hurt by the therapist—is critical. Several studies have shown that communication is less effective under low than under high trust conditions (e.g., Schlenker, Helm, & Hedeschi, 1973), and that trust facilitates open discussion of problems and attitudes (Johnson & Matross, in press). Yet the development of trust is a topic which has received no formal attention in the behavioral literature.

Extrapolating from experimental findings, Johnson and Matross (in

press) have specified an operational model for building trust in a cooperative problem-solving situation such as behavior therapy. In response to
the client disclosing problems, the therapist shows warmth, accurate
understanding, and cooperative intentions. The third step in promoting
trust involves reciprocity of self-disclosure by the therapist with respect
to his or her perceptions of the client. Consistent with social exchange
theory (Thibaut & Kelley, 1959), Davis and Skinner (1974) found that
self-disclosure by an interviewer was significantly more effective in producing self-disclosure by the interviewee than either exposure to a self-
disclosing model or simple request to self-disclose. However, intimacy of
client disclosure can be reduced by self-disclosure from high status figures
such as professional therapists (Chaikin & Derlega, 1974). Self-disclosure
of personal information not obviously germane to the client's concerns
should be done cautiously, at least early in therapy (Carkhuff, 1969);
perhaps the guiding principles could be whether the therapist's disclosure
provides using information for the client to model and whether the
disclosure will help to clarify the therapeutic situation so that the client's
experiences may be more carefully structured and focused (Mahoney,
1974).

DIRECT INTERPERSONAL INFLUENCE ON BEHAVIOR CHANGE

Thus far we have considered certain interpersonal behaviors that are
prerequisites for behavior therapy. The therapist-client relationship, as
revealed in the discussion of self-disclosure, involves the therapist's interpersonal behaviors in interaction with those of the client. Therapeutic
relationships are not static—the nature of these interpersonal behaviors
changes over time—nor are they very characteristic of normal dyadic
relationships in everyday life. For one thing, the level of involvement
is asymmetrical, with the therapist usually much less committed than
the client; for another, the commercial, or at least consultative, nature of
the relationship renders it, in Kurth's (1970) terms, a "friendly relation"
rather than a "friendship." Because it is atypical, some commentators
(e.g., Bandura, 1969, p. 79) have argued that there is probably little generalization from the therapeutic relationship to the client's natural relationships. This does not mean, however, that the interpersonal behaviors
making up the relationship are not powerful sources of behavior influence,
particularly as the professional character of the interaction results in an
otherwise unique social situation in which the needs of the therapist
are subordinated to those of the client. Rather than attempting to specify,

in their complexity, all the components of the interaction, we will outline some of the social learning mechanisms whereby the relationship is
thought to exert its direct therapeutic influences.

The Therapist as Counterconditioner

A very major part of the relationship in effective therapy is that the
therapist communicate to the client, both verbally and non-verbally,
unconditional positive regard, or warmth. If the clients learn that they
are accepted as individuals, there is good evidence that their feelings of
self-worth are considerably enhanced and their tolerance for non-punitive
but negative feedback from the therapist regarding specific, maladaptive
behavior is greatly increased (Bierman, 1969). For certain kinds of problems, these dual experiences provide strong antidotes: if the self-concept
repertoire is changed, so is the way in which others respond to that individual; and verbal communications from the therapist regarding the
client's behavior will result in significant relabeling and reasoning repertoires in that individual (Staats, 1972)—commonly known as cognitive
therapy.

It has long been hypothesized that the client, in talking about anxiety-
evoking material, may be desensitized in the presence of the non-threat-
ening, calm, reassuring therapist. In an attempted rapprochement between
client-centered and learning theory approaches to therapy, Martin (1971a)
has theoretically analyzed this process. He relies heavily on the notion
of certain anxieties being by-products of internal conflicts between approach tendencies and avoidance tendencies resulting from earlier social
punishment. This orientation has been somewhat neglected recently,
probably because the theoretical rationale is similar to that proposed by
Dollard & Miller (1950) and Shoben (1949), all of whose ideas have been
criticized by the more radically behavioral sectors of modern behavior
therapy. However, Martin's analysis has considerable appeal in providing
a learning rationale for the direct, anxiety-reducing effect of the therapeutic relationship: "My definition of relationship as a counter-condition-
ing agent means only that behaviors provided by the therapist that have
an effect on the client provide, in some way, a rewarding or pleasant
situation. . . . For many clients these rewarding behaviors can be described
as permissiveness, nonpossessive warmth, . . . congruence, respect, or
prizing. . . . It seems most likely that the behaviors we associate with
'good relationships' most adequately meet the criteria of 1) being strongly
reinforcing (and of a social nature), and 2) being precisely applicable

at the moment the client attempts an approach response to the elements of his conflict" (Martin, 1971b, p. 149). On the basis of this model, Martin is then able to give explicit suggestions regarding appropriate therapist behavior during the course of verbal interactions with the client.

The Therapist as a Personal Role Model

Just as counterconditioning can occur through certain experiences arranged by the therapist (systematic desensitization) or can occur implicitly within the context of the therapist/client verbal interactions, so modeling can be explicitly evoked (as in teaching assertive and other social skills) or may occur implicitly and sometimes haphazardly during therapy interactions. As the degree to which an observer (client) imitates depends in part on the model (therapist) having qualities of attractiveness, status, and so forth, implicit modeling is almost certainly an inevitable consequence of a good therapeutic relationship. Depending upon what characteristics are imitated, this source of social influence places a considerable burden on the competencies of the therapist.

Advocating the development of broadly based coping skills and problem-solving competencies in clients, Mahoney (1974) favors viewing the therapist as a personal model. In particular, "multimodal" modeling of behavioral, affective, and cognitive reactions—including appropriate self-disclosure by the therapist of his own coping strategies—should constitute a significant aspect of the therapeutic influence. In the cognitive realm, for example, Mahoney suggests that the therapist provide problem-solving expertise by "thinking out loud." Some empirical support for the efficacy of this strategy is provided by Meichenbaum's (1971) finding that a model who verbalized thoughts and feelings during the performance of a behavioral task exerted more influence on observers than a model who did not.

Awareness of this source of influence, whether deliberately fostered or not, raises a number of intriguing questions. To what extent, for instance, must the therapist be a well-adjusted, effective problem-solver in his own right? Mahoney notes that the modeling research on the coping-versus-mastery distinction suggests that therapists who try to appear perfectly adjusted may be undermining their therapeutic impact. But being a less-than-perfect fallible human (Ellis, 1970) is one thing; lacking good social judgment or being unduly hampered by one's own personal problems is another. Even given well-adjusted therapists who can provide appropriate models of interpersonal functioning, there will be numerous other features of their behavior which should not be imitated by their clients. This concern, taken in conjunction with the task of facilitating generalization beyond the therapist's office, makes it important to direct the client's attention to available role models in the natural environment. All therapists should avoid the temptation of presenting themselves, implicitly or explicitly, as idealized human beings to be emulated in all situations.

Developing Therapeutic Expectancies

Although behavior therapy is characterized by the scientific approach to self-management and effective coping, as well as by adherence to the empirical method, enthusiasm for new techniques and procedures has not always been tempered with scientific caution. As Klein, Dittman, Parloff, and Gill (1969) observed, behavior therapists try to develop expectations of therapeutic gain in their clients. The role of expectancy in behavioral change has been increasingly recognized (e.g., Lick & Bootzin, 1975; Wilkins, 1976), and it is important to attempt a theoretically consistent integration of the expectancy effect with more formal techniques of behavior therapy. Ullmann and Krasner (1969) defined expectancy as a "verbal description of a role enactment likely to be reinforced in a given situation" (p. 72). This definition refers to the aspects of expectancy in which role-appropriate behaviors occur. Following Bandura's social learning model, Mahoney (1974) offers a more cognitive view of expectancy as "a complex of mediational processes which influence selective attention, response utilization, and anticipated consequences" (p. 275).

The significance of expectancies within social learning theory is considerable. By fostering in the client realistic expectations of ultimate success, the therapist bridges the gap between the immediate, often taxing, tasks required and the eventual improvement (Mischel, in press). Another consequence of increased expectancy is the elicitation of positive emotional states, such as hope, which can counteract feelings of demoralization and helplessness (Frank, 1961). One way of reducing demoralization is by having clients relabel or reinterpret the reasons for their distress. Behavioral explanations of emotional disorders often decrease anxiety by plausibly attributing problems not to illness, but to learning experiences which the client can oppose by re-learning (e.g., Meichenbaum & Smart, 1971). Davison (1969) has called this "assessment therapy," and it is, in itself, very helpful when anxiety about the problem behavior is an important maintaining variable (Evans, 1972).

Since it is likely that clients enter treatment with expectancies not only of outcome but of what the therapeutic process will entail, incongruities between what they expect and what they receive could impede progress or result in premature termination of therapy (Baekeland & Lundwill, 1975). Related to this latter process is Rosen's (1972) suggestion that the following two variables affect a client's continuation of the therapeutic relationship. The first is stimulus-response congruence —the extent to which the therapist's responses inform clients that their communications are understood. Congruence is viewed as a generalized secondary reinforcer, incongruence as a secondary aversive stimulus. The second is content relevance—the extent to which the content of the therapist's response is perceived by clients as pertinent to their preconceptions of crucial therapeutic issues. At a more practical level, Goldfried and Davison (1976) describe how the therapist might attempt to "shape" congruent expectancies about therapy, while Fish (1973) discusses a number of ways in which behavioral methods can be presented to different clients based on the therapist's knowledge of their interests, attitudes, and expectations—an important clinical skill.

The most sophisticated attempt to tie the expectancy effect to the more formal components of a behavioral technique has been the research on the active ingredients of systematic desensitization. It appears reasonable to conclude that induced expectancies can enhance the technique's therapeutic effects (cf., Borkovec, 1973; Emmelkamp, 1975; Lick & Bootzin, 1975; Wilson & Davison, 1975), although the precise manner in which expectancies contribute to fear reduction is still controversial. Borkovec (1973) contends that therapeutic expectancy communications act as external demand characteristics, and, as such, are effective with mildly fearful but not clinically phobic individuals. The possibility remains, of course, that more elaborate "demands" might then be developed for clinical cases. More recently, Borkovec (in press) has reported that subjects given information about the therapeutic purpose of the procedures they received showed lower heart rate throughout therapy sessions than subjects given contrary information. Borkovec maintains that "this effect represents the only demonstration to date relating expectancy manipulations to an objectively measured and potentially important therapy process variable"—positive expectancies possibly augmenting desensitization by way of their arousal-reducing effects. Rosen's (1974) findings are consistent with this position, and he has hypothesized that therapy set, or expectancy, helps subjects relax, thereby facilitating nonreinforced exposure to the aversive stimuli.

In developing therapeutic expectancies, the therapist has to maintain what is sometimes a delicate balance. On the one hand, positive expectancies appear to facilitate outcome; on the other hand, if expectancies are built up too high and success does not immediately follow, the client may see in his failure yet another affirmation of the hopelessness of his plight, with concomitant feelings of depression and resignation. The behavior therapist might be well-advised to make explicit to the client what is implicit in most behavioral strategies—the desirability of *gradual* change. Thus Brickman and Hendricks (1975) found that people who expected gradual rather than sudden improvement showed superior on-task performance, improved their performance more when it appeared that they were failing, and felt more comfortable following success.

Finally, in helping the client to develop positive but realistic outcome expectancies, it is suggested that the therapist anticipate difficulties and discuss possible pitfalls. Research on susceptibility to influence and counter-influence indicates that forewarned is forearmed (McGuire, 1964), and the client should be prepared to persist in the face of initial failure. Even so, positive expectancy will not suffice to sustain durable behavior change in the absence of other suitable maintaining variables. Direct influence procedures, such as maintaining positive expectations, have to be integrated into wider behavioral treatment programs.

THE THERAPEUTIC RELATIONSHIP AS AN INDIRECT
ENHANCEMENT IN BEHAVIOR CHANGE

In this section we will analyze the relationship per se as a source of increased therapist influence over the client such that behaviors may be more efficiently arranged to have positive, therapeutic interactions with the environment. Since much of active behavior therapy involves asking the client to *do* something—imagine a scene, relax in a chair, self-monitor daily caloric intake, refuse to accede to unreasonable requests, squeeze a partner's penis, or whatever—ensuring the potency of the therapist's requests is important. Lest this statement should appear too Machiavellian, there are three important provisos to consider. One of these is the now commonplace observation that unilateral therapist control over a client is actually quite limited. The second is the important observation that therapists' behaviors are also considerably influenced by their clients' interpersonal interactions. The third concern is the ultimate undesirability of trying to increase the therapist's ability to manipulate clients, even for their own good, rather than fostering relative independence from social influence. In an important argument critiquing some of the social influence studies being drawn upon in this section, Argyris (1975) described the typical model of applied social psychology (Model 1) which sanctions the right of some people to control others, and contrasted it with a second model (Model 2) which involves the sharing of power "with anyone who has competence and who is relevant in describing or implementing the action . . . Model 2 couples articulateness and advocacy with an invitation to others to confront one's views, to alter them, in order to produce the position that is based on the most complete, valid information possible, to which people involved can become internally committed" (Argyris, 1975, p. 482). Although some of the following examples of enhancing influence appear to involve Model 1 strategies, behavior therapy ideally, by attempting to involve the client as explicitly as possible in the total therapeutic experience, can be consistent with Model 2 theories of practice.

Interpersonal Attraction

Staats' A-R-D model of human motivation (Staats, 1968) provides one convenient way of analyzing the effect of the therapeutic relationship on the therapist's ability to elicit therapeutically desirable behavior from the client. The A-R-D model supposes that the therapist's emotional value (A), reinforcing properties (R), and ability to elicit specific behavior (D) are mutually interlinked. Thus one way of enhancing the instigative influence of the therapist is to increase personal attractiveness to the client. It can be argued that there are basically two means of producing client attitudes favorable to the therapist (Berscheid & Walster, 1969). One is to equip the therapist with the personal skills likely to enhance attractiveness. The other is to attempt to make the therapist and client more similar by matching them in terms of criteria designed to increase mutual attractiveness.

Although certain social skills have already been mentioned, the client's liking for the therapist is more complex than the consequence simply of the therapist's personal qualities. For one thing, the therapist's instigative ability is not just a function of liking, but also of prestige, status, perceived competence, and so forth (Goldstein et al., 1966). Then, secondly, one must assume that liking for the therapist increases over time, so that the therapist's greatest influence may occur towards the end of therapy when the client should be gaining independence and initiating new behaviors without direct instigation from the therapist. Thirdly, as Johnson and Matross (in press) concluded from the experimental findings on attitude change, the therapist's ability to influence the client is more a function of what the therapist does than the social niceties of interpersonal characteristics. Among the more important of these activities is the overall treatment plan—it is a truism that clients like those therapists who are successful, which is one of the logical problems of research reporting that the efficacy of behavior therapy is correlated with the clients' positive feelings for their therapists (Ryan & Gizynski, 1971).

Although therapist attractiveness can be developed, there are also occasions, perhaps most predominantly during the initial phases of therapy, when the direct match between therapist and client may be important. Instead of deliberate therapist-client matching, which is difficult with what Goldstein (1973) has termed the non-YAVIS client, behavior therapy has attempted to create a similar effect by emphasizing the triadic model of non-professional mediators (Tharp & Wetzel, 1969). The involvement of parents, teachers, peers, and even former clients who have special experience with different problem areas, would appear to have unique advantages. Self-help groups like Alcoholics Anonymous, Take Off Pounds Sensibly (TOPS), Mothers Anonymous (for child-abusing mothers), and even a group of exhibitionists, have advocated this policy; behavioral programs for obesity (Levitz & Stunkard, 1974) and alcoholism (Wiens, Montague, Manaugh, & English, 1974) have employed TOPS chapter leaders and recovered alcoholics respectively.

Yet the actual value of relying upon mediators who are similar to the client has never been fully determined. Levitz and Stunkard (1974) showed that their weight reduction program was significantly more effective when administered by the professional behavior therapists. In their behavioral consultation program for parents and teachers of children with conduct problems, Kent and O'Leary (in press) found no difference between the effectiveness of Ph.D. level behavior therapists and B.A. level paraprofessionals (e.g., former teachers). Subjective ratings, however, did show that teachers preferred working with the paraprofessionals.

Social Reinforcement

In addition to the attitudinal value of a stimulus, its function as a reinforcer is a determinant of approach behavior (Staats, 1968), and it is obvious that a therapist's careful use of social reinforcement is a major factor in the instigation of behavior change. Explicit social reinforcement is well-established as a primary behavior change method in the natural environment (O'Leary & O'Leary, 1972; Tharp & Wetzel, 1969). Behavior therapists are probably ultra careful in their use of social attention (particularly with depressed individuals or clients with recurring emotional upsets), and attempt to arrange contingencies of social reinforcement to discourage dependency and foster self-initiated, appropriate behavior.

The role of therapist-delivered reinforcement during adult behavior therapy is much less certain. Several studies have demonstrated the effect of social reinforcement on limited behaviors in both therapeutic (e.g., Kanfer & Phillips, 1970) and contrived settings (e.g., Salzinger, 1959). Truax (1966) even proposed that the "therapist-offered" conditions of empathy, warmth, and genuineness derive their importance, at least in part, from their function as differential reinforcers of positive client self-concepts. Such was the early enthusiasm for verbal conditioning and its presumed significance for psychotherapy that Krasner (1962) referred to the therapist as a "social reinforcement machine." Today, however, the limitations of verbal conditioning are more apparent and the meaningful generalization of its effects still indeterminate.

A major issue is how awareness of an explicit social reinforcement contingency affects the client's behavior. It has become increasingly difficult to argue that verbal conditioning is feasible without subjects' awareness of what is being reinforced (Page, 1972; Spielberger & DeNike, 1966). Insko and Cialdini (1971) have reviewed a number of studies supporting a two-factor theory of verbal reinforcement: "the positive verbal stimulus, 'good' provides information regarding the experimenter's attitude . . . and causes the subject to like the experimenter. The subject then responds consistently with the experimenter's attitude because of a tendency to agree with the liked other" (p. 18). Social reinforcement seems to act not so much as an automatic strengthener of human behavior as a source of information and incentive (Bandura, 1974; Mahoney, 1974), and is strongly affected by the personal characteristics of both therapist and client. Consider, for example, the client who becomes aware of the therapist-imposed social contingency and thereafter deliberately avoids performing the target behavior. Davison (1973 labeled this oppositional behavior "countercontrol" and attempted to analyze it within the social learning framework. He cited a study by Davis (1971) in which more verbal conditioning was obtained if the experimenter first disagreed with the subject and then agreed, as opposed to agreeing or disagreeing all the time—an arrangement which also results in greater liking by the subject (Aronson, 1969). Drawing on Haley's (1973) communications analysis, Davison interpreted these results as showing the importance of the subject perceiving himself as being in a position where he is not manipulated and is able to exert some influence over the experimenter's behavior. Conversely, some clients become so concerned about pleasing the therapist and eliciting reinforcement that they falsify record keeping or the outcomes of assignments. In such cases they have to be helped to become less dependent on such specific approval and able to find alternative sources of reinforcement.

Overcoming Resistance: Obtaining Client Compliance

Although attitudinal and reinforcement conditions appear to be optimal, it is sometimes the case that clients will still not do what their therapists suggest (Davison, 1973; Levy & Carter, in press). Confronted with this clinical problem, the behavior therapist might first explore with the client their mutual relationship. To check that the client is not distrustful or lacking confidence in the treatment program embarked upon, it is recommended that the therapist occasionally encourage subjective feedback regarding the client's feelings (cf., Lazarus, 1971). If, in the course of this exploration, hidden feelings of resentment or anger are uncovered, the occasion could also be used as an opportunity for training in more assertive behavior. In the event that this feedback is unrevealing, and noncompliance with the therapist's request persists, logical analysis of possible causes is needed.

One basic reason may be that the behavior is not sufficiently well established in the client's repertoire. Resistance is not necessarily volitional; it may be that the client *cannot* respond at that level of difficulty. Similarly, the task demands may be impractical given the current situation and mood of the client; instructing an obese client to consistently count calories might be too demanding because of interfering anxieties and depression. Fear of social disapproval and guilt may often counteract the therapist's instigative influence. The client's motivation to perform assigned tasks is sometimes diminished by anticipation of failure. A history of prior failures, leading to minimal or negative outcome expectancies, is no rarity in behavior therapy as it is still customary for many clients to be referred to behavior therapists only after continued unresponsiveness to more traditional forms of intervention.

Several strategies exist for combating client resistance (see also Davison, 1973; Levy & Carter, in press). If the client does not possess the necessary behavioral repertoire, direct training and rehearsal of assignments is required. A carefully graded approach can help overcome competing negative influence in the client's natural environment. Prompting the client to make a specific statement of interest or commitment to a well-defined task increases the probability of compliance. One method of obtaining commitment is to draw up a formal contract; another is to offer a pair of equally important therapeutic assignments that the client is asked to choose between (Mahoney, 1974), which is somewhat similar to one of Haley's (1973) useful strategies known as "providing a worse alternative." To the extent that clients perceive themselves as having *choice* it is possible that what Brehm (1966) has called psychological reactance is reduced. Reactance is assumed to be aroused when individuals perceive their choices as being restricted or threatened by an external authority. In a related proposition, Johnson and Matross (in press) argue that clients will be less resistant to influence they attribute as deriving from themselves rather than from the therapist. These authors suggest that instead of directly rewarding or punishing clients, the therapist, by providing expertise and direction within a problem-solving discussion, might foster self-attribution of influence and thereby increase compliance. A Model 2 (Argyris, 1975) approach, however, would be preferable: teaching clients self-management strategies that would eventually reduce their social compliance.

CONCLUSION

Unlike most other forms of psychotherapy, behavior therapy emphasizes the development of specific treatment techniques. Moreover, it appears that many of these techniques have been effective even when administered by therapists differing widely in personal style and background (Leitenberg, 1976; O'Leary & Wilson, 1975). The efficacy of behavior therapy techniques has been further highlighted by successful self- or client-administration, enhancing thereby self-regulated improvement in naturalistic settings.

This aspect of behavior therapy—self-administered methods, bibliographic materials, and tape-recorded programs—has undoubtedly contributed to an image of behavior therapy as mechanistic or impersonal. Yet, as we have tried to illustrate, behavior therapy is surely as personally challenging as psychotherapy and requires considerable interpersonal skill, social sensitivity, and clinical acumen for effective application. Much of the documented efficacy of behavior therapy attests to the fact that behavior therapists generally possess these skills. Direct study of their therapeutic behavior confirms this impression, as does the more biased reports of contented clients: O'Leary, Turkewitz, and Tafel (1973) found that virtually all parents whose children were treated at the Stony Brook child guidance clinic rated their behavior therapists as understanding, warm, sincere and interested.

Another factor responsible for the mechanistic stereotype of behavior therapy has been the attitude of many of its practitioners: insufficient attention has been focused on relationship variables in favor of an emphasis on more easily measurable—but occasionally trivial—procedural details. And last, but perhaps not least, the use of mechanistic metaphors describing the therapist as a "social reinforcement machine," a "behavioral engineer," and a behavioral "programmer" has helped perpetuate an unflattering image. The use of these terms not only tarnishes the public image (Woolfolk, Woolfolk, & Wilson, in press), but also reflects a simplistic image of man dominated by environmental factors beyond his control (cf., Bandura, 1974).

The theme of this paper—that relationship variables are extremely important and that they can be fruitfully conceptualized and integrated into the social learning formulation of behavior therapy—is in fundamental disagreement with the increasingly common view that behavior therapists are really only skilled technicians (e.g., London, 1972) and that, therefore, only formal procedures should be evaluated. Martin (1974), for example, argues that it would "make more sense to certify procedures rather than people because all the persons involved do not come under the control of any one profession. Individuals running structured learning programs might be licensed in psychology, psychiatry, education, sociology, social work or other professions" (p. 21). This view reveals a limited understanding of the essence of behavior therapy, which does not lie merely in a set of techniques. Quality control will be most assured if professionals who practice behavior therapy are well-versed in its scientific foundation *and* are possessed of the clinical/interpersonal skills we have described. Technicians are merely mediators of behavior change in the Tharp and Wetzel (1969) sense. If the continued lop-sided preoccupation with so-called "treatment techniques" continues without serious consideration of the kinds of complex variables discussed here, the stereotype of behavior therapy as clinically naive will become increasingly difficult to dispute.

REFERENCES

AGRAS, W. S. Toward the certification of behavior therapists? *Journal of Applied Behavior Analysis,* 1973, 6, 167-171.

ANNON, J. S. *The Behavioral Treatment of Sexual Problems, Volume 1: Brief Therapies.* Honolulu, Hawaii: Kapiolani Health Service, 1974.

ARGYRIS, C. Dangers in applying results from experimental social psychology. *American Psychologist,* 1975, 30, 469-485.

ARONSON, E. Some antecedents of interpersonal attraction. In M. J. Arnold & D. Levine (Eds.), *Nebraska Symposium on Motivation.* Lincoln: University of Nebraska Press, 1969.

BAEKELAND, F. & LUNDWILL, L. Dropping out of treatment: A critical review. *Psychological Bulletin,* 1975, 82, 738-783.

BANDURA, A. Behavior theory and the models of man. *American Psychologist,* 1974, 29, 859-869.

BEGELMAN, D. A. Ethical and legal issues of behavior modification. In M. Hersen, R. M. Eisler, & R. M. Miller (Eds.), *Progress in Behavior Modification. Vol. 1.* New York: Academic Press, 1975, pp. 159-187.

BERSCHEID, E. & WALSTER, E. H. *Interpersonal Attraction.* Reading, Mass.: Addison-Wesley, 1969.

BIERMAN, R. Dimensions of interpersonal facilitation in psychotherapy or child development. *Psychological Bulletin,* 1969, 72, 338-352.

BORKOVEC, T. D. The role of expectancy and physiological feedback in fear research: A review with special reference to subject characteristics. *Behavior Therapy,* 1973, 4, 491-505.

BORKOVEC, T. D. Investigations of fear and sleep disturbance: Methodological, measurement, and theoretical issues in therapy outcome research. In G. E. Schwartz and D. Shapiro (Eds.), *Conscious and Self-Regulations Advances in Research.* New York: Plenum Press, in press.

BREHM, J. M. *A Theory of Psychological Reactance.* New York: Academic Press, 1966.

BRICKMAN, P. & HENDRICKS, M. Expectancy for gradual or sudden improvement and reaction to success and failure. *Journal of Personality and Social Psychology,* 1975, 32, 893-900.

CARKHUFF, R. R. *Helping and Human Relations.* New York: Holt, Rinehart and Winston, 1969.

CHAIKIN, A. L. & DERLEGA, V. J. *Self-disclosure.* Morristown, N. J.: General Learning Press, 1974.

DAVIS, J. D. *The Interview as Arena.* Stanford: Stanford University Press, 1971.

DAVIS, J. D. & SKINNER, A. E. G. Reciprocity of self-disclosure in interviews: Modeling or social exchange? *Journal of Personality and Social Psychology,* 1974, 29, 779-784.

DAVISON, G. C. An appraisal of behavior modification techniques with adults in institutional settings. In C. M. Franks (Ed.), *Behavior Therapy: Appraisal and Status.* New York: McGraw-Hill, 1969.

DAVISON, G. C. Counter-control in behavior modification. In L. A. Hamerlynck, L. C. Handy, and E. J. Mash (Eds.), *Behavior Change: Methodology, Concepts and Practice.* Champaign, Ill.: Research Press, 1973.

DAVISON, G. C. Homosexuality: The ethical challenge. *Journal of Consulting and Clinical Psychology,* 1976, 44, 157-162.

DAVISON, G. C. & WILSON, G. T. Attitudes of behavior therapists towards homosexuality. *Behavior Therapy,* 1973, 4, 686-696.

DOLLARD, J. & MILLER, N. E. *Personality and Psychotherapy: An Analysis in Terms of Learning, Thinking and Culture.* New York: Institute for Rational Living, 1970.

EMMELKAMP, P. M. G. Effects of expectancy on systematic desensitization and flooding. *European Journal of Behavioral Analysis and Modification*, 1975, 1, 1-11.

EVANS, I. M. A conditioning model of a common neurotic pattern—fear of fear. *Psychotherapy: Theory, Research and Practice*, 1972, 9, 238-241.

EVANS, I. M. & NELSON, R. O. A curriculum for the teaching of behavior assessment. *American Psychologist*, 1974, 29, 598, 606.

EVANS, I. M. & NELSON, O. R. The assessment of child behavior problems. In A. Ciminero, K. S. Calhoun, and H. E. Adams (Eds.), *A Handbook of Behavior Assessment*. New York: Wiley, in press.

EYSENCK, H. J. *Fact and Fiction in Psychology*. Baltimore: Penguin, 1965.

FISH, J. M. *Placebo Therapy*. San Francisco: Jossey Bass, 1973.

FRANK, J. D. *Persuasion and Healing*. Baltimore: Johns Hopkins University Press, 1961.

FRANKS, V. & BURTLE, V. (Eds.). *Women in Therapy: New Psychotherapies for a Changing Society*. New York: Brunner/Mazel, 1974.

GOLDFRIED, M. R. & DAVISON, G. C. *Clinical Behavior Therapy*. New York: Holt, Rinehart and Winston, 1976.

GOLDSTEIN, A. P. *Structured Learning Therapy*. New York: Pergamon, 1973.

GOLDSTEIN, A. P., HELLER, K., & SECHREST, L. B. *Psychotherapy and the Psychology of Behavior Change*. New York: Wiley, 1966.

HALEY, J. *Uncommon Therapy*. New York: Norton, 1973.

INSKO, C. A. & CIALDINI, R. B. *Interpersonal Influence in a Controlled Setting: The Verbal Reinforcement of Attitude*. Morristown, N. J.: General Learning Press, 1971.

JOHNSON, D. W. & MATROSS, R. Interpersonal influence in psychotherapy. In A. S. Gurman and A. M. Razin (Eds.), *The Therapist's Contribution to Effective Psychotherapy: An Empirical Approach*. New York: Pergamon Press, in press.

KANFER, F. H. & PHILLIPS, J. S. Behavior therapy: A panacea for all ills or a passing fancy? *Archives of General Psychiatry*, 1966, 15, 114-128.

KANFER, F. H. & PHILLIPS, J. S. *Learning Foundations of Behavior Therapy*. New York: Wiley, 1970.

KENT, R. N. & O'LEARY, K. D. Treatment of conduct problem children: B.A. and/or Ph.D. therapists. *Behavior Therapy*, in press.

KLEIN, M. H., DITTMAN, A. T., PARLOFF, M. B., & GILL, M. M. Behavior therapy: Observations and reflections. *Journal of Consulting and Clinical Psychology*, 1969, 33, 259-266.

KRASNER, L. The therapist as a social reinforcement machine. In H. H. Strupp and L. Luborsky (Eds.), *Research in Psychotherapy* Vol. II. Washington, D. C.: American Psychological Association, 1962.

KURTH, S. B. Friendships and friendly relations. In G. J. McCall (Ed.), *Social Relationships*. Chicago: Aldine, 1970.

LANG, P. J., MELAMED, B. G., & HART, J. A psychophysiological analysis of fear modification using an automated desensitization procedure. *Journal of Abnormal Psychology*, 1970, 76, 220-234.

LAZARUS, A. A. *Behavior Therapy and Beyond*. New York: McGraw-Hill, 1971.

LAZARUS, A. A. & FAY, A. *I Can If I Want to*. New York: Morrow, 1975.

LEITENBERG, H. *Handbook of Behavior Modification and Behavior Therapy*. Englewood Cliffs, N. J.: Prentice-Hall, 1976.

LEVITZ, L. S. & STUNKARD, A. J. A therapeutic coalition for obesity: Behavior modification and patient self-help. *American Journal of Psychiatry*, 1974, 131, 424-427.

LEVY, R. L. & CARTER, R. D. Obtaining client compliance with practitioner instigations: An explorative literature review. *Social Work*, in press.

LICK, J. & BOOTZIN, R. Expectancy factors in the treatment of fear: Methodological and theoretical issues. *Psychological Bulletin*, 1975, 82, 917-931.

LONDON, P. The end of ideology in behavior modification. *American Psychologist*, 1972, 27. 913-920.

MAHONEY, M. J. *Cognition and Behavior Modification*. Cambridge, Mass.: Ballinger, 1974.

MARTIN, D. G. *Learning-Based Client-Centered Therapy*. Belmont, California: Brooks/Cole, 1971. (a)

MARTIN, D. G. *Introduction to Psychotherapy*. Belmont, California: Brooks/Cole, 1971. (b)

MARTIN, R. *Behavior Modification: Human Rights and Legal Responsibilities*. Champaign, Ill.: Research Press, 1974.

McGUIRE, W. J. Inducing resistance to persuasion. In L. Berkowitz (Ed.), *Advances in Experimental Social Psychology*. Vol. I. New York: Academic Press, 1964, pp. 191-229.

MEICHENBAUM, D. Examination of model characteristics in reducing avoidance behavior. *Journal of Personality and Social Psychology*, 1971, 14, 298-307.

MEICHENBAUM, D. & SMART, I. Use of direct expectancy to modify academic performance and attitudes of college students. *Journal of Counseling Psychology*, 1971, 18, 531-535.

MEYER, V. The impact of research on the clinical application of behavior therapy. In T. Thompson and W. S. Dockens, III. (Eds.), *Applications of Behavior Modification*. New York: Academic Press, 1975.

MEYER, V. & CRISP, A. H. Some problems in behavior therapy. *British Journal of Psychiatry*, 1966, 112, 367-381.

MISCHEL, W. *Personality and Assessment*. New York: Wiley, 1968.

MISCHEL, W. Processes in delay of gratification. In L. Berkowitz (Ed.), *Advances in Experimental Social Psychology*. Vol. 7. New York: Academic Press, in press.

O'LEARY, K. D. & O'LEARY, S. G. *Classroom Management*. New York: Pergamon Press,

O'LEARY, K. D., TURKEWITZ, H., & TAFFEL, S. J. Parent and therapist evaluation of behavior therapy in a child psychological clinic. *Journal of Consulting and Clinical Psychology*, 1973, 41, 279-283.

O'LEARY, K. D. & WILSON, G. T. *Behavior Therapy: Application and Outcome*. Englewood Cliffs, N. J.: Prentice-Hall, 1975.

O'NEILL, N. & O'NEILL, J. *Open Marriage*. Philadelphia: Lippincott, 1972.

PAGE, M. M. Demand characteristics and the verbal operant conditioning experiment. *Journal of Personality and Social Psychology*, 1972, 23, 372-378.

RICE, J. K. & RICE, D. G. Implications of the women's liberation movement for psychotherapy. *American Journal of Psychiatry*, 1973, 130, 191-196.

ROSEN, A. The treatment relationship: A conceptualization. *Journal of Consulting and Clinical Psychology*, 1972, 38, 329-337.

ROSEN, G. M. Therapy set: Its effect on subjects' involvement in systematic desensitization and treatment outcome. *Journal of Abnormal Psychology*, 1974, 83, 291-300.

RYAN, V. L. & GIZYNSKI, M. N. Behavior therapy in retrospect: Patients' feelings about their behavior therapies. *Journal of Consulting and Clinical Psychology*, 1971, 37, 1-9.

SALZINGER, K. Experimental manipulation of verbal behavior: A review. *Journal of General Psychology*, 1959, 61, 65-95.

SCHLENKER, B. R., HELM, B., & TEDESCHI, J. T. The effects of personality and situational variables on behavioral trust. *Journal of Personality and Social Psychology*, 1973, 25, 419-427.

SHOBEN, E. J., JR. Psychotherapy as a problem in learning theory. *Psychological Bulletin*, 1949, 46, 366-392.

SOBELL, M. & SOBELL, L. Individualized behavior therapy for alcoholics. *Behavior Therapy*, 1973, 4, 49-72.

SPIELBERGER, C. D. & DENIKE, L. D. Descriptive behaviorism versus cognitive theory in verbal operant conditioning. *Psychological Review*, 1966, 73, 306-326.

STAATS, A. W. Social behaviorism and human motivation: Principles of the A-R-D system. In A. G. Greenwald, T. C. Brock, and T. M. Ostrom (Eds.), *Psychological Foundations of attitudes*. New York: Academic Press, 1968.

STAATS, A. W. Language behavior therapy: A derivative of social behaviorism. *Behavior Therapy*, 1972, 3, 165-192.

STAPLES, F. R., SLOANE, R. B., WHIPPLE, K., CRISTOL, A. H., & YORKSTON, N. T. Differences between behavior therapists and psychotherapists. *Archives of General Psychiatry*, 1975, 32, 1517-1522.

THARP, R. G. & WETZEL, R. J. *Behavior Modification in the Natural Environment*. New York: Academic Press, 1969.

THIBAUT, J. W. & KELLY, H. H. *The Social Psychology of Groups*. New York: Wiley, 1951.

TRUAX, C. B. Reinforcement and nonreinforcement in Rogeran psychotherapy. *Journal of Abnormal and Social Psychology*, 1966, 71, 1-9.

TRUAX, C. B. & MITCHELL, K. M. Research on certain therapist interpersonal skills in relation to process and outcome. In A. E. Bergin and S. L. Garfield (Eds.), *Handbook of Psychotherapy and Behavior Change*. New York: Wiley, 1971, pp. 229-344.

ULLMAN, L. P. & KRASNER, L. *A Psychological Approach to Abnormal Behavior*. Englewood Cliffs, N. J.: Prentice-Hall, 1969.

WIENS, A. H., MONTAGUE, J. R., MANAUGH, T. S., & ENGLISH, C. J. Pharmacologic aversive counterconditioning to alcohol in the private hospital: One year followup. Unpublished manuscript, University of Oregon Medical School, 1974.

WILKINS, W. Expectancy of therapeutic gain: An empirical and conceptual critique. *Journal of Consulting and Clinical Psychology*, 1973, 40, 69-77.

WILSON, G. T. Towards specifying the "nonspecific" factors in behavior therapy: A social learning analysis. Paper presented at the Association for Advancement of Behavior Therapy, San Francisco, December 1975.

WILSON, G. T. & DAVISON, G. C. "Effects of expectancy on systematic desensitization and flooding": A critical analysis. *European Journal of Behavioral Analysis and Modification*, 1975, 1, 12-14.

WILSON, G. T. & EVANS, I. M. The therapist-client relationship in behavior therapy. In A. Gurman and A. Razin (Eds.), *The Therapist's Contribution to Effective Psychotherapy: An Empirical Approach*. New York: Pergamon Press, in press.

WILSON, G. T., HANNON, A. E., & EVANS, W. I. M. Behavior therapy and the therapist-patient relationship. *Journal of Consulting and Clinical Psychology*, 1968, 32, 103-109.

WOOLFOLK, A. E., WOOLFOLK, R. L., & WILSON, G. T. A rose by any other name . . . : Labeling bias and attitudes toward behavior modification. *Journal of Consulting and Clinical Peychology*, in press.

35

BEHAVIORAL APPROACHES TO MARITAL DISCORD AND CONFLICT

Steven E. Greer and

Thomas J. D'Zurilla

State University of New York at Stony Brook

This paper reviews the empirical research in behavioral approaches to marital therapy. The level of product of current research designs has not yet advanced significantly beyond the non-factorial single-group design, and the breadth of treatment populations employed thus far has been restricted. The power of the behavioral method is found in its theoretical base, observational and treatment-relevant assessment, procedural specificity, and quantification of outcome. The outcomes of treatment, though relatively small in number, thus far, have been almost universally positive and encouraging.

In the last two decades there has been a fundamental departure from traditional views of the nature, cause, and treatment of behavior disorders. A new socio-behavioral orientation has asserted that behavior which is maladaptive or varies widely from accepted social and moral

Reprinted with permission from *Journal of Marriage and Family Counseling*, October, 1975, 299-315.

The research reviewed in this paper covers the period from 1968-1974.

principles should be viewed not only as symptomatic of an underlying "disease" process but as a learned coping response to environmental, interpersonal, or self-imposed demands. Within this model, treatment is viewed as a problem in social learning rather than one in the psychodynamic domain (Bandura, 1969). The various methods for treating behavioral dysfunction conceptualized in these social learning terms have been subsumed under the label "behavior modification" or "behavior therapy."

The rapid proliferation of theory, research, and practice in the field of behavior modification has been a development of dramatic proportions. However, one of the products of the movement—the behavioral approach to marital discord and conflict—is currently only in its embryonic stages of development, as evidenced by the fact that the first published social learning-based treatment for marital discord did not appear until 1968 (Lazarus, 1968). One possible reason for the lag in applying the behavioral approach to marital problems is that behavior modification typically has been defined as the application of principles derived from general experimental psychology (especially learning theory and research) to the changing of undesirable behaviors (Krasner, 1969) and, therefore, has tended to focus on the individual, with relatively little work dealing with group or dyadic processes.

Marital behavioral therapy (MBT) has, nevertheless, emerged, but it has come in as a back-door enterprise. Most of the work to be reviewed in this paper has developed as a by-product of work with other types of problems and other treatment populations, especially children. That is, behavior therapists—like family therapists—have embraced the marital dyad as a culmination of the realization that a child's behavior problems cannot be treated in an individual, non-familial vacuum. All relationships in the family—including the marital relationship—potentially contribute to the environmental conditions maintaining deviant behavior. If, as Ferber, Mendelsohn, and Napier (1973) assert, family therapy is defined not by the number of family members in the room during a session but by the interests and allegiance of the therapist toward the whole family, then MBT may be called family therapy both in theory and in practice.*

---

* Although the behavioral treatment of sexual inadequacy (e.g., Masters & Johnson, 1970; LoPiccolo & Lobitz, 1973) is often a part of MBT, a review of the work in this area would require a separate paper and will not be included here.

CONCEPTUALIZATION

The conceptual framework for analysis of dyadic interactions in MBT has been derived from social learning theory—that "loosely organized body of literature dealing with the changes in learning, or performance, which occur as a function of contingencies which characterize social interaction" (Patterson, 1969). This literature reflects two major areas of theory and research: a) the mechanisms of behavior influence derived from social psychological principles, such as persuasion, modeling, and conformity; and b) a second set of mechanisms derived from laboratory investigations of reinforcement principles as they apply to social interactions. These two primary sources have been tapped by Patterson and Reid (1970) and Patterson and Hops (1972) in conceptualizing parent-child and husband-wife dyads, respectively, in terms of two hypothesized social reinforcement mechanisms—*reciprocity* and *coercion*. Reciprocity describes a dyadic exchange in which two persons reinforce each other at an equitable rate, positive reinforcers maintaining the behavior of both parties. Coercion refers to interaction in which both persons provide aversive stimuli which control the behavior of the other person, negative reinforcement resulting from the termination of this aversive stimulation maintaining the behavior of both parties.

To illustrate the coercion mechanism, consider an example of the usual demand-compliance interaction. Mr. Jones demands sexual responsiveness from Mrs. Jones and is rewarded by her compliance. Also, Mrs. Jones' compliant behavior is maintained by positive reinforcers, such as "I love you," from Mr. Jones. The coercive interaction subverts this positive process: Mr. Jones again emits the same demand; however, Mrs. Jones now fails to comply, acting as if she were asleep instead. There is now a noticeable rise in the intensity level of Mr. Jones' demand as he resubmits the demand. Mrs. Jones' reply is no longer likely to be passive noncompliance; instead, she is likely to reply in kind, with aversive stimulation in the form of some misdirected verbalization counterattacking the previous demand by her husband, such as "You know you're a lousy lover." This rising crescendo of aversive demand-counterdemand may continue for several more exchanges until Mrs. Jones finally emits some form of pseudo-compliant behavior, such as engaging in sex passively. After years of training in marital coercion, Mrs. Jones will have also learned to pseudo-comply by making some vague promise to comply with the demand in the future, or if this tactic is perceived by Mr. Jones as noncompliant and results in rising aversive stimulation, the initial demand may serve as a discriminative stimulus setting the occasion for immediate compliant or pseudo-compliant behavior.

Patterson and Reid (1970) maintain that it is likely that as one member uses aversive stimuli to control behavior, the other member of the dyad will also introduce this method of control. Their coercion hypothesis asserts that equity is generally established in the exchange of aversive stimuli; their analysis of family interactions showed a median correlation of .65 between the proportion of aversive stimulation given and received. Therefore, this hypothesis would predict that in most coercive marital interactions the aversive cycle of demand and counterdemand moves well beyond compliance, or submission, in the early rounds of the sequence. As Lederer and Jackson (1968) so aptly phrased it: "nastiness begets nastiness." The effective by-product of mutual aversive control of dyadic interactions is an increase in unpleasantness and concomitant reduction in the ability of either party to change the behavior of his spouse; coercion effectively sidetracks the couple from any possible solution of the problem originally posed by one partner's demand. Patterson and Hops (1972) define marital *conflict* in terms of this interaction pattern as a dyadic interchange in which one party fails to comply with explicit or implicit demands for immediate changes in behavior with accompanying escalation of aversive stimulation until one person gives in (complies or pseudo-complies) or leaves the situation (withdrawal). The result of conflict is an increment in the number of unchanged behaviors, an increase in the number of bitter fights, and an increasingly punitive marital relationship up to some point at which one or both members agree to terminate the marriage.

The concepts of conflict, coercion, and reciprocity as defined above have been the main theoretical constructs used for the conceptualization of marital discord in the MBT literature. Though not described in social learning terminology, these same constructs have also formed the bedrock of the family role theory of psycho-pathological disorders advanced by Tharp and Otis (1966). Family therapists more familiar with the latter formulation will realize that social learning theorists have simply translated Tharp and Otis role-theory constructs into the language of reinforcement theory. It is significant to note that Tharp now prefers the social learning terminology (Tharp & Wetzel, 1969).

ASSESSMENT

Virtually all of the currently available MBT approaches employ observational methodology in the assessment of marital conflict and/or in the evaluation of treatment. Sociologists working in the area of marriage and family research have, likewise, required research instruments for the assessment of marital and familial interaction processes and have increasingly begun to use observational methodology rather than relying on the more traditional interview and self-report data (Olson & Ryder, 1970; Olson & Straus, 1972). As a consequence, instruments derived from these sociological endeavors have been available for adaptation to the field of MBT.

The impetus for the observational approach to the study of marital and family interaction has been the heuristic work with families of psychiatric patients by workers such as Bateson et al. (1956), Laing and Esterson (1964), and their associates. An important antecedent of the observational assessment technique was Stodtbeck's Revealed Differences Technique (Stodtbeck, 1951), which for years has been used to observe marital interaction in a relatively unstructured way. Spouses simply filled out a questionnaire individually and discussed disagreements jointly; meanwhile, of course, they are being observed by raters or recorded for later rating. Olson and Ryder developed the Inventory of Marital Conflicts (IMC) to override some of the complications of data analysis with the Revealed Differences Technique and ended up developing a 29-category coding system for verbal interactions of couples engaged in conflict-resolution discussions. However, no in vivo observers are required for this device since the only data afforded is audio-taped conversation.

Going a step further, sociologists Murphy and Mendelson (1973) compared typescript and videotaped codings of interactions between young married couples (based upon Thematic Apperception Test cards as the stimuli for discussion) with self-report data from the Locke-Wallace Marital Adjustment Scale (Locke & Wallace, 1959). Reliabilities among pairs of videotape-coders were significantly greater than those for typescript-coders. Murphy and Mendelson evaluated this finding as validational support for the use of observational methodology in the study of live marital communication.

Similarly, Olson and Straus (1972) describe a standardized lab procedure called the Simulated Family Activity Measurement (SIMFAM) for the diagnostic measurement of family and marital interactions. In a gameroom setting requiring a minimum of apparatus, the couple or family is confronted with a shuffleboard-like game and instructed to begin playing and to learn the rules themselves by attending to feedback from red and green lights monitoring the appropriateness of their spontaneous actions from behind a one-way mirror. Feedback is manipulated artificially to produce an experimental crisis halfway through the 24-minute game by drastically increasing the frequency of red (failure) signals. With this system, individuals, couples, or families may be coded according to some standard categories (e.g., assertiveness = number of verbalizations intended to modify the behavior of another person; power = number of assertive statements which succeed in modifying behavior, and so on). The authors even suggest that certain variables generated by the code may be used in pre-post assessment of the outcome of therapy. These coding methods bear a striking resemblance to observational coding methods frequently used by behavioral observers. One such code, the Marital Interaction Coding System (MICS), has been the primary assessment instrument of an important group of MBT researchers (Hops et al., 1972).

Perhaps the most extensive behavioral assessment procedures currently employed in the field have been those developed by Patterson and his associates at Oregon. These assessment procedures have been of the self-report, self-observational and observational variety. The self-report techniques include: 1) the Locke-Wallace Scale of Marital Adjustment, a traditional measure included to allow for comparison between the Oregon sample and others reported in the literature; 2) the Willingness to Change Scale (W-C), an instrument designed to pinpoint conflict by asking each spouse to indicate on a seven-point scale whether his partner should engage in specified activities much less, no change, or much more; 3) the Marital Activities Inventory (MAI), surveying 85 common leisure-time activities by asking the spouse to estimate the frequency of occurrence of these activities in the past month and whether he was alone, with spouse, or with others at the time, thus estimating his patterns and sources of social reinforcement; and 4) the Pleasurable-Displeasurable count (P's and D's), an extremely comprehensive listing of specific pleasant or aversive behaviors in several marital categories with the instruction to record frequency of these behaviors over a two-week baseline period.

Birchler (1972) and Vincent (1972) studied various aspects of these instruments in samples of distressed and nondistressed couples selected and differentiated on the basis of their Locke-Wallace, W-C, and interview rating scores. Distressed couples were significantly different from non-distressed couples in their P and D rates, with significantly higher D's and significantly lower P's among distressed couples. It was also found that distressed couples reported a significantly lower mean percentage of recreational activities shared with the spouse as reported on the MAI, in spite of the fact that distressed and nondistressed couples did not differ in their absolute range of activities.

Since most investigations of marital interaction have employed global ratings of self-reported marital satisfaction or "happiness," Wills, Weiss, and Patterson (1974) sought to determine the behavioral determinants of these ratings. Seven paid volunteer couples recorded daily P's and D's in two broad categories, instrumental and affectational events. Instrumental actions are taken to accomplish some end (e.g., taking out the garbage), while affectational actions refer to overt displays of affection or love. In addition, they recorded the extent to which outside (nonspouse related) events of the day were pleasurable. By means of multiple regression analysis these five measures were related to global daily ratings of marital satisfaction. Interestingly, Wills et al. found that instrumental P's and affectional P's were the main contributors to the daily satisfaction ratings for husbands and wives, respectively. However, D events in both categories accounted for more of the variance of satisfaction ratings than did P events, suggesting that satisfaction ratings are more sensitive to aversive events, possibly because couples are more skilled at perceiving and remembering D events.

The observational techniques employed in assessment by the Oregon group included: 1) a structured interview used as a sample of marital distress in which the interviewer makes a continuous record of positive and negative exchanges and a final rating on a seven-point scale of marital distress; 2) coded samples of ongoing problem-solving interactions using the MICS; and 3) home observations employing the Patterson Family Observation System developed in work with families of children with conduct problems (Patterson & Hops, 1972).

Of the above techniques, the MICS provides the bulk of the information for assessment and evaluation of outcome of treatment. To use this method, short (10-minute) interactions of husband and wife trying to solve problems raised in the structured interviews or selected from the MAI are videotaped and played back for scoring by trained coders. Both verbal and nonverbal aspects of the behavior of both spouses are scored in 30-second units to a minimum interrater agreement of 70 percent. Thirty behavior categories or codes are used. Some examples of verbal codes are Agree, Approval, Problem Description, Problem Solving, and Put Down. Examples of nonverbal codes are Attention, Laugh, Positive Physical Contact, and Compliance. Coders were graduate and undergraduate students trained for at least two weeks of daily sessions, two to three hours in length. Typically, two laboratory observation sessions are recorded for each treated couple during a two-week, pre-treatment baseline and two more following treatment.

Research reported by Weiss, Hops, and Patterson (1973) indicates that during baseline only one MICS category in 30 showed an increase approaching significance $(p < .10)$, a result well within statistical expectation; that the discussion of major versus minor problems does have a specific effect on certain codes during baseline; and that significant within-session favorable change in problem-solving codes (a set of three categories) was evident during intervention. In short, MICS is sensitive to behavior change in short samples of interaction both within and between sessions (Hops, Patterson, & Weiss, 1973; Weiss, Patterson, & Hops, 1973).

TREATMENT

This section will focus upon the work of Patterson, Hops, and Weiss, and their associates at the University of Oregon and the Oregon Research Institute as the most advanced current example of MBT. Maley (1973) has described this work as "basically a conceptual effort, with enough preliminary data presented to convince the reader that this technology has great promise for the treatment of marital discord." However, Patterson and associates have not been the pioneers in MBT. The work of other behaviorally-oriented clinicians has undoubtedly contributed to the present cumulative product in the Oregon work, and these efforts will be reviewed as well. Forgetting about origins for the moment, it is useful to note that one theoretical construct unifies all of these behavioral treatments (at least, implicitly), the construct of reciprocity of reinforcement between spouses. The remainder of this paper will endeavor to explore the development of treatments involving this central concept and the various research designs within which these treatments have been tested.

Individual Case Studies

Considering the abundance of anecdotal case studies perennially encountered in the marital therapy literature it would seem appropriate to begin our review with similar early literature. Liberman (1970) criticized the confusion in the rationales and techniques underlying some forms of family and marital therapy, specifically the belief that the vital communications in all forms of psychotherapy are intuitive, affective, unspoken, and unconscious. Having bombarded tradition in a manner all too reminiscent of the behavior modification literature of the early 1960's, Liberman presented a fairly adequate operant rationale in terms of reciprocal social reinforcement of individual deviancy within families of dysfunctional communication patterns between spouses. Three of the four cases he reported involved marital discord, but the account is anecdotal and provides no data. In two of these cases, treatment began with a single, referred patient, but a functional analysis of the patient's symptoms revealed that certain spouse behaviors were maintaining symptomatic behavior. In each of these cases, an effort was made to increase the rate of positive social reinforcement emitted by each spouse and to redirect inappropriate attention from deviant behavior to more appropriate alternative behavior. As such, the dyad was only indirectly involved as a consequence of the aversiveness of the patient's symptoms and the marital unhappiness thus produced. In only one of the four cases was there a presenting problem of marital discord. In this instance, treatment involved a negotiated exchange of behaviors without the mediation of a formal contract; essentially, the therapist served as stimulus for keeping the agreement, which remained unwritten. Such a treatment is the immediate predecessor of the formal contractual-exchange methods used in most of the studies reported in the remainder of the paper.

Arnold A. Lazarus (1968) was the first behavior therapist to suggest the applicability of the armamentarium of behavioral techniques for many forms of marital discord. His paper's significance lies in the then novel suggestion that behavioral techniques developed for implementation with individual clients (e.g., systematic desensitization, behavioral rehearsal, assertive training, and co-therapeutic modeling) could be modified for use with marital difficulties. As with the first two cases presented by Liberman (1970), Lazarus' "techniques" approach would seem to be most appropriate for dealing with the problem of isolated symptomatic behavior of individual spouses contributing to, or resulting from marital conflict. In short, such an approach largely ignores the marital dyad and focuses on its individual members' personal problems.

Knox (1971) has advanced a similar position but has incorporated the relationship-oriented technique of exchange contracting among the more individually-oriented methods. Knox's work best illustrates the "shotgun" behavioral approach, the utilization of any and all techniques currently employed by behavior therapists in individual therapy. His book continues to be the only lengthy publication of the behavioral approach to MBT available to those not familiar with the broader literature. Knox produces a categorical listing of common problems in marriage, analyzing problem areas into more specific categories and mapping some potentially applicable behavioral techniques onto these categories in the context of actual case reports from his files. Though some data are presented, the account is once again largely anecdotal. The end result is a "cookbook," a rather ingenious enumeration of tactics for the ad hoc generalization of existing behavioral procedures to the individual members of the dyad.*

More recent case studies have focused more exclusively on the dyadic relationship per se. Rappaport and Harrell (1972) have reported a case which goes much further than previous reports in providing procedural detail as well. They used a behavioral-exchange model based upon negotiation skills training and successive fading of therapist involvement in the process, i.e., negotiating skills were the goal of therapy. Sessions were initially educational, with cotherapists providing information concerning behavioral principles and channeling this information into examples of pertinent marital interactions modeled by the co-therapists. After training the couple to label desirable and undesirable behavior specifically, a behavioral-exchange contract was negotiated with continuous therapist supervision. These authors then encouraged negotiation of contracts outside the session, with telephone monitoring by the therapist if necessary. The couple finally learned to identify and renegotiate any poor contracts they made on their own. Although the reader is assured that the treatment was a success, again little data are provided to confirm the assertion.

Hickok and Komechak (1974) present a similar case study. The conflict for their couple centered around the husband's demands for sexual cooperation from his wife and the wife's demands for less dependent behavior on the part of her husband. These demands were converted to specific, pinpointed behaviors, and a token economy was initiated in which the husband earned tokens for allowing his wife to leave the house while he watched the children, while the wife earned tokens for engaging in husband-initiated sexual behavior. Although these authors used a reversal (ABA) design to illustrate the changes in behavior produced by therapy, the target behaviors continued to improve during the two-week removal of the token economy. As such, the reversal failed in a technical sense to provide evidence that the token economy was responsible for the changes in this couple's behavior, but it did show

---

* Knox has recently published a similar volume for the layman (Knox, 1975).

that something which occurred in the six-week token period prior to removal was generalized even to the two-week removal period.

Another study focusing on a single couple but using a multiple baseline design was reported recently by Wieman, Shoulders, and Farr (1974). As the authors were endeavoring to employ Stuart's (1969b) behavioral exchange approach, they encountered a difficult, but not atypical, obstacle. More communication time was requested from the husband and improvement in sexual activities was desired by both, but the husband in this case could not communicate with his wife on an acceptable level, and both spouses were unable to initiate and maintain sexual activity in an appropriate and mutually satisfying way; in other words, behavioral skill deficits were present. This occasioned a considerable amount of didactic counseling, the content of which was only grossly described in the article. The targeted pairs of behaviors were exchanged one-by-one over the 24 weeks of therapy with those involving skill deficits being introduced for exchange only after appropriate didactic procedures promised greater readiness. Spouse observations and self-report instruments were, once again, singularly positive following the introduction of behavioral exchange. However, changes were variable, and targeted behaviors without initial deficit tended to show greater increases than targeted behaviors with initial deficits, which casts some doubt on the efficacy of the didactic counseling procedures.

In spite of the reports of success at follow-up in these two reports (Hickok & Komechak, 1974; Wieman, Shoulders, & Farr, 1974), lasting behavioral change might be more effectively achieved in general through direct training in negotiation and contracting skills, which the couple can carry with them far beyond the termination of therapy. For the moment, however, let us turn our attention to a very different research and endeavor prior to a consideration of more elaborate and comprehensive contractual methods.

Apparatus-Oriented Experimental Analog Research

This approach to MBT makes no claim of comprehensiveness but focuses on very specific problems of communication, both verbal and nonverbal, and employs apparatus not generally available to most practitioners. This research is characteristically exploratory, technological, and suggestive of clinical application. The implication is that these mechanical systems may be employed in MBT as adjunctive procedures for the assessment and modification of dysfunctional patterns of communication.

Eisler, Hersen, and Agras (1973a) reported the use of videotaped observation of interpersonal interactions for the assessment of nonverbal interpersonal behavior. Most previous work had concerned itself with videotaping as a psychotherapeutic tool of "self-confrontation." In a similar vein, Lazarus (1968) suggested the value of co-therapeutic modeling, a procedure in which the cotherapists spend time learning the point-of-view of an individual spouse in order to confront the clients with a role-played interaction highlighting the essential inanity of their typical interaction. This is virtually equivalent to videotaped replay without the convenience of the camera. Eisler and his associates, on the other hand, initially sought only to reliably rate nonverbal interpersonal behaviors—especially eye contact and smiling—due to the reported and intuitive significance of these behaviors in interpersonal warmth and approval (Mehrabian, 1969). The videotape method of assessment showed very high inter-rater agreement for these categories of behavior. This pilot study, however, involved only six couples, none of whom were receiving or seeking any sort of treatment for marital problems and in which the husband was a hospitalized psychiatric patient. Obviously, there is ample reason to doubt the external validity of the method to non-psychiatric couples seeking marriage counseling, and thus, the analog nature of this work.

A second study by these investigators (Eisler, Hersen, & Agras, 1973b) with a similar population of couples and identical nonverbal dependent variables attempted to modify the nonverbal behavior of the couples through intervention procedures involving a factorial combination of videotape feedback of the immediately preceding session and novel instructions focusing upon the particular nonverbal behavior to be modified, thus yielding four experimental groups ($N = 3$ couples per treatment): videotaped feedback alone, focused instructions alone, feedback and instructions combined, and a no-treatment control (watching irrelevant television). Although the procedures lend themselves to criticism on methodological grounds (e.g., discussion topics for the videotaped interactions were client-selected and, therefore, varied across baseline and treatment sessions) and the statistical analysis failed to test for significance due to the small N, the conclusions were suggestive: 1) irrelevant television had no effect, 2) videotaped feedback alone produced trivial increases in the target behavior (eye contact), 3) focused instructions alone were just as effective as the combined condition in increasing eye contact, but 4) the combined condition also produced an increase in smiling, even though the instructions did not mention this behavior.

The fact that these couples were not seeking assistance or motivated to change their behavior and that they were exposed to less than an hour of interaction and feedback suggests the possibility of even greater improvement under more optimal clinical conditions. However, similar evaluations of verbal behavior have not been performed by this group of workers.

A series of studies conducted by Carter and Thomas at the University of Michigan complements Eisler, Hersen, and Agras' non-verbal procedures in the *verbal* sphere. Over the past few years a sequence of increasingly sophisticated reports have appeared concerning a device called SAM, Signal System for the Assessment and Modification of Behavior (Thomas, Carter, & Gambrill, 1971; Carter & Thomas, 1973a; 1973b). SAM is a system consisting of client button-boxes for transmitting light signals; client light-boxes for receiving signals; a therapist control-box for regulation of the system's circuits, monitoring of client signals, and transmission of signals from the therapist to either client; and various counters, event recorders, tape recorders, and timers for the collection of data. A wooden blind is used to eliminate visual cues between interacting clients. SAM therefore provides a minute-by-minute record of verbal and signal behavior which may be subjected to functional analysis. Verbal behaviors to be assessed may include problems in decision-making or problem-solving, bizarre psychotic speech, specificity of referential speech, and the relative occurrence of verbal reinforcers, aversive stimuli, and cues. In the assessment of signaling behavior, meaningful patterns of conversational control are disclosed in the asymmetrical usage of lights, which are assigned specific meanings (e.g., red = stop talking; green == you talk) depending upon the target behavior and client-therapist configuration.

Thomas, Carter, and Gambrill (1971) present data for a single case focusing upon two important aspects of marital communication during a problem-solving session: *conversational control* and *specificity of problem description*. Conversational control was assessed using measures of *signal use*, the number of red or green signals activated by a spouse, and *signal control*, signal use which can be shown to influence the partner's verbal behavior. Specific signal control measures employed were *giveover control*, the percentage of green signals inducing a partner to start talking, and *takeover control*, the percentage of red signals inducing the partner to stop talking. An asymmetrical pattern of conversational control favoring the husband was modified using corrective feedback and instructions; that is, the asymmetrical pattern was described in detail along with its adverse consequences for the couple's interactions, and specific instructions for changing the pattern of control were advanced by the therapist. Parity was increased significantly for all measures defined above. Specificity of problem description was similarly rated by two coders scoring transcripts of sessions and revealed very low baseline levels of denotativeness in problem descriptions. Before the next session, the couple was instructed to be specific, concrete, and oriented toward problem description. In the subsequent interaction, the therapist signaled with the green light for specific talk and provided no signal for non-specific references, thus reinforcing the former. Rated specificity showed a marked increase from 18 percent to 60 percent in a single 24-minute session.

Carter and Thomas (1973a) extended the method to nine couples but only report data for two. With procedures very similar to those reported above, interventions to modify interrogative and opinionated behavioral asymmetries in one couple and nonspecificity in another were explored. In each case, couples were referred through social workers employed by the host agency on the basis of real communication problems discovered in the course of family and marital therapy. An inductive stance was adopted in the selection of target behaviors producing a case-specific precision that is largely lacking in other current approaches to marital discord. A by-product of this individualization process was a 27-category set of explicit verbal problems typically encountered in MBT. This useful tool was subsequently formalized and published as a separate instrument by Thomas, Walter, and O'Flaherty (1974).

Carter and Thomas (1973b) have since reported the first nonexperimental application of SAM with a single case. The apparatus was easily introduced to the couple, readily accepted by them, and viewed as an integral component of therapy by the clients. The authors contend that SAM may prove useful not only as a specialized apparatus for direct intervention but as an adjunctive procedure to yield diagnostic information about problems that lend themselves best to modification by other means. For example, they found that by virtue of SAM-intervention to enhance specificity in the discussion of sexual problems this couple was enabled to produce more relevant information concerning the responses and controlling conditions involved in their sexual problems. This information then facilitated progress in concurrent psychotherapy.

Non-Factorial Single-Group Studies

Early outcome studies. Some of the earliest studies of MBT differ from later studies in that, though they prescribe a particular approach to the treatment of marital discord, their procedures are not modular; that is, they focus on the use of one main technique or several relatively independent techniques rather than employing an interdependent series of treatment units, or modules.

Goldstein and Francis (1969) and Goldstein (1971) completed two non-modular studies employing a total of 15 volunteer couples, but involving therapeutic contact with the wives only. This one-sided intervention is usually considered inadvisable on a routine basis, and most marital behavior therapists do not prefer to make themselves the agent of a single member of the dyad. In fact, Goldstein's favorable outcomes and their maintenance at follow-up are somewhat surprising in view of this unidirectional intervention. Although this approach is somewhat atypical of MBT in general, it seems to have received considerable attention because he did, nevertheless, find that by training wives to identify and selectively reinforce desirable husband behaviors and ignore undesirable behaviors, a significant change in response rate for desirable behaviors occurred in eight of 10 cases (overall $p < .001$). Satisfactory change had been maintained at 3-7 month follow-up for six of the seven successful couples contacted. However, there is little evidence provided to support the assertion that the overall quality of the marital relationship had improved, since there was no assessment of the wives' behavior, which may very well have remained highly aversive to the spouse in spite of the training the wives received in responding to the husband's behavior in very specific situations. The next studies give the reader more confidence that the dyad had been properly treated.

Richard Stuart's delineation of a conceptual framework for an operant-interpersonal treatment of marital discord was the first data-based indication that behavior modification could be a productive endeavor within a dyadic conceptualization. Though initially reported in rather simplified form as a portion of the proceedings of an annual convention (Stuart, 1969a), a fuller account has since appeared (Stuart, 1969b). What emerged from this paper was the first sophisticated behavioral analysis of discordant interaction based upon the conceptual model developed by Patterson and Reid (1970), a stepwise outline for a unitary treatment procedure, and group data for four couples without unnecessary anecdotal commentary.

Stuart's assumptions are: 1) that an exact pattern of interaction between spouses at any point in time is never accidental, but is representative of the best balance that can be achieved between individual and mutual rewards and costs; 2) that a "quid pro quo" arrangement (viz.

Lederer & Jackson, 1968), or reciprocity, underlies successful marriage; and 3) that it is essential to train each spouse to mediate rewards for the other. The goals of treatment encompass this trio of assumptions by endeavoring to train spouses in the fine art of negotiation and contingency contracting as encountered above (Rappaport & Harrell, 1972; Hickok & Komechak, 1974; Wieman, Shoulders & Farr, 1974).

For cases in which continuous and persistent patterns of coercion and withdrawal are likely to make reciprocity difficult to achieve, it is necessary to more precisely intervene in the exchange procedure by arranging for immediate forms of continuous token reinforcement. Stuart (1969a, b) presents data for four couples seeking treatment as a last ditch effort prior to divorce in each of which the wife complained that her husband neglected her conversational needs while the husband complained that his sexual advances were singularly refused. Tokens were dispensed by the wife contingent upon criterion levels of conversation and were redeemable at the husband's request for various sexual favors. The average daily hours of conversation and weekly rate of sexual behavior were vastly increased over a ten-week treatment period and maintained themselves without decrement at a 3-9 month follow-up. Though conversational and sexual complaints are common in marital therapy, Stuart's paper is obviously reporting the application of the behavioral (operant-interpersonal) approach to a very specific dyadic dysfunction. Other studies have applied essentially the same approach (minus tokens) to a more diverse spectrum of marital conflicts.

Modular package studies. Frequent reference has been made to the work of the Oregon group of researchers, with particular emphasis upon the level of sophistication and control inherent in their work. Several investigators have provided theoretical and methodological precedents for this modular package. First, the extensive family studies conducted at the National Institute of Mental Health (e.g., Olson & Ryder, 1970; Ryder, 1970) in conjunction with the family observation studies of Patterson and Reid (1970) provided fuel for the development of the MICS. Second, these workers described their dependence upon the "quid pro quo" procedures so well delineated by Lederer and Jackson (1968)—so well delineated, in fact, that clients are assigned readings in this excellent book for laymen. Thirdly, the contingency contracting methods suggested by the successful studies of Stuart (1969a, b) are the most essential part of the package. Short of being absolutely innovative, therefore, the Oregon package is the current culmination of dyadic behavioral approaches. The modus operandi is the module, a standardized training component of the total package having a limited, specific purpose and contributing to the other modules that follow it sequentially.

The six treatment modules comprising the Oregon package are designed to accomplish the retraining of the couple's interactional repertoire in the areas of affectional exchanges, problem-solving, and behavior change attempts. The modules (more fully presented in Weiss, Hops, & Patterson, 1973) are: 1) Presenting Problem, 2) P and D Spouse Observation, 3) Pinpointing and Discrimination Training, 4) Communication, 5) Behavioral Utilities, and 6) Negotiation Training and Contracting. For example, the Behavioral Utilities module involves being able to specify the utility, or value, of pinpointed behaviors prepared for exchange in the previous modules. Clients specify the consequences they wish to employ in later contract negotiation according to the values (positive or negative), the source of the consequence (husband, wife, environment, or therapist), and its recipient in such a way that reward and penalty equity is assured.

Weiss, Hops, and Patterson (1973) have also made an important distinction between "If you do X, I'll do Y" contracts and contracts of the form "X and Y; if X then W+, if Y then H+.X and Y represent the target behaviors stated in accelerated format for husband and wife, respectively, while H+ and W+ represent contingent rewards to husband and wife. The latter type of contract establishes *independent control* for X and Y so that a failure of the wife to perform X does not sabotage the entire contractual exchange, nor does the failure of the husband to perform Y keep the wife from completing her half of the contract and being rewarded. In the less-preferred "If X, then Y" contract, the mutual dependency of reward fosters a "you go first" attitude that can virtually program most distressed couples for failure from which they may not recover.

However, even in the preferred form of contract, if a reward system alone is ineffective in changing behavior, it is advisable to build in the penalties generated in the Behavioral Utilities module as well. These penalties should originate from the environment or therapist, since otherwise, they would result in the undesirable condition of the spouses mediating aversiveness for one another in an effort to change their behavior in such a way that they mediate less aversiveness for one another. The latter principle of contracting is known as the avoidance of *cross-linking consequences*. An excellent discussion of the principles of negotiation and behavioral contracting may be found in a recent paper by Weiss, Birchler, and Vincent (1974).

Therefore, the final product of training in all of these modules is a reciprocal, independently-controlled, mutual exchange of the complaint behaviors that led to therapy in the first place—recast in pinpointed, utilitarian terms.

Weiss, Hops, and Patterson (1973) summarized the results of two as yet unpublished studies completed as a part of the ongoing evaluation of the package (Hops, Patterson, & Weiss, 1973; Weiss, Patterson, & Hops, 1973). The first study involved five young couples (ages: 21-33; married: 1.5-8 years). MICS data obtained during baseline problem-solving sessions were compared to post-intervention sessions. Increases approaching significance ($p < .10$) were found in MICS categories reflecting compromise statements and simple verbal activity, while decreasing trends were found in three categories presumed to be counterproductive: talking about problems, disagreeing with each other's statements, and using demeaning "put-down" statements. Similarly, while there was a significant decrease in mean rates of Pleasures reported over the two weeks of baseline, there was a significant increase in mean Pleasures for the post-intervention period ($p < .01$).

The second study allowed a more complete report of the changes in the dependent variables because of less missing data than in the previous study. Also, the five couples involved in this second study were somewhat older and had been married longer than the couples in the first study. Rather than analyzing the MICS by individual category, the 30 categories were reduced to six combined codes. Repeated measures analysis of variance revealed highly significant change in the favorable direction for all six combined codes: Problem Solving increased ($p < .001$), Problem Description decreased (p < .001), Negative Verbal and Negative Nonverbal Behaviors decreased ($p < .05$ and $p < .005$, respectively), and Positive Verbal and Positive Nonverbal Behaviors increased ($p < .005$ and $p < .025$, respectively). The self-report and self-observation measures were consistent with the above results. The Locke-Wallace and Willingness-to-Change measures showed favorable changes ($p < .01$ and $p < .05$, respectively); there was an increase in percentage of time spent with spouse on MAI for seven of 10 spouses though the overall change was not significant; and Pleasures increased ($p < .01$), while Displeasures decreased ($p < .02$).

These data help to strengthen the hypothesis that the MBT package is effective in producing the kinds of change deemed most appropriate by the reciprocity model: more problem-solving, more positive verbal and nonverbal behavior, greater reported Pleasures, more time spent with spouse, and consequently, greater global satisfaction. However, due to the small N and the absence of necessary control procedures, only correlational conclusions can be drawn; no cause-effect relationship has been established. That is, while it has been shown that positive changes in marital behavior occurred along with participation in the MBT program, it was not demonstrated unequivocally that the MBT program caused these changes, since the possible influence of such variables as time, extra-therapy life-experiences, problem-solving set, and such non-specific factors as suggestion, expectation of help and attention were not controlled for.

At this point a marriage counselor reading this paper may have been impressed with the amount of data generated by treating such a small number of cases and the elegance and specificity of the modular approach, but, nevertheless, may be wondering how he is supposed to translate the MICS into a viable assessment device when he has no videotape equipment, not to mention research assistants for coding (even if he had time to train them); when he does not have the staff to conduct home observation visits; and when he rarely has clients cooperative enough to spend their time and money completing assessment instruments or daily reports or P's and D's.

Fortunately, a similar approach which may be more realistic for the average marriage counselor has been developed independently by Azrin, Naster, and Jones (1973). Though a precise week-by-week sequence of therapeutic activities is carefully outlined by these authors, it would require too much space to reproduce this outline here. Let it suffice to say that the treatment modules are parallel to those of the Oregon package: negotiating and contracting skills remain central. However, there are several important differences which make the Azrin package far more immediately practical. This approach does not employ technical terms (such as "reinforcement" and "extinction") in instructing clients. Rather, more common terms such as "happiness," "frustration," and "appreciation" are used. This has the immediate advantage of making the approach more broadly applicable with less sophisticated couples. While oriented toward specific behaviors and pinpointing skills, the approach is rather traditional in its dependence upon the marital partners' "happiness" ratings as the dependent variable in marital therapy, thus reducing the somewhat cumbersome assessment requirements of the research-oriented, data-based Oregon package to manageable proportions. Although the approach retains the behavioral demand for quantification of outcome, the need for clients to keep extensive records is minimized. The package does contain one drawback, the use of the "If X, then Y" format as opposed to the "X and Y; if X then W+, if Y then H+" format in contracting.

One decided methodological improvement has been introduced by Azrin—a single-group design which includes an own-control placebo counseling procedure against which to compare the reciprocity counseling. This placebo procedure, labeled "catharsis counseling," encouraged the clients to communicate their feelings to each other and the therapist in discussing various problem areas in marriage. For the six one-hour "catharsis" sessions, the therapist was non-directive, supportive, and interrupted only to discourage physical aggression. Couples were given no differential expectations concerning the efficacy of the catharsis and reciprocity procedures, indeed, they were never led to believe that they were in any way distinct. Scores of 12 couples on a self-report "Marital Happiness Scale" constructed for the study were significantly higher on the average during reciprocity counseling than during the catharsis procedure ($p < .005$), and significantly greater at one-month follow-up than during catharsis or reciprocity counseling ($p < .005$). Scores for individual clients showed that 96 percent of the clients reported a higher level of happiness during the last week of reciprocity counseling than on the day before reciprocity counseling. Also, for each of the nine specific marital problems reported in the scale, happiness increased during reciprocity counseling, with the largest gains for communication and sexual categories.

By using a placebo-control condition, Azrin et al. (1973) have produced a higher level of product than previous studies, which strengthens the hypothesis of a cause-effect relationship involving an MBT package. However, the conclusions which can be drawn are still limited to some degree by the fact that such variables as repeated treatments, repeated testing, therapist characteristics, and extended treatment time period, and time alone may have had some effect on the obtained positive results. Moreover, it is possible that marital happiness may have been significantly *decreased* by the catharsis counseling procedure, as suggested by the statement of the authors that "The only point at which the therapist interrupted communication was when the clients were becoming physically angry with each other." The result of such an effect would be to inflate the significance of the increase in happiness during the reciprocity counseling procedure. To control for the possible confounding effects noted above, a matched no-treatment control group and independent placebo group would be needed.

FUTURE DIRECTIONS

In reviewing the field of marital therapy, Gurman (1973) concluded that although marital therapy has been with us for a long time, the empirical investigation of this area of clinical service is still open for the development of even more potent change methods. At the time of Gurman's review (October, 1972), some of the MBT studies reviewed in the present paper were not available. Therefore, Gurman was forced to assess the effectiveness of behavioral approaches based upon three early studies (Goldstein, 1971; Goldstein & Francis, 1969; Stuart, 1969a). He detected the following improvement rates: group, 71 percent; conjoint, 68 percent; and behavioral, 93 percent. This apparent superiority of behavioral approaches, he contended, must be tempered due to the small number of actual cases involved ($N = 19$). Since then, data from the Patterson and Azrin groups have more than doubled this number. These would seem to go at least some of the way toward "untempering" Gurman's viewpoint regarding effectiveness.

Given that the single-group design with an own-control placebo treatment has been the highest level-of-product research to date, however, we must still be cautious in our conclusions about MBT at the present time; designs which include matched no treatment groups and placebo control groups are still needed before a definite cause-effect relationship can be concluded. Weiss, Hops, and Patterson (1973) asserted that they were currently completing "waiting-list control" designs similar to that of Azrin (1973) and that, given some moderate degree of success in these, the next step would be to develop treatments for more severely distressed populations. While this would surely help to improve confidence in their results, the aforementioned controls would still be needed before definite conclusions about the effectiveness of their package would be possible.

Turner's (1972) work is another as yet uncompleted venture which promises to advance the current level-of-product. He purportedly intends a factorial treatment of several substantive issues in MBT, including the relative advantages of: 1) having one or both spouses in therapy, 2) a married therapist team versus a single therapist, and 3) positive versus negative behavioral contingencies. He apparently plans to use $N = 10$ couples (subjects) per cell in this 2×2×2 design, thus yielding a total of 80 new cases, more by far than have been reported in the total MBT literature to date. This is indeed an extensive undertaking and could go a long way toward advancing the field when finally finished. All of the above would appear to argue well for a continuing advance of the current momentum in the field of marital behavior therapy.

CONCLUDING COMMENT

It is hoped that the present review will have served to give those having non-behavioral orientations a comprehensive perspective of current work in MBT. An unstated theme running through this review has been the potential for cross-fertilization of theory, research, and practice in family therapy and behavior therapy, especially as they intersect with a treatment population of increasingly mutual interest—married couples in distress.

REFERENCES

AZRIN, N. H., NASTER, B. J., & JONES, R. Reciprocity counseling: A rapid learning-based procedure for marital counseling. *Behav. Res. & Ther.*, 1973, 11, 365-382.

BANDURA, A. *Principles of Behavior Modification.* New York: Holt, Rinehart, & Winston, 1969.

BATESON, G. D., JACKSON, D. D., HALEY, J., & WEAKLAND, J. Toward a theory of schizophrenia. *Behav. Sci.*, 1956, 1, 251-264.

BIRCHLER, G. R. Differential patterns of instrumental affiliative behavior as a function of degree of marital distress and level of intimacy. Unpublished doctoral dissertation, University of Oregon, 1972.

CARTER, R. D. & THOMAS, E. J. Modification of problematic marital communication using corrective feedback and instruction. *Behav. Ther.*, 1973, 4, 100-109. (a)

CARTER, R. D. & THOMAS, E. J. A case application of asignaling system (SAM) for the assessment and modification of selected problems of marital communication. *Behav. Ther.*, 1973, 4, 629-645. (b)

EISLER, R. M., HERSEN, M., & AGRAS, W. S. Videotape: A method for the controlled observation of nonverbal inter-personal behavior. *Behav. Ther.*, 1973, 4, 420-425. (a)

EISLER, R. M., HERSEN, M., & AGRAS, W. S. Effects of videotape and instructional feedback on nonverbal marital interaction: An analog study. *Behav. Ther.*, 1973, 4, 551-558. (b)

FERBER, M., MENDELSOHN, M., & NAPIER, A. *The Book of Family Therapy.* Boston: Houghton Mifflin, 1973.

GOLDSTEIN, M. K. Behavior rate change in marriages: Training wives to modify husbands' behavior. *Diss. Abs. Int.*, 1971, 32 (1-B), 559.

GOLDSTEIN, M. K. & FRANCIS, B. Behavior modification of husbands by wives. Paper presented at the National Council on Family Relations, Washington, D. C., 1969.

GURMAN, A. S. The effects and effectiveness of marital therapy: A review of outcome research. *Family Process*, 1973, 12, 145-170.

HICKOK, J. E. & BOMECHAK, M. G. Behavior modification in marital conflict: A case report. *Family Process*, 1974, 13, 111-119.

HOPS, H., PATTERSON, G. R., & WEISS, R. L. A social learning approach to reducing marital conflict. Unpublished manuscript, University of Oregon, 1973.

HOPS, H., WILLS, T. A., PATTERSON, G. R., & WEISS, R. L. The marital interaction coding system (MICS). Unpublished manuscript, University of Oregon, 1972.

KNOX, D. *Marriage Happiness.* Champaign: Research Press, 1971.

KNOX, D. *Dr. Knox's Marital Exercise Book.* New York: McKay, 1975.

KRASNER, L. Behavior modification—values and training: The perspective of a psychologist. In C. M. Franks (Ed.), *Behavior Therapy: Appraisal and Status.* New York: McGraw-Hill, 1969, pp. 537-566.

LAING, R. D. & ESTERSON, A. *Sanity, Madness and the Family.* New York: Basic Books, 1964.

LAZARUS, A. A. Behavior therapy and marriage counseling. *J. Amer. Soc. Psychosom. Dent. Med.,* 1968, 15, 49-56.

LEDERER, W. & JACKSON, D. D. *The Mirage of Marriage.* New York: W. W. Norton, 1968.

LIBERMAN, R. Behavioral approaches to family and couples therapy. *Amer. J. Orthopsychiat.,* 1970, 40, 106-118.

LOCKE, H. J. & WALLACE, K. M. Short marital adjustment and prediction tests: Their reliability and validity. *Marr. Fam. Liv.,* 1959, 21, 251-255.

LoPICCOLO, J. & LOBITZ, W. C. Behavior therapy of sexual dysfunction. In L. A. Hamerlynck, L. C. Handy and E. J. Mash (Eds.), *Behavior Change: Methodology, Concepts and Practice.* Champaign, Ill.: Research Press, 1973, 343-358.

MALEY, R. F. A book review. *Behav. Ther.,* 1973, 4, 725-727.

MASTERS, W. H. & JOHNSON, V. E. *Human Sexual Inadequacy.* Boston: Little, Brown, 1970.

MEHRABIAN, A. The significance of posture and position in the communication of attitude and status relationships. *Psychol. Bull.,* 1969, 71, 359-372.

MURPHY, D. C. & MENDELSON, L. A. Use of the observational method in the study of live marital communication. *J. Marr. Fam.,* 1973, 35, 256-263.

OLSON, D. & RYDER, R. G. Inventory of marital conflicts (IMC): An experimental interaction procedure. *J. Marr. Fam.,* 1970, 32, 443-448.

OLSON, D. & STRAUS, M. A. A diagnostic tool for marital and family therapy: The SIMFAM technique. *Family Coordinator,* 1972, 21, 251-258.

PATTERSON, G. R. Behavior techniques based upon social learning: An additional base for developing behavior modification techniques. In C. M. Franks (Ed.), *Behavior Therapy: Appraisal and Status.* New York: McGraw-Hill, 1969, 341-374.

PATTERSON, G. R. & HOPS, H. Coercion, a game for two: Intervention techniques for marital conflict. In R. C. Ulrich and P. Mountjoy (Eds.), *The Experimental Analysis of Social Behavior.* New York: Appleton-Century-Crofts, 1972, pp. 424-440.

PATTERSON, G. R., HOPS, H., & WEISS, R. L. A social learning approach to reducing rates of marital conflict. In R. Stuart, R. Lieberman, and S. Wilder (Eds.), *Advances in Behavior Therapy.* New York: Academic Press, 1973.

PATTERSON, G. R. & REID, J. B. Reciprocity and coercion: Two facets of social systems. In C. Neuringer and J. L. Michael (Eds.), *Behavior Modification in Clinical Psychology.* New York: Appleton-Century-Crofts, 1970, 133-176.

RAPPAPORT, A. F. & HARRELL, J. A behavioral-exchange model for marital counseling. *Family Coordinator,* 1972, 21, 203-212.

RYDER, R. G. A topography of early marriage. *Family Process,* 1970, 9, 385-402.

STODTBECK, F. Husband-wife interaction over revealed differences. *Amer. Sociol. Rev.,* 1951, 16, 468-473.

STUART, R. Token reinforcement in marital treatment. In R. Rubin and C. M. Franks (Eds.), *Advances in Behavior Therapy.* New York: Academic Press, 1969, pp. 221-230. (a)

STUART, R. Operant-interpersonal treatment for marital discord. *J. Cons. Clin. Psychol.,* 1969, 33, 675-682. (b)

THARP, R. G. & OTIS, G. D. Toward a theory for therapeutic intervention in families. *J. Cons. Psychol.,* 1966, 30, 426-434.

THARP, R. G. & WETZEL, R. J. *Behavior Modification in the Natural Environment.* New York: Academic Press, 1969.

THOMAS, E. J., CARTER, R. D., & GAMBRILL, E. D. Some possibilities of behavioral modification of marital problems using SAM. In R. Rubin, A. Fensterheim, A.

Lazarus, and C. Franks (Eds.), *Advances in Behavior Therapy*. New York: Academic Press, 1971, pp. 273-287.

THOMAS, E. J., WALTER, C. L., & O'FLAHERTY, K. A verbal problem check-list for use in assessing family verbal behavior. *Behav. Ther.*, 1974, 5, 235-246.

TURNER, J. Couple and group treatment of marital discord. Paper presented at the Sixth Annual Meeting of the Association for the Advancement of Behavior Therapy, New York, October, 1972.

VINCENT, J. P. The relationship of sex, degree of intimacy, and degree of marital distress to problem solving behavior and exchange of social reinforcement. Unpublished doctoral dissertation, University of Oregon, 1972.

WEISS, R. L., BIRCHLER, G. R., & VINCENT, J. P. Contractual models for negotiation training in marital dyads. *J. Marr. Fam.*, 1974, 36, 321-330.

WEISS, R. L., HOPS, H., & PATTERSON, G. R. A framework of conceptualizing marital conflict: A technology for altering it, some data for evaluating it. In L. A. Hamerlynck, L. C. Handy, and E. J. Mash (Eds.), *Behavior Change: Methodology, Concepts and Practice*. Champaign: Research Press, 1973, pp. 309-342.

WEISS, R. L., PATTERSON, G. R., & HOPS, H. Toward the development of a modular-social learning approach to marital discord: Clinical assessment and intervention data. Unpublished manuscript, University of Oregon, 1973.

WIEMANN, R. J., SHOULDERS, D. I., & FARR, J. H. Reciprocal reinforcement in marital therapy. *J. Behav. Ther. Exp. Psychiat.*, 1974, 5, 291-295.

WILLS, T. A., WEISS, R. L., & PATTERSON, G. R. A behavioral analysis of the determinants of marital satisfaction. *J. Cons. Clin. Psychol.*, 1974, 42, 802-811.

36

SECONDARY ORGASMIC DYSFUNC-
TION. II. CASE STUDY

Arden Snyder,

Private Practice, Eugene, Oregon

Leslie LoPiccolo and

Joseph LoPiccolo

*Department of Psychiatry and Behavioral Science,
State University of New York at Stony Brook*

The treatment of a case of secondary orgasmic dysfunction is described. In this case, a direct behavioral retraining program was employed to increase the couple's repertoire of effective sexual behaviors. An extinction and successive approximation procedure was used to transfer orgasmic responsiveness from solitary masturbation to heterosexual coitus. Since other data have indicated that nonsexual marriage problems contribute to the maintenance of secondary orgasmic dysfunction, a direct, confrontive intervention into the marital relationship was made concurrent with the sexual retraining program. Outcome data are presented to illustrate the effectiveness of the treatment procedures.

Reprinted with permission from *Archives of Sexual Behavior*, Vol. 4, No. 3, 1975, 277-283.

INTRODUCTION

McGovern et al. (1975) indicate that cases of secondary orgasmic dysfunction tend to be associated with a disturbed marital relationship and narrow stimulus control over the occurrence of orgasm. These data also indicate that the usual sexual retraining program leads to marked increase in self-report measures of sexual satisfaction, compatibility, and happiness, but not to increases in the rate of orgasm in intercourse. Because of this failure to accomplish the most direct goal of therapy, and following their data analysis, McGovern, Stewart, and LoPiccolo recommended two changes in the training program. In the past, the sexual therapy program involved focusing exclusively on sexual problems and avoiding intervention into nonsexual marital problems as much as possible. Thus the therapists would notice but not respond to nonsexual marital pathology except as was absolutely necessary to keep the clients following the sexual training program. Since it now appears that this procedure does not work with cases of secondary orgasmic dysfunction, a directive approach to marriage counseling was employed. The second focus of therapy in this case was to attempt to break the rigid and narrow stimulus control of orgasm which characterized the female client, as is typical in cases of secondary orgasmic dysfunction.

CASE HISTORY

The clients were a young couple in the early 20s, married for 6 months when first seen by the therapists. At intake, Mrs. A. was able to reach orgasm while masturbating, but not during genital manipulation by her husband or in coitus. She masturbated digitally, in a rigidly constrained manner. Orgasm could be attained only during masturbation while standing, and the client had masturbated in this manner since early adolescence.

Mrs. A. had initially enjoyed intercourse with her husband, which they began 6 months prior to marriage. However, due to her subsequent inability to reach coital orgasm she gradually came to find all sexual activity aversive. The frequency of intercourse had dropped from three or four times a week prior to marriage to approximately two times a month on entering treatment.

Mrs. A.'s sexual history indicated no unusual or traumatic experiences in childhood. Her parents did make it clear they were against premarital intercourse, and Mrs. A. did not engage in intercourse until she was in college and met Mr. A.

Mr. A.'s sexual history was relatively unremarkable. His previous sexual experiences included masturbation and petting; however, he did not engage in intercourse until meeting Mrs. A.

The couple began engaging in intercourse a few months after they met. Their first attempts were unpleasant experiences, due to the fear of parental discovery and pregnancy.

After several months of intercourse and concurrent with beginning oral contraceptives, Mrs. A. experienced a lessening in sexual responsiveness and mild depression. On advice of her gynecologist, the oral contraceptives were discontinued but her previous sexual responsiveness did not return.

At intake Mrs. A. reported that she thought she had been orgasmic on 40-50 percent of coital occasions prior to marriage, but had not experienced coital orgasm during the last several months. As treatment progressed, however, it became clear to the therapists that while Mrs. A. had been highly aroused, it was unlikely that she had ever experienced coital orgasm. She was unable to describe any of the physiological correlates of orgasm during coitus, although she was able to clearly describe these phenomena as occurring when she masturbated. As previously reported, this tendency to misperceive the orgasmic response is common in women with orgasmic difficulties (McGovern et al., 1975).

COURSE OF TREATMENT

The clients were seen together for 17 sessions over a 15-week period by a male-female cotherapy team (A.S. and L.L.). During history taking, it became clear to the therapists that, in addition to the couple's sexual dysfunction, there was also a good deal of marital disharmony. While this is consistent with the findings of McGovern et al. (1975), it was quite surprising in this case as both Mr. and Mrs. A's pretreatment scores on the Locke-Wallace Marital Adjustment Test (1959) were well into the range considered to indicate satisfactory marital adjustment. On the basis of the clinical material, however, the therapists decided to focus treatment on three issues: 1) training in sexual technique, 2) breaking the narrow stimulus control of orgasm, and 3) dealing with the marital problems. Despite the fact that these were carried out more or less concurrently, they will be presented separately in the interest of clarity.

Sexual Technique Training

Treatment emphasized reduction of performance anxiety, increase in verbal feedback, and acquisition of more effective sexual techniques. Since the approach is well described elsewhere (Masters & Johnson, 1970; Lo-Piccolo & Lobitz, 1974), it will not be elaborated on here. Briefly, the clients were initially forbidden to engage in sexual intercourse. They were then given "homework" assignments each week. During the first week, only hugging, kissing, and body massage were permitted. This assignment allowed the couple to focus on sensual pleasure without anticipating, with anxiety, sexual intercourse. In subsequent weeks, the couple gradually moved toward intercourse by successively adding behaviors such as breast touching and genital stimulation by manual, oral, and electric vibrator means. Intercourse was introduced in a series of successive approximations starting with partial penile insertion with no movement, penile insertion with female movement, and finally full insertion with mutual pelvic thrusting and ejaculation. To eliminate performance anxiety, these behaviors were introduced only when both partners felt comfortable with the next step.

Breaking Stimulus Control of Orgasm

Annon (1971) has suggested that women who have narrow stimulus control over orgasm in their masturbation can learn new means of reaching orgasm by gradually switching from their restricted method to positions and techniques of masturbation which approximate coitus. Rather than follow this gradual stimulus generalization procedure in this case, the therapists decided to simply extinguish the stimulus response link between standing masturbation and orgasm. Mrs. A. was forbidden to continue in her pattern of standing while masturbating. The therapists explained that discontinuing her current practice was necessary in order for her to learn to respond to a wider variety of sexual stimulation. She was therefore started on a 9-step program of masturbation designed to result in coital orgasm (LoPiccolo & Lobitz, 1972). This program begins with visual and tactile exploration of the pelvic region, to locate sensitive areas, progresses to manipulation of these areas, and eventually (step 6) involves stimulation of the clitoral region with an electric vibrator. To break the previously established pattern of orgasm only while standing, the client was instructed to engage in each step of this program while lying down. Initially while learning to masturbate in this new way, the client was not aroused, but she did eventually become orgasmic. Once orgasm in masturbation while lying down was well established, the final three steps of the masturbation program were used to transfer orgasmic response to coitus (LoPiccolo & Lobitz, 1972). In subsequent weeks, Mrs. A. masturbated with her husband watching her, masturbated with her husband kissing, caressing, and embracing her, and then guided her husband's manipulation of her genitals. At this point, she began to experience orgasm during her husband's manipulation of her genitals with the vibrator. All that remained at this point was to instruct the clients to continue clitoral stimulation *during* coitus, and shortly Mrs. A. became orgasmic in intercourse.

Teaching a woman to switch, via successive approximation, her masturbation from the clitoris to the vaginal opening as Annon (1971) advocates may be inefficient, given the Kinsey et al. (1953) and the Masters and Johnson (1966) data that clitoral stimulation is the focus of female orgasm. Annon's procedure, involving successive changes in masturbatory focus from the clitoral shaft to the mons area, to the vulva area, and to vaginal stimulation when orgasm is imminent may, furthermore, reinforce a client's erroneous belief in the now generally discredited concept of vaginal orgasm. It may be more effective to simply teach clients to have coital orgasms through maintaining active manual stimulation of the clitoris during intercourse, as was done in this case. Annon's procedure is, however, well thought out and is reported to have produced results with one client (Annon, 1971).

Marital Problems

After emphasizing to the couple the positive aspects of their relationship, the therapists pointed out that Mrs. A.'s dissatisfaction with her career prospects was having a negative influence on their sexual adjustment. The therapists shared their impression that Mrs. A. wanted either to attend graduate school or to secure employment in some field related to her art major, rather than take a menial job to support her husband and remain professionally stagnant for 4 years while he pursued his graduate career. The legitimacy of Mrs. A.'s discouragement over what she felt was expected of her was supported by the therapists openly indicating their belief that women should be permitted the same opportunity to develop their potential as men. Meanwhile, Mr. A.'s attentive listening and expressions of concern for his wife's feelings were mentioned and reinforced with praise. This strategy was aimed at minimizing his defensiveness and maintaining her esteem for him.

The therapists informed Mr. and Mrs. A. that they were convinced that until this issue was resolved the sexual problem would probably not be alleviated. It was suggested that they thoroughly talk out their

TABLE 1
Outcome Data

	Pretreatment	Posttreatment	Follow-up
Frequency of intercourse	1 or 2 times a month	twice a week	twice a week
Duration of foreplay	15-30 min	30-60 min	16-30 min
Duration of intercourse (from entry of penis until male reaches ejaculation)	4-7 min	7-10 min	7-10 min
Percentage of female orgasm through genital stimulation by male	0	100	100
Percentage of female orgasm in coitus with concurrent clitoral stimulation	0	50	100

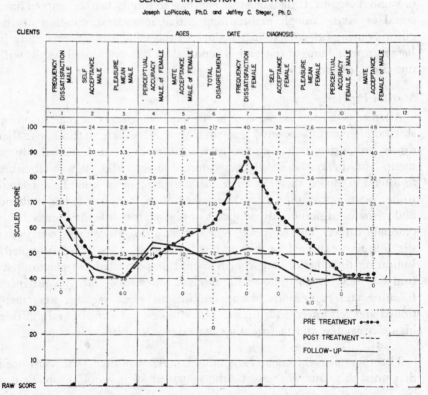

SEXUAL INTERACTION INVENTORY

Joseph LoPiccolo, Ph.D. and Jeffrey C. Steger, Ph.D.

Fig. 1. Sexual Interaction Inventory profile for Mr. and Mrs. A.

thoughts and feelings about the issue and rate their conversations on a 1 to 10 scale along a "constructive-descriptive" continuum. Mrs. A. was also encouraged to write out what she felt she "should do" and what she "wanted to do" in order to insure that her value conflict would be clearly expressed in their discussions.

Several other marital problems emerged at this point: Mrs. A. felt negative about their spending too much time with their parents. She also resented the subtle pressure from Mr. A.'s mother to take a menial job to support Mr. A. She also expressed dissatisfaction with Mr. A.'s constant compliance with his parents' wishes. In response to these issues, the therapists were directive and confrontive and informed the clients that satisfying sexual relations were dependent on redefining their family as the two of them. They were encouraged to ask "What is best for *us*?"

As the couple became more aware of the interrelatedness of their difficulties, it was recommended that they begin to identify the possible courses of action for their future and start constructing a branching tentative plan (Tyler, 1969). In subsequent interviews, the clients were assisted in exploring possibilities, constructing a plan, identifying choice points, and dealing with parental attitudes. As a result of this plan construction, they were able to disengage from their parents, and agree that Mrs. A. would pursue a graduate career in art.

OUTCOME DATA

Assessment data were collected from the couple before and after treatment and at 3 months following termination of therapy. A number of scores from this assessment battery are presented in Table 1. These data indicate that gains were made in all aspects of the sexual relationship. Additionally, at termination Mr. and Mrs. A. reported they were each initiating sexual intercourse about equally often, in marked contrast to their pretherapy pattern of Mr. A.'s usually initiating. In response to the questionnaire item "Overall, how satisfactory to you is your sexual relationship?" both Mr. and Mrs. A. responded "extremely satisfactory" at the close of treatment in comparison to their responses of "slightly unsatisfactory" (Mr. A.) and "moderately unsatisfactory" (Mrs. A.) prior to treatment.

As Figure 1 indicates, Mr. and Mrs. A. made significant gains in their sexual relationship as measured by scores on the Sexual Interaction Inventory (LoPiccolo and Steger, 1974). For those scales that indicated the most pathology at intake (scales, 6, 7, 8), posttreatment scores changed in the desired direction and improved by more than 1 SD.

Scores on the Locke-Wallace Marital Adjustment Test (1959) showed that the overall marital relationship improved following treatment. Mr. A.'s score increased from 132 to 146 and at follow-up was 142. Mrs. A.'s score increased from 120 to 134 and at follow-up was 128.

DISCUSSION

In this case, a directive and confrontive marital therapy plus a direct, simplistic approach to breaking stimulus control of orgasm led to a successful treatment outcome. As reported by McGovern et al. (1975), the usual sex therapy program had previously failed to increase the orgasmic response in coitus of six successive secondary inorgasmic women. Two other couples with secondary orgasmic dysfunction have since been seen by other therapy teams, and in both cases following the procedures outlined in this article has led to regular coital orgasm. While treatment of only three cases clearly does not "prove" the effectiveness of a set of procedures, it is hoped that this report will lead other therapists to experiment with this therapeutic strategy.

REFERENCES

ANNON, J. S. The therapeutic use of masturbation in the treatment of sexual disorders. Paper presented at the Fifth Annual Meeting of the Association for the Advancement of Behavior Therapy, Washington, D.C., September, 1971.

KINSEY, A. C., POMEROY, W. B., MARTIN, C. E., & GEBHARD, P. H. Sexual Behavior in the Human Female. Philadelphia: W. B. Saunders, 1953.

LOCKE, H. J. & WALLACE, K. M. Short marital adjustment and prediction tests: Their reliability and validity. Marriage Family Living, 1959, 21, 251-255.

LoPICCOLO, J. & LOBITZ, W. C. The role of masturbation in the treatment of primary orgasmic dysfunction. Arch. Sex. Behav., 1972, 2, 163-171.

LoPICCOLO, J. & LOBITZ, W. C. Behavior therapy of sexual dysfunction. In L. A. Hamerlynck, L. C. Handy, and E. J. Mash (Eds.), Behavior Change: Methodology, Concepts, and Practice. Champaign, Ill.: Research Press, 1974.

LoPICCOLO, J. & STEGER, J. C. The Sexual Interaction Inventory: A new instrument for assessment of sexual dysfunction. Arch. Sex. Behav., 1974, 3, 585-595.

MASTERS, W. H. & JOHNSON, V. E. Human Sexual Response. Boston: Little, Brown, 1966.

MASTERS, W. H. & JOHNSON, V. E. Human Sexual Inadequacy. Boston: Little, Brown, 1970.

McGOVERN, K. B., STEWART, R., & LoPICCOLO, J. Secondary orgasmic dysfunction. I. Analysis and strategies for treatment. Arch. Sex. Behav., 1975, 4, 265-275.

TYLER, L. The Work of the Counselor. New York: Appleton-Century-Crofts, 1969.

SECTION X: CLINICAL ISSUES, INNOVATIONS
AND CASE STUDIES

37

SELF-DIRECTED IN VIVO TREATMENT OF AN OBSESSIVE COMPULSIVE CHECKING RITUAL

Barbara G. Melamed and Lawrence J. Siegel

Psychology Department, Case Western Reserve University
Cleveland, Ohio

Summary—A multiple treatment program including operant reinforcement, disruption of the chain of ritualistic behaviors, systematic desensitization of related fears, and response prevention was successful in the elimination of ritualistic checking in a 63-year-old man. The program was carried out by the client *in vivo* with minimal assistance from the therapist. The report correlates in the week-by-week changes in checking time with the changes in treatment strategy. The advantage of a multiple treatment approach and the need for consideration of motivational aspects are discussed.

Obsessive-compulsive disorders are generally very difficult to treat, having a high incidence of recurrence (Ingram, 1961; Kringler, 1965). Within the last several years, a number of behavioral techniques have been used in the treatment of compulsive rituals with varying degrees of success. Encouraging results have attended the use of modeling and flooding (Hodgson, Rachman, & Marks 1972; Rainey, 1972; Boulougouris

Reprinted with permission from *Journal of Behavior Therapy and Experimental Psychiatry*, Vol. 6, 31-35, 1975.

& Bassiakos, 1973); response prevention (Meyer, 1966; Levy & Meyer, 1971; Mills, Agras, Barlow, & Mills, 1973); and systematic desensitization (Rackensperger & Feinberg, 1972).

The following is a detailed account of a multiple treatment program for an obsessive-compulsive checking ritual using operant reinforcement, disruption of the chain of ritualistic behaviors, systematic desensitization of related fears and response prevention. Most behavioral treatments of compulsive rituals have veen carried out under the close supervision of trained personnel, often in hospital settings. The present treatment was conducted *in vivo* by the client and his wife.

CASE HISTORY

Mr. R., 63 years old, had developed an extensive checking ritual that he performed each evening before going to bed. Not only was this problem time-consuming and very frustrating, but it also created much conflict between him and his wife. In fact, it was his wife who initiated contact with the behavior therapist.

The compulsive checking began approximately 9 months before the initial assessment interview. This behavior first occurred in reaction to a minor malfunction in the gas line. Despite reassurance from a repairman that the automatic shut-off valve would prevent any accidents, Mr. R.'s concern about a possible fire or explosion led him to engage in a ritualistic trip to the basement to check that the pilot light in the furnace was still on before he could go to sleep. In the course of the next few weeks the checking behavior generalized to the entire house. He was spending more than 3 hours each evening checking such things as electrical appliances to make sure that they were turned off, wall sockets and wires to see if they were touching anything, windows and doors to make sure that they were locked, and ash trays to clean them of any cigarette ashes. He was also inspecting all cupboards in the house to make sure that the pots and pans were so placed that they would not fall and make a loud noise that might frighten him. This generalized to any object which might fall off a shelf or table.

Each evening, at approximately the same time, Mrs. R. would go to her bedroom and get ready for bed. Mr. R. would then begin his checking in a very systematic manner, examining each room in the house in the same order every night. Mrs. R. had to be in her bedroom before the checking could begin, because Mr. R. was afraid that she might use something after he had checked it or that she might leave her cigarettes burning in an ashtray that he had already cleaned. This behavior was extremely annoying to Mrs. R., and she refused his repeated requests to assist him in his checking.

Mr. R. was afraid to be home by himself, and was, therefore, very reluctant to let his wife go away and leave him home alone. Furthermore, he constantly checked on her while she worked in the basement on her hobbies to assure himself that nothing had happened to her. This behavior caused Mrs. R. to feel very restricted in her own activities. Mr. R. was also severely limited in his social activities. For example, each Sunday he would drive by himself to visit his sister who lived in another state. It took him more than 3 hours to drive there, but he would return home as soon as possible, often after only 10 minutes visit, because he was concerned that something might happen to his wife while she was alone in the house. These fears and concerns resulted in Mr. R. becoming extremely withdrawn from social contacts. In addition, he became quite nervous which necessitated his taking tranquillizers for about 5 months prior to therapy. The tranquillizers were prescribed by a psychiatrist with whom Mr. R. had had one therapy contact. In addition, the psychiatrist recommended hospitalization and insulin shock treatment which Mr. R. rejected.

It is interesting to note that Mr. R.'s occupation involved detailed checking behavior. He worked at a railroad repair yard and was responsible for checking airbrakes on each of the railroad cars. Therefore, it was important that a treatment program designed to eliminate checking behavior build in a discrimination for settings where such behavior was inappropriate.

In addition to the compulsive checking behavior, Mr. R. had a hernia that was in need of surgical repair. It caused him much pain and discomfort, but he was afraid to have the surgery because he feared that he would not awaken from the anesthetic after the operation. Medical fears and fear of dying were reflected in his response to similar items on the Fear Survey Schedule (Wolpe & Lang, 1964) as causing "much" or "very much" fear or unpleasant feelings. Mr. R. had been scheduled for surgery several months prior to therapy, but because of these fears he cancelled his admission to the hospital so that surgery was never performed.

PROCEDURE AND RESULTS

Week 1—Baseline Period

During the first week the Fear Survey Schedule and the Minnesota Multiphasic Personality Inventory (MMPI) were administered, and the

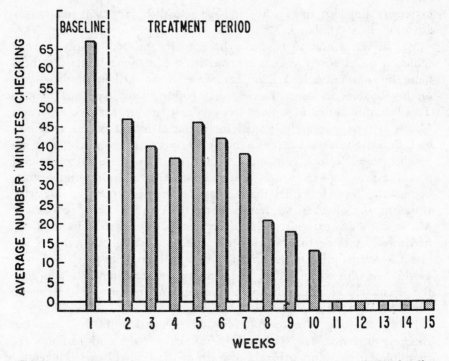

FIG. 1. Average number of minutes spent daily in ritualistic checking during baseline and treatment.

client baseline data were obtained. Mr. R. was given a stop-watch and asked to keep a record of the time he spent checking each room of the house. He was also told to keep a record of the exact time that he began and completed the checking. He was to list things he liked that might serve as effective reinforcers. There were few of these available. Since the onset of the behavior problem he had become so withdrawn socially that he would not even read a newspaper or watch television for fear of seeing something that might upset him. The solitary activity of working crossword puzzles was the only accessible reinforcer.

Figure 1 illustrates week-by-week changes in the total time he spent checking. Baseline data indicated that the client was spending an average of 67 minutes each evening checking various rooms in the house before he went to bed. There is reason to believe that the client's observing and recording his own behavior (during the baseline period) helped decrease the amount of time he regularly spent checking, since both he and his wife had intimated that he usually spent more than 3 hours each evening in checking activities. In addition, Mr. R. had remarked upon receiving the stop-watch during the first session that he was going to try to "beat his time" each evening.

Psychological test results indicated that Mr. R. would be a good candidate for behavior therapy. His Fear Survey Schedule showed two circumscribed clusters of fears: one related to the prospect of a surgical operation and the fear of dying; the other reflecting strong feelings of inadequacy by high anxiety on such items as fear of failure, being watched working, being criticized, making mistakes, and feeling disapproved of. The MMPI profile was within normal limits with peak elevations on depression (t score = 68) and psychasthenia (t score = 64) indicating obsessive-compulsive characteristics.

Week 2

Mr. R. was told to discontinue checking the living room because his baseline record had indicated that he was spending the least amount of time in this room (less than 3 minutes). In addition, he was asked to do his checking in less than 60 minutes. This time was selected because it was several minutes less than his mean baseline checking and it was felt that he could reasonably succeed at this goal. Each evening he completed checking in under 60 minutes, he received a hug and a kiss from his wife and could work on a crossword puzzle. His wife remarked that on the first night he succeeded they resumed sexual relations which had been suspended 10 years previously.

The results indicated that Mr. R. was able to eliminate the living room from his checking. Each evening he was spending an average of 47 minutes checking, which was a substantial decrease from the baseline period.

Although Mr. R. reported significant relief in anxiety following completion of his checking, he still experienced some tension which made it difficult for him to fall asleep. He was, therefore, trained to relax several muscle groups and instructed during week 3 to continue practicing for 15 minutes each evening before going to bed.

Week 3

Mr. R. was also told to discontinue checking the bedroom where he was spending less than 5 minutes each evening. If he was able to spend less than 50 minutes in total checking each evening, he was to reinforce himself with a crossword puzzle and as an added incentive could earn $1 reduction in the clinic fee each day he succeeded in this goal. After he completed his checking, he was to practice muscle relaxation using the remainder of the muscle groups that he had been taught to relax during the weekly session.

There was a further decrease in his checking behavior during the third week. He was spending an average of 40 minutes inspecting the various rooms of the house except the living room and bedroom which he had eliminated. He earned a $5 reduction in the clinic fee.

Week 4-Week 7

For the remaining treatment program, Mr. R. was to continue leaving out the living room and bedroom from his checking. In addition, he was given a list (arranged in random order), of the three rooms he checked, that he was to follow each evening in his room inspection. If the checking ritual can be conceptualized as a chain of behaviors, with each component maintained by the terminal reinforcer of relief from anxiety, then interference with this chain might further decrease the amount of checking behavior. He was also to continue to practice relaxation for 15 minutes after completing the checking.

Requiring Mr. R. to check the rooms in a different order each evening did not produce a decrease in the time he was spending in each room. His average weekly time for this period was 40 minutes. In the fifth week of the program, there was a slight increase in his average checking time, coinciding with Mrs. R.'s going out of town on four consecutive days and returning late each evening. As a result, Mr. R. was anxious about being left alone in the house and was unable to begin his checking until much later in the evening when Mrs. R. returned home.

Week 8-Week 9

Desensitization of Mr. R.'s fears of hospitalization was conducted during the eighth through tenth sessions. During this period, he was asked to eliminate another room from his checking ritual. He decided on the basement since it had the advantage of a door that he could close and thereby remind himself not to go down to check. In addition, he was to practice muscle relaxation 15 minutes before beginning checking, to reduce his apparent anticipatory anxiety. After checking he was to continue muscle relaxation.

There was a substantial decrease in checking behavior during this period. Mr. R. was spending 50 percent less time checking compared with the mean checking time of the previous period. Because he was able to eliminate the basement from his checking ritual, the room in which he had been spending the most time, it was possible to decrease his average checking time to 21 minutes and to 18 minutes for weeks eight and nine respectively. Mr. R. also had spent more than 3 hours visiting his sister and had joined a card game with a group of men he had avoided for years.

Week 10

At a joint session with Mr. R. and his wife, a response prevention program was explained indicating that it had worked successfully with others who had similar problems. Furthermore Mr. R.'s hospitalization for surgery would be important in response prevention since it would be the first time he would be away from the house overnight and unable to check before going to bed. Mr. R. was also told that when he returned home from the hospital he would no longer feel the need to check as no aversive consequences would have occurred. He was encouraged to eliminate checking completely at least one evening during the week. In this his wife was to assist him by escorting him to the bedroom after he had checked the doors of the house. He had to close his bedroom door and remain there for the rest of the night and practice muscle relaxation for at least 15 minutes. In addition, he could call the therapist if he felt the need to check, but was not to leave his bedroom once the door was closed.

Mr. R. was able to begin the response prevention for two evenings before his hospitalization, by going to his bedroom and remaining there until the next morning without any checking. He did not find it necessary to phone the therapist. His average checking time for the tenth week was 13 minutes.

Week 11

Mr. R. was admitted to hospital and operated on for a hernia during the eleventh week, and remained there for 7 days. The day before he was discharged the therapist visited him in the hospital, when he and his wife were reminded of the response prevention program to be continued for at least a week after Mr. R. was returned home. Mrs. R. was to continue to escort her husband to his bedroom each evening where he was to remain until the next morning. It is interesting to note that, while in hospital, Mr. R. did not experience or express concern about not being able to check.

Weeks 12-15

Response prevention remained in effect during the twelfth week when he returned home from the hospital. Mr. R. was contacted by phone once a week to obtain reports on the frequency of his checking behavior. A final session was held during the fifteenth week with both Mr. R. and his wife. Mr. R. reported that he no longer had the urge to check and was able to discontinue taking tranquilizers indicating that he no longer experienced the extreme anxiety that in the past had necessitated relief through checking.

Follow-Up

At a 1-month follow-up, Mr. R. was still free of symptomatic behavior, feeling much more relaxed than in the last year, his social contacts having increased significantly. In addition, he had not used tranquilizers since the treatment program had terminated. Mrs. R. was now able to leave the house without his being concerned about being left home alone. He was no longer checking on her while she worked in the basement, and Mrs. R. reported that she was more comfortable about leaving the house because it would no longer upset her husband as it had in the past. The test battery was repeated at the 1-month follow-up and interesting results were obtained. The Fear Survey Schedule had not one rating in either the "much" or "very much" fear category. This reduction included those items referring to feelings of inadequacy as well as target fears of injury and death. The MMPI profile revealed marked decreases on both the depression (t score $= 55$) and psychasthenia scales (t score $= 51$). The client contacted the therapist at 4 months to report a fear of reinstatement of the urge to check, although the previous maladaptive pattern of checking did not recur. He was again instructed in response prevention for 1 week. At an 8-month follow-up he remained symptom free, and no longer reported an urge to check.

DISCUSSION

It is not possible to determine the relative contribution of each procedure in eliminating the symptomatic behavior, though this multiple treatment approach effectively produced a change in the compulsive checking ritual. Although some decrease in frequency of the checking ritual can be attributed to the operant reinforcement, complete elimination did not occur until response prevention was introduced, further supporting it as a technique for the treatment of obsessive-compulsive disorders. Interfering with the chain of ritualistic behaviors, by requiring the client to perform the checking in a different order each evening, not only did not contribute to the results but increased the anxiety.

Muscle relaxation facilitated the client's ability to refrain from checking and decreased the frequency of this behavior. He continued to experience some discomfort even after the checking had been completed. This reported anxiety is consistent with the findings of Roper, Rachman, and Hodgson (1973) who found that compulsive checkers were more likely to experience anxiety after checking than were compulsive hand washers after completing their ritualistic behavior. Practicing muscle relaxation after completing his checking had enabled the client to overcome this anxiety.

Further progress in the treatment program was obtained by the client's eliminating the basement from his checking. He was able to achieve this goal despite the fact that he had spent the most time inspecting this room. The client would become so upset about his inability to stop the checking that he would dread the thought of night time. As a result, he would begin the checking, having built up a great deal of anxiety. Achieving deep muscle relaxation before beginning his checking, therefore, resulted in a sufficient decrease in this anticipatory anxiety, and may account for the ease with which he was able to refrain from checking the most anxiety provoking room in the house. Indeed, both the client and his wife expressed amazement at this particular achievement.

Motivation is certainly an important factor in enlisting the cooperation of the client for a self-directed treatment program of the kind described in this case report. However, as Marks (1973) has indicated, even where the desire for behavior change is strong, it is frequently necessary that continuous supervision by trained personnel be provided for persons exhibiting extensive checking rituals. If various components in the chain of compulsive checking behaviors are gradually eliminated the client may be able to assume the major responsibility for changing his own compulsive behavior, thereby facilitating its *in vivo* treatment, and decreasing the probability that it will recur. The client's ability to attain the goals of the treatment program, through a self-directed, graduated elimination of checking behavior, provides the opportunity to reinstate a sense of self-control and mastery over his own behavior. In the present case study, the issue of self-control was particularly important since the client perceived the problem as basically a "loss of his self-confidence." In addition, with systematic desensitization he was also able to enter the hosptal and achieve success in this previously avoided area, further enhancing his self-mastery feelings. Not only was this multiple treatment strategy effective in eliminating the compulsive checking behavior, but it enabled the client to regain a sense of control over his own behavior and a concomitant improvement in his self-concept.

REFERENCES

BOULOUGOURIS, J. C. & BASSIAKOS, L. Prolonged flooding in cases with obsessive-compulsive neurosis. *Behaviour Research and Therapy*, 1973, 11, 227-232.

HODGSON, R., RACHMAN, S., & MARKS, I. M. The treatment of chronic obsessive-compulsive neurosis: Follow-up and further findings. *Behaviour Research and Therapy*, 1972, 10, 181-189.

INGRAM, I. M. The obsessional personality and obsessional illness. *American Journal of Psychiatry*, 1961, 117, 1016-1019.

KRINGLER, E. Obsessional neurotics. *British Journal of Psychiatry*, 1965, 3, 709-722.

LEVY. R. & MEYER, V. New techniques in behavior therapy. *Proceedings of the Royal Society of Medicine*, 1971, 64, 1115-1118.

MARK, I. M. New approaches to the treatment of obsessive-compulsive disorders. *Journal of Nervous and Mental Diseases*, 1973, 156, 420-426.

MEYER, V. Modification of expectations in cases with obsessional rituals. *Behaviour Research and Therapy*, 1966, 4, 273-280.

MILLS, H. L., AGRAS, W. S., BARLOW, D. H., & MILLS, R. J. Compulsive rituals treated by response prevention. *Archives of General Psychiatry*, 1973, 28, 524-529.

RAINEY, C. An obsessive-compulsive neurosis treated by flooding *in vivo*. *Journal of Behavior Therapy and Experimental Psychiatry*, 1972, 3, 117-122.

RACKENSPERGER, W. & FEINBERG, A. Treatment of severe handwashing compulsion by systematic desensitization: A case report. *Journal of Behavior Therapy and Experimental Psychiatry*, 1972. 3, 123-128.

ROPER, G., RACHMAN, S., & HODGSON, R. An experiment on obsessional checking. *Behaviour Research and Therapy*, 1973, 11, 271-277.

WOLFE, J. & LANG, P. J. A fear survey schedule for use in behavior therapy. *Behaviour Research and Therapy*, 1964, 2, 27-30.

SECTION X: CLINICAL ISSUES, INNOVATIONS
AND CASE STUDIES

38

SELF-CONTROL OVER INTRUSIVE EXPERIENCES

E. B. Fisher, Jr.

Washington University

and

Robin C. Winkler

University of New South Wales, Sydney, Australia

An undergraduate's presenting problem consisted of re-current, frightening, and uncontrollable visual sensations. Agreeing that the major problem with the sensations was their intrusive nature, the client cooperated in exercises designed to increase her control over the production and dismissal of them. The exercises involved producing, maintaining, and dismissing the sensations at the verbal signals of the therapist. Praise was given contingent on the client's ability to produce and dismiss the sensations faster and to maintain them longer. With two sensations of a particularly frightening nature, exercises were carried out after a relaxation induction. At both the 45- and 85-day follow-up, the client reported substantially reduced incidence of the sensations and no anxiety attributable to them. Data gathered during the exercise sessions indicate that improvement

Reprinted with permission from *Journal of Consulting and Clinical Psychology*, Vol. 43, No. 6, 1975, 911-916. Copyright 1975, American Psychological Association.

This article is based on a case seen by the first author under the supervision of the second author while both were at the State University of New York at Stony Brook, Stony Brook, New York.

was attributable to practice and to other manipulations involved in the exercise sessions themselves. The relationship between the increased control over the sensations and the reduction of their incidence and disturbing nature is discussed.

A recurrent phenomenon in therapy is the client who reports that experiences or thoughts intrude on his/her consciousness, with the result that the client feels he or she is losing control, losing his/her mind, or going insane. The most obvious example of this type of apparently involuntary, intrusive experience is the hallucination. Obsessive thoughts and compulsive behavior may be regarded in this light also.

Behavior modification techniques for hallucinatory experiences have been largely derived from operant procedures (Ayllon & Haughton, 1964; Ayllon & Michael, 1959; Liberman, Teigen, Patterson, & Baker, 1973; Meichenbaum, 1966, 1969; Rutner & Bugle, 1969; Schaefer & Martin, 1969; Wincze, Leitenberg, & Agras, 1970): They have typically been used with hospitalized psychotics and have differentially reinforced behavior that is traditionally understood to be indicative of hallucinatory or psychotic experience. Working from a counterconditioning orientation, Slade (1972) has reported a treatment of auditory hallucinations employing the desensitization of anxiety cues found to be temporally associated with the hallucinatory behavior. However, neither the operant nor counterconditioning approaches have dealt directly with the intrusive experiences, as was attempted in the procedures reported here.

The techniques used in this case were derived from the literature that shows that if a subject can or believes he/she can control the onset and/or offset of an aversive stimulus, then the ability of that stimulus to produce anxiety or to disrupt normal activity is greatly reduced (Geer, Davison, & Gatchel, 1970; Staub, Tursky, & Schwartz, 1971). If an intrusive sensation is conceptualized as an aversive event that produces fear and disturbance, then it should be less disturbing if the client can be taught how to control its onset and/or offset. If the client is able to turn the intruding sensation on and off at will, not only will the experience of being out of control of one's mind be gone but the sensation can be terminated quickly if it does occur. Thus, if the sensation is not disturbing and is under control, the question arises as to whether the sensation remains a problem. Furthermore, if the client can be taught to control the onset and offset of the previously intrusive experience, it is possible that the skills so learned can be used to prevent onset, thus removing the experience altogether. Procedures derived from these conceptualizations were tested with a client who referred herself to the

Psychological Services Unit at the State University of New York at Stony Brook.

Client Background

The client was an 18-year-old female who had been raised in a suburb of New York. Previous therapy consisted of contact with two psychiatric social workers during both her first and second year at the university. Both of these contacts centered on her social adjustment and sex role identity.

Upon intake, the client complained of severe feelings of depersonalization and unreality. According to her report, these feelings were largely caused by several repetitive visual sensations that frightened her, making her afraid that she was going insane. The most regular of these involved flashes of dark colors when she closed her eyes at bedtime, the perception of people and objects as varying in size and distance from her, heads of screaming dogs and cats, a black and white geometric pattern with a spot of light at the center that "comes in and out and flashes around," and the sensation of "tiny white pinpoints moving around like dust" when she looked at the sky in daylight. She reported little control over the occurrence of these sensations with the exception of sometimes being able to stop the variation in size and distance of people and objects by "clearing my head and straightening up" and being able to stop the tiny white pinpoints by looking away from the sky. Prior to intake, the specific sensations had increased in frequency, resulting in increased feelings of depersonalization and desperation and in her becoming convinced that "there's something really wrong with me."

METHOD

Therapy commenced with the therapist reflecting and clarifying the client's experiences in order to reduce her anxiety as well as to satisfy both of them that he fully appreciated what she was experiencing. After the therapist felt he had gained her trust, conversation within therapy was directed toward the need to establish some control over the upsetting sensations. At this point, the client mentioned that the major source of disturbance was not the sensations themselves but their intrusive quality. The therapist strongly supported this idea, pursuing its discussion with the suggestion that her therapy might include exercises directed toward gaining control over the intrusiveness of the sensations. The client readily agreed to this. Therefore, part of each of the next four sessions was set aside for these exercises. The rest of these sessions were spent in discussion of the client's feelings and current functioning, still directed toward reassurance and support.

The exercises were conducted with the client seated in a relaxed manner in a lounge chair. Mild relaxation suggestions were given. Additionally, relaxation training of the type used in systematic desensitization (Wolpe, 1973) was used for the final two exercise sessions in which the sensations being dealt with were not only intrusive but disturbing in content (flashing colors and heads of screaming dogs). For clients with particularly disturbing sensations, use of the present techniques in conjunction with more extended relaxation training seems advisable.

Each exercise session consisted of the client practicing the production and dismissal of the various intrusive sensations. Each exercise trial was commenced with the therapist giving the direction, "Start." After this, the client produced, as fast as she could, a given sensation and signaled success by *raising* an index finger. Then the therapist repeated several times "Hold it" and then directed the client to "Stop!" after which she dismissed the sensation as rapidly as possible, signalling success by *lowering* the index finger. The only exception to this procedure was for the flashes of light that the client experienced as instantaneous. For these sensations, the exercises consisted of practicing only the production of the sensations.

The therapist used a stopwatch to time all trials. The "onset latency" was the time that elapsed between the therapist's command to produce the sensation and the client's signal that she had succeeded in doing so. The "exposure duration" was the time between her signal that she had produced the sensation and the therapist's direction to dismiss it. The "offset latency" was measured from the therapist's direction to dismiss the sensation to her signal that she had done so. Feedback on the development of control was provided by moving on to the next sensation and by praise, both of which were contingent on decreased onset and offset latencies.

The client initially reported being unable to produce the sensation of screaming dog and cat heads. Since this sensation was upsetting not only because of its intrusive qualities but also because of its disturbing content, an approach hierarchy, similar to that used in desensitization, was used. After unsuccessfully attempting to imagine "a brown dog" for 60 seconds, she was directed to imagine walking through a wooded area. In the course of narrating this imagery, the therapist directed her to imagine seeing a boy in a field at the edge of the woods and then to imagine a dog next to him. She was able to do this and in the following session to imagine a dog standing alone. In the third and fourth sessions in which this sensation was addressed, the client was relaxed as for desensitization (Wolpe, 1973) and was able to complete the exercise, progressing through images of pleasant and natural dog heads, dog heads with bared teeth, and finally heads with the mouth open as if screaming.

The exposure duration varied between 5 and 20 seconds during the course of the exercises. It was found that offset latency was less for shorter exposure durations. If the client had trouble dismissing a sensation, the exposure duration was shortened and, after some improvement, lengthened gradually so that she could work up to quickly dismissing sensations after relatively long exposure durations.

The sensation of flashing colors was practiced in two sessions with a total of 22 trials. The sensation of screaming dog heads was practiced for 25 trials in four sessions. The sensation of people and objects varying in size and distance received 12 trials spread over two sessions, with the client focusing on producing changes in her perception of a table lamp in the interview room. The black and white patterns were given only 2 trials during one session. The sensation of tiny white pinpoints, reported by the client to occur when she looked at the sky, was dealt with by informing her that this was a normal sensation, of no cause for alarm.

In dealing with occurrences of the intrusive experiences or with situations in which their occurrence was likely, the client was encouraged to use the skills being developed through the exercises. However, she was not given instructions to practice the exercises at other times.

Therapy was temporarily terminated at the end of the school semester. The client was seen for six more sessions during summer school. She reported very little disturbance from the sensations at that time so no more exercises were carried out. Therapy continued, however, with attention being given to her general social adjustment and to her vaguer feelings of depersonalization.

In summary, the client was seen for a total of 12 sessions, 6 during the regular school year (the last 4 of which were devoted to the exercises described above) and 6 sessions during the summer. Follow-up of the effects of the exercises was gathered during the first and last of the 6 sessions during the summer—45 and 85 days after the last session during which the exercises were practiced.

RESULTS

The client reported zero incidence of the flashing colors and screaming animal head sensations 45 days after the last practice session. A further check at 85 days after the last practice session again showed zero inci-

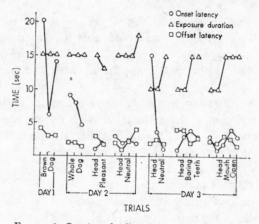

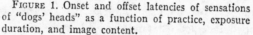

FIGURE 1. Onset and offset latencies of sensations of "dogs' heads" as a function of practice, exposure duration, and image content.

RESULTS

The client reported zero incidence of the flashing colors and screaming animal head sensations 45 days after the last practice session. A further check at 85 days after the last practice session again showed zero incidence. At the 45-day follow-up, she reported that the sensation of people and objects varying in size and distance had not decreased in frequency but had instead become only "a little" upsetting to her. After 85 days, she felt that the sensation was a little less frequent, adding, "I don't pay much attention to it . . . [and] can make it go away more easily." She indicated that she felt she could disperse the sensation by not letting it bother her. The sensation of black and white patterns was said to occur "rarely" after 45 days and "every couple of weeks, maybe" after 85 days. It was also less troublesome in that the only aspect of it that occurred after treatment was the light in the center of the pattern.

Figure 1 shows the latencies of onset and offset and exposure durations as the client moved along the hierarchy directed toward her image of screaming dog heads. Onset latency was initially high but quickly dropped with practice. Offset latency for all images was short, even from the start. Figure 1 also shows how for each new image toward the top of the hierarchy, duration was kept short at first, then increased when offset latencies remained low.

Figure 2 shows the decrease in the onset latency of the sensation of flashing lights over 22 trials in two sessions. It also shows that improvement continued over trials, regardless of the color that the client was

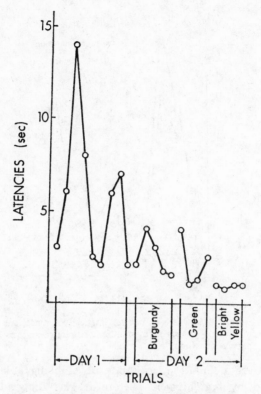

FIGURE 2. Onset latencies of sensations of flashing colors as a function of practice.

directed to imagine. (She experienced the flashes as instantaneous events, so no exposure time or offset latency data were obtained.)

Figure 3 shows the change in latencies over practice trials for the sensation of the table lamp in the office moving closer to and farther away from the client. (This was the particular form used of the general sensation of people and objects varying in size and distance.) Inspection of Figure 3 shows that onset latencies were initially minimal (2 seconds) and remained short (2-5 seconds) throughout the 12 trials. The offset latency was initially high (29 seconds) but was shortened by reducing the exposure duration from 20 to 5 seconds. After several trials at shorter exposure durations, the exposure was increased, and the client was able to retain control of dismissal in the sense of maintaining short offset latencies. As can be seen from the figure, throughout most of the trials, offset latency paralleled exposure duration, increasing when exposure increased and decreasing when exposure decreased. This pattern indicates

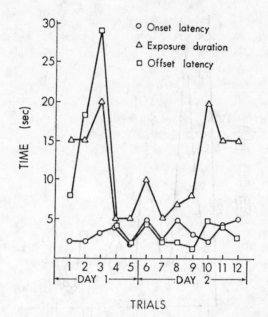

FIGURE 3. Onset and offset latencies of sensations
of moving objects as a function of practice and exposure duration.

that control over a sensation, in the sense of being able to dismiss it,
may be aided by "catching it" before it gets too well formed and
developed.

The general results of treatment were positive. The procedure reported
here was terminated after the sixth session at the end of the regular
school year. At this point, the client's fear that she was going insane was
greatly reduced and remained so when she was seen in Session 7 at the
start of summer school. By the termination of therapy at the end of
summer school, her feelings of depersonalization had abated and she
was functioning well. One year after termination, she was still in school
and reported doing "fine."

DISCUSSION

The treatment results reported here suggest that practicing the control
of onset and offset of intrusive sensations may be effective in reducing
both the frequency of such sensations and the amount of disturbance
caused by the sensations when they do occur. The importance of the
specific procedures used here is suggested by the data showing onset
latencies to decrease with increasing practice and by the data showing

offset latencies to be positively related to exposure duration early in the practice sessions. Additionally, the client's statements to the effect that increased control over the intrusive experiences eliminated some of them and markedly reduced the frequency and troublesomeness of the others attests to the importance of practicing this control in therapy. The results are consistent with research on the effects of actually being able to control (Staub et al., 1971) or of perceiving oneself as able to control the occurrence or characteristics of aversive stimulation (Geer et al., 1970).

Several other frameworks exist from which the present results may be understood. In a recent discussion of self-control, Kanfer (1975) mentioned that many self-monitoring procedures impose a break in a behavior chain by requiring the client to record the occurrence of some member of the chain. In the present case, the client's signals of sensation onset and offset may have served such a function, causing a subsequently lowered probability of the chain occurring in an unbroken and, subjectively, uncontrolled manner.

It might be suggested that either "thought stopping" or massed practice procedures are similar to those used in the present case. However, in thought stopping (Cautela, 1969) the emphasis is primarily on offset of the thought with less emphasis on controlling onset. Further, Cautela's rationale for thought stopping makes little reference to research indicating the value of perceived control in reducing responses to aversive stimuli. Indeed, it may be that thought stopping is a special case of the general self-control approach exemplified in the present procedure. In comparison to "massed" or "negative" practice (Yates, 1958, 1970), the present procedure involves much fewer repetitions of a given response and much longer intervals between repetitions. Nevertheless, it remains an open question as to whether similar processes account for both those effects reported here as well as those reported with massed practice.

Another perspective is suggested by the client's report that although the frequency of the sensations was reduced following the sessions in which their control was practiced, she was not aware of being particularly vigilant as to their occurrence or of actively preventing their onset. It may be that the practice sessions demonstrated that the sensations were controllable, thereby reducing their intrusive potency by helping the client to see them as natural and not bizarre or inexplicable experiences. In this sense, it is important to note that in encouraging her to view as problematic and to work at controlling their *intrusive* characteristics, the therapist emphasized and reassured the client that the *content* of her sensations was not pathological or sufficient cause for labeling herself "crazy." The advisability of such a tactic is supported perhaps by the client's statement at follow-up that even though some of the experiences had not ceased altogether she felt she could control them and, consequently, was not bothered by them.

This approach is supported by several other case studies. For example, Davison (1966) eliminated a paranoid delusional system by leading a client to believe that his headaches resulted from tension as opposed to "a spirit either inside or outside his body, helping him to make decisions." Similarly, Neale (Note 1) reported a case in which anxiety and fears of homosexuality were eliminated by convincing the client that the apparent shortness of his penis was a function of it being foreshortened by lying in the plane of his own vision of it. Valins and Nisbell (1971) have integrated these findings with laboratory research on the role of attribution in self-perception. They concluded that much psychopathology can be considered a function of attributing normal but private events to mysterious causes instead of to oneself or to natural causes. It is possible that the procedure reported here achieved success through altering the client's attributions of her behavior by teaching her that her experiences were of her own, controllable production rather than a function of being "crazy" or possessed.

This procedure should be seen within the context of behavior therapy's increasing emphasis on self-control procedures. Goldfried (1971, 1973) has suggested that desensitization may be presented as a means of learning to "relax away" responses to anxiety- and fear-evoking stimuli. Sharing much of Goldfried's orientation, Meichenbaum (1972) has indicated the utility of teaching clients to control their fears by controlling their self-verbalizations and by inhibiting those self-verbalizations that tend to evoke anxiety. In the case presented here, the client was taught to control the occurrence or evocation of *sensations* and, by such control, to reduce their attendant fear and discomfort.

The procedure may be applicable to a wide range of intrusive experiences that lead the client to believe she or he is going insane. It may be that the procedure will be most effective early in the development of the intrusive experiences before the client has accepted that he or she is out of control (has attributed the experiences to being insane) or has been forced to develop new behaviors to cope with or "explain" the intrusive experiences.

REFERENCE NOTE

1. NEALE, J. M. Case study presented in informal meeting of clinical psychology students and faculty, State University of New York at Stony Brook, Fall 1969.

REFERENCES

AYLLON, T. & HAUGHTON, E. Modification of symptomatic verbal behavior of mental patients. *Behav. Res. & Ther.*, 1964, 2, 87-97.

AYLLON, T. & MICHAEL, J. The psychiatric nurse as a behavioral engineer. *J. Exp. Anal. Behav.*, 1959, 2, 323-334.

DAVISON, G. C. Differential relaxation and cognitive restructuring in therapy with a "paranoid schizophrenic" or "paranoid state." *Proc. 74th Ann. Con. Amer. Psychol. Assn.*, 1966, 1, 177-178. (Summary.)

CAUTELA, J. R. Behavior therapy and self-control: Techniques and implications. In C. M. Franks (Ed.), *Behavior Therapy: Appraisal and Status.* New York: McGraw-Hill, 1969.

GOLDFRIED, M. R. Systematic desensitization as training in self-control. *J. Cons. Clin. Psychol.*, 1971, 37, 228-234.

GEER, J. H., DAVISON, G. C., & GATCHEL, R. I. Reduction of stress in humans through nonveridical perceived control of aversive stimulation. *J. Pers. Soc. Psychol.*, 1970, 16, 731-738.

GOLDFRIED, M. R. Systematic desensitization as training in self-control. *J. Cons. Clin. Psychol.*, 1971, 37, 228-234.

GOLDFRIED, M. R. Reduction of generalized anxiety through a variant of systematic desensitization. In M. R. Goldfried and M. Merbaum (Eds.), *Behavior Change Through Self-Control.* New York: Holt, Rinehart & Winston, 1973 .

KANFER, F. H. Self-management methods. In F. H. Kanfer & A. P. Goldstein (Eds.), (Eds.), *Helping People Change.* Elmsford, N. Y.: Pergamon Press, 1975.

LIBERMAN, R. P., TEIGEN, J., PATTERSON, R., & BAKER, V. Reducing delusional speech in chronic, paranoid schizophrenics. *J. Appl. Behav. Anal.*, 1973, 6, 57-64.

MEICHENBAUM, D. H. Effects of social reinforcement on the level of abstraction in schizophrenics. *J. Abnorm. Psychol.*, 1966, 71, 354-362.

MEICHENBAUM, D. H. The effects of instructions and reinforcement on thinking and language behaviors of schizophrenics. *Behav. Res. & Ther.*, 1969, 7, 101-114.

MEICHENBAUM, D. H. Cognitive modification of test anxious college students. *J. Cons. Clin. Psychol.*, 1972, 39, 370-380.

RUTNER, I. T., & BUGLE, C. An experimental procedure for the modification of psychotic behavior. *J. Cons. Clin. Psychol.*, 1969, 33, 651-653.

SCHAEFER, H. H. & MARTIN, P. L. *Behavioral Therapy.* New York: McGraw-Hill, 1969.

SLADE, P. D. The effects of systematic desensitization on auditory hallucinations. *Behav. Res. & Ther.*, 1972, 10, 85-92.

STAUB, E., TURSKY, B., & SCHWARTZ, G. E. Self-control and predictability: Their effects on reactions to aversive stimulation. *J. Pers. Soc. Psychol.*, 1971, 18, 157-162.

VALINS, S. & NISBETT, R. E. Attribution processes in the development and treatment of emotional disorders. In E. E. Jones, D. E. Kanouse, H. H. Kelley, R. E. Nisbett, S. Valins, and B. Weiner (Eds.), *Attribution: Perceiving the Causes of Behavior.* Morristown, N. J.: General Learning Press, 1971.

WINCZE, J. P., LEITENBERG, H., & AGRAS, W. S. A sequential analysis of the effects of instructions and token reinforcement in the modification of delusional verbal behavior in chronic psychotics. *Proc. 78th Ann. Con. Amer. Psychol. Assn.*, 1970, 5, 737-738. (Summary.)

WOLPE, J. *The Practice of Behavior Therapy* (2nd ed.). New York: Pergamon Press, 1973.

YATES, A. J. The application of learning theory to the treatment of tics. *J. Abnorm. Soc. Psychol.*, 1958, 56, 175-182.

YATES, A. J. *Behavior Therapy.* New York: Wiley, 1970.

SECTION X: CLINICAL ISSUES, INNOVATIONS
AND CASE STUDIES

39

SELF-CONTROL TECHNIQUES AS AN ALTERNATIVE TO PAIN MEDICATION

Philip Levendusky and Loren Pankratz

Veterans Administration Hospital, Portland, Oregon

A 65-year-old retired army officer with a productive work history was admitted to a psychiatric ward with symptoms of chronic abdominal pain and social withdrawal. For several years his pain had been managed with Talwin (Pentazocine), which was self-administered intramuscularly six times per day. The patient was taught self-control of his

Reprinted with permission from *Journal of Abnormal Psychology*, Vol. 84, No. 2, 1975, 165-168. Copyright 1975, American Psychological Association.

This article was written while Philip Levendusky was a Postdoctoral Fellow, Department of Psychology, State University of New York at Stony Brook. Loren Pankratz is V.A. Investigator MRIS #6901. The authors wish to thank John Lipkin, Henry Grass, and the staff of Ward 5-B for their assistance and helpful formulations with this patient. For their comments of earlier versions of this manuscript, we also thank Gerald C. Davison, Vincent Glaudin, Marvin R. Goldfried, and Yoram Jaffe.

Editor's Note. This case report raises some ethical considerations because of the use of deception in dealing with the patient and his symptoms. Therefore, I invited a number of psychologists who are concerned with ethical issues in psychological practice to comment on this aspect of the seemingly successful treatment of this case. Stuart W. Cook served as Chairman of the committee that drafted *Ethical Principles in the Conduct of Research with Human Participants,* which is now part of the ethics code of the American Psychological Association (1973). Herbert Kelman also served on that committee and has in the past spoken forthrightly about the use of deception in social psychological experiments.—LEONARD D. ERON, *Editor*

846

pain through a program of relaxation, covert imagery, and cognitive relabeling. He was then withdrawn from medication by diluting the Talwin with increasing proportions of normal saline. Follow-up showed the patient to be socially active, without medication, and more successfully controlling his pain. Results are discussed in terms of punishment, self-attribution of change, the nature of pain, and the ethical issues involved in instituting a treatment procedure without the completely informed consent of the patient.

Salter (1941) suggested that self-controlled hypnotic induction can effectively increase pain tolerance. More recent experimental evidence shows that this tolerance can be facilitated when the subject has control of a competing set of cues (Kanfer & Seidner, 1973), is given task-motivating instructions (Barber & Calverley, 1963), or receives self-attributed rather than externally attributed coping skills (Davison & Valins, 1969). In a recent review, Goldfried and Merbaum (1973) concluded that self-control procedures have considerable potential for increasing pain tolerance. The present case exemplifies the use of relaxation, covert imagery, and cognitive relabeling as self-control procedures for the management of pain related to a medical problem.

METHOD AND PROCEDURE

History

Mr. X was a 65-year-old retired army officer with a history that included significant military achievement, a productive teaching and research career, and numerous social accomplishments. Medically, the patient had had frequent abdominal operations for gallstones, postoperative adhesions, and bowel obstructions. At the time of his voluntary hospitalization, he was complaining of continued abdominal pain, loss of weight, and social withdrawal.

A mental status exam revealed an oriented, intact man with excellent higher mental functions. His mood was somewhat depressed, and he was unkempt and had poor personal hygiene. He explained that because of the difficulty controlling his abdominal pain over the past 2½ years, it had become impossible for him and his wife to remain socially active. For example, to control his pain while in social situations with friends, he would often assume awkward or embarrassing postures.

The patient's reliance on Talwin (Pentazocine, a weak narcotic antagonist with some narcotic-like properties) had begun more than 2 years prior to the current treatment. It had been initially prescribed to control pain following abdominal surgery. Mr. X was convinced that this medication was essential for the control of pain and he had spent considerable effort adjusting dosage to his optimal level of 1.25 cc, self-administered intramuscularly, six times daily. Because of the resultant excessive tissue and muscle damage, it had become difficult to find injection sites. The patient insisted that any less than 1.25 cc was almost useless and that more was of no additional value. He had read the early drug literature and was quick to cite evidence that Talwin was not addictive. In addition, Mr. X had no difficulty obtaining his medication by prescription.

Mr. X's primary goal for therapy was to "get more out of life in spite of my pain." He also verbalized the need to control Talwin, but had become highly resistant to any change in his medication regime.

The Setting

The patient was admitted to a newly opened inpatient psychosomatic ward. The therapy program of this ward used many of the principles described by Fordyce, Fowler, Lehmann, and DeLateur (1968) in treating patients with chronic pain. Basically, these are methods for rearranging the contingencies for pain behavior. For example, pain verbalization was not reinforced with staff attention. It should be noted that it was no easy task for ward personnel to ignore pain behavior and to abstain from psychological tug-of-war over symptoms. In addition, adjustment of pain medication was an explicit expectation of the setting, which further included individual behavior therapy programs, daily group therapy, ward government, social activities, and brief sessions for time-limited discussion of symptoms.

Training Program

Mr. X was started on a program of self-controlled relaxation. Relaxation training sessions were monitored by polygraph recordings, and the patient was given feedback on his performance. He was able to achieve states of deep relaxation as indicated by both the physiological measures and his verbal report. He further reported that during the sessions and for a short time after, his abdominal discomfort was somewhat reduced. These effects were reinforced as a clear indication of his growing personal conquest of pain.

The patient also learned to control his experience of pain through visual imagery. Images were devised that were familiar and meaningful to him because of his engineering background. For example, he visualized his pain sensations as being caused by tightening steel bands, which he could loosen, and as electrical impulses traveling over circuits, which he could manipulate. After a short period of visualization training, Mr. X was able to use this procedure, which provided him with new cognitive labels for his physiological cues.

Additionally, attempts were made to help him lengthen the time between injections. The patient was instructed to use his newly developed relaxation skills at the onset of abdominal pain as an alternative technique for managing his discomfort. Although he initially resisted schedule changes, eventually he was able to sleep through the night and reduce Talwin intake to 6-hour intervals. In addition to this lengthening of medication intervals, the patient's self-report indicated that the relaxation training sessions, visual imagery, and self-relaxation efforts were becoming increasingly successful in helping him cope with his physical discomfort.

Drug Withdrawal

Shortly after entering the hospital, Mr. X was shifted to a time-contingent rather than a pain-contingent medication schedule. Fordyce et al. (1968) suggested that the usual pain-contingent schedules amount to little more than reinforcement for pain behavior. Mr. X was placed on a 4-hour interval between his 1.25 cc Talwin injections. This was essentially equal to his self-administration schedule. Although he had admitted himself to a ward where medication adjustment was an explicit expectation, he resisted direct modification of his Talwin dosage levels. He reported numerous past-developed attempts to modify his regime, and each time he became more convinced of the importance of the medication. Once the 6-hour injection interval (mentioned above) had been reached there seemed to be a plateau beyond which no progress was made. The staff then wrestled with the task of reducing Talwin dosage in a patient who had great apprehension about accomplishing such a goal. Our solution was to attempt withdrawal without the patient's knowledge, and while this decision was reached after much discussion with colleagues, it was thought that such a strategy would increase the probability of the patient's achieving his goal of better control over the pain and medication.

The actual withdrawal procedure entailed a gradual dilution of Talwin with normal saline at the rate of .25 cc over the four injections each day. Therefore, after 5 days Mr. X was receiving injections of 100 percent normal saline four times daily. The patient experienced with-drawal symptoms of nausea, diarrhea, and cramps, but he misattributed these symptoms to Elavil (Amitriptyline), which had been introduced at the same time the Talwin dilution began. The Elavil was prescribed to ease the withdrawal symptoms, and while it was not given to deceive him, the timing fortuitously caused him to misattribute these symptoms. Mr. X continued to be unaware of dosage adjustment, and his verbal report indicated that abdominal pain was relieved by injections. Elavil was discontinued after 5 days, but the saline was administered for 3 more weeks. Concurrently, self-control training was successfully continued and the interval between injections was gradually expanded to 12 hours.

RESULTS

After 3 weeks of saline injections, the patient was aware of the changes in intervals, but he knew nothing of the adjusted dosage. In a special session, his therapist told him of the medication changes. Mr. X responded with a brief reaction of incredulity and some anger. He quickly indicated, however, that saline could not have been an effective agent in reducing his pain and asked that it be discontinued. In addition, he requested continued relaxation and covert imagery training and attributed the recent management of his discomfort to these techniques. In place of medication, Mr. X continued the self-control and socialization programs in the hospital for 20 more days.

At the time of discharge, the patient reported that he continued to experience abdominal pain but that the magnitude of this discomfort could be moderated more effectively with the self-control techniques than had been possible with Talwin. In addition, Mr. X had become very involved in both on- and off-ward social interactions.

A 6-month follow-up found that the patient had implemented his post-hospital plans, including a return to club activities, tournament bridge, and part-time teaching, and that he was still using the relaxation techniques. Furthermore, Mr. X was making plans for a lengthy summer excursion and was attempting to teach his wife self-control procedures to help her control her migraine headaches.

DISCUSSION

While there is a growing literature to suggest that drug dependency can be modified through the use of aversive conditioning, it is our judgment that there is an advantage to treatment strategies which avoid the use of these techniques and that most behaviors can be changed by other means. The effects of punishment are highly variable (Church, 1963), and its use entails numerous practical difficulties (Rachman & Teasdale, 1969). In addition, aversive conditioning procedures make it more difficult for the individual to attribute his change in behavior to himself. Furthermore, aversive treatment techniques modify the patient-therapist relationship in unknown ways; it is difficult for the therapist to know at what level the patient is cooperating with treatment. For example, Lang and Melamed (1969) reported how they were initially outsmarted by an infant during aversive conditioning of a vomit reflex.

In the case of Mr. X, it is doubtful that we would have obtained his cooperation for aversive treatment. He had a fixed belief that he needed a chemical agent to reduce abdominal pain. His anxiety about any change was so acute that he engaged in avoidance behavior, which frustrated treatment. The treatment strategy we employed provided him with an alternative set of behaviors for reducing pain under conditions which made cognitive sense to him. An important feature of this strategy was the emphasis on substituting internal control (relaxation) and cognitive self-attribution for external control (medication). This is in line with the research by Davison and Valins (1969) and Davison, Tsujimoto, and Glaros (1973), whose experimental evidence suggests a greater persistence of therapeutic gain when change is attributed to one's own effort rather than to an external agent. In addition, the effective cognitive relabeling of pain cues would be consistent with the Schachter and Singer (1962) assertion that the evaluation of physiological states may be controlled by cognitive factors. Nisbett and Schachter (1966) more specifically suggested that the intensity of naturally occurring pain states is also subject to cognitive manipulations, within certain limits. Therefore, our patient was not only able to shift from medication to self-control of his pain but also to relabel the physiological experience.

While the subjective sensation of pain may be a function of pain-receptor stimulation and autonomic responsiveness, there also appear to be relevant environmental and cognitive factors. Fordyce, Fowler, Lehmann, DeLateur, Sand, and Treischmann (1973) described most chronic pain behaviors as operants that are susceptible to contingency management, and they reported considerable therapeutic success using this paradigm. While Mr. X was involved in a similar program, he was also trained in a procedure that helped him reinterpret his physiological sensations and put them into a framework that enabled him to conceptualize a considerable degree of active, covert control of the pain experience.

This result is consistent with the growing body of literature that suggests the importance of considering environmental and cognitive factors in pain control.

The combination of our delay in informing the patient of the drug dilution schedule and his misattributing withdrawal symptoms to the side effects of a second drug permitted the use of an effective treatment program that otherwise would have been rejected as incompatible with the patient's assumptions and beliefs. However, in using a partially blind withdrawal procedure the staff chose an alternative with definite ethical implications. Mr. X admitted himself to a ward, where medication adjustment was an explicit expectation, for treatment of debilitating pain and drug dependency. However, because of his apprehension about direct intervention, we decided that informing him specifically of the withdrawal program would only increase his resistance. Therefore, withdrawal was started surreptitiously but under close medical monitoring concurrent with a self-control treatment program that he agreed was helpful. The Talwin was gradually diluted, Elavil was prescribed to ease withdrawal symptoms, and the process was reversible at any point. In short, Mr. X had been informed that a modification of his medication regime would be undertaken, but the details of his withdrawal was not specified.

Mr. X was our patient and not a subject in an experiment. We felt ethically obliged to use a treatment that had a high probability of success. To withhold the procedure may have protected some standard of openness but may not have been in his best interests. We saw no option without ethical problems. Although it is precarious to justify the means by the end, we felt most obliged to use a procedure designed to help the patient achieve a personally and medically desirable goal. Similar ethical decisions may become more common and more complex as health care professionals treat other dependencies, addictions, or self-destructive behaviors. One can only hope that the individual will be included in as much of his case planning as possible and that treatment goals will be made in an open arena where the staff can freely discuss and contribute to the decision-making process.

REFERENCES

BARBER, T. X. & CALVERLEY, D. Toward a theory of hypnotic behavior: Effects on suggestibility of task motivating instructions and attitudes toward hypnosis. *J. Abnorm. Soc. Psychol.*, 1963, 67, 557-565.

CHURCH, R. The varied effects of punishment. *Psychol. Rev.*, 1963, 70, 369-402.

DAVISON, G. C., TSUJIMOTO, R. N., & GLAROS, A. G. Attribution and the maintenance of behavior change in falling asleep. *J. Abnorm. Psychol.*, 1973, 82, 124-133.

DAVISON, G. C. & VALINS, S. Maintenance of self-attributed and drug-attributed behavior change. *J. Pers. Soc. Psychol.*, 1969, 11, 25-33.

FORDYCE, W. E., FOWLER, R. S., LEHMANN, J. F., & DELATEUR, B. Some implications of learning in problems of chronic pain. *J. Chronic Dis.*, 1968, 21, 179-190.

FORDYCE, W. E., FOWLER, R. S., LEHMANN, J. F., DELATEUR, B., SAND, P., & TREISCHMANN, R. Operant conditioning in the treatment of chronic pain. *Arch. Physical Med. Rehab.*, 1973, 54, 399-408.

GOLDFRIED, M. R. & MERBAUM, M. *Behavior Change Through Self-Control.* New York: Holt, Rinehart, & Winston, 1973.

KANFER, F. H. & SEIDNER, M. L. Self-control: Factors enhancing tolerance of noxious stimulation. *J. Pers. Soc. Psychol.*, 1973, 25, 381-389.

LANG, P. S. & MELAMED, B. G. Case report: Avoidance conditioning therapy of an infant with chronic numerative vomiting. *J. Abnorm. Psychol.*, 1969, 74, 1-8.

NISBETT, R. E. & SCHACHTER, S. Cognitive manipulation of pain. *J. Exp. Soc. Psychol.*, 1966, 2, 227-236.

RACHMAN, S. & TEASDALE, J. D. Aversion therapy: An appraisal. In C. M. Franks (Ed.), *Behavior Therapy: Appraisal Status.* New York: McGraw-Hill, 1969.

SALTER, A. Three techniques of autohypnosis. *J. Gen. Psychol.*, 1941, 24, 423-438.

SCHACHTER, S. & SINGER, J. E. Cognitive, social, and physiological determinants of emotional state. *Psychol. Rev.*, 1962, 69, 379-399.

40

WAS DECEPTION JUSTIFIED — AND WAS IT NECESSARY? COMMENTS ON "SELF-CONTROL TECHNIQUES AS AN ALTERNATIVE TO PAIN MEDICATION"

Herbert C. Kelman

Harvard University

Ethical issues raised by the use of placebos in clinical practice are discussed in connection with the case of a patient undergoing self-control training, who was withdrawn from antipain medication without his knowledge by substitution of a placebo. Ethical problems resulting from the use of deception in this case center on the patient's right to informed consent, on the quality of the patient-therapist relationship, and on potential damages to the patient's self-concept. On the other hand, a number of mitigating factors may well have justified the use of deception in this particular case. Nevertheless, the question is raised whether deception was really necessary and might have been avoided by a therapeutic model that goes beyond the control of

Reprinted with permission from *Journal of Abnormal Psychology*, Vol. 84, No. 2, 1975, 172-174. Copyright 1975, American Psychological Association.

* My own thinking about these issues was greatly stimulated by Sissela Bok's recent paper (Bok, 1974). I am very grateful to Dr. Bok for showing me the manuscript and discussing some of the issues with me.

specific behaviors and views the treatment as part of a
larger process designed to enhance the patient's capacity to
cope with his life situation.

The case report by Levendusky and Pankratz (1975) provides a good
starting point for considering some of the subtler ethical issues raised
by the use of placebos in clinical practice.* The authors describe the
case of a patient who underwent a training program in self-control of
severe pain through the use of relaxation, visual imagery, and cognitive
labeling. He was highly resistant, however, to giving up his antipain
medication, on which he had come to rely. The authors decided to withdraw him from the medication without his knowledge by substituting
increasing proportions of a placebo for the medication. The deception
involved was clearly designed to benefit the patient, and it apparently
did contribute to a successful treatment program. Moreover, the indications are that the decision to use deception was taken responsibly, rather
than casually. Thus we are obviously dealing with a benign deception,
which makes it easier to focus on the ethical implications of deception
as such, even where it does not cause any readily apparent harm to the
patient.

The use of deception in the case reported here raises several ethical
questions:

1. Does the therapist have a right to decide what treatment is in the
patient's best interest without obtaining the patient's informed consent?
It is apparent from the report that Mr. X was a competent individual,
who had voluntarily admitted himself to the hospital and who was
well aware of the fact that the medication was an unsatisfactory solution
to his chronic pain and was having a debilitating effect on him. By
tricking him into a course of treatment that they could not persuade
him to follow, the therapists deprived him of the freedom of choice to
which he was entitled. Even though the patient's resistance may have
been based on irrational fears, and even though the treatment may have
been not only medically indicated but also consistent with the patient's
own goals, there is much potential for abuse in the view that the therapist
is better able to decide what is good for the patient than the patient
himself. Thus, the sidestepping of informed consent represents a dangerous practice, although, alas, not an unprecedented one in hospital
settings.

2. Does the use of deception undermine the quality of the relationship
between therapist and patient? Clearly, there is the danger that a patient,

once deceived, even though it may have been "for his own good," will no longer be able to fully trust the therapist, and that the therapist's future effectiveness may thereby suffer. The authors report that Mr. X when informed of the deception, responded with some incredulity and anger, but there are no indications that the experience undermined the future course of treatment. Nevertheless, the possibility of such an effect cannot be discounted, particularly when we keep in mind that deception has a tendency to escalate and to spread into different areas of the relationship. The difficulty in containing deception is illustrated in the present case by the fact that the introduction of the placebo was accompanied by a second deception. As the dilution of the patient's medication began, a second drug was prescribed to ease his withdrawal symptoms (which, incidentally, seemed to play an important part in the success of the procedure, because Mr. X attributed the withdrawal symptoms that he did experience to the effects of this drug). The authors do not say what they told Mr. X about the purpose of this drug, but they obviously did not reveal its true purpose—to ease withdrawal—since he had not been told that he was undergoing withdrawal.

3. Does the use of deception have potentially damaging consequences for the patient's self-concept? For many patients, a central or at least a derivative concern engendered by their symptoms is their inability to control their own lives. The brief history presented in the report suggests that this was a major issue for Mr. X, a man of many professional, intellectual, and social accomplishments, who found himself unable to lead the kind of life he wanted because of his chronic pain and drug dependence. One of the great virtues of the self-control training he received was that it helped to restore the sense of personal efficacy that he had lost. There is, in my judgment, a real danger that the discovery that he has been tricked and manipulated might confirm the patient's sense of dependence and powerlessness and prove a setback in his efforts to regain control over his own life. There is no indication in the case report that this happened to Mr. X, but the possibility of such subtly damaging consequences must be considered before we conclude that a deception is entirely benign.

On the other side of the ledger, one can cite a number of mitigating factors that might serve to justify the use of deception in the present case:

1. The therapists were confronted with an ethical dilemma. Though concerned with the ethical implications of deceiving the patient, they

"felt most obliged to use a procedure designed to help the patient achieve a personally and medically desirable goal." Mr. X's dependence on his medication was clearly destructive, as the patient himself realized, yet his resistance to giving up the drug was apparently overwhelming. What was needed was a dramatic demonstration that he could, in fact, do without it. The therapists made the clinical judgment that the only way they could provide this demonstration was to withdraw him without his knowledge and then to confront him with this fact. Their report suggests that this clinical judgment was validated by the success of the treatment and the apparent absence of psychologically damaging effects. It might be argued that the deception in this case did not deprive the patient of the opportunity to choose between different forms of treatment, involving different arrays of costs and benefits, but merely helped to overcome a barrier to a form of treatment that the patient really wanted but was afraid to enter into.

2. In support of the last point, the authors could cite the fact that the patient admitted himself to a ward in which "adjustment of pain medication was an explicit expectation of the setting." The patient did know, for example, that the medication schedule and the interval between injections were being modified. Thus, it can be argued that the deception was only partial and involved only the details and the timing of the treatment rather than the fact that such a treatment would be undertaken. Although there is no question that the patient was deceived, the treatment did seem to be within the range of possibilities to which he had at least implicitly given his consent.

3. A further mitigating factor is the way in which the decision to use deception was reached in this case. Indications are that it was not a routine or casual decision, based on the therapists' interest in making the job easier for themselves. The authors report that the staff wrestled with the task of reducing the drug dosage in light of the patient's great apprehension, and that they reached the decision to proceed without the patient's knowledge only after much discussion. Such a careful and responsible approach counteracts the potentially damaging long-term effects that the use of deception might otherwise have on hospital practices. It communicates the principle that deception can be countenanced only under very special circumstances and makes it less likely that such procedures will be legitimized, routinized, and institutionalized.

On balance, I find it difficult, despite my real misgivings, to take an absolute stand against the use of deception in the case reported here.

And yet I wonder whether the deception was really necessary. The patient seems to be a man who was highly motivated, had considerable ego strength, and showed an ability to accept objective evidence. Moreover, he gradually developed skills in controlling his pain and recognized the effectiveness of these skills. Might it have been possible, as his confidence in these self-control efforts grew, to obtain his consent to a procedure whereby the pain medication would be gradually withdrawn, with the understanding that (in the interest of counteracting resistance) he would not be told the exact timing and amount of withdrawal and that he would be closely monitored to deal with possible side effects of the procedure? I do not know to what extent the therapists tried or considered such a procedure. They apparently concluded that, once they reached the 6-hour injection interval, they could not obtain the patient's consent for further adjustments in the medication, because of his acute anxiety about any change, his conviction that he needed the medication, and his overt resistance to efforts in this direction.

It would be presumptuous of me to second-guess the authors' clinical judgment, since I was not there, I am not familiar with the technique they used, and I am not even a clinician. All I can do, therefore, is to raise the question and to point out that it is precisely the role of the outsider to raise the kinds of questions that may not emerge from an insider's perspective. From my reading of the authors' own description of the patient and the treatment, I come away with the feeling that they may have underestimated Mr. X's coping abilities. They do so, perhaps, because they work within a model that emphasizes specific behaviors (self-controlled relaxation, covert imagery, cognitive relabeling, causal attribution) without sufficient attention to the person responsible for those behaviors. I do not wish to minimize the value of the training techniques they employ; in fact I am greatly impressed with their apparent effectiveness. I do not dismiss them on the grounds that they "merely" deal with symptoms, nor do I regard them as incompatible with the personal dignity of the patient. But I think it is important to keep in mind that the training program, for the patient, is part of a larger process of coping with his life situation. Thus, while Mr. X was obviously concerned with controlling his pain, he was also concerned with regaining control over his life, with fulfilling his potential, and with repairing a damaged self-concept. It seems reasonable to assume that, as he learned to control his pain, his self-confidence and sense of efficacy also grew.

Let me suggest—and I do so with no sense of certainty—that the course of treatment might have been different if the therapists had been prepared to work with the broader motives that the patient brought to the treatment and to draw on the increasing coping capacities that the patient developed as the treatment proceeded—in other words, to deal with him as a whole person. They might have found that deception was not necessary to initiate the withdrawal procedure. They might even have concluded that deception was more likely to retard than to advance the treatment process.

REFERENCES

Bok, S. The ethics of giving placebos. *Scientific American,* 1974, 231 (5), 17-23.
Levendusky, P. & Pankratz, L. Self-control techniques as an alternative to pain medication. *J. Abnorm. Psychol.,* 1975, 84, 165-168.

SECTION X: CLINICAL ISSUES, INNOVATIONS
AND CASE STUDIES

41

BIOFEEDBACK TREATMENT OF A
CASE OF RAYNAUD'S DISEASE

Edward B. Blanchard and Mary R. Haynes

*University of Mississippi Medical Center,
Jackson, Mississippi*

Summary—A patient with long-standing moderately severe
Raynaud's disease was successfully treated with biofeedback
procedure based on finger tip surface temperature. Control
conditions in the experiment isolated the feedback training
as the important element in the treatment. Follow-up data
at two, four and seven months with booster treatment sessions are presented.

Raynaud's disease has been described by Spittell (1972) as a condition
"without associated and contributing conditions or disease" in which the
patient suffers from "episodes of constriction of the small arteries or
arterioles of the extremities, such as pallor, cyanosis, or both. Following
the episodes of constriction, hyperemia may produce a red color" (p.
388). In somewhat less technical terms it is a functional disorder of the
cardiovascular system in which the patient experiences painful episodes
of vasoconstriction in the hands, and possibly the feet, which leave the
extremities cold to the touch.

Reprinted with permission from *Journal of Behaviour Therapy and Experimental
Psychiatry*, Vol. 6, 1975.
This research was supported in part by a grant from the National Heart and Lung
Institute, HL 14906-03.

Several cases of this disease have recently been reported in which a biofeedback procedure played some role in treatment (Surwit, 1973; Jacobson, Hackett, Surman and Silverberg, 1973; Peper, 1973; Schwartz, 1972). In two cases, Jacobson et al. (1973) and Schwartz (1972), the treatment was a success and follow-up revealed continued success. In two other cases, Peper (1973) and Surwit (1973), there was initial success and symptomatic relief, but follow-up revealed a fairly rapid relapse. In the final case, Schwartz (1972), treatment was unsuccessful.

All of the above cases but one (Jacobson et al., 1973) present difficulties in interpretation because little or no systematic data are reported on the patients as they progressed through the treatment, little or no pretreatment data are presented, and frequently other forms of treatment accompanied the biofeedback training. In the case described by Jacobson et al. (1973) systematic data were apparently collected and part of them are reported. Unfortunately, the specific effects of biofeedback training cannot be assessed since it was used in combination with hypnosis and other forms of therapy.

As most of the previous investigators of this phenomenon have mentioned, emotional factors frequently play a part in Raynaud's disease. However, no controls for placebo or expectancy effects have been used in the above mentioned cases although Schwartz (1972) readily acknowledged the possible role of such factors in his successful case.

The case report described below is an improvement over previous reports because (1) systematic data on the chief dependent variable, skin temperature, are presented; and (2) baseline and control phases are included as well as biofeedback training phases to assess the ability of the patient to control the response in the absence of feedback.

CASE HISTORY

The patient, a 28-year-old female, was married and had no children. She was a registered nurse and worked as an instructor at a local school of nursing. The patient related that she had had cold hands and feet "for as long as she could remember." Her mother had a similar condition. During her nursing education she recognized her problem as a case of Raynaud's phenomenon and had sought medical help upon occasion without any apparent benefit. Her case can be described as moderately severe Raynaud's disease, that had not warranted a medical trial. She claimed to wear gloves sometimes in her office which was described as "chilly" due to the air conditioning. Actual episodes of painful vasoconstriction were relatively infrequent, about once per month.

Apparatus

A complex Wheatstone bridge circuit was constructed in which thermistors (material whose electrical resistance varies radically with changes
in temperature) constituted two arms of the circuit. A 1½ V battery
provided a constant voltage across the circuit. This circuit was connected
to a d.c. voltmeter which could be switched to read either the absolute
temperature of one of the thermistors or the temperature difference between the two thermistors. This circuit was also connected to a Grass
Model 7 Polygraph with two channels recording the voltage simultaneously with 7P1 DC Preamplifiers.

The thermistors were attached with paper tape to the ventral side of
the most distal digit of the right index finger and to the middle of the
forehead. With the circuit and the polygraph, continuous recordings were
made of both the absolute temperature of the finger and the difference
between the finger and the forehead temperatures. The thermistor circuit
and the polygraph were calibrated so that these temperatures could be
read to within 0.2°F.

Procedure

There then followed, under all conditions, a 40-minute session which
was divided into three parts. The first 15 minutes were devoted to adaptation. Next followed a five-minute session-baseline during which the
polygraph readings were recorded. Finally there was a 20-minute experimental trial in each session. The activity during this part of the session
varied from condition to condition in an A-B-A-B design and is described
below:

Experimental Conditions

Baseline. The first four sessions were baseline trials during which the
patient continued to sit quietly with instructions to relax.

Self-control. During the next six sessions the patient was asked to try
to make her hands become warmer through "mental means." She was
told that this was the first phase of treatment. This phase thus controlled
for expectancy effects and constituted an instructed no-feedback control
phase which other workers in the biofeedback area have mentioned as
the best condition against which to compare feedback effects (Blanchard
& Young, 1973).

Feedback-training. In the next six sessions the patient was given analog visual feedback of the difference in temperature between her hand and her forehead and instructed to try to raise the temperature of her hand to that of her forehead as indicated by the moving pen on the meter.

Self-control. The next six sessions constituted a return to the instructed no-feedback condition and served as a control phase for the effects of feedback training.

Feedback training. The final six sessions were a return to the feedback training condition to complete the experimental analysis of the A-B-A-B design. At the conclusion of treatment, the patient was advised to use newly learned ability whenever her hands felt cold. However, no specific home practice regimen was instituted.

Follow-up. Two months after the completion of treatment we contacted the patient and asked her to return to the laboratory. She was first given two self-control sessions. These were followed by four feedback training sessions as a booster.

Four months after the completion of treatment she was given one self-control session, followed by four more booster feedback sessions and a final self-control session.

Finally, seven months after the completion of treatment the patient was seen again for 10 sessions over a three-week period of time. After three self-control sessions, she received five more booster feedback-training sessions, followed by two more self-control sessions.

RESULTS

The principal dependent variable in this study is the difference between the temperature rcorded from the finger electrode and that recorded from the forehead electrode. To take into account individual daily fluctuations in both room and body surface temperature, a change score was calculated for each session by subtracting the temperature difference recorded at mid-point of the session baseline from the greatest temperature difference recorded during the experimental trial. These differences, with the appropriate sign (positive values represent a warming of the hands relative to forehead) are presented graphically in Figure 1 for each phase of the study on a session by session basis.

Inspection of Figure 1 reveals that the hands tended to drop in temperature during the baseline phase when the patient continued to sit quietly relaxed. This decrease ranged from 0 to 1.6°F.

Initial attempts at self-control yielded somewhat inconsistent results:

four sessions led to increases in temperature, two to essentially no change. The overall average increase was 1.1°F.

Interestingly, not only was the patient able consistently to increase the temperature of hand during the feedback phase, but the latency with which the maximum increase was obtained decreased during this phase. The maximum increase required 17 minutes to achieve a 1.6°F increase in trial 1 as compared to three minutes to achieve a 4.8°F increase by the end of the phase. This indicated that although there seemed to be a physiological limit to how great an increase could be obtained, learning was still taking place with repeated trials as the patient learned to make the response more quickly. Again, results were somewhat inconsistent from session to session but the overall average increase was 3.4°F.

In the return to self-control, the dependence on the feedback was demonstrated to some degree. Although three sessions yielded sizeable increases in temperature, three others did not. The overall average increase was 1.4°F.

Completing the experimental analysis, the final return to feedback training led to consistent increases in hand temperature which averaged 3.7°F.

At the first follow-up the patient could show little self-control of hand temperature. Four booster treatment sessions seemed to reestablish the hand warming response and led to an overall increase of 2.0°F. At the second follow-up, some degree of self-control remained. Again four booster sessions were given which led to an overall increase of 1.6°F.

At the third follow-up, seven months after the conclusion of initial treatment, self-control of handwarming was initially variable. Five booster feedback training sessions again led to rapid re-instatement of her ability to warm her hands by an average of 2.2°F.

Absolute Hand Temperature and Self-Report

During interviews with the patient at the end of treatment and at each follow-up, she reported using mental means (certain mental imagery she had identified as helpful during treatment) outside of treatment to make her hands warmer when they seemed cold, and having less trouble in her "cold" office. Also, she stated that both hands became warm when she tried mentally to warm them and she was even getting some transfer to her feet (they felt warmer). Finally, she reported that the clinical problem of the Raynaud's disease was mostly abated.

In order to determine whether the improvement the patient was report-

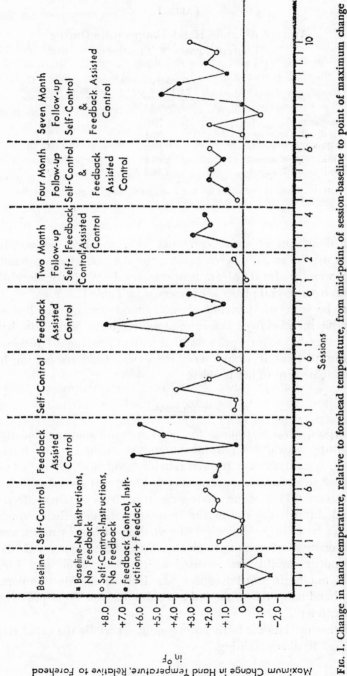

FIG. 1. Change in hand temperature, relative to forehead temperature, from mid-point of session-baseline to point of maximum change in experimental phase of session, on a session by session basis, for all phases of treatment.

TABLE 1

Average Absolute Hand Temperature During
Different Phases of Treatment

Phase of treatment	Average absolute hand temperature from session-baseline (*F)	Number of sessions on which average is based*
Baseline	79.0	4
Feedback-Training—2	91.1	3
Follow-up: 2 months	89.9	3
Follow-up: 4 months	86.8	2
Follow-up: 7 months	88.3	3

Note: * Average is calculated on last 2 or 3 sessions of a phase except for
Baseline for which all 4 sessions were used.

ing had significant objective correlates (i.e., whether she was feeling
better because of actually being better), the data on absolute hand temperature were analyzed. Mean temperatures from the session-baseline
recordings from several phases are presented in Table 1.

As can be seen, the patient's absolute hand temperature had shown
considerable increase from before to after treatment during the baseline
portion of each session (prior to the patient's trying to increase the
temperature). Thus it would seem there was good reason for her to
report an abatement of her problem.

DISCUSSION

This report serves to confirm the previous work showing that biofeedback training provides a possible alternative treatment for Raynaud's
disease. In certain ways, it is more reliable "evidence" for the efficacy of
biofeedback treatment than previous cases because of several experimental
design features: 1) baseline trials were run, 2) expectancy effects were
controlled through the use of the instructional, no-feedback condition,
3) no other forms of psychological intervention such as hypnosis, assertive
training, or psychotherapy were given concurrently, 4) systematic data on
the dependent variable are reported which clearly show that improvement did not begin until feedback was introduced. Most importantly,
absolute hand temperature showed a reliable increase from pre-treatment
to post-treatment.

The follow-up data are fairly encouraging, especially the rapid response
to "booster" feedback training.

REFERENCES

BLANCHARD, E. B. & YOUNG, L. D. Self-control of cardiac function: A promise as yet unfulfilled. *Psychol. Bull.,* 1973, 79, 145-163.

JACOBSON, A. M., HACKETT, R. P., SURMAN, O. S., & SILVERBERG, E. L. Raynaud's phenomenon: Treatment with hypnotic and operant technique. *J. Amer. Med. Assn.,* 1973, 225, 739-740.

PEPER, E. Frontiers of clinical biofeedback. In L. Birk (Ed.), *Seminars in Psychiatry,* Vol. 5. New York: Grune & Stratton, 1973.

SCHWARTZ, G. E. Clinical applications of biofeedback: Some theoretical issues. In D. Upper and D. S. Goodenough (Eds.), *Behavior Modification with the Individual Patient: Proceedings of Third Annual Brockton Symposium in Behavior Therapy.* Nutley, N. J.: Roche, 1972.

SPITTEL, J. A. Chapter 19 in J. F. Fairbairn, J. L. Juergens, and J. A. Spittell (Eds.), *Peripheral Vascular Diseases.* (4th Ed.). Philadelphia: W. B. Saunders, 1972.

SURWIT, R. S. Biofeedback: A possible treatment for Raynaud's disease. In L. Birk (Ed.), *Biofeedback: Behavioral Medicine.* New York: Grune & Stratton, 1973.

42

BEHAVIORAL TREATMENT OF FUNCTIONAL APHONIA

Robert C. Marshall and Mary T. Watts

*Veterans Administration Hospital, Portland, Oregon;
Portland State University*

Summary—This case report describes the procedures employed and problems encountered in a vocal rehabilitation program for a man 48 years old with a 3-year history of functional aphonia. Results suggest that the speech pathologist, using a combination of voice and behavior therapy techniques, can successfully treat the patient with functional aphonia. The patient exhibited a normal voice at the end of a 30-session program and at 2 and 6 months' follow-ups.

Functional aphonias and dysphonias have commonly been divided into two etiologic classifications (Aronson, Peterson & Litin, 1964), comprising disorders resulting from improper use of the vocal mechanism and disorders that have an alleged psychoneurotic origin. In the first instance improper use of the vocal organ may lead to or result from histological changes in the larynx such as vocal nodules, contact ulcers or polyps. Treatment ordinarily consists of vocal rest, surgical removal of the nodule or polyp by the laryngologist, re-education in the appro-

Reprinted with permission from the *Journal of Behaviour Therapy and Experimental Psychiatry*, Vol. 6, 75-78, 1975.

This study was conducted at the V.A. Hospital, Portland, Oregon, while the second author was involved in a clinical traineeship sponsored by the Veterans Administration.

priate use of the vocal mechanism by the speech pathologist or some combination of voice rest, surgery and voice therapy. In the second classification the patient's voice problem is disproportionately severe to any recognized degree of laryngeal involvement or there may be no apparent alteration in structure detected by laryngoscopic examination. Aronson, Peterson and Litin furthermore suggest that a number of functional voice disorders reflect changes in psychoneurotic or psychotic mental states. These include spastic dysphonia (Critchley, 1939; Heaver, 1959; Kiml, 1963), ventricular dysphonia (Jackson & Jackson, 1935; Brodnitz, 1959; Freud, 1962) and hysterical aphonia (Winkelman, 1937; Clerf & Braceland, 1942; Barton, 1960; Wilson, 1962). Treatment may include physical manipulation and stimulation of the laryngeal mechanism by the laryngologist (MacMahon, 1932; Babcock, 1942; Froschels, 1955), referral by the laryngologist to the psychiatrist (Barlow, 1930; Barton, 1960) or referral by the laryngologist or psychiatrist to the speech pathologist (Ellis, 1959; Wilmore, 1959).

Recently several speech pathologists have reported on the benefits of voice therapy in conjunction with behavior therapy techniques with functional aphonia cases (Bangs & Freidinger, 1950; Walton & Black, 1959; Wolski & Willy, 1965; Gray, England & Mahoney, 1965; Boone, 1966). These encouraging results suggest that the speech pathologist, skilled in the use of voice and behavior therapy techniques, may be helpful in the treatment of functional aphonia cases. This paper describes the treatment and results of a verbal rehabilitation and behavior modification program for a patient with a 3-year history of functional aphonia and the rather unique problems encountered in administering such a program within a hospital environment.

CASE HISTORY

Edward, 48 years old, was initially referred to the Speech Pathology Service by a hospital otolaryngology resident. Edward's aphonia had begun shortly following an incident during which he was overcome by carbon monoxide while working as a heavy equipment operator. His medical records indicated that he had been hospitalized and treated for laryngitis and bronchitis, the symptoms of which were inspiratory and expiratory dyspnea, cough and hoarseness. Edward failed to respond, however, to prescribed medications of tetracycline, aminophylline, sodium iodide and steroids; his dyspnea subsequently increased and he began to develop difficulty expelling non-purulent secretions. Direct laryngoscopy on the sixth hospital day revealed a partial paralysis of the left true vocal cord, and a tracheostomy was performed. Although subsequent diagnostic tests to determine the cause of the paresis were non-conclusive, his condition improved with time. A second laryngoscopic examination 10 days following tracheostomy showed no evidence of the vocal cord paresis. The tracheostomy was removed without incidence on the sixteenth hospital day and Edward was discharged 2 days later.

In the 3-year period prior to being referred to our clinic, Edward had sought medical attention on twelve occasions for symptoms of shortness of breath, dyspnea and dysphonia. After one of these incidents, another direct laryngoscopic examination revealed "a normal glottic chink" and no evidence of vocal paralysis. Shortly before being referred to us he had also been hospitalized for symptoms of epigastric pain, vomiting and nocturnal enuresis. After another series of non-conclusive clinical and laboratory tests his problems were thought to have a functional basis. A psychiatric consultation attributed Edward's gastrointestinal difficulties to situational stresses, but described him as a poor treatment candidate in view of his past medical history, his stated reluctance to accept treatment and the impossibility of involving his family in any treatment program because of their distance from the hospital.

SPEECH AND VOICE EVALUATION

When first seen by the Speech Pathology Service, Edward could best be described as having "intermittently phonated—whispered speech" similar to patients described by Aronson, Peterson and Litin (1964, 1966). Our impression was that Edward's vocal symptoms as well as his past medical and social history were reasonably typical of functional aphonia cases (Barton, 1960; Aronson, Peterson & Litin, 1964; Aronson, 1969). As the onset of his aphonia closely followed an incident of near asphyxiation, he may have had temporary vocal cord paresis. Although indirect laryngoscopy performed the day before his speech and voice evaluation revealed mildly edamatous true and false vocal cords, his voice problem was too severe for such a minor laryngeal problem. He also exhibited a wide range of vocal qualities and a substantial degree of laryngeal hyperfunction. When speaking, his voice was unusually high pitched and strained and his body excessively tense. Finally, his aphonia appeared to provide him with gains both primary (he was medically retired and received a pension because of his voice problem) and secondary (he received much attention from individuals who sympathized with him and/or tried to determine the cause of his problems). Although Edward expressed a strong desire to speak normally, he also expressed delight in the knowledge that numerous medical and paramedical professionals had attempted to find out "what was wrong with him."

TREATMENT AND RESULTS

Phase 1

We felt that any type of vocal rehabilitation program with Edward would be unsuccessful if he continued to receive professional attention for problems other than his aphonia. Since no organic basis had been clearly substantiated for most of his physical complaints we consulted his attending physician who agreed to ignore, whenever possible, his somatic complaints during one month of voice therapy. At the same time we needed to liberally reinforce (socially) any effort by Edward to improve his voice. We informed Edward that his laryngeal examination had shown nothing structurally wrong with his vocal mechanisms to account for his voice problem and that with proper instruction and hard work, he could learn to speak normally.

Initial treatment sessions were devoted to teaching Edward the use of progressive relaxation techniques (Jacobson, 1951). Efforts were made to achieve general body relaxation and then relaxation of the laryngeal musculature as well. In a relaxed state Edward was asked to say after the clinician, various vowels, words and phrases designed to facilitate normal vocal production. He followed instructions readily and in the second treatment session produced 25 short vowels of essentially normal quality. As a carryover technique he was taught to say "Hi" normally and was reinforced for using this word to greet staff clinicians whenever they came into his ward. In the fourth treatment session his voice improved so dramatically that the clinician called another staff member to listen to Edward speak normally, producing a variety of vowels, words and sentences. Immediately following this session, however, Edward rushed to the nurse's station complaining of a chest pain and a tingling sensation in his right arm, hand, and shoulder. While he received a substantial amount of sympathy from other patients on his ward, his pleas were largely ignored by the staff and he soon stopped complaining.

From the 5th through the 10th treatment sessions Edward continued to exhibit improved, and essentially normal voice quality in the clinic. During the 9th session, however, he began to stutter. Over this same time span we also noted an increase in the number of somatic complaints documented in his medical chart. For example Edward reported falling down on a number of occasions and frequently requested medications for a variety of ailments. After a brief staff conference we decided to ignore the stuttering and to continue reinforcing Edward's efforts to improve his voice. The falling behavior was attributed to the fact that Edward's right leg was 1¼ inches shorter than his left. This was treated by building up his right shoe, use of a right leg brace, issuing him a cane, and warning him to be careful. At this point we were pleased that Edward was able to use a normal voice in the clinic but disappointed with his increased number of somatic complaints and the fact he spent most of the time in bed, interacting minimally with other patients and seldom leaving the hospital setting.

Phase 2

The next major step in Edward's treatment program was to begin to reinforce him for behaviors which were incompatible with somatic complaints and inactivity. We decided to praise Edward for increased physical and recreational activity and for socially interacting with other patients. Comments such as "It's good to see you up and about," "I like the way you're keeping up with me" were used routinely. Almost immediately Edward requested that his pain medication be discontinued. He began to move freely about the hospital, to play cards and to socialize with other patients. While he had only one leave of absence during the first 2 weeks of his treatment program he requested and received 11 leaves of absence during the second 2 weeks of his treatment. At the same time we noted a decrease in the number of somatic complaints documented in his medical chart. From the 11th through the 25th treatment sessions Edward continued to use a normal voice in the clinic and also exhibited increased proficiency in his ability to employ this voice outside the treatment setting. He often stated that he would maintain a normal voice when he left the hospital, and finally asked to return home. His treatment was terminated at the end of the 30th session when he was discharged from the hospital.

MAINTENANCE AND FOLLOW-UP

As a portion of a maintenance program, we told Edward that he had improved so markedly that we wanted him to return to our clinic on a periodic basis. We stressed that he should be talking normally when he returned for these checkups since we wanted to make a tape recording of his voice and demonstrate to our students what could be accomplished in a vocal rehabilitation program. We hypothesized that the reinforcement Edward received from these visits would facilitate his continuing to use a normal voice. Also we felt that by having Edward return to the hospital for something positive might minimize the chance of his returning for some somatic complaint. Two months following completion of his treatment program, Edward returned to the clinic speaking normally. He also reported entering a marriage counseling group with his wife and embarking on verbally oriented activities such as using his short wave radio. A 6-month follow-up visit found Edward continuing to speak normally; he was asked to return for another check-up again in six months.

DISCUSSION

This case report illustrates that the speech pathologist using voice and behavior therapy techniques can readily improve the communication of the patient with functional aphonia. Perhaps the primary argument against a speech pathologist treating the functional aphonic has been the fear that removing a symptom may be harmful to the patient. This long standing belief that a patient stripped of his symptom may undergo a conversion has been questioned by psychiatrists (Spiegel, 1967). In our case alleviation of the patient's aphonia resulted in improving his social functioning both in the hospital and at home.

A number of clinicians have reported that a normal voice can be rapidly achieved with functional aphonia cases. Aronson (1969) reported restoring normal or near normal voice in 39 of 40 functional aphonia cases in a single treatment session of about one hour's duration. Interestingly, Edward seemed reluctant to use his normal voice. This may have been due to the reinforcement he received in medical attention for his aphonia and associated problems. At one point during his treatment program Edward actually had the best of two worlds by being reinforced in the clinic for talking normally, and by seeking attention for his somatic ailments on the ward. It was not until he was praised for physical and social activity that his somatic complaints subsided.

Though Edward had been reluctant to become involved in a program of psychotherapy he readily responded to symptomatic voice therapy and the behavioral modification procedures associated with his vocal rehabilitation program. It is possible that the speech pathologist was less threatening to Edward than a laryngologist, psychiatrist or psychologist and afforded him a convenient opportunity to discard his aphonia for a normal voice.

REFERENCES

ARONSON, A. E. Speech pathology and symptom therapy in the interdisciplinary treatment of psychogenic aphonia. *J. Speech Hear. Dis.*, 1969, 34, 321-341.

ARONSON, A. E., PETERSON, H. W., JR., & LITIN, E. M. Voice symptomatology in functional dysphonia and aphonia. *J. Speech Hear. Dis.*, 1964, 29, 367-380.

ARONSON, A. E., PETERSON, H. W., JR., & LITIN, E. M. Psychiatric symptomatology in functional dysphonia and aphonia. *J. Speech Hear. Dis.*, 1966, 31, 115-127.

BABCOCK, M. Speech therapy for certain vocal disorders. *J. Laryngol. Otol.*, 1942, 62, 101-112.

BANGS, J. & FREIDINGER, A. A case of hysterical dysphonia in an adult. *J. Speech Hear. Dis.*, 1950, 15, 316-323.

BARLOW, R. A. A newer concept of functional aphonia. *Trans. Amer. Lar. Assn.*, 1930, 52, 23-34.

BARTON, R. T. The whispering voice syndrome of hysterical aphonia. *Annls. Oto. Rhin. Laryngol.*, 1960, 69, 156-164.

BOONE, D. Treatment of functional aphonia in a child and adult. *J. Speech Hear. Dis.*, 1966, 31, 69-74.

BRODNITZ, F. S. *Vocal Rehabilitation.* American Academy of Ophthalmology and Otolaryngology, 1959.

CLERF, L. F. & BRACELAND, F. J. Functional aphonia. *Annls. Otol. Rhino. Laryngol.*, 1942, 51, 905-915.

CRITCHLEY, M. Spastic dysphonia ("inspiratory speech"), *Brain*, 1939, 62, 96-103.

ELLIS, M. Remarks on dysphonia. *J. Laryngol. Otol.*, 1959, 73, 99-103.

FREUD, E. D. Functions and dysfunctions of the ventricular folds. *J. Speech Hear. Dis.*, 1962, 27, 334-340.

FROSCHELS, E. Method of therapy for paralytic conditions of the mechanism of phonation. *J. Speech Hear. Dis.*, 1955, 20, 365-370.

GRAY, B. F., ENGLAND. G., & MAHONEY, J. Treatment of benign vocal nodules by reciprocal inhibition. *Behav. Res. & Ther.*, 1965, 3, 187-193.

HEAVER, L. Spastic dysphonia II. *Logos*, 1959, 2, 15-24.

JACKSON, C. & JACKSON, C. L. Dysphonia plicae ventricularis: Phonation with ventricular bands. *Arch. Otolar.*, 1935, 21, 157-167.

JACOBSON, E. *Progressive Relaxation.* Chicago: University of Chicago, 1951.

KIML, J. Le classement des aphonics spastiques. *Folia Phoniat.*, 1963, 15, 269-277.

MACMAHON, C. Treatment of functional aphonia. *J. Lar. Otol.*, 1932, 47, 243-246.

SPIEGEL, H. Is symptom removal dangerous? *Amer. J. Psychiat.*, 1967, 123, 1279-1282.

WALTON, D. A. & BLACK, H. The application of modern learning theory to the treatment of aphonia. *J. Psychosom. Res.*, 1959, 3, 303-311.

WILLMORE, L. The role of speech therapy in voice cases. *J. Lar.*, 1959, 73, 104.

WILSON, M. S. Hysterical aphonia. *Amer. J. Psychiat.*, 1962, 119, 80.

WINKELMAN, N. W. Diagnosis and treatment of hysterical aphonia. *Med. Clins. N. Amer.*, 1937, 21, 1211-1220.

WOLSKI, J. & WILEY, J. Functional aphonia in a 14-year-old boy. *J. Speech Hear. Dis.*, 1965, 30, 71-75.

43

ATTEMPTED SUICIDE AS AN OPERANT BEHAVIOR

Tudor Bostock

*Royal Hobart Hospital, Mental Health Services
Commission, Australia*

and

Christopher L. Williams

University of Tasmania, Australia

In the light of the increased incidence of attempted suicide and the stress this imposes on medical resources, alternative approaches to management need to be considered.
Where it can be established that the suicidal behavior has
an operant component, management according to behavioral
principles would appear relevant.
The behavior of a 20-year-old woman who exhibited repeated suicidal behavior was managed within a ward program by means of operant principles. After 27 months of
follow-up, there has been no recurrence for 18 months.

The incidence of suicidal behavior, if not actual suicide, has increased
markedly in recent years (1-3). Analyses of this behavior have made it
clear that suicidal behavior is not a unitary phenomenon. Consequently,

Reprinted with permission from *Archives of General Psychiatry*, Vol. 31, October,
1974, 482-486. Copyright 1974, American Medical Association.
Prof. J. D. Frank, Prof. M. Rosenbaum, and Prof. A. S. Henderson aided in this
study.

the management of the suicidal individual may involve several treatment methods, each concerned with a different aspect of the presenting behavior. We wish to focus on one aspect of suicidal behavior, and indicate what we consider appropriate management.

In the light of the rapid growth of the principles and procedures of behavior modification, it is surprising that such scant attention has been paid to the problem of suicidal behavior. A behavioral formulation has also been attempted recently (4). Arriving at this, there appears to be concordance of opinion among workers who focus on the consequences of suicidal behavior. Where the suicidal behavior apparently serves the purpose of generating an active response from the environment, a low rating of intent has been inferred (5). High ratings of intent have correlated significantly with depth of depression (6). Similarly, where suicidal behavior provokes desired effects (defined as the patient's efforts to affect modifications in the attitudes or a change in his relationships with persons important to him through making a suicide attempt) (7), the severity of the suicidal behavior in terms of self-damage tends to be minimal. Conversely, suicidal behavior where no desired effect is evident is relatively severe, with a high probability that death is intended (8, 9). It is considered that those patients who manipulate by means of suicidal behavior are prone to make future attempts because they discover the power that this class of behavior commands in social maneuvers (10, 11).

The unwitting reinforcement of abnormal symptomatic behavior has been well documented (12). It appears that some classes of suicidal behavior are maintained by unwitting reinforcement from environmental contingencies. As part of the environment a therapist is in an invidious position, since often he may be provoked to respond inappropriately. Some go so far as to speculate on the possibility that some types of suicide prevention services may specifically reinforce suicidal behavior since such behavior gains entry to the care-giving system (4).

Suicidal behavior almost invariably invokes a response from the environment, and it has been pointed out that theoretically any response may reinforce the behavior. Since the behavior is aversive to others, it may evoke negative responses that could also serve as positive reinforcement. Similarly, positive responses such as care, concern, and attention from significant others may be likely to increase the probability that similar behavior will recur. However, whereas care, concern, and attention are appropriate responses to people in distress, they are appropriate for this reason alone and not because the distress is communicated by suicidal behavior. This distinction is pertinent, but often not made by the patient because the responses are contiguous in time with the suicidal behavior. The patient then learns that his inappropriate behavior elicits certain consequences from his environment. Therapy then demands that the patient learn new behavior, a new set of response contingencies, and appropriate behaviors that will elicit caring responses from his environment.

Behavior that is specified in terms of its consequences is defined as operant (13). The consequent interpersonal manipulations following suicidal behavior are seen in some instances as the reinforcing consequences that maintain this particular behavior. We propose that a large proportion of suicidal behavior takes this form, and the prevalence of this behavior may be increased by traditional intervention procedures and the immediate response of the environment.

Operant conditioning principles have been employed successfully in the modification of a diverse range of clinical problems, including many deviant social behaviors (14-16). While many of these studies lack replicative control features, they consistently report favorable outcomes. The present communication describes a case of repeated suicidal behavior that was identified as generating an active response from important people in the patient's environment, and that appeared to represent an attempt to effect a change in their attitude and behavior toward the patient. The suicidal behavior was modified by operant shaping within a ward program, both by extinction of the inappropriate behavior and by the introduction of response-contingent rewards for adaptive and coping behavior. In association with this, individual therapy was conducted by a combined behavioral and dynamic approach involving two therapists. The two therapists were in close collaboration, as they were with the nursing staff who were responsible for the ward program.

REPORT OF A CASE

The patient was a 20-year-old single woman, a university student, the eldest child of a medical practitioner. From the age of 9 she became overly involved in her parents' problems. Their marriage broke in her early teens when her mother left the home. She had considerable anger toward her father, who never took sufficient notice of her, and toward her mother, who was lacking in adequate affection. As a child she was witness to her mother's uncontrolled emotions, and to her mother's dramatic episodes of attempted suicide. Her mother received psychiatric treatment over an extended period. She remarried in 1968, but has no

878 ANNUAL REVIEW OF BEHAVIOR THERAPY

other children. Her father remarried in April 1970, a much younger woman, aged 24. This woman was introduced to the home where her father was living with the children of his first marriage. Their first child was born in February 1971.

As a schoolgirl the patient was exceptional. She entered a university in 1968, where she did well in her first year, but less well in her second. In 1970 she failed to complete the university year.

In 1969, at a time when her father was courting his new wife, the patient became involved in a heterosexual relationship. This relationship came to an end in April 1970, at the time when the father remarried.

Initial Presentation

The first episode of self-poisoning occurred in April 1970. The patient took tablets after she had attended a birthday party. She did not awaken until the next night, when she took more tablets and phoned home 120 miles away. Shortly, friends were on her doorstep.

The second episode occurred the night before the start of the second term of 1970. She had been home during the vacation, had felt very restless, and had been angry with her father. Again she rallied to the concern of friends. In May 1970 she was referred to a psychiatrist whom she saw once or twice weekly for two months before breaking off therapy. She dropped out of the university and drifted between states in an aimless existence. To control her feelings of tension and discomfort she relied on medications, both prescribed and proprietary.

She returned home for Christmas 1970, a period that was distinguished by a loss of affective tone and responsivity. Feeling lonely, she first cut her wrist in January 1971, the day another friend got married.

In February 1971 her stepbrother was born. Two weeks later she returned to the university. She sought much reassurance from her colleagues and peers. The weekend before classes started she cut her wrist twice, on successive days. She went to the general hospital and was referred to her previous psychiatrist. She cut her wrist again, and was admitted to hospital on March 10, 1971.

First Hospitalization

She was admitted to the psychiatric unit of a general hospital. This unit functions as a therapeutic community, with the expectation that all patients will behave normally and appropriately. She was looked after by a senior resident medical officer. Eight days after admission, when all the other patients were at a social function, she was found deeply unconscious on her bed after further self-poisoning. After resuscitation she was returned to the ward where she was welcomed by large sheaths of flowers and the display of much concern. Her mother visited from another state. Two weeks later she told a student-nurse that she was going to shave her legs, and half-an-hour later the nurse found she had cut her wrist.

She was discharged the next day to return to the university. Contact with the senior resident was maintained, seeing him thrice weekly. The senior resident was attempting "relationship therapy" within a time limit defined at the outset. In their relationship concentration was on the expression of feelings. Her behavior was demanding, provocative, and seductive. No medication was used. Preparation for separation commenced well before the event. During this period she cut her wrist and took a minor overdose of tablets in one episode, precipitating a brief overnight admission to hospital. She was in receipt of much concern from her peers.

As separation became imminent she became increasingly miserable, indecisive, and care-seeking. Plans were laid for her transfer to another doctor. On the day of separation she cut her wrist more severely, without damage to deep structures but requiring sutures. She was readmitted on May 7, 1971, and came into the care of one of us.

Second Hospitalization

The patient had repeated suicidal behavior (Figure 1). It was formulated that the patient had learned two maladaptive behaviors for coping with her feelings and tensions. It appeared that she responded to depressive feelings predominantly by self-poisoning, and to states of tension by superficial wrist-cutting. Both behaviors were associated with considerable attention-getting. Furthermore, wrist-cutting was apparently self-reinforcing in that it was associated with considerable release from tension.

The treatment program was defined during the first week of admission. Initially the patient was allowed considerable freedom of movement; her father visited from another part of the state; she telephoned her mother interstate. She was seen by the psychiatrist twice weekly at specified times, where the main emphasis was on appropriate verbalizations and the treatment alliance. She was seen by the behavior therapist three times weekly, for relaxation training and systematic desensitization of fears related to rejection. The nursing staff were involved in the operant

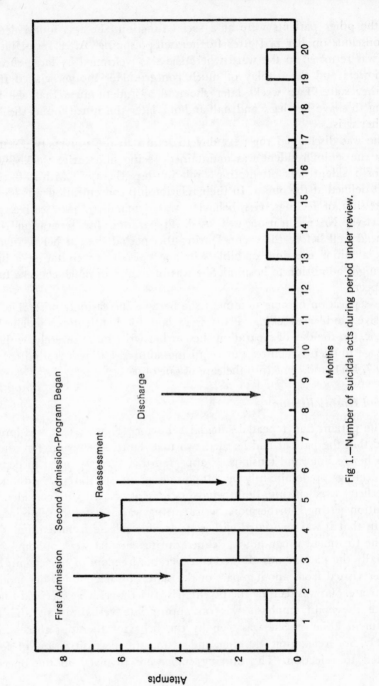

Fig 1.—Number of suicidal acts during period under review.

shaping of behavior within a ward program: initially by the nonreinforcement of attention-seeking behaviors by the withdrawal of attention. Detailed records were kept of daily progress, including the occurrence of maladaptive behavior and the response of the staff. Behavior termed maladaptive included suicidal acts, verbalizations concerning suicide, and clear-cut attention-seeking behavior. Figure 2 presents the frequency of maladaptive behavior during the treatment program.

The response to this was an increase in the frequency and intensity of attention-seeking and demanding behaviors, which became apparent approximately one week following the institution of the program. She ostentatiously handed in razor blades and pieces of glass. She went out drinking. When her demands were not met she became angry and went on a five-day fast. She cut her wrist repeatedly, even though it now did not bring any relief of tension. She threatened to jump from the ninth floor of the building, thereupon demanding to see a doctor. (She was sedated with intramuscular chlorpromazine hydrochloride.) She constantly demanded to see her two therapists, despite the clearly defined program. She expressed marked aggression and hostility toward the psychiatrist. She was anxious, cold, and demanding in her behavior toward the nursing staff. She again threatened to jump, and cut three times in two days.

The ward staff were exhorted to continue with their consistent management, ignoring maladaptive behavior, and rewarding any appropriate behavior. In particular this entailed the withdrawal of reinforcement of wrist-cutting and other attention-seeking behaviors. When she cut her wrist, it was inspected by a senior nurse, dressed, and then ignored as far as was practicable. She responded by verbal attention-seeking, making statements about her great desires to cut, meanwhile assiduously practicing her relaxation exercises.

One week later she cut her wrist more severely and then demanded her discharge. She telephoned her father who visited the next day. Her father was initially uncertain, but in a joint interview backed the psychiatrist when he stated emphatically that he would have no hesitation in certifying the patient under the Mental Health Act if she insisted on being discharged in her dangerous mood. She appeared stunned by this information, but retired to bed early after doing her relaxation exercises.

The next week the patient started attending the university again. On her request she was given weekend leave and her discharge was entertained.

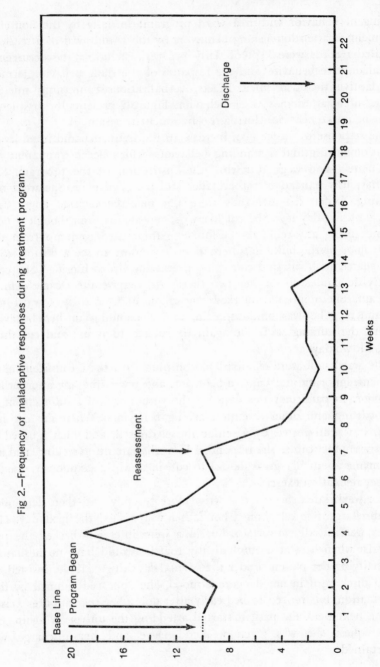

Fig 2.—Frequency of maladaptive responses during treatment program.

She felt frustrated and unhappy at what she felt to be the enormity of the demands made on her and the expectation that she control herself and accept full responsibility for her own behavior both on the ward and in the university environment. She had by now made no suicidal gestures for two weeks. On weekend leave she was asked to demonstrate that she could cope further with the outside world so that her discharge could be expedited. That weekend she cut her wrist again.

Before her next appointment with the psychiatrist, other personnel were communicating to him their concern. The patient was communicating to them with great intensity and conviction that she was going to kill herself. In interview she repeated her argument in unanswerable fashion.

Reassessment

It was formulated that the suicidal behaviors had been partially extinguished. Following the withdrawal of social attention there had been an escalation of attention-seeking behavior, followed by a diminution (Figure 2). Wrist-cutting was no longer associated with relief from tension, and continued at a diminished rate. Yet whether these behaviors would follow an extinction curve only the further elapse of time would tell. At that time the patient was ignoring all our rewards for her achievements, and emitting no further behaviors that were adaptive and could be reinforced.

It was decided to continue the ward program but that stricter environmental control was desirable: in order to control the present crisis, to exclude inappropriate reinforcement, and to facilitate more efficient reinforcement of adaptive behavior. The patient was told to go to her room, where she was voluntarily confined. The room was stripped bare of all furniture and fittings except a bed and bed clothes. She was allowed out of her room for toilet privileges only. A nurse sat outside her door, which was kept shut. The nurse's main function was to observe the patient throughout the day and record her observations.

The behavior therapist continued his previously planned course of treatment, seeing her three times weekly. The psychiatrist saw the patient daily, carefully shaping her verbal behavior. Also tangible rewards were dispensed daily immediately following the interview with the psychiatrist, after consultation with the behavior therapist. The tangible rewards were the return of personal possessions and normal privileges.

Period of Confinement

The reinforcement schedule proved to be comparatively straightforward and behavior gains were consolidated by an intermittent schedule. Each day she produced about 20 minutes of appropriate verbalization. Considered appropriate were those verbalizations about feelings, their appropriate expression and adequate control, and these were reinforced by therapist attention. Verbalizations of symptoms were discouraged by the withdrawal of therapist attention. Immediately after the interview she received her tangible reward, variously a bath, a clean nightdress, or cigarettes with meals. The rewards were graded according to their perceived value to the patient. Contingent on her increased appropriate social behavior, from the sixth day she was progressively allowed increasing periods of time in the day-ward in the company of other patients. From the 16th day she had progressed to spending the major part of the day in the day-ward, dressed in her own clothes; except for two periods (10:30 a.m. to 12:30 p.m. and 2 p.m. to 4 p.m.) in her own room under her own sanctions. These periods were used for practicing her desensitization program and thinking. She was still not allowed makeup, perfumes, or deodorants.

Further Progress in the Hospital

With the return to living predominantly on the day-ward, less control could be exerted over environmental contingencies, but increased concern was given to the shaping of her social behavior by rewarding the appropriate behavior that was now replacing previous undesirable responses. The patient was allowed weekend leave. She made progress, but more slowly. With the return to the realities of life on the ward, the psychiatrist reverted to seeing her twice weekly.

One month later the patient cut her wrist again, and she was confined to her room under her own sanctions for a further six days. She was allowed to the day-ward progressively from the third day. While confined she was again seen daily by the psychiatrist.

She then worked determinedly to win leave from the hospital to celebrate her 21st birthday at home with her family. In order to facilitate generalization of adaptive behaviors learned on the ward, she was allowed graded exposure to problem situations, both real and imagined. Contingent on her continued progress she was granted leave for ten days, and her makeup returned. She coped with this period well, and then set her sights on discharge from the hospital in a further month's time.

The psychiatrist contracted to see her weekly following discharge, as separately did the behavior therapist. She was discharged on October 1, 1971.

OUTPATIENT FOLLOW-UP

The patient demonstrated exquisite sensitivity to rejection experiences, both real and imagined. The paradigm was in her relationship with both her parents, which she transferred to all important later relationships. She transferred identical feelings to her therapist and to ward staff, constituting a major resistance to treatment. As an outpatient she was seen at weekly intervals by both therapists. At all times she had a firm treatment contract with each therapist, and with both a strong relationship.

Despite the intensity of the treatment program, there were three further episodes of suicidal behavior, which were in response to perceived rejection by important others. However, these episodes were all minor, of a different quality, and quite lacking in their previous intensity. The first two episodes occurred relatively soon after discharge, and involved very superficial cutting. The third occurred in July 1972, and involved minor self-poisoning that did not require medical treatment. Early in 1973, in response to a further rejection experience, suicidal behavior was covertly threatened but not acted on.

To an increasing degree she has been coping well socially and academically. She completed her university degree in 1972, achieving excellent grades. She completed an honors course in 1973. In her social relationships she behaves more assertively and exhibits a broader repertoire of skills. In individual therapy she relates more openly and warmly. She has a higher threshold to rejection experiences.

For 18 months there has been no suicidal behavior. The patient is no longer receiving active treatment.

COMMENT

Clearly many other things were happening in therapy and in relationships with this young woman than have been recounted here, and in no sense would we wish to discount these. Therapy has many components, and the present case has a large operant component that is the one here recorded. What we wish to point out is that, all else apart, where it can be established that a behavior is an operant maintained by environmental contingencies, behavioral principles afford a coherent rationale, and consistent management by all concerned according to such principles yields an apparently successful outcome.

Our behavioral formulation recognized that the attention of the psychiatrist, in particular, was a potent reinforcer. Similarly, we recognized that the social attention provided by hospitalization may unwittingly reinforce much undesirable behavior. In both situations, of individual therapy and ward program, great care was exercised to make explicit just what behavior was being rewarded, with the provision of continual feedback to the patient about her performance. From the beginning of therapy attention was repeatedly paid to the treatment alliance and what might be reasonable expectations for the patient to hold of therapy. Because we perceived the patient to be in receipt of so much inappropriate social reinforcement, initial therapy tended to concentrate on the withdrawal of social attention and not responding to maladaptive behavior. Nevertheless at a climax of their interaction the psychiatrist was provoked to respond with the threat of commitment. It is of considerable interest that the patient perceived all our maneuvers as indexes of the extent to which we cared for her.

It must be clear that the psychiatric problem of this young patient would most frequently be defined as "hysterical personality disorder." Other conceptualizations aiding the understanding and treatment of such behavior would similarly emphasize the necessity of withstanding the patient's infantile rage and anger, of repudiating anticipated and provoked rejection, and continuing to offer appropriate help and new solutions to problems and conflicts. However, it would appear that a behavioral conceptualization most parsimoniously encompasses the observable data, and is communicated most readily as a rationale for treatment.

The implementation of a ward program requires appropriately trained staff, clear communication among all members of the treatment team, and adequate control over the reinforcers operating in the environment. The importance of accurate assessment of what are extraordinarily complex behaviors cannot be overemphasized (17). During a behavioral assessment, the target behaviors requiring change are specifically delineated in terms of their frequency, duration, intensity, and their antecedent and consequent events. Further explication of the reinforcers maintaining the target behavior, and identification of positive reinforcers that can be used to reward adaptive and coping behavior are essential. A process of continuous assessment allows monitoring of the efficacy of the treatment program and the constant readjustment of the reinforcement schedule.

An important question to ask of any therapeutic technique is how much it costs in relation to the benefit it provides. The present study was expensive in both staffing and therapeutic time. Our justification is that, apart from the interest it afforded the major therapists, it appeared to indicate a more general technique. Foster appears to demonstrate that an operant technique may eventually prove more efficient than traditional intervention procedures (18).

Most psychiatric treatment techniques are intensely verbal and presuppose the patient's ability to transform his "symptoms" into appropriate verbalizations. It is our experience that many patients appear unable to do this, and we would argue the need for nonverbal treatment techniques in some of these instances. Even when it is conceptualized that suicidal behavior has a large communicational component, it seems to us important to control to a significant degree the aberrant behavior by behavioral means before placing too great reliance on verbalizations.

A case study and a treatment technique are described following these aims. Contemporaneously with the management designed to bring under control the suicidal behavior, other more verbal techniques focused on other problems and difficulties experienced by the patient, with a view to their alleviation.

REFERENCES

1. AITKEN, R. C. B., BUGLASS, D., & KREITMAN, N. The changing patterns of attempted suicide in Edinburgh, 1962-67. *Brit. J. Prev. Soc. Med.*, 1969, 23, 111-116.
2. HETZEL, B. S. The epidemiology of suicidal behavior in Australia. *Aust. N.Z. J. Psychiat.*, 1971, 5, 156-166.
3. OLIVER, R. G., ET AL. The epidemiology of attempted suicide as seen in the casualty department, Alfred Hospital, Melbourne. *Med. J. Aust.*, 1971, 1, 833-839.
4. FREDERICK, C. J. & RESNICK, H. L. P. How suicidal behaviors are learned. *Amer. J. Psychother.*, 1971, 25, 37-55.
5. HENDIN, H. Attempted suicide: A psychiatric and statistical study. *Psychiat. Q.*, 1950, 24, 39-46.
6. SILVER, M. A., ET AL. Relation of depression to attempted suicide and seriousness of intent. *Arch. Gen. Psychiat.*, 1971, 25, 573-576.
7. RUBENSTEIN, R., MOSES, B., & LIDZ, T. On attempted suicide. *Arch. Neurol. Psychiat.*, 1958, 79, 103-112.
8. DORPAT, T. L. & BOSWELL, J. W. An evaluation of suicidal intent in suicide attempts. *Compr. Psychiat.*, 1963, 4, 114-125.
9. GLASER, K. Attempted suicide in children and adolescents: Psychodynamic observations. *Amer. J. Psychother.*, 1965, 19, 220-228.
10. SIFNEOS, P. E. Manipulative suicide. *Psychiat. Q.*, 1966, 40, 525-537.
11. FAWCETT, J., LEFF, M., & BUNNEY, W. B.: Suicide clues from interpersonal communication. *Arch. Gen. Psychiat.*, 1969, 21, 129-137.

12. AYLLON, T. & MICHAEL, J. The psychiatric nurse as a behavioral engineer. *J. Exp. Anal. Behav.*, 1959, 2, 323-334.
13. SKINNER, B. F. *The Behavior of Organisms: An Experimental Analysis.* New York: Appleton-Century-Crofts, Inc., 1938.
14. HALL, R. V., LUND, D., & JACKSON, D. Effects of teacher attention on study behavior. *J. Appl. Behav. Anal.*, 1968, 1, 1-12.
15. MARKS, I. M., CAMERON, P. M., & SILBERFELD, M. Operant therapy for an abnormal personality. *Brit. Med. J.*, 1971, 1, 647-648.
16. MILBY, J. M. Modification of extreme social isolation by contingent social reinforcement. *J. Appl. Behav. Anal.*, 1970, 3, 149-152.
17. KANFER, F. H. & SASLOW, G. Behavioral diagnosis. In C. M. Franks (Ed.), *Behavior Therapy: Appraisal and Status.* New York: McGraw-Hill Book Co., 1969.
18. FOSTER, J .The economics of behavior modification programs. Read before the Annual Meeting of the American Psychological Association, Washington, D. C., September 1969.

REFERENCES TO EDITORS' COMMENTARIES

AGRAS, W. S., BARLOW, T. H., CHAPIN, H. N., ABEL, G. G., & LEITENBERG, H. Behavior modification of anorexia nervosa. *Archives of General Psychiatry*, 1974, 30, 279-286.

AINSLIE, G. Specious reward: A behavioral theory of impulsiveness and impulse control. *Psychological Bulletin*, 1975, 87, 463-496.

ALABISO, F. Operant control of attention behavior: A treatment for hyperactivity. *Behavior Therapy*, 1975, 6, 39-43.

ALEXANDER, J. F. & PARSONS, B. V. Short-term behavioral intervention with delinquent families: Impact on family process and recidivism. *Journal of Abnormal Psychology*, 1973, 81, 219-225.

American Psychological Association. Committee on Ethical Standards in Psychological Research. *Ethical Principles in the Conduct of Research with Human Participants*. Washington, D. C., 1973.

ANNON, J. S. The Therapeutic Use of Masturbation in the Treatment of Sexual Disorders. Paper presented at the Annual Meeting of the Association for Advancement of Behavior Therapy, Washington, D. C., 1971.

ANNON, J. S. *The Behavioral Treatment of Sexual Problems, Volume I, Brief Therapy*. Honolulu: Enabling Systems, 1975.

ANNON, J. S. *The Behavioral Treatment of Sexual Problems, Volume II, Techniques*. Honolulu: Enabling Systems, 1976.

ANNON, J. S. & ROBINSON, C. H. The Use of Vicarious Learning in the Treatment of Sexual Concerns. Paper presented at the annual meeting of the American Psychological Association, Chicago, September, 1975.

ARAGONA, J., CASSADY, J., & DRABMAN, R. Treating overweight children through parental training and contingency contracting. *Journal of Applied Behavior Analysis*, 1975, 8, 269-278.

ARGYRIS, C. Dangers in applying results from experimental social psychology. *American Psychologist*, 1975, 30, 469-485.

ARMOR, D. J., POLICH, J. M., & STAMBUL, H. B. *Alcoholism and Treatment*. Santa Monica, Cal.: The Rand Corporation, 1976.

ASHER, J. Sociobiology: Behavior from a gene's point of view. *APA Monitor*, 1975, 6, Dec., 4-5.

ATTHOWE, J. M., JR. Controlling nocturnal enuresis in severely disabled and chronic patients. *Behavior Therapy*, 1972, 3, 232-239.

ATTHOWE, J. M. Token economies come of age. *Behavior Therapy*, 1973, 4, 646-654.

ATTHOWE, J. M. Legal and ethical accountability in everyday practice. *Behavioral Engineering*, 1975, 3, 35-38.

AXELROD, S. Comparison of individual and group contingencies in two special classes. *Behavior Therapy*, 1973, 4, 83-90.

AYERS, S. K. B., POTTER, R. E., & McDEARMON, J. R. Using reinforcement therapy and precision teaching techniques with adult aphasics. *Journal of Behavior Therapy and Experimental Psychiatry*, 1975, 6, 301-305.

AYLLON, T. & ROBERTS, M. Eliminating discipline problems by strengthening academic performance. *Journal of Applied Behavior Analysis*, 1974, 7, 71-76.

AZRIN, N. H., & FOXX, R. M. A rapid method of toilet training the institutionalized retarded. *Journal of Applied Behavior Analysis*, 1971, 4, 147-156.

AZRIN, N. H. & WESOLOWSKI, M. D. The use of positive practice to eliminate persistent floor sprawling by profoundly retarded persons. *Behavior Therapy*, 1975, 6, 627-631.

AZRIN, N. W. & WESOLOWSKI, M. D. Theft reversal: An analysis of the effects on students and teacher. *Journal of Applied Behavior Analysis*, 1974, 7, 577-582.

BACHMAN, J. A. Self-injurious behavior: A behavioral analysis. *Journal of Abnormal Psychology*, 1972, 80, 211-224.

BAER, D. M., WOLF, M. M., & RISLEY, T. R. Some current dimensions of applied behavior analysis. *Journal of Applied Behavior Analysis*, 1968, 1, 91-97.

BAKER, S. B., HOFFMAN, A. M., & SHUTE, R. E. Weight loss through variations in the coverant control paradigm. *Journal of Consulting and Clinical Psychology*, 1975, 43, 68-72.

BALCH, P. & ROSS, A. W. Predicting success in weight reduction as a function of locus of control: A unidimensional and multidimensional approach. *Journal of Consulting and Clinical Psychology*, 1975, 43, 119.

BALCH, P. & ROSS, A. W. A behaviorally oriented didactic-group treatment of obesity: An exploratory study. *Journal of Behavior Therapy and Experimental Psychiatry*, 1974, 5, 239-243.

BANCROFT, J. H. *Deviant Sexual Behavior*. Oxford: Oxford University Press, 1974.

BANDER, K. W., STEINKE, G. V., ALLEN, G. J., & MOSHER, D. L. Evaluation of three dating-specific treatment approaches for heterosexual dating anxiety. *Journal of Consulting and Clinical Psychology*, 1975, 43, 259-265.

BANDURA, A. Self-reinforcement: Theoretical and methodological considerations. *Behaviorism*, 1976, in press.

BANDURA, A. *Principles of Behavior Modification*. New York: Holt, Rinehart and Winston, 1969.

BANDURA, A. Psychotherapy based on modeling principles. In A. E. Bergin & S. L. Garfield (Eds.), *Handbook of Psychotherapy and Behavior Change*. New York: Wiley, 1971. Pp. 653-708.

BANDURA, A. The ethics and social purposes of behavior modification. In C. M. Franks & G. T. Wilson (Eds.), *Annual Review of Behavior Therapy: Theory and Practice*, Vol. III. New York: Brunner/Mazel, 1975. Pp. 13-20.

BANDURA, A. & BARAB, P. G. Processes governing disinhibitory effects through symbolic modeling. *Journal of Abnormal Psychology*, 1973, 82, 1-9.

BANDURA, A., MAHONEY, M. J., & DIRKS, S. J. Discriminative activation and maintenance of contingent self-reinforcement. *Behaviour Research and Therapy*, 1976, 4, 1-6.

BARKER, R. G. *Ecological Psychology: Concepts and Methods for Studying the Environment of Human Behavior*. Stanford, Cal.: Stanford University Press, 1968.

BARLOW, D. H., AGRAS, W. S., ABEL, G. G., BLANCHARD, E. B., & YOUNG, L. D. Biofeedback and reinforcement to increase heterosexual arousal in homosexuals. *Behaviour Research and Therapy*, 1975, 13, 45-50.

BARLOW, D. H. & HERSEN, M. Single case experimental designs. *Archives of General Psychiatry*, 1973, 29, 319-325.

BARRON, F. H. Behavioral decision theory: A topical bibliography for management scientists. *Interfaces, The Bulletin of the Institute of Management Sciences*, 1974, 5, 50-62.

BASSIN, A. Red, white and blue poker chips: An AA behavior modification technique. *American Psychologist*, 1975, 30, 695-696.

BECKER, H. G. & COSTELLO, C. G. Effects of graduated exposure with feedback of exposure times on snake phobias. *Journal of Consulting and Clinical Psychology*, 1975, 43, 478-484.

BEECH, H. R. *Obsessional States*. London: Methuen, 1974.

BELLACK, A. S. Behavior therapy for weight reduction. *Addictive Behaviors*, 1975, 1, 73-82.

BELLACK, A. S. & HERSEN, M. Use of self-reports inventories in behavioral assessment. In J. D. Cone & R. P. Hawkins (Eds.) *Behavioral Assessment: New Directions in Clinical Psychology.* New York: Brunner/Mazel (in press).

BELLACK, A. S., SCHWARTZ, J., & ROZENSKY, R. H. The contribution of external control to self-control in a weight reduction program. *Journal of Behavior Therapy and Experimental Psychiatry*, 1974, 5, 245-249.

BEM, D. J. Constructing cross-situational consistencies in behavior: Some thoughts on Alker's critique of Mischel. *Journal of Personality*, 1972, 40, 17-26.

BEM, D. J. & ALLEN, A. On predicting some of the people some of the time: The search for cross-situational consistencies. *Psychological Review*, 1974, 81, 506-519.

BERGIN, A. E. The evaluation of therapeutic outcomes. In A. E. Bergin & S. L. Garfield (Eds.) *Handbook of Psychotherapy and Behavior Change.* New York: Wiley, 1971. Pp. 217-270.

BERLYNE, D. E. Behaviourism? Cognitive theory? Humanistic Psychology?—To Hull with them all! *Canadian Psychological Review*, 1975, 16, 69-80.

BERNSTEIN, D. Modification of smoking behavior: An evaluative review. *Psychological Bulletin*, 1969, 71, 418-440.

BERNSTEIN, D. A. & BORKOVEC, T. D. *Progressive Relaxation Training.* Champaign, Ill.: Research Press, 1973.

BERNSTEIN, D. A. & PAUL, G. L. Some comments on therapy analogue research with small animal "phobias." *Journal of Behavior Therapy and Experimental Psychiatry*, 1971, 2, 225-237.

BERNSTEIN, P. H. & HAMILTON, S. B. Token rewards and straw men. *American Psychologist*, 1975, 7, 780-781.

BERNSTEIN, T. Electrical safety in aversive conditioning of humans. *Behavioral Engineering*, 1975, 2, 31-34.

BERSOFF, D. N. Silk purses into sow's ears: The decline of psychological testing and the suggestion for its redemption. *American Psychologist*, 1973, 28, 892-899.

Biofeedback therapy with electronic teaching aids. *Patient Care, August* 1, 1975, 1-16.

BIRCHLER, G. R., WEISS, R. L., & VINCENT, J. P. Multimethod analysis of social reinforcement exchange between maritally distressed spouse and stranger dyads. *Journal of Personality and Social Psychology*, 1975, 31, 349-360.

BIRK, L. *Biofeedback: Behavioral Medicine.* New York: Grune and Stratton, 1973.

BIRNBRAUER, J. S., PETERSON, C. R., & SOLNICK, J. V. Design and interpretation of studies of single subjects. *American Journal of Mental Deficiency*, 1974, 79, 191-203.

BLAKE, B. G. The application of behavior therapy to the treatment of alcoholism. *Behaviour Research and Therapy*, 1965, 3, 75-85.

BLANCHARD, E. B. The relative contributions of modeling, information influences, and physical contact in the extinction of phobic behavior. *Journal of Abnormal Psychology*, 1970, 76, 55-61.

BLANCHARD, E. B. & HAYNES, M. R. Biofeedback treatment of a case of Raynaud's disease. *Journal of Behavior Therapy and Experimental Psychiatry*, 1975, 6, 230-234.

BLANCHARD, E. B., YOUNG, L. D., & HAYNES, M. R. A simple feedback system for the treatment of elevated blood pressure. *Behavior Therapy*, 1975, 6, 241-245.

BLECHMAN,-BECK, E. A. Objectives and procedures believed necessary for the success of a contractual approach for family intervention. *Behavior Therapy*, 1976, 7, in press.

BLECHMAN, E. A., OLSON, D. H. L., & HELLMAN, I. D. Stimulus control over family problem-solving behavior. *Behavior Therapy*, 1976, 7, in press.

BLOM, B. E. & CRAIGHEAD, W. E. The effects of situational and instructional demand on indices of speech anxiety. *Journal of Abnormal Psychology*, 1974, 83, 667-674.

BLOOD, M. R. Spin-offs from behavioral expectation scale procedures. *Journal of Applied Psychology*, 1974, 59, 513-515.

BODNER, S. E. The role of assessment in assertion training. *The Counseling Psychologist*, 1975, 5, 90-96.

BONEAU, C. A. Paradigm regained? Cognitive behaviorism restated. *American Psychologist*, 1974, 29, 297-309.

BORKOVEC, T. D. Effects of expectancy on the outcome of systematic desensitization and implosive treatments for analogue anxiety. *Behavior Therapy*, 1972, 3, 29-40.

BORKOVEC, T. D. The role of expectancy and physiological feedback in fear research: A review with special relevance to subject characteristics. *Behavior Therapy*, 1973, 4, 491-505.

BORKOVEC, T. D. Heart-rate process during systematic desensitization and implosive therapy for analogue anxiety. *Behavior Therapy*, 1974, 5, 636-641.

BORKOVEC, T. D. Cognitive Extensions of Two-Factor Theory. Paper presented at the 9th annual meeting of the Association for Advancement of Behavior Therapy, San Francisco, December, 1975.

BORKOVEC, T. D., KALOUPEK, D. G., & SLAMA, K. The facilitative effect of muscle-tension release in the relaxation treatment of sleep disturbance. *Behavior Therapy*, 1975, 6, 301-309.

BORKOVEC, T. D. & NAU, S. D. Credibility of analogue therapy rationales. *Journal of Behavior Therapy and Experimental Psychiatry*, 1972, 3, 257-260.

BOSTOCK, T. & WILLIAMS, C. L. Attempted suicide: An operant formulation. *Australian and Zealand Journal of Psychiatry*, 1975, 9, 107-110.

BOUDEWYNS, P. A. Implosive therapy and desensitization therapy with inpatients: A five-year follow-up. *Journal of Abnormal Psychology*, 1975, 84, 159-160.

BOWERS, K. S. Situationalism in psychology: An analysis and a critique. *Psychological Review*, 1973, 80, 307-336.

BRANDEIS, R. & LUBOR, R. E. Conditioning without awareness—again. *Bulletin of the Psychonomic Society*, 1975, 5, 36-38.

BRAUKMANN, C. J. & FIXSEN, D. L. Behavior modification with delinquents. In R. M. Eisler and P. M. Miller (Eds.) *Progress in Behavior Modification, Volume I.* New York: Academic Press, 1975.

BRAUKMANN, C. J., FIXSEN, D. L., PHILLIPS, E. L., & WOLF, M. M. Behavioral approaches to treatment in the crime and delinquency field. *Criminology*, 1975, 13, 299-331.

BRAUN, S. H. Ethical issues in behavior modification. *Behavior Therapy*, 1975, 6, 51-62.

BRENTON, M. Profile of a sex and marriage clinic. *Sexual Behavior*, 1972, 2, 28-32.

BREWER, W. F. There is no convincing evidence for operant or classical conditioning in adult humans. In W. E. Werner & D. S. Palermo (Eds.) *Cognition and the Symbolic Process.* Hillsdale, N. J.: Lawrence Erlbaum Associates, 1974.

BRIDDELL, D. W. & NATHAN, P. E. Behavior assessment and modification with alcoholics: Current status and future trends. In M. Hersen, R. M. Eisler & P. M. Miller (Eds.) *Progress in Behavior Modification, Vol. 2.* New York: Academic Press, 1976.

BROOK, P., DEGUN, G., & MATHER, M. Reality orientation, a therapy for psychogeriatric patients: A controlled study. *British Journal of Psychiatry*, 1975, 127, 42-45.

BROWN, H. H. Role of expectancy manipulation in systematic desensitization. *Journal of Consulting and Clinical Psychology*, 1973, 41, 405-411.

BROWN, P. Paper presented at the Second Annual Conference of Behavior Therapy, Wexford, Ireland, 1972.

BROWN, R. A. & WILLIAMS, R. J. Internal and external cues relating to fluid intake in obese and alcoholic persons. *Journal of Abnormal Psychology*, 1975, 84, 666-672.

BURCHARD, J. D., HARIG, P. T., MILLER, R. B., & ARMOUR, J. New strategies in community-based intervention. In E. Ribes-Inesta & A. Bandura (Eds.) *Analysis of*

Delinquency and Aggression. Hillsdale, N. J.: Lawrence Erlbaum Associates, 1976.

BURT, D. W. A behaviorist looks at A.A. *Addictions,* 1975, 22, 56-69.

BUSHNELL, D., WROBEL, P. A., & MICHAELIS, M. L. Applying "group" contingencies to classroom study behavior of pre-school children. *Journal of Applied Behavior Analysis,* 1968, 1, 55-61.

BUTTERFIELD, W. H. Electric shock-safety factors when used for the aversive conditioning of humans. *Behavior Therapy,* 1975a, 6, 98-110.

BUTTERFIELD, W. H. Electric shock-hazards in aversive shock conditioning of humans. *Behavioral Engineering,* 1975b, 3, 1-28.

BYKOV, K. M. *The Cerebral Cortex and the Internal Organs.* New York: Chemical Publishing Co., 1957.

CANTELE, J. R. & UPPER, D. The process of individual behavior therapy. In M. Hersen, R. M. Eisler, & P. M. Miller (Eds.) *Progress in Behavior Modification, Vol. 1.* New York: Academic Press, 1975.

CAPLAN, A. Ethics, evolution and the milk of human kindness: A review of the reviews of E. J. Wilson's "Sociobiology." *The Hastings Center Report,* 1976, 6, 20-25.

CARLSON, C. G., HERSEN, M., & EISLER, R. M. Token economy programs in the treatment of hospitalized adult psychiatric patients. *Journal of Nervous and Mental Disease,* 1972, 155, 192-204.

CARPENTER, A. & ARMENTI, N. Some effects of ethanol on human sexual and aggressive behavior. In B. Kissin & H. Begleiter (Eds.) *The Biology of Alcoholism, Vol. 2.* New York: Plenum Press, 1971.

CARTER, R. D. & THOMAS, E. J. A case application of a signaling system (SAM) for the assessment and modification of selected problems of marital communication. *Behavior Therapy,* 1973, 4, 629-645.

CASH, W. M. & EVANS, I. M. Training pre-school children to modify their retarded siblings' behavior. *Journal of Behavior Therapy and Experimental Psychiatry,* 1975, 6, 13-16.

CATALDO, M. F. & RISLEY, T. R. Evaluation of living environments: The MANIFEST description of ward activities. In P. O. Davidson, F. W. Clark, & L. A. Hamerlynck (Eds.) *Evaluation of Behavioral Programs in Community, Residential and School Settings.* Champaign, Ill.: Research Press, 1974.

CATANIA, C. A. The myth of self-reinforcement. *Behaviorism,* 1975, 3, 192-199.

CAUDILL, B. D. & MARLATT, G. A. Modeling influences in social drinking: An experimental analogue. *Journal of Consulting and Clinical Psychology,* 1975, 43, 405-415.

CAUTELA, J. R. The treatment of overeating by covert conditioning. *Psychotherapy: Theory, Research, and Practice,* 1972, 9, 211-216.

CAUTELA, J. R. & ROSENTIEL, A. K. The use of covert conditioning in the treatment of drug abuse. *The International Journal of the Addictions,* 1975, 10, 277-303.

CAUTELA, J. R. & UPPER, D. The process of individual behavior therapy. In M. Hersen, R. M. Eisler & P. M. Miller (Eds.), *Process in Behavior Therapy,* Vol. 1. New York: Academic Press, 1975, 276-305.

CHAPMAN, C. & RISLEY, T. R. Anti-litter procedures in an urban high-density area. *Journal of Applied Behavior Analysis,* 1974, 7, 377-384.

CHESNEY, M. A. & TASTO, D. L. The development of the menstrual symptom questionnaire. *Behaviour Research and Therapy,* 1975, 13, 237-244.

CHRISTENSEN, A., ARKOWITZ, H., & ANDERSON, J. Practice dating as a treatment for college dating inhibitions. *Behaviour Research and Therapy,* 1975, 13, 321-331.

CHRISTY, P. R. Does use of tangible rewards with individual children affect peer observers? *Journal of Applied Behavior Analysis,* 1975, 7, 187-196.

CIMINERO, A. R., DOLEYS, D. M., & DAVIDSON, R. S. Free-operant avoidance of alcohol. *Journal of Behavior Therapy and Experimental Psychiatry,* 1975, 6, 242-245.

COATES, B. & PUSSER, H. E. Positive reinforcement and punishment in "Sesame Street" and "Mister Rogers." *Journal of Broadcasting,* 1975, 19, 143-151.

COHEN, M., LIEBSON, I. A., FAILLACE, L. A., & ALLEN, R. P. Moderate drinking by chronic alcoholics. *Journal of Nervous and Mental Disease*, 1971, 153, 434-444.

COLLINS, R. W. & PLASKA, T. Mowrer's conditioning treatment for enuresis applied to geriatric residents of a nursing home. *Behavior Therapy*, 1975, 6, 632-638.

CONE, J. D. Assessing the effectiveness of programmed generalization. *Journal of Applied Behavior Analysis*, 1973, 6, 713-715.

COOK, S. W. Comments on ethical considerations in "self-control techniques as an alternative to pain medication." *Journal of Abnormal Psychology*, 1975, 84, 169-171.

COPELAND, R. E., BROWN, R. E., & HALL, R. V. The effects of principal-implemented techniques on the behavior of pupils. *Journal of Applied Behavior Analysis*, 1974, 7, 847-860.

COURSEY, R. D. Electromyograph feedback as a relaxation technique. *Journal of Consulting and Clinical Psychology*, 1975, 43, 825-834.

CRIDER, A., SCHWARTZ, G. E., & SHNIDMAN, S. On the criteria for instrumental autonomic conditioning: A reply to Katkin and Murray. *Psychological Bulletin*, 1969, 84, 169-171.

CUMMINGS, L. I. & SCHWAB, D. *Performance in Organizations: Determinants and Appraisal.* Glenview, Ill.: Scott, Foresman, 1973.

CURRAN, J. P. Social skills training and systematic desensitization in reducing dating anxiety. *Behaviour Research and Therapy*, 1975, 13, 65-68.

CURRAN, J. P. & GILBERT, F. S. A test of the relative effectiveness of a systematic desensitization program and interpersonal skills training program with date anxious subjects. *Behavior Therapy*, 1975, 6, 510-521.

DAVIDS, A. Therapeutic approaches to children in residential treatment: Changes from the mid-1950's to the mid-1970's. *American Psychologist*, 1975, 30, 809-814.

DAVIDSON, P. O., CLARK, F. W., & HAMERLYNCK, L. A. (Eds.). *Evaluation of Behavioral Programs in Community, Residential and School Settings.* Champaign, Ill.: Research Press, 1974.

DAVIDSON, W. S. & ROBINSON, M. J. Community psychology and behavior modification: A community-based program for the prevention of delinquency. *Journal of Corrective Psychiatry and Behavior Therapy*, 1975, 21, 1-12.

DAVIDSON, W. S. & SEIDMAN, E. Studies of behavior modification and juvenile delinquency: A review, methodological critique, and social perspective. *Psychological Bulletin*, 1974, 81, 98-101.

DAVISON, G. C. Systematic desensitization as a counterconditioning process. *Journal of Abnormal Psychology*, 1968, 73, 91-99.

DAVISON, G. C. & STUART, R. B. A statement on behavior modification from the Association for the Advancement of Behavior Therapy, *AABT Newsletter*, May, 1974, 2-3.

DAVISON, G. C. & WILSON, G. T. Processes of fear reduction in systematic desensitization: Cognitive and social reinforcement factors in humans. *Behavior Therapy*, 1973, 4, 1-21.

deCHARMS, R. *Personal Causation: The Internal Affective Determinants of Behavior.* New York: Academic Press, 1968.

DECI, E. L. Effects of externally mediated rewards on intrinsic motivation. *Journal of Personality and Social Psychology*, 1971, 18, 105-115.

DECI, E. L. Intrinsic movitation, extrinsic reinforcement, and inequity. *Journal of Personality and Social Psychology*, 1972a, 22, 113-120.

DECI, E. L. The effects of contingent and non-contingent rewards and controls on intrinsic motivation. *Organizational Behavior and Human Performance*, 1972b, 8, 217-229.

DIAMENT, C. & WILSON, G. T. An experimental investigation of the effects of covert sensitization in an analogue eating situation. *Behavior Therapy*, 1975, 6, 499-509.

DRABMAN, R., SPITALNIK, R., & O'LEARY, K. D. Teaching self-control to disruptive children. *Journal of Abnormal Psychology*, 1973, 82, 10-16.

DRABMAN, R. S., SPITALNIK, R., & SPITALNIK, K. Sociometric and disruptive behavior as a function of four types of token reinforcement programs. *Journal of Applied Behavior Analysis*, 1974, 7, 93-101.

DULANY, D. E. On the support of cognitive theory in opposition to behavior theory: A methodological problem. In W. B. Weimer & D. S. Palermo (Eds.) *Cognition and the Symbolic Process*. Hillsdale, N. J.: Lawrence Erlbaum Associates, 1974.

DYKMAN, R. A. Conditioning as sensation. *The Pavlovian Journal of Biological Science*, 1976, 11, 24-36.

D'ZURILLA, T., WILSON, G. T., & NELSON, R. A preliminary study of the effectiveness of graduated prolonged exposure to the treatment of irrational fear. *Behavior Therapy*, 1973, 4, 672-685.

EDDY, G. L. & SINNETT, R. Behavior setting utilization by emotionally disturbed college students. *Journal of Consulting and Clinical Psychology*, 1973, 40, 210-216.

EISLER, R. M. The behavioral assessment of social skills. In M. Hersen & A. S. Bellack (Eds.) *Behavioral Assessment: A Practical Handbook*. New York: Pergamon Press, 1976.

EISLER, R., HERSEN, M., & MILLER, P. Shaping components of assertive behavior with instructions and feedback. *American Journal of Psychiatry*, 1974, 131, 1344-1347.

ELLIOT, C. H. & DENNEY, D. R. Weight control through covert desensitization and false feedback. *Journal of Consulting and Clinical Psychology*, 1975, 43, 842-850.

ELLIS, A. *Reason and Emotion in Psychotherapy*. New York: Lyle Stuart, 1962.

EMMELKAMP, P. M. G. Effects of expectancy on systematic desensitization and flooding. *European Journal of Behavioural Analysis and Modification*, 1975a, 1, 1-11.

EMMELKAMP, P. M. G. Face validity and behavior therapy. *European Journal of Behavioural Analysis and Modification*, 1975b, 1, 15-19.

EMMELKAMP, P. M. G. & EMMELKAMP-BENNER, A. Effects of historically portrayed modeling and group treatment on self-observation: A comparison with agoraphobics. *Behaviour Research and Therapy*, 1975, 13, 135-139.

EMMELKAMP, P. M. G. & ULTEE, C. A. A comparison of "successive approximation" and self-observation" in the treatment of agoraphobia. *Behavior Therapy*, 1974, 5, 605-613.

EMMELKAMP, P. M. G. & WESSELS, H. Flooding in imagination vs. flooding *in vivo*: A comparison with agoraphobics. *Behaviour Research and Therapy*, 1975, 13, 7-15.

ERIKSSON, J. H., GOTESTAM, K. G., MELIN, L., & OST, L. A token economy treatment of drug addiction. *Behaviour Research and Therapy*, 1975, 13, 113-125.

EVANS, W. I. M. Theoretical and experimental aspects of the behavior modification approach to autistic children. In Michael Rutter (Ed.) *Infantile Autism: Concepts, Characteristics and Treatment*. London: Churchill Livingstone, 1971. Pp. 229-251.

EYSENCK, H. J. The effects of psychotherapy: An evaluation. *Journal of Consulting Psychology*, 1952, 16, 319-324.

EYSENCK, H. J. The effects of psychotherapy. In H. J. Eysenck (Ed.), *Handbook of Abnormal Psychology*. New York: Basic Books, 1961.

EYSENCK, H. J. A theory of the incubation of the anxiety/fear response. *Behaviour Research and Therapy*, 1968, 6, 309-321.

EYSENCK, H. J. & BEECH, H. R. Counterconditioning and related methods. In A. E. Bergin & S. L. Garfield (Eds.) *Handbook of Psychotherapy and Behavior Change*. New York: Wiley, 1971. Pp. 543-611.

FAIRWEATHER, G. W. *Social Psychology in Treating Mental Illness: An Experimental Approach*. New York: Wiley, 1964.

FAIRWEATHER, G. W., SANDERS, D. H., CRESSLER, D. L., & MAYNARD, H. *Community Life for the Mentally Ill*. Chicago: Aldine, 1969.

FAULK, M. Frigidity—a critical review. *Archives of Sexual Behavior*, 1973, 2, 257-266.

FEINGOLD, B. D. & MAHONEY, M. J. Reinforcement effects on intrinsic interest: Undermining the overjustification hypothesis. *Behavior Therapy*, 1975, 6, 367-397.

FEINSTEIN, A. R. The measurement of success in weight reduction: An analysis of methods and a new index. *Journal of Chronic Diseases*, 1959, 10, 439-456.

FELDMAN, M. P. & MacCULLOCH, M. J. *Homosexual Behavior: Therapy and Assessment.* New York: Pergamon, 1971.

FERSTER, C. B. & SKINNER, B. D. *Schedules of Reinforcement.* New York: Appleton-Century-Crofts, 1957.

FIELD, G. D. & TEST, M. A. Group assertive training for severely disturbed patients. *Journal of Behavior Therapy and Experimental Psychiatry,* 1975, 6, 129-134.

FO, W. S. O. & O'DONNELL, C. R. The Buddy System: Relationship and contingency conditions in a community intervention program for youth with nonprofessionals as behavior change agents. *Journal of Consulting and Clinical Psychology,* 1974, 42, 163-169.

FO, W. S. O. & O'DONNELL, C. R. The Buddy System: Effect of community-intervention on delinquent offenses. *Behavior Therapy,* 1975, 6, 522-524.

FORD, J. D. & FOSTER, S. L. Extrinsic incentives and token-based programs: A reevaluation. *American Psychologist,* 1976, 31, 87-90.

FORDYCE, W. E. *Behavioral Methods for Chronic Pain and Illness.* St. Louis: C. V. Mosby, 1976.

FORDYCE, W., FOWLER, R., LEHMANN, J. & DELATEUR, B. Some implications of learning in problems of chronic pain. *Journal of Chronic Diseases,* 1968, 21, 179-190.

FOREYT, J. P. & HAGEN, R. L. Covert sensitization: Conditioning and suggestion? *Journal of Abnormal Psychology,* 1973, 82, 17-23.

FOREYT, J. P., ROCKWOOD, C. E., DAVIS, J. C., DESVOUSGES, W. H., & HOLLINGSWORTH, R. Benefit-cost analysis of a token economy program. *Professional Psychology,* 1975, 6, 26-33.

FOXX, R. M. & AZRIN, N. H. *Toilet Training the Retarded.* Champaign, Ill.: Research Press, 1973.

FRANK, L. B. The cognitive behaviorism of Boneau may help to integrate the work of Skinner and Szasz. *American Psychologist,* 1975, 30, 942-943.

FRANKL, V. E. Paradoxical intentions: A logotherapeutic technique. *American Journal of Psychotherapy,* 1960, 14, 520-535.

FRANKS, C. M. & WILSON, G. T. (Eds.). *Annual Review of Behavior Therapy: Theory and Practice,* Vol. I. New York: Brunner/Mazel, 1973.

FRANKS, C. M. & WILSON, G. T. (Eds.). *Annual Review of Behavior Therapy: Theory and Practice,* Vol. II. New York: Brunner/Mazel, 1974.

FRANKS, C. M. & WILSON, G. T. (Eds.). *Annual Review of Behavior Therapy: Theory and Practice,* Vol. III. New York: Brunner/Mazel, 1975.

FRANKS, V. Gender and psychotherapy. In E. Gomberg & V. Franks (Eds.) *Gender and Disordered Behavior.* New York: Brunner/Mazel (in press).

FEDERIKSEN, L. W., EPSTEIN L. H., & KOSEVSKY, B. Reliability and controlling effects of three procedures for self-monitoring smoking. *Psychological Record,* 1975, 25, 255-264.

FREMOUW, W. J. & HARMATZ, M. G. A helper model for behavioral treatment of speech anxiety. *Journal of Consulting and Clinical Psychology,* 1975, 43, 652-660.

FRIEDMAN, P. R. Legal regulation of applied behavior analysis in mental institutions and prisons. *Arizona Law Review,* 1975, 17, 39-104.

GALASSI, J. P. & GALASSI, M. D. Validity of a measure of assertiveness. *Journal of Counseling Psychology,* 1974, 21, 248-250.

GALASSI, J. P., DELO, J. S., GALASSI, M. D. & BASTIEN, S. The college self-expression scale: A measure of assertiveness. *Behavior Therapy,* 1974, 5, 165-171.

GAMBRILL, E. D. Role of behavior modification in community mental health. *Community Mental Health Journal,* 1975, 11, 307-315.

GARCIA, J., McGOWAN, B. K., & GREEN, K. F. Biological constraints on conditioning. In M. E. P. Seligman & J. L. Hager (Eds.) *Biological Boundaries of Learning.* New York: Appleton-Century-Crofts, 1972. Pp. 21-34.

GAUL, D. J., CRAIGHEAD, W. E., & MAHONEY, M. J. Relationship between eating rates and obesity. *Journal of Consulting and Clinical Psychology,* 1975, 43, 123-125.

GAY, M. L., HOLLANDWORTH, J. G., & GALASSI, J. P. An assertiveness inventory for adults. *Journal of Counseling Psychology*, 1975, 22, 340-344.

GAYLIN, W. & BLATTE. H. Behavior modification in prisons. *The American Criminal Law Review*, 1975, 13, 11-35.

GELDER, M. G., BANCROFT, J. H. J., GATH, D., JOHNSTON, D. W., MATTHEWS, A. M., & SHAW, P. M. Specific and non-specific factors in behavior therapy. *British Journal of Psychiatry*, 1973, 123, 445-462.

GELFAND, D. M. & HARTMANN, D. P. *Child Behavior Analysis and Therapy*. New York: Pergamon, 1975.

GERTZ, H. O. Paradoxical intention in obsessives. *American Journal of Psychiatry*, 1966, 23, 548-553.

GLASGOW, R. E. & ARKOWITZ, H. The behavioral assessment of male and female social competence in dyadic heterosexual interaction. *Behavior Therapy*, 1975, 6, 488-498.

GOFFMAN, E. *Asylums: Essays on the Social Situation of Mental Patients and Other Inmates*. Harmondsworth, England: Pelican, 1961.

GOLDBERGER, D. Court challenges in prison behavior modification programs: A case study. *The American Criminal Law Review*, 1975, 13, 37-68.

GOLDIAMOND, I. Singling out behavior modification for legal regulation: Some effects on patient care, psychotherapy, and research in general. *Arizona Law Review*, 1975, 17, 105-126.

GOLDFRIED, M. R. Systematic desensitization as training in self-control. *Journal of Consulting and Clinical Psychology*, 1971, 37, 228-234.

GOLDFRIED, M. & DAVISON, G. C. *Clinical Behavior Therapy*. New York: Holt, Rinehart & Winston, 1976.

GOLDFRIED, M. R. & D'ZURILLA, T. J. A behavioral analytic model for assessing competence. In C. D. Spielberger (Ed.) *Current Topics in Clinical and Community Psychology*. New York: Academic Press, 1969.

GOLDFRIED, M. R. & KENT, R. N. Traditional versus behavioral personality assessment: A comparison of methodological and theoretical assumptions. *Psychological Bulletin*, 1972, 77, 409-420.

GOLDFRIED, M. R. & POMERANZ, D. Role of assessment in behavior modification. *Psychological Reports*, 1968, 23, 75-87.

GOLDFRIED, M. R. & SOBOCINSKI, D. Effect of irrational beliefs on emotional arousal. *Journal of Consulting and Clinical Psychology*, 1975, 43, 504-510.

GOLDFRIED, M. R. & SPRAFKIN, J. N. *Behavioral Personalities Assessment*. Morristown, N.J.: General Learning Press, 1974.

GOLDSTEIN, A. P. *Psychotherapeutic Attraction*. New York: Pergamon, 1971.

GOODSTEIN, L. D. Self-control and therapist-control: The medical model in behavioral clothing. *Journal of Abnormal Psychology*, 1975, 84, 178-180.

GORDON, B. N. & KOGAN, K. L. A mother-instruction program: Analysis of intervention procedures. *Family Process*, 1975, 14, 205-221.

GORMALLY, J., HILL, C. E., OTIS, M., & RAINEY, L. A micro-training approach to assertion training. *Journal of Consulting Psychology*, 1975, 22, 299-303.

GORMEZANO, I. & TAIT, R. W. The Pavlovian analysis of instrumental conditioning. *The Pavlovian Journal of Biological Science*, 1976, 11, 37-55.

GREEN, G. Instrumentality theory of work motivation: Some experimental results and suggested modifications. *Journal of Applied Psychology Monograph*, 1969, 53, 2 part 2.

GREEN, L. The temporal and stimulus dimensions of self-monitoring in the behavioral treatment of obesity. Unpublished Ph.D. dissertation, Rutgers University, 1976.

GREENBERG, D. J., SCOTT, S. B., PISA, A., & FRIESEN, D. D. Beyond the token economy: A comparison of two contingency programs. *Journal of Consulting and Clinical Psychology*, 1975, 43, 498-503.

GREENSPOON, J. & BROWNSTEIN, A. J. Awareness in verbal conditioning. *Journal of Experimental Research in Personality*, 1967, 2, 295-308.

GRELLER, M. M. The consequences of feedback. Unpublished Ph.D. dissertation, Yale University, 1975a.

GRELLER, M. M. Supervisory Evaluation in the Context of Alternative Sources of Feedback. Paper presented at the 35th Annual Meeting of the Academy of Management, New Orleans, 1975b.

GRELLER, M. M. & HEROLD, D. M. Sources of feedback: A preliminary investigation. *Organizational Behavior and Human Performance*, 1975, 13, 244-256.

GUERNEY, B. G. Filial therapy: Description and rationale. *Journal of Consulting Psychology*, 1964, 28, 304-310.

GURMAN, A. S. The effects and effectiveness of marital therapy: A review of outcome research. *Family Process*, 1973, 12, 145-170.

GURMAN, A. S. Some theoretical implications of marital therapy research. In A. S. Gurman & D. Rice (Eds.) *Couples in Conflict*. New York: Aronson, 1975.

HACKMANN, A. & McLEAN, C. A comparison of flooding and thought stopping in the treatment of obsessional neurotics. *Behaviour Research and Therapy*, 1975, 13, 263-269.

HACKMAN, J. R. & OLDHAM, G. R. Development of the job diagnostic survey. *Journal of Applied Psychology*, 1975, 60, 159-170.

HALL, S. M. Performance of two self-managed treatments of overweight in university and community populations. *Journal of Consulting and Clinical Psychology*, 1974, 42, 781-786.

HALL, S. M., HALL, R. G., BORDEN, B. L., & HANSON, R. W. Follow-up strategies in the behavioral treatment of overweight. *Behaviour Research and Therapy*, 1975, 13, 167-172.

HALL, S. M., HALL, R. G., HANSON, R. W., & BORDEN, B. L. Permanence of two self-managed treatments of overweight. *Journal of Consulting and Clinical Psychology*, 1974, 42, 781-786.

HAMBURG, S. Behavior therapy in alcoholism: A critical review of broad-spectrum approaches. *Journal of Studies on Alcohol*, 1975, 36, 69-87.

HAMNER, W. C. & FOSTER, L. F. Are intrinsic and external rewards addictive: A test of Deci's cognitive evaluation theory of task motivation. *Organizational Behavior and Human Performance*, 1975, 14, 398-415.

HARRIS, D. E. & LICHTENSTEIN, E. The contribution of nonspecific social variables to a successful behavioral treatment of smoking. Paper presented at the annual meeting of the Western Psychological Association, San Francisco, April, 1971.

HARRIS, V. W. & SHERMAN, J. A. The use and analysis of the "Good Behavior Game" to reduce disruptive behavior. *Journal of Applied Behavior Analysis*, 1973, 6, 405-417.

HARRISON, B. G. The books that teach women to say "no." *McCall's, November*, 1975, 24-32.

HARTMAN, D. P. & ATKINSON, C. Having your cake and eating it too: A note on some apparent contradictions between therapeutic achievement and design requirements in N = 1 studies. *Behavior Therapy*, 1973, 4, 589-591.

HAUSERMAN, N., WALEN, S. R., & SEHLING, M. Reinforced racial integration in the first grade: A study in generalization. *Journal of Applied Behavior Analysis*, 1973, 6, 193-200.

HAYES, S. C., JOHNSON, V. S., & CONE, J. D. The marked item technique: A practical procedure for litter control. *Journal of Applied Behavior Analysis*, 1975, 8, 381-386.

HAYES-ROTH, F., LONGABAUGH, R. & RYBACK, R. The problem-oriented medical record and psychiatry. *British Journal of Psychiatry*, 1972, 121, 27-34.

HAYNES, S. N., GRIFFIN, P., MOONEY, D., & PARISE, M. Electromyographic biofeedback and relaxation instruction in the treatment of muscle contraction headaches. *Behavior Therapy*, 1975, 6, 672-678.

HEDBERG, A. G. & CAMPBELL, L., III. A comparison of four behavioral treatments of alcoholism. *Journal of Behavior Therapy and Experimental Psychiatry*, 1974, 5, 251-256.

HEIMAN, G. W. A note on "operant conditioning principles extrapolated to the theory of management." *Organizational Behavior and Human Performance*, 1975, 13, 165-170.

HENDERSON, S. & WILLIAMS, C. L. On the prevention of parasuicide. *Australian and New Zealand Journal of Psychiatry*, 1974, 8, 2, 237-240.

HEPNER, A. & CAUTHEN, N. R. Effect of subject control and graduated exposure of snake phobias. *Journal of Consulting and Clinical Psychology*, 1975, 43, 297-304.

HERMAN, C. P. & POLIVY, J. Anxiety, restraint, and eating behavior. *Journal of Abnormal Psychology*, 1975, 84, 666-672.

HERMAN, S. H., BARLOW, D. H., & AGRAS, W. S. An experimental analysis of exposure to "explicit" heterosexual stimuli as an effective variable in changing arousal patterns of homosexuals. *Behaviour Research and Therapy*, 1974, 12, 335-345.

HERMAN, S. H. & PREWETT, M. An experimental analysis of feedback to increase sexual arousal in a case of homo- and heterosexual impotence: A preliminary report. *Journal of Behavior Therapy and Experimental Psychiatry*, 1974, 5, 271-274.

HERMANN, J. A., deMONTES, A. I., DOMINGUES, B., MONTES, F., & HOPKINS, B. L. Effects of bonuses for punctuality on the tardiness of industrial workers. *Journal of Applied Behavior Analysis*, 1973, 6, 563-570.

HERSEN, M. & BELLACK, A. S. Assessment of social skills. In A. R. Ciminero, K. S. Calhoun, & H. E. Adams (Eds.) *Handbook of Behavioral Assessment*. New York: Wiley, 1976.

HERSEN, M., EISLER, R. M., & MILLER, P. M. An experimental analysis of generalization in assertive training. *Behaviour Research and Therapy*, 1974, 12, 295-310.

HIGGINS, R. L. & MARLATT, G. A. Fear of interpersonal evaluation as a determinant of alcohol consumption in male social drinkers. *Journal of Abnormal Psychology*, 1975, 84, 644-651.

HIGGINS, R. L. & MARLATT, G. A. The effects of anxiety arousal on the consumption of alcohol by alcoholics and social drinkers. *Journal of Consulting and Clinical Psychology*, 1973, 41, 426-433.

HODGSON, R. J. & RACHMAN, S. The effects of contamination and washing in obsessional patients. *Behaviour Research and Therapy*, 1972, 10, 111-117.

HOEFLER, S. A. & BORNSTEIN, P. H. Achievement Place: An evaluative review. *Criminal Justice and Behavior*, 1975, 2, 146-168.

HORAN, J. J., BAKER, S. B., HOFFMAN, A. M., & SHUTE, R. E. Weight loss through variations in the coverant control paradigm. *Journal of Consulting and Clinical Psychology*, 1975, 43, 68-72.

HORAN, J. J., HACKETT, G., NICHOLAS, W. C., LINBERG, S. E., STONE, C. I., & LUKASKI, H. C. Rapid smoking: A cautionary note. Paper presented at the annual meeting of the American Educational Research Association, San Francisco, April 20, 1976.

HUNT, S. M. & AZRIN, N. H. The community-reinforcement approach to alcoholism. *Behaviour Research and Therapy*, 1973, 11, 91-104.

HUNT, W. A. & MATARAZZO, J. D. Three years later: Recent developments in the experimental modification of smoking. *Journal of Abnormal Psychology*, 1973, 81, 107-114.

JABLONSKY, S. F. & DeVRIES, D. L. Operant conditioning principles extrapolated to the theory of management. *Organizational Behavior and Human Performance*, 1972, 7, 340-358.

JACOBSON, A. M., HACKETT, T. P., SURMAN, O. S., & SILVERBERG, E. L. Raynaud phenomenon. Treatment with hypnotic and operant technique. *Journal of the American Medical Association*, 1973, 225, 739-740.

JACOBSON, E. *Progressive Relaxation*. Chicago: University of Chicago Press, 1938.

JEFFMAR, M. & JEFFMAR, C. A system approach to cognition. *General Systems*, 1975, 20, 65-69.

JEFFREY, D. B. Treatment evaluation issues in research on addictive behaviors. *Addictive Behaviors*, 1975, 1, 23-36.

JOHNSON, S. M. & BOLSTAD, O. D. Methodological issues in naturalistic observation: Some problems and solutions for field research. In L. A. Hamerlynck, L. C. Handy & E. J. Mash (Eds.), *Behavior Change: Methodology, Concepts and Practice.* Champaign, Ill.: Research Press, 1973.

JOHNSON, W. G. & TURIN, A. Biofeedback treatment of migraine headache: A systematic case study. *Behavior Therapy*, 1975, 6, 394-397.

JONES, N. B. (Ed.). *Ethological Studies of Child Behaviour.* Cambridge: Cambridge University Press, 1972.

JONES, R. J. & AZRIN, N. H. An experimental application of a social reinforcement approach to the problem of job finding. *Journal of Applied Behavior Analysis*, 1973, 6, 345-353.

JONES, R. T. & KAZDIN, A. E. Programming response maintenance after withdrawing token reinforcement. *Behavior Therapy*, 1975, 6, 153-164.

JORDAN, H. A. & LEVITZ, L. S. Behavior modification in the treatment of childhood obesity. In M. Winick (Ed.), *Childhood Obesity.* New York: Wiley, 1975, pp. 141-150.

JORAVSKY, D. Russian psychology (Book review of Soviet psychology). *Contemporary Psychology*, 1975, 20, 774-776.

KAGEL, J. H., BATTALIO, R. C., WINKLER, R. C., FISHER, E. B., MILES, C. C., BASMAN, R. L., & KRASNER, L. Income consumption and saving in controlled environments: Further economic analysis. In C. G. Miles (Ed.) *Experiments in Controlled Environment.* Toronto: Addiction Research Foundation 1975.

KANFER, F. H., KAROLY, P., & NEWMAN, A. Reduction of children's fear of the dark by competence-related and situational threat-related verbal cues. *Journal of Consulting and Clinical Psychology*, 1975, 43, 251-258.

KANFER, F. H. & PHILLIPS, J. S. *Learning Foundation of Behavior Therapy.* New York: Wiley, 1970.

KANFER, F. H. & SASLOW, G. Behavioral diagnosis. In C. M. Franks (Ed.) *Behavior Therapy: Appraisal and Status.* New York: McGraw-Hill, 1969.

KAROLY, P. Ethical considerations in the application of self-control techniques. *Journal of Abnormal Psychology*, 1975, 84, 175-177.

KATZ, R. C. & WOOLLEY, F. R. Improving patients' records through problem orientation. *Behavior Therapy*, 1975, 6, 119-124.

KATZ, R. C. & ZLUTNICK, S. (Eds.). *Behavior Therapy and Health Care: Principles and Applications.* New York: Pergamon, 1975.

KAZDIN, D. E. Methodological and assessment consideration in evaluating reinforcement programs in applied settings. *Journal of Applied Behavior Analysis*, 1973, 6, 517-536.

KAZDIN, D. E. & KOPEL, S. A. On resolving ambiguities of the multiple-baseline design: Problems and recommendations. *Behavior Therapy*, 1975, 6, 601-608.

KENT, R. A methodological critique of "interventions for boys with conduct problems." *Journal of Consulting and Clinical Psychology*, 1976, 44, 297-299.

KIMMEL, H. D. Reflex "habituality" as a basis for differentiating between classical and instrumental conditioning. *Conditional Reflex*, 1973, 8, 10-27.

KIMMEL, H. D. Are operant and classical conditioning the same or different? *The Pavlovian Journal of Biological Science*, 1976, 11, 1-2.

KING, R. D., RAYNES, N. V., & TIZARD, J. *Patterns of Residential Care—Sociological Studies in Institutions for Handicapped.* London: Routledge & Kegan Paul, 1971.

KIRK, S. A. & THERRIEN, M. E. Community mental health myths and the fate of former hospital patients. *Psychiatry*, 1975, 38, 209-217.

KIRSCH, I., WOLPIN, M., & KNUTSON, J. L. A comparison of *in vivo* methods for rapid reduction of "stage-fright" in the college classroom: A field experiment. *Behavior Therapy*, 1975, 6, 165-171.

KLONOFF, H. & COX, B. A problem oriented system approach to analysis of treatment outcome. *American Journal of Psychiatry*, 1975, 132, 836-841.

KOCKOTT, G., DITTMAR, F., & NUSSELT, L. Systematic desensitization of erectile impotence: A controlled study. *Archives of Sexual Behavior*, 1975, 4, 493-500.

KOHLENBERG, R. & PHILLIPS, T. Reinforcement and the rate of litter depositing. *Journal of Applied Behavior Analysis*, 1973, 6, 391-396.

KOHLENBERG, R., PHILLIPS, T., & PROCTOR, W. A behavioral analysis of peaking in residential electrical-energy consumers. *Journal of Applied Behavior Analysis*, 1976, 9, 13-18.

KOPEL, S. & ROSEN, R. C. Carbon monoxide monitoring: Clinical and research utility for smoking reduction. Paper presented at the Annual Meeting of the Association for Advancement of Behavior Therapy, San Francisco, December, 1975.

KORNHABER, R. C. & SCHROEDER, H. E. Importance of model similarity on extinction of avoidance behavior in children. *Journal of Consulting and Clinical Psychology*, 1975, 43, 601-607.

KRASNER, L. What are the variables necessary for training environmental designs? In C. S. Miles (Ed.) *Experiments in Controlled Environment*. Toronto: Addiction Research Foundation, 1975.

KRASNER, L. & KRASNER, M. Token economies and other planned environments. In C. E. Thoresen (Ed.) *Behavior Modification in Education: The Seventy-Second Yearbook of the National Society for the Study of Education*. Chicago, Ill.: University of Chicago Press, 1973. Pp. 351-381.

KUNKEL, J. D. *Behavior, Social Problems and Change: A Social Learning Approach*. Englewood Cliffs, N. J.: Prentice-Hall, 1975.

LANDAU, P. A guide for the assertive book buyer. *Human Behavior*, May, 1976, 64-71.

LANDO, H. A. An objective check upon self-reported smoking levels: A preliminary report. *Behavior Therapy*, 1975, 6, 547-549.

LANDO, H. A. A comparison of excessive and rapid smoking in the modification of chronic smoking behavior. *Journal of Consulting and Clinical Psychology*, 1975a,

LANG, P. J. Learned control of human heart rate in a computer directed environment. In P. A. Obrist, A. H. Black, J. Brener & L. V. Dicara (Eds.) *Cardiovascular Psychophysiology*. Chicago: Aldine, 1974.

LANG, A. R., GOECKNER, D. J., ADESSO, V. J., & MARLATT, G. A. Effects of alcohol on aggression in male social drinkers. *Journal of Abnormal Psychology*, 1975, 84, 508-518.

LANG, P. J., MELAMED, B. G., & HART, J. A psychophysiological analysis of fear modification using an automated desensitization procedure. *Journal of Abnormal Psychology*, 1970, 76, 220-234.

LANGE, A. J. & JAKUBOWSKI, P. *Responsible Assertive Behavior: Cognitive Behavioral Procedures for Trainees*. Champaign, Ill.: Research Press, 1976.

LANYON, R. I. & LANYON, B. J. Behavioral assessment and decision making: The design of strategies for therapeutic behavior change. In M. P. Feldman & A. Broadhurst (Eds.) *Theoretical and Experimental Bases of the Behaviour Therapies*. London: Wiley, 1976.

LATHAM, G. P. & BALDES, J. J. The "practical significance" of Locke's theory of goal-setting. *Journal of Applied Psychology*, 1975, 60, 122-124.

LATHAM, G. P. & KINNE, S. Improving job performance through training in goal-setting. *Journal of Applied Psychology*, 1974, 59, 187-191.

LAZARUS, A. A. *Multimodal Behavior Therapy*. New York: Springer, 1976.

Least Restrictive Alternative. *Law and Behavior*, 1976, 1, No. 1, 5.

LECOMPTE, W. F. Behavior setting: The structure of the treatment environment. *Proceedings of the Environmental Design & Research Association Conference*, Vol. I. University of California, 1972.

LEITENBERG, H. The use of single case methodology in psychotherapy research. *Journal of Abnormal Psychology*, 1973, 82, 87-107.

LEITENBERG, H. Behavioral approaches to treatment of neuroses. In H. Leitenberg

(Ed.) *Handbook of Behavior Modification and Behavior Therapy.* Englewood Cliffs, N. J.: Prentice-Hall, 1976.

LEITENBERG, H., AGRAS, W. S., ALLEN, R., BUTZ, R., & EDWARDS, J. Feedback and therapist praise during treatment of phobia. *Journal of Consulting and Clinical Psychology,* 1975, 43, 396-404.

LELAURIN, K. & RISLEY, T. R. The organization of day care environments: "Zone" vs. "man-to-man" staff assignments. *Journal of Applied Behavior Analysis,* 1972, 5, 225-232.

LEPPER, M. R. & GREEN, D. On understanding "overjustification": A reply to Reiss and Sushinsky. *Journal of Personality and Social Psychology,* 1976, 33, 25-35.

LEPPER, M. R., GREEN, D. & NISBETT, R. E. Undermining children's intrinsic interest with extrinsic rewards: A test of the "overjustification hypothesis." *Journal of Personality and Social Psychology,* 1973, 28, 129-137.

LESTER, D. Self-mutilating behavior. *Psychological Bulletin,* 1972, 78, 119-128.

LEVENDUSKY, P. & PANKRATZ, L. Ethical issues considered within the context of the milieu: Comments on the reviews of a case study. Unpublished manuscript, 1976.

LEVINE, F. M. & FASNACHT, G. Token rewards may lead to token learning. *American Psychologist,* 1974, 29, 816-820.

LEWINSOHN, P. M. A behavioral approach to depression. In R. J. Friedman & M. M. Katz (Eds.) *The Psychology of Depression: Contemporary Theory and Research.* New York: Wiley, 1974.

LEWINSOHN, P. M. The behavioral study and treatment of depression. In M. Hersen, R. M. Eisler & P. M. Miller (Eds.) *Progress in Behavior Modification, Vol. I.* New York: Academic Press, 1975.

LEWIS, S. A comparison of behavior therapy techniques in the reduction of fearful avoidance behavior. *Behavior Therapy,* 1974, 5, 648-655.

LIBERMAN, R. P., FERRIS, C., SALGADO, P., & SALGADO, P. Replication of the Achievement Place model in California. *Journal of Applied Behavior Analysis,* 1975, 8, 287-299.

LICHTENSTEIN, E. Aversive control and the treatment of cigarette smoking. Paper presented at the annual meeting of the Association for Advancement of Behavior Therapy, San Francisco, December, 1975.

LICHTENSTEIN, E., HARRIS, D. E., BIRCHLER, G. R., WAHL, J. H., & SCHMAHL, D. P. Comparison of rapid smoking, warm smoky air, and attention placebo in the modification of smoking behavior. *Journal of Consulting and Clinical Psychology,* 1973, 40, 92-98.

LICK, J. Expectancy, false galvanic skin response feedback, and systematic desensitization in the modification of phobic behavior. *Journal of Consulting and Clinical Psychology,* 1975, 43, 557-567.

LICK, J. & BOOTZIN, R. Expectancy factors in the treatment of fear: Methodological and theoretical issues. *Psychological Bulletin,* 1975, 82, 917-931.

LICK, J. R. & UNGER, T. E. External validity of laboratory fear assessment: Implications from two case studies. *Journal of Consulting and Clinical Psychology,* 1975, 43, 864-866.

LICKORISH, J. R. A behavioral interactional model for assessing family relationships. *Family Process,* 1975, 14, 535-558.

LIPINSKI, D. P., BLACK, J. L., NELSON, R. O., & CIMINERO, A. R. Influence of motivational variables on the reactivity and reliability of self-recording. *Journal of Consulting and Clinical Psychology,* 1975, 43, 637-646.

LIRA, F. T., NAY, W. R., McCULLOUGH, J. P., & ETKIN, M. W. Relative effects of modeling and role playing in the treatment of avoidance behaviors. *Journal of Consulting and Clinical Psychology,* 1975, 43, 608-619.

LITOW, L. & PUMROW, D. K. Brief review of classroom group-oriented contingencies. *Journal of Applied Behavior Analysis,* 1975, 8, 341-347.

LLOYD, R. W., JR. & SALZBERG, H. C. Controlled social drinking: An alternative to abstinence as a treatment goal for some alcohol abusers. *Psychological Bulletin,* 1975, 82, 815-842.

LOBITZ, W. C. & LOPICCOLO, J. New methods for the behavioral treatment of sexual dysfunction. *Journal of Behavior Therapy and Experimental Psychiatry,* 1972, 3, 265-271.

LOCKE, E. A. Toward a theory of task motivation and incentives. *Organizational Behavior and Human Performance,* 1968, 3, 157-189.

LOCKE, H. J. & WALLACE, K. M. Short marital adjustment and prediction tests: Their rehabilitation and validity. *Marriage and Family Living,* 1959, 21, 257-265.

LOGAN, D. L. & TURNAGE, J. R. Ethical consideration in the use of faradic aversion therapy. *Behavioral Engineering,* 1975, 3, 29-34.

LONDON, P. The end of ideology in behavior modification. *American Psychologist,* 1972, 27, 913-920.

LONGIN, H. E. & ROONEY, W. M. Teaching denial assertion to chronic hospitalized patients. *Journal of Behavior Therapy and Experimental Psychiatry,* 1975, 6, 219-222.

LOPICCOLO, J. & LOBITZ, W. C. The role of masturbation in the treatment of orgasmic dysfunction. *Archives of Sexual Behavior,* 1972, 2, 163-171.

LOPICCOLO, J. & STEGER, J. C. The Sexual Interaction Inventory: A new instrument for assessment of sexual dysfunction. *Archives of Sexual Behavior,* 1974, 3, 589-595.

LOTT, D. R. & MURRAY, E. J. The effect of expectancy manipulation on outcome in systematic desensitization. *Psychotherapy: Theory, Research and Practice,* 1975, 12, 28-32.

LOVITT, T. C. Applied behavior analysis and learning difficulties. Part I. Characteristics of ABA, general recommendations and methodological limitations. *Journal of Learning Disabilities,* 1975, 8, 33-50.

LOVITT, T. C. Applied behavior analysis and learning disabilities: Specific research recommendations and suggestions. *Journal of Learning Disabilities,* 1975, 8, 36-50.

LUBORSKY, L., SINGER, B., & LUBORSKY, L. Comparative studies of psychotherapies: Is it true that everyone has won and all must have prizes? *Archives of General Psychiatry,* 1975, 32, 995-1008.

LUTHANS, F. & KREITNER, R. *Organizational Behavior Modification.* Glenview, Ill.: Scott, Foresman & Co., 1975.

LYNCH, W. C., HAMA, H., KOHN, S., & MILLER, N. E. Instrumental learning of vasomotor responses: A progress report. Proceedings of the Biofeedback Research Society, 1974, 68 (Abstract).

MAHONEY, M. J. *Cognitive Behavior Modification.* Cambridge, Mass.: Ballinger, 1974.

MAHONEY, M. The obese eating style: Bites, beliefs and behavior modification. *Addictive Behaviors,* 1975, 1, 47-53.

MAHONEY, M. J. The behavioral treatment of obesity: A reconnaissance. *Biofeedback and Self-Regulation,* 1976, 1, 127-133.

MAI, N. Mathematical models for evaluation of therapies. In J. C. Brengelmann (Ed.) *Progress in Behavior Therapy.* Berlin: Springer Verlag, 1975.

MANDLER, G., MANDLER, J. M., & UVILLER, E. T. Autonomic feedback: The perception of autonomic activity. *Journal of Abnormal and Social Psychology,* 1958, 56, 367-373.

MARCIA, J. E., RUBIN, B. M., & EFRAN, J. S. Systematic desensitization: Expectancy change or counterconditioning. *Journal of Abnormal Psychology,* 1969, 74, 382-387.

MARGOLIN, G., CHRISTENSEN, A., & WEISS, R. L. Contracts, cognition and change: A behavioral approach to marriage therapy. *The Counseling Psychologist,* 1975, 5, 15-26.

MARHOLIN, D., PLIENIS, A. J., HARRIS, S. D., & MARHOLIN, B. L. Mobilization of the community through a behavioral approach: A school program for adjudicated females. *Criminal Justice and Behavior,* 1975, 2, 130-145.

MARKS, I. M. *Fears and Phobias.* New York: Academic Press, 1969.

MARKS, I. Management of sexual disorders. In H. Leitenberg (Ed.) *Handbook of*

Behavior Modification and Behavior Therapy. Englewood Cliffs, N. J.: Prentice-Hall, 1976.

MARKS, I. M., RACHMAN, S., & HODGSON, R. Treatment of chronic obsessive-compulsive neurosis by *in-vivo* exposure. *British Journal of Psychiatry,* 1975, 127, 349-364.

MARLATT, G. A. Training responsible drinking with college students. Paper presented at the annual meeting of the American Psychological Association, Chicago, September, 1975.

MARLATT, G. A., KOSTURN, C. F., & LANG, A. R. Provocation to anger and opportunity for retaliation as determinants of alcohol consumption in social drinkers. *Journal of Abnormal Psychology,* 1975, 84, 652-659.

MARSTON, M. V. Compliance with medical regimens: A review of the literature. *Nursing Research,* 1970, 19, 312-323.

MARTIN, R. Ethical and legal implications of behavior modification in the classroom. Paper presented at the First Annual Conference in School Psychology, Temple University, Philadelphia, Pa., June, 1972.

MARTIN, R. *Behavior Modification: Human Rights and Legal Responsibilities.* Champaign, Ill.: Research Press, 1974.

MARTIN, R. *Legal Challenges to Behavior Modification: Trends in Schools, Corrections, and Mental Health.* Champaign, Ill.: Research Press, 1975.

MASH, E. J. & McELWEE, J. D. Situational effects on observer accuracy: Behavioral predictability, prior experience, and complexity of coding categories. *Child Development,* 1974, 45, 367-377.

MASH, E. J. & TERDAL, L. G. Behavior therapy assessment: Diagnosis, design and evaluation. *Psychological Reports,* 1974, 35, 587-601.

MASTERS, W. & JOHNSON, V. *Human Sexual Inadequacy.* Boston: Little, Brown, 1970.

MAWHINNEY, T. C. Operant terms and concepts in the description of individual work behavior: Some problems of interpretation, application, and evaluation. *Journal of Applied Psychology,* 1975, 60, 704-712.

MAY, J. G., RISLEY, T. R., TWARDOSZ, S., FRIEDMAN, P., BIJOU, S., WEXLER, D., et al. *Guidelines for the Use of Behavioral Procedures in State Programs for Retarded Persons.* Arlington, Texas: National Association for Retarded Citizens, 1975.

McCLANNAHAN, L. E. & RISLEY, T. R. Design of living environments for nursing-home residents: Increasing participation in recreation activities. *Journal of Applied Behavior Analysis,* 1975, 8, 261-268.

McCUTCHEON, B. A. & ADAMS, H. E. The physiological basis of implosive therapy. *Behaviour Research and Therapy,* 1975, 13, 93-100.

McFALL, R. M. & HAMNER, C. L. Motivation, structure and self-monitoring: Role of nonspecific factors in smoking reduction. *Journal of Consulting and Clinical Psychology,* 1971, 37, 80-86.

McFALL, R. & LILLESAND, D. B. Behavior rehearsal with modeling and coaching in assertion training. *Journal of Abnormal Psychology,* 1971, 77, 313-323.

McFALL, R. & TWENTYMAN, C. T. Four experiments on the relative contributions of rehearsal, modeling, and coaching to assertion training. *Journal of Abnormal Psychology,* 1973, 81, 199-218.

McGOVERN, K. B., STEWART, R. C. & LoPICCOLO, J. Secondary orgasmic dysfunction, 1. Analysis and strategies for treatment. *Archives of Sexual Behavior,* 1975, 4, 265-275.

McLAUGHLIN, T. F. A review of applications of group-contingency procedures used in behavior modification in the regular classroom: Some recommendations for school personnel. *Psychological Reports,* 1974, 35, 1299-1303.

McLAUGHLIN, T. F. & MALABY, J. E. Elementary school children as behavioral engineers. In E. A. Ramp & G. Semp (Eds.) *Behavior Analysis: Areas of Research and Application.* New York: Prentice-Hall, 1975. Pp. 319-328.

McLEAN, P. D. & MILES, J. E. Evaluation and the problem oriented record in psychiatry. *Archives of General Psychiatry,* 1974, 31, 622-625.

McREYNOLDS, W. T. & PAULSEN, B. K. Stimulus control as the behavioral basis of weight loss procedures. In B. J. Williams, S. Martin & J. P. Foreyt (Eds.), *Obesity: Behavioral Approaches to Dietary Management*. New York: Brunner/Mazel, 1976. Pp. 43-64.

McReynolds, W. T., Barnes, A. R., Brooks, S., & Rehagen, N. J. The role of attention-placebo influences in the efficacy of systematic desensitization. *Journal of Consulting and Clinical Psychology*, 1973, 41, 86-92.

Meichenbaum, D. Examination of model characteristics in reducing avoidance behavior. *Journal of Personality and Social Psychology*, 1971, 17, 298-307.

Meichenbaum, D. H. Cognitive factors in behavior modification: Modifying what clients say to themselves. In C. M. Franks and G. T. Wilson (Eds.) *Annual Review of Behavior Therapy: Theory and Practice*. New York: Brunner/Mazel, 1973. Pp. 416-431.

Meichenbaum, D. *Cognitive Behavior Modification*. Morristown, N. J.: General Learning Press, 1974.

Meichenbaum, D. Toward a cognitive theory of self-control. In G. Schwartz & D. Shapiro (Eds.) *Consciousness and Self-Regulation: Advances in Research*. New York: Plenum Press, 1975.

Meichenbaum, D. A cognitive-behavior modification assessment approach. In M. Hersen & A. Bellack (Eds.), *Behavioral Assessment: A Practical Approach*. New York: Pergamon (in press).

Meichenbaum, D., Gilmore, J., & Fedoravicius, A. Group insight versus group desensitization in treating speech anxiety. *Journal of Clinical and Consulting Psychology*, 1971, 36, 410-421.

Meichenbaum, D. H. & Goodman, J. Training impulsive children to talk to themselves: A means of developing self-control. *Journal of Abnormal Psychology*, 1971, 77, 115-126.

Melzack, R. *A Puzzle of Pain*. New York: Basic Books, 1973.

Meyers, A. W., Craighead, W. E., & Meyers, H. H. A behavioral preventive approach to community mental health. *American Journal of Community Psychology*, 1974, 2, 275-285.

Meyers, H., Nathan, P. E., & Kopel, S. A. Effects of a token reinforcement system on journal reshelving. *Journal of Applied Behavior Analysis* (in press).

Milby, J. B., Pendergrass, P. E., & Clarke, C. H. Token economy versus control word: A comparison of staff and patient attitudes toward ward environment. *Behavior Therapy*, 1975, 6. 22-29.

Miles, C. S. (Ed.). *Experimentation in Controlled Environment: Its Implication for Economic Behaviour and Social Policy Making*. Toronto: Addiction Research Foundation, 1975.

Milford, J. *Kind and Usual Punishment: The Prison Business*. New York: Knopf, 1973.

Milich, R. S. A critical analysis of Schachter's externality theory of obesity. *Journal of Abnormal Psychology*, 1975, 84, 586-588.

Miller, P. M. & Hersen, M. Research on addictive behaviors: Current needs. *Addictive Behaviors*, 1975, 1, 1-2.

Miller, P. M., Hersen, M., Eisler, R. M., & Hemphill, D. P. Electrical aversion therapy with alcoholics: An analogue study. *Behaviour Research and Therapy*, 1973, 11, 491-497.

Miller, S. B. The contribution of therapeutic instructions to systematic desensitization. *Behaviour Research and Therapy*, 1972, 10, 159-170.

Mischel, W. *Personality and Assessment*. New York: Wiley, 1968.

Mischel, W. Toward a cognitive social learning reconceptualization of personality. *Psychological Review*, 1973, 80, 252-283.

Mitchell, W. S., Mowat, E. M., & Stoffelmayr, B. E. Effects of social deprivation and satiation on the reinforcing properties of social stimulation in chronic male hospitalized schizophrenics. *Journal of Abnormal Psychology*, 1975, 84, 494-497.

Moos, R. H. *Evaluating Treatment Environments: A Social Ecological Approach.* New York: Wiley, 1974.

Moos, R. H. *Evaluating Correctional and Community Settings.* New York: Wiley, 1975.

Moos, R. H. *The Human Context: Environmental Determinants of Behavior.* New York: Wiley, 1976.

Morganstern, K. P. Implosive therapy and flooding procedures. *Psychological Bulletin.* 1973, 79, 318-334.

Morris, H. Persons and punishment. *The Monist,* 1968, 52, Oct., 475-501.

Mowrer, O. H. & Ullman, A. D. Time as a determinant in integrative learning. *Psychological Review,* 1945, 52, 61-90.

Mumford, S. J., Patch, I. C. L., Andrews, N., & Wyner, L. A token economy ward program with chronic schizophrenic patients. *British Journal of Psychiatry,* 1975, 126, 60-72.

National Research Council News Report, 1976, 26, No. 4, 10-11 (Benefit-Cost Analysis).

Nau, S. D., Caputo, J. A., & Borkovec, T. D. The relationship between therapy credibility and simulated therapy response. *Journal of Behavior Therapy and Experimental Psychiatry,* 1974, 5, 129-133.

Nelson, R. O., Lipinski, D. P., & Black, J. L. The effects of expectancy on the reactivity of self-recording. *Behavior Therapy,* 1975, 6, 337-349.

Newcomb, H. *How to Be a Man: A Book for Boys.* Boston: Gould, Kendall and Lincoln, 1847.

Newton, J. R. & Stein, L. I. Implosive therapy in alcoholism: Comparison with brief psychotherapy. *Quarterly Journal of Studies on Alcohol,* 1974, 35, 1256-1265.

Ney, P. G. Uses and abuses of operant conditioning. *Canadian Psychiatric Association Journal,* 1975, 20, 119-132.

Nisbett, R. Hunger, obesity, and the ventromedial hypothalamus. *Psychological Review,* 1972, 79, 433-470.

Noll, J. Needed—A bill of rights for clients. *Professional Psychology,* 1974, 1, 3-12.

Notz, W. W. Work motivation and the negative effects of intrinsic rewards: A review of implications for theory and practice. *American Psychologist,* 1975, 30, 884-890.

Nunes, J. S. & Marks, I. M. Feedback of true heart rate during exposure *in vivo.* *Archives of General Psychiatry,* 1975, 32, 933-936.

O'Leary, K. D., Becker, W. C., Evans, M. B., & Saudargas, R. A. A token reinforcement program in a public school: A replication and systematic analysis. *Journal of Applied Behavior Analysis,* 1969, 2, 3-13.

O'Leary, K. D. & Drabman, R. Token reinforcement programs in the classroom: A review. *Psychological Bulletin,* 1971, 75, 379-398.

O'Leary, K. D., Poulos, R. W., & Devine, V. T. Tangible reinforcers: Bonuses or bribes? *Journal of Consulting and Clinical Psychology,* 1972, 38, 1-8.

O'Leary, K. D. & Wilson, G. T. *Behavior Therapy: Application and Outcome.* Englewood Cliffs, N. J.: Prentice-Hall, 1975.

O'Leary, S. G. & O'Leary, K. D. Behavior modification in the school. In H. Leitenberg (Ed.) *Handbook of Behavior Modification.* Englewood Cliffs, N. J.: Prentice-Hall, 1976. Pp. 475-515.

Ornstein, H. & Carr, J. Implosion therapy by tape-recording. *Behaviour Research and Therapy,* 1975, 13, 177-182.

Orr, F. E., Mitchell, K. R., & Hall, R. F. Effects of reductions in social anxiety on behavior in heterosexual situations. *American Psychologist,* 1975, 10, 139-148.

Osarchuk, M. & Goldfried, M. R. A further examination of the credibility of therapy rationales. *Behavior Therapy,* 1975, 6, 694-695.

Page, S., Caron, P., & Yates, E. Behavior modification methods and institutional psychology. *Professional Psychology,* 1975, 9, 175-181.

Paivio, A. Neomentalism. *Canadian Journal of Psychology,* 1975, 29, 263-291.

PATTERSON, G. R. & GULLION, M. E. *Living with Children: New Methods for Parents and Teachers*. Champaign, Ill.: Research Press, 1971.

PATTERSON, G. R., WEISS, R. L., & HOPS, H. Training of marital skills: Some problems and concepts. In H. Leitenberg (Ed.) *Handbook of Behavior Modification and Behavior Therapy*. Englewood Cliffs, N. J.: Prentice-Hall, 1976.

PAUL, G. L. *Insight versus Desensitization in Psychotherapy*. Stanford: Stanford University Press, 1966.

PAUL, G. L. Outcome research in psychotherapy *Journal of Consulting and Clinical Psychology*, 1967, 31, 109-118.

PAUL, G. L. Behavior modification research: Design and tactics. In C. M. Franks (Ed.) *Behavior Therapy: Appraisal and Status*. New York: McGraw-Hill, 1969a.

PECK, C. L. Current legislative issues concerning the right to refuse versus the right to choose hospitalization and treatment. *Psychiatry*, 1975, 38, 303-317.

PETERSON, D. R. *The Clinical Study of Social Behavior*. New York: Appleton-Century-Crofts, 1968.

PIERCE, C. H. & RISLEY, T. R. Improving job performance of Neighborhood Youth Core aides in an urban recreation program. *Journal of Applied Behavior Analysis*, 1974, 7, 207-215.

PIORKOWSKI, G. K. & MANN, E. T. Issues in treatment efficacy research with alcoholics. *Perceptual and Motor Skills*, 1975, 41, 695-700.

POLLOCK, D. D. & LIBERMAN, R. P. Behavior therapy of incontinence in demented inpatients. *The Gerontologist*, 1974. 14, 488-491.

POMERLEAU, O., BASS, F., & CROWN, V. Role of behavior modification in preventative medicine. *The New England Journal of Medicine*, 1975, 292, 1277-1282.

POPPER, K. R. *Conjectures and refutations*. New York: Harper and Row, 1963.

PORTER, L. W. & LAWLER, E. E. *Managerial Attitudes and Performance*. Homewood, Ill.: Irwin-Dorsey, 1968.

QUILITCH, H. R. A comparison of three staff-management procedures. *Journal of Applied Behavior Analysis*, 1975, 8, 59-66.

QUILITCH, H. R. & RISLEY, T. R. The effects of play materials on social play. *Journal of Applied Behavior Analysis*, 1973, 6, 573-578.

RACHLIN, H. Self-control. *Behaviorism*, 1974, 2, 94-107.

RACHLIN, H. & GREEN, L. Commitment, choice and self-control. *Journal of the Experimental Analysis of Behavior*, 1972, 17, 15-22.

RACHMAN, S. *The Effects of Psychotherapy*. New York: Pergamon Press, 1971.

RACHMAN, S. Treatment by prolonged exposure to high intensity stimulation. *Behaviour Research and Therapy*, 1969, 7, 295-302.

RACHMAN, S. & HODGSON, R. Synchrony and desynchrony in fear and avoidance. *Behaviour Research and Therapy*, 1974, 12, 311-318.

RACHMAN, S., HODGSON, R., & MARKS, I. M. The treatment of chronic obsessive-compulsive neurosis. *Behaviour Research and Therapy*, 1971, 9, 237-247.

RACHMAN, S. & TEASDALE, J. *Aversive Therapy and Behavior Disorders*. Coral Gables, Fl.: University of Miami Press, 1969.

RAMP, E. & SEMB, G. (Eds.). *Behavior Analysis: Areas of Research and Application*. Englewood Cliffs, N. J.: Prentice-Hall, 1975.

RAMSAY, R. W. Comments on G. L. Thorpe's article. *European Journal of Behavioural Analysis and Modification*, 1975, 1, 45-46.

RANGEL, C. B. Symposium on behavior modification in prisons. Introduction: Behavior modification. *The American Criminal Law Review*, 1975, 13, 3-9.

RAY, R. D. Conditions conditioning conditioning. Paper presented to the Southeastern Psychological Association meeting, New Orleans, April, 1973.

RAY, R. D. & BROWN, D. A. A systems approach to behavior. *The Psychological Record*, 1975, 25, 459-478.

RAY, R. D. & BROWN, D. A. The behavioral specificity of stimulation: A systems approach to procedural distinctions of classical and instrumental conditioning. *The Pavlovian Journal of Biological Science*, 1976, 11, 3-23.

RAY, R. D. & RAY, M. R. A systems approach to behavior, II. The ecological description and analysis of human behavior dynamics, *Biological Record*, 1976, 26, 147-180.

RAZRAN, G. The observable unconscious and the inferable conscious in current Soviet psychophysiology: Interoceptive conditioning, semantic conditioning and the orienting reflex. *Psychological Review*, 1961, 68, 81-147.

REAVLEY, W. The use of biofeedback in the treatment of writer's cramp. *Journal of Behavior Therapy and Experimental Psychiatry*, 1975, 6, 335-338.

REID, J. B. Reliability assessment of observation data: A possible methodological problem. *Child Development*, 1970, 41, 1143-1150.

REID, J. B. & PATTERSON, G. R. Follow-up analyses of a behavioral treatment program for boys with conduct problems: A reply to Kent. *Journal of Consulting and Clinical Psychology*, 1976, 44, 299-302.

REINKING, R. H. & KOHL, M. L. Effects of various forms of relaxation training on physiological and self-report measures of relaxation. *Journal of Consulting and Clinical Psychology*, 1975, 43, 595-600.

REISS, S. & SUSHINSKY, L. W. The competing response hypothesis of decreased play effects: A reply to Lepper and Green. *Journal of Personality and Social Psychology*, 1976, 33, 233-244.

REISS, S. & SUSHINSKY, L. W. Undermining extrinsic interest. *American Psychologist*, 1975a, 7, 782-783.

REISS, S. & SUSHINSKY, L. W. Overjustification, competing responses, and the acquisition of intrinsic interest. *Journal of Personality and Social Psychology*, 1975b, 31, 1116-1125.

REPPUCCI, N. D. & SAUNDERS, J. T. Social psychology of behavior modification: Problems of implementation in natural settings. *American Psychologist*, 1974, 29, 649-660.

REVENSTORFF, D. A mathematical model for the analysis of therapies. In J. C. Brengelmann (Ed.) *Progress in Behaviour Therapy*. Berlin: Springer-Varlag, 1975.

RICHARDS, C. S. Behavior modification of studying through study skills advice and self-control procedures. *Journal of Counseling Psychology*, 1975a, 22, 431-436.

RICHARDS, C. S. The politics of a token economy. *Psychological Reports*, 1975b, 36, 615-621.

RIMM, D. C. & MASTERS, J. C. *Behavior Therapy: Techniques and Empirical Findings.* New York: Academic Press, 1974.

RIMM, D. C., SAUNDERS, W. D., & WESTEL, W. Thought stopping and covert assertion in the treatment of snake phobics. *Journal of Consulting and Clinical Psychology*, 1975, 43, 92-93.

ROBERTS, A. H., SCHULER, J., BACON, J., & ZIMMERMAN, R. L. Individual differences and autonomic control: Absorption, hypnotic susceptibility and the unilateral control of skin temperature. *Proceedings of the Biofeedback Research Society*, 1974, 67 (Abstract).

ROBIN, A. S., ARMEL, S., & O'LEARY, K. D. The effects of self-instruction on writing deficiencies. *Behavior Therapy*, 1975, 6, 178-187.

ROMANCZYK, R. G. & GOREN, E. R. Severe self-injurious behavior: The problem of clinical control. *Journal of Consulting and Clinical Psychology*, 1975, 43, 730-739.

ROMANCZYK. R. G., KENT, R. N., DIAMENT, C., & O'LEARY, K. D. Measuring the reliability of observational data. A reactive process. *Journal of Applied Behavior Analysis*, 1973, 6, 175-184.

ROMANCZYK, R. G., TRACEY, D. A., WILSON, G. T., & THORPE, G. L. Behavioral techniques in the treatment of obesity: A comparative analysis. *Behaviour Research and Therapy*, 1973, 11, 629-640.

ROPER, G., RACHMAN, S., & MARKS, I. Passive and participant modelling in exposure treatment of obsessive-compulsive neurotics. *Behaviour Research and Therapy*, 1975, 13, 271-279.

ROSEN, G. M. Subjects' initial therapeutic expectancies towards systematic desensitization as a function of varied instructional sets. *Behavior Therapy*, 1975, 6, 230-237.

Rosen, G. M. Therapy set: Its effects on subjects' involvement in systematic desensitization and treatment outcome. *Journal of Abnormal Psychology*, 1974, 83, 291-300.

Rosen, R. C. Suppression of penile tumescence by instrumental conditioning. *Psychosomatic Medicine*, 1973, 35, 509-514.

Rosen, R. C., Shapiro, D., & Schwartz, G. Voluntary control of penile tumescence. *Psychosomatic Medicine*, 1975, 37, 479-483.

Rosenbaum, A., O'Leary, K. D., & Jacob, R. B. Behavioral intervention with hyperactive children: Group consequences as a supplement to individual contingencies. *Behavior Therapy*, 1975, 6, 315-323.

Rosenzweig, S. A transvaluation of psychotherapy—a reply to Hans Eysenck. *Journal of Abnormal and Social Psychology*, 1954, 49, 298-304.

Ross, M. Salience of reward and intrinsic interest. *Journal of Personality and Social Psychology*, 1975, 32, 245-254.

Russell, R. R., Miller, D. E. & June, L. N. A comparison between group systematic desensitization and cue-controlled relaxation in the treatment of test anxiety. *Behavior Therapy*, 1975, 6, 172-177.

Rybolt, G. A. Token reinforcement therapy with chronic psychiatric patients: A three-year evaluation. *Journal of Behavior Therapy and Experimental Psychiatry*, 1975, 6, 188-191.

Sachs, D. A. Behavioral techniques in a residential nursing home facility. *Journal of Behavior Therapy and Experimental Psychiatry*, 1975, 6, 123-127.

Salter, A. *Conditioned Reflex Therapy*. New York: Farrar, Straus, 1949.

Sarason, I. J. Test anxiety and the self-disclosing coping model. *Journal of Consulting and Clinical Psychology*, 1975, 43, 148-153.

Sand, P. L., Trieschmann, R. B., Fordyce, W. E., & Fowler, R. S. Behavior modification in the medical rehabilitation setting: Rationale and some applications. *Rehabilitation and Practice Review*, 1970, 1, 11-24.

Scales, E. J. & Johnson, M. S. A psychiatric POMR for use by a multidisciplinary team. *Hospital and Community Psychiatry*, 1975, 26, 371-373.

Schachter, S. Some extraordinary facts about obese humans and rats. *American Psychologist*, 1971, 25, 129-144.

Schachter, S., Goldman, R., & Gordon, A. Effects of fear, food deprivation and obesity on eating. *Journal of Personality and Social Psychology*, 1968, 10, 91-97.

Schaeffer, H. H., Sobell, M. B., & Mills, K. C. Some sobering data on the use of self-confrontation with alcoholics. *Behavior Therapy*, 1971, 2, 28-39.

Schmahl, D. P., Lichtenstein, E., & Harris, D. E. Successful treatment of habitual smokers with warm, smoky air and rapid smoking. *Journal of Consulting and Clinical Psychology*, 1972, 38, 105-111.

Schnelle, J. F. & Lee, F. J. A quasi-experimental retrospective evaluation of a prior policy change. *Journal of Applied Behavior Analysis*, 1974, 7, 483-496.

Schrier, A. M. & Stollnitz, F. (Eds.). *Behavior of Nonhuman Primates: Modern Research Trends*. Vol. 4. New York: Academic Press, 1971.

Schwab, D. P., Heneman, H. G., & DeCotiis, T. A. Behaviorally anchored rating scales: A review of the literature. *Personnel Psychology*, 1975, 28, 549-562.

Schwartz, G. E. Biofeedback as therapy: Some theoretical and practical issues. *American Psychologist*, 1973, 28, 666-673.

Schwartz, G. E. Toward a theory of voluntary control of response patterns in the cardiovascular system. In P. A. Obrist, A. H. Black, J. Bruner, & L. V. Diccara (Eds.) *Cardiovascular Psychopyhsiology: Current Issues in Response Mechanisms, Biofeedback and Methodology*. Chigaco: Aldine (in press).

Schwartz, J. & Bellack, A. S. A comparison of a token economy with standard inpatient treatment. *Journal of Consulting and Clinical Psychology*, 1975, 43, 107-108.

SCHWITZGEBEL, R. K. A contractual model for the protection of the rights of institutionalized mental patients. *American Psychologist*, 1975, 30, 815-820.

SCHWITZGEBEL, R. K. Use and regulation of psychological devices. *Behavioral Engineering*, 1975, 2, 44-46.

SELIGMAN, M. E. P. Phobias and preparedness. *Behavior Therapy*, 1971, 2, 307-320.

SELIGMAN, M. E. P. *Helplessness*. San Francisco: W. H. Freeman, 1975.

SERBER, M. The employment of videotape recording as an adjunct to the treatment of sexual dysfunction. *Archives of Sexual Behavior*, 1974, 4, 377-380.

SHAPIRO, D. & SURWIT, R. S. Learned control of psychological function and disease. In H. Leitenberg (Ed.) *Handbook of Behavior Modification and Behavior Therapy*. Englewood Cliffs, N. J.: Prentice-Hall, 1976.

SHERMAN, A. R., MULAC, A., & McCANN, M. S. Synergistic effect of self-relaxation and rehearsal feedback in the treatment of subjective and behavioral dimensions of speech anxiety. *Journal of Consulting and Clinical Psychology*, 1974, 42, 819-827.

SHOEMAKER, J. E. & TASTO, D. L. The effects of muscle-relaxation on blood pressure of essential hypertensives. *Behaviour Research and Therapy*, 1975, 13, 29-43.

SIDDALL, J. W., VARGAS, J. M., & ADESSO, V. J. Standards of safety for electrical apparatus used in aversion therapy. *Behavior Therapy*, 1975, 6, 272-273.

SIDMAN, M. *Tactics of Scientific Research*. New York: Basic Books, 1960.

SIPICH, J. F., RUSSELL, R. K., & TOBIAS, L. L. A comparison of covert sensitization and "nonspecific" treatment in the modification of smoking behavior. *Journal of Behavior Therapy and Experimental Psychiatry*, 1974, 5, 201-203.

SKINNER, B. F. *Beyond Freedom and Dignity*. New York: Knopf, 1971.

SKINNER, B. F. The steep and thorny way to a science of behavior. *American Psychologist*, 1975, 30, 42-49.

SKINNER, B. F. *About Behaviorism*. New York: Knopf, 1974.

SLOVENKO, R. & LUBY, E. D. On the emancipation of mental patients. *Journal of Psychiatry and Law*, 1975, 3, 191-213.

SLOANE, R. B., STAPLES, F. R., CRISTOL, A. H., YORKSTON, N. J., & WHIPPLE, K. *Psychotherapy vsrsus Behavior Therapy*. Cambridge, Mass.: Harvard University Press, 1975.

SMITH, P. S., BRITTON, P. G., JOHNSON, M., & THOMAS, D. A. Problem involved in toilet-training profoundly mentally handicapped adults. *Behaviour Research and Therapy*, 1975, 13, 201-307.

SMITH, W. E. The effects of social and monetary rewards on intrinsic motivation. Unpublished manuscript, Cornell University, 1974.

SNYDER, L. K., LOVITT, T. C., & SMITH, J. O. Language training for the severely retarded: Five years of behavior analysis research. *Exceptional Children*, 1975, 42, 7-15.

SOBELL, M. B. & SOBELL, L. C. Second year treatment outcome of alcoholics treated by individualized behavior therapy: Results. *Behaviour Research and Therapy*, 1976, 14, 195-215.

SOBELL, L. C. & SOBELL, M. B. Outpatient alcoholics give valid self-reports. *Journal of Nervous and Mental Disease*, 1975b, 161, 32-42.

SOBELL, M. B. & SOBELL, L. C. A brief technical report on the Mobat: An inexpensive portable test for determining blood alcohol concentration. *Journal of Applied Behavior Analysis*, 1975a, 8, 117-120.

STAHL, J. R., THOMSON, L. E., LEITENBERG, H., & HASAZI, J. E. Establishment of praise as a conditioned reinforcer in socially unresponsive psychiatric patients. *Journal of Abnormal Psychology*, 1974, 83, 488-496.

STAMPFL, T. G. & LEVIS, D. J. Essentials of implosive therapy: A learning theory approach. *Journal of Abnormal Psychology*, 1967, 72, 496-503.

STAPLES, F. R., SLOANE, R. B., WHIPPLE, K., CRISTOL, A. H., & YORKSTON, N. J. Differences between behavior therapists and psychotherapists. *Archives of General Psychiatry*, 1975, 32, 1517-1522.

STEFFEN, J. J. Electromyographically induced relaxation in the treatment of chronic alcohol abuse. *Journal of Consulting and Clinical Psychology*, 1975, 43, 275.

STEIN, T. J. Some ethical considerations of short-term workshops in the principles and methods of behavior modification. *Journal of Applied Behavior Analysis*, 1975, 8, 113-115.

STEINMARK, S. W. & BORKOVEC, T. D. Active and placebo treatment effects on moderate insomnia under counterdemand and positive demand instructions. *Journal of Abnormal Psychology*, 1974, 83, 157-163.

STEPLETON, J. V. Legal issues confronting behavior modification. *Behavioral Engineering*, 1975, 2, 35-43.

STERN, R. & MARKS, I. Brief and prolonged flooding: A comparison of agoraphobic patients. *Archives of General Psychiatry*, 1973, 28, 270-276.

STOLZ, S. B. Ethical issues in research on behavior therapy. In W. S. Wood (Ed.), *Issues in Evaluating Behavior Modification: Proceedings of the First Drake Conference on Professional Issues in Behavior Analysis, 1974.* Champaign, Ill.: Research Press, 1975.

STONE, N. M. & BORKOVEC, T. D. The paradoxical effect of brief CS exposure on analogue phobic subjects. *Behaviour Research and Therapy*, 1975, 13, 51-54.

STOYVA, J. Self-regulation: A context for biofeedback. *Biofeedback and Self-Regulation*, 1976, 1, 1-6.

STRUPP, H. H. The outcome problem in psychotherapy: A rejoinder. *Psychotherapy*, 1964, 1, 101.

STUART, R. B. Behavioral control of overeating. *Behaviour Research and Therapy*, 1967, 5, 357-365.

STUART, R. B. Operant interpersonal treatment for marital discord. *Journal of Consulting and Clinical Psychology*, 1969, 33, 675-682.

STUART, R. B. & DAVIS, B. *Slim Chance in a Fat World.* Champaign, Ill.: Research Press, 1972.

STUART, R. B. & STUART, F. *Marital Pre-Counseling Inventory.* Champaign, Ill.: Research Press, 1972.

STUMPHAUZER, J. S. Modifying delinquent behavior: Beginnings and current practices. *Adolescence.* In press, 1976.

STUNKARD, A. Satiety is a conditioned reflex. *Psychosomatic Medicine*, 1975, 37, 383-387.

STUNKARD, A. J. *The Pain of Obesity.* Palo Alto, Cal.: Bull Publishing Co., 1976.

SUEDFELD, P. & IKARD, F. F. Use of sensory deprivation in facilitating the reduction of cigarette smoking. *Journal of Consulting and Clinical Psychology*, 1974, 42, 888-895.

SULZER-AZAROFF, B., THAW, J., & THOMAS, C. Behavioral competencies for the evaluation of behavior modifiers. In W. S. Wood (Ed.), *Issues in Evaluating Behavior Modification: Proceedings of the First Drake Conference on Professional Issues in Behavior Analysis, 1974.* Champaign, Ill.: Research Press, 1975.

SURWIT, R. S. Biofeedback, a possible treatment for Raynaud's disease. *Seminars in Psychiatry*, 1973, 5, 484-490.

SURWIT, R. S. & SHAPIRO, D. Skin temperature feedback and concomitant cardiovascular changes. *Proceedings of the Biofeedback Research Society*, 1974, 69 (Abstract).

SUTHERLAND, A., AMIT, Z., GOLDEN, M., & ROSEBERGER, Z. Comparison of three behavioral techniques in the modification of smoking behavior. *Journal of Consulting and Clinical Psychology*, 1975, 43, 443-447.

TAVORMINA, J. B. Basic models of parent counseling: A critical review. *Psychological Bulletin*, 1974, 81, 827-835.

THARP, R. G., WATSON, D., & KAYA, J. Self-modification of depression. *Journal of Consulting and Clinical Psychology*, 1974, 42, 624.

THARP, R. G. & WETZEL, R. J. *Behavior Modification in the Natural Environment.* New York: Academic Press, 1969.

THORESEN, C. E. & COATES, T. J. Behavioral self-control: Some clinical concerns. In
    M. Hersen, R. M. Eisler, P. M. Miller (Eds.) *Progress in Behavior Modification*,
    Vol. 2. New York: Academic Press, 1976.
THORESEN, C. E. & MAHONEY, M. J. *Behavioral Self-Control*. New York: Holt, Rine-
    hart and Winston, 1974.
THORPE, G. L. Desensitization, behavior rehearsal, self-instructional training and
    placebo effects on assertive-refusal behavior. *European Journal of Behavioural
    Analysis and Modification*, 1975, 1, 30-44.
TONDO, T. R., LANE, J. R., & GILL, K. Suppression of specific eating behaviors by
    covert response cost: An experimental analysis. *The Psychological Record*, 1975,
    25, 187-196.
TORI, C. & WORELL, L. Reduction of human avoidant behavior: A comparison of
    counterconditioning, expectancy, and cognitive information approaches. *Journal
    of Consulting and Clinical Psychology*, 1973, 41, 269-278.
TURNER, J. Couple and group treatment of marital discord. Paper presented at the
    Annual Meeting of the Association for Advancement of Behavior Therapy, New
    York, 1972.
TWARDOSZ, S., CATALDO, M. F., & RISLEY, T. R. An open environment design for infant
    and toddler day care. *Journal of Applied Behavior Analysis*, 1974, 7, 529-546.
TWENTYMAN, C. T. & McFALL, R. M. Behavioral training of social skills in shy males.
    Journal of Consulting and Clinical Psychology, 1975, 43, 384-395.
U.S. *Department of Health, Education and Welfare, Children's Bureau, Juvenile
    Court Statistics, 1965*. Washington, D. C.: Government Printing Office, 1966.
VAN DER KOOY, D. & WEBSTER, C. D. A rapidly effective behavior modification pro-
    gram for an electively mute child. *Journal of Behavior Therapy and Experi-
    mental Psychiatry*, 1975, 6, 149-152.
VINCENT, J. P., WEISS, R. L., & BIRCHLER, G. R. A behavioral analysis of problem-
    solving in distressed and nondistressed married and stranger dyads. *Behavior
    Therapy*, 1975, 6, 475-487.
VOGLER, R. E., COMPTON, J. V., & WEISSBACH, T. A. Integrated behavior change tech-
    niques for alcoholics. *Journal of Consulting and Clinical Psychology*, 1975, 43,
    233-243.
VOGLER, R. E., FERSTL, R., KRAEMER, S., & BRENGELMANN, J. C. Electrical aversion con-
    ditioning of alcoholics: One year follow-up. *Journal of Behavior Therapy and
    Experimental Psychiatry*, 1975, 6, 171-173.
VOGLER, R. E., LUNDE, S. E., JOHNSON, G. R., & MARTIN, P. L. Electrical aversion con-
    ditioning with alcoholics. *Journal of Consulting and Clinical Psychology*, 1970,
    34, 302-307.
VON BERTALANFFY, L. *General System Theory: Foundations, Development, Applica-
    tions*. London: Allen Lane/Penguin Press, 1971.
VROOM, V. H. *Work and Motivation*. New York: Wiley, 1964.
WAHLER, R. G. Some structural aspects of deviant child behavior. *Journal of Applied
    Behavior Analysis*, 1975, 8, 27-42.
WALKER, H. M. & BUCKLEY, N. K. Programming generalization and maintenance of
    treatment effects across time and setting. *Journal of Applied Behavior Analysis*,
    1972, 5, 209-224.
WATKINS, J. G. The expanding fist: A behavioral approach to riot prevention and
    rehabilitation. *The Journal of Psychiatry and Law*, 1974, 8, 437-453.
WEATHERS, L. & LIBERMAN, R. P. Contingency contracting with families of delinquent
    adolescents. *Behavior Therapy*, 1975, 6, 356-366.
WEED, L. L. *Medical Records, Medical Education, and Patient Care*. Cleveland: Case
    Western Reserve University Press, 1971.
WEIGEL, R. G. & UHLEMANN, M. R. Developing individualized behavior change goals
    with clients. *Journal of Contemporary Psychotherapy*, 1975, 7, 91-95.

WEIMER, W. B. Overview of cognitive conspiracy: Reflections on the Volume. In W. B. Weimer & D. S. Palermo (Eds.) *Cognition and the Symbolic Process*. Hillsdale, N. J.: Lawrence Erlbaum Associates, 1974.

WEIN, K. S., NELSON, R. O., & ODOM, J. V. The relative contributions of reattribution and verbal extinction to the effectiveness of cognitive restructuring. *Behavior Therapy*, 1975, 6, 459-474.

WEINSTEIN, M. S. Two, four, six, eight—everyone evaluate! *Canadian Psychological Review*, 1975, 16, 134-138.

WEISS, C. H. Where politics and evaluation meet. *Evaluation*, 1973, 1, 37-45.

WEISS, R. L., HOPS, H., & PATTERSON, G. R. A framework for conceptualizing marital conflict, a technology for altering it, some data for evaluating it. In L. A. Hamerlynck, L. C. Handy & E. J. Mash (Eds.) *Behavior Change: Methodology, Concepts and Practice*. Champaign, Ill.: Research Press, 1973.

WENDER, P. H. *Minimal Brain Dysfunction in Children*. New York: Wiley-Interscience, 1971.

WENDT, G. R. An analytic study of the conditional knee jerk. *Archives of Psychology*, 1930, 19, No. 123.

WEXLER, D. Token and taboo: Behavior modification, token economies and the law. *California Law Review*, 1973, 61, 81-109.

WEXLER, D. B. Token and taboo: Behavior modification, token economies and the law. *California Law Review*, 1973, 7, 151-165.

WEXLER, D. B. Behavior modification and other behavior change procedures: The emerging law and the proposed Florida guidelines. *Criminal Law Bulletin*, 1975a, 11, 600-616.

WEXLER, D. B. Behavior modification and legal developments. *American Behavioral Scientist*, 1975b, 18, 679-684.

WEXLEY, K. N. & NEMEROFF, W. F. Effectiveness of positive reinforcement and goal setting as methods of management development. *Journal of Applied Psychology*, 1975, 60, 446-450.

WHATMORE, R., DURWALD, L., & KUSHLICK, A. Measuring the quality of residential care. *Behaviour Research and Therapy*, 1975, 13, 227-236.

WHITEHEAD, W. E., RENAULT, R. F., & GOLDIAMOND, I. Modification of human gastric acid secretion with operant-conditioning procedures. *Journal of Applied Behavior Analysis*, 1975, 18, 147-156.

WILKINS, W. Expectancy of therapeutic gain: An empirical and conceptual critique. *Journal of Consulting and Clinical Psychology*, 1973, 40, 69-77.

WILLEMS, E. O. An ecological orientation in psychology. *Merrill-Palmer Quarterly of Behavior and Development*, 1965, 11, 317-343.

WILLEMS, E. O. Planning a rationale for naturalistic research. In E. P. Williams & H. L. Raush (Eds.) *Naturalistic Viewpoints in Psychological Research*. New York: Holt, Rinehart & Winston, 1969.

WILLEMS, E. O. The interface of the hospital environment and patient behavior. *Archives of Physical Medicine and Rehabilitation*, 1972, 53, 115-122.

WILLS, T. A., WEISS, R. L., & PATTERSON, G. R. A behavioral analysis of the determinants of marital satisfaction. *Journal of Consulting and Clinical Psychology*, 1974, 42, 802-811.

WILSON, E. O. *Sociobiology: The New Synthesis*. Cambridge, Mass.: Harvard University Press, 1975.

WILSON, G. T. Innovations in the modification of phobic behaviors in two clinical cases. *Behavior Therapy*, 1973, 4, 426-430.

WILSON, G. T. Effects of false feedback on avoidance behavior: "Cognitive" desensitization revisited. *Journal of Personality and Social Psychology*, 1973, 28, 115-122.

WILSON, G. T. Toward specifying the "non-specifics" in behavior therapy: A social learning analysis. Paper presented at the Annual Meeting of the Association for Advancement of Behavior Therapy, San Francisco, December, 1975.

WILSON, G. T. & DAVISON, G. C. Processes of fear-reduction in systematic desensitization: Animal studies. *Psychological Bulletin*, 1971, 76, 1-14.

WILSON, G. T. & DAVISON, G. C. Effects of expectancy on systematic desensitization and flooding: A critical analysis. *European Journal of Behavioural Analysis and Modification*, 1975, 1, 12-14.

WILSON, G. T. & EVANS, I. M. The therapist-client relationship in behavior therapy. In A. S. Gurman & A. M. Razin (Eds.) *The Therapist's Contribution to Effective Psychotherapy: An Empirical Approach*. New York: Pergamon (in press).

WILSON, G. T. & LAWSON, D. M. Expectancies, alcohol and sexual arousal in male social drinker. *Journal of Abnormal Psychology*, in press.

WILSON, G. T., LEAF, R. C., & NATHAN, P. E. The aversive control of excessive alcohol consumption by chronic alcoholics in the laboratory setting. *Journal of Applied Behavior Analysis*, 1975, 8, 13-26.

WILSON, G. T. & TRACEY, D. A. An experimental analysis of aversive imagery versus electrical aversive conditioning in the treatment of chronic alcoholics. *Behaviour Research and Therapy*, 1976, 14, 41-51.

WINETT, R. A. & WINKLER, R. C. Current behavior modification in the classroom: Be still, be quiet, be docile. *Journal of Applied Behavior Analysis*, 1972, 5, 499-504.

WOLFF, W. T. & MERRENS, M. R. Behavioral assessment: A review of clinical methods. *Journal of Personality Assessment*, 1974, 38, 3-16.

WOLLERSHEIM, J. P. The effectiveness of group therapy based upon learning principles in the treatment of overweight women. *Journal of Abnormal Psychology*, 1970, 76, 462-474.

WOLPE, J. *Psychotherapy by Reciprocal Inhibition*. Stanford: Stanford University Press, 1958.

WOLPE, J. & LANG, P. J. A fear survey schedule for use in behavior therapy. *Behaviour Research and Therapy*, 1964, 2, 27-30.

WOLPE, J. & LAZARUS, A. A. *Behavior Therapy Techniques*. New York: Pergamon Press, 1966.

WOOLEY, O. W. & WOOLEY, S. C. The experimental psychology of obesity. In T. Silverstone (Ed.), *Obesity: Its Pathogenesis and Management*. Lancaster, England: Medical and Technical Publishing, 1975.

WOOLEY, S. C. & BLACKWELL, B. A behavioral probe into social contingencies on a psychosomatic ward. *Journal of Applied Behavior Analysis*, 1975, 8, 337-339.

YATES, A. J. *Behavior Therapy*. New York: Wiley, 1970.

YATES, A. J. *Theory and Practice in Behavior Therapy*. New York: Wiley, 1975.

YOUELL, K. J. & McCULLOUGH, J. P. Behavioral treatment of mucous colitis. *Journal of Consulting and Clinical Psychology*, 1975, 43, 740-745.

YUKL, G. A. & LATHAM, G. P. Consequences of reinforcement schedules and incentive magnitudes for employee performance: Problems encountered in an industrial setting. *Journal of Applied Psychology*, 1975, 60, 294-298.

YUKL, G. A., LATHAM, G. P., & PURSELL, E. D. The effectiveness of performance incentives under continuous and variable ratio schedules of reinforcement. *Personnel Psychology*, 1976 (in press).

YUKL, G. A., WEXLEY, K. N., & SEYMORE, J. D. Effectiveness of pay incentives under variable ratio and continuous reinforcement schedules. *Journal of Applied Psychology*, 1972, 56, 19-23.

ZEMORE, R. Systematic desensitization as a method of teaching a general anxiety-reducing skill. *Journal of Consulting and Clinical Psychology*, 1975, 43, 157-161.

ZIMMERMAN, J. If it's what's inside that counts, why not count it? I. Self recording of feelings and treatment by "self-implosion." *The Psychological Record*, 1975, 25, 3-16.

ZIMMERMAN, J. & LEVITT, E. E. Why not give your client a counter: A survey of what happened when we did. *Behaviour Research and Therapy*, 1975, 13, 333-337.